THE VICTORIA HISTORY
OF THE
COUNTIES OF ENGLAND

—

A HISTORY OF
STAFFORDSHIRE

VOLUME III

THE VICTORIA HISTORY
OF THE
COUNTIES OF ENGLAND

EDITED BY R. B. PUGH

THE UNIVERSITY OF LONDON
INSTITUTE OF
HISTORICAL RESEARCH

Oxford University Press, Ely House, 37 Dover Street, London, W.1

GLASGOW NEW YORK TORONTO MELBOURNE WELLINGTON
CAPE TOWN SALISBURY IBADAN NAIROBI DAR ES SALAAM LUSAKA ADDIS ABABA
BOMBAY CALCUTTA MADRAS KARACHI LAHORE DACCA
KUALA LUMPUR SINGAPORE HONG KONG TOKYO

INSCRIBED TO THE

MEMORY OF HER LATE MAJESTY

QUEEN VICTORIA

WHO GRACIOUSLY GAVE THE TITLE TO

AND ACCEPTED THE DEDICATION

OF THIS HISTORY

LICHFIELD CATHEDRAL FROM THE SOUTH-WEST, 1961
To the north-east of the cathedral is the former bishop's palace, and to the south is Minster Pool. To the east is Stowe Pool, with St. Chad's Church, at the top of the photograph, beside it.

A HISTORY OF THE COUNTY OF

STAFFORD

EDITED BY M. W. GREENSLADE

VOLUME III

PUBLISHED FOR

THE INSTITUTE OF HISTORICAL RESEARCH

BY

OXFORD UNIVERSITY PRESS

1970

Distributed by Oxford University Press until 1 January 1974
thereafter by Dawsons of Pall Mall

CONTENTS OF VOLUME THREE

CONTENTS OF VOLUME THREE

LIST OF ILLUSTRATIONS

The following are thanked for permission to use material in their possession and for the loan of photographs: the Treasurer and Masters of the Bench of the Honourable Society of Gray's Inn; the Bishop of Lichfield; the Dean and Chapter of Lichfield; the National Monuments Record; the Ministry of Public Building and Works; the Cardinal Archbishop of Westminster; the Trustees of the William Salt Library, Stafford; and the Wolverhampton Public Libraries.

The map on p. 138 was drawn by K. M. Wass from a draft prepared by G. C. Baugh and M. W. Greenslade and based on the Ordnance Survey with the sanction of the Controller of H.M. Stationery Office, Crown Copyright reserved.

LIST OF ILLUSTRATIONS

EDITORIAL NOTE

A GENERAL account of the Victoria History is to be found in an article entitled 'The Structure and Aims of the *Victoria History of the Counties of England*' in the *Bulletin of the Institute of Historical Research*, Volume XL, May 1967. The present volume is the sixth to appear in the Staffordshire set. Like Volumes II, IV, V, and VIII, it has been prepared under the auspices of the Staffordshire Victoria History Committee. The Committee, as explained in the Editorial Note to Volume IV, was the outcome of a partnership formed in 1950 between the University of London and a group of Staffordshire local authorities. Two changes have taken place in the constitution of the committee in recent years. In 1966 the County Borough of Smethwick became part of the new County Borough of Warley, and Warley has taken Smethwick's place on the committee. The County Borough of Dudley, which was transferred from Worcestershire to Staffordshire in 1966, has been represented on the committee since 1969. The University would like once more to express its gratitude to the Staffordshire authorities, particularly as they have again generously increased the scale of their financial help. The local editorial arrangements have remained unchanged since the publication of Volume II: the county editor is Mr. M. W. Greenslade and the assistant county editors are Mr. D. A. Johnson and Mr. G. C. Baugh.

On the contents of the present volume, it may be helpful to state that the detailed history of the Close at Lichfield and the detailed architectural description of the cathedral have not been included in the article on the cathedral but are reserved for the volume of the *History* covering the City of Lichfield. Similarly the architectural descriptions of the royal free chapels are reserved for the relevant topographical volumes; in the case of Penkridge the description is to be found in *V.C.H. Staffs.* Volume V. As is normal in volumes of the Victoria History devoted to ecclesiastical history in general, the religious houses in the present volume are the medieval houses; modern religious houses are dealt with in the article on Roman Catholicism or reserved for the relevant topographical volumes.

Special thanks for extensive help in the preparation of this volume are rendered to the Very Revd. W. S. Macpherson, Dean of Lichfield from 1954 to 1969, and to the Cathedral Chapter; to Mr. M. B. S. Exham, Diocesan Registrar and Chapter Clerk; and to Miss Marjorie Anderson and Dr. D. B. Robinson, successively assistant archivists at the Lichfield Joint Record Office. Thanks are also due to a number of other people and organizations who have helped. The services of some of them are acknowledged in the list of illustrations and in the footnotes to the articles on which their help was given. In addition mention must be made of Mr. H. Appleyard, Lichfield City Librarian, and his staff; Prebendary H. Baylis, Lichfield Cathedral Librarian; Professor C. N. L. Brooke of Westfield College in the University of London; Mr. B. M. Cocks, formerly Librarian at Gray's Inn; Mr. P. Draper of the Courtauld Institute of Art in the University of London; the Revd. A. R. Duncan-Jones, Head Master of St. Chad's Cathedral School, Lichfield; Miss M. E. Macdonald, Staffordshire County Librarian, and her staff; the Revd. J. D. McEvilly, Archivist to the Archbishop of Birmingham; Miss Elisabeth Poyser, Archivist to the Archbishop of Westminster; Mr. R. J. Sherlock, Archaeological Assistant to the Staffordshire County Planning and Development Officer, and his staff; and Mr. F. B. Stitt, William Salt Librarian and Staffordshire County Archivist, and his staff.

STAFFORDSHIRE
VICTORIA COUNTY HISTORY COMMITTEE

as at 1 January 1970

Mr. G. C. W. Jones, Chairman — Representing the West Bromwich County Borough Council

Alderman H. Barks, o.b.e., Vice-Chairman — Representing the Stoke-on-Trent City Council

Councillor C. H. Stafford Northcote, Vice-Chairman — Representing the Staffordshire County Council

Alderman J. F. Amery, O.B.E.
Alderman J. E. Roberts
Alderman F. N. Salmon
Councillor A. L. Garratt
Councillor P. E. McEllin
Councillor F. W. Savill
Councillor A. G. Ward
Mr. R. D. Birch
Mr. S. A. H. Burne
Mr. S. O. Stewart
Mr. N. W. Tildesley
} Representing the Staffordshire County Council

Mr. K. F. Stanesby — Representing the Burton-upon-Trent County Borough Council

Councillor Mrs. G. Homer — Representing the Dudley County Borough Council

Mr. K. D. Miller — Representing the Stoke-on-Trent City Council

Councillor W. W. Dean-Myatt
Mr. F. N. Bowler
} Representing the Walsall County Borough Council

Councillor K. A. Fletcher — Representing the Warley County Borough Council

Councillor Mrs. E. H. Allen
Councillor R. J. Dallow
Mr. F. Mason
} Representing the Wolverhampton County Borough Council

Co-opted Members

Mr. F. B. Stitt
Mr. P. Styles

Mr. A. Taylor Milne
Professor M. J. Wise, m.c.

Professor R. B. Pugh — Editor, *Victoria History of the Counties of England*
Mr. T. H. Evans, c.b.e., d.l. — Honorary Secretary
Mr. E. H. Bugg — Honorary Treasurer

xv

CLASSES OF DOCUMENTS IN THE
PUBLIC RECORD OFFICE
USED IN THIS VOLUME
WITH THEIR CLASS NUMBERS

Chancery
    Proceedings
C 1   Early
C 2   Series I
    Six Clerks Series
C 5   Bridges
C 6   Collins
C 8   Mitford
C 12   1758–1800
C 22   Country Depositions, 1649–1714
C 33   Decrees and Orders, Entry Books
C 47   Miscellanea
C 66   Patent Rolls
C 93   Proceedings of Commissioners for Charitable Uses: Inquisitions and Decrees
C 142   Inquisitions post mortem, Series II
C 143   Inquisitions ad quod damnum
C 145   Miscellaneous Inquisitions

Duchy of Lancaster
D.L. 27   Deeds, Series LS
D.L. 37   Chancery Rolls
D.L. 42   Miscellaneous Books

Exchequer, Treasury of the Receipt
E 21   Surrenders and Annexations to Cardinal College
E 28   Council and Privy Seal Records
E 36   Books

Exchequer, King's Remembrancer
E 101   Accounts, Various
E 106   Extents of Alien Priories
E 117   Church Goods
E 134   Depositions taken by Commission
E 135   Ecclesiastical Documents
E 159   Memoranda Rolls
E 178   Special Commissions of Inquiry
E 179   Subsidy Rolls etc.
E 210   Ancient Deeds, Series D

Exchequer, Augmentation Office
E 301   Certificates of Colleges and Chantries
E 315   Miscellaneous Books
E 319   Particulars for Grants etc. for Schools etc.
E 321   Proceedings of Court of Augmentations

E 322   Surrenders of Monasteries
    Ancient Deeds
E 326   Series B
E 327   Series BX
E 329   Series BS

Exchequer, First Fruits and Tenths Office
E 331   Bishops' Certificates of Institutions to Benefices

Exchequer, Lord Treasurer's Remembrancer's and Pipe Offices
E 358   Miscellaneous Accounts, Pipe Office
E 372   Pipe Rolls
E 377   Recusant Rolls, Pipe Office Series

Home Office
H.O. 129   Census Papers, Ecclesiastical Returns

Justices Itinerant etc.
J.I. 1   Eyre Rolls, Assize Rolls, etc.

Court of King's Bench (Crown Side)
K.B. 26   Curia Regis Rolls
K.B. 27   Coram Rege Rolls

Exchequer, Office of the Auditors of Land Revenue
L.R. 2   Miscellaneous Books

Privy Council Office
P.C. 2   Registers

Court of Requests
Req. 2   Proceedings

Special Collections
S.C. 1   Ancient Correspondence
S.C. 6   Ministers' Accounts
S.C. 12   Rentals and Surveys, Portfolios

State Paper Office
    State Papers Domestic and Foreign
S.P. 1   Hen. VIII, General Series
S.P. 7   Wriothesley Papers
    State Papers Domestic
S.P. 12   Eliz. I
S.P. 14   Jas. I
S.P. 16   Chas. I

Court of Star Chamber
Sta. Cha. 2   Proceedings, Hen. VIII

CLASSES OF OFFICIAL DOCUMENTS IN THE STAFFORDSHIRE RECORD OFFICE
USED IN THIS VOLUME

Court of Quarter Sessions

Q/SO	Sessions Order Books, main series
Q/SR	Sessions Rolls

CLASSES OF DOCUMENTS IN THE LICHFIELD JOINT RECORD OFFICE
FORMERLY IN THE LICHFIELD DIOCESAN REGISTRY AND USED IN THIS VOLUME

Archdeacons' Visitation Records

A/V/1	Visitation Books

Bishop's Administrative Records

B/A/1	Bishops' Registers
B/A/3	Presentation Deeds and Grants of Advowson
B/A/4	Subscription Books and Papers
B/A/9	Non-residence Licences and Papers
B/A/13	Benefice Papers
B/A/17	Miscellaneous Parliamentary Returns (including clergy taxation)

Bishop's Court Records

B/C/1 and 2	Consistory Court Books
B/C/5	Consistory Court Cause Papers
B/C/10	Consistory Court Probate Act Books

Bishop's Visitation Records

B/V/1	Visitation Books
B/V/5	Primary Visitation Parish Returns and Churchwardens' Presentments to Articles of Inquiry

Dean and Chapter Court Records

DC/C/1	Court Books

NOTE ON ABBREVIATIONS

Among the abbreviations and short titles used the following may require elucidation:

B.A.A.	Birmingham Archdiocesan Archives, Archbishop's House, Birmingham
C.C.	Church Commissioners
C.R.S.	*Catholic Record Society*
D. & C. Lich.	Dean and Chapter of Lichfield
Dugdale, *Warws.*	W. Dugdale, *The Antiquities of Warwickshire* (1730 edn.)
E.E.T.S.	Early English Text Society
Erdeswick, *Staffs.*	S. Erdeswick, *A Survey of Staffordshire*, ed. T. Harwood (1844)
Handbk. of Brit. Chron.	*Handbook of British Chronology*, ed. F. M. Powicke and E. B. Fryde (2nd edn.)
Harwood, *Lichfield*	T. Harwood, *The History and Antiquities of the Church and City of Lichfield* (1806)
Hibbert, *Dissolution*	F. A. Hibbert, *The Dissolution of the Monasteries, as illustrated by the suppression of the religious houses of Staffordshire* (1910)
Lich. Dioc. Regy.	Lichfield Diocesan Registry
S.H.C.	Staffordshire Record Society (formerly William Salt Archaeological Society), *Collections for a History of Staffordshire*
S.R.O.	Staffordshire Record Office
Shaw, *Staffs.*	Stebbing Shaw, *The History and Antiquities of Staffordshire* (2 vols., 1798, 1801)
Staffs. Cath. Hist.	*Staffordshire Catholic History* (the Journal of the Staffordshire Catholic History Society)
T.N.S.F.C.	North Staffordshire Field Club, *Transactions*
T.O.S.S.	Stafford Historical and Civic Society (formerly Old Stafford Society), *Transactions*
T.R.H.S.	Royal Historical Society, *Transactions*
W.S.L.	William Salt Library, Stafford
Wilkins, *Concilia*	*Concilia Magnae Britanniae et Hiberniae*, ed. D. Wilkins (1737)

ANALYSIS OF SOURCES

PRINTED IN

COLLECTIONS FOR A HISTORY OF STAFFORDSHIRE

(STAFFORDSHIRE RECORD SOCIETY)

AND USED IN THIS VOLUME

ANALYSIS OF SOURCES

ANALYSIS OF SOURCES

THE MEDIEVAL CHURCH

I

THE continuous history of Christianity in Staffordshire seems to begin no earlier than 653. It has been surmised[1] that the population of this part of the country was largely British in the early 7th century, but there is no evidence, apart from the place-name Eccleshall, to show that it was Christian.[2] In 653, however, Peada, sub-king of Middle Anglia, married the daughter of Oswiu, King of Northumbria, a match which was permitted only on condition that Peada and his subjects became Christian.[3] And so half a century after Augustine's mission arrived in England the Midlands were infiltrated by their first recorded evangelists, but from Northumbria and the Celtic Church, not from Kent and Rome.

With his wife and his newly converted retinue Peada brought back to his Midland territory four missionaries, three of them English and one, Diuma, an Irishman. The adjoining region of Mercia, kingdom of his father Penda, was probably visited by some of these men or their assistants, for, though Penda was a pagan, Bede records that he raised no obstacles to missionaries in his land. The proselytizing activities in Mercia must have increased when Peada succeeded his father as king in 654, and still more on Peada's own death in 656 when Mercia came under the direct control of his father-in-law, Oswiu of Northumbria. It was by Oswiu's command that Diuma was ordained first bishop of the Middle Angles, the Lindisfaras and the Mercians; he was thus responsible for a region extending from the Lincolnshire coast to Warwickshire and Worcestershire and from the Humber to the Severn. Diuma's tenure was fruitful but brief, as was that of his successor, Ceollach, also an Irishman, who soon retired to Iona. It may be that Ceollach's departure was less voluntary than Bede implies, for it seems to have occurred about 657 when Northumbrian political control of Mercia was terminated by Wulfhere, Peada's brother; certainly Ceollach was not Wulfhere's bishop, and his successor, Trumhere, was appointed by the new king. Perhaps as a further sign of independence Trumhere was the first English bishop of this region, though ordained in the Celtic Church.[4] Some time before 665 Trumhere had been succeeded by Jaruman who in that year was described as Bishop of the Mercians and was sent by Wulfhere to recover the lapsed East Saxons for the Church; in this his tact and tireless travelling, which ensured success, suggest a Celtic training, if not a Celtic origin.[5] Jaruman lived until 667,[6] but even before this another bishop had been simultaneously at work in Mercia, Wilfrid of York.

For the first ten years of its Christian history Mercia had been dominated by bishops and missionaries who were either Celtic-born or Celtic-trained, men whose notions of ecclesiastical organization and customs derived from Bishop Finan and ultimately,

[1] H. P. R. Finberg, *Lucerna*, 5, 73, 75.

[2] W. H. C. Frend, 'The Christianization of Roman Britain,' *Christianity in Britain 300–700*, ed. M. W. Barley and R. F. C. Hanson, 37–49; K. Cameron, 'Eccles in English Place-Names', ibid. 87–92. The theory that there was a Christian community at Wall in late-Roman times (*S.H.C.* 1950–1, 144–5) is based on an erroneous interpretation of a Welsh poem: J. Gould, '*Letocetum:* the name of the Roman settlement at Wall, Staffs.' *Trans. Lichfield and S. Staffs. Arch. & Hist. Soc.* v. 52.

[3] Bede, *Historia Ecclesiastica*, bk. iii, chap. xxi.

[4] Ibid. chaps. xxi, xxiv.

[5] Ibid. chap. xxx.

[6] *Handbk. of Brit. Chron.* 242.

I

through Aidan, from Columba. Perhaps the Celtic background of the missionaries commended the new religion in an area where British survival may have been significant and where, it has been speculated,[7] even the royal dynasty may have had British origins. It is hard to discern what the missionaries achieved during this decade, apart from the conversion of the people. We know of no Celtic monasteries in Staffordshire at this date, but then we know of Repton in neighbouring Derbyshire only because it enclosed St. Guthlac and was therefore celebrated by his biographer; other houses, still to be identified, were doubtless established by this date.[8] That the diocese was vast and lacked an episcopal seat is clear.

At the end of this decade the synod of Whitby (663 or 664) reconciled the Celtic Church in England to Roman uses. Wulfhere, who had married a Kentish princess and may even have been himself baptized at Canterbury, was perhaps aware of the synod's conclusions and troubled by Jaruman's orders and outlook. He induced Wilfrid, the Roman champion at Whitby, to fulfil various episcopal functions in Mercia at intervals between 666 and 669; moreover, in his eagerness to assist the work of the reform movement and for the good of his soul, he gave Wilfrid many lands 'on which he soon established monasteries'.[9] Indeed it is likely that most of the estates which belonged to the bishopric in the 11th century were given by Wulfhere to Wilfrid or to Jaruman's successor, Chad. This is probable both from Wulfhere's known generosity to them[10] and from the proximity of the episcopal estates to the royal estates out of which they had evidently been carved;[11] unfortunately no extant charters record these donations. Among them was Lichfield, soon to become at Wilfrid's suggestion the seat of the bishopric.[12]

In 669 Archbishop Theodore appointed Wilfrid to the see of York, from which he had just deposed Chad for irregular consecration. Impressed by Chad's humility and confronted by a request from Wulfhere for a successor to the recently deceased Jaruman, Theodore appointed Chad as Bishop of Mercia and Lindsey.[13] It would be rash to see unequivocal evidence of Chad's missionary journeys in churches dedicated to him (as at Barton Blount and Longford in Derbyshire) or in place-names which recall his memory (like Chadkirk in Cheshire and Chadwick in Lancashire), but they may represent local recollections of his pastoral visits.[14] Characteristically, when free from preaching and other duties, Chad used to withdraw to a retreat near the church at Lichfield with several companions to pray and study.[15] He died in 672 and was buried at Lichfield, close to the church of St. Mary. When St. Peter's was built 28 years later, Chad's bones were transferred there and wrought miracles which, with his life, won for him a renown denied to all his successors.[16] In his combination of austerity and humility he surpassed, in these pre-eminently Celtic virtues, all his predecessors, though ironically he was the first Mercian bishop to acknowledge the authority of Canterbury.

Chad was succeeded as Bishop of Mercia, Middle Anglia, and Lindsey by Wynfrith who had been his deacon *non pauco tempore*. Wynfrith, however, was soon deposed by Theodore for disobedience.[17] A proposal to increase the number of bishoprics was discussed at the synod of Hertford in 672, and it was at this same council or within the

---

[7] Nora K. Chadwick, *Celt and Saxon*, 336.

[8] *Felix's Life of St. Guthlac*, ed. B. Colgrave, 84, 178; *The Life of Bishop Wilfrid by Eddius Stephanus*, ed. B. Colgrave, chap. li.

[9] *Life of Wilfrid*, chaps. xiv, li; and see below n. 27. For monasteries which have been associated with Wulfhere and his family see below pp. 135, 240.

[10] He had given Chad extensive lands at 'Adbarwe',

possibly Barrow (Lincs.): Bede, *Hist. Eccles.* bk. iv, chap. iii; *V.C.H. Lincs.* ii. 2.

[11] *V.C.H. Staffs.* iv. 8.   [12] *Life of Wilfrid*, chap. xv.

[13] Bede, *Hist. Eccles.* bk. iv, chaps. ii, iii.

[14] *V.C.H. Derb.* ii. 2; *V.C.H. Warws.* ii. 1.

[15] See below p. 135.

[16] Bede, *Hist. Eccles.* bk. iv, chap. iii; see below p. 140.

[17] Bede, *Hist. Eccles.* bk. iv, chaps. iii, vi.

next three years that Wynfrith was expelled from his see.[18] The common assumption that he was in fact deposed for resisting the division of the diocese is difficult to sustain, since the diocese was not divided on his departure, whenever that was, but remained intact effectively until about 679. In his place was appointed Seaxwulf, who may have been a Middle Anglian since Bede regarded him as *constructor et abbas* of Medeshampstede (the later Peterborough);[19] before he died (about 691–2) the diocese was divided and truncated. In 678 Eadhed was appointed the first Bishop of Lindsey, which had recently been severed from Mercia by Northumbria.[20] When, however, Ethelred of Mercia recovered Lindsey about 679, Theodore translated Eadhed to Ripon and reunited Lindsey to Mercia under Seaxwulf.[21] Meanwhile Hereford had probably already been taken from the Mercian diocese, although there is no secure evidence for this. After Ethelred's ravaging of Rochester and other Kentish monasteries in 676 Seaxwulf granted to Putta, the ejected Bishop of Rochester, some land and a church where he lived out his days serving God and teaching divine songs. Although Bede does not credit Putta with a see in Mercia,[22] the much later appendix to Florence of Worcester places him first in the list of bishops of Hereford, and the third of his successors, Wahlstod, is named by Bede as Bishop of Hereford in 731.[23] It thus seems likely that Putta became Bishop of Hereford only when the Mercian diocese was severally divided.

The appendix to Florence of Worcester's chronicle records that Mercia was divided in 679 into the five sees of Lichfield, Lindsey, Leicester, Worcester, and Dorchester. This source, however, is alone in recording this division; moreover it omits Hereford, includes Dorchester, and confuses the holders of Lichfield and Leicester. These errors, quite apart from the chronicle's remoteness from the events, may raise doubts about the other parts of the story — not least the simultaneous creation of five sees.[24] Nevertheless, although this is nowhere confirmed by Bede or the Anglo-Saxon Chronicle, it is nowhere impugned by their information. Moreover the statement in the appendix to Florence that Theodore created one of these sees in response to a request from Ethelred of Mercia and Oshere, sub-king of the Hwicci,[25] better accords with the realities of ecclesiastical politics at that time than the view that Theodore was the guiding force. From about 679 until the Viking disruptions a regular succession of bishops can be established for each of those sees except Leicester and Dorchester, both of which are omitted from Bede's list of sees and their holders in 731. It seems that when Cuthwine of Leicester died at some uncertain date the see of the Middle Anglians was reunited with that of the Mercians under Seaxwulf.[26] Then in 692 Wilfrid, again in exile from Northumbria, returned to familiar territory and to the protection of his friend, King Ethelred, and served as Bishop of the Middle Anglians for a number of years, probably until about 702 when he departed for Rome.[27] Headda, who had succeeded Seaxwulf as Bishop of the Mercians, then assumed control of Leicester as well and in this capacity visited and consecrated the oratory of St. Guthlac at Crowland.[28] No separate bishop of Leicester is heard of again until 737.[29] Why Leicester

---

[18] For the detailed and conflicting sources see A. W. Haddan and W. Stubbs, *Councils and Eccles. Documents*, iii. 118–22, 127–30.

[19] Bede, *Hist. Eccles.* bk. iv, chap. vi.

[20] *Anglo-Saxon Chron.* ed. Dorothy Whitelock, D. C. Douglas, and S. I. Tucker, 22.

[21] Bede, *Hist. Eccles.* bk. iv, chap. xii; *Monumenta Historica Britannica*, ed. H. Petrie and J. Sharpe, i. 624.

[22] Bede, *Hist. Eccles.* bk. iv, chap. xii.

[23] Ibid. bk. v, chap. xxiii; *Mon. Hist. Brit.* i. 621.

[24] *Mon. Hist. Brit.* i. 622; Haddan and Stubbs, *Councils*, iii. 129. [25] *Mon. Hist. Brit.* i. 624.

[26] Bede, *Hist. Eccles.* bk. v, chap. xxiii. For a different interpretation of the evidence relating to Cuthwine see R. I. Page, 'Anglo-Saxon Episcopal Lists', *Nottingham Medieval Studies*, ix. 92–93.

[27] A chronology of Wilfrid's life is given in *Venerabilis Baedae Opera Historica*, ed. C. Plummer, ii. 316–20.

[28] Felix's *Life of St. Guthlac*, 142–3. But see *Nottingham Medieval Studies*, ix. 92–93.

[29] Haddan and Stubbs, *Councils*, iii. 129.

should suffer this fate may be explicable only by inscrutable personal reasons; political affairs certainly shed no light on it. Dorchester seems to have been created in recognition of Mercia's advance to the Thames and to have vanished with the recovery of that area by Wessex;[30] no holder of the see is known between about 660 and the 9th century when the bishop of Leicester fled there from the Danes.

About 679, therefore, and more by royal instigation than archiepiscopal initiative, the great see of Mercia had been shorn of its farther members and now comprised the centre of that extensive kingdom.[31] By the middle of the 8th century the bishopric of Lichfield had been reduced to boundaries probably not unlike those which defined it in the later Middle Ages; vastly curtailed, it was still an immense diocese, covering Derbyshire, Staffordshire, and Cheshire and spilling over into Warwickshire and Shropshire; when the area between the Ribble and the Mersey was wrested from Northumbria about 923, it too was added to the Lichfield diocese.[32]

About the disposition of churches within these boundaries, still less within Staffordshire, we know little. The church of St. Mary at Lichfield and the later church of St. Peter there have been mentioned above.[33] None of the numerous monasteries endowed for Wilfrid by Wulfhere[34] has ever been located; the only religious houses of the period in Staffordshire are the doubtfully attested foundations at Burton and Stone and the nunnery at Hanbury.[35] In the 8th century, when Bede has stopped writing and the Anglo-Saxon Chronicle is more interested in, and more knowledgeable about, Wessex affairs, our knowledge of the Church in Staffordshire is still more sporadic and thin. Even in the time of Offa information becomes considerable, though still remarkably defective, only on the controversial elevation of Lichfield into an archbishopric.

In 787, at a council at Chelsea, amid much discord Offa deprived Jaenberht, Archbishop of Canterbury, of part of his province or jurisdiction and chose Hygeberht, until then merely Bishop of Lichfield, to exercise metropolitical authority over the severed portion. In seeking papal approval for this move and a pallium for the new Archbishop of Lichfield, Offa represented to Pope Hadrian I that this was the unanimous wish of the English, the land being so vast and the province of Canterbury, therefore, so impracticable.[36] That this was a lie is apparent not only from the Anglo-Saxon Chronicle which calls the synod 'contentious', but also from the statement of the next King of Mercia, Cenwulf, that Offa created a new province because he hated Jaenberht and the Kentish people. The fierce hostility of Kent to Offa's ambitions and its proximity to his enemy, Charlemagne, easily explain and confirm Cenwulf's assertion,[37] but the version of that late and dubious source, the 'Vita Offae' of St. Albans, that Jaenberht had promised Charles and his forces a favourable reception in the south-east, while it adds point to Cenwulf's claim, is clearly trying to establish a worthy case for one who was the founder of St. Albans.[38] That Hadrian I accepted Offa's statement suggests that the papal legates, George and Theophylact, who were then in England, were not present at the Chelsea synod, or they would surely have disabused him.[39] In 788 Hygeberht received his pallium and duly changed his title from bishop to archbishop when witnessing charters.[40] How wide his province was is known only

---

[30] See the suggestions in *Venerabilis Baedae Opera Historica*, ed. Plummer, ii. 245–6.

[31] The assertion of a 14th-cent. writer that Mercia was divided into 5 sees only in 724 (H. Wharton, *Anglia Sacra*, i. 427–8) does not bear scrutiny.

[32] *V.C.H. Lancs.* i. 270; *Anglo-Saxon Chron.* ed. Whitelock, Douglas, and Tucker, 67.

[33] See above p. 2; see also below p. 140.

[34] See above p. 2.

[35] See below pp. 135, 199, 240. T. Tanner, *Notitia Monastica*, gives the nunnery supposedly founded by St. Modwen at 'Streneshale' (Dugdale, *Mon.* ii. 365) as in Staffs. but makes no mention of her association with an early house at Burton.

[36] Haddan and Stubbs, *Councils*, iii. 523–5.

[37] Ibid. 521–3.

[38] J. W. Lamb, *Archbishopric of Lichfield*, 14–15.

[39] But see Haddan and Stubbs, *Councils*, iii. 443–6. [40] Ibid.

from William of Malmesbury, who managed to confuse the holders of the sees, and from the derivative 'Vita Offae';[41] if any confidence can be placed in these, the Thames and the Humber separated the province of Lichfield from those of Canterbury and York.

In 792 Jaenberht died and was replaced by a Mercian abbot, Æthelheard, who was consecrated by Hygeberht in 793.[42] Hygeberht continued to appear in charters as Archbishop of Lichfield until 799,[43] but already his authority was being undermined. Offa had died in 796, and during the following two years his successor Cenwulf, admitting Offa's base motives, was seeking to transfer the archbishopric from Lichfield to London, in conformity with Gregory I's original scheme; but Pope Leo III, while doubting the metropolitan authority of Lichfield, refused to countenance that of London.[44] In addition to this, Æthelheard, consecrated Archbishop of Canterbury by Hygeberht, was also seeking ways of abolishing the archbishopric of Lichfield. About 797 he sought the advice of Alcuin and was urged to consult his fellow bishops and the Archbishop of York and so to arrange things that, while Hygeberht (not mentioned by name) should keep his pallium, the consecration of bishops should revert to Canterbury.[45] That Æthelheard appears in five charters between 793 and 796 alongside other bishops, but without Hygeberht, is hardly evidence that he was intent at that time on diminishing the authority of Lichfield,[46] for only one of those charters has more than four other episcopal witnesses.[47] Hygeberht's absence, therefore, need not be sinister, especially since he continued to witness charters as archbishop from 794 until 799.[48] The professions of obedience made by diocesan bishops to Archbishop Æthelheard,[49] the earliest known, certainly derive from Canterbury's anxiety about his authority, but they are not dated and seem more likely to follow from, rather than to precede, Alcuin's advice. They cannot plausibly be dated earlier than 798 and may well have been made after Æthelheard had been to Rome and back in 801–2,[50] though even before that time Leo III's doubts about Lichfield's primacy were probably well known. A charter dated 801 which describes Hygeberht merely as a bishop and includes his successor, also described as bishop, among its witnesses is known only from a late-14th-century copy and is therefore a dubious guide to the events of the 9th century.[51] All that is certain is that as a result of a visit by Æthelheard to Rome Leo III in 802 issued a decree restoring all the rights of Canterbury as its archbishop enjoyed them in 787; no doubt the details of this reorganization were conveyed to Æthelheard verbally, for Leo's decree is otherwise extraordinarily brief.[52] In the following year in a synod at Clovesho, attended by all the prelates and presided over by Cenwulf, the archbishopric of Lichfield was solemnly and publicly dismantled, the original papal grant being condemned and abrogated; and among other signatories of this act was an Abbot Hygeberht.[53] Lichfield was never again so important ecclesiastically, but then never again was Mercia so influential politically.

The 9th century saw the political eclipse of Mercia, weakened by succession

[41] Ibid. 446–7; Wilkins, *Concilia*, i. 152.

[42] W. Levison, *Eng. and the Continent in the Eighth Cent.* 244–5.   [43] Haddan and Stubbs, *Councils*, iii. 443–6.

[44] Ibid. 501–3, 523–5.

[45] Ibid. 518–20; *Eng. Hist. Docs.* i, ed. Dorothy Whitelock, 788–90. Although these two differ on the date, the first preferring 798 and the second 797, the advice was clearly given during Æthelheard's exile from Canterbury and Kent 796–8 since it urges him to return to his see (see below n. 50).

[46] As Lamb, *Archbishopric of Lichfield*, 26–29, thinks.

[47] *Cart. Sax.* ed. Birch, i, pp. 369–71, 379, 387, 388–9.

[48] Haddan and Stubbs, *Councils*, iii. 443–6.

[49] viz. Lindsey, Dunwich, Hereford, Worcester, and Sherborne: ibid. 506–7, 511, 525, 528–30.

[50] Ibid. 533–4. Æthelheard was in exile from 796 to 798 as a result of the Kentish revolt against Mercian rule: F. M. Stenton, *Anglo-Saxon Eng.* (2nd edn.), 223–4. Stenton (ibid. 226–7) favours 798 as the date of the earliest of the professions; Levison, *Eng. and the Continent in the Eighth Cent.* 20, and J. Godfrey, in *Studies in Church Hist.* i, ed. C. W. Dugmore and C. Duggan, 149, prefer 796.

[51] Haddan and Stubbs, *Councils*, iii. 531. Lamb, *Archbishopric of Lichfield*, 36, argues the existence of a coadjutor bishop from this evidence.

[52] Haddan and Stubbs, *Councils*, iii. 536–7.   [53] Ibid. 542–4.

problems, truncated by the Northumbrians and then by the Danes. The Danes were at Nottingham in 868, and in 874 they expelled Burgred from his kingdom and replaced him by a puppet, Ceolwulf; in the 890s they three times traversed Mercia and probably Staffordshire.[54] Although this had some important political consequences, in other ways Mercia flourished: in the early part of this century Mercian sculpture achieved a distinguished maturity, while Lichfield, like Evesham and Worcester, is believed to have been a notable literary centre; and it was from Mercia that Alfred drew such scholars and reformers as Plegmund.[55] According to a 14th-century writer, it was during this period, in 822, that the community at Lichfield was organized as a body of canons under a provost. Though this accords with the 8th-century scheme of Chrode-gang of Metz for cathedrals, it is unsupported in Anglo-Saxon records, and such a community had certainly vanished before 1066.[56] It is difficult to complete the episcopal succession for the later part of the century and indeed until the reign of Athelstan (924–39); yet it is by no means sure that the continuity was in fact broken, though Staffordshire was certainly a battleground during that time.

During the next century there is evidence in Staffordshire of the religious fervour seen elsewhere in England at that period. Despite frequent campaigns in the West Midlands in the earlier and late 10th century and early in the next,[57] the county seems to have escaped the worst afflictions of warfare and shows signs, ecclesiastically, of consolidation. The communities at Gnosall, Penkridge, Stafford, Tamworth, Tetten-hall, and Wolverhampton probably all originated in the 10th century;[58] Burton Abbey was founded just after the year 1000.[59] It may be that some of the monastic foundations of Æthelwold, which were attacked and dispersed in 975 by Alfhere, Ealdorman of Mercia,[60] were located in Staffordshire, but there is no confirmation of this. Elsewhere in the county there are a number of stone crosses, which have been variously assigned to the 9th and 10th centuries. In six instances, at Checkley, Leek, Ilam, Heaton, Swythamley, and Alstonefield, they may indicate late-Saxon centres of worship other-wise unrecorded.[61]

By 1086 there were probably 40 churches in Staffordshire. Besides the cathedral at Lichfield and the communities of priests noted above, Domesday Book implies 25 churches in the county;[62] the evidence of sculptured crosses perhaps adds six more. In addition monasteries had been founded at Burton and probably Tutbury. The recorded priests seem to be distributed in proportion to the population. In this thinly peopled county with its extremes, on the one hand, of unproductive gritstone uplands, forest, and gorse, and, on the other hand, of rich claylands and fertile river valleys, Christianity was by now firmly rooted. At Lichfield a cathedral already four hundred years old housed five canons, not yet a chapter, and was endowed with lands in several counties, extensive enough to support the bishop and his church. If it was among the poorest bishoprics in the country in 1066, its bishops were far from indigent.[63]

[54] *Anglo-Saxon Chron.* ed. Whitelock, Douglas, and Tucker, 46, 48, 56, 57.

[55] L. Stone, *Sculpture in Brit. in the Middle Ages*, 21–25; D. Talbot Rice, *Eng. Art 871–1100*, 87–89, who is much less sure about the date of the sculpture; R. Vleeskruyer, *The Life of St. Chad* (Amsterdam, 1953), 40–41, 44, 51–61; Margaret Rickert, *Painting in Brit. in the Middle Ages*, 16–17; Stenton, *Anglo-Saxon Eng.* 268.

[56] See below p. 140.

[57] *Anglo-Saxon Chron.* ed. Whitelock, Douglas, and Tucker, 59, 64, 66–67, 71, 80, 94, 96.

[58] See below pp. 298, 303, 309–10, 315–16, 321; *V.C.H. Staffs.* iv. 128.

[59] See below p. 199.

[60] *Anglo-Saxon Chron.* ed. Whitelock, Douglas, and Tucker, 78.

[61] T. Pape, 'The Round-Shafted Pre-Norman Crosses of the N. Staffs. Area', *T.N.S.F.C.* lxxx; T. Pape, 'The Rectangular-Shafted Pre-Norman Crosses of N. Staffs.' *T.N.S.F.C.* lxxxi; S. A. Jeavons, 'Anglo-Saxon Cross Shafts in Staffs.' *Trans. Birm. Arch. Soc.* lxvi; H. M. Taylor, 'Anglo-Saxon Architecture and Sculpture in Staffs.' *N. Staffs. Jnl. of Field Studies*, vi. 7, 10 n. 1; Stone, *Sculpture in Brit.* 239; Talbot Rice, *Eng. Art 871–1100*, 138.

[62] See *S.H.C.* 1916, 186 sqq.; *V.C.H. Staffs.* iv. 20, 24. The figures exclude Alveley and Worfield, then in Staffs, but now in Salop.

[63] See below pp. 15, 18.

The last Anglo-Saxon bishop of Lichfield was a very different character from the first. Leofwine, appointed in 1053, had been Abbot of Coventry, and he had a wife and children. He had the misfortune to live on into a more demanding age; summoned to a legatine council in 1070 to answer charges about his family, he refused to appear, and after excommunication resigned his see to the king as a last act of defiance.[64] Archbishop Lanfranc committed the oversight of Lichfield to Wulfstan, Bishop of Worcester; this was done no doubt as much for political as for ecclesiastical reasons, since Wulfstan was a collaborating Saxon and the area was regarded as remote and intransigent.[65]

II

Wulfstan's biographer believed that the diocese covered only Shropshire, Cheshire and Staffordshire,[66] but in this he was either ignorant of ecclesiastical geography or was recording a transitory arrangement. It would not have been difficult for Wulfstan during his administration of the see to annex to his own diocese the Lichfield territory in Warwickshire, but it is unlikely. Indeed it is most improbable that the boundaries changed at all between their advance to the Ribble about 923 and the severance of the archdeaconry of Chester in 1541, but a long and now inscrutable process of definition must have taken place as the area was sown with parish churches and monastic houses. In 1236, for example, papal delegates were ordered to define the recently disputed limits of the three sees of Coventry and Lichfield, Worcester, and St. Asaph.[67] The dispute with Worcester was no doubt the one solved by a papal decree in 1238 which declared that the whole of Dudley and its churches and their lands were within Worcester diocese but that the site of the castle and the priory were in Staffordshire and belonged to the jurisdiction of the Bishop of Coventry and Lichfield.[68] The point of conflict with St. Asaph can only be deduced, and perhaps not accurately, from the complaint in 1282 that the Bishop of St. Asaph was illegally confirming children and performing other episcopal functions within the diocese of Coventry and Lichfield, an encroachment which in that year may well have been connected with Llewelyn's revolt and probably concerned the parts of Lichfield diocese in Flintshire and Denbighshire.[69] In the next century the diocese clearly comprised Staffordshire, Cheshire, Derbyshire, part of Warwickshire (including Coventry), part of Shropshire, and Lancashire south of the Ribble.[70]

If the shape of the diocese remained stable throughout the later Middle Ages, the location of the episcopal see has a much more complicated history. In 1075 Lanfranc, in accord with his policy of transferring bishoprics to important centres, moved the see from Lichfield, which half a century later was described as *villa exigua*,[71] to the substantial town of Chester,[72] where the bishop already had considerable property.[73] In 1085 Robert de Limesey became bishop,[74] and in 1102, *secularibus intentus magis quam divinis*,[75] he moved the see yet again, this time to Coventry, solely, according to one chronicler, in order to appropriate the wealth of that abbey.[76] His act may have been prompted rather by the turbulent state of Cheshire.[77] Yet even before this, and soon

[64] F. Barlow, *The Eng. Church 1000–1066*, 218–19.
[65] William of Malmesbury, *Vita Wulfstani* (Camd. Soc. 3rd ser. xl), 26.
[66] Ibid.
[67] *S.H.C.* 1924, p. 186; *Cal. Papal Regs.* i. 150.
[68] *Annales Monastici* (Rolls Ser.), iv. 429; *V.C.H. Worcs.* ii. 159–60.
[69] *S.H.C.* 1924, p. 186; G. Ormerod, *Hist. of the County Palatine and City of Chester* (1882 edn.), i. 108.
[70] *Eulogium Historiarum* (Rolls Ser.), ii. 180.

[71] William of Malmesbury, *De Gestis Pontificum Anglorum* (Rolls Ser.), 307.
[72] Wharton, *Anglia Sacra*, i. 433.
[73] See below p. 15.
[74] *Anglo-Saxon Chron.* ed. Whitelock, Douglas, and Tucker, 161.
[75] *Ann. Mon.* ii. 223.
[76] Malmesbury, *De Gestis Pontificum*, 309–10.
[77] *The Church in Chester, 1300–1540* (Chetham Soc. 3rd Ser. vii), 4–5.

after his election to the see, Robert had been reproved by Lanfranc for oppressing the monks of Coventry,[78] and William of Malmesbury gives a detailed account of the bishop's plundering of Coventry's abundant possessions.[79] While the date of this transfer is uncertain,[80] the papal bull of approbation is dated 1102,[81] and it may well be that the diocesan business which Robert conducted in Rome that year, while he was there for the king against Anselm, concerned this matter.[82] The see continued to be located at Coventry under his two successors, Robert Peche (1121–6) and Roger de Clinton (1129–48), but these two each contributed to the resurgence of Lichfield; the first began the rebuilding of the cathedral church, the latter apparently completed the work and also established a chapter at Lichfield on Norman lines.[83] When Coventry Priory was destroyed and converted into a castle by Robert Marmion about 1143,[84] a temporary migration of the see to Lichfield may well have occurred; there is, however, no evidence to corroborate this beyond Clinton's fortification of the castle at Lichfield and his strengthening of the town's defences.[85]

Despite their claims on Coventry and their interest in Lichfield, Peche and Clinton, like Limesey, thought of themselves as bishops of Chester; the next bishop, Walter Durdent (1149–59), a Benedictine, was the first to use the title Coventry, and he used no other. More than this, perhaps prompted by the challenge of the newly established chapter at Lichfield to Coventry's primacy, he secured from Eugenius III in 1152 confirmation of Paschal II's original approval of the move to Coventry.[86] In view of his own monastic career at Christ Church, Canterbury, Durdent's preference for the Benedictine house at Coventry, where he was buried in 1160, is hardly surprising.[87] Yet under his secular successors, Richard Peche, Gerard Pucelle, and even Hugh de Nonant, who replaced the monks at Coventry by secular canons and codified the statutes and endowed the deanery of the Lichfield chapter, no attempt was made to shift the see or change the title.[88]

But Coventry's claim to pre-eminence was unlikely to survive long against the claims of Lichfield. Lichfield was conveniently situated for the administration of the diocese. In addition it was the centre of a large episcopal estate, and this became more important as the relations of Coventry Priory and the bishop were more closely defined.[89] To the administrative argument was added that of tradition, for the church of Lichfield housed the shrine of St. Chad, had enjoyed five centuries' precedence in the diocese and was four centuries older than Coventry. The challenge to Coventry's primacy was developed with growing vigour by the new Lichfield chapter's persistent and resolute claim to participate in, though not to conduct exclusively, the election of the bishop. These electoral claims of Lichfield, which had been bitterly resented and grudgingly conceded by the monks and tacitly acknowledged and cynically exploited by the Crown since the 1160s or at least the 1180s, received *de jure* recognition in 1228. How this occurred has never been fully told.

The first recorded canonical election to the see was in 1149 when Durdent succeeded Clinton. Of his Anglo-Norman predecessors the first, Peter, was a royal courtier

[78] *Regesta Regum Anglo-Normannorum*, ed. H. W. C. Davis, i. 73.

[79] E. A. Freeman, *Norman Conquest*, iv. 420, declares that Rob.'s arrival at Coventry 'partook strongly of the nature of a raid or storm'.

[80] 1100 in *Ann. Mon.* ii. 40; less precisely as Hen. I's time ibid. 223; 1095 in the 14th-cent. Lichfield source printed in Wharton, *Anglia Sacra*, i. 434.

[81] Joan C. Lancaster, 'The Coventry Forged Charters', *Bull. Inst. Hist. Res.* xxvii. 134.

[82] *Ann. Mon.* ii. 41; Eadmer, *Hist. Novorum in Anglia* (Rolls Ser.), 131–2.

[83] See below pp. 141, 143.

[84] John de Oxenedes, *Chronica* (Rolls Ser.), 53.

[85] Wharton, *Anglia Sacra*, i. 434.

[86] *S.H.C.* 1924, pp. 126–7.

[87] A. Saltman, *Archbp. Theobald*, 57–59, 288–9, 447–9, 535–8; Wharton, *Anglia Sacra*, i. 434.

[88] The statement in *D.N.B.* that Peche moved the see back to Chester in 1175 lacks both probability and evidence and is at best a misinterpretation of a brief sojourn there for part of that year.

[89] See below pp. 18–20.

rewarded by the king with the see of Lichfield in 1072;[90] Robert de Limesey, a royal clerk, was appointed at a synod of the archbishop and clerics, following the Christmas court at Gloucester in 1085;[91] Robert Peche's appointment was conducted in a manner unrecorded, but as he had previously been an official of the royal household,[92] it is unlikely that the canons of Chester or the monks of Coventry were involved; and Clinton is reputed to have bought the see for 3,000 marks.[93] Clearly the efforts of Anselm and the compromise of 1107 had had very little effect on the manner in which the bishops of this see were chosen. It is therefore a measure of the changes un-obtrusively wrought in Stephen's reign that an undeniably canonical election occurred in 1149, though the fact that the choice fell upon Durdent, who had been Theobald's protégé and servant in the diocese of Canterbury,[94] might suggest that the wishes of the primate bore heavily upon the electors; it is even possible that Theobald offered them the chance to establish their right to elect in return for nominating his candidate.

It is indisputable that in 1149 there was an election by a local chapter, but who in fact could and did elect was a controverted point. By the mid 12th century there were three possible electoral bodies: the canons of Chester, the monks of Coventry, and, since Clinton had established a chapter there, the canons of Lichfield. The Chester canons had little claim to participate in an election in 1149, apart from the tenacity with which the bishops continued to use the style of Chester; only two bishops had had their see at Chester, and neither of them throughout his episcopate. The recently created chapter at Lichfield founded its claims on the cathedral's antiquity, but these were scarcely likely to prevail if no bishop had resided there since about 1100; and the evidence which suggests that Clinton may have temporarily deserted Coventry for Lichfield is inconclusive.[95] The 14th-century Lichfield account, therefore, which reports how Stephen licensed the monks of Coventry and the canons of Lichfield to proceed to an episcopal election and, when they failed to agree, gave the see to Durdent, requires cautious acceptance, if any.[96] A Coventry account of 1215 tells how the monks, summoned to Leicester by the archbishop, chose Durdent, and how, after the canons of Lichfield and Chester had appealed to the Pope against their exclusion, the Prior of Coventry himself travelled to Rome to secure the quashing of the appeal and the confirmation of Durdent's election.[97] It is unlikely that in 1149 anyone would have thought of inviting Chester and Lichfield to participate, and the 1215 account, although written in a polemical atmosphere, derives plausibility from the long lapse between Clinton's death and Durdent's consecration, delayed as that consecration must have been by an appeal.[98] That Lichfield had failed to share in the election seems probable from the statement in the same 1215 account that after enthronement at Coventry Durdent found the doors at Lichfield locked against him, whereupon he excommuni-cated the canons;[99] they may, however, merely have been protesting against his enthronement at Coventry first. Whatever their success it was improbable that the canons of Lichfield would neglect this chance, the first available, to press their claims, and once they did so Chester was unlikely to remain passive.

Of the election of his successor, Richard Peche, in 1161 there are two conflicting accounts, the Coventry one of 1215 baldly stating that he was elected by the prior and monks,[1] and the Lichfield and later one asserting that the canons and monks jointly

[90] Ann. Mon. i. 185; Wharton, Anglia Sacra, i. 433.
[91] Anglo-Saxon Chron. ed. Whitelock, Douglas, and Tucker, 161.
[92] Malmesbury, De Gestis Pontificum, 310–11; Eadmer, Hist. Nov. 293.
[93] Symeon of Durham, Historia Regum (Rolls Ser.), ii. 283.
[94] Saltman, Archbp. Theobald, passim.
[95] See above p. 8.
[96] Wharton, Anglia Sacra, i. 434.
[97] Dugdale, Mon. vi(3), 1242.
[98] See Saltman, Archbp. Theobald, 116, for the conson-ance of the archbp.'s itinerary with the Coventry version.
[99] Dugdale, Mon. vi(3), 1242.
[1] Ibid.

agreed on his election, *voluntate regis Henrici II mediante*.[2] The Lichfield report seems more circumstantial and more persuasive, with its claim to participation and not exclusive right, and with its reference to royal intervention; the Coventry source would obviously be eager to pass over in silence any successful assertion by Lichfield of its electoral claims. Moreover the procedure at the next election adds weight to the claims that Lichfield participated in this one. In 1183 the king while in France was reminded by the archbishop of some pressing vacancies, Coventry among them. Henry ordered the Dean and Chapter of Lichfield to send five or six of their canons, to Caen, sufficiently empowered to proceed to an election;[3] no doubt a similar mandate or invitation went to the monks of Coventry. Once again the Coventry tradition eschews all mention of the Lichfield participation,[4] while the Lichfield historian acknowledges the role of the monks.[5] He does, however, strain credulity by stating that the monks and canons elected Gerard Pucelle *concorditer*, though perhaps this was just possible in the presence of the king at Caen.

As with Pucelle, so with the election of his successor, Hugh de Nonant, in 1185. The Coventry source makes no mention of the canons.[6] The later Lichfield writer, however, asserts that the monks and canons elected jointly,[7] and his testimony is corroborated by a capitular letter to the king. This was in reply to his mandate to the chapter to send a delegation (in fact the dean and three canons) with full powers to represent it at an election in consultation with the king.[8] In view of the documentary silence about the part of the monks, it is suggestive of some integrity in the Lichfield writer that he did in fact report their participation. That the choice of candidate was entirely free, however, is cast in doubt by the testimony of Gervase of Canterbury,[9] by the resultant bishop's character and career, and by the common practice of that time.

About the election of the next bishop, Geoffrey Muschamp, in 1198 the best contemporary authority states that he was consecrated on 21 June at Canterbury by Archbishop Hubert Walter on petition and presentation by the Prior of Coventry, no mention being made of the canons of Lichfield.[10] Since this omission is to be found in a secular source we need not be surprised that the Coventry tradition ascribes electoral rights solely to the monks, stating that because Prior Joybert was sick and unable to travel two of the brethren were sent to the archbishop with letters empowering him to make the choice on Coventry's behalf.[11] Although the Lichfield author is alone in stating that the canons as well as the monks, at the archbishop's bidding, jointly elected Muschamp and gets the date and place of consecration wrong,[12] it is hard to believe that Lichfield had no share in this election. The Coventry source itself admits that the canons were present at the election, against the wishes of the monks, and takes the opportunity of attacking the rude behaviour of one of them, the Archdeacon of Stafford.[13] It does not, however, allow that they had any part in the election and attempts to show that Muschamp was elected against their wishes. It relates how at the consecration the prior refused to read his postulation while the canons were present and how they were then summarily ejected by order of the archbishop, who told them: 'Nolite impedire nos; satis audivimus protestationem vestram.'[14] The archbishop,

---

[2] Wharton, *Anglia Sacra*, i. 435.
[3] *S.H.C.* 1924, p. 181.
[4] Dugdale, *Mon.* vi(3), 1242.
[5] Wharton, *Anglia Sacra*, i. 435.
[6] Dugdale, *Mon.* vi(3), 1242.
[7] Wharton, *Anglia Sacra*, i. 435.
[8] *S.H.C.* 1924, p. 180.
[9] Gervase of Canterbury, *Opera Historica* (Rolls Ser.), i. 326.
[10] Ibid. 554, 556; Ralph de Diceto, *Opera Historica*

(Rolls Ser.), ii. 162–3.
[11] Dugdale, *Mon.* vi(3), 1242.
[12] Wharton, *Anglia Sacra*, i. 436.
[13] Dugdale, *Mon.* vi(3), 1242. When the archbishop announced his choice one of the monks began to sing the *Te Deum*. The archdeacon asked him: 'Who made you cantor here?' and was told by the monk: 'I am cantor here, not you.'
[14] Ibid.

acting on papal authority, had just restored Coventry to monastic control,[15] so that he may have been especially sensitive and indulgent to the rights and claims of the monks. Yet Muschamp for his part would hardly have been a monastic choice. He may well have enjoyed the Lichfield chapter's support; later he was certainly a benefactor to Lichfield, creating another prebend out of the moiety of Wolvey church and granting the common fund 20 marks a year for the provision of ale for the canons.[16] On his death in 1208 he was buried by his own wish at Lichfield — the first bishop to be buried there since the Conquest — despite the protests and appeals of the Coventry monks.[17]

Muschamp died during the Interdict and no successor was elected until 1214; in that year William Cornhill, described by the Prior of Coventry as *vir simplex et liberalis, fidelis regi et utilis regno*,[18] was elected both by the monks and by the canons, so the Bishop of Winchester informed the Archbishop of Canterbury.[19] The manoeuvres for this election had begun some years before and not long after Muschamp's death.[20] In 1209 the monks, on Innocent III's mandate, had elected their prior, Joybert, as bishop; but the king had seized the monastery and, charging the prior with simony, forced him to pay a fine of 300 marks before resuming his priorate.[21] Later in that year, according to the Coventry source, the monks and the canons, whose participation was insisted on by the Crown, elected the king's chancellor, Walter de Gray.[22] Afterwards this election was quashed by the archbishop because of the way in which the king had forced Gray upon the unwilling monks. The papal legate then took the initiative and put before them the names of four candidates, one of whom was William Cornhill, another Hugh, Abbot of Beaulieu.[23] It was for Abbot Hugh that he chiefly attempted to get the monks' approval. According to the Coventry chronicler the legate solemnly denied that he was the proctor of the Lichfield canons,[24] although a certificate of the legate himself records that, to trump Coventry's objection to their electoral rights, the canons had appointed him their proctor in this matter.[25] Furthermore it was believed at Dunstable that the canons had already chosen the Abbot of Beaulieu.[26] Suspicious of surrendering to Lichfield's choice, the Coventry monks firmly resisted the pressure of legate and archbishop and opted instead for William Cornhill; the legate eventually acquiesced in this choice. It seems exceedingly unlikely that if the Lichfield canons had shared in no previous election they would have been successively encouraged by a king and a legate to do so now. It is even more unlikely that they would ultimately have succeeded in establishing their right if they had neglected to assert it during the 12th-century elections.

The election which followed the death of Cornhill in 1223 involved five parties: the canons of Lichfield, the monks of Coventry, the archbishop, the king, and the Pope. As soon as Cornhill died, both chapters sought a *congé d'élire*; this was read out to the dean and prior by Hubert de Burgh and expressly empowered all those to elect who should and were accustomed to do so, thus begging a vital question which was challenged at once by both parties. The prior spurned a suggestion by the dean of a joint election, and the dean immediately announced before the king and assembled magnates his intention to appeal to the archbishop to withhold confirmation from anyone elected by

[15] *V.C.H. Warws.* ii. 53.

[16] Wharton, *Anglia Sacra*, i. 436; *S.H.C.* 1924, pp. 212–213.

[17] Dugdale, *Mon.* vi(3), 1243.

[18] Ibid.

[19] *S.H.C.* 1924, p. 181.

[20] Dugdale, *Mon.* vi(3), 1243–4, gives a detailed account of the events between Muschamp's death and Cornhill's election, from the Coventry point of view.

[21] *V.C.H. Warws.* ii. 54; *Cal. Papal Regs.* i. 32; C 47/19/2(2).

[22] Dugdale, *Mon.* vi(3), 1243.

[23] Hugh, the first abbot of John's Cistercian foundation at Beaulieu, acted as an intermediary between the king and the Pope during the Interdict. He later became Bishop of Carlisle: *V.C.H. Hants*, ii. 140–1.

[24] Dugdale, *Mon.* vi(3), 1243.

[25] *S.H.C.* 1924, pp. 180–1.

[26] *Ann. Mon.* iii. 38.

the monks alone.[27] The dean duly appeared before Archbishop Langton at Mortlake in the autumn of 1223, announced the death of Cornhill, and then lodged an appeal at the papal curia for Lichfield's right of co-election with the monks; about Michaelmas the dean appealed again to the archbishop lest the monks should proceed alone.[28] Undaunted the monks went ahead and elected their prior, Geoffrey; Langton delayed his confirmation because of the Lichfield appeal and wrote to the king for his reaction, since the monks had not yet obtained royal approval. He then summoned the canons before him at Lambeth to show why the election was invalid, and, when they had done so, on the grounds of their customary right to participate, he quashed the election in November 1223.[29] Meanwhile the king himself had appealed to Rome on behalf of the canons,[30] and in October the monks too had lodged a counter-appeal with the Pope. After hearing the proctors of both parties the Pope confirmed the quashing of the election of Prior Geoffrey[31] and after much cajolery induced them to let him provide a candidate to the see. Each party protested that it did not deserve to forfeit its electoral right in this way, but since neither would yield to the other, and since time and litigation cost money, the Pope held the trump card. He duly provided to the see a clerk of the papal camera, Alexander Stavensby, who was consecrated bishop in Rome on Easter Day (14 April) 1224.[32]

Provision solved the vacancy but did nothing about the rights of the rival electors; indeed the Pope had been careful in his provision to include the phrase 'saving the rights of each church'.[33] One thing he had done: he had upheld Langton's quashing of Geoffrey's election, and he notified the dean and chapter of this in May 1224.[34] Battle began again in Rome between the proctors of each party late in May of that year; judges delegate were appointed to hear and settle the case or to refer it back to Rome.[35] They heard proceedings intermittently at Abingdon from August 1224 until January 1225,[36] and at Westminster from May 1225 or 1226 until April 1227 when, on Stavensby's advice and for the purpose of examining papal privileges produced in evidence, the case was recalled to Rome.[37] After further disputation there, when both parties were weary and eager to save expense, Gregory IX in March 1228 decreed that both chapters were henceforth to elect alternately at Coventry and Lichfield, the prior always voting first and the dean second.[38] The electoral rights of Lichfield were now fully acknowledged by Pope and monks, and the rights of Coventry by the canons. In token of this Stavensby abandoned the title used by his predecessors, from Durdent to Cornhill, and replaced 'Coventry' by 'Coventry and Lichfield', a title consistently used by his successors for over 400 years, though variations were for long employed by others. It was, however, one thing to get the electors to agree to a method, quite another to secure agreement on a candidate, and still more difficult to achieve unity on how to resolve such disputes.

The first election under the new papal arrangement took place in 1239–40. Stavensby died in December 1238, the royal *congé d'élire* was issued in May 1239, and a bishop elected in July 1240.[39] The time which elapsed at once casts doubt on the Lichfield account which implies that Hugh Pattishall was easily and instantly elected.[40] Matthew Paris gives quite a different version. He depicts the monks of Coventry about September

[27] Wharton, *Anglia Sacra*, i. 437–8.
[28] *S.H.C.* 1924, p. 204.
[29] Ibid. pp. 220–4. This provides persuasive evidence of the canons' earlier participation in the elections.
[30] Wharton, *Anglia Sacra*, i. 438.
[31] *S.H.C.* 1924, p. 220.
[32] Wharton, *Anglia Sacra*, i. 438; *Ann. Mon.* ii. 299.
[33] *Ann. Mon.* iii. 90.
[34] *S.H.C.* 1924, p. 220.
[35] Ibid. pp. 186–7.
[36] Ibid. pp. 187, 188–9.
[37] Ibid. pp. 198–203.
[38] *Ann. Mon.* iii. 104; *S.H.C.* 1924, pp. 361–2; Wharton, *Anglia Sacra*, i. 438.
[39] *S.H.C.* 1924, p. 3; Wharton, *Anglia Sacra*, i. 439; *Ann. Mon.* iii. 152; iv. 86.
[40] Wharton, *Anglia Sacra*, i. 439.

1239 appreciating that to elect a man unwelcome to the king would merely incur his objections and would inflict upon their church great expense *per morosam expectationem*; and as a consequence they unanimously elected William Raleigh, a favourite clerk and lawyer of the king.[41] Raleigh, however, was already a candidate for the vacant see at Norwich, and he preferred to remain 'with the English in England rather than amid the untamed Welsh on the borders of Wales'.[42] His election to Norwich was approved, and the monks of Coventry sought a fresh candidate; they settled on the learned Nicholas Farnham. The canons of Lichfield had resented these unilateral decisions and approaches by Coventry and, although they approved of Farnham, they elected their own dean, William of Mancetter. Uproar broke out on this, and the dean, to allay it, *exaltando vocem publico* declined the election and urged unanimous support for Farnham. The united invitation, however, only brought a refusal from Farnham; 'realizing that the election was highly litigious and seeing that the bishopric lay in the borderlands of England', he excused himself as unworthy to undertake the perilous charge of so many souls and withdrew — to find subsequently another, and a richer, border see, Durham.[43] In July 1240 the monks and canons, apparently unanimously, elected Hugh Pattishall,[44] a canon of St. Paul's and the king's treasurer, who acquiesced in this elevation only after long consideration and out of pity, if one chronicler be believed.[45] In the Dunstable Annals, where the record is extremely brief, it is said that Robert of Lexington and Farnham were both elected and both resigned, whereupon Pattishall was chosen;[46] it may be that Lexington was approached after Farnham's refusal, or that he had been the first choice of the canons when Raleigh was the monks'. At any rate it is evident that more than one assembly took place in the chapter-house at Coventry to fill the vacancy, though the sources offer no exact chronology.

Following the death of Pattishall in December 1241, a *congé d'élire* was issued in June 1242,[47] but the see was not filled until July 1245 when Roger Weseham was papally provided.[48] The election took place, as scheduled, at Lichfield, and while the monks chose their precentor, William of Montpellier, the canons yielded to the king's suggestion and named the Abbot of Evesham, Richard le Gras, who was then keeper of the Great Seal.[49] Undaunted by this alliance of king and canons, the monks remained adamant in their choice. As a result they incurred royal condemnation for a whole variety of offences and apparently the distraint of their goods, for the convent dispersed to other Benedictine houses, the prior and some monks being liberally entertained at St. Albans for over a year;[50] or they may have been attempting to save money and gather funds for litigation at the Curia. They had some hope of avoiding this when about 1243 they heard of the death of the Abbot of Evesham and enlisted in support of their candidate, Montpellier, some of the canons of Lichfield, no doubt eager for a solution. The king, however, was implacably opposed to the rival of his own late nominee and proposed another candidate, unnamed in the sources, who was supported by the rest of the Lichfield canons.[51] The extravagant and protracted lawsuit begun at the Curia in 1243[52] was only resolved when two years later Montpellier, discouraged by the strength of his opponents and to save Coventry further costs, resigned into the Pope's hands such right as he had in the election.[53] Innocent IV seized the opportunity

[41] Matthew Paris, *Chron. Majora* (Rolls Ser.), iii. 525.
[42] Ibid. 531–2.
[43] Ibid. 540–2; Marion Gibbs and Jane Lang, *Bishops and Reform, 1215–72*, 189, 194–5.
[44] *Ann. Mon.* iii. 152.
[45] Paris, *Chron. Majora*, iii. 542–3; iv. 1–2. In the first of these references he is described as chancellor.
[46] *Ann. Mon.* iii. 149.
[47] *S.H.C.* 1924, p. 3.
[48] Ibid. pp. 133–4; *Cal. Papal Regs.* i. 218.
[49] Paris, *Chron. Majora*, iv. 171–2.
[50] Ibid. 172.
[51] Ibid. 237; Matthew Paris, *Hist. Anglorum* (Rolls Ser.), ii. 469.
[52] Paris, *Chron. Majora*, iv. 237; *Cal. Papal Regs.* i. 203.
[53] Paris, *Chron. Majora*, iv. 424; Paris, *Hist. Anglorum*, ii. 505; *Ann. Mon.* iii. 168; *S.H.C.* 1924, pp. 133–4.

to provide to the see Grosseteste's dean and protégé, Roger Weseham. The king was no doubt satisfied to see Montpellier defeated, but a papal provision was not greatly welcome. Although Weseham was consecrated by the Pope at Lyons in 1245, where he was attending the council,[54] it was only in 1246 that Henry III, *precibus amicabilibus mitigatus*, restored the temporalities of the see.[55] Among the new bishop's benefits to his diocese was his appointment of arbitrators in 1248 to reconcile the Coventry and Lichfield chapters on further electoral problems.[56] Their suggestion that in future elections, whatever the numerical proportions of their personnel, the chapters were to be reckoned as equal in numbers, was confirmed by the chapters and by the bishop in 1255.[57] This arrangement forestalled decision by majority where one chapter was numerically superior to the other, but it made some unjustifiable assumptions about the exclusive solidarity of each.

By now the electoral relations of the two chapters were at last defined to the satisfaction of both, and the next election in January 1257 was the most amicable and the quickest of the century.[58] The monks and canons assembled at Coventry for two days and agreed to proceed by scrutiny; before this the king had been urging on them his treasurer Philip Lovell, and the queen, with the help of Richard, Earl of Cornwall,[59] had been advocating the king's nephew, Roger Meuland (or Longespee).[60] The scrutiny found all the monks and most of the canons in favour of Meuland, a result which persuaded the dean and six canons to withdraw their support for Ralph, Chancellor of Salisbury, two other canons to abandon their treasurer, and another to drop his support of the Archdeacon of Salop. Meuland was carried from the church, various ceremonies were completed, and the prior then published to the clergy and people the unanimous election.[61] It was in fact a canonical, if not entirely free, election, proceeding by scrutiny and ending in unanimity.

It is hard to believe that the election in 1296 of Walter Langton, Edward I's treasurer, was the free and spontaneous choice of the monks and canons which it appears to have been, but at least it was completed without any recorded dispute or complication within six months of Meuland's death.[62] Nearly forty years had passed since the previous election, and fifty since an electoral dispute, so that the monks and canons who met together in 1296 must have been largely unfamiliar with the contentious atmosphere of the early 13th century; this may explain the surprising tranquility of 1296. It was very different in 1321 when the monks, denying their earlier agreement that both the chapters should be counted as numerically equal, elected their prior, and the canons appealed to the Pope at Avignon, where litigation continued for at least twelve more years.[63] The Pope soon filled the see by the provision of Roger Northburgh, but the outcome of the lawsuit remains unknown and, significantly enough, unimportant, for by then episcopal appointments by free canonical capitular elections were a thing of the past; in Coventry and Lichfield, as elsewhere, from the mid 14th century, indeed from the very appointment of Northburgh, the role of the local chapters was merely nominal beside the bargaining of king and pope. No bishop of this see after Langton was a local choice; if no electoral disputes marred the relations of the two chapters after 1321 it was because the choice was no longer theirs.

[54] Wharton, *Anglia Sacra*, i. 439–40.
[55] Paris, *Chron. Majora*, iv. 552.
[56] *S.H.C.* 1924, pp. 111–12.
[57] Ibid. pp. 11–12, 284.
[58] Wharton, *Anglia Sacra*, i. 440–1; *Ann. Mon.* i. 377–80.
[59] *Ann. Mon.* iii. 202.
[60] Paris, *Chron. Majora*, v. 613.

[61] *Ann. Mon.* i. 377–80. Meuland accompanied Ric. of Cornwall when he sailed for Germany in Apr. to be crowned King of the Romans: *Cal. Pat.* 1247–58, 589; N. Denholm-Young, *Richard of Cornwall*, 90.
[62] *S.H.C.* 1924, pp. 3–4, 291, 305.
[63] See below p. 155.

III

By the time of Domesday Book the estates of the Bishop of Chester were to be found in five counties. Considerable property had accrued to the see in Cheshire in Anglo-Saxon times; in 1086 this comprised 56 burgages and the collegiate church of St. John in Chester, certain profitable customs in the city, and 6 manors elsewhere in the county.[64] The bishop held 6 manors (including Prees) in Shropshire and 16 burgages and the collegiate church of St. Chad in Shrewsbury.[65] Three manors (including Bishop's Tachbrook) in Warwickshire, 7 burgages in Warwick,[66] and two Derbyshire manors (including Sawley)[67] complete the list of the bishop's lands outside Staffordshire. In this county the bishop held 12 manors; these included Lichfield, Eccleshall, and Sugnall, each of which contained many villages and hamlets.[68]

It is clear that many changes affected the endowment of the bishopric during the century after the compilation of Domesday Book: despite some subinfeudation the extent and relative importance of the episcopal estates in Staffordshire increased, while property was lost in the other four counties. In Shropshire 5 of the 6 episcopal manors were subinfeudated or alienated in the earlier 12th century,[69] and one of the 2 Derbyshire manors was subinfeudated during the same period.[70] In Warwickshire 2 manors had been lost by the mid 12th century,[71] but against these losses must be set the acquisition in the mid 12th century of the manors of Chadshunt and Itchington from the estates of Coventry Priory.[72] In Cheshire 2 of the 6 episcopal manors were subinfeudated,[73] probably during the 12th century.

In Staffordshire part of the royal manor of Cannock had been acquired by 1152,[74] and thereafter the episcopal estates in the county steadily increased at the expense of those of the Crown. In 1153–4 Henry, Duke of Normandy and Aquitaine, granted Longdon and all its appurtenances to the bishop, at the same time confirming all the episcopal lands in Cannock Forest and all the assarts made there by the bishops before Pentecost 1153.[75] Confirmation of at least part of this grant may have been necessary after Henry's accession to the throne, for in 1155 he granted the bishop 1,500 acres around Lichfield and elsewhere in Cannock Forest, including 80 acres at Brewood; this land was said to consist of assarts made since 1135.[76] In 1189 Richard I, about to go on crusade, sold the royal manors and churches of Cannock and Rugeley to Bishop Nonant. The churches were soon granted by the bishop to the Lichfield chapter, but the manors were retained; they became, with Longdon, the nucleus of the great area of free chase taken from the royal forest of Cannock by the bishops.[77]

In the 13th century the episcopal estates were subject to no changes comparable with

[64] *The Domesday Survey of Cheshire* (Chetham Soc. N.S. lxxv), 26–28, 79, 86–93. A seventh manor entered as part of the bishop's holding belonged to St. John's Church.

[65] *V.C.H. Salop.* i. 290, 310–11. A seventh manor entered as part of the bishop's holding belonged to St. Chad's Church.

[66] *V.C.H. Warws.* i. 273, 302.

[67] *V.C.H. Derb.* i. 298, 334.

[68] *V.C.H. Staffs.* iv. 10, 41–43.

[69] Two were granted by Clinton to Buildwas Abbey (for the foundation of which see below p. 23), and some of the Shrewsbury burgages may have been lost with them: R. W. Eyton, *Antiquities of Shropshire*, vi. 321–3, 359–60. A third passed to Shrewsbury Abbey at an early period, though episcopal claims may have been revived by Clinton: ibid. 181–3; and see below p. 21. Two other manors passed into lay hands: Eyton, op. cit. viii. 200, 205.

[70] It was subinfeudated before 1135 and passed, after partition between heiresses in 1196–7, to the Gresley and

Sacheverell families: *S.H.C.* i. 147, 152–3; ibid. ii(1), 68, 69–70. When, towards the end of Nonant's episcopate, the estates of the bishopric were forfeited to the Crown, Sawley was evidently the only Derbyshire manor from which the see drew any income: *Chanc. R.* 1196 (P.R.S. N.S. vii), 206.

[71] *V.C.H. Warws.* iv. 40; v. 84.

[72] See below n. 19.

[73] G. Ormerod, *Hist. of the County Palatine and City of Chester* (1882 edn.), ii. 327–8, 806.

[74] *V.C.H. Staffs.* v. 53.

[75] *S.H.C.* 1924, p. 10; ibid. x. 23–24. Beaudesert (in Longdon), the site of an episcopal palace, is mentioned among the bishop's possessions in 1259: ibid. 1924, p. 101.

[76] Ibid. 1924, p. 9; *V.C.H. Staffs.* ii. 337, 342. When the land mentioned in this grant was delivered to the bishop, its bounds were marked by the royal forest officials.

[77] *S.H.C.* 1924, p. 8; *V.C.H. Staffs.* i. 226; ii. 342–3; v. 53, 58–59, 63, 154, 158, 162; see below pp. 16–17.

those of the 12th century. The estates which the bishop held in 1195–6[78] were those which he held in 1297–8 when a survey of the episcopal lands was made.[79] At both dates the bishop held the manors of Burton, Farndon, Tarvin, and Wybunbury in Cheshire, as well as certain property in Chester;[80] in Shropshire the manor of Prees; in Warwickshire the manors of Bishop's Tachbrook, Chadshunt, and Bishop's Itchington;[81] and in Derbyshire the manor of Sawley. In 1195–6 and 1297–8 the Staffordshire estates still in the bishop's hands consisted of the manors of Lichfield, Eccleshall,[82] Haywood, Baswich, Longdon, Brewood, Cannock, and Rugeley. The 1297–8 survey also reveals that the bishop's income was then enlarged by mineral workings at Rugeley, Cannock, and Prees and by stone quarries at Baswich. The extent of the episcopal estates remained unchanged for the rest of the Middle Ages.[83]

The bishops acquired town houses in London and Coventry in the 12th and 13th centuries. Nonant was not the first bishop of the diocese to frequent the king's court, but he was the first to acquire a permanent base in London. In 1188 he purchased a house at Newgate for 140 marks, no small one judging by the price, and in the next few years he bought land next to it and rented land outside Newgate.[84] In 1191 he granted all this property to his successors in the bishopric 'to save them begging the favour of hospitality' and specified that it was not to be alienated.[85] Nevertheless this seems to have been done, though by whom is not clear. By about 1259 Meuland was acquiring in perpetuity buildings and land in the parish of St. Mary le Strand, extending from the Strand to the Thames, with a right to make a quay up to that of his neighbour the Bishop of Worcester.[86] It was here that Bishop Langton built his palace.[87] A *pied à terre* was acquired at Coventry in 1224–5 when the prior and convent granted Stavensby land outside their graveyard as a site for a residence.[88] This was no doubt an attempt to avert his sojourns in the priory.

The value and extent of the episcopal estates were increased by various grants of privileges from the Crown. About 1151 King Stephen granted the bishop a mint at Lichfield;[89] this was confirmed in 1154 by Henry, Duke of Normandy and Aquitaine.[90] In 1153 Stephen granted the bishop Sunday markets at Lichfield and Eccleshall.[91] The Eccleshall market was confirmed in October 1189 by Richard I together with toll and team, sac and soc, infangentheof, and the right to judge by the ordeals of water and fire and by duel.[92] In November Richard confirmed Stephen's grant of the mint at Lichfield[93] and gave the bishop quittance, for all his manors, lands, and men, from suit of shire and hundred, sheriff's aids, pleas and regards of the forest, castle work,[94] and common fines imposed for murder and larceny.[95] In December Richard sold to the bishop the manors and churches of Cannock and Rugeley with liberties in 'wood and

[78] *S.H.C.* ii(1), 54, 59–60, 63–64.
[79] S.R.O., D.(W.) 1734/J.2268.
[80] The 1195–6 Pipe Roll makes no mention of the bishop's Cheshire manors (*S.H.C.* ii(1), 63), but they almost certainly then consisted of these four.
[81] In 1195–6 the bishop also held property in Coventry and the Warws. manors of Hardwick and Southam: ibid. 59–60, 64. These, however, were gains at the expense of the temporarily suppressed Coventry Priory and were later restored: *V.C.H. Warws.* v. 137; vi. 221; and see below p. 24. *S.H.C.* ii(1), 64, wrongly states that the bishop held Whichford (Warws.) in 1195–6; it seems simply to have been an escheat accounted for by the same official as the bishop's forfeited estates: *V.C.H. Warws.* v. 205.
[82] Sugnall had been absorbed into Eccleshall: S.R.O., D.(W.) 1734/J.2268.
[83] See *Valor Eccl.* (Rec. Com.), iii. 128.
[84] *S.H.C.* 1924, pp. 26–27, 28–29.

[85] Ibid. pp. 27–28.
[86] Ibid. pp. 95, 152–3.
[87] Harwood, *Lichfield*, 126.
[88] *V.C.H. Warws.* viii. 316.
[89] *S.H.C.* 1924, pp. 219–20.
[90] Ibid. p. 219. Hen. was by then Stephen's recognized heir: A. L. Poole, *From Domesday Bk. to Magna Carta*, 164–6.
[91] *S.H.C.* 1924, p. 78.
[92] Ibid. p. 101. These rights were apparently modelled on those 'enjoyed by the church of Lichfield in the market of Lichfield'.
[93] Ibid. p. 220. The mint seems to have worked only a short time after 1189: G. C. Brooke, *Eng. Coins from the Seventh Cent. to the Present Day* (3rd edn.), 106.
[94] Actually quittance from work on castles, fishponds, or pools.
[95] *S.H.C.* 1924, p. 10.

plain'. These manors, lying between the episcopal estates at Baswich and Lichfield and doubtless near the assarts in Cannock Forest granted by Henry II, were confirmed to the bishop in 1230. From that time successive bishops claimed to hold a large area of woodland entirely free from the king's forest. The Crown did not, however, recognize this right until 1290, when the bishop surrendered his claims and received them back as a grant on payment of a large sum of money.[96] In 1259 Henry III granted the bishop free warren in all his demesne lands, weekly markets and annual fairs at Brewood, Cannock, Rugeley, Itchington, Prees, and Sawley, and an annual fair at Eccleshall.[97]

The bishop was called upon to establish his title to some of his estates and franchises in the late 13th century. By that time, in addition to the possessions and franchises specifically granted by royal charters, other privileges were claimed on the episcopal estates by prescription. The purpose of these prescriptive claims was evidently twofold: maintenance of the privileges acquired from the Crown in the 12th century[98] in face of the administrative changes of a century, and clarification of the obsolescent terms in which these privileges had been defined. During the *quo warranto* proceedings in Derbyshire in 1281 the bishop claimed prescriptive right to view of frankpledge, fines for offences against the assize of bread and ale, infangentheof, gallows, and waif. In effect these rights amounted to a court co-ordinate with the sheriff's tourn, the power to hang 'handhaving' thieves, and the power to seize felons' goods which were normally accounted for by the sheriff.[99] The grant of these privileges had probably been intended by Richard I in his charter of 1189, and the bishop doubtless claimed prescriptively because of the uncertain wording of the charter and the tolerance of prescriptive claims by the royal justices.[1] During the Warwickshire proceedings of 1285 a jury allowed episcopal claims which were the same as those put forward four years earlier in Derbyshire but which were now based on Richard I's charter as well as on prescriptive right.[2]

During the Shropshire proceedings of 1292 and the Staffordshire proceedings of 1293 prescriptive right and charters were adduced by the bishop to support his claim to all the articles of the sheriff's tourn, infangentheof, gallows, and waif. Plainly the intention was to maintain the immunity of the bishop's estates from the increasing jurisdiction of the sheriff. This seems clear from the uncertainty which the bishop's advisers evidently felt about the propriety of claiming the plea *de vetito namio*:[3] though expressly disclaimed during the Shropshire proceedings, the plea was claimed as part of the bishop's franchise in Staffordshire in the following year. At the time when Richard I had freed the bishop's estates from shrieval jurisdiction the plea *de vetito namio* had belonged to the king's courts; by the later 13th century, however, it was part of the sheriff's jurisdiction, and it thus became necessary to claim this plea in order to keep out the sheriff. In 1293, however, the jury found that the plea had been usurped by the bishops since the limit of legal memory.[4]

In 1299 Edward I granted the bishop in clear and unambiguous terms those franchises which had been claimed in 1292 and 1293. A charter of that year, granted for Bishop Langton's good services to the Crown, virtually completed the exclusion of

[96] Ibid. p. 8; *V.C.H. Staffs.* i. 226; v. 53, 58–59, 154, 158; *Ann. Mon.* iii. 361.

[97] *S.H.C.* 1924, pp. 101–2; *Cal. Chart. R.* 1257–1300, 18–19.

[98] *V.C.H. Staffs.* iv. 62.

[99] *Plac. de Quo Warr.* (Rec. Com.), 436; Sir F. Pollock and F. W. Maitland, *Hist. Eng. Law* (2nd edn.), i. 558–60, 580–2; Helen M. Cam, *The Hundred and the Hundred Rolls*, 178.

[1] D. W. Sutherland, *Quo Warranto Proceedings in the Reign of Edw. I, 1278–1294*, 78–79.

[2] *Plac. de Quo Warr.* 781, 783.

[3] This plea is often confused with the plea of withernam but was in fact a distinct action: G. E. Woodbine, 'A Case of Misnomer', *Columbia Law Review*, xliv. 65–70.

[4] *Plac. de Quo Warr.* 677, 710–11; *S.H.C.* vi(1), 243–4; W. A. Morris, *The Medieval Eng. Sheriff to 1300*, 197–8.

the sheriff from the bishop's estates and erected them into a private shire by the franchise of return of all royal writs;[5] the other privileges included in the grant were pleas *de vetito namio*, the chattels of felons and fugitives, and the fines and amercements of all men and tenants on the episcopal estates.[6]

The bishop now possessed, therefore, a substantial liberty firmly based on royal charters. The privileges claimed for his manor of Sawley during the Derbyshire *quo warranto* inquiry of 1330[7] probably give a good idea of those claimed throughout the episcopal estates by this time: toll and team, sac and soc, infangentheof, and halimote;[8] quittance from suit of shire and hundred, sheriff's aids, pleas and regards of the forest, castle work, and common fines imposed for murder and larceny;[9] the right of free warren and a market and fair;[10] return of all royal writs, pleas *de vetito namio*, the chattels of felons and fugitives, and the fines and amercements of all the bishop's men and tenants;[11] view of frankpledge twice a year with all its appurtenances, waif, wreck, treasure trove, and quittance from tolls at markets and fairs throughout the kingdom and from all scot, geld, Danegeld, wardpenny, burghpenny, and lastage.[12]

Alongside these developments another process of definition had been taking place. By the time of the *quo warranto* proceedings the bishop's estates had become clearly distinguished from those of his cathedral churches. In the 12th century, however, it appears that there was no clear division of property between the bishop on the one hand and his cathedral and collegiate churches on the other. Lichfield Cathedral, the oldest of the bishop's sees and the one with fewest claims to independence from him, evidently held no property distinct from that of the bishop at the time of Domesday Book. This still seems to have been the case in the earlier 12th century: Stephen's grant of the mint at Lichfield and the confirmations of his grant by Duke Henry and Richard I[13] were made to the church of St. Chad, Lichfield, as well as to the bishop. Stephen's grant of the markets at Eccleshall and Lichfield[14] was made in similar terms. Papal bulls issued in 1139 and 1144, however, suggest that from at least Bishop Clinton's time the church of Lichfield achieved a measure of independent control over property granted to it by the bishops and others.[15]

At Coventry the history of the bishop's control over the priory estates is more complex, for not until the death of Abbot Leofwine (in or shortly before 1095) could the bishop hope for any control over the estates of this independent monastery. After Leofwine's death, however, Robert de Limesey, anxious to obtain the wealth of Earl Leofric's foundation for his bishopric, secured custody of the house as well as removing his see from Chester to Coventry.[16] In 1100 Henry I 'gave' Coventry to Bishop Limesey;[17] Henry also granted the bishop a charter recognizing his claims to toll and team, sac and soc, infangentheof, and the right to halimote on all the estates of Coventry Priory.[18] Roger de Clinton divided the income from the priory's estates between himself,

[5] For the significance of return of writs see M. T. Clanchy, 'The Franchise of Return of Writs', *T.R.H.S.* 5th ser. xvii. 59–79.

[6] *Cal. Chart. R.* 1257–1300, 476. Langton had then been Treasurer for 3½ years: *Handbk. of Brit. Chron.* 100.

[7] For the rest of this para. see *Plac. de Quo Warr.* 149–50.

[8] For these privileges the bishop produced a charter of Hen. II (see below p. 19) in an *inspeximus* of Edw. I (*Cal. Chart. R.* 1257–1300, 346–7).

[9] For these privileges the bishop produced Ric. I's charter of 1189 (see above p. 16) in the *inspeximus* of Edw. I (*Cal. Chart. R.* 1257–1300, 348).

[10] For these privileges the bishop produced Hen. III's charter of 1259 (see above p. 17).

[11] For these privileges the bishop produced Edw. I's charter of 1299 (see above). Later 15th-cent. account rolls show the bishop's bailiff accounting mainly for forfeited chattels: S.R.O., D.(W.) 1734/3/2/2.

[12] These privileges were claimed by prescriptive right. For later confirmations of the bishop's rights see *Cal. Pat.* 1422–9, 357–8; 1441–6, 58.

[13] See above p. 16.

[14] See above p. 16.

[15] *S.H.C.* 1924, pp. 128, 214–15.

[16] H. Wharton, *Anglia Sacra*, i. 433 n., 463; see above p. 7.

[17] *Ann. Mon.* ii. 40.

[18] *S.H.C.* 1924, p. 9. These were stated to be the liberties possessed by the monks in the time of Edward the Confessor and Earl Leofric. There is evidence that the monastery enjoyed some of them in the Conqueror's reign: *Royal Writs in Eng. from the Conquest to Glanvill* (Selden Soc. lxxvii), pp. 425–6.

the secular canons at Lichfield, and the monks of Coventry.[19] This arrangement was made on the advice of certain abbots and of certain bishops who ruled over monastic cathedrals; it evidently gave the bishop rights not only over the property of the priory but also over its internal government. Papal approval for the arrangement was granted by Innocent II in 1139 and Lucius II in 1144.[20] In 1152, however, the Cistercian Pope, Eugenius III, ratified an agreement made in his presence between the bishop and the monks; this seems to suggest that the earlier settlement had not lasted. Although Eugenius, like his predecessors, enjoined the monks to obey the bishop, he nevertheless granted them some protection against arbitrary episcopal government. Moreover he decreed that in future, despite anything to the contrary in the bulls of his two predecessors, the monks were to enjoy the endowments granted to them by their founder Earl Leofric or by any others of the faithful.[21] Although the Pope may have intended to undo the work of Bishop Clinton by restoring the monks' property,[22] in fact no restoration appears to have been made.

The bishops seem to have maintained control of the priory's estates and to have assigned a sufficient portion of the revenues to the monks. This arrangement, clearly approved by Innocent II and Lucius II, was not ruled out by the ambiguous phrasing of Eugenius III's bull. In the royal grants of the period it was the bishop to whom the various judicial liberties belonging to the priory's estates were confirmed, and it was the bishop who was responsible to the Crown for the knight service due from the estates. In 1155 Henry II confirmed his grandfather's recognition of the bishop's right to the liberties belonging to the priory estates.[23] In 1188, just a few days before his consecration, Hugh de Nonant was granted all the possessions, liberties, and free customs, including knights' fees and tenants' fealties, belonging to the priory, to hold as fully as Bishop Clinton and his predecessors had held them. The grant was approved by Archbishop Baldwin, by Cardinal Bobo the papal legate, and by Clement III. In 1189 it was confirmed by Richard I,[24] possibly on payment of 300 marks.[25] In the same year the Prior of Coventry formally surrendered the demesne and barony of the monastery to the bishop in the presence of the Archbishop of Canterbury and the bishops of London and Rochester.[26]

By this time the personal feud between Bishop Nonant and the monks of Coventry had culminated in the temporary dissolution of the priory (1190–8), and in 1190–1 the priory itself was in the bishop's hands.[27] After the restoration of the monks by Celestine III and Innocent III[28] episcopal interference with their property seems to have ceased. Two papal confirmations of the monks' possessions, granted in 1221,[29] show that there had been no restoration of early-12th-century acquisitions by the canons of Lichfield or by the bishop. Nevertheless all the property held by the monks when their priory was dissolved had been restored, and Eugenius III's rules governing relations between

[19] S.H.C. 1924, p. 216; Wharton, Anglia Sacra, i. 434. The manor of Chadshunt (then including Gaydon), which belonged to the monks of Coventry until the mid 12th century, then passed to the bishop; the advowson was about the same time attached to the precentor's prebend in Lichfield Cathedral, and in 1297 it was stated that the advowson 'spectat ad dominum episcopum et pertinet ad prebendam cantarie': V.C.H. Warws. v. 31, 33, 88–89; S.R.O., D.(W.) 1734/J. 2268, f. 8; S.H.C. 1924, p. 126. The manor and advowson of Itchington seem to have devolved in the same way: V.C.H. Warws. vi. 122, 124.

[20] S.H.C. 1924, pp. 216–17. Innocent's bull praised Clinton's efforts to raise the observance of religious life in the priory and enjoined on the monks 'the same obedience as is rendered to the bishops of Winchester, Ely, and Worcester by their monks'.

[21] Ibid. pp. 126–7.

[22] There is some evidence that the monks at least regarded the bull as a restoration of the property which had passed to the canons of Lichfield and to the bishop: V.C.H. Warws. v. 31; vi. 122.

[23] S.H.C. 1924, p. 9.

[24] Ibid. pp. 78, 215, 284.

[25] Gervase of Canterbury, Opera Historica (Rolls Ser.), i. 461.

[26] Helena M. Chew, Eng. Eccles. Tenants-in-Chief and Knight Service, 164; Rot. Cur. Reg. (Rec. Com.), i. 66.

[27] Red Bk. Exch. (Rolls Ser.), i. 74.

[28] See below p. 24.

[29] V.C.H. Warws. ii. 54–55.

the monks and the bishop were evidently re-established. It was doubtless to prevent bishops from diminishing the revenues of the see and from misappropriating the property of the cathedrals of Coventry and Lichfield that from at least the early 13th century no grant by a bishop from the episcopal lands and no licence for appropriation of churches in the diocese was binding on his successors unless it had been first approved by both of his chapters and their attested confirmation obtained.[30] This requirement endured to the end of the Middle Ages.[31] In the king's courts in the 14th century the authenticity of an episcopal grant was tested by its capitular confirmations.[32] After the dissolution of Coventry Priory in the 16th century an Act of Parliament was necessary to eliminate the need for Coventry's confirmation; the need for Lichfield's was reaffirmed in the same Act.[33]

While they were strengthening their control over the estates of Coventry Priory the bishops seem also to have been trying to annex the property of various collegiate churches in the diocese. The bishops' claims on the churches of Coventry, Lichfield, Chester, and St. Chad's, Shrewsbury, doubtless sprang from their having been episcopal foundations or cathedral churches at various times.[34] In the 12th century, however, there arose episcopal claims on other collegiate churches in the diocese; these seem to have originated in the reign of Stephen. In 1136 Stephen granted to Bishop Clinton, and to his cathedral churches at Lichfield and Coventry, the royal free chapels of Penkridge and Stafford with all their lands, chapels, tithes, and appurtenances and with toll and team, sac and soc, and infangentheof. These churches were confirmed to the bishop and to the church of Lichfield by Innocent II in 1139. In 1139 too Stephen added the royal free chapel of Wolverhampton to his earlier grant, and in 1144 all three chapels were confirmed to the bishop by Lucius II. At some later date, however, Stephen revoked this grant of Wolverhampton and restored the church to Worcester Priory, the rightful owner.[35] The church of Gnosall, belonging to the Crown in 1086, probably passed to the bishop during Stephen's reign; it had certainly done so by 1140.[36] In 1152 Eugenius III confirmed to the bishop (among the other possessions of his see) the collegiate churches of Chester, St. Chad's, Shrewsbury, Gnosall, Penkridge, and Stafford.[37] The bishop's possession of Penkridge and Stafford, however, was short-lived; Henry II recovered these churches, and they became once more royal free chapels.[38] The collegiate churches of Chester and Shrewsbury remained in the bishop's patronage until their dissolution in the 16th century.[39] The church of Gnosall seems to have failed to attain true collegiate status; it remained simply a church of four portioners or prebendaries who were collated by the bishop.[40]

For his barony the bishop rendered the king a *servicium debitum* of 15 knights, the bishopric being so assessed in 1070.[41] By 1135 he had distributed $12\frac{7}{8}$ knights' fees among 19 tenants, and he subsequently enfeoffed another 6 to supply $1\frac{4}{7}$ knight; the deficit was made up out of the episcopal chamber and not from the demesne.[42] In 1166[43] and in the early 13th century[44] the bishop still owed 15 knights, but by 1284–5,

[30] *Chartulary or Reg. of the Abbey of St. Werburgh, Chester, Pt. I* (Chetham Soc. N. S. lxxix), pp. 130–1, 133–6; *S.H.C.* 1937, pp. 36, 41, 42, 48–49, 52, 68; *Cal. Papal Regs.* i. 510.
[31] *Cal. Papal Regs.* iv. 532–3 (1394); Lich. Dioc. Regy., B/A/1/14, f. 94v. (1509).
[32] *S.H.C.* xiii. 132–4.
[33] 33 Hen. VIII, c. 30.
[34] In Domesday Bk. the property of St. John's, Chester, and St. Chad's, Shrewsbury, was counted among the bishop's possessions: see above notes 64, 65.
[35] See below pp. 298, 303, 322.
[36] *V.C.H. Staffs.* iv. 128.
[37] *S.H.C.* 1924, pp. 126–7.   [38] See below pp. 298, 303.
[39] For St. John's, Chester, see e.g. *S.H.C.* N.S. x(2), 165; during vacancies in the see the patronage lapsed to the Prince of Wales: ibid. 8–9, 162. For St. Chad's, Shrewsbury, see H. Owen and J. B. Blakeway, *Hist. of Shrewsbury*, ii. 188; in the later 14th cent. the Crown tried unsuccessfully to make good a claim to the patronage: ibid. 197–8.
[40] *V.C.H. Staffs.* iv. 128.
[41] Chew, *Eng. Eccles. Tenants-in-Chief*, 3.
[42] *S.H.C.* i. 146–8, 152–9.
[43] Ibid. 147–8.   [44] *Red Bk. Exch.* i. 183.

in common with all ecclesiastical tenants-in-chief, he claimed to hold his barony for a vastly reduced *servicium debitum*: two knights for royal campaigns in Wales only.[45] By 1166 no more knights had been enfeoffed than were due to the king, and there had clearly been little of that exploitation of episcopal lands for kinsmen of the bishops which had occurred at York, Lincoln, and Chichester.[46] But the relatives of the bishops of Coventry were not wholly without episcopal succour: Robert de Limesey established the mother of his son, Richard, and Noel, who had married his daughter Celestria, as tenants on his lands;[47] the Durdent family evidently came to Staffordshire in the wake of Bishop Durdent settling at Wall and Fisherwick, as well as at Itchington and 'Cleithul';[48] and in 1166 Geoffrey Peche held ¼ fee in Little Pipe near Lichfield of Bishop Peche.[49] These, however, were not alienations of episcopal or cathedral lands such as Clinton retrieved[50] and Muschamp was authorized to recover.[51]

Certain of the temporalities, like the income from the mill at Tachbrook,[52] were earmarked for the episcopal *mensa*. Bishops Stavensby and Pattishall between them bought the advowson of Wybunbury church (Ches.) for 120 marks;[53] in 1240 Pattishall appropriated it for personal use,[54] and it was later attached to the *mensa*.[55] In 1241 St. Michael's, Coventry, was appropriated for the increase of the *mensa*.[56] In 1345 the bishop was permitted to reserve to his own collation four livings worth 30 marks, or four without cure worth 20 marks, one each in the gift of Coventry and Kenilworth priories and Chester and Shrewsbury abbeys.[57] Still inadequately supported, his *mensa* was enriched in 1395 by the appropriation of Denford rectory (Northants.).[58]

The men who were supported in this way were chiefly the bishop's chaplains and secretaries. In the 13th century these were almost indistinguishable,[59] but by the 15th century the definition was clearer: the secretaries were usually notaries,[60] who were not necessarily in major orders and were perhaps even married. Over them was the bishop's registrar, the late-medieval successor to Wigfrith, *vir librarius*, or secretary, of Bishop Headda about the turn of the 7th century.[61] By the later Middle Ages the bishop's chancellor had little connexion with the episcopal chancery and was simply the bishop's principal legal adviser; there are no letters extant appointing the chancellor, but that he sometimes (and perhaps usually) acted as vicar general suggests his legal role.[62] The other members of the episcopal household included chamberlains, butlers, almoners, bailiffs, marshals,[63] and sundry gentlemen, like John Harcourt, 'esquire', of Eccleshall who belonged to Bishop Heyworth's household in 1444.[64] Among all these the bishop's kinsfolk were sometimes found: Roger and Rabel Durdent in Bishop Walter's time;[65] Gilbert and Geoffrey Peche, respectively chamberlain and steward of Bishop Richard;[66] Richard and Alan Stavensby who witnessed some of the acts of Bishop Alexander;[67]

[45] *Feud. Aids.* v. 2, 5, 6, 7; Chew, *Eng. Eccles. Tenants-in-Chief*, 31–32.

[46] Chew, *Eng. Eccles. Tenants-in-Chief*, 115–17, 119.

[47] T. Hearne, *Hist. of Glastonbury* (1722), 293–4; *S.H.C.* iv(1), 264–5.

[48] In 1166 Rabel Durdent held Wall, and a Durdent also held Fisherwick: *S.H.C.* i. 47. In 1284–5 Rob. Durdent is given as holding ⅕ knight's fee in Fisherwick of the bishop: *Feud. Aids.* v. 8. For Itchington and 'Cleithul' see *S.H.C.* 1924, pp. 93, 290, 291; *V.C.H. Warws.* vi. 122.

[49] *S.H.C.* i. 48, 147, 149. In 1284–5 the ¼ fee was held by 'the son of Richard Pecche': *Feud. Aids.* v. 8.

[50] *S.H.C.* 1924, pp. 216–17.

[51] Ibid. p. 209.

[52] T. Madox, *Formulare Anglicanum* (1702), pp. 44, 177.

[53] *S.H.C.* 1924, pp. 252, 253.

[54] Ibid. p. 257.

[55] *Valor Eccl.* iii. 128.

[56] *Cal. Papal Regs.* i. 198; *Les Registres de Grégoire IX*, ed. L. Auvray (Bibliothèque des Écoles Françaises d'Athènes & de Rome, 2nd ser. ix), iii, col. 523.

[57] *Cal. Papal Regs.* iii. 176.

[58] Ibid. v. 369, 473–4; vi. 417.

[59] e.g. *S.H.C.* 1924, p. 251; *Coucher Bk. of Whalley Abbey, vol. i* (Chetham Soc. x), p. 38.

[60] e.g. *Cal. Papal Regs.* xi. 49.

[61] *Felix's Life of St. Guthlac*, ed. B. Colgrave, 142–3.

[62] e.g. in 1459 and 1488: *Cal. Papal Regs.* xi. 533; Lich. Dioc. Regy., B/A/1/12, ff. 174v., 175.

[63] *S.H.C.* 1924, pp. 52, 211, 239; *S.H.C.* xi. 312–13.

[64] *Cal. Pat.* 1441–6, 262.

[65] *S.H.C.* 1924, p. 87.

[66] *S.H.C.* iii(1), 186; xi. 312–13; 1924, p. 239.

[67] *Whalley Coucher Bk.* p. 144; Madox, *Form. Angl.* pp. 303–4.

and William Blythe was one of the wardens of Beaudesert palace in 1507, during Bishop Blythe's time.[68]

The administration of the estates required a large staff. The first known officer in charge of episcopal lands is Ralph, lord of Harborne (now in Birmingham), the steward under Durdent in the late 1150s.[69] Successors appear in the records throughout the 13th century,[70] but only in 1322 are any of the steward's tasks or powers detailed: the appointment and removal of constables, bailiffs, and serjeants.[71] By the 15th century the office had been divided, one steward being responsible for the lands in Staffordshire and Shropshire, the other for those in Warwickshire; the lands in Cheshire and Derbyshire were presumably leased out.[72] It is from this century too that most of the evidence for the other officers comes. Eccleshall had a bailiff, who held for life and was also keeper of the gaol;[73] in addition there was a constable of the castle, in 1453 an armigerous gentleman, appointed for life and paid £5 a year.[74] Each of the palaces with its grounds was supervised by a keeper, a post which by the end of the Middle Ages was usually granted jointly to two men, paid at the rate of 1d. or so a day, for the life of the longer liver.[75] Cannock Chase required a keeper and an *equitator*.[76] Apart from the estates there were the liberties, administered in the time of Bishop Hales by a bailiff.[77] One clerk for £3 6s. 8d. a year acted for all the various secular courts that were held on the bishop's lands in Staffordshire and Shropshire.[78] The fees paid to all these keepers, bailiffs, and stewards, as well as to the receiver general who supervised the whole system, amounted in 1535 to £92 12s. 4d., almost a seventh of the whole annual yield of the temporalities, and almost £20 more than the bishop's total income from spiritual sources.[79]

There is no doubt that despite all his lands and liberties the bishop was not devoid of financial worries. It is a measure of its poverty that in 1070 the bishopric was assessed, like Hereford, for a *servicium debitum* of 15 knights; only three bishoprics owed less.[80] Despite the acquisitions in the intervening centuries, in 1535 the position was no better: according to the *Valor Ecclesiasticus* the spiritual and temporal revenues of thirteen English sees exceeded Lichfield's, and only two, Rochester and Chichester, received less. The survey of 1535 shows a net income of £703 from a total of £796;[81] the difference between the two figures is accounted for only by the fees of the estate officers and makes no allowance for the multifarious claims on episcopal money indicated rather more fully by the accounts of the receiver general for 1464–5, when a gross income of £921 left a net total of only £359.[82] Out of this the bishop had to support his household and maintain hospitality, which in 1461 cost an average of 10s. a day or £180 a year;[83] then there were travelling expenses, household fees, the cost of furniture and equipment, and the regular drain of taxation, which amounted in 1484–5 to £37 14s. for the temporalities in Staffordshire, Middlesex, and Cheshire alone.[84] There were furthermore the palaces to maintain, though in 1448, with archiepiscopal permission, the bishop decided to demolish all his residences except those at Coventry, Lichfield, Eccleshall, Haywood, and Beaudesert and in the Strand, repairing these from the materials of the others,[85] which doubtless included Tachbrook in Warwickshire and

[68] Lich. Dioc. Regy., B/A/1/14, f. 76.
[69] S.H.C. 1924, p. 146.
[70] Ibid. pp. 166, 176, 178, 214, 304.
[71] B/A/1/3, f. iv.
[72] Ibid. /12, ff. 124, 130v., 164.
[73] Ibid. /13, f. 224.   [74] Ibid. /11, f. 44.
[75] Ibid. ff. 49v., 91v.; ibid. /12, ff. 127v., 142v., 154v.; /14, f. 76.
[76] V.C.H. Staffs. v. 59–60.

[77] B/A/1/12, f. 125; and see above n. 11.
[78] B/A/1/10, f. 80.   [79] Valor Eccl. iii. 128–30.
[80] Chew, Eng. Eccles. Tenants-in-Chief, 3.
[81] Valor Eccl. iii. 128, 129.
[82] S.R.O., D.(W.) 1734/J.1948.
[83] D.(W.) 1734/3/3/264.
[84] Lich. Dioc. Regy., B/A/1/12, f. 177.
[85] Cal. Papal Regs. x. 471–2. Papal permission was granted in 1450.

Prees in Shropshire and possibly Sawley in Derbyshire. Even as far back as 1364 the house at Coventry with its gardens had been leased to two citizens for four years at £2 6s. 8d. a year and the repairs, provided the bishop and his household could use it for the annual synod there.[86] The loss of the archdeaconry of Chester in 1541 entailed a diminution of the episcopal revenues, and this was followed in 1546 by the surrender to the king of the episcopal manors of Baswich, Haywood, Longdon, Cannock, and Rugeley,[87] which ten years earlier had accounted for a fifth of the bishop's temporal income.[88]

IV

That its comparative poverty may have deterred some nominees from accepting the see of Lichfield is very probable, even when its Welsh character is the ostensible reason.[89] Roger de Clinton (1129–48), however, is reputed to have bought the see for 3,000 marks.[90] A nephew of Henry I's 'new man' Geoffrey de Clinton,[91] he was noted for his martial vigour during the civil war of Stephen's reign when he was among those bishops who, 'girt with swords and wearing magnificent suits of armour, rode on horseback with the haughtiest destroyers of the country and took their share of the spoil';[92] but before he died on crusade at Antioch in 1148,[93] he had conferred some notable benefits on his diocese. Surviving charters show him solving disputes about the relationship of a mother-church to its chapels,[94] confirming the possessions of his uncle's foundation at Kenilworth[95] and those of Shrewsbury Abbey,[96] and holding synods at Lichfield.[97] He is, however, best remembered for establishing a chapter on Norman lines at Lichfield, where he also continued his predecessor's work of rebuilding the cathedral. Clinton was moreover the founder of Buildwas Abbey (Salop.), the nunnery at Farewell, and possibly St. John's Hospital at Lichfield, and he assisted the foundation of Radmore Abbey. He approved the establishment of houses at Blithbury and Canwell, and it may have been during his tenure of the see that Brewood nunnery was founded on the episcopal estate there.[98]

None of his successors in the 12th century, though more canonically elected, seems to match his diligence. Walter Durdent (1149–59), who had served twelve successful years as Prior of Christ Church, Canterbury,[99] left few traces of his tenure apart from his kinsfolk installed on episcopal estates.[1] Richard Peche (1161–82) completed Gerard fitz Brian's foundation of the priory of St. Thomas the Martyr near Stafford and retired there on renouncing his see,[2] but he left little other impression on the diocese or on his own times. Gerard Pucelle (1183–4), possibly the most learned and virtuous holder of the bishopric during the 12th century, died within a year of his election and only a few months after his consecration.[3] He was succeeded by Hugh de Nonant (1185–98), a politician and administrator,[4] whose statutes for Lichfield are the earliest extant for any English cathedral chapter.[5]

[86] Lich. Dioc. Regy., B/A/1/5, f. 45v.

[87] For this see below pp. 51–52.

[88] *Valor Eccl.* iii. 128–9.   [89] See above p. 13.

[90] Symeon of Durham, *Hist. Regum* (Rolls Ser.), ii. 283. This is probably merely gossip; the sum is grotesque in relation to the value of the bishopric.

[91] R. W. Southern, 'The Place of Hen. I in Eng. History', *Proc. Brit. Acad.* xlviii. 136–9.

[92] *Gesta Stephani*, ed. K. R. Potter, 104.

[93] *Ann. Mon.* ii. 233.

[94] Saltman, *Archbp. Theobald*, 348.   [95] Ibid. 361.

[96] Ibid. 472.   [97] Ibid. 512–13; *S.H.C.* xi. 322.

[98] See below pp. 141, 214, 220, 222, 225, 279; Dugdale, *Mon.* v. 355, 356.

[99] Saltman, *Archbp. Theobald*, 57–59, 288–9, 447–9, 535–8.

[1] See above p. 21.   [2] See below p. 261.

[3] Ralph de Diceto, *Opera Historica* (Rolls Ser.), ii. 21; *Materials for Hist. of Thos. Becket* (Rolls Ser.), iii. 525. For a survey of his career and writings see S. Kuttner and Eleanor Rathbone, 'Anglo-Norman Canonists of the 12th Cent.' *Traditio*, vii. 296–303.

[4] *D.N.B.*   [5] See below p. 142.

Nonant was elected bishop in 1185 though he was not consecrated until January 1188. He had an almost pathological hatred of monks[6] and as early as February 1188 had led an attack at the council of Geddington on the Canterbury monks.[7] The Prior of Coventry surrendered his demesne and barony in 1189.[8] Soon after this Hugh invaded the priory, put the prior to flight, assaulted some of the monks as they fled to the church, imprisoned others, broke up the altars, and burnt the muniments.[9] One chronicler records that Hugh first sowed discord between the prior and his monks to occasion scandal and then, to extinguish it, expelled them all by armed force.[10] At the synod at Westminster in October 1189 Hugh complained that the monks had assaulted him with a cross from their church and shed his blood before the high altar, a version not irreconcilable with those of the other chroniclers; he had therefore expelled most of them and now sought from the assembled bishops written support for his complaint to the Pope.[11] Armed with this support from his colleagues for the excommunication of the monks and their replacement by secular canons, Hugh set out for Rome in March 1190.[12] Clement III allowed six months for the monks to lodge an appeal, and, when they had failed to do so, the papal legate at the council of Westminster in October 1190 ordered their expulsion and replacement by canons with prebends.[13] Clement's approval was later claimed by Innocent III to have been obtained by misrepresentation of the facts.[14] With royal, papal, and episcopal approval for the change, Nonant quickly set about the destruction of the church at Coventry and the building of a new one for his canons, whose prebends were carved out of the monastic estates, though he kept two manors for his own use. Some of the prebends, it was said, were given in perpetuity to papal cardinals to disarm subsequent opposition. All the canons were absentees, but they built themselves large houses around the church and employed vicars.[15] It was only in 1191 that Moses, the prior, left for Rome with an appeal,[16] but nothing was reversed that year. Probably the cardinal-canons, a change of pope, and Count John's confirmation of the secular establishment at Coventry[17] (perhaps a political bribe to Hugh) explain the futility of this mission of the prior, if the failure of the monks to respond before Clement III's term of six months does not. The canons were expelled and the monks restored early in January 1198 by the Archbishop of Canterbury, the Bishop of Lincoln, and Samson, Abbot of Bury, acting on a mandate from Celestine III;[18] and a new mandate for the monks' restoration was issued the following June by Celestine's successor, Innocent III.[19] Nonant died as a monk at Bec, in March, bitterly repenting, and doing penance for, his evil work at Coventry.[20]

Easily the most outstanding bishops of this diocese in the 13th century, and perhaps, after Chad, throughout the Middle Ages, were the two appointed by papal provision, Alexander Stavensby and Roger Weseham. The first bishop of the century, Geoffrey Muschamp (1198–1208), was an ecclesiastical administrator;[21] he seems to have been worthy but otherwise unmemorable. William Cornhill (1214–23), a royal adminis-

[6] *Chron. of Ric. of Devizes*, ed. J. T. Appleby, 71: 'numquam monacos mordere quievit'.

[7] *D.N.B.*

[8] See above p. 19.

[9] Gervase, *Op. Hist.* i. 461. This probably explains why there is so little Coventry evidence for the 12th-cent. elections.

[10] *Chronicles of the reigns of Stephen, Hen. II and Ric. I* (Rolls Ser.), i. 393–5.

[11] *Chron. Ric. of Devizes*, 8; *Rot. Cur. Reg.* (Rec. Com.), i. 66.

[12] Gerald of Wales, *Opera* (Rolls Ser.), iv. 64–67; *Chron. Stephen, Hen. II and Ric. I*, i. 393–5; *Chron. and Memorials, Ric. I* (Rolls Ser.), ii. 324.

[13] *Chron. Stephen, Hen. II and Ric. I*, i. 395; ii. 392.

[14] *Cal. Papal Regs.* i. 2.

[15] *Chron. Ric. of Devizes*, 69–70.

[16] Gervase, *Op. Hist.* i. 488.

[17] *S.H.C.* 1924, p. 59.

[18] Gervase, *Op. Hist.* i. 550; Roger de Hoveden, *Chronica* (Rolls Ser.), iv. 35–37 (perhaps a Bury source); *Ann. Mon.* i. 194–5 (dependent on Hoveden); *Chron. of Jocelin of Brakelond*, ed. H. E. Butler, 94–95, 155–6.

[19] *Cal. Papal Regs.* i. 2; Roger of Wendover, *Flores Historiarum* (Rolls Ser.), i. 274–6.

[20] Gervase, *Op. Hist.* i. 552; Wendover, *Flores Hist.* i. 273–4.

[21] *D.N.B.*

trator,[22] is notable for his diocesan constitutions[23] and his conferment on the Lichfield chapter of the right to elect its own dean.[24] Alexander Stavensby (1224–38) was very different: an experienced diplomat, he was at home in the papal court and when treating with kings and barons; he had been a regent of theology at Toulouse where he taught St. Dominic, and he was influenced by Grosseteste.[25] He was a firm and imaginative bishop who, despite many political calls upon his talents, spent much of his time in his diocese.[26] Besides promoting the solution of the chronic electoral dispute between the chapters of Coventry and Lichfield and establishing his right to visit Coventry Priory,[27] he addressed to his subjects some notable decrees.[28] His successor, Hugh Pattishall (1239–41), died before he could exercise in his diocese much of the vigour and skill which he had displayed in the royal Exchequer.[29] If anything, Roger Weseham (1245–1256) surpassed even Stavensby as a diocesan of the highest order. A learned and distinguished theologian who had lectured to the Franciscans at Oxford[30] and had served under Grosseteste as an archdeacon and then as the Dean of Lincoln, he ruled Lichfield as Grosseteste would have done. Thus he addressed to his clergy clear instructions about their teaching to the laity,[31] arbitrated between Haughmond and Ranton in 1247,[32] investigated a parochial pension due to Lenton Priory in the same year,[33] ordered a careful inquiry into the endowment of a private chapel in Hillmorton (Warws.) also in 1247,[34] appointed arbitrators to solve further electoral problems in 1248,[35] increased the existing prebends at Lichfield, and in 1253 annexed Bolton to the archdeaconry of Chester.[36] By 1251 he was already unwell,[37] and in 1253 he was licensed to appoint a coadjutor;[38] but, despite ill health, in 1252 he organized a searching inquiry into the parochial life of his diocese,[39] and further acts of his date from 1254 and 1255.[40] Exhausted, paralysed, and mortally ill, he resigned his see in 1256[41] and died in the summer of 1257.[42]

Roger Meuland, or Longespee (1257–95), a kinsman of Henry III, urged upon the chapters by the queen and Richard, Earl of Cornwall,[43] presents a striking contrast with Weseham. The evidence against his integrity is considerable and varied: for appropriating Bradbourne church to Dunstable Priory he received 200 marks 'for alms';[44] he arranged for his cook and barber to receive annuities of 40s. a year and accommodation from Tutbury Priory and St. Thomas's Priory near Stafford;[45] and in defiance of canon law he divided the church of Uttoxeter.[46] In 1280 Archbishop Pecham's list of Meuland's abuses ranges from the extortion of excessive probate fees and the misappropriation of the goods of intestates to his frequent absence from the diocese as a result of which 'an infinite multitude' of his subjects were unconfirmed;[47] it concludes with an order to appoint a suffragan and a coadjutor. When in 1290 Meuland secured part of Cannock Forest on payment of a large fine he levied this from

[22] Gibbs and Lang, *Bishops and Reform*, 187.
[23] Ibid. 108–9. [24] See below p. 145.
[25] Wendover, *Flores Hist.* ii. 281, 309, 348, 361; iii. 79; Gibbs and Lang, *Bishops and Reform*, 29–31. For the tradition that he founded the Franciscan house at Lichfield see below p. 268.
[26] e.g. *S.H.C.* vi(1), 22; *S.H.C.* 1924, pp. 227, 241, 312, 344; *S.H.C.* 4th ser. iv, p. 48; *Chron. Abbatiae de Evesham* (Rolls Ser.), 274, 278; Matthew Paris, *Chron. Majora* (Rolls Ser.), iii. 518.
[27] *Cal. Papal Regs.* i. 151, 153.
[28] C. R. Cheney, *Synodalia*, 42, 119; *Councils and Synods*, ed. F. M. Powicke and C. R. Cheney, ii. 207–26.
[29] Paris, *Chron. Majora*, iv. 2, 171; *Ann. Mon.* iii. 143, 152.
[30] Paris, *Chron. Majora*, iv. 552; *Monumenta Franciscana* (Rolls Ser.), i. 38.

[31] Cheney, *Synodalia*, 149–52.
[32] See below p. 253. [33] *S.H.C.* 1924, p. 166.
[34] Ibid. p. 61. [35] See above p. 14.
[36] See below p. 143.
[37] Paris, *Chron. Majora*, v. 225.
[38] *Cal. Papal Regs.* i. 289.
[39] *Ann. Mon.* i. 296–8. No returns are known to exist.
[40] *S.H.C.* 1924, p. 30; *S.H.C.* 4th ser. iv, p. 37.
[41] *Ann. Mon.* i. 376–7; Paris, *Chron. Majora*, v. 588.
[42] *Ann. Mon.* i. 408.
[43] Ibid. iii. 202; Wharton, *Anglia Sacra*, i. 440n.
[44] *Ann. Mon.* iii. 279–80; J. C. Cox, *Notes on the Churches of Derbs.* ii. 427, 437.
[45] See below pp. 263–4, 333.
[46] *Reg. Epist. Fratris Johannis Peckham* (Rolls Ser.), i. 175–6.
[47] Ibid. 167–8, 183–4, 203–5; ii. 479–80.

his clergy, 3s. in the mark from those in Derby archdeaconry, 1s. in the mark else-where.[48] Even before the reforming influence of the archbishop was felt, however, Meuland had created new prebends at Lichfield, ordained a vicarage at Shirley in Derbyshire (1268), and enlarged the endowment of the vicarage at Lapley (1266); whether his influence is to be discerned in the dean and chapter's ordination of vicarages at Brewood (1275), Colwich and Rugeley (1276), and whether his official's settlement of the endowments of Prestbury, Eastham, and St. Oswald's, Chester, can be attributed to this period is less certain.[49] That the first known episcopal register of the diocese dates from his time, though it is no longer extant, might be due to Pecham's influence or to the coadjutor's initiative, for the only references to it concern institutions of 1285 and 1292.[50]

The impact of Walter Langton (1296–1321) on the diocese was limited by his preoccupations as Treasurer of the realm until 1307 and again in 1312, by his inter-mittent imprisonment in 1307–9, and by his absence at Avignon in 1312–13 when trying to reverse Archbishop Winchelsey's sentence of excommunication upon him.[51] Nevertheless he celebrated orders in the diocese in 1300, 1303, 1304, 1309, 1310, and 1311.[52] Only from 1314 to 1321 was he regularly active in his diocese.[53] His lavish building projects, of episcopal residences and the Lady Chapel at Lichfield, and his beneficence to his cathedral do something to redeem the years of neglect.[54] By contrast the political career of Roger Northburgh (1321–58) ended, either by choice or necessity, when he was provided, at Edward II's urgent request, to Coventry and Lichfield in 1321. Although he was occasionally involved in politics thereafter, negotiating with the Scots in 1327 and with the French in 1330 and 1337 and holding the office of Treasurer in 1328 and 1340,[55] he spent most of his time in his diocese. His two full registers record alongside the smoothly working machinery of diocesan administration his searching visitations of monastic houses in 1322, 1323, 1334, 1347, and 1351.[56] Long before his death it seems that failing health and advancing years had prompted him to seek a licence to appoint a coadjutor.[57] Under the next bishop, Robert Stretton (1358–85), the records show more of his officers' activity than his own; only the Black Prince's intemperate and persevering patronage induced the Pope finally to agree to the appointment of a man who had been three times examined and found unable to read.[58] He did in fact celebrate ordinations between 1360 and 1367 and visited Repton in 1364, as it turned out at the risk of life and limb.[59] Walter Skirlaw was consecrated in January 1386, six months after his provision, but in August he was translated to Bath and Wells.[60] His successor, Richard le Scrope (1386–98), was a graduate in arts and law of Oxford and Cambridge, with legal experience in the diocese of Ely and in the papal curia, who before his translation to York in 1398 coupled his episcopal duties and visitations[61] with diplomatic missions to the Scots in 1392 and 1394 and to the Pope in 1387.[62]

[48] Ann. Mon. iii. 361; V.C.H. Staffs. ii. 343; ibid. v. 59.

[49] See below p. 144; V.C.H. Staffs. iv. 149–50; ibid. v. 40, 162; S.H.C. 1924, pp. 43–44, 294; Chartulary of Abbey of St. Werburgh, Pt. I, pp. 119, 128, 130.

[50] S.H.C. N.S. viii. 96, 128.

[51] D.N.B.; Alice Beardwood, 'The Trial of Walter Langton, Bishop of Lichfield, 1307–1312', Trans. American Philosophical Soc. N.S. liv(3).

[52] Lich. Dioc. Regy., B/A/1/1, ff. 92, 93v., 96v., 98, 100, 109v., 111v., 112, 112v., 114; S.H.C. 1937, p. 115.

[53] S.H.C. 1924, pp. 44–45, 115–16, 132, 159, 160, 182–3, 191–2, 243–4, 249–50, 279, 306–7, 347; Lich. Dioc. Regy., B/A/1/1, ff. 53, 117–141v.

[54] See below pp. 157, 159; Wharton, Anglia Sacra, i. 447.

[55] D.N.B.

[56] Lich. Dioc. Regy., B/A/1/3, ff. 5, 29, 33, 34v., 38v.–39, 56, 68, 71, 81v.–82, 110, 126v., 136; see below pp. 205, 207, 208, 221, 224, 249, 264, 280. And see below p. 253 for his attempted visitation of Ranton c. 1357.

[57] Cal. Papal Regs. iii. 176.

[58] Wharton, Anglia Sacra, i. 44; S.H.C. N.S. viii, p. ix. His inability to read may have been due to defective sight; by 1381 he was blind.

[59] S.H.C. N.S. viii. 103–4, 159 sqq.; Lich. Dioc. Regy., B/A/1/6, ff. 140–58v. For orders celebrated by a suffragan in 1366 see below p. 40.

[60] Le Neve, Fasti Ecclesiae Anglicanae, 1300–1541 (new edn.), x. 2.

[61] e.g. of Stafford archdeaconry in 1391: B/A/1/6, f. 106.

[62] D.N.B.

Of the seven bishops between 1398 and 1490 three were regulars and three (including one of the regulars) came from the entourage of Margaret of Anjou or of her allies the dukes of Suffolk and Somerset. John Burghill (1398–1414), Richard II's Dominican confessor who was translated from Llandaff,[63] spent sixteen busy and unremarkable years in the diocese though he rarely ordained.[64] John Catterick (1415–19), translated from St. David's, spent almost the whole of his tenure at the Council of Constance, and there is no evidence that he was ever in his diocese; he is buried in the church of Santa Croce, Florence.[65] After this virtual interregnum, the rule of William Heyworth (1419–47) must have taken the diocese rather by surprise; he had been Abbot of St. Albans at an unusually early age,[66] and he showed his qualities in the diocese by his visitations both of religious houses[67] and of parishes, as in the archdeaconry of Coventry in 1424.[68] William Booth (1447–52), a Suffolk candidate, was little concerned with affairs of his see.[69] Nicholas Close, translated from Carlisle in August 1452, died in November.[70] Reynold Boulers (1453–9), formerly an Abbot of Gloucester, who had risen by the patronage of Suffolk to the see of Hereford, was translated by the influence of Somerset to Coventry and Lichfield;[71] but there, perhaps because it was by then both difficult and dangerous to promote Somerset's cause, his diligence in visiting religious houses almost rivalled Heyworth's,[72] and his register is one of the fullest and most interesting of the century. Yet another member of Queen Margaret's party succeeded him, her chaplain John Hales (1459–90), a professional theologian and Dean of Exeter.[73] By the time he obtained the see his party was near its eclipse. Perhaps for this reason he passed most of his long tenure in his diocese, apart from the brief return of the Lancastrians in 1470–1 when he served as Keeper of the Privy Seal;[74] he was at Coventry in 1459, at Eccleshall in 1465, 1468, 1469, and 1489 (usually in the early months of the year), at Haughmond in 1468, Colwich and Kenilworth in 1469, Chester in 1486, Beaudesert in 1488, and Manchester in June 1490.[75] Until 1476 he quite frequently celebrated orders, but rarely afterwards. By 1488 he was already ill,[76] and two years later he died.[77] The most remarkable record of his time is a household account book for the period from 24 May to 2 October 1461,[78] which shows him entertaining suffragans, choristers, vicars choral, estate officers and tenants, parish clergy, his vicar general, carpenters, bell-ringers, labourers, inhabitants of Lichfield, travellers *en route* from Scotland, and at the end of May Edward IV himself. Though guests were not entertained daily, there were often between ten and twenty a day, and on the feast of the Assumption he welcomed at his table the clergy of the cathedral, the officers of the diocese, and various men of Lichfield, altogether totalling sixty.

Hales was the last medieval bishop of the diocese who was in any real sense a pastor and whose episcopal attention was undisturbed by urgent political or secular responsibilities. Four bishops held the see between 1492 and 1543, three of them for some years

[63] Thomas Walsingham, *Ypodigma Neustriae* (Rolls Ser.), 380.

[64] B/A/i/7.

[65] Ibid. /8, f. 1; *Cal. Papal Regs.* vii. 134; see below plate facing p. 60.

[66] Thomas Walsingham, *Gesta Abbatum Monasterii S. Albani* (Rolls Ser.), iii. 494.

[67] B/A/i/9, ff. 117–18, 135v.–138v., 175–179v., 197–202; see below pp. 205, 207, 208. [68] E 326/8926.

[69] *D.N.B.* For conflicting accounts of his character and career see *Political Poems and Songs* (Rolls Ser.), ii. 225–9; *Historians of the Church of York and its Archbishops* (Rolls Ser.), ii. 435–6, 487.

[70] Le Neve, *Fasti* (new edn.), x. 2.

[71] A. B. Emden, *Biog. Reg. of Univ. of Oxford to A.D. 1500*, i. 228–9.

[72] B/A/i/11, ff. 52, 56–60v., 76, 78, 80v., 90, 103; see below pp. 207, 208, 209.

[73] Emden, *Biog. Reg. Oxford*, ii. 856–7. Like Bps. Pecock of Chichester and Lyhert of Norwich, also members of the court party, Hales had been a member of Oriel College, which has been called 'a nursery of Lancastrian bishops': E. F. Jacob, 'Reynold Pecock, Bp. of Chichester', *Proc. Brit. Acad.* xxxvii. 126, 131–2.

[74] *Cal. Pat.* 1466–77, 233; Emden, *Biog. Reg. Oxford*, ii 856.

[75] B/A/i/12.

[76] Ibid. f. 163.

[77] Le Neve, *Fasti* (new edn.), x. 3.

[78] S.R.O., D.(W.) 1734/3/3/264.

President of the Council of the Marches of Wales,[79] and the other, John Arundel (1496–1502), a member of Prince Arthur's council.[80] William Smith enjoyed the revenues of the see for over 18 months before he was provided in 1492; he departed to Lincoln in 1496.[81] Geoffrey Blythe, who succeeded Arundel in 1503, became President of the Council in 1512 but in previous years had had considerable royal employment; his last seven years until 1531 were free from such distractions, and in 1527 he was planning a visitation of his diocese.[82] Rowland Lee too was concerned in politics, though he had previously been Blythe's vicar general,[83] and his register is the most laconic and jejune of all. Nevertheless their Welsh responsibilities brought these bishops to the diocese more than would otherwise have been likely. Blythe in particular has left two manuscript books, apart from his register, testifying to his administrative energy on behalf of his church; one records heresy trials in 1511–12[84] and the other monastic visitations in various years between 1516 and 1525.[85] These men, though far removed from the stature of Weseham and even from the serene paternalism of Hales, avoided gross neglect of their episcopal responsibilities and conformed to the general pattern of their colleagues in other sees. Moreover the sophisticated machinery for diocesan administration, which had developed principally in the 14th century, meant that the absence of a bishop did not entail laxity, chaos, or corruption.

V

The administrative machinery of the diocese had to keep pace with the institutional development, but a time lag was almost unavoidable. Each new parish church or chapel and each new religious house increased the responsibilities of the bishop. But whereas few new churches and religious communities were founded after 1300, it was only in the late 14th century, and after some baffling fluctuation, that the scope and relations of the major diocesan offices, some in being since the 12th century, were firmly defined.

There were some 40 places in Staffordshire where there were evidently priests, churches, or abbeys in 1086.[86] If to these are added other parishes where 12th-century architectural features still survive, there must have been some 80 parish churches in Staffordshire by 1200, and doubtless others which have left no trace.[87] In 1291 the *Taxatio*, which is notoriously incomplete, listed 84 parish churches.[88] Omissions are difficult to discover on the evidence of earlier charters and of later tax lists, based as these latter were until the 1520s on the 1291 list.[89] The survey of 1535 yields similar figures.[90] Eighty parish churches, even allowing for some omissions, may seem an inadequate number; there were, however, chapels of ease, and in addition much of Staffordshire was thinly populated. By 1261, for example, Penkridge had dependent chapels at Cannock, Coppenhall, Shareshill, and Stretton.[91] In the parish of Stoke-

---

[79] Caroline Skeel, *Council of the Marches of Wales*, 287.

[80] Emden, *Biog. Reg. Oxford*, i. 50–51.

[81] Le Neve, *Fasti* (new edn.), x. 3; *Handbk. of Brit. Chron.* 234, 236.

[82] B/A/1/14, f. 2.   [83] See below p. 35.

[84] J. Fines, 'Heresy Trials in the Dioc. of Coventry and Lichfield', *Jnl. Eccles. Hist.* xiv.

[85] Lich. Dioc. Regy., B/V/1/1.

[86] See above p. 6.

[87] S. A. Jeavons, 'The Pattern of Ecclesiastical Building in Staffs. during the Norman Period', *Trans. Lichfield & S. Staffs. Arch. & Hist. Soc.* iv. 5–22. The list of claimed Norman dedications on p. 22 would add another 18

churches or parishes to those existing before 1200, but there is no discussion of the evidence and the claims still await rigorous examination.

[88] *Tax. Eccl.* (Rec. Com.), 242–4.

[89] e.g. 81 churches are given in a list of 1300/1 (D. & C. Lich., M.4), 80 in 1381 (E 179/15/8b), and 81 *temp*. Hen. VII (E 36/58).

[90] *Valor Eccl.* (Rec. Com.), iii. 99–152.

[91] See below p. 300. Cannock, however, was disputed with the Dean and Chapter of Lichfield: see below pp. 299, 300. A chapel at Pillaton was mentioned in 1272, and a chapel had been built at Dunston by 1445: see below pp. 300, 302.

upon-Trent six chapels of ease were built during the Middle Ages.[92] Some chapels themselves became parish churches; Blore and Grindon, for example, became independent of Ilam about 1180.[93] By the end of the 13th century, if not a hundred years earlier, the medieval parochial pattern seems to have been more or less complete. In the remaining centuries before the Reformation, however, some important changes occurred in the value and status of parish livings.

The majority of the Staffordshire religious houses dated from the 12th century, although the most important remained the 11th-century monasteries at Burton and Tutbury. Staffordshire was a county which attracted neither Premonstratensians[94] nor Cluniacs but one which could offer the Cistercians the solitude which they particularly sought. The friars *suo more* found their way to the main urban centres.

Religious houses were rarely founded without modifying episcopal jurisdiction by various forms of exemption. They could be free from episcopal control and subject only

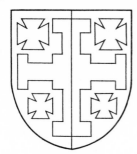

THE SEE OF LICHFIELD

Per pale gules and argent, a cross potent quadrate per pale argent and or between four crosses formy, those on the dexter argent and those on the sinister or. The charges were borne in Bishop Smith's time, 1492–6: B.M. Seal Cast lvii. 55.

to the head of their order by rule, as were the Cistercians and the friars; they could be specially exempted from episcopal control and placed under papal protection, like St. Werburgh's, the Benedictine house at Chester; or the abbot could exercise over the abbey's dependent churches and their parishioners all the normal jurisdiction of a bishop, though the house itself might still be subject to episcopal visitation. The Abbot of Burton in the late 11th or early 12th century was granted the spiritual franchise of the parish of Burton.[95] Here the abbot's court was to replace the courts of the arch-deacon and the bishop, and in it the abbot was to hear all spiritual causes, including testamentary and matrimonial causes. The only qualification was 'so long as justice is not wanting', implying apparently that appeal was to the bishop. Confirmed subse-quently by Archbishops Theobald, Becket, Langton, and Pecham, this ordinary jurisdiction seems to have included Abbots Bromley and Mickleover (Derb.) and was disputed, vainly, in the 13th and 14th centuries by Bishops Weseham, Northburgh, and Stretton and the Archdeacons of Stafford and Derby. Similar privileges were conferred in the 12th century on the Augustinian houses at Rocester, Stone, and Trentham,[96] and by the mid 13th century Bishop Weseham was complaining to the Pope that the Abbot of Burton and certain other Benedictine and Augustinian houses were claiming matri-monial and other spiritual jurisdiction in his diocese.[97] Some of the collegiate churches also secured exemption from the bishop's jurisdiction. Their immunity was strongly challenged by Bishop Meuland, and the dispute was eventually settled in 1281 when the royal free chapels of Stafford, Penkridge, Tettenhall, Wolverhampton, Bridgnorth, and

[92] *V.C.H. Staffs.* viii. 188.
[93] *S.H.C.* 1937, pp. lxiv–lxv.
[94] For an abortive plan to found a Premonstratensian house at Tamworth in 1283 see below p. 295.
[95] See below pp. 209–10.
[96] See below pp. 241, 247, 256.
[97] *S.H.C.* 1924, p. 193.

St. Mary's, Shrewsbury, with their chapels, clergy, and parishioners, were recognized as exempt from episcopal control and subject directly to Rome. The bishop was left with no more than the right to be honourably received and to be allowed to preach, ordain, consecrate, and confirm within their peculiars.[98]

Nor was this all. In 1396, after protracted resistance by the chapter, the bishop established his right to visit the Dean and Chapter of Lichfield at ten-yearly intervals; this was reduced to seven years in 1428. The right, however, was limited to visitation of the chapter only and in no way concerned the prebendal and common fund parishes. Under the statutes of 1191 each prebendary had archidiaconal jurisdiction over his church and its parishioners. The dean had jurisdiction over the common fund churches and the city and churches of Lichfield, and he could visit the prebendal churches, receive procurations there, and hear the causes of parishioners devolving upon him by appeal.[99] Only when the deanery was vacant did its jurisdiction lapse to the bishop, as in 1336.[1] All in all a significant number of Staffordshire parishes was exempt from the bishop's jurisdiction.

In the 12th century, especially in Clinton's and Durdent's time, the bishops had relied notably on the heads of local religious houses to witness their acts.[2] Already in the 12th century, however, they were being displaced in diocesan affairs as increasing use was made of the seculars who were remunerated with capitular dignities and prebends and with rich parish churches. It is true that the bishops continued to repose confidence in the religious, but more for the management of their personal affairs than those of the diocese. In 1274, for example, Bishop Meuland, about to depart for the Council of Lyons, left his affairs in the hands of the Prior of St. Thomas's and Gilbert de Kirkeby.[3] The monasteries were also valued as safe places for the bishops' valuables. When Bishop Langton was arrested in 1307 the Abbots of Combermere and Haughmond and the Prior of St. Thomas's were among those who were required to give information about any hoards of money or treasure which the bishop might have left with them.[4] At the time of Langton's death in 1321 one of the keys to his treasure chest in Eccleshall castle was held by the Prior of Ranton.[5] By the early 14th century, however, the religious were playing little part in diocesan government as the cathedral chapter at Lichfield provided a reservoir of talent.

The earliest of the secular officers to emerge were the archdeacons, who can be traced in this diocese for the first time in the late 11th century. Herbert Grammaticus was probably Archdeacon of Salop in the 1080s,[6] and Robert, Archdeacon of Stafford, witnessed a charter of about 1130.[7] Three archdeacons, probably from this diocese, witnessed an act of Bishop Clinton which can be dated 1136–40.[8] The Archdeacons of Derby, Salop, and Chester are mentioned in a document of 1151,[9] and the Archdeacon of Coventry occurs a few years later with the other four.[10] It would be as unwise to assume that these chance survivals indicate the dates of administrative developments as

[98] Ibid. pp. 251–2; see below pp. 301, 305, 316, 323, 324.
[99] See below pp. 155, 163; *Statutes of Lincoln Cathedral*, ed. H. Bradshaw and C. Wordsworth, ii(1), 16, 24, 26, 27.
[1] Lich. Dioc. Regy., B/A/1/2, f. 159.
[2] *S.H.C.* iii(1), 183; vi(1), 15; 1924, pp. 79, 133, 147.
[3] *Cal. Close*, 1272–9, 117. The prior was obviously a man of administrative ability: in 1273 and 1274 he audited the accounts and surveyed the lands of Jas. de Audley, the late Justice of Chester, and in 1274 he was appointed a commissioner to treat on the king's behalf with Llewelyn, Prince of Wales: *Cal. Pat.* 1272–81, 5, 47, 48, 67.
[4] Alice Beardwood, 'The Trial of Wal. Langton, Bp. of Lichfield', *Trans. American Philosophical Soc.* N.S. liv(3), 26.

[5] Ibid. 40.
[6] R. W. Eyton, *Antiquities of Shropshire*, i. 110. Two grants of Rog., Earl of Shrewsbury, to Shrewsbury Abbey were witnessed by 'Herbert the archdeacon' (Dugdale, *Mon.* iii. 518, 522); he was almost certainly the Herbert who was one of the earl's 'three wise clerks' (Ordericus Vitalis, *Historiae Ecclesiasticae Libri XIII*, ed. A. Le Prévost, ii (1840), 220).
[7] *S.H.C.* ii(1), 205.
[8] Ibid. 1924, p. 79. And see *S.H.C.* xi. 322, for an act of 1139–45 also witnessed by 3 archdeacons.
[9] *S.H.C.* 1937, p. 11.
[10] Ibid. 1924, p. 281.

to accept some of the unsupported identifications of Le Neve.[11] It would be equally unwise to ascribe their origin to the time when Wulfstan supervised the see simply because it is during his tenure of Worcester that archdeacons are first discerned there.[12] All that is certain is that by Henry II's accession archidiaconal development in the diocese was clearly complete.

Archdeacons were much used in the daily administration of the diocese in the 12th century; they were constantly in attendance on the bishop, witnessing, assisting, and advising,[13] and this continued in the 13th and succeeding centuries. Some indeed combined their archdeaconry with the office of bishop's official; for example, Robert de Bosco was Archdeacon of Coventry and official in the 1220s,[14] Richard of Gloucester, Archdeacon of Coventry in 1231, was official in 1228 and 1231,[15] and Peter of Radnor, Archdeacon of Salop in the 1240s and 1250s, was official in 1241.[16] In the next century Robert de Radewell, Archdeacon of Chester, acted as Langton's vicar general.[17] In the 15th century Roger Wall, secretary and a continual commensal member of Heyworth's household, held the archdeaconry of Coventry from 1442 to 1488 when he was succeeded by Thomas Milley, registrar of Boulers and in 1482 vicar general of Hales.[18] The close liaison that existed between the archdeacons and the bishops throughout the later Middle Ages was further assisted by the habit of some bishops of appointing their relatives to the archdeaconries; Muschamp,[19] Stretton,[20] Heyworth,[21] and Hales[22] all did this, but not on the same scale as Blythe who in the early 16th century collated three of his kinsmen to Coventry and Stafford.[23]

With the growing exploitation of provisions by the popes the office of archdeacon was increasingly prone to be filled by aliens, though only Chester had a prebend attached (Bolton)[24] and none was remunerated on a scale likely to attract the attention of aliens for long. Rayner de Vichy, who died Archdeacon of Stafford in 1301, was the first of the aliens there, and he was succeeded by John, son of Octavian de Brunforte and a member of the papal *familia*.[25] Coventry also was occupied by Italians from the beginning of the 14th century until 1335.[26] Derby from 1328 to 1338 was held by Anthony de Monte Peliologo, a prominent Italian in England.[27] Chester had no aliens except for Peter Gomez (1342–8),[28] and Salop escaped altogether.[29] The archdeaconries ceased to be filled by papal provision after 1355, and indeed the only alien after 1348 seems to have been Master Joachim Bretunne at Salop from 1515 to 1523.[30] Alongside foreigners who were rarely, if at all, in England, there were also men who, while largely resident in the diocese, on occasion were despatched overseas or occupied elsewhere. Peter of Radnor, Archdeacon of Salop, was in Rome on the business of episcopal election in 1245 and 1248;[31] Robert de Stafford, Archdeacon of Coventry from 1299, was in Rome in that year[32] and one of his successors who held a variety of other diocesan posts, Richard de Birmingham, was at Rome in the mid 1360s.[33]

[11] e.g. that of Ric. Peche to Chester: *Fasti* (1854 edn.), i. 565, 573. Peche is also given as Archdeacon of Chester, without any source, by *D.N.B.* and by Stubbs in Ralph de Diceto, *Opera Historica* (Rolls Ser.), i, p. xxvii.

[12] *Vita Wulfstani of William of Malmesbury* (Camden Soc. 3rd ser. xl), pp. xxv, xxvi. For Wulfstan's administration of the diocese see above p. 7.

[13] *S.H.C.* iii(1), 180–3; xi. 316, 322; 1924, pp. 79, 80, 83, 87, 147, 240, 281.

[14] Ibid. 1924, p. 179; *S.H.C.* 4th ser. iv, p. 32 n.

[15] *S.H.C.* 1939, 6–8; 1924, p. 251.

[16] Ibid. 1939, 10–15.

[17] Lich. Dioc. Regy., B/A/1/1, ff. 27–30v., 42v.; Le Neve, *Fasti* (new edn.), x. 12.

[18] B/A/1/11, f. 84; /12, ff. 38, 105, 115; *Cal. Papal Regs.* ix. 296; Le Neve, *Fasti* (new edn.), x. 15.

[19] *S.H.C.* 1924, p. 179.

[20] Le Neve, *Fasti* (new edn.), x. 15, 16.

[21] Ibid. 15.

[22] Ibid. 17, 18.

[23] Ibid. 16, 20.

[24] See below p. 143.

[25] Le Neve, *Fasti* (new edn.), x. 18; *Cal. Papal Regs.* i. 596.

[26] Le Neve, *Fasti* (new edn.), x. 14.

[27] Ibid. 16.

[28] Ibid. 13.

[29] Ibid. 17–18.

[30] Ibid. 12–20.

[31] *S.H.C.* 1939, 10–15.

[32] Lich. Dioc. Regy., B/A/1/1, f. 3.

[33] B/A/1/5, ff. 46v.–47; and see below pp. 34, 35.

These preoccupations and remote domiciles made some neglect or delegation of duties inescapable. Personal visitation was a declining feature by 1246 when archdeacons of this diocese were prohibited from collecting procurations unless they visited in person.[34] As early as the 1160s the Archdeacons were employing clerks or *ministri*,[35] who may have been their deputies. Archdeacons' officials *eo nomine*, however, first occur in Stafford with Master Zachary of Chebsey about 1210–11;[36] and his successors are found in 1223–9,[37] 1239,[38] and 1257.[39] An official of the Archdeacon of Salop occurs in 1249[40] and 1303.[41] For all the archdeaconries of the diocese officials are recorded in the first decade of the 14th century. They are mentioned in induction mandates, which are normally addressed to the archdeacons and their officials.[42] It seems clear, however, that the office was firmly established by the 13th century, and probably earlier. Appointed by the archdeacon, on assuming office the official took an oath of obedience to the bishop, promising to execute faithfully all mandates directed by him or his ministers to the archdeacon.[43] Such officials are found inducting incumbents,[44] installing abbots,[45] and hearing causes in the archdeacon's court;[46] they presumably also visited parishes.

The archdeacon's jurisdiction was exercised on his visitations and in his court, where instance and *ex officio* business was heard. The records of such courts are few, and consequently details of the frequency and place of the sessions and of the length and cost of litigation are wanting. Even the competence of any particular archdeacon cannot be taken for granted; some could hear causes, such as matrimonial, usually reserved to the bishop, but their powers varied from time to time as special concessions were made or not renewed. The Archdeacon of Chester from the 13th until the early 16th century, by a separate agreement with each bishop and for an annual pension of £20 or £40, exercised within his archdeaconry exclusive first instance jurisdiction even in reserved cases;[47] but no such extensive authority seems to have been conferred upon the other archdeacons of this diocese if the absence of disputes, compromises, and pensions is any guide. Some parishes were exempt from archidiaconal supervision. Those belonging to the Dean and Chapter of Lichfield in 1231 had their exemption from the archdeacon's control confirmed by episcopal charter: Cannock, Rugeley, and Arley (now in Worcs.) from the Archdeacon of Stafford; Bakewell and Hope, with its chapel of Tideswell, from the Archdeacon of Derby.[48] All the prebendal churches were similarly exempt.[49] The charter of 1231 in no way deterred the Archdeacon of Derby from vainly contesting the exemption, his protest finally being rejected in 1255.[50] Similar exemption was claimed by Burton Abbey for Mickleover (Derb.), Burton, and Abbots Bromley, but here again the enjoyment of this was subject to challenge and assault by the Archdeacons of Derby and Stafford.[51]

No doubt these disputes are symptomatic of the time when the archdeacons were at their most aggressive about their rights and powers, but they also reflect the difficulties of defining jurisdiction, and they occur at a time when the bishops themselves were trying to encroach upon the immunities of the Dean and Chapter of Lichfield and the Abbot and Convent of Burton. On the whole the proverbial greed and corruption of

[34] *S.H.C.* 1924, p. 193.
[35] T. Madox, *Formulare Anglicanum* (1702), p. 294; *Letters of John of Salisbury*, ed. W. J. Millor, H. E. Butler, and C. N. L. Brooke, i. 169–71.
[36] *S.H.C.* 1924, p. 152.
[37] Ibid. 1937, p. 38.
[38] Ibid. p. 41.
[39] *Annales Monastici* (Rolls Ser.), i. 401–2.
[40] S.R.O., D.593/A/1/35/3.
[41] Ibid./9.
[42] B/A/1/1, ff. 34v., 56v., 70.
[43] e.g. B/A/1/2, ff. 201v., 212v., 225.
[44] *S.H.C.* 1924, p. 152.
[45] Ibid. 1937, pp. 179–80.
[46] Ibid. p. 123.
[47] See P. Heath, 'The Medieval Archdeaconry and Tudor Bishopric of Chester', *Jnl. Eccles. Hist.* xx. 243–52.
[48] *S.H.C.* 1924, pp. 210–11.
[49] *Lincoln Cathedral Statutes*, ii(1), 24.
[50] *S.H.C.* 1924, pp. 11–12, 47.
[51] See below p. 210.

archdeacons is not easily illustrated from this diocese, apart from the attempt of the Archdeacon of Derby in the 1160s to extort money for the chrism oil[52] and the accusation against the Archdeacon of Stafford in 1322 of eluding and defrauding the bishop's jurisdiction.[53]

The office of archdeacon had certain disadvantages from the point of view of the bishop. First, since it was a benefice, the bishop was unable to dispossess the holder at pleasure; secondly, the appointment of the archdeacons was increasingly exploited by the king and by the Pope; and thirdly, the jurisdiction of the archdeacon was geographically circumscribed, and this made the whole system cumbersome. The bishop had a need for officers whom he could appoint and remove at pleasure, whose competence he could extend or limit, who had specialized responsibilities and yet were capable of assisting each other. The change to a more flexible system probably began about 1200 with the appearance of the official. The first to occur in the records of this diocese was Master Alan in Bishop Muschamp's time (1198–1208).[54] Others quickly followed; Robert de Bosco in 1222, Richard of Gloucester in 1228 and 1231, and Peter of Radnor in 1241.[55] In the 1270s Meuland's official, Master Simon de Baliden,[56] is found fixing the portion of the Vicar of Prestbury (Ches.), increasing the vicar's portions at Eastham (Ches.) and St. Oswald's, Chester, and hearing and judging a tithe suit concerning Prestbury church.[57] The first extant description of the powers and duties of this office dates only from a commission of 1313.[58] From then onwards (there are no extant commissions between 1322 and 1453) the official is empowered to hear and determine causes, to inquire into and punish all crimes and excesses, and to process all that came within the jurisdiction of the bishop's consistory court.[59] Thus, although probate is not mentioned at all and matrimonial and divorce causes only specifically in 1453 and 1458,[60] there is no ground for believing that the official's competence here was in any way less than the bishop's. Similarly the omission of powers of correction in the commission of 1534 is countered by the grant of 'all things known to belong to the office'.[61]

The officials were all appointed during the bishop's pleasure and not, or never explicitly, just for his absence, but this by no means meant that they held office until the bishop vacated the see. Richard de Birmingham, for example, in 1382 received a commission as official, an office which he had already held earlier in the same episcopate, between 1362 and 1375.[62] By 1453 the title had been expanded from 'official' to 'official principal',[63] perhaps to distinguish him from the archdeacon's official; in 1503 the bishop appointed two men as officials, but they were designated jointly 'official principal'.[64]

Vicars general were appointed in the diocese of Coventry and Lichfield from the early 14th century at least, the first recorded being in 1307.[65] Invariably until 1503, and perhaps even after this, they were appointed during the bishop's absence *in remotis*, whether he was away on business for the Church,[66] in London at Convocation,[67] in Westminster at Parliament,[68] attending at the royal palace,[69] abroad on the king's

[52] *Letters of John of Salisbury*, ed. W. J. Millor, H. E. Butler, and C. N. L. Brooke, i. 171.
[53] Lich. Dioc. Regy., B/A/1/3, f. 9v.
[54] *S.H.C.* 1924, p. 180.
[55] See above p. 31.
[56] *S.H.C.* 1924, p. 185.
[57] *Chartulary or Reg. of Abbey of St. Werburgh, Pt. I* (Chetham Soc. N. S. lxxix), pp. 119, 128, 130; *Pt. II* (Chetham Soc. N. S. lxxxii), p. 474.
[58] Lich. Dioc. Regy., B/A/1/1, f. 47.
[59] Ibid. ff. 8, 47; ibid. /14, ff. 10v.–11.

[60] Ibid. /11, ff. 19, 94v.
[61] Ibid. /14, ff. 10v.–11.
[62] *S.H.C.* N.S. viii. 119, 122, 127, 133–4; N.S. x (2), 28, 49, 176.
[63] B/A/1/11, f. 19.
[64] Ibid. /14, f. 1v.
[65] Ibid. /1, f. 27.
[66] Ibid. /2, f. 3.
[67] Ibid. /6, f. 76v.; /9, ff. 22, 146v.
[68] Ibid. /9, ff. 7, 23v.
[69] Ibid. /6, f. 76v.

business,[70] going to the Scottish campaign with the magnates,[71] or even, like Scrope in 1391, going to visit his father in the north of England.[72] The act books of Robert de Radewell and Ralph of Leicester, Langton's vicars general in 1307 and 1312 respectively, and the record of licences and graces issued by Richard de Birmingham, Scrope's vicar general 1385–9, survive as part of the bishops' registers;[73] by contrast, the whole register of Catterick from 1415 to 1419 is that of his vicar general, Walter Bullock.[74] But already by the end of the 14th century[75] the vicar general himself was not always resident in the diocese, so that Heyworth was particularly careful on most occasions[76] to name as well as the vicar general one or two others who could exercise the office during his absences.[77] Usually the office was committed to one man *pro hac vice*, who was by no means always reappointed on the next occasion. Bishop Arundel began the habit of appointing vicars general to act 'as often as we are absent from our diocese', but even this did not inhibit him from changing his officers quite rapidly, for the phrase occurs in the commissions to William Duffield in 1496, to Richard Salter in 1497 and to John Voysey in 1498.[78] Although Ralph Cantrell was appointed vicar general by Blythe 'during our pleasure' in 1503, his commission was dated from Westminster,[79] and Thomas Fitzherbert is found acting as vicar general for Blythe in 1515–16, 1521, 1523, and 1524.[80] On some of these occasions Fitzherbert was conducting an episcopal visitation, and it is uncertain that Blythe was in fact *in remotis*, the appointment presumably being made expressly for the visitation. When Bishop Lee appointed David Pole vicar general during pleasure in 1534, Lee, though present in his diocese a great deal, was in terms of his episcopal interest and attention *in remotis*.[81]

The responsibilities of the vicar general are recorded with varying fullness in the extant commissions, which all conclude with the phrase 'to do all those things which are known to belong to the office'. Obviously the powers are primarily administrative, being concerned with such matters as admissions, institutions, elections, and appointments, but some of these powers, for example the authority to licence absenteeism, are on occasions withheld,[82] and others, as for the enforcement of residence, are sometimes explicitly conferred.[83] Under Catterick, of course, the limitations on his vicar general's power were merely nominal. The other part of the office was judicial. That this aspect varied with the man and the time is probable; but that such variations are accurately reflected in the commissions is not. Thus, while correction powers are first mentioned in 1360, they are omitted in 1420; conversely, instance jurisdiction, unmentioned in 1360, is specified in the latter year; both are included from 1448 to 1452, neither from 1453 to 1503.

There is no evidence that before the 1490s one man usually held the two offices of official principal and vicar general simultaneously; it was prima facie unlikely so long as the first was usually held for a number of years and the latter was a severely limited appointment with rapidly changing personnel, on occasions even shared by two or three. Sometimes an official did act as vicar general as well,[84] but only by Bishop Arundel was the same man appointed on the same day to both offices — William Duffield on 21 November 1496 and Richard Salter on 9 December 1497.[85] Once begun

---

[70] Ibid. /2, ff. 21v., 23v., 102; /6, f. 1.
[71] Ibid. /6, f. 80.
[72] Ibid. f. 76v.
[73] Ibid. /1, ff. 27–30, 31–33; /6, ff. 122–125v.
[74] Ibid. /8.
[75] e.g. ibid. /6, f. 80 (1392).
[76] Except e.g. 1438: ibid. /9, f. 36v.
[77] Ibid. ff. 14, 22, 39 (1424, 1428, 1449).
[78] Ibid. /13, ff. 200, 238v., 240.
[79] Ibid. /14, f. 1v.

[80] Ibid. f. 67; B/V/1/1.
[81] B/A/1/14, f. 10 (2nd nos.); see above p. 28.
[82] B/A/1/6, f. 1v.
[83] Ibid. /9, f. 1.
[84] John Fox, official principal from at least 1464 to 1479, was vicar general in 1473; on the other hand, in 1465 Thos. Heywood, vicar general, presided over the consistory court in Fox's absence: B/C/1/1, ff. 16v., 48, 53, 76v.; ibid. /2, *passim*; B/A/1/12, f. 48.
[85] B/A/1/13, ff. 200v.–201, 238v.

the conjunction apparently continued in the 16th century. Blythe appointed Cantrell in 1503 solely as vicar general, but jointly with Salter as official principal;[86] Rowland Lee held both offices in 1515,[87] and Fitzherbert appears to have done so in 1524–5.[88] In 1534 Lee appointed David Pole on 20 April to both offices.[89]

The commissary general's duties often seem indistinguishable from those of the official principal. In 1265 the Prior of St. John's Hospital, Lichfield, acted as deputy to the official principal in certain causes.[90] When therefore Meuland in or before 1269 appointed the prior judge for all causes in the consistory court,[91] it might be supposed that he had become the official principal. On this occasion, however, he may have been deputizing in the court for the commissary general, for he is described as commissary of the cathedral treasurer who is known to have been commissary general in 1272.[92] Meanwhile Robert of St. Peter, who in 1271 heard a pension suit in the consistory court, was then described as commissary general.[93] Other men are similarly described in 1276,[94] 1302,[95] and 1311.[96] The earliest extant definition of the duties and powers of the office occurs in 1322 when Master Ralph de Holebech was authorized to hear and conclude causes *ex officio* and instance, to investigate and correct crimes and excesses, to issue letters dimissory, and to do all that pertained to the office.[97] To these were added in 1325 the appointment and removal of apparitors and rural deans, the issue of citations, and the power to deprive clerks of their benefices and offices; furthermore his jurisdiction was defined as over all cases in the bishop's consistory of Lichfield.[98] Clearly these are powers almost indistinguishable from the official's, and in 1368 the bishop, perhaps seeking to rationalize the position, revoked all his appointments of commissaries and transferred their powers to his official, Master Richard de Birmingham, who from 1373 occurs as the bishop's official and as a commissary.[99] When the office holders were next recorded, in 1447, the official and commissary were different persons and they remained so thereafter, but their powers were still confusingly similar: in 1493 two men were appointed jointly commissary general with powers to hold consistories, to hear and try all causes, and to investigate and correct crimes and excesses, though this time no mention was made of the appointment of apparitors.[1] As early as 1311 the commissary general had been licensed to prove the wills of people whose goods were valued at less than £30, but whether this was more than a personal grant to Geoffrey de Blaston no evidence shows;[2] no probate powers are mentioned thereafter except when the commissary general was also the sequestrator general.[3] Although there is no indication of duration in the commissions until 1493,[4] from the changing personnel of the office even during the time of a single bishop it is clear that appointments were during pleasure.

The competence of the sequestrator general, who appears frequently in the records from Edward I's time,[5] was different in kind and extent from that of the *ad hoc* sequestrators of intestates' goods, vacant livings, or vacant archdeaconries,[6] and even from that of the sequestrators in each deanery of the diocese whom he himself was empowered to appoint and remove at will in the mid 14th century.[7] When fuller details are given in 1360 he has authority to correct and punish the excesses of lay subjects

[86] Ibid. /14, f. 1.   [87] Ibid. f. 106.   [96] Lich. Dioc. Regy., B/A/1/1, f. 44.

[88] Ibid. f. 67 (1524, vicar general); B/C/2/1, f. 1ov. (1525, official principal).   [97] Ibid. /3, f. 1.   [98] Ibid. f. 13.

[89] B/A/1/14, ff. 1v.–2, 10 (2nd nos.).   [99] S.H.C. N.S. viii. 119, 127; N.S. x(2), 49, 176.

[90] S.H.C. 1924, p. 341.   [1] B/A/1/10, f. 38v.; /13, f. 138.   [2] Ibid. /1, f. 44.

[91] Ibid. pp. 137–8.   [92] Ibid. p. 361.   [3] Ibid. /12, ff. 7, 31v., 32.   [4] Ibid. /13, f. 138.

[93] Ibid. 1937, pp. 69–70.   [5] S.R.O., D.593/A/1/35/2; *Cat. Anct. D.* iii. A 4433,

[94] Ibid. p. 79.   4583; B/A/1/1, ff. 59, 73; /3, ff. 2v., 3, 76v.

[95] Ibid. pp. 116–17.   [6] B/A/1/2, ff. 28v., 75v.; /3, f. 143v.; /9, f. 2v.

[7] Ibid. /3, f. 108.

and to appoint rural deans and apparitors,[8] but probate and instance jurisdiction are not yet mentioned. Since the work of probate would seem to have been his *raison d'être*, its mention might have been rendered otiose by common knowledge or common assumption. Instance jurisdiction was more appropriately an attribute of the commissary general, and it was only after the two offices were combined that it was itemized in the commissions. When the offices were first linked is uncertain, but that this may have been from 1360 is a strong possibility; Robert Primme, who was appointed sequestrator general in that year, had in 1359, when the see was vacant, been authorized to hear all causes before the consistory court,[9] and although no title was conferred on him then, this was a recognizable attribute of the commissary general, and indeed of the official principal. By 1427 the offices were certainly combined[10] and were never separated thereafter.[11] When in 1447 the next commission occurs, probate jurisdiction is included, as well as the sequestration of the goods of vacant benefices and of intestates, the correction of absentees, the punishment of illicit farming of benefices, and the examining of witnesses for the official of the consistory.[12] In 1453 instance jurisdiction is mentioned for the first time and the duty to hold synods in Coventry and Lichfield and elsewhere, as well as the power to appoint commissaries (i.e. deputies) in any part of the diocese.[13] All these items appear in the remaining medieval commissions.[14] Something of the importance and of the essence of the office of sequestrator general can be gathered from the account of Master John Clone for the year 1463–4, where he is found collecting Peter's Pence and synodals, pensions from churches, fees for probate, and the revenues of vacant livings.[15] Three years later the total receipts of the sequestrator general, Master Thomas Reynold, came to £171 3s. 7d. and his expenditure to £151 9s. 10d.; arrears amounted to some £29, Peter's Pence to £63, pensions from churches to £27, probate fees to £44, and the fruits of vacant livings to £8.[16] By 1542, with probate fees unrecorded and the income from vacancies and Peter's Pence abolished, the total revenue was £64.[17]

All these four officers shared in the work of the consistory court. Originally the bishop's own, this court was in theory, and could at any time be literally, *coram episcopo*;[18] but more usually, even in the 13th century, the official presided.[19] Occasionally the commissary general deputized,[20] and perhaps even his commissary.[21] At the end of the Middle Ages the same pattern is observable: from 1464 to 1479 the official principal, Master John Fox, usually presided over the court, but in his absence he was replaced by such deputies as the vicar general, Thomas Heywood, in September 1464,[22] or the sequestrator and commissary general, Thomas Reynold,[23] in 1467, 1469, 1473, and 1476;[24] usually Reynold was assisted by Roger Wall, a confidant of the bishop and Archdeacon of Coventry.[25] The same pattern is repeated in the early 16th century. Rowland Lee, the official principal, was occasionally relieved, as in 1525, by Master Ralph Cantrell, a previous official principal;[26] Ralph Snede, Lee's successor as official, was relieved by Cantrell and John Blythe jointly in 1529 and by Ralph Withed alone

[8] *S.H.C.* N.S. viii. 3–4; but see also notes 44 and 55 below.
[9] *S.H.C.* N.S. viii. 3–4, 93; N.S. x(2), 7.
[10] B.M., Harl. MS. 2179, f. 34v.
[11] See e.g. W.S.L., S.MS.335(1); S.R.O., D.(W.) 1734/3/4/201; D.(W.) 1734/4/3/1; D.(W.) 1734/J.1948; and notes 12–14 below. From 1360 to 1447 no commission for either office is known, and there are only very sparse references to the officers by name. Between 1447 and 1542 the commissions or holders are regularly recorded.
[12] Lich. Dioc. Regy., B/A/1/10, f. 38v.
[13] Ibid. /11, ff. 18v.–19.
[14] Ibid. /13, ff. 139v. (1493), 200v. (1496); /14, f. 1v. (c. 1503).
[15] S.R.O., D.(W.) 1734/J.1948.
[16] D.(W.) 1734/3/2/4.
[17] D.(W.) 1734/J.1949.
[18] As in 1295: *S.H.C.* 1924, pp. 307–8.
[19] Ibid. 1937, pp. 78, 87.
[20] Ibid. pp. 69–70.
[21] See above p. 35.
[22] Lich. Dioc. Regy., B/C/1/1, f. 16v.
[23] Who held these offices jointly from at least 1466 to 1480: B/A/1/12, ff. 7, 31v., 32; S.R.O., D.(W.) 1734/3/2/4.
[24] Lich. Dioc. Regy., B/C/1/1, ff. 153, 233v.; /2, ff. 95v., 107, 118, 124v., 140, 144, 159v., 236v., 254v.
[25] See above p. 31.
[26] B/C/2/1, f. 16v.; see above p. 35.

on other occasions in the same year.[27] During a vacancy in the see, such as obtained from the end of 1532 to the early part of 1534, the consistory met under officers deputed by the Archbishop of Canterbury[28] or under the guardians of the spiritualities of the vacant see.[29] And during the vacancy of 1532–4 the court met as regularly as usual.[30] As well as the president a considerable number of other lawyers were present as consultants in matrimonial causes. Hales inhibited the Archdeacon of Chester's jurisdiction in such matters because it was necessary to have a body of *jurisperiti* present.[31] When the official promulgated a sentence of divorce in the consistory court in 1458, at least five canon lawyers were there, including the dean of the cathedral, the Archdeacons of Coventry and Stafford, and the bishop's receiver general.[32] In 1496 the official pronounced a divorce sentence, *de consilio jurisperitorum cum quibus mature communicavimus.*[33]

The court usually sat at Lichfield. In 1295 the official heard a pension suit in the cathedral there,[34] possibly in the chapel of St. Peter on the south side of the cathedral where much church business was transacted.[35] In the early 15th century the official cited an offender to appear before him, or another commissary of the bishop, in the prebendal church of Eccleshall, and once, in 1530, a sitting of the consistory court was prorogued to the prebendal church of Longdon.[36] There seem to have been no local branches of the consistory court, nor does it appear that the court itinerated in what was, after all, a most extensive diocese.[37] The only local courts, apart from those in the peculiars of the dean and prebendaries of Lichfield, the deans of the royal colleges, the abbots of Burton and Rocester and the priors of Stone and Trentham, were the traditional ones of the archdeacons; of their regularity and even of their existence we know little, except in the case of Chester whose history is entirely untypical.[38]

In the late 13th century, at least for instance business, the court appears to have met as necessary from Monday to Friday inclusive.[39] In the late 15th and early 16th centuries, for which several instance act books survive, more detail is available. From 1464 to 1479 the court sat on average 13 or 14 days a year, little more in fact than once a month, August in every year save one being entirely free.[40] In two or three months of the year it sat twice, most years in July to clear up business before the summer recess, which was usually from the last week of July until the last week of September (about the 24th or 25th). Throughout these years it was only on very rare occasions that the meeting was held on any other day than Tuesday; Monday or Wednesday was usually the other day. Between 1525 and 1533 the court rarely sat less than 15 days a year and often nearer 20, so that with August still in recess there were two meetings in most months, three usually in July, and in some years as many as four.[41] Tuesday was still the usual day, but there was growing recourse to Mondays, Wednesdays, and Saturdays as well.

The records make it clear that litigation in this court was seldom, by medieval standards, greatly protracted, though with so few meetings progress was slow and a suit could take several months. Entirely exceptional was the divorce case heard, *sede vacante*, in 1415 by the Rector of Tatenhill, a bachelor of decrees, at St. John's, Chester, and

[27] B/C/2/3, ff. 57v., 90v., 95.
[28] Ibid. ff. 172, 224v.; B/A/1/14, f. 1v. (2nd nos.); *Handbk. of Brit. Chron.* 234. When the archbishopric itself was vacant, officers were deputed by the Prior and Chapter of Canterbury: B/C/2/3, f. 192.
[29] B/C/2/3, f. 175.
[30] Ibid. ff. 172–224v.
[31] B/A/1/12, f. 140.
[32] Ibid. f. 158.
[33] Ibid. /14, f. 70.
[34] *S.H.C.* vi(1), 27.

[35] In 1254 it was stated that the business of the church was frequently transacted in this chapel: ibid. 1924, p. 19.
[36] B.M., Harl. MS. 2179, f. 34v.; Lich. Dioc. Regy., B/C/2/3, f. 115v.
[37] Wills were sometimes proved locally: Lich. Dioc. Regy., B/C/10/I.
[38] See above p. 32.
[39] See references in notes 92, 93, 18–20, and 34 above.
[40] B/C/1/1 and 2.
[41] B/C/2/1–3.

completed from the citation of parties to the certification of the sentence in eleven days, or just under three weeks from the original petition.[42] The volume of business in this court at the end of the Middle Ages is misleadingly reflected in the greater frequency of court days in the 1520s, for without the inclusion of some *ex officio* cases a considerable decline would be evident, especially marked in causes of *fidei laesio* (or perjury), and to a lesser degree in matrimonial causes which had been declining even in the 1470s. It should also be remembered that the court's *ex officio* business is recorded in no such comprehensive records; it must have met on many other days of the year to cope with what was probably the greater, though the less complex, part of its business.

There appears to have been an apparitor for each archdeaconry; in 1457 we hear of those for Salop, Coventry, and Derby,[43] though none appears in the records for Stafford and Chester. Their appointment was granted to the commissary general in 1325 and to the sequestrator general in 1360,[44] evidently temporary concessions, for the power was normally exercised by the bishop.[45] Over the whole diocese there was the apparitor general, invariably from the first record in 1350[46] appointed by the bishop. In the late 15th century at least he was appointed for life, or if there were two men jointly appointed, as in 1453, 1461, and 1484,[47] for the life of the longer liver. Each apparitor and apparitor general swore an oath which was the same in 1458 as in 1350:[48] to be faithful to the bishop and humbly to execute whatever his officers canonically enjoined; to keep the secrets of the consistory court; to visit often the diocese or archdeaconry for which he was responsible; to report news of excesses to the registrar of the consistory or to the bishop's ministers; neither to conceal anyone defamed nor to cite anyone not accused, whether for money, love, hate, or favour; not to impede any action against the defamed but to resist all prayers and impediments.

For some purposes of communication the bishops and archdeacons relied on the rural deans. Theirs was possibly an ancient office, but it is first discernible in this diocese in 1151 when three deans, Aschetill, Pain, and Adam, are among the witnesses of a lease.[49] References occur in the time of Bishop Richard Peche (1161–82) to the dean of Stone and in the 1220s to Silvester, dean of the chapter of Alton.[50] In 1224 a chronicler lists seven deaneries within the archdeaconry of Stafford (as against 9 in Chester, 2 in Salop, 6 in Derby, and 4 in Coventry): Stafford, Lapley, Trysull, Newcastle, Alton, Tamworth, and Tutbury.[51] These arrangements, however, were evidently fluid. In the 1291 *Taxatio* the number of deaneries in the archdeaconry was reduced to five with the linking of Lapley and Trysull and of Tamworth and Tutbury.[52] By the early 14th century the linking of Stafford and Newcastle had reduced the number of deaneries to four: Lapley and Trysull, Stafford and Newcastle, Alton and Leek, and Tamworth and Tutbury.[53] These four deaneries were probably identical with those which existed in 1535, though by then the deanery of Stafford and Newcastle had become known as the deanery of Newcastle and Stone.[54] The rural deans were apparently appointed by the

[42] B.M., Harl. MS. 2179, f. 37.   [43] B/A/1/11, ff. 86v., 87.

[44] See above pp. 35, 36. This power was included in the sequestrator general's first commission of 1360 but not in the second: see below n. 55.

[45] *S.H.C.* N.S. viii. 4; B/A/1/11, f. 86v.

[46] B/A/1/2, f. 2v.

[47] Ibid. /11, f. 44v. (when a father and son shared the office); /12, f. 130 (when one of the bp.'s *familiarii* was among them); /13, f. 154v.

[48] Ibid. /2, f. 2v.; /11, f. 91v.

[49] *S.H.C.* 1937, p. 11.

[50] Ibid. vi(1), 20; ibid. 1937, p. 38.

[51] Bartholomew de Cotton, *Hist. Anglicana* (Rolls Ser.), 406.

[52] *Tax. Eccl.* 242–3.

[53] D. & C. Lich., M.5, M.7, M.9. What are fairly obviously the same 4 deaneries are called Alton, Lapley, Stafford, and Tamworth in a document of 1300/1: ibid., M.4.

[54] *Valor Eccl.* iii. 99, 107, 123, 149. An account of subsidy paid by the clergy of Stafford archdeaconry in 1381 (E 179/15/8b) lists incumbents under the 4 deaneries of Stafford and Newcastle, Alton and Leek, Lapley and Trysull, and Tamworth. It also, however, lists the assessments of churches under six deaneries called Stafford, Newcastle, Alton, Tamworth, Lapley, and Trysull. The latter 'deaneries' were perhaps merely circuits convenient for the collectors.

bishop during pleasure.[55] They were not just agents of communication, for, as well as executing citations to parties to appear in the consistory court,[56] from 1311 they proved the wills of their subjects whose goods were valued at less than £5 and granted administration to the executors.[57]

The penitentiaries, who first appeared in the diocese in the mid 14th century as auxiliaries to the parish clergy in a time of plague and resulting panic, participated in both the pastoral and the disciplinary work of the diocese. Drawn from mendicants, canons regular, and cathedral and parish clergy, they were appointed at first for periods varying from a few weeks to a few years, and for areas varying from one parish to, on rare occasions, the whole diocese. They were empowered to hear confessions, grant absolution, and award penances in most cases. The exceptions were usually those listed in 1363: homicide, assault on the clergy, corruption of nuns, apostasy, contraction of prohibited marriage, sacrilege, the unlawful detention of others' goods, and injury to the bishop or his property.[58] In 1406 two penitentiaries were appointed for one year for each archdeaconry except Chester, which had four.[59] In 1421 the vicar general appointed penitentiaries throughout the diocese during pleasure. The Rector of Stoke was appointed penitentiary for the archdeaconry of Stafford and, apparently under him, the Vicar of Colwich for Stafford rural deanery, the Abbot of Rocester for Alton and Leek, the Rector of Bradley and the parish priest of Kinver jointly for Lapley and Trysull, and the parish priest of Burton for Tamworth and Tutbury.[60] These territorial penitentiaries are distinguishable from the numerous confessors licensed at that time by their competence in some of the cases reserved *de jure* to the bishop and — though this is strangely omitted from the terms of their commissions — by their special responsibility for confessing the clergy.[61]

The duties of the suffragan bishop were entirely pastoral and sacramental. He was usually a religious consecrated to an Irish see or to a see *in partibus infidelium* which is not always identifiable. As the ordinary's spiritual deputy he was a man of great importance to the well-being of the diocese. Appointed during pleasure by the bishop or his vicar general, he was responsible, when required, for ordaining clergy; consecrating, dedicating, and reconciling churches; blessing *inter alia* altars, bells, and vestments; administering confirmation; hearing confessions, awarding penances, and absolving, even in cases usually reserved to the bishop. Throughout the later 15th century preaching in Latin or English to the clergy and people in churches and other fit places was added to his obligations.[62]

About the suffragans' suitability for, and acquittance of, these tasks, comment must await much more biographical research; a pre-requisite is to establish their names and dates. The earliest found working in the diocese is Eugenius, Bishop of Ardmore, who was employed in 1184 during the vacancy in the see after Bishop Pucelle's death.[63] In 1280 Bishop Meuland, who had evidently neglected his episcopal duties in the diocese, was instructed to appoint a coadjutor and a suffragan.[64] This suffragan's name, however, is not known, and it is not certain what arrangements were generally made before 1300[65]

[55] The power to appoint rural deans, included in the sequestrator general's commission in 1360, may well have been temporary; it was made by the vicars general before Stretton's consecration. A commission issued shortly after the consecration mentions only the power to appoint substitutes in the deaneries. See *S.H.C.* N.S. viii. 3-4, 93.

[56] *S.H.C.* 1937, pp. 69, 80.

[57] Lich. Dioc. Regy., B/A/1/1, f. 44v.

[58] Ibid. /5, f. 8v.; and see /7, f. 158 (1406), and /9, f. 3 (1421); see also below p. 273.

[59] B/A/1/7, f. 158.

[60] Ibid. /9, f. 3.

[61] Lyndwood, *Provinciale*, lib. v, tit. 16, c. 1; *Reg. Edmundi*

Lacy, episcopi Herefordensis (Cant. & York Soc.), i. 21.

[62] B/A/1/11, f. 192; /13, f. 139.

[63] *S.H.C.* i. 115, 117, 121, 124. He was paid 5s. a day from the revenues of the vacant bishopric.

[64] See above p. 25.

[65] Llewelyn de Bromfield, Bishop of St. Asaph, ordained at Coleshill in 1295: C. Lynam, *Abbey of St. Mary, Croxden*, chronicle, p. v. The clearest evidence for the activities of the suffragans is provided by the ordination lists in the episcopal registers; the earliest of these, preserved in Langton's register, is dated 4 June 1300: B/A/1/1, f. 92.

during vacancies in the see and the absence or incapacity of the diocesan bishop. A clearer picture emerges during the years of Bishop Langton's episcopate after 1300:[66] John of Halton, Bishop of Carlisle, was commissioned to ordain in the diocese in 1301 and 1302;[67] Thomas Dalton, Bishop of Whithorn, was celebrating orders as suffragan in 1305 and 1306;[68] and Gilbert O Tigernach, Bishop of Annadown, was ordaining as suffragan in 1308, 1309, and 1312.[69] The last-named was commissioned again in 1322 before Northburgh's consecration.[70] In Northburgh's later years, when infirmity was overtaking him, several suffragans are found: Richard, Bishop of Glendalough (*Bisaciensis*), in 1347 and 1348; Thomas of Brakenberg, Bishop of Leighlin, in 1349; Roger Cradock, Bishop of Waterford, in 1351 and 1352; and Thomas, *episcopus Magnassiensis*, from 1353 until Northburgh's death in 1358.[71] In 1359 the last of these was commissioned by the Archbishop of Canterbury to ordain in the diocese,[72] and in 1360 he received from Stretton's vicars general a fuller commission to perform a much wider range of episcopal functions.[73] Stretton, however, was consecrated in September 1360, and during the next seven years, except in 1366 when he was assisted by Robert, *episcopus Vosporiensis*,[74] he seems to have been able to do without the services of a suffragan.[75] In January 1368 Robert Worksop, *episcopus Prissinensis*, was commissioned to act as suffragan, and thereafter Stretton ordained only once;[76] for the rest of his episcopate he was evidently dependent for the performance of his episcopal duties on a succession of suffragans. Worksop was employed until 1375[77] and was succeeded in that year by William, *episcopus Bellenensis*;[78] after a few months, however, this bishop's orders were found to be doubtful, and Worksop returned to continue as suffragan for a further two years (1376-8).[79] Philip, Bishop of Leighlin, ordained once in 1379,[80] and Robert Hyntlesham, Bishop of Sebastopol, acted as suffragan during 1380.[81] Hyntlesham was succeeded early in 1381 by William Northbrugge, Bishop of Hvar (*Pharensis*), who remained working in the diocese until 1398.[82]

The system thus established during the 14th century, of employing an almost unbroken succession of suffragans, was continued in the 15th century. Only under Bishop Hales was there any considerable break in the series. From 1398 to 1414 Bishop Burghill employed John Stokes, Bishop of Kilmore.[83] Stokes was still working in the diocese in 1415 as suffragan to the absent Bishop Catterick,[84] but he was succeeded in that year by Simon, Bishop of Tripoli. In 1416 the Bishop of Tripoli was succeeded by

---

[66] For the events necessitating Langton's employment of a suffragan see above p. 26.

[67] B/A/1/1, ff. 95v., 96.

[68] Ibid. ff. 101, 102, 103.

[69] Ibid. ff. 104v., 105, 106v. He was a Franciscan: *Handbk. of Brit. Chron.* 345.

[70] B/A/1/3, f. 1v.

[71] Ibid. /1, ff. 199–216; *S.H.C.* i. 287. Brakenberg and Cradock were Franciscans: *Handbk. of Brit. Chron.* 335, 340. Thomas, *episcopus Magnassiensis*, was a Cistercian of Merevale Abbey (Warws.): W. Stubbs, *Registrum Sacrum Anglicanum*, 196. There are no ordination lists between Sept. 1345 (B/A/1/1, f. 197v.) and Sept. 1347 (ibid. f. 199). In Dec. 1345 John Kirkby, Bishop of Carlisle, was licensed to ordain 3 of his household clerks in the diocese, and the licence included permission to ordain such beneficed and religious clerks of Coventry and Lichfield diocese as had letters dimissory: ibid. /3, f. 117v. Another (undated) licence of the same kind to Kirkby may also belong to these years: ibid. f. 74. A similar licence granted to the Bishop of St. Asaph may date from 1329: ibid. f. 22.

[72] *S.H.C.* N.S. x(2), 11–13, 15–16, 18.

[73] Ibid. N.S. viii. 3.

[74] Ibid. 199–203, 204–5.

[75] Ibid. 159–99, 203–4, 205–12; ibid. N.S. x(2), 19. An unnamed suffragan was appointed in June 1364 and also made penitentiary general of the diocese (ibid. N.S. viii. 102), but there is no evidence of his activity in the ordination lists of that time.

[76] Ibid. N.S. viii, pp. ix, 212–14. Worksop was an Augustinian friar: Stubbs, *Registrum Sacrum Anglicanum*, 196.

[77] *S.H.C.* N.S. viii. 214–96.

[78] Ibid. 296–308.

[79] Ibid. pp. ix, 308–43.

[80] Ibid. 343–5.

[81] Ibid. 345–56, 356–8. He was a Carmelite friar.

[82] Ibid. 356, 358–96; B/A/1/6, ff. 140–58; /7, f. 1. Simon, Bishop of Achonry, a Cistercian, is said to have worked in the diocese in 1387: *Handbk. of Brit. Chron.* 269.

[83] B/A/1/7, ff. 160, 212–236v. He was a Benedictine: *Handbk. of Brit. Chron.* 271.

[84] B/A/1/8, f. 35. He had been employed during the vacancy after Burghill's death: *Reg. Chichele*, ed. E. F. Jacob, iii. 311, 326–35.

Robert Mulfield, Bishop of Killaloe, who worked in the diocese under Catterick and his successor, Heyworth, until 1447.[85] Mulfield was employed during the vacancy in the see after Heyworth's death,[86] but in 1447 Bishop Booth commissioned John, *episcopus Insulensis*, to act as his suffragan. This bishop was employed until Booth's translation to York.[87] During the vacancy of 1452–3, after the death of Bishop Close, ordinations were carried out by John, Bishop of Sodor and Man, and by Richard Wolsey, Bishop of Down and Connor.[88] Wolsey was employed by Close's two successors almost continuously until 1462.[89] Bishop Hales then seems to have done without the services of a suffragan for 13 years; in 1475, however, he began to employ Robert Wellys, Bishop of Achonry, who remained working in the diocese for the remainder of Hales's episcopate and during 1491 when the see was vacant.[90] In 1492 Richard, Bishop of Cloyne, was celebrating orders in the diocese,[91] but Bishop Smith soon afterwards appointed Thomas Ford, Bishop of Achonry and Prior of Stone, as his suffragan.[92] Ford worked in the diocese during the vacancy of 1496 but subsequently left to continue as Smith's suffragan in the diocese of Lincoln.[93] In 1496 Smith's successor, John Arundel, commissioned Thomas Weell, Bishop of Panados, as his suffragan; Weell worked as suffragan until Arundel's translation in 1502.[94] John Bell, Bishop of Mayo, was working in the diocese in 1503, probably during the vacancy in the see.[95] Bishop Weell, however, was recommissioned in that year by Arundel's successor, Geoffrey Blythe, and worked in the diocese until 1520.[96] In 1521 Roger Smyth, Bishop of Lydda and a former Prior of Ranton, was employed as suffragan.[97] Before the end of that year, however, William Sutton, Weell's successor as Bishop of Panados, had taken over the suffragan's duties which he continued to carry out during the remainder of Blythe's episcopate.[98] He occurs again in 1532 during the vacancy after Blythe's death.[99] Sutton may perhaps be considered the last of the medieval suffragans, for Henry VIII's break with Rome meant the end of the system of employing men provided by the Pope to Irish or foreign sees. In 1538 Bishop Lee appointed as his suffragan

[85] B/A/1/8, ff. 35–44; /9, ff. 205–243v. Mulfield was a Cistercian of Meaux Abbey (Yorks. E.R.): Stubbs, *Registrum Sacrum Anglicanum*, 207. See also *Cal. Papal Regs.* vii. 7–8, 279. The last ordination recorded in Heyworth's reg. is dated Mar. 1444: B/A/1/9, f. 243v. Nevertheless the fact that Mulfield was still being employed during the vacancy after Heyworth's death (see below), argues that he was suffragan during Heyworth's last years.

[86] B/A/1/10, f. 5v.

[87] Ibid. ff. 105–114v. This bishop, who was Vicar of Dunchurch (Warws.) from 1449 to 1450 (Dugdale, *Warws.* i. 284), is most probably to be identified with John Grene, Bishop of Scattery Island and formerly (Augustinian) Prior of Leighs (Essex); Grene's provision to this see, however, was conditional on his exercising his episcopal rights only in Ireland: see *Handbk. of Brit. Chron.* 334 and n. 2. This, coupled with the fact that a few years later John, *episcopus Sodorensis* (who also might have been called *Insulensis*: see ibid. 202–3), is known to have worked in the diocese (see below), may create some doubt about the identification. It is, however, evident that Grene lived in England despite his conditional provision: *Cal. Papal Regs.* xi. 181. He has sometimes been wrongly included in the series of bishops of Kilfenora and of Sodor and Man: *Handbk. of Brit. Chron.* 328 n. 5; Stubbs, *Registrum Sacrum Anglicanum*, 212.

[88] B/A/1/11, ff. 4–6. Wolsey was a Dominican friar: *Handbk. of Brit. Chron.* 316.

[89] B/A/1/11, ff. 93, 97–108v., 114–117v.; /12, ff. 5–6, 9, 178–87. Wolsey seems not to have been active in 1457 and the earlier part of 1458; episcopal duties were performed by Boulers himself, by John, *episcopus Insulensis*, and by Thomas, Bishop of Sodor and Man: ibid. /11, ff. 83v., 86, 109v.–113.

[90] Ibid. /12, ff. 210–245v., 255–91; /13, ff. 121v., 122–9. Bishop Wellys, a Franciscan, was Rector of Waters Upton (Salop.) from 1477 to 1483: *Trans. Shropshire Arch. and Nat. Hist. Soc.* 2nd ser. ix. 32; *Handbk. of Brit. Chron.* 344.

[91] B/A/1/13, f. 136v.

[92] Ibid. ff. 139, 178, 180, 183–189v.; see below p. 247. Ford was also Rector of Edgmond (Salop.) in 1494: *Trans. Shropshire Arch. and Nat. Hist. Soc.* 2nd ser. i. 283.

[93] B/A/1/13, f. 198; *Handbk. of Brit. Chron.* 269.

[94] B/A/1/13, ff. 201, 235, 239, 258–296v.

[95] *Handbk. of Brit. Chron.* 271; D. & C. Lich., Bp. Blythe's ordination reg. (where the first ordination is dated 23 Sept. 1503, a few days after Blythe's consecration). He was an Austin friar.

[96] B/A/1/14, f. 1v.; D. & C. Lich., Bp. Blythe's ordination reg. He was Vicar of Nuneaton (Warws.) from 1505 until his death in 1521: Dugdale, *Warws.* ii. 1086. In his will he styles himself Suffragan of Coventry: Stubbs, *Registrum Sacrum Anglicanum*, 200. His title is variously given as *Pavidensis* (B/A/1/13, f. 201), *Pavadensis* (ibid. f. 259v.), and *Panadensis* (ibid. ff. 268v. sqq.); the last seems to be the correct form.

[97] D. & C. Lich., Bp. Blythe's ordination reg.; and see below p. 255 and n. 84.

[98] D. & C. Lich., Bp. Blythe's ordination reg. He was (Benedictine) Prior of Alvecote (Warws.): Stubbs, *Registrum Sacrum Anglicanum*, 202.

[99] B/A/1/14, ff. 3v., 4v. (2nd nos.).

John Bird, Bishop of 'Penreth',[1] one of the new suffragan sees created by Act of Parliament in 1534.[2]

VI

It would be facile to suppose that this administrative superstructure had little to do with the religious life of the diocese, for virtue, piety, and orthodoxy are easily imperilled by inefficiency. There were, however, men more obviously and intimately responsible for nurturing the faith — the parish clergy. Their condition had been seriously impaired by the practice of appropriation. This had already begun in Staffordshire by about 1175,[3] but it became a significant habit, or was merely better recorded, only after the Fourth Lateran Council in 1215. A 1531 taxation list[4] reveals 41 rectories and 38 vicarages; in addition there were some 18 churches served by stipendiary curates, of which 9 were appropriated to houses of Augustinian canons, one to the Benedictine priory of Sandwell, one to the college of St. Mary, Stafford, one to the Cistercian abbey of Bordesley (Worcs.), and 6 to Lichfield Cathedral. Most of the curates in these 18 churches received 4 marks yearly for their labours. Of the ordained vicarages only 2 were worth £10, and 32 were worth less than £7. Half the rectories exceeded £10 and only 10 were worth less than £7; the richest in the county was Hanbury at £33 6s. 8d., and only 5 exceeded £20. The consequences of this conspicuous poverty can only be the subject of speculation in the absence of parochial visitation returns and injunctions, such as the answers to Bishop Weseham's comprehensive inquiry of 1252.[5]

Some indication of the faith of the parishioners is given by the persistent demand for private altars and ancillary confessors which reached a peak between the mid 14th and mid 15th centuries.[6] The main cause may well have been the Black Death,[7] but to what extent the explanation is economic, psychological, or religious cannot be known without more detailed investigation. The history of indulgences (often inducements to necessary public works and charity[8]), obits, and chantries reveals no distinctive trend in Staffordshire.

Chantries first appeared in this diocese, as in others, in the late 12th century, but apart from one in Burton Abbey[9] none is known in Staffordshire before the mid 13th century.[10] From the 1240s, however, the cathedral at Lichfield began to accommodate a large number.[11] At least 13 were founded before the end of the century, and there were 20 in 1335. Shortage of funds and amalgamation reduced the cathedral chantries to 14 in the early 15th century, though by 1535 there were 17.[12] In the parishes too the later 13th century had witnessed numerous foundations which were afterwards supplemented or replaced by yet more. In addition to those serving chantries in monastic

---

[1] Ibid. f. 15 (2nd nos.); A. B. Emden, *Biog. Reg. of Univ. of Oxford to A.D. 1500*, i. 191; *D.N.B.* Bird was a Carmelite of Coventry. 'Penreth' is not to be confused with Penrith (Cumb.); it was probably a Welsh place, now no longer identifiable: G. Watson, 'A Misappropriated Bishop', *Trans. Cumb. and Westmld. Antiquarian and Arch. Soc.* xv. No record of ordinations during Lee's episcopate has so far been found.

[2] Lewis Thomas, consecrated Bp. of Shrewsbury in 1537, acted as suffragan to the Bp. of St. Asaph: D. R. Thomas, *Hist. of the Dioc. of St. Asaph*, i. 243.

[3] *S.H.C.* 4th ser. iv, p. 30.

[4] Lich. Dioc. Regy., B/A/17/1. It is much fuller than the *Valor Eccl.*

[5] See above p. 25.

[6] B/A/1/5–11.

[7] For plague in the diocese *temp.* Bp. Stretton see *S.H.C.* N.S. viii. 16, 99, 109, 141. For Staffs. religious houses where there was a change of head in 1349 see below pp. 219, 239, 240, 246, 251, 255.

[8] B/A/1/11, ff. 67v., 71v., 91v., 92, 94v.

[9] See below p. 208 and n. 87.

[10] The chantries referred to in Trentham parish in 1229 and Leek a little later (see below p. 257; *S.H.C.* N.S. ix. 312) were clearly private chapels and not commemorative foundations in the strict sense of the word *cantaria*; for this distinction see K. L. Wood-Legh, *Perpetual Chantries in Britain*, 1.

[11] *S.H.C.* 1924, pp. 15–19, 29–30, 70–78.

[12] See below pp. 149, 156, 165.

houses, there were at least 145 chantry priests in Staffordshire by the beginning of the 16th century.[13] During the years 1545–8 some 74 were still at work in the county, about 10 of whom also kept a school.[14] There were some 112 chantries endowed at altars in parish churches or chapels of ease; another 39 chantry chapels existed some distance from parish churches or chapels of ease.[15]

There is ample evidence of the existence and persistent survival of heresy in the diocese in the 15th and 16th centuries. During the vacancy in the see in 1414–15 the keepers of the spiritualities were particularly ordered to seek out Lollards and the preachers of unsound doctrine.[16] In 1424 the eccentric, if not heterodox, preachings of a hermit called John Grace were causing some unrest in Coventry and South Staffordshire, and his arrest was ordered by the Council.[17] Other examples of heresy occur at Tamworth in 1454,[18] Burscough (Lancs.) in 1455,[19] Adbaston in 1473–4,[20] Coventry in the 1480s[21] and notably in 1511,[22] Bolton (Lancs.) in 1503,[23] and Atcham (Salop.) in 1526–8.[24] But all this only underlines the general orthodoxy of Staffordshire which escaped notoriety in the early days of Lollardy and whose later Lollards were few and guilty of sortilege and sorcery more often than of Wycliffite errors.

The Reformation, therefore, found the people of this county little inclined to religious change. The clergy were apparently neither worse nor better equipped than elsewhere, even if they were a little poorer. As for the dissolution of religious houses, it was no unfamiliar experience for Staffordshire people by the 1530s.[25]

From one point of view the most striking event of the dissolution in the diocese was the suppression of Coventry Priory in 1539, which left the Lichfield chapter as the sole electoral body.[26] More significant, however, was the separation of Chester archdeaconry in 1541.[27] Chester had been the seat of the diocese from 1075 to 1102, its title officially until Durdent's time and unofficially until Lee's.[28] From the 13th century its archdeaconry had enjoyed a degree of administrative autonomy, complicated by the palatine status of the county, which had embarrassed the relations of successive bishops and archdeacons. Its loss, however, entailed some diminution of episcopal revenues, and this was followed in 1546 by the surrender to the king of substantial episcopal estates, whose value was much higher than those granted in return by the Crown.[29] The post-Reformation bishops, therefore, ruled over a diminished see and with resources far smaller than their predecessors had enjoyed. But the shape of their responsibilities and endowments they inherited very largely from the 7th century, the parochial structure mainly from the 12th century, and their administrative machinery chiefly from the 14th century.

[13] *S.H.C.* 1915, pp. xxxiii–xxxiv.

[14] Ibid. p. xxxiv. There are 85 priests listed ibid. pp. 361–4 (Lists 1–4), but 11 of these must be excluded as they were guild priests (4), or incumbents of chapels of ease (3) or hospitals (4). The total of 74 includes 5 chantry priests who resigned their chaplaincies between 1545 and 1548: ibid. p. 364.

[15] Ibid. p. xxxiv, where the editor gives a total of 43 chantries existing at some distance from parish churches and chapels of ease; this figure, however, includes 4 hospitals. Some of the chantries without chaplains were probably served by parochial curates: ibid. pp. 364–5.

[16] *Reg. Chichele*, ed. E. F. Jacob, i, p. xcviii; iii, p. 291.

[17] *The Coventry Leet Bk. Pt. I* (E.E.T.S. cxxxiv), 96–97; *Cal. Pat.* 1422–9, 275–6; B.M., Harl. MS. 2179, f. 16. He claimed that he had the bishop's licence to preach and that

he had preached in the Close at Lichfield 'among the canons'.

[18] B/A/1/11, ff. 50v.–52.   [19] Ibid. f. 55.
[20] Ibid. /12, f. 142.   [21] Ibid. ff. 166–169v.
[22] Ibid. /14, ff. 98–100; J. Fines, 'Heresy Trials in the Dioc. of Coventry and Lichfield', *Jnl. Eccles. Hist.* xiv.
[23] B/A/1/14, f. 72.
[24] Ibid. ff. 51–52.
[25] See below pp. 135–6.
[26] See below p. 166. For Bp. Lee's attempt in 1539 to save Coventry, as being his 'principal see and head church', in order that 'I may keep my name', see *V.C.H. Warws.* viii. 316.
[27] See below p. 44.
[28] *L. & P. Hen. VIII*, vi, p. 619; xiii(1), p. 385.
[29] See above p. 23 and below pp. 51–52.

THE CHURCH OF ENGLAND SINCE THE REFORMATION[1]

The year 1541 brought the first major change in the boundaries of the diocese of Coventry and Lichfield for over six hundred years.[2] Under Henry VIII's plan for the creation of new bishoprics[3] the archdeaconry of Chester, which covered Cheshire, some parishes in North Wales, and Lancashire south of the Ribble, was taken from Coventry and Lichfield and united with the archdeaconry of Richmond,[4] from the diocese of York, to form the new diocese of Chester.[5]

Richard Sampson, translated from Chichester in 1543, was the first bishop appointed to the reduced bishopric.[6] Like his predecessor, Rowland Lee, Sampson was a cleric whose services as an administrator and agent of the Crown had been rewarded by ecclesiastical preferment; he was the last such bishop to hold the see. He was a conservative in religious matters, but like most of the other bishops he accepted, though probably with little enthusiasm, the changes that were taking place.[7] Despite his obvious lack of sympathy with the more extreme reformers he kept his bishopric under Edward VI, though it is possible that he found it necessary to safeguard his position by buying favour at Court.[8]

The conformist attitude of Bishop Sampson and his predecessor[9] seems to have been reflected in Staffordshire. There is, on the one hand, no evidence to suggest that in its early stages the Reformation found any enthusiastic supporters in the county. Staffordshire had been little affected by the Lollard tradition which, despite the attacks of a succession of bishops, persisted at Coventry into the early 16th century.[10] Thomas Becon, who with Robert Wisdom preached the Reformed doctrines in the diocese in the mid 1540s, thought the Staffordshire laity less 'superstitious' than those in Derbyshire, but he was unimpressed by the clergy.[11] On the other hand the Henrician and Edwardian reforms encountered little or no opposition.[12] The religious houses were dissolved without difficulty, and local men joined in the scramble for the spoils.[13] There was no popular protest when the few pilgrimage shrines were swept away: it proved to be as easy to remove the long-established shrines of St. Chad at Lichfield and St. Modwen at Burton[14] as to pull down the statue of St. Erasmus in a recently-

[1] The writer wishes to acknowledge Mr. D. A. Johnson for providing extensive material on the period up to the Restoration and also the details from the 18th-century visitations.

[2] For the last major change see above pp. 4, 7.

[3] A. G. Dickens, *The Eng. Reformation*, 149.

[4] The archdeaconry of Richmond comprised north-west Yorks., north Lancs., south Cumb., and south Westmld.

[5] Act for transferring the bishoprics of Chester and Man to the province of York, 33 Hen. VIII, c. 31. Another Act of the same year constituted the Dean and Chapter of Lichfield, who had previously joined with the prior and convent of the dissolved priory of Coventry in episcopal elections, 'the entire and sole chapter' of the bishopric: see below p. 166.

[6] For this para. see, unless otherwise stated, *D.N.B.*; L. B. Smith, *Tudor Prelates and Politics, 1536–58*, passim.

[7] Sampson was not among the 8 bishops who voted against the Prayer Book of 1549: *L.J.* i. 331a.

[8] For a considerable grant of episcopal property by Sampson to a confidential agent of the Duke of Somerset see below p. 52.

[9] Lee's sympathies were conservative, but he did not balk at any of Hen. VIII's ecclesiastical policies: *D.N.B.*

[10] See above p. 43.

[11] A. G. Dickens, *Lollards and Protestants in the Diocese of York, 1509–58*, 195; T. Becon, *The Catechism, with other pieces written by him in the reign of Edw. VI* (Parker Soc. 1844), 423.

[12] It is likely that in the early stages of the Reformation most people found it difficult to comprehend the implications of the changes that were taking place: for examples of those who thought it possible that the dissolved religious houses might be revived see below p. 137.

[13] See below p. 137.

[14] See below pp. 168, 210, 212.

built pilgrimage chapel at Ingestre.[15] In 1537 Dr. David Pole, Archdeacon of Salop, assured Bishop Lee that he knew of no priest in the diocese who supported papal claims or approved of the Pilgrimage of Grace.[16] Six Staffordshire incumbents resigned in the last years of Henry VIII's reign; but there is no evidence that they did so on conscientious grounds, and during the following reign the parochial clergy appear to have conformed without exception.[17] Although about 85 chantry priests were dispossessed in 1548 most of them obtained livings or curacies, remained as schoolmasters in the places where they had served their chantries, or were granted pensions.[18]

It is evident nevertheless that at times the proceedings of the chantry commissioners provoked resentment. Such was the case at Tamworth, where the college was suppressed in 1548.[19] The collegiate church was the parish church, and there was considerable dissatisfaction in the town when the commissioners discharged the clergy and seized all the church goods. The townspeople petitioned the Duke of Somerset, and on 2 May 1548 he wrote to the commissioners expressing his amazement that they had 'had no further consideration than to leave a number of people to so loose a disorder'. They were instructed to restore to St. Edith's such ornaments and utensils as were necessary for services. Two days later a selection of vestments and plate was given back to the church.[20]

The inventory of church goods drawn up in 1552 shows, however, that it was not only royal agents who laid their hands on plate, bells, and vestments. In a number of cases the parish authorities were responsible. At Shareshill a bell was sold 'by the assent of the whole people for £4, whereof 40s. was paid to the bishop for his licence to bury and 30s. to his officers for the compositions';[21] at Rushton Spencer a chalice and a bell were sold to provide funds for the repair of Hug Bridge;[22] at Tamworth two of the five sacring bells were disposed of for the benefit of the free school.[23] Elsewhere individuals had done the same. At Newcastle-under-Lyme Richard Norton, a churchwarden, had sold two brass candlesticks;[24] at St. Mary's, Stafford, John ap Harry, Prebendary of Coton, had taken a set of vestments.[25] Changes had also been made to suit the Prayer Book services. At St. Michael's, Lichfield, some of the money acquired by the sale of ornaments had been used to buy a Bible, a Book of Common Prayer, and Erasmus's *Paraphrase* of the New Testament; at Handsworth two chalices had been made into a single large one for administration to the laity.[26] The final stage was reached in 1553, when a commission was issued for the confiscation of church goods. The commissioners spared only what they judged necessary for the new services. At Wednesbury, for instance, they took 3 pairs of silk vestments, 8 altar cloths, 6 houseling napkins, 2 corporals, an altar cross, and 2 candlesticks. The church kept a chalice and paten for the communion table, and a surplice for use by the curate. It also kept the four bells in the tower and the sanctus bell, though the use of the latter was forbidden.[27]

Bishop Sampson swore allegiance to Mary[28] and probably found the ecclesiastical climate of the first months of the new reign more congenial to him. After receiving the queen's order for the deprivation of married clergy he acted promptly. His com-

[15] H. E. Chetwynd-Stapylton, *Chetwynds of Ingestre* (1892), 133–4; *S.H.C.* N.S. xii. 150; *L. & P. Hen. VIII*, xiii(2), p. 203. The chapel was frequented by pilgrims who visited a nearby medicinal spring.

[16] *L. & P. Hen. VIII*, xii(1), p. 335.

[17] *S.H.C.* 1915, pp. xl–xli. A canon of Lichfield was deprived in 1546 for refusing to pay tithes to the Crown: see below p. 169.

[18] *S.H.C.* 1915, pp. xxxiii–xxxiv, 361–6.

[19] See below p. 314.

[20] E 117/12/5/1 and 2. Somerset ordered the commis-

sioners to make similar restitution wherever necessary throughout Staffs.

[21] *S.H.C.* N.S. vi(1), 173.

[22] S. W. Hutchinson, *Archdeaconry of Stoke-on-Trent* (1893), 186.

[23] *S.H.C.* N.S. vi(1), 182; ibid. 1915, 267.

[24] Hutchinson, *Archdeaconry of Stoke*, 10.

[25] *S.H.C.* N.S. vi(1), 186; ibid. 1915, 240–1.

[26] Ibid. N.S. vi(1), 178, 183.

[27] F. W. Hackwood, *Religious Wednesbury* (Dudley, 1900), 38.

[28] *D.N.B.*

missioners cited and deprived at least 42 married clergy in the diocese: among them were the Dean of Lichfield, two of the vicars choral of the cathedral, and eleven other priests with Staffordshire benefices.[29] In numerical terms the upheaval was not nearly so striking as that which had occurred when the chantries were dissolved; but, unlike the former chantry priests, the deprived married clergy who were not prepared to put away their wives were left with no prospect of any future employment in the Church.

Sampson died in 1554.[30] His successor, Ralph Baynes, was a distinguished Hebrew scholar, and one of those who reintroduced the study of that language to England. He was also a zealous Catholic, who had been an opponent of Latimer at Cambridge, spent the previous reign abroad teaching at the University of Paris, and was now to assist at the trials of Hooper, Rogers, and Taylor for heresy. His activity against the Protestants, with whom he saw that there could no longer be any compromise, naturally earned him the hatred of later Protestant writers: the only thing that Fuller could find in his favour was that he was not as bad a bishop as Bonner.

Few records survive of Baynes's work as diocesan, but presumably he did his best to see that the old forms of worship were restored and that any recalcitrants were disciplined. His diocese was not one of those in which Protestantism was already strong and well established, but the new doctrines were evidently spreading into it. Under Mary at least 7 people were burnt in the diocese: 3 at Lichfield, 3 at Coventry, and 1 at Derby.[31] Among the Lichfield victims was Joyce Lewis, daughter of Sir Thomas Curzon of Croxall and niece of Latimer; one of those who suffered at Coventry was Laurence Saunders, who had given divinity lectures in Lichfield Cathedral during Edward's reign.[32] Despite this it is evident that Warwickshire, and especially Coventry, remained the real reservoir of Protestant strength in the diocese and that Reform had won few fervent adherents in Staffordshire.[33] Only two Staffordshire incumbents are definitely known to have been deprived during Baynes's episcopate, and the surviving records of his episcopal visitation of 1558 reveal no traces of heresy in the county. A few churches, notably Wolstanton, were in disrepair, but otherwise there were few causes for complaint.[34]

The process of imposing the Elizabethan Settlement on the clergy began with the royal visitation of 1559.[35] Baynes was deprived by the commissioners and died later in the year, and between 1559 and 1562 the composition of the cathedral chapter was much altered as a result of deprivation and resignation.[36] Although the parochial clergy were generally conformist, between 1559 and 1561 seven resigned or were deprived.[37] Five of these did not subscribe to the Acts of Uniformity and Supremacy in 1559; two of the five, who were also canons of Lichfield, are known to have been recusants,[38] and

[29] J. Strype, *Ecclesiastical Memorials* (1816 edn.), iv. 174–5; vii. 42–44. Strype lists 43 deprived clergy, but the J. Garleke who appears early in the list may be the same man as the John Garlyke who occurs later.
[30] For this para. see *D.N.B.*; Smith, *Tudor Prelates and Politics*, 135–6.
[31] Strype, *Eccl. Mem.* vii. 416–19, printing a contemporary list of the burnings during Mary's reign found among Burghley's papers. For the list see Dickens, *Eng. Reformation*, 266.
[32] W. Beresford, *Lichfield*, 218; J. Foxe, *Acts and Monuments*, ed. J. Pratt, viii. 401–5; see below p. 167. Saunders was sent for execution from London to Coventry; he had been Vicar of All Hallows' in Bread Street: *V.C.H. Warws.* ii. 34.
[33] Six of the martyrs in the list printed by Strype are stated to be from Warws. and one from Derbs. Coventry appears to have been the only part of Warws. where the religious changes under Mary aroused active opposition: *V.C.H. Warws.* ii. 33–34.

[34] *S.H.C.* 1915, p. xli, supplemented by Strype, *Eccl. Mem.* iv. 174–5; Lich. Dioc. Regy., B/V/1/2. This last contains only a *liber cleri* and some *comperta*, however, and no office court books or papers survive to supplement it. The only presentment of a suspected heretic among the *comperta* comes from Bridgnorth (Salop.).
[35] For this royal visitation of the southern province see H. Gee, *Elizabethan Clergy and the Settlement of Religion, 1558–64*, 97–98.
[36] *D.N.B.*; see below p. 169.
[37] For the remainder of this para. see, unless otherwise stated, *S.H.C.* 1915, p. xlvii.
[38] They were Thos. Chedulton and Dr. Ant. Draycott. Chedulton was a canon of St. Mary's, Stafford, first vicar of the reorganised church there from 1548, Prebendary of Pipa Parva from 1552, Master of St. John's Hospital, Stafford, from 1556, and probably Vicar of Worfield (Salop.) from 1545 (ibid. 243, 245). Draycott was Rector of Checkley and of Grindon, Prebendary of Longdon, and Baynes's vicar general (ibid. pp. l, 58, 110, 368).

the other three, also including a canon, may reasonably be regarded as such. The other two, who did subscribe, may have had a speedy change of heart, but there is no proof of this. Twelve more who subscribed in 1559 had by 1571 resigned, been deprived, or vacated their livings for some unknown cause, but probably not because of death; some of these may have been recusants.

The alterations to the pattern of worship also entailed yet another review of church furnishings. Thus at a metropolitical visitation of the diocese held early in 1560, during the vacancy in the see, various groups of churchwardens, including those of Biddulph, Church Eaton, Sandon, and Stone, were ordered to destroy the altars in their churches. Although in some other churches altars had evidently already been replaced by communion tables, the process was still not complete five years later.[39]

The new bishop, Thomas Bentham, consecrated in 1560, exemplified the changes of the new reign. A zealous Protestant, he had been deprived of his Oxford fellowship on Mary's accession and had gone abroad, to Zürich, Basle, and Geneva, to join other exiles. Later in the reign he had been recalled to head the persecuted Protestant congregation in London. He was, like Baynes, a leading Hebrew scholar: he helped with the translation of the Geneva Bible and was the translator of part of the later Bishops' Bible.[40] Otherwise the two men had virtually nothing in common. Bentham was one of a number of bishops appointed in the first years of Elizabeth's reign whose sympathies were with the Puritans; he was, for example, on excellent terms with Anthony Gilby, one of the leading Puritan divines, and, when a bishop, was prepared to submit to Gilby's admonitions.[41] In the first Convocation of Elizabeth's reign he voted against the retention of ecclesiastical vestments, and as a diocesan he was reluctant to punish ministers who, on grounds of conscience, refused to wear the surplice.[42] By contrast he was one of the first bishops to take action against those who retained popish ceremonial in their Rogation perambulations. The carrying of crosses and banners on these occasions was forbidden, and those who transgressed were brought before the consistory court.[43]

Bentham's Puritan sympathies cannot have endeared him to the queen. Nor was his reputation as a diocesan improved by evidence that the papists in his diocese were far from crushed.[44] In 1562 the recusancy commissioners reported that in parts of Staffordshire and Derbyshire the old religion remained very strong and was maintained by several families of gentry. Apparently the Bench could not be relied upon to act with the requisite vigour in these cases: when, in 1564, Bentham submitted to the government an analysis of the religious affiliations of 17 Staffordshire J.P.s he pointed out that no fewer than 10 were 'adversaries of religion'[45] and that the county as a whole was 'too much hinderly in all good things pertaining to religion'. Bentham's standards were high, but it is obvious that as other bishops reduced their dioceses to order the inertia and opposition in Staffordshire was becoming more noticeable.

Finally, in 1565,[46] following a rebuke from the queen or the Council, Bentham

[39] Lich. Dioc. Regy., B/V/1/3; see below p. 48.

[40] D.N.B.; Dickens, Eng. Reformation, 268, 273, 288; P. Collinson, Elizabethan Puritan Movement, 61. Bentham was the first married bishop of the see, and his wife bore him a child four days before his consecration as bishop: Diary of Hen. Machyn (Camd. Soc. xlii), 229.

[41] Collinson, Elizabethan Puritan Movement, 105.

[42] F. O. White, Lives of the Elizabethan Bishops (1898), 141; Letters of Thos. Wood, Puritan, 1566–77, ed. P. Collinson (Bull. Inst. Hist. Res. Special Supplement 5), 20.

[43] Lich. Dioc. Regy., B/V/1/5, Acta 22 Jan. 1562 (Office v. John Stanley, Vicar of Alton). In 1560 Grindal, then Bp. of London, had ordered his archdeacons to see that

no banners or 'other like monuments of superstition' were carried during the perambulations: E. Grindal, Remains (Parker Soc. 1843), 241.

[44] For the remainder of this para. see S.H.C. 1915, 367–371; and below p. 99.

[45] There were 27 Staffs. J.P.s in 1564. Of the 10 not mentioned by Bentham 5 lived outside the county; the other 5 were Bentham himself, the Earl of Shrewsbury, the Lords Audley and Paget, and Wm. Robinson of Drayton Bassett.

[46] For the following three paras. see, unless otherwise stated, Visitation Articles and Injunctions of the Period of the Reformation, vol. iii (Alcuin Club Colls. xvi), 163–70.

attempted to purge the diocese of the 'disorders' alleged against his clergy. In the visitation which he held that year yet another attempt was made to root out the remnants of popery. The injunctions enjoined clergy to destroy surviving Latin service-books, to adhere rigidly to the Communion service as set out in the Prayer Book, to forbid the carrying of candles at funerals, and to ensure that there was no ringing for the dead, save for thirty minutes at the time of death and a short knell before burial. Parishioners were to be constantly urged to throw away their rosaries,[47] forbidden to set down corpses by wayside crosses as they brought them to burial, and reminded that they were not to pray for the dead. They were also to be reminded that they must work as usual on those holy days which had been abolished by Act of Parliament. The churches themselves were to be purified. Any remaining altars were to be destroyed, rood-lofts were to be taken down 'unto the lower beams', such things as holy-water stoups, handbells, and 'sepulchres which were used on Good Friday' were to be thrown away, the bases upon which statues had stood were to be smashed, and niches in the church walls filled in. When this had been done the interior of the church was to be whitewashed and the building was to be refurnished with a communion table, a 'crest or vault' erected upon the cross-beam of the dismantled rood-loft, and a 'table of the Commandments' set up where the Sacrament used to hang, 'with other godly sentences which be lately set forth'. Before Michaelmas each church was to have a Bible, a *Paraphrase*, a Book of Common Prayer, a psalter, a copy of the royal Injunctions of 1559, the Declaration, and the Homilies.

The injunctions also show that Bentham hoped for standards of pastoral care that were rather higher than those normally required of the parochial clergy: his demand that clergy should say morning and evening prayer in public every day was, for example, one of the few attempts to enforce a neglected Prayer Book rubric.[48] He was also determined that congregations should hear sermons regularly: whereas the royal Injunctions of 1559 allowed clergy unable to preach the obligatory quarterly sermon the option of reading one of the authorized Homilies,[49] Bentham demanded that such men should contribute annually a thirtieth of the net value of their livings towards the maintenance of a preacher. Communion was to be celebrated on the first Sunday of every month, and the bishop wished parishioners to communicate at least four times a year; both requirements were more than was usually demanded. Finally clergy were required to present at the visitation all children who were 'full seven years of age' and still unconfirmed; this is the lowest age mentioned for confirmation in any articles or injunctions of the period.

Bentham showed interest in both old and new methods of enforcing church discipline. He wished to revive or reinvigorate the office of rural dean: the dean would sit quarterly at one of the churches in his deanery and incumbents would present all fornicators and adulterers from their parishes to him. The bishop also called for the establishment in each parish of groups of between four and eight 'of the most substantial and honest men', charged with the task of keeping order in church. Persistent troublemakers were to be marched by these men 'up unto the chancel door and set . . . with their faces looking down towards the people for the space of one quarter of an hour'. Those who visited alehouses before or during service-time were to be brought into church by the 'honest men' and suffer the same punishment.

The extent to which Bentham's reforms succeeded in Staffordshire is difficult to

---

[47] Clergy were to 'diligently note and mark' those people who wore rosaries, and penalties were laid down for persistent offenders.

[48] *Elizabethan Episcopal Administration, vol. i* (Alcuin Club Colls. xxv), pp. cv–cvi.

[49] *Visitation Articles and Injunctions, iii,* 10.

determine. It is probable, however, that in a number of parishes his injunctions were either quickly forgotten or never fully obeyed. Thus in 1573 almost twenty churches lacked their full complement of books,[50] and in 1576 there were complaints about infrequent sermons and celebrations: at Audley, for example, it was alleged that the congregation had heard only four sermons in ten years.[51] The low standard of the parochial clergy under Bishop Overton, Bentham's successor (see below), suggests that Bentham did not leave behind him a flourishing ministry.

Bentham and his officers were also unable to sway the allegiance of many of the Staffordshire recusants: a return of recusants which the bishop made to the Privy Council in 1578 shows the extent of their failure.[52] The lack of success may to some extent be due to the fact that the county had as yet seen little of the organized Protestant missionary work which Bentham found so useful in other parts of the diocese. In 1576, when the official reaction against 'prophesyings' was setting in, he reported to Archbishop Grindal on the three which had been established in his diocese, emphasizing their success in combating popery and superstition.[53] There was none in Staffordshire, however, and although in the following year John Aylmer, Bishop of London, suggested to Burghley that some Puritan ministers should be sent as missionaries to Staffordshire and other counties where the Church was weak,[54] by then the climate of official opinion rendered such a move virtually impossible. 'Prophesyings' were suppressed, and by 1579, when Bentham died, the views which he had held were generally out of favour among the episcopate.[55]

Bentham's successor was William Overton (1580–1609), treasurer of Chichester Cathedral, an ecclesiastical careerist who had been accumulating benefices since the early 1550s.[56] The early years of his episcopate were stormy. He owed his bishopric mainly to the influence of one of his patrons, the Earl of Leicester.[57] Another of Leicester's clerical protégés was a Dr. John Beacon. Overton had promised that, if Beacon helped him to a bishopric by speaking to the earl on his behalf, he would show his gratitude, and when he became bishop he duly appointed Beacon to the chancellorship of the diocese.[58] A rift soon occurred, however, and he began to try to edge Beacon out,[59] appointing a local man, Zachary Babington, first as joint chancellor with Beacon and then as sole chancellor. Beacon stood firm, and by 1582 the situation was out of Overton's control. There was at least one scuffle in the cathedral, Beacon and Babington held rival courts, and Beacon began to sue the bishop in every possible court, from Quarter Sessions to Star Chamber. Overton was at the same time trying to quell a revolt among the cathedral chapter. At his primary visitation he had demanded a *subsidium charitativum* from the clergy of the diocese. The chapter had refused to pay this, and when Overton retaliated by vilifying the dean and trumping up

[50] Lich. Dioc. Regy., B/V/1/8, *Comperta*. The *Paraphrase* was the book most commonly missing.

[51] Ibid. B/V/1/10, *Comperta*. It was also alleged that the vicar neither catechized nor celebrated 3 times a year.

[52] *S.H.C.* 1915, 373–5.

[53] B.M. Add. MS. 29546, ff. 51v.–52v. Bentham maintained that the meetings, which were held at Coventry, Shrewsbury, and Southam (Warws.), increased learning in the simple and kept ministers on their mettle, and that their effect was broadened by the way in which those who attended spread reports of the proceedings in their own parishes.

[54] A. F. Scott Pearson, *Thos. Cartwright and Elizabethan Puritanism, 1535–1603*, 234. Salop. was another of the counties mentioned by Aylmer. In 1576 there was a 'prophesying' at Shrewsbury, but it had been active for less than 3 years: B.M. Add. MS. 29546, f. 52.

[55] Collinson, *Elizabethan Puritan Movement*, 193, 196, 201.

[56] *D.N.B.*; White, *Elizabethan Bishops*, 271–3. The *D.N.B.* wrongly states that he became Vicar of Eccleshall in 1553 and Rector of Swynnerton in 1555, and that he held the rectories of Stoke-upon-Trent and Hanbury before becoming bishop. For the incumbents of these livings see *S.H.C.* 1915, 88, 115, 249, 265.

[57] J. Strype, *Annals of the Reformation* (1824 edn.), iii(2), 210.

[58] *Cal. S.P. Dom.* 1547–80, 651; White, *Elizabethan Bishops*, 272–3; *D.N.B. sub* Becon.

[59] For the remainder of this para. see Strype, *Annals*, iii(1), 131–8; iii(2), 202–11; Strype, *Life of Whitgift* (1822 edn.), i. 199–213; Strype, *Life of Grindal* (1821 edn.), 404–10; Lambeth Palace Libr., Reg. Grindal, i, ff. 139v.–143v.; and below p. 171.

charges against two of the canons the chapter counter-attacked by accusing him of disregarding its privileges and of using the endowments of the see to reward his son-in-law. This affair and that of the chancellorship eventually drove Grindal, early in 1583, to order a metropolitical visitation of the diocese. It was conducted by John Whitgift, Bishop of Worcester, and three other commissioners; with some difficulty the contending parties were brought to an agreement, and the visitation ended in June.

Overton's own visitation of his diocese in 1584 brought him further trouble. The articles of inquiry which he published for the visitation contained nothing new, and no exception was taken to them.[60] Some of the measures put forward in the subjoined 'advertisements' were, however, Puritan in tone and often controversial. The most far-reaching were the establishment of a diocesan board of examiners, responsible for the compulsory public examination of candidates for the ministry and clerks presented to benefices, and the requirement that the latter, having satisfied the examiners, should spend a month in their new cures as probationers before institution. Four of the examiners were to be preachers, and in the eyes of the government Overton compounded his offence by his choice of preachers: at least two of those whom he named as examiners were well-known Puritans. Overton claimed, in a letter to the Privy Council, that he was merely acting in accordance with the spirit of the Council's recent demand for the removal of 'insufficient' ministers; but Whitgift, by then Archbishop of Canterbury, denounced the association of four preachers with the bishop and his officers as 'a kind of seignory', and the scheme was vetoed.

Overton's motives for his proposals are obscure. His earlier career as one of Leicester's protégés indicates Puritan sympathies, and as bishop he was prepared to compromise with Puritans. Thus in 1582 he told the rigid Puritan William Axton, Rector of Moreton Corbet (Salop.), that he need not make the sign of the Cross at baptism, and that no further proceedings would be taken against him for not wearing the surplice if he would undertake to wear it once.[61] There is, nevertheless, no evidence that Overton was a convinced reformer. It is possible that the initiative came from John Beacon. He had drawn up a similar, though more ambitious, scheme when chancellor of the diocese of Norwich,[62] and he was acting with Babington as Overton's chancellor again by the summer of 1584, before the visitation began.[63] Overton's readiness to acquiesce in such proposals and to defend them later could thus be explained by his eagerness to win back Leicester's favour, which he had forfeited by his earlier behaviour to Beacon.[64]

Leicester's reaction is uncertain. Burghley, another of Overton's patrons, had, however, completely lost patience with his former client and certainly did not see him

---

[60] For this para. see *Elizabethan Episcopal Administration, vol. iii* (Alcuin Club Colls. xxvii), 161–74; B.M., Eg. MS. 1693, f. 118; *Seconde Parte of a Register*, ed. A. Peel, i. 260–7; Collinson, *Elizabethan Puritan Movement*, 183–4. At his primary visitation in 1581 Overton had circulated printed 'advertisements' for the 'public examination of ministers to be ordered, instituted, or admitted to cures' (Strype, *Whitgift*, i. 200, 207). No copy of these appears to have survived, and it was claimed (ibid.) that in any case Overton had done little or nothing to implement them.

[61] *Seconde Parte of a Register*, i. 68–74. Axton refused the compromise and was deprived of his living. The editor of the *Seconde Parte* dates the proceedings 1570 and identifies the unnamed bishop as Bentham; but Axton was not admitted to the rectory until 1580 (Lambeth Palace Libr., Reg. Grindal, ii, f. 438), and the proceedings culminating in his deprivation can be traced in Lich. Dioc. Regy.,

B/V/1/13, *Acta* 31 Aug., 20 Sept., 21 Nov. 1582; B/C/3/10 18 Jan. 1583. For Overton's willingness later in his episcopate to license Puritans silenced by other bishops see below p. 55.

[62] Collinson, *Elizabethan Puritan Movement*, 183, 184.

[63] Beacon was acting as chancellor again by July 1584: Lich. Dioc. Regy., B/C/3/10, 5 July 1584. The visitation was held in the late summer or the autumn: B/V/1/16 and 17. At a case held before Beacon in 1585 a key role was evidently played by 4 preachers, one of whom had also been named by Overton as an examiner: B/C/3/10, 5 Feb. 1585 (Office *v.* John Barwell, Rector of Seckington, Warws.).

[64] Leicester accused Overton of 'apostasy': Strype, *Annals*, iii(2), 207, 208. Beacon could also have been responsible for the 1581 'advertisements', for which see above n. 60.

as a genuine reformer eager to raise the standards of the ministry. In 1585 he spoke contemptuously of Overton as the bishop 'who made seventy ministers in one day for money, some tailors, some shoemakers, and others craftsmen'.[65] Above all, the Puritan propagandists regarded Overton, possibly unfairly, as an enemy and a persecutor.[66] In the late 1580s he was held up to ridicule in the Marprelate Tracts,[67] accused of having obtained his bishopric by simony,[68] and subjected, with Babington, to a violent attack in an unpublished Puritan treatise, according to which his 'new device' of 1584 was merely a pretext to make money: 'swarms of ministers', wrote the author, echoing Burghley, were 'made hand over head . . . and payments hansed [levied] from 2s. 6d. to 16s. or 17s. apiece'.[69]

Overton's need to raise money was in fact indisputable. He arrived at Lichfield heavily in debt, and some of his difficulties during the early years of his episcopate were undoubtedly the result of his desperate attempts to recoup the expenses incurred in obtaining his bishopric. The charge of simony was no doubt a malicious fabrication, but in 1583 Overton himself claimed that he had paid more than £1,300 in first-fruits, fees, liveries, and other necessary expenditure before he even set foot in his diocese.[70]

Overton's plight was not exceptional. Bentham's finances had also been strained: according to Overton he had died over £1,100 in debt to the Crown and £250 in debt to the see.[71] By this period in fact the bishops of Coventry and Lichfield, like most other bishops, were finding their resources inadequate for their commitments.[72] Above all they were beginning to feel the effect of the alienation of substantial portions of the temporalities of the see which had been forced upon their predecessors in the 1530s and 1540s.

Even the medieval bishops had, considering the size of the area under their jurisdiction, been comparatively poor: in 1535, before the alienations began, the bishop's net annual income was just over £700.[73] The losses under Bishop Lee were disturbing but not severe. In 1537 he was forced by the king to give his London house to the queen's brother, Viscount Beauchamp (later Duke of Somerset), but received from the Crown in exchange the rectory of Hanbury, the richest in Staffordshire.[74] The amputation of the archdeaconry of Chester in 1541[75] meant the loss of a steady source of income from fees and dues of various kinds.

The worst depredations were suffered during Sampson's episcopate. In 1546 he was compelled to surrender to the king for the benefit of Sir William Paget, one of the Secretaries of State, a large block of property north of Lichfield. This included Beaudesert and Haywood, two of the bishop's three country houses in Staffordshire,

[65] Conyers Read, *Lord Burghley and Queen Elizabeth*, 302–3; and see below p. 54. For Burghley as Overton's patron see e.g. Strype, *Annals*, iii(2), 209–10.

[66] Several cases in the early years of his episcopate could have been held against him. Besides the deprivation of Axton, whose own version (*Seconde Parte of a Register*, i. 68–74) shows that Overton was prepared to concede much of what was asked, there was, for example, the case of Rob. More, Vicar of Rushall, forced in 1586 to do penance for refusing the sacraments to those who knelt: Lich. Dioc. Regy., B/C/3/10, 6 Aug. 1586.

[67] *Marprelate Tracts, 1588, 1589*, ed. W. Pierce, 90, 155–6, 187, 217.

[68] B.M. Add. MS. 48064, f. 48; Collinson, *Elizabethan Puritan Movement*, 400. Overton was accused of having paid 1,000 marks to an unnamed individual for his bishopric and of having granted a Wm. Plased a £20 annuity for further help.

[69] *Seconde Parte of a Register*, ii. 16–17. Taken in isolation this might be regarded merely as a reflection of a

Puritan dislike of ordination fees; but the same accusation had earlier been made both by the dean and chapter and by Burghley: Strype, *Whitgift*, i. 207; see above.

[70] E 135/9/6. Besides this Overton spent another £1,300 in lawsuits and other matters connected with the bishopric: ibid. He later stated that when he first went to Lichfield he was so heavily in debt that he could not even pay his servants' wages or his lawyers' fees: B.M. Add. MS. 48064, f. 48.

[71] E 135/9/6.

[72] The almost complete loss of the see's estate and financial archives for the late 16th and early 17th cents. makes it impossible to trace in detail the bishops' finances. For episcopal finances in general see C. Hill, *Economic Problems of the Church*, esp. chap. 2.

[73] See above p. 22.

[74] *L. & P. Hen. VIII*, xii(1), pp. 357, 363, 440, 526; xii(2), p. 346; xiii(1), p. 63; xiv(1), pp. 403, 404. For the value of Hanbury rectory see above p. 42.

[75] See above p. 44.

and the manors of Haywood, Baswich, Longdon, Cannock, and Rugeley. In 1547, under the terms of Henry VIII's will, Sampson was granted as compensation the appropriation of six rectories, three chapels, and the church of Gnosall;[76] although this was an apparently fair exchange, it was one which meant that the see received a fixed asset in return for one which was to appreciate in value as the years went by. Earlier in 1547 Sampson had granted some Warwickshire properties, the manors of Bishop's Tachbrook, Bishop's Itchington, Chadshunt, and Gaydon, and the advowsons of Bishop's Tachbrook, Bishop's Itchington, and Fenny Compton, to Thomas Fisher, a confidential agent of the Duke of Somerset. The suggestion that Sampson made the grant in the hope of gaining a friend at Court is strengthened by the fact that whereas originally a £50 rent-charge was agreed upon, in 1548 the bishop abandoned all claim to this.[77] In 1548 Sampson also surrendered his manorial rights in Lichfield to the burgesses in return for a £50 rent-charge.[78] Other manors, such as Prees (Salop.), Farndon (Ches.), and Sawley (Derb.), were granted away at low rents on long leases or in fee-farm.[79]

Bishop Baynes forced Thomas Fisher to disgorge the advowson of Fenny Compton and to agree to pay a rent-charge of £82 10s. for the rest of the property granted to him by Sampson.[80] Neither Baynes nor Bentham could, however, regain any of the other losses. In 1583 Overton stated that his income from temporalities, pensions, and appropriated churches was some £560;[81] this apparently represents his gross income from these sources and compares with a gross revenue of about £760 from the same sources in 1535.[82] The income from spiritualities is unlikely to have risen appreciably, and after the loss of the archdeaconry of Chester may even have declined. Thus in about 50 years, and during a period of steadily rising prices, the value of the see had dropped by some £200 a year. Economies were virtually impossible. The bishop's responsibilities, temporal as well as ecclesiastical, remained vast and undoubtedly proved increasingly expensive; and although the loss of a number of his estates meant that he could dispense with the services of a few minor officials he now usually had a wife to maintain in proper style and children to educate and to place or marry.

Overton's debts led him to make vigorous attempts early in his episcopate to restore the finances of the see. He sued Thomas Fisher's son Edward who, having found a legal flaw in his father's agreement with Bishop Baynes, had refused to pay the stipulated rent-charge; Overton soon obtained an Act confirming his right to the £82 10s. a year.[83] He challenged Sampson's grant to the burgesses of Lichfield[84] and sued Lord Paget and others for rights or property which he claimed they illegally detained from the see.[85] His efforts no doubt helped to make him unpopular at Lichfield and among the gentry of the diocese, but they apparently achieved nothing else. He could do little to increase the regular yield from his temporalities, however much he might fall back on that mainstay of bishops and ecclesiastical corporations, the

[76] S.H.C. 1939, 110–11, 132–3; Cal. Pat. 1547–8, 179–80. The appropriated churches were the rectories of Wolstanton, Belgrave (Leics.), Pytchley, Long Buckby, and Towcester (all Northants.), and Towyn (Merioneths.), 3 chapels dependent on Towyn, and Gnosall. For the status of Gnosall see V.C.H. Staffs. iv. 128. The net yearly value was given as some £183.
[77] Cal. Pat. 1548–9, 403; 1549–51, 19–20; Dugdale, Warws. i. 349; D.N.B. sub Fisher.
[78] Harwood, Lichfield, 336.
[79] Lich. Dioc. Regy., C.C. 124100, pp. 6, 7; C.C. 282222.
[80] Ibid. C.C. 124095.

[81] E 135/9/6. In 1582 Overton had stated in a letter to the Privy Council that his living was 'scantly four hundred pounds by the year, for these first years': Strype, Annals, iii(2), 217. This may have been an understatement (the letter was designed to win sympathy) or may represent what was left after Overton had paid some of his debts but before he had paid his officers.
[82] Valor Eccl. iii. 128–30.
[83] Cal. S.P. Dom. 1581–90, 8; E 135/9/6; Lich. Dioc. Regy., C.C. 124068, 124095.
[84] Acts of P.C. 1581–2, 447–8; E 135/9/6.
[85] E 135/9/6.

manipulation of long leases in return for high entry fines.[86] At his primary visitation he resorted, as has been seen, to extraordinary taxation of his clergy; the dean and chapter claimed that the visitation brought him in between £400 and £500, and although they were hostile witnesses the estimate is not unreasonable.[87] He was also accused, in 1586, of having plundered the bishopric by felling timber worth almost £1,000, of selling offices, and of countenancing corruption among his officers.[88] Little appears to be known of his finances during the latter part of his episcopate, but the see remained impoverished, and Overton himself died heavily in debt to the Crown.[89]

Overton's jaundiced reports in the 1580s concerning the state of his diocese may be partly explained by the fact that he had set an influential section of the clergy and the laity against him. He may also have been trying to find excuses for his own short-comings. When, for example, he told Walsingham in 1581 that he had the stubbornest diocese in the land, with the most parsimonious and unpatriotic clergy, he was trying to explain away the fact that he had been able to collect only half of a subsidy recently demanded from his clergy.[90]

Nevertheless it is evident that the see was a difficult one to administer and that Staffordshire was one of the most troublesome parts of it. In 1582 Overton alleged that as a diocesan Bentham had been 'touched with too much idleness, or at least with too much softness',[91] but pointed out that Bentham's attempts to maintain discipline, as well as his own, had been hindered by the existence of a large number of peculiars into which episcopal officers could not penetrate. He complained of the lax way in which peculiar jurisdictions in the diocese were administered, singling out those in Staffordshire for particular condemnation.[92] The existence of the peculiars had helped to make the diocese 'the den of fugitives, the very receptacle of all the refuse that is thrown out of other dioceses round about me'.[93] The fugitives no doubt included Roman Catholics, whose presence would have helped to reinforce the strong recusant element in Staffordshire. If the county had had a sufficient number of zealous and well-trained clergy the threat to the Church might not have been serious; but in 1584 Overton reported that 'in Stafford archdeaconry, where are about one hundred and fifty cures, there is scarce the thirtieth parish furnished with a tolerable preacher'. In general the county was, he stated, 'dangerous and superstitious'.[94]

The standard of the parochial clergy in Staffordshire rose little, if at all, during Overton's long episcopate, and the county always remained relatively ill-served.[95] Graduate clergy, for example, seem to have been rarer than they were in most other English counties.[96] Returns of Staffordshire parochial clergy, all incomplete in some

---

[86] In Oct. 1582 the dean and chapter alleged that since Overton's appointment 'the demises of leases already have been worth to him about £400': B.M., Lansd. MS. 36, f. 130. Whether renewal fines would generally average about £200 a year, or whether Overton was offering favourable renewals of unexpired leases in return for cash down it appears to be impossible to decide. A survey of episcopal property made in 1623 seems to suggest that few of the more valuable leases fell in during Overton's episcopate: Lich. Dioc. Regy., C.C. 124100, pp. 1–10. For his involvement in the glass industry at Eccleshall see *V.C.H. Staffs.* ii. 225 and note.

[87] B.M., Lansd. MS. 36, f. 128. The procurations received at an undated visitation during Overton's episcopate amounted to almost £250: Lich. Dioc. Regy., B/V/1/12. If this was the normal figure the *subsidium charitativum* would bring the total up to that alleged.

[88] *Seconde Parte of a Register*, ii. 16–17. The anonymous author of this attack is violently prejudiced against Overton, but the reckless sale of timber was certainly one of the expedients favoured by impoverished bishops: Hill,

Econ. Problems, 11, 310–12.

[89] *Cal. S.P. Dom.* 1603–10, 505.

[90] Ibid. 1581–90, 18. The clergy's reluctance to pay is not surprising. In 2 years they had paid 2 sets of procurations and, 'with murmuring and repining', the charitative subsidy to Overton: B.M., Lansd. MS. 36, f. 128.

[91] Strype, *Annals*, iii(2), 212.

[92] Ibid. 211, 212, 213, 214. Overton concentrated his attack mainly on the dean and chapter's peculiar jurisdiction in Lichfield, and to some extent his complaint was a move in his struggle with the chapter (see above p. 49). Nevertheless, the problem of peculiars had already been raised by Bentham in 1564, and in 1638 was spotlighted by Bp. Wright: *S.H.C.* 1915, 369; *Cal. S.P. Dom.* 1638–9, 118–19. [93] Strype, *Annals*, iii(2), 217.

[94] B.M., Eg. MS. 1693, f. 118.

[95] Hill, *Econ. Problems*, 207.

[96] In 1603 Coventry and Lichfield had proportionately fewer graduate clergy than any other diocese in Eng. and Wales: R. G. Usher, *Reconstruction of the Eng. Church*, i. 207, 241.

respect, survive for 1593,[97] 1602,[98] and 1604.[99] Of the 109 clergy about whom definite information is given in 1593 14 were graduates; of the remaining 95 eleven had studied at Oxford or Cambridge but appear not to have taken their degrees.[1] Nine years later 20 of the 91 clergy listed had degrees and 69 were non-graduates,[2] while in 1604 about 22 ministers were graduates, about 95 were not, and most of the remaining 53 were probably non-graduates.[3] Some of the graduate clergy were evidently men of learning: Everard Digby, for example, who was Rector of Hamstall Ridware for a few years in the mid-1580s and again in the 1590s, was the author of works on science and philosophy.[4] Among the non-graduates, many of whom had probably received a grammar-school education, there were marked variations in ability. Thus in 1593 Richard Mitchell, incumbent of Horton, was described as 'in sacris litteris bene exercitatus',[5] whereas George Horden, Vicar of Penkridge, was found to be 'penitus illiteratus'.[6]

The percentage of clergy licensed to preach was low, as it was elsewhere in the country. In 1593 16 of the 109 clergy listed were preachers,[7] in 1602 21 were preachers and 68 non-preachers,[8] and in 1604 45 were preachers and 112 non-preachers.[9] Moreover not all preachers could be counted upon: in 1604 10 of the preachers listed in the return were described as non-resident, while of others the Puritan compilers made such remarks as 'very slow in preaching', 'preacheth very seldom', and 'weak'. It was claimed that as many as 118 congregations in the county had no preachers, 'neither have had (for the most) now more than 40 years'.[10]

In some places it was probably impossible to obtain a supply of well-qualified clergy because no adequate stipend could be offered.[11] Poor chapelries were frequently served by lay readers: in 1604 Chapel Chorlton (in Eccleshall), where the stipend was 40s., had a miller as lay reader and Billington (in Bradley), where the stipend was 16 groats, a husbandman.[12] The county as a whole suffered from the large number of impropriations. In 1604 it was estimated that there were at least 75 impropriated livings in Staffordshire,[13] and the incomes of those who served them were on the whole meagre. At Leek, for example, where the rectory was valued at £400 a year, the vicar received only £10; at Penkridge, worth £250 a year, the vicar received £16; at Cannock, worth £50 a year, the curate's stipend was £8.[14] A few of these clergy supplemented their incomes by practising trades or professions: at Madeley the vicar was stated to be a weaver, and at Checkley the curate was 'a practitioner in physic but seldom in divinity'.[15]

[97] In a diocesan return, now Lambeth Palace Libr., C.M. XIII/37. This and the following 2 returns are utilized in S.H.C. 1915, which also contains a discussion of them (pp. 398–400).

[98] In a diocesan return, printed as 'An Elizabethan Clergy List of the Diocese of Lichfield', ed. J. C. Cox, Jnl. Derb. Arch. and Nat. Hist. Soc. vi.

[99] Printed as 'A Puritan Survey of the Church in Staffs. in 1604', ed. A. Peel, E.H.R. xxvi.

[1] S.H.C. 1915, p. xxxvi.

[2] The 91 include 3 readers and a preacher. Nothing has been discovered about the academic status of 2 of the clergy. The figures given in the return have been supplemented from S.H.C. 1915. [3] Ibid. p. xxxvi.

[4] Ibid. 113; D.N.B. He was also the author of the earliest treatise on swimming published in England. The notable scholar Hadrian a Sarravia was Rector of Tatenhill 1588–96, and evidently resided for a time in the parish: S.H.C. 1915, 276, 278–9. [5] S.H.C. 1915, 130.

[6] Ibid. 205, 210. [7] Ibid. p. xxxviii.

[8] The totals have been obtained by collating the returns of 1602 and 1604, supplemented by inf. from S.H.C. 1915,

which, however, gives (p. xxxviii) the totals as 17 preachers and 61 non-preachers.

[9] The total of preachers given here includes Dr. Sam. Heron, Rector of Cheadle, but not the Archdeacon of Coventry, who was included in the return as a prebendary. S.H.C. 1915, p. xxxviii, omits Heron and gives 44 preachers.

[10] E.H.R. xxvi. 341–52, esp. pp. 344, 347, 352.

[11] For the curates of Bilston, Pelsall, and Willenhall see below p. 326. [12] E.H.R. xxvi. 345, 346.

[13] Ibid. 352. [14] Ibid. 342, 346, 347.

[15] Ibid. 344. The stipend in both cases was £10. It has been pointed out (Hill, Econ. Problems, 217–18) that although a minister was required to promise not to engage in 'any artificers' occupations' if his living were worth £6 13s. 4d. a year or more the promise was often broken; artisans who entered the ministry were sometimes prepared to accept low stipends, relying for the bulk of their income upon what they earned during the week. It is also suggested that the 70 craftsmen whom Burghley accused Overton of ordaining in a day (see above p. 51) were probably men of this type.

There appears to be no evidence that Puritanism was as yet widespread in Staffordshire. The 'prophesyings' which had been held elsewhere in the diocese in the 1570s can have affected the county only marginally, and there appears to be only one Staffordshire example of an 'exercise', the type of gathering devised by Puritan clergy in an attempt to evade the ban on 'prophesyings'. This was held at Burton-upon-Trent in the 1590s and during the first decade of the 17th century; it achieved a certain fame, and in its later years was attended by at least two notable Puritan divines, William Bradshaw and Arthur Hildersham. Their activity in the diocese reveals Overton's laxity or toleration: although both had been silenced by their former diocesans Overton granted them licences to preach.[16] The influence of the Burton gatherings upon Staffordshire clergy from neighbouring parishes is difficult to estimate. It is possible, for example, that there were sympathizers at Clifton Campville, where in 1604 the rector and his two curates were all licensed preachers; a group of three resident preachers in a parish was unusual in Staffordshire, and the censorious compilers of the 1604 return had nothing unfavourable to say about any of the three.[17] Nevertheless it is obvious that in the early years of the 17th century there were few Puritan clergy in the county, and probably none that was regarded by authority as dangerous.[18]

The Jacobean and Caroline bishops were in general more vigorous diocesans than Bentham and Overton had been. After the brief episcopate of George Abbot, who succeeded Overton in 1609 and was bishop for only a month before translation to London and then to Canterbury,[19] came that of Richard Neile (1610–14). Neile, translated from Rochester, was a severe disciplinarian and a dedicated opponent of the Puritans. He attempted to maintain a rigid orthodoxy in the diocese, and it was during his episcopate that a layman was burnt at Lichfield for heresy.[20] His successors continued the struggle against nonconformity with less extreme means. John Overall (1614–18), a theologian who had been a leading figure at the Hampton Court Conference and had subsequently been one of those responsible for the revision of the Authorized Version of the Bible, was a moderate man; Fuller described him as 'a discreet presser of conformity'. Thomas Morton (1619–32) was another moderate, a low churchman who as Bishop of Chester had tried to win over both recusants and nonconformists and continued to pursue this policy after his translation to Coventry and Lichfield. Much of his published work consisted of refutations of Roman Catholic doctrines; but these were calm and scholarly in tone and content. Robert Wright (1632–43), who was translated from Bristol, was, unlike Morton, a supporter of Laudian principles; as a diocesan he shared Laud's concern for the proper maintenance of churches and, like the archbishop, endeavoured to enrich and dignify services.

For all the early-17th-century bishops save Wright the see was a stepping-stone to wealthier and more desirable bishoprics. It remained comparatively poor. A brief survey drawn up in 1623[21] shows that more than half of the surviving episcopal manors and 6 out of 9 appropriated rectories had been leased in the previous century either in fee-farm or for terms of 50 years and over; the rents were in most cases below the valuations given in 1535. Although the long leases would gradually have fallen in, and the bishop would have been able to demand substantial fines for renewing them, there appeared to be no real prospect of putting episcopal finances upon a sound footing. In the late 1630s, moreover, Wright was complaining that the bishops lacked even a

[16] *D.N.B.* *sub* Bradshaw, Hildersam; Collinson, *Elizabethan Puritan Movement*, 168, 209, 438. Neither Bradshaw nor Hildersham lived in Staffs., although Bradshaw's home was just over the border in Stapenhill (Derbs.).

[17] *E.H.R.* xxvi. 349.

[18] Usher, *Reconstruction of Eng. Church*, i. 249–51; ii. 4 n.2.

[19] For this para. see *D.N.B.*

[20] In this case, however, Neile cannot be held solely responsible: see below p. 59.

[21] Lich. Dioc. Regy., C.C. 124100, pp. 1–10.

suitable house. According to him the palace at Lichfield was not only dilapidated but also partly inhabited by tradesmen and other tenants to whom his predecessors had leased portions of the building; he was left with the choice of returning to 'moist Eccleshall, *sepulchrum episcoporum*', or of going to Coventry, where the palace had been on long lease since 1545.[22]

Wright accumulated a considerable private fortune through his ecclesiastical preferments.[23] Nevertheless he evidently judged that his regular income from the bishopric was insufficient, and his method of overcoming this problem was a common one. In 1637 Laud reported to the king that Wright had disregarded the prohibition on the cutting of timber on episcopal estates and had been 'making waste of the poor woods there remaining'. Ten years later it was stated that in two years Wright had felled and sold timber at Brewood worth over £130.[24]

Another expedient, also common, had been adopted by the Crown to relieve Wright's three predecessors.[25] On his election to the see Neile had been granted a dispensation to hold *in commendam* livings to the value of £133 6s. 8d. on the ground that the income of his new bishopric was 'insufficient'. Neile already held one rectory *in commendam*, and in 1612 the king presented him to another, Clifton Campville, which was to be held only during his tenure of the see. The king's right of presentation was challenged by two claimants to the patronage of the living and, as the case developed, wider issues were raised. Finally James's personal intervention, his coercion of the judges, and his dismissal of Coke, the only recalcitrant, combined to make the Case of *commendams* one of major political and constitutional importance. Clifton Campville had by this time passed from Neile to Overall; after the king's victory Overall and Morton held it *in commendam*, apparently without disturbance, throughout their episcopates.

If the financial condition of the bishops was precarious that of some of their parochial clergy was desperate. Sir Nathaniel Brent, Laud's vicar general, reporting to the archbishop in 1635 on the results of that year's metropolitical visitation of the southern province, noted that the Staffordshire clergy were 'exceeding poor'.[26] In fact at the outbreak of the Civil War many vicars and curates were receiving little more than their predecessors had been getting some forty years earlier. Thus in the 1640s the stipend of the Curate of Barlaston was £10 a year, an increase of only £4 since 1604, while at Weston-upon-Trent the curate's income had risen from £6 in 1604 by a mere 8s. 8d.[27] In some parishes the augmentations had been rather more substantial, though still insufficient. The Curate of Adbaston, for example, received £8 in 1604 and £14 in the 1640s, and the Curate of Maer, who received £6 in 1604, was getting £20 in the 1640s.[28] Bishop Morton was prominent among those who urged the augmentation of poor vicarages, but, doubtless owing to opposition from vested interests, he could achieve virtually nothing.[29] It was at his request, however, that in 1630 the Puritan Feoffees for

[22] *Cal. S.P. Dom.* 1638–9, 119; W. Laud, *Works*, ed. W. Scott and J. Bliss, v. 360, 364; C.C. 124100, p. 9. The lease of the Coventry palace, which had been for 99 years, had reserved to the bishops the right to use the palace whenever they were at Coventry. And see above p. 23.
[23] *D.N.B.*
[24] Laud, *Works*, v. 346; S.R.O., 547/M/1/173.
[25] For this para. see *Eng. Reps.* lxxx. 290–313; S. R. Gardiner, *Hist. of Eng. 1603–42* (1883–4 edn.), iii. 13–19; J. R. Tanner, *Constitutional Docs. of the Reign of Jas. I*, 175–6, 192–8; *S.H.C.* 1915, 68. Overton occurs as Rector of Stoke-upon-Trent 1602–4 and as Rector of Swynnerton 1604 (*S.H.C.* 1915, 249, 265), but in each case the tenure was brief.

[26] *Cal. S.P. Dom.* 1635, p. xxxvii. Brent is reporting on his visit to Stafford and is speaking of 'the clergy of this division'. This presumably means the clergy of the archdeaconry of Stafford: his report from Lichfield is concerned only with the cathedral and some peculiars, while other reports by him cover the 3 other archdeaconries in the diocese (ibid. pp. xxxvi–xxxvii, xxxvii–xxxix).   [27] *S.H.C.* 1915, 23, 312.   [28] Ibid. 5, 187.
[29] He augmented the vicarage of one of the Northants. livings appropriated to the bishopric in 1547, and Wright augmented another. After his translation to Durham Morton continued his campaign with rather more success: White Kennett, *Case of Impropriations* (1704), 230–1, 243–248.

the Purchase of Impropriations granted the Curate of St. Chad's, Stafford, what appears to be an augmention of his stipend.[30]

By Morton's time the parochial clergy in the county were becoming, for the first time, a body consisting predominantly of graduates. Between 1619 and 1631 43 of the 48 clergy instituted to Staffordshire livings were graduates, while a few surviving ordination lists of 1623–31 show that of 23 men who subsequently obtained livings in the county 20 had degrees. The trend towards a graduate clergy was a national one, and Morton, himself a patron of young scholars, no doubt welcomed it and fostered it in his own diocese.[31]

Records of visitations in the 1620s and 1630s reveal little about the state of parish life in Staffordshire that could not easily be paralleled elsewhere.[32] At the metropolitical visitation of 1635, for example, most parishes had little to report save the names of local recusants, the fornications and adulteries of some of the parishioners, and the misdemeanours of Sabbath-breakers and other black sheep of the community. What the vicar general singled out for special condemnation was the state of the parish churches. Staffordshire churches and churchyards were, he reported, 'kept very undecently'. At Uttoxeter 'the walls of the chancel were almost quite covered with verses made by one Mr. Archbold . . . in commendation of divers learned divines whom he hath heard preach in that church, which I ordered to be wiped out and divine sentences of Scripture to be put in their place, whereat the old gentleman was much offended'. Several churches near Stafford had been turned into barns 'or worse'.[33] Certainly at least one church had recently been turned into a barn: by 1635 William Brooke had depopulated Haselour and converted the chapel 'to profane uses, as putting hay, furzes, or such like into it or keeping cattle there &c.'[34] Elsewhere the Laudian visitation brought to light examples of the neglect of church fabrics: thus in the north of the county the chancel at Barlaston was 'far out of repair', and work needed to be done on the chancel at Waterfall and the roof at Wetton.[35] Evidence from visitation records shows that churchyards too were commonly ill-kept.

By the 1630s militant Puritanism had become endemic in parts of Staffordshire; bishops now had to contend not only with a vocal minority of recalcitrant clergy but also with a growing number of dissident laymen. The development should not be over-emphasized: to zealous Protestants from more favoured parts of England Staffordshire remained, spiritually, a barren and backward county ripe for missionary endeavour. Nevertheless the ground was being prepared for that flowering of sectarian activity which was to occur in the county during the Interregnum.[36] Some of the influences at work are obscure. Staffordshire was, for example, one of the counties in which London Puritans founded or augmented schools in the hope that they would thereby help to combat not only ignorance but also popery;[37] but it is virtually impossible to assess the extent to which schoolmasters in fact contributed to the work of conversion.

[30] *Activities of the Puritan Faction of the Church of England, 1625–33*, ed. Isabel M. Calder, pp. xxii, 40. For the Feoffees' work in Staffs. see below p. 58.

[31] *S.H.C.* 1915, p. xxxvi. For some statistics from other dioceses relating to the emergence of a graduate clergy see e.g. Hill, *Econ. Problems*, 207 and n. 1; M. H. Curtis, *Oxford and Cambridge in Transition, 1558–1642*, 184.

[32] Lich. Dioc. Regy., B/V/1/52, 55, and 61; these are respectively the visitation bks. of Bp. Morton (1629), Abp. Laud (1635), and Bp. Wright (1636).

[33] *Cal. S.P. Dom.* 1635, p. xxxvii. Mr. Archbold had also cluttered up the chancel at Uttoxeter with 'his intended monument, and a box wherein a book of his verses were kept'.

[34] S.P. 16/287, f. 40. This is part of a survey of various peculiars in the diocese (not merely in Salop., as stated in *Cal. S.P. Dom.* 1635, 37, no. 20) submitted by the bishop in 1635 for the attention of the visitors. Brent probably had this example in mind when he wrote his comment.

[35] Lich. Dioc. Regy., B/V/1/55, pp. 38, 94, 95. Lay impropriators were responsible for the maintenance of the chancels at Barlaston and Waterfall: see e.g. *E.H.R.* xxvi. 343, 345.

[36] See below pp. 116–18.

[37] W. K. Jordan, *Charities of London, 1480–1660*, 311.

The short-lived Puritan group known as the Feoffees for the Purchase of Impropria-tions[38] was active in Staffordshire in the late 1620s and early 1630s, and its work probably provides the best example of organized Puritan endeavour in the county. In 1629 the Feoffees bought a lease of the rectory of Tipton, appropriated to the Lichfield prebend of Prees. Next they were approached by the inhabitants of Kinver, who 'desired to have a good preacher and a schoolmaster'. Money was raised locally and transferred to the Feoffees, who in 1630 were able to lease part of the impropriate rectory of Kinver, including the right to appoint the curate and the schoolmaster. Finally in 1631 the Feoffees acquired the advowson of Mayfield.[39] In each case they found suitable men to hand. At Tipton Robert Atkins, curate since at least 1621,[40] was a Puritan; at Kinver there was a Puritan reader, John Cross;[41] at Mayfield there was an able Puritan vicar, William Barton.[42] The Feoffees were suppressed by the Crown in 1633, and Atkins was silenced as a result of the Laudian visitation.[43] Barton, however, retained his vicarage until his ejection by royalists in 1643,[44] and Cross, who in 1635 was attracting people from neighbouring parishes with his Sunday-afternoon dis-courses, was still Curate of Kinver in 1646.[45]

Atkins had probably remained unmolested until 1635 because Tipton was a Lichfield peculiar; centres of Puritanism and nonconformity were to be found in other Stafford-shire peculiars, of whose lax administration bishops had complained since at least the 1560s.[46] During the Laudian visitation Puritan clergy were also ejected at Weeford, another Lichfield peculiar,[47] and Wolverhampton. The latter parish, one of the largest and most undisciplined of the peculiars, was under the jurisdiction of the holder of the joint deaneries of Windsor and Wolverhampton and had been neglected for many years prior to the 1630s. Then two successive deans, Matthew Wren and his brother Christopher, made vigorous attempts to eradicate Puritanism from St. Peter's church and the peculiar as a whole.[48] The parish had, however, been allowed to remain untouched for too long. Local Puritans did not take it kindly when, in 1635, Richard Lee, a popular preacher, and the only prebendary who did not neglect his cure, was suspended from his prebend in St. Peter's because of his Puritan views. Nor were they overawed when, later in the same year, Laudian ritual and furnishings were introduced, with much publicity, into St. Peter's; the solemn service during which the communion table was dedicated as an altar succeeded only in bringing to their support some of the abler Puritan pamphleteers.[49] Some continued to hold religious gatherings in private and went to other parishes to hear congenial preachers whenever Sunday services at St. Peter's did not include a sermon. In 1641, when the government had been forced on to the defensive, a group of townspeople took action against what they considered to

---

[38] For an account of the Feoffees and their work see *Activities of the Puritan Faction.*

[39] Ibid. pp. xvi, xvii, xxi, 9, 10, 14, 38, 87.

[40] *S.H.C.* 1915, 289.

[41] Ibid. 141, 143.

[42] Although the Feoffees themselves later stated that Mayfield was acquired in Dec. 1631 (*Activities of the Puritan Faction*, pp. xvii, 10), it was presumably effectively in their hands by Mar., when Rowland Heylyn, a leading Feoffee, was patron and presented Barton: *S.H.C.* 1915, 190, 191. For Barton see *D.N.B.*

[43] S.P. 16/287, f. 40.

[44] After his ejection he published a verse translation of the Psalms and several volumes of hymns: *D.N.B.* His influence may have prompted the attack which a few young zealots made in 1642 upon the character of the apparently harmless, if easy-going, John Hill, vicar of the neighbour-ing parish of Ellastone: *Staffs. and the Great Rebellion*, ed. D. A. Johnson and D. G. Vaisey, 41–43.

[45] *Staffs. and the Great Rebellion*, 9; *S.H.C.* 1915, 141, 143.

[46] See above p. 53 and n.92.

[47] S.P. 16/287, f. 40; *Cal. S.P. Dom.* 1635, p. xxxvi. At Weeford the curate, a Mr. Pegge, was ordered by the visitors to read the Book of Sports, and it seems probable that he refused. He had been replaced by 1639: *S.H.C.* 1915, 308.

[48] See below p. 327. In 1635 Bp. Wright stated that Wolverhampton had been 'very faulty heretofore in harbouring papists and nonconformists', but that since the death of 'old Mr. Bailie' the dean had begun the refor-mation of the peculiar: S.P. 16/287, f. 40. Wm. Bailey, the official of the peculiar, died in 1633, during the deanship of Matt. Wren: *S.H.C.* 1915, 329, 333.

[49] *S.H.C.* 1915, 331, 344, 347; G. P. Mander and N. W. Tildesley, *Hist. of Wolverhampton*, 72–74; and see below p. 327.

be idolatry: they entered St. Peter's, broke down the communion rail, dragged the altar out of the chancel, and placed it in the nave.[50]

In a succession of punitive actions the bishops, from Neile onwards, attempted, with ever-diminishing success, to restrain the Puritans. In 1611, for example, Neile suppressed the 'exercises' at Burton; in 1617 Overall silenced Bradshaw.[51] The suppression of the Burton exercises may have been hastened by the earliest and most spectacular, but probably also the least typical of the cases of nonconformity dealt with by these bishops, that of Edward Wightman.[52] Wightman, who is said to have been a Burton mercer, attended, uninvited, the Burton exercises, where he aired his heterodox views on various subjects, including infant baptism. The ministers who attended the exercises tried to wean him away from his opinions, but early in 1611 he presented James I with a manuscript treatise which purported to refute the Nicolaitan heresy and was in fact heretical itself. He was imprisoned and cross-examined by Neile and others, including Laud, then Neile's chaplain; the cross-examination revealed that he not only denied the orthodox doctrine of the Trinity but also held certain blasphemous prophetic views about himself. He was consequently brought before the Court of High Commission and then the consistory court at Lichfield, where he was excommunicated and handed over to the secular authorities. In March 1612 he was led to the stake in Lichfield market-place, but after the fires had been lit he cried out that he recanted and the crowd pulled away the burning faggots. Soon afterwards, however, he reasserted his heresies, and on 11 April he suffered at Lichfield, the last heretic to be burnt in England.

Enough evidence survives to make it plain that during the following thirty years the bishops had to deal with insubordinate ministers and laymen from many parts of the county. Thus, besides the examples cited above, there occur in the 1620s the cases of William Fenner, Vicar of Sedgley, ejected about 1627 for his Puritan opinions;[53] Simeon Ashe, later a leading Presbyterian minister in London, said to have been deprived in Staffordshire for refusing to read the Book of Sports;[54] and of Francis Capps, Vicar of Wolstanton, accused in 1629 of refusing to wear the surplice or to administer Communion to those who knelt to receive it.[55] In 1633 Wright suppressed various unidentified monthly lectures in the diocese and also 'the running lecture, so called because the lecturer went from village to village, and at the end of the week proclaimed where they would have him next, that his disciples might follow'.[56] The bishop's zeal sometimes led him to see Puritanism or nonconformity where none existed,[57] but by 1636 even his cathedral was not safe from Puritan protest.[58]

[50] A. G. Matthews, *Congregational Churches of Staffs.* 9–11; *Staffs. and the Great Rebellion*, 15.

[51] *D.N.B. sub* Hildersam, Bradshaw.

[52] For what follows see *D.N.B.*; C. Burrage, *Early Eng. Dissenters*, 216–20; Harwood, *Lichfield*, 304–5. There is a MS. account entitled 'The Proceedings at Lichfield in 7 court days against Edward Wightman in case of blasphemy and heresy . . .' in Bodl. MS. Ashmole 1521 (B) VII, ff. 1a, 1–43.

[53] *D.N.B.*; *S.H.C.* 1915, 226.

[54] *D.N.B.*; A. G. Matthews, *Calamy Revised*, 16, stating wrongly that Ashe was Vicar of Rugeley. Ashe was curate at Rugeley *c.* 1627–9: *Rugeley Par. Reg.* (Staffs. Par. Reg. Soc.), p. xi. Presumably this was the place from which he was ejected.

[55] *Staffs. and the Great Rebellion*, 8. A parishioner was excommunicated for refusing to kneel to receive Communion: ibid. Since Capps appears to have held the vicarage until his death in 1643 (*S.H.C.* 1915, 316), he presumably submitted.

[56] Laud, *Works*, v. 320, stating also: 'They say this lecture was ordained to illuminate the dark corners of that diocese.' The king commented: 'If there be dark corners in this diocese it were fit a true light should illuminate it, and not this that is false and uncertain': ibid.

[57] Thus in 1635 he reported to the Laudian visitors that complaints had often been made about nonconformity at Cannock; the visitors, however, found that the only complaint about the curate was that 'he preacheth too long': S.P. 16/287, f. 40.

[58] In 1636 the fanatic Lady Eleanor Davies smeared tar and water over the hangings of the cathedral altar, apparently as a protest against the introduction of the hangings and the placing of candlesticks on the altar. Among her accomplices were the wife of the town clerk of Lichfield and the wife of one of the cathedral clergy: *Cal. S.P. Dom.* 1637–8, 219. For Lady Davies see *D.N.B. sub* Davies, Sir John; Laud, *Works*, v. 346.

Wright, who acted with Laud in the ecclesiastical crises of 1640 and the following years, was one of the twelve bishops arrested for protesting in December 1641 against their exclusion from Parliament. He was imprisoned in the Tower, brought to the bar of the House of Lords in February 1642, and eventually ordered to return to his diocese. On the outbreak of the Civil War he was at Eccleshall castle, and he died there in August 1643 while the parliamentarians were besieging it.[59] Diocesan organization had already broken down.[60] Accepted Frewen, President of Magdalen College, Oxford, was consecrated in his college chapel as Wright's successor in April 1644; but by then the parliamentarians were in control of practically all his diocese, and he appears to have had no opportunity of entering it.[61]

The cathedral was severely damaged during the course of the war, and the chapter was scattered. Most of the parochial clergy conformed during the Interregnum, though about 20 were ejected from their livings for such offences as using the Book of Common Prayer or placing the communion table altarwise.[62] The attitude of many of the conformists is uncertain. Although some may have continued to hold Anglican services without detection, it is obvious that others felt little or no regret for the passing of the old order. Thus a number of ministers who had been instituted to their livings before the outbreak of the war were among those who signed the Presbyterian Staffordshire *Testimony* of 1648.[63]

Attempts were made during the Interregnum to increase the stipends of the more poorly-paid parochial clergy out of confiscated episcopal and cathedral estates and out of the pockets of lay impropriators. At Barlaston, for example, the lay impropriator was ordered to increase the curate's stipend from £10 a year to £50; at Weston-upon-Trent the curate was allotted £47 a year, to be taken from the impropriator, in lieu of his former £6 8s. 8d. Altogether over 70 Staffordshire benefices were augmented, but the orders were constantly changed and probably some of the clergy did not receive their augmentations.[64]

In 1653 civil marriage was introduced; it was enacted that thenceforth only marriages solemnized before a J.P. were to be lawful.[65] Banns were usually still published in church, but at Newcastle and Cheadle they were called by the town-crier at the market cross on three market-days, an alternative permitted by the Act. Charles Worsley, major-general for Lancashire, Cheshire, and Staffordshire, reported in 1656 that he had 'inflicted deserved punishment upon several persons unduly and pretendedly married contrary to the law, and the persons that married them'; this was a reference presumably to those who still sought a religious ceremony.

The Restoration led to the ejection of at least 44 Staffordshire clergy: first those who were dispossessed in favour of former royalist incumbents returning from exile, and then those, mainly Presbyterians, whom the Act of Uniformity forced to relinquish their livings.[66] The Restoration also brought a new bishop. Frewen was translated to York in 1660 and was succeeded the following year by John Hacket, a canon of Lincoln and of St. Paul's, and a divine who had been prominent in the ecclesiastical discussions

[59] *D.N.B.*

[60] The bishop's consistory court seems to have ceased to function during 1642: see e.g. Lich. Dioc. Regy., B/C/2/73; B/C/3/18; B/C/5.

[61] *D.N.B.*

[62] See below pp. 174–5; *S.H.C.* 1915, pp. lii–lvii; R. S. Bosher, *Making of the Restoration Settlement, 1649–62*, 284–94; A. G. Matthews, *Walker Revised*, 322–5.

[63] The ministers of Alstonefield, Biddulph, Blore Ray, Draycott-in-the-Moors, Elford, Ilam, Kingswinford,

Leek, Madeley, Uttoxeter, and Wombourn: Matthews, *Cong. Ch. Staffs.* 18n.; *S.H.C.* 1915, *passim*. For the *Testimony* see below p. 116.

[64] *S.H.C.* 1915, pp. lxii, 23, 312.

[65] For this para. see *Acts and Ords. of Interregnum*, ed. C. H. Firth and R. S. Rait, ii. 715–18; *V.C.H. Staffs.* viii. 11; R. Plant, *Hist. of Cheadle* (1881), 245; *D.N.B.*; W. H. Hutton, *Eng. Church from Accession of Chas. I to Death of Anne*, 160.

[66] See below p. 118.

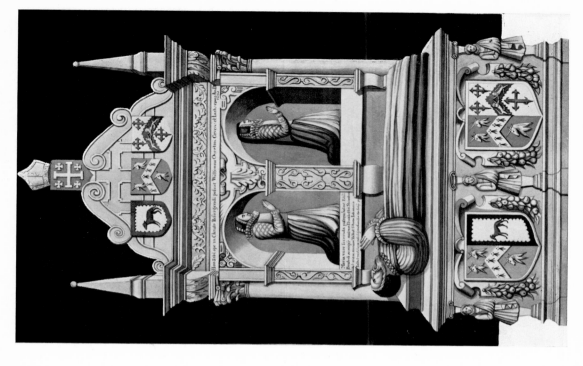

Tomb of William Overton, Bishop of Coventry and
Lichfield 1580–1609, in Eccleshall Church

Tomb of John Catterick, Bishop of Coventry and
Lichfield 1415–19 and of Exeter 1419, in the Church
of Santa Croce, Florence

THOMAS WOOD, BISHOP OF LICHFIELD AND
COVENTRY 1671–92

FREDERICK CORNWALLIS, BISHOP OF LICHFIELD
AND COVENTRY 1750–68

GEORGE SELWYN, BISHOP OF LICHFIELD 1868–78

AUGUSTUS LEGGE, BISHOP OF LICHFIELD
1891–1913

of the early 1640s. He was the first bishop to use the title 'Lichfield and Coventry' instead of 'Coventry and Lichfield'.[67]

Hacket is best known for his work in restoring the ruined cathedral.[68] He also made great efforts to revive church life and ecclesiastical discipline in the diocese. Although he was almost 70 when he came to Lichfield and suffered from bad health,[69] he proved a vigorous and active diocesan. In November 1664 he informed Archbishop Sheldon that since the beginning of the summer he had 'visited in my own person above 26 parish churches, to take order that the communion table and font be well placed (beside other reformations)'.[70] Between 31 May and 16 June 1665 he preached at Stafford and seven towns in Shropshire and confirmed 5,384 persons, being 'marvellously resorted to everywhere'.[71] The articles of inquiry at his second triennial visitation of 1668 indicate the standard of churchmanship that he sought to achieve. They included: 'Doth your parish maintain a lecturer? Is he a virtuous and orthodox divine? Is he licensed by the bishop? Doth he read the full service of Common Prayer once a month at least, wearing a surplice?' 'Do your parishioners behave reverently in church, men and youths with their hats off?' 'Do they engage in bodily labours on Sundays and Holy Days?' 'Are the king's arms set up?'[72] Although Hacket was a staunch opponent of dissent and did his best to root it out of his diocese, his attitude seems to have been a positive one. When, for example, the anthem which followed the sermon in services at the cathedral was replaced by a congregational psalm and critics objected that the practice smacked of puritanism, Hacket first defended the change on the grounds that it was 'no innovation, it was so in this Church *ab antiquo*, and but of late omitted', and then justified it on the grounds that it was popular with the congregation as a whole — the Church must 'feed lambs as well as sheep, let babes have milk as well as men strong meat, gain souls to Christ by all means that are lawful. Too much rigidness brought our late confusions upon us'.[73]

Hacket died in 1670. He did not have a worthy successor in Thomas Wood, who became bishop in 1671. Wood had been Dean of Lichfield since 1664 and had succeeded in infuriating Hacket and setting the chapter in a turmoil.[74] Having obtained the bishopric by making court to the Duchess of Cleveland,[75] he refused to live in his diocese. Archbishop Sancroft, having in vain ordered him to return in 1681, decided to take judicial action in 1684. Several clergymen testified that they had been forced to undertake long journeys to secure ordination. Confirmation was neglected. Even when he was in residence at Lichfield the bishop, through going early to buy cheap vegetables in the market, 'came very seldom or never to prayers'. The people of Lichfield complained that his absences and his failure to maintain due hospitality lost them £2,000 a year. He was also alleged to have sold timber set aside for rebuilding the palace at Lichfield destroyed in the Civil War.[76] Sancroft suspended Wood until he should 'make a full and becoming submission to His Grace the present Lord Arch-

---

[67] Lich. Dioc. Regy., B/A/1/17. For Hacket see *D.N.B.*; T. Plume, *Life of Bp. Hacket*, ed. M. Walcott (1865). Hacket was nominated by the Crown to be Bp. of Coventry and Lichfield but from the start of his episcopate used the new title. The series of *congés d'élire*, royal letters missive, monitions from the dean, mandates from the Archdeacon of Canterbury, and allied documents concerning the election and installation of Hacket and his successors (D. & C. Lich., Q4 sqq.), and the relevant bishops' registers (Lich. Dioc. Regy., B/A/1/17 sqq.) show, however, that the new title took almost a century to become universally accepted. It is not until the appointment in 1750 of Fred. Cornwallis that all the relevant papers give the title as 'Lichfield and Coventry'.

[68] See below pp. 175–6.

[69] 'I am always sickly in autumn, if not downright sick': Bodl. MS. Tanner 45, f. 26 (Hacket to Abp. Sheldon, 20 Sept. 1665).

[70] Bodl. MS. Tanner 47, f. 203 (Hacket to Sheldon, 9 Nov. 1664).

[71] Bodl. MS. Tanner 45, f. 13 (Hacket to Sheldon, 17 June 1665).

[72] J. H. Overton, *Life in the Eng. Church, 1660–1714*, 182 n. 3, 191, 201, 318.

[73] Bodl. MS. Tanner 131, f. 13 (Hacket to Thos. Browne, 14 Apr. 1666); see below pp. 119, 181.

[74] See below pp. 177–8.

[75] G. D'Oyly, *Life of Sancroft* (1840 edn.), 116.

[76] Lambeth Palace Libr., Depositions in Reply to a Commission *in partibus*, 1684.

bishop of Canterbury for his absence from his diocese and the neglect of his duty and all other crimes'. He was also ordered to pay £2,600 towards the rebuilding of the palace.[77] Wood had influence enough to recover his revenues by 1686 and held the see until his death in 1692.

Wood's successor, William Lloyd (1692–9), was translated from St. Asaph, where he had become notorious by combining toleration for dissent with strict discipline for the clergy and laity of the Church. His continuance of this policy, especially after Wood's lax rule, was bitterly resented, and he remained very unpopular until translated to Worcester in 1699.[78] He disliked the new palace and let it to a tenant. Later bishops continued this practice, Anna Seward, the authoress, living there from 1754 until her death in 1809.[79] Lloyd himself rebuilt Eccleshall castle where he and his successors resided.[80]

The first three bishops of the 18th century were scholars. John Hough (1699–1717) was the President of Magdalen College, Oxford, who had withstood James II in 1687 and been rewarded with the bishopric of Oxford in 1690. While Bishop of Lichfield he further remodelled Eccleshall castle. After declining the primacy in 1715, he was translated to Worcester.[81] Edward Chandler (1717–30) was among the most studious prelates of the century and known almost entirely as a writer, particularly against the Deists. He does not seem to have had an enemy or a disparager during his episcopate and was conscientious in his duties. In 1722 he reported to Archbishop Wake that Wolverhampton, 'being very populous and without confirmation these twenty-seven years, will afford business for two or three days'; he had been forced to postpone his visitation of Derbyshire for a month 'to give his body some refreshment, for what with bad ways, travelling to so many different places, and the ordinary duties at each place, he was sufficiently wearied'.[82] He was translated to Durham and succeeded by Richard Smalbroke (1731–49), translated from St. David's. Smalbroke was also a writer against the Deists, and having ingeniously calculated that, when the legion (6,000) of devils was expelled from the demoniac into the Gadarene swine, each pig received no more than three devils, he was commonly nicknamed 'split-devil Smalbroke'. He displayed some of the characteristics of contemporary bishops. Horace Walpole referred to a caricature of him bowing obsequiously at the passing ministerial coach, and Samuel Pegge the elder, a canon of Lichfield from 1757 to 1796, accused him of 'filling the Church at Lichfield with his relations'.[83]

After the Restoration the Church of England experienced a religious revival, one result of which was the formation of societies to encourage the fulfilment of religious duties and secure a reformation of manners. Bishop Hough expressed the hope that 'those sincere, and upright, and hearty endeavours . . . will in time, with God's blessing, give a new face to the moral world'.[84] Out of such societies came the Society for Promoting Christian Knowledge, founded in 1699. It worked through local groups, and in its early days in Staffordshire 16 clergy met each market-day at Newcastle for a conference, followed by a service in the church which was well attended.[85] In 1704, to assist poorly endowed benefices, annates were transferred from the Crown to the Governors of Queen Anne's Bounty. Between 1715 and 1740 they made 43 grants of

[77] Ibid., Sentence Book B.10.
[78] A. Tindal Hart, *William Lloyd, 1627–1717*, 138, 145.
[79] Ibid. 145; *D.N.B.*; Hesketh Pearson, *The Swan of Lichfield*, 14.
[80] Tindal Hart, *Lloyd*, 145–6.
[81] *D.N.B.*
[82] Ibid.; C. J. Abbey, *The Eng. Church and its Bishops, 1700–1800*, ii. 25–26; N. Sykes, *Church and State in Eng.*

in the Eighteenth Cent. 120, 144.
[83] *D.N.B.* sub Pegge, Smalbroke; H. Walpole, *Letters*, ed. P. Cunningham, i. 66; J. Nichols, *Literary Anecdotes of the Eighteenth Cent.* (1812), i. 405.
[84] J. Hough, *A Sermon preach'd . . . before the Societies for Reformation of Manners* (1705), 18 (copy in W. S. L. Pamphs.).
[85] Hutchinson, *Archdeaconry of Stoke*, 15.

£200 each to 42 churches and chapels in Staffordshire to meet in each case £200 or its equivalent, locally raised.[86]

The period was also marked by ecclesiastical strife, particularly as religion and politics could not be separated. The few Staffordshire clergymen who became non-jurors included Thomas Wagstaffe, deprived of the chancellorship of Lichfield Cathedral and consecrated Bishop of Ipswich by the nonjuring bishops in 1694.[87] William Binckes, Dean of Lichfield from 1703 to 1712, was one of the leaders of the Lower House of Convocation in its violent disputes with the Upper House and from 1704 to 1707 was its prolocutor. He caused a storm by preaching on 5 November 1704 that the papists were no longer dangerous and had earlier been censured by the House of Lords for a sermon preached on 30 January 1702 in which he drew a forced and virtually blasphemous analogy between the execution of Charles I and the crucifixion of Jesus.[88] The Sacheverell case aroused excitement in Staffordshire. Sacheverell had personal friends at Lichfield, and it is not surprising, therefore, that when he visited the city during his triumphal tour of the Midlands in 1710 he was received by the corporation and presented with three dozen bottles of wine.[89]

Little is known about the majority of Staffordshire parish clergy at this period, but it is evident that as usual a number of the less fortunate lived in poverty or near it. In 1664 Bishop Hacket had written to Archbishop Sheldon: 'The lower part of the clergy, and they by far the greatest, are very poor. In this diocese of Lichfield, containing 500 benefices with cure (besides petty chapelries), not 50 in the whole diocese [are] of value to maintain a scholar in a competent maintenance and a tolerable library.'[90] Bishop Lloyd's visitation of the cathedral in 1693 had revealed the extent to which the canons had neglected their prebendal churches and the churches of the common fund; it also showed the meagreness of the stipends allotted to some of the clergy who served these livings. In his cathedral statutes of 1694 Lloyd laid down that in future lessees of cathedral rectories were to covenant to pay the vicars or curates who served the rectories at least £26 13s. 4d. a year; a sliding scale of stipends, based on the number of households in the parish served, brought the salary of a man serving a parish of 600 households or more to £60 a year.[91]

Although the surviving parochial returns drawn up in 1718 for Bishop Chandler's primary visitation are so few that no general picture of clerical life in the diocese can be obtained from them, it is evident that several of the ten Staffordshire clergy whose replies survive were barely making ends meet.[92] Thomas Prince's perpetual curacies of Waterfall and Cauldon and chapelry of Calton brought him in about £30 a year, including the value of the house at Calton in which he lived; he also taught a private school 'for the better increase of my living and support of myself and family'. John Peploe ruefully noted the 'poor income' of his perpetual curacies of Castle Church and Penkridge, and the Mr. Phillips who served the chapelries of Newborough and Marchington obviously regarded his stipend of £13 a year merely as a supplement to his income as a schoolmaster at Uttoxeter.

[86] C. Hodgson, *An Account of the Augmentation of Small Livings by the Governors of the Bounty of Queen Anne* (1826 edn.), 352–9.

[87] G. Hickes, *Memoirs of the Life of Mr. John Kettlewell* (1718), pp. xxiv–xxv; *D.N.B.*; Hutton, *Eng. Church from Chas. I to Anne*, 240.

[88] *D.N.B.*; H. E. Savage, *Dr. Binckes, in Convocation and the Deanery* (Lichfield, 1929; copy in W. S. L. Pamphs.); Beresford, *Lichfield*, 257 n.1.

[89] A. L. Reade, *Johnsonian Gleanings*, iii (1922, priv. print.), 67–71, discussing also the story (J. Boswell, *Life of Dr. Johnson*, ed. G. B. Hill and L. F. Powell, i. 39) that

Johnson, 'not quite three years old', was carried to the cathedral on his father's shoulders to listen to Sacheverell. Reade considers it possible that this occurred in 1710, the date of Sacheverell's only recorded visit to Lichfield. J. L. Clifford, *Young Samuel Johnson*, 21–22, considers it 'an amusing story, but doubtful'.

[90] Bodl. MS. Tanner 47, f. 201v. (Hacket to Sheldon, 29 Oct. 1664).

[91] See below pp. 179–80.

[92] For the next two paras. see Lich. Dioc. Regy., B/V/5/ 1718.

The case of Nathanael Williams, perpetual curate of Keele since 1696, affords a striking example of the poor parish priest dependent on the whims of his patron and slighted by his parishioners. The living was a poor one. The patrons and impropriators, the Sneyds of Keele Hall, allowed the minister £10 a year and the small tithes, which were worth about £12 a year more. Williams stated that in addition 'the minister (if a single man) usually has his diet at the Hall, or if a married man and not living at the Hall he has £10 a year more given him in consideration of his diet; but I have nothing allowed me in consideration of mine'. Williams was not even provided with a house, though he was in constant residence at Keele: within a few months of his appointment the minister's house had been added to the Keele Hall demesne and turned into a farm. The living had not been augmented by the Governors of Queen Anne's Bounty 'for the Queen's Bounty was neglected by the patron and parishioners'; Williams himself had spent 40s. in his efforts to attract the governors' attention 'which the wardens promised to repay him, but they have not done it, nor will it ever be done unless the Lord Bishop order the new churchwardens to pay him'. The management of the parish charities had also passed out of his hands into the control of a John Stubbs of Keele. Nor was Williams happy about the spiritual life of his parish: there were few communicants, it was very seldom that anyone came to him for exhortation, and parents were remiss in sending their children to be catechized.

At Keele Williams held two services every Sunday and celebrated Communion four times a year, but it is difficult to decide from the surviving evidence how typical this pattern of worship was in Staffordshire in 1718. At Newcastle there were services on Wednesdays and Fridays and twice on Sundays, and at least seven celebrations a year, while at Uttoxeter the newly-arrived curate, deputizing for an old and infirm vicar, had a morning service every day, two services on Sundays, and monthly celebrations. At Caverswall there were services twice on Sundays and once on holy days, with communion seven times a year. Thomas Loxdale, who held the livings of Seighford and Ellenhall, generally had two Sunday services in each parish with additional services on holy days and on Wednesdays and Fridays in Lent; he celebrated six times a year at Seighford and four times a year at Ellenhall.

The mid-century years saw two new developments in Staffordshire — industrialization and evangelicalism.[93] Wednesbury was an early evangelical centre, to which John Wesley recorded over thirty visits, beginning in January 1743. The vicar, Edward Egginton, was at first friendly to the Methodists; but owing to what Wesley described as the 'inexcusable folly' of an itinerant Methodist lay preacher, whose sermons in the town contained violent attacks on the Anglican clergy, his attitude changed. When John Wesley paid his second visit the following April he found Egginton an open enemy. The vicar delivered an impassioned sermon against Methodism, and two days later, at an open-air meeting held by Wesley, there was a drunken attempt by a local clergyman to interrupt Wesley's sermon and ride down the listening crowd. The following months a succession of anti-Methodist riots broke out in the neighbourhood. The Staffordshire evangelicals, as elsewhere, failed to gain episcopal sympathy; indeed Wesley himself commented that he would not have been surprised 'if, after the advices they had so often heard from the pulpit, as well as from the episcopal chair, the zealous High Churchmen had rose and cut all that were called Methodists in pieces'.[94] Smalbroke, having noted in his charge of 1735–6 'extraordinary efforts' to spread

---

[93] For Wesley and the early history of Methodism in Staffs. see below pp. 124–5.
[94] J. Wesley, *Journal* (Everyman edn.), i. 411, 421–2, 424; Anon. *Some Papers giving an Account of the Rise and* *Progress of Methodism at Wednesbury in Staffs., and other Parishes adjacent: as likewise of the late Riots in those Parts* (1744), 10–11 (copy in W.S.L.); J. F. Ede, *Hist. of Wednesbury*, 204–11; see below pp. 124–5.

popery in his diocese, devoted his charge of 1741 to an attack on 'modern Enthusiasts'. In 1744–5 he noted with disapproval how 'these new itinerant preachers seem to copy after the popish pattern of the regulars in their contests with the secular priests in the thirteenth century'.[95] Before long, however, there were evangelicals among the clergy of the county. In 1752 Wesley met at Wednesbury a clergyman who, 'since he has known the pardoning love of God . . . has been swiftly going on from faith to faith and growing not in knowledge only, but in love'.[96] The evangelicals of Wolverhampton had the support of Benjamin Clement, head master of the grammar school and Vicar of St. John's.[97] In 1773 Edward Best, Vicar of Wednesbury, another opponent of Methodism, deplored the activity of 'some clergymen, regularly ordained, who hold Methodistical doctrines and take every opportunity they can of preaching and poisoning the minds of the people in this populous part of the country in every church they can gain admittance into'.[98]

The leading evangelical layman in the county was William Legge, Earl of Dartmouth (d. 1801), of whom Cowper wrote in *Truth*:

> We boast some rich ones whom the Gospel sways,
> And one who wears a coronet and prays.

He was converted by Lady Huntingdon in 1756, six years after succeeding to the title. He used his immense wealth lavishly in good works and in helping needy clergymen, while he bestowed the livings in his gift on evangelicals and secured preferment for them from others. He offered the living of West Bromwich to William Romaine, Lady Huntingdon's chaplain; Romaine refused it, but it was accepted by Edward Stillingfleet, great-grandson of the eminent Bishop of Worcester (1689–99) and son of James Stillingfleet of Hotham (Yorks. E.R.), a notable evangelical scholar and a devoted pastor. Edward Stillingfleet, who had been, like Wesley, a Fellow of Lincoln College, Oxford, was also chaplain to Lord Dartmouth, whose seat, Sandwell Hall, was in the parish; in 1786 he became the first secretary of the Church of England Sunday School Society. Another evangelical, William Jesse, was incumbent of West Bromwich from 1790 to 1814.[99]

The parochial returns for the primary visitations of Bishop Frederick Cornwallis in 1751 and Bishop North in 1772–3 have survived in greater numbers than those for 1718: about 70 Staffordshire parishes and chapelries have returns for 1751 and about 60 for 1772–3. They provide what is probably a fair sample of parish clergy and religious observance, both in the country and in the towns, in the mid-18th century.[1] In 1773, for example, the clergy included wealthy absentees such as George Taylor, Rector of Church Eaton, who held at least one other living besides his post as domestic chaplain to Lord Grosvenor and appears to have made a net profit of about £110 a year from Church Eaton after paying his curate's stipend; parsons such as William Sawrey, Rector of Elford, whose £200 a year enabled him to live in comfort; and a variety of more or less poorly-paid curates.

In both 1751 and 1773 the surviving returns show a majority of churches with two

[95] R. Smalbroke, *Charge delivered . . . in 1735 and 1736* (1737), 1 (copy in W.S.L. Pamphs.); *Charge delivered . . . in 1741* (1744; copy in W.S.L. Pamphs.), speaking (p. 60) of his fear that 'the contagion may soon spread in this diocese' and adding in a footnote: 'That this was then spoken too prophetically appears from the progress of Methodism in Staffordshire and elsewhere in this diocese'; *Charge delivered . . . in the years 1744 and 1745* (1746), 37 (copy in W.S.L. Pamphs.). [96] Wesley, *Journal*, ii. 217.
[97] L. E. Elliott-Binns, *The Early Evangelicals*, 294.
[98] Lich. Dioc. Regy., B/V/5/1772–3; Ede, *Wednesbury*, 199; and see below p. 124.

[99] Elliott-Binns, *Early Evangelicals*, 139–40, 293 sqq., 314, 380; *D.N.B.* sub Legge, Wm.; [A. C. H. Seymour], *Life and Times of Selina, Countess of Huntingdon* (1839), i. 380; *Gent. Mag.* 1815, lxxxv(1), 87–88. For the Earl of Dartmouth's patronage of the local Methodists see below p. 125.
    For the following paras. see Lich. Dioc. Regy., [1]B/V/5/1751, 1772–3. The articles for the latter visitation are dated 1772, but all the dated Staffs. returns were drawn up in 1773. For a survey of general parochial practice at this period see e.g. Sykes, *Church and State*, chap. 6.

Sunday services; one sermon was the rule, though occasionally, as at Audley in 1773, there were two. The churches with only one Sunday service were on the whole small or remote chapelries, generally held in plurality: thus in 1751 a Mr. Turner served three chapels of ease in the Moorlands, Meerbrook, Quarnford (or Flash), and Rushton, and with some help from neighbouring clergy generally managed to hold a service every Sunday in each of his chapels.[2] As was usual at this period, weekday prayers were the exception rather than the rule. In 1751 Joseph Dickenson, Rector of St. Mary's, Stafford, was the only incumbent who held morning prayers daily throughout the year, and no example at all of this practice is found in 1773.[3] A few clergy had retained the habit of reading prayers on Wednesdays and Fridays — those at Blithfield, Newcastle, Stone, Forton, and Ilam in 1751, and those at Cheadle, Kinver, Tamworth, and Wednesbury in 1773 — while at Leek in 1751 there were prayers on Wednesdays and Saturdays. About half the churches in 1751 and the majority of churches in 1773 had prayers on all or some of the recognized saints' days and public holy days; at St. Mary's, Stafford, for example, holy days were marked in 1751 by afternoon prayers in addition to the daily morning prayers. At Hanley in 1751 the incumbent noted that he had prayers 'upon some holy days when I can hope for a congregation'. The Rector of Blore at the same date was even less sanguine; he rarely served his church except on Sundays, 'for I have found by experience that a congregation cannot be depended upon except on the Lord's Day'. Lent was marked by additional services at 10 or 11 churches in 1751 and at about 16 of those whose returns have survived for 1773. These additional services generally took the form of services on Wednesdays and Fridays throughout Lent and daily services during Passion Week and are mentioned only in the returns from churches which did not have regular weekday prayers in any case. In some of the more active churches the incumbents created other opportunities of gathering a congregation: at Leek, for example, there were in 1751 more than 20 lectures and occasional services a year besides those on Sundays and the prayers on Wednesdays, Saturdays, and holy days, while at West Bromwich in 1773 Edward Stillingfleet gave a weekly sermon at 6 p.m. on Wednesdays 'for the instruction of the inhabitants after their hours of work are over'.

Stillingfleet was also careful and methodical in his catechizing. The children were catechized publicly before the congregation on Sundays in Lent and privately at the church on Wednesdays and Fridays during the summer, with Stillingfleet expounding the Catechism to them and giving them written questions and answers 'which they repeat to me the next time we meet, till I have gone through a regular course of instruction in the fundamental doctrines and precepts of the Christian religion'. In general Lent was the most favoured time for catechizing, though some incumbents preferred the summer for practical reasons. The 1751 return from Stoke, for example, stated that the curate catechized in May and June every year 'on account of the length of the days and the extensiveness of the parish'. In 1773 the Vicar of Caverswall reported that although he usually catechized in Lent 'I find it will be more convenient after Easter when the days are longer: a greater number may then be had'. The problem of finding a suitable time for catechizing within the pattern of services was touched on in 1751 by John Daintry, Vicar of Leek. Originally, he wrote, he had catechized during the afternoon service every Sunday in Lent and had afterwards lectured on some part of the Catechism to the congregation and the children; 'but this drawing the afternoon

---

[2] For an account of the exertions of a clergyman who served these 3 chapels in the early 19th cent. see Beresford, *Lichfield*, 272 and n. 1.

[3] There is, however, no return from St. Mary's, Stafford, for 1773.

service out to an unreasonable length I changed the time and now catechize the children on Saturday evenings through Lent, and have by this means an opportunity of talking more freely and particularly to the children'. Daintry gives no clue to what books, if any, he used in his catechizing; in 1773 William Sawrey of Elford catechized 'with extempory exposition' while Simon Collins of Drayton Bassett preferred to rely on Dr. Richard Bundy's *Apparatus Biblicus* and Archbishop Wake's *Principles of the Christian Religion Explained*. Other books of this type favoured by Staffordshire clergy in 1773 included Bishop Beveridge's *Church Catechism Explained* and Thomas Stackhouse's *New and Practical Exposition of the Creed*. In most cases attendance at the catechizing appears to have been adequate, though in 1773 there were complaints from both Keele and Milwich that parishioners did not send their children, and in 1751 some incumbents were finding it difficult to persuade servants to attend. At Kingsley, for example, 'custom and a false shame prevents servants and others who are at men and women's estate being sent for instruction to the ministers', while at Cheddleton 'the more grown-up servants only hear the children say their Catechism: they will not be prevailed upon to say the Catechism themselves'.

In both 1751 and 1773 Holy Communion was being administered 4 times a year in about 40 per cent. of the churches for which returns have survived. Another 40 per cent. had between 5 and 10 celebrations a year, while the remaining 20 per cent. were divided almost equally between those with fewer than 4 celebrations a year and those with more than ten. Four Sacrament Sundays a year was the general standard for country churches of the period. Typical Staffordshire examples were Ingestre and Keele, which in 1751 had celebrations on the three great festivals of the Church and on the nearest Sunday to Michaelmas. At Maer at the same date there was a fifth celebration on Palm Sunday, while at Haughton there was in addition a sixth celebration on Good Friday. Churches in which Communion was administered twelve times or more a year were chiefly town churches: Leek, Newcastle, St. Mary's, Stafford, and Stone in 1751, and Kinver, Tamworth, and Walsall in 1773. Monthly Communion was, however, the practice in some country churches: Forton and Norton-in-the-Moors in 1751 and West Bromwich in 1773. This was evidently due to the energy of the incumbents. William Oakeley, Rector of Forton, was one of the relatively few Staffordshire country clergy who maintained Wednesday and Friday prayers (see above), while Timothy Keene, the curate at Norton-in-the-Moors, was a man who kept a watchful eye on the devotions of his flock: 'I cannot be particular in the precise number of communicants, but always observe a considerable number. And if any neglect I am not wanting to instruct 'em in the necessity of better observing their duty, which exhortation hath mostly had its due effect'. Stillingfleet's conscientious ministry at West Bromwich has already been mentioned.

The 1751 returns show that in general a high proportion of adult parishioners communicated, especially in rural parishes. At Bradley near Stafford, for example, the curate estimated the number of communicants in the parish as about 170, of whom 120 received at Easter and over 60 at Whitsun; at Forton about 100 of the 150 communicants received at Easter and Whitsun and about 40 at other times; at Weston-under-Lizard 45 or 46 of the 60 communicants received at Easter, about 30 at Whitsun, and about 23 or 24 at other times. This state of affairs was, however, by no means universal: at Blore, for example, the rector explained that he celebrated only three times a year because of the poor response from his parishioners; there were seldom as many as 10 to receive in a parish with about 80 communicants, and some of the 10 came from other parishes.

The aristocratic bishops of Lichfield in the later 18th century were unlikely either to understand evangelicals or to meet the needs of this rapidly changing part of the country. Frederick Cornwallis (1750–68), a younger son of Charles, Baron Cornwallis (d. 1722), held the deanery of St. Paul's *in commendam* from 1766 and was translated to Canterbury. John Egerton (1768–71), son of Henry Egerton, Bishop of Hereford, and Lady Elizabeth Bentinck, daughter of the Earl of Portland, was translated from Bangor, held a residentiaryship in St. Paul's *in commendam* and was translated to Durham.[4] Brownlow North (1771–4), son of Francis North, Earl of Guilford (d. 1790), was consecrated to Lichfield and Coventry at the age of thirty; his rapid preferment was due to his half-brother, Frederick, Lord North, who observed that his brother was doubtless young to be a bishop but when older would not have a brother prime minister. Bishop North seems to have been a dignified, generous and popular man. He had private means and held the vicarages of Lydd and Bexley in Kent *in commendam*, a fact which was criticized by Fox when attacking Lord North in the House of Commons in 1772. He was translated to Worcester and then to Winchester.[5] An explanation of such pluralism and short episcopates is to be found in a valuation of the church preferments in the gift of the Crown drawn up for George III in the early years of his reign, in which Lichfield and Coventry is classed among those sees worth £1,000–£1,400 a year, while wealthier sees such as Canterbury, York, Durham, Winchester, or Worcester had £3,000–£7,000.[6]

By 1774 the revenues of the see had risen to £1,800 a year, but even so the new bishop, Richard Hurd, found his finances severely strained by the necessary costs of £502 16s. 6d. attendant upon his promotion.[7] Hurd was born in 1720 at Congreve in the parish of Penkridge; he was educated at Brewood grammar school and went to Cambridge as a 'poor scholar'. He attracted the attention in 1749 of William Warburton, then chaplain to Frederick, Prince of Wales, and Bishop of Gloucester from 1759 to 1779, and his later patrons included Lord Mansfield, C.J., on whose recommendation he was nominated to the bishopric. Upon his elevation to the episcopate his courtly manners soon made him the favourite bishop of George III, who respected him as a spiritual counsellor and valued him as a friend and in 1776 made him preceptor to the Prince of Wales and the Duke of York. He was a moderate and orthodox Churchman, suspicious of religious enthusiasm.[8] Before he came to Lichfield, he had expressed his views in a sermon at Norwich in 1752 on such 'exorbitancies of ungoverned piety' and regretted that this 'groundless and ill-directed zeal' could not perform its 'true service to religion' by submitting to 'the guidance of well-interpreted Scripture and sober piety'.[9] He followed the tradition usual among 18th-century bishops of summer retirement to their sees, when they held their ordinations, irrespective of the canonical embertides. On nomination to the see he asked William Arnald of St. John's College, Cambridge, to serve him as chaplain, promising to 'consult his time and ease as much as possible' if he would 'oblige him with his company at Eccleshall for some part of the summer, and particularly for a fortnight or three weeks about Michaelmas, when his principal ordination would be'; and George III, when he translated him to Worcester in 1781, expressed the 'hope that he would allow Hartlebury to be a better summer residence than Eccleshall'.[10]

---

[4] *D.N.B.*

[6] Sykes, *Church and State*, 61.

[7] Ibid. 150. Hurd himself, a few days after he had received the news of his elevation to the episcopate, had written to tell a friend that, financially, Lichfield was 'on all accounts an eligible see': F. Kilvert, *Memoirs of the Life and Writings of the Rt. Rev. Ric. Hurd, D.D.* (1860), 123.

[5] Ibid.

[8] *D.N.B.*; Abbey, *Eng. Church and its Bishops*, ii. 223–7. In some quarters he was irreverently known as 'the Beauty of Holiness': W. Derry, *Dr. Parr*, 82.

[9] R. Hurd, *The Mischiefs of Enthusiasm and Bigotry: a Sermon Preached at Norwich Assizes* (1752), 6, 7 (copy in W.S.L. Pamphs.).

[10] Sykes, *Church and State*, 95, 100.

The last bishop of the century was James Cornwallis (1781–1824), third son of Charles, 1st Earl Cornwallis, and younger brother of Charles, 1st Marquess Cornwallis, Governor General of India and Lord Lieutenant of Ireland. During his long episcopate he held *in commendam* the deanery of Windsor from 1791 and that of Durham from 1794.[11] At Eccleshall he lived in state, and, though the castle adjoined the churchyard, he would not walk through the shrubbery to the church but drove with four horses through the village and solemnly marched from the gates to the church door, bewigged and hat in hand, while after service no one left before him.[12] Having taken exception to a turnpike put up near his gate, he lived for many years in Richmond (Surr.); Eccleshall castle was let to a farmer who used some rooms as granaries.[13] Confirmations were still held, according to Canon 60, 'in the bishop's visitation every third year', and Cornwallis is said to have confirmed 'upwards of 1,200 persons' at St. Mary's, Stafford, in 1795 and 'about 700 young persons' at Tamworth in 1797.[14] In Wolverhampton, still outside the jurisdiction of the diocesan, over 3,000 persons were confirmed on Saturday, 19 July 1788, by the dean of this peculiar, Bishop John Douglas, who had halted there on his northward journey to his diocese of Carlisle.[15]

Such an episcopal standard did not set a high example for the Staffordshire clergy. Tales of scandalous clergy are few, the most notorious being William Moreton, incumbent of Willenhall from 1789 to 1834, fined for poaching in 1791, often drunk, and a frequenter of cock-fighting and bull-baiting.[16] Examples of pluralism and non-residence are more common. Alexander Haden, Vicar of Wednesbury from 1782 to 1829, became a lecturer at the collegiate church of Wolverhampton, Rector of Saddington (Leics.) in 1802, and minister of Ware (Herts.) in 1811, and towards the end of his life lived at Tettenhall.[17] Since the early 18th century the deans of Lichfield had held the rectory of Tatenhill, 9 miles distant, and in the early 19th century Dean Woodhouse was also Rector of Stoke and of Donington (Salop.).[18] The curates who cared for the parishes of such absentee incumbents were not always well paid. Benjamin Johnson, curate of Weston-upon-Trent (Staffs.) from 1809 to 1819 under a non-resident vicar, had to keep a school for boys in the kitchen, and his wife one for girls in the scullery, of the four-roomed cottage in which they lived with their six children.[19]

Most serious was the failure to provide more churches for the growing population of the county; in many places the nonconformists were better served. Only seven new post-Reformation churches or chapels were built in North Staffordshire before 1800: Broughton, 1633;[20] Bucknall, 1718;[21] Endon, 1730;[22] Hanley, 1738;[23] Quarnford, 1744;[24] Lane End, 1762;[25] and Cotton, in the parish of Alton, 1795.[26] Many churches were not kept in proper repair. Stone church was rebuilt in 1758, after becoming so ruined that a large part fell down in 1749; before Willenhall church was rebuilt in 1750 it was 'so decayed that the inhabitants, when they met together, were in great danger of being killed'.[27] To provide for more worshippers galleries were built and pews

---

[11] *D.N.B.*

[12] Beresford, *Lichfield*, 276.

[13] J. G. Lonsdale, 'The Church in Staffs. during the Nineteenth Cent.' *Staffs. Advertiser*, 5 Jan. 1901.

[14] J. L. Cherry, *Stafford in Olden Times* (Stafford, 1890), 55; H. C. Mitchell, *Tamworth Parish Church* (1935), 53.

[15] Sykes, *Church and State*, 120. Many years later Bp. Selwyn heard the story from 'an aged member of the Church at Wolverhampton' who had been one of the 3,000: H. W. Tucker, *George Augustus Selwyn*, ii. 361. In 1722 Bp. Chandler stated that there had been no confirmation at Wolverhampton for 27 years: see above p. 62.

[16] F. W. Hackwood, *Annals of Willenhall* (Wolverhampton, 1908), 98, 100–104; N. W. Tildesley, *Hist. of Willenhall* (Willenhall, 1952), 45–51.

[17] J. F. Ede, *Hist. of Wednesbury*, 199.

[18] See below pp. 181, 184, 185.

[19] *Trent Valley Parochial Mag.* v(2), 6.

[20] *S.H.C.* 1915, 89.

[21] J. Ward, *Borough of Stoke-upon-Trent* (1843), 527.

[22] White, *Dir. Staffs.* (1851).

[23] *V.C.H. Staffs.* viii. 154.

[24] White, *Dir. Staffs.* (1851).

[25] *V.C.H. Staffs.* viii. 233.

[26] White, *Dir. Staffs.* (1851).

[27] W. H. Bowers and J. W. Clough, *Researches into Hist. of Stone* (Birm., 1929), 44 sqq.; Tildesley, *Willenhall*, 18, 20

crowded into existing churches. As early as the 17th century Bishop Hacket was complaining that 'some great man will be content to set up a new pew for his own use, but stick at all other new building'.[28] The new church at Stone was partly financed by the sale of the freehold of sittings in it. The same arrangement was adopted when Hanley church was rebuilt in 1790; out of about 1,200 sittings only 80 were free together with 300 for children in the aisles and galleries. The church was kept in repair by an annual levy on the pews.[29] In 1831 only about a third of the sittings in Staffordshire were free.[30]

The impetus necessary for reform in the Church in Staffordshire came through the episcopate of Henry Ryder (1824–36). His appointment to Gloucester in 1815 and translation to Lichfield were regarded as examples of Lord Liverpool's disinterested use of patronage, by which he 'elevated unpretending merit and excellence to high places in the Church'.[31] Though Ryder was to be the first of the new bishops of the diocese, he was also the last of the old, for he was the youngest son of Nathaniel Ryder, 1st Baron Harrowby, of Sandon. He had been ordained to the curacy of Sandon in 1800.[32] At Gloucester he was the first evangelical raised to the episcopate, and his appointment aroused protests. His tact and humility had ensured against a repetition of this at Lichfield, but people came 'to see this great curiosity, a religious bishop', and, a local clergyman wrote, 'many have expressed their astonishment that a person could be an ultra-religionist without being the morose and violent ascetic they expected'.[33] He was not a scholar or administrator but had a high reputation for piety and energy and was helped by belonging to a leading county family. Though conscientious, he held the deanery of Wells *in commendam* from 1812 until 1831, when he took instead a less valuable prebend at Westminster, which he held until his death.[34] The see had remained one of the less wealthy ones. Since the 1770s the bishop's income had more than doubled; during the three years 1829, 1830 and 1831 Ryder's average annual net income was almost £4,000, virtually the same as that of the Bishop of Salisbury. But other episcopal incomes had also gone up, and there were still 14 English and Welsh bishops (including the Bishop of Salisbury) whose average annual net income exceeded Ryder's.[35]

The diocese gave Ryder scope for his energies, and he had a genuine concern for its workpeople. In his charge of 1832, after noting that Wolverhampton had church accommodation for about a fifth of its population, he exclaimed: 'How often must the Urbicus of our days have to exclaim, in the bitterness of his heart, "Where, alas! are those my stray sheep — stray from compulsion in the wilderness of this evil world; those poor whom I might instruct, in hope, according to the promise, of making them wise unto salvation".'[36] Helped by his friend George Hodson, Archdeacon of Stafford, he founded the Diocesan Church Building Society, launched in 1835 with over £10,000 in donations and £600 in annual subscriptions.[37] The first new church built

[28] Plume, *Hacket*, 88.
[29] Bowers and Clough, *Stone*, 44 sqq.; Ward, *Stoke*, 350, 358–9; *V.C.H. Staffs.* viii. 154.
[30] *Authorized Rep. of the Church Congress held at Wolverhampton, 1867*, 20–22.
[31] R. H. Eden, 2nd Baron Henley, *A Plan of Church Reform* (8th edn., 1832), 59. [32] *D.N.B.*
[33] G. R. Balleine, *Hist. of the Evangelical Party*, 152. Ryder's appointment to Gloucester had aroused great indignation; Abp. Manners Sutton and the Dean and Chapter of Gloucester resisted the demand for consecration for several months: J. W. C. Wand, *The Second Reform*, 47.
[34] W. L. Mathieson, *Eng. Church Reform 1815–40*, 111–12.

[35] *Rep. Com. Eccl. Revs.* [67], pp. 2–7, H.C. (1835), xxii.
[36] H. Ryder, *Charge addressed to the Clergy of the Diocese of Lichfield and Coventry at his third Visitation, 1832* (1832), 31 (copy in W.S.L. Pamphs.).
[37] *D.N.B.*; *Rep. of Proceedings at a Meeting of the Nobility, Gentry and Clergy of the Diocese of Lichfield and Coventry held at Dee's Royal Hotel, Birmingham, on Tuesday the 27th of January, 1835, for the purpose of forming a Church Building Society for the Diocese of Lichfield and Coventry* (Birm., 1835), 29 (copy in W.S.L. Pamphs.). For the aims and objects of the society see *A Summary View of the Object, Plan and Operations of the Church Building Society for the Diocese of Lichfield and Coventry, with Instructions for Carrying its Designs into Effect* (Lichfield 1835; copy in W.S.L. Pamphs.).

in the diocese in the 19th century was at Hanford in Trentham in 1827, and in 1839 Archdeacon Hodson said that since Ryder's accession about 30 new churches and chapels had been built in Staffordshire or were in the process of being built. These, with enlargements to existing churches, had added up to 35,000 new sittings, making a total of about 125,000.[38] Church building had become recognized as a national need, and the county received help from the agencies established to promote it. In 1818 and 1824 the government voted grants, and the Commissioners for Building New Churches spent about £37,000 on churches in the Potteries: St. Mark's, Shelton, and St. James's, Longton (£10,000 each), St. Paul's, Burslem (£8,000), St. George's, Newcastle (£6,000), and Christ Church, Tunstall (£3,000).[39] The Church Building Society, founded in 1818, also made grants, and private contributions were considerable: £1,000 at Tunstall and about £1,500 at St. Paul's, Burslem.[40]

The new churches of this period were uniform in plan and furnishing, typical being the new church of Stoke-upon-Trent, which replaced the ruinous old one in 1830.[41] In plan it was 'a quadrangle without interruption of its floor except by the pillars supporting galleries on the north, south and west sides', the western gallery accommodating the Sunday-school children with the organ and choir in front. 'In the chancel there were no seats, but both the galleries and body were filled with pews, some of them at the east end, square-shaped with spring cushions to the seats and embroidered linings within the fastening doors.' These pews were appropriated with fixed rents according to their position, the free seats for the poor being at the west end of the south side. 'The pulpit stood a few feet west of the chancel arch on the centre line of the church'; it was three stories high, with the parish clerk's seat, a reading-desk accommodating two and the preacher's place at the top, so that the altar was obstructed from most positions in the church.[42] Money was not so freely forthcoming to endow the new churches, and pew-rents were necessary to pay the incumbent. In the early 1840s the stipend at Tunstall was only £200 from 639 appropriated pews out of 1,000 and at Shelton £220 from 1,600 out of 2,100.[43] Ryder deeply regretted that in 1832 free sittings were still less than a quarter of the total in the diocese.[44]

Ryder was also 'one of the evangelical bishops who did much to reform the method of conducting confirmations'.[45] In order to emphasize the meaning of the rite he sent a printed letter beforehand to the parents and god-parents of every candidate; Archdeacon Hodson gave a second letter to each candidate as he rose after the imposition of hands, and the bishop concluded with a short pastoral address from the pulpit.[46]

Overwork shortened Ryder's life, and he was succeeded by Samuel Butler (1836–9), head master since 1798 of Shrewsbury School, which under him had acquired a high reputation. He was 62 when he became bishop and suffered much ill-health, but he administered the diocese with great energy and was popular with the clergy.[47] It was a shrunken diocese that he had to rule. Although he was consecrated Bishop of Lichfield and Coventry in 1836, later in the same year the newly founded Ecclesiastical Commissioners annexed the Archdeaconry of Coventry to the see of Worcester by

---

[38] Hutchinson, *Archdeaconry of Stoke*, 141; G. Hodson, *Charge delivered to the Clergy of the Archdeaconry of Stafford, 1839* (Rugeley, 1839), 25 (copy in W.S.L. Pamphs.). Hodson estimated that at least another 100,000 sittings were needed.
[39] *V.C.H. Staffs.* viii. 23, 93, 123, 155, 234; White, *Dir. Staffs.* (1851).
[40] Ward, *Stoke*, 91, 247.
[41] *V.C.H. Staffs.* viii. 190.

[42] F. D. How, *Bp. Lovelace T. Stamer*, 68–69.
[43] Ward, *Stoke*, 92, 425, stating, however, that when all the sittings at Shelton were taken the income from pew-rents would rise to almost £600.
[44] Ryder, *Charge of 1832*, 31.
[45] Wand, *The Second Reform*, 47.
[46] Beresford, *Lichfield*, 282–3.
[47] *D.N.B.*

Order in Council. Butler was left as Bishop of Lichfield with a stipend of £4,500.[48] The building and restoration of churches did not slacken. Butler raised £6,000 in an appeal for the Diocesan Church Building Society in 1838.[49] He did not, however, favour some of the methods of church extension countenanced under his predecessor. The Church Building Act of 1831[50] permitted the establishment of new churches, the patronage of which could be exercised by trustees. Ryder had welcomed 'the stimulus of the grant of patronage under proper guards and limitations' and considered it 'an opportunity of promoting esteemed ministers and securing personal edification'.[51] Butler, however, had misgivings about the Act, 'which if not acted upon with the greatest care might become one of the most oppressive and obnoxious to patrons, incumbents, and bishops that I know of, and in many cases might create or perpetuate party spirit and party feuds'. He particularly disliked 'the very increasing patronage of small livings among trustees over whom the bishop has no control and in whose election he has no voice' and the fact that 'the sum provided for the establishment of such livings [is] far too small'.[52] Again, Archdeacon Hodson, a friend of Charles Simeon, had been appointed in 1837 one of the trustees who exercised the patronage of the livings purchased by the evangelical leader;[53] but Butler considered that the sale of livings was 'the greatest of all the evils in our Church Establishment' and that 'the system of trustee patronage' had been 'carried too far already'.[54]

The establishment of a Diocesan Board of Education and of a teachers' training college for men at Lichfield during Butler's episcopate marked a major step in the improvement of the Church's educational work in the diocese. Bishop Ryder had pointed out the need for more and better organized schools in the expanding industrial towns and had stressed the importance of the role which the clergy should play in the education of the poor.[55] It was necessary, however, that the work of church schools should be co-ordinated and supervised; this task was undertaken by the Diocesan Board of Education, formed in November 1838 and publicly launched at a meeting at Lichfield the following January, when Sir Robert Peel was among the distinguished speakers from various parts of the diocese who pledged their support for the venture.[56] By June 1840 the organization of the Board's system of subordinate District Boards was complete, a training college for schoolmasters had been set up at Lichfield, and an inspector of the Staffordshire schools in union with the Board had been appointed. Plans were also in hand for the extension of church education to 'that important section of the people known by the name of the middle classes'. It was admitted that the educational needs of these people had hitherto generally been ignored by the Church. Middle-class parents, because they were considered capable of paying for the education of their children, had been left to their own devices and forced to seek schools where they could; a situation which often left the children of Anglican parents in the hands of dissenters 'or in quarters where religion was of little or no account and worldly advancement is considered all in all'. The remedy for this was, it was suggested, the establishment where necessary of Anglican 'commercial' or 'middle' schools for the children of tradesmen and farmers: a successful one had already been opened at Lichfield and similar schools had appeared at Wolverhampton and Bridgnorth

[48] *Orders in Council ratifying Schemes of the Ecclesiastical Commissioners for England*, i. 44–47; *V.C.H. Warws.* viii. 317. The severance of the archdeaconry of Coventry from the diocese was completed on 24 Jan. 1837: S. Butler, *Life and Letters of Dr. Samuel Butler* (1896), ii. 224.

[49] Beresford, *Lichfield*, 280–1.

[50] 1 & 2 Wm. IV, c. 38.

[51] Ryder, *Charge of 1832*, 16.

[52] Butler, *Samuel Butler*, ii. 301.

[53] A. J. Tait, *Charles Simeon and his Trust*, 53, 61.

[54] Butler, *Samuel Butler*, ii. 263, 289.

[55] H. Ryder, *Charge delivered to the Clergy of the Diocese of Lichfield and Coventry at the Second Visitation of that Diocese* (Stafford, 1828), 42–45 (copy in W.S.L. Pamphs.).

[56] *Staffs. Advertiser*, 26 Jan. 1839.

(Salop.).[57] By 1846 271 schools of all kinds were in union with the Diocesan Board and there was an average daily attendance of 11,824 children.[58]

Another notable advance during Butler's episcopate was the division of the diocese into rural deaneries.[59] In some dioceses the office of rural dean had never lapsed;[60] in others it had recently been revived. At Bishop Ryder's last meeting with his arch-deacons before his death it had been agreed unanimously that a similar revival in the diocese of Lichfield and Coventry would be desirable; it had, however, been 'thought advisable to defer carrying it into execution till we could learn the course which would be adopted by the Church Commissioners and Parliament on the subject'. Such prudence turned out to be unnecessary, for both Parliament and the Ecclesiastical Commissioners favoured the general revival of the office, and in 1836 Butler was able to announce to the clergy of the diocese in his primary visitation charge that he would shortly be appointing his first rural deans. The first appointments were made the following year. Staffordshire was initially divided into 13 deaneries, but the abolition of peculiar and exempt jurisdictions in 1846 (see below) enabled Bishop Lonsdale to raise the number to twenty-one.

Another reform of this period was the gradual reduction of pluralism. In 1804 46 licences for non-residence were registered for Staffordshire; in 1824, 10; in 1844, 5; and in 1864, 1.[61] Its elimination would come, as Ryder said, when the provision of a stipend 'adequate, according to the most moderate estimate, to the sustenance of a married clergy can be assigned to each parish',[62] and meanwhile Butler did his best to see that the parishes did not suffer. He insisted in 1836 that the absentee incumbent of Chapel Chorlton must appoint a curate 'to reside on the spot, and to take . . . good care of the school and of the congregation' and provide 'two full services each Sunday'.[63] At the same time Butler was anxious that the standard of the clergy should not fall. He dis-liked ordaining 'candidates who have never resided at college and thus had no regular academic education, but have merely gone up for a few days to answer and pass at a general examination', and he expected 'that all candidates should be at least A.B. of one of our English universities (Durham included), or if of T.C.D. that they shall have been born of English parents'. He objected strongly to the policy of the evangelical Pastoral Aid Society in employing lay preachers, 'which militates against my notion of Ecclesiastical Polity'.[64]

Butler's death in 1839 was followed by the even shorter episcopate of James Bow-stead, translated from Sodor and Man. He encouraged the work of church extension and drew up rules for the office of rural dean, but he was disabled by illness nearly all the time that he held the see and died in 1843.[65] He was succeeded by John Lonsdale (1843–67), a fine scholar and one of the promoters of King's College, London; he had

[57] H. E. J. Howard, *Charge delivered at the Triennial Visitation of the Peculiars under the Jurisdiction of the Cathedral Church of Lichfield, 1840* (Lichfield, 1840), 14–16 (copy in W.S.L. Pamphs.).

[58] G. Hodson, *The Danger of Receding from the Principles of the Protestant Reformation: a Charge delivered to the Clergy of the Archdeaconry of Stafford, 1846* (1846), 8 (copy in W.S.L. Pamphs.). Hodson vigorously advocated better pay for schoolteachers: 'We must pay for good schoolmasters and mistresses if we would have them: and in this, as in other kinds of barter, if you will pay for a good article you will get one . . . Men must have a competency. They cannot prosecute with vigour and cheerfulness an occupation which, more than most, requires both to perform it well, if they are struggling with poverty, oppressed by domestic cares, or worn out by hopeless and endless labour': Hodson, *Diocesan Union the Strength and Ornament of the Church: a Charge delivered to the Clergy of the Archdeaconry of Stafford, 1847* (1847), 20 (copy in W.S.L. Pamphs.).

[59] For this para. see, unless otherwise stated, S. Butler, *Charge delivered . . . at his Primary Visitation, 1836* (1836), 14–15 (copy in W.S.L. Pamphs.); Lich. Dioc. Regy., B/A/1/30, pp. 75–82, 86–88; Hodson, *Charge of 1847*, 10, 41.

[60] e.g. it had survived in the archdeaconry of Surrey: W. Dansey, *Horae Decanicae Rurales* (1835), ii. 359.

[61] Lich. Dioc. Regy., B/A/9.

[62] Ryder, *Charge of 1832*, 14.

[63] Butler, *Samuel Butler*, ii. 198.

[64] Ibid. 206–7, 262.

[65] Beresford, *Lichfield*, 281, 285; obituary, *Staffs. Advertiser*, 21 Oct. 1843.

become its third principal in 1839, a post offered to him on its creation but then declined, and the college flourished under him. His habitual modesty probably prevented him from becoming Provost of Eton in 1840 and Archbishop of Canterbury in 1848 and made him at first decline the offer of Lichfield by Sir Robert Peel. He was an able bishop, moderate in his views and popular in his diocese, though his strict attention to his episcopal duties prevented him from taking that part in the national affairs of the Church of England for which he was well qualified. In addition his reticence allowed him to deal only rarely with the questions of the day in his visitation charges; nor were any of his charges published.[66] It was during his episcopate that, by Order in Council in 1846, the deanery of Bridgnorth was transferred to the diocese of Hereford.[67]

Another Order in Council in 1846 brought under the bishop's control all peculiar and exempt jurisdictions in the diocese;[68] their holders were left only with such relics of their former independence as the power to grant probate and administration, which they retained until the general extinction of such rights in 1858.[69] Bishop Ryder had regarded such peculiars as 'a remnant of popery' contrary to the bishop's 'just exercise of general authority and control', and he had looked forward to their abolition.[70] Archdeacon Hodson rejoiced in the abolition of peculiars as a reform which was long overdue: the bishop was now in complete control of his diocese, and it would thenceforth be possible for all his clergy to co-operate fully and effectively in diocesan work.[71]

Under Lonsdale the building of new churches was at its height. An appeal by Bowstead for the Diocesan Society in 1841 had brought in £16,000, and one by Lonsdale in 1846 brought in £19,000. During his episcopate £65,000 was raised for the Society, of which he himself gave £3,700. He consecrated 156 new churches in the diocese during those 24 years, an average of one every 8 weeks.[72] Efforts were stimulated by the report of the Midland Mining Commission published in 1843, which showed the scarcity of churches and clergy in parts of Staffordshire. At Rowley Regis, for instance, the commissioners found that there was then neither resident clergyman nor magistrate among its 12,000 inhabitants, of whom 8,000 were employed in mining or some branch of the iron industry.[73] The religious census of 1851, which enumerated 317 Anglican places of worship in the county, indicated that 129 had been built or acquired since 1801 and that 82 of these had been added between 1841 and 1851.[74] Church extension was facilitated by the 'Peel Act' of 1843,[75] which made the creation of new ecclesiastical parishes easier and cheaper. Isaac Clarkson, Vicar of Wednesbury from 1829 to 1855, and a great church builder who raised nearly £1,000 a year during his incumbency for this purpose, took advantage of the Act to form the three new districts of St. John's, St. James's, and All Saints', Moxley.[76] A total of 31 'Peel Districts' were formed in Staffordshire between 1844 and 1932.[77]

The 1851 religious census also showed, however, that despite its achievements in Staffordshire the Church could not afford to relax its efforts or to lapse into complacency.[78] The printed tables showed that of a population of 608,716 only 66,264

[66] *D.N.B.*; F. J. C. Hearnshaw, *Centenary Hist. of King's College, London,* 48, 152–65; E. B. Denison, *Life of John Lonsdale, Bp. of Lichfield* (1868).

[67] *Orders in Council ratifying Schemes of the Eccl. Commrs.* v. 284–7.

[68] *Lond. Gaz.* 18 Sept. 1846 (pp. 3317–19), exempting only Lichfield Cathedral and Close. For a list of the peculiars in the diocese in the early 19th cent. see below pp. 93–94.

[69] Under the terms of the Act of the previous year, 20 & 21 Vic. c. 77.

[70] Ryder, *Charge of 1832,* 18, 19.

[71] Hodson, *Charge of 1847,* 5–9.

[72] Denison, *Lonsdale,* 136; Beresford, *Lichfield,* 281.

[73] *1st Rep. Com. Midland Mining (S. Staffs.)* [508], p. clii (1843), xiii.

[74] *Census, 1851: Religious Worship, Eng. and Wales, Rep. and Tables,* p. ccxlvii.

[75] Act to make better provision for the spiritual care of populous parishes, 6 & 7 Vic. c. 37.

[76] Ede, *Wednesbury,* 297–8.

[77] *Lich. Dioc. Dir.* (1955–6), 126–33.

[78] For the following para. see *Census, 1851: Religious Worship,* p. ccxxii; H.O. 129/15/367–81; see below pp. 131–2.

attended Anglican places of worship on the morning of Census Sunday, 44,331 in the afternoon, and 26,319 in the evening. Although this meant that over half the worshippers of all denominations who attended morning and afternoon services on that day were Anglicans, it also revealed the very large task which still faced the Church, especially among the urban proletariat. In two great industrial centres, the parliamentary boroughs of Stoke-upon-Trent and Wolverhampton, Anglican worshippers on Census Sunday were comparatively few and were outnumbered by the nonconformists. The census returns reveal some of the obstacles facing the provision of services for the poor. One was still the appropriation of pews. At Pattingham there were 15 free sittings and the remaining 400 were appropriated under a deed of apportionment of 1806; at Burton-upon-Trent, out of over 1,000 sittings, only 'benches in the aisles' were free, and 'half the pews are unoccupied owing to illegal traffic in pews. The poor are excluded because they cannot afford to pay for a pew'. Another was Sunday work. At St. James's, Wednesbury, 'the parishioners consist almost exclusively of miners and colliers and labourers — too many of whom are compelled to Sunday labour'.

Lonsdale's episcopate was contemporaneous with important developments in the Church of England. Tractarianism, having developed from an academic movement into a religious system with its own conception of worship and the sacraments, was spreading from the universities into the country. A. J. B. Beresford Hope, a man of great wealth, who had become a warm supporter at Cambridge of J. M. Neale, Benjamin Webb, and the Cambridge Camden Society, later the Ecclesiological Society, appointed Webb as incumbent of his living of Sheen in 1851 and employed William Butterfield to rebuild the church. He later wrote to Webb that he was wondering 'whether Sheen could not be brought into the market as a religious watering-place'.[79] Similarly the patron from 1855 to 1884 of St. James's, Wednesbury, Colonel J. N. Bagnall, was a member of the English Church Union and the Confraternity of the Blessed Sacrament. In 1856 he presented to the living the assistant curate, Richard Twigg (d. 1879), who had worked as a layman under Dr. W. F. Hook of Leeds, the introducer of tractarian and Wilberforcian principles into an industrial parish. Twigg was the pioneer of mission services in Staffordshire and came to be known as 'the Apostle of the Black Country'. After enlarging and adorning the chancel of St. James's in 1857, he introduced an altar cross and lights, and in 1866 there were protests in the parish against the wearing of 'Popish vestments' in the church.[80] Other early tractarian clergymen in the county were F. E. Paget, Rector of Elford from 1835, and William Gresley, Canon of Lichfield from 1841. Both were writers of religious stories published by A. C. Lomax of Lichfield, one of whose apprentices, Joseph Masters, went to London to become the leading tractarian publisher of the time.[81]

A feature of early tractarianism was the revival of daily services. Joseph Masters's *Guide to Daily Prayers* shows that in 1849 in Staffordshire only the cathedral, Harborne, and Hixon had daily matins and evensong; Elford had daily matins, with evensong on Wednesdays and Fridays and in Lent; Baswich, Cheadle, and Uttoxeter had daily matins; and St. Mary's and St. John's, Wolverhampton, both had matins on holy days.[82] In 1854 5 churches had daily matins and evensong;[83] 4 others daily

[79] G. Wakeling, *Oxford Church Movement* (1895), 276–7; H. W. and I. Law, *Book of the Beresford Hopes*, 128–32, 184 sqq.; *P.O. Dir. Staffs.* (1860). The Lichfield Soc. for the Encouragement of Ecclesiastical Architecture, an ecclesiological group, had been founded as early as 1841: see below p. 193.

[80] Hackwood, *Religious Wednesbury*, 117–20; Ede, *Wednesbury*, 310–13.

[81] Wakeling, *Oxford Church Movement*, 221, 271, 299.

[82] [J. Masters], *Masters's Guide to the Daily Prayers of Eng., Wales and Scotland* (3rd edn., 1849).

[83] Cathedral; Berkswich; Harborne; Sheen; St. Mary's, Wolverhampton. These and the following details are taken from *Masters's Guide to the Churches where the Daily Prayers are said in Eng., Wales, Scotland and Ireland* (16th edn., 1854).

matins;[84] St. James's, Wednesbury, daily evensong; Aldridge daily matins, with evensong on holy days; Cheadle daily matins, with evensong on Wednesdays and Fridays; Clifton Campville daily matins, with evensong on the vigils of holy days; Colton daily matins, with evensong on Fridays; Elford daily matins, with evensong on Thursdays and holy days; and King's Bromley and Uttoxeter daily matins, with an additional morning service on holy days.

The tractarians also desired more frequent celebrations of Holy Communion. In the early 19th century it was still common practice for incumbents to have only about four celebrations a year. Bishop Butler sympathized with those who felt that in populous parishes this was inadequate. In 1838 he told an incumbent who had forbidden one of his curates to celebrate more frequently: 'Surely, Sir, you cannot think monthly sacraments too frequent in a population of about ten thousand souls; you cannot intend that such a vast body of people should live without the means of grace offered them oftener than four times a year.'[85] Masters's *Guide* showed that in 1850 only the cathedral had a weekly celebration; but by 1858 there were also weekly celebrations at Clifton Campville, Elford, Ilam, Sheen, and St. James's, Wednesbury.[86] The religious census of 1851 suggested that congregations did not always want more frequent celebrations, for the incumbents of St. Paul's, Burslem, and St. Chad's at Stowe near Lichfield indicated that as the day, Sunday, 30 March 1851, was their 'Sacrament Sunday', congregregations were 'smaller than usual'.[87]

Another development of the time was the introduction of evening worship, though here the Church of England was slower than the nonconformists. Bishop Butler had not very enthusiastically tolerated the development. Informing an incumbent in 1836 that there must be two Sunday services in larger parishes, he said: 'The canonical hour is three, but if a better attendance can be obtained, and the expense of lighting the church can be defrayed by the congregation voluntarily, I do not object to the change to six. If you give a third service it will be a gratuitous act.'[88] The census of 1851 showed that the evening service was most common in the towns, being held, for instance, in every church in Wolverhampton and West Bromwich for which details were given.[89] By the end of the century the evening service was usual, and Bishop Kempthorne in 1918 urged the clergy to continue it despite war-time restrictions because it was 'the service at the only hour after midday at which many of our people are able to attend'.[90]

The most notable effect of early tractarianism on the conduct of worship was to increase the use of music. The evangelical revival had made its contribution to this. Hanley church, when rebuilt in 1790, acquired an organ, though this was much disliked by the elderly incumbent, John Middleton, who called it a 'hurdy-gurdy', and at Tamworth the chanting of psalms and canticles by Sunday-school children and congregation was begun in 1793.[91] Masters's *Guide* showed only the cathedral and Sheen church as having choral services in 1855 and 1860, but gradually surpliced choirs and sung services were introduced; during Lonsdale's episcopate, largely through the efforts of Canon John Hutchinson, Vicar of Blurton and precentor of the cathedral, the Diocesan Choral Association was formed and held festivals in the cathedral, the first in 1856 being attended by 26 Staffordshire church choirs.[92]

Though there were several crises in the Church of England during Lonsdale's

---

[84] St. Leonard's, Bilston; St. Mary's, Handsworth; St. Mary's, Stafford; St. Peter's, Wolverhampton.

[85] Butler, *Samuel Butler*, ii. 293–4.

[86] *Masters's Guide* (5th edn., 1850); *Lich. Dioc. Church Calendar* (1859).

[87] H.O. 129/15/370/3/1; 377/1/13.

[88] Butler, *Samuel Butler*, ii. 179.

[89] H.O. 129/15/379/4/1; /381/3/1.

[90] *Lich. Dioc. Mag.* 1918, 140–1.

[91] Ward, *Stoke*, 354; Mitchell, *Tamworth Parish Church*, 53.

[92] *Lich. Dioc. Mag.* 1897, 107; 1906, 115–16; and see below p. 192.

episcopate, these had few repercussions in the diocese, apart from some local incidents, such as high feeling and anti-Puseyite pamphleteering caused in 1843 by the refusal of the Rector of Cheadle to bury a child who had been baptized by a Methodist minister.[93] This peaceful atmosphere was due very largely to Lonsdale himself. A younger contemporary, the classical scholar B. H. Kennedy, said of him: 'He was a High Churchman of the old school, broadened by experience, and inclining always to moderation and comprehension.' He had little sympathy with tractarian clergy, complaining once that there was only one in the diocese who ever obeyed him, and another time saying: 'I don't know what you think of the high-church theology; I don't believe in it a bit.' After the Wolverhampton Church Congress of 1867, at which he presided, some members subscribed to present him with a pastoral staff, but without his consent, and a friend of his expressed the opinion that 'he would much rather be presented with an umbrella'.[94] He protested against F. D. Maurice's dismissal from King's College, London, in 1853 and in 1864 wrote that he shared the wish of Archbishop Tillotson and many others that 'we were well rid of the damnatory clauses in the Athanasian creed'.[95] He never repeated these clauses himself in Eccleshall church, nor did he turn eastwards to say the creeds. He made one obeisance in the creeds, but not at the *Gloria Patri* or elsewhere. At the same time he condemned the low-church practice of saying the words of administration in Holy Communion collectively to a row of communicants.[96] 'He was absolutely without party spirit. . . . Above all things he was a lover of good men.'[97] Like Bishop Butler he opposed the party patronage exercised by trustees, since in his opinion it usually forced upon a parish clergymen of extreme opinions, and he sought to replace meetings of clergy of the same party by a revival of the ruridecanal chapters. Such a character gained him universal esteem. 'In this diocese we are singularly united', said Lord Dartmouth at the Wolverhampton Church Congress, 'but if it had not been for the wise and temperate rule of our bishop, I do not think we should be the united diocese we are.'[98]

The most controversial episode of Lonsdale's episcopate was the establishment of Lichfield theological college. It was one of several such colleges founded in cathedral cities and largely inspired by Pusey's pamphlet, *Remarks on the Prospective and Past Benefits of Cathedral Institutions, in the promotion of sound religious knowledge, occasioned by Lord Henley's Plan for their Abolition*, of 1833.[99] A college at Lichfield was proposed early in 1852 by E. J. J. G. Edwards and E. T. Codd, the incumbents of Trentham and Cotes Heath, and an address in its favour was presented to Lonsdale by the dean, the Archdeacons of Stafford and Salop, and others; but two of the three existing theological colleges were tractarian, and there was opposition in the diocese. The college was finally opened in 1857, but only after an unsuccessful attempt to stop it by a bill in Chancery. Lonsdale supported it throughout, though he feared that the dissension might harm the diocese, and was rewarded by its success before his death.[1] It was modelled on the colleges at Chichester and Wells rather than on Bishop Wilberforce's 'diocesan seminary' at Cuddesdon (Oxon.), as its only building was the principal's house and its students lived in lodgings. It differed, however, from previous colleges in that, though primarily offering graduates theological and devotional preparation for the ministry, it sought also to meet the needs of the diocese by training non-graduates.

[93] Plant, *Cheadle*, 112–13.

[94] Denison, *Lonsdale*, 120–1, 207–8, 240; see also *Lich. Dioc. Mag.* 1883, 43.

[95] Denison, *Lonsdale*, 111; F. W. Cornish, *Hist. of the Eng. Church in the Nineteenth Cent.* ii. 160; *D.N.B.*

[96] Denison, *Lonsdale*, 113–14.

[97] Obituary, *The Guardian*, 23 Oct. 1867.

[98] Denison, *Lonsdale*, 74, 247; *Authorized Rep. of the Church Congress held at Wolverhampton, 1867*, 284.

[99] F. W. Bullock, *Hist. of Ridley Hall, Cambridge*, i. 1–17, esp. 10, 11–12.

[1] Denison, *Lonsdale*, 57–65. There are some pamphlets by supporters and opponents of the proposed college in W.S.L. Pamphs. *sub* Lichfield.

About these 'the question was not whether they should be admitted to Holy Orders, but whether they should pass through a regular course of training and preparation previously to their offering themselves to the bishop for examination'. In its first ten years the college trained 35 such students, of whom 31 were ordained to curacies in the diocese.[2]

Besides the theological college it was proposed to found a training college for women teachers at Lichfield, but eventually this was established at Derby in 1853. Lonsdale supported a plan for extending the existing men's training college at Lichfield and offered it a site near his palace. In 1861, however, it was arranged that the diocese of Worcester training college at Saltley (Warws.) should also serve the dioceses of Lichfield and Hereford, and the Lichfield college was closed.[3]

Lonsdale died suddenly in 1867. His successor was George Augustus Selwyn, Primate of New Zealand since 1841, during which time he had established self-government and flourishing institutions for the Church in the colony. He accepted translation to Lichfield, at first unwillingly, while he was in England for the first Pan-Anglican conference of 1867.[4] His appointment was popular. *Punch* commemorated it in some verses entitled, 'The Right Bishop in the Right Place; or Selwyn among the Blacks', for he had been brought from 'the savage o'er sea to the savage at home'.[5] Selwyn had a dominating personality and great organizing ability, which New Zealand had enabled him to exercise fully. Archbishop Tait called him 'a veritable king of men' and said that 'an electric force attended his presence wherever he went' — though he added that 'perhaps some of those who had to do with him in his administration of the diocese of Lichfield might have liked the calmer and more prosaic modes of administration to which they had been accustomed'.[6] Selwyn admitted that his temper was not always under control; and his clergy found particularly trying his habit of appearing at some church unexpectedly just before service began and commenting on it afterwards to the officiating ministers.[7]

Selwyn was not, however, an autocrat. He believed in enlisting the counsel of the diocese through regular conferences. Bishop Phillpotts had summoned a diocesan synod at Exeter in 1851 to consider the Gorham judgement, but this was of clergy only. Bishop Browne summoned the first diocesan conference of clergy and laity at Ely in 1865. Bishop Lonsdale had been prevented by death from doing the same in 1867, but Selwyn, who had introduced such self-government into the Church in New Zealand, enthusiastically carried out the project.[8] He overcame local opposition, saying when Lord Harrowby objected to the proposed title of synod: 'I would rather be in a conference with Lord Harrowby than in a synod without him'; and the first diocesan conference was held at Lichfield in June 1868 on the eve of Selwyn's departure for a six months' farewell visit to New Zealand.[9] Though many felt that all the clergy should be summoned, the conference consisted of an equal number of clerical and lay representatives, as well as the lords lieutenant, members of parliament, patrons of benefices, and government inspectors of church schools of the diocese.[10]

Selwyn told this first diocesan conference: 'We shall want a diocesan fund, not restricted to special objects but available, under the direction of the diocesan council, for church works and needs of every kind.'[11] This was the more necessary as parishes

[2] Tucker, *Selwyn*, ii. 275. For a brief hist. of the college's first 70 years see E. C. Inman, *Hist. of Lichfield Theological College, 1857–1927* (Lichfield, 1928).
[3] Denison, *Lonsdale*, 65–66.
[4] *D.N.B.*; Tucker, *Selwyn*, ii. 235 sqq.
[5] *Punch*, 14 Dec. 1867.
[6] Tucker, *Selwyn*, ii. 248; R. T. Davidson and W.

Benham, *Life of Abp. Tait*, ii. 495.
[7] H. Anson, *Looking Forward*, 161; J. G. Lonsdale, 'The Church in Staffs. during the Nineteenth Cent.' *Staffs. Advertiser*, 5 Jan. 1901.
[8] S. C. Carpenter, *Church and People 1789–1889*, 257–8.
[9] Tucker, *Selwyn*, ii. 254.   [10] How, *Stamer*, 84–85.
[11] Tucker, *Selwyn*, ii. 256.

were having to adjust their finances. Church rates had long been under fire. In the early 1840s there was 'a violent spirit of opposition' to church rates among 'a large portion' of the inhabitants of Stoke-upon-Trent, and no rate had been levied since a proposal by the churchwardens in 1837 for a rate of a penny in the pound had been defeated by the vestry. At Wednesbury in 1851 the churchwardens, after great opposition and an inconclusive poll, levied a rate of sixpence in the pound, which it was estimated would produce £700, to enlarge the churchyard, but only £378 was collected; this was the last attempt at Wednesbury to levy a church rate.[12] Ryder had insisted in 1832 on the continuance of church rates, it being 'of the very essence of an established Church that substantial repairs of the churches, the maintenance of their decent state, both within and without, and the expense generally attendant upon our divine worship, should be defrayed by the whole parish'. Butler in 1837, however, considered that 'the public voice will have a change' and feared that 'by trying to support what indeed is not, but what in public opinion is, an unjust tax, far more may be lost than could in any case be gained. Only see what the principle of non-concession adopted by the Duke of Wellington did in the Reform Bill'. Lonsdale hoped in 1861 for 'a legislative measure, which, while it would secure to the Church her indisputable and immemorial right of raising rates . . . would exempt . . . those who do not belong to her communion from contributing to them'.[13] In 1868 the Compulsory Church Rate Abolition Act was passed.[14] On Selwyn's advice parishes gradually instituted offertories to replace rates, and in 1875 the offertories at St. Matthew's, Walsall, totalled £1,000, half of which was collected in pence.[15] Bishop Legge found, however, in 1892 that 'the weekly offertory is not yet general in the diocese'.[16] Selwyn persevered with his plan for a general diocesan fund, and one of his last actions before his death was to fix the first 'Diocesan Sunday' in January 1878. Collections were then to be made in all the churches of the diocese to help, through the fund, the theological college, the diocesan inspection of schools, the Poor Benefice Fund, the Clergy Widow and Orphan Fund, and the Clergy Pension Fund; £2,278 was raised on that Sunday.[17]

After pioneering in New Zealand Selwyn chafed at much in the diocese. He disliked the worldly state which an English bishop had to maintain. He refused to live at Eccleshall, which was abandoned as an episcopal residence. He announced that he would live at Lichfield 'in the old palace . . . now inhabited for the first time by a Bishop of Lichfield', and added that 'public opinion unanimously supports us in declining to live at Eccleshall castle, twenty-five miles from Lichfield. The country-house heresy is losing ground'.[18] He also disliked being unable to apply existing resources to increase the episcopate. He wished to divide the diocese into two or three sees; but the Ecclesiastical Commissioners, since £4,200 was the minimum income of a bishop of an old see, would not let him give more than £300 of his stipend of £4,500 to a new bishopric, which itself had to have not less than £3,000 a year. Selwyn contrasted this with 'colonial bishops, happy, useful, respected, upon less than a third of that income, with needs tenfold greater than can befall a Church by law established'.[19] And so, though originally favourable to a revival of bishops suffragan, he now felt that it would be totally inadequate to meet the Church's difficulties, and that a far more drastic measure of reform was needed.[20] He was, however, assisted by his old friends

[12] Ward, *Stoke*, 495; Ede, *Wednesbury*, 298–9.

[13] Ryder, *Charge of 1832*, 22–23, suggesting also ways of safeguarding parishioners from the levying of excessive church rates; Butler, *Samuel Butler*, ii. 220; Denison, *Lonsdale*, 79. [14] 31 & 32 Vic. c. 109.

[15] G. H. Curteis, *Bp. Selwyn of New Zealand and of Lichfield*, 396.

[16] *Lich. Dioc. Mag.* 1892, 119.

[17] Tucker, *Selwyn*, ii. 369; *Diocese of Lichfield: Rep. of the Diocesan Institutions, 1878* (1879), 161.

[18] Tucker, *Selwyn*, ii. 241.

[19] Ibid. 358–65.

[20] Davidson and Benham, *Tait*, ii. 54.

Charles John Abraham and Edmund Hobhouse, formerly bishops in New Zealand, who acted as coadjutors in the diocese,[21] and in 1877 he succeeded where Lonsdale had failed, in dividing Staffordshire into two archdeaconries; the northern half of the archdeaconry of Stafford became the archdeaconry of Stoke-upon-Trent, and Sir Lovelace Stamer, Rector of Stoke-upon-Trent, became the first Archdeacon of Stoke.[22]

On his return from New Zealand one of Selwyn's first changes in diocesan arrangements had been to hold confirmations more frequently than triennially. He instituted annual confirmations in the large parishes and one every two or three years in the smaller. He tried also 'to induce the parents and sponsors of the children to attend as witnesses of their confirmation and to meet the bishop afterwards at the Holy Communion', and he adopted the practice, copied by Bishop Moberly of Salisbury, of sitting to confirm, usually one candidate at a time, and of requiring 'the separate answer of each candidate to the great question asked in the service'.[23]

Another change was made by Selwyn from 1874, when he provided devotional preparation before his ordinations. He kept the examination in the week before ordination but required the candidate to attend early matins in the cathedral and evensong in his palace chapel daily. The examination finished on Thursday, and the result was published early on Friday. The candidates spent Friday and Saturday in interviews with Selwyn and his coadjutors and in hearing pastoral addresses. On Sunday they attended matins at the cathedral; the ordination followed, and here again the questions were answered by each candidate separately.[24]

Selwyn also wished to increase the importance of the cathedral in the diocese. When a young curate at Windsor, he had put forward a bolder and more detailed plan than Pusey's for the cathedrals, in which he foresaw much of the part played by modern cathedrals in diocesan life: he wanted the members of the chapter to be in continual residence and not to hold any parochial charge, so that each canon could perform some task such as training ordinands or organizing the diocesan societies.[25] At Lichfield he sought to put this into practice. In 1869 he summoned a meeting of the general chapter of the cathedral to consider what reforms and reorganization were needed, and it achieved at least one major success, the revision and translation of the ancient statutes, completed in 1875.[26] The choral festival, by now triennial, was so successful that Selwyn arranged similar festivals to alternate with it in the vacant two years: the 'Diocesan Home Mission Festival' in aid of Church defence societies, Sunday schools, and district visiting, and the 'Diocesan Foreign Mission Festival'. Each consisted of a service in the cathedral followed by a meeting in the palace garden.[27]

Above all Selwyn wished to improve training for the ministry. Referring in the first days of his episcopate to 'the hopes which I formed thirty years ago as a juvenile writer on cathedral reform', he was glad that Lichfield had 'a theological college with thirty students'.[28] And in 1870 in a pastoral letter to the clergy and laity he stated, after the experience of two years and nine ordinations, that the diocese's most urgent need was the extension and improvement of clerical education. The rapid increase of town population, the division of parishes, and the multiplication of benefices demanded more curates than the universities could provide. In a speech at Wolverhampton, however, Selwyn said that he was determined not 'to lower the standard of clerical education and

[21] *Lich. Dioc. Ch. Cal.* (1871, and subseq. edns.); Tucker, *Selwyn*, ii. 78, 273, 350.
[22] How, *Stamer*, 161–6.
[23] Tucker, *Selwyn*, ii. 268–9; C. A. E. Moberly, *Dulce Domum*, 223.
[24] Curteis, *Selwyn*, 370–2. But see below p. 82 for the practice at the beginning of the next episcopate.
[25] Tucker, *Selwyn*, i. 30–43.   [26] See below p. 191.
[27] Curteis, *Selwyn*, 399–401; Tucker, *Selwyn*, ii. 314.
[28] Tucker, *Selwyn*, ii. 241.

to abridge the period of probation', for 'raw recruits and untrained levies are the first to shrink from the hardships of real warfare. So will the untrained curate shrink from the daily and hourly work of our town parishes'.[29] Instead he urged that the Church should recruit its ministry much more widely and believed that if the clergy would 'encourage the more promising of the young men who attended their ministrations', the diocese could have as clergy 'its own servants, drawn from its own people, educated in its own college, proved in its own ministry'.[30] The admission by Lichfield theological college of non-graduates had his approval, and in 1870 he secured a house to give the unmarried students the benefits of collegiate residence; but in his pastoral letter he said he was often asked to ordain 'men who have neither obtained a university degree nor a testimonium from a theological college' through lacking 'the means of maintaining themselves at college'. He therefore evolved his 'probationer system' by which such young men, after a preliminary test, studied for two years while remaining at their work or acting for a small stipend as lay deacons in a parish, before coming to the theological college for a final year's course of training for ordination.[31]

During this time excitement over matters of worship continued. Selwyn himself favoured the High Churchmen. He accepted a pastoral staff presented to him by his New Zealand flock.[32] While believing the black gown illegal, he declared himself unwilling to proceed against clergy contravening the Purchas judgement of 1871 which declared vestments, the eastward position, wafers, and the mixed chalice illegal.[33] Although his own wish was 'that in all the churches in my diocese, the rubrics . . . should be strictly observed', he felt that 'great caution should be used in enforcing prompt obedience upon an unwilling congregation, by legal proceedings'. He insisted, however, that if even a minority of parishioners objected to alterations to the services as appointed by law the incumbent was bound to perform, for their benefit and in their own parish church, 'the services of the Church . . . in a strictly legal manner, at certain convenient times, at which they may be able to attend, without seeing or hearing anything to offend their conscientious scruples'.[34] In 1871, when a dispute arose between vicar and congregation over the services at St. George's, Wolverhampton, he placed his son John, who had been ordained for only 18 months, in charge; John remained there until he went to the Pacific to join the Melanesian Mission in 1873.[35] The solution favoured by Selwyn for these problems was a revision of the Prayer Book rubrics, and in 1875 he circularized his clergy about this through the ruridecanal chapters; two-thirds did not reply and the rest, by a majority of nearly two to one, desired 'that the ornaments rubric should remain unaltered'. This was also the attitude taken by Convocation, where Selwyn received support only from Bishop Durnford of Chichester.[36]

Upon Selwyn's death in 1878 William Dalrymple Maclagan became bishop. He was appointed by Disraeli, who commented: 'It seems a success with all "schools of Church thought", *alias* Church nonsense.'[37] Brought up a Scottish Presbyterian, Maclagan had, before going to Cambridge, soldiered in India, and he drew a military pension for the rest of his life. He was experienced in practical and pastoral work, having been incumbent of St. Mary's, Newington, in South London, and of St. Mary Abbot's, Kensington.[38] He was also energetic, and in 1882 Archbishop Tait on his deathbed warned him 'against tryin to do too much'.[39] Some in the diocese missed

---

[29] Ibid. 275–7.
[30] Ibid. 256, 329.
[31] Ibid. 277 sqq.; Carpenter, *Church and People*, 282.
[32] *Staffs. Advertiser*, 20 Apr. 1878.
[33] Tucker, *Selwyn*, ii. 350–1.
[34] Ibid. 346–7.

[35] F. D. How, *Bp. John Selwyn*, 26–32. For other ritual disputes during Selwyn's episcopate see below pp. 82–83.
[36] Curteis, *Selwyn*, 391–5.
[37] W. F. Monypenny and G. E. Buckle, *Life of Disraeli* (1929 edn.), ii. 1175. [38] *D.N.B.* 1901–11.
[39] Davidson and Benham, *Tait*, ii. 594–5.

Selwyn's extraordinary power, but others were relieved to exchange his rather stern rule for Maclagan's sympathy and moderation.[40]

At the outset of Maclagan's episcopate Derbyshire had been transferred to the see of Southwell under the Bishoprics Act of 1878.[41] This was, however, merely an enabling Act. An endowment sufficient to support the new bishopric had to be created before the latter could come into existence, and between 1878 and 1884, when the diocese of Southwell was finally founded by Order in Council, the diocese of Lichfield raised over £28,000 for the Southwell Bishopric Endowment Fund. This effort was, moreover, made at a time of agricultural depression when landowners and others were not so eager to dip into their pockets for subscriptions.[42]

In some directions Maclagan developed Selwyn's reforms. He sought to arrange his confirmations so that parishes might present candidates annually, and to assist him he had Sir Lovelace Stamer appointed in 1888 bishop suffragan of Shrewsbury.[43] Maclagan sat at the chancel step to confirm, two at a time. He declared himself very unwilling to confirm 'in churches where there are square pews or high partitions between the seats', because it was 'very undesirable that the candidates should sit facing each other, and part of them turning their backs upon the person addressing them', while all 'should be able to kneel easily and devoutly'.[44]

Reforms were also made at ordinations. At his first ordination Maclagan found that the names of the successful candidates in the examination were announced only at 10 o'clock on the Saturday night before the ordination on Sunday. From 1880 he therefore separated the examination from the ordination by several weeks to prevent last-minute rejections and to leave the Ember Days for devotional retirement, a rule of silence obtaining all Saturday and Sunday morning. The candidates lodged in the palace, in which Maclagan forbade smoking.[45] In 1888, after he had ordained 450 deacons, Maclagan declared that 'the preparation of our candidates in general for Holy Orders seems to me to be lamentably insufficient'; he considered that 'every graduate desiring to take Holy Orders should pass one year at a theological college after taking his degree' and looked forward to 'such a training becoming the rule instead of the exception'. He announced at the same time that in future, 'with very rare exceptions', he would ordain only graduates and students of Lichfield theological college and required three months' notice from any candidate so that he might make inquiries and direct the candidate's preparation. One of his rules was that no deacon might preach in his parish church more than a monthly sermon, which was to be sent to the examining chaplain; he preferred a diaconate of two years and refused deacons to incumbents unlikely to help them.[46]

Early in his episcopate Maclagan was faced with several attempts by the Church Association to take proceedings under the Public Worship Regulation Act of 1874.[47] Maclagan, who publicly expressed his regret that the Act had ever been passed,[48] was himself a moderate High Churchman. In 1883 he accepted a pastoral staff from his clergy for himself and his successors.[49] After his death a friend said of him: 'Extreme ritual never appealed to the late Archbishop, and he had an almost excessive horror of anything approaching conformity with Roman observances.'[50] Yet he met ritual cases in Staffordshire with conciliation and moderation. In 1876–8 Charles Bodington, Vicar

[40] F. D. How, *Archbp. Maclagan*, 195.
[41] 41 & 42 Vic. c. 68.
[42] 'The Bishopric of Southwell', *Lich. Dioc. Yr. Bk. 1883* (1884), 77–103.
[43] How, *Maclagan*, 264–6; *Lich. Dioc. Mag.* 1890, 19. A Bishop Suffragan of Shrewsbury was consecrated in 1537 but did not work in the diocese: *Dict. of Eng. Ch. Hist.* ed. S. L. Ollard and G. Crosse (1948 edn.), 334. Bp. Stamer

resigned the title in 1905: How, *Stamer*, 300.
[44] How, *Maclagan*, 245; *Lich. Dioc. Mag.* 1883, 55.
[45] How, *Maclagan*, 211–12, 227, 324–5.
[46] Ibid. 212–13, 227, 229; *Lich. Dioc. Mag.* 1888, 4–5; 1889, 159–61.
[47] 37 & 38 Vic. c. 85.
[48] *Rep. of the Chief Institutions and Yr. Bk. of the Dioc. of Lichfield, 1881*, 117.
[49] *Lich. Dioc. Mag.* 1883, 57–58.
[50] How, *Maclagan*, 162.

of St. Andrew's, Wolverhampton, had been charged with the use of illegal vestments and of altar lights, celebrating in the eastward position and facing east at the Lord's Prayer and Collect for Purity, elevating the consecrated elements, using the mixed chalice and waferbread, kneeling and bowing in the Prayer of Consecration, making the sign of the cross towards the congregation, holding illegal processions, and singing the *Agnus Dei*. As the Bishop of Lichfield was patron of the living, Archbishop Tait had to act. He vetoed the prosecution, as Bodington was ready to submit to Selwyn's request that he provide a plain midday celebration monthly, and Maclagan concurred with this decision.[51] Selwyn had agreed in 1877 to proceedings against Herbert Gardner, Vicar of St. Matthew's, Smethwick, for similar causes as well as making the sign of the cross in administering the elements; Maclagan asked Gardner to abandon the latter practice but did not allow proceedings against him. Proceedings against Edward Glover, Vicar of Christ Church, Wolverhampton, had been vetoed by Selwyn, and Maclagan asked him to cease using altar lights, the mixed chalice, and wafers.[52]

Though disliking controversy Maclagan believed that the Church should express itself through periodicals. Parish magazines were becoming common. Stamer had been a pioneer in Staffordshire by starting one at Stoke-upon-Trent in 1859, but it lasted only until the end of the year and was not revived until 1874. Meanwhile Twigg had started one at St. James's, Wednesbury, in 1867, and in January 1869 the clergy of the parishes of Colwich, Fradswell, Gayton, Great Haywood, Salt, Sandon, Stowe, Tixall, and Weston had begun to publish the monthly *Trent Valley Parochial Magazine*.[53] There was also a monthly publication, the *Lichfield Diocesan Churchman*, established in 1871 as the earliest of all diocesan periodicals. It had a circulation of 2,000 but was unofficial, and Maclagan persuaded the Diocesan Council to authorize an official *Lichfield Diocesan Magazine*, the first number of which appeared in 1880.[54] For this he wrote a series of letters 'Ad Clerum', which attracted much attention, the representative of *The Times* sometimes sitting at the local printing-office until midnight taking down his latest letter.[55] These letters were widely read because Maclagan expressed himself on the questions of the day. In 1886, for instance, he wrote on worship, holding it 'a serious responsibility for a clergyman to introduce into the service usages to which his people have not been accustomed, unless they should be merely such as help to greater reverence without exciting suspicion or leading to distraction'. On a particular point, he said that it was 'a widespread and perhaps at one time universal custom in the Church to turn to the east in saying the creeds . . . as significant of the unity of the faith', but for doing the same at 'the *Gloria* at the end of every psalm . . . there is no such authority nor any such reason . . . and the occasional frequency of its recurrence tends rather to diminish than to increase the reverence of the service. The same may be said of the continual repetition of acts of obeisance towards the Holy Table'.[56]

Maclagan sought to bring the clergy together in synods and retreats and founded the 'Pastoral Order of the Holy Ghost', the 'great object' of which was to help clergy 'in the more perfect fulfilment of their duties and obligations as the ministers of Christ's Church'.[57] He encouraged mission and teaching work and in 1890 appointed W. S.

[51] Ibid. 191–2; Tucker, *Selwyn*, ii. 333–49; Davidson and Benham, *Tait*, ii. 254–62; W. H. B. Proby, *Annals of the 'Low Church' Party in Eng. down to the death of Archbp. Tait*, ii. 352–3, 395–6; G. B. Roberts, *Hist. of the Eng. Church Union, 1859–1894*, 197–8, 210–11.

[52] Proby, *Low Church Party*, ii. 353–5, 398.

[53] How, *Stamer*, 81; Hackwood, *Religious Wednesbury*, 121; *Trent Valley Par. Mag.* 1869 and subseq. edns. (set in W.S.L.).

[54] An earlier diocesan publication with official sanction was the *Church Calendar and General Almanac for the Diocese of Lichfield*. The first editor was the Revd. E. J. J. G. Edwards of Trentham, one of the advocates of a diocesan theological college (see above p. 77), and the first issue was that for 1856. From 1887 to 1937 it appeared as the *Lichfield Diocesan Church Calendar*. Since 1938 it has appeared as the *Lichfield Diocesan Directory*.

[55] How, *Maclagan*, 201–2.

[56] *Lich. Dioc. Mag.* 1886, 144–5.

[57] Ibid. 1884, 152–3, printing the rules of the Order.

Swayne, later Bishop of Lincoln, as diocesan preacher and lecturer in theology and C. W. Carrington, later Dean of Christchurch, New Zealand, as diocesan preacher and assistant diocesan missioner.[58] In 1892 Charles Gore conducted a mission at Walsall; it was of a teaching rather than evangelistic nature, as has since become more common.[59] This was also a work in which Maclagan believed the laity could assist. He stressed the importance of recruiting working-class laymen to do missionary work among members of their own class,[60] telling his clergy that 'we want men who can speak to their fellows in their own language, knowing what their difficulties and temptations are'.[61] In 1882 he reorganized the two classes of lay helpers which had hitherto existed in the diocese, lay deacons and lay readers, into a single order of lay readers,[62] while in the same year H. A. Colvile, once a Salvation Army leader, was appointed Diocesan Lay Missioner to organize missions in the Potteries and Black Country.[63] As a result of the success of Colvile and his workers it was decided to establish a diocesan training house for lay evangelists. One was opened at Hanley in 1887,[64] but it did not become firmly established there, and it was not until 1892 that a permanent Diocesan Training Home, at Wolverhampton, was formally opened. Colvile became the first warden and held the post until his retirement in 1904.[65] An additional link between the lay evangelists in the diocese had been forged in the late 1880s when they were formed into an Evangelist Brotherhood.[66] In 1887 Maclagan licensed lay catechists to help the clergy in instructing children.[67]

Indeed by the end of the century the Church in Staffordshire had done much to meet the needs of the times. This was accomplished not only by outstanding bishops but also by a number of capable parish clergy. Sir Lovelace Stamer, Rector of Stoke-upon-Trent from 1858 to 1892, found one curate when he came to the parish but had seven, eight, or nine before he left.[68] Richard Twigg, Vicar of St. James's, Wednesbury, from 1856 to 1879, of whom it was said that he had 'buried talents which would have won the admiration of the world in the smokiest dens of the Black Country', was succeeded by Charles Bodington, Vicar of St. Andrew's, Wolverhampton, who became Canon Missioner of the diocese in 1888. By contrast John Winter, Rector of St. John's, Wednesbury, was a noted Broad Churchman.[69]

Tractarianism had brought about the revival of religious communities, and in 1863 the Sisterhood of the Good Samaritans (now the Community of the Holy Rood) of Middlesbrough (Yorks. N.R.) established a cottage hospital at Walsall. Shortly after its foundation it was placed under the charge of Dorothy W. Pattison (1832–78), a sister of Mark Pattison and usually known as Sister Dora. She eventually severed her connexion with the Community but spent her life at the hospital, caring for the sick and teaching her patients the Christian faith.[70] During the later years of the century other sisterhoods were at work in the county. The Society of All Saints (Sisters of the Poor) had a mission house at Wolverhampton, and so had the Society of the Sisters of Bethany at Burton-upon-Trent; the Community of St. Peter managed the County Home at Stafford, a refuge at Lichfield, and St. Winifred's Home for criminally assaulted children at Wolverhampton.[71]

[58] W. S. Swayne, *Parson's Pleasure*, 117–20, 132; *Lich. Dioc. Mag.* 1890, 138.
[59] G. L. Prestige, *Life of Chas. Gore*, 140–1.
[60] K. S. Inglis, *Churches and the Working Classes in Victorian Eng.* 44.
[61] *Lich. Dioc. Mag.* 1883, 4.
[62] Ibid. 1882, 18–19.
[63] Ibid. 1883, 7; How, *Maclagan*, 234–6.
[64] *Lich. Dioc. Mag.* 1886, 150–1; 1887, 31.
[65] Ibid. 1892, 123; 1904, 19.
[66] Ibid. 1888, 192.
[67] Ibid. 1887, 7–8, 44–45; How, *Maclagan*, 207–8.
[68] How, *Stamer*, 77, 227.
[69] Hackwood, *Religious Wednesbury*, 117–20, 122.
[70] Margaret Lonsdale, *Sister Dora* (1880); P. F. Anson, *The Call of the Cloister* (1964 edn., revised and ed. A. W. Campbell), 372.
[71] Anson, *Call of the Cloister*, 324, 367, 411.

Throughout the century three successive earls of Harrowby were the leading Anglican laymen in the county. Dudley Ryder, 2nd Baron and 1st Earl (d. 1847), urged the augmentation of benefices and was largely responsible for the Curates Act of 1813;[72] Dudley Ryder, 2nd Earl (d. 1882), a strong Protestant, actively supported Lord Shaftesbury's reforms; and Dudley Francis Stuart Ryder, 3rd Earl (d. 1900), an earnest but moderate Churchman, was believed to have influenced Disraeli's ecclesiastical appointments and as Vice-President of the Committee of Council on Education supported voluntary schools and religious instruction.[73]

The 2nd Earl of Harrowby was responsible, during the passing of the Burial Laws Amendment Act of 1880, for an amendment allowing any form of Christian service in churchyards.[74] Great controversy preceded this. Selwyn was a vigorous opponent of the measure; a few months before his death he said: 'I have no concessions to offer, no compromises to accept. I hold that our burial-grounds belong to the National Church, to be governed by its laws; not to the nation, to be dealt with as they please. If Parliament wish to take them, they must take them by force; and then, as dutiful and loyal citizens, we submit.' In 1878 he was chosen to present to the Archbishop of Canterbury a declaration against Lord Harrowby's proposal signed by 15,000 clergymen and more than 30,000 eminent laymen.[75] Lord Harrowby, however, through his friendship with Tait, secured the archbishop's support for his amendment, which the government accepted.[76] Stamer, in his primary charge as archdeacon in 1877, supported the Bill 'in the direction of Lord Harrowby's amendment', despite a protest from the rural deans.[77] Maclagan, though he regarded it not 'as the redress of a real grievance, but rather as a move in the game of politics', told his clergy in 1880: 'I would earnestly advise you to throw no impediments in the way of the operation of the Act.'[78] Seven years later, as President of the Church Congress at Wolverhampton, he declared that the effect of the Act had been 'remarkable', for 'our churchyards are as peaceful and orderly as they were twenty years ago', and 'the Act, in the main, has made very little difference after all the alarm and foreboding which it excited before it passed into law'.[79]

The beginning of Maclagan's episcopate saw a decline in the income of the Diocesan Church Extension Society. Since its foundation in 1835, an appeal for its funds had been made by the bishop every fifth year. Selwyn raised £20,000 for it in 1875, but Maclagan only £16,000 in 1880; in 1850 its annual subscriptions were nearly £800, but in 1880 only £200.[80] Church building had, however, passed its peak, and the Society's achievements had been considerable. At first it made grants for building and enlarging churches, to which it added successively grants for parsonage houses, mission chapels and temporary churches, for poor benefices and for curates. Between 1835 and 1880 it had aided the building of 173 new churches in the diocese and the enlargement of 252, with a consequent increase of 132,000 sittings, augmented 221 parish endowments and provided 96 additional clergy.[81] By 1893, as a result of this and similar efforts, of the 123 churches in the archdeaconry of Stoke, 48 had been built and 17 rebuilt or enlarged during the century.[82] Church restoration also had been widespread. This had not been done without loss; at the restoration of Wednesbury parish church in 1827–8 fifteen

---

[72] Act for the further Support and Maintenance of Stipendiary Curates, 53 Geo. III, c. 149.

[73] For the earls of Harrowby see *D.N.B.*; for the 1st Earl see also G. F. A. Best, *Temporal Pillars, passim.*

[74] 43 & 44 Vic. c. 41.

[75] Tucker, *Selwyn,* ii. 367.

[76] Davidson and Benham, *Tait,* ii. chap. 29, esp. pp. 387–8, 411–12.

[77] How, *Stamer,* 168–75.

[78] How, *Maclagan,* 203–4.

[79] *Rep. of Church Congress held at Wolverhampton, 1887,* 16–17.

[80] *Lich. Dioc. Mag.* 1881, 152. The decline was no doubt due partly to agricultural depression and partly to the effort of raising money for the Southwell Bishopric Endowment Fund: see above p. 82.

[81] *Lich. Dioc. Mag.* Sept. 1880, 3–5.

[82] Hutchinson, *Archdeaconry of Stoke,* 37–149.

medieval stalls, the mouldings of the nave arches, and all the ancient glass were destroyed.[83] But often restoration was very necessary; when George Gilbert Scott restored St. Mary's, Stafford, in the early 1840s, the four piers of the central tower were so unsound that the tower was saved only with great difficulty.[84] Largely through the efforts of John Hutchinson, the precentor, the cathedral was restored.[85] By 1867 Archdeacon Moore could say that in Staffordshire 'few . . . of our churches are unseemly and very many of them [have been] brought back to their original excellence and beauty'.[86]

An effect of church building and restoration was the gradual disappearance of galleries and high pews. Whereas in the late 18th and early 19th centuries faculties for the erection of galleries were common, from the 1860s faculties were requested for their removal. Church extension made them unnecessary; in 1865, for example, a faculty was granted for the removal of galleries holding 80 people from Stowe church, the population of the parish having declined from 1,200, when they were built, to 432, following the creation of the new districts of Hixon and Great Haywood.[87] Moreover contemporary ideas were hostile to both high pews and galleries. Thus it was complained in 1872 that the pews at Madeley made it difficult for most of the congregation to kneel and in 1875 that the benches for the poor at Holy Trinity, Smethwick, were not only mean but constituted 'a very marked distinction between the richer and poorer members of the congregation'.[88] In 1896 it was said of the galleries at Rugeley that 'it is found almost impossible to preserve due order in them and to prevent the young people, who crowd into them at an evening service, from behaving in an irreverent and unseemly manner'.[89] During this period there was also a movement for the abolition of appropriated pews: thus in 1857 Twigg instituted a weekly offertory instead of pew rents at St. James's, Wednesbury.[90] In the later part of the century, however, a large proportion of appropriated pews had still to be freed, for in Staffordshire in 1882, out of about 190,000 sittings in the 488 churches, 70,000 were still appropriated.[91]

New ways of worship produced other changes in the churches. The three-decker pulpit disappeared. At the outset of his incumbency at Stoke Stamer removed the pulpit to the corner of the chancel arch,[92] and others did the same. The organ was often removed from the west gallery to a transept, as at All Saints', West Bromwich, in 1871–2 and St. Bartholomew's, Wednesbury, in 1885.[93] Often, at the same time, a surpliced choir was formed, as at Christ Church, West Bromwich, in 1876.[94]

Most of the severe church restorations in the county took place during the last 40 years of the 19th century; a pictorial survey of Staffordshire churches, made between 1857 and 1860, shows that most were then still virtually untouched by the new influence.[95] The gradual change in the character of church interiors, both old and new, was, nevertheless, under way in the county by the late 1850s and early 1860s. In 1857 alterations to Christ Church, Fenton, built as recently as 1838–9,[96] 'at a period when Gothic architecture was at a low ebb, that is to say before the revival of that graceful

[83] Ede, *Wednesbury*, 304; Hackwood, *Religious Wednesbury*, 105.

[84] Sir George Gilbert Scott, *Personal and Professional Recollections* (1879), 99, 413–14.

[85] See below pp. 193–5.

[86] *Authorized Rep. of Church Congress at Wolverhampton, 1867*, 24.

[87] Lich. Dioc. Regy., B/C/2, Consistory Ct. Act Bk. 1856–65, p. 502.

[88] Ibid. 1871–5, pp. 95, 588.

[89] Ibid. 1891–9, p. 277; *V.C.H. Staffs.* v. 165.

[90] Hackwood, *Religious Wednesbury*, 118.

[91] Beresford, *Lichfield*, 295.

[92] How, *Stamer*, 72.

[93] Mary Willett, *Hist. of West Bromwich* (West Bromwich, 1882), 69; Hackwood, *Religious Wednesbury*, 106.

[94] *Lich. Dioc. Mag.* 1929, 17.

[95] S. A. Jeavons, 'Staffs. Church Interiors during the years 1857–1860', *Trans. Lich. Arch. and Hist. Soc.* ii. The article is based upon a collection of watercolours (in the Cathedral Libr., Lichfield) painted between 1857 and 1860 by a Mrs. Moore and her sister, showing interior and exterior views of Staffs. churches.

[96] *V.C.H. Staffs.* viii. 214.

style had fairly set in', included the demolition of 'the former apology for a chancel' and the erection of a new one 'of considerable size', with side aisles and vestry. Galleries were removed, the east window was filled with stained glass and the other windows with painted glass. Further improvements in 1861–2 included the installation of a reredos.[97] During 1861–2 the chancel of Hanford church was also enlarged and a reredos and stained glass installed.[98] A church in the new idiom was G. E. Street's All Saints', Denstone. Bishop Lonsdale, when he consecrated it in 1862, stressed the fact that it was especially a church for the poor, and noted that all the sittings were free. This did not, however, mean that the church was plain or sparsely furnished. Street himself explained that the ritual arrangements were 'very complete'. There were carved oak stalls in the chancel for the clergy and choir, the altar stood forward in the centre of the apse and had a reredos of marble and alabaster, sculptured and painted, the altar cloths were richly embroidered, and the plate and linen were of the best. The chancel walls were furnished with arcades, sedilia, piscina, and credence, the pulpit and the font were of marble and alabaster, and all the windows were filled with stained glass.[99]

Upon Maclagan's translation to York in 1891 the Hon. Augustus Legge became bishop. He had very close connexions with the county. He was born at Sandwell Hall, West Bromwich, the fifth son of William Legge, Earl of Dartmouth (d. 1853). After graduating at Oxford, he was trained at Lichfield theological college in 1863 and served as curate at St. Mary's, Handsworth, before being beneficed in South London.[1] Though brought up in evangelical surroundings, his own inclinations were High Church, and in 1894 he accepted a cope for himself and his successors given by the diocese. He did not possess the great gifts of his immediate predecessors, but he was industrious and travelled continually through his diocese, using carriage, train, bicycle, and finally motor-car.[2] For many years one of his examining chaplains was W. R. Inge, whose family also had local connexions. Inge later described Bishop Legge as 'a Christian gentleman of the very best type. He did his work thoroughly without any fuss and was trusted and respected by everybody'.[3]

In administration Legge continued the policy of his predecessors. Thus in 1909, on the death of his lifelong friend Bishop Anson, who had served him as assistant bishop since 1901, he had Dr. E. A. Were, Bishop Suffragan of Derby, appointed as the first Bishop Suffragan of Stafford. Since it was intended that Bishop Were's new duties should lie chiefly in Staffordshire it was considered appropriate that he should take his title from the county town, leaving the suffragan see of Shrewsbury, held until 1905 by Bishop Stamer, vacant until such time as it should be considered necessary to appoint a second suffragan for the diocese.[4] Maclagan had proposed in 1890 the formation of a diocesan sisterhood of deaconesses with a training house in the cathedral close.[5] Legge formed such a sisterhood in 1894. He based its rules on those of the diocese of Rochester, in which he had worked. Its training house was at Walsall, and in 1896 it opened an institution at Longton for women's work.[6] Legge provided confirmations on Sundays for candidates unable to attend an afternoon or early-evening service on week-days.[7] In 1900 he inaugurated a Twentieth Century Million Shilling Fund — £50,000 — for church extension, which produced just over £8,000 in the year; and his

[97] *Lich. Dioc. Ch. Cal.* (1863), 140–1.
[98] Ibid. 144.
[99] Ibid. 141–3, including Street's descrip. of the church.
[1] Obituary, *The Times*, 17 Mar. 1913; obituary, *Staffs. Advertiser*, 22 Mar. 1913.
[2] *Lich. Dioc. Mag.* 1894, 65; obituary, ibid. 1913, 44–48.
[3] W. R. Inge, *Diary of a Dean*, 19.
[4] *Lich. Dioc. Mag.* 1909, 94–95, 145. Shrewsbury was not revived until 1940: *Staffs. Advertiser*, 28 Oct. 1939; *Lich. Dioc. Mag.* 1940, 5, 25.
[5] *Lich. Dioc. Mag.* 1890, 155.
[6] Ibid. 1894, 24–25; 1896, 159.
[7] Ibid. 1905, 163.

quinquennial appeal for the Church Extension Society in 1906 raised £18,500 of which £2,300 was given by the clergy.[8]

The most difficult problem facing him was that of clerical stipends, which had been becoming increasingly serious. This was so in the whole Church of England, but in Staffordshire the situation was particularly affected by church building and the division of parishes. During the 19th century, for example, the ancient parish of Stoke-upon-Trent was divided into 26 parishes, Stone into 7, and Wolstanton into 7 besides contributing to 4 other composite parishes. Whereas in the district comprising the archdeaconry of Stoke from 1877 there were 51 parishes in 1800, by 1893 there were 123 with 120 beneficed clergy.[9] This development had not taken place without some misgivings. Bishop Butler had declared himself 'very sorry to diminish the income of the mother-church' at Wolverhampton but recognized that new churches were necessary 'on account of the dissenters' competition'.[10] In 1859 Bishop Lonsdale wrote that 'the question whether it be best to divide large parishes into independent districts or to leave them under the care of one incumbent with several curates under him . . . admits, as it seems to me, weighty arguments on both sides'.[11] The religious census of 1851 revealed that many parishes, both old and new, were badly endowed. The incumbent of St. Chad's, Stafford, gave the income of his church as just under £67 a year and stated: 'From the small amount of the endowment [there is] only one service though the religious necessities of the town require a second.'[12] Similarly at Hilderstone, where a new church had been built in 1833 by Ralph Bourne, the lord of the manor, the incumbent's stipend was only £80 a year from Queen Anne's Bounty and £15 in pew-rents, and he commented: 'It is scarcely necessary to remark that this cure without private means is totally inadequate to support a clergyman.'[13]

The result was that in 1880 there were 249 benefices in the diocese worth under £200 a year.[14] Maclagan in 1887 urged parishes to revive the ancient custom of Easter offerings either for their own incumbent or for an Easter Offerings Fund which he established for poor clergy; but Legge in 1904 stated that 136 of the 336 parishes in Staffordshire had no Easter offering.[15] In 1895 there were in the diocese 22 benefices worth under £100, 48 worth between £100 and £150, and 75 worth between £150 and £200; the raising of these stipends was one of the objects of Legge's quinquennial appeal on behalf of the Diocesan Church Extension Society that year.[16] Local effort was supplemented by the foundation of the Queen Victoria Clergy Fund, of which a diocesan branch was set up in 1897; in 1898 the diocesan conference agreed to amalgamate this with the Easter Offerings Fund.[17] The Queen Victoria Clergy Fund was based upon the method of re-endowment adopted by the Church of Ireland after disestablishment. The diocese doubled parochial contributions, which were again doubled by the Ecclesiastical Commissioners. In 1898 £1,958 was distributed in amounts from £5 to £35 to the incumbents of 103 benefices in the diocese worth under £200 a year; but declining local contributions steadily reduced the sum — £1,159 in 1904, £1,025 in 1905 and £672 in 1909.[18] As for the unbeneficed clergy, the average stipend assigned to curates licensed to Staffordshire parishes in the 19th century were: 1814 just over £65; 1834 about £86; 1854 almost £87; 1874 just over £120; 1894 almost £131.[19] Of the £34,000 contributed to the stipends of assistant clergy in the diocese in

[8] Ibid. 1900, 41–42; 1902, 58; 1911, 5.
[9] Hutchinson, *Archdeaconry of Stoke*, 17, 149.
[10] Butler, *Samuel Butler*, ii. 239–40.
[11] How, *Stamer*, 83.
[12] H.O. 129/15/367/1/9.
[13] Ibid. /368/1/3; White, *Dir. Staffs.* (1851).
[14] *Lich. Dioc. Mag.* Sept. 1880, 4.

[15] Ibid. 1887, 64; A. Legge, *Charge to the Clergy of the Diocese . . . at his Second General Visitation, Oct. 1904* (Lichfield, 1904), 46 (copy in W.S.L. Pamphs.).
[16] *Lich. Dioc. Mag.* 1895, 181.
[17] Ibid. 1897, 68; 1898, 175.
[18] Ibid. 1898, 93; 1904, 79; 1905, 100; 1909, 89.
[19] Lich. Dioc. Regy., B/A/11a.

1904 £10,286 was in grants from the Ecclesiastical Commissioners and church societies, £13,983 in subscriptions and collections, and £10,416 paid by incumbents.[20]

Legge died in 1913 and was succeeded by John Augustine Kempthorne, then aged 49, who had held livings in the North of England, including Liverpool and Gateshead, and had been Bishop Suffragan of Hull since 1910.[21] Archbishop Lang said of him: 'His face alone counted for much, and his preaching and speaking were admirably clear and strong. Everybody liked looking at him and listening to him.'[22] Archbishop Davidson said that he was the most pastorally minded bishop of his day.[23] His episcopate was a time of development in the organization of the Church, which he enthusiastically supported. He presided in 1918 over a meeting in Walsall addressed by William Temple on the Life and Liberty Movement. It was, Temple reported, a 'decidedly good' meeting; 'the bishop was strongly in our favour'.[24] Later Kempthorne supported Temple in urging that women should be admitted members of the new Church Assembly.[25] In 1918 Kempthorne became the first chairman of the executive committee of the newly-formed Industrial Christian Fellowship, a union of the Navvy Mission and the Christian Social Union.[26] In 1926, during the coal stoppage which lasted nearly seven months after the General Strike, he led a number of bishops and nonconformists in negotiating with the miners and drawing up a memorandum of terms, a move that was not received favourably by Archbishop Davidson.[27] Kempthorne was also anxious that his diocese should co-operate in the changes in the Church. In 1920 he was 'devoutly thankful that the Enabling Bill is now safe' and urged that it was 'of the utmost importance that every parish should now proceed to the election of such [parochial church] councils'.[28] The next year he allowed a diocesan collection for the Central Church Fund.[29]

There was a reorganization of diocesan finance at the beginning of Kempthorne's episcopate. In 1914 the Diocesan Sunday Fund, supported by an annual collection in churches throughout the diocese and divided annually by the Diocesan Council between the various church organizations in the diocese, was replaced by a Finance Committee of the Diocesan Council. This now budgeted annually for funds to be raised by parochial quotas.[30] In 1914 433 parishes and districts out of the 455 into which the diocese was divided for budgetary purposes made contributions towards the £8,000 for which the Finance Committee asked them, raising £6,901, or 86 per cent. of the target. The budget remained £8,000 between 1914 and 1918, but in no year did contributions reach £7,000.[31] Finance was a problem between the wars. For 1922 and 1923 the diocesan budget was £10,700, but only £8,462 was raised in 1922 and £7,953 in 1923.[32] In 1931 the diocese paid to the Church Assembly Fund only £2,135 of the £4,742 that it was asked to contribute, and in the following year diocesan receipts fell by £633.[33] Even in 1938, after two years in which the income of the diocese had shown 'a most appreciable increase', the total was still £665 short of the budget, and all departments received only 90 per cent. of their requirements.[34]

One reform which Kempthorne failed to secure was the further division of the diocese. Several parishes in South Staffordshire, including Smethwick and Harborne, had been transferred to the see of Birmingham under the Southwark and Birmingham

[20] *Lich. Dioc. Mag.* 1905, 182.
[21] *Crockford's Clerical Dir.* (1914); *Staffs. Advertiser*, 3 May 1913. [22] J. G. Lockhart, *Cosmo Gordon Lang*, 206.
[23] *Lich. Dioc. Mag.* 1947, 107.
[24] F. A. Iremonger, *William Temple*, 255–6.
[25] Ibid. 257.
[26] R. Lloyd, *Church of England in the Twentieth Cent.* ii. 96.

[27] G. K. A. Bell, *Randall Davidson*, ii. 1317–18.
[28] *Lich. Dioc. Mag.* 1920, 3–5.
[29] Ibid. 1921, 46.
[30] Ibid. 1913, 152–5, 163.
[31] Ibid. 1916, 68; 1917, 65; 1918, 79; 1919, 55.
[32] Ibid. 1924, 63.
[33] Ibid. 1933, 60.
[34] Ibid. 1938, 30, 31.

Bishoprics Act of 1904.[35] Legge thought that the whole of Shropshire (part of which was in the diocese of Hereford) should be a separate diocese,[36] and after the First World War it was proposed to make it so. Kempthorne spoke in 1922 of 'the splendid possibilities which await the new diocese of Shropshire with a bishop who can really know his people'.[37] The Shrewsbury Bishopric Measure was passed by the Church Assembly but was rejected by the House of Lords in 1926, largely through a speech by Hensley Henson, Bishop of Durham and formerly Bishop of Hereford, who disliked 'breaking up the great historic sees and substituting a number of little bishoprics which, while confessedly too small for effective diocesan administration, would still be too large for direct pastoral ministry'. He could not agree that 'because Lichfield is too large for efficient administration, Hereford should be made too small' and considered that 'the addition of northern Shropshire to the diocese of Hereford would give to Lichfield all the relief that the present measure offers, and it would ensure the unity of Shropshire under a single bishop'.[38]

Two years later, when the House of Commons rejected the Prayer Book Measure, Kempthorne called a diocesan synod of the clergy. They agreed that the bishop should be guided at his discretion by the provisions of the 1928 Book, including the authorization of reservation. If both parochial church council and incumbent agreed, he should allow deviations from the 1662 Book, although the alternative communion service was to be permitted only in exceptional circumstances.[39]

Kempthorne resigned in 1937 and died in 1946.[40] He was succeeded by Edward Sydney Woods, Bishop Suffragan of Croydon since 1930. When an undergraduate at Cambridge in the 1890s Woods had been a leading member of the evangelical Inter-Collegiate Christian Union, but after the First World War, as Vicar of Holy Trinity, Cambridge — where his 'saintliness of life and power of preaching had quickly made him a force in post-war Cambridge' — his outlook broadened.[41] Archbishop Lang described him as 'always genial, popular and able'.[42] He supported Archbishop Temple's campaign to secure recognition of the importance of Christianity in all aspects of human life and had an enthusiasm for evangelism and religious education.[43] He made constant 'pilgrimages' through his diocese, having made five to rural deaneries and visited 300 parishes by the end of the first two years of his episcopate. He continued them on foot during the petrol shortage of the Second World War.[44] After the war he urged the revival of evangelistic work, and from 1948 he and the diocesan Evangelistic Director held conferences with the parochial church councils.[45]

In January 1939 the Bishop's Campaign for New Churches was launched and had raised over £90,000 by the end of the Second World War.[46] Finance improved during the war, and in 1941 there was an excess of income over expenditure of £1,879, the total diocesan income being £15,534, of which the quotas raised £12,365.[47] This continued after the war. In 1946 only in one of the 29 rural deaneries of the diocese did

[35] 4 Edw. VII, c. 30. The new see was constituted by Order in Council on 12 Jan. 1905: *V.C.H. Warws.* ii. 50. The area transferred from the bishopric of Lichfield was the deanery of Handsworth, consisting of the pars. of Birchfield, Hamstead, St. Mary's, Handsworth, St. Michael's, Handsworth, St. James's, Handsworth, St. Peter's, Harborne, St. John's, Harborne, Perry Barr, Smethwick Old Church, St. Mary's, Smethwick, St. Matthew's, Smethwick, St. Michael's, Smethwick, St. Paul's, West Smethwick, Holy Trinity, Smethwick, St. Chad's, Smethwick, and St. Stephen's, Smethwick: *Lich. Dioc. Ch. Cal.* (1905). After the transfer to Birmingham the deanery was divided into two deaneries, Handsworth and Harborne: *V.C.H. Warws.* ii. 50. And see below p. 98.

[36] *Lich. Dioc. Mag.* 1905, 187.
[37] Ibid. 1922, 131.
[38] H. H. Henson, *Retrospect of an Unimportant Life,* ii. 90–91, 94–97.
[39] *Lich. Dioc. Mag.* 1928, 239–40.
[40] Ibid. 1946, 33–34; obituary, *Staffs. Advertiser,* 2 Mar. 1946.
[41] J. C. Pollock, *A Cambridge Movement,* 144, 147, 197–8.
[42] Lockhart, *Lang,* 331.
[43] Obituary, *The Times,* 12 Jan. 1953.
[44] *Lich. Dioc. Mag.* 1938, 90; 1939, 192.
[45] Ibid. 1950, 106.
[46] Ibid. 1939, 3, 43–45; 1945, 44.
[47] Ibid. 1942, 53–55.

every parish meet its obligations fully, but 11 deaneries did so in 1949 and 18 in 1950. In this latter year the diocese raised £23,473.[48] In 1966 it raised £179,463, of which £143,675 represented contributions from the 472 parishes in the diocese.[49]

Clerical stipends, however, were still a problem. In 1916 218 benefices in the diocese were worth under £250, but in 1925 all benefices were raised to a minimum of £280 with £20 for each child, and the minimum for curates was fixed at £220 with a similar child allowance.[50] Post-war inflation, the nationalization of coal and railways, and reduction of interest on securities worsened the situation. In 1947 195 benefices in the diocese were worth below £400, and it was decided to begin by raising them to that figure, £14,000 a year being required for this.[51] By 1956 the diocesan standard stipend had been raised to £600 a year. In 1966 the minimum stipend was £1,025, or £1,065 for an incumbent in charge of more than one parish.[52] An increasing number of parishes have been united, especially since the Pastoral Reorganization Measure of 1949.[53]

The number of curates in the county has also declined.[54] In 1859 167 Staffordshire incumbents were without curates, 99 had one, 13 had two, 6 had three (Holy Trinity, Burton-upon-Trent; Coseley; St. Mary's, Lichfield; St. Mary's, Stafford; Tamworth; St. Matthew's, Walsall), and one had four (St. Peter's, Wolverhampton). In 1966 248 incumbents were without curates, 49 had one, 16 had two, 5 had three (Bucknall with Bagnall; Bushbury; St. Peter's, Stoke-upon-Trent; St. Matthew's, Walsall; St. Peter's, Wolverhampton), and one had seven (St. Luke's, Cannock).

Bishop Woods died in 1953 and was succeeded by Canon Arthur Stretton Reeve, Vicar of Leeds.[55] Bishop Reeve decided to live not in the palace but in a house in the cathedral close. In 1954 the palace was handed over by the Church Commissioners to the dean and chapter for use by St. Chad's School, at which the cathedral choirboys are educated.[56]

---

[48] Ibid. 1951, 53.

[49] Lich. Dioc. Board of Finance, *Rep. and Accounts 1966–7*, 3–4, 16.

[50] *Lich. Dioc. Mag.* 1916, 174; 1925, 9–10.

[51] Ibid. 1947, 54, 95–97.

[52] Ibid. 1956, 51; Lich. Dioc. Board of Finance, *Rep. and Accounts 1966–7*, 4–5.

[53] Between 1921 and 1963 33 Staffs. benefices were united under the Union of Benefices Act, 1919, and the Union of Benefices Measure, 1923, while between 1951 and 1963 5 pluralities were effected in the county under the Pastoral Reorganization Measure: *Lich. Dioc. Dir.* (1964).

[54] For the following para. see *Lich. Dioc. Ch. Cal.* (1859); *Lich. Dioc. Dir.* (1966). The figs. for 1966 include vacant incumbencies (21) but not vacant curacies (8).

[55] *Lich. Dioc. Mag.* 1953, *passim*.

[56] Ibid. 71; 1954, 83; and see below p. 197. Kempthorne left the palace in the early 1920s, and until 1932 it was used as a hostel for students from the Theological College: *Lich. Dioc. Ch. Cal.* (1921–2), 20; (1923), 18; (1931), 263; (1932), 259.

DEANERIES

Until the later 19th century the archdeaconry of Stafford coincided approximately with the county of Stafford. The most noteworthy discrepancies were on the western borders where the archdeaconry included the Shropshire parishes which had formed part of Staffordshire in 1086.[1] In the south of the county Amblecote (in Old Swinford, Worcs.) and Rowley Regis (in the otherwise detached Staffordshire parish of Clent) were in the diocese of Worcester. In the north-west Balterley (in Barthomley, Ches.) was in the archdeaconry of Chester (in the diocese of Chester from 1541), and Tyrley (in Market Drayton, Salop.) was in the archdeaconry of Salop.[2] On the other hand Woore, the Shropshire portion of Mucklestone parish, Rudge, the Shropshire portion of Pattingham parish, and the parts of Tamworth parish that lay in Warwickshire, were all in the archdeaconry of Stafford.

In 1224 the archdeaconry consisted of seven deaneries: Stafford, Lapley, Trysull, Newcastle, Alton, Tamworth, and Tutbury.[3] By 1291 these had been reduced to five: Stafford, Newcastle, Alton and Leek, Tamworth and Tutbury, and Lapley and Trysull. The union of Stafford and Newcastle by the early 14th century reduced the number to four.

The fullest lists of the constituent parishes of the medieval deaneries are those in the *Taxatio Ecclesiastica* of 1291 and the *Valor Ecclesiasticus* of 1535. These documents, however, do not make any systematic attempt to distinguish the parishes subject to the jurisdictions of the archdeacon and the rural dean from those subject to a peculiar jurisdiction. The peculiar jurisdictions within the archdeaconry were in fact very numerous. The most notable were those of the royal free chapels and of the dean and chapter and certain prebendaries of Lichfield Cathedral. In addition Burton Abbey exercised a peculiar jurisdiction over the parishes belonging to it,[4] and in the 12th century the Augustinian houses of Rocester, Stone, and Trentham were granted privileges modelled on those of Burton.[5] The extent of these monastic jurisdictions, however, is difficult to define, and in the following lists parishes subject to a monastic jurisdiction are included in the deaneries to which they are assigned by the *Taxatio* or the *Valor*. The other peculiars are noted separately.

In 1291 the deanery of Stafford consisted of the parishes of Abbots Bromley, Blithfield, Chebsey, Cheswardine (Salop.), Draycott-in-the-Moors, Milwich, Sandon, Seighford, Standon, Stone, Stowe, Swynnerton, and Weston-upon-Trent.[6] The deanery of Newcastle consisted of the parishes of Audley, Biddulph, Madeley, Maer, Mucklestone, Stoke-upon-Trent, Trentham, and Wolstanton.[7] As already seen Stafford and Newcastle were soon afterwards formed into a single deanery. In 1535 this united deanery (by then known as Newcastle and Stone) also included the parishes of Ashley, Barlaston, and Gayton, none of which was mentioned in 1291, and Haughton, which

---

[1] i.e. Cheswardine, Quatt, Sheriff Hales, and Worfield, and Alveley and Claverley in the peculiar jurisdiction of Bridgnorth: *V.C.H. Staffs.* iv. 1–2, and map between pp. 36 and 37; *Valor Eccl.* (Rec. Com.), iii, map of Coventry and Lichfield diocese between pp. 508 and 509.

[2] See map on p. 138. Clent itself is now in Worcs. The detached Staffs. parish of Broom (now in Worcs.) was also in Worcester diocese.

[3] For this para. see above p. 38.

[4] See above p. 29 and below pp. 209–10.

[5] See below pp. 241, 247, 256.

[6] *Tax. Eccl.* (Rec. Com.), 242. Adbaston was valued under this deanery; it was, however, appropriated to the Dean of Lichfield (*S.H.C.* 1924, pp. 11, 116–19) and was almost certainly subject to his peculiar jurisdiction.

[7] *Tax. Eccl.* 242–3.

was in the deanery of Lapley and Trysull in 1291.[8] By 1535 Abbots Bromley was in the deanery of Tamworth and Tutbury.

The deanery of Alton and Leek in 1291 consisted of the parishes of Alstonefield, Alton, Caverswall, Cheadle, Checkley, Cheddleton, Dilhorne, Ellastone, Grindon, Ilam, Kingsley, Kingstone, Leek, Leigh, Mayfield, Rocester, and Uttoxeter.[9] In 1535 the deanery also included the parishes of Blore, Bramshall, Croxden, and Gratwich, none of which was mentioned in 1291.[10]

The deanery of Tamworth and Tutbury in 1291 consisted of the parishes of Aldridge, Burton-upon-Trent, Clifton Campville, Elford, Hamstall Ridware, Hanbury, Handsworth, Rolleston, Shenstone, Tamworth, Tatenhill, Tutbury, Walsall, Wednesbury, West Bromwich, and Yoxall.[11] In 1535 the deanery also included Colton,[12] Darlaston, Drayton Bassett, Rushall, and Thorpe Constantine, none of which was mentioned in 1291, and Abbots Bromley, which was in the deanery of Stafford in 1291.[13]

The deanery of Lapley and Trysull in 1291 consisted of the parishes of Blymhill, Bradley, Bushbury, Church Eaton, Enville, Forton, Gnosall, Haughton, Kingswinford, Kinver, Lapley, Norbury, Pattingham, Penn, Quatt (Salop.),[14] Sedgley, Sheriff Hales (now in Salop.), Weston-under-Lizard, Wombourn, and Worfield (Salop.).[15] In 1535 the deanery also included Himley (not mentioned in 1291), but Haughton had by then passed into the deanery of Newcastle and Stone.[16]

In the 16th century the following peculiar jurisdictions also lay within the limits of the archdeaconry:

the royal free chapel of St. Mary Magdalen, Bridgnorth (Salop.), comprising the Shropshire parishes of Alveley, Bridgnorth St. Leonard, Claverley, and Quatford, and the Staffordshire chapelry of Bobbington;[17]

the royal free chapel of St. Michael, Penkridge, covering the parish of Penkridge;[18]

the royal free chapel of St. Mary, Stafford, comprising the parishes of Castle Church, Ingestre, Stafford St. Mary, and Tixall;[19]

the royal free chapel of St. Michael, Tettenhall, covering the parish of Tettenhall;[20]

the royal free chapel of St. Peter, Wolverhampton, covering the parish of Wolverhampton;[21]

the peculiar jurisdictions of the dean and chapter and certain prebendaries of Lichfield Cathedral comprising, in addition to the Close, the parishes of Adbaston, Alrewas, Armitage, Berkswich, Brewood, Cannock, Colwich, Eccleshall, Edingale, Farewell

[8] *Valor Eccl.* iii. 107–22.
[9] *Tax. Eccl.* 243.
[10] *Valor Eccl.* iii. 123–8 (where the deanery is called Leek and Alton).
[11] *Tax. Eccl.* 243. Wednesbury, although noted separately in 1291, was in fact a chapelry of Walsall at that date; it seems gradually to have acquired the status of a parish church: J. F. Ede, *Hist. of Wednesbury*, 54–69.
[12] Colton was evidently in the deanery of Stafford and Newcastle in the early 14th cent.: *S.H.C.* i. 248.
[13] *Valor Eccl.* iii. 148–52.
[14] Quatt may have been in Worcester diocese in the 11th cent.: J. F. A. Mason, 'South-East Shropshire in 1086', *Trans. Shropshire Arch. Soc.* lvii. 158.
[15] *Tax. Eccl.* 243. Upper Arley was valued under this deanery; it was, however, appropriated to the dean and chapter of Lichfield (*S.H.C.* 1924, pp. 11, 12) and was almost certainly subject to their peculiar jurisdiction. Tipton too was valued under this deanery; by the 16th cent. at least it was a peculiar of the Prebendary of Prees: see below.
[16] *Valor Eccl.* iii. 99–106.

[17] Ibid. 199. Bobbington was part of Claverley parish: Eyton, *Antiquities of Shropshire*, iii. 172–3. Quatford, like Bridgnorth itself (originally in Morville parish), seems earlier to have been in Hereford diocese: *Trans. Shropshire Arch. Soc.* lvii. 158. In 1291 Bridgnorth was valued under Stafford archdeaconry, and Quatford under Hereford diocese, but by the 16th cent. both were considered territorially part of Coventry and Lichfield diocese, although the peculiar jurisdiction meant that this had little practical consequence: *Tax. Eccl.* 166, 243; Eyton, *Shropshire*, i. 118, n. 59.
[18] See below p. 302. During the Middle Ages Shareshill was part of Penkridge parish, and the peculiar jurisdiction of the former royal free chapel over Shareshill survived until the 19th cent.: see below pp. 300, 302; *V.C.H. Staffs.* v. 178–9; *Valor Eccl.* iii. 510.
[19] *Valor Eccl.* iii. 117–20; see below p. 307.
[20] *Valor Eccl.* iii. 510. During the Middle Ages Codsall was part of Tettenhall parish (*S.H.C.* 1915, 71–72; see below p. 319), and the peculiar jurisdiction of the former royal free chapel over Codsall survived until the 19th cent.
[21] *S.H.C.* 1915, 325, 326.

(from 1527), Harborne, Haselour, High Offley, Hints, King's Bromley, Lichfield St. Chad, Lichfield St. Mary, Lichfield St. Michael, Longdon, Mavesyn Ridware, Norton Canes, Pipe Ridware, Rugeley, Stafford St. Chad, Tipton, Upper Arley (now in Worcs.), Weeford, and Whittington.[22]

The peculiar jurisdictions belonging to the dean and chapter and prebendaries of Lichfield survived until the 19th century. Peculiar jurisdictions exercised by the royal free chapels until their dissolution also survived until the 19th century, with the exception of that which had belonged to St. Mary's, Stafford.[23] The only monastic peculiar to survive the Dissolution, however, was that which the Paget family acquired in Burton parish after the suppression of Burton College; this too survived until the 19th century.[24]

The four rural deaneries survived as divisions of the archdeaconry until the 19th century.[25] Rural deans, however, ceased to be appointed in the 16th century.[26]

With the revival of rural deans in the diocese in 1837 the archdeaconry of Stafford was divided into 13 deaneries; this number was increased to 21 when the peculiar and exempt jurisdictions were abolished in 1846.[27] In 1851 the composition of the deaneries was as follows:[28]

Alstonefield: Alstonefield, Blore, Butterton, Calton, Cauldon, Elkstone, Grindon, Ilam, Longnor, Quarnford, Sheen, Warslow, Waterfall, Wetton.

Brewood: Blymhill, Brewood, Bushbury, Codsall, Shareshill, Sheriff Hales (now in Salop.), Tettenhall, Weston-under-Lizard.

Cheadle: Alton, Bradley, Caverswall, Cheadle, Cotton, Dilhorne, Draycott, Freehay, Kingsley, Oakamoor.

Eccleshall: Adbaston, Ashley, Broughton, Chapel Chorlton, Chebsey, Cheswardine (Salop.), Cotes Heath, Croxton, Eccleshall, Ellenhall, Forton, Gnosall, High Offley, Knightley, Maer, Moreton, Mucklestone, Norbury, Standon.

Himley: Brierley Hill, Brockmoor, Coseley, Ettingshall, Lower Gornal, Upper Gornal, Himley, Kingswinford Holy Trinity (Wordsley), Kingswinford St. Mary, Pensnett, Quarry Bank, Sedgley.

Leek: Biddulph, Brown Edge, Cheddleton, Endon, Horton, Ipstones, Leek St. Edward, Leek St. Luke, Meerbrook, Norton-in-the-Moors, Onecote, Rushton, Wetley Rocks.

Lichfield: Alrewas, Burntwood, Edingale, Farewell, Gentleshaw, Hammerwich, Hints, King's Bromley, the Lichfield parishes of St. Chad, St. Mary, St. Michael, and Christ Church, Shenstone, Weeford, Whittington.

Newcastle-under-Lyme: Audley, Betley, Burslem St. John, Burslem St. Paul, Chesterton, Cobridge, Goldenhill, Keele, Kidsgrove, Mow Cop, Newcastle St. Giles, Newcastle St. George, Newchapel, Sneyd, Talke, Tunstall, Wolstanton.

---

[22] *S.H.C.* 1915, under the parishes here listed. See also above notes 6, 15. Not all the churches appropriated to the dean and chapter came under their peculiar jurisdiction: *S.H.C.* 1915, 56 (Chebsey), 81 (Dilhorne). For Farewell see below p. 224.

[23] *Valor Eccl.* iii. 510, 511; see above p. 74 and below pp. 302, 308, 320, 329–30.

[24] *Valor Eccl.* iii. 510; see below p. 210. Other peculiars in the county were the probate jurisdictions exercised by the lords of the manors of Pattingham, Sedgley, and Tyrley: A. J. Camp, *Wills and Their Whereabouts*, 70, 87, 116; F. W. Hackwood, *Sedgley Researches* (Dudley, 1898), 42–43; *S.H.C.* 1945–6, 36–37, 116, 144–5, 193–4, 273–87; J. E. Auden, 'The Local Peculiar Courts of Shropshire', *Trans. Shropshire Arch. and Nat. Hist. Soc.* 4th ser. xii. 301–2. Gnosall, said in 1816 to be a peculiar jurisdiction of

the Bishop of Lichfield and Coventry (*Valor Eccl.* iii. 510), may have been a manorial peculiar of this type: Camp, op. cit. 68.

[25] See e.g. Lich. Dioc. Regy., B/V/1/55 (1635, where Newcastle and Stone deanery is called Stafford and Stone); A/V/1/2–4 (1830).

[26] An attempt by Bishop Bentham in 1565 to revive the office of rural dean was unsuccessful: see above p. 48.

[27] See above pp. 73, 74. The new deaneries were at first unnamed: Lich. Dioc. Regy., B/A/1/30, pp. 75–78, 191, 195. The 21 are named in G. Hodson, *Diocesan Union the Strength and Ornament of the Church: a Charge delivered to the Clergy of the Archdeaconry of Stafford, 1847* (1847), 41 (copy in W. S. L. Pamphs.).

[28] Based on White, *Dir. Staffs.* (1851), 42–44 (but omitting the chapels of ease included there).

Penkridge: Acton Trussell, Bednall, Bradley, Church Eaton, Coppenhall, Dunston, Lapley, Penkridge, Stretton, Wheaton Aston.

Rugeley: Armitage, Blithfield, Brereton, Cannock, Colton, Colwich, Great Wyrley, Hamstall Ridware, Hixon, Longdon, Mavesyn Ridware, Norton Canes, Pipe Ridware, Rugeley.

Stafford: Berkswich, Castle Church, Forebridge, Haughton, Ingestre, Marston, Ranton, Salt, Seighford, Stafford St. Mary, Stafford St. Chad, Stafford Christ Church, Tixall, Whitgreave.

Stone: Aston, Fradswell, Fulford, Gayton, Hilderstone, Milwich, Sandon, Stone St. Michael, Stone Christ Church, Stowe, Swynnerton, Weston-upon-Trent.

Stoke-upon-Trent: Bucknall, Edensor, Etruria, Fenton, Hanley, Hartshill, Hope, Lane End, Longton, Northwood, Penkhull, Shelton, Stoke-upon-Trent, Trent Vale, Wellington.

Tamworth: Clifton Campville, Drayton Bassett, Elford, Fazeley, Harlaston, Stonnall, Tamworth, Thorpe Constantine, Wigginton, Wilnecote (Warws.).

Trentham: Barlaston, Blurton, Butterton, Hanford, Madeley, Trentham, Whitmore, Woore (Salop.).

Trysull: Bobbington, Enville, Kinver, Patshull, Pattingham, Penn, Quatt (Salop.), Trysull, Upper Arley (now in Worcs.), Wombourn, Worfield (Salop.).

Tutbury: Barton-under-Needwood, Burton-upon-Trent St. Modwen, Burton Holy Trinity, Burton Christ Church, Hanbury, Marchington, Needwood, Newborough, Rolleston, Tatenhill, Tutbury, Wychnor, Yoxall.

Uttoxeter: Abbots Bromley, Bramshall, Checkley, Croxden, Ellastone, Gratwich, Kingstone, Leigh, Mayfield, Rocester, Tean, Uttoxeter.

Walsall: Aldridge, Bloxwich, Darlaston St. Lawrence, Darlaston St. George, Great Barr, Moxley, Pelsall, Rushall, Walsall St. Matthew, Walsall St. Paul, Walsall St. Peter, Walsall Wood, Wednesbury St. Bartholomew, Wednesbury St. John, Wednesbury St. James.

West Bromwich: Handsworth St. Mary, Handsworth St. James, Harborne, North Harborne, Perry Barr, Smethwick, Tipton St. Martin, Tipton St. Mark (Ocker Hill), Tipton St. Paul, the West Bromwich parishes of All Saints, Christ Church, Holy Trinity, and St. James.

Wolverhampton: Bilston St. Leonard, Bilston St. Mary, Bilston St. Luke, Wednesfield, Willenhall St. Giles, Willenhall St. Stephen, Willenhall Holy Trinity, the Wolverhampton parishes of St. Peter, St. John, St. George, St. Paul, St. Mary, St. James, St. Mark, and St. Matthew.

A few parts of the county were still outside the archdeaconry of Stafford in the mid 19th century.[29] Amblecote and Rowley Regis remained in Worcester diocese, although both were now independent of their mother parishes.[30] Balterley was in Chester diocese, and Tyrley was still in the archdeaconry of Salop. Bobbington was added to Hereford diocese in 1846.

In 1877 the archdeaconry of Stafford was divided.[31] By this time it consisted of 20 deaneries, Stone having been divided between Stafford and Trentham.[32] Eight of these were formed into the new archdeaconry of Stoke-upon-Trent — Alstonefield, Cheadle, Eccleshall, Leek, Newcastle-under-Lyme, Stoke-upon-Trent, Trentham, and Uttoxeter. The archdeaconry of Stafford now consisted of the remaining twelve —

[29] For this para. see White, *Dir. Staffs.* (1851); *V.C.H. Worcs.* iii. 50, 53, 221; *Lond. Gaz.* 25 Dec. 1846, p. 5961.
[30] Rowley Regis now consisted of two ecclesiastical parishes.

[31] For this para. see *Lich. Dioc. Ch. Cal.* (1878); above p. 80.
[32] Stone deanery disappears from the *Dioc. Ch. Cal.* after the edn. of 1860.

Brewood, Handsworth (formerly West Bromwich), Himley, Lichfield, Penkridge, Rugeley, Stafford, Tamworth, Trysull, Tutbury, Walsall, and Wolverhampton.

The deaneries were extensively reorganized in 1894.[33] In the archdeaconry of Stafford two further deaneries were created: West Bromwich out of Handsworth, and Wednesbury out of Walsall and Handsworth. The deanery of Brewood was abolished, and most of its parishes were assigned to Penkridge.[34] In the archdeaconry of Stoke the deanery of Hanley was created out of the northern part of Stoke-upon-Trent deanery.[35] In addition a number of parishes in both archdeaconries were reassigned to new deaneries.

In 1905 there were further changes. The deanery of Handsworth was transferred to the new diocese of Birmingham.[36] Rowley Regis too was added to Birmingham from the diocese of Worcester.[37] Upper Arley, which had been added to Worcestershire in 1895, was now transferred to Worcester diocese.[38] Bobbington was transferred from Hereford diocese to Lichfield.[39]

In the mid 1960s the archdeaconry of Stafford still comprised 12 deaneries consisting of the following parishes:[40]

Himley: Brierley Hill, Brockmoor, Coseley Christ Church, Coseley St. Chad, Lower Gornal, Upper Gornal, Himley, Kingswinford Holy Trinity (Wordsley), Kingswinford St. Mary, Pensnett, Quarry Bank, Sedgley All Saints, Sedgley St. Mary (Hurst Hill).

Lichfield: Alrewas with Fradley, Burntwood, Canwell, Chasetown, Farewell, Gentleshaw, Hammerwich, Hints, King's Bromley, the Lichfield parishes of St. Chad, St. Mary, St. Michael, and Christ Church, Little Aston, Longdon, Ogley Hay with Brownhills, Shenstone, Stonnall, Wall, Weeford, Whittington, Wychnor, Yoxall.

Penkridge: Acton Trussell with Bednall, Bishop's Wood, Blymhill with Weston-under-Lizard, Brewood, Codsall, Coven, Dunston with Coppenhall, Gailey with Hatherton, Lapley with Wheaton Aston, Penkridge with Stretton, Shareshill.

Rugeley: Abbots Bromley, Armitage, Blithfield, Brereton, Cannock with Chadsmoor, Colton, Colwich, Great Haywood, Great Wyrley, Hamstall Ridware with Pipe Ridware, Hednesford, Hixon, Mavesyn Ridware, Norton Canes, Rugeley.

Stafford: Berkswich with Walton, Bradley, Castle Church, Church Eaton, Forebridge, Gayton with Fradswell, Haughton, Ingestre with Tixall, Marston with Whitgreave, Milwich, Moreton, Rickerscote, Salt, Sandon, Seighford with Derrington and Creswell, the Stafford parishes of St. Mary, St. Chad, Christ Church, St. Thomas, and St. John, and Weston-upon-Trent.

Tamworth: Clifton Campville with Chilcote, Drayton Bassett, Edingale, Elford, Fazeley, Harlaston, No Man's Heath, Tamworth with Glascote and Hopwas, Thorpe Constantine, Wigginton, Wilnecote (Warws.).

Trysull: Bobbington, Enville, Kinver, Patshull, Pattingham, Penn, Pennfields, Swindon, Tettenhall, Tettenhall Wood, Trysull, Wombourn.

Tutbury: Anslow, Barton-under-Needwood, Branston, the Burton-upon-Trent parishes of St. Modwen, Holy Trinity, Christ Church, St. Paul, All Saints, St. Chad, and St. Aidan (Shobnall), Dunstall, Hanbury, Hoar Cross, Horninglow, Needwood, Newborough, Rangemore, Rolleston, Stretton with Wetmoor, Tatenhill, Tutbury.

[33] For this para. see ibid. (1895); *Lich. Dioc. Mag.* 1895, 3-4, 15.
[34] The exceptions were Bushbury with Essington, which was added to Wolverhampton deanery, and Sheriff Hales, which was added to Edgmond deanery in Salop archdeaconry.
[35] It disappears from the *Dioc. Ch. Cal.* after the edn. of 1920; its parishes returned to Stoke deanery.
[36] See above pp. 89–90 and n. 35.
[37] *Crockford* (1906); *Lond. Gaz.* 11 Aug. 1905 (pp. 5538, 5539).
[38] *Lich. Dioc. Ch. Cal.* (1906), preface; *V.C.H. Worcs.* iii. 5.
[39] *Lich. Dioc. Ch. Cal.* (1906), preface. Quatt and Worfield were transferred from Lichfield to Hereford
[40] *Lich. Dioc. Dir.* (1966).

Walsall: Aldridge, Blakenhall Heath, Bloxwich, Great Barr, Pelsall, Rushall, Streetly, the Walsall parishes of St. Matthew, St. Peter, St. John (The Pleck), St. Michael, St. Paul, St. George, St. Andrew, St. Mary and All Saints (Palfrey), St. Mark, and St. Gabriel, and Walsall Wood.

Wednesbury: Darlaston St. Lawrence, Darlaston All Saints, Darlaston St. George, Moxley, the Tipton parishes of St. Martin, St. John, St. Paul, St. Mark (Ocker Hill), St. Michael (Tividale), and St. Matthew, the Wednesbury parishes of St. Bartholomew, St. John, St. James, St. Paul, and St. Luke.

West Bromwich: the West Bromwich parishes of All Saints, Christ Church, St. James (Hill Top), Holy Trinity, St. Peter, St. John, St. Andrew, St. Paul (Golds Hill), St. Philip, the Good Shepherd, and St. Francis.

Wolverhampton: Bentley, Bilston St. Leonard, Bilston St. Mary, Bilston St. Luke, Bradley, Bushbury, Essington, Ettingshall, Heath Town (Wednesfield Heath), Oxley, Short Heath, Wednesfield St. Thomas, Wednesfield St. Gregory, Willenhall St. Giles, Willenhall St. Stephen, Willenhall St. Anne, and the Wolverhampton parishes of St. Peter with St. Mary, St. John, St. George, St. Paul, St. Mark, St. Matthew, St. Luke, St. Andrew, Christ Church, St. Jude, All Saints, St. Stephen, St. Chad, and St. Martin.

At the same time the archdeaconry of Stoke-upon-Trent consisted of 9 deaneries, Stoke North having been formed out of parts of Newcastle-under-Lyme and Stoke-upon-Trent deaneries in 1963; the 9 deaneries consisted of the following parishes:[41]

Alstonefield: Alstonefield, Butterton, Calton, Cauldon, Grindon, Ilam with Blore Ray and Okeover, Longnor, Quarnford, Sheen, Warslow with Elkstone, Waterfall, Wetton.

Cheadle: Alton, Bradley-in-the-Moors, Caverswall, Cheadle, Dilhorne, Draycott-in-the-Moors, Forsbrook, Foxt with Whiston, Freehay, Kingsley, Meir, Oakamoor with Cotton, Upper Tean, Werrington.

Eccleshall: Adbaston, Ashley, Broughton with Croxton, Chapel Chorlton, Chebsey, Cotes Heath, Eccleshall, Ellenhall with Ranton, Forton, Gnosall with Knightley, High Offley, Maer, Mucklestone, Norbury, Standon.

Leek: Biddulph, Biddulph Moor, Brown Edge, Cheddleton, Endon with Stanley, Horton, Ipstones, Knypersley, Leek St. Edward, Leek St. Luke, Leek All Saints (Compton), Longsdon, Meerbrook, Milton, Norton-in-the-Moors, Onecote with Bradnop, Rushton Spencer, Wetley Rocks.

Newcastle-under-Lyme: Alsager Bank, Audley, Basford, Betley, Chesterton, Clayton, Cross Heath, Keele, Kidsgrove, Knutton, Madeley, Newcastle-under-Lyme St. Giles with Butterton, Newcastle St. George, Newcastle St. Paul, Porthill, Silverdale, Talke St. Martin, Talke St. Saviour, Westlands, Wolstanton.

Stoke North: Birches Head, Burslem St. John, Burslem St. Paul, Burslem St. Werburgh, Chell, Cobridge, Goldenhill, Hanley St. John with Hope, Mow Cop, Newchapel, Northwood, Smallthorne, Sneyd, Sneyd Green, Tunstall Christ Church, Tunstall St. Mary, Tunstall St. Chad, Wellington.

Stoke-upon-Trent: Bucknall with Bagnall, Dresden, Edensor, Etruria, Fenton, Hanley St. Jude, Hanley All Saints, Hartshill, Longton St. James, Longton St. John, Longton St. Mary and St. Chad, Meir Heath, Normacot, Penkhull, Shelton, Stoke-upon-Trent, Trent Vale.

Trentham: Aston, Barlaston, Blurton, Fulford, Hanford, Hilderstone, Oulton, Stone St. Michael, Stone Christ Church, Swynnerton, Tittensor, Trentham, Whitmore.

Uttoxeter: Checkley, Croxden with Hollington, Denstone, Ellastone with Stanton,

---

[41] Ibid.; inf. from the Chapter Secretary, Stoke North Deanery (1968).

Gratwich, Kingstone, Leigh, Marchington with Marchington Woodlands, Mayfield, Rocester, Stowe, Stramshall, Uttoxeter with Bramshall.

More of the ancient county lay outside the diocese of Lichfield in the mid 1960s than a century before, mainly as a result of the transfer of Handsworth deanery to Birmingham diocese in 1905.[42] The deanery had been much altered: there was now a separate deanery of Smethwick (which included Rowley Regis), and Harborne was in Edgbaston deanery.[43] Amblecote remained in Worcester diocese, Balterley in Chester, and Tyrley in the archdeaconry of Salop.

[42] For this para. see *Crockford* (1965–6).

[43] North Harborne was in Smethwick deanery.

ROMAN CATHOLICISM[1]

During the earlier stages of the Reformation there seems to have been little reluctance to conform in Staffordshire.[2] The Elizabethan Settlement too met with little opposition from the parochial clergy, though there was evidently some time-serving.[3] The higher clergy, however, were less willing to conform in 1559,[4] while the laity of the county were particularly noted for their recusancy under Elizabeth.[5]

The lists of recusants in the bishop's return of 1577,[6] the Quarter Sessions records of the 1580s,[7] the Recusant Rolls of the 1590s,[8] and a return made by the parish clergy to the bishop in 1607[9] are full of the names of yeomen, husbandmen, craftsmen, labourers, and servants. But it was naturally the nobility and gentry who were most influential. The strength of recusancy in much of Staffordshire and Derbyshire in the early 1560s was attributed by the recusancy commissioners to 'the example of Sir Thomas Fitzherbert, John Sacheverell, and John Draycott esquires, being by us committed to prison and so remaining' and to 'the bearing and supporting of their wives, friends, kinsfolk, allies, and servants'.[10] In 1585 Sir Ralph Sadler, keeper of Mary, Queen of Scots, analysed the papists of Staffordshire and Derbyshire into three types: voluntary recusants, those who were poor and ignorant, and those who were 'fearful to displease their landlords or masters for worldly respects by doing other than they do'.[11]

Thomas, Lord Paget, provides a good example of the sort of influence that a Roman Catholic landowner could exert. According to the bishop's return of 1577 he was 'thought never to come unto the church nor any of the servants',[12] and in 1580 he was declared by the Privy Council to have 'perverted to popery' by his example many people in Staffordshire who had hitherto conformed. He was duly committed to the custody of the Dean of Windsor for persuasion 'from his error and blindness', and after 14 weeks of imprisonment he promised to conform.[13] In May 1582, however, the bishop was complaining that Paget was using his official position in the county to molest good churchmen and had chosen the time of the Easter communion to send his officers into Colwich church to arrest certain people against whom writs had been issued some time before. He also caused trouble at Burton the same Easter: 'for that the Lord Paget being bound to find the parishioners communion bread, his officers would have forced them to use little singing cakes, after the old popish fashion, varying nothing at all in form from the massing bread, save only somewhat in the print'.[14] Paget was suspected of complicity in the Throckmorton Plot and fled abroad in 1583,[15] but his local influence continued a few years more. In 1586 Sir Amias Paulet, who had secured the stewardship of the confiscated Paget estates in Staffordshire, wrote to Walsingham that 'it is too

[1] The writer wishes to acknowledge the late Brig. T. B. Trappes-Lomax whose MS. account of Roman Catholicism in Staffs. (annotated copy in possession of the editor, V.C.H. Staffs.) has provided much material for this article.

[2] See above p. 44.

[3] See above pp. 46–47. Bp. Bentham's injunctions of 1565 (see above pp. 47–48) indicate the survival of popish customs and objects among clergy as well as laity.

[4] See above pp. 46–47.

[5] In addition to the examples in the next paras. see above p. 49.

[6] P. Ryan, 'Diocesan Rets. of Recusants for Eng. and Wales, 1577', C.R.S. xxii. 88–92.

[7] S.H.C. 1929, 36–62, 123–42.

[8] Ibid. 1915, 384–8, where the Recusant Rolls quoted are wrongly dated 1590–3 instead of 1593–6.

[9] See below n. 59.

[10] S.H.C. 1915, 367.

[11] Shaw, Staffs. i, App. p. 20.

[12] C.R.S. xxii. 88. Thomas's brothers, including the 2nd Baron Paget, are stated to have been Catholics in Complete Peerage, x. 280 n., but no reference is given.

[13] S.H.C. 1915, 375–6; Acts of P.C. 1580–1, 134, 157.

[14] J. Strype, Annals of the Reformation (1824 edn.), iii(2), 215–16; Complete Peerage, x. 282 n.

[15] Complete Peerage, x. 282.

true that divers of the better calling of the late servants of the Lord Paget's are ill-affected in religion, come seldom to the church, and that for fashion's sake only, and come not to the communion at all'. He declared that he had desired the stewardship largely to keep the tenants 'in better obedience to Her Majesty's laws and proceedings in matter of religion, wherein they had been greatly seduced by the Lord Paget and his ministers', and added that he had had some success.[16]

Recusancy thus tended to focus on a squire who collected Catholic tenants and servants around himself[17] and whose house provided a refuge for priests and thus became a mass-centre. Typical families were the Biddulphs of Biddulph, the Comberfords of Comberford, Tamworth and Wednesbury, the Draycotts of Paynsley in Draycott-in-the-Moors, the Fitzherberts of Swynnerton, the Fowlers of St. Thomas near Stafford, the Giffards of Chillington in Brewood, the Heveninghams of Aston in Stone, the Levesons of Wolverhampton, and the Macclesfields of Maer.[18]

It is clear that the slack enforcement of the penal laws had much to do with this persistence of recusancy. The laws indeed were in themselves not easy to enforce,[19] nor were the local agents of the government on whom the enforcement depended reliable. Justices and jurors could be unwilling to persecute friends and relations, indifferent to the government's policy, and even recusants or near-recusants themselves. Bishop Bentham, in submitting a list of recusants to the Privy Council in 1578, complained that he could 'find few trusty to deal with and fewer willing to utter what they know'.[20] Ten out of the 17 Staffordshire justices listed by Bentham in 1564 were 'adversaries of religion',[21] while 2 of the 9 recusant gentry summoned before the Privy Council in 1575 were justices, and a third was allowed to go back to Staffordshire for several weeks because he had to sit on a local commission.[22] The recusant Thomas, Lord Paget, was frequently employed by the Privy Council on matters concerning the queen's peace in Staffordshire,[23] and, as seen above, he used his official position to harass the parishioners of Colwich in 1582. Nor was lack of co-operation confined to the gentry. Bentham complained in 1564 that 'the greatest disorder within my whole diocese hath been in great towns corporate; for there when I have required the assistance of the bailiffs or other officers I have found open resistance in matters of charge, whereof it is needful to place good men in office there'. He also stated that 'many offenders are either borne with by mastership, which I alone cannot redress, or else fly into exempt places and peculiar jurisdictions and so avoid ordinary correction'.[24] This problem of exempt

[16] S.H.C. 1915, 378, 379. The Paget heir was brought up a Protestant so that the family no longer provided a focal point for recusancy.

[17] In Brewood until the earlier 19th century most of the tenants of the Giffards were Catholics: White, *Dir. Staffs.* (1834; 1851). But in the 18th cent. at least the tenants of several Catholic landowners in Staffs. were far from being all Catholics: Marie Rowlands, 'Catholics in Staffs. from the Revolution to the Relief Acts 1688–1791' (Birm. Univ. M.A. thesis, 1965), 140–1. At Swynnerton in 1830 a Catholic (formerly the parish clerk) was holding a weekly school in the parish church with the sanction of Thos. Fitzherbert; at the visitation that year the archdeacon ordered 'a stop to be put to the profanation of the south chancel by teaching a weekly school in it': Lich. Dioc. Regy., A/V/1/2, no. 87.

[18] The detailed history of centres is reserved for treatment in the relevant topographical volumes of this *History*.

[19] For the technical legal difficulties see *S.H.C.* 1929, pp. xxxii–xxxvi. And see Bp. Overton's complaint to the Privy Council in 1582 about his adversaries in the diocese: 'If I correct them for religion . . . they sit out the excommunications willingly and are glad they have so good occasion

to be cut off from the church; thinking to avoid the penalty of the statute because we forbid them *ingressum ecclesiae*, when indeed they meant not to come there at all though they had been bidden never so much': Strype, *Annals of the Reformation*, iii(2), 217.

[20] *S.H.C.* 1915, 373.

[21] See above p. 47.

[22] *Acts of P.C.* 1575–7, 13 sqq. One of the justices was John Giffard of Chillington, who had entertained Elizabeth during her recent progress through Staffs. It seems likely that signs of recusancy in the county had come to the queen's notice during the progress and that the Privy Council summons followed as a result. Giffard was allowed to return temporarily 'to his house, being, as he alleged, by reason of Her Majesty's late being there, out of order and unfurnished': ibid. 18; *S.H.C.* N.S. v. 127–30.

[23] *Complete Peerage*, x. 282 n.

[24] 'Coll. of Original Letters from the Bishops to the Privy Council' (*Camden Misc.* ix), 41. For a borough official who engineered the escape of a priest at Stafford *c.* 1612 see M. Greenslade, *St. Austin's, Stafford* (Stafford, 1962), 7. For the problem of peculiar jurisdictions see above p. 53.

jurisdictions was raised again with the Privy Council by Bishop Overton in 1582,[25] while a Puritan survey of the county in 1604 singled out parishes within the exempt jurisdiction of the Dean and Chapter of Lichfield as particular centres of popery.[26]

Even the bishops did not escape criticism. In 1573 the Earl of Shrewsbury, reporting the arrest of Thomas Comberford and two mass priests to Burghley, expressed the wish 'that bishops and others of authority . . . would have more regard unto their charges and not suffer such dangerous vagabonds [mass priests] to rest unpunished in their jurisdiction'.[27] In 1585 Sir Ralph Sadler, reporting to Walsingham on the number of papists in the Tutbury district, urged that Bishop Overton should be admonished by the queen 'to look better to his flock, so as they may be induced to come to the church according to the law, or else that they feel the smart of the same'.[28]

In 1581 the authorities had trouble with jurors. In November the Privy Council ordered the sheriff to arrest fifteen jurymen impanelled for the finding of recusants and to take bonds for the jurors' appearance before the Court of Star Chamber the same month 'to answer their disordered proceedings'. In December the Council complained that at the last assizes the grand jury of Staffordshire had either ignored the bishop's certificate of recusants in the diocese or been completely careless of their duty: they had only 'found the Bill of some of the number certified and put out other some at their pleasure, such as are known to be the most obstinate and dangerous recusants of that county'. The jurors were ordered to acknowledge their offence at the next assizes or else be brought before Star Chamber.[29]

In 1588 it was the turn of the Staffordshire recusancy commissioners. The Earl of Shrewsbury wrote a stinging letter accusing them of indifference or negligence in making returns, these having contained the names only 'of the most ignorant and base people'. 'I find the trust reposed in you so corrupted as, if my own knowledge could not reveal more worthy apprehension than your barren certificate hath brought forth, Her Majesty's commandment might return frustrate. . . . Be more willing henceforth to make amends, otherwise I must discharge my duty and will not fail to charge you with forgetfulness of yours towards Her Majesty'. The commissioners were ordered to apprehend all recusants in a list sent by the earl.[30] Even when severity was practised, popular opinion could intervene. A group of laymen, mostly gentry, were condemned for being present at Robert Sutton's mass in Stafford gaol in 1588; Sutton was executed, but the rest were let off with a fine, 'the judge seeing the people flock about them much lamenting for them, for they were well beloved in the town'.[31]

A list of notable Staffordshire recusants compiled in 1592[32] shows in fact how varying was the treatment meted out. John Draycott of Paynsley, Francis Gatacre of Swynnerton, William and John Stapleton of Bradley, Philip Draycott of Leigh, Sampson Erdeswick of Sandon, and William Macclesfield of Maer were at liberty. Humphrey Comberford of Comberford, Erasmus Wolseley of Wolseley, and Hugh Erdeswick of Sandon were in prison. John Giffard of Chillington and Brian Fowler of St. Thomas were at liberty on bond.

The Marian priests who first ministered to the recusant congregations were re-inforced by priests returning from seminaries on the Continent from 1574 and including Jesuits from 1580. An early example of the activities in Staffordshire of this new wave of

[25] See above p. 53.
[26] S.H.C. 1915, 385.
[27] Ibid. 371.
[28] Ibid. 377.
[29] Acts of P.C. 1581–2, 256, 270–1. The Council took the opportunity to commend the bishop for 'his godly and

dutiful proceedings' and promised that he would be remembered to the queen 'to his comfort and benefit': ibid. 271–2.
[30] S.H.C. 1915, 383–4.
[31] Ibid. 384. For Sutton see below p. 102.
[32] V.C.H. Staffs. i. 249.

clergy is to be found in the Privy Council's order of 1579 to three Staffordshire justices for the searching out of priests, the Council being 'informed that within the said county do lurk certain mass priests disguised in serving men's apparel or like other lay persons and are secretly received and entertained in sundry men's houses'.[33] In 1581 'one Worsley in the county of Stafford', perhaps Erasmus Wolseley, was among those who were to be examined in connexion with the harbouring of Edmund Campion and whose houses were to be searched for 'books and other superstitious stuff'.[34] Dr. Henshawe, a secular priest, claimed in November 1582 that he and two Jesuits, William Holt and Jasper Heywood, had spent three months in Staffordshire and converted 228 persons.[35] In 1588 there occurred at Stafford the execution of Robert Sutton. Born in 1544 at Burton-upon-Trent the son of a carpenter, he resigned the rectory of Lutterworth (Leics.) in 1577 and studied for the priesthood at Douai. He worked in Stafford borough where he was arrested in 1588 while saying mass in the gaol; he was executed later the same year.[36] The Jesuit John Gerard seems to have passed through the county in 1591, visiting a relative there, possibly one of the Gerards of Gerrard's Bromley.[37]

It seems unlikely that the recusants of Staffordshire were ever politically dangerous, especially after the removal of Mary, Queen of Scots, in 1586.[38] Her arrival at Tutbury in 1585[39] aroused some Protestant fears and Catholic hopes. Her keeper, Sir Ralph Sadler, wrote to Walsingham that the Tutbury district was 'a perilous country, for both men and women of all degrees are almost all papists'.[40] Later the same year Sir Amias Paulet, Mary's new keeper at Tutbury, told Walsingham that 'this country is so ill-affected . . . as I think no man of judgment would willingly take the charge of this queen in any house in this shire out of this castle'.[41] Philip II of Spain was informed in 1586 that in Staffordshire 'the gentry and common people are strong Catholics, and all are devoted to the Queen of Scotland'.[42] One of Mary's agents advised that if possible she should not leave Staffordshire which was 'altogether in her favour',[43] and it was because of 'the unsoundness of that country' that Elizabeth had Mary moved to Fotheringhay in Northamptonshire.[44]

It is true that Thomas, Lord Paget, was implicated in the Throckmorton Plot of 1583,[45] but it seems that the worst to be feared was normally no more than an occasional quarrel or riot if tempers ran high. This seems, for example, to have been the extent of the trouble at Sandon in May 1582, despite a highly coloured report by Bishop Overton to the Privy Council. The justices, including the bishop, were meeting in Sandon churchyard in the presence of 'a great part of the county', when Hugh Erdeswick, lord of the manor of Sandon and 'the sorest and dangerousest papist one of them in all England', struck one of the justices with his crabtree staff. 'Whereupon', reported the bishop, 'immediately began a number of swords and daggers to be drawn, and had we not with diligence applied ourselves forthwith to appease the outrage, or rather had not God blessed our business at that time and stayed the hands and hearts of the people from further mischief, I think there had been such a bloody day as hath not been seen

[33] Acts of P.C. 1578–80, 57. The justices were ordered to collect the facts from the Vicar of Hanbury, a gentleman of the Earl of Shrewsbury named Edw. Thorn, and Thos. Shifford of Hanbury and to make search accordingly, always taking the constable of the place with them and searching only where they had good reason to think they would find something.
[34] Ibid. 1580–1, 163–4.
[35] F. Roberts, 'The Society of Jesus in Staffs.' Staffs. Cath. Hist. iii. 1. Jasper Heywood's brother Elizaeus vacated a prebend at Lichfield early in Eliz. I's reign and became a Jesuit: D.N.B.
[36] D. M. Rogers, 'Ven. Robert Sutton of Stafford',

Biographical Studies, 1534–1829, ii; Greenslade, St. Austin's, Stafford, 5–6, 34.
[37] John Gerard, Autobiography, ed. P. Caraman, chap. 6.
[38] For orders of 1585 and 1592 for the confiscation of recusants' arms see W.S.L., S.MS. 315.
[39] For Mary's periods of imprisonment in Staffs. between 1569 and 1586 see V.C.H. Staffs. i. 250–2.
[40] S.H.C. 1915, 377.
[41] Ibid. 378.
[42] Cal. S.P. Spanish, 1580–6, 610.
[43] V.C.H. Staffs. i. 249.
[44] S.H.C. 1915, 379–80.
[45] See above p. 99.

this great while in Staffordshire'. Erdeswick was bound for £200 to appear at the next assizes.[46] In addition a pursuivant was sent to bring him before the Council, and a month later his house was ordered to be searched for a priest named Dr. John Price and other suspects and for 'popish trumpery'.[47]

Overton hinted at a deeper plot, but he was unduly alarmist. A report to the Privy Council in 1586[48] shows several Roman Catholics of the county, from the gentry down to 'a poor serving man' at Hamstall Ridware, as willing to come to terms with the government by compounding their fines. They would thus 'be discharged of the peril and penalty of the law' and so enabled to practise their religion in peace; this doubtless represented the extent of their ambitions. In November 1588 John Giffard of Chillington, for all his recusancy, acknowledged Elizabeth as 'his only lawful and undoubted sovereign lady and queen'.[49] It is true that Stephen Littleton of Holbeche House, Kingswinford, was involved in the Gunpowder Plot of 1605 and that the fleeing conspirators were overpowered at Holbeche on 7 November; the operation against them was conducted by the Sheriff of Worcestershire, and the sheriff and gentry of Staffordshire were noted as conspicuous by their absence.[50] But as elsewhere the general run of Catholics in Staffordshire seem not to have been involved in the Plot.[51]

The Elizabethan pattern continued into Stuart times with the gentry supporting numerous recusant centres served by resident or itinerant priests and the authorities applying the penal laws haphazard. Numerous presentments were made at Quarter Sessions in 1608, 1609, and 1619.[52] In 1624 certain recusants accused the Sheriff of Staffordshire of being over hasty in seizing their goods. The justices wrote to the Privy Council denying this; they stated that such people were always ready to slander the king's faithful servants and urged that an example be made of some who were 'rich in the attributes of the Devil', as it would 'make the high crests of the residue fall somewhat lower'.[53] By 1625 the justices and the grand jury were involved in a dispute 'touching the not finding of the petty constables' presentments by the grand jury, which doth now appear to be the only cause why the Clerk of the Peace would not proceed to the indictment of recusants'; at Michaelmas 1625 the justices 'ordered the grand jury to find true bills thereafter'.[54] In November the deputy lieutenants were complaining to the Council that directions for disarming recusants came so slowly that they were divulged before they were received. The deputy lieutenants also inquired whom they should take for convicted recusants and who might be justly suspected, and expressed the fear that some of those who had taken the oath of allegiance would now refuse it.[55] A year later the justices were required by the Attorney General to ensure that at the next sessions recusants were indicted and proceeded against and that the ministers,

[46] Strype, *Annals of the Reformation*, iii(2), 214–15. Overton's letter, concerned with the state of the diocese, seems to exaggerate generally. The Council in reply told Overton that he and the other J.P.s should have dealt with the matter in the first instance and required him to do so in future 'in like cases, wherewith their lordships have not always convenient leisure to deal, neither can conveniently upon general informations do the same': *Acts of P.C.* 1581–2, 432. Erdeswick had been in trouble the previous year for having 'very violently used' a pursuivant and having 'unreverently reviled' the bishop: ibid. 30–31.

[47] *Acts of P.C.* 1581–2, 425, 437.

[48] *S.H.C.* 1915, 380–1. See also *S.H.C.* N.S. v. 138–9.

[49] *Cal. S.P. Dom.* 1581–90, 561. Unlike others who were with him before the Council for recusancy in 1575 Giffard had promised to conform: *Acts of P.C.* 1575–7, 46–47. He was however in trouble again for recusancy in 1580: ibid. 1580–1, 178–9. After 2 months in the Fleet in 1575–6 Fra. Gatacre agreed to conform: ibid. 1575–7, 41, 75. For Lord Paget's promise in 1580 after 14 weeks' imprison-

ment see above p. 99.

[50] *V.C.H. Staffs*. i. 254–5; G. P. Mander and N. W. Tildesley, *Hist. of Wolverhampton to the Early Nineteenth Cent.* 63–66. Geo. Littleton of Holbeche had two-thirds of his property seized for recusancy in 1599 (E 377/8), and the estate was finally forfeited by the family after the Plot: *Cal. S.P. Dom.* 1611–18, 292.

[51] Many people took the oath of allegiance of 1606 repudiating the papal claim to depose princes: S.R.O., Q/SR Mich. 1606, nos. 50, 52; Epiph. 1606/7, nos. 41, 42, 43; Mich. 1607, no. 26; *S.H.C.* 1948–9, 84, 111–12, 171.

[52] *S.H.C.* 1948–9, 80, 163–6; S.R.O., Q/SR East. 1619, nos. 1–3.

[53] *Cal. S.P. Dom.* Addenda, 1623–5, 359.

[54] S.R.O., Q/SO 2, f. 148v. The bishop had written to the justices 'concerning recusants absent from church upon Sundays', and at Michaelmas the justices ordered the letter 'to be executed according to the statute': ibid. f. 145.

[55] *Cal. S.P. Dom.* 1625–6, 143, 157.

churchwardens, and constables of the parishes concerned discharged their duty; otherwise they were to be reported by the justices.[56]

Under Charles I Catholics were recognized as a useful source of revenue and were allowed to compound their fines. Fifty-two people compounded in Staffordshire in 1629–30 for sums varying between £20 and £2 a year.[57] In 1634 Peter Giffard agreed with the recusancy commissioners to pay £180 a year in lieu of fines due for refusal to attend church. In 1638, however, he was petitioning for relief from proceedings taken against him for supporting priests and hearing mass, and two years later the 'Officers of the Exchequer much wondered that Mr. Giffard should be troubled for transgressing penal statutes made against recusants, seeing that he pays to the king the greatest rents of any recusant saving two or three'.[58]

Some indication of the size of the recusant population in the mid 17th century is given by two Quarter Sessions returns (which do not, however, cover the whole county) of 1641 and 1657 giving 1,069 and 1,019 recusants respectively.[59] Wolverhampton was a particularly strong centre of recusancy. Papists were declared to be very numerous in 1604.[60] In 1624 Richard Lee, a canon of St. Peter's with Puritan sympathies, declared of the district that he 'never knew any part of the kingdom where Rome's snaky brood roosted and rested themselves more warmer and safer and with greater countenance than in our country'.[61] By the 1650s Wolverhampton was 'by many styled little Rome'.[62] Catholic influence was sufficiently strong at the beginning of the century to secure the removal of the master of the grammar school. After taking up his appointment as master in 1605 Richard Barnes insisted that all pupils, including those with recusant parents, should attend the services of the Established Church. The Catholics claimed that this was a reversal of previous practice, and, although Barnes secured the support of the trustees and a number of the townsmen, the pressure of Catholic opinion was such that the trustees dismissed him in 1610.[63]

There were ten secular priests working in the county in 1610.[64] By 1631 Staffordshire and Cheshire together formed an archdeaconry served by 13 priests.[65] These seculars were now reinforced by the Jesuits who first settled in the county about 1613, very possibly at Biddulph under the wing of the Biddulph family.[66] By about 1620 there was a Jesuit school at Ashmore, the house of 'Mr. Leveson' near Wednesfield in Wolverhampton parish. In 1635 the priest and his eight pupils were arrested; the boys were soon sent home but the Jesuit was imprisoned.[67] Staffordshire became a separate Jesuit 'residence', dedicated to St. Chad, in 1661 and a self-contained 'college', also St. Chad's, in 1669–70.[68] The establishment of the Jesuits evidently aroused hostility among the secular priests. In 1634 Richard Button, Archdeacon of Staffordshire and Cheshire[69]

---

[56] Q/SO 3, f. 29. A letter of Feb. 1626 from the Attorney General to the Clerk of the Assizes ordering the indictment and conviction of recusants at the forthcoming Assizes (ibid. f. 20) appears to have been common form.

[57] C.R.S. liii. 332–5.

[58] V.C.H. Staffs. i. 255–6; S.H.C. N.S. v. 174–6.

[59] For these returns see Ann J. Kettle, 'A List of Staffs. Recusants 1641', Staffs. Cath. Hist. v; S.H.C. 4th ser. ii. For a much less complete return made by the parish clergy in 1607 see M. W. Greenslade, 'The 1607 Return of Staffs. Catholics', Staffs. Cath. Hist. iv; this gives 275 recusants and 19 half-recusants or church papists, i.e. those who attended the parish church but did not receive the sacrament.

[60] S.H.C. 1915, 388. Wolverhampton was within the exempt jurisdiction of the collegiate church of St. Peter.

[61] G. P. Mander, Wolverhampton Antiquary, i. 305.

[62] See below p. 106.

[63] G. P. Mander, Hist. of Wolverhampton Grammar School, 59 sqq.

[64] B.A.A., transcript of Old Brotherhood Archives.

[65] Archives of the Archbp. of Westminster, xxiv, p. 613, declaration of Aug. 1631 by the priests that all or most of the laity of the 2 counties were opposed to the recent declaration against the Bp. of Chalcedon, the archpriest. The archdeaconry included Derbs. as well by 1692 and probably by 1667: C.R.S. ix. 108; B.A.A., C. 2135(b).

[66] Staffs. Cath. Hist. iii. 1–2.

[67] Ibid. 18–19 (which mentions only 4 pupils); Cal. S.P. Dom. 1625–49, 611 (evidently wrongly dated); ibid. 1635, 303, 590.

[68] Staffs. Cath. Hist. iii. 2.

[69] Archives of the Archbp. of Westminster, xxiv, p. 613. In 1613 the Privy Council ordered a pursuivant 'to repair to Stafford Castle or any other place where he shall understand of Richard Button alias Haughton alias Williamson' and bring him before the Council: Acts of P.C. 1613–14, 59.

and a man strongly prejudiced against the Jesuits, wrote: 'About 30 years ago, when I first came to these parts, no member of a religious order lived in or visited Cheshire or Staffordshire. At that time the secular clergy administered religion in great charity and peace. Concord reigned not only among the priests but also the laity. And so for about 10 years matters continued and the cause of God smoothly prospered' until the Jesuits were introduced.[70] Details of the disguises worn by priests are given in an account of a case of alleged possession in 1620 at Bilston, a place described as 'much infected with popery and infested with popish priests'. One of the three priests who visited the possessed boy wore 'a greenish suit, his doublet opened under the armpits with ribbons', another 'a kind of russet coloured suit with a sword by his side', and the third 'a horseman's coat'.[71]

During the Civil War Roman Catholics were naturally royalist or neutral.[72] The Catholics of Staffordshire and Shropshire lent the king between £4,000 and £5,000 at the beginning of the war.[73] Several Catholic houses were garrisoned against the parliamentarians. Chillington Hall was taken after a two-day siege in 1643, and Peter Giffard, his two sons, some 80 other people and an old seminary priest were captured.[74] Wootton Lodge, taken from Sir Richard Fleetwood in 1643, was described by the parliamentarians as 'one of the strongest places in that county, exceeding well provided of all necessaries and manned with such a company of obstinate papists and resolute thieves as the like were hardly to be found in the whole kingdom'.[75] Stafford Castle was held for a time in 1643 by Lady Stafford who, according to the commander of the attacking force, was acting under 'the pernicious counsel of some priest, Jesuits or other incendiaries about her, who delight in nothing but fire and sword'.[76] Either Alton Castle or Alton Lodge seems to have been held by a Catholic garrison; the latter was in parliamentarian hands by early 1644.[77] Biddulph Hall was taken from Francis Biddulph in 1644.[78] Patshull Hall was captured in 1645 with Walter Astley the owner, a Jesuit, 12 gentlemen, and some 60 soldiers.[79] In 1644 the Parliamentary Committee at Stafford banned papists from the town and its neighbourhood, but the order was twice repeated that year,[80] a fact which suggests that it was difficult to enforce. Numerous papists had had their property sequestered by this time,[81] and some 59 Catholic land-owners in Staffordshire were under sequestration in the early part of 1648.[82] Several local Catholics played a part in the escape of Charles II through south-west Staffordshire after the battle of Worcester in 1651.[83]

New laws against papists were passed during the Commonwealth and Protectorate, but their enforcement varied from time to time.[84] At Wolverhampton in 1654 the two ministers reported:[85]

[70] Staffs. Cath. Hist. iii. 1. For a Benedictine in the county in 1618 see F. Roberts, 'Staffs. Benedictine Monks', Staffs. Cath. Hist. i. 14.

[71] R. Baddeley, The Boy of Bilson (1622), 61, 63, 64, 72.

[72] S.H.C. N.S. vi(2), 331, 332; S.H.C. 4th ser. i, p. xvii. A broadsheet printed in London in connexion with the death of Lord Brooke, the parliamentary commander during the first siege of Lichfield Close in 1643, prayed God for protection from 'the wolf-like cavaliers and bloody-minded papists': V.C.H. Staffs. i. 259.

[73] V.C.H. Staffs. i. 259.

[74] S.H.C. N.S. v. 176–7; S.H.C. 1941, 138–9; S.H.C. 4th ser. i, p. lxv. Peter was given permission to return to Chillington from prison on payment of a fine and security: ibid. 296–7.

[75] Shaw, Staffs. i, Gen. Hist. p. 57; M. T. Fortescue, Hist. of Calwich Abbey, 64–68.

[76] Greenslade, St. Austin's, 11–12; V.C.H. Staffs. v. 83.

[77] Staffs. Cath. Hist. iii. 16, 18; S.H.C. 4th ser. i. 62.

[78] Shaw, Staffs. i, Gen. Hist. p. 59; S.H.C. 4th ser. i, p. lxv; ibid. 4th ser. ii. 7. His father John, 'a recusant of Staffordshire', was killed at the Battle of Hopton Heath in 1643: S.H.C. 4th ser. ii. 7; V.C.H. Staffs. i. 260.

[79] A Perfect Diurnal of some Passages in Parliament, no. 81, 10–17 Feb. 1644/5. This also includes a report which mentions 2 Jesuits.

[80] S.H.C. 4th ser. i. 125–6, 150, 204. Earlier that year the Committee ordered that 'papists living in the lodge on this side of the castle do depart'; they were to be replaced by people whose houses on the Green and in Foregate had been demolished in the interests of the town's defence: ibid. 67.

[81] Ibid. passim.

[82] S.H.C. N.S. vi(2), 331, 332; S.H.C. 1915, 389–92.

[83] V.C.H. Staffs. i. 264–5.

[84] S.H.C. 4th ser. ii. 72–74.

[85] S.H.C. 1915, 327–8.

The state of this miserable town is so much the more sad in regard it swarms with papists (and thence is by many styled little Rome), there being besides many of inferior rank above 20 families of recusants of the rank of the gentry by whom many are drawn to popery; and some of them were so turbulent the last summer and guilty of such high riots that could not be suppressed by the justices at their monthly meeting or a smaller party of soldiers without further assistance from a whole troop of horse.

In August the Council acted on information of meetings of papists, Jesuits, and ill-affected persons at Wolverhampton and took steps to prevent such meetings, arrest dangerous persons and proceed against priests and Jesuits.[86] In the new attack on recusants in 1657 several Staffordshire Catholics took the oath of 1643 abjuring numerous Catholic doctrines, and an extensive presentation of papists was made at the Michaelmas Sessions.[87]

The Restoration did not bring as much relief as expected. In 1675 Lord Aston, in reporting to Secretary Williamson expectations of a general election, mentioned that 'some, who believe that the papists in this country have a great interest in many of the electors, are endeavouring to persuade that it is not the Protestant party but the Episcopal Prelatical party . . . which is at this time the cause of putting the penal statutes rigorously in execution against them'. He went on to report that local Roman Catholics considered that 'this country . . . is more severely prosecuted than any other in this circuit', despite the fact that it was there that 'His Majesty was preserved'; even 'Whitgrave and the Pendrells who were so eminent loyal in his preservation are now prosecuted for being papists'. Later the same year, however, the king put a stop to proceedings against these and other Catholic families who had helped in his escape in 1651.[88]

Persecution was renewed during the Popish Plot scare that began in 1678. At the August Assizes in 1679 Chief Justice Scroggs described Staffordshire as 'swarming with priests; like scurvy elsewhere, papism was there spread about by a mere touch'.[89] In that year nine men accused of being priests were imprisoned at Stafford, and at the Assizes Scroggs condemned two of them to death for being seminary priests. These were the young Andrew Bromwich, a native of Perry Barr (in Handsworth, now in Birmingham), and the aged Jesuit William Atkins. The sentences were not in fact carried out; Bromwich was eventually released, but Atkins died in gaol in 1681.[90] Nearly all the Staffordshire Jesuits were arrested; in addition to Atkins one died in 1679 as a result of ill-treatment by his captors and another was executed at Tyburn the same year.[91] It was in Staffordshire that the evidence was secured against William Howard, Viscount Stafford, which led to his execution for high treason in 1680.[92] William Southall of Penkridge, one of the coroners and an active priest-hunter,[93] persuaded Stephen Dugdale, bailiff of the Catholic Lord Aston of Tixall, to turn informer and reveal highly dubious details of a plot to kill the king. This had allegedly been hatched at Tixall and involved Lord Stafford. At Michaelmas 1681 the under-sheriff of Staffordshire stated that he had levied £1,300 from popish recusants in the county.[94] At the end of 1683 there were nine laymen (including John Giffard, father and son) in Stafford gaol for failure to pay their recusancy fines. They then petitioned the Privy Council for their

[86] Cal. S.P. Dom. 1654, 307.
[87] S.H.C. 4th ser. ii. 72 sqq.
[88] Cal. S.P. Dom. 1675–6, 87; Cal. Treas. Bks. 1672–5, 756. Subsequently, and even in 1679, these families were granted exemption from penalties imposed on Catholics: A. Fea, The Flight of the King, 329–30; R. Ollard, The Escape of Charles II, 141.
[89] J. Warner, 'Hist. of Eng. Persecution of Catholics and the Presbyterian Plot, Pt. I,' C.R.S. xlvii. 308.
[90] Ibid. 307–8; F. Grady, 'Andrew Bromwich', Staffs. Cath. Hist. ii. 9–10; Staffs. Cath. Hist. iii. 5–6. Scroggs had difficulty in securing witnesses against Bromwich,

who had not long been back in England. In 1683 Bromwich petitioned the Privy Council for release; he stated that he had taken the oaths of allegiance and supremacy: P.C. 2/70, p. 43.
[91] Staffs. Cath. Hist. iii. 3, 5–6, 8–9, 10, 13–14, 16, 18.
[92] See S. A. H. Burne, Trial of Wm. Howard, Visc. Stafford (copy in W.S.L.).
[93] Priest-hunting proved financially profitable to him: in 1679 he was paid £20 for each of 3 priests whom he had taken: ibid. 4–5; Cal. Treas. Bks. 1679–80, 66, 67, 771.
[94] Cal. Treas. Bks. 1681–5, 334.

liberty, and in view of their poverty the Council ordered the lords of the Treasury 'to take particular care to relieve them'.[95]

The one lasting feature of the short-lived Roman Catholic revival under James II was the re-establishment of a regular system of Catholic church government. In 1685 a vicar apostolic, John Leyburn, was appointed for England, and in 1688 the country was divided into four districts, each with its own vicar apostolic.[96] Staffordshire was within the Midland District, whose first vicar was the notable Bonaventure Giffard (1642–1734), the son of Andrew Giffard of Wolverhampton.[97] Bishop Leyburn came to Staffordshire during his confirmation tour of 1687 — the first time that a Catholic bishop had been available to administer this sacrament in England since 1631; 417 people were confirmed in the new chapel at Stafford, 5 in the Fowler family's chapel at St. Thomas two miles outside the town, and 37 at Wolverhampton. The 499 who were confirmed at Edgbaston just over the Warwickshire border probably included many from South Staffordshire.[98]

Another feature of this time was the growing organization among the local clergy. As early as 1676 a clerical benevolent fund was established known as 'the Fund or Common Purse of Staffordshire'.[99] Its purpose was 'the relief of priests in this district who by any accident are in real want and have showed themselves true clergy men by . . . acknowledging the Dean and Chapter'.[1] Members were to leave money to the fund; gifts were also made by laymen. The archdeacon and others were to check the accounts annually and on this occasion make any rules that were needed, subject to the consent of the brethren. Money from this fund was evidently paid to priests in Stafford gaol during the Popish Plot persecution. In 1686 the 19 secular priests working in Staffordshire drew up 22 articles of association.[2] These articles were concerned mainly with the organization of pastoral work in the county, under a superior chosen from among the priests. The common purse was now to be entrusted to a treasurer and an assistant, both to be elected; accounts were to be presented annually at the meetings of the brethren. It was also provided that 'every brother will promote the common purse what he can and yearly add to it 10 or 20 shillings if he can spare it'. In addition the superior was empowered 'to appoint a contribution among the brethren' for the relief of any brother in want. Each priest was to leave some of his books to maintain 'a public library or two in the county'. It was also agreed 'that we endeavour for youths of our own county to be sent to colleges that a succession may follow us in the mission'.

By 1688 there was a flourishing Jesuit mission at Wolverhampton. Six Jesuits were living at the Deanery House in Horse Fair and maintained a large, much frequented chapel and also a school where nearly 50 local boys were taught.[3] At Stafford too the reign of James II saw the opening of a chapel and school — possibly by the secular Daniel Fitter, chaplain at St. Thomas.[4] Politics and religion became entangled at Stafford in 1687 when James II had a Catholic appointed as alderman and later the same year had him elected mayor.[5]

[95] P.C. 2/70, p. 43. The Giffards had evidently been in prison since 1681; in a petition of Aug. 1683 they stated that they were imprisoned for refusing the oaths: ibid. p. 35.

[96] See B. Hemphill, *Early Vicars Apostolic of Eng.* chaps. 1 and 2.

[97] Ibid. 18–20; *S.H.C.* N.S. v. 167, 188; Mander and Tildesley, *Wolverhampton*, 62; *Notes and Coll. relating to Brewood* (Wolverhampton, 1860), 109–13. When Jas. II expelled the Protestant fellows of Magdalen College, Oxford, in 1687, Bonaventure Giffard was appointed president and his brother Andrew was elected one of the fellows: *D.N.B.*

[98] M. Greenslade, 'Bp. Leyburn at Stafford and Wolverhampton', *Staffs. Cath. Hist.* ii.

[99] B.A.A., A. 586.

[1] The chapter was that established in the 1620s; though never officially recognized by the Pope, it governed the English Catholics from 1631 until the appointment of a vicar apostolic in 1685: Hemphill, *Early Vicars Apostolic*, 4 sqq.

[2] M. Greenslade, 'The Association of the Staffs. Clergy, 1686', *Staffs. Cath. Hist.* ii.

[3] *Staffs. Cath. Hist.* iii. 3, 19.

[4] Greenslade, *St. Austin's*, 7, 10.

[5] Ibid. 8 (where the date is wrongly given as 1686).

The Revolution of 1688 brought this revival to an end.[6] Staffordshire Catholics, however, showed few signs of Jacobitism either then or in the years that followed. Informers in the mid 1690s alleged a Jacobite meeting at Paynsley in 1691, at which a number of Staffordshire gentry had been present. Instructions for a search of several houses were given in March 1696, and in August Sir James Simeon of Aston near Stone and Sir Robert Howard of Hoar Cross (in Yoxall) were ordered to the Fleet.[7] Catholics were excluded from the Toleration Act of 1689, but persecution was now almost entirely financial. The chief method was the imposition in 1692 of double land tax in place of fines for non-attendance at church.[8] Even Catherine of Braganza, the queen dowager, was assessed for this on her Staffordshire lands; humble people too are found paying it. In 1723 a special levy was made on Catholics according to the amount of papist estate registered; Staffordshire had the heaviest assessment after Yorkshire.[9] This levy evidently imposed a severe strain on Catholics,[10] but on the whole the financial persecution seems to have been unjust rather than burdensome. The 1692 assessment came to bear less and less relation to the real value of land. Nor were industrial interests much affected. And evasion of double tax was possible — by passing on the actual expense to tenants or by vesting the estate in a sympathetic Protestant as Lord Shrewsbury had done by the early 1720s in Totmonslow Hundred.[11] Certainly the Catholic gentry of Staffordshire were not impoverished; they enjoyed security of tenure in practice, and the 18th century was a period of increasing prosperity for them.[12]

Indeed this century saw a general improvement in the position of Staffordshire Catholics. Numbers rose from some 1,100 in 1706 to just under 3,000 in 1767, when the whole of the diocese of Lichfield and Coventry numbered only 2,000 more.[13] Much the same centres occur on both occasions, with Wolverhampton and Brewood the largest. The climate in fact was one of growing toleration. Caution, however, was the mark of the Catholic community. In 1749 Bishop Stonor, the vicar apostolic, considered that Alban Butler, the new priest at Paynsley, should not be 'too forward and busy in conversions and disputes, especially in regard of parsons'.[14] In 1754 the Catholics of Wolverhampton were eager to contribute towards the building fund of the new Anglican church of St. John both because 'they depend on their Protestant neighbours for trade' and because 'if troublesome times should come again 'twill keep the mob from molesting our chapel, breaking the windows, etc.'[15] It was later recalled that in the 18th century Wolverhampton Catholics were obliged to go to their chapel stealthily 'in small parties, or rather singly, and by different and circuitous routes, to avoid observation and the consequences which often attended detection'.[16] There were no outbreaks in Staffordshire during the Gordon Riots in London in 1780, but there were some fears on that score. At Cobridge near Burslem work on the new chapel was

---

[6] For the destruction of the Jesuit mission at Wolverhampton see *Staffs. Cath. Hist.* iii. 19.

[7] Marie Rowlands, 'Catholics in Staffs. from the Revolution to the Relief Acts 1688–1791' (Birm. Univ. M.A. thesis, 1965), 133, 134, 154–6.

[8] Marie Rowlands, 'The Iron Age of Double Taxes', *Staffs. Cath. Hist.* iii.

[9] Marie Rowlands, 'Staffs. Papists and the Levy of 1723', *Staffs. Cath. Hist.* ii. The second heaviest assessment was that for Northumberland and Durham combined.

[10] Rowlands, 'Catholics in Staffs.' 152–3.

[11] See *Staffs. Cath. Hist.* iii. 30, 34, 38, 42, 43–44; Rowlands, 'Catholics in Staffs.' 131, 179. Strictly, from the reign of Anne it was illegal to pass on the expense of the tax to tenants.

[12] Rowlands, 'Catholics in Staffs.' 158 sqq. Sir Jas. Simeon was able to uphold his right to Aston near Stone and to Pipe Hall near Lichfield against Chris. Hevening-ham, his wife's cousin, in the late 17th and early 18th centuries; Thos. Fleetwood was able to vindicate his right to Gerrard's Bromley and other property against the Duke of Hamilton in 1710–11: ibid. 159–60.

[13] Ibid. 100–1 and App. 1; Marie Rowlands, 'Staffs. Papists in 1767, Pt. I', *Staffs. Cath. Hist.* vi. 2.

[14] B.A.A., C. 363.

[15] B.A.A., C. 591.

[16] 'Catholic Chapels in Staffs.' *Cath. Mag.* 1834, 306, based on the memories 'in better times' of 'the late Mr. Green, who was one of the most respectable Catholics in Wolverhampton and had lived there for more than half a century'.

temporarily suspended.[17] William Ward, whose father had let Park Hall at Sedgley for a Catholic school nearly twenty years before, grew anxious for his property and reluctantly served notice to quit if there were 'the least suspicion of disturbance'.[18] The friendly attitude normally shown by the Wards was perhaps a sign of growing tolerance. Another example is to be found at Saredon in Shareshill where on 21 June 1780 Thomas Whitgreave was married in his home. The Catholic chaplain from Moseley officiated. On 22 June, to comply with the law, the bride, groom, chaplain, and guests went to the Anglican church at Bushbury where the curate performed a second ceremony. He then accompanied the party to Saredon for dinner, and afterwards the chaplain, curate, and groom's father left for home together.[19] John Byng, visiting Moseley in 1792, saw 'a sneaking priest glide by me' and commented: 'of what should they fear now?'[20]

The influence of the gentry as the mainstay of Roman Catholicism, though still important, declined in the 18th century. When Catholic gentry moved away from an area, the fact no longer meant the automatic extinction of Catholic life there. St. Thomas ceased to be a Catholic centre by the 1730s, but whereas there were only 23 Catholics returned for the parish of Baswich in 1705, in 1780 44 were recorded.[21] The growing organization of the clergy meant that leadership was passing more and more to them. Thus the chapel and house built at Wolverhampton in 1723–34 owed much to the financial support of the Giffards, but the initiative seems to have come from the clergy themselves.[22] Similarly Daniel Fitter's endowment of an itinerant priest in the late 17th century was specifically designed to free such a priest from being 'confined to any gentleman's house'.[23] Furthermore a new class of influential people was emerging among the laity, particularly in a county like Staffordshire which was becoming increasingly industrialized.[24] Among those contributing to the new chapel at Cobridge, the first Roman Catholic chapel in the Potteries, were Catholic potters — the names Bagnall, Blackwell, Bucknall, Warburton occur — and the agent to the Grand Trunk Canal Company as well as the gentry — the Macclesfields and the Biddulphs.[25] The gentry were, however, still influential through their continuing maintenance of a number of priests; although the bishop had the power of appointment, the patrons in fact exercised extensive control for it was they who paid the chaplains' salaries. Thus in 1792 John Kirk was dismissed from Pipe Hall near Lichfield by the patron, Thomas Weld of Lulworth Castle (Dors.),who objected to Kirk's Gallican attitude in the Relief Bill dispute.[26]

From 1688 until the earlier 19th century the vicars of the Midland District were largely resident in Staffordshire. Bonaventure Giffard, the first, may well have lived in his native Wolverhampton where his family had a house in Cock Street.[27] George Witham, who succeeded him in 1703, lived at St. Thomas until his translation to

[17] V.C.H. Staffs. viii. 272.
[18] F. C. Husenbeth, Hist. of Sedgley Park School, 12, 14–15; W. Buscot, Hist. of Cotton College, 29, 33–35, 43–44. The warning was withdrawn in 1781: ibid. 45–46. No formal lease was granted: Husenbeth, op. cit. 21.
[19] W.S.L., D. 1808, Whitgreave's diary 1780–1. Bushbury (in which Moseley was situated) was a Catholic area; in 1767 a priest and 116 other Catholics were recorded there: Staffs. Cath. Hist. vi. 22.
[20] Torrington Diaries, ed. C. Bruyn Andrews, iii. 145.
[21] Rowlands, 'Catholics in Staffs.' App. 1.
[22] Marie Rowlands, 'The Building of a Public Mass House in Wolverhampton 1723–34', Staffs. Cath. Hist. i.
[23] See below p. 110.
[24] Rowlands, 'Catholics in Staffs.' 178 sqq.

[25] T. M. Leith, 'Records of the Mission of St. Peter, Cobridge' (MS. at St. Peter's, Cobridge), ff. 43, 46, 47. All 4 potter families occur among the people confirmed at Cobridge in 1773: B.A.A., C. 667. For these potters see W. Mankowitz and R. G. Haggar, Concise Encyclopedia of Eng. Pottery and Porcelain, 25–26, 230, 269; V.C.H. Staffs. viii. 330.
[26] Rowlands, 'Catholics in Staffs.' 22–23; and see below p. 111.
[27] Mander and Tildesley, Wolverhampton, 62, 127. Even after his translation to the London District in 1703 Bp. Giffard continued to take an interest in Staffs. ecclesiastical affairs (Rowlands, 'Catholics in Staffs.' 9) and in his will left £20 to poor Catholics in Wolverhampton and its neighbourhood: B.A.A., A. 1061.

the Northern District in 1716.[28] When John Hornyold became vicar apostolic in 1756 he was living at Longbirch on the Chillington estate, and this remained the home of the vicars for nearly fifty years.[29] Both Hornyold and his successor Thomas Talbot enlarged the farm attached to the house, Talbot in particular having both the knowledge and the money to run it successfully. His successors, however, found the expense too much; as Bishop Milner put it, 'the expense of keeping a *gentleman's farm* (as is unavoidable in the situation of a bishop) and entertaining all visitors with their horses must make it a loosing [*sic*] concern to any bishop who has not a plentiful fortune of his own, not to speak of the remoteness of the situation, and the difficulty of procuring letters, victuals etc.' Milner therefore moved from Longbirch to Wolverhampton in 1804, making his home at the house attached to the church of St. Peter and St. Paul. His successor, Thomas Walsh, moved to Birmingham in 1841.

The number of secular priests working in the county rose from 10 in 1692[30] to at least 13 in 1701.[31] This was down to 9 again in 1725,[32] but by 1791 there were 15 seculars.[33] There were 4 Jesuits in Staffordshire in 1705 and 5 in 1738; at the suppression of the Society of Jesus in 1773 there were only three.[34] Benedictines served Tixall and Swynnerton for short periods during the 18th century, and there was a Franciscan at Hoar Cross in 1758.[35] A new departure was the endowment of a priest who was not to be 'confined to any gentleman's house' but free to go wherever he was needed. This scheme was instituted by Daniel Fitter, the priest at St. Thomas (d. 1700). In his will he left £20 a year for the support of such a priest, £10 for 'diet' and £10 for salary, and stipulated: 'I would have him table in some convenient place in the county that he may be ready to help any poor whom other priests cannot help; as also if any priest die in the county this priest may supply his place and residence till another priest shall come to supply the place.'[36] Bishop Giffard (d. 1734) made a similar endowment; in his will he left £30 a year for a second priest at Wolverhampton who would serve the outlying areas of Sedgley, Gornalwood, Dudley, and Bilston.[37]

The seculars continued to develop their organization.[38] The association of Staffordshire clergy in 1686 was presumably dissolved when an English branch of the *Institutio Clericorum Secularium in Communi Viventium* was established in England before the end of the century. It was divided into London and Staffordshire Districts, the second covering Staffordshire, Derbyshire, Shropshire, and Worcestershire.[39] Most of the original members of the Staffordshire District were Staffordshire clergy, and Daniel Fitter was elected first provincial president and procurator. The Common Purse

[28] Marie Rowlands, 'An Inventory of the Chapel of St. Thomas', *Staffs. Cath. Hist.* ii. 27.

[29] For the rest of this para. see *V.C.H. Staffs.* v. 38, 44–45; Buscot, *Cotton College*, 139; B.A.A., C. 1679, p. 5. And see B.A.A., A. 868, for Milner's request to Rome to move 'la sua Residenza dall' angolo rimoto dello stesso Distretto, ove è situata, alla Metropoli nella vicinanza di Londra'; permission was granted in 1808. Hornyold had built a house at Oscott for the use of the vicars apostolic in case they should ever be forced to leave Longbirch by the expiry of the lease; the house became the first Oscott College in 1794: R. H. Kiernan, *Story of the Archdiocese of Birmingham*, 22.

[30] *C.R.S.* ix. 108. There may also have been priests just over the Salop. border at Madeley Court and Albrighton: ibid. 114.

[31] B.A.A., A. 664. This was the number of Staffs. seculars who gave up membership of the Institute of Secular Clergy in 1701: see below p. 111.

[32] B.A.A., R. 12. The next largest figures in the Midland District were for Worcs. and Lincs. with 6 each.

[33] See below p. 112. One was an ex-Jesuit. For the triennial meetings of the clergy of a number of Midland counties at the home of the vicar apostolic from at least 1782 see B.A.A., C. 1136, 1679, 2121. For a meeting in 1758 see A. 1303. The meetings became annual in 1822: A. 611, C. 1679.

[34] *Staffs. Cath. Hist.* iii. 3.

[35] Rowlands, 'Catholics in Staffs.' 94 and App. 3. The Franciscans at Edgbaston served the Catholics of Handsworth and Harborne (then in Staffs., now in Birmingham): ibid. 94; *V.C.H. Warws.* vii. 398–9.

[36] B.A.A., A. 522.

[37] B.A.A., A. 9, A. 475.

[38] For this para. see, unless otherwise stated, Rowlands, 'Catholics in Staffs.' 44 sqq.

[39] It is stated ibid. that the Staffs. District covered Staffs., Derb., Salop., Worcs. and Warws. In 1744, however, Thos. Berington stated that it covered Staffs. and 3 neighbouring counties (B.A.A., C. 2121, note on flyleaf), and Thos. Brockholes's survey of the 3 clergy funds in 1741 (B.A.A., A. 590 and R. 20) implies that Warws. was not included since only Staffs., Derb., Salop. and Worcs. enjoyed rights in the former Institute funds.

funds passed to this district. The Institute, however, aroused much jealousy, and it was dissolved in the opening years of the 18th century. The Common Purse remained available to the priests of the four counties of the former Staffordshire District; the money was assigned to those saying masses for the souls of benefactors, their families, and their friends as directed by the administrators and trustees of the fund.[40] Another part of the former Institute funds was administered separately to help any priests of the same four counties who were in need; from the name of an early administrator, John Johnson, priest at Longbirch, it became known as the Johnson Fund.[41] A third fund, the Common Fund, was established in 1702 for the secular clergy of the whole of the Midland District; subscribers promised to leave to it in their wills, 'our debts being first paid, a third part of what remains which we shall have acquired by our ecclesiastical functions and die possessed of'.[42] The Common Fund and the Johnson Fund had a chequered early history of mismanagement and disputes with the vicar apostolic over control, but by the later 18th century the administration of all three funds was in an orderly state.[43]

Besides help from these sources priests received direct support from the laity. A family chaplain was paid a salary of between £20 and £30 a year. Thomas Berington, at St. Thomas from about 1711, received £20 from William Fowler.[44] In 1727 Peter Giffard was paying the Chillington priest 'a voluntary pension of £20 per annum besides the keeping of a horse and washing of his linen'. There was a further £3 6s. 8d. from a share in an endowment settled by an earlier Giffard for three priests to say one mass each a week.[45] The centre at Paynsley was endowed by Philip Draycott by will of 1697. He settled £15 a year 'for the perpetual maintenance of a secular priest to assist the family of Paynsley and the tenants and neighbourhood of Draycott and Paynsley'. The priest was to say two masses a week for the soul of Philip Draycott, and when the fund was finally established in 1706 the trustees stipulated that the priest should live at Paynsley if the owner required and anyhow in the neighbourhood.[46] The income of the priest in 1729 was the £15, a further £6 without any obligations attached and dating from Philip Draycott's time, and £5 from the widow of Sir William Goring for a weekly mass for his soul. The priest lived at Leesehouses to the north-west of Paynsley Hall; the people there, he wrote just after his arrival, 'seem to be good civil obliging folks enough and keep a very sufficient table, for which with washing, fire and candle and strong drink I'm to pay £12 per annum'.[47] John Kirk, who was at Pipe Hall near Lichfield from 1788 to 1792, received £20 and his board from the tenant on the instructions of the owner, Thomas Weld; Kirk, however, had 'to find his washing and supply the altar'.[48]

The later 18th century saw the establishment of Roman Catholic education in the county. Mention has been made above of the short-lived schools in Wolverhampton and its neighbourhood and at Stafford in the 17th century. As a rule Catholic boys, if they attended a school, were sent abroad to Douai and to the Jesuit college at St. Omer. Over 20 Staffordshire boys occur at Douai during the period 1689–1774.[49] Edward, son of Sir James Simeon of Aston, after leaving St. Omer continued his education in France from 1698 to 1701 in the company of the Jesuit George

[40] B.A.A., A. 590.
[41] B.A.A., A. 590, C. 2121.   [42] B.A.A., A. 664.
[43] Two new funds had been added. For the appointment of administrators of the Common Purse and the Johnson Fund at triennial clergy meetings from 1782 see B.A.A., C. 1136.
[44] B.A.A., A. 173; Rowlands, 'Catholics in Staffs.' App. 2.

[45] B.A.A., A. 184. Peter Giffard paid the rest of the income from the mass endowment to the priests at Longbirch and Tamworth.   [46] B.A.A., A. 163.
[47] B.A.A., A. 203. For the furnishings of the chapel see letter of 1721, ibid. C. 359.   [48] B.A.A., C. 1226.
[49] Rowlands, 'Catholics in Staffs.' 200–3. See above p. 107 for the Staffs. clergy's efforts to maintain a supply of church students in 1686.

Webb.[50] Several Staffordshire girls were sent to the schools at York and Hammersmith run by the Ladies of the Institute of the Blessed Virgin Mary.[51] Such schools, however, were mainly for the gentry.[52] In the mid 18th century attention was given to the needs of the middle classes. John Hornyold, while still coadjutor to Bishop Stonor, had hopes of starting a school first at Oscott and then in 1754 at Longbirch.[53] In fact it was Bishop Richard Challoner of the London District (1758–81) who was responsible for starting the school.[54] He was anxious to provide secondary education for middle-class boys, including students for the priesthood, and he entrusted the task of founding such a school to William Errington, one of his priests in London. After two failures in Buckinghamshire and Wales Errington opened the school at Betley in north-west Staffordshire in 1762 as a temporary measure. The next year, with two masters and 15 boys,[55] the school removed to larger premises at Sedgley Park, rented from Lord Ward with the help of Thomas Giffard of Chillington. Within 5 years it had over 100 pupils and continued to attract boys from all over England. In 1873 it moved to Cotton Hall (in Alton) in the north-east of the county[56] where it continues. In the 1767 returns of papists five women in Staffordshire are described as schoolmistresses. They were presumably keeping dame schools, but these were probably not specifically Catholic establishments.[57]

In 1791, under the Relief Act allowing Roman Catholic worship in registered places, 12 Staffordshire chapels were registered and the names of 15 priests recorded.[58] Soon after this *emigré* priests and nuns began to arrive in England, and several of these settled in Staffordshire. The first to do so was Louis Martin de Laistre. He came to Mucklestone about 1794 as tutor to the rector's children and said mass for a time in the house of a Catholic farmer at Napley Heath. In 1796 he took charge of the mission at Ashley.[59] The first religious house to be opened in the county after the Reformation was the convent of Benedictine nuns from Ghent established at Caverswall castle in 1811 by Walter Hill Coyney and his Catholic wife.[60]

During the 1790s the Staffordshire clergy were notable for their marked Gallican tendencies.[61] In 1790, on the initiative of Anthony Clough, chaplain at Chillington, and Joseph Berington at Oscott, all 15 Staffordshire priests signed an address to their vicar apostolic, Thomas Talbot, in support of the oath which the Catholic Committee was proposing for inclusion in the Relief Bill. This oath was above all a repudiation of papal claims to temporal authority. Talbot himself was in favour of it, but he hesitated to commit himself publicly. Although the oath was not in fact included in the Relief Act of 1791, the controversy continued, and over the next few years the Staffordshire clergy clashed with all the vicars apostolic except their own. Talbot died in 1795 and was succeeded by his coadjutor Charles Berington, whose faculties, however, were delayed by Rome because of his views. He at first refused to retract, and the Staffordshire clergy circulated a memorial supporting him. He eventually retracted in 1797, though he later regretted his action. By this time many of the original upholders of the

[50] Rowlands, 'Catholics in Staffs.' 204–6.
[51] Ibid. 195.
[52] John Perry (born at Bilston 1742) was educated at Douai out of the Common Fund; he later served as a priest in Staffs., mainly at Sedgley: ibid. 208 and App. 2. For the suggestion that a daughter of the Warburtons, the potters, was educated at the York convent see ibid. 195.
[53] B.A.A., C. 590.
[54] For what follows on Sedgley Park see F. Roberts, 'Early Hist. of Sedgley Park', *Staffs. Cath. Hist.* i.
[55] This is the number recalled by Jas. Tasker, one of the boys: B.A.A., C. 1620.
[56] W. Buscot, *Hist. of Cotton College*, 208–9, 262. Cotton

had been used as a preparatory school for Sedgley Park since 1868: ibid. 251–2.
[57] *Staffs. Cath. Hist.* vi. 4.
[58] S.R.O., Q/SO Trans. 1791. The figures include the vicar apostolic and also the chapel and priest at Oscott in Handsworth, now in Birmingham. In a return to Rome made in 1787 13 chapels were mentioned: B.A.A., A. 961.
[59] M. Josephine Bailey, 'Ashley', *Staffs. Cath. Hist.* iv. 33.
[60] *V.C.H. Staffs.* viii. 272; W. Pitt, *Topographical Hist. of Staffs.* 232–3.
[61] For this episode see Rowlands, 'Catholics in Staffs.' 14–17, 62 sqq.

'Staffordshire Creed' had left the county or died. The dispute was kept alive largely by the interference of Charles Walmesley, Vicar Apostolic of the Western District, who had led the opposition to the oath, and by Berington's sudden death in 1798 without a coadjutor. No successor was appointed until 1801, and the Vicar Apostolic of the London District claimed jurisdiction. The dispute was finally settled in 1801 when George Stapleton, the new Vicar Apostolic of the Midland District, secured a retraction which satisfied everyone.

With the rapid growth of population the size of the Catholic community now began to rise, at any rate in the towns. Irish immigration was contributing to this rise as early as the 1820s; in 1827 the priest at Cobridge, appealing for help for his mission, wrote: 'I plead for the English and the Irish.'[62] The first half of the 19th century produced 14 new churches in the Staffordshire towns.[63] A return made by the clergy to the vicar apostolic in 1847 gave the number of Catholics in the county as 17,695. The largest congregations were those at Wolverhampton, Walsall, and West Bromwich (each 2,000), Bilston (1,694), Longton with Stoke (1,510), Cobridge (1,350), and Brewood (1,200).[64] By 1851 there were 33 Catholic churches and chapels in Staffordshire, and some 8,500 people heard mass there on 30 March.[65] Schools too were being provided.[66]

Such expansion, however, taking place in poor areas, brought great financial problems.[67] At Cobridge the enlargement of the church in 1816–17 produced a debt of £200, in 1820 an organ was installed at a cost of £120, and the school opened in 1822 involved further expense. Yet in 1834 the priest's weekly income was only 12s., mainly from seat rents; the offertory collection was not introduced until some ten years later. The *emigré* priest who served the mission from 1813 gave French lessons to raise extra money; he also received £40 a year as confessor to the Earl of Shrewsbury; bazaars were held in 1827 and 1833. In 1834 a parish committee fixed the seat rents at 4s. a year, and those who did not rent a seat were expected to contribute according to their means as they entered the church. By 1842 the priest's income had been raised to some £120 a year. But the priest who took over the mission in 1851 found the building and church furnishings in such a poor state that he had to spend £600 on repairs and refurnishing.

During this period Staffordshire was at the centre of some of the developments marking the 'Second Spring'. John, Earl of Shrewsbury (1827–52), is an example on the grand scale of the influential Catholic landowner.[68] Premier earl and leading Catholic layman, he was also the patron of A. W. N. Pugin and provided generously for the building of churches designed by him. In 1832 the earl engaged Pugin to work on his home at Alton Towers; this work included a private chapel on a lavish scale. In 1839 the small church at Uttoxeter was opened, described by Pugin as 'the first Catholic structure erected in this country in accordance with the rules of ancient ecclesiastical architecture since the days of the pretended Reformation'. In 1840 the first part of the 'hospital' of St. John was opened in Alton; intended to be 'a perfect revival of a Catholic hospital of the old time', this included a chapel and a school as well as the

[62] *Laity's Dir.* (1828). For a further reference to Irish immigration by the Cobridge priest in 1851 see M. W. Greenslade, 'Staffs. Catholics in the 1851 Religious Census', *Staffs. Cath. Hist.* viii. 27.

[63] See details given in the 1851 Religious Census: *Staffs. Cath. Hist.* viii.

[64] Reference supplied by the late T. B. Trappes-Lomax in the 1950s from the Birm. Archdioc. archives. In 1966 the document could not be traced.

[65] *Staffs. Cath. Hist.* viii. The total population of Staffs. in 1851 was 608,716.

[66] For the school at Wolverhampton (1814) see Kiernan,

Archdioc. of Birm. 44–45; for that at Stafford (1818) see Greenslade, *St. Austin's*, 27–28; for that at Cobridge (1822) see *V.C.H. Staffs.* viii. 272, 313.

[67] For this para. see M. Greenslade, *Brief Hist. of the Catholic Church in Stoke-on-Trent* (Stoke-on-Trent, 1960), 19–20.

[68] For this para. see D. Gwynn, *Lord Shrewsbury, Pugin and the Catholic Revival*; F. G. Roberts, *Church and Parish of St. Wilfrid's, Cotton*; D. Gwynn, *Father Dominic Barberi*. With the death of Earl John's nephew and heir in 1856 the title and estates passed after a law suit to the Protestant Earl Talbot of Ingestre.

almshouse.[69] The highly ornate church at Cheadle was finished and consecrated in 1846; Pugin considered it 'a perfect revival of an English parish church of the time of Edward I'. A church was completed in 1848 at Cotton where in 1846 Lord Shrewsbury had presented the hall and attached estate to the convert Frederick Faber and his Brothers of the Will of God; the cost of the church was met by Lord Shrewsbury and three members of the community. Lady Shrewsbury built the village school. In 1848 the Brothers joined the Oratorian order, and Cotton became the first Oratory in England, with John Henry Newman as superior. The following year, however, most of the community moved to Birmingham, and in 1850 Cotton was taken over by the Passionists. This Italian order, one of whose aims was the conversion of England to Roman Catholicism, had already settled at Aston near Stone in 1842 under Blessed Dominic Barberi, who had proceeded to found the mission at Stone.[70]

These advances did not escape opposition, particularly in 1828–9 when Catholic Emancipation was under discussion and in 1850–1 as a result of the restoration of the Catholic hierarchy. Strongly supported petitions and meetings were organized in 1828–9 in many parts of the county, country districts as well as towns, in order to oppose Catholic Emancipation on the ground that in a Protestant state and in view of the Pope's temporal pretensions Roman Catholics should not enjoy political power.[71] It is perhaps worth noting that toleration had progressed far enough for the Wolstanton petition to disclaim any desire for legislative interference with Roman Catholic doctrines and their peaceful dissemination.[72] The clergy of the Archdeaconry of Stafford organized a petition,[73] but the bishop voted for the Catholic Emancipation Bill, stating that the dangers were highly exaggerated and that the measure would have the good effect of alerting Protestant vigilance.[74]

The outcry of 1850–1 against the 'papal aggression' was very much more vehement and widespread.[75] A wave of highly charged Protestant patriotism produced crowded meetings, petitions, lectures, sermons, and burnings in effigy in Staffordshire as elsewhere. The agitation culminated in a $4\frac{1}{2}$-hour county meeting in the shire hall in January 1851 which was attended by upwards of 1,000 people; the proceedings ended with three cheers for the queen, followed by ' "three groans for the Pope" which also were given with a heartiness truly Protestant'.[76] Dissenters often joined forces with the Established Church, and the opportunity was frequently seized of attacking the tractarians as 'a traitorous party' within the Church of England. Catholics themselves attended some of the meetings but with little effect. Two of the three Catholic priests present at the Bilston meeting in November 1850 were allowed to speak 'at considerable length', but the Catholic group 'left completely defeated, having received from one of the laymen of the Dissenters a challenge to public disputation'.[77] Special fears were aroused at Hanley late in 1850 by a party of soldiers who were carrying out a survey for the Board of Ordnance. They erected a temporary structure on the top of Hanley church, and several old ladies assumed that this was connected with the papal aggression. A rumour went round that 'the soldiers have come to build a barrack on the steeple and intend to occupy it as a guard till the dispute is settled'.[78]

---

[69] See plate on facing page.

[70] It was Dominic Barberi who received John Henry Newman into the Roman Catholic Church in 1845 at Littlemore.

[71] *Staffs. Advertiser*, 27 Dec. 1828–4 Apr. 1829, *passim*.

[72] Ibid. 7 Feb. 1829. The Norton-in-the-Moors petition disclaimed all animosity against Roman Catholics: ibid. 27 Dec. 1828. The Biddulph petition, however, referred to Roman Catholicism as 'a mere political institution,

formed for the purpose of obtaining power through the ignorance and superstition of its votaries': ibid. 31 Jan. 1829.

[73] Ibid. 21, 28 Mar., 4 Apr. 1829.

[74] Ibid. 18 Apr. 1829.

[75] Ibid. 26 Oct. 1850–8 Mar. 1851, *passim*.

[76] Ibid. 1 Feb. 1851.

[77] Ibid. 23 Nov. 1850.

[78] Ibid. 21 Dec. 1850.

PUGIN'S DRAWING FOR ST. JOHN'S HOSPITAL, ALTON, 1842

ECCLESHALL CASTLE IN 1837, THEN THE BISHOP'S PALACE

STATUE OF CHARLES II, FORMERLY ON THE
WEST FRONT OF LICHFIELD CATHEDRAL

The outcry had died down by the spring of 1851, and the Roman Catholic life of Staffordshire continued to develop. The county, which in 1850 became part of the bishopric of Birmingham,[79] had 33,643 Catholics in 1884 and 51 churches.[80] The religious orders continued to establish houses, devoting themselves particularly to education and the care of the aged. The Dominicans are now the most widely represented order. Their convents at Stone and Stoke, founded by Mother Margaret Hallahan, were opened in 1853 and 1857; the convent at Brewood dates from 1920.[81] In 1894 Dominican friars settled at Hawkesyard (in Armitage), a house and estate left to them by Josiah Spode (d. 1893). A priory was built, into which they moved in 1897, and the house was then occupied by a series of schools; in 1954 it was opened as a conference centre under the name of Spode House.[82] In 1967 there were some 95,000 Catholics in the county with 124 churches, chapels, and mass-centres.[83]

The pattern of development during the last 100 years or so has in fact been similar to the pattern elsewhere in England, with new churches and schools above all in the towns and suburbs. Hanley is typical.[84] A church was opened there in 1860 with its own resident priest after a period during which mass had been said in a nearby carriage works by the priest at Cobridge. A school was opened in the church in 1861. With a Catholic population probably of about 1,000 a second church was also planned, but the poverty of the mission delayed its building until 1889–91;[85] a new school was built nearby in 1893. A convent was opened in 1890 by the Little Sisters of the Poor, who stayed in Hanley for two years and then moved to Cobridge. By the end of the century the Catholic population had reached some 3,300. In 1915 a mission served from Hanley was started at Birches Head in a building which had the chapel on the first floor and a school on the ground floor. Birches Head became a separate parish in 1923, and a new church was opened five years later. The parish priest at Birches Head opened a mass-centre and school at Abbey Hulton in 1938, and the area became a parish in 1941; the new church was consecrated in 1966. Its priest opened a mass-centre in the community hall on the Bentilee housing estate in 1956, and the same year Bentilee became a separate parish. An infants' school was opened in 1958 and a church in 1960. A mass-centre served by the Abbey Hulton priest was opened at the Greenway Inn, Baddeley Green, in 1958 and a church in 1967. In 1964 a secondary school was opened at Birches Head mainly for these four parishes, whose total Catholic population in 1967 was some 5,500.

[79] When the vicariates were reorganized in 1840, Staffs. had become part of the new Central District. Birmingham became an archbishopric in 1911; the first archbishop was Edw. Ilsley, a native of Stafford, who had become Bishop of Birmingham in succession to Wm. Ullathorne: Kiernan, *Archdioc. of Birm.* 46.

[80] B.A.A., Status Dioecesis Birminghamiensis anno 1884. Warws. was the next largest county in the diocese with 32,346 Catholics and 42 churches.

[81] Sister Mary Cecily, O.P., and Sister Mary Barbara, O.P., *Mother Margaret Hallahan in Staffs.* (Staffs. Cath. Hist. x).

[82] Columba Ryan, O.P., *Guide and Hist. of Hawkesyard Priory and Spode House* (1962). The estate was left to the Dominicans subject to the life-interest of Spode's niece

Helen Gulson; she, however, handed the house over to the friars and then built the priory.

[83] *Archdiocese of Birm. Cath. Dir.* (1968). The chapels include those of eight religious houses and the chapel at the University of Keele. The figures do not include the area covered by the ancient parishes of Handsworth and Harborne, which were formerly in Staffs. and are now in Birm.; they account for some 16,000 more Catholics.

[84] For what follows see *V.C.H. Staffs.* viii. 274, 276, 318, 325, 327; *Archdiocese of Birm. Cath. Dir.* (1965), 194; ibid. (1967), 203; ibid. (1968), *passim;* inf. from the parish priests at Abbey Hulton and Bentilee (1966).

[85] The first church remained in occasional use until its sale c. 1940.

PROTESTANT
NONCONFORMITY

For practical purposes the history of organized Protestant nonconformity in Staffordshire begins with the Interregnum. It is true that Puritan ministers were to be found in the county from at least the 1580s and that Puritan discontent with the Church began to manifest itself strongly in a few localities from about the 1620s.[1] Puritans were not, however, necessarily separatists, and few took the final step of breaking completely with the Established Church. One who evidently did so was Thomas Wood of Checkley, who confessed in 1632 that he had been guilty of 'absenting himself from church . . . and using and frequenting disordered and unlawful conventicles and assemblies under pretence and colour of exercise of religion'.[2] Another was John Collins, a Lapley tailor, who in 1637 attempted unsuccessfully to draw another tailor from that 'swine-sty', the Church of England.[3] Richard Baxter, who came to Dudley in 1638, found 'many private Christians thereabouts that were nonconformists'.[4] Apart from the case of Thomas Wood, however, there is no evidence that Staffordshire nonconformists were organized; nor is it known to which sect Wood belonged.

Diocesan administration in the county collapsed in the early stages of the Civil War[5] and was not replaced by any alternative system of comprehensive church government. In 1648 36 ministers and two schoolmasters signed the Staffordshire *Testimony*, in which they expressed their full consent to the confession of faith which the Westminster Assembly had promulgated. The authorities in Staffordshire, however, unlike those in the neighbouring counties of Derbyshire, Shropshire, and Warwickshire, appear to have made no effort to organize the county into classes or presbyteries.[6] Nor was a voluntary association of ministers formed in Staffordshire, as was done in various other parts of the country. Nevertheless the idea was discussed, and seven ministers from the county joined the Worcestershire Association, which was headed by Baxter.[7]

It appears to have been Presbyterianism rather than Independency which found most support among clergy serving the parish churches during the Interregnum.[8] By 1660 Staffordshire had a substantial number of Presbyterian parochial clergy, some large and loyal congregations, and a group of influential Presbyterian gentry. By contrast there seem to have been only a few parochial clergy whose leanings were towards Independency.

Outside the parish churches the more radical sects were at work up and down the county. The first evidence of Baptist activity comes from Ipstones, in the north, where in 1644 a Captain John Garland and a James Cokayne were preaching against infant baptism, the separation of the soul from the body at death, and the calling of the clergy, and claiming that 'we may keep any day for the Sabbath as well as the day we keep'. The

[1] See above p. 51 n. 66, and pp. 57–59.
[2] W.S.L., S.MS. 407(ii), p. 286.
[3] *Staffs. and the Great Rebellion*, ed. D. A. Johnson and D. G. Vaisey, 14–15.
[4] *Reliquiae Baxterianae*, ed. M. Sylvester (1696), pt. i, 13; *D.N.B.*
[5] See above p. 60.

[6] A. G. Matthews, *Congregational Churches of Staffs.* 18–20; Matthews, *Calamy Revised*, 557.
[7] Matthews, *Cong. Ch. Staffs.* 28; *Reliquiae Baxterianae*, pt. i, 90.
[8] For this para. see Matthews, *Cong. Ch. Staffs.* 33, and below p. 119.

two men were examined by order of the Parliamentary Committee at Stafford, though the result is not known.[9] In the following years the Baptists increased in strength, and by the early 1650s there was a considerable congregation at Stafford, including the military governor, Col. Henry Danvers, who became a Baptist while in the town during these years. The minister, Henry Haggar, was a noted controversialist, as was Thomas Pollard, the Baptist minister at Lichfield. The latter engaged Richard Farnworth, one of the early Quaker missionaries, in public debate at Harlaston in 1654, and with Haggar's aid he subsequently took part in a minor pamphlet war with Farnworth.[10] Addresses to Cromwell in 1651 and 1654 reveal the existence of other congregations at Walsall, Burton-upon-Trent, and Berry Hill.[11]

During the 1650s the Quakers became firmly established in the county. The records of their missionary activity, including an account of the beginnings of Quakerism in Staffordshire drawn up for the Staffordshire Quarterly Meeting in 1680,[12] not only help to identify the centres where Quakerism was strongest but also give some idea of other sects working in the county at the time. In 1651, shortly after his release from Derby gaol, George Fox preached near Burton-upon-Trent and then went on to Lichfield; he relates how he 'went up and down the streets, crying with a loud voice "Woe to the bloody city of Lichfield!" ... And no one laid hands on me. But as I went thus crying through the streets there seemed to me to be a channel of blood running down the streets, and the market-place appeared like a pool of blood.'[13] Some time in this or the following year Fox journeyed to Cauldon, in the Moorlands, 'and gave a report of the Gospel to the people there'.[14] By 1654 the Quakers were active around Leek and throughout the Moorlands. In May of that year Richard Hubberthorne, a Quaker missionary, wrote to Fox informing him that 'about Congleton and Leek there is a people drawing in, where we have had some meetings, and many high separates [persons opposed both to episcopacy and to presbyterianism] and strong oaks that ways are convinced by the power of truth'; he then asked for reinforcement.[15] Later in 1654 Richard Hickock, another prominent early Quaker, came to the Moorlands and preached with considerable success in and around Leek. Several meetings were established despite strong opposition from the Leek magistrates, who objected to Hickock's activities in the town and posted armed men at the doors of the house where he was preaching, to keep the townspeople out.[16] Some time during the same year Fox visited the area and stayed with the most noted of the local converts, Thomas Hammersley of Basford (in Cheddleton). He disputed there with 'the Ranters of that country' and succeeded in winning many over.[17] In 1655 two Quakers were imprisoned for preaching 'the excellency and spirituality of the true Gospel-worship' at Leek.[18]

[9] Matthews, *Cong. Ch. Staffs.* 34, quoting Bodl. MS. Tanner lxi, f. 110. In Dec. 1644 Capt. Garland was being held in custody by order of the Parliamentary Committee, but this appears to have been because he had not paid the people upon whom he had been quartered for his meals: *S.H.C.* 4th ser. i. 222.

[10] Matthews, *Cong. Ch. Staffs.* 34–35.

[11] Ibid. 36.

[12] Account written at end of Quarterly Meeting Min. Bk. 1672–1743 (hereafter Q.M.M.B.), in possession of Society of Friends, Staffs. Monthly Meeting, to whom acknowledgement is made for permission to use this material. This reference has been supplied by Mr. D. G. Stuart of the Dept. of Adult Educ., Keele University, who has placed at the disposal of the V.C.H. his notes and transcripts relating to the early history of the Society of Friends in Staffs.

[13] Fox, *Journal* (1694 edn.), 53–54. For a discussion of Fox's visit to Lichfield and his vision there see W. C. Braithwaite, *The Beginnings of Quakerism* (1955 edn.), 56, 549–50.

[14] Account in Q.M.M.B.

[15] Quoted in Braithwaite, *Beginnings of Quakerism*, 124.

[16] Ibid. 392. On his first visit to Leek Hickock attempted to preach in the church but was 'violently thrown down backwards and his head break and then haled out into the graveyard and thrown off the graveyard wall into the street': account in Q.M.M.B.

[17] Fox, *Journal*, 130–1. Thos. Hammersley, formerly a leading Baptist and a signatory of the 1651 address to Cromwell (Matthews, *Cong. Ch. Staffs.* 36), was stated to be of Cheddleton parish in 1668 (Lich. Dioc. Regy., B/V/1/75) and of Basford in Cheddleton in 1675 (S.R.O., Q/SR T. 1675, no. 23). The Hammersley family was probably responsible for introducing Methodism to Leek in the following century: J. B. Dyson, *Brief Hist. of Rise and Progress of Wesleyan Methodism in Leek Circuit* (Leek, 1853), 8.

[18] M. H. Miller, *Olde Leeke*, i (Leek, 1891), 306.

Three years later Hickock stated that he had recently visited the Ranters at Leek twice and silenced them; the only opposition he had found there had come from a woman belonging to the Family of Love.[19]

Quaker success alarmed some of the other Protestant sects. It would seem that the Quakers drew most of their converts from Ranter and Baptist congregations and similar groups: in 1658 Hickock wrote of the Baptists' dismay on hearing of the great Quaker meetings in market-towns and elsewhere throughout the county. According to his account there was scarcely a weekly meeting in the county with an attendance of less than 100, and sometimes there were over 200 present. By then he had extended his activities as far west as Newcastle-under-Lyme, holding two meetings there and finding the prospects quite favourable.[20] A group arose in the district, the leading member of which was Humphrey Wolrich, a former Baptist. In or before 1659 he baptized, at her request, a woman convert who also had been a Baptist; this seems to be the only example of baptism in early Quaker history.[21]

Soon after the establishment of Quakerism in North Staffordshire missionaries from that area began work in the south of the county. In 1653–4 Miles Bateman came to Stafford 'out of the north'. He began to preach in the streets but was taken before the mayor, whipped, and imprisoned before he had time to make any firm converts. Shortly afterwards Humphrey Wolrich visited the town and convinced a waverer whom Bateman had left behind him; he also planted Quakerism at Eccleshall, Chebsey, and Shallowford. In 1655 Edward Burrough and Francis Howgill converted one of the South Staffordshire gentry, Francis Comberford of Comberford, his wife, and two of his children. Comberford offered his house as a meeting-place. 'He was', it was later noted, 'a valiant man for the truth and in the time of persecution stood faithful'. Other missionaries are found at work at Lichfield, and around Lynn (in Shenstone) and Uttoxeter.[22] By the Restoration there appears to have been a substantial body of Quakers in Staffordshire; in 1661, for example, 183 were imprisoned. A few years later, however, Hickock, 'suffering his mind to be drawn aside by the enticement of the wicked and giving way to the imaginations of his own heart, was drawn into whimsies'. He left the sect, and his defection lost it many of the converts that he had made.[23]

Soon after the Restoration clergy who had been ejected during the Interregnum began to petition the Crown, asking either for the return of their livings or for other preferment. After the 1660 Act for Confirming and Restoring of Ministers at least eight Staffordshire ministers were forced to relinquish their livings in favour of their sequestered predecessors. Nearly four times as many were ejected as a result of the 1662 Act of Uniformity, and at least 44 Staffordshire incumbents lost their livings in the early 1660s.[24] Of those dispossessed three, Henry Bee of Hanbury, Thomas Buxton of Tettenhall, and Richard Hincks of Tipton, were later licensed as Congregationalists in Staffordshire,[25] while Richard Astley of Stowe-by-Chartley became a member of the Congregational church at Hull in 1669 and was licensed in that town in 1672 as an Independent. Thomas Bakewell of Rolleston was later licensed as a Presbyterian and then as a Congregationalist.[26] The bulk of the ejected ministers were Presbyterian. Sixteen were later licensed as such; these included, besides Bakewell, William Turton of Rowley Regis, who became pastor of what was later called the Old Meeting at Birmingham, and Joseph Eccleshall of Sedgley, the first minister of what was after-

[19] Braithwaite, *Beginnings of Quakerism*, 392.
[20] Ibid.
[21] Ibid. 392–3; *V.C.H. Staffs.* viii. 56; R. Simms, *Bibliotheca Staffordiensis*, 524.
[22] Account in Q.M.M.B.

[23] Ibid.; Braithwaite, *Beginnings of Quakerism*, 391, 392.
[24] Matthews, *Calamy Revised*, p. xiii.
[25] Ibid. 44, 95, 267–8.
[26] Ibid. 17, 24.

wards known as Coseley Old Meeting.[27] At least two of those who appear not to have taken out licences made successful careers for themselves in other ways. Richard Morton, ejected from Kinver in 1662, studied medicine and later became a Fellow of the College of Physicians and physician in ordinary to William III; Thomas Pool, ejected from Talke, found a coalmine on his land nearby and became a prosperous coalmaster.[28]

During the years after 1662 the ejected ministers could count on the sympathy, if not more, of a considerable proportion of the Staffordshire gentry. A list of the county gentry compiled in 1662–3 when there were rumours of secret meetings and signs of discontent reveals that 27, and possibly 30, were Presbyterians, 3 were Baptists, and one, Francis Comberford, was a Quaker. John Chetwode of Oakley (in Mucklestone) was labelled simply 'fanatic'.[29] John Swynfen of Swinfen (in Weeford), described as 'a rigid Presbyterian of the Long Parliament', was an active M.P. after the Restoration[30] and appears to have influenced some of the other gentry. William, Lord Paget, was a Presbyterian stated to be 'governed by Mr. Swynfen',[31] and Sir Thomas Wilbraham of Weston-under-Lizard was also alleged to be under Swynfen's influence.[32] Sir Thomas and his wife sheltered various nonconformist ministers at Weston; another refuge was at Prestwood House, Kingswinford, where Philip Foley at different times had at least three Presbyterian ministers as chaplains and one as his steward.[33]

Some ministers, however, suffered persecution. William Grace, for example, who was ejected from Shenstone in 1662, was presented in 1665 for holding conventicles at his house there and later was imprisoned for a time at Stafford. John Mott, ejected from Abbots Bromley in 1662, subsequently lived for a time at Stafford 'in a very afflicted, troublesome condition, frowned upon by the magistrates'.[34] Bishop Hacket (1661–70) was a zealous hammer of nonconformity. His successor Bishop Wood (1671–92) appears to have favoured the nonconformists, but during the period of Wood's suspension in the mid 1680s Lancelot Addison, Dean of Lichfield, took up Hacket's work in and around Lichfield.[35] Hacket's inquiries revealed a sprinkling of nonconformity even among reputed conformists, and in 1665 and 1668 almost 150 people were excommunicated for offences which either prove or suggest that they were dissenters.[36] The churchwardens' presentments at Hacket's visitation of the diocese in 1668 show nonconformists scattered throughout the county. They are mainly described as Quakers or Baptists, though two Muggletonians are mentioned at Ilam.[37]

A magistrate particularly diligent in seeking out nonconformists in the years immediately after the passing of the Act of Uniformity was Sir Brian Broughton of Broughton. Between 1663 and 1666 he sent a number of letters to the Government giving information about the existence of pockets of discontent in the county and emphasizing the links between dissent and political unrest. The nonconformists, however, continued to hold their conventicles, especially in the area of Burton-upon-Trent, which was a nonconformist stronghold and a convenient meeting-point for people thoughout the north-west Midlands. Broughton scored a success when in November 1663 he reported a large conventicle there; as a result Thomas Bakewell

[27] Ibid. 21, 24, 25, 60, 109, 178–9, 196, 211, 231, 242, 267, 327, 350, 473, 498, 529.
[28] Ibid. 357, 395; *V.C.H. Staffs.* ii. 74.
[29] *S.H.C.* 4th ser. ii. 3–41.
[30] He was M.P. for Stafford 1660, Tamworth 1661–79, 1679, 1681, and Bere Alston (Devon) 1690–4: ibid. 29; *S.H.C.* 1920 and 1922, 76–78. His younger brother, Ric., was ejected from the rectory of Mavesyn Ridware in 1660: Matthews, *Calamy Revised*, 473; Matthews, *Cong. Ch. Staffs.* 43.

[31] *S.H.C.* 4th ser. ii. 40.
[32] Ibid. 32–33.
[33] *V.C.H. Staffs.* iv. 174; Matthews, *Calamy Revised*, 132, 267, 287, 383.
[34] Matthews, *Calamy Revised*, 231, 358.
[35] Matthews, *Cong. Ch. Staffs.* 51–56, 69–75, 79–80; see above p. 61.
[36] Matthews, *Cong. Ch. Staffs.* 51–53, 56.
[37] Lich. Dioc. Regy., B/V/1/75.

and Thomas Ford, a minister who had never held a living, were imprisoned for ten weeks at Stafford.[38]

The numerical strength of dissent in the county in the years before the Toleration Act of 1689 is difficult to determine. The churchwardens' presentments of 1668 give the impression that there were many small groups scattered throughout the county, often in ones and twos. It must be remembered, however, that the returns depended on the energy or thoroughness of individual churchwardens, some of whom may have sympathized with dissenters or been unwilling to cause trouble for friends or neighbours. In most cases too the returns show only the hard core of dissent. Moreover the presentments, given as they are parish by parish, probably accentuate the impression of small, scattered groups; dissenters were not restricted by parish boundaries, and individuals from a number of adjacent parishes could easily be brought together for a meeting. A report on a Quaker meeting at Leek in 1675 shows that of the 14 people present 9 came from the parish of Leek, 2 (one of whom was Thomas Hammersley) from the parish of Cheddleton, 2 from the parish of Horton, and one from the parish of Ipstones.[39] Similarly at a Quaker meeting held at Bradley, near Stafford, in 1670 there were people present from the parishes of Bradley, Brewood, Chebsey, Haughton, Ingestre, Kingswinford, and Wolverhampton.[40] Some of the 1668 presentments, however, show fair-sized groups of dissenters in individual parishes; besides the 21 Quakers reported at Leek, for example, there were 38 persons, probably dissenters, who refused to attend church at Checkley and 18 'sectaries' at Uttoxeter. Further south there were groups which did not attend church at Lapley (28), in and around Burton-upon-Trent (45), and at Handsworth (48). Groups of more than ten were found at Norton-in-the-Moors (11 'Anabaptists'), Tamworth (12 absentees from church), Tutbury (12 'sectaries'), and Darlaston (12 absentees).[41]

In 1669, when Archbishop Sheldon conducted his inquiry into the extent of nonconformity in the country, it was reported that conventicles were being held at 24 places in the archdeaconry of Stafford and that 41 persons were allowing their houses to be used for this purpose. Presbyterians were the most prominent, the largest of their gatherings being those at Burton (over 300), Walsall (over 300), Wednesbury (200 to 300), Darlaston (100 to 200), and Sedgley (about 200). At Burton there was also a sizeable conventicle of 'Anabaptists' and at Colton and Hanbury there were smaller meetings similarly described. John Wade, at whose house in Stafford 300 to 400 conventiclers met and who was described as one of the heads of the meeting, is said to have been a Baptist. Quakers met at Leek and at five other places in the neighbourhood; the largest gathering was at Horton, where the number is given as 100. There was a group of Quakers at Bramshall, and at Shenstone two conventicles are described respectively as of Quakers and Brownists. The names of the 24 heads or teachers at the different conventicles are given. Eleven were ministers who had been ejected from Staffordshire livings, and there were six who had been ejected from livings in other counties.[42] Numbers were, apparently, not so great as they had been: in October 1669 the county magistrates sent a loyal address to the king thanking him for his 'most gracious and seasonable Proclamation for quickening the execution of the laws against unlawful conventicles' and assuring him that it had brought great benefit to the county, 'very many of the said unlawful meetings being altogether suppressed and the rest very much abated of their former numbers'.[43]

[38] Matthews, *Cong. Ch. Staffs.* 56–62.
[39] S.R.O., Q/SR T. 1675, no. 23.
[40] Ibid. M. 1670, no. 19.
[41] Lich. Dioc. Regy., B/V/1/75.

[42] *Original Returns of Early Nonconformity*, ed. G. L. Turner, i. 60–63.
[43] S.R.O., Q/SR M. 1669, no. 5.

Another indication of the strength of nonconformity is given in 1672 by the number of licences granted under the terms of the Declaration of Indulgence.[44] During the year that this was in operation 21 'teachers' were licensed in Staffordshire: Thomas Bakewell for a joint meeting of Presbyterians and Congregationalists at Longdon, three others as Baptists, two as Congregationalists, and the rest as Presbyterians. Four of the Presbyterians and one of the Baptists were teachers 'in general and at large', allowed to minister in any licensed building; the others were licensed only for specified places. Besides the places mentioned in these personal licences there were about 50 houses licensed throughout the county, of which at least 30 were for Presbyterian worship. The places mentioned in the licences are mostly in towns and the more populous parts of the county. There were 5 meeting-places at Lichfield, for example, 4 each at Burton-upon-Trent, Eccleshall, and Wolverhampton, and 3 each at Kingswinford, Stafford, Walsall, and Wednesbury. One of the earliest nonconformist academies in the country was opened at Sheriff Hales (now in Salop.) by John Woodhouse, who used the manor-house as a school from at least 1676 until his departure for London in 1696.[45]

In 1672 the Quakers were holding 'particular meetings', or meetings for worship (usually held weekly), at seven centres in the county: Fould (in Leek), Knutton (in Wolstanton), Lynn (in Shenstone), Morridge (in Ipstones), Stafford, Uttoxeter, and Whitehough (in Ipstones).[46] The four meetings in North Staffordshire were combined for purposes of discipline, organization, and administration into the Leek Monthly Meeting, while Stafford, Lynn, Uttoxeter, and the meetings which later developed at places such as Burton, Tutbury, and Wolverhampton combined to form the Stafford Monthly Meeting. The two monthly meetings together joined to form the Staffordshire Quarterly Meeting. It has been estimated that in the mid 1670s there were probably at least 140 Quaker families in the county, of which 60 came under the discipline of the Leek Monthly Meeting and 80 under that of the Stafford Monthly Meeting. Scattered references between 1660 and 1689 add the names of another 25 families.

The Compton Census of 1676 contains returns for almost 70 per cent. of Staffordshire parishes and chapelries, including all the towns in the county except Lichfield, Rugeley, and Wolverhampton.[47] The incompleteness of the Staffordshire returns makes it impossible to give an accurate assessment of the numerical strength of nonconformity in the county in 1676. It is, however, possible to draw a few conclusions from the returns. There was evidently a considerable body of nonconformists in the south of the county. No figures are available for Wolverhampton, but 200 dissenters were returned at Walsall, 200 at Sedgley, 45 at Wednesbury, and 20 at Rushall, in addition to smaller groups at West Bromwich, Penn, Darlaston, Kingswinford, Wombourn, Himley, Kinver, and Handsworth. Nonconformity was also vigorous in its well-established centres along the eastern borders of the county: the Census lists 32 dissenters at Uttoxeter, 25 at Tutbury, 65 at Burton, 62 at Tamworth, and 20 in the parish of Shenstone, besides small groups in such parishes and chapelries as Marchington, Hanbury, Newborough, Tatenhill, Rolleston, Barton-under-Needwood, Elford, Clifton Campville, and Thorpe Constantine. Groups of nonconformists are also to be found in central Staffordshire. At Stafford itself, where 155 dissenters are listed, there was evidently a significant nonconformist minority, and there were smaller nonconformist groups around Abbots Bromley, where 31 dissenters are listed, Colton (30 dissenters), and Cheslyn Hay (20 dissenters). In the north of the county the appearance of 73 dissenters

[44] See lists printed in Matthews, *Cong. Ch. Staffs.* 91–93.

[45] Ibid. 98–101; Matthews, *Calamy Revised*, 544.

[46] This para. is based on Q.M.M.B. and inf. from Mr. Stuart.

[47] W.S.L., S.MS. 33, pp. 371–2, 376, 377, 378–80. The returns as printed in *S.H.C.* 1915, pp. lxix–lxxii (the figs. followed by Matthews, *Cong. Ch. Staffs.* 79) are incomplete and have been supplemented from the MS.

in the return for Ipstones, 43 in that for Grindon, 40 in that for Audley, and 27 in that for Leek proves that dissent had become well-rooted in that area, thanks to the missionary work of Quakers and others. Except possibly in the north of the county nonconformity appears to have been predominantly an urban phenomenon; its comparative strength in such parishes as Audley and Abbots Bromley may be connected with the existence of coalmining and ironworking.[48]

Soon after the Toleration Act Presbyterians and Congregationalists, joining together in a short-lived 'Happy Union', formed a Fund Board designed to relieve needy ministers, to help young men to prepare for the ministry, and to encourage the preaching of the gospel in places which had no fixed ministry. A nation-wide survey was begun in 1690 to discover which congregations were in need of assistance.[49] The reports from Staffordshire show that several of the ministers ejected in the 1660s were still active. Richard Hilton, for example, was minister at West Bromwich and maintained a lecture at Walsall, while various other ministers were stated to be able to go out preaching every Sunday. Some, however, were aged and infirm, and at least three of these were living in poverty. In addition to the Walsall lecture there were lectures at Lichfield, Longdon, Tamworth, and Wolverhampton. There was much activity in and around Uttoxeter and two ministers were working in the neighbourhood; there had, however, been some rivalry and disagreement between the congregation in the town and the congregations in the surrounding countryside. In the north of the county it was planned to set up a meeting at Seabridge, a hamlet some two miles south-west of Newcastle.[50] There seem to have been no Presbyterian or Congregational meetings in the Staffordshire Moorlands; possibly this reflects the success of Quakerism in that area. The Quakers had established the Leek town meeting in a 'meeting cottage' in 1673, and in 1694 they bought the plot of ground in the town upon which the present meeting-house was built.[51] A Quaker school had been established at Leek by 1699.[52]

Despite the easing of the situation by the passing of the Toleration Act the position of nonconformists could still be hazardous. During the summer of 1715 there were outbreaks of rioting in various parts of the country encouraged, if not fomented, by Jacobite sympathizers; the mobs professed a devotion to High Church principles and found nonconformist meeting-houses obvious targets for attack. Staffordshire was one of the counties in which the disturbances were widespread and violent.[53] Meeting-houses[54] were demolished at Newcastle, Pensnett,[55] Stafford, Stone, Walsall, West Bromwich, and Wolverhampton, and damaged at Burton,[56] Leek, Coseley,[57] and Uttoxeter.[58] The government subsequently paid out about £5,234 in damages to

[48] V.C.H. Staffs. ii. 74, 112.

[49] Matthews, Cong. Ch. Staffs. 95–98, 106.

[50] A house at Seabridge had been licensed as a Presbyterian meeting-place in 1672: V.C.H. Staffs. viii. 56.

[51] Records, Leek Meeting House; deeds in poss. of Society of Friends, Staffs. United Charities Trustees.

[52] Inf. from Mr. Stuart.

[53] For a brief account of the riots in Staffs. and their aftermath see Matthews, Cong. Ch. Staffs. 102–5; Matthews, 'Some Notes on Staffs. Nonconformity', Trans. Congregational Hist. Soc. xii. 5–9. See also G. P. Mander, Wolverhampton Antiquary, i. 27–30; F. W. Willmore, Hist. of Walsall (1887), 352–3.

[54] The following list of meeting-houses demolished or damaged is based upon the lists in Cal. Treas. Bks. 1717, 185–7; Dr. Williams's Libr., Thompson MS. (printed in Matthews, Cong. Ch. Staffs. 128).

[55] Thompson MS. lists this as Cradley, and the meeting was frequently so named; the meeting-house was, however, on Pensnett Chase (in Kingswinford) until 1796, when a new building was erected at Cradley (in Halesowen,

Worcs.): G. E. Evans, Midland Churches (Dudley, 1899), 89 sqq.

[56] Thompson MS. states that £45 was subsequently allotted for the repair of Burton meeting-house. Burton is not mentioned in the other list which, however, notes that a Dorothy Pike of Newcastle (not listed in Thompson MS.) lost goods and chattels to the value of £45: Cal. Treas. Bks. 1717, 185. According to a contemporary account the Presbyterian meeting-house at Burton was gutted by the mob: W.S.L., S.MS. 370/viii/II, pp. 489–90 (transcript of Flying Post, 2–4 Aug. 1715).

[57] Thompson MS.; Trans. Cong. Hist. Soc. xii. 9.

[58] Thompson MS. states that £37 11s. was subsequently allotted for the repair of Uttoxeter meeting-house. Uttoxeter is not mentioned in the other list which, however, notes that a Hen. Bradshaw of Newcastle (not listed in Thompson MS.) lost goods and chattels to the value of £37 11s.: Cal. Treas. Bks. 1717, 185. According to a contemporary account the Uttoxeter meeting-house was one of those attacked: W.S.L., S.MS. 370/viii/II, p. 489 (transcript of Flying Post, 30 July–2 Aug. 1715).

sufferers in eight English and Welsh counties. Payments in Staffordshire accounted for £1,722 2s. 6d., by far the largest total for any county.[59]

A survey of the dissenting interest made in 1717[60] listed eleven Presbyterian meetings in the county which had their own ministers — Burton, Leek, a joint meeting of Lichfield and Longdon, Newcastle, Pensnett, Stafford, Stone, Tamworth, Uttoxeter, Walsall, and Wolverhampton. West Bromwich shared its minister with Birmingham, Coseley was served by an itinerant preacher who visited the meeting once a fortnight, and there were eleven small meetings served by itinerants. It was estimated that the Presbyterian congregations amounted to about 4,560 people. The only non-Presbyterian meeting included in the survey was a Baptist meeting at Delves (in Wednesbury). The survey is, however, evidently little concerned with the Baptists, and it totally ignores the Quakers, who were well-established in various parts of the county, though possibly not very numerous. The few surviving parochial returns drawn up in 1718 for Bishop Chandler's primary visitation[61] supplement the 1717 survey to a certain extent. They appear to confirm the view that numerically the Presbyterians were the strongest nonconformist body in the county. At Newcastle the incumbent stated that there were 30 Presbyterian families (the 1717 survey gives a congregation of 300), and at Uttoxeter the incumbent reported 14 Presbyterian families (the 1717 survey gives a congregation of 200).[62] When account is taken of worshippers coming into the two towns from adjacent parishes the two sets of figures would appear to tally. The returns also show that there were a few Baptists in the north of the county at Caverswall and Keele and in eastern Staffordshire in the Newborough-Marchington area,[63] in addition to those who attended the meeting at Delves.

The first two decades of the 18th century were marked by the consolidation and expansion of nonconformity, but the fact that only two or three meeting-houses were opened during the next 50 years illustrates the stagnation that followed among the older sects. By the later 18th century Presbyterianism had become extremely weak in the county as some congregations dwindled and others drifted towards Unitarianism. In 1748 Stafford and Stone were joined together as one pastorate, while the Lichfield meeting-house was closed in 1753 and that at Uttoxeter in 1760. In 1773 the Unitarian minister at Tamworth visited once a fortnight the few worshippers who still met at Longdon. Coseley and Pensnett had also become Unitarian and other congregations were proceeding along the same path, which for two of them, Burton and Newcastle, ended in the closure of their meeting-places early in the 19th century. Of Wednesbury it was stated in 1773 that 'anyone preaches, they can often get no one', while the Bilston building was rarely open and then only for the use of Methodists. There had been an orthodox secession at Walsall which had left the chapel in the hands of the Unitarians, and at Wolverhampton and Leek the congregations were Arian.[64] Dwindling membership among the Quakers led to a remodelling of their organization in the county. In 1783 Staffordshire ceased to have a separate Quarterly Meeting and was joined with Cheshire in the Staffordshire and Cheshire Quarterly Meeting. The two Monthly Meetings in the county were amalgamated, though Stafford, Leek, and Uttoxeter

[59] Cal. Treas. Bks. 1717, 184–5. The figures printed in Matthews, Cong. Ch. Staffs. 128, show some slight differences from the official totals, and the figure given there for total damages throughout the country includes the expenses (about £345) incurred by the agents nominated by the sufferers in making out the claims.

[60] Matthews, Cong. Ch. Staffs. 105–7, 129, giving total congregation as 4,480. Tamworth, with a congregation of 80, is presumably omitted since the town lay partly in Warws.

[61] Lich. Dioc. Regy., B/V/5/1718.
[62] Ibid.; Matthews, Cong. Ch. Staffs. 129.
[63] Lich. Dioc. Regy., B/V/5/1718.
[64] Matthews, Cong. Ch. Staffs. 110–11, mentioning Bilston and Wednesbury as meeting-houses built after 1720. To these must be added the Quaker meeting-house at Tamworth, described as 'newly erected' when it was registered in 1757: S.H.C. 4th ser. iii. 121.

held Preparative Meetings on the day preceding the joint Monthly Meeting.[65]

A survey of the state of the parishes in the diocese of Lichfield and Coventry was undertaken for Bishop North in 1772–3. From this about 60 Staffordshire returns survive.[66] They provide further confirmation of the decline among the older dissenting denominations. In many rural parishes there were stated to be no dissenters, and where dissenters appear it seems that their numbers were either declining or stagnating. At Keele, for example, where there had been a few Quakers and a Baptist in 1718, dissent was stated to be extinct in 1773.[67] At Kingswinford, where there were 71 dissenters in 1773, the incumbent noted that 'they are of late lessened in number, there having been within eight years last past three separate meeting-houses, and now there is not one'.[68] In several cases the dissenters attended the parish church, possibly because the nearest congregation of their denomination was difficult of access or because the social pressure on a few dissenting families in an otherwise Anglican community became overwhelming. Thus a family of Baptists at Abbots Bromley, some Presbyterians and a Baptist at Cheadle, and all the dissenters, save the Baptists, at Kingswinford were regular or occasional church-goers.[69]

By this date, however, the coming of Methodism had breathed new life into nonconformity, and it is evident from the remarks of some incumbents that they found the vigour and 'enthusiasm' of early Methodism much less congenial than the older forms of dissent. At Wednesbury the vicar considered that Wesley had instituted the circuit system, with itinerant preachers, 'as the most likely means to tickle itching ears and keep his flock from deserting him'; nevertheless he admitted the increase of Methodism in Wednesbury and the surrounding parishes.[70] By the early 1770s Wednesbury had in fact become the stronghold of Methodism in the Staffordshire Black Country. The town contained the earliest Methodist society in the county. Charles Wesley visited Wednesbury in September 1742 and made some converts. The following January John Wesley came and preached seven times in three days with great success. When he moved on he left behind him a society of about 100 members. By May the number of Methodists at Wednesbury had increased to 300, and in the same month anti-Methodist riots broke out, spreading within the next few weeks to include Wednesbury, Darlaston, Walsall, and West Bromwich. The riots and attacks on individual Methodist families continued at intervals until early 1744. When John Wesley visited the town in October 1743 he was mobbed, but won the crowd over by his courageous behaviour.[71] It appears that the mob was incited against the Methodists by various local gentry and clergy. An observer at Tamworth remarked that in his opinion the rioters had been 'spirited on to do those riotous and wicked acts by some of the higher rank who keep behind the curtain at present. As to their pretence of suppressing the Methodists, 'tis only a pretence, for these mobsters seldom frequent any place of worship. . . . A Staffordshire mob comprised of colliers, nailers, and brick makers are but ill judges in matters of religion'.[72]

In 1745 John Wesley preached at Tipton Green and Wednesbury, and although

[65] Inf. from Mr. Stuart. In 1854 a further reorganization united Staffs., Warws., Leics., and Rutland in one Quarterly Meeting: inf. from Mr. Stuart.

[66] Lich. Dioc. Regy., B/V/5/1772–3. Although the printed questionnaire is dated 10 Apr. 1772 it would appear that all surviving rets. made by Staffs. incumbents date from 1773.

[67] Ibid. 1718, 1772–3.

[68] Ibid. 1772–3.   [69] Ibid.

[70] Ibid.; and see above p. 65.

[71] J. Wesley. Journal (Everyman edn.), i. 411, 421–2,

424–5, 438–44, 453–7; Anon. Some Papers giving an Account of the Rise and Progress of Methodism at Wednesbury in Staffs., and other Parishes adjacent: as likewise of the late Riots in those Parts (1744), 10–11 (copy in W.S.L.); J. F. Ede, Hist. of Wednesbury, 204–11; R. F. Wearmouth, Methodism and the Common People of the 18th Cent. 159–63.

[72] Ede, Wednesbury, 211; Wearmouth, Methodism and Common People of 18th Cent. quoting letter from Sam. Crossland to Sir Thos. Abney, 13 Feb. 1744. For the hostility of some of the local clergy towards Methodism see above pp. 64–65.

there was some clod-throwing the former hostility had died away.[73] Subsequent visits to Wednesbury were comparatively peaceful. In October 1749, for example, after meeting violent opposition at Dudley, Wesley proceeded to Wednesbury and preached to 'a nobler people'.[74] It was nearly eighteen months before he came into the neighbourhood again; this time he was greeted by a large congregation at Wednesbury and had a much better reception at both Dudley and Darlaston.[75] Many more visits to Staffordshire followed, almost always with Wednesbury as one of the places where he preached.[76] In 1760, when he preached in the newly-built meeting-house in the town, he noted that 'few congregations exceed this either in number or seriousness. . . . Indeed hunger after the word has been from the beginning the distinguishing mark of this people'.[77] When the country was first divided into circuits, at the 1746 Methodist Conference, Wednesbury was included in the Evesham Circuit. Two years later a Staffordshire Circuit was in existence. Wednesbury became its head and remained the head of a circuit until the 1780s, becoming a circuit headquarters once more in 1801.[78] The Wednesbury Methodists enjoyed the patronage of one of the more notable local landowners, William, 2nd Earl of Dartmouth (d. 1801), of Sandwell Hall, West Bromwich. He attended their meetings, and his park keeper, James Bayley, was a leader of West Bromwich Methodism.[79]

Wesley first visited Burslem in 1760,[80] thus bringing the Methodist revival to the Potteries at the moment when the rapid industrialization of the area was beginning. He and his lieutenants preached at Burslem frequently during the next 25 years and Methodism grew rapidly in the area.[81] There had been a society at Leek since at least 1754[82], and elsewhere in the county Methodism was carried to all the towns. At Stafford, for example, Dr. Thomas Coke, one of Wesley's disciples, was the first Methodist to preach. His visit, in 1779, led to the formation of a small society at which Wesley preached annually from 1783 to 1786 and again in 1788.[83] At Wolverhampton Wesley began to preach in 1760, and by 1763 the local society had erected a small meeting-house.[84]

Methodism, aimed as it was at remedying some of the deficiencies of the Established Church, made its most striking advances in the expanding industrial towns, where the existing parochial organization was incapable of catering for the increasing population.[85] Other notable workers in this field were the preachers who carried on missionary work under the patronage of Selina, Countess of Huntingdon. Although the Countess of Huntingdon's Connexion itself never became firmly established in Staffordshire it was due to her preachers and their followers that Congregationalism made headway in the county. Between 1743 and 1754 George Whitefield, the most eminent of the countess's preachers, visited several places in Staffordshire, including Gornal, Wednesbury, and Wolverhampton. The work he started was continued by Jonathan Scott, who was responsible for the founding of many churches in Staffordshire. Among the places where he preached was Hanley, where a chapel was built in 1784 and called The Tabernacle after Whitefield's Tabernacle in London. The first

[73] Wesley, *Journal*, i. 498–9.
[74] Ibid. ii. 130. [75] Ibid. 190–1.
[76] He visited the town 33 times and preached on at least 27 of these visits: Ede, *Wednesbury*, 211.
[77] Wesley, *Journal*, ii. 496.
[78] J. S. Simon, *John Wesley and the Methodist Societies*, 324; Simon, *John Wesley and the Advance of Methodism*, 87; F. W. Hackwood, *Religious Wednesbury* (Dudley, 1900), 75.
[79] A. G. Cumberland, 'Protestant Nonconformity in the Black Country, 1662–1851' (Birm. Univ. M.A. thesis,

1951), 115. For the Earl of Dartmouth see also above p. 65.
[80] Wesley, *Journal*, ii. 500.
[81] *V.C.H. Staffs.* viii. 276.
[82] Dyson, *Wesleyan Methodism in Leek Circuit*, 8–9.
[83] A. L. P. Roxburgh, *Stafford*, 125; Wesley, *Journal*, iv. 266, 275, 308, 338, 422.
[84] G. P. Mander and N. W. Tildesley, *Hist. of Wolverhampton*, 131.
[85] For the next two paras. see Matthews, *Cong. Ch. Staffs.* chap. v, unless otherwise stated.

resident minister of the Hanley chapel was James Boden, who introduced Congregationalism into Stafford in 1786.[86] George Burder, who began preaching in Staffordshire in the 1770s, was another notable pioneer of Congregationalism in the county. John Underhill, yet another who had come under Whitefield's influence, worked at Gornal, where in 1777 a chapel was built for the congregation he had gathered. Among the preachers of the Countess of Huntingdon's Connexion who were active in the county towards the end of the 18th century, especially in the Black Country, were William Boddily and Thomas Grove.

By the end of the century Congregationalism had become firmly rooted in Staffordshire. In the northern half of the county there were churches at Cheadle, Hanley, Leek, Newcastle, Stafford, Stone, Tutbury, and Uttoxeter. In the south there were churches at Bilston, Burton, Gornal, Longdon, Walsall (Bridge Street), Wednesbury, West Bromwich (Ebenezer and Mayer's Green), and Wolverhampton (Pountney's Fold and Temple Street).

The rising tide of nonconformity, and especially of Methodism, in Staffordshire was not held back by the schisms which occurred in the Methodist movement after the death of John Wesley. Of these the most important, leading to the formation of the Methodist New Connexion and Primitive Methodism, had strong links with the Potteries. Alexander Kilham, the founder of the Methodist New Connexion, visited Hanley after his expulsion by the 1796 Methodist Conference and spent several days with 'some valuable friends'. He preached to large congregations in the chapels and out of doors and stated: 'If the preachers will not accede to the measures of the friends they are determined to separate and build two or three chapels for us in that neighbourhood.'[87] His hopes were speedily fulfilled. Before the end of 1797 there were five societies of his Connexion in the Potteries: at Burslem, Etruria, Hanley, Longton, and Sneyd Green. Hanley Circuit, formed of these societies and those at Newcastle, Silverdale, and Werrington, was one of the ten original New Connexion circuits established that year. The Connexion flourished, and by 1822 Hanley Circuit had 19 societies, 17 chapels, 5 circuit preachers, 39 local preachers, and a membership of 1,916.[88]

Primitive Methodism, the second of the denominations which broke away from the Wesleyan Methodists, had its origins in the Potteries themselves and in the moorlands to the north and east. In 1799 Hugh Bourne, a carpenter from Bemersley, joined the Wesleyan Methodists,[89] and in 1801 he began evangelistic work among the colliers at Harrisea Head. He achieved great success, and a 'revival' took place.[90] This period saw the appearance of one of the ideas which was to lead to the open-air 'camp meetings' — the distinguishing feature of early Primitive Methodism and the immediate cause of its secession from Wesleyan Methodism. One of the instruments of the Harrisea Head revival was the weekday evening prayer-meeting. There were sometimes complaints that these were too short, and on one such occasion Daniel Shubotham, a collier whom Bourne had converted, remarked: 'You shall have a meeting upon Mow [Mow Cop, a ridge on the Staffordshire–Cheshire border] some Sunday and have a whole day's praying, and then you'll be satisfied.' Although nothing was done then, the idea took root among the Harrisea Head converts. In 1802 Bourne persuaded the group to join the

86 See J. F. Amery, 'Brief Hist. of the Congregational Church, Stafford' (TS. in poss. of Mr. Amery).
87 W. Salt, *Memorial of the Wesleyan Methodist New Connexion* (Nottingham, 1822), 27 (copy in W.S.L.).
88 Ibid. 172, 218; *V.C.H. Staffs.* viii. 276–7.
89 J. Petty, *Hist. of the Primitive Methodist Connexion* (1864 edn.), 5; H. Bourne, *Hist. of the Primitive Methodists* (Bemersley, 1823), 4 (copy in W.S.L.). For Bourne see J. T. Wilkinson, *Hugh Bourne. V.C.H. Staffs.* viii. 277, incorrectly mentions a 'John Bourne' as one of the pioneers of Primitive Methodism when it is Hugh Bourne who is meant. 90 Bourne, *Primitive Methodists*, 5.

Wesleyan Methodists, and a chapel was built at Harrisea Head. Preachers at the new chapel opposed the idea of an open-air prayer-meeting; but their sermons were not such an effective means of evangelization as the previous prayer-meetings had been, and the impetus of the revival slackened. Meanwhile Methodist magazines which began to circulate in the area mentioned the success of open-air meetings in the U.S.A. and thus kept alive the idea of a meeting on Mow Cop besides introducing the term 'camp meeting'.[91]

In 1804 there was a further revival around Harrisea Head. It spread throughout the Potteries, and among those converted at a class at Tunstall led by James Steele was William Clowes, a potter; both Steele and Clowes were to become prominent members of the early Primitive Methodist Connexion.[92] The new revival at Harrisea Head began to flag in 1806, and after there had been no conversions for about a year many of the local Methodists began to press for a Sunday meeting on Mow Cop, in the hope that this would bring in converts. At this date Lorenzo Dow, an American Methodist who was an enthusiastic advocate of camp meetings, was conducting revival campaigns in England. He visited Harrisea Head in April 1807, and as a result of his visit Bourne decided to hold a camp meeting at Norton-in-the-Moors in August, at the time of the wakes. As he himself subsequently explained, his plan was to hold the meeting during the first few days of the wakes, thereby providing a rival attraction, especially for young people, 'until the heat of the wake should be gone past'.[93]

When Bourne asked the Harrisea Head Methodists for their help at Norton he found that they had already decided to hold a camp meeting themselves. Bourne agreed to this, and the first English camp meeting was held on Sunday 31 May on the Cheshire side of Mow Cop. There was a large crowd present when the meeting began at 6 a.m., and more people flocked in later. By the early afternoon there were four preaching stands, at which the services 'were carried on with singing, prayer, preaching, exhortations, speaking experience, relating anecdotes, &c.' There were also two permanent 'praying companies'. The meeting went on without a break until 8.30 p.m. Bourne subsequently attributed the success of this and later meetings to the fact that they were not merely open-air sermons but included 'a variety of exercises'. Old-fashioned field-preaching, based on Wesley's example, was in his opinion 'nearly worn out'. Before the meeting broke up further meetings were announced, for Mow Cop in July and for Norton in August; both were intended to act as counter-attractions to wakes.[94]

Although Methodist leaders in the area immediately denounced camp meetings, the second Mow Cop meeting was held as planned on the 19–21 July and attracted large crowds. The effects of opposition from official Methodism were, however, already beginning to be felt.[95] At the first camp meeting Bourne and his associates had been assisted by many Wesleyan Methodist preachers and laymen and by several preachers from the Methodist New Connexion.[96] The meeting had in fact been started some time before Bourne and his Harrisea Head supporters arrived.[97] At the second meeting Bourne was supported by numerous New Connexion Methodists and by a number of Wesleyan laymen, including William Clowes, but official disapproval kept away many of the local Wesleyan leaders. Bourne's difficulties were increased by a resolution of the 1807 Wesleyan Methodist Conference banning camp meetings.[98]

[91] Ibid. 5–7.
[92] Ibid. 7–8; Petty, *Primitive Methodist Connexion*, 7–8, 14–15. For Clowes see J. T. Wilkinson, *William Clowes*.
[93] Bourne, *Primitive Methodists*, 8–9.
[94] Ibid. 9–11, 19.
[95] Ibid. 12–13.
[96] Ibid. 14.
[97] Ibid. 10.
[98] Ibid. 14. It has been suggested that one of the motives which led the Conference to ban camp meetings was the realization by the staunchly loyalist Methodist leadership of the political danger inherent in bringing together large masses of people at a time of hardship and distress: R. F. Wearmouth, *Methodism and the Working-Class Movements of Eng., 1800–50*, 58.

A further meeting was held at Brown Edge (in Norton-in-the-Moors) on 16 August, and the Norton meeting which Bourne had planned took place on 23–25 August; this latter meeting was later regarded by Bourne as marking the firm establishment of camp meetings in England.[99] Soon numbers of small independent camp meetings began to be held, and during the following year Bourne and his brother James travelled in North Staffordshire, Cheshire, Lancashire, and Shropshire propagating their ideas. A prominent use of the camp meeting remained that of drawing people away from wakes and other popular entertainments. On their travels the Bournes formed several Methodist societies, which became affiliated to the Wesleyan Methodists.[1]

Despite his loyalty to the Wesleyans Bourne's defiance of the 1807 Conference resolution made him too dangerous a man to countenance, and in June 1808 he and his brother were expelled from the Connexion. During the next two years they continued to preach and to hold camp meetings. Their aim was 'conversion' rather than the formation of a separate sect, and those whom they converted usually joined the Wesleyans.[2] In 1810, however, the Wesleyans refused to admit a society which the Bournes had formed at Stanley (in Leek), and the brothers found themselves responsible for its maintenance. From then on they were virtually the leaders of an independent Connexion.[3]

Later in 1810 the Wesleyans in the Potteries began a purge of Bourne's sympathizers.[4] William Clowes, who had attended a camp meeting at Ramshorn (in Ellastone), was first suspended from duty as a local preacher and then expelled from the Connexion. Clowes was a popular figure and the leader of two classes in the Potteries, and when he was expelled by the Wesleyans his Tunstall class followed him. The numbers increased, and from December 1810 two local sympathizers, both working potters, provided Clowes with enough money to enable him to become a full-time preacher. Early in 1811 James Steele was also ejected from the Wesleyan Connexion because of his associations with Clowes and the Bournes, and he brought most of the Sunday-school teachers and children with him. A room was taken in Tunstall, and the efforts of Steele and Clowes met with such success that a chapel was built, the first belonging to the Connexion.

Meanwhile the Bournes were gradually building up new societies. When they became responsible for Stanley they were supplying preachers regularly to six places in North Staffordshire: Lask Edge (in Leek), Tean (in Checkley), Wootton and Ramshorn (in Ellastone), Cauldon, and Stanley. They employed a travelling preacher, and six other unpaid preachers helped them. The Bournes provided about £30 a year to keep the Connexion solvent and therefore 'had to be diligent in their temporal business'.[5] In the summer of 1810 Hugh Bourne extended his activities to South Staffordshire, preaching in and around Wyrley Bank (in Cheslyn Hay) and laying the foundations of what was to become the Darlaston Circuit.[6] After further expansion in North Staffordshire and Cheshire it was decided to construct an organizational framework on traditional Methodist lines. In May 1811 the printing of quarterly tickets for the Connexion was ordered. At a meeting at Tunstall in July it was decided that in future the Connexion should be financed by regular contributions from the various societies.[7]

[99] Bourne, *Primitive Methodists*, 15–18.

[1] Ibid. 19–24. In Shropshire 'there had existed, time out of mind, an evil custom of multitudes assembling on the top of Wrekin on the first Sunday in May, and spending the day in iniquity'. The Bournes therefore held a meeting on the Wrekin on Sunday, 1 May 1808, and attracted a large number of people from the merrymaking: ibid. 22.

[2] Ibid. 24–29.

[3] Ibid. 29–31.

[4] For this para. see ibid. 31, 33–37, 40–41.

[5] Ibid. 30.

[6] Ibid. 31–32.

[7] Ibid. 37–41; Petty, *Primitive Methodist Connexion*, 46–48.

At a further meeting held at Tunstall in February 1812 the Connexion adopted the name of Primitive Methodists. A new plan of Tunstall Circuit was issued; it contained 34 preaching-places and 23 preachers.[8] The Connexion grew rapidly. In 1811 it was estimated that there were in all some 200 members. By 1818 there were several circuits in England, and Tunstall Circuit alone had 690 members. Two years later the membership of the circuit had risen to 1,703 and it was divided into separate Tunstall and Darlaston circuits. During the following year Tunstall created a Manchester Circuit and in 1821–2 two further circuits headed by Belper (Derb.) and Burton-upon-Trent. In 1822–3 Tunstall formed the Ramshorn, Burland (Ches.), and Oakengates (Salop.) circuits. By 1823 the Connexion had 46 circuits and over 29,000 members.[9]

The Primitive Methodists undoubtedly owed some of their success[10] to the vigorous and colourful nature of their services, camp meetings, and other activities. This fervour appealed to working-class audiences, and the report of a commissioner inquiring into child employment in the Black Country in the early 1840s describes Primitive Methodist success in the drab industrial regions of the area.[11] In Sedgley parish the commissioner found that 'the great majority' of working-class people were Primitive Methodists; in each village in the parish there were 'two or three Primitive Methodist chapels . . . all regularly attended, and often densely crowded, by the poorest class'. There were many 'sacred days', on some of which the congregations would march in procession through the streets, singing and praying. After the procession had returned to the chapel a short play with a religious theme would be performed. 'The children of the working classes, as it may readily be supposed, are but too happy to vary the dull monotonous round of their daily labours by attending such spectacles as these, to which they look forward with excitement, and it is doubtless one cause, among the many causes, of the greater numbers of children and young persons who attend the chapels and schools of the Primitive Methodists than those of any other of the sects.'[12]

Among other factors which contributed to the comparative success of Primitive Methodism among the urban proletariat were the working-class origins of the Connexion and its democratic constitution.[13] The Bournes, Clowes, and the other pioneers were working men who appealed to their audiences in simple, unambiguous terms, and when the constitution of the new Connexion was drawn up control both locally and centrally was placed in the hands of the laity.[14] Bourne, however, was careful to ensure that this system of democratic lay control should not lead to an alliance between the Connexion and political Radicalism. There were undoubtedly unofficial links between the Radicals and some of the New Connexion[15] and Primitive Methodists; but when the 1821 Primitive Methodist Conference seemed on the point of making these links official Bourne intervened, ejected a Radical-minded delegate from the conference, and ensured that the Connexion should remain free of political affiliations.[16]

[8] Bourne, *Primitive Methodists*, 42; Petty, *Primitive Methodist Connexion*, 49–53.

[9] Bourne, *Primitive Methodists*, 41, 64, 65, 67, 68.

[10] It has been pointed out that Primitive Methodist success, in Staffs. and elsewhere, should not be exaggerated. The statistics provided in the religious census of 1851 indicate that despite their democratic organization and atmosphere (for which see below) 'their power to attract the inhabitants of the densest parts of England was by no means as strong as that of the original body': K. S. Inglis, 'Patterns of Religious Worship in 1851', *Jnl. Eccles. Hist.* xi. 86; see below pp. 131–2.

[11] *2nd Rep. Com. Child. Employment, App. Pt. 2* [432], pp. Q79, Q80, H.C. (1843), xv.

[12] Ibid. p. Q80, describing one such play. In a footnote the commissioner notes the similarity between these dramas and the medieval Miracle Plays. Primitive Methodist processions, with bands and banners, flourished at Stafford until the outbreak of the First World War: P. C. Murcott, 'The Ranters: some Aspects of Primitive Methodism in Stafford' (TS in W.S.L.), 49–50.

[13] Wearmouth, *Methodism and Working-Class Movements*, 208.

[14] Ibid.; Bourne, *Primitive Methodists*, 62–63.

[15] New Connexion Methodists were prominent in reform agitation in Hanley in 1819–20: Wearmouth, *Methodism and Working-Class Movements*, 211.

[16] Ibid. 211–12.

Another chapter in the history of late-18th- and early-19th-century Staffordshire nonconformity which was of national significance was the protracted dispute over the ownership of the old Presbyterian meeting-house in John Street, Wolverhampton.[17] This meeting-house, the first to be built in the town, had been erected in 1701–2[18] for a Presbyterian congregation and conveyed to a body of trustees. During the course of the 18th century the congregation gradually drifted towards Unitarianism. There was trouble in the 1740s with a minister who was 'orthodox in principles but not in practice'.[19] Philip Holland, minister about 1750,[20] held Arian views and preached them openly; his successor John Cole (minister 1759–81) appears to have held similar views but preached sermons acceptable to both Unitarians and Trinitarians. A section of the congregation, including a minority of the trustees, remained staunchly Trinitarian, and when Cole resigned in 1781 this group invited a Trinitarian to become the new minister. The Unitarians, however, succeeded in barring him from the chapel and installing a more congenial minister. The John Street ministers remained Unitarians until 1816, when the incumbent, John Steward, announced his conversion to Trinitarianism. Although the congregation tried to force his resignation, he resisted them with the help of Benjamin Mander, one of the Trinitarian trustees of 1781, who had not worshipped at John Street since the defeat of his candidate. The Unitarians were unable to expel Steward, and Mander opened proceedings in Chancery in 1817 with the object of proving that he himself was a trustee of the chapel and that, since a unanimous vote of all the trustees was necessary for the appointment of a new trustee, no appointment made since 1781 was valid. Sir Samuel Romilly, appearing for Mander, argued that the Unitarians had no rights in the chapel since it had been founded by and for Presbyterians; moreover, Unitarianism itself had not been legalized until 1813, when that part of the Blasphemy Act of 1698 which had been aimed at it was repealed.[21] The Lord Chancellor issued an order forbidding the Unitarians to take any steps to regain possession of the chapel until the further order of the court; he proposed that there should be a more detailed inquiry, but this does not appear to have been held.

The case gave birth to a vigorous pamphlet warfare between Trinitarians and Unitarians. The latter risked losing not only the John Street chapel but also a number of other nonconformist chapels which had come into their hands in similar circumstances. Proceedings in Chancery were reopened in 1822, but no further progress was made. Meanwhile the ejected Unitarian congregation flourished in premises elsewhere in Wolverhampton. The congregation remaining at John Street was small and divided within itself, and in 1829 the chapel was temporarily closed. In the 1830s and early 1840s the case was again argued in Chancery. In 1835 judgment was given against the Unitarians, and in 1842, after the House of Lords had found against the Unitarians in a similar case, the Lord Chancellor dismissed the appeal.

The Wolverhampton Meeting-house Case and the decision of the House of Lords aroused fears among Unitarians that other denominations might attempt to recover property which had been peacefully enjoyed by Unitarians for many years. In 1844 the position was regularized by the passage of the Dissenters' Chapels Act,[22] which laid down that deeds were to be interpreted not in historical terms but as though all the

[17] For the next three paras. see, unless otherwise stated, Cumberland, 'Protestant Noncon. in the Black Country', 104–10; Matthews, *Cong. Ch. Staffs.* 152–64.

[18] *S.H.C.* 4th ser. iii. 113.

[19] Quoted in Matthews, *Cong. Ch. Staffs.* 152.

[20] Cumberland, 'Protestant Noncon. in the Black Country', 105, gives the dates of Holland's pastorate as

1745–54; Matthews, *Cong. Ch. Staffs.* 152, as 1750–4; Mander and Tildesley, *Wolverhampton*, 130, as 1748–54. No refs. are given for any of these statements. *D.N.B.* does not give the dates of Holland's pastorate.

[21] 9 Wm. III, c. 35; 53 Geo. III, c. 160.

[22] 7 & 8 Vic. c. 45.

relevant statutes passed prior to 1844 had been in force at the time when the deeds were drawn up. The doctrinal requirements in the foundation deed were to be ignored if the existing congregation could prove 25 years' uninterrupted use of the chapel. The John Street chapel, so long a bone of contention, never recovered its former importance as a nonconformist place of worship. In 1863 it passed into the hands of the Church of England, becoming a chapel of ease to St. Peter's, Wolverhampton; finally in 1890 the building became part of the works of Mander Bros.

The religious census of 1851 shows that Staffordshire was no exception to the general rule that, so far as attendance at church or chapel was concerned, there was an 'alarming number of . . . non-attendants'.[23] The county had a population of 608,716. On Sunday 30 March 1851 129,962 people attended public worship in the morning, 83,404 in the afternoon, and 83,881 in the evening. Of these there were 54,918 Protestant nonconformists in the morning, 36,266 in the afternoon, and 52,917 in the evening.[24] The Methodists were overwhelmingly the most numerous of the nonconformist bodies in the county. Between them the various Methodist connexions (excluding the Welsh Calvinistic Methodists) had 377 places of worship in Staffordshire; by contrast the Congregationalists had 63 and the Baptists 35. There were 39,878 Methodists attending public worship in the morning, 30,604 in the afternoon, and 39,182 in the evening. Of the various Methodist connexions the Wesleyan (or Original Connexion) Methodists were the strongest numerically. They had 191 places of worship, and morning, afternoon, and evening attendances were given as respectively 23,991, 13,998, and 15,284. The Primitive Methodists had 128 places of worship and attendances of 7,834, 11,294, and 14,505; the New Connexion Methodists had 54 places of worship and attendances of 7,691, 4,992, and 8,430. The Wesleyan Methodist Association and the Wesleyan Reformers (two small groups which had recently split away from the parent body) had between them 4 places of worship and a total allegiance of perhaps 1,000. Congregationalism, with its 63 places of worship and morning, afternoon, and evening attendances of 9,192, 2,573, and 7,749, was numerically the next strongest of the nonconformist denominations. There were 35 Baptist places of worship, with combined morning, afternoon, and evening attendances of 4,595, 2,300, and 4,577. Of these 26 belonged to the Particular Baptists, 4 to the General (New Connexion) Baptists, and 5 to Baptists whose allegiance is unstated. The other nonconformist denominations were numerically insignificant: there were 6 Quaker meeting-houses, with 70 worshippers in the morning and 29 in the afternoon; 6 Unitarian places of worship, with, at the 3 which sent in returns, 340 attenders in the morning, 280 in the afternoon, and 78 in the evening; 4 places of worship belonging to the Presbyterian Church in England, with an attendance of 359 in the morning and 398 in the evening; one Welsh Calvinistic Methodist place of worship, with an attendance of 150 in the afternoon and 150 in the evening; one Swedenborgian place of worship, with an attendance of 30; 5 places of worship belonging to the Brethren, with 65 attenders in the morning and 151 in the evening; 8 isolated congregations with undisclosed affiliations and attendances of 389 in the morning, 330 in the afternoon, and 632 in the evening; and 5 Mormon places of worship, with afternoon attendances of 234 and evening attendances of 192.[25]

In the three large towns — the parliamentary borough of Stoke-upon-Trent (population 84,027), the municipal borough of Walsall (population 25,680), and the

---

[23] *Census, 1851: Religious Worship, Eng. and Wales, Rep. and Tables*, p. clviii.
[24] Ibid., p. ccxxii, stating that attendance-figures were lacking for 37 (out of 863) places of worship. Of these 24 belonged to the Church of England, 4 to the Independents

(Congregationalists), 1 to the Particular Baptists, 3 to the Unitarians, 2 to the Wesleyan Methodists, 1 to the Primitive Methodists, 1 to an unidentified Protestant nonconformist sect, and 1 to the Roman Catholics.
[25] Ibid.

parliamentary borough of Wolverhampton (population 119,748) — the Wesleyan Methodists were again the largest nonconformist denomination.[26] At Walsall and Wolverhampton they dominated the nonconformist scene in terms of numbers; at Wolverhampton they appear to have outnumbered all the other nonconformists put together, and at Walsall the proportions were almost as striking. At Stoke they had no such superiority; there the New Connexion was almost as strong, the Primitive Methodists and the Congregationalists each had about a third the strength of the Wesleyans, and the Wesleyan Methodist Association had a considerable body of supporters. At Walsall the Particular Baptists, Congregationalists and Primitive Methodists each had about the same amount of support, and there were smaller bodies of General Baptists and unaffiliated Baptists. At Wolverhampton the Primitive Methodists and the Congregationalists appear to have had congregations of approximately the same size, and there were slightly smaller groups of Particular Baptists and New Connexion Methodists. At Stoke and Wolverhampton nonconformist worshippers considerably outnumbered those belonging to the Church of England. At Stoke, where no returns of attendance were made for two of the 18 Anglican churches and chapels, 8,073 nonconformists attended worship in the morning, 3,730 in the afternoon, and 9,968 in the evening; the respective Anglican figures are 5,681, 2,852, and 2,331. At Wolverhampton, where there were no returns from three of the 23 Anglican churches and chapels and three of the 69 nonconformist places of worship, 13,777 nonconformists attended worship in the morning, 8,412 in the afternoon, and 13,934 in the evening; the Anglican figures are 11,578, 2,455, and 8,966. At the smaller town of Walsall Establishment and Dissent were more evenly balanced. At the 12 out of 13 nonconformist places of worship for which returns of attendance were made there were 2,043 worshippers in the morning, 600 in the afternoon, and 1,954 in the evening. The Anglican figures were 2,158, 1,395, and 1,075.

In the large towns in Staffordshire, therefore, the nonconformists, especially the Methodists, were performing essential and much-needed work for which the structure and organization of the Church of England were not well suited, even after twenty or thirty years of attention to the problem.[27] Nonconformist success must, however, be seen in perspective. Throughout the country most people in the large manufacturing towns, despite the efforts of all denominations, did not go to church or chapel, and both Stoke and Walsall conformed to the typical low attendance-rate for such towns.[28] Wolverhampton was, however, one of the few large manufacturing towns where attendance was above the urban average; and there, as in similar towns, it was evidently the nonconformist contribution which made the difference.[29]

The Census also shows the extent to which the nonconformists were striving to keep abreast of the rising tide of population by building new chapels and acquiring new places of worship. In several cases the figures may be somewhat misleading,[30] but it is evident that the years 1831–51 were a peak period of expansion. At least 93 of the 191 places of worship in the county belonging to the Wesleyan Methodists in 1851 had been built or acquired since 1831. At least 86 of the Primitive Methodists' 128 places of

[26] For the following para. see ibid., pp. cclxix, cclxxi, cclxxii.

[27] For a summary of the nonconformist contribution in large towns in 1851 see *Jnl. Eccles. Hist.* x. 84–86.

[28] Ibid. It has been estimated from the census returns that in Longton slightly less than a ninth of the population attended a nonconformist place of worship on Census Sunday, while at Hanley and Shelton the proportion was a tenth: *V.C.H. Staffs.* viii. 278.

[29] *Jnl. Eccles. Hist.* x. 84.

[30] *Census, 1851: Religious Worship*, p. ccxxxix, pointing out that 'in the case of some Dissenting Bodies places only recently occupied for religious worship have been returned with the date of their erection instead of that of their first appropriation to such uses. So too of chapels which have passed from one denomination to another.' The extent of the 1831–51 expansion would thus be minimized. In some cases also the date of erection or acquisition of a building was not given in the return.

Hugh Bourne, 1772–1852, pioneer of Primitive Methodism

Bonaventure Giffard, Bishop of Madura, Vicar Apostolic of the
Midland District 1688–1703

The chapel of 1813

The new building of 1866

QUEEN STREET CONGREGATIONAL CHURCH, WOLVERHAMPTON

worship dated from the same period, and at least 30 of the 54 belonging to the Methodist New Connexion. The Congregationalists had built or acquired at least 24 of their 63 places of worship since 1831, the Baptists (all denominations) 18 of the 35 belonging to them in 1851.[31] The rapid growth of the Potteries and the Black Country, however, meant that in 1851 the nonconformists could provide accommodation for only about 25 or 26 per cent. of the population in Stoke and for about 17 per cent. of the population in Wolverhampton.[32]

The later 19th century was a period of prosperity and expansion for Staffordshire nonconformity: at Wolverhampton in 1891 a secularist lecturer could raise a laugh by suggesting that the advice 'sell what thou hast, and give to the poor' was not followed by the leading Congregational minister in the town and the rich who went to his chapel.[33] Nonconformists had for many years made their mark in the industrial and commercial life of the county. In the Potteries, for example, supporters of the Methodist New Connexion in the early 19th century included the Ridgways of Cauldon Place, Shelton, while in the Black Country there had for long been prominent dynasties of nonconformist ironmasters, manufacturers, and tradesmen.[34] With the removal of all legal obstacles nonconformists began to play their full part in civic life; at Wolverhampton members of the Queen Street Congregational Church held the mayoralty 12 times between 1869 and 1909.[35] Denominations which had a few decades before been frowned upon not only by members of the Church of England but also by more 'respectable' nonconformists became accepted. Thus, although it was still felt in some quarters that membership of a Primitive Methodist chapel was inappropriate for a middle-class family,[36] in general barriers were crumbling. Three of the sons of Mrs. Elizabeth Brownhill, formerly Elizabeth Johnson, one of the early Primitive Methodist women preachers, became Primitive Methodist mayors of Walsall.[37] Among all denominations increased prosperity and expanding congregations led to the building of new chapels, larger and often more architecturally ambitious than their predecessors. At Wolverhampton, for example, the plain Queen Street Congregational chapel of 1813 was demolished in 1864 and replaced by a larger and more richly decorated building, opened two years later.[38] In the Potteries the period 1870–1900 was the golden age of chapel building.[39]

The later 19th century also saw a decline among nonconformists of the previously held view that pleasure as such was immoral — an attitude typified earlier by the decision of the elders of a Wolverhampton chapel to expel from membership a family which had held a private dance in its own home and remained unrepentant.[40] It was the Black Country which saw the birth of 'the most systematic attempt to attract new working-class worshippers by offering them consecrated pleasure'. In 1875 John Blackham, a Congregationalist deacon at West Bromwich, invented the Pleasant Sunday Afternoon. This took the form of a regular Sunday afternoon meeting in a chapel or public hall at

[31] Ibid. p. ccxlvii. For the decade 1821–31 the figures are: Wesleyan Methodists 33, Primitive Methodists 18, New Connexion Methodists 11, Congregationalists, 8, Baptists (all denominations) 1.

[32] These figures are obtained by deducting from the total percentages of dissenting accommodation (given ibid. p. ccxcvii) the Roman Catholic total.

[33] K. S. Inglis, Churches and the Working Classes in Victorian Eng. 101.

[34] V.C.H. Staffs. viii. 277, 294; Cumberland, 'Protestant Noncon. in the Black Country', 115–19, noting among other ironmasters the Quaker families of Parker (Tipton) and Parkes (Wednesbury), and the Baptist families of Green (Coseley) and Thompson (Ettingshall). Another notable ironmaster, John Wilkinson of Bradley (in Bilston),

was also well-disposed towards nonconformists, though his exact religious allegiance is difficult to determine: ibid. 119.

[35] H. A. May, Queen St. Congregational Church, Wolverhampton: the Story of a Hundred Years, 1809–1909, 94–95.

[36] Thus, when in Arnold Bennett's The Old Wives' Tale Samuel Povey transfers his allegiance from the Primitive Methodists to the Wesleyan Methodists, the move has a social as well as a religious significance.

[37] J. Ritson, Romance of Primitive Methodism, 145–6.

[38] May, Queen St. Cong. Church, 27, 29–31; see plate on facing page.

[39] V.C.H. Staffs. viii. 278–9.

[40] May, Queen St. Cong. Church, 19.

which the programme included communal hymn-singing, sacred solos, duets, or quartets, prayers, Bible readings, and short religious or moral addresses. During the next ten years the idea was taken up in and around West Bromwich. In 1885 Blackham inspired the foundation of a P.S.A. Society in Derby, and subsequently the movement spread rapidly throughout the North and Midlands and gained a footing in parts of London. In 1891 the P.S.A. Society at Wolverhampton had over 1,000 members and that at Hanley, described as one of the largest in the country, 1,680 members.[41]

During the 20th century, and especially since the first World War, the nonconformist churches have faced common problems of declining membership,[42] which have sometimes forced a policy of retrenchment upon them. In general, however, the chapels which have been closed have been old buildings, difficult to maintain and situated in town centres where resident population is dwindling, and their closure has made available funds for the construction of chapels and halls in the new suburbs. A feature of the period has been the renewal of old links among the various denominations and the forging of new ones; the most notable advance has been the reunion of the Methodist churches. A sign of more extensive co-operation among the Free Churches has been the formation of councils to discuss and consider matters of common interest to the various denominations; for example, the Stafford Free Church Union was formed in 1895 and a Free Church Council was founded in the Potteries in 1934.[43]

In the early 1960s there were in Staffordshire 42 churches belonging to the Methodist Church, with a total membership of over 34,500. They were divided between 4 districts: Birmingham (7 Staffordshire churches, with a membership of 3,821), Wolverhampton and Shrewsbury (17 Staffordshire churches, with a membership of 16,147), Nottingham and Derby (3 Staffordshire churches, with a membership of 2,238), and Chester and Stoke-on-Trent (15 Staffordshire churches, with a membership of 12,340).[44] The Staffordshire Congregational Union had 59 places of worship divided between a Northern District and a Southern District, with a total adult membership of 3,635.[45] There were 36 Baptist churches in the county affiliated to the East Midland Association and the West Midland Association, with a total adult membership of 2,930.[46] Several smaller denominations, including the Presbyterian Church of England (6 churches and 980 communicants),[47] the Quakers, and the Unitarians, were represented in the county, and there was a considerable number of evangelistic and undenominational bodies.

[41] Inglis, *Churches and the Working Classes*, 79–85.

[42] In 1915 it was stated that attendance at nonconformist churches at Tipton was 'at a very low ebb'; the writer dated the beginning of the decline to *c.* 1890: J. Parkes, *Hist. of Tipton* (Tipton, 1915), 212 (copy in W.S.L.). A study of the decline of a Stafford chapel after 1918 is to be found in Murcott, 'The Ranters', 54–59.

[43] *Staffs. Advertiser*, 29 June 1895; *V.C.H. Staffs.* viii.

279.

[44] *Mins. of Methodist Conf. 1964.* The figures given are those of the Dec. 1963 visitation.

[45] *Congregational Yr. Bk. 1964–5.* The figures given are for Jan. 1964.

[46] *Baptist Handbk. 1964.* The figures given are for 1 Jan. 1963.

[47] *Presbyterian Ch. of Eng. Official Handbk. 1962–3.*

RELIGIOUS HOUSES

The earliest religious communities in Staffordshire are largely subjects of legend, but it would seem that they dated from the period of the conversion of Mercia in the later 7th century. Bede describes how St. Chad, Bishop of the Mercians (669–72), established his see at Lichfield and built a house near the church, retiring there when his work permitted with a number of companions for prayer and study.[1] Wulfhere, King of Mercia (657–74), is said to have founded a monastery at Stone;[2] his daughter St. Werburgh was Abbess of Hanbury and was buried there about 700.[3] If there is anything in the legend that the Irish abbess St. Modwen founded a community at Burton-upon-Trent, the foundation probably dated from this period.[4] The Danish invasions from the later 9th century must have brought any existing religious houses to an end. The fate of Hanbury is recorded in the story that St. Werburgh's body remained incorrupt until the approach of the Danes in 874 when it crumbled away lest it should fall into their hands; the nuns of Hanbury then fled to Chester with the saint's relics.[5]

There seems to have been some revival in the 10th century. The later royal free chapels of Staffordshire may have originated in foundations of that time; St. Peter's, Wolverhampton, may indeed have existed as a monastery by 994, and there is mention of a community at Tamworth in Wulfric Spot's will about ten years later.[6] The county's monastic history, however, may really be said to begin with the foundation of Burton Abbey at the beginning of the 11th century. This house, the last in Staffordshire to be surrendered at the Reformation, was also the wealthiest and largest.

The Norman Conquest produced only one new house in the county, Tutbury Priory, although by that time there may possibly have been a cell of St. Rémy at Lapley. Most of the Staffordshire houses dated from the 12th century; six houses of Augustinian canons, two Benedictine priories for men and three for women, and two Cistercian abbeys were founded at that time. The nobility and gentry and the bishops of Coventry were the main patrons. In the 13th century two more Cistercian houses[7] and three friaries were founded, and the Templars established a preceptory at Keele. After this there was only one more foundation, the Austin friary at Stafford in 1344.

Few of these monasteries had more than local significance, and some of them lacked even that. Several did not survive until the Reformation. The first Cistercian house, at Radmore in Cannock Forest, lasted only some 10 years and was then transferred to Stoneleigh in Warwickshire by Henry II at the monks' own request. The Benedictine nunnery at Blithbury seems to have been amalgamated with that at Brewood by the 14th century. The first suppression was in 1308 when the preceptory at Keele came to an end. The next was in 1415 when the small alien priory at Lapley was dissolved. There were further suppressions in the 1520s when the tiny communities at Canwell and Sandwell and the nunnery at Farewell were dissolved by Wolsey. The Augustinian priory at Calwich, which had only one canon left in 1530, was suppressed in

---

[1] Bede, *Historia Ecclesiastica*, bk. iv, chap. iii. And see below p. 140.
[2] See below p. 240.
[3] F. A. Hibbert, *Monasticism in Staffs.* 10; *Chartulary or Reg. of Abbey of St. Werburgh, Chester, Pt. I* (Chetham Soc. N.S. lxxix), pp. viii–xiv. For the mistaken tradition that St. Werburgh founded a monastery at Trentham see below p. 255 and note 2.

[4] See below p. 199.
[5] *Chartulary of Abbey of St. Werburgh, Pt. I*, pp. xiii–xiv.
[6] See below pp. 310, 321.
[7] For the abortive foundation at Wolverhampton see below pp. 322–3.

1532; unlike the previous dissolutions, this resulted in the secularization of the priory's property. The rest of the monasteries were dissolved in the later 1530s. Burton Abbey was given a new lease of life as a college in 1541, but it survived for only four years. The five remaining colleges were suppressed under the Act of 1547. Wolverhampton was revived by Mary I in 1553 and survived until the 19th century.

None of the medieval hospitals in the county was of particular importance; indeed for several of them the evidence is minimal.[8] There was at least one monastic hospital, that of St. Anne at Ranton Priory in the later 13th century. There may have been others at Dieulacres and Burton: 'poor bede women' were given alms at the dissolution of Dieulacres in 1538, and four bedesmen received wages of 25s. each when Burton College was suppressed in 1545.[9] In 1548 the chantry commissioners listed four towns in the county as having most need of hospitals for the relief of the poor: Stafford, Walsall, Tamworth, and Burton.[10] The hospitals at Stafford and Tamworth had probably ceased to maintain any poor, but they were suppressed and not reformed; the Crown made no provision for eleemosynary foundations in any of these towns.[11]

A number of hermits and anchorets occur in the county during the Middle Ages. The earliest is the legendary Anglo-Saxon saint, Bertelin, who is said to have had a hermitage on the island of Bethnei, the later Stafford; according to legend he subsequently left Bethnei for a mountainous area, perhaps near Ilam, where he ended his days.[12] It has been suggested that Holy Austin Rock on Kinver Edge was the cave dwelling of a recluse.[13] Several hermits seem to have settled in remote places which became the sites of 12th-century religious houses: Calwich in Dovedale, Radmore in Cannock Forest, Blithbury, Farewell, and Sandwell; the early-13th-century abbey at Dieulacres north of Leek may also have been near a former hermitage.[14] At Sandwell and probably Farewell the hermitages were associated with a spring; similarly the possessions of Trentham Priory in 1162 included 'the hermitage of the well of Dunstall' (probably near the priory itself) and land there cultivated by Walter the hermit.[15] Also in the later 12th century there was a hermitage at Ranton, a hermit living in the wood of Sutton (in Forton), and two hermits living in the wood of Hamstall Ridware.[16] A hermitage chapel had probably been established on the site of the present Armitage church by the 12th century; although still known as 'the hermitage of Handsacre' in the mid 13th century, the chapel then seems no longer to have been a hermitage.[17] A hermitage at Agardsley in Needwood Forest was given to Tutbury Priory by William,

[8] In addition to the hospitals treated separately in this volume there may have been a leper hospital near Gunstone (in Brewood): V.C.H. Staffs. v. 20. A 'house' in Tamworth, dedicated to St. John, was inhabited by 'brethren' in 1227–8 (S.H.C. iv(1), 70), and this too may have been a hospital.

[9] See below pp. 233–4, 252, 297, 298. For the 13th-century 'house of stone next to the church for the reception of the poor' at Burton see below p. 212.

[10] A. F. Leach, Eng. Schools at the Reformation, 1546–8, pt. ii, 210.

[11] See below pp. 292, 294, 295. At Walsall an almshouse had been founded by William Harpur by the early 16th century: 9th Rep. Com. Char. H.C. 258, p. 579 (1823), ix; Shaw, Staffs. ii. 64. The history of this charity is reserved for a future volume of this History.

[12] The Church of St. Bertelin at Stafford, ed. A. Oswald, 6–7, 9. After St. Bertelin perhaps the best known medieval recluse connected with the county was Katherine of Ledbury, sometimes called 'Saint'; she was the daughter of John Giffard of Brimpsfield (Glos.) and the wife of Nicholas de Audley (d. 1299). Katherine, however, established her anchorage at Ledbury (Herefs.) and so falls outside the scope of this survey. See Rotha M. Clay, The

Hermits and Anchorites of Eng. 74–75, 218–19.

[13] Clay, Hermits and Anchorites, 48.

[14] See below pp. 216, 220, 222–3, 225, 230, 237, 240.

[15] S.H.C. xi. 303; see below p. 256. In 1537 there were lands near the priory called Over, Middle and Nether Tunstall (S.C. 6/Hen.VIII/3352, m. 3); it seems likely that the hermitage was situated here rather than at Holly Wall in Tunstall (in Wolstanton) as suggested in V.C.H. Staffs. viii. 93. For the holy well at Lichfield see below n. 25.

[16] F. A. Hibbert, 'Ronton Priory', T.N.S.F.C. l. 95, 97; Dugdale, Mon. vi(1), 257–8; V.C.H. Staffs. iv. 107; Shaw, Staffs. i. 153; S.H.C. xvi. 232–3.

[17] Shaw, Staffs. i. 207, *208, *209. Armitage parish church, before its rebuilding in the 1840s, was undoubtedly of Norman origin: S. A. Jeavons, 'The Pattern of Ecclesiastical Building in Staffs. during the Norman Period', Trans. Lichfield & S. Staffs. Arch. & Hist. Soc. iv. 11, 14, 15, 16; W.S.L., Staffs. Views, i, pp. 82, 86, 87, 92, 94. In the mid 13th cent. the church was held by John, the parson of Colton: B.M. Add. Ch. 24239; and see F. P. Parker, Some Account of Colton and of the De Wasteneys Family, 196; S.H.C. iv(1), 211–12.

Earl of Derby (1190–1247).[18] The hermitage of 'Gutheresburn' in Kinver Forest was granted by Henry III in 1248 to Brother Walerand of Kidderminster to celebrate divine service there for the souls of the king and queen, the king's ancestors and heirs, and the faithful departed.[19] The existence of an anchoress in the church of Newcastle-under-Lyme in 1227[20] shows that the solitary religious life was not confined to remote places.

Evidence of recluses in the county becomes scarcer in the later Middle Ages, though it is clear that they continued to exist, notably in the towns. Commissions to suffragans in the later 14th century included the duties of professing hermits and enclosing anchorets.[21] An anchoret at Stafford occurs among the many anchorets and hermits throughout the country to whom Henry, Lord Scrope, left money in 1415.[22] In 1424 a hermit called John Grace was preaching in the south of the county.[23] There was a hermit at Newcastle-under-Lyme in 1465[24] and an anchoret named John Mede in 1504 at Stowe near Lichfield, where 'the Ancker's House' in the churchyard occurs in 1571.[25] At the Reformation there was a 'hermitage chapel' in the collegiate church of Wolverhampton.[26]

The suppression of the monasteries produced little opposition in Staffordshire; rather there were several local men eager for the spoils and only too ready to press their claims even before the actual suppressions.[27] There are, however, a few signs of sympathy for the religious. In 1536 Sir Simon Harcourt put in a plea for Ranton, founded by his ancestors to secure prayers for ever, and he offered to pay for its preservation; but he added a further plea that, if his first request were not granted, he should be given the house on its dissolution.[28] Rowland Lee, Bishop of Coventry and Lichfield, acted in the same way over St. Thomas's Priory.[29] In 1537 Lord Stafford, who had been trying to secure a grant of Stone Priory, reported the Prior of Stone's optimism about the survival of his house, 'whereof the country is glad'.[30] The priory was nevertheless dissolved in the same year; Lord Stafford then removed his family monuments from the priory to the Austin friary in Forebridge, Stafford, evidently supposing that this would survive.[31] Richard Ingworth, Bishop of Dover, the special visitor for friars, wrote in 1538 that the friars in North Wales and the West Midlands, including Staffordshire, 'have many favourers, and great labour is made for their continuance. Divers trust to see them set up again, and some here have gone up to sue for them'.[32] An example of this hope of revival is the bequest made by Margaret Sutton of Stafford in 1556: 'I will that my fyne kercher be made a corporas and geven to the freres if it go up againe.'[33] Similarly the Cistercian Thomas Whitney, the last Abbot of Dieulacres, who died in 1558, stipulated in his will that his chalice was to be restored to Dieulacres if the monastery 'be hereafter re-edified'.[34]

[18] See below p. 332.

[19] Cal. Pat. 1247–58, 20. It is not known whether this was in the Staffs. or the Worcs. portion of the forest.

[20] Clay, Hermits and Anchorites, 246–7. This also mentions a hermit at Newcastle in 1355, but the source (S.H.C. N.S. viii. 154) gives 'Novus Burgus', perhaps Newport (Salop.).

[21] S.H.C. N.S. viii. 131, 200, 356; Lich. Dioc. Regy., B/A/1/7, ff. 160, 212.

[22] F. D. S. Darwin, The Eng. Mediaeval Recluse, 60–61; T. Rymer, Foedera (1740 edn.), iv. 132. The sum left to the Stafford anchoret was 13s. 4d.

[23] See above p. 43. It was rumoured that Grace had been successively monk, friar, and recluse.

[24] Clay, Hermits and Anchorites, 246–7.

[25] D. & C. Lich., Chapter Act Bk. iii, f. 82v.; Cal. Pat. 1569–72, p. 398. The anchoret's house was built against the north-west corner of the church; nearby is the spring known as St. Chad's Well: P. Laithwaite, Hist. of St. Chad's Church, Lichfield, Staffs. (1938), 15–16, 28 (copy in W.S.L. Pamphs. sub Lichfield); W.S.L., Staffs. Views, v, pp. 194, 200.

[26] S.H.C. 1915, 322. For some evidence of a hermitage by the bridge over the Dove at Tutbury see Shaw, Staffs. i. 57.

[27] See below pp. 210, 254.

[28] See below p. 254.

[29] See below pp. 265–6.

[30] See below p. 246.

[31] See below p. 274.

[32] L. & P. Hen. VIII, xiii(2), p. 67.

[33] S.H.C. 1926, p. 12.

[34] See below p. 234. The fate of the dispossessed clergy is not easy to trace; some are found as parish clergy, others continued to live locally: see below pp. 222 n.45, 229, 230 n.93, 234, 250 n.57, 251 n.95, 254, 266, 308, 329.

RELIGIOUS HOUSES

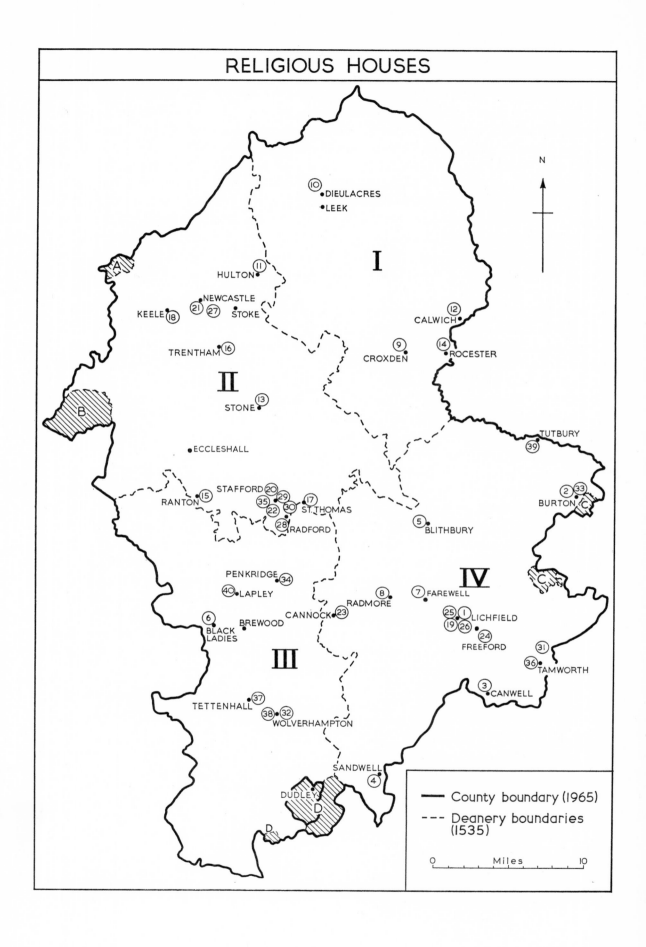

I

II

III

IV

N

•DIEULACRES
⑩
•LEEK

HULTON• ⑪

NEWCASTLE
㉑ ㉗
KEELE•⑱ STOKE•

TRENTHAM•⑯

STONE•⑬

ECCLESHALL•

CALWICH
⑫

⑨
CROXDEN•

⑭
ROCESTER•

TUTBURY
㊴

STAFFORD•⑳
㉟ ㉙
RANTON•⑮ ㉒ ㉚• ⑰
ST.THOMAS•
㉘
•RADFORD

② ㉝
BURTON•Ⓒ

⑤
•BLITHBURY

PENKRIDGE
• ㉞
㊵•LAPLEY

⑧
RADMORE•
⑦•FAREWELL

Ⓒ

CANNOCK• ㉓

㉕ ①
LICHFIELD•
⑲ ㉖
⑥
BLACK
LADIES• BREWOOD•

FREEFORD
㉔

㉛

㊱•TAMWORTH

③
•CANWELL

㊲
TETTENHALL•
㊳• ㉜
WOLVERHAMPTON•

SANDWELL•
④

DUDLEY•
Ⓓ
Ⓓ

Ⓐ

Ⓑ

	County boundary (1965)
- - -	Deanery boundaries (1535)

0   Miles   10

KEY TO MAP OF RELIGIOUS HOUSES

SECULAR CANONS
1. Lichfield Cathedral

BENEDICTINE MONKS
2. Burton Abbey
3. Canwell Priory
4. Sandwell Priory

BENEDICTINE NUNS
5. Blithbury Priory
6. Brewood Priory (Black Ladies)
7. Farewell Priory

CISTERCIAN MONKS
8. Radmore Abbey
9. Croxden Abbey
10. Dieulacres Abbey
11. Hulton Abbey

AUGUSTINIAN CANONS
12. Calwich Priory
13. Stone Priory
14. Rocester Abbey
15. Ranton Priory
16. Trentham Priory
17. St. Thomas's Priory near Stafford

KNIGHTS TEMPLARS
18. Keele Preceptory

FRIARS
19. Lichfield Franciscans
20. Stafford Franciscans
21. Newcastle-under-Lyme Dominicans
22. Stafford Augustinians

HOSPITALS
23. Cannock, St. Mary
24. Freeford, St. Leonard
25. Lichfield, Dr. Milley's
26. Lichfield, St. John the Baptist
27. Newcastle-under-Lyme
28. Radford, St. Lazarus or the Holy Sepulchre
29. Stafford, Forebridge, St. John the Baptist
30. Stafford, Forebridge, St. Leonard
31. Tamworth, St. James
32. Wolverhampton, St. Mary

COLLEGES
33. Burton, Christ and St. Mary
34. Penkridge, St. Michael
35. Stafford, St. Mary
36. Tamworth, St. Edith
37. Tettenhall, St. Michael
38. Wolverhampton, St. Peter

ALIEN HOUSES
39. Tutbury Priory
40. Lapley Priory

RURAL DEANERIES
I. Leek and Alton
II. Newcastle and Stone
III. Lapley and Trysull
IV. Tamworth and Tutbury

NOTE: the boundaries of the rural deaneries are based on the *Valor Ecclesiasticus* of 1535. They are to some extent notional since there were also large areas of peculiar jurisdiction, not shown on this map (see above pp. 93-94).

The shaded areas represent:

A part of the archdeaconry of Chester
B part of the archdeaconry of Salop
C part of the archdeaconry of Derby
D part of the diocese of Worcester

1. THE CATHEDRAL OF LICHFIELD[1]

Early History

ST. WILFRID, who at the request of King Wulfhere performed episcopal duties in Mercia at various times between 666 and 669, received many grants of land from the king. Lichfield was one of these grants, and Wilfrid decided that it should become the seat of the hitherto peripatetic bishops of the Mercians.[2] St. Chad, Bishop of the Mercians from 669 to 672, was the first to have his seat at Lichfield, and when he died he was buried there 'close to the church of St. Mary'.[3] This church was probably on the site of the present cathedral;[4] about half a mile to the north-east, on the site of the present St. Chad's Church next to Stowe Pool, is the spot where Chad is traditionally supposed to have preached to the people.[5] The first church definitely known to have stood on the site of the present cathedral was that built by Bishop Headda and consecrated in December 700. Chad's bones were transferred to a wooden shrine in the new cathedral and became a popular object of pilgrimage.[6] The dedication of this cathedral presents some problems. Bede's statement that it was dedicated to St. Peter[7] appears to be the only early reference to such a dedication. By the time of Domesday Book the cathedral was 'the church of St. Chad',[8] and this remained its popular name.[9] The present dedication, to St. Mary and St. Chad, is found from at least the late 1150s.[10] The dedication to the Virgin may represent a 12th-century accretion.[11] Alternatively, since Bede states that Chad's cathedral was dedicated to St. Mary, it may have formed part of the dedication of Headda's cathedral and have been overshadowed by the cult of the local saint until the 12th-century revival of the cult of the Virgin.[12]

Nothing is known of the administration of the cathedral until 822 when, according to the Lichfield Chronicle,[13] Bishop Æthelweald set up canons in the cathedral for the first time. There were 20 of them, including a provost — 11 priests and 9 deacons.[14] The date of this event suggests that Æthelweald was introducing the *decretulum* of Bishop Chrodegang of Metz, a rule of common life drawn up for his cathedral clergy about 755. A characteristic of this rule was the placing of a provost at the head of the body of canons.[15] A rule similar to that of Chrodegang was introduced at Canterbury in 813, but, apart from Lichfield, there is no evidence that the rule was adopted in other English cathedrals until shortly before the Norman Conquest.[16]

The history of the cathedral from 822 until the episcopate of Roger de Clinton (1129–48) is obscure — so obscure that Clinton, who reorganized the cathedral, was thought by a 13th-century Prior of Coventry to have been the first to introduce canons at Lichfield.[17] The tradition was that before Clinton's time there had been only five priests, *deservientes quinque capellis, singuli singulis*.[18] This is supported by the entry for Lichfield in Domesday Book which says that there were on the bishop's manor five canons holding three ploughs.[19] The break-up of common life and the division of great parts of the common estates and goods into separate portions or prebends for the canons were common tendencies in cathedrals during the 10th and 11th centuries;[20] at Lichfield the Danish invasions of the 9th and 10th centuries and the transference of the bishop's see to Chester in 1075 and thence to Coventry in 1102[21] must have contributed to the disintegration of the communal life instituted by Æthelweald.

A late-16th-century history of the cathedral wrongly ascribed to Æthelweald the foundation of prebends to support his canons.[22] The earliest canons were more probably supported by estates held in common. Traces of these estates may possibly be found in Domesday Book where some of the estates held by the bishop in 1086 are said to have belonged to the cathedral ('the church of St. Chad') before the Conquest.[23] In one case, that of Tachbrook (Warws.), the bishop was the tenant-in-chief, but it was said that the land belonged to (*est de*) the church of St. Chad.[24] Portions of several of the manors, such as Baswich, Brewood, and Eccleshall, were said to have been held by the cathedral and are known to have become prebends by the end of the 12th century. It seems likely, however, that

---

[1] Thanks are due to Dr. Kathleen Edwards for reading and commenting on this article in draft, and to Mr. J. H. Harvey for help with the sections which deal with the architectural history of the cathedral in the Middle Ages.

[2] See above p. 2.

[3] Bede, *Historia Ecclesiastica*, bk. iv, chap. iii.

[4] Such appears to be the implication of the relevant passage in Bede. According to this, Chad 'sepultus est primo quidem iuxta ecclesiam sanctae Mariae; sed postmodum constructa ibidem ecclesia beatissimi apostolorum principis Petri, in eandem sunt eius ossa translata': ibid. It is, however, possible that Chad's church was at Stowe.

[5] H. Wharton, *Anglia Sacra*, i. 459. Stowe, and in particular St. Chad's Well to the west of the church, remained a sacred spot: *S.H.C.* 1924, p. 51; Leland, *Itin.* ed. L. Toulmin Smith, ii. 99; see above p. 137.

[6] Bede, *Hist. Eccles.* bk. iv, chap. iii; Wharton, *Anglia Sacra*, i. 428; Hester Jenkins, 'Lichfield Cathedral in the 14th Cent.' (Oxford Univ. B. Litt. thesis, 1956), i. 1–2.

[7] See above n. 4 and below n. 12.

[8] *V.C.H. Staffs.* iv. 41 (no. 70), 42 (nos. 75, 79), 50 (no. 168).

[9] See e.g. *S.H.C.* 1924, pp. 10, 51, 219–20, 246, 281–2, 285.

[10] Ibid. p. 281.

[11] The double dedication is attributed to Bp. Clinton ibid. pp. xxviii–xxix.

[12] Leland (*Itin.* ii. 101–2), who makes King Oswiu the founder of the cathedral, states that the original dedication was to St. Mary and St. Peter and that 'of far later times' the cathedral was rebuilt and rededicated to St. Mary and St. Chad.

[13] This was written by Alan of Ashbourne during the first half of the 14th cent.; it was published by Wharton in *Anglia Sacra*, i. 423 sqq. but wrongly ascribed to Thos. Chesterfield: see H. E. Savage, *The Lichfield Chronicles* (1915) and *The Book of Alan de Assheborn* (1922). These are two of a series of addresses by Dean Savage on the history of the cathedral given on St. Chad's Day (2 Mar.) 1913–34, and subsequently printed as pamphlets; there is a set in W.S.L. Pamphs. *sub* Lichfield.

[14] Wharton, *Anglia Sacra*, i. 431.

[15] Kathleen Edwards, *Eng. Secular Cathedrals in the Middle Ages* (1949 edn.), 4, 139.

[16] Ibid. 9.

[17] Dugdale, *Mon.* vi(3), 1242.

[18] Ibid.

[19] *V.C.H. Staffs.* iv. 42, no. 80.

[20] Edwards, *Eng. Secular Cath.* 5.

[21] See above p. 7.

[22] Wharton, *Anglia Sacra*, i. 444–5. The list obviously dates from the 13th cent.

[23] *V.C.H. Staffs.* iv. 41 (nos. 66, 67, 70), 42 (nos. 75, 79, 80).

[24] *V.C.H. Warws.* i. 302.

an earlier beginning of the prebendal system is to be seen in the tradition, found from the 13th century, that the holders of five prebends had the special duty of ministering at the high altar;[25] these prebends were named in the 16th century as Freeford, Stotfold, Longdon, Hansacre, and Weeford.[26] These are all places in or near Lichfield, and it is possible that the prebends were in existence by 1086 and were held by the five canons mentioned in Domesday Book; if so, they would provide a link between the early cathedral organization and the reconstituted chapter of the 12th century.

The date at which a full prebendal system was introduced at Lichfield is obscure. At Lincoln, Salisbury, and York this took place in the 1090s,[27] but it would be unwise to argue by analogy in the case of Lichfield as it is impossible to know the effects of the transference of the see to Chester and then to Coventry. The most likely theory is that a full prebendal system was created by Roger de Clinton in the 1130s when he reorganized the cathedral. Apart from the five possibly pre-Conquest prebends already mentioned, none of the prebends can be definitely dated to before 1130.[28] On the other hand the Lichfield Chronicle says that Roger de Clinton increased the number of prebends,[29] a statement which suggests that the prebendal system was in existence before his time. His eight new prebends, however, all consisted of the churches and tithes of manors in Warwickshire which had been granted to Coventry Priory on its foundation in 1043 and the administration of which had been taken over by Bishop Clinton.[30] Only one of these new prebends, Ufton, survived;[31] the remaining churches were presumably recovered by Coventry, probably by 1152.[32] It seems likely that the other prebends of whose foundation there is no evidence apart from the tradition that they were of Saxon origin were formed from churches and tithes on the bishop's estates in Staffordshire, Warwickshire, and Derbyshire at about the same time. These were Brewood, Bishopshull, Curborough, Eccleshall, Gaia, and Whittington and Berkswich in Staffordshire, Bishop's Itchington and Tachbrook in Warwickshire, and Sawley in Derbyshire.[33] A few additional prebends were formed during the later 12th century: Harborne was made a prebend about 1165,[34] and the prebend of Alrewas was presumably formed some time after the royal grant of the church to the cathedral and the bishop in the 1190s.[35]

Bishop Clinton reconstituted the cathedral chapter in the 1130s, forming a *collegium canonicorum* along the same lines as those founded at Lincoln, Salisbury, and York some forty years previously.[36] It has been suggested that his motive

in setting up a secular chapter at Lichfield was to obtain support against the monastic chapter at Coventry.[37] The new chapter was headed by four dignitaries, the usual 'four-square' constitution found in all English secular cathedrals by the late 12th and the 13th centuries. It has been questioned whether any Norman cathedral could have been the precise model for this sort of constitution, at least for those chapters formed in the late 11th century.[38] The Lichfield chapter, however, was based on that of the cathedral of Rouen, for Bishop Richard Peche (1161–82) ordered that 'the institutions of the church of Rouen, on which this church was originally modelled, so far as they are sound and possible, shall be strictly observed, both in choir and chapter, and in the degrees and dignities of the *personae* and the canons'.[39] The Rouen connexion may account for the fact that in the earliest statutes of the cathedral, drawn up in 1191,[40] the order of precedence of the four dignitaries differs from that of other English cathedrals, the Lichfield order being dean, precentor, treasurer, and chancellor.[41] By the mid 13th century, however, the order of treasurer and chancellor had been reversed to conform to the usual English practice.[42]

A dean of Lichfield, William, first appears about 1140 as a witness to the foundation charter of Farewell Priory; a fellow-witness was Odo, the treasurer.[43] The dignity of precentor is not mentioned by name until about 1177 when Bishop Peche granted the office to his clerk, Matthew; Matthew, however, succeeded Walter Durdent, the clerk and probably the kinsman of Bishop Durdent (1149–59), who in his turn had succeeded William de Vilers, Archdeacon of Chester.[44] The chancellor is first mentioned by name about 1200 when he was granted a messuage in the Close.[45] A subdean is found about 1165 when Bishop Peche constituted the prebend of Harborne for him.[46] The deanery was first endowed with lands and tithes from the bishop's estates, but in or just after 1176 Bishop Peche found that it was necessary to re-endow the deanery which had been 'ruined during the time of war'. He gave to it tithes in Lichfield, including a tithe of the fish from the bishop's ponds, a tithe of the farms of the archdeaconry of Derby, various pieces of land, and also the prebend of Brewood.[47] In 1192 these widely scattered endowments of land and tithes (with the exception of the prebend of Brewood) were replaced by the church of Adbaston which had previously been attached to the prebend of Eccleshall; in 1291 the deanery was worth £26 13s. 4d. a year.[48] The precentorship was endowed with the prebend of Bishop's Itchington, formed from property in Warwickshire belonging to Coventry Priory and

[25] Dugdale, *Mon.* vi(3), 1257.
[26] Muniments of Dean and Chapter of Lichfield (hereafter referred to as D. & C. Lich.), uncatalogued 17th-cent. misc. bk., loose-leaf note; Harwood, *Lichfield*, 267.
[27] Edwards, *Eng. Secular Cath.* 13.
[28] See, however, H. E. Savage, *The Prebendal System* (1921), 7–10, for an opposing view.
[29] Wharton, *Anglia Sacra*, i. 434.
[30] Ibid.; *S.H.C.* 1924, pp. 216–17; *Cod. Dipl.* ed. Kemble, iv, pp. 254, 273. The prebends were Priors Hardwick, Honington, Priors Marston, Offchurch, Wasperton, Southam, Ufton, and Holy Trinity, Coventry.
[31] By 1241 it had been divided into two prebends: D. & C. Lich., xiii, f.3. (The muniments of the D. & C. were catalogued by J. C. Cox in 1886; a summary of their contents was given by him in *S.H.C.* vi, pt. 2).
[32] *S.H.C.* 1924, pp. 126–7.

[33] Jenkins, 'Lich. Cath.' ii. 13–18.
[34] *S.H.C.* 1924, pp. 205–6.   [35] Ibid. p. 358.
[36] Dugdale, *Mon.* vi(3), 1242; Edwards, *Eng. Secular Cath.* 12.
[37] H. E. Savage, *The Chapter in the 12th Cent.* (1917), 13.
[38] Edwards, *Eng. Secular Cath.* 15.
[39] *S.H.C.* 1924, p. 13.
[40] See below.
[41] Dugdale, *Mon.* vi(3), 1256; *S.H.C.* 1924, p. xxvi.
[42] *S.H.C.* 1924, p. xxvi.
[43] Dugdale, *Mon.* iv. 111.
[44] *S.H.C.* 1924, pp. 82–83, 87.
[45] Ibid. p. 190.
[46] Ibid. pp. 205–6.
[47] Ibid. p. 240. For the property at Brewood see *V.C.H. Staffs.* v. 35, 40.
[48] *S.H.C.* 1924, p. 118; *Tax. Eccl.* (Rec. Com.), 243.

worth £40 in 1291.[49] The treasurer had the prebend of Sawley, in 1291 worth £66 13s. 4d. and the richest prebend in the cathedral.[50] The chancellor first held the prebend of Gaia, but by 1255 he had been given instead the richer prebend of Alrewas, worth £20 in 1291.[51]

The duties and privileges of the four dignitaries are described in the first statutes of the cathedral, dating from the episcopate of Bishop Nonant (1185–98). These, the earliest surviving statutes of any English cathedral, were probably drawn up by the dean and chapter for the bishop in 1191 when the establishment of a secular cathedral at Coventry necessitated a written statement of the Lichfield organization and customs to supply a model for the new cathedral.[52] In form the statutes follow closely Bishop Osmund's *Institutio* of 1091 for Salisbury and are very similar to the constitutional part of Richard le Poore's *Tractatus de Officiis* — it is possible that an earlier version of part of the *Tractatus* was lent to Lichfield in the 1190s.[53] The dean was entrusted with the direction and correction of the canons and vicars and had the right of visitation of the prebends and of the Lichfield city clergy. He was also in charge of the cathedral livings, and new prebendaries received their prebends from him and were assigned a stall by him.[54] The precentor was the deputy of the dean in choir, being in charge of the cathedral services, with the duty of instructing the *rectores chori* before every solemn festival. He was also responsible for choosing boys for the choir and for their *instructio et disciplina*. The duties of the treasurer are described in elaborate detail: he was the custodian of the treasures of the cathedral and responsible for the lighting of the church and for maintaining, through his deputy the sacrist, the supply of candles, bread, wine, incense, water, coals, and rushes. The chancellor was the legal and literary officer of the cathedral; he kept the seals and wrote the letters of the chapter and was also expected to run a school. He was also responsible for the standard of reading in services and had the right to preach as often as he wished in the cathedral, except on the two days a year reserved for the dean. The statutes make no mention of the archdeacons of the diocese, and at Lichfield, as at Hereford, no special place or precedence was ever assigned to the archdeacons in the choir or in the chapter-house unless they held prebends. The prebend of Bolton (Lancs.) was annexed permanently to the office of Archdeacon of Chester in 1253, but the archdeacons never lived within the Close for soon after the annexation took place they were assigned a house in Beacon Street by the dean and chapter.[55]

The 1191 statutes start with an outline of the daily services in the cathedral with the hours at which they were to be performed and variations in their sequence on different occasions.[56] There are very few details of the ritual involved, but there is frequent reference for details to the Consuetudinary and the Ordinal; these are in fact the earliest allusions in England to the Ordinal.[57] The section on services also contains some notes on the 'Representations', spectacular ceremonies which took place under the direction of the subchanter on the great festivals — 'as is contained in the books about these and other things'. The Ordinal of Rouen Cathedral contains full directions for three of these ceremonies: the Shepherds at Christmas, the Pilgrims at Easter (the scene at Emmaus), and the Nebulae at Whitsuntide. This is another indication of the connexion between Lichfield and Rouen.[58] At the end of the statutes is a long and detailed scheme for the ringing of the various bells which announced the different services; this section is peculiar to the Lichfield statutes.[59]

It is impossible to estimate how many canons were actually resident at the end of the 12th century; non-residence, however, was evidently becoming such a problem that sometimes there were not enough canons in residence to staff the cathedral properly. The rules of residence laid down at Archbishop Hubert Walter's legatine visitation of Lichfield in 1195 were designed to remedy this situation and are the earliest surviving statutes of residence for any English cathedral.[60] They laid down that each of the 22 canons should reside for a minimum of 3 months, or a quarter of the year. Each quarter was allotted to one of the 4 dignitaries and the rest of the canons were divided into four groups: 5 resided with the dean during the first *stadium* or quarter, beginning at Michaelmas; 5 with the precentor during the second quarter; 4 with the treasurer during the third quarter; and 4 with the chancellor during the fourth quarter. In this way at least 5 canons were always in residence. No canon was to be absent except on the business of the church or other necessary affairs, and any canon failing to keep his residence was to pay a fine totalling a fifth of the value of his prebend into the common fund. This elaborate system, very similar to one in force at Salisbury,[61] seems to have been difficult to put into practice from the first.[62]

The main reason for the growth of non-residence must have been the smallness of the common fund

[49] *S.H.C.* 1924, p. 87; *Tax. Eccl.* 241.
[50] Jenkins, 'Lich. Cath.' ii. 14; *Tax. Eccl.* 246. The prebend of Eccleshall, later divided (see below p. 144), was also worth £66 13s. 4d. in 1291: *Tax. Eccl.* 243.
[51] *S.H.C.* 1924, pp. 11, 17; *Tax. Eccl.* 243.
[52] H. E. Savage, *The Earliest Statutes of the Cathedral* (1920), 15–16.
[53] Ibid. 9; Edwards, *Eng. Secular Cath.* 54.
[54] Bp. Nonant's statutes are printed in Dugdale, *Mon.* vi(3), 1255–7. There is another edn., based on a 14th-cent. MS. in Lincoln Cathedral, in *Statutes of Lincoln Cathedral*, ed. H. Bradshaw and C. Wordsworth, ii (1), 11–25.
[55] Edwards, *Eng. Secular Cath.* 252, 255; *S.H.C.* 1924, pp. 57, 314.
[56] Dugdale, *Mon.* vi(3), 1255.
[57] Savage, *Earliest Statutes*, 7. The packing leaves of the original binding of the 14th-cent. *Magnum Registrum Album* are from a discarded missal in which the form of services does not correspond in certain features with any of the known English Uses: *S.H.C.* 1924, p. xxv; and see below p. 146.
[58] Savage, *Earliest Statutes*, 8. During the Nebulae light wheaten cakes were scattered from the triforium into the choir. It has been suggested that the 'Shrewsbury Fragments', a single actor's part for 3 church plays (*The Non-Cycle Mystery Plays* (E.E.T.S. Extra Ser. civ), 1–7), may be extracts from a 13th- or 14th-cent. version of the Lichfield 'Representations': W. L. Smoldon, 'Liturgical Drama', *New Oxford Hist. of Music*, ii. 189; E. D. Mackerness, *Social Hist. of Eng. Music*, 25, 26.
[59] Savage, *Earliest Statutes*, 10. Some further statutes following this section are ascribed to Nonant in Dugdale, *Mon.* vi(3), 1267, but are really part of Bp. Pattishall's code of statutes: Savage, *Earliest Statutes*, 10–12.
[60] They are printed in Wilkins, *Concilia*, i. 501.
[61] *V.C.H. Wilts.* iii. 162.
[62] See below p. 145.

at Lichfield. The chapter had accumulated very little communal property by the end of the 12th century. Bishop Clinton had endowed it with 'churches, tithes, lands, and other property', its possession of which was confirmed by successive popes;[63] and in 1149 King Stephen restored to it the church of Gnosall which it had held under Henry I — the sale of Gnosall prebends helped to augment the common fund.[64] Bishop Richard Peche found that the common fund had been reduced to nothing, and to augment it he ordered that when a prebend fell vacant the dean and chapter should appoint a keeper who would apply its revenues to the common fund for a year. The same bishop confirmed to the chapter a number of endowments which consisted largely of small rent-charges in money or goods on the bishop's property.[65] Many grants to the chapter during this century were of the same sort, such as the grant of lands by the bishop to his steward in the 1150s in return for an annual payment of 4s. for the lighting of the high altar of the cathedral.[66] There were also some gifts by individuals, such as the grant of a burgage in Lichfield to the common fund by Peter Giffard in 1176.[67] The chapter in the 1160s and 1170s also successfully defended its right to part of the revenues of two churches, Bradley and Shenstone, of which it had been deprived by the religious houses of Stone and Osney (Oxon.).[68] In the 1170s two more churches were appropriated to the common fund: Adam and Sybil de Port gave the chapter their church of Arley (now in Worcs.), and Robert Marmion gave it his church of Thornton (Lincs.).[69] The most important donations to the common fund, however, did not begin until the 1190s.[70]

Of the cathedral buildings little definite is known before the rebuilding in the 13th century. The Saxon cathedral, consecrated in 700,[71] was replaced after the Conquest. Bishop Robert de Limesey (1085–1117) is said to have used money obtained from Coventry for *magnas aedificationes* at Lichfield;[72] his successor, Robert Peche (1121–6), is also said to have been *magnarum apud Licetfeld edificationum inchoator*.[73] The Norman cathedral was probably completed by Bishop Clinton, *qui ecclesiam Lichesfeldensem erexit tam in fabrica quam in honore*.[74] During the 19th-century restoration of the cathedral the foundations of the Norman church were discovered under the choir.[75] This church originally had an apse with an ambulatory at the east end and probably one or more radiating chapels; a square-ended chapel, 38 feet long and 21 feet wide, was added to the east end of the apse in the mid 12th

century, probably in the time of Bishop Clinton. In the course of the 12th-century rebuilding a deep moat was dug on three sides of the Close, and the excavations probably provided stone for the new cathedral.[76] A further rebuilding of the choir and the tower crossing probably began during the last years of the 12th century.[77]

The Thirteenth Century

The 1190s marked the end of the period of reconstruction of cathedral life begun by Bishop Clinton, and the 13th century was the time of the most rapid advance in the cathedral's history. The chapter grew in wealth, independence, and influence. The number of prebends was increased, there was a succession of important donations to the common fund, and the chapter acquired several pensions. There were some important developments in the organization of the chapter, which in this period asserted both its right to take part in the election of the bishop and its independence of him. The 13th century also saw the emergence of minor corporations in the cathedral and the beginning of the complete rebuilding of the church.

The prebend of Wolvey was formed about 1200 by Bishop Muschamp.[78] Bishop Stavensby founded the prebend of Wellington (Salop.) in 1232,[79] and when he annexed Burton-in-Wirral (Ches.), a prebend *ab antiquo*, to his new hospital for the shipwrecked at Denhall (Ches.) in the early 1230s, he created in its place a prebend from the church of Tarvin (Ches.).[80] Prees (Salop.), also known as Pipa Minor, became a prebend soon after 1235.[81] Bishop Pattishall formed the prebends of Colwich and Meresbury (Ches.) in 1241; the latter apparently had only one holder and then lapsed.[82] The two Warwickshire prebends of Bobenhull and Ryton were founded in 1248 after the churches had been granted to Bishop Weseham (1245–56) by the Prior of Coventry.[83] Bolton (Lancs.), the prebend attached to the Archdeaconry of Chester, was formed in 1253 after the church had been given to the bishop by Mattersey Priory (Notts.).[84] In addition the two small prebends of Dernford and Dasset Parva (Warws.) were in existence by 1255.[85]

The confirmation in 1255 by Bishop Weseham to the chapter of all its existing prebendal endowments marks the virtual end of the construction of the prebendal system at Lichfield. In 1255 there were 26 prebends with endowments of churches or land, and an additional 3 'bursarial' prebends.[86]

[63] *S.H.C.* 1924, pp. 128, 214–15.
[64] Ibid. pp. 79, 80.
[65] Ibid. pp. 13, 165.
[66] Ibid. pp. 146–7.
[67] Ibid. p. 53.
[68] Ibid. p. 79; see below p. 241. By 1223 the share in Bradley had passed to the Stafford family, who compensated the church of Lichfield with a pension: *S.H.C.* 1924, p. 15.
[69] *S.H.C.* 1924, pp. 152, 247.
[70] See below p. 146.
[71] See above p. 140.
[72] Wharton, *Anglia Sacra*, i. 445.
[73] William of Malmesbury, *De Gestis Pontificum Anglorum* (Rolls Ser.), 311.
[74] Wharton, *Anglia Sacra*, i. 434.
[75] R. Willis, 'On Foundations of Early Buildings recently discovered in Lichfield Cathedral', *Arch. Jnl.* vol. xviii, no. lxix. In 1932 the remains of a Saxon bishop's throne and

of a Norman font were unearthed in the Close: *S.H.C.* 1931, 272–4.
[76] *V.C.H. Staffs.* ii. 185.
[77] Savage, *Chapter in the 12th Cent.* 20; A. R. Dufty, 'Lichfield Cathedral', *Arch. Jnl.* cxx. 294 and plan facing (reproduced from *The Builder*, 7 Feb. 1891).
[78] Wharton, *Anglia Sacra*, i. 436; Jenkins, 'Lich. Cath.' ii. 19.
[79] R. W. Eyton, *Antiquities of Shropshire*, ix. 51–53.
[80] Wharton, *Anglia Sacra*, i. 446; *S.H.C.* 1924, pp. 342–3. The modern spelling of the prebend, which will be used hereafter, is Tervin.
[81] Savage, *Prebendal System*, 12.
[82] Ibid. 11, 12.
[83] Ibid. 12.
[84] *S.H.C.* 1924, pp. 237–8, 314. Mattersey retained the advowson of the church.
[85] Jenkins, 'Lich. Cath.' ii. 15.
[86] *S.H.C.* 1924, p. 11.

These latter were formed by Bishop Stavensby and were in the nature of retaining fees for suitable canons until a full prebend should fall vacant.[87] At first the stipends of 3 or 4 marks were paid from the bishop's own purse; under Weseham they were paid from the Peter's pence collected in the Archdeaconry of Derby.[88] Bishop Meuland (1257–95) replaced the bursarial prebends by the three normal prebends of Sandiacre (Derb.), Flixton (Lancs.), and Pipa Parva.[89] The chapter was not anxious to accept these additional prebends, fearing that the new canons might become a charge on the common fund; Meuland therefore agreed that the three new prebendaries should not be allowed to go into residence until they had arranged to augment the common fund by £40 a year each.[90] The chapter was eventually forced to agree to Meuland's request that the holders of the three new prebends should be admitted before the augmentation was carried out, but these were the last new prebends to be constituted.[91] There were a few changes in the existing prebends; Meresbury lapsed,[92] and in 1279 Harborne was assigned to the common fund.[93] Two other prebends were divided: Gaia into Gaia Major and Gaia Minor before 1279,[94] and Eccleshall into Eccleshall (later sometimes called Johnson) and Offley in 1332.[95]

After this final division there were 32 prebends in the cathedral.[96] In 1535 their combined value was under £400, much less than that of other, larger cathedrals; at Salisbury, for example, the deanery alone was worth over £200 in 1535.[97] The Lichfield prebends then ranged in value from Sawley, worth £56 13s. 4d., to Dasset Parva, worth 3s. 4d. Only three were worth £40 and above, five were worth between £20 and £40, eight between £10 and £20, and the rest under £10. There were two types of prebend. The first, of which there were 24, consisted of appropriated parishes, from which the prebendary received the tithes and other income and where he often had peculiar jurisdiction. The second type consisted solely of property, partly land and partly tithes; of these there were eight, seven of them endowed from land and tithes in Lichfield and carrying with them responsibilities in the city churches.

The members of the 12th-century chapter are shadowy figures who usually occur as mere names in lists of witnesses to charters. With the 13th century, however, it is possible to discover something more about the personnel of the cathedral. Most of the elements which are regarded as typical of medieval secular chapters can be found at Lichfield.[98] Royal clerks and officials were granted prebends and dignities in the cathedral. Thus in 1214 Ralph Nevill, a royal clerk and later Bishop of Chichester and Chancellor of England, was nominated to the vacant deanery by the king;[99] in 1223 Luke des Roches, chaplain of Hubert de Burgh, was granted the chancellorship;[1] Thomas Wymondham, who became Treasurer of England in 1265, was precentor of the cathedral in 1241 and held the post until his death in 1278.[2] In addition other canons are described as king's clerks — notably John of Derby, an influential royal clerk who was elected dean in 1280 and who in 1282 is found going abroad on the king's business.[3] Ralph de Hengham, the judge, occurs as a canon in 1286 and gave some vestments to the cathedral;[4] both Anthony Bek (d. 1311) and his brother Thomas (d. 1293) were canons in 1280.[5] Some canons acquired places in the chapter through their services to the bishop: among them was Richard of Gloucester, who after being the official of Bishop Stavensby became Archdeacon of Coventry and successively chancellor and treasurer of the cathedral.[6] Richard was only one of a contingent of secular clerks from Gloucester who held prebends or dignities at Lichfield in the earlier years of the 13th century. This link with Gloucester seems to have been begun by Alexander de Swereford, the notable Exchequer official and a chaplain to Bishop Cornhill, who in 1235 resigned his prebend at Lichfield in favour of his nephew, Simon of Gloucester.[7] Compared with other cathedrals Lichfield seems to have had few connexions with the schools and universities in the 12th and 13th centuries, though the canonist Simon of Southwell, who became treasurer in 1203, had lectured at Bologna, Paris, and probably Oxford, Dean Sempringham had been Chancellor of Oxford, and Luke of Ely, who became chancellor in 1292, was a distinguished Oxford theologian. Alfredus Anglicus de Sareshel, author of a treatise 'De motu cordis' and translator of at least two works from the Arabic, probably held a prebend at Lichfield in the early 13th century.[8]

From the sparse records which survive of the activities of the chapter in the 13th century there emerge some figures who played important parts in the development of the cathedral but whose activities were confined to Lichfield. Outstanding among these was William of Mancetter, the first elected dean and one of the most notable men to have held the office.[9] Others were Ralph of Chaddesden, treasurer (c. 1259–c. 1276) and a great mediator in disputes, who in 1276 bequeathed £100 for the development (promocio) of the cathedral,[10] and Ralph de Lacok (d. 1257), the last subdean to be found at Lichfield and

[87] Savage, *Prebendal System*, 14.
[88] *S.H.C.* 1924, p. 343. [89] Ibid. p. 242. [90] Ibid.
[91] Savage, *Prebendal System*, 14–15; *S.H.C.* 1924, pp. 242, 301–2.
[92] Savage, *Prebendal System*, 11.
[93] *S.H.C.* 1924, pp. 22–24.
[94] Savage, *Prebendal System*, 11.
[95] Ibid.; *Ecclesiastical Documents* (Camden Soc. viii(2)), 73–74.
[96] For this para. see Jenkins, 'Lich. Cath.' i. 160–70.
[97] *V.C.H. Wilts.* iii. 182 n. 82.
[98] For the system at Salisbury see ibid. 161–2.
[99] *D.N.B.*; *S.H.C.* 1924, p. 341.
[1] *Pat. R.* 1216–25, 386; *S.H.C.* 1939, 5.
[2] *S.H.C.* 1924, pp. 29–30, 54; Le Neve, *Fasti* (1854 edn.), i. 578; *Handbk. of Brit. Chron.* 100.
[3] *Cal. Pat.* 1281–92, 12; Jenkins, 'Lich. Cath.' ii, App. F.
[4] *Radulphi de Hengham Summae*, ed. W. H. Dunham Jr.,

p. xlix; *S.H.C.* vi(1), 165; ibid. vi(2), 209; ibid. 1924, p. 334.
[5] See below p. 147. Anthony was Bp. of Durham 1283–1311; Thomas was Bp. of St. David's 1280–93.
[6] *S.H.C.* 1939, 6.
[7] Ibid.; *Cal. Pat.* 1232–47, 75, 106, 120. For Swereford see *D.N.B.*
[8] S. Kuttner and Eleanor Rathbone, 'Anglo-Norman Canonists of the 12th Cent.' *Traditio*, vii. 317–21, 326–7; *S.H.C.* 1939, 23; Jenkins, 'Lich. Cath.' ii, App. F; A. B. Emden, *Biog. Reg. of Univ. of Oxford to A.D. 1500*, iii. 1669; J. C. Russell, *Dict. of Writers of 13th Cent. Eng.* (1936 edn.), 18–19. The first and last of these references have been supplied by Dr. Rathbone.
[9] See below p. 145; H. E. Savage, *William de Mancetter, Dean* (1921).
[10] *S.H.C.* 1924, p. xxxv; H. E. Savage, *A Cathedral Library* (1934), 18.

a man active in the service of the cathedral for over 25 years.[11]

Information about developments within the chapter during the 13th century comes mainly from two sets of statutes: those of Bishop Pattishall, dated 1241, and those of Bishop Meuland, dated 1294.[12] In spite of the increase in the number of prebends non-residence continued to be a problem. In 1224 it seems that certain canons were avoiding their terms of residence by a subterfuge (*dissimulacione*), and Bishop Stavensby reinforced the penalties imposed by Archbishop Walter.[13] In 1241 Bishop Pattishall repeated the residence regulations in his code of statutes, fitting the prebends created since 1191 into the scheme and setting out the amount of the fine to be levied for non-residence from each prebend.[14] Each canon was allowed to take up to 30 days' leave during his term of residence, thus reducing each *stadium* to two months only. The scheme was given flexibility by the provision that any canon could reside for the whole year, or for half the year, if he wished. Hubert Walter's regulations appear for the last time in the statutes of Bishop Meuland;[15] when the statutes were revised in the 16th century all references to the scheme were removed. In fact the system seems to have been unworkable from the start, and the usual practice was for certain canons to reside the whole year, although occasionally they would be joined by other canons residing only for one quarter or two.[16] Until the act books begin in the 14th century it is impossible to know how many canons were usually in residence; the number of canons witnessing 13th-century charters ranges from between three or four to nearly twenty and is probably not a reliable guide to the numbers of canons in residence.[17]

The most important constitutional development in the 13th century was the establishment by the chapter of its right to elect a dean. The first deans were probably appointed by the bishop,[18] but when Richard of Dalham died in 1214 the see was vacant. King John claimed the right to nominate and sent his legate to see that his clerk, Ralph Nevill, was appointed. The chapter had already discussed the election of a dean but agreed to accept the king's choice on condition that it did not prejudice the chapter's right of election in the future.[19] A few years later it obtained from Bishop Cornhill a charter granting it the right to elect its own dean in perpetuity.[20] In 1222 the chapter exercised its new privilege for the first time when William of Mancetter was elected dean,[21] and the right of election was exercised without interruption until 1325.[22]

Under William of Mancetter the office of dean became more powerful. In the statutes of Bishop Pattishall, which were probably drafted by Dean Mancetter himself, the importance of the office was stressed: in the cathedral the dean was second only to the bishop — all were to rise when he entered the church or the chapter. He exercised archidiaconal jurisdiction in the cathedral, the city of Lichfield, the prebendal parishes, and the parishes of the common fund churches.[23] In the statutes of Bishop Meuland 50 years later it was laid down that the dean had the right to visit prebendal churches every three years with a 'reasonable' train — about ten horsemen.[24] In both sets of statutes it was laid down that the dean should be in residence for the whole year; the other dignitaries need keep only their quarterly residence.[25] According to Meuland's statutes the dean was also to receive double commons while he was in residence — the bishop too was to have double commons when in the city.[26]

At Lichfield daily commons seem to have been paid wholly in money rather than partly in kind from at least the 1240s.[27] Under Bishop Pattishall the rate of commons was 4*d.* daily to each residentiary, 6*d.* on feast days, 12*d.* on solemn feast days, and 5*s.* at Christmas, the feast of St. Chad, Easter, and the Assumption.[28] Fifty years later Bishop Meuland raised the daily commons, which were then 6*d.*, to 12*d.*, with 2*s.* on solemn feast days and 10*s.* on the four principal feasts.[29] The common fund was managed by one or two canons elected by the chapter at Michaelmas. These communars were forbidden to convert the money of the chapter to their own use or to lend it without permission. They had to render a yearly account to the chapter, and any surplus after the payment of commons and other expenses was to be divided among the resident canons according to the number of quarters during which they had been in residence.[30] The common fund met the expenses of lawsuits dealing with the property of the cathedral, but the expenses of any case involving only a prebend had to be paid by the prebendary concerned.[31]

From at least the end of the 13th century the resident chapter met every Friday morning. The dean had to give a day's notice of any other meeting of the chapter, unless the business was extremely urgent.[32] Provision was made in Meuland's statutes for the appointment of a chapter clerk to write the chapter's letters under the supervision of the chancellor and to deal with legal business on behalf of the dean and chapter; he was to be paid a salary from the common fund.[33] There was also to be a chest for the common seal and the *privilegia* of the chapter; keys to it were to be held by the four dignitaries.[34] The statutes of 1241 are concerned more with directing the services of the cathedral

[11] *S.H.C.* 1924, p. xxxv; and see below p. 279.
[12] D. & C. Lich., xiii, f.5. This vol. contains the portions of statutes, including date clauses, omitted in the 16th-cent. revision. Dugdale, *Mon.* vi(3), 1257, wrongly attributes part of Pattishall's set to Bp. Nonant: see above n. 59.
[13] *S.H.C.* 1924, p. 209.
[14] D. & C. Lich., xiii, f.3. The fines ranged from 7 marks from Sawley to 5*s.* from Bishopshull.
[15] Ibid. f.5.
[16] Jenkins, 'Lich. Cath.' i. 72.
[17] See e.g. *S.H.C.* 1924, pp. 312–13.
[18] Wharton, *Anglia Sacra*, i. 437.
[19] *S.H.C.* 1924, p. 341.
[20] Ibid. p. 166. The charter was confirmed by the Pope in 1221: ibid. p. 208.
[21] Wharton, *Anglia Sacra*, i. 437.

[22] Jenkins, 'Lich. Cath.' i. 47. Lichfield was one of the last secular cathedrals to secure the right of electing its own dean: Edwards, *Eng. Secular Cath.* 122.
[23] Dugdale, *Mon.* vi(3), 1257. For the attribution of the statute to Pattishall see n. 12 above.
[24] Dugdale, *Mon.* vi(3), 1260.
[25] Ibid.; D. & C. Lich., xiii, f.3.
[26] Dugdale, *Mon.* vi(3), 1260.
[27] See Edwards, *Eng. Secular Cath.* 44–45.
[28] D. & C. Lich., xiii, f.3v.
[29] Wharton, *Anglia Sacra*, i. 447; Dugdale, *Mon.* vi(3), 1260.
[30] Dugdale, *Mon.* vi(3), 1261.
[31] Ibid. 1260.
[32] Ibid. 1261.
[33] Ibid.
[34] Ibid. 1260.

than with the workings of the chapter. The ceremony for admitting and installing a new canon is described and the order of stalls in the choir is given. Instructions are also given for movements in the choir during the daily services and for the wearing of the appropriately coloured copes on the various feast days. The saints' days which were to be specially observed at Lichfield are listed and details of services on feast days given.[35] All this went to make up the Use of Lichfield.

Between 1190 and 1220 the chapter was given several important churches. In 1192 Bishop Nonant granted those of Cannock and Rugeley to the common fund; he had been sold the manors and churches by Richard I three years previously.[36] In 1535 the two churches were worth £32 a year.[37] Also in 1192 John, Count of Mortain (later King John), gave the chapter the Derbyshire church of Bakewell, on condition that it should always be served by three priests and that the chapter should appoint a priest-prebendary to say a daily mass for the king's well-being and in due course for the king's soul.[38] John also gave Bishop Nonant the neighbouring church of Hope with the chapel of Tideswell to be assigned either to the church of Coventry or to that of Lichfield. Bishop Muschamp granted to the Lichfield chapter, 'considering the extreme meagreness of the common fund', 20 marks a year from Hope and its chapelries for the provision of ale. About 1220 Bishop Cornhill granted Hope and Tideswell outright to the chapter 'to provide commons of bread and ale'.[39] Bakewell, Hope, and Tideswell, known collectively as the Peak parishes,[40] were the chapter's most valuable possession; in 1535 they and their thirteen chapels[41] were worth over £200 a year, nearly half the total revenue of the chapter.[42] In the 1280s Edward I tried to take back the advowson of Bakewell but was finally persuaded that his claim was false — at a cost to the chapter of 1,000 marks.[43] The common fund acquired another Derbyshire church in 1290 when Bishop Meuland granted it Kniveton, formerly a chapelry of Ashbourne.[44] A further Staffordshire church, Dilhorne, had been appropriated to the fund by at least 1272.[45]

Thus most of the chapter's income came from appropriated churches. The usual procedure with the churches of the common fund, and with many of the prebends, was the appointment of a farmer, who might be one of the canons. The farmer collected the chapter's share of the tithes and held the rectory lands in return for an annual rent and the duty of keeping the church and rectory buildings in repair. The chapter ordained a vicarage in many of the prebends and appropriated parishes and gave the vicar an income independent of the farm;[46] the farmer was, however, often the vicar himself. Where there was no vicar, it was usual for the farmer to appoint a chaplain. Included in the statutes of

Bishop Meuland were several regulations about the granting of farms. Whoever held a farm, whether a canon or not, was to have a five-year lease only. This could be renewed by five-year terms to a limit of 20 years, but no lease was to be renewed at a loss. The lease was to be withdrawn if the farmer did not pay his rent promptly, and the farmer was to keep the buildings in proper repair. No farmer was to have jurisdiction of any sort.[47] These regulations were probably the result of papal action: in about the 1280s the Dean of Salisbury was ordered to investigate allegations that the Lichfield chapter had been leasing its property, under pressure and at serious loss, to various clerks and laymen for life or for long terms, or even in fee farm.[48]

The Peak parishes provide an example of one of these long leases. In the earlier 13th century the chapter leased to Robert of Lexington, the judge and a prebendary of Southwell (Notts.), the churches of Bakewell and Hope, with all their appurtenances except the chapel of Tideswell, for life at a rent of 125 marks.[49] Subsequently the lease was transferred to Robert's brother, Henry, who surrendered it when he became Bishop of Lincoln in 1254.[50] The chapter evidently continued the policy of farming out Bakewell and Hope;[51] in Tideswell, however, it seems to have employed a proctor to collect its revenues.[52]

The Peak parishes were the cause of almost continuous litigation during the 13th century. In 1113 William Peverel, an illegitimate son of the Conqueror, had given to the newly founded priory of Lenton (Notts.) two-thirds of the tithes of various lordships including Bakewell and Tideswell, two-thirds of the tithes of pasture in the lordship of the Peak, and various other tithes. Under Henry II the Peverel estates escheated and were given to the Count of Mortain; the churches of Bakewell, Hope, and Tideswell had passed into the hands of the chapter by the early 1220s.[53] The subsequent disputes centred on three issues: the extent of the lordship of William Peverel, whether he had the right to grant tithes of land not under cultivation in his lifetime, and how far the charters of the Count of Mortain overrode those of William Peverel.[54] By the 1220s there was already a 'long-standing controversy' between the chapter and the priory about the tithes of Bakewell. A composition was then made by which the priory was to have two-thirds of the tithes from land then or afterwards cultivated within the former demesne of William Peverel and two-thirds of the tithes of lead; the remaining third of both tithes was to go to the dean and chapter.[55]

There were occasional disagreements after this settlement,[56] and in 1250 a major dispute broke out again. In that year the chapter complained that the monks of Lenton had seized its tithes of wool and lambs in Tideswell, and the following year it

---

[35] Ibid. 1258–9.
[36] S.H.C. 1924, pp. 8, 359; V.C.H. Staffs. v. 53, 154, 162.
[37] Valor Eccl. (Rec. Com.), iii. 132.
[38] S.H.C. 1924, pp. 60, 210.   [39] Ibid. pp. 211–13.
[40] Tideswell became a separate parish c. 1254: Jenkins, 'Lich. Cath.' ii. 10.
[41] Listed ibid. 11.
[42] Valor Eccl. iii. 133, 134.
[43] S.H.C. 1924, pp. 60–61; Cal. Pat. 1281–92, 67.
[44] J. C. Cox, Notes on the Churches of Derbs. ii. 596–7.
[45] Jenkins, 'Lich. Cath.' ii. 8.
[46] See e.g. the ordination of Rugeley vicarage in 1276: S.H.C. 1924, p. 43.

[47] Dugdale, Mon. vi(3), 1261.
[48] S.H.C. 1924, p. 136. In particular complaints were made about leases in the prebend of Harborne.
[49] Ibid. pp. 58–59.
[50] S.H.C. vi(2), 18; S.H.C. 1924, p. 34.
[51] S.H.C. vi(2), 18–19.
[52] J. C. Cox, 'Ancient Documents relating to Tithes in the Peak', Jnl. Derb. Arch. Soc. v. 156.
[53] Ibid. 129–30; see above.
[54] Jnl. Derb. Arch. Soc. v. 130.
[55] S.H.C. 1924, pp. 123–4.
[56] Ibid. pp. 62–63.

ordered the sheep to be folded in the church for safety. The monks broke into the church and took away some of the lambs by force; during the fight some of the chapter's servants were wounded and the church was polluted with blood.[57] The chapter appealed to the Pope, and with the help of two papal commissioners an agreement was reached in 1253. The priory was to return what had been wrongly taken and to pay the chapter 100 marks in four half-yearly instalments to cover damages and expenses. The chapter was to have all the tithes in Tideswell, except two-thirds of the tithe on lead and the tithes of the stud-farm and chase in the parish. The former agreement on tithes in Bakewell and Hope was to stand, but the chapter was to give the priory 14 marks of its yearly share of these tithes, and the priory was to receive in future two-thirds of the tithes on newly-cultivated land.[58]

In the 1270s the chapter was complaining that this agreement was very disadvantageous to it and petitioned the Pope to cancel it.[59] In 1278 a band of 35 men led by a Lichfield canon, William Wymondham, was accused of seizing the tithes of the priory stored at Bakewell and of raiding the prior's house at Haddon; Wymondham and one of the Bakewell chaplains were seized by the Sheriff of Nottinghamshire and imprisoned for a while.[60] In 1280 Anthony Bek and his brother Thomas, both canons of Lichfield, negotiated a new agreement. Under the terms of this the arrangement of 1253 was confirmed, the priory was to pay 75 marks owing to the chapter and an additional sum of 280 marks, and was also to give to Lichfield half the advowson of Handsworth church.[61] This agreement remained in force for the rest of the Middle Ages, although the division of tithes on newly-cultivated land occasionally caused fresh disputes.[62]

During the 13th century the chapter was also involved in years of litigation with Halesowen Abbey (Worcs.) over the right of presentation to the church of Harborne[63] and with the collegiate church of Penkridge over the church of Cannock.[64]

Much of the chapter's income was made up of annual pensions from churches which had been appropriated to religious houses. Before the bishop could allow any church to be appropriated, the permission of the Lichfield and Coventry chapters had to be obtained; the price of this permission was often a pension to both chapters. The earliest example of the acquisition of a pension by the chapter is in the 1170s when the chapter challenged the appropriation of the church of Shenstone to Osney Abbey and was awarded a pension of 10s. a year from the church.[65] Most of the chapter's pensions, however, were acquired in the 13th century: £10 from Dunchurch (Warws.) in 1229,[66] £6 13s. 4d. from Abbots Bromley a few years later,[67] and £10

from Leamington Hastings (Warws.) in 1232.[68] Three other pensions were to cause much litigation in the 14th century: a grant by the bishop in 1231 of 25s., raised to 24 marks in 1248, from the rich church of Winwick (Lancs.) to supplement the 'inadequate resources' of the common fund;[69] a pension acquired in 1248 from the church of Southam (Warws.) which was not appropriated but whose rector was under obligation to pay £20 a year;[70] and 20 marks from Aston (Warws.) granted in 1253.[71] Three more pensions were acquired in the 13th century: 10 marks from Mayfield by 1255,[72] 10 marks from Stowe-by-Chartley in 1278 to augment the common fund,[73] and £2 from Alspath (Warws.) by 1291.[74]

The growing power and influence of the Lichfield chapter is shown most clearly by its successful assertion of its right to a share in the election of the bishop.[75] Its long feud with the Coventry chapter centred on the status of the Lichfield chapter after the see was transferred first to Chester and then to Coventry. Lichfield did not claim the sole right of election but only an equal voice with Coventry; the monks of Coventry denied that the canons had the right to any representation at all. The first evidence of a dispute occurs in 1149, when Walter Durdent became bishop. It continued until 1228 when the canons' persistence was finally rewarded. Gregory IX then decreed that all future elections should be made jointly by Lichfield and Coventry — the first to take place at Coventry with both chapters sitting together, the next at Lichfield, and so on alternately. The Prior of Coventry was to have the first vote in each election. This judgement was a notable victory for Lichfield, since at the beginning of the struggle it seemed to have little chance against the richer and more influential Coventry. A further refinement was added in 1255 when it was agreed that at future elections the two chapters should be reckoned equal in number, even though one might in fact be more numerous than the other.

During most of the 13th century the chapter's relations with the bishop were cordial. No prebend was attached to the bishopric, so that the bishop was not a regular member of the chapter. He had the right, however, of choosing and instituting the canons and of making statutes in conjunction with the chapter.[76] He was also occasionally called in to settle a dispute: in 1264 he mediated between the chapter and the priory of St. Thomas near Stafford in a controversy over tithes,[77] and in 1279 he tried to settle a quarrel between the chapter and one of the canons.[78] The chapter was not, however, prepared to allow the bishop the right of visitation, either of the chapter itself or of its prebends and common fund churches. Coventry Priory finally acknowledged the bishop's right of visitation in 1283 after a dispute lasting 50 years.[79] There may

[57] *Jnl. Derb. Arch. Soc.* v. 131, 146–7.
[58] *S.H.C.* 1924, pp. 67–70.
[59] Ibid. p. 124.
[60] Ibid. p. 122.
[61] Ibid. pp. 119–22.
[62] Jenkins, 'Lich. Cath.' i. 122.
[63] *S.H.C.* 1924, pp. 23–24, 81–82, 135–6, 171.
[64] See below pp. 299, 300.
[65] *Cartulary of Oseney Abbey, vol. v* (Oxford Hist. Soc. xcviii), 68, 69–70.
[66] Dugdale, *Warws.* i. 284.
[67] *S.H.C.* 1924, p. 213.
[68] Ibid. p. 227.
[69] Ibid. pp. 226, 228.

[70] Ibid. pp. 111–12.
[71] Dugdale, *Warws.* ii. 873–4.
[72] *S.H.C.* 1924, p. 11.
[73] Ibid. pp. 155–6, 311–12, 322–3. The pension is wrongly given as £10 in *Tax. Eccl.* (Rec. Com.), 242.
[74] *Tax. Eccl.* 242. In 1535 the vicars choral were receiving a pension of £1 from Alspath: *Valor Eccl.* (Rec. Com.), iii. 136.
[75] For a detailed account of the struggle between Lichfield and Coventry see above pp. 8–14.
[76] Dugdale, *Mon.* vi(3), 1256, 1258.
[77] *S.H.C.* 1924, p. 137.
[78] Ibid. pp. 22–23.
[79] Ibid. pp. 224, 305–6.

have been a similar attempt to visit the Lichfield chapter during this period. In the 1240s the chapter was trying to find out whether any of the other secular cathedrals were visited by their bishops,[80] and the agreement about visitation between the Bishop of Lincoln and his dean and chapter in 1261 was entered in Lichfield's Great Register.[81] The problem of visitation did not, however, come to a head until the 14th century. No resistance was shown to the occasional visitations of the Archbishop of Canterbury; when Archbishop Pecham fulminated in 1280 against the provision made by the chapter for the spiritual care of Bakewell, the chapter simply ignored his ordinance as illegal. One of the conditions of a compact made with the parishioners of Bakewell in 1315 was that Pecham's ordinance should be declared void.[82] The only serious dispute between the bishop and the chapter during the 13th century concerned the extent of the bishop's jurisdiction over the canons' tenants in the city of Lichfield, and this was settled amicably by arbitration in 1252.[83]

The 13th century saw the development of bodies of lesser clergy in the cathedral. Vicars were first mentioned in the statutes of Hugh de Nonant when non-residence of canons was already becoming a problem.[84] Bishop Meuland's statute in the 1290s that every canon, whether resident or not, was to appoint a vicar merely enforced a *consuetudinem diutius usitatam*;[85] in the 1240s it was laid down that any canon who had no vicar was to pay the equivalent of a vicar's salary to the chapter.[86] The first statutes for the vicars were made in 1241.[87] All the vicars were to be continuously resident in Lichfield and were not to be absent from services on pain of expulsion; one of them was to be appointed to note the absences and defects of his fellows. Five at least were to be priests; these were the vicars of the five canons who had the traditional duty of ministering at the high altar.[88] Those with duties at the high altar were to be entered on the weekly table of services and were to receive a fee of 6d. from the hebdomadary. In addition to the vicars who were priests there were a number of secular clerks, known as 'clerk vikars', whose duties were to attend mass *sine murmure et chachinno* and to sing anthems at services with *cantationibus dulcibus, sine organis* on feast days.[89] These vicars were to be paid a salary of at least 20s. a year by their canons and were, according to custom, to be paid quarterly; vicars who were priests were to be paid higher salaries.[90] In addition the vicars received daily commons, evidently 1d. a day,[91] from the chapter; their commons were paid twice a day, apparently according to attendance at services.[92]

Each new vicar was presented to the dean by his canon and tested in reading and singing by the precentor; in 1294 it was necessary to order that new vicars should not be forced to make gifts to the other vicars.[93] There is little evidence that the vicars led an organized common life before the 14th century; the chapter, however, is said to have assigned them a house in the 1240s,[94] and under Bishop Meuland a house at Stowe was set apart for old and infirm vicars.[95] The subchanter, one of the two leading vicars, had a house of his own in the city during the 13th century.[96] The subchanter and the other leading vicar, the sacrist, are both mentioned in the earliest statutes of the cathedral. The subchanter was the precentor's deputy and in his absence had the task of arranging all cathedral services, as well as the special duty, peculiar to Lichfield among English cathedrals, of arranging the 'Representations' at major feasts.[97] The sacrist was the treasurer's deputy and was responsible for the physical property of the church and for maintaining the supply of candles, bread, and wine for services; in return he was entitled to some of the candles used in various services.[98]

From the earlier 13th century the vicars owned and probably managed their own property. In the time of Bishop Stavensby they were given control of the lands attached to the martiloge;[99] this was the place, probably a small chapel off the south aisle of the choir,[1] where the relics of St. Chad and other saints were kept. The martiloge had its own property from at least the beginning of the 13th century when many small grants of lands and rents were made to it.[2] When this property was placed in the charge of the vicars it was kept separate from their other property and managed by vicars called keepers of the martiloge.[3] Grants of property, mainly burgages in Lichfield, were also made to the vicars, usually with the condition that they should keep the obit of the donor.[4] The vicars acquired at least one pension: £5 a year was allotted to them from the church of Bolton (Lancs.) as part of the arrangements made in 1253 by Bishop Weseham for the establishment of the new prebend of Bolton.[5] In addition the sacrist was, by the end of the century, receiving pensions from Berrington (Salop.), Youlgreave (Derb.), and Wigan (Lancs.).[6] The vicars who ministered at the mass of the Virgin in the cathedral were granted a pension of £2 by Dale Abbey (Derb.) in 1237,[7] acquired a pension of £1 from the church of Walsall in 1248,[8] and benefited from a further endowment when the chantry of Peter of Radnor was established in 1277.[9]

[80] Ibid. p. 182.
[81] Ibid. p. 195.
[82] Ibid. pp. 39–42; H. E. Savage, *The Great Register of Lichfield* (1923), 16–17.
[83] *S.H.C.* 1924, pp. 171–6.
[84] Dugdale, *Mon.* vi(3), 1256; see above p. 142.
[85] Dugdale, *Mon.* vi(3), 1260.
[86] Ibid. 1258.
[87] Ibid. 1257–8.
[88] Ibid. 1260; see above p. 141.
[89] Dugdale, *Mon.* vi(3), 1258.
[90] Ibid.
[91] In 1311 the rate was increased by ½d. to 1½d.: see below p. 156.
[92] Dugdale, *Mon.* vi(3), 1258.
[93] Ibid. 1258, 1261.
[94] Wharton, *Anglia Sacra*, i. 446.
[95] Dugdale, *Mon.* vi(3), 1261.
[96] *S.H.C.* 1924, p. 54.
[97] Dugdale, *Mon.* vi(3), 1255, 1257; Edwards, *Eng. Secular Cath.* 174; see above p. 142.
[98] Dugdale, *Mon.* vi(3), 1256–7. In 1328 the sacrist's rights were more exactly defined: *S.H.C.* 1924, pp. 338–9.
[99] *S.H.C.* 1924, pp. 174–5.
[1] See below p. 150.
[2] See e.g. *S.H.C.* 1924, pp. 47–51, 196–7.
[3] Ibid. pp. 174–5.
[4] See e.g. ibid. p. 47. See also *S.H.C.* vi(2), 171–2, 177, 178, 179, 181, 183, 184, 186.
[5] *S.H.C.* 1924, pp. 237–8, stating that the pension was for the augmentation of their commons. For the prebend of Bolton see above p. 143.
[6] *S.H.C.* 1924, pp. 11, 164, 338; Cox, *Churches of Derb.* ii. 316.
[7] *S.H.C.* 1924, p. 357.
[8] Ibid. pp. 287–8.
[9] Ibid. p. 114. Radnor's chantry was founded at the altar of the B.V.M., and it was stipulated that the masses celebrated by the chantry chaplain were not to interfere with the mass of the Virgin celebrated there every morning. Four vicars, in addition to the usual four, were to assist at the mass of the Virgin every day, each receiving ½d. a day.

LICHFIELD CATHEDRAL: VIEW OF THE WEST FRONT PUBLISHED IN 1656
The building on the left is the late-15th-century library.

The chapter-house

The nave looking east

LICHFIELD CATHEDRAL

Many bishops and canons left lands in trust to provide payments for the vicars who observed their obits: for example, in 1208 Bishop Muschamp left one mark a year to the vicars who kept his obit,[10] and in 1249 Dean Mancetter arranged with Coventry Priory that it should pay 40s. to the vicars for his obit from lands bought with money given by him.[11] In Bishop Pattishall's statutes the keepers of the martiloge were ordered to record the attendances of the vicars at obits so that the money could go to those who had fulfilled their duty.[12]

During the 13th century at least thirteen chantries were founded in the cathedral, and all but Roger Weseham's chantry at Stowe[13] were attached to one of the ten lesser altars around the high altar.[14] These chantries were endowed by their founders either directly with lands and rents or by giving enough money to a religious house to buy lands to produce a yearly sum to support the chantry; the endowment had to be enough to provide a salary for a priest and to buy candles for the altar. Examples of the former sort of endowment were the chantry of Canon Hugh de Sotesby at the altar of St. Radegund, founded in 1242,[15] and that of Canon Reynold de Cleydon established at the altar of St. Katherine a few years later.[16] On the other hand the chantry of Bishop Pattishall, founded in 1254 at the altar of St. Stephen,[17] and that of Dean Mancetter, founded in the same year at the altar of St. Peter,[18] were both supported by payments from Kenilworth Priory (Warws.). During the 13th century most of the chaplains who ministered at the chantries were vicars; it is only at the end of the century that a separate body of chantry chaplains begins to emerge.[19] Three vicars had chantries permanently attached to their stalls: the subchanter had that of Bishop Pattishall,[20] the sacrist that of Canon Ralph of Chaddesden,[21] and the vicar of the Archdeacon of Chester that of Canon Thomas de Bradford.[22] There were also two chantries for the souls of the kings of England; they were attached to the altar of St. John and were in the charge of the prebendaries of Dernford and Ufton, though probably held by their vicars.[23]

Of the other body of cathedral personnel, the choristers, little is known for this period. From 1265 there seem to have been six of them, chosen by the bishop; they were then given a pension of 10 marks from the church of Wigan, to be collected for them by the sacrist.[24] By statute their musical education was in the hands of the precentor, whose deputy, the subchanter, supervised the song schoolmaster.[25] A Master Peter occurs in 1272; variously called Rector and Master of the Scholars of Lichfield,[26]

he probably taught the boys grammar under the general direction of the chancellor.

The cathedral itself was much rebuilt during the 13th century, and the work done then and in the following century shaped the plan of the building as it is today. It is, however, difficult to date exactly the different stages of construction. There are no surviving medieval fabric accounts, and the chapter act books, which do not begin until the early 14th century, contain comparatively little information concerning the fabric. Although stylistic evidence supplements what can be gleaned from documentary sources, even this is sometimes difficult to assess. The medieval cathedral was built of a soft sandstone which weathers badly, and the extensive rebuilding and restoration which was necessary in the 17th, 18th, and 19th centuries has also to some extent hampered investigation.

The task of rebuilding the choir and the tower crossing was probably finished by 1208.[27] There is then no further evidence of work on the cathedral until 1221, when the king gave the chapter 20 oaks from Cannock Forest; these, it was stated, were to be used for rafters and timber for the church,[28] and the gift may indicate that the rebuilding of the transepts, the next stage of the reconstruction, was already under way.[29] Building operations must have been almost continuous during the deanery of William of Mancetter (1222–54). The major work was initially on the transepts. The king aided it with gifts of wood and stone from Cannock Forest: in 1231 he gave timber from Ogley Hay for ladders[30] and in 1235 and 1238 permission to use a quarry in Hopwas Hay which had already provided stone for the cathedral.[31] At least one of the transepts was evidently completed by the early 1240s: Henry III, who was at Lichfield in 1235, 1237, and 1241,[32] admired the high wooden roof of 'the new work at Lichfield', carved and painted to resemble stonework, and in 1243 ordered the construction of a similar roof for the royal chapel at Windsor.[33]

The agreement with Coventry on joint elections made it necessary for Lichfield to have a chapter-house large enough to accommodate both chapters. A chapter-house is mentioned in the statutes of Bishops Nonant and Pattishall, and it has been suggested that it stood in the angle between the north transept and the nave.[34] The new chapter-house, in the angle between the north transept and the choir, was built in the 1240s;[35] in 1244 the chapter was granted 40 oaks from the bishop's woods *ad operationem ecclesie*, presumably for this purpose.[36] It resembles the chapter-house at Lincoln but is of two storeys, of which the lower was used as

---

[10] Ibid. p. 52.   [11] Ibid. p. 113.
[12] Dugdale, *Mon.* vi(3), 1258.
[13] Founded in 1257 and allotted to the vicars some time before 1311: *S.H.C.* 1924, pp. 317, 318–19.
[14] See Jenkins, 'Lich. Cath.' ii. 1–6.
[15] *S.H.C.* 1924, pp. 70 sqq.   [16] Ibid. pp. 97–98.
[17] Ibid. pp. 106–7.
[18] Ibid. pp. 17–19.
[19] Jenkins, 'Lich. Cath.' i. 108; ii. 1–6.
[20] Ibid. ii. 1.
[21] *S.H.C.* 1924, p. 115.
[22] Ibid. p. 57.
[23] Jenkins, 'Lich. Cath.' ii. 2.
[24] *S.H.C.* 1924, p. 164.
[25] Dugdale, *Mon.* vi(3), 1257; see above p. 142.
[26] *S.H.C.* 1924, pp. 360, 361.
[27] Savage, *The Chapter House* (1919), 4; A. R. Dufty, 'Lichfield Cathedral', *Arch. Jnl.* cxx. 294.

[28] *Rot. Litt. Claus.* (Rec. Com.), i. 465. See also *V.C.H. Staffs.* ii. 342 (where note 10 should begin: 'Ibid. 465').
[29] It has been suggested that the rebuilding of the S. transept began c. 1220 and that of the N. transept c. 1240: P. Brieger, *Eng. Art, 1216–1307*, 184. For the view that the N. transept is the earlier see H. E. Savage, 'The Architectural Story of Lichfield Cathedral', *T.N.S.F.C.* xlviii. 115–16.
[30] *Close R.* 1227–31, 471 (gift of timber for making 4 ladders). Four oaks were taken: C 47/11/1/23.
[31] *Close R.* 1234–7, 103; 1237–42, 46.
[32] Ibid. 1234–7, 141, 502; 1237–42, 330.
[33] Ibid. 1242–7, 39. See also Brieger, *Eng. Art*, 184–5; *Hist. of the King's Works*, ed. H. M. Colvin, i. 123; ii. 868.
[34] Savage, *The Chapter House*, 11.
[35] J. H. Harvey, *Eng. Mediaeval Architects*, 345. For a view see plate on facing page.
[36] *Close R.* 1242–7, 175.

a chapter-house and the upper as the chapter's treasury and library. The design, an elongated octagon with a ten-celled roof vaulted from a central pillar, is unusual; it is possible that it was originally planned to have the entrance in the north transept but that this scheme was abandoned to avoid interfering with St. Stephen's altar and the grave of Bishop Pattishall. Instead a door was cut through the north wall of the choir aisle, and a vestibule built to the entrance of the chapter-house in the west face of the octagon.[37] The vestibule, with its row of canopied stalls along the west wall, remains one of the outstanding features of the cathedral.

Another work dating from Mancetter's deanery was the chapel, dedicated to St. Peter, for his chantry; this was said in 1254 to be 'attached to the church on the south side' and has been identified as the room now used as the consistory court.[38] Above it was a chapel, later known as the Chapel of St. Chad's Head, which was probably used as the martiloge.[39]

The rebuilding of the nave dates from the episcopate of Roger Meuland (1257–95), and features of the design reflect Henry III's new work at Westminster Abbey.[40] Building was evidently in progress by 1270, when the king granted the chapter timber from Kinver Forest for the cathedral fabric, and the eight bays were probably finished about 1285.[41] Work on a new west front began shortly afterwards. It was built in at least three stages, of which only the lowest is 13th-century. This was completed during the 1290s, possibly by about 1295; work on the west front may then have ceased for a few years, for the next stage shows the hand of a new architect.[42]

Little is known about how these works were carried out or how they were financed. The cathedral's master mason in the 1230s and 1240s was probably Thomas the mason,[43] who was succeeded in the 1250s and 1260s by his son, William the mason (or William fitz Thomas).[44] In the 1270s a Thomas Wallace was variously described as 'Mason of the Church of Lichfield' and 'Master of the Work in the Mother Church of Lichfield'.[45] Building material was obtained locally. In addition to the

gifts of timber and quarrying rights already mentioned the chapter had its own sources of supply. Some stone no doubt came from around the cathedral itself. Also, during the deanery of Ralph of Sempringham (1254–80), the chapter bought the right to dig for sand in a piece of ground on the Longdon road;[46] both this transaction and the purchase at an unknown date of a quarry at 'Hoppelee'[47] may be connected with the rebuilding of the nave. Money for the cathedral buildings went into a separate fabric fund which had its own keepers, the keepers of the fabric; they first occur in 1272,[48] and the first mentioned by name are two vicars in 1283.[49] The only known sources of income for the fabric fund in the 13th century are a pension of £3 paid by Halesowen Abbey from its appropriated church of Walsall[50] and a few rent-charges.[51] The congregations of the churches of the diocese contributed to the support of the fabric by the payment of Pentecostals, known as Chad-farthings and levied at the rate of a farthing a year from each household,[52] and by the alms which were collected annually for the fabric fund by the *questores* of the brotherhood of St. Chad.[53] The cost of rebuilding the cathedral could obviously not have been met from these sources alone, and the chapter must have relied largely on unrecorded gifts and legacies.

An undated survey of the Close,[54] written before it was surrounded by a stone wall, describes it as enclosed by banks and ditches; the moat, which drew its water from the bishop's fish-pool, was probably the work of Roger de Clinton.[55] In 1299 licence was granted for the building of a crenellated stone wall round the Close.[56] In the north-west corner of the Close was the site of the bishop's palace, 320 feet long and 160 feet wide. Next to it was the dean's *locus* exactly half the size, and the canons each had a portion half the size of the dean's. In all there were 26 houses in the Close.[57] The canonical houses in the Close were assigned by the bishop to canons when they first came into residence, and they were then responsible for keeping them in repair.[58] Each canon had authority over his own household, and every member of a canonical household was entitled to be buried in the Close cemetery.[59] At some time before 1280 the Close had

[37] Savage, *The Chapter House*, 13–15 (describing the plan of the chapter-house as an irregular decagon); Brieger, *Eng. Art*, 124.
[38] *S.H.C.* 1924, pp. xxvii–xxviii, 19.
[39] *T.N.S.F.C.* xlviii. 115.
[40] Brieger, *Eng. Art*, 185–6.
[41] *Close R.* 1268–72, 199; *T.N.S.F.C.* xlviii. 118.
[42] J. T. Irvine, 'The West Front of Lichfield Cathedral', *Jnl. Brit. Arch. Assoc.* xxxviii. 349–50. Subsequent research has endorsed Irvine's dating: inf. from Mr. J. H. Harvey. It has sometimes been stated that the lowest stage was completed by 1293, the year in which Thos. of Leighton made the wrought-iron hinges for the central door: see e.g. [H. E. Savage], *Story of Lichfield Cathedral* (Lichfield, 1925 and subseq. edns.; copies in W.S.L. Pamphs. *sub* Lichfield). The hinges (of which the 2 upper pairs survive) belong to this period and help to date the lowest stage; but although they are stylistically close to Leighton's only dated work, the iron grille for Queen Eleanor's tomb in Westminster Abbey, finished in 1293 (*Hist. of the King's Works*, i. 481), there appears to be no documentary evidence either that they were made in 1293 or that they are by Leighton.
[43] *S.H.C.* 1924, pp. 15–16, 17, 48, 99; Harvey, *Eng. Med. Architects*, 263–4.
[44] *S.H.C.* 1924, pp. 15–16, 99, 109, 241, 244; Harvey, *Eng. Med. Architects*, 106.
[45] *S.H.C.* 1924, pp. 53, 110, 197, 265, 268; Harvey, *Eng.*

Med. Architects, 275. Three other masons who occur at Lichfield in the 1270s, Phil. de Harpel, Gilb. de Babenham, and Nic. de Eyton (*S.H.C.* 1924, pp. 245, 265; Harvey, op. cit. 103), were probably also employed on the cathedral.
[46] *S.H.C.* 1924, p. 268.   [47] Ibid.
[48] Ibid. p. 57.
[49] Ibid. p. 267.
[50] Ibid. pp. 287–8.
[51] Ibid. pp. 57, 264–7, 267–8.
[52] Lich. Dioc. Regy., B/A/1/3, f. 127. Although this describes the position in 1352 it is stated that the practice is that traditional in the diocese.
[53] Ibid. ff. 10v.–11, stating that from Advent until Easter Week no *questores* save those of the brotherhood are allowed to collect alms in the churches of the diocese. Although this describes the position in 1322 it is stated that the practice is that traditional in the diocese.
[54] In Wharton, *Anglia Sacra*, i. 459; the copy in Dugdale, *Mon.* vi(3), 1242, has some mistakes.
[55] Wharton, *Anglia Sacra*, i. 434.
[56] *S.H.C.* 1924, pp. 141–2; *Cal. Pat.* 1292–1301, 408, 409.
[57] Wharton, *Anglia Sacra*, i. 459.
[58] *S.H.C.* 1924, p. 347; Dugdale, *Mon.* vi(3), 1261.
[59] Dugdale, *Mon.* vi(3), 1261. In 1272 all canonical houses, inside and outside the Close, were freed by the king from all livery of hospitality: *S.H.C.* 1924, p. 243.

been provided with a piped water-supply from Maple Hayes, two miles west of the city: in that year the Archdeacon of Chester, who lived outside the Close,[60] was given permission to pipe water for his own use from the chapter's 'great conduit' which passed through his land.[61]

The Fourteenth Century

The systematic compilation of capitular records of various kinds began in the early years of the 14th century. The man chiefly responsible for this seems to have been Walter of Leicester, a former sacrist; he was specially appointed to take charge of the treasury, the treasurership being held at the time by an absentee.[62] Under him an active scriptorium was built up composed of professional scriveners and vicars with literary and legal ability.[63] One of these vicars, Alan of Ashbourne, wrote the Lichfield Chronicle; he began work in 1323 and continued until his death in 1334. By 1345 his chronicle was on display in the choir as one of the treasures of the cathedral with the Anglo-Saxon St. Chad's Gospels, which had belonged to the cathedral from at least the 10th century.[64] Another vicar, John of Aston, also wrote a chronicle, of which only fragments survive in a 16th-century copy.[65]

Even more important for the history of the cathedral was the compilation, between 1317 and 1328, of the *Magnum Registrum Album*, an invaluable collection of transcripts of documents bearing on the cathedral's privileges and property.[66] The Great Register was followed by at least two other minor registers: a *Parvum Registrum*, which has been lost, and a *Registrum Tercium*, which is a list of pensions belonging to the cathedral and a cartulary of the Peak parishes.[67] In addition the chapter acts began to be recorded in a permanent form; the first surviving entry in the earliest act book is dated 22 April 1321.[68]

Another aspect of this activity was the assembling of a library at Lichfield. When the new chapter-house was completed it was decided to use the room above it as a library as well as a treasury, and about 1260 the chapter acquired copies of the Burton and Chester Annals for the new library.[69] Alan of Ashbourne must have been able to draw upon an extensive collection when compiling his chronicle, since he uses not only the records of the cathedral itself but also other historical works, such as the chronicles of William of Malmesbury.[70]

As with most of the other English secular cathedrals a notable feature of the Lichfield chapter in the 14th century was the non-residence of the dignitaries.[71] Between 1320 and 1390 the deans spent less than 10 years in Lichfield; it was only with the election of Thomas Stretton in 1390 that the dean became once more permanently resident. The precentor was also non-resident for much of the century; holders of the office included a Frenchman, three Italians, and a clerk of the king's pantry. The 14th-century chancellors were more often resident than other dignitaries, and it was only after 1364 that the office was held by non-residents. Nearly all the treasurers, however, were non-resident; two of them, Cardinal Gaucelin Johannis Deuza (1317–1348) and Hugh Pelegrini (1348–70), were distinguished papal officials.

The main reason for the non-residence of the dignitaries was the growth of papal provisions, which brought about a great change in the personnel of the chapter as a whole.[72] Ninety-four, or about a third, of the 14th-century canons were provided by the Pope. The number of provisions reached its height in the middle of the century: of 98 canons installed under Bishop Northburgh (1321–58) 47 were provided, while of 47 installed between 1385 and 1400 only 6 were provided. In the first half of the century most of the provisions were direct, resulting mainly from the Pope's appointment of members of the chapter to other benefices. The first such provision was to the richest prebend in the cathedral, that attached to the treasurership, which became vacant in 1316. Usually provisors had little trouble in obtaining possession of their prebends, but there were two long-drawn-out suits when the king and the Pope both claimed the right to collate to the prebends of Colwich and Tervin; in the former the Pope upheld his right of provision, while the latter case established the important principle that if a canon died at the papal court during a vacancy of the see the king had the right to present to his prebend. In the second half of the century the number of direct provisions decreased and the number of provisions by expectation rose. Under the system of expectations a clerk was granted a canonry in the cathedral and was admitted into the chapter, but without income or rights; he then waited until he was granted a vacant prebend. The records of expectations are incomplete, but it seems that during the century about 50 clerks obtained their Lichfield prebends by expectation, while at least 75 held expectancies but never obtained prebends; few of those obtaining expectations were foreigners. The statutes of 1351 and 1353 had little effect, although they did cause some provisions to be challenged. The 1390 legislation, however, had an

---

[60] See above p. 142.
[61] *S.H.C.* 1924, p. 317. See also Harwood, *Lichfield*, 296–7.　　[62] *S.H.C.* 1924, p. xxi.
[63] Ibid. pp. xxi–xxii. In 1335 John of Leicester, a notary, was appointed his assistant in the custody of the cathedral muniments: Savage, *Book of Alan de Assheborn*, 12.
[64] *S.H.C.* 1924, p. xvi. For the history of the St. Chad's Gospels see H. E. Savage, *The St. Chad's Gospels* (1931).
[65] *S.H.C.* 1924, p. xxi.　　[66] Ibid. pp. xiv–xv.
[67] Ibid. pp. xviii–xx. The third reg. is now in the Brit. Mus. (Harl. MS. 4799).
[68] Some folios are missing from the beginning of the book; it has been suggested that it was started after the election of Stephen Segrave as dean in 1319: *S.H.C.* 1924, pp. xvii–xviii. This first act book is in the Bodleian Libr. (MS. Ashmole 794).
[69] *S.H.C.* 1924, p. xxii. Both sets of annals are bound up with the Great Register.

[70] Savage, *Book of Alan de Assheborn*, 16, 19–20. An inventory of the treasury made in 1345 lists 60 books, mainly service books (*S.H.C.* vi(2), 204–5). The only survivor of the medieval library at Lichfield, apart from the St. Chad's Gospels, is a 13th-cent. copy of Gregory VII's Decretals: *Medieval Libraries of Great Brit.* ed. N. R. Ker (1964 edn.), 115. It was presumably from the library that in 1406 Wm. Neuhawe, parson of Tilston (Ches.), stole a chained 'Catholicon' valued at £30: *Procs. before J.P.s in the 14th and 15th Cents.* ed. Bertha H. Putnam, 323.
[71] For this para. see Jenkins, 'Lich. Cath.' i. 47–54; Le Neve, *Fasti Ecclesiae Anglicanae, 1300–1541* (new edn.), x. 5–12.
[72] For this para. and for a detailed discussion of the effect of papal provisions on the chapter see Jenkins, 'Lich. Cath.' i. 182–201.

instant effect; the last admission by expectation was in 1389 and the last by direct provision in 1391.

As a result of papal provisions the 14th-century non-resident chapter was unusually distinguished.[73] There were 27 foreign canons, most of them members of the papal court or members of prominent French or Italian families with papal connexions. Among them were eight cardinals, notably John XXII's relative Cardinal Gaucelin Johannis Deuza, a leading cardinal for 30 years, and Cardinal John Gaetani de Urbe who was one of the principal papal agents in the struggle against the Emperor Henry VII and the antipope. In the second half of the century there were the Cardinals Francis de Teobaldeschi and Pileus de Prata, the latter being largely responsible for bringing about the Agreement of Bruges in 1375 between the Pope and Edward III.

The composition of the rest of the non-resident chapter followed the usual pattern. Leading royal servants, such as William of Wykeham, Richard of Bury, and William Ayermine, and great numbers of household and chancery clerks were given prebends by royal presentation. There were also a number of clerks of the nobility, such as John de Kynardessey, the clerk of Thomas, Earl of Lancaster, who tried to hide his master's treasure in Tutbury Priory before Boroughbridge.[74] There were several clerks whose careers were solely ecclesiastical; most of these were in the service of the bishops of Lichfield. Some of the non-resident canons had successful careers at Oxford or Cambridge, such as Richard Tonworth, Principal of Hart Hall and Black Hall, and William of Gotham, Master of Michaelhouse and Chancellor of Cambridge.

The resident chapter was composed mainly of men who had retired to Lichfield after active careers in the service of the Crown or the Church or at the universities. Hugh of Hopwas had been in the service of the Black Prince before coming to Lichfield where he was a leading member of the chapter for some 30 years until his death in or before 1384. Richard de Birmingham, official of Bishop Stretton, was an effective member of the chapter from 1366 to 1386, and John of Merton, a Fellow of University (later Clare) Hall, Cambridge, and an advocate in the Court of Arches, did much legal business for the chapter in the 1370s. There was also a group of men who spent short periods of their lives as resident canons at Lichfield before being given bishoprics or deaneries; among them were John Sheppey, from a great family of Coventry wool merchants and a noted lawyer and diplomat, Stephen Segrave, a civil servant and leading churchman, and Edmund Stafford, Keeper of the Privy Seal and Chancellor of England. The most famous resident canon during the 14th century was undoubtedly Richard Fitz-

Ralph, who was provided to the deanery by the Pope in 1336 and held it until he became Archbishop of Armagh in 1346. One of the most important theological writers of the century, he spent about three years in residence at Lichfield, and there survive twenty sermons which he preached at the cathedral and in the neighbouring parishes.[75]

The survival of some accounts from the 1290s and the beginning of the act books make it possible to discover the size of the resident chapter for the first time. Some fragments of commons rolls for the 1290s show an average of six canons in residence during each quarter, usually the four dignitaries in continual residence joined by two or three other canons for one or more quarters.[76] The only communars' account for the 14th century — in fact the only more or less complete medieval account roll of the chapter to survive — is for the year Michaelmas 1325 to Michaelmas 1326 and shows that the size of the resident chapter had increased considerably.[77] There were then ten or eleven canons resident in each quarter, six of them resident the whole year and the rest resident for one or more quarters. This account shows quite clearly that the attempt to impose quarterly residence had broken down altogether and that more canons wished to reside the whole year. There was already considerable concern about the growing number of residents, and in 1301 measures had been taken to restrict it.[78] Canons were to give at least 40 days' notice of their intention to take up residence, so that the chapter could discuss their admission. No canon was to be allowed to take up residence unless he was prepared to spend at least £40 a year of his own money at Lichfield, 'lest, like a drone among bees or like a thief entering upon the labours of others, he should seem to eat the honey from which those labouring day and night in the vineyard of the Lord ought to be sustained and should so destroy the apiary'.[79] This ordinance seems to have resulted in the imposition of a fee of £40 on new canons on their first beginning residence.[80] In 1396 regulations were made laying down that new canons were to pay 100 marks to the dean for cathedral use on beginning residence and that no canon was to be admitted who was not prepared to spend 100 marks a year.[81]

The reason for these measures seems to have been the chapter's fear that unless new residentiaries had an adequate private income they would be unable to meet the expenses of the hospitality to which they were obliged by statute without making impossible demands on the common fund. This anxiety may have been caused by the general rise in prices during the century and by the reduction in the size of each canon's share in the yearly surplus caused by the rise in the number of residentiaries. Certainly the surviving communars' account shows that very

[73] For this and the following paras. see ibid. 71–82, 210–23. See ibid. ii, App. F, for detailed biographies of 14th-cent. canons.

[74] For this episode see also below p. 334.

[75] See also H. E. Savage, *Richard FitzRalph, sometime Dean* (1928); G. Leff, *Richard FitzRalph*.

[76] D. & C. Lich., I. 1–3. These are arrears rolls and therefore do not contain the names of canons absent for more than 30 days in a quarter as they were not entitled to a share of the arrears.

[77] D. & C. Lich., I. 4. In the early 17th cent. there was a complete set of commoners' rolls from the beginning of the 15th cent. and six 13th- and 14th-cent. rolls; only that for 1325–6 survived the Civil War: see list in D. & C.

Lich., 17th-cent. misc. bk., f. 133.

[78] This measure was later included in the statutes of Bp. Langton made in 1300 (see Dugdale, *Mon.* vi(3), 1262); it was in fact a separate ordinance made in Jan. 1300/1: D. & C. Lich., xiii, f. 6.

[79] Dugdale, *Mon.* vi(3), 1262; translation by Edwards, *Eng. Secular Cath.* 64.

[80] In 1385 the £40 fee paid on beginning residence by Thos. Stretton was put into the fabric fund: D. & C. Lich., Chapter Act Bk. (hereafter cited as C.A.) i, f. 9.

[81] D. & C. Lich., C.A. i, f. 48. These regulations were included in Bp. Heyworth's statutes in 1428: Dugdale, *Mon.* vi(3), 1262; D. & C. Lich., xiii, f. 7v.

small sums were being distributed at the annual division of the year's surplus: in 1327 there was a £40 surplus, and a canon residing the whole year received only 73s.[82] The rising cost of residence was a problem common to all the secular cathedrals at this time and was met by them in different ways;[83] the entrance qualifications imposed at Lichfield seem to have been successful in halting the increase in the number of residentiaries which remained at an average of 10 for the rest of the century.[84]

As well as restricting the number of residents the chapter was concerned to collect the statutory fees from non-resident canons.[85] In 1322 it was decided to levy contributions for non-residence for the last five years and canons in arrears were to have their goods sequestrated. At a general meeting of the chapter in 1325 it was again decided to collect non-residence fees with the further provision that in future the statute about non-residence was to be read to the chapter yearly so that no one could plead ignorance. In the year 1325–6 'contributions' from non-residents amounted to almost £25.[86] There was a further effort to collect arrears in 1357 when it was decided that those who disregarded sequestration orders should be excommunicated, and in 1368 the chapter ordered that expenses incurred in levying the fees should be met from the common fund. At the same time the vicars were warned that if they did anything to impede the collection of the fees they would be deprived of their dinners in the canons' houses. In 1369 the non-residents petitioned against the fees, and there were no more concerted efforts to levy them, although occasional sequestration orders were still issued by the chapter.

Financial affairs too are illuminated by the beginning of chapter records. In the early part of the century a vicar and the chapter clerk were usually put in charge of the common fund under the supervision of the chancellor,[87] but later in the century there was only one communar, a canon.[88] The communars' duties included collecting the revenues of the chapter — tithes, rents, pensions, non-residence fees — and paying the salaries of cathedral officials and the expenses of such people as messengers and proctors employed on chapter business. They also distributed commons to the canons and vicars, noting absences and making small payments to canons who came into residence for only one or two days during general chapters.[89] They were also responsible for collecting arrears of revenue and arranging for their division among resident canons.[90] In 1325–6 the total income of the chapter was £429; of this £104 6s. went to pay commons, £98 to pay arrears of commons, and £127

to pay salaries and other expenses.[91] At some time during the century it was decided to set aside a sum of money in what was called the *baga de Whalley*, which was put in a *cista gratiae* with four keys held by four elected vicars. If a communar did not have enough money to pay the commons of the canons and vicars he could borrow from the deposited money, provided he repaid the sum during his term of office; if the money was ever alienated the bishop was given authority to raise £20 for the *baga* from three churches of the common fund.[92]

The finances of the chapter must have been embarrassed by certain transactions with Edward II and Edward III. In 1321 Bishop Langton left the chapter 904 marks to complete the Lady Chapel; in July 1322 Edward II seized this money and extorted a further £257 19s. 11d. from the chapter for the expenses of his Scottish campaign. He undertook to repay the full sum of £860 13s. 3d. from the farms of the towns of Shrewsbury, Nottingham, Oxford, and Bridgnorth,[93] but in 1332 the chapter claimed that £65 was still unpaid.[94] In addition the chapter made a loan of £100 to Edward III, which it was still trying to recover in 1388.[95] In 1390 it had to pawn a chalice to the vicars to raise £20 to lend to Sir Walter Bagot who was going on crusade to 'Lettow' (Lithuania) with Henry, Earl of Derby (later Henry IV).[96] Apart from these financial transactions the chapter was little affected by politics. The disturbances of 1321 and 1322 caused alarm, and the chapter made elaborate plans to guard the Close.[97] The Close was defended again in 1329 when two prominent local knights, Sir Ralph Bassett and Sir Robert Mauvesyn, moved in.[98] There were several royal visits to Lichfield: in 1323 the king stayed for one night in the bishop's palace and the queen in the dean's house, while Richard II visited Lichfield in 1386, 1397, and 1398 and as a prisoner in 1399.[99]

There were few constitutional developments in the chapter during the century. The statutes of Bishop Langton, promulgated in 1300,[1] were mainly concerned to curb the powers of the dean.[2] He was to give proper notice of his visitations, and it was emphasized that jurisdiction in the prebends and churches of the common fund belonged to the dean and chapter, not to the dean alone; nor had the dean alone authority to dismiss a vicar.[3] Only the treasurer was to have a key to the treasury, and the dean was not to meddle in his affairs or those of the other dignitaries.[4] When the dean was not in residence it was usual for him to appoint one or more *locum tenentes*; in 1365, however, the chapter decided that it was against the statutes to have such a person and

---

[82] D. & C. Lich., I. 4. In 1293 the arrears of revenue divided among resident canons alone totalled over £300 (ibid. I. 2), but this was probably an unusually large sum: see I. 2 and 3.
[83] See Edwards, *Eng. Secular Cath.* 62–67.
[84] Jenkins, 'Lich. Cath.' i. 71.
[85] For this para. see ibid. 84–86; *S.H.C.* vi(2), 61, 62.
[86] D. & C. Lich., I. 4.
[87] In 1325 the communars were Rob. Bernard, the chapter clerk (see *S.H.C.* 1924, p. xx), and a vicar, John of Polesworth (see ibid. p. 96): D. & C. Lich., I. 4.
[88] Jenkins, 'Lich. Cath.' i. 61.
[89] D. & C. Lich., I. 4.
[90] Ibid. I. 1–3.
[91] Ibid. I. 4.
[92] In 1397 200 marks left by Bp. Langton were given to the bag of Whalley and the arrangements were given statutory authority: Dugdale, *Mon.* vi(3), 1253–4;

Wharton, *Anglia Sacra*, i. 451; D. & C. Lich., C.A. i, f. 16.
[93] *Cal. Pat.* 1321–4, 180–1. Langton's will is printed in Alice Beardwood, 'The Trial of Walter Langton', *Trans. American Philosophical Soc.* N.S. liv(3), 39–40.
[94] Jenkins, 'Lich. Cath.' i. 12.
[95] D. & C. Lich., C.A. i, f. 16.
[96] Ibid. f. 23v.
[97] Jenkins, 'Lich. Cath.' i. 6–7; *Cal. Close*, 1318–23, 424.
[98] Jenkins, 'Lich. Cath.' i. 7.
[99] Ibid. On the last occasion he seems to have stayed in the house of the Archdeacon of Chester outside the Close: D. & C. Lich., C.A. i, f. 56v.
[1] D. & C. Lich., xiii, f. 6.
[2] The dean, John of Derby, was non-resident in 1300: Jenkins, 'Lich. Cath.' ii, App. F.
[3] Dugdale, *Mon.* vi(3), 1261.
[4] Ibid.

after *diversis allegationibus et responsionibus* chose instead a president of the chapter.[5] In 1329 it was ordered that the common seal of the chapter was to be used only if there were two canons present.[6] In 1393 there was some concern about the secrecy of chapter meetings and the dean, with the authority of the whole chapter, solemnly warned each canon not to reveal the proceedings of the chapter.[7] Apart from financial business and the regulation of chapter property, meetings were concerned mainly with disciplining vicars and settling disputes between the chapter and individual canons.[8] In the 1340s there was some concern because the citizens of Lichfield were claiming a right of way through the Close, and the chapter had to obtain letters patent from Edward III restricting transit to members of the church and their servants.[9] The chapter was also obliged by statute to see that the water supply was properly regulated and the aqueduct inspected.[10]

One of the chapter's regular concerns was to see that the priests who served the three city churches received weekly instructions from the subchanter about services.[11] Bishop Langton's statutes contain regulations about the celebration of major feasts,[12] but there is little new information in the 14th century about the Use of Lichfield. In 1311 the dean and chapter of the collegiate church of Upholland (Lancs.) were ordered by the bishop to follow as far as possible the Lichfield Use in divine service;[13] but when a chantry was founded in the prebendal church of Colwich in 1341 its breviary was ordered to be that of the Use of Salisbury.[14] In 1398 the Convocation of Canterbury ordered that the feast of St. Chad should be observed throughout the province and thus it came to be included in the Salisbury Use. According to the Salisbury breviary the canonical hours on that day were to be according to the Use of Lichfield.[15]

The chapter acquired only two more churches for its common fund during the 14th century. Chebsey, together with the tithes of Slindon, a township in Eccleshall, was in the hands of the chapter by 1321.[16] The second appropriation, that of Worfield (Salop.), came later in the century. In 1318 Bishop Langton acquired the advowson from Edward II in exchange for the manor of Greenford (Mdx.) which Langton had intended to use to found a chantry for the soul of Edward I.[17] In 1371, however, Edward III accused Langton's successors of fraudulently retaining the advowson.[18] In 1394 Bishop Scrope granted the church to the chapter, after founding a chantry from its revenues.[19] The cost of the appropriation to the chapter was 200 marks, which was found by a levy of one-tenth of the value of every prebend for two years and the assignment of part of a new canon's entrance fee.[20]

All the churches of the common fund, with the exception of those of the Peak parishes, were farmed out during the century.[21] There was a great differ-

ence in their value: the highest farm was that of Chebsey which reached £40 at the end of the century, and the lowest that of Rugeley, farmed for 10 marks. There was a general tendency for the value of the churches to fall between 1291 and 1535, but the value of the farms fluctuated only very slightly during the 14th century. It is probable that the farming of churches was not very profitable for it was not unusual for farmers to be in arrears. In 1386 the Vicar of Chebsey said that he could no longer pay the same farm; the chapter, wishing to keep up the value of the farm, asked the same rent but agreed to remit him £2 at the end of each year. Sometimes it was difficult to find anyone willing to take on a farm: in 1356 the chapter was trying to find a farmer for Thornton, and in 1382 it was still having to arrange the sale of produce and repair of buildings itself.

Farms were only rarely held by canons, although Cannock was held for many years by John of Melbourne, the president of the chapter. Occasionally farms were given to other ministers of the cathedral: in 1323 two vicars choral were given Kniveton, and in 1359 the tithes of Harborne were farmed to the chapter clerk. Farms were more usually held by the vicar of the church or a local resident: for example, in the 1320s Arley was farmed by Thomas de Arley who had been given the farm at a reduced rate because the chapter thought him well qualified to look after its woodland there. The upkeep of the chancel of the church was supposed to be the responsibility of the farmer, but in many cases the chapter itself had to undertake repairs: for example, in 1382 the Vicar of Dilhorne was warned that the chapter clerk was coming with a carpenter to repair the chancel and the farmer was asked to help meet the cost. The parishioners of the chapter's churches were supposed to provide their own chalice and missal while the chapter supplied books and ornaments, and occasional gifts and loans by the chapter from its own considerable collection of ornaments, service books, and vestments are recorded in the act books.[22]

Individual canons farmed their prebends in the same way and on the same sort of terms. A roll of receipts and expenses of the deanery which has survived for the year 1333–4 gives some idea of how a canon managed his property.[23] The dean received £40 from the farmer of his prebend of Brewood and Adbaston and various smaller sums from rents of other property and perquisites such as mortuary dues. There was obviously some difficulty over the farm of this prebend as the dean employed messengers to take letters to the farmer and to the Vicar of Brewood and the Abbot of Lilleshall (Salop.) 'touching the farm of Brewood'; he also sent a representative to Brewood to inspect defects in the houses there.

Unlike the other churches of the common fund

[5] Jenkins, 'Lich. Cath.' i. 61.
[6] Bodl. MS. Ashmole 794, f. 33.
[7] D. & C. Lich., C.A. i, f. 37.
[8] See e.g. the dispute between the chapter and Ric. Tysho: ibid. f. 31.   [9] *Cal. Pat.* 1348–50, 56.
[10] Dugdale, *Mon.* vi(3), 1261.
[11] Jenkins, 'Lich. Cath.' i. 25, 59.
[12] Dugdale, *Mon.* vi(3), 1261.
[13] *S.H.C.* 1924, pp. 184–5.
[14] Jenkins, 'Lich. Cath.' i. 24.
[15] Ibid.   [16] Ibid. ii. 8, 10.
[17] *S.H.C.* 1924, pp. 262–3. As part of the exchange

Langton was also granted the advowson of Chesterton (Warws.). This was granted to the vicars choral in the 15th cent.: see below p. 164.
[18] *Cal. Close,* 1369–74, 240–1.
[19] *Cal. Pat.* 1391–6, 427; Jenkins, 'Lich. Cath.' i. 118–19.
[20] Wharton, *Anglia Sacra,* i. 451; D. & C. Lich., C.A. i, ff. 47v.–48.
[21] For this and the following para., unless otherwise stated, see Jenkins, 'Lich. Cath.' i. 122–30.
[22] For an inventory of the goods in the treasury see the sacrist's roll for 1345: *S.H.C.* vi(2), 199–221.
[23] D. & C. Lich., I. 7.

those of the Peak parishes were administered directly by the chapter in the 14th century; this was a change from its policy in the previous century when some of the parishes were leased.[24] The chapter had a proctor to safeguard its rights to the Peak, usually a prominent local knight. In the 1350s the proctor was Sir John Cockayne of Ashbourne; in 1370 he was succeeded by Sir Godfrey Foljambe, steward of the honor of Tutbury,[25] who was followed in 1376 by Sir Nicholas Stafford, holder of the manor of Tideswell in the right of his wife. As well as a proctor the chapter had an agent to do the routine work and present accounts to it. The mineral tithes were farmed out: in 1358 Robert de Hethcote of Tideswell was granted them at 24 marks a year for ten years. The chapter received a very large income from the Peak parishes. In 1339, for example, the tithes of grain were worth £218, mineral tithes £18 10s., and mortuaries £23; the tithes of wool and lambs, which were accounted for separately, may have been worth at least £200. The chapter kept a close watch on the Peak parishes. In 1376 the chapter clerk, who was taking some vestments to Bakewell, was ordered to inquire into the value of lambs and the prospects for the sale of the autumn harvest; two weeks later two canons were sent to Bakewell to look for buyers of grain, wool, and lambs. In 1382 the chapter clerk was again sent to Bakewell to deal with merchants about the price of wool. Sometimes the chapter had difficulty in disposing of the wool. In 1375 it was decided that the wool unsold by 15 August should be brought to Lichfield and distributed there; in 1382 and 1383 the wool from Bakewell was stored in the chapter-house.

During the century the chapter acquired at least 20 new pensions, the price of appropriations to religious houses.[26] They ranged from 5 marks from the church of Condover (Salop.)[27] to 20d. from the church of Weston-upon-Trent,[28] but few of them were worth more than a mark. Occasionally the payment of pensions fell into arrears: in 1305 the chapter started a suit to recover arrears of 140 marks from the Priory of St. Thomas near Stafford for the pension from Stowe-by-Chartley, and in 1318 the officers of Pipewell Priory (Northants.) were excommunicated for being in arrears with their pension from Dunchurch.[29] Three large 13th-century pensions, those of Southam, Winwick, and Aston, caused the chapter endless trouble and continual litigation throughout the 14th century,[30] and there were also less serious disputes over the pensions from Wigan and Leamington Hastings.[31]

The relations of the chapter with the bishop during this century were determined more by the personality of the bishops than by any issues of privilege or authority. With Bishop Langton (1296–1321), a benefactor *munificentissimus* to the cathedral, its relations were very good apart from a protracted dispute over the visitation of certain prebends.[32] In 1302-3, when Langton was suspended by Boniface VIII for suspected adultery, murder, simony, and pluralism, the chapter wrote to the Pope in his defence, testifying that he was devoted to his ministry and had performed notable services for the cathedral.[33] After his death the quarrel between Lichfield and Coventry over the right of election flared up once more. The election took place at Coventry, and when the two sides failed to reach agreement, the monks denied that both chapters should be counted as equal in numbers and elected their prior. The canons of Lichfield appealed to the Pope who meanwhile had provided Roger Northburgh to the see; the case dragged on at Avignon for at least twelve years, and the final decision probably only confirmed the arrangement which had been worked out in the 13th century.[34]

The relations of the chapter with Bishop Northburgh (1321–58) were unhappy in every way. Soon after his consecration he announced his intention of visiting the chapter, a move which led to a protest from the dean.[35] In 1323 the chapter refused to recognize the bishop's right to excommunicate the Archdeacon of Chester on the ground that the disciplining of the chapter was the duty of the dean.[36] A few months later the dean publicly abused the bishop's steward, who had earlier been arraigned before the chapter for attempting to test the weights used by some of the canons, 'disgracing him and railing against the bishop'.[37] After the appointment of Dean Segrave to the archbishopric of Armagh in 1324, Northburgh claimed jurisdiction in the deanery during the vacancy and the chapter hurriedly inquired into the customs of other secular cathedrals during vacancies.[38] The chapter was united against him, and it was more than once decided that any canon or minister of the church prosecuted by the bishop should be defended from the common fund. In 1329 seven cases were pending in the Court of Arches between the bishop and the chapter, and the question of visitation was later taken to the papal court.[39] After Northburgh's death the relations between chapter and bishop were peaceful, although the question of visitation was revived in the 1390s. Bishop Scrope attempted to conduct a visitation in 1390 and announced one in 1396; after protests from the chapter he then agreed that he and his successors should visit the chapter only once every ten years and that the rest of the cathedral should be exempt from their jurisdiction. He visited the chapter in 1397, but the question of episcopal visitation was not finally resolved for over thirty years.[40]

Much of the work of running the cathedral was in the hands of the vicars at this period. With the precentor almost continually non-resident the subchanter was permanently in charge of the cathedral services, while the sacrist replaced the treasurer as custodian of the goods of the cathedral. In addition the vicars supplied the chapter with communars, keepers of the fabric, chapter clerks, and scribes; they served on commissions for the chapter,

---

[24] For this para. see Jenkins, 'Lich. Cath.' i. 130–4.
[25] R. Somerville, *Hist. of Duchy of Lancaster*, i. 381.
[26] See Jenkins, 'Lich. Cath.' i. 20–24.
[27] *S.H.C.* 1924, pp. 249–50.
[28] Ibid. p. 364.
[29] Jenkins, 'Lich. Cath.' i. 149.
[30] For a full discussion of these disputes see ibid. 149–59.
[31] *Cal. Close*, 1349–54, 281–2; D. & C. Lich., C.A. i, f. 50.
[32] *S.H.C.* 1924, p. 354.

[33] Jenkins, 'Lich. Cath.' i. 36–39; *S.H.C.* 1924, p. 307.
[34] Jenkins, 'Lich. Cath.' i. 30.
[35] *S.H.C.* 1924, pp. 353–4.
[36] Ibid. p. 354.
[37] Ibid.
[38] Ibid. pp. 353, 355–7.
[39] Jenkins, 'Lich. Cath.' i. 40–41.
[40] D. & C. Lich., C.A. i, ff. 22, 48–49v.; Wharton, *Anglia Sacra*, i. 451; see below pp. 162–3.

acted as proctors for absent canons, and even represented the chapter at the papal court.[41] In 1311 the commons of the vicars were raised from 1*d.* to 1½*d.* a day with double payments on 14 feast days; in 1325–6 the commons of 29 vicars cost the chapter £67.[42] In 1361 the vicars began a campaign to have their commons increased; they complained to the chapter that they did not have enough to live on, what with the price of food, linen, and wool, but the chapter replied that their complaint was *minus vera.*[43] In 1374 the commons were doubled to 3*d.* a day on condition that the vicars gave up their right to dinner with the canons and provided themselves with a suitable dining-hall;[44] this arrangement was confirmed by the bishop in 1390.[45]

The vicars continued to accumulate small grants of property in Lichfield and the surrounding area.[46] In 1348 they acquired their first appropriated church, that of Penn, from Bishop Northburgh. In return they were to say two masses a year for Edward III and one for Ralph, Lord Stafford; those attending these services were to be given special payments, and after pensions for the bishop and the chapter had been deducted from the revenues of the church, the rest was to be distributed among the vicars for their vestments and other clothing.[47] Little is known about the way in which the vicars managed their property, but they had a common seal by at least 1315 and were accustomed to appoint proctors to act for them by 1324.[48] They continued to receive gifts of money, such as a share of the 200 marks left to the cathedral by Bishop Stretton,[49] and pensions, such as £1 from the church of Tibshelf (Derb.) in 1319 and £1 6*s.* 8*d.* from the church of Lullington (Derb.) in 1341.[50]

From the beginning of the century the vicars lived in common. In 1315 Bishop Langton, concerned about the dangers to the vicars of lodging outside the Close in lay people's houses,[51] gave them a plot of land in the north-west corner of the Close that had formerly belonged to one of the canons.[52] On this site some houses were evidently built by individual vicars, since in 1330 John of Aston was given permission to finish the house which he had begun and two other vicars received permission to rebuild their house; a condition was made that both houses should revert to the chapter on the death of the vicars.[53] The chapter allotted rooms to the vicars — usually two vicars shared a room — and there were occasional complaints: in 1326, for example, the vicar of Gaia Minor complained that his room was not suitable to his status.[54] The vicars had some of their meals together from early in the century, for in 1329 they were ordered to repair their kitchen and

hall, but they had their dinners with the canons until later in the century.[55]

The vicars' behaviour was a constant problem for the chapter. In 1321 the dean gave them a stern lecture in their common hall on the theme *de vita et honestate clericorum.*[56] An unruly vicar of that time was Richard of Elmhurst, who in 1324 was indicted before the king's court for attacking royal officers in Gaia Lane;[57] in 1330 he was accused by the chapter of being a dealer in chickens and cattle and of having a fire in his room to the peril of other vicars.[58] The most usual offence of the vicars was incontinence, punishable by a fine to the fabric fund. In 1359 seven vicars, including the subchanter, were accused of it; in the case of the subchanter five women were involved.[59] In 1383 the chapter made regulations for the behaviour of the vicars, forbidding them to go outside the Close after nine in the evening or to have any *suspectam mulierem* in their rooms; they were to dress properly and follow the canonical hours, day and night.[60] In 1394 it was decided by the chapter that any vicars who attempted to interfere with punishments imposed by the chapter by calling in lay people should be suspended for three months.[61]

Little is known about the choristers at this time. They wore surplices and caps, were paid 1*d.* each for attending certain special services, and received in addition various unspecified payments from the communar of the chapter.[62] The pensions allotted to them, amounting to 13 marks a year, were collected for them by the sacrist, and one 14th-century sacrist left them a small legacy.[63]

The number of chantries in the cathedral decreased during the century: in 1335 there were 20 chantries, including the one at Stowe, but by the beginning of the 15th century only 14 were still being served.[64] A few new chantries were founded during the century. Bishop Langton established chantries at the altars of St. Mary and St. Nicholas and endowed them both with pensions.[65] In 1321 the prior and brethren of St. John's Hospital, Lichfield, founded a chantry at the altar of St. Thomas for the soul of Canon Philip de Turvill, to be served by one of their community.[66] In 1325 the vicars founded a chantry for the soul of the chancellor, William de Bosco, which was served by all the vicars, each taking a week's turn.[67] By the 1330s the condition of the chantries was causing concern to the chapter. There had already been an inquiry in 1311 into the condition of the chantry at Stowe which the vicars had allowed to become dilapidated,[68] and in 1335 the chapter ordered a full-scale inquiry into all the chantries; the subchanter and five other vicars were to find out what chantries

[41] Jenkins, 'Lich. Cath.' i. 93; see above p. 153. In 1325 two vicars were absent at the papal court: D. & C. Lich., I. 4.
[42] D. & C. Lich., I. 4; Vicars' Mun. A. 3; Jenkins, 'Lich. Cath.' i. 88.　　[43] Jenkins, 'Lich. Cath.' i. 89.
[44] D. & C. Lich., Vicars' Mun. A. 7.
[45] D. & C. Lich., C.A. i, f. 19v. (the year here wrongly given as 1389: see D. & C. Lich., K.4).
[46] See *S.H.C.* vi(2), 171–94.
[47] Jenkins, 'Lich. Cath.' i. 90–91.
[48] *S.H.C.* 1924, p. 96; ibid. vi(2), 196.
[49] Wharton, *Anglia Sacra,* i. 449.
[50] Jenkins, 'Lich. Cath.' ii. 22, 23.
[51] The vicars may have previously lodged in some buildings in Gaia Lane mentioned in 1315: *S.H.C.* 1924, p. 96.

[52] D. & C. Lich., K. 2.
[53] Jenkins, 'Lich. Cath.' i. 97.
[54] Ibid. 97–98.
[55] Ibid. 98; see above p. 153.
[56] Jenkins, 'Lich. Cath.' i. 98–99.　　[57] *S.H.C.* x(1), 52.
[58] Jenkins, 'Lich. Cath.' i. 103.
[59] Ibid. 100.　　[60] Ibid. 99.
[61] D. & C. Lich., C.A. i, f. 41v.
[62] Jenkins, 'Lich. Cath.' i. 114; D. & C. Lich., I. 4.
[63] D. & C. Lich., I. 8; Jenkins, 'Lich. Cath.' i. 114.
[64] Jenkins, 'Lich. Cath.' ii, App. A; D. & C. Lich., C.A. i, f. 113v.
[65] Jenkins, 'Lich. Cath.' i. 107–8; *S.H.C.* 1915, 156, 157.
[66] *S.H.C.* 1924, p. 365.
[67] Ibid. pp. 331–2.
[68] Ibid. pp. 318–19.

there were and who officiated at each.[69] They discovered that only five of the 20 chantries were being properly served. There were many complaints: in one case the chaplain celebrated frequently but did not know for whose soul, in another the chaplain celebrated for someone other than the founder of the chantry, and in one case the holder said he was too infirm to celebrate. The most frequent complaint was that the endowment of the chantry was insufficient to maintain the services laid down in its ordination. A typical example was the chantry of Ralph of Sempringham whose chaplain reported that his salary was not sufficient for a daily celebration and that he was allowed by the chapter to celebrate every other day — it was said that in fact he celebrated only once a year. The chapter could do little to reform the chantries apart from ordering the chaplains to celebrate properly in future under penalty of a fine to the fabric fund.

Some of the smaller chantries seem to have lapsed later in the century, usually because their endowment was insufficient. One poor chantry, that of Reynold de Cleydon, was refounded by its chaplain in 1364, two years after he had been given permission to hold services only three days a week, the revenue being insufficient for daily service *modernis temporibus*.[70] In another case, that of Bishop Weseham's chantry at St. John's altar, it was the unusual ordination that the prebendary of Bobenhull should celebrate in person which led to the suspension of the chantry; the prebendaries refused to serve the chantry and the case was taken to the Court of Arches in the 1350s.[71] During the century vicars came to be displaced as the holders of chantries by special chantry chaplains, and when Bishop Scrope founded a chantry in 1386 one of the conditions was that it should not be served by a vicar.[72]

At about the same time the chapter made its first regulations for chantry chaplains; they were to dress like other members of the choir and were to attend services on Sundays and feast days.[73] The chaplains did not yet live in common, and several of the chantries had houses in Lichfield attached to them. The chantry at St. Katherine's altar had a house in Gaia Lane, in which the chaplain was keeping a mistress in 1357.[74] In the same lane there was a house belonging to Dean Mancetter's chantry, whose chaplain claimed in 1335 to be celebrating the

chantry services *in hospitio suo*.[75]

The heavy building programme which had been started in the 13th century was continued during much of the fourteenth. It included the completion of the west front with its two stone spires, and the building of the central spire, probably also in stone. It is impossible to date this work precisely: the central spire, possibly the first to be built, was destroyed during the Civil War, while the northwest spire and the upper part of the tower on which it stands are later in date than the rest of the west front and possibly represent a late-14th- or 15th-century addition or rebuilding.[76] It is, however, probable that work on the front was taken up again about 1300, and it has been suggested that by the time of Bishop Langton's death building had progressed as far as the string-course below the belfry-stage.[77] It may have been even further advanced: a brief description of the cathedral by a friar who visited it in 1323[78] suggests that one at least of the western spires must by then have been complete or virtually complete.[79] It is in fact possible that by 1323 the west front, with its spires, window,[80] and rows of statues, was already finished, and that for some reason the north-west spire had later to be rebuilt.

Meanwhile work on the eastern arm of the church was also in hand. Bishop Langton, whose gifts to the cathedral during his lifetime included a magnificent shrine worth £2,000 for the relics of St. Chad,[81] had persuaded the chapter to build a Lady Chapel to the east of the choir and had left over £600 in cash and plate to finish it.[82] From stylistic evidence it has been suggested that work on the chapel may have started about 1310 or, more probably, about 1315.[83] Its plan, a rectangle of three bays with a three-sided east end, is unique among English cathedrals. In 1322 the architect, William de Eyton, the cathedral's master mason, had seven masons working under him, and an agreement of 1323 for the quarrying of stone for the chapel *noviter construenda* implies that work was being continued despite the king's confiscation of Langton's bequest.[84] The chapel had evidently been finished to Eyton's designs by 1336, when two keepers of its fabric were appointed.[85] Possibly the date of completion was a year or two earlier, since Eyton, who probably died during the winter of

[69] The rep. of the vicars, from Bodl. MS. Ashmole 794, is transcribed in Jenkins, 'Lich. Cath.' ii, App. A.

[70] Jenkins, 'Lich. Cath.' i. 111.

[71] Ibid. 111–12.

[72] Ibid. 112; D. & C. Lich., C.A. i, f. 38.

[73] D. & C. Lich., C.A. i, f. 41v.

[74] Jenkins, 'Lich. Cath.' i. 108.

[75] Ibid. 108–9.

[76] It has been suggested that the N.W. tower and spire may have been rebuilt between 1522 and 1533, under Dean Denton (J. T. Irvine, 'The West Front of Lichfield Cathedral', *Jnl. Brit. Arch. Assoc.* xxxviii. 353), but the evidence offered in support of this suggestion seems very slender.

[77] Ibid. 350.

[78] He found it 'mire pulcritudinis, turribus lapideis sive campanilibus altissimis, picturis, sculpturis, et aliis ecclesiasticis apparatibus excellenter ornata atque decorata': *Itinerarium Symonis Semeonis ab Hybernia ad Terram Sanctam*, ed. M. Esposito, 24–26. This reference has been supplied by Mr. J. H. Harvey.

[79] There is some evidence that 'turris' could mean a spire, or at any rate a steeple: see J. H. Harvey, 'Had Winchester Cathedral a Central Spire?' *Winchester Cathedral Record*, no. 27 (1958). Stone spires were,

moreover, sufficiently uncommon to be worth noting, whereas to remark that a cathedral's towers were of stone would have been superfluous: inf. from Mr. Harvey.

[80] The original W. window has been attributed to the same phase of building as the S.W. spire: *Jnl. Brit. Arch. Assoc.* xxxviii. 351. Its tracery, as shown in a 17th-cent. view of the W. front (see above plate facing p. 148), is consistent with a date shortly before 1323: inf. from Mr. Harvey.

[81] Wharton, *Anglia Sacra*, i. 442; *S.H.C.* vi(2), 199. The shrine was made in Paris: Alice Beardwood, 'The Trial of Walter Langton', *Trans. American Philosophical Soc.* N.S. liv(3), 27.

[82] *Trans. Amer. Phil. Soc.* N.S. liv(3), 40; *Cal. Pat. 1321–4*, 180–1.

[83] J. H. Harvey, *Eng. Medieval Architects*, 103; A. R. Dufty, 'Lichfield Cathedral', *Arch. Jnl.* cxx. 295; inf. from Mr. Harvey. Langton was imprisoned by Edw. II in 1307 but was free and celebrating orders in his diocese 1309–11; he was active in the diocese again from 1314 until his death, especially after his final dismissal from office in 1315: see above p. 26; *D.N.B.*

[84] Bodl. MS. Ashmole 794, ff. 2v., 5v. For the chapter's forced loan of the bequest to Edw. II see above p. 153.

[85] Bodl. MS. Ashmole 794, f. 55.

1336–7, was also responsible for the first stages of the construction of a new presbytery running west from the Lady Chapel. The outer walls of this for three bays westwards on the north and four bays on the south are his work; they could have been built outside the existing early-13th-century eastern arm of the cathedral without interfering with it.[86]

In May 1337 the chapter engaged William of Ramsey, the king's master mason, as consultant architect.[87] Ramsey's work on the cathedral, which is marked by its distinctive new Perpendicular style, consists of the main arcades and upper levels of the presbytery, the linking bays of the aisle walls to north and south, and the upper levels of the choir. The main arcades of the choir were virtually untouched, though Ramsey remodelled the eastern pillars to match the new work and mask the change of styles.[88] The Lady Chapel had not been built on the same axis as the choir and the rest of the church,[89] but Ramsey solved this problem by modifying the axis of the main arcades of the presbytery one bay at a time.[90] When he died in 1349 no major work remained to be done on the eastern arm of the church.[91]

Work on the fabric after Ramsey's death can be traced only from incidental references. It was almost certainly interrupted by the Black Death but, according to Bishop Northburgh, had been resumed by 1352. This later work may merely have concerned the embellishment of the choir and the new presbytery; but since something more substantial seems to be implied by the bishop's statement it may have included the revaulting, in stone, of the transepts and tower crossing.[92] In 1357 a glazier from Lenton (Notts.) was employed to glaze three large and four small windows of 'the new work'.[93]

There is evidence of what may have been quite extensive work on the fabric in the 1380s. For several years after 1380, when each residentiary was ordered to give the fabric fund 10s. a quarter from his commons for a year,[94] the expenses involved evidently strained the chapter's resources. Work of

some kind was being done on the choir in 1382. In May it was agreed that each existing residentiary and each new residentiary should give £10 *ad reparacionem chori*,[95] and in June that each residentiary should contribute 30s. a quarter from his commons *ad opus chori perficiendum*.[96] The other two references to the fabric that year also concern the choir.[97] Three years later work was still in progress, though no mention was then made of the part of the cathedral affected.[98] In March 1385 Gilbert Mason was appointed for life as the cathedral's master mason,[99] and in June John Douve of Lichfield was appointed master carpenter.[1] New residentiaries were now being ordered to pay their entrance fees into the fabric fund.[2] Despite this, money was running short, and in October the chapter had to borrow in order to pay the masons' wages during the winter.[3] The work, whatever it was, was probably finished during the next few years, for there is little subsequent reference to the fabric in the act books.

The bulk of the money for building probably came from individual gifts and bequests and from contributions, voluntary or compulsory, by the residentiaries. In addition the keepers of the fabric had a small but steady income from pensions, rents, and fines from cathedral clergy.[4] There were also the receipts of the Chad-farthings and the alms brought in each year by the *questores* of the brotherhood of St. Chad.[5] At times both these sources evidently produced less than they should have done. In 1322, for example, Northburgh warned his archdeacons that *questores* collecting for other causes had bribed parish priests to let them into their churches during the months reserved for the brotherhood. In 1352 he threatened to excommunicate laymen who were in arrears with their Chad-farthings and archdeacons' officials, rural deans, apparitors, and parish clergy who had embezzled money that had been collected.[6] During the later 14th century both collections were normally farmed out: thus in 1389 John de Outheby, Archdeacon of

[86] Harvey, *Eng. Med. Architects*, 103; J. H. Harvey, 'The Origin of the Perpendicular Style', *Studies in Building History*, ed. E. M. Jope, plan on p. 151; inf. from Mr. Harvey.
[87] Bodl. MS. Ashmole 794, f. 57v. Ramsey was to receive a fee of £1 a visit, with 6s. 8d. for his travelling expenses from London. For Ramsey see Harvey, *Eng. Med. Architects*, 215–18.
[88] Harvey, *Eng. Med. Architects*, 217, 345; *Studies in Building History*, 152, and plan and diagrams on p. 151; inf. from Mr. Harvey.
[89] The misalignment was caused by the northward swing of the shelf of sandstone on which the building rests: *S.H.C.* 1950–1, 165.
[90] H. E. Savage, *The 14th-cent. Builders* (1916), 7; A. Clifton-Taylor, *Cathedrals of Eng.* 191.
[91] There is no trace of later medieval work in this part of the cathedral: inf. from Mr. Harvey.
[92] Early in 1352 Northburgh stated that the dean and chapter, 'newly setting to work, are trying, with God's help and at great expense, to restore to modern elegance (*ad novitatis decorem*) the work that pious antiquity built in its own style (*suo more*)': Lich. Dioc. Regy., B/A/1/3, f. 127. The vaulting is probably work of the later 14th cent.: *Arch. Jnl.* cxx. 295.
[93] Bodl. MS. Ashmole 794, ff. 105v., 108v. In 1375 work was in progress on the reredos of the high altar: ibid. f. 155v.
[94] Ibid. f. 182.
[95] Ibid. f. 190. The money was to be paid in 3 yearly instalments.
[96] Ibid. f. 190v. Only 5 marks of each residentiary's yearly contribution was, however, to go 'ad domum chorum'.

[97] In Mar. a vicar's executors gave 20 marks 'ad reparacionem unius nove fenestre chori', and in Dec. it was after the chapter had had a discussion 'super reparacione chori' that residentiaries made provisional arrangements to pay the wages of Master Wm. Driffeld and at least 2 other masons for 9 months out of their own pockets: ibid. ff. 189v., 194.
[98] The order in Oct. 1385, subsequently rescinded, that all masons save Driffeld and one other should be laid off until the summer suggests work on the exterior of the fabric, though obviously financial considerations were also involved: D. & C. Lich., C.A. i, f. 9; see below.
[99] His salary was 40s. a year, with an additional 3s. 4d. a week for the periods when he was actually at work on the fabric: ibid. f. 2v., stating that he later agreed to accept a salary of 30s. a year.
[1] Ibid. ff. 5v.–6. He was retained for life at a salary of 20s. a year, with an additional 2s. 6d. a week for the periods when he was actually at work on the fabric. When there was no work to be done on the fabric the residentiaries were to have first call on his services for their private work.
[2] Ibid. ff. 4, 7, 9.
[3] Ibid. f. 9. The decision to keep all the journeymen on was taken after Mason had sworn that he had chosen them carefully and that they all knew the 'formas et signa' by which stones were carved and worked and which it would take other masons a year to learn.
[4] Jenkins, 'Lich. Cath.' i. 17.
[5] See above p. 150.
[6] Lich. Dioc. Regy., B/A/1/3, ff. 10v.–11, 127.

Derby, took the farm of the collections in the archdeaconry of Coventry, paying £10 down and £4 a year.[7]

Langton's building operations were not confined to the cathedral itself. He fortified the Close, constructing a stone perimeter wall[8] with massive gatehouses at the south and west entrances.[9] He was responsible for the Bird Street and Dam Street causeways, set up about 1310 across the bishop's fish-pool; the stretch of water between them forms the present Minster Pool, south of the Close.[10] He also built himself a large new palace in the Close,[11] in which at the end of the 16th century Sampson Erdeswick found 'a goodly large hall, wherein hath been excellently well painted, but now much decayed, the coronation, marriage, wars, and funeral of Edward I'.[12]

The Later Middle Ages

The full extent of the destruction of the cathedral's records during the Civil War[13] becomes apparent when an attempt is made to write the history of the cathedral for the period between 1400 and the Restoration. There are no records of chapter acts between 1439 and 1480 and very few after 1553; nor are there any communars' or fabric accounts for any part of the period, and only a handful of leases have survived.

Such records as have survived, however, seem to show that the 15th and early 16th centuries saw the development of tendencies already apparent in the fourteenth. The resident chapter shrank in size as the revenues of the chapter shrank in value. There were no great issues to be contested or projects to be finished: relations with the bishop were usually cordial, no constitutional innovations were necessary in the chapter, and the cathedral building had already been more or less completed. The chapter confined itself to the task of straightening out anomalies in administration and liturgy and, in the realm of building, to enriching the interior of the church. In addition there was a new concern to see that the lesser bodies of cathedral clergy — the vicars, choristers, and chantry priests — were properly housed and disciplined.

The cessation of papal provisions meant that the 15th-century non-resident chapter was less colourful than that of the previous century. The only papal official was John de Gigliis, papal collector, admitted

to the prebend of Bishopshull in 1481.[14] Otherwise the non-resident chapter was composed of much the same elements as before. A few eminent royal servants and rising churchmen held prebends: for example, Henry Chichele (Archbishop of Canterbury 1414–43) was Prebendary of Wellington from 1400 to 1407,[15] and Thomas Bourchier (Archbishop of Canterbury 1454–86) held the prebend of Colwich from 1429 to 1435.[16] Other prebendaries who later became bishops included John Arundel (Bishop of Chichester 1459–77), Lawrence Booth (Bishop of Durham 1457–76), and Richard Sampson, who was dean from 1533 to 1536 and Bishop of Lichfield from 1543 to 1554.[17] Others, such as Andrew Holes, Chancellor of Salisbury,[18] and John Nottingham, a Chancellor of the Exchequer and Treasurer of York,[19] achieved distinction in other cathedral chapters. The resident chapter also included the same mixture of retired royal servants, lawyers, and bishops' and noblemen's clerks.[20] In the second half of the century an effort was made by Bishop Hales (1459–90) to change the character of the chapter by introducing and promoting scholars.[21] These included George Strangeways, D.Th., Richard Salter, B.C.L., D.Cn.L., and Thomas Mills (or Milley), who became Hales's registrar.[22] Of the 15th- and early-16th-century deans none was so distinguished as Richard FitzRalph, although John Yotton (1493–1512) was a theologian of some note[23] and James Denton (1522–33) had a distinguished career as a royal chaplain and as almoner and later chancellor of Princess Mary, sister of Henry VIII.[24] Thomas Heywood, dean from 1457 to 1492, was undoubtedly the most important figure in the history of the 15th-century chapter, but he had no career outside Lichfield.[25]

There were nine residentiaries present at the installation of Bishop Burghill in 1398,[26] and the same number were resident in the Close in 1417.[27] By the 1530s, however, the normal number of residentiaries had dropped to six and earlier in the 16th century had been as low as four.[28] The reason for this reduction in numbers was undoubtedly the stringent entrance qualifications imposed by the chapter as a result of the drop in value of its revenues. The entrance qualifications imposed at the end of the 14th century[29] were incorporated in the statutes of Bishop Heyworth in 1428;[30] further regulations were then added stipulating that the 100 marks paid by new canons on beginning residence were to be used partly for the fabric and partly for

[7] D. & C. Lich., C.A. i, f. 20, mentioning 'Chad-halfpennies' (*oboli Sancti Cedde*). The farm excluded gifts or bequests to the brotherhood or the fabric worth more than 10s.; these were to be handed to the keeper of the fabric. For Outheby see Le Neve, *Fasti Ecclesiae Anglicanae, 1300–1541* (new edn.), x. 16, and for other farms of the collections see Jenkins, 'Lich. Cath.' i. 18.

[8] Wharton, *Anglia Sacra*, i. 442; see above p. 150. The tower at the N.W. angle of the Close, on which his statue stood in the 1390s (D. & C. Lich., C.A. i, f. 33v.), was presumably his work. For the site of this tower see below p. 276 n. 5.

[9] Harwood, *Lichfield*, 11. The W. gatehouse was completed and the moat round the Close redug during Northburgh's episcopate, in both cases at the chapter's expense: Wharton, *Anglia Sacra*, i. 447.

[10] S.H.C. 1950–1, 162 and map on p. 154.

[11] See plan in W. Beresford, 'Lichfield Close in the Middle Ages', *The Reliquary*, vii. 249.

[12] Erdeswick, *Staffs.* 281–2.

[13] See below p. 174.

[14] Le Neve, *Fasti* (new edn.), x. 22; D. & C. Lich., C.A.

ii, f. 3v. For his career see *D.N.B. sub* Gigli, Giovanni.

[15] Le Neve, *Fasti* (new edn.), x. 66; C.A. i, f. 57.

[16] Le Neve, *Fasti* (new edn.), x. 26.

[17] Ibid. 33, 41, 48, 60.

[18] Ibid. 38; *V.C.H. Wilts.* iii. 178, 179, 183, 383.

[19] Jenkins, 'Lich. Cath.' ii, App. F.

[20] See ibid. for biographies of e.g. Rob. Wolveden, John de Outheby and Thos. de Herdewyk.

[21] Wharton, *Anglia Sacra*, i. 454; Savage, *The Lichfield Chronicles*, 12–14.

[22] Wharton, *Anglia Sacra*, i. 454, calling Salter 'utriusque legis professor'; A. B. Emden, *Biog. Reg. of Univ. of Oxford to A.D. 1500*, iii. 1633, 1795–6.

[23] Wharton, *Anglia Sacra*, i. 454.

[24] D.N.B.

[25] See H. E. Savage, *Thomas Heywode, Dean* (1925).

[26] Wharton, *Anglia Sacra*, i. 451.

[27] D. & C. Lich., C.A. i, f. 94v.

[28] H. E. Savage, *The Cathedral and the Chapter, 1530–55* (1927), 4.

[29] See above p. 152.

[30] Dugdale, *Mon.* vi(3), 1262; D. & C. Lich., xiii, f. 7v.

ornaments for the church and that the money was to be kept in a special chest with two locks, one key held by the keeper of the fabric and the other by a canon elected by the chapter.[31] These new rules were necessary as the chapter had been dividing the fees between the canons resident in the Close.[32] At the time when Bishop Heyworth's statutes were made the chapter was finding it very difficult to manage its finances. In 1428 the communar was forced to ask Dean Stretton's executors to return 19s. 1½d. to the common fund as the dean had died in the middle of a quarter.[33] The communars had been borrowing heavily from the *baga de Whalley*,[34] which had been augmented by many legacies.[35] When in 1429 it was found that there was still not sufficient money to meet the expenses of the church it was decided that the canons should be allowed an absence of 40 days in each quarter of the following year.[36] Even with this measure or relief for the common fund the chapter still had to borrow from the newly-established fund of entrance fees to pay the chantry chaplains their salaries.[37]

By the 1490s, when the number of residentiaries seems to have been reduced to five,[38] the communar was again borrowing heavily from the *baga de Whalley*.[39] In 1528 the chapter decided, after considering the meagreness of the cathedral revenues and the expenses incurred in the last few years, that for the time being no new residentiary should be admitted.[40] An exception was made in the case of Richard Strete in consideration of his hard work for the cathedral,[41] but when in April 1530 the chancellor, Ralph Whitehead, announced his intention of coming into residence, the chapter refused to admit him.[42] It argued that it could not afford to maintain another residentiary: it had recently been forced to pawn jewels to raise a loan of £100 for the king, the Mortuaries Act had meant a reduction of £40 or more in its annual revenues, and then there were the costs of a suit against the bishop, and the high price of provisions.[43] A few months later Whitehead invited all the canons to an entrance feast, hoping it would persuade them to change their minds, and in September he was admitted at the bishop's request.[44]

There were few changes in chapter procedure in this period, and the four codes of statutes issued by Bishops Heyworth (1428), Boulers (1454), Hales (1465), and Blythe (1526) were concerned mainly with straightening out existing procedures and removing anomalies. The relations of the dean with his chapter were generally smooth, although the election of John Verney in 1432 was challenged by a non-residentiary whose proctor had not voted for him and the case was taken as far as the papal court.[45] In 1512, after the death of Dean Yotton, the chapter acted with a certain degree of independence. Having fixed a date for the election of the next dean the residentiaries sequestrated the income of the deanery and made arrangements for a capitular visitation *decanatu vacante*; the president and two residentiaries then visited the prebends in and around Lichfield.[46] In 1533, when Dean Sampson appointed a notorious pluralist as his *locum tenens*, the chapter refused to accept the nomination of such a certain absentee to an irremovable post and instead appointed him president during good behaviour.[47] The statutes of 1428 and 1454 laid down the procedure for settling disputes between members of the chapter, and the latter laid down severe penalties against canons who involved laymen in their disputes with fellow canons;[48] the statutes of 1465 forbade any canon to employ a servant dismissed by another canon.[49]

According to the 1428 statutes canons had been neglectful about attending chapter meetings, and it was ordered that in future all residentiaries were to be present when chapter business was being discussed.[50] Later statutes and chapter acts emphasized the need for secrecy about chapter business.[51] The statutes of 1526 ordered that the common seal *ad causas* should be kept in the custody of three residentiaries and that a communar's seal should be cut. The common seal was not to be used without the permission of the whole chapter.[52] In 1527 the communar's seal, a new common seal *ad causas*, and a chest with three locks were shown to the chapter.[53] There was also concern that the statutes should be readily available for inspection: in 1465 it was ordered that they should be rewritten in a parchment book to which all the canons were to have access.[54]

Apart from the management of chapter property and the disciplining of the ministers of the cathedral, chapter meetings were concerned with many aspects of cathedral life. Business ranged from the general order in 1483 that all ministers of the church were to 'reform' their tonsures to ensure that their ears were showing,[55] to the occasional admission of notables, such as Humphrey, Earl of Stafford (1429), and Richard, Earl of Warwick (1434), into confraternity.[56] There were also officials to be appointed, ranging from proctors and attornies at common law[57] to keepers of the clock.[58] In some of the appointments outsiders took an interest; thus in 1483 Thomas Rigley was appointed sergeant, or verger, at the request of the Duke of Buckingham.[59] Canons had also to nominate to vacant benefices and chantries in the gift of the chapter, and at the beginning of the 16th century an elaborate scheme was worked out by which the residentiaries nominated in rotation, the order being determined by lot.[60]

[31] Dugdale, *Mon.* vi(3), 1262.
[32] D. & C. Lich., C.A. i, f. 94v.
[33] Ibid. f. 128. In 1426 the chapter had pawned a chalice to the executors for £18: ibid. f. 115.
[34] Ibid. f. 134v.
[35] Ibid. f. 91v.; D. & C. Lich., xiii, f. 37.
[36] C.A. i, f. 134v.
[37] Ibid. f. 136.
[38] C.A. iii, f. 1.
[39] Ibid. f. 9v.
[40] Ibid. iv, f. 53.
[41] Ibid. f. 58.
[42] Ibid. f. 64.
[43] Ibid.
[44] Ibid. f. 67, 67v.
[45] *Cal. Papal Regs.* ix, 117–18.
[46] D. & C. Lich., C.A. iii, f. 105.
[47] Ibid. f. 107.
[48] Dugdale, *Mon.* vi(3), 1262, 1263–4; D. & C. Lich., xiii, ff. 7v., 8.
[49] Dugdale, *Mon.* vi(3), 1264; D. & C. Lich., xiii, f. 8v.
[50] Dugdale, *Mon.* vi(3), 1263.
[51] Ibid. 1264; D. & C. Lich., C.A. iv, f. 63.
[52] Dugdale, *Mon.* vi(3), 1265.
[53] D. & C. Lich., C.A. iv, f. 41.
[54] Dugdale, *Mon.* vi(3), 1264.
[55] D. & C. Lich., C.A. ii, f. 11.
[56] Ibid. i, ff. 132, 145.
[57] Ibid. ii, f. 1; iv, f. 95v.
[58] Ibid. i, f. 58; iii, f. 70. The keeper of the clock received 20s. a year; from 1503 he also received food and drink.
[59] Ibid. ii, ff. 9, 18v.
[60] Ibid. iii, f. 110; iv, ff. 20v.–21, 73v.

The chapter was also much concerned with the regulation of the Close, except for the allotment of canonical houses which was the privilege of the bishop. The statutes of 1465 laid down that all refuse was to be carried out of the Close and that canons were not to put piles of wood outside their houses.[61] There was a graveyard in the Close, but in the 1530s the chapter had to enforce the rule that only those living in the Close were entitled to be buried there.[62] The water-supply also caused trouble in the late 15th century when the chapter accused Sir Humphrey Stanley of breaking the conduit and depriving the Close of water; the case was finally taken before the king's council.[63] The Close was not always popular with the city, and in 1436 a body of citizens attempted to break open the gates and attacked members of the church.[64] As a result of this and further attacks the dean and chapter were given extensive privileges within the Close in 1441: no royal official was to be allowed beyond the gates, and the dean and chapter were to have the return and execution of all writs and were to be justices of the peace for the Close.[65] In 1532 the subchanter and sacrist asked a county justice to issue a warrant against one of the canons but withdrew the request on being warned by the chapter that this would infringe the privileges of the Close.[66] A special guard was employed to keep the gates of the Close, which were not opened before seven in the morning.[67] In 1532 there occurred what was probably the last case of sanctuary in the Close when a thief took refuge there.[68]

The statutes of 1428 ordered that services in the cathedral were to follow the Salisbury Use,[69] but there is no evidence that this order was imposed. During the 15th century there were repeated demands that all ministers of the church should be properly habited for services,[70] and in 1487 some regulations were made about the administration of sacraments in the cathedral.[71] There was, however, no consistent attempt to reform the cathedral liturgy until the time of Dean Denton. Bishop Blythe at his visitation of 1523 found that cathedral services still differed in many ways from the Salisbury pattern, and his statutes laid down that in future that Use was to be followed for all services, except for those on the feasts of St. Chad, St. Katherine, and St. Nicholas and on the Monday, Tuesday, and Wednesday of Pentecost, when observances were to be those most convenient.[72] As a result several chapter orders were issued about particular services: vicars were ordered that whenever they said requiems for the dead according to the Salisbury Use they were to say immediately afterwards the *commendaciones animarum in conventu*, and that in future the saying of the Confession at compline and prime was to be according to the Use

of Salisbury and not according to the Lichfield Use.[73] In 1532 some of the canons complained that they were being overburdened with duties in the choir, and the chapter agreed that the ancient Use of the cathedral should be followed until the dean found out the practice of Salisbury in this connexion.[74] In a dispute over ritual the following year both sides cited the Salisbury Use, differing only in their interpretation of it.[75]

The drive for conformity at Lichfield was not confined to the form of the liturgy. By ancient cathedral custom silk copes were not worn in procession at Candlemas because of the expense of replacing them if they should be spoilt by burns or candle-wax. In 1523 Dean Denton, overriding the protests of at least one of the canons, persuaded the chapter to abolish this custom and bring Lichfield into line with other English cathedrals; he promised to give £40 to cover possible damage.[76] A levy from the prebends was later ordered to renew the copes.[77] In 1528 four processionals had to be obtained as the cathedral had no suitable ones.[78]

Another apparent innovation of these years was the arrangement made for the administration of the sacraments to servants and those lodging temporarily in the Close. In 1523 it was decided that a curate should be appointed to hear their confessions, receiving 2d. from each servant at Easter and the mortuaries of laymen dying within the Close; a chantry chaplain was nominated to the post.[79] In 1528 this arrangement was confirmed, with the proviso that if any of those in the charge of the curate of the Close fell sick of the plague they were to be visited instead by the curate who ministered to the sick of Lichfield under the Vicar of St. Mary's.[80] Two years later fear of the plague led to a more complete isolation of the Close. The confessions of all servants and laymen living within the Close were to be heard in one of the chapels in the cathedral by the Vicar of St. Mary's, but no inhabitants of the city were to be admitted to receive *viaticum* in the cathedral unless they belonged to the household of a canon, were cathedral servants, or had been granted a special licence by the chapter.[81]

In 1401, following his metropolitical visitation, Archbishop Arundel confirmed the possessions of the cathedral.[82] There was little change in the property of the chapter during the later Middle Ages. The few churches that were appropriated to the cathedral were given to the vicars or choristers.[83] The chapter acquired eight new pensions, but their total value was not much over £2.[84] In the later 15th century Dean Heywood bought some land at Alrewas and King's Bromley and conveyed it to the chapter;[85] in 1535 this property was the only temporality of the chapter (as opposed to the churches of the common fund which were

[61] Dugdale, *Mon.* vi(3), 1264.
[62] D. & C. Lich., C.A. ii, f. 14; iv, ff. 95v.–96.
[63] D. & C. Lich., OO. 2; 17th-cent. misc. bk., ff. 54v.–55.
[64] *Cal. Pat.* 1436–41, 84. The dean and chapter decided that the attack was a matter for the whole chapter, the costs to be met from the common fund: D. & C. Lich., C.A. i, f. 145v.
[65] *Cal. Pat.* 1441–6, 31–32. The grant was confirmed in 1461: ibid. 1461–7, 141.
[66] D. & C. Lich., C.A. iv, f. 98.
[67] Ibid. iii, f. 135v.; iv, f. 8v.
[68] Ibid. iv, ff. 93v., 94v.
[69] Dugdale, *Mon.* vi(3), 1263.
[70] Ibid. 1262, 1264.

[71] D. & C. Lich., C.A. ii, f. 14v.
[72] Dugdale, *Mon.* vi(3), 1264.
[73] D. & C. Lich., C.A. iii, ff. 138, 139.
[74] Ibid. iv, f. 95.
[75] Ibid. f. 101.
[76] Ibid. iii, ff. 138v.–139.
[77] Dugdale, *Mon.* vi(3), 1256; see below p. 168.
[78] C.A. iv, f. 54v.
[79] Ibid. iii, f. 138.
[80] Ibid. iv, f. 54v.
[81] Ibid. f. 63v.
[82] Ibid. i, f. 59.
[83] See pp. 164–5.
[84] Jenkins, 'Lich. Cath.' i. 20–24.
[85] Savage, *Thomas Heywode*, 19.

spiritualities) and was valued at 51s. 5¾d.[86] According to the *Valor Ecclesiasticus* Lichfield was the poorest of the secular cathedrals in 1535,[87] with a common fund worth £436 10s. 3¼d. gross a year, of which £160 17s. 1d. was earmarked for the payment of vicars' commons, chantry priests' salaries, and other fees and expenses.[88] The Peak parishes and their chapels yielded £215 15s. 9½d. a year, while the rest of the appropriated churches yielded a total of £125 a year;[89] 37 pensions from churches in six counties brought in a yearly total of £93 3s.[90] The total annual value of the prebends and dignities was given as £390 1s. 10¾d.[91] The assessments of the individual prebends, which are generally supposed to give the minimum rental value of the property,[92] show considerable variations from the values given in 1291.[93] The deanery had increased in value from £26 13s. 4d. to £40, but the treasurership had dropped from £66 13s. 4d. to £56 13s. 4d. Some of the prebends had nearly doubled in value, such as Flixton which had risen from £4 13s. 4d. to £7; others had fallen considerably, such as Longdon, which was assessed at £20 in 1291 and only £8 in 1535. The variations in value are too erratic to allow any conclusions to be drawn about changes in the value of cathedral property between 1291 and 1535.[94]

Very little is known about how the chapter managed its property during this period since little more than a dozen leases have survived, all but two of them from the early years of the 16th century. What evidence there is suggests that the 14th-century policy was continued. It seems likely that the farmers of cathedral property found their leases less profitable; in 1481 the farmer of Worfield asked for a remission of rent because of his great losses during the year.[95] In the Peak parishes the mineral tithes were leased as before: in 1482 the lead tithes in the Peak were leased for five years at a rent of £11 a year.[96] In addition the other tithes (with the exception of the wool tithes) and the lands in the Peak were leased, and the chapter appointed an attorney to collect its rents.[97]

The chapter continued to collect the wool tithes and dispose of the wool directly. The tithes were collected by local men, either by the vicars of the churches or by specially appointed agents, and sold by them; the proceeds, after the expenses of the collectors had been deducted, were given to the communar of the chapter. In 1427 the Vicar of Bakewell accounted for £20, the proceeds of the

sale of fleeces at 8d. each.[98] In 1481 the chapter leased the wool tithes for five years to its subproctor in the Peak,[99] but by the end of the 1480s the communar was administering the tithes again and in one year the chapter's agents collected 3,365 fleeces.[1]

In the early 15th century leases were still being made for short periods only, usually 5 years, according to the statutes.[2] Where a comparison is possible the rents paid seem to have been lower than the annual value of the property given in the *Valor*;[3] it would be necessary, however, to know the size of entry fines before an assessment could be made of the efficiency of the chapter's estate management.[4] At the beginning of 1523 the manner of making leases came under discussion; it was decided that the granting of leases should be a matter for the whole chapter and that a draft of the lease should be available for alteration before a decision was made.[5] Another matter which was causing concern was the growing practice by which canons procured leases for themselves or their relations on favourable terms and then sublet the property. It was ordered that no canon was to have a lease unless he paid as much rent as an outsider would give and that canons were themselves to occupy the property which they leased.[6] If, however, a canon wanted a lease he was to be preferred to outsiders.[7] In 1535 the chapter was paying fees to six officials concerned in the collection of its revenues: a receiver-general, a collector of pensions, an auditor, a steward of courts, glebes, and rectories, and a bailiff and a steward of the Peak.[8]

In June 1400 there was a metropolitical visitation of the cathedral by Archbishop Arundel at which a levy of one-tenth of the value of all the prebends for three years was ordered; the proceeds were to be used to provide new vestments and to make stalls in the choir.[9] The chapter was reluctant to take any action; several general chapter meetings were called to discuss the matter, but no non-residentiaries attended and the levy was not agreed to until nearly two years after the visitation. Even then it does not seem to have been collected.[10] A few years later the question of the bishop's right of visitation was reopened. The chapter seems to have resisted Bishop Burghill's attempt to visit it in 1407,[11] and in 1423 it obtained an inhibition from the court of Canterbury against Bishop Heyworth who had announced his intended visitation.[12] Heyworth complained to the Pope who restored him to 'the office of

[86] *Valor Eccl.* (Rec. Com.), iii. 132.
[87] *V.C.H. Wilts.* iii. 182.
[88] *Valor Eccl.* iii. 132–5.
[89] Ibid. 132–3.
[90] Ibid. 133–4. The substantial pension from Winwick, about which there had been litigation in the 14th and 15th centuries (see above p. 155; D. & C. Lich., C.A. ii, ff. 22–23v.) is not listed.
[91] *Valor Eccl.* iii. 130–2.
[92] See *V.C.H. Wilts.* iii. 182.
[93] For a comparison of the assessments see Jenkins, 'Lich. Cath.' ii. 13–19.
[94] See *V.C.H. Wilts.* iii. 182.
[95] D. & C. Lich., C.A. ii, f. 4v.
[96] Ibid. f. 5v.; see above p 155.
[97] *S.H.C.* vi (2), 19.
[98] D. & C. Lich., C.A. i, f. 122v.
[99] Ibid. ii, ff. 1v., 2.
[1] Ibid. ff. 46 sqq. This account must date from Ric. Sherborne's second term as communar in 1487–8.
[2] Ibid. iii, f. 108; *S.H.C.* vi(2), 20; see above p. 146.

[3] E.g. the rectory of Tideswell was leased in 1509 for 26s. 8d. a year (C.A. iii, f. 108), while in 1535 its value is given as 45s. 1d. (*Valor Eccl.* iii. 133); in 1521 Cannock, valued in 1535 at £28 (*Valor Eccl.* iii. 132), was farmed for £16 a year (C.A. iii, f. 127v.).
[4] There is a record of a £10 entry fine paid in 1523 for property with an annual rental of £1 6s. 8d.: *S.H.C.* vi(2), 20.
[5] D. & C. Lich., C.A. iii, f. 139v.
[6] Ibid. iv, f. 8v. An example of this practice was the leasing in 1521 by Canon Ralph Cantrell and his brother of Thornton, valued at £3 6s. 8d. in 1535, for 40s. a year: C.A. iii, f. 128v.; *Valor Eccl.* iii. 132.
[7] Dugdale, *Mon.* vi(3), 1264.
[8] *Valor Eccl.* iii. 135.
[9] Wharton, *Anglia Sacra*, i. 452; H. E. Savage, *Bishop John Burghull* (1924), 11. By this time the rebuilding of the choir must have been completed: see above p. 158.
[10] Savage, *Bishop John Burghull*, 12; D. & C. Lich., C.A. i, ff. 60, 62v.–63.
[11] C.A. i, f. 70. [12] *Cal. Papal Regs.* vii. 294–5.

visitation and reformation which his predecessors have neglected to exercise'.[13] In 1427 two vicars were appointed to note the defects of the residentiary canons according to new arrangements for visitation by the bishops,[14] and these arrangements were sealed by the bishop and the chapter during a visitation in October 1428.[15] Visitations were to take place only at seven-year intervals and were to be of the chapter only; the other cathedral clergy and the churches of the common fund and the prebends were, except in cases of scandalous neglect, to be exempt. Any money arising from the visitation was to go to the fabric or the ornaments of the church. Apart from Hereford, which resisted visitation until after the Reformation, Lichfield was the last of the English secular cathedrals to submit to episcopal visitation.[16]

After the settlement of the visitation dispute the relations between bishop and chapter appear to have been good, although occasionally storms blew up. The last years of Bishop Blythe's episcopate were marked by unsuccessful attempts by both parties to encroach on each other's privileges. The first, in 1529–30, was over the bishop's claim to the patronage of St. Mary's, Lichfield; the case was hotly contested, and Blythe showed his displeasure by ostentatiously snubbing the chapter when he passed through Lichfield on his way to London in June 1530.[17] The matter was settled by arbitration later that year,[18] only to be succeeded by a fresh dispute arising out of an attempt by the chapter to prevent Blythe from visiting St. John's Hospital, Lichfield.[19]

By the beginning of the 15th century the subchanter had emerged as the *ex officio* president of the vicars.[20] The statutes of 1428 ordered the subchanter and the vicars of the three other dignitaries to wear special amices trimmed with calabar fur; they were to have 6s. 8d. above their usual salaries to pay for them.[21] The same statutes laid down regulations for ensuring that a vicar's stall was filled within a few months of a vacancy but also stipulated that all new vicars were to be examined to make sure that they could chant to an organ.[22] By the end of the century the chapter was imposing a year's probation on new vicars,[23] and in 1530 a probationer was dismissed because he was old and had lost his voice.[24] The following year some of the vicars claimed that they were being impoverished as a result of the custom whereby a vicar fully admitted after his probationary year had to provide a feast, called 'ly seynyfest'.[25] The chapter ordered an investigation and found that for many years the vicars had been illegally demanding an entrance fee, or 'interest money', of 20s. from new vicars and two further payments of

26s. 8d.; these sums were said to impoverish newcomers and sometimes discouraged those with musical ability from taking vicarships.[26] The chapter decided that the entrance fee should remain but gave the vicars £20 to buy lands to provide 10s. towards each vicar's 'interest money'.[27] Ten years earlier the vicars had been told that they must give the dean and chapter a quarter's notice if they intended to give up their stalls.[28]

The vicars' behaviour was a constant problem to the chapter. Absenteeism was a continually recurring offence. The statutes of 1465 imposed a fine of 2d. to the fabric fund on unlicensed absentees,[29] and in January 1496 the fine for being outside the Close after the gates were shut in the evening was fixed at 12d.[30] The latter order apparently led to fears for the safety of the porter and his assistant, and in February a scale of fines was drawn up for various types of attack on them.[31] Another common offence was incontinence, and in 1496 a vicar accused of fornication was forbidden to leave the Close except to practise archery with his fellow-vicars outside the city.[32] Some vicars were sportsmen who bred dogs in the Close and went out hunting at night, and in 1512 the chapter was forced to order the removal of all dogs from the Close and to forbid vicars to go hunting.[33] There were also the usual minor misdemeanours — vicars dealing with their own private affairs during services and roaming around the Close and city improperly dressed.[34] An unusual case was that of Robert Bendbow who was summoned before the chapter in 1523 for dicing and card-playing instead of attending services; he was stated to have obtained his stall on the petition of his father, in spite of the fact that he was so young that a tutor had to be appointed to look after him.[35] The vicars were subject to visitation by the dean and chapter,[36] who appointed one of them as *intitulator* to report on the absences and other offences of his fellows;[37] this post was an unpopular one.[38]

In 1513 the chapter's attempts to control and discipline the vicars led to a short-lived strike. The vicars refused to take part in services until the chapter agreed to accept their traditional usage as to rest days and to reinstate one of their number who had been excommunicated. After two or three days the chapter succeeded in breaking down their resistance and the ringleaders were punished.[39] Another dispute arose between the two bodies in 1526 when the vicars drew up several articles of complaint against the chapter.[40] They alleged that they were not being paid commons during reasonable absences; that the chapter made statutes for them without their consent; that they were summoned

[13] Ibid.
[14] C.A. i, f. 129.
[15] Wilkins, *Concilia*, iii. 508–11.
[16] Edwards, *Eng. Secular Cath.* 133–4.
[17] C.A. iv, ff. 61, 61v., 62, 64, 65v. He avoided the delegation waiting to greet him because 'of the dislike he felt for the canons residentiary'.
[18] Ibid. f. 70.
[19] See below pp. 281–2. At the same time there was a dispute over jurisdiction in the parish of Chebsey: C. A. iv, f. 74v.
[20] This situation was unique among the secular cathedrals: Edwards, *Eng. Secular Cath.* 174.
[21] Dugdale, *Mon.* vi(3), 1263.
[22] Ibid. 1262, 1263.
[23] D. & C. Lich., C.A. iii, ff. 25v., 26, 30v.
[24] Ibid. iv, f. 66v.
[25] Ibid. f. 76v.
[26] Ibid. ff. 96v.–97.

[27] Ibid.
[28] Ibid. iii, ff. 126, 128.
[29] Dugdale, *Mon.* vi(3), 1264.
[30] C.A. iii, f. 29. The rule applied to both vicars and choristers.
[31] Ibid. Again the rule applied to both vicars and choristers.
[32] Ibid. f. 30.
[33] Ibid. f. 104v.
[34] Ibid. ff. 135, 138.
[35] Ibid. f. 139v.
[36] E.g. ibid. f. 84v.
[37] Ibid. ff. 9v., 82, 138.
[38] Ibid. f. 87.
[39] Ibid. ff. 115v.–116v., 117v.–118, 118v.–119v. The rest days were called 'ly Stene' and must have been in origin days for bleeding.
[40] Ibid. iv, ff. 26v.–27.

before the chapter for trifling offences in spite of the fact that they could be expelled after only three admonitions; that the chapter had reduced the number of vicars from 27 to 21 or less and was pocketing the stipends of vacant stalls;[41] and that vicars were having to perform the duties of hebdomadaries without receiving any extra salary.[42] They carried their complaints to the bishop, and at the beginning of 1527 Wolsey appointed a legatine commission to investigate the dispute; in April, after the statutes had been revised, the vicars agreed to a settlement.[43]

In 1528 the vicars made a bid for greater independence by applying for a royal licence of incorporation. This step was taken without the knowledge of the chapter, although the vicars claimed afterwards that the suggestion had come from John Veysey, Bishop of Exeter and formerly Archdeacon of Chester. The chapter used its influence to prevent the granting of the licence, which it said would be injurious to the cathedral and the vicars themselves. It advised the vicars to ask the help of Sir Anthony Fitzherbert, the judge, in drawing up another charter of incorporation, which it would then consider; nothing more was heard of incorporation, however, until after the Reformation.[44]

Unlike vicars in other cathedrals the Lichfield vicars were not allowed to hold any preferments apart from their stalls. In 1400 Bishop Burghill changed this custom and allowed vicars to accept any benefices other than those requiring continual residence, but this concession was cancelled by Archbishop Arundel at his metropolitical visitation later the same year.[45] In 1412 Burghill obtained licence to appropriate to the vicars their second church, Chesterton (Warws.), 'as the possessions of the vicars are at present much deteriorated and many intend to depart for lack of maintenance';[46] in 1505 the income from the church totalled £10 10s. 10d.[47] In 1535 the vicars' gross income was just over £200 a year; apart from nearly £100 from the chapter for commons, the greater part of the income, £65, came from rents of property in and around Lichfield.[48] By the early 16th century, when they owned about 250 houses and an even larger number of single pieces of land, the vicars must have been the major landowners in the city.[49] To manage their property they had a bailiff or rent-collector and a receiver-general.[50] An ordinance made at the end of the 15th century laid down that both these officials were to be elected by the whole body of vicars and

that the receivership was to be held by a vicar and the collectorship by either a vicar or a layman.[51] In 1528 the chapter decreed that in future no vicar was to hold the latter office.[52] The property was farmed under the management of the subchanter; in 1524 it was discovered that he had been leasing property out at low rates and had failed to see that the rents were collected properly.[53]

In the earlier 15th century the vicars' houses were repaired and a common hall was built for them by Canon Thomas Chesterfield (d. 1452) with the help of Bishop Heyworth and two Oxford burgesses.[54] Dean Heywood, a generous benefactor to the vicars, completed the repair of their houses and in 1474 built them an infirmary or rest-house, which contained a small chapel and a muniment room. It was laid down that the building was not to be let or occupied privately by any vicar.[55] The conduct of the vicars in their common buildings was regulated by a set of statutes which they themselves drew up.[56] They were to behave well at table and not to refuse the food put in front of them; they were not to gamble in hall, except for ale; they were to keep their rooms in good repair and free from fire, water, women, and hunting-dogs. To manage their common hall they had their own steward and butler.[57] In the 15th century two funds, the 'chest of charity' (1419) and the 'bag of grace' (1490), were established to provide vicars with extra money for such things as food, repairs, and obits.[58]

The number of choristers had risen to twelve by 1535.[59] During the 1520s their part in the cathedral services was greatly increased: they attended every bishop's obit and were ordered to be present at the services held in the middle of the night.[60] A master of the choristers was appointed *pro instruccione seu doctrina eorum*; in addition he taught them 'priksong et descant' and sometimes, by special arrangement, to play the organ.[61] The boys were not restricted to sacred music. Visitors to the Close were sometimes entertained by *cantilenae vel ballettae* sung by the choristers, and in 1522 the chapter laid down the way in which any rewards received after such performances were to be divided.[62] In the 1520s and 1530s a boy bishop, presumably one of the choristers, was being appointed on Innocents' Day (28 December);[63] there appears to be no other evidence concerning the history of this custom at Lichfield. Bishop Hales (d. 1490) left money to build a house for the choristers,[64] but they did not live in common until the late 1520s. In 1527 the Crown granted

[41] The reduction in the numbers of vicars had been brought up at the 1516 episcopal visitation (Lich. Dioc. Regy. B/V/1/1, p. 2); in 1527 (C.A. iv, between ff. 37 and 38) and in 1535 (*Valor Eccl.* iii. 137–8) there were 21 vicars, 7 of them laymen.

[42] Harwood, *Lichfield*, 259–60. The 5 hebdomadary vicarships, carrying extra commons, were said by the chapter to have been abolished, but it was not known what had happened to their stipends: D. & C. Lich., 17th-cent. misc. bk., loose-leaf notes.

[43] Harwood, *Lichfield*, 260–1; C.A. iv, ff. 38, 41.

[44] C.A. iv, f. 53; see below p. 167. Fitzherbert was one of the Fitzherberts of Norbury (Derb.) and an acquaintance of Dean Denton: D.N.B. In 1530 he was one of the arbitrators in the dispute between the chapter and the bishop: C.A. iv, f. 70; see above p. 163. For Veysey see D.N.B.

[45] Savage, *Bishop John Burghull*, 10–12.

[46] *Cal. Pat.* 1408–13, 456. For Chesterton see V.C.H. Warws. v. 46; above p. 154 n. 17.

[47] D. & C. Lich., C.A. iii, f. 85.

[48] *Valor Eccl.* iii. 136–8.

[49] Jenkins, 'Lich. Cath.' i. 91.

[50] *Valor Eccl.* iii. 136. There was also an auditor.

[51] D. & C. Lich., 17th-cent. misc. bk., ff. 82v.–83v.

[52] C.A. iv, f. 54v.   [53] Ibid. f. 13v.

[54] Savage, *Thomas Heywode*, 7; Shaw, *Staffs.* i. 306.

[55] Savage, *Thomas Heywode*, 19.

[56] D. & C. Lich., 17th-cent. misc. bk., ff. 75–77. These undated statutes start with the regulations for payment of entrance money.

[57] Ibid. f. 76; C.A. iv, f. 19.

[58] D. & C. Lich., 17th-cent. misc. bk., ff. 78–79v.; Bodl. MS. Ashmole 1521, pp. 1–2.

[59] *Valor Eccl.* iii. 135. Dean Denton had increased their number by 4: Wharton, *Anglia Sacra*, i. 455.

[60] C.A. iv, ff. 9, 12v., 75.

[61] Ibid. f. 124v.

[62] Ibid. iii, f. 137v.

[63] Hist. MSS. Com. *Middleton*, 346, 351, 364, 379, 386; *Valor Eccl.* iii. 154.

[64] C.A. iii, f. 37.

the church and property of the dissolved nunnery at Farewell to the chapter for the support of the choristers. At the same time Bishop Blythe assigned the choristers a house on the north side of the Close; with the help of Dean Denton it was repaired and a cook installed.[65] In 1535 the choristers had an income of £39; their property was managed by the chapter, and fees were paid from their income to a receiver-general, a bailiff, and a steward.[66] Their net income of £25 was not sufficient to feed and clothe twelve boys, and they were being allowed an additional £20 a year by the chapter.[67]

The chantry chaplains numbered seventeen in 1535. Their only common property consisted of some lands left to pay for obits, worth about £7 a year.[68] They were principally supported by the endowments of their chantries, of which there were seventeen left in the cathedral, worth about £95 a year in all.[69] In 1411 Bishop Burghill gave the thirteen chantry priests without official houses a site on the south side of the Close, and after his death in 1414 his executor built them the 'New College'.[70] In 1468 this building was improved by Dean Heywood, who added a bakehouse and a brewhouse, glazed the windows, and supplied the common hall with a stove and a table-cloth.[71] Under Dean Denton the chantry priests, like the choristers, were given permission to draw water from the aqueduct.[72] Their duties were laid down in 1428: they were to celebrate their masses each day in turn from the sixth to the tenth hour, and after the consecration during high mass one of them was to say mass for the benefit of travellers.[73] They were not to absent themselves without permission and were to submit their disputes to the dean and chapter for settlement.[74]

In 1535 the seventeen chantries were being served at thirteen altars.[75] Many of the chantries founded in the 13th and 14th centuries had disappeared, for of the seventeen survivors four had been founded during the 15th and early 16th centuries.[76] The most elaborate of these new foundations was the chantry of Jesus and St. Anne, founded in 1468 by Dean Heywood; its organization forms an interesting contrast to the simpler arrangements of earlier centuries. The chaplain was supported by annual payments from Lilleshall Abbey (Salop.) and, after 1471, from Dale Abbey (Derb.); the Lilleshall pension included a stipend to the New College so that Heywood's chaplain could live with the other chantry priests. Heywood furnished the chantry chapel with statues of the Saviour and St. Anne, stalls for a choir, and an organ, and supplied all the necessary ornaments and vestments. In 1473 he added to the ordination of the chantry; there was to

be in addition a cursal mass, celebrated by the vicars, a week each at a time. Every Friday morning there was also to be sung in the chantry chapel a mass of the Name of Jesus followed by a requiem mass for all the bishops, deans, and canons of Lichfield. Moreover on Friday evening after compline in the choir a suitable antiphon was to be sung before the Saviour's statue; people were to be called to this latter devotion by the ringing of the great bell of the cathedral during the saying of compline. The object of this new service was to draw lay people into the cathedral for special devotions; in 1473 Heywood obtained from Archbishop Bourchier an indulgence of 100 days to all penitents of Canterbury Diocese attending the Friday services and similar indulgences of 40 days from the bishops of the southern province. In 1482 he obtained from Rome further indulgences for pilgrims attending first and second vespers in the chapel on various specified occasions.[77] In 1483 it was decided that offerings given at the chantry should be used first to maintain its ornaments and then for the maintenance of the cathedral ornaments and fabric. A *custos oblacionum de Jhesu* was appointed to account annually to the chapter for the proceeds of the chantry, which by the 1490s was producing a steady income.[78]

It was only at the beginning of the 15th century when the great work of rebuilding the cathedral had been completed that the duties of the keeper of the fabric were given statutory confirmation.[79] The fabric fund was to be kept separate from the common fund, although fabric money could be borrowed by the chapter if it was promptly repaid; also all entry fees were to be used for the fabric. No extensive or special work on the fabric of the church was to be undertaken without the permission of the dean and chapter.

In fact no major work was undertaken before the Reformation, and the fabric money was used only to maintain the church.[80] During this period the interior of the cathedral was enriched and beautified, but this was at the expense and on the initiative of individual deans rather than as a consistent policy. Dean Heywood did much to improve the appearance of the church: he adorned the chapter-house with coloured glass, paintings, and panelling and bought for the cathedral a great organ and a bell called the 'Jesus Bell' which alone cost £100.[81] While he was dean a fine stone screen was erected at the entrance of the Lady Chapel.[82] Another benefactor was Dean Denton, a man of great liberality who, among other things, spent £160 in roofing-over the market cross at Lichfield 'for poor market folks to stand dry in'.[83] In 1524 he offered to have the vaults at the west end of the nave newly built in stone at his own expense

[65] D. & C. Lich., C.A. iv, ff. 43, 46, 47; ibid. L.2; Lich. Dioc. Regy., B/A/1/14, f. 97; see below p. 224. In front of the house was a gatehouse with the inscription: 'Domus pro choristis extructa 1531': *Gent. Mag.* 1782, lii, 558–9.
[66] *Valor Eccl.* iii. 135; C.A. iv, ff. 47, 57v.
[67] *Valor Eccl.* iii. 135.
[68] Ibid. 139, 141.
[69] Ibid. 139–41. There was also the chantry at Stowe, worth £5 a year: ibid. 141.
[70] Savage, *Bishop John Burghull*, 17.
[71] Savage, *Thomas Heywode*, 9.
[72] Wharton, *Anglia Sacra*, i. 455; C.A. iv, f. 76v.
[73] Dugdale, *Mon.* vi(3), 1262. For the order of celebration see C.A. i, f. 113v.
[74] Dugdale, *Mon.* vi(3), 1262, 1263, 1264.
[75] *Valor Eccl.* iii. 139–41; S.H.C. 1915, 153–9.
[76] See *Cal. Pat.* 1446–52, 549; Savage, *Thomas Heywode*,

8–18; *L. & P. Hen. VIII*, i (1920 edn.), p. 934.
[77] See Savage, *Thomas Heywode*, 11–18; J. C. Cox, 'Benefactions of Thomas Heywood', *Archaeologia*, lii(2), 627–9; *Cal. Papal Regs.* xiii(1), 117, 264–9; *Regs. of Rob. Stillington and Ric. Fox* (Som. Rec. Soc. lii), p. 101. The chantry was probably situated in the chamber above the vestibule of the chapter-house, now the annex to the library.
[78] D. & C. Lich., C.A. ii, ff. 8v.–9, 11; iii, ff. 8v., 25v., 32v.
[79] In Heyworth's statutes: Dugdale, *Mon.* vi(3), 1262.
[80] See e.g. C.A. i, ff. 58v., 73v., 105v.–106, 136. In 1531 the keeper of the fabric was directed to repair the service books: ibid. iv, f. 75v.
[81] Savage, *Thomas Heywode*, 19–20.
[82] [H. E. Savage], *The Sedilia* (1914), 7–8.
[83] Leland, *Itin.* ed. L. Toulmin Smith, ii. 100.

if the chapter would provide the stone; the offer was evidently accepted.[84] It was probably at this time that Bishop Blythe contributed 50 oaks and £20 towards the repair and restoration of the cathedral and a further £20 for the decoration of the nave.[85]

At the end of the 15th century a new detached library was built on the north side of the Close beside the north transept. In 1490 Dean Heywood gave £40 towards this library, then in the course of construction, and it was finished in 1500 by Dean Yotton at his own expense.[86] At the same period three of the residentiaries, Thomas Milley, Henry Edyall, and George Strangeways, were building themselves new houses in the Close.[87]

The Reformation

The Reformation brought no basic change to the constitution of the chapter. Only one prebend was lost, that of Bolton, which was granted to the king in 1541 with the archdeaconry of Chester to form part of the new bishopric of Chester.[88] The constitutional relationship of bishop and chapter remained unchanged, though with the dissolution of Coventry Priory the existence of two separate chapters came to an end. In 1541 it was enacted that the Dean and Chapter of Lichfield should be 'the full entire and sole see and chapter of the said bishopric of Coventry and Lichfield'.[89] As a result the chapter had the sole right to confirm grants made by the bishop, and since it had proved expensive to obtain the privilege the chapter recouped some of its expenses by charging the bishop a fee of 40s., in addition to that claimed by the chapter clerk, for confirming small grants and more for those of greater value.[90]

The right of collating to prebends remained with the bishop. Rowland Lee (1534–43) and Richard Sampson (1543–54) either sold, or were persuaded to give, many presentations to prebendal stalls to laymen. In 1536 Lee sold to Thomas, Duke of Norfolk, the first two vacant appointments to Bishop's Itchington or Gaia Minor, and in 1538, in answer to Thomas Cromwell's request for a good prebend, he gave him the presentation to Eccleshall; in 1540 he sold two reversions to a syndicate which included Cromwell's nephew, Sir Richard Cromwell.[91] Bishop Sampson, who alienated much episcopal property, made a practice of selling reversions of benefices and in 11 years disposed of 19 presentations to prebendal stalls.[92] A possible explanation of this traffic in prebends was the need to find places for dispossessed monks, for many of whom the lay impropriators were legally bound to provide pensions.[93] During the vacancy after Lee's

death the Crown had presented Stephen Sagar, who had been the last Abbot of Hailes (Glos.), to one of the Ufton prebends, and in 1547, probably at Sagar's instigation, the bishop appointed Philip Brode, who had been a monk at Hailes, to the prebend of Dernford. At the beginning of 1550 the two former colleagues combined to purchase from the bishop the next assignments of five of the canonical houses in the Close, thus obtaining partial control of possible candidates for residentiaryships. The following year one of the pre-Reformation canons, Arthur Dudley, Prebendary of Colwich, bought from the bishop the right of nomination to four of the remaining houses to prevent the ex-monks from gaining complete control of the chapter.[94]

As was common at other cathedrals the medieval statutes, so recently revised, remained in force, those enjoining 'popish' practices being quietly ignored.[95] Royal visitation of cathedral chapters, a short-lived innovation, was exercised at Lichfield in 1547 and 1559.[96] The Edwardian visitors did little except deliver the standard injunctions concerning preaching, vestments, education, and discipline. English was to be used for anthems and the liturgy, and the Bible was to be read in English during services; one criticism which the visitors made was that members of the cathedral body had not been as 'studious and diligent in reading of the Bible' as they should have been. Excessive hospitality was forbidden and not more than £20 was to be exacted in fines at the beginning of residence. The vicars choral were to have one month's leave of absence a year, and the master of the choristers was to take over from the precentor and subchanter the duty of choosing and managing the choristers.[97] The visitation of 1559 added nothing apart from an order that married canons and vicars were entitled to commons and an injunction that a register of leases was to be kept.

The 1559 injunction about the register was no doubt intended as a curb on the chapter. A drastic change in the chapter's policy on the length of leases had taken place in the 1540s and 1550s. During these years the statute of 1294 limiting leases to a term of 20 years was ignored. A great number of fee-farms were granted,[98] and in addition there were a number of leases for long terms, such as 80 or 99 years.[99] These leases were usually to local gentlemen and were not confined to the property of the common fund: in 1550 the manor of Farewell, belonging to the choristers, was granted to William, Lord Paget, in fee-farm.[1] The most notable example of a local family which acquired fee-farms of chapter property is the Gell family of Hopton in Derbyshire. Before 1559 Ralph Gell acquired leases of land and tithes in many of the Peak parishes and their chapelries

[84] C.A. iv, f. 9; J. T. Irvine, 'The West Front of Lichfield Cathedral', *Jnl. Brit. Arch. Assoc.* xxxviii. 353, suggesting also (pp. 352–3) that a rebuilding of the upper part of the N.W. tower may have taken place during Denton's deanery.

[85] Wharton, *Anglia Sacra*, i. 455.

[86] Ibid.; Savage, *Thomas Heywode*, 20; C.A. iii, f. 1; see above plate facing p. 148.

[87] Wharton, *Anglia Sacra*, i. 454.

[88] D. & C. Lich., C.A. iv, ff. 130–131v., 132.

[89] Act for confirmation of the authority of the Dean and Chapter of Lichfield, 33 Hen. VIII, c. 30. Coventry Priory was dissolved in 1539: *V.C.H. Warws.* ii. 58.

[90] D. & C. Lich., C.A. iv, f. 127.

[91] H. E. Savage, *The Cathedral and the Chapter, 1530–1553* (1927), 8; *L. & P. Hen. VIII*, xiii(1), p. 17.

[92] Savage, *Cathedral and Chapter*, 9.

[93] Ibid.

[94] Ibid. 10–11.

[95] See above p. 160 and below p. 178.

[96] C.A. iv, ff. 145v., 164v.; 17th-cent. misc. bk., ff. 97v.–101, 101v.–104.

[97] In 1538 the subchanter refused to present for admittance a suitable chorister and was forced to do so by the chapter: C.A. iv, f. 118v.

[98] See abstracts of leases in D. & C. Lich., 17th-cent. misc. bk., ff. 60v.–74. For the statute of 1294 see above p. 146.

[99] 17th-cent. misc. bk., ff. 71, 73.

[1] C.A. iv, f. 156v.

either in perpetuity or for very long terms of years, and the family continued to accumulate leases up to the time of the Civil War.[2] In 1550 Ralph Gell and his heirs were granted the office of receiver-general and collector of the farms, rents, and profits of the chapter, with the exception of the tithes of wool and lambs, in the Bakewell jurisdiction. For this office and the fee-farm of Kniveton Gell paid a fine of £120.[3] Other beneficiaries included the Vernon family, which in 1543 acquired the farm of the grain and hay tithes in the Peak at an annual rent of £37 and was still paying the same in 1649.[4] There are several possible explanations for these grants of fee-farms and long leases; the most probable is that the chapter needed ready money and could charge large entrance fines for such grants.[5] It is evident that by the late 1540s the chapter was having to consider ways of eking out its reduced revenues. In 1548 it decided that canons could be absent for up to 40 days in each quarter and still receive commons for the time of their absence; the object of this was to persuade residentiaries to spread their residence more evenly through the year and lessen the burden of hospitality.[6] In 1553, however, it was decided that the measure was dishonourable and contrary to the statutes, and it was revoked.[7] The Act of 1559 limiting the term of leases granted by archbishops and bishops seems also to have applied to deans and chapters; leases, except those to the Crown, were in future to be for 21 years or for the term of three lives only and the rents charged were to be no lower than the 'old, accustomed' ones.[8]

As a result of the Edwardian visitation a new post was created at the cathedral, that of divinity lecturer. The first lecturer, Dr. John Ramridge, Prebendary of Hansacre, appeared before the chapter with his letter of appointment from Archbishop Cranmer at the beginning of 1548. He was to lecture in the choir three times a week, receiving annually £10 from the chapter, 5 marks from the chancellor, and board for himself and a servant. Ramridge then offered to undertake the residentiaries' preaching turns as well if his stipend from the dean and chapter were raised to £20; it was agreed that he should receive £20 and whatever payments he could obtain from the residentiaries, but no board.[9] In July 1548 the Duke of Somerset ordered Ramridge's removal, presumably because of his lack of zeal for reform, and replaced him with Laurence Saunders, later a Marian martyr.[10] The post lapsed during Mary's reign, and an injunction delivered at the royal visitation of 1559 ordered the reappointment of a divinity lecturer.[11]

The most notable change in the personnel of the cathedral during the years of the Reformation came with the dissolution of the cathedral's chantries in 1548 and the consequent disappearance of the body of chantry chaplains.[12] In April 1549 the royal commissioners arrived to inquire into the possessions of the seventeen chantries and the arrangements for obits and lights.[13] There is no direct reference in the records of the cathedral to the destruction of the chantries, but at the end of the year the residentiaries were dividing amongst themselves the altar ornaments and various vestments.[14] During the following years the property of the chantries was sold off, mainly to London speculators, although much of it came eventually into the hands of local landowners, such as the Levesons and the Pagets.[15] Some of the endowments of the chantries had been lost even before their dissolution in 1548 with the sale of the property of the abbeys which had provided them with pensions. In 1544 and 1546 the chapter had made strenuous efforts to recover the endowments of Dean Heywood's chantries, invested with the abbeys of Halesowen, Lilleshall, and Dale, from the laymen to whom the abbeys had been granted; the report of the commissioners in 1548 shows that this effort was unsuccessful.[16] The chantry chaplains' college was sold to London speculators and came eventually into the hands of the corporation of Lichfield.[17] The chantry chaplains for the most part disappeared without trace, although some of them are found later in receipt of pensions, and one or two of them may have obtained Staffordshire livings.[18]

At the Reformation the vicars were brought more closely under the control of the dean and chapter; this was a direct reversal of the position in the early years of the century when the vicars had been demanding, and obtaining, more independence.[19] In February 1539 a royal commission, consisting of the bishop, the president of the chapter, and two laymen, drew up new statutes for the vicars.[20] Any statutes made by the vicars themselves were to be disregarded, and all new statutes were to be made by the dean and chapter and were not to be changed without their knowledge and consent. The *intitulator* was to keep a strict watch on the movements of the vicars and all absences were to be reported.[21] Regulations were made for the payment of tenths and first fruits by the vicars, and it was decided that no vicar should be allowed to act as bailiff or collector. None of their property was to be leased for a term of lives or for more than 15 years without the knowledge and consent of the dean and chapter, and the vicars were not to dispose

[2] 17th-cent. misc. bk., ff. 60–63v.; D. & C. Lich., D. 32.
[3] 17th-cent. misc. bk., f. 60.
[4] D. & C. Lich., liv, f. 4.
[5] See C. Hill, *Econ. Problems of the Church from Abp. Whitgift to the Long Parliament*, 6–8, 15–18.
[6] C.A. iv, f. 148.
[7] Ibid. f. 159v. In the 1550s there were stated to be 5 residentiaries: Bodl. MS. Ashmole 855, p. 107.
[8] Act for giving authority to the Queen's Majesty, upon the avoidance of any archbishoprics or bishoprics, to take into her hands certain of the temporal possessions thereof, 1 Eliz. I, c. 19; Hill, *Econ. Problems of the Church*, 14–16.
[9] C.A. iv, f. 147v.; Le Neve, *Fasti* (1854 edn.), i. 612.
[10] C.A. iv, f. 154; *D.N.B.* Ramridge became dean in 1554 on the deprivation of Dean Williams: see below pp. 169, 197.
[11] D. & C. Lich., 17th-cent. misc. bk., f. 103.
[12] See *S.H.C.* 1915, 153–9, for a detailed survey of the chantries and their chaplains in 1548.

[13] C.A. iv, f. 148.
[14] Ibid. f. 154v.; Savage, *Cathedral and Chapter*, 18–19.
[15] *Cal. Pat.* 1548–9, 234–5, 391, 420; 1549–51, 16, 125, 126, 361; 1553, 216, 234; 1553–4, 205. See also S.R.O., D.(W.)1734/2/1/760–2, /2/2/72–74, /2/3/86 (records of chantry of St. Radegund acquired by Paget family).
[16] Savage, *Cathedral and Chapter*, 14.
[17] *Cal. Pat.* 1548–9, 392. For the later history of the New College, on the site of which part of the Theological College now stands, see Savage, *Bishop John Burghull*, 18–19.
[18] See *S.H.C.* 1915, 153–9, 175–6; E 178/3239.
[19] See above p. 164.
[20] There is a copy of these statutes in D. & C. Lich., 17th-cent. misc. bk., ff. 117–19v.
[21] The subchanter and vicars presented a petition to the commissioners on the subject of lawful absences: ibid. f. 119.

of any of their goods without the chapter's permission; if called upon they were to make a yearly account to the chapter. It seems that the funds which had been established for the vicars[22] had become depleted, and the commissioners allowed the vicars a year to restore them to their former amounts. There were in addition the usual regulations about attending services and not introducing suspect women into the Close, and also an order forbidding the vicars to sell water from the aqueduct. In 1544 the vicars were given a 'friendly warning' to mend their ways; otherwise the statutes would be applied in their full vigour.[23]

The vicars narrowly escaped losing all their property at the beginning of 1549 under the terms of the Chantries Act of 1547. A *prima facie* case was made out against them that they were 'incorporated by the name of a college' and that all their possessions should be confiscated. The chantry commissioners, however, found that in fact the vicars were 'united and consolidated to the corporation of the dean and chapter', and they were confirmed in their possessions by letters patent later in the year.[24]

Several of the vicars took advantage of the Edwardian Act permitting clerical marriage. On Mary's accession two priest vicars were deprived for marriage, and in August 1558 Thomas Bagot, a lay vicar whose wife had just died, was ordered to return to live in common with the other vicars.[25] The 1559 injunctions laid down that married vicars were to be permitted to receive commons even if they lived outside the Close.[26]

Very little is known of the choristers during the years of the Reformation. They were put directly under the control of the master of the choristers, and they retained their property which continued to be administered for them by the chapter.[27] The 1547 and 1559 injunctions ordered that each chorister should be given an annual pension of £3 6s. 8d. for five years after his voice had broken to enable him to attend a grammar school.[28]

The most damaging loss to the cathedral at the Reformation was the destruction or removal of many of its treasures. St. Chad's shrine, which was said to bring in an annual income of £400,[29] was among those destroyed in the general attack on pilgrimage shrines in 1538. The statues, jewels, and other ornaments were seized by the Crown, but Bishop Lee persuaded the king to grant the shrine itself to the cathedral for its own uses,[30] while St. Chad's bones were smuggled away by Canon Arthur Dudley.[31] In March 1548 the chapter ordered the removal of the statues on the high altar and elsewhere in the cathedral in accordance with the royal decree of 21 February,[32] and by the end of 1549 the chantry chapels had been dismantled.[33] The body of

the cathedral seems to have survived undamaged, and it appears from later descriptions that much of the medieval glass and most of the monuments were left intact.[34] Hardly any evidence survives concerning work on the fabric between 1538 and the Civil War, though it is known that in 1543 Robert Hodd of Ludlow (Salop.) was appointed to gild the reredos for £40, and in 1550 Dean Williams, who had won Henry VIII's favour through his skill as an architect, came to an agreement with John Osbaston of Abbots Bromley for the repair of the central tower, which had been struck by lightning.[35]

The vestments, plate, and service-books of the cathedral were dispersed during Edward VI's reign. In 1549 the residentiaries divided among themselves the albs and the money received for 'ly canopy', and in the following year the chapter sold all the books in the choir, having first defaced them, and divided the proceeds, each canon receiving 5s. 4d.[36] Despite all this the cathedral was still thought worthy of the Crown's attention. At the end of April 1553 five commissioners visited Lichfield and seized all remaining vestments and ornaments; the best were locked away under seal in the cathedral and the rest sold. On 18 May Edward Littleton, one of the commissioners, returned to collect what had been left behind — silver plate, crosses, and thuribles, the best copes, and two mitres. Having poured the consecrated oil from three silver cruets on the ground, he loaded everything into a cart and took it away.[37] Of the cathedral's furnishings all that appears to have been left behind were 2 silver-gilt chalices with patens, 6 cloths for the communion table, 24 old cushions, a brass lectern, and the 12 bells in the towers.[38]

It is impossible to estimate the extent of this loss since the only full surviving inventory of the goods of the cathedral is that made in 1345.[39] By the early 16th century some of the vestments were evidently shabby. In 1523 Bishop Blythe ordered a levy from the revenues of the prebends to help renew the copes.[40] The move appears to have had no success, however, for in 1531 the chapter put restrictions on the use of the copes on the grounds that they were almost worn out by long use and no resources (*facultates*) existed for their repair.[41] At the same time it was directed that the service-books in the choir, which were also worn out through age and long use, should be repaired.[42] The value of the plate and church ornaments lost must, however, have been considerable. The accession of Mary and the restoration of the old forms of worship found the cathedral lacking most of the furniture for divine service. The shifts to which the chapter was put when it reviewed the situation in October 1553 are revealing. There were no service-books left and all

[22] See above p. 164.   [23] C.A. iv, f. 137v.
[24] 17th-cent. misc. bk., ff. 125–6; Harwood, *Lichfield*, 262; *S.H.C.* vi(2), p. ii after p. 196.
[25] Savage, *Cathedral and Chapter*, 17; C.A. iv, f. 163v.
[26] 17th-cent. misc. bk., f. 104.
[27] C.A. iv, ff. 111, 153, 156v., 159v.; see above p. 166.
[28] 17th-cent. misc. bk., ff. 99, 103.
[29] *L. & P. Hen. VIII*, x, p. 137.
[30] Wharton, *Anglia Sacra*, i. 457–8; Savage, *Cathedral and Chapter*, 8.
[31] For the history of the relics, which are now in the Roman Catholic Cathedral at Birmingham, see H. Foley, *Records of the English Province of the Society of Jesus*, ii. 230–3; ibid. iii. 794–7; *Hist. of St. Chad's Cathedral, Birmingham (1841–1904)*, 106–17.

[32] D. & C. Lich., C.A. iv, f. 148; Savage, *Cathedral and Chapter*, 18.
[33] See above p. 167.
[34] Harwood, *Lichfield*, 51–56.
[35] C.A. iv, ff. 130, 156v.; Savage, *Cathedral and Chapter*, 17.
[36] C.A. iv, ff. 155, 156.
[37] Ibid. ff. 158v., 159.
[38] *Annals of the Diocese of Lichfield*, iv. 68–69 (copy in W.S.L. Pamphs. *sub* Lichfield).
[39] See above p. 154 n. 22.
[40] Dugdale, *Mon.* vi(3), 1265.
[41] C.A. iv, ff. 75v.–76.
[42] Ibid.

that could be procured by the chapter clerk were two breviaries: a large one which he obtained from Humphrey Swynnerton and a damaged one given by Sir Thomas Fitzherbert. Vestments were also in short supply, and one of the prebendaries contributed a chasuble and two tunicles.[43] More were evidently collected later: in 1579 the Privy Council ordered the destruction of 'certain copes, vestments, tunicles and such other Popish stuff' which the dean had reported to be in the cathedral.[44]

The doctrinal changes between the 1530s and the 1550s seem to have caused few crises of conscience at Lichfield. A good example of the conforming attitude of the chapter is the career of Henry Sydall, B.C.L., a prebendary from 1541 and holder of Dean Yotton's chantry. In 1548 he was deprived of his chantry but ordered to continue to preach at Lichfield; he was an equally zealous conformist under Mary when he helped to persuade Cranmer to recant, and on the accession of Elizabeth he was one of the first to take the Oath of Supremacy.[45] One prebendary was deprived in 1546 for refusing to pay tithes to the king,[46] and the dean and two prebendaries were deprived for marriage on the accession of Mary.[47] The biggest upheaval came in 1559 after the accession of Elizabeth I.[48] The dean, John Ramridge, who had been divinity lecturer under Edward VI and had obtained the deanery under Mary, was imprisoned in the Tower; he was released on bail and escaped to Flanders. He was succeeded by Lawrence Nowell, the Anglo-Saxon scholar, who was rarely resident at Lichfield. Also deprived were the precentor, Henry Comberford, who was accused in February 1559 of 'lewd preaching and misdemeanour' by the bailiffs of Lichfield,[49] and the chancellor, Alban Langdale, said to be 'learned and very earnest in papistry'; the treasurer took the Oath of Supremacy in 1559 but resigned the following year. The chancellor and the precentor were replaced by extreme Protestants who were, however, rarely, if ever, resident at Lichfield. Of the canons residentiary one was deprived, one retired, and the other four conformed; it was probably due to these four that there were no violent innovations after 1558. Of the other prebendaries three were deprived in 1559 and three more in 1562.

The Cathedral under Elizabeth I and the Early Stuarts

The period after Elizabeth I's accession must have been a time of considerable adjustment for the chapter, both to a new liturgy and to a reduction in revenues. Very few records of chapter acts have, however, survived between 1560 and the Civil War. It is therefore impossible to draw any definite conclusions about the character of cathedral life

during this period, and any generalizations are based on very fragmentary evidence.

Notes made for the guidance of the communars in the 1580s give an idea of the revenues of the chapter at this period and how they were accounted for.[50] The total revenue of the common fund was just over £360 a year. Of this £137 13s. 8d. came from leases of chapter property, £3 7s. from rents of the land given by Dean Heywood, and £161 14s. 3½d. from the Peak parishes; in addition there should have been £110 a year from pensions, but it was usually possible to collect only some £60 of this. The revenue of the farm of the tithes of wool and lambs from the Peak seems to have been divided among the chapter separately.[51] Out of these receipts there had to be paid the commons of the residentiaries at the rate of £21 9s. each for a full year's residence, and the commons of the bishop and dean at double the rate. Each vicar was paid £4 11s. 3d. a year in commons. Over £70 went to the queen in payment of subsidies and tenths. Another £53 went in fees and salaries to the chapter clerk, the organist, the porter, the collector of the Bakewell revenues, and other officials, and in augmentation of the stipends of the vicars of the Peak parishes. Finally there were unspecified foreign expenses; in the years 1574–85 these varied between £3 15s. 10d. in 1575 and £130 17s. 1d. in 1581. It was estimated in the mid 1580s that the average income of the chapter was about £364 and the average expenditure was about £383, if 5 canons were in residence and there were 17 or 18 vicars. This deficiency involved the communars in extensive borrowings from the chapter's reserve fund, the *baga de Whalley*.[52]

The income of the fabric fund was kept separate from that of the common fund and consisted of some £5 18s. in rents from various fabric lands, together with receipts from 'stall money' paid by prebendaries without vicars, burials in the cathedral,[53] and various other fees. From this income the cathedral had to be kept in good repair and fees paid to a clerk of the fabric, a clocksmith, a plumber, a bellringer, an organ-blower, and other officials.[54] The income from the choristers' property, which amounted to about £58 a year, was also managed separately. This money was used to pay the stipends of the eight choristers at £1 each a year and a fee of 26s. 8d. to the master of the choristers.[55] From it also came annual payments of £6 13s. 4d. for the boys' clothing and 26s. 8d. for fuel.

There is little evidence about the policy which the chapter pursued in managing its estates, for, although the 1559 injunctions ordered the keeping of registers of leases, such registers survive only from 1631.[56] Where a comparison is possible it appears that during the later 16th century the farms charged by the chapter corresponded more or less

[43] Ibid. f. 159v.
[44] *Acts of P.C.* 1578–80, 208.
[45] See *D.N.B.* and *S.H.C.* 1915, 175–6. The holder of the chantry had to be a graduate in divinity or in civil law: *S.H.C.* 1915, 159.
[46] C.A. iv, f. 142.
[47] Ibid. f. 159v.; Savage, *Cathedral and Chapter*, 17.
[48] For the rest of this para. see H. E. Savage, *The Cathedral under the Elizabethan Settlement* (1930), 10–19.
[49] *Acts of P.C.* 1558–70, 64.
[50] D. & C. Lich., 17th-cent. misc. bk., ff. 104v.–115.
[51] See below p. 170.
[52] 17th-cent. misc. bk., ff. 141–143v. In 1564 there were Chancery proceedings over a loan from this fund: *S.H.C.*

N.S. ix. 223–5. A list of pensions drawn up in 1560 by the communar, with copies of the grants and some other material relating to the cathedral, is now at Emmanuel College, Cambridge (MS. 77(II)).
[53] This could be an expensive privilege; for rates see C.A. v, f. 53.
[54] 17th-cent. misc. bk., ff. 104v.–105. The keeper of the fabric for 1599–1600 stated that he had received only £2 4s. 10d. during the year and had spent £16 16s. 2d. on necessary work about the cathedral: Lich. Dioc. Regy., DC/C/1/1, 3 Oct. 1600 (giving total receipts incorrectly as 40s. 10d.).
[55] 17th-cent. misc. bk., f. 105v.
[56] *S.H.C.* vi(2), 100.

to the annual values given in the *Valor Ecclesiasticus*.[57] Although the chapter continued to suffer financially from the effects of long leases granted in the 1540s and 1550s,[58] after 1559 most of the surviving leases were for 21 years, with occasional leases for three lives.[59]

From the 1560s the chapter even leased the tithes of wool and lambs in the Peak, the collection of which it had kept in its own hands for so long. In 1566 the tithes were leased to Sir Edward Littleton at a rent of £115 a year; the lease was for 20 years, renewable for another 20 years in 1586.[60] By the 1630s the farm of these tithes had passed into the hands of the Gell family, the most notable farmers of the chapter's property.[61] Even after the Restoration the tithes were still being leased for only £115 a year,[62] although it had been found in 1649 that they were usually worth £450 a year.[63] The rent, which was paid half-yearly, was not added to the common fund but was divided immediately among the residentiaries.[64]

Much money was lost because impropriators of churches formerly appropriated to monastic houses were reluctant to pay pensions due to the chapter. It has been seen above how nearly half of the income from pensions was proving impossible to collect in the 1580s. In 1612 25 of the chapter's 45 pensions were in arrears, most of them from Henry VIII's reign. The chapter decided to sue the impropriators, when it could discover who they were, in the Exchequer and Court of Arches, and it asked a lawyer to draw up a general bill against them for payment of arrears from 1534–5.[65] Evidently it met with little success as many of the pensions had virtually lapsed by the 18th century.[66]

By the 1590s it was apparent that the common fund could no longer support a full chapter of a dean and six residentiaries, and in 1596 Bishop Overton's statutes laid down a new system of residence, as complicated as that drawn up at the end of the 12th century.[67] The year, running from Michaelmas, was thenceforth to be divided into halves. Three residentiaries were to be in residence in each half of the year; the dean was allowed to choose which half he preferred for his residence. Every canon was to reside at least 12 full weeks in his half. Any surplus revenue was still to be divided according to quarters (*stadia*), but this was now an artificial concept. Canons in residence between Michaelmas and the Annunciation were to lose their dividend for one quarter if they were absent more than 93 days, for 2 quarters if they were absent more than 114 days, for 3 quarters if they were absent more than 135 days, and for the whole year if they were absent more than 156 days. A similar

scale was laid down for those resident in the second half. One of the canons in residence during the first half was obliged to provide hospitality within the Close during the twelve days of Christmas, and one of those in residence during the second half was responsible for hospitality during Easter Week and at Whitsun; the burden of hospitality thus fell on each canon once every three years.[68] Even with a reduction in commons the cathedral's revenues were insufficient to maintain a dean and six residentiaries, and it was laid down that the number of residentiaries was to be reduced to four when the death or resignation of the existing canons permitted it. The scheme of residence was then to be altered to two senior canons in residence for the first half and two junior canons resident in the second. These changes were later attributed to the reduction in revenues caused by grants of fee-farms and leases for long terms at 'very small' reserved rents,[69] presumably those of the 1540s and 1550s. A fragmentary act book for the last years of the 16th century provides confirmation of the chapter's financial embarrassment at that period. In 1598, for example, Bishop Overton agreed to take no more than £13 6s. 8d. a year for his commons in order to lighten the burden on the cathedral's finances,[70] while the following year the canons gave a tenth of the income of their prebends to the cathedral after the dean had appealed to them for help.[71]

The estate policy of the chapter in the early 17th century differed little from that which had damaged its revenues in the previous century; in common with other ecclesiastical corporations of the time, long leases at uneconomic rents in return for high entry fines were still the rule.[72] In 1634 the Lichfield chapter, with the chapters of other cathedrals and collegiate churches, was warned by the Crown to stop converting leases for years into leases for lives. It was ordered that in future no leases were to be made for more than 21 years and no leases at all were to be made by deans after their appointment to a 'better' deanery or a bishopric; in this way it was hoped that chapters could be prevented from depriving their successors of entry fines or the benefits of increased rents.[73] The full extent of the chapter's mismanagement of its property can be seen in the reports of the commissioners appointed to survey the chapter estates under the terms of the Act of 1649 'for the abolishing of deans, deans and chapters, and canons'.[74] The unfavourable leasing of wool tithes in the Peak parishes has already been mentioned. The mineral tithes of the Peak, which were farmed by the chapter before the Reformation,[75] had been lost completely by the cathedral to a lay impropriator, Sir John Gell; in 1649 the

---

[57] Compare *Valor Eccl.* iii. 132, with 17th-cent. misc. bk., ff. 109v.–110. Cannock, which was valued at £28 in 1535, was leased to the chapter clerk for £18 a year in 1545: *S.H.C.* vi(2), 12.

[58] See above pp. 166–7.

[59] 17th cent. misc. bk., ff. 66v.–73v.

[60] Ibid. f. 69; the copy of the indenture is wrongly headed 1550.

[61] D. & C. Lich., D. 32. For the Gell family as farmers of chapter property see above pp. 166–7.

[62] *S.H.C.* vi(2), 22, 23.

[63] D. & C. Lich., liv, ff. 2–3. The tithes had been leased in 1640 to Sir Edw. Leech of Shipley (Derb.) at the fixed rent of £115 a year.

[64] D. & C. Lich., D. 37; 17th-cent. misc. bk., ff. 135v.–137v.

[65] D. & C. Lich., I. 9.

[66] See below p. 179.

[67] The best copy of Bp. Overton's statutes is in 17th-cent. misc. bk., ff. 95–97.

[68] Canons were also to keep 'canons' days' (when they waited on the vicars at table according to ancient custom) and to distribute alms to the poor every Thursday.

[69] *Statuta et Consuetudines Ecclesiae Cathedralis Lichfieldiae* (1863, priv. print.), 41 (copy in W.S.L. Pamphs. *sub* Lichfield).

[70] Lich. Dioc. Regy., DC/C/1/1, 24 July 1598.

[71] Ibid. 11 Dec. 1599.

[72] Hill, *Econ. Problems of the Church*, 6–8.

[73] D. & C. Lich., C.A. vi, ff. 92v.–93.

[74] D. & C. Lich., liv, lv.

[75] See above p. 162.

tithes of lead ore were said to be worth nearly £1,000 a year.[76] Sir John Gell held the office of receiver in the Peak under the lease of 1550 and was found to be taking tithes of woodland but not accounting for them to the chapter.[77] Even when the lease was a recent one the terms benefited only the canons who shared the entry fine: the glebe of Tideswell was leased in 1637 for £12 whereas it was estimated in 1649 to be worth £46 a year.[78] In many cases the rents charged were still the same as the annual values given in the *Valor Ecclesiasticus*. In 1650, for example, the rectory of Edgbaston was being farmed for 53s. 4d. a year, the 1535 value, when it was in fact worth £47 6s.[79] The rest of the chapter property was under-exploited in the same way. Whereas the lands given to the cathedral by Dean Heywood and the property belonging to the fabric fund produced rents totalling only £11 a year, the commissioners considered them to be worth £135 a year.[80] The same inadequate rents were found in the case of prebendal properties. The dean's prebend of Brewood had been leased in 1628 for three lives at a rent of £30, but the total value of the lands, profits, and tithes was £185 a year in 1649; the prebend of Flixton was leased on the same terms in 1620 at a rent of £16 and was worth £122 in 1649, and the prebend of Tervin had been leased for 90 years in 1559 at a rent of £1 a year and was worth £14 10s. in 1649.[81]

A few of these leases were used by the chapter to reward its officers. The chapter clerk, for example, held land in Lichfield on favourable terms and paid a peppercorn rent for a house in the Close which the commissioners valued at £4 a year.[82] The clerk by this period was responsible for the routine administration of the chapter estates and many of the prebendal estates: in the 1620s, for example, Thomas Glazier transacted business for both residentiaries and non-residentiaries, collecting rents and tithes, paying wages and dues, repairing houses, and arranging for proctors.[83]

The chapter's relations with the bishop were generally harmonious during this period, though there was a sharp clash early in Bishop Overton's episcopate.[84] Shortly after his appointment in 1580 the bishop, heavily in debt[85] and harassed by lawsuits, demanded from the clergy of the diocese a *subsidium charitativum* of a twentieth of their revenues. The cathedral clergy refused to pay on the grounds that such a claim had never been made to enable a bishop to meet his normal expenses, and that they were exempt in any case. The bishop threatened the canons with a suit under the writ *de scandalis magnatum* and arrested two of them. When his case collapsed he obtained an order from the Court of High Commission directing two of the

canons to lend him £100 each or appear before the court. One of the canons, who was 70 years old and confined to his room, gave in under the threat; the other went to London with the dean, but Overton managed to obtain an order for £30 costs against him. There were further disputes over the bishop's refusal to recognize the cathedral statutes as valid and the reluctance of the dean and chapter to confirm grants of leases, offices, and annuities which the bishop had made to one of his sons-in-law; the chapter's explanation of its action was that the possessions of the bishopric should not be squandered. These quarrels led Archbishop Grindal to order a visitation of the cathedral by John Whitgift, then Bishop of Worcester; this took place at the beginning of 1583. It resulted in the reappointment of a divinity lecturer[86] and the appointment of four canons, the 'best learned and affected to religion', to visit the chapter peculiars and report on the ministers' 'sufficiency and worthiness'. Relations between Overton and George Boleyn, the dean who had led the opposition to him, were still bad in 1587 when Boleyn complained that the bishop refused to quit the Deanery; Boleyn had been living in a canonical house which he had promised to give up to the Earl of Essex.[87]

During James I's reign deans began to be appointed by the Crown under a *congé d'élire*.[88] Unlike some other deaneries Lichfield was not greatly sought-after: in 1625 the Chancellor of Salisbury asked for the deanery of either Salisbury or Rochester 'or at least of poor Lichfield, which is hardly worth £100 *per annum*'.[89] Yet it proved during the early 17th century a good stepping-stone to further ecclesiastical preferment. Of the seven deans appointed between 1603 and the Civil War three moved to bishoprics and two to more lucrative deaneries;[90] Dean Tooker, who remained at Lichfield from 1605 until his death in 1621, is said to have narrowly missed receiving the bishopric of Gloucester,[91] and Dean Higgs's career was interrupted by the outbreak of war.

Bishop Overton's statutes do not seem to have been strictly observed during the period before the Civil War. Though by the 1630s the residentiary chapter had been reduced to a dean and four canons the elaborate system of residence had broken down and the five residentiaries were dividing the year into five sections and residing in turn; any canon who failed to perform his residence forfeited his commons for the whole year.[92] Overton's statutes appear, indeed, to have been unknown to, or ignored by, Bishop Wright, who in 1638 informed Laud that the cathedral statutes had not been renewed since 1526 and were 'very capable of reformation'.

---

[76] D. & C. Lich., liv, ff. 16, 40. In the 1620s Gell was involved in a lawsuit over the payment of tithes with the miners of Bakewell, Hope, and Tideswell: *V.C.H. Derb.* ii. 331. [77] D. & C. Lich., liv, f. 4; see above p. 167.
[78] D. & C. Lich., liv, f. 14.
[79] Ibid. f. 51; *Valor Eccl.* iii. 132.
[80] D. & C. Lich., liv, ff. 54–91.
[81] Ibid. lv, ff. 11–27, 41, 97.
[82] Ibid. liv, ff. 53, 98.
[83] D. & C. Lich., II. 3, *passim*. The chapter clerk was not always the person chosen by prebendaries to act as their man of business: thus in the 1590s the treasurer, Wm. Barlow, was employing Gabriel Newman, a London goldsmith, to collect the rent of his prebend of Sawley, leased to the Earl of Shrewsbury for £66 13s. 4d. a year: E 135/5/15/3–5, 7, 9–21.

[84] For this para. see Savage, *Cathedral under the Elizabethan Settlement*, 25–28; J. Strype, *Life and Acts of Whitgift* (1718 edn.), 99–106; H. E. Savage, *Letters Patent of James I* (1933), 18–19.
[85] For an estimate by Overton of the expenses which he incurred on becoming a bishop, see E 135/9/6.
[86] See below p. 173.
[87] W.S.L., C. B. Lichfield, copy of letter of 20 June 1587 from Geo. Boleyn to Ric. Bagot. For the connexion of the Devereux earls of Essex with Lichfield see Harwood, *Lichfield*, 340–2. [88] *Statuta et Consuetudines*, 28.
[89] *Cal. S.P. Dom.* 1625–6, 149.
[90] See below p. 197. Dean Montague subsequently became Bp. of Bath and Wells and then of Winchester: *D.N.B.* [91] *D.N.B.*
[92] D. & C. Lich., C.A. vi, ff. 87v.–88.

Laud himself had apparently commended the work of revision to Wright and the chapter during his metropolitical visitation of the diocese .in 1635. Several drafts were prepared and additions were made from the recent Canterbury statutes; but when Wright attempted to impose the new statutes upon the cathedral some two years later he was opposed by Dean Fell. The dean complained to Laud that the bishop's additions were prejudicial to the cathedral and added that if Wright and his successors were to make a habit of producing new statutes at their visitations it would probably lead to confusion. Laud, evidently impressed by the argument, reminded the bishop that 'as the course of the kingdom now stands, 'tis requisite that all statutes which are binding to such a body should be under the Broad Seal'. He forbade Wright to impose his new statutes upon the cathedral until the whole body of Lichfield statutes had been revised by an independent panel of royal commissioners. This intervention appears to have stifled the attempt at revision.[93]

The number of vicars tended to decrease during the later 16th century. In 1568, owing to the age and weakness of some vicars and the lack of musical ability among the priest vicars, there were not enough vicars to carry on the services properly. The chapter therefore decided that lay vicars should in future be appointed to two stalls usually reserved for priest vicars and called epistolers' stalls.[94] At this time, out of a total of 18 or 19 vicars, 6 were laymen, compared with 14 priests and 7 laymen in 1535; by 1616 only 4 of the 16 vicars were priests.[95] Little is known of the late-16th-century or early-17th-century vicars. Robert Tarentyre, admitted as a lay vicar in 1595 after the chapter had received letters of recommendation from the queen, was a singer (*psaltes*) in the Chapel Royal and presumably a good musician. He remained a member of the Chapel Royal, however, so that his Lichfield appointment was evidently intended merely as a sinecure; there is no evidence that he was ever in residence or took part in the services. In April 1598 the chapter granted him £10 a year while he remained in the queen's service, since he was unable to come to Lichfield and therefore received no commons or dividend. By the following September, however, he was dead.[96] A musician who did come to Lichfield was the composer Michael East. East, whose music forms one of the links between that of the great English madrigalists and that of the school which produced Purcell, became master of the choristers at some date between 1610 and 1618 and remained at Lichfield until his death in 1648. Compositions

which he published during his years at Lichfield include anthems presumably composed for use at the cathedral.[97]

There is little evidence concerning the corporation of vicars as a whole, but it is evident that by the 1590s the statute of 1539 which stated that no vicar should act as bailiff for the corporation was virtually a dead letter. When in 1595 the subchanter and a minority of the vicars complained to the chapter about the election by a majority of the vicars of one of their number, John Ballard, as bailiff, the chapter merely appointed another vicar, Raphael Potter, to the post.[98] Although the estate policy of the vicars is even more sparsely documented than that of the chapter it would seem that they too failed to exploit their property to the full. In 1616 their yearly revenues totalled £148, from which they had to pay subsidies to the king, chief rents to various lords, and the cost of repairing their hall and houses. They had also to pay the fees of a collector and a bailiff and to defend lawsuits; the yearly accounts, or 'restore', of the vicars include such items as 'Mr. Bearsley's charges to Hampton to serve Mr. Levison with [a] process'.[99] In 1632 the vicars were warned by the chapter not to grant leases for longer than a term of 20 years renewable every five years, and in 1634 the chapter was reminded by the Crown that the royal order against leases for lives applied also to the vicars.[1] On the balance of the revenues supplemented by the commons paid by the chapter sixteen vicars subsisted; in 1616 only one of the four priest vicars held any other benefice.[2] There were the usual problems caused by vicars' unruliness. In 1591, for example, two vicars were indicted at Quarter Sessions for having gathered a mob and assaulted one of their colleagues in the Close. In 1598 another vicar was summoned before the chapter to answer for his daily visits to alehouses and his drunkenness and blasphemies.[3] In the 1630s their absences from services were being carefully noted by the chapter and fines imposed. Laud after his visitation ordered the expulsion from the Close of three laymen who had been living with the vicars in order to avoid holding public office in the city.[4]

By at least the 1580s the number of choristers had been reduced to eight, and by that date they were evidently no longer living in common. In 1582 their house was let on condition that the boys should have access to the privy and to the butts in the garden. The tenant was also to give up the hall, buttery, and kitchen 'if it fortune the dean and chapter to take order that the choristers shall keep commons together in such manner as heretofore they were accustomed'.[5] The choristers were taught in a room

[93] *Cal. S.P. Dom.* 1637–8, 316, 352; W. Laud, *Works*, ed. W. Scott, vii. 415.
[94] 17th-cent. misc. bk., loose-leaf note on vicars; D. & C. Lich., xiii, f. 38. In 1594 the subchanter and vicars petitioned the chapter, apparently without effect, that no layman be given a priest vicar's stall: Lich. Dioc. Regy., DC/C/1/1, 18 Nov. 1594.
[95] 17th-cent. misc. bk., loose-leaf note; D. & C. Lich., Vicars' Mun. D. 9; *Valor Eccl.* iii. 137–8. For lists of vicars in the mid 16th cent. see *S.H.C.* 1915, 159–65.
[96] Lich. Dioc. Regy., DC/C/1/1, 16 June 1595, 8 Apr., 15 Sept. 1598.
[97] M. East, *Fifth Set of Books* (1618), and subsequent sets of *Books*; *D.N.B.*; *Grove's Dict. of Music and Musicians* (3rd edn.), ii. 136; E. H. Fellowes, *Eng. Madrigal Composers* (2nd edn.), 252; *Abstracts of Probate Acts in the Prerogative Court of Canterbury*, ed. J. and G. F. Matthews, iv. 329. A. G. Matthews, *Walker Revised*, 5, stating that

East the composer was granted £3 in 1656 by the Trustees for Maintenance of Ministers, confuses East with his son, also named Michael, who became a vicar choral at the cathedral. Elias Ashmole, who was a chorister for a time before leaving Lichfield in 1633, states that he was taught singing by East and keyboard music by Hen. Hinde, the cathedral organist: E. Ashmole, *Diary*, ed. R. T. Gunther, 10, 11.
[98] Lich. Dioc. Regy., DC/C/1/1, 18 and 26 July 1595. For the 1539 statutes see above p. 167.
[99] D. & C. Lich., Vicars' Mun. C. 1, D. 9; acct. for 1593–4 printed in Harwood, *Lichfield*, 268–71. During the reign of Jas. I the vicars resisted the payment of first fruits: Harwood, *Lichfield*, 263–4.
[1] C.A. vi, ff. 87, 95. [2] Vicars' Mun. D. 9.
[3] *S.H.C.* 1930, 142; Lich. Dioc. Regy., DC/C/1/1, 7 Oct. 1598. [4] C.A. vi, ff. 87, 94v.; Wilkins, *Concilia*, iv. 520.
[5] 17th-cent. misc. bk., ff. 67v., 105v.

somewhere in the Close which, by the 1620s, was proving 'very loathsome not only unto them but also unto gentlemen which have resorted thither to hear music'; as a result the master of the choristers built them a schoolroom above the adjoining gateways of two canonical houses.[6] In 1635 Laud ordered the chapter to try to recover the lease of the choristers' house and take the building into its own hands again, presumably so that the choristers could once more live in common, but no such move appears to have been made.[7] It is possible that by the end of the 16th century the cathedral could no longer afford to pay choristers retirement pensions on the scale laid down in the 1547 and 1559 injunctions, for in 1600 a chorister who was leaving the cathedral was paid only 30s.[8]

There was no divinity lecturer at the cathedral in 1583, when Whitgift carried out his visitation. This was reported to the Privy Council and the chapter was ordered to appoint 'some able, sufficient person, learned in the tongues and otherwise qualified for the place, to have continual residence there'; the lecturer was to have a salary of at least £40 a year.[9] The chapter decided that the stipend should be provided by a levy of a tenth on all prebendal incomes, though in the case of canons with prebends worth less than £10 a year the first year's levy on a new tenure was to be paid from the common fund.[10]

Without complete act books it is impossible to trace any liturgical changes in services at the cathedral, but by the time of Bishop Wright it is evident that services had become richer and more elaborate. Some visitors in 1634 noted that 'the organs and voices were deep and sweet, their anthems we were much delighted with, and of the voices two trebles, two counter-tenors, and two basses, that equally on each side of the choir most melodiously acted and performed their parts'. In the vestry they saw 'three old rich copes of cloth of tissue, a fair communion cloth of cloth of gold for the high altar and the plate belonging thereunto, rich and fair, answerable and fit for such a sacred place'.[11] Laud himself found little to complain of during his metropolitical visitation the following year. He ordered the repair of the bell-frame and also of the two organs which were 'much defective' and which he suggested should be combined and made into a 'chair organ'.[12] He found 'too many seats' in the body of the church, and Lichfield became one of the few cathedrals where Charles I's order for the removal of pews from cathedrals was carried out completely.[13] Finally, the Close was to be tidied up: the churchyard walls were to be repaired and the Close was not to be made a highway for carriages or profaned in any other way.[14]

The visitors in 1634 were shown, amongst other things, the Lady Chapel 'where they have their 6 of

the clock prayers' — a reference to an early-morning service regularly held there at 6 a.m. on weekdays; this time of day was regarded as the most convenient for servants, workmen, and shopkeepers. The subsacrist had the duty of ringing the bell and cleaning the chapel, and one of the priest vicars officiated. After the service the dean and residentiaries provided hospitality for the vicars.[15] A service of matins at 6 a.m. had been enjoined by the 1547 injunctions. By 1559 matins was evidently celebrated later in the morning, but the injunctions of that year ordered an early-morning service as well, at 6 a.m. in winter and 5 a.m. in summer, 'to the intent that the scholars of the grammar [school] and all other well-disposed people and artificers may daily resort thereunto'.[16] By 1634 the service was held at 6 a.m. all the year round.[17]

The chapter's jurisdiction over the Close was threatened twice by the city authorities in the earlier 17th century.[18] In 1622 James I granted a new charter to the city and, it seems by accident, the traditional clause guaranteeing the independent liberty of the Close was omitted. The chapter, under the leadership of Dean Curle, complained, and a charter which it obtained from the Crown in 1623 not only ratified and confirmed the privileges granted in 1441 but also amplified them. The Close was to be entirely separate from the city and exempt from the jurisdiction of any of the city officials, with the one minor proviso that the bailiffs of Lichfield should be allowed to have their maces borne before them when they attended services at the cathedral. No citizen was to lose his civic rights by living in the Close; conversely no craftsman working at the cathedral was to be refused permission by the city authorities to live freely in Lichfield. The cathedral officers, defined in the charter as the vicars choral, the two chapter clerks, the two clerks of the fabric, the bailiff of the liberty of the Close, and the collector of pensions, were to be exempt from jury-service. At the request of the dean and chapter the bishop, Robert, Earl of Essex (for life), the dean and residentiaries, and the bishop's vicar general were made sole J.P.s within the Close, taking two oaths, that of a J.P. and that of fidelity to the cathedral. County coroners were to have the right to hold inquests in the Close. Three days after the issue of the capitular charter the city received a revised version of its own charter in which all the passages exempting the Close from civic jurisdiction were restored.

The second threat came in 1635, when the city authorities petitioned the Privy Council that laymen living in the Close should be required to contribute towards Lichfield's ship-money assessment or that the city's assessment should be reduced.[19] In a counter-petition the chapter, in conjunction with the

---

[6] D. & C. Lich., L. 5.   [7] Wilkins, *Concilia*, iv. 520.
[8] Lich. Dioc. Regy., DC/C/1/1, 25 Nov. 1600. For the pensions laid down in 1547 and 1559 see above p. 168.
[9] Savage, *Eliz. Settlement*, 28; Strype, *Whitgift*, App. p. 39.
[10] Savage, *Eliz. Settlement*, 28.
[11] *A Relation of a Short Survey of 26 Counties, 1634*, ed. L. G. Wickham Legg, 56–57.
[12] Wilkins, *Concilia*, iv. 520; *Cal. S.P. Dom.* 1635, p. xxxvi, noting also that the pulpit and pulpit cloth were 'exceeding mean'. The chapter ordered a new organ from Rob. Dallam in 1636 at a cost of £315: *S.H.C.* vi(2), 40. For Dallam see *D.N.B.*
[13] *Cal. S.P. Dom.* 1635, p. xxxvi; Hill, *Econ. Problems of*

the Church, 179.
[14] Wilkins, *Concilia*, iv. 520.
[15] *Relation of a Short Survey*, 57; *Statuta et Consuetudines*, 103–5, which probably sets out the vicars' duties as they were before the Civil War.
[16] 17th-cent. misc. bk., ff. 99, 103.
[17] *Statuta et Consuetudines*, 103; see below p. 180.
[18] For the following para. see Savage, *Letters Patent of James I*, 5–6, 10–15, citing, however, Edw. IV's confirmation of the 1441 grant as the original. For the 1441 grant see above p. 161.
[19] For the following para. see *Cal. S.P. Dom.* 1635, 454–5, 462; 1635–6, 12; 1636–7, 493, 494; 1638–9, 137. For laymen living in the Close see above p. 172.

officials of the diocesan consistory court, alleged that this move was merely part of a general attack by the city authorities on clerical privileges. Many people coming to the cathedral to appear before the consistory court as plaintiffs or witnesses were, the counter-petition claimed, unjustly arrested as they passed through the city, while the corporation had recently begun to tax the inhabitants of the Close and to distrain upon their goods for non-payment. The corporation admitted that the Close was not in the county of the city but argued that it was within the city and that the inhabitants should join with them in paying the city's ship-money. The Close was in fact assessed separately, and in 1638 the Solicitor-General gave his opinion that the Close was in neither the city nor the county of Lichfield.

During the Civil War Lichfield suffered more than any other cathedral. The Close was a natural strongpoint and was besieged three times, with consequent damage to the cathedral and its surrounding houses. At the beginning of the war a body of local gentry and Lichfield burgesses under the leadership of the Earl of Chesterfield and Sir Richard Dyott garrisoned the Close for the king. On 2 March 1643 parliamentary forces under Lord Brooke, who was killed in the course of the siege, opened a bombardment which, after three days, forced the surrender of the garrison. The cathedral, already battered by artillery fire, appears to have been further mishandled by the parliamentary soldiers who, according to Dugdale, smashed windows and destroyed monuments, carvings, and muniments. Having wrecked the church,

> they stabled their horses in the body of it, kept courts of guard in the cross-aisles, broke up the pavement, polluted the choir with their excrements, every day hunted a cat with hounds throughout the church, delighting themselves in the echo from the goodly vaulted roof, and to add to their wickedness brought a calf into it wrapped in linen, carried it to the font, sprinkled it with water, and gave it a name in scorn and derision of that holy sacrament of baptism.[20]

The following month Prince Rupert arrived to dislodge the parliamentarians. After ten days during which his artillery was unable to breach the walls of the Close he drained the moat and sprang two mines; one was successful, and after some fierce fighting the garrison surrendered.[21] The Close remained a royalist stronghold until 1646; it finally fell after a destructive siege lasting from March until July during which the central spire of the cathedral was destroyed.[22]

A report made in July 1649 by the parliamentary commissioners surveying the lands and property of the chapter shows how much damage the three sieges had caused. The cathedral itself was 'exceedingly ruinated; much lead and iron was taken away whilst it was a garrison, and much lead and other materials is taken away since, and is continually by evil persons stolen away in the night'. Much of the roofing was gone, and the report stated that if speedy action were not taken the rest of the lead would soon disappear and the whole roof would collapse.[23] The library was a wreck, and the gatehouse at the east end of the Close in ruins. Of the 14 houses in the Close belonging to the chapter (including those leased to the chapter clerk and the verger), 8 had been entirely destroyed or were out of repair. The vicars' common hall and their communal 'boghouse' had been destroyed, and 5 of their 20 houses were in ruins or out of repair.[24] The bishop's palace, according to a survey made a few years later, was badly damaged, and orchards, gardens, and walls in and around the Close had been 'digged up to make works and trenches'.[25] The ruin of the cathedral itself was completed in October 1651 when, under a parliamentary order of the previous April, Col. Henry Danvers, Governor of Stafford, had the remaining lead stripped off the roof and sold.[26] This sale and that of other material from the cathedral appear to have raised some £1,200. Much of the money vanished into private pockets; well over two years later £600 assigned to Stafford for the relief of the poor there had not been paid, while as late as 1658 the Warwickshire authorities were still making inquiries about £200 due to them.[27] Minor acts of destruction continued after 1651. By the following year some of the bells had been broken and others carried off, and in 1653 Dugdale noted the destruction of the Jesus Bell by 'a Presbyterian pewterer who was the chief officer for demolishing of that cathedral'.[28] The communion plate and linen had been carried off by the defeated parliamentary commander after the second siege of 1643.[29] The books and manuscripts were destroyed or scattered.[30]

The varying fates of canons during the Civil War and Commonwealth suggest that at the outbreak of war a fairly wide range of political and ecclesiastical loyalties may have been represented in the chapter. Some of the canons adapted themselves to the new order and even displayed a real or feigned zeal for it: in 1648, for example, Alexander How signed the *Testimony* of the Staffordshire Presbyterian ministers and John Bisby that of the Shropshire ministers.[31]

[20] D. R. Guttery, *The Great Civil War in Midland Parishes*, 34, 37–38; Harwood, *Lichfield*, 20–25; W. Dugdale, *A Short View of the Late Troubles in England* (1681), 559–60.
[21] Guttery, *Great Civil War*, 41–42; Harwood, *Lichfield*, 25.
[22] Guttery, *Great Civil War*, 119; W. Hamper, *Life of Dugdale* (1827), 97–98. There is a sketch of the cathedral without its central spire labelled 'Mr. Dugdale's draught' in Bodl. MS. Ashmole 1521, p. 147.
[23] D. & C. Lich., liv, f. 99.
[24] Ibid. ff. 92–100. The vicars lost 52 of their houses in Lichfield, said to be worth £2,500: Bodl. MS. Ashmole 1521, p. 105.
[25] S.R.O. 547/1/106–10.
[26] *Cal. S.P. Dom.* 1653–4, 407; Bodl. MS. Ashmole 826, f. 125; Hamper, *Dugdale*, 98. Some 5 tons of the lead were used for repairs to Stafford gaol: S.R.O., Q/SR M. 1655, no. 63.

[27] *Cal. S.P. Dom.* 1653–4, 407; Hamper, *Dugdale*, 98 n. In 1652 the parliamentary commissioners complained that owing to the dishonesty and carelessness of the officers put in charge of the Close great quantities of lead had disappeared from the cathedral: S.R.O. 547/1/109.
[28] S.R.O. 547/1/109; Hamper, *Dugdale*, 99–100.
[29] Dugdale, *Late Troubles*, 560.
[30] N. R. Ker, 'Patrick Young's Catalogue of the Manuscripts of Lichfield Cathedral', *Mediaeval and Renaissance Studies*, ii. 151. Some of the MSS. were saved by Precentor Higgins and Jeffery Glazier, the chapter clerk (Hamper, *Dugdale*, 320, 333), and some were recovered from parliamentary soldiers by Elias Ashmole: H. E. Savage, *Reconstruction after the Commonwealth* (1918), 18. The chronicle history of the cathedral painted on folding wooden leaves in the south transept was destroyed in 1643 by 'our good baily, Sir John Gell': Hamper, *Dugdale*, 320; Savage, *The Lichfield Chronicles*, 10, 15.
[31] Matthews, *Walker Revised*, 303, 323.

By steering a wary course Richard Love, a friend of Col. Valentine Walton the regicide, succeeded not only in retaining his preferments during the Interregnum but in obtaining the deanery of Ely in 1660.[32] Others made no secret of their royalist sympathies. James Fleetwood became chaplain to the regiment of John, Earl Rivers, and distinguished himself at the battle of Edgehill. He was subsequently granted the rectory of Sutton Coldfield (Warws.), from which he was later ejected by Parliament.[33] The precentor, William Higgins, was taken prisoner after Edgehill and imprisoned at Coventry for three months. He was taken prisoner again when the Close surrendered in 1646 and on his release maintained himself and his family by teaching. When this was forbidden in 1655 he is stated to have been reduced to penury.[34] Another zealous royalist, John Arnway, was taken prisoner when Shrewsbury fell to Parliament in 1645 and is said to have fled first to Oxford, then to The Hague, and finally to Virginia, where he died.[35] Some of the cathedral body appear to have remained in or around Lichfield; in the late 1650s the Trustees for Maintenance of Ministers made various grants to relieve some of the vicars choral.[36] What connexions they retained with the cathedral appears to be unknown. Parliament appointed a lecturer to serve the cathedral in July 1646, shortly after the third siege, and in 1655 the minister serving the cathedral in place of the dean and chapter received a salary increase of £50.[37] No details concerning services at the cathedral during the Interregnum appear to have survived.

From the Restoration to 1700

At the Restoration there were two main tasks: the reconstitution of the chapter and the rebuilding of the cathedral. Most of the work in the first few months fell upon Precentor Higgins; the new dean, Dr. William Paul, was not appointed till February 1661, and there was no bishop to oversee proceedings between Frewen's translation to York in September 1660 and Bishop Hacket's arrival at Lichfield in August 1662.[38] Of the 27 prebends at least 15, and possibly 18, were vacant at the Restoration. Bishop Frewen soon began to send in nominations, and in September 1660 Higgins formed a chapter with two of the surviving canons, John Mainwaring

and Thomas Tudman, and admitted seven of the bishop's nominees.[39] Between then and the following January a further eight canons were admitted.[40] The completion of the residentiary chapter took longer and was rather more complicated. In the absence of a dean Precentor Higgins chose three new residentiaries. In April 1661 Dr. Paul was installed as dean; a few days later he produced a letter from the king which voided the recent appointments and ordered that in future no residentiary was to be admitted without the dean's consent. Higgins naturally disagreed with this but was overridden by Dr. Paul, who the following day admitted on his own authority three royal nominees, including the chancellor, Richard Harrison, one of those whom Higgins had admitted. The dispossessed canons appealed to the Court of Arches, but without success.[41] The chapter was meanwhile building up the number of vicars choral: there were 7 by 1661, 9 by 1663, and 14 by 1664.[42]

The systematic restoration of the cathedral began with Dean Paul's arrival, though there are indications that some temporary repairs had been carried out by Higgins. When services at the cathedral began again in 1660 the chapter-house and the vestry were the only parts of the church which were still roofed; later a makeshift choir may have been prepared in the nave or the Lady Chapel.[43] Large sums of money were needed for the full-scale restoration of the church, and as an opening move the canons petitioned the Crown late in 1660, asking that improved rents from property belonging to prebends might be devoted to the repair of the cathedral and the canonical houses in the Close.[44] In April 1661 a subscription list was opened, and shortly afterwards a Mr. Fisher was engaged as 'surveyor' or architect.[45] Work was pressed on energetically, and in September 1665 Bishop Hacket wrote that the Lady Chapel, choir, chancel, transepts, and nave had been roofed and leaded 'and the side aisles, by God's blessing, shall be covered by Christmas'. The central spire was more than half completed.[46] By April 1666 Hacket could boast to Sheldon that 'we have at Lichfield the stateliest spire and the goodliest window in stone to the west that is in England', adding ruefully: 'I would they were paid for'.[47] The glass for the west window was apparently put up later the same year.[48] The west front was further adorned by a statue of Charles II, which has been attributed to Sir William Wilson; this was placed in the central

[32] D.N.B.
[33] Ibid. After the Restoration he became chaplain in ordinary to Charles II, Provost of King's College, Cambridge (1660), and Bishop of Worcester (1675).
[34] Matthews, Walker Revised, 305.
[35] Ibid. 303; Le Neve, Fasti (1854 edn.), i. 570.
[36] Matthews, Walker Revised, 5.
[37] W. A. Shaw, Hist. of the Eng. Church during the Civil Wars and under the Commonwealth, ii. 329; Cal. S.P. Dom. 1655-6, 52.
[38] H. E. Savage, Reconstruction after the Commonwealth (1918), 8-9. Wm. Bates, a leading Presbyterian divine, was offered the deanery by the king in Sept. or Oct. 1660 but refused it; Edmund Calamy, another prominent Presbyterian, similarly refused the bishopric: F. Bate, The Declaration of Indulgence, 1672, 15-16.
[39] Savage, Reconstruction, 10; D. & C. Lich., C.A. vii, ff. 1-4v.
[40] Savage, Reconstruction, 10; C.A. vii, ff. 5 sqq.
[41] Savage, Reconstruction, 10-14.
[42] D. & C. Lich., lxiv, accts. for 1660-4.
[43] Savage, Reconstruction, 14-15; Browne Willis, Survey of the Cathedrals of York, Durham, Carlisle, Chester, Man,

Lichfield, Hereford, Worcester, Gloucester, and Bristol (1727), 379. In 1663 it was discovered that the chapter-house itself was in a dangerous condition and repairs were ordered: Lich. Dioc. Regy., DC/C/1/2, chapter acts 3 Dec. 1663.
[44] Cal. S.P. Dom. 1660-1, 396. In 1665 £149 8s. 4d. was received from the king and divided among the holders of the 8 prebendal houses: D. & C. Lich., II. 4.
[45] Savage, Reconstruction, 15.
[46] Bodl. MS. Tanner 45, f. 26 (Bp. Hacket to Abp. Sheldon, 20 Sept. 1665).
[47] Ibid. f. 71 (Hacket to Sheldon, 21 Apr. 1666). The tracery of this new W. window differed considerably from that of the medieval window. For the medieval window see above plate facing p. 148; for Hacket's window see e.g. Shaw, Staffs. i, plate facing p. 235. During his restoration of the cathedral (see below pp. 194-5) Scott replaced the 17th-cent. window by one which he considered 'more in character, though possibly a little too late in detail': G. G. Scott, Personal and Professional Recollections (1879), 296.
[48] Bodl. MS. Tanner 45, f. 84 (Hacket to Sheldon, 11 July 1666).

niche of the apex.[49] Two years later the bishop was occupied with the furnishings and complaining that 'it is come most cross unto our work that the maker of our organ, by all report a most sufficient artist, is detained about the organ of Whitehall'. The organ-builder was the famous Bernard Smith ('Father Smith').[50] The cathedral was finally rededicated on Christmas Eve 1669.[51]

The work was not, however, complete. Hacket's last contribution to the restoration before his death in 1670 was a peal of six bells to be placed in the south-west tower. Only three had been cast before his death and only the tenor had been hung. The three smallest bells were not hung until 1673, and by the late 1680s it was agreed that all six were 'bad and useless'. A subscription was opened in 1687 to pay for the recasting of the bells into a peal of ten, and Henry Bagley of Ecton (Northants.) was engaged as bell-founder. Various difficulties were encountered, and it was not until 1691 that all ten bells were ready.[52] Another addition was an elaborate Classical reredos, completed about 1678. A much-admired specimen had recently been installed in the Chapel Royal at Whitehall, and Dean Smalwood decided to obtain a replica for Lichfield. He engaged the three master-craftsmen responsible for the Whitehall reredos, Thomas Kinward the joiner, Henry Phillips the carver, and Robert Streeter the painter, and instructed them to produce another for the cathedral, identical in its general pattern and ornamentation though somewhat smaller than the original. The final cost, after some haggling, was about £310, of which the three craftsmen's fees amounted to £230.[53] Another £100 was spent in 1680 when Smith enlarged the organ.[54] Even so, as late as 1693 the precentor estimated that to restore the cathedral to the state in which it was before the Civil War would cost at least another £5,000.[55]

The leading part in the work of restoration was played by Bishop Hacket. While it is true that reconstruction was under way when he arrived at Lichfield in 1662 and continued after his death, it is also obvious that the chapter owed much to his energy and generosity and that the traditional picture of him as virtually the builder of a new cathedral is substantially correct. Of the £2,729 paid into the restoration fund by July 1663 Hacket

gave £1,160, the chapter itself raised some £965, and just over £604 came in gifts from individual subscribers and from collections made in various parishes in the diocese.[56] Of a further £835 3s. 2d. added by September 1665, when Hacket undertook the management of the fund, the bishop himself contributed £523 12s.[57] By July 1666 he was 'drawn dry and driven to work upon my credit', and a final estimate of his expenditure shows that by his death he had given £3,500 towards the restoration of the cathedral fabric, £1,300 for bells, and £230 for plate and ornaments.[58] Besides giving so generously himself, he was also endowed with all the gifts of an expert fund-raiser. A month before his death he claimed to have collected about £15,000 for the restoration fund,[59] and his correspondence with Sheldon shows him appealing to the Duke and Duchess of York for contributions and asking that the plight of the cathedral be brought to the notice of M.P.s.[60] According to one contemporary he raised much of the money 'by barefaced begging. No gentleman lodged, or scarce baited in the city, to whom he did not pay his respects by way of visit, which ended in plausible entreaties for some assistance towards rescuing his distressed church from ruin'.[61] Some of his schemes have a very modern flavour. In 1667 Sir Edward Bagot of Blithfield was informed that for £8 he could buy one of the 52 stalls to be erected in the choir; his name would be set on an escutcheon over the stall, so that 'among the chiefest nobility and most ancient gentry . . . your memorial may be recorded; a patronage to the Church, and for your own honour, easily purchased'. His wife was asked for a contribution towards the £600 needed for the organ, which was 'to be called the Ladies' Organ, with his Majesty's approbation, because none but the honourable and most pious of that sex shall contribute to that sum'.[62] Hacket appears to have been unsuccessful with Lady Bagot, but he obtained ten distinguished subscribers to the organ fund, including Frances, Duchess of Somerset, who later bequeathed to the cathedral some 1,000 volumes of her late husband's library.[63]

The bishop's palace in the Close had suffered badly during the sieges and from decay and looting during the years that followed. In 1652 the parliamentary commissioners had found it 'a large and

[49] H. M. Colvin, *Biog. Dict. Eng. Architects, 1660–1840*, 680; see above plate facing p. 114. It was removed in the 19th cent.: see below p. 195. The king had contributed 100 trees from Needwood Forest towards the repair of the cathedral: *Cal. S.P. Dom.* 1661–2, 487.
[50] Bodl. MS. Tanner 44, f. 47 (Hacket to Sheldon, 31 Oct. 1668); H. E. Savage, *Last Quarter of the 17th Century* (1932), 19; *D.N.B.*
[51] Bodl. MS. Tanner 131, ff. 40 sqq. (Hacket to Sheldon, 18 Jan. 1670, enclosing copy of form of service of rededication); Harwood, *Lichfield*, 65–66.
[52] D. & C. Lich., lviii, p. 47; Harwood, *Lichfield*, 65, 66–67, 68–70, 71; *Diary of Elias Ashmole*, ed. R. T. Gunther, 170–1; Savage, *Last Quarter*, 16–18.
[53] D. & C. Lich., O. 8, Hen. Phillips to Smalwood, 27 Oct. 1677, stating that work is going well; Savage *Last Quarter*, 6–9 and plate facing p. 8 (reproducing Jas. Wyatt's scale drawing of the reredos). The Whitehall prototype was removed in 1686 and the Lichfield reredos was destroyed during Wyatt's alterations to the cathedral: Savage, *Last Quarter*, 7–8; and see below p. 188.
[54] Savage, *Last Quarter*, 19; Bodl. MS. Tanner 131, f. 58.
[55] D. & C. Lich., unnumbered papers, Bp. Lloyd's Visitation 1693–4, f. 4.
[56] D. & C. Lich., lviii, pp. 1–6.

[57] Ibid. pp. 19–23; Savage, *Reconstruction*, 16.
[58] Bodl. MS. Tanner 45, f. 84 (Hacket to Sheldon, 11 July 1666); MS. Tanner 131, f. 44.
[59] Bodl. MS. Tanner 131, f. 45 (Hacket to Sheldon, 28 Sept. 1670).
[60] Ibid. ff. 11, 20 (Hacket to Sheldon, 6 Jan. 1666, 4 Apr. 1668); MS. Tanner 45, f. 84 (Hacket to Sheldon, 11 July 1666). The Duke of York (later Jas. II) paid for the glazing of the great west window: Harwood, *Lichfield*, 74. A few months after Hacket's arrival at Lichfield he and the chapter were appealing for funds to 'the nobles and gentry and other well-disposed who have good lands and hereditaments within the diocese': B.M., Harl. MS. 7001, f. 248 (Hacket and chapter to Sir Hen. Puckering, 3 Feb. 1663).
[61] R. North, *Lives of the Norths*, ed. A. Jessopp, i. 185.
[62] [Wm. Bagot, 2nd Baron Bagot], *Memorials of the Bagot Family* (1824, priv. print.), 73, printing letter of 5 Sept. 1667 from Hacket to Bagot.
[63] Harwood, *Lichfield*, 67–68; Savage, *Last Quarter*, 5–6. 'Corban, or Gifts to the Temple', a register (apparently unfinished) of subscribers to the cathedral restoration fund drawn up in 1675 by Ant. Nichols, Chapter Registrar, with additions dated 1682, is now B.M. Add. MS. 43857.

fair edifice built all with stone and a great part leaded on the roof' but 'very much ruinated',[64] and when Hacket arrived at Lichfield he evidently did not consider it worth repairing. Instead he leased one of the prebendal houses from the chapter, and at a cost of over £800 repaired it and so enlarged it by adding a gallery, a dining-room, other rooms, and outbuildings that in later years it was converted into two houses.[65] The work was almost complete by March 1667, when Hacket expressed the opinion that although the house was not large 'no bishop in England . . . will have a more commodious seat'. Although he appears to have made efforts to secure the house for himself and his successors, at the time of his death it was still only rented from the chapter, which, however, appears to have been willing to settle it on the bishops.[66] Hacket's successor, Thomas Wood, was not satisfied with it and by 1672 was suing the bishop's son and executor, Sir Andrew Hacket, for compensation for the decay caused by the negligent treatment of the former palace, which had been used as a source of material for other buildings.[67] The new bishop, whose relationship with Hacket had been stormy (see below), appears to have acted through a mixture of spite and avarice; and when the case was finally settled by arbitration in 1684 it was laid down that Wood was to pay £2,600 towards the reconstruction of the palaces in the Close and at Eccleshall and Sir Andrew Hacket £1,400. It was at this time that Wood was suspended, and the responsibility for building a new palace in the Close fell on Archbishop Sancroft, who chose Edward Pierce (or Pearce) as architect and delegated the task of organizing work at Lichfield to the dean, Dr. Addison. The foundations were laid on the site of the old palace in the north-east corner of the Close in May 1686 and the building was completed in October 1687. Pierce's dignified Classical house of brick with stone dressings remains unaltered save for the two wings added in the 19th century by Bishop Selwyn.[68]

In general relations between the chapter and Hacket were cordial; at the bishop's instigation, for example, the chapter agreed in the mid 1660s that each canon should contribute to the restoration fund a quarter of the fine he received whenever he leased any of his prebendal property. The only difficulty that arose was with Dr. John Cornelius, Prebendary of Hansacre, who despite having agreed to the measure subsequently refused to contribute.[69] Both chapter and bishop suffered when in 1663 Dean Paul was made Bishop of Oxford,[70] for his successor

at Lichfield, Thomas Wood, was a constant source of annoyance. He was appointed through influence at Court,[71] and appears to have done all he could to make himself objectionable to the bishop and the canons. Hacket complained of his long absences at London and elsewhere and of his meanness:[72] thus he promised £50 towards the restoration but then announced his intention of spending it on the reconstruction of the chapter's consistory court in the cathedral, the only part of the restoration which Hacket had proposed to leave to the chapter. The bishop, who had allotted Wood's £50 to the repair of the pavements, remarked bitterly that 'in effect he shall escape with nothing contributed to the great fabric out of the public stock'.[73] The dean even went into open opposition; whether out of conviction or in an attempt to embarrass Hacket he encouraged the Protestant nonconformists in Lichfield to such an extent that the bishop wrote angrily of 'the phrenetic dean, who sides altogether with Puritans and told me to my face I did more harm than good in re-edifying this church'.[74] In fact, the bishop declared, 'I never met in one man with such an ingredient of maliciousness, pride, rudeness, covetousness, and ignorance. I must endure him as an affliction sent by God'.[75]

Wood aroused similar feelings among the chapter, whom he appears to have treated with a mixture of arrogance and indifference. In January 1668 Hacket informed the archbishop that three residentiaries (Richard Harrison, Thomas Browne, and Henry Greswold) had presented a petition against the dean. Wood, it was alleged, had refused to call chapter meetings, had ransacked the muniments and removed some documents, had taken away the accounts of the keeper of the fabric, and had refused to confirm a list of preachers drawn up by the residentiaries on the bishop's instructions. He had refused several times to appear before Hacket to answer the charges and on the last occasion had locked the doors of the chapter-house against the bishop, compelling him to force the lock. Hacket excommunicated him, and he caused a disturbance in the cathedral.[76] Thomas Browne wrote to Sheldon supporting the bishop; the dean was, he said, 'the strangest man that ever I have had anything to do with'.[77] Despite Hacket's protests Wood was absolved by the archbishop, and by the end of January a reconciliation of some sort had been patched up between him and the chapter. It would, however, seem that he still maintained his unconstitutional claim to a right of veto in capitular

[64] S.R.O. 547/1/106–10.
[65] Bodl. MS. Tanner 131, f. 68; Cal. S.P. Dom. 1672, 279, stating that the house contained about 35 rooms; Gent. Mag. 1783, liii(1), 120.
[66] Bodl. MS. Tanner 45, f. 18 (Hacket to Sheldon, 25 Mar. 1667); MS. Tanner 131, f. 84; Cal. S.P. Dom. 1672, 279, 280.
[67] Cal. S.P. Dom. 1672, 279–80.
[68] Savage, Last Quarter, 10–12; Colvin, Biog. Dict. Eng. Architects, 455; Bodl. MS. Tanner 131, f. 199 (Addison to Sancroft, 29 May 1686); Lich. Dioc. Regy., C.C. 123828 (Addison's accts. for building the palace); see below p. 195. There is a brief account of the building and architecture of the palace, with illustrations, in O. Hill and J. Cornforth, Eng. Country Houses: Caroline, 1625–85, 184–6.
[69] Bodl. MS. Tanner 131, f. 11 (Hacket to Sheldon, 6 Jan. 1666); MS. Tanner 45, ff. 82, 84 (Hacket to Sheldon, 11 July 1666, with enclosure from 3 canons).
[70] Le Neve, Fasti (1854 edn.), i. 563.

[71] A. G. Matthews, Congregational Churches of Staffs. 70.
[72] Bodl. MS. Tanner 45, ff. 26, 71 (Hacket to Sheldon, 20 Sept. 1665, 21 Apr. 1666).
[73] Ibid. f. 288 (Hacket to Sheldon, 4 Mar. 1668).
[74] Matthews, Cong. Churches Staffs. 71–72; Bodl. MS. Tanner 44, f. 66 (Hacket to Sheldon, 12 Dec. 1668).
[75] Bodl. MS. Tanner 45, f. 278 (Hacket to Sheldon, 15 Feb. 1668).
[76] Bodl. MS. Tanner 131, ff. 18–19v. (Hacket to Sheldon, 20 Jan. 1668); Lich. Dioc. Regy., DC/C/1/2, Dean Wood's protest 18 Jan. 1668. According to this protest the trouble arose because Wood, relying on his right of veto, refused to call a chapter for the collation of a man whom he regarded as unsuitable to the vicarage of Harborne. The disturbance at Wood's excommunication came to Pepys's notice: Pepys, Diary, ed. H. B. Wheatley, vii. 299.
[77] Bodl. MS. Tanner 45, f. 255 (Browne to Sheldon, 22 Jan. 1668); Le Neve, Fasti (1854 edn.), i. 628.

business,[78] and the quarrel continued to simmer. He persisted in his refusal to call chapter meetings — according to Hacket because the residentiaries quoted the statutes at him in Latin, which he did not understand — and though he remained in the Close he appears to have cut himself off almost completely from cathedral life.[79] Hacket went to the aid of the chapter by making a statute empowering three residentiaries who had asked the dean to call a chapter meeting to summon such a meeting themselves if, after three weeks, he had not done so. A month before his death Hacket was still threatening to sue and suspend the dean.[80]

The elevation of Wood to the bishopric of Lichfield as Hacket's successor in 1671 brought no obvious disadvantages to the chapter, though it was disastrous for the diocese. Dr. Matthew Smalwood, his successor as dean, was a capable administrator who took over Hacket's role as organizer of the restoration work and managed cathedral business with little or no reference to the chapter. The residentiaries were, on the whole, content to allow him a free hand; on one occasion the precentor, Henry Greswold, protested at this but his protest was overridden.[81]

As the affairs of the cathedral returned to normal, however, the chapter became less and less willing to leave all important decisions to the dean, and this led to a series of disputes with Smalwood's successor, Dr. Lancelot Addison, father of the essayist Joseph. The official copy of the cathedral statutes had been destroyed in the Civil War. Though a satisfactory text had been produced under Bishop Hacket it had never been promulgated officially, and Addison appears to have preferred to base his claims upon the precedents set by his predecessors, Dr. Paul and the masterful Dr. Smalwood. The residentiaries, headed by Precentor Greswold, to whom Hacket had committed the revision of the statutes, and Christopher Comyn, Prebendary of Bishopshull, began to campaign for the restoration of their statutory right of consultation.[82] In 1689, feeling that it would be useless to approach Bishop Wood, they sent a petition to William Lloyd, Bishop of St. Asaph, explaining the situation and asking for his advice. Lloyd appears to have avoided becoming committed and to have recommended a direct appeal to the dean, but it was inevitable that when he was translated to Lichfield in 1692 he should have been prejudiced against Addison.[83] The visitation of the cathedral which he held in 1693 and 1694 allowed Addison's opponents to bring out their complaints against him. As was to be expected, these mainly concerned occasions on which Addison had acted without consulting the chapter: he had, for example, dismissed the librarian and appointed another on his own authority and in the same way had assigned seats in the cathedral himself. Some accusations, of drunkenness and peculation, were obvious attempts to blacken his character but were nevertheless accepted or investigated by the bishop. On the whole

the dean's opponents were successful in humiliating him.[84]

One important result of the visitation was the promulgation of a new code of statutes. In 1668 Hacket had asked the residentiaries to 'compile a form of statutes out of the old ones . . . adding such new ones as may conduce to the true worship of God, to laudable government in the church, and to a fair and unfailing way of unity among yourselves'. The work was given to Precentor Greswold; obsolete pre-Reformation statutes ('ea omnia . . . quae papisticis temporibus accommodata Ecclesiae reformatae non convenirent') were dropped and the remaining statutes were sorted out and, where necessary, revised. The regulations concerning residence, for example, were simplified. The dean and the four residentiary canons were each to reside at least 90 days in the year — which, as before, ran from Michaelmas to Michaelmas and was divided into four quarters. The dean was privileged to reside in whichever part of the year he wished and had to pay a 10s. fine to the fabric fund for each day's residence he missed; the four canons, whose fine for a day's absence was 5s., divided the four quarters among themselves according to the rule laid down in the 1596 statutes, the two senior taking the first two quarters and the two junior the last two quarters. The usual practice at the time when the statutes were being revised and one which, it was stated, was to be followed as far as possible was that the senior canon took the first quarter, the second senior the next quarter, and so on. Canons were to be permitted to reside for each other, so long as everyone personally performed 90 days' residence.[85]

Nothing remained to be done at the time of Hacket's death, but the collection still needed the bishop's assent and it was impossible to proceed further under Bishop Wood. On Bishop Lloyd's arrival the draft *Collectio Hacketiana* was submitted once more to the dean and chapter and they, after having made a few changes and additions, approved it. It was sealed by Lloyd in February 1694.[86] In addition the bishop supplemented the ten chapters of Hacket's code with eleven chapters of his own, promulgated just under a fortnight later in March.[87] Various of these settled disputes which had arisen between the dean and his opponents among the residentiaries; all the settlements emphasized the corporate responsibility of the residentiary chapter and limited the independence of the dean. It was declared, for example, that seats and benches in the cathedral were to be assigned jointly by the dean and the residentiary chapter.[88] More important were Lloyd's last two statutes, forced through despite considerable opposition in the general chapter and a public protest from Addison. The most bitterly contested controversy between the dean and the residentiaries had been provoked by the attempts of Dr. John Willes, Prebendary of Ufton Decani, to force himself into the residentiary chapter after the deprivation of the non-juring Thomas Browne

[78] Bodl. MS. Tanner 45, ff. 265, 269 (Hacket to Sheldon, 27 and 29 Jan. 1668).
[79] Bodl. MS. Tanner 131, f. 22 (Hacket to Sheldon, 1 Feb. 1669).
[80] Ibid. f. 45 (Hacket to Sheldon, 28 Sept. 1670).
[81] Savage, *Last Quarter*, 3–5; see above pp. 61–62.
[82] Savage, *Last Quarter*, 13–18.
[83] Ibid. 19–20, 24.
[84] Ibid. 24–27, 28–30; D. & C. Lich., Bp. Lloyd's

Visitation 1693–4, *passim*.
[85] D. & C. Lich., xiv, loose-leaf letter from Hacket to residentiaries, 13 Aug. 1668 (*S.H.C.* vi(2), 96 n. 1, wrongly gives date as 1660); *Statuta et Consuetudines*, 2–4, 44–45. For the 1596 statutes see above p. 170.
[86] *Statuta et Consuetudines*, 4–5, 88–89.
[87] Ibid. 120, 125–6.
[88] Ibid. 112–13.

in 1690. Dr. John Mainwaring, Prebendary of Weeford, the newly elected residentiary, never came into residence and Willes tried to take his place. In this he was resisted by the whole residentiary chapter. When, however, in 1692 Dr. Mainwaring died and an election was held for a new residentiary the chapter was split, two, including the dean, voting for Thomas White, Prebendary of Longdon, and two for Willes. Addison gave his casting vote for White and declared him elected. Willes's two supporters protested, and Willes himself sued the dean and chapter in the Exchequer for loss of his commons. The case was in progress at the time of Lloyd's visitation, and the two controversial statutes, ostensibly aimed at preventing the recurrence of a similar situation, were undoubtedly aimed at the dean. The first laid down that if in future the residentiary chapter could not come to a unanimous decision about the election of a new residentiary, the matter was to be transferred to the general chapter, which was to make the election by a majority vote. The second abolished the dean's casting vote in the residentiary chapter by decreeing that no decision could be taken, save in the hebdomadary chapter, without the approval of at least three of those present. The bishop's action in thus diminishing the dean's powers and his open support for Willes evidently influenced the court. Willes won his case and duly became a residentiary.[89]

Lloyd also took measures to augment the cathedral's income. In 1660–1 the revenues of the common fund had amounted to some £404, of which about £164 came from fee-farms, about £118 from other farms, just over £110 from pensions, and the remainder from rents and Peak revenues. The real income, however, amounted to only some £333, the chapter having been unable to collect over £71 of the money. By 1664–5 the chapter had succeeded in raising the real income to some £448, partly by pushing the revenue from farms up to £179 and partly by reducing the arrears of payment to £12. Pensions were always in arrears and continued to be so throughout the rest of the 17th and the whole of the 18th centuries. After the payment of commons, fees, salaries, royal dues, and various other expenses there was every year a surplus to be divided, ranging from over £23 in 1661–2 to just under 30s. in 1664–5. Over the next 35 years the annual revenue of the common fund varied between £460 and £491. There was a surplus each year except for 1665–6 and 1666–7 (deficits of over £11 and almost £31), and between 1671–2 and 1691–2 the annual surplus never dropped below £60, rising in 1681–2 to over £107. In 1692–3 the heavy expenses incurred in fighting the Willes case brought the annual surplus down to under £10, and from then until the end of the century it did not rise above £57.[90] In addition there were of course entry fines for leases of the common property. These could be substantial,[91] and in his 1694 statutes Lloyd decreed that future residentiaries were to lay aside a proportion of the fine paid whenever the lease of any of the property belonging to the common fund was renewed; in this manner a fund could be raised to endow two more residentiaryships, thus bringing the number up to the seven which existed before Bishop Overton's reform.[92]

From the evidence given at Lloyd's visitation of 1693 it appears that virtually all the prebendal property was leased, either for years or for three lives. It is impossible to estimate the incomes of individual canons, but it is evident from some of the complaints that several were suffering because predecessors had granted leases on favourable terms, either because of family considerations or in return for large entry fines. Francis Ashenhurst, Prebendary of Ufton Cantoris, having acquired the existing lease of the prebendal property, which was for years, transformed it in 1685 into a lease for the lives of three of his sons. When Edmund Lees became Prebendary of Bobenhull in 1686, he found that the rectory of Bubbenhall, which had at one time brought in a yearly income of £60, had been leased by a predecessor for three lives at £3 6s. 8d. a year.[93] Addison noted that some canons failed to register their leases as required by statute, and the visitation revealed at least one example.[94] Some canons were careless of the rights of jurisdiction attached to their prebends. Willes and Palmer, the two Ufton prebendaries, had 'neglected to assume the jurisdiction belonging to their prebends'; it had therefore been exercised by the dean and chapter.[95] Although one of Bishop Meuland's statutes laid down that *nullus firmarius habeat cognicionem causarum*, Dr. Edmund Diggle, treasurer from 1660 to 1688, leased his prebend for three lives with all the jurisdictions, courts, and perquisites of courts belonging to it.[96]

The 1693 visitation further revealed that the spiritual life of the prebendal parishes had suffered as a result of the canons' neglect. Most of the evidence pointed that way. Dean Addison claimed that the only canon who preached in the parish church within his prebend was Richard Wood of Stotfold. The churchwardens of Sandiacre (Derb.) complained about the way in which their church was being served.[97] In general the stipends which farmers were compelled under the terms of their leases to pay curates were not generous, and where no specific sums were mentioned payment was low. A canon noted that there was 'very mean provision' for the curates of some of the prebendal churches and churches of the common fund.[98] At St. Chad's, Stafford, the curate received only the £7 a year specified in the farmer's lease.[99] In Derbyshire the rectories of Sawley and Wilne, leased by Dr. Diggle, were valued at about £530 a year; the lease laid

[89] Ibid. 121–6; Savage, *Last Quarter*, 21–30.
[90] D. & C. Lich., lxiv, communars' accts. 1660–1700, *passim*.
[91] In 1663, for example, the chapter received £600 for the lease of Cannock: Lich. Dioc. Regy., DC/C/1/2, chapter acts 3 Dec. 1663.
[92] *Statuta et Consuetudines*, 90–92, fixing the amount to be set aside at twice the annual rent.
[93] D. & C. Lich., Bp. Lloyd's Visitation, ff. 16, 20v.
[94] Ibid. ff. 3v., 16.
[95] Ibid. f. 12.
[96] Ibid. f. 8v. For Meuland's statute see above p. 146.

[97] D. & C. Lich., Bp. Lloyd's Visitation, ff. 3, 14v. The precentor stated that there had been great neglect among the prebendaries who were 'parcel rectors' of St. Michael's, Lichfield, until the arrival of Dean Addison, who frequently preached and catechized there: ibid. f. 5.
[98] Ibid. f. 22v., specifying Adbaston, where the curate received £10 a year, and Bubbenhall, where the curate's stipend was £8. At Adbaston the tenant was bound by the terms of his lease to allow the curate 'a competent maintenance', and no sum was mentioned in the Bubbenhall lease: ibid. ff. 3v., 20v.
[99] Ibid. f. 14.

down that the tenant was to provide ministers for the two parish churches and their three chapels, Breaston, Long Eaton, and Risley, and was to pay them stipends amounting in all to at least £34 a year. The visitation revealed that there was, and had been for many years, only a single curate to serve all five churches and chapels. The farmer paid him £36 a year, of which £7 4s. went in tax. In addition to his stipend he had only surplice fees and what he could make out of the perquisites of court — he acted as the farmer's official with regard to the improperly leased prebendal jurisdiction.[1] The affluent curate, such as the man at Tipton who held the lease of the rectory, worth £80 a year, was definitely the exception.[2] Contemporary opinion realized the danger that an impoverished parochial clergy might bring the Established Church into disrepute; Bishop Lloyd considered that the stipends of some of the clergy who served cathedral livings were so poor as to make them *contempti et abjecti*.[3] In the second of his eleven statutes he laid down that in future each lease of a rectory was to make provision for a stipend of at least 40 marks (£26 13s. 4d.) for the vicar or curate. A sliding scale was added, under which a man who served a parish containing 100 households was to receive £30 a year, a man serving a parish of 200 households £40 a year, a man serving one of 400 households £50 a year, and a man with one of 600 households or more £60 a year. Special arrangements were made for the Vicar of St. Mary's, Lichfield, whose stipend of £30 had become inadequate; the dean and those canons whose prebends lay partly in St. Mary's parish were to transfer the small tithes of the prebends to the bishop for the vicar's use.[4]

Lloyd also took steps to reorganize the finances of the vicars choral. Since the outbreak of the Civil War the corporation had suffered several losses, of which the most important was that of the almshouse at Stowe for sick or aged vicars.[5] Two customary payments made to vicars by the chapter or by individual canons had lapsed: the 'interessem' or 'perdition money' divided among the vicars 'for the greater encouragement of such as come to church most and do their duty best', and the 'litany money', paid until about 1692.[6] Moreover by the time of Lloyd's arrival at Lichfield the stipends themselves had become inadequate, and the vicars had been forced to look for supplementary sources of income, laymen for jobs and clergy for benefices. To increase the stipends the reserved rents from the vicars' property had to be raised; Lloyd ordered that the income from this source should be raised to £480, which would give each vicar £40 a year. Until this was done the vicars were forbidden to renew leases

of any portions of their common property without doubling the reserved rent. When each vicar had been provided with £40 a year in this way none was to take any additional job or benefice.[7]

Little evidence appears to have survived concerning services at the cathedral in the years immediately following the Restoration. As was commonly the case throughout the country at this period,[8] celebrations of Holy Communion appear to have been rare. In October 1664 the dean and chapter ordered that 'for the present' there should be at least four celebrations a year, on Christmas Day, Easter Day, Whit Sunday, and the first Sunday after Michaelmas. Other celebrations were to be held 'as there shall be occasion and as the dean and chapter shall think fitting'.[9] The following year, at a meeting presided over by Hacket, it was decided that in future there should be a celebration on the first Sunday in each month,[10] presumably in addition to the four celebrations laid down in 1664. How long this practice lasted is unknown. It had evidently lapsed by 1683, when Addison informed Archbishop Sancroft that he had begun a monthly Communion which he hoped to continue 'with comfort'; but, he added, he could not 'promise anything of success should I attempt it oftener'.[11]

In 1663 Dr. Paul's visitation articles for the vicars choral asked them what they remembered of the 6 a.m. weekday services 'in order to the restoration thereof when God shall please to fit the church'.[12] Nothing, however, appears to have been done, and it was not until the beginning of Lloyd's episcopate that the early-morning service in the Lady Chapel was revived. The bishop gave instructions that morning prayers were to be read 'after the parochial manner' in the chapel as before the war; the hour, however, was altered to 7 a.m. between Michaelmas and the Annunciation and the residentiaries' duty of hospitality to the vicars was commuted for an annual payment of £12 10s., £2 10s. of which was allotted to the subsacrist.[13] Matins was to be celebrated at 10 a.m. and evensong at 4 p.m.[14] Lloyd also laid down that in future the first part of the Litany was to be sung by a priest vicar or by a priest vicar and a lay vicar together instead of by two lay vicars – the traditional Lichfield practice embodied in Hacket's code. He further lifted Hacket's restrictions on priest vicars who did not hold priests' stalls and who, under Hacket's statutes, were allowed to take only lay parts in services.[15]

The cathedral music appears to have been fully restored by 1663. There were nine vicars in residence and a number of choristers, and the choristers' music school had been reopened.[16] The only hint of past

[1] Ibid. ff. 8v.–9.
[2] Ibid. f. 14.
[3] G. F. A. Best, *Temporal Pillars*, 13–15; *Statuta et Consuetudines*, 92, stating also that the stipends set a bad example to lay patrons.
[4] *Statuta et Consuetudines*, 92–98. Nevertheless, 11 years later an unknown correspondent assured Abp. Tenison that vicars and curates serving the cathedral's churches were still 'scandalously provided for': Lambeth Palace Libr. MS. 640, p. 635.
[5] In 1663 Dean Paul asked what had become of it: Lich. Dioc. Regy., DC/C/1/2, articles of inquiry for Dean Paul's visitation of vicars, June 1663.
[6] Ibid.; C.A. vii, ff. 132, 178.
[7] *Statuta et Consuetudines*, 98–100. In 1667 two vicars who had been keeping alehouses in the Close were forbidden to do so: Lich. Dioc. Regy., DC/C/1/2, chapter acts 27 May 1667.

[8] N. Sykes, *Church and State in Eng. in the 18th Cent.* 22–23.
[9] Lich. Dioc. Regy., DC/C/1/2, chapter acts Oct. 1664.
[10] Ibid., chapter acts 5 Oct. 1665.
[11] Bodl. MS. Tanner 131, f. 83 (Addison to Sancroft, 17 Nov. 1683).
[12] Lich. Dioc. Regy., DC/C/1/2, Dean Paul's articles of inquiry, June 1663.
[13] *Statuta et Consuetudines*, 103–6. For the service see above p. 173. [14] *Statuta et Consuetudines*, 107.
[15] Ibid. 100–2. Dean Addison's order in 1687 that priest vicars should not chant the Litany because 'parochial reading of the Litany is rubric' had been one of the articles of complaint laid against him: Savage, *Last Quarter*, 20–21.
[16] Lich. Dioc. Regy., DC/C/1/2, scrutiny of candidate vicars, 19 June 1663, and Dean Paul's articles of inquiry, June 1663.

uncertainties comes with an inquiry into the behaviour of the organist: did he, as was the ancient custom, play a voluntary before the first lesson after the psalmody? 'And is it grave or apt? For ye know how he hath been accused that hath been in that office.'[17] Of the ability of the vicars and choristers it is impossible to judge; it may be noted, however, that after a trial of candidate vicars in June 1663 the man chosen as a probationer by the chapter was one whom eight of the nine vicars had pronounced unsuitable for the post. He was dismissed sixteen months later.[18] By 1665 the cathedral possessed, in addition to ten folio service books, six books containing 'all the ditties of the anthems in print';[19] but a few months later Bishop Hacket intervened to replace the customary anthem after the sermon by a psalm. There were objections from members of the chapter at this interference with cathedral services. It was claimed that the alteration gave offence to gentry and clergy, with the further comment that 'it is not difficult to foresee how nauseous church music and common prayer will again become if Hopkins and Sternhold's rhythms may jostle out our anthems, and a long pulpit-prayer seduce the devotions of the common people'. The bishop, however, appears to have got his way.[20] Things seem to have been back to normal by 1676. Roger North later considered that a Sunday service which he had attended at the cathedral at that date had been performed 'with more harmony and less huddle than I have known it in any church in England, except of late in St. Paul's'.[21]

From 1700 to the Cathedrals Act

Between 1700 and the Cathedrals Act of 1840 there were various changes in the constitution of the cathedral. The most important of these related to the number of residentiaries. Bishop Lloyd's scheme for raising an endowment to provide for the re-establishment of the two residentiaryships abolished by Bishop Overton was abandoned in 1703. At a general chapter held in September of that year Dr. William Binckes, the newly-elected dean, put forward a plan of his own. Under this adequately endowed additional residentiaryships would be created by bestowing more than one prebend on a canon, to whom the bishop would then assign a prebendal house in the Close. The chapter approved the plan; but since it affected the bishop's patronage and required parliamentary sanction it was referred to Bishop Hough. The dean and chapter pointed out to the bishop that the cathedral revenues could not be raised sufficiently to provide for further residentiaries and asked for his support in obtaining an Act to consolidate several prebends. They wished

to raise the number of residentiaries to eight or more, and appointed a standing committee to co-operate with the bishop in the matter and to act on their behalf.[22]

In 1706 an Act was obtained which aimed at bringing the residentiary chapter up to nine. The bishop was empowered to confer two or more prebends on one person, provided that the total of the reserved rents of such prebends did not exceed £70 a year; anyone collated to a second prebend was to bind himself to perform the residence required by the cathedral statutes from the time that he got his prebendal house and a £45 a year income from reserved rents. In view of the low income of the deanery the Duchy of Lancaster rectory of Tatenhill was vested, from its next vacancy, in the dean. Prebends worth less than £4 a year in reserved rents were to be vested in the dean and chapter when they fell vacant and were to become part of the common fund property. The bishop, for his part, was to receive the prebend of Eccleshall for himself and his successors when it next fell vacant.[23]

Whether by accident or design the Act was drafted in a way which worked very much to the disadvantage of the residentiaries appointed under the new scheme.[24] These canons residentiary of the New Foundation were allotted by the Act neither a vote in the residentiary chapter nor a share in the common revenues of the chapter, and successive local statutes emphasized the fact that they were, so to speak, the poor relations of the residentiaries of the Old Foundation. Bishop Chandler's 1720 statutes, for example, reserved to the residentiaries of the Old Foundation the election of residentiaries, the appointment of the chapter clerk and the verger, and the management of the common fund; they also laid down that the fabric fund was to be managed solely by the Old Foundation and was not to be touched by the New. In the cathedral hierarchy residentiaries of the New Foundation were to be placed after the Old Foundation residentiaries, and they were to pay only half the admission fees demanded of residentiaries of the Old Foundation. If in course of time they became residentiaries of the Old Foundation the £30 which they had paid into the fabric fund at the time of their original admission was to be transferred to the common fund together with an additional £36 13s. 4d. to make up the traditional 100-mark entry fine.

The residentiaries of the New Foundation thus faced all the disadvantages of residence with none of the compensating advantages, and Chandler's statutes had to make provision against the possibility that a man with the necessary qualifications would refuse to accept a residentiaryship.[25] In the opinion of residentiaries of the Old Foundation the new

---

[17] Ibid., Dean Paul's articles of inquiry, June 1663.

[18] Ibid., scrutiny of candidate vicars, 19 June 1663, and chapter acts 20 June 1663, 11 Oct. 1664.

[19] Ibid., inventory of cathedral furnishings, 9 Nov. 1665.

[20] Bodl. MS. Tanner 131, f. 14 (Canon Thos. Browne to Sheldon, 18 Apr. 1666, with Hacket's justification for the change). 'Hopkins and Sternhold's rhythms' refers to the metrical version of the Psalms by John Hopkins and Thos. Sternhold.

[21] North, *Lives of the Norths*, i. 185.

[22] H. E. Savage, *Dr. Binckes, in Convocation and the Deanery* (1929), 20–21; D. & C. Lich., C.A. vii, f. 116v.; ibid., H. 12. Binckes assured Bp. Hough in 1703 that 'the statute of doubling the rents for the increase of the number of residentiaries is impracticable': D. & C. Lich., EE.4/Bp.

Hough's visitation of the cathedral, 1703. For Bp. Lloyd's scheme see above p. 179.

[23] Act for augmenting number of Canons Residentiary in Cathedral Church of Lichfield, 4 & 5 Anne, c. 33 (priv. act).

[24] For this para. see preamble to Act to explain and amend an Act of 4 & 5 Anne, 37 Geo. III, c. 20 (priv. act); *Statuta et Consuetudines*, 131–3. Chandler evidently envisaged that the residentiaries of the New Foundation would have a say in some day-to-day business, for he laid down that each was to have only 1 vote in the hebdomadary and other chapters even if he had 2 or 3 prebends: ibid. 131.

[25] *Statuta et Consuetudines*, 132.

residentiaries were merely there to aid and assist them, chiefly by lightening the burden of compulsory residence. Under Chandler's statutes the new residentiaries were obliged to reside 45 consecutive days a year if the income of their prebends amounted to £55 or 38 consecutive days if it did not. The actual dates were to be settled at the residentiary chapter's main yearly meeting, the Michaelmas audit. By the time of Bishop Frederick Cornwallis's statutes of 1752 there were three residentiaries of the New Foundation, and the statutes laid down more exact arrangements. In each of the four quarters into which the year was still divided a residentiary of the Old Foundation was to be in residence for two consecutive calendar months and a residentiary of the New Foundation for one calendar month. A residentiary of the Old Foundation was to pay a 5s. fine to the fabric fund each time he was absent from a cathedral service during his first month's residence and 2s. 6d. for each absence during his second month's residence; a residentiary of the New Foundation was to pay 5s. for absence during his month. With the four residentiaries of the Old Foundation and the three residentiaries of the New this ensured that there would be a canon in residence for eleven months of the year; the remaining month was to be filled by the three New Foundation residentiaries in rotation until the creation of a fourth residentiary of the New Foundation. During this month fines for absence were reduced to 2s. 6d. to maintain equality with the arrangements for Old Foundation residentiaries. As for periods of residence, the New Foundation residentiaries had to wait until the others had made their choice. The only advantage they gained from the statutes was a decision that they should join in presenting to lay vicars' stalls in future.[26]

This unsatisfactory state of affairs, with the New Foundation residentiaries receiving nothing from the common fund and having no say in most of the important capitular decisions, persisted until almost the end of the 18th century. Finally, at the 1796 audit, the chapter decided to ask leave to bring in a Bill to explain and amend the 1706 Act, make further provision for the residentiaries, and provide an addition to the fabric fund.[27]

The preamble to the 1797 Act revising the constitution of the cathedral pointed out the disadvantages which the last Act had brought with it and emphasized the benefits which would follow if all residentiaries participated in the work of the residentiary chapter. The revenues of the residentiary chapter were, as things stood, insufficient to maintain even four residentiaries, but if an addition were made to the income of the residentiaries of the Old Foundation by amalgamating prebends it would be possible to establish six residentiaries with equal shares in the revenues of the common fund. The Act therefore laid down that the residentiary chapter was to consist of the dean and of six canons who were to have the powers and authority of the four existing residentiaries of the Old Foundation. The dean was to receive annually one fifth of the income of the common fund, plus

£42 18s. for his commons (the existing arrangement); after the deduction of these sums the income of the common fund was to be divided equally among the six residentiaries. The bishop, not the chapter, was to appoint the residentiaries; a man so appointed was to be installed forthwith by the dean and residentiary chapter, without any election. The residentiaryships were to be known as the 1st, 2nd, 3rd, 4th, 5th, and 6th residentiaryships; each residentiary was allotted a house in the Close and a sixth of the annual dividend from the common fund. The First Residentiary was to hold the prebend of Colwich, and that of Bishop's Itchington, with the precentorship, when it fell vacant; the Second was to have the prebends of Alrewas (with the chancellorship) and Weeford, when they fell vacant; the Third was to hold the rich prebend of Sawley, with the treasurership; the Fourth was allotted the prebends of Ryton and Prees; the Fifth those of Offley and Flixton; and the Sixth those of Freeford and Hansacre. The Act was to come into effect when either the prebend of Alrewas or that of Weeford fell vacant. Each of the six was to be in residence for two calendar months each year under the same conditions as those applying to the existing residentiaries of the Old Foundation.

Various financial concessions were made to the new residentiary chapter. The prebendal house in the Close which had been occupied by the late Richard Jackson, Prebendary of Colwich and Prees, was to become part of the property of the fabric fund, as were the prebends of Tervin and Stotfold when they next fell vacant. In addition future treasurers were to give the fabric fund a fifth of all fines, rents, and other receipts from their prebend of Sawley after the deduction of the traditional reserved rent of £66 13s. 4d. and of the profits of the rectory of St. Philip's, Birmingham. Members of the residentiary chapter were encouraged to spend their own money on repairs or improvements to their houses in the Close by a clause laying down that if any dean or canon, with the bishop's approval, should spend between £100 and £800 in this way he or his heirs might recover a proportion of the cost from his successor. The bishop, whose patronage was diminished by the Act, received as compensation the advowsons of certain vicarages belonging to the dean and chapter — Colwich, Bishop's Itchington (Warws.), Tachbrook (Warws.), Longdon, High Offley, and Tarvin (Ches.).[28]

The Act came into force with the death of Richard Farmer, the chancellor and Prebendary of Alrewas, in the autumn of 1797[29] and regulated the constitution of the residentiary chapter until the Cathedrals Act of 1840. The various minor adjustments which accompanied the major reform appear to have been made smoothly. The 1799 audit, for example, reorganized the system of chapter patronage so as to provide presentations for the new residentiaries; and when in 1803 the prebends of Tervin and Stotfold became part of the fabric property on the death of Dr. Samuel Smalbroke, that year's audit ordered a survey of the two prebends and a reallotment of the preaching turns.[30]

[26] Ibid. 131, 137–8.
[27] D. & C. Lich., C.A. ix, ff. 6v.–7. A sum of £200 was allotted for the expenses of obtaining the Act.
[28] 37 Geo. III, c.20 (priv. act). For the attachment of St. Philip's, Birmingham, to the prebend of Sawley in 1708

see *V.C.H. Warws.* vii. 377.
[29] Le Neve, *Fasti* (1854 edn.), i. 586.
[30] D. & C. Lich., C.A. ix, f. 25v., pp. 56–57; Le Neve, *Fasti* (1854 edn.), i. 628, 631.

A printed sheet of about 1796, arguing the case for a revision of the Act of 1706, noted amongst other things that the residentiaries of the New Foundation, not having been allowed any powers in the residentiary chapter, were seldom in residence; indeed two of their houses were ruinous.[31] Non-residence was not, however, confined to the New Foundation residentiaries. At Bishop Hough's visitation in 1703 the dean asked that the statute allowing one residentiary to perform another's residence might be interpreted in such a way as to allow one month's personal residence to suffice, with the rest being performed by another residentiary. In 1738 during his visitation of the cathedral Bishop Smalbroke censured the non-residence of certain of the residentiaries, which had been 'too frequently practised for long intervals of time, to the great offence of many observing persons'. The act books of the hebdomadary chapter, starting in 1709, reveal much absenteeism throughout the 18th century and the early part of the nineteenth. Between 1748 and 1772, for example, very little business was done in the hebdomadary chapter, the dean and all the residentiaries sometimes being away at the same time.[32] Those who had no particular business in Lichfield avoided residence and saved paying the statutory fines by persuading other, more amenable, colleagues to perform part at least of their residence for them. This practice drew a formal protest from the precentor, Thomas Smalbroke, in 1754.[33] His argument was that residentiaries who resided by proxy were virtually defrauding the fabric fund by avoiding payment of fines for non-residence; and when, from 1758 to 1761, the practice was forbidden the chapter's declared reason was the bad state of the fabric and the need to supplement the fabric fund.[34] When the demands on the fabric fund were not so heavy, residence was not so strictly enforced; in 1778 and 1781, for example, the dean and residentiaries were often away, and between mid-November 1805 and April 1806 all the members of the residentiary chapter were absent.[35] At the 1837 audit 'the probability of some of the canons being prevented by illness from keeping their residences . . . formed the subject of conversation'. It was duly decided that, 'if on any future occasion of this nature it should be proposed by any member of the chapter not keeping his residence to offer pecuniary compensation to any other canon willing to keep his residence for him, it be understood that such an arrangement will not be objected to by the body'.[36] The residentiaries were not, however, willing to grant others the latitude they allowed themselves; in 1759 the divinity lecturer was warned that he must be in constant residence according to the terms of foundation of the lectureship.[37]

Relations between the chapter and the bishop were generally good during the period. The only serious breach occurred during Smalbroke's prolonged visitation of the cathedral from 1737 to 1739. Besides the non-residence of certain of the canons the bishop found numerous causes for complaint, such as the canons' failure to register prebendal leases,[38] the chapter's reluctance to provide an adequate stipend for the Vicar of St. Mary's, Lichfield,[39] and the negligence of the sacrist.[40] The bishop's persistence, his complaints about the slowness with which the chapter answered his articles of inquiry and the imprecision of their answers, and his apparent intention to conduct a visitation of the vicars choral, provoked the chapter into an assertion of its rights. It denied that the jurisdiction of the dean and chapter over the vicars choral was suspended during an episcopal visitation or that the regular capitular visitation of the cathedral body devolved upon the bishop during his visitation. An episcopal visitation did not, it was claimed, extend to the profits or ecclesiastical jurisdiction of any member of the chapter, save in cases of neglect or default. 'If it were otherwise your Lordship might from time to time find some cause or other for adjournment of your visitation and thereby make it perpetual and entirely destroy the jurisdiction of the dean as well as dean and chapter, which we neither apprehend your Lordship intends nor the Composition [of 1428] or local statutes of the church'.[41] Smalbroke in reply insisted that the chapter had entirely misunderstood his intentions. He was asking for nothing but his canonical rights when he claimed that all inferior jurisdictions were suspended during an episcopal visitation and that several branches of the chapter's jurisdiction devolved upon him during a visitation; it was in fact questionable 'whether the denial of such a power can be excused by any thing but by an unacquaintance with the Canon Law', especially when the denial was accompanied by such a misinterpretation of his motives.[42]

The chapter maintained friendly relations with the Lichfield authorities during these years. In some instances concern for the feelings of local tradesmen coincided with concern for the dignity of the Close. Some time after the Civil War the Lichfield guild of corvisors and curriers had complained to the chapter about a 'foreigner' who had set up business in the Close. Their petition was probably successful, for in 1717 the dean forbade one of the inhabitants of the Close to take a bridle-cutter into his house, saying that he 'would not admit any person that followed a trade to come into the Close to live'.[43] No attempts appear to have been made to infringe the liberty of the Close, and the chapter continued to appoint its own J.P.s and overseers of the poor.[44] In 1738 it was stated that £13 was distributed

[31] D. & C. Lich., uncatalogued packet X (residentiary canons), printed sheet.
[32] D. & C. Lich., EE.4/Bp. Hough's visitation 1703; ibid./ injunctions as to residence, 4 Oct. 1738; D. & C. Lich., x (acts of hebdomadary chapter), 1726–58, 1758–72, *passim*.
[33] D. & C. Lich., C.A. viii, ff. 28v.–29.
[34] Ibid. ff. 37, 40, 41v.
[35] D. & C. Lich., x, 1772–85, 1802–20.
[36] C.A. x, p. 345.
[37] C.A. viii, f. 40.
[38] D. & C. Lich., EE.4/Bp. Smalbroke's visitation of the cathedral 1737–8, f. 4; ibid./injunctions as to leases, 5 Oct. 1738.

[39] Ibid./visitation 1737–8, f. 4v.; ibid./articles of inquiry, 10 July 1739;/articles of inquiry, 2 Oct. 1739;/acts of visitation, 1739; *Statuta et Consuetudines*, 134–5, ordering that the Vicar of St. Mary's and his curates at St. Mary's, St. Chad's, and St. Michael's are each to have stipends of not less than £30 a year.
[40] D. & C. Lich., EE.4/visitation 1737–8, f. 5.
[41] Ibid./chapter's answers to articles of inquiry, 3.
[42] Ibid./articles of inquiry, 2 Oct. 1739.
[43] D. & C. Lich., PP.9; D. & C. Lich., x, 1709–26, 1 Nov. 1717.
[44] C.A. vii, f. 157v.; D. & C. Lich., x, 1726–58, composite entry for 30 Dec. 1748, 6 and 13 Jan. 1749.

annually among the poor of the Close in bread-money; the poor also benefited from 'an hospitality not to be named'.[45] The payment of bread-money ceased in 1767 because the weekly payments to the poor of the Close far exceeded the offering money and there was a deficiency of £23.[46]

In the early 1720s there was a brief squabble with the parishioners of St. Michael's, Lichfield. Canons who had a statutory duty to deliver a certain number of afternoon sermons at the church *vel per se vel per alium* found it inconvenient to walk to the church in bad weather and asked the churchwardens for permission to ride up to the church door in a coach. The request was turned down. The canons retaliated by taking refuge in the letter of the statute and sending one of the vicars (whom they provided with 'a set of very good printed sermons for the whole year') to preach in their place, a move which greatly annoyed the parishioners. Finally the matter came to the ears of the bishop, the churchwardens were persuaded to rescind their ban, and harmony was restored.[47]

The period saw little change in the cathedral's estate policy, which remained essentially unaltered, with the chapter and the individual canons continuing to lease their estates as before. Most improvements to prebendal estates can probably be attributed to the efforts of the farmers. In the years between 1694 and 1739, for example, the estates in and around Lichfield were 'generally improved nine parts in twelve' by inclosure; the acreage of arable land was 'vastly increased' and that of pasture declined. The farmers benefited from increased corn and grain tithes and the Vicar of St. Mary's, Lichfield, to whom the tithes of wool and lambs were allotted, suffered proportionately.[48] The chapter reaped the benefits of agricultural improvements through increased entry and renewal fines rather than by higher rents. When in 1766 it was decided that the lease of the tithes of Litton (Derb.) should not be renewed but instead offered to the highest bidder, the reason given was that the existing tenant had refused to increase the fine although the commons had recently been inclosed and ploughed, thereby swelling his yield from corn and grain tithes and diminishing the chapter's wool and lamb tithes.[49] The general rule appears to have been that up to 1755 the entry fine was equivalent to a year's return, at current valuation, from the property leased. In that year, because of the lowering of the rate of interest and the consequent increase in the value of leases, the chapter decided that in future lessees should pay fines of 1¼ year's value. This was raised to 1½ year's value for septennial renewals in 1778 and for all leases in 1783.[50]

The problems of management were similarly unchanged. Complaints came at intervals during the earlier 18th century about the failure of canons to register leases of their prebendal estates in the chapter lease-book. In 1703, for example, it was reported that no fewer than six canons had failed to register leases, while in 1738 Bishop Smalbroke ordered the institution of systematic inspection and registration, with tenants being ordered to bring in terriers or surveys to be deposited in the registry.[51] Sufficient information always appears to have been available, however, at least for the more accessible parts of the capitular estates; Smalbroke himself was well-informed about the property around Lichfield.[52] In 1775 the chapter was employing a land-surveyor, John Renshaw.[53]

Between 1700 and 1800 the revenues of the common fund from fee farms, other farms, pensions, Peak revenues, and rents remained virtually static, seldom falling below £460 a year and only once rising over £500. The surplus for division after the payment of commons and other charges generally varied between £60 and £90, though it occasionally dropped as low as £15 and in at least one year exceeded £100.[54] Commons and dividend, however, formed only a comparatively small part of the residentiaries' income; far more important were the fines received from lessees of the common property. Even so, Lichfield was not a wealthy cathedral. About 1796 it was estimated that over the past 10 years the four residentiaryships of the Old Foundation had each been worth, upon an average, £124 1s. 7½d. a year, and it was argued that one of the merits of the proposed Act (of 1797) would be the creation of five residentiaryships worth about £300 a year each and a sixth, the treasurership, which on account of the increased value of the prebend of Sawley would be worth much more.[55]

The figures published in 1835 by the royal commission inquiring into ecclesiastical revenues show that during the three years ending in 1831 the average annual income of the common fund was £1,638 gross, £1,311 net. Just over £1,000 of the gross income came from fines, some £560 from reserved rents, and the remainder from various other unnamed minor sources.[56] Lichfield had the smallest common fund of any English cathedral save Chester, though it is true that the common fund of York provided only some £40 net a year more.[57] From it the dean drew annually an average of £279 in commons and dividend and each of the six residentiaries an average of £172.[58] The individual prebendal estates differed widely in value. The dean was by far the wealthiest member of the chapter, with an average net annual income from his prebend and the annexed rectory of Tatenhill of just over £1,500; next came the treasurer, with some £670 a year from the prebend of Sawley, and then the Fourth Residentiary with about £340. The other canons — the precentor, the chancellor, the Fifth and Sixth Residentiaries, and the 14 non-residentiaries — received regularly little more than nominal reserved rents from their prebendal estates: the precentor £23, the chancellor £46, the Fifth

[45] D. & C. Lich., EE.4/answers to articles of inquiry, 1738.
[46] C.A. viii, f. 53.
[47] D. & C. Lich., uncatalogued envelope XXXIV, Bp. Chandler to Dean Walmisley, 19 Sept. 1724.
[48] D. & C. Lich., EE.4/articles of inquiry, 10 July, 2 Oct. 1739.
[49] C.A. viii, f. 52v.   [50] Ibid. ff. 32, 89v., 100.
[51] D. & C. Lich., EE.4/Bp. Hough's visitation 1703;/Bp. Smalbroke's injunctions as to leases, 5 Oct. 1738.

[52] See ibid./articles of inquiry, 10 July, 2 Oct. 1739.
[53] C. A. viii, f. 79.
[54] D. & C. Lich., lxiv, *passim*; D. &. C. Lich., un-numbered papers, communars' accts. 1733–1800.
[55] D. & C. Lich., uncatalogued packet X (residentiary canons), printed sheet.
[56] *Rep. Com. Eccl. Revs.* [67], p. 18, H.C. (1835), xxii.
[57] Ibid. 10–26. The average income of the Chester common fund was £2,135 gross but only £634 net.
[58] Ibid. 19.

Residentiary £44, the Sixth Residentiary £51, and none of the non-residentiaries more than £20. Income from fines was considerable but irregular; in the three years ending in 1831 the dean received nothing from this source while the precentor received a total of £1,295, the chancellor £895, and the treasurer £1,350.[59] This did not of course exhaust the sources of income available to the canons. All the residentiaries and all, save apparently two, of the non-residentiaries were pluralists. Dean Woodhouse's rich rectory of Stoke-upon-Trent (which he resigned in 1831) brought him a net annual income of over £2,500 and the rectory of Donington (Salop.) another £573. Similarly the precentor, Anthony Hamilton, held the rectories of Loughton (Essex) and St. Mary-le-Bow (London), together worth over £800 net, besides the archdeaconry of Taunton (Som.) with its annexed stall at Wells.[60]

During this period the organization and status of the vicars remained virtually unchanged. Shortly after the Restoration their numbers had settled at twelve — five priest vicars, including the subchanter, and seven lay vicars, including the organist — and no alteration was subsequently made.[61] In general they were a well-behaved body. There were occasional black sheep,[62] but there is little to compare with the more spectacular misdoings of previous centuries.

The chapter's chief ground for complaint was absenteeism. Each vicar was entitled to one day off duty a week (the 'sine' or 'ensign' days), but for some this was evidently insufficient. In 1734, on Bishop Smalbroke's orders, the subchanter delivered a lecture to the vicars on the evils of absenteeism. As he subsequently reported to the bishop, most of the vicars performed their duties conscientiously. The trouble was caused mainly by a minority of absentees over whose movements he appears to have had little or no control despite the fact that penalties for absence were being strictly enforced. The chief offender was the sacrist, Henry Perkins, 'nominal or pretended rector' of Barwick in Elmet (Yorks. W.R.). He was away from Lichfield for more than two-thirds of the year, seldom attended services when he was resident, and had infringed the cathedral statutes by not appointing another vicar to act as his deputy. A second vicar was a chronic invalid and often available for only three months in the year; two more had been away from Lichfield for some time. Thus whenever any of the remaining vicars failed to attend a service

the choir was left 'almost destitute'. The subchanter promised that there would be a further tightening of discipline, and the chapter ordered Perkins to return to his duties on pain of deprivation.[63] In 1753 it was decided that any vicar absent from duty for more than a week should lose his commons until his return to duty, even if he had obtained leave of absence; if he stayed away for more than a fortnight he was in addition to pay a fine of 2d. a day into the fabric fund. A vicar who was in Lichfield and missed a cathedral service was to lose his commons for the day and pay a 2d. fine.[64] In 1770, 1774, and 1777 the vicars were officially warned to attend services more regularly and their attention was drawn to the oath which they had taken upon their admission.[65] From 1779 vicars had to submit the reasons for any absence in writing to the chapter.[66]

There appears to have been no marked increase in the revenue of the corporation. Despite Bishop Lloyd's attention to the revenue from reserved rents[67] this rose very little. In 1718 priest vicars were still receiving a dividend of only £14 3s. 3d. from reserved rents and lay vicars one of £12 3s. 3d. With each vicar receiving about £7 17s. in commons, pensions, stall-money, and other payments, priests had a basic income of about £22 and laymen one of about £20.[68] Bishop Chandler's statute of 1720, which laid down that in future the vicars were not to lease any of their common property unless a quarter or a fifth were added to the existing reserved rent, also allowed various exceptions from this rule: when, for example, the leases were of land worth less than £10 a year attached to houses in Lichfield paying customary rents.[69] All this marked a retreat from Lloyd's instructions to double the reserved rents, and income from this source never approached the target of £480 a year which Lloyd had set. In a period of nearly 50 years, from 1732 to 1780, it rose from just over £194 a year to some £242; by about 1830 it was still only £253 a year.[70] There were also fines, which evidently provided the greater part of the vicars' corporate income. In the years 1828–31 the vicars had an average annual income of £804 gross, £770 net; of the gross income £551 came from fines and the rest from reserved rents. The net revenues were divided equally save that the five priest vicars each received £2 more than the seven lay vicars from the reserved rents. The only member of the corporation with an additional income was the subchanter, who received various annual payments

[59] Ibid. 48–53.
[60] Ibid. 48–49, 201, 475, 501, 661; *V.C.H. Staffs.* viii. 186, 190 (where the date of Woodhouse's resignation from Stoke is wrongly given as 1832). Hamilton was cited in 1831 as an example of 'the measureless rapacity that directs the disposal of church-preferment': [John Wade], *The Extraordinary Black Book* (1831), 26. Dean Woodhouse's predecessor, Dean Proby, had held the valuable rectory of Doddington (Cambs.) and the rectory of Thornhaugh-with-Wansford (Northants.), and at the time of his death the income from his preferments amounted, according to one contemporary, to £3,500 a year: *Gent. Mag.* 1807, lxxvii(1), 183, 275.
[61] C. A. vii, f. 131v.; *Rep. Com. Eccl. Revs.* 19. Though there were 14 in 1664 (see above p. 175) this number was evidently not maintained long.
[62] See e.g. D. & C. Lich., EE.4/Bp. Hough's visitation 1703; C.A. vii, f. 143v. In 1728 Thos. Cottrell, an organ-builder of Halesowen (Worcs.), deposed that Geo. Lamb, the organist, had tried to persuade him to remove several pipes from a little organ in the Lady Chapel to make him a house organ, saying that 'they [the chapter] would

never miss them': D. & C. Lich., P.2.
[63] D. & C. Lich., uncatalogued envelope XL, John Stephenson to Bp. Smalbroke, 13 July 1734.
[64] Savage, *Dr. Binckes*, 26; C.A. viii, f. 27.
[65] C.A. vii, ff. 264, 265v. (bis); C.A. viii, f. 65.
[66] C.A. viii, ff. 90v.–91. [67] See above p. 180.
[68] D. & C. Lich., uncatalogued envelope XII, statement of quarterly dividends for vicars, 1718.
[69] *Statuta et Consuetudines*, 130–1. The modifications were inserted in answer to a petition from the vicars, who feared that if they were forced to raise the rents of their houses in Lichfield when the leases ran out, many of their tenants, who lived in 'old decayed buildings', would fail to do any repairs and then move when the existing leases expired: D. & C. Lich., uncatalogued envelope XII, petition of vicars choral, 1720; uncatalogued envelope XXXIV, Bp. Chandler to Dean Walmisley, 1 July 1720. A survey of the vicars' leases and rents made c. 1700 (uncatalogued envelope XII) shows that at that date over two-thirds of the vicars' income from property came from houses and pieces of land in Lichfield.
[70] C.A. vii, ff. 210v., 269; *Rep. Com. Eccl. Revs.* 18.

amounting to £7.[71] Individual vicars thus received between £60 and £70 a year, in addition to their houses and the commons provided by the dean and chapter.

When the dean and chapter visited the vicars in 1723 the latter stated that they had one church, Chesterton, appropriated to them, adding 'there may [be] some others have been lost for aught we know, but how or where to recover them we know not'.[72] In fact the appropriated church of Penn appears to have been lost at some date between 1706 and 1714.[73] The appropriation was later recovered, however,[74] and during the greater part of the 18th century and in the early 19th century the vicars seem to have organized their affairs quite efficiently, keeping their houses in the Close in good repair[75] and, between 1756 and 1759, building themselves a 'new, commodious muniment house'.[76]

The early years of the 19th century saw various changes with regard to the choristers. In 1806 the number was reduced from ten to eight,[77] and in late 1817 or in 1818 a choristers' school was established with the help of a gift of £100 from Dean Woodhouse. Here the choristers were taught reading, writing, and arithmetic and had a specially-appointed master in charge of them. The organist continued to be personally responsible for their musical education.[78] During the 18th century the organist or his deputy had taught the boys singing, and mention is made of a singing school in the ante-room of the cathedral library in 1772, and of a practice room for the older boys in the Vicars' College in 1802;[79] but there appears to be no definite evidence concerning the boys' general education. Possibly, since all were local boys, they were taught in Lichfield itself. They each received £2 a year until 1770, when their stipends were increased to £3. In 1800 it was decided that newly-admitted choristers should receive £3 a year but that as the older boys left the choir the stipends of the younger boys should be increased, according to their merit, on the recommendation of the subchanter. Since the previous year the boys had received supplementary payments of 14s. or 15s. each a year from chapter funds.[80] When in 1806 the number of choristers was reduced to eight, the stipends were considerably increased for the older boys: the two eldest each received £10 a year, the next pair £8, the next pair £6, and the two youngest £4. Further increases followed in 1812 and 1825.[81] Apart from this the boys came to the chapter's attention only when their surplices were grubby or their behaviour in church fell below the required standard.[82]

Except when there was a sermon, the choir was the only part of the cathedral used for services. This caused difficulties until the time of Wyatt's restoration of the building; his scheme of throwing the choir and the Lady Chapel together was welcomed by the chapter, since it provided greater accommodation for the congregation and enabled sermons to be preached in the choir. It is in fact probable that the idea came from the chapter.[83] Previously, whenever there was a sermon, the inhabitants of the Close were obliged to move from the choir into the nave in order to hear it, 'a circumstance very awkward, disagreeable, and troublesome'. A large number of people also came up from the city, where sermons appear to have been infrequent. Afterwards those who intended to communicate returned into the choir, 'the sacrament being administered there every Sunday if there is a proper number of communicants'.[84]

In 1752 Bishop Frederick Cornwallis made various adjustments to the hours of services. The early morning prayers were in future to be celebrated in the Lady Chapel at 7.30 a.m. from Michaelmas to the Annunciation and at 6.30 a.m. during the rest of the year. On weekdays matins was to be at 10.30 a.m. from Michaelmas to the Annunciation and at 10 a.m. during the rest of the year. Evensong remained at the usual time, 4 p.m. On Sundays matins was to begin at 10.30 a.m. all the year round and evensong at 4.30 p.m.[85] In 1779 new regulations were laid down for Passion Week services: the organ was not to be used and services were to be read 'in a parochial way'.[86]

The 18th century saw an increased insistence on decorum in the conduct of services. Though it was stated at the beginning of the century that a customary rule allowed vicars to be credited with attendance at a service if they reached their stalls before the first *Gloria* of the psalms,[87] steps were taken a few years later to ensure that once they were in their stalls they stayed until the end of the service. Dean Kimberley considered it 'very scandalous and offensive' that many vicars should leave the church when prayers ended and before the sermon began; in future, he directed, vicars were to stay for the sermon.[88] The Sacheverell affair evidently had its repercussions in Lichfield, for in 1710 the chapter moved to prevent the preaching of inflammatory or controversial sermons in the cathedral.[89]

The later 18th century evidently saw a marked improvement in the cathedral's music. Probably this is to be attributed to the efforts of John Alcock, organist and master of the choristers 1749–60, for the standard of musicianship before his arrival seems to have been somewhat undistinguished.[90] In 1723 the vicars reported that although they knew of no

[71] *Rep. Com. Eccl. Revs.* 18–19.   [72] C.A. vii, f. 176v.
[73] Ibid. ff. 131, 143.   [74] *Rep. Com. Eccl. Revs.* 492.
[75] See e.g. ibid. ff. 210v., 218.   [76] Ibid. ff. 235v., 238v.
[77] C.A. ix, p. 81. Numbers had varied; there were 8 in Oct. 1732 (C.A. vii, f. 211) and 9 in Sept. 1799 (C.A. ix, f. 27). This presumably happened as voices broke, though in 1771 John Alcock, the former cathedral organist (see below), noted that 'many of the lads are continued in their places for ten, twelve, or fourteen years, and long after their voices are broke': J. E. West, *Cathedral Organists Past and Present* (1899 edn.), 45.
[78] C.A. ix, p. 215; *Gent. Mag.* 1818, lxxxviii(2), 6–7.
[79] C.A. viii, f. 28; D. & C. Lich., x, 1772–85, 31 July 1772; C.A. ix, pp. 50–51.
[80] C.A. viii, f. 64; C.A. ix, ff. 27, 36v.
[81] C.A. ix, pp. 81, 159; C.A. x, p. 95.
[82] C.A. vii, ff. 144, 236; C.A. viii, f. 89.
[83] Shaw, *Staffs.* i. 259, 260. For Wyatt's restoration see below pp. 187–8.
[84] Shaw, *Staffs.* i. 259, 260.
[85] *Statuta et Consuetudines*, 139.
[86] C.A. viii, f. 91. The custom of playing the organ in Passion Week may have been one of John Alcock's innovations (see below); it certainly lapsed after he left the cathedral in 1760: West, *Cathedral Organists*, 45.
[87] Savage, *Dr. Binckes*, 26.
[88] D. & C. Lich., x, 1709–26, 15 Nov. 1717.
[89] D. & C. Lich., II. 9.
[90] Several vicars were, however, founder-members of the select Lichfield Musical Club, which was formed in 1739 and met in the vicars' hall. By 1747 the club had acquired the scores of instrumental music by Geminiani, Corelli, Vivaldi, Tessarini, Handel, and John Humphries: W.S.L., S.MS. 24(iv), rules and account book of the club 1739–48. W.S.L., S.MS. 370(iv), pp. 275–311, is an annotated transcript of this.

occasion on which a candidate had been admitted through bribery 'sometimes we have had reason to think some of our body's judgements much biassed and their testimonies too partial' — apparently a hint that some unsatisfactory singers had been accepted. Nine years later they were more positive about the choristers: the boys were quite well-behaved, 'but as to their natural abilities with respect to music they are not the most promising'.[91] In 1732 the vicars reported that 'the organ is out of repair, all our books imperfect, and no dinner for the preacher on a Sunday'.[92] Alcock, a competent and experienced musician and a former pupil of the blind organist John Stanley, appears to have brought with him new efficiency. His *Divine Harmony*, published in 1752, contained a collection of 55 chants which he had composed for the use of the cathedral, and he noted in the preface that these were 'not much more than half the number I've composed for this church'. He had also accumulated a valuable collection of services and anthems by various composers, which he doubtless put to use at Lichfield.[93] Eventually a breach of some sort occurred between him and the other vicars. In 1760 his colleagues formally complained that he spoilt the services 'by playing improperly, indecently, and perversely on the organ with design to confound and prevent the vicars from the due performance of their duty in singing the said services and anthems'. The chapter admonished him to behave in future and he left the cathedral.[94] The choir continued, however, to be well-served. Boswell was 'very much delighted' with the music when he attended a service at the cathedral in 1776. Vicars visited London to sing in oratorios and public concerts there, and when a visitor called at the cathedral in 1799 he noted that several of the vicars were 'names of celebrity in the musical world' and that the choristers sang 'exceeding well'.[95] When lay vicars were required in the early 19th century the chapter advertised not only in the Birmingham newspapers but also in those at London and Bath.[96]

The cathedral fabric needed little work done upon it, apart from care and maintenance, for a hundred years after the 17th-century restoration. During the 1730s, for example, payments out of the fabric fund were usually small, and in 1738 Bishop Smalbroke was informed that the building was in good repair 'except in the roof, where there is some defect'.[97] In 1749 many of the statues on the west front were removed, in 1758 the rose-window on the south face of the south transept was restored, and in 1765–6 the upper part of the north-west spire was rebuilt;[98] but no large-scale work was begun until the 1770s. By 1772 the roof had become dangerous. At least two surveys were made of it in that year and the next, and various plans for making it safe were submitted to the chapter. That finally adopted appears to have been the one proposed by Thomas Webb, somewhat modified by William Newbolt. The lead was gradually stripped from the roof and sold, while the timber framework, evidently the cause of the anxiety, was removed and replaced. The new framework lowered the pitch of the roof and reduced its area by over 6,000 sq. ft.; this, and the replacement of the lead covering by Westmorland slates, must have lessened the cost of reconstruction considerably. Even so, the work, which went on from 1774 to 1778, involved the chapter in heavy expense: £525 10s. was paid for 205 tons of slates, and at least £547 10s. was spent 'on account of the roof' and for timber. Nevertheless the sale of the lead which had formerly covered the roof may have enabled the chapter to recoup the cost, with enough money left to lay a new floor and clean the inside of the cathedral, as had been planned in 1772.[99]

Soon after the reroofing had been completed the chapter was considering further restoration and reconstruction. In 1781 it asked the Staffordshire-born James Wyatt to make a survey of the proposed alterations in the nave, the choir, and the Lady Chapel, and it was under his direction that the work was completed between 1788 and 1795.[1] The period between the first approach to Wyatt and the beginning of the work was spent by the chapter in fund-raising. Bishop James Cornwallis took a keen interest in the proposed 'improvements' and was a liberal subscriber, while members of the chapter not only subscribed themselves but were urged to rouse local support. Cornwallis estimated that the scheme would cost £4,000; Wyatt, however, stated that the cost would be over £5,950. By 1788 £5,200 had been raised by subscription. To this the chapter added £1,800 which it had borrowed, and Wyatt could begin.[2]

Lichfield was the first cathedral in which Wyatt's plans for restoration were actually carried out, and his aims — uniformity of style and the creation of sweeping, uncluttered 'vistas' — were those which he later pursued elsewhere.[3] His work here, as at

[91] C.A. vii, ff. 177v., 211.
[92] Ibid. f. 211v.
[93] J. Alcock, *Divine Harmony, or a Collection of Fifty-five Double and Single Chants for Four Voices* (Birmingham, 1752), preface and advertisement; *D.N.B.* For the subsequent history of Alcock's collection see C. H. Phillips, *The Singing Church*, 160.
[94] C.A. viii, f. 41v.; West, *Cathedral Organists*, 45–46.
[95] Boswell, *Life of Johnson*, ed. G. B. Hill and L. F. Powell, ii. 466; C.A. viii, f. 84; *Gent. Mag.* 1800, lxx(1), 16. When Hugh Bourne, the founder of Primitive Methodism, visited the cathedral in 1807 he was delighted by the singing, though he 'saw much lightness and sin among the parsons': J. T. Wilkinson, *Hugh Bourne*, 51.
[96] D. & C. Lich., x, 1802–20, 10 Nov. 1815, 15 and 22 Jan. 1819.
[97] D. & C. Lich., uncatalogued envelope XIII, no. 13; D. & C. Lich., EE.4/answers to Bp. Smalbroke's articles of inquiry, 1738.
[98] Harwood, *Lichfield*, 73; J. G. Lonsdale, *Recollections of Work done in and upon Lichfield Cathedral from 1856 to 1894* (Lichfield, 1895), 35–36 (copy in W.S.L. Pamphs. sub Lichfield); *Aris's Birmingham Gazette*, 29 Sept. 1766.

[99] C. Bodington, 'The Roofs of the Cathedral', *Lich. Dioc. Mag.* (1893), 21–23; D. & C. Lich., x, 1772–85, 7 Aug 1772; C.A. viii, ff. 77, 79, 84; see below. The 'housing' marks of the former high-pitched roof are still visible on the central tower of the cathedral. In 1780 it was noted that slates had been substituted for lead 'on account of the narrow revenues left to maintain this venerable pile': T. Pennant, *Journey from Chester to London* (1811 edn.), 145. The removal of the lead had aroused the anger of Dr. Johnson, who mistakenly imagined that the canons intended to divide among themselves the money received from the sale of the lead; in the original version of his *Journey to the Western Islands* he referred to the chapter as 'a body of men . . . longing to melt the lead of an English cathedral. What they shall melt, it were just that they should swallow': Boswell, *Life of Johnson*, v. 502.
[1] C.A. viii, f. 97; H. M. Colvin, *Biog. Dict. Eng. Architects, 1660–1840*, 722, 727.
[2] D. & C. Lich., x, 1785–1802, 7 Feb., 23 Mar. 1787; Shaw, *Staffs.* i. 259–60.
[3] A. Dale, *James Wyatt* (1956 edn.), 99; Colvin, *Biog. Dict. Eng. Architects*, 724.

other cathedrals, was later savagely criticized; but his contemporaries agreed that restoration work was urgently needed at Lichfield[4] and his clients not only approved of his alterations to the cathedral but in fact probably dictated them. The principal object of the restoration was to enlarge the choir, so that it could contain the whole congregation. Wyatt effected this by removing the 'elegant stone screen' between the choir and the Lady Chapel, and also Dean Smalwood's Classical reredos which stood before it.[5] The latter, which Celia Fiennes had admired in 1697,[6] was now regarded as a monstrosity; Pennant in 1780 considered that 'the beauty of the choir was much impaired' by it, and Stebbing Shaw agreed, calling it 'a sad mass of deformity'.[7] The materials of the stone screen were repaired and used as a base for the organ. The new choir, formed out of the choir and the Lady Chapel, provided the required accommodation and did not in general offend the aesthetic susceptibilities of a Gothicizing public, though before long there were complaints that it was too long — 'it is all seeing and no hearing'.[8] The pews and pulpit were removed from the nave, the stalls in the choir were repainted, new floors were put in — Derbyshire stone in the nave and grey and white marble in the choir — and a new freestone altar, 'elegantly sculptured', was put at the east end of the former Lady Chapel.[9] To render the new, enlarged choir more self-contained and easier to keep warm, Wyatt blocked up the four easternmost arches on both sides of the choir, the only ones which were still open, by building a plain walled screen flush with the inner arches.[10]

In other parts of the cathedral he undertook some substantial rebuilding. The weight of the stone vaults in the roof of the nave was threatening to bring down the walls; this was remedied by taking down five of them and replacing them by plaster, 'in consequence of which the walls . . . have not now a twentieth part of the weight to sustain'.[11] The roofs of the aisles were raised; much of the central spire was taken down and rebuilt; windows, doors, pillars, and capitals were restored; walls and roof were scraped and whitewashed; new glass was inserted; and two great buttresses were erected to support the south transept.[12] The restoration, which cost in all some £8,000, was completed in 1795 with the addition of a stained glass window after a design by Sir Joshua Reynolds at the east end of the cathedral.[13]

At least one other architect appears to have been employed under Wyatt's general supervision to carry out part of the work: at the 1794 audit it was agreed that Joseph Potter of Lichfield should repair and secure the 'south spires' of the cathedral and be allowed his reasonable expenses.[14] Francis Eginton of Handsworth was responsible for the stained glass. He executed the east window and was commissioned by the chapter to do other work in the cathedral.[15]

The restoration left the fabric fund about £2,700 in debt,[16] and various other alterations now made necessary were paid for out of the common fund; the bishop's consistory court, for example, had been removed during Wyatt's restoration of the interior of the cathedral, and the chapter had to fit up a new one in the vestry in the south aisle.[17] In 1797 Dean Proby came to the chapter's aid with a loan which enabled it to pay the bills still due on the fabric account.[18] In 1799, however, it was decided to erect a screen in front of the organ and glaze it 'in order to render the choir less inconvenient during the winter months'; the cost, £180, had to be defrayed by £20 subscriptions from the residentiaries and the proceeds of a public appeal.[19]

The most notable addition to the cathedral came shortly after 1800. While travelling on the Continent in 1801 Sir Brooke Boothby of Ashbourne (Derb.) purchased for £200 340 panels of mid-16th-century stained glass which had come from the dissolved Cistercian abbey of Herckenrode, some 2 miles from Hasselt in what is now Belgium. The Peace of Amiens the following year enabled him to bring the glass to England and some time before the Michaelmas audit he offered it to the chapter at cost price. The offer was gratefully accepted, as was Wyatt's offer in 1804 to give advice on the placing of the glass in the cathedral. Preparations for installing it were begun in 1803, when 'a machine for new leading the painted glass was ordered to be procured from Birmingham'. It was finally decided to fill seven windows in the Lady Chapel. The Revd. W. G. Rowland of Shrewsbury was responsible for the actual arrangement, and John (later Sir John) Betton of Shrewsbury had the work of putting up the glass.[20] In 1814 some remaining pieces were placed in the south window of the east aisle of the transept.[21]

A visitor to the cathedral in 1818 noted that the interior presented 'a most interesting and gratifying sight to the lover of neatness, harmony, and preservation. Every part is clean, sound, and beautiful'. Externally, however, the building had suffered from the action of the weather on a bad

---

[4] Shaw, *Staffs.* i. 259; *Gent. Mag.* 1800, lxx(1), 17, stating that whatever might be thought of the restored cathedral 'one thing is certain, that it wanted repair'.

[5] Shaw, *Staffs.* i. 260. For the reredos see above p. 176.

[6] *The Journeys of Celia Fiennes*, ed. C. Morris, 111.

[7] Pennant, *Journey*, 146; Shaw, *Staffs.* i. 260.

[8] *Gent. Mag.* 1795, lxv(2), 785, 924 (attacks on Wyatt's restorations at Hereford and Lichfield).

[9] Shaw, *Staffs.* i. 260, stating that the old altar was removed to Stowe Church; Dale, *Wyatt*, 100; Harwood, *Lichfield*, 93.

[10] Dale, *Wyatt*, 99–100.

[11] Ibid. 99; Shaw, *Staffs.* i. 260; *Lich. Dioc. Mag.* (1893), 22, printing an extract from a report of 1844 which ascribes the ruinous condition of the south nave clerestory wall to the thrust of the old roof.

[12] Dale, *Wyatt*, 99; Shaw, *Staffs.* i. 261, noting that though the buttresses were ugly they would have been much more expensive if built 'to correspond with the general elegance of the building'.

[13] Shaw, *Staffs.* i. 260.

[14] C.A. viii, f. 123; Colvin, *Biog. Dict. Eng. Architects*, 469.   [15] Shaw, *Staffs.* i. 260; *D.N.B.*

[16] C.A. ix, f. 4v.; D. & C. Lich., uncatalogued packet X (residentiary canons), printed sheet of c. 1795 showing state of fabric fund.

[17] C.A. viii, f. 118; C.A. ix, ff. 7v., 14.

[18] C.A. ix, f. 14v.

[19] Ibid. ff. 25v.–26. The screen was put up in 1801: Harwood, *Lichfield*, 90. Earlier in the century John Alcock stated that he had developed rheumatism through having to play the organ 'in the severest cold weather when, very often, there was only one vicar, who read the service, and an old woman at church besides the choristers': West, *Cathedral Organists*, 45.

[20] D. & C. Lich., x, 1802–20, 22 July 1803; *Staffs. Advertiser*, 16 Nov. 1811; H. Bright, *The Herckenrode Windows in Lichfield Cathedral* (Lichfield, 1932), 7–12 (copy in W.S.L. Pamphs. *sub* Lichfield). Bright (pp. 12–19) gives a description of the windows, attributing them to Lambert Lombard.

[21] C.A. ix, p. 176.

sandstone, and considerable alterations were by this time going on under the direction of Joseph Potter the younger of Lichfield. One of the works proposed was a thorough repair and restoration of the west front, 'which at present is sadly mutilated'.[22] This proposed restoration took place in the early 1820s and was executed principally in Roman cement. Much of the remaining sculpture on the west front was defaced or destroyed in the course of the work, which was immediately attacked as 'patching and plastering'.[23]

Apart from work on the cathedral, there was some rebuilding going on in the Close throughout the period. Dean Binckes, for example, reconstructed the deanery at the beginning of the 18th century. The building, which dated from the 15th or early 16th century and had been badly damaged during the Civil War, was given a new front 'with good brickwork and well set off with uniform windows'.[24] It was probably Binckes who planted lime-trees along the north and east sides of the Close, forming 'The Dean's Walk'.[25]

At that time the Close must have presented a somewhat unkempt appearance. In 1706 it was reported that there were two alehouses within the precincts, the pavement was broken up in various places, a horse was sometimes kept in the churchyard, and there was a dunghill near the south door of the cathedral.[26] By 1714 the alehouses were gone but the pavements were still broken up and sometimes horses and cows were turned into the churchyard to graze.[27] In the 1720s and 1730s there were renewed complaints about the pavements and the general condition of the Close,[28] but from the middle of the century the chapter showed a new concern about the tidiness and general appearance of the precincts. Provision was made for cutting the trees in the walks formed earlier in the century, and steps were taken to keep the Close free from weeds and rubbish.[29] In 1759 part of the churchyard was levelled, provoking a protest from Precentor Smalbroke, who did not think that the bones of the dead should be disturbed.[30] In 1775 the north doorway of the cathedral was cleared and the road to it gravelled; in 1781 the sundial in the Close was taken down, the paths round the cathedral were widened and gravelled, and the road to the deanery was made into a carriage road.[31] This concern for tidiness led to one ludicrous episode. The sight of the conduit which stood on the cathedral green gave offence to two of the dignitaries, and in 1786 they persuaded the chapter to have it taken down and

replaced by a reservoir and pump.[32] A local humorist told the story of the demolition and its sequel. A workman summoned up from Lichfield swore that a reservoir would give as good a water supply as the conduit. He was ordered to pull the conduit down.

> Great was thereof the fall,
> Of water few have complement,
> The Bishop none at all.
> What can be done in such a case,
> How will they make amends?
> E'en build another in its place,
> And so the frolic ends.[33]

No replacement appears to have been built, however, until in 1803 an octagon brick conduit, equal in size and capacity to the one demolished, was erected in a corner of the Close.[34]

The quest for elegance and uniformity resulted in the destruction of several of the medieval buildings in the Close. The most notable loss was the late-15th-century half-timbered library on the north side of the cathedral,[35] which as early as 1724 was thought to be 'a mean structure'.[36] In 1757 the chapter ordered the destruction of the building, which also contained the chapter clerk's house, on the ground that its proximity to the cathedral threatened the latter in case of fire.[37] The room above the chapter-house was fitted with shelves and became the cathedral library once more.[38] In 1772 the choristers' house was pulled down and rebuilt by the lessee 'in an elegant style'.[39] The south gateway to the Close was demolished in the mid 18th century,[40] and in 1800 Bishop Langton's other gateway, at the west entrance to the Close, 'was, with a barbarous taste, pulled down, and the materials applied to lay the foundation of a pile of new buildings, for the residence of necessitous widows of clergymen'.[41]

All this is, perhaps, a reflection of the extent to which the Close had become one of the leading centres of polite society in the county, despite the fact that none of the 18th- or early-19th-century bishops of the diocese lived in their palace at Lichfield.[42] Gilbert Walmesley (d. 1751), the bishop's registrar and a man of taste and learning, was for many years tenant of the palace. There he was the head of a group of local literati and there both Johnson and Garrick received help and encouragement from him in their youth.[43] A few years after Walmesley's death Thomas Seward, Prebendary of Pipa Parva (d. 1790), moved into the palace with his family. Seward achieved a modest distinction as an author and as editor of the plays

[22] *Gent. Mag.* 1818, lxxxviii(2), 511. For Potter see Colvin, *Biog. Dict. Eng. Architects*, 469.
[23] *Gent. Mag.* 1824, xciv(2), 295–6 (attack on restoration of the cathedral by 'B'), 390–1 (reply by 'A.C.' of Lichfield defending the work), 582–3 (rejoinder by 'B' attacking the 'tasteless havoc' wrought at Lichfield by 'the profane hand of James Wyatt').
[24] Savage, *Dr. Binckes*, 21–22. Additional alterations were made to the building in 1808, 1876, and 1893: ibid. 23.
[25] Ibid. 23.
[26] C.A. vii, f. 132.
[27] Ibid. f. 144, complaining also that the Close was 'very much troubled with vagrants and beggars'.
[28] Ibid. ff. 178, 211v., both complaining also about vagrants and beggars.
[29] C.A. viii, ff. 21v., 23.
[30] Ibid. f. 40v.
[31] Ibid. ff. 79v., 97; D. & C. Lich., x, 1772–83, 31 Aug. 1781.
[32] C.A. viii, f. 107.

[33] W.S.L., S.MS. 341, MS. poem written by Nat. Lister. Lister married the daughter of John Fletcher, chapter clerk: R. Simms, *Bibliotheca Staffordiensis* (Lichfield, 1894), 284.
[34] C.A. ix, pp. 35–36, 58.   [35] See above p. 166.
[36] B.M. Add. MS. 5829, f. 2v.
[37] C.A. viii, f. 35v.
[38] Ibid. ff. 35v., 47.
[39] *Gent. Mag.* 1782, lii. 558, and facing plate, which shows the gatehouse of the demolished building. There is another description of the gatehouse in S. Pegge, *Sylloge of Authentic Inscriptions relative to the Erection of our Eng. Churches* (1787), 97–98.
[40] Harwood, *Lichfield*, 11.
[41] Ibid.; C.A. ix, ff. 26v.–27. The new building was Newton's College, the charitable foundation of Andrew Newton.
[42] For the bishops' preference for Eccleshall castle see above p. 62.
[43] *D.N.B.*; J. L. Clifford, *Young Samuel Johnson*, 92 sqq.

of Beaumont and Fletcher, and the palace again became 'the resort of every person in that neighbourhood who had any taste for letters'. Seward's daughter Anna, 'the Swan of Lichfield', who became a far more eminent figure in the literary world, lived on at the palace until her death in 1809.[44] Another author with a home in the Close was Erasmus Darwin, who from 1758 to 1781 lived in a house facing Beacon Street.[45]

Reform and Reconstruction, 1840 to 1900

The conditions revealed by the 1835 Report on Ecclesiastical Revenues and similar parliamentary reports led to an era of reform in the Church of England. In the rapidly growing industrial towns money was needed to augment poor livings and to endow new parishes, and it was felt that part of this money could well come from capitular revenues.[46] The Cathedrals Act of 1840 reduced the establishments of cathedrals and collegiate churches and by a general reorganization of cathedral finances and patronage made a considerable sum available to a newly formed body, the Ecclesiastical Commissioners, to be redistributed where it was most needed.

Lichfield, despite its comparative poverty as a cathedral, did not escape the workings of the Act.[47] It was laid down that the cathedral was to lose two of the six residentiaryships. Sawley, the richest of all, was to be detached from the rectory of St. Philip's, Birmingham, and suspended when it next fell vacant; the first of the other residentiaryships to become vacant, which in fact proved to be that of Freeford and Hansacre,[48] was likewise to be suspended. The endowments of the two prebends, less the sum customarily paid out of the prebend of Sawley into the fabric fund, were to be used by the Ecclesiastical Commissioners to provide stipends for two Birmingham incumbents, the Rector of St. Philip's and the perpetual curate of Christ Church. At the next vacancy of the deanery the annexed estates were to be transferred to the common fund or used by the Commissioners to make proper provision for the new dean who, it was laid down, was to have an average income of £1,000 a year. The four remaining residentiaries were each to have an average of £500 a year. Non-resident prebendaries were to be abolished and the endowments of their prebends transferred to the Commissioners; in place of the non-residentiaries the bishop was to be allowed to appoint up to 24 honorary canons and dignitaries, who would be non-resident and receive no emoluments. Minor canons (the term used in the Act to describe vicars choral) appointed after the passage of the Act were to receive not less than £150 a year and, if priests, were to hold no benefice situated more than six miles from the cathedral.

Under the terms of the Act the Crown retained the right of appointing the dean, who was in future to be in residence at least eight months a year. No alteration was made to the method of electing residentiaries, who were to reside at least three months a year. Rights of patronage held by individual members of the chapter by virtue of their tenure of certain dignities or prebends were to be vested in the bishop; livings belonging to the common fund were to be given only to members of the chapter, to archdeacons of the diocese, to honorary canons of the cathedral, or, if they were willing to leave their previous posts within a year of institution, to clergy who had been for at least five years minor canons or lecturers in the cathedral, incumbents or curates in the diocese, or public tutors at Oxford or Cambridge. Should common fund livings not be filled within six months the right of presentation was to lapse to the bishop. Regulations were also laid down concerning property in the Close. For the disposal of surplus prebendal houses or for the raising of mortgages on canonries in order to improve the remaining residences the chapter now had to obtain the permission not only of the bishop but also of the Ecclesiastical Commissioners.

The cathedral was thus placed more firmly than ever before under episcopal and parliamentary control. It remained hard-pressed financially. In 1852 the chapter had an income of some £2,941, over half of which came to it from the fabric fund. By comparison Durham, the richest of the English cathedrals, had an income that year of almost £58,000. Lichfield's relative position was even worse when considered over the seven-year period 1846–1852. Salisbury, which was the only English cathedral in 1852 to have an income lower than that of Lichfield, had an average annual income for the seven years of over £5,300; Lichfield was the poorest English cathedral, with an average annual income of about £3,167.[49] Between 1857 and 1863 the chapter's average annual income from its corporate property was only some £1,550. Rents were evidently being pushed up gradually, but as usual the chapter relied chiefly upon entry fines to keep up the average income. In the year 1860–1, for example, when the chapter received no entry fines, its income was only some £881, whereas in the following year fines of £2,170 brought the total up to some £3,059.[50]

Under an Order in Council of 1852 provision was made for securing fixed incomes for future deans and residentiaries of Lichfield.[51] Deans appointed after the making of the Order were to have incomes of £1,000 and residentiaries of £500 a year. Any surplus decanal or canonical income was to be paid to the Ecclesiastical Commissioners, who were in turn to make up any deficiencies. In 1876 the dean and chapter transferred all their property, except the cathedral and its precincts, the deanery, the canonical houses, the chapter clerk's house, their ecclesiastical and educational patronage, the property held in trust for the choristers, and about 10 acres of land in Lichfield, to the Ecclesiastical Commissioners. In return they were guaranteed £5,250 a year until the death or resignation of

[44] D.N.B.; Le Neve, *Fasti* (1854 edn.), i. 621; Hesketh Pearson, *The Swan of Lichfield*, 14–34; E. V. Lucas, *A Swan and her Friends*.

[45] Anna Seward, *Memoirs of the Life of Dr. Darwin* (1804), 14–15; D. King-Hele, *Erasmus Darwin*, 18, 31.

[46] G. F. A. Best, *Temporal Pillars*, 331–47.

[47] For this and the following para. see Cathedrals Act, 3 & 4 Vic. c. 113.

[48] *Statutes of the Cathedral Church of Lichfield, 1875* (priv. print.), 5on.

[49] *1st Rep. Cath. Com.* [1822], pp. 44–45, 48–49, H.C. (1854), xxv.

[50] D. & C. Lich., unlisted 19th-cent. corresp. concerning commutation of capitular property: account of chapter income 1857–63.

[51] For this para. see C.A. xiv, pp. 8–9, 10, 13–23, 35; Savage, *Dr. Binckes*, 24, 25.

Canon Henry Ryder, the last of the pre-1852 residentiaries, and £5,500 a year thereafter. This provided incomes of £1,000 a year for the dean and £500 a year for the residentiaries (only £250 for Canon Ryder, who still enjoyed his customary share of the capitular income) and £2,500 a year for the maintenance of the cathedral and other expenses. The chapter clerk was allotted a further £120 a year, the value of some property in the Close and Dam Street, Lichfield. Since the chapter had refrained from renewing certain leases on parts of the property to be transferred it was compensated for loss of fines by a grant of £3,000. A further lump sum of £15,000 was allotted to it to be spent under the supervision of the Ecclesiastical Commissioners on repairs and restoration at the cathedral. With this arrangement of 1876 begins the modern pattern of the cathedral's finances. Meanwhile various measures taken to regulate the financial position of the deanery according to the terms of the 1852 Order resulted in the loss to the dean of the rectories of Brewood and Adbaston in 1867, on the death of Dean Howard, and that of Tatenhill in 1875, on the death of Dean Champneys.

The loss of two residentiaries under the provisions of the Cathedrals Act had reduced the residentiary chapter to a dean and four residentiaries by the mid 1850s. When the prebend of Sawley was suspended on the death of Dr. Lawrence Gardner in 1845 the treasurership also fell into abeyance, thus leaving the cathedral with only three dignitaries.[52] Among the suggestions made by the chapter to the Cathedral Commissioners in the mid 1850s was one calling for the treasurership to be revived and conferred upon one of the remaining residentiaries; the chapter considered that to the post there could be attached the cure of souls in the parish of the Close and possibly the office of principal of the proposed theological college at Lichfield (opened in 1857).[53] Bishop Selwyn (1867–78), who thought that a cathedral chapter should ideally be a body of men devoted to the training of ordinands and the organization of diocesan work,[54] favoured a more ambitious scheme. In 1869 he summoned a general chapter of residentiaries and honorary canons to consider reforms and reorganization at the cathedral in the light of reports by the Cathedral Commissioners,[55] and in 1871 the general chapter proposed that the two suspended residentiaryships should be revived[56] — a move probably taken at the bishop's instigation and undoubtedly meeting with his full approval. The residentiary chapter, however, felt that the proposal was injudicious and in 1872 informed Archbishop Tait on its own authority that it did not think it desirable to alter the existing number of residentiaries.[57] The residentiaries thought that it would be difficult, if not impossible, to endow two further residentiaryships; and though Selwyn, who had hoped that one of the revived canonries would be held by a coadjutor bishop and the other by the principal of the Lichfield Theo-

logical College, fought hard for his proposals, in the end nothing was done.[58] The treasurership was finally revived in 1906 by Order in Council. It was, however, to be held by the prebendary of Offley and Flixton, and the treasurer's former prebend of Sawley remained suspended.[59]

Although Selwyn failed to enlarge the residentiary chapter, he effected other reforms. It was he, for example, who reinstated the general chapter as a regular supervisory body for the cathedral. Though its recommendations regarding the residentiaryships came to nothing, it achieved one major success during his episcopate: the revision and translation between 1869 and 1875 of the cathedral statutes.[60] In 1863 Bishop Lonsdale had printed *Statuta et Consuetudines Ecclesiae Cathedralis Lichfieldiae*. This collection contained the statutes of Bishops Hacket, Lloyd, Hough, Chandler, Smalbroke, and Frederick Cornwallis, and Lonsdale's own statute of 1863 concerning the vicars choral, the first statute issued to the cathedral in English. A number of the older statutes, especially those concerning property, had been rendered meaningless by the passage of time and the operation of the Cathedrals Act and subsequent measures. Selwyn was determined to produce an intelligible modern body of statutes. The work was completed in December 1875, and the bishop wrote to a friend: 'On December 21, when the whole document had been printed, we met *pro forma* to sign and seal; and so came to pass the euthanasia of the old Composition [of 1428] and all of the unintelligible stuff which has been sworn to for "four or five centuries."'[61] These English statutes have formed the basis of all subsequent versions of the cathedral statutes.

The passage of the Cathedrals Act and the widespread attacks upon clerical absenteeism forced the residentiaries to take their obligations of residence far more seriously. In 1840, shortly after the Act had been passed, the dean and chapter, 'having witnessed with much pain and concern the very imperfect state of the residence directed by the statutes on the part of the several canons of this cathedral and the consequent failure of attendance on the services of the church', adopted certain resolutions to bring the practice at Lichfield into line with that at other cathedrals. It was decided that, if any residentiary was unable to perform his statutory residence, his duties might be carried out by another residentiary, or by one of the honorary canons if no residentiary would help. The substitute was to be paid £100 a year by the absentee and, if an honorary canon, was to have such of the privileges of a residentiary 'as may be deemed expedient'. All the residentiaries save one agreed to abide by these rules, and it was expected that two, who were in bad health, would take advantage of them promptly.[62] In general this arrangement appears to have worked satisfactorily; in 1873, however, Bishop Selwyn used as one of his arguments for enlarging the residentiary chapter the fact that at that time it was reduced virtually to

[52] *1st Rep. Cath. Com.* 20; C.A. xvi, p. 300.
[53] *1st Rep. Cath. Com.* App. p. 606.
[54] See above p. 80.
[55] H. W. Tucker, *George Augustus Selwyn*, ii. 273.
[56] C.A. xiii, p. 239.   [57] Ibid. p. 240.
[58] Ibid. pp. 239–67; Tucker, *Selwyn*, ii. 284–5. Selwyn also suggested as suitable persons to hold the revived residentiaryships the diocesan inspector of schools, the chancellor of the diocese, the vice-principal of the

theological college, and the archdeacons of the diocese: C.A. xiii, p. 245.
[59] C.A. xvi, pp. 295–302, transcribing Order in Council of 22 Oct. 1906. The prebend of Sawley remained suspended at the time of writing (1964): *Lich. Dioc. Dir.* (1964).
[60] Tucker, *Selwyn*, ii. 273–4.
[61] Ibid.
[62] C.A. xi, pp. 43–45, 48, 49.

three members by the unauthorized absence of Canon Henry Ryder.[63] The 1875 statutes laid down that the dean and residentiaries were each to keep at least three months' residence a year. On at least 45 days of this period attendance at both matins and evensong was required; during the remainder of the three months attendance at one service a day sufficed. Attendance by proxy — another residentiary or 'in case of need' an honorary canon — was permitted.[64] The rule remained unaltered in 1905.[65]

A noticeable feature of the changes after 1840, and one example of the increased vigour of cathedral life, was the greater number of services and celebrations of Holy Communion.[66] The cathedral was also becoming once more a centre of diocesan life, and this was reflected in the number of special services held there. In the mid 1850s there were two services daily, except on the six days a year during which the building was closed for cleaning. Services were at 10.30 a.m. and 4.30 p.m. on Sundays and 10 a.m. and 4 p.m. on week-days, except for Christmas Day, Good Friday, and some special occasions. All services were choral except on 'days of humiliation', when the organ was not played. There was a service of Holy Communion every Sunday and on Christmas Day and Ascension Day. Sermons were preached at matins every Sunday and on holy days and other special occasions; the duties of the divinity lecturer had been commuted into that of preaching on certain saints' days.

By 1880 the number of services had increased still more.[67] Holy Communion was celebrated at 8 a.m. every Sunday, and there was also a midday celebration on the first, third, and, when it occurred, the fifth Sunday of every month. There were two celebrations on all great festivals and one on all saints' days and on various diocesan occasions. Sunday services remained at the same times, with the Litany as a separate service at 2.30 p.m. whenever there was a midday Communion. Weekday services were at 10 a.m. and 4 p.m. between Lady Day and Michaelmas and on holy days, and at 10.30 a.m. and 4 p.m. during the rest of the year. All services were choral except the 2.30 p.m. Litany, evensong whenever there was a special evening service, and Holy Communion, which was choral only at midday celebrations and on the great festivals. Various extra services were held, notably during Advent and Lent. There were two sermons each Sunday, those at the morning service being preached by the dean, one of the residentiaries, or one of the honorary canons, and those in the afternoon by the dean or the canon in residence. On saints' days sermons were preached by the divinity lecturer or some other member of the cathedral body; there were sermons preached by diocesan clergy at special weekday services during Advent and Lent, and 'addresses' delivered at other times such as Good Friday and Holy Week.

By 1880 the cathedral was being used regularly for diocesan gatherings of various kinds.[68] Among the more notable of these were the Diocesan Choir Gatherings; Lichfield was the first cathedral to hold such a festival, and it was subsequently copied in almost every other diocese in England. John Hutchinson, the precentor, was responsible for the first gathering, held on 14 October 1856, when 26 parish choirs joined the cathedral choir in morning and evening services. The Bishops of Lichfield and of Sodor and Man, the cathedral chapter, and about 150 diocesan clergy were present, and the congregation numbered in all nearly 3,000 people.

The increased number of cathedral services and the growing diocesan use of the building made the ability and efficiency of the vicars choral far more important than it had been previously, and various moves were made after 1840 to improve the musical side of cathedral worship.[69] In 1842 the chapter informed the vicars that in future at least three vicars were to be present at each morning or evening service, one representing each part of the choir; no vicar would be allowed leave beyond that laid down by statute unless he had previously found a substitute. Applications for leave were to be made, whenever possible, to the hebdomadary chapter instead of simply to the canon in residence, so that daily services might be arranged 'with greater precision'. Five years later, however, it was reported that the order limiting the number of vicars who might be absent from any one service had been 'habitually disregarded'.

The chief problem facing those who wished to improve the quality of the choir was the vicars' freehold. Once appointed a vicar held office until he died or resigned, and a number of elderly vicars whose voices had decayed clung to their posts and forced the chapter to various shifts to maintain the quality of the singing. In the early 1850s, for example, it was employing two supernumerary lay vicars because two octogenarian vicars were no longer able to sing with the choir.[70] Precentor Hutchinson submitted to the Cathedral Commissioners in 1853 that more vicars were required; it was impossible to ask men to sing twice a day throughout the year, and leave and infirmity left gaps in the choir. Unpaid assistance would be unreliable; but he felt that a salary less than half that received by the existing vicars would secure the three supernumeraries necessary to bring the choir to full efficiency. The organist was less sanguine: 'Nothing but salary can accomplish what you wish . . . If you were to double the number of lay vicars you would not improve the choir but would have *more noise* and less music. Good musicians and good voices are scarce things and are not to be found in this city'.[71] Finally, in 1861, six supernumerary lay vicars were appointed, all resident in Lichfield, and it was agreed that up to £12 a year should be distributed among such of them as required some payment.[72]

In 1863 Bishop Lonsdale promulgated new statutes for the vicars. The number of vicars was, it was stated, no longer sufficient for the due performance of services if vicars were to be allowed 'reason-

[63] C.A. xiii, p. 266.
[64] *Statutes, 1875*, 23–24.
[65] *Statutes of the Cathedral Church of Lichfield, 1905* (priv. print.), 23–24.
[66] For this para. see *1st Rep. Cath. Com.* App. pp. 243, 244.
[67] For this para. see *Rep. Cath. Com. Lichfield* [C. 4238], App. p. 8, H.C. (1884–5), xxi.

[68] For this para. see J. G. Lonsdale, *Recollections of the Internal Restoration of Lichfield Cathedral* (Lichfield, 1884), 5, 9 (copy in W.S.L. Pamphs. *sub* Lichfield); 'A Day at Lichfield', *Churchman's Companion*, Nov. 1856.
[69] For this para. see C.A. xi, pp. 94, 289.
[70] *1st Rep. Cath. Com.* App. pp. 243–4, 703.
[71] Ibid. App. p. 703.
[72] C.A. xii, p. 168.

able relaxation and occasional necessary absence'; and since the value of their property had increased, thus making more funds available, their numbers were duly raised from 12 (5 priest vicars and 7 lay vicars) to 14 (4 priest vicars and 10 lay vicars). Any vicar incapable of performing his duties was to provide a duly qualified substitute; the existing vicars were allowed the option of paying instead an annual sum to the chapter.[73] These reforms were evidently insufficient, for in the early 1880s Bishop Maclagan, the dean, and the chapter were united in agreeing that the corporation of vicars should be dissolved and replaced by a body of stipendiary vicars who could be dismissed or pensioned off when their voices were no longer adequate.[74] The Cathedral Commissioners recommended this in their report on the cathedral in 1884,[75] but nothing was done.

The financial arrangements of the corporation followed the same general pattern as those of the chapter. The vicars, who in 1840 were managing their own estates, had by the end of the century transferred their property to the Ecclesiastical Commissioners in return for a fixed annual payment. In the seven years 1846–52 the average gross annual income of the corporation was about £1,500; the income varied between £2,010 in 1849 and £882 in 1851. On an average rack-rents amounted to about £110 a year, while reserved rents on leases came to about £234 a year; commons from the chapter provided a regular £54 12s. a year, and the rest was made up of entry fines. This provided the subchanter with an income which varied between £179 4s. in 1849 and £84 17s. 8d. in 1851; some of the vicars, both priest and lay, received over £165 each in 1849, while in 1851 one of the priest vicars was paid as little as £67 12s. 3d. and one of the lay vicars £63 6s. 7d.[76] The 1863 cathedral statutes laid down that none of the existing vicars was to suffer financially because of the increase in numbers.[77] In 1872 the vicars transferred all their property, with the exception of the twelve vicarial houses in the Close, to the Ecclesiastical Commissioners in return for an annual payment of £2,160.[78] From this in 1880 the six 'older' vicars, those appointed before the 1863 statutes, received sums varying from £171 1s. 8d. to £176 15s. 4d.; the eight 'younger' vicars, those appointed since 1863, received £128 14s. 4d. each, except for the dean's vicar, who was paid £2 6s. more. Upon the death of every 'older' vicar the salaries of the remaining vicars were augmented. It was estimated that when all the 'older' vicars had died or retired the fourteen vicars would each receive £152 4s. a year and their commons. In addition twelve of the vicars had vicarial houses in the Close.[79] The financial position of Lichfield vicars in the last quarter of the 19th century compared very favourably with that of

vicars at other English cathedrals, and in 1906 the dean informed them that their stipend of about £150 'with one or possibly two exceptions . . . is the largest in England'. He added that whenever there was a vacancy at Lichfield there were many applicants from other cathedrals, not only because of the stipend offered 'but also because of the advantageous terms enjoyed in retirement'.[80]

The number of choristers remained at eight until December 1861, when it was increased to ten.[81] In addition there were generally four or six supernumerary boys on probation. The boys continued to be maintained on the proceeds of property managed on their behalf by the residentiary chapter; by 1879 the property — houses and land — produced about £360 a year. In the mid 1850s the boys received stipends ranging from £7 to £20 a year. When the numbers were increased in 1861 the scale of stipends was revised.[82] Choristers and probationers received free education from the schoolmaster provided for them by the chapter; the school was in the Close, and in 1866 a newly-appointed schoolmaster was given permission to take up to 14 probationers in addition to the choristers.[83] When choristers left they were generally given a bonus payment to be used as an apprenticeship fee, the amount varying according to their past behaviour and general usefulness in the choir.[84]

The major work undertaken by the chapter during these years was perhaps the full-scale restoration of the cathedral. To some extent this was rendered necessary by decay and the deterioration of poor-quality stone used in previous rebuilding; but it is evident from contemporary evidence that what weighed more heavily with the chapter was the changing taste in ecclesiastical architecture and the consequent dissatisfaction with the state of the cathedral as Wyatt[85] and Potter had left it. Moreover the greater use being made of the cathedral and the need to accommodate larger congregations rendered the 18th-century arrangements, which isolated the choir and the Lady Chapel from the rest of the building, totally inadequate.

Ecclesiology reached Lichfield early. The pioneering Cambridge Camden Society was founded in 1839,[86] and in 1841 there appeared the Lichfield Society for the Encouragment of Ecclesiastical Architecture, a body with similar, though rather less ambitious, aims and ideals. It had close connexions with the cathedral: the dean and chapter were among its vice-presidents, and its first chairman was William Gresley, Prebendary of Wolvey. At the first annual general meeting, held in January 1843, Gresley offered the society's help in 'the restoration of the west front or even the whole of Lichfield Cathedral; if only the dean and chapter will accept our services and the diocese will place twenty or thirty thousand pounds at our disposal'.[87] Although

[73] Statuta et Consuetudines, 144–5, 147.
[74] C.A. xiv, pp. 261–3; C.A. xv, leaflet attached between pp. 391 and 392; Rep. Cath. Com. Lichfield, App. pp. 9, 10.
[75] Rep. Cath. Com. Lichfield, 4–5.
[76] 1st Rep. Cath. Com. App. pp. 671–2.
[77] Statuta et Consuetudines, 151–2.
[78] C.A. xiv, pp. 230, 235, 261 (which incorrectly gives annual payment as £2,100).
[79] Ibid. pp. 235–6.
[80] C.A. xvi, p. 283.   [81] C.A. xii, p. 180.
[82] 1st Rep. Cath. Com. App. p. 243; Rep. Cath. Com. Lichfield, App. p. 3; C.A. xii, p. 180.
[83] 1st Rep. Cath. Com. App. p. 243; C.A. xiii, p. 7.

[84] 1st Rep. Cath. Com. App. p. 243; Rep. Cath. Com. Lichfield, App. p. 3.
[85] Pugin, who had an unreasoning hatred of Wyatt and his work as a restorer, remarked after seeing Lichfield: 'This monster of architectural depravity — this pest of cathedral architecture — has been here. Need I say more?': B. F. L. Clarke, Church Builders of the 19th Cent. 66.
[86] Ibid. 75.
[87] 1st Rep. Lich. Soc. for Encouragement of Eccl. Architecture (Rugeley, 1843), 19, 27 (copy in W.S.L. Pamphs. sub Lichfield). The date of the society's foundation is given as 1841 in its 4th Rep. (Lichfield, 1850), 6 (copy in W.S.L. Pamphs. sub Lichfield).

such a task was, and remained, outside the society's powers it is highly probable that its activities focussed attention on the cathedral and strengthened the position of those who wished to see a thorough-going restoration of the building.

In fact work on the cathedral began shortly after the society's foundation. In September 1842 a report on the state of the fabric was submitted to the chapter by Sydney Smirke, a younger brother and pupil of the more famous Sir Robert Smirke, and he was authorized to spend £1,000 during the ensuing year on such repairs and restorations 'as appear to him of the most urgent importance'.[88] Between 1842 and 1846 Smirke restored the south aisle of the nave at a cost of some £3,000. Large-scale work was then brought to an end for lack of funds, though the chapter retained two workmen to carry out urgently needed repairs and Smirke remained consultant architect to the cathedral.[89]

Work was resumed on a rather larger scale in the late 1850s, thanks mainly to the enthusiasm and powers of persuasion of Precentor Hutchinson. After Hutchinson had visited Ely Cathedral, and one or two other churches which had recently been restored, Dean Howard, a cautious man, was finally persuaded that similar restoration was needed at Lichfield.[90] The work immediately involved was chiefly the opening out and rearrangement of the choir, for which Smirke and George Gilbert (later Sir Gilbert) Scott submitted plans in April 1855.[91] Early in 1857 the chapter considered Smirke's drawings for the proposed restoration of the choir; it then asked Scott and Benjamin Ferrey, diocesan architect for Bath and Wells, who had been associated with the two others in some of their earlier proposals, to prepare schemes for its consideration.[92] Ferrey having declined to compete, Scott's and Smirke's proposals were considered later in the year, and the verdict went to Scott.[93]

One of the canons later painted a gloomy picture of the cathedral as it was before Scott started his work.[94] The whole of the interior was 'one uniform, dead, yellowish whitewash, many coats thick'. The nave was 'quite unused — indeed, except during service hours the verger's silver key alone gave admission to any part of the church. During morning and evening prayers the nursery maids, it was said, used to walk up and down with babies in their arms; nay, it is reported that the smell of a cigar has been detected in the nave while service was being sung in the choir'. As a result of Wyatt's work nave and choir were completely separated by a high stone screen, filling the whole of the first bay of the choir. On this screen was placed the organ, surmounted by a glass screen going up to the roof. Since the arches between the choir and the choir aisles had been filled in with plaster, there had thus been created what was virtually a self-contained church within a church.[95] In the choir itself, with its altar at the east end of the Lady Chapel, there were oak pews, lined with green baize and studded with brass nails, and, in the three bays eastward from the screen, stalls 'composed of plaster, wood, rope, nails, and much else, with canopies of the same material over them, which the old verger of that day used to call "beautiful tabernacle work."'

The work of demolishing the plaster between the choir and the choir aisles, which had been begun in 1856, evidently under Smirke's direction,[96] was continued by Scott, together with that of pulling down the stalls and canopies in the choir. In 1858 the organ was moved into the nave, which was temporarily equipped for services, and the screen upon which it had stood was demolished. The arches between the transept aisles and the choir aisles were opened out, and in both choir and transepts whitewash was scraped off and plaster replaced by stone. Mouldings, figures, and capitals were renewed. It had originally been intended to confine the restoration to the choir; the chapter subsequently decided, however, that a whitewashed nave would look strange against a restored choir and Scott was instructed to complete the restoration of the whole of the interior. When the work in the choir was sufficiently advanced the organ was moved back and Scott turned his attention to the nave. Comparatively little needed to be done there beyond the removal of the whitewash and the restoration of some stonework; Scott was urged to replace Wyatt's plaster groining with stone but refused, saying that the walls would not bear it.[97]

Among the furnishings installed during the course of the restoration was a new organ presented by Josiah Spode of Hawkesyard Park, Armitage; it was placed in the north transept aisle.[98] A metal screen designed by Scott was erected between the nave and the choir. It was the first of its type; later examples included those at the cathedrals of Worcester and Hereford.[99] Similarly the pavement tiles within the altar rails containing Old Testament subjects worked in pottery ware by Minton and Co. of Stoke-upon-Trent and presented by the firm to the cathedral were the first of their kind in modern times and were later copied in other churches.[1] The cathedral was officially reopened on 22 October 1861, though services had been held in the building virtually throughout the restoration.[2]

[88] C.A. xi, p. 93. For S. Smirke see Clarke, *Church Builders of 19th Cent.* 262.
[89] C.A. xi, pp. 131, 189–93, 221–3, 244–8; C.A. xii, p. 30. [90] Lonsdale, *Internal Restoration*, 5, 6.
[91] C.A. xii, p. 37.
[92] Ibid. pp. 55, 71. For Ferrey see Clarke, *Church Builders of 19th Cent.* 112–13.
[93] C.A. xii, p. 79. Scott himself later stated that he succeeded Smirke rather against his will: Sir George Gilbert Scott, *Personal and Professional Recollections* (1879), 291–2. [94] Lonsdale, *Internal Restoration*, 7–8.
[95] One of the deans sarcastically referred to this long narrow apartment as 'the first drawing-room in Europe': *Lich. Dioc. Church Cal.* (1862), 139.
[96] Lonsdale, *Internal Restoration*, 9; Scott, *Recollections*, 291–2, stating that Smirke 'had restored the south aisle of the nave and had really commenced upon the choir'.
[97] Lonsdale, *Internal Restoration*, 9–17; Scott, *Recollections*, 291–7. Scott also wished to retain Wyatt's plaster reredos at the E. end of the Lady Chapel but was overruled by the chapter: Lonsdale, *Internal Restoration*, 24.
[98] Lonsdale, *Internal Restoration*, 18, stating that Spode bought the old organ and placed it in Armitage church; J. G. Lonsdale, *Recollections of Work done in and upon Lichfield Cathedral from 1856 to 1894* (Lichfield, 1895), 24–25 (copy in W.S.L. Pamphs. *sub* Lichfield), stating that the new cathedral organ, first used in 1861, was reconstructed and enlarged 20 years later, the work being completed in 1884.
[99] Lonsdale, *Internal Restoration*, 18–19; Scott, *Recollections*, 293.
[1] Lonsdale, *Internal Restoration*, 20–21, stating that the idea of using pottery ware for such subjects was suggested by some old tiles found at Chertsey Abbey (Surr.) and deposited in the Victoria and Albert Mus.
[2] Ibid. 21.

The reopening did not, however, mark the end of work on the cathedral. Restoration went on almost continuously for another forty years, first under G. G. Scott and then under his son J. O. Scott. The interior of the cathedral occupied the chapter's attention during the years immediately following 1861. The plaster arcading on either side of the nave was replaced by stone, similar work was carried out in the choir aisles, the chapter-house and library were repaired, Wyatt's plaster reredos was removed from the Lady Chapel, some new glass was inserted to match the Herckenrode windows, and the consistory court was cleaned and restored. With this last task, completed in 1880, the restoration of the interior was virtually finished and the chapter could concentrate on external repairs.[3]

Work had already begun in 1877 on the west front to remove Potter's much-criticized Roman cement and replace it by stone. It was also decided to replace with new statues the numerous figures which had formerly adorned the west front and of which only two survived. The distribution of the statues followed in general the former pattern, though a statue of Christ replaced one of Charles II in the central niche of the apex. The cost of these statues, some £5,000, was borne by individual donors and the Ecclesiastical Commissioners agreed that the £15,000 which they had laid aside in 1876 for use on the fabric, together with the interest which had accumulated on it, should be devoted to the restoration of the west front; the chapter itself raised a further £15,000 by subscription. The work, which included not only the west front but also the refacing of both the west towers and considerable repairs to them and their spires, was completed in 1884.[4] Other major work completed later included the repair and restoration of the exterior of the Lady Chapel, repairs to the central tower and spire, the rebuilding of the north and south ends of the transepts, and the restoration of St. Chad's Chapel.[5] In March 1901 a Thanksgiving Festival for the complete restoration of the cathedral was celebrated.[6]

After the 18th-century demolitions and rebuilding in the Close there were comparatively few major alterations to the domestic buildings in the 19th century. When in the late 1870s Bishop Selwyn decided to live in Lichfield, after many years during which the bishops had used Eccleshall castle as their sole residence, two wings were added to the 17th-century palace in the Close.[7] Otherwise the only important work appears to have been the provision, south of the cathedral, of quarters for the theological college, which was opened in 1857.[8]

The Twentieth Century

During the present century the life and work of the cathedral and the chapter have been further modified to harmonize with changing conditions. The most notable alteration to the constitution of the cathedral body came in 1934 with the dissolution of the ancient corporation of the subchanter and vicars choral under the terms of an Order in Council of that year.[9] Even this, however, was not a startling event; at intervals for many years the corporation had been attacked by bishops and chapter as an anachronism in a modern cathedral,[10] and it is not surprising that when, under the provisions of the Cathedrals Measure of 1931, the minor corporations of other English cathedrals were dissolved[11] the Lichfield corporation shared their fate. The rights of existing vicars were safeguarded, and the property of the corporation, consisting chiefly of two annuities from the Ecclesiastical Commissioners amounting to £2,260 a year, was transferred to the dean and chapter.[12] The 1937 cathedral statutes laid down a new scheme under which there were to be nine lay vicars and not more than four priest vicars. All were to be appointed by the residentiary chapter, except for one of the priest vicars who was to be appointed by the dean. Vicars were to have a written contract of employment including the provision of three months' notice on either side. Lay vicars were to attend all sung services at the cathedral; each was to have one free day a week, still known in the traditional fashion as his sine day, and in addition an annual holiday of 21 days.[13] In 1964 there were nine lay vicars but only two priest vicars.[14]

Under the 1905 cathedral statutes and the Order in Council of the following year reviving the treasurership the residentiary chapter consisted of the dean and four canons, including the precentor, chancellor, and treasurer; they allotted annually amongst themselves the offices of commoner (with responsibility for auditing chapter accounts), fabric keeper or *custos* (with responsibility for the cathedral building), and director of ceremonies (with responsibility for the arrangements on ceremonial occasions).[15] The 1937 statutes, while leaving the number of residentiaries at five, made the post of *custos* one of the cathedral dignities, thus giving each residentiary a dignity.[16] The terms of residence were at the same time slightly altered. In lieu of the three months' residence a year required by the 1905 statutes, a distinction was now made between 'residence', during which attendance at both morning and evening services was not obligatory, and 'close residence', corresponding to the periods of residence required by previous cathedral statutes, when the residentiary was to be present daily at

---

[3] Ibid. 22, 24–25. In the mid 1890s the modern glass in the Lady Chapel was replaced by more 16th-century glass, purchased on behalf of the chapter by C. E. Kempe. This fills the 2 westernmost windows on the N. and S. sides of the Lady Chapel. See C.A. xv, pp. 310–11.

[4] Lonsdale, *Recollections*, 26–29; *Staffs. Advertiser*, 31 May 1884, reporting dedication of restored W. front. C.A. xiv contains two photographs of the W. front taken in 1881, when the restoration was half-completed. The cost of the 1856–61 and 1877–84 restorations was *c.* £80,000: *Lichfield Cathedral: Completion of the Works of Reparation* (leaflet, no date, but 1901; copy inserted into C.A. xvi between pp. 387 and 388). For the statue of Chas. II see above pp. 175–6.

[5] Lonsdale, *Recollections*, 29–35; *Lichfield Cathedral: Completion of Works of Reparation.*

[6] C.A. xvi, p. 110.

[7] H. E. Savage, *The Last Quarter of the 17th Cent.* (1932), 11.

[8] Tucker, *Selwyn*, ii. 275, 277; see above pp. 77–78.

[9] C.A. xx, p. 230, citing Order in Council of 20 Dec. 1934.

[10] See e.g. above pp. 192–3.

[11] See e.g. *V.C.H. Wilts.* iii. 206.

[12] C.A. xx, pp. 193–4, 201.

[13] *Statutes of Cathedral Church of Lichfield, 1937* (priv. print.), 13–14.

[14] Inf. from the Dean (1964).

[15] *Statutes of Cathedral Church of Lichfield, 1905* (priv. print.), 5, 25–27; see above p. 191.

[16] *Statutes, 1937*, 1.

matins and evensong. It was laid down that in future the dean was to be in close residence for 45 days a year and a canon residentiary for three consecutive months a year; residence of at least 240 days a year was enjoined on dean and canons.[17]

The present century has seen at Lichfield, as in all English cathedrals, a great reduction in the number of sung services.[18] Whereas about 1900 morning and evening prayer were sung daily except on Wednesdays, in 1964 the only sung services were those on Sundays, matins every Friday, and evensong four week-day evenings a week. The reasons for this change are chiefly economic. Whereas previously a lay vicar's chief source of income was his stipend from the cathedral, which he could eke out with money from part-time jobs such as music-teaching, today it is usually necessary to find a lay vicar a full-time job, and the money which he receives from the cathedral simply supplements his main income. The cathedral has been fortunate in finding a number of local employers who are prepared to allow men time off for services and rehearsals, but it is obviously impossible to have sung services as frequently as before. This new pattern of employment was one of the factors which in 1951 persuaded the chapter to change the time of evensong to the present 5.30 p.m., thus making it easier for lay vicars to come to the cathedral when they finished work in the afternoon. Meanwhile the number of special services and diocesan gatherings held at the cathedral continues to increase. There has, for example, been an annual service for Young Farmers in the diocese since 1962, while services for the combined diocesan Sunday Schools, for the Darby and Joan clubs in the diocese, and on such occasions as Commonwealth Youth Sunday fill the cathedral with congregations of about 2,000 people at a time.

Shortly after the beginning of the century there was a brief dispute over vestments and ritual. A chapter order that copes should be worn at celebrations of Holy Communion in the cathedral on and after Christmas Day 1901[19] gave rise to some dissension among the residentiaries. The chancellor, J. G. Lonsdale, objected and was granted an exemption because of his advanced age (he had been a canon of the cathedral for over forty-five years). Another residentiary, Canon C. Mortimer, refused to obey the order. At a meeting of the residentiary chapter in May 1902 Dean Luckock announced that he was advised that the order for the wearing of copes was lawful, as were the newly-introduced practices of taking the Ablutions at the altar and of singing a hymn during the cleansing of the chalice, about which another canon had complained. Two months later, at another chapter meeting, Lonsdale announced that both he and Mortimer would wear copes, though 'it seemed to them hard that after being so long in Orders they should be called upon to adopt a dress that had been so rarely used in

cathedrals' and they did not acknowledge the soundness of the legal opinion given to the dean. Luckock, anxious to avoid further friction within the chapter, proposed that instead the exemption already granted to Lonsdale should be extended to Mortimer; this was unanimously agreed[20] and appears to have closed the matter. In 1918, 'in view of the extremely unsatisfactory nature of the only bread now available for altar use', the chapter decided to adopt the use of wafer bread in the cathedral, and the Sisters of the Community of St. Peter, Horbury (Yorks. W.R.), were asked to supply the wafers.[21]

The maintenance and repair of the cathedral fabric continues to be one of the chapter's chief preoccupations. One major improvement of the past half-century has been the installation, in 1930, of electric lighting in the cathedral[22] to replace the gas lights which had been in use since at least 1861.[23] Some restoration work was undertaken in the 1920s,[24] and since the Second World War a more extensive and ambitious scheme has been embarked upon.[25] In the early 1950s the central spire was strengthened. Shortly afterwards it was discovered that the roof of the cathedral had been badly damaged by the death-watch beetle, and in 1956 the chapter launched an appeal for funds to enable it to repair the roof and complete other necessary repairs and improvements. Since then it has been able to proceed steadily with the work. The roofs of the nave, choir, presbytery, Lady Chapel, and north and south transepts have been restored; the two spires at the west end have been strengthened; some exterior stonework has been restored; glass has been releaded; the cathedral has been rewired throughout; and in 1964 the west side of the south transept, omitted from the 19th-century restoration, was being restored. The chapter itself has had to raise all the money for this work, and it has been greatly helped in this task by the efforts of the Friends of Lichfield Cathedral, an organization founded in 1937 to support and assist the cathedral. In recent years the Friends have not only contributed to the appeal fund in general but have also made grants towards the cost of such things as the rebinding of the St. Chad's Gospels, the provision of new copes, the purchase of new altar books, and the cleaning of monuments in the cathedral. At present there are about 1,300 members of the organization.

The most important recent development in the Close has resulted from the expansion and transformation of the choir school.[26] By the 1930s the number of choristers had risen to 18, and there were 36 boys (two sets of 18) receiving free education at the chapter's expense. The financial burden on the chapter was causing it concern in the late 1930s, and the position worsened after the outbreak of the Second World War. In 1941 it was decided to reorganize the school. In the following year it was reopened as a preparatory school in the house in the

[17] Statutes, 1905, 23; Statutes, 1937, 10–11.
[18] This para. is based on inf. from the Dean and on C.A. xxiii, p. 35.
[19] C.A. xvi, pp. 124–5, also decreeing that on and after Christmas Day 1901 the altar lights are to be lit for all celebrations of Holy Communion.
[20] Ibid. pp. 138–40, 146–9.
[21] C.A. xvii, p. 352.
[22] C.A. xix, pp. 333, 348, 349. The use of electric lights had been proposed as early as 1909: C.A. xvii, p. 12.

[23] Lonsdale, Internal Restoration, 21; Staffs. Advertiser, 26 Oct. 1861.
[24] C.A. xviii, pp. 366, 377; C.A. xix, pp. 152–3.
[25] The rest of this para. is based on inf. from the Dean; C.A. xx, pp. 304, 313, 320; Friends of Lichfield Cathedral Ann. Rep. 1964 (copy in W.S.L. Pamphs. sub Lichfield).
[26] This para. is based on inf. from the Dean; Lich. Dioc. Mag. 1941, 96, 105–6; Staffs. Advertiser, 10 May 1941; Friends of Lichfield Cathedral Ann. Rep. 1964; above p. 91.

Close previously assigned to the chancellor. It was renamed St. Chad's Cathedral School, and fee-paying non-choristers were admitted. Since 1955 the school has also occupied the former Bishop's Palace in the Close, last used by Bishop Woods and handed over to the dean and chapter in 1954; the present bishop lives in a smaller house in the Close. There are at present some 80 boys at the school, most of them Midlanders. Of the boys 18 are choral scholars whose fees are paid by the chapter.

Another feature of the modern Close is the Dean Savage Library, founded and endowed in 1924[27] by the dean whose name it bears, a notable historian of the cathedral. It occupies part of one of the houses in the Close and contains his library of history and theology and some of his notes and transcripts.

DEANS OF LICHFIELD

William, occurs about 1140.[28]

Master Hamon, occurs about 1170.[29]

William de Lega, occurs by 1173.[30]

Richard of Dalham, succeeded William de Lega 1176, occurs about 1210–11.[31]

Ralph Nevill, appointed 1214, Bishop of Chichester 1222.[32]

Master William of Mancetter, elected 1222, died 1254.[33]

Ralph of Sempringham, D.Th., elected 1254, died 1280.[34]

Master John of Derby, elected 1280, died 1319.[35]

Stephen Segrave, D.Cn.L., elected 1319, Archbishop of Armagh 1324.

Roger de Convenis, provided 1324, exchanged the deanery with John Garssia for a canonry in Lerida, Spain, 1328.

John Garssia, provided 1328, Bishop of Marseilles 1335.

Richard FitzRalph, D.Th., provided 1335, Archbishop of Armagh 1346.

John Thoresby, B.C.L., provided 1346, Bishop of St. David's 1347.

Master Simon Brisley, provided 1347, Dean of Lincoln 1349.

John Buckingham, admitted 1350, Bishop of Lincoln 1363.

William Manton.

Laurence Ibstock, Lic.C.L.

Anthony Rous.

> Papal licence was granted for the king to nominate to the deanery in 1363. Manton occurs in 1364. Ibstock was elected in February 1369, but Manton was presented by the king to the deanery in September. Rous died as dean in 1370.

Francis de Teobaldeschi, Cardinal priest of St. Sabina, admitted 1371 after provision, died 1378.

William Pakington, installed 1381 after provision, resigned by April 1390.

Thomas Stretton, B.C.L., elected 1390, died 1426.

Robert Wolveden, elected 1426, died by September 1432.

John Verney, elected 1432, died 1457.

Thomas Heywood, B.C.L., D.Cn.L., elected 1457, died 1492.

John Yotton, D.Th., elected 1493, died by August 1512.

Ralph Colyngwood, D.Th., elected 1512, died 1521.

James Denton, D.C.L., installed 1522, died 1533.

Richard Sampson, D.Cn.L., D.C.L., elected 1533, Bishop of Chichester 1536.

Henry Williams, B.Th., elected 1536, deprived for marriage 1553.[36]

John Ramridge, D.D., installed 1554, deprived shortly after the accession of Elizabeth I.[37]

Lawrence Nowell, M.A., installed 1560, died 1576.[38]

George Boleyn, D.D., installed 1576, died 1603.

James Montague, D.D., installed 1603, Dean of Worcester 1604.[39]

William Tooker, D.D., installed 1605, died 1621.

Walter Curle, D.D., installed 1621, Bishop of Rochester 1627.

Augustine Lindsell, D.D., installed 1628, Bishop of Peterborough 1632.

John Warner, D.D., appointed 1633, Bishop of Rochester 1637.

Samuel Fell, D.D., appointed 1637, Dean of Christ Church, Oxford, 1638.

Griffith Higgs, D.D., appointed 1638, died 1659.

William Paul, D.D., installed 1661, Bishop of Oxford 1663.

Thomas Wood, D.D., appointed 1664, Bishop of Lichfield and Coventry 1671.

Matthew Smalwood, D.D., appointed 1671, died 1683.

Lancelot Addison, D.D., appointed 1683, died 1703.

William Binckes, D.D., appointed 1703, died 1712.

Jonathan Kimberley, D.D., appointed 1713, died 1720.

William Walmisley, M.A., appointed 1720, died 1730.

Nicholas Penny, D.D., appointed 1730, died 1745.

John Addenbrooke, D.D., appointed 1745, died 1776.

Baptist Proby, D.D., appointed 1776, died 1807.

John Chappel Woodhouse, D.D., appointed 1807, died 1833.

Hon. Henry Edward John Howard, D.D., appointed 1833, died 1868.[40]

[27] C.A. xvii, pp. 319, 351–2; C.A. xix, p. 369.

[28] Dugdale, *Mon.* iv. 111; *S.H.C.* xi. 313.

[29] J. Nichols, *Hist. and Antiquities of Leics.* iii (2), 1003; *S.H.C.* 1924, pp. 205–6. Hamon had been appointed subdean c. 1165.

[30] *Letters and Charters of Gilbert Foliot*, ed. A. Morey and C. N. L. Brooke, p. 322 n.

[31] *S.H.C.* 1924, pp. 53, 151, 240, 290, 291.

[32] Ibid. p. 341; Savage, *William de Mancetter*, 7; Le Neve, *Fasti* (1854 edn.), i. 240.

[33] Wharton, *Anglia Sacra*, i. 448.

[34] Ibid.; *S.H.C.* 1924, p. 12; A. B. Emden, *Biog. Reg. of Univ. of Oxford to A.D. 1500*, iii. 1669.

[35] The list from John of Derby up to and including Hen.

Williams is taken from Le Neve, *Fasti Ecclesiae Anglicanae, 1300–1541* (new edn.), x. 5–7. For Heywood's degrees see Emden, *Biog. Reg. Oxford*, ii. 897–8.

[36] Savage, *Cathedral and Chapter*, 17.

[37] Ibid. 18; *S.H.C.* 1915, pp. l, 367; Le Neve, *Fasti* (1854 edn.), i. 562; J. Foster, *Alumni Oxonienses, 1500–1714*, iii. 1230.

[38] The list from Lawrence Nowell up to and including John Chappel Woodhouse is taken from Le Neve, *Fasti* (1854 edn.), i. 562–4. For degrees not given by Le Neve see J. and J. A. Venn, *Alumni Cantabrigienses to 1751*; Foster, *Alumni Oxonienses, 1500–1714*; ibid. *1715–1886*.

[39] Le Neve, *Fasti*, i. 563, incorrectly stating that he became Dean of Winchester; ibid. iii. 71.   [40] *D.N.B.*

William Weldon Champneys, M.A., appointed 1868, died 1875.[41]

Edward Bickersteth, D.D., appointed 1875, resigned 1892.[42]

Herbert Mortimer Luckock, D.D., appointed 1892, died 1909.[43]

Henry Edwin Savage, D.D., appointed 1909, died 1939.[44]

Frederic Athelwold Iremonger, D.D., appointed 1939, died 1952.[45]

William Stuart Macpherson, M.A., appointed 1954.[46]

The earliest reference to capitular seals occurs in Bishop Nonant's statutes of 1191, according to which the chancellor was the keeper of the chapter's seals *ad causas et negocia*.[47] With one probable exception no impression of a pre-Restoration common seal is known, though there are several examples of the more frequently used seals *ad causas*. By at least the late 15th century the seal *ad causas* was being used for sealing leases and other grants, and Bishop Blythe, in his statutes of 1526, made rules concerning its safe custody and proper use.[48]

A chapter seal, probably the common seal, in use between at least 1267 and 1309, is a pointed oval about $2\frac{5}{8}$ by about $1\frac{3}{4}$ in.[49] It depicts a crowned female figure (presumably the Virgin) wearing a gown with long pendant sleeves. The hands are held together, probably in prayer. The figure stands in front of what appears to be a building; this has a central tower with a high-pitched roof rising from a flat-roofed façade. On either side of the standing figure there is in the façade a window or fragment of arcading rising to twin semi-circular arches. Legend, lombardic:

SIGILLU[M] ... LDENSIS ...

The chapter seal in use since the Restoration is a pointed oval $2\frac{1}{2}$ by $1\frac{3}{4}$ in.[50] The design, with one small modification, is a replica of that of the seal *ad causas* in use before the Civil War (see below). It depicts the Virgin, crowned and holding a sceptre in her right hand, seated under a Gothic canopy of three arches. In the base, between two pillars, is St. Chad in pontificals, full-face and holding a pastoral staff with both hands. Legend, roman:

SIGILLUM COMMUNE DECANI ET CAPITULI
ECCLESIAE CATHEDRALIS LICHFEILDIAE

A new matrix, an exact replica of that just described, was cut in 1959 and first used in 1960. It is now in the possession of the chapter clerk.[51]

A seal *ad negocia* in use between at least 1224 and 1276 had the legend:

OMNIBUS HOC SIGNO LEVIORA NEGOCIA SIGNO

No impression is known.[52]

A seal *ad causas* in use between at least 1333 and 1550 is a pointed oval $2\frac{3}{4}$ by $1\frac{5}{8}$ in. depicting the Virgin and Child under a pointed trefoiled arch.[53] In the field are a crescent and an estoile. In the base, under a two-spired church and a rounded trefoiled arch, is St. Chad in pontificals seated on a throne, lifting his right hand in benediction and holding a pastoral staff in his left. Legend, lombardic:

SIGILLUM DECANI ET CAPITULI ECCLESIE
SANCTE MARIE ET SANCTI CEDDE LYCHEFELDIE
AD CAUSAS

A small seal *ad causas* in use between at least 1378 and 1409 is a pointed oval about $1\frac{1}{2}$ by about 1 in.[54] It depicts a figure, apparently mitred, seated under a pointed trefoiled arch and holding a book in his lap. In the base is a kneeling figure, possibly a bishop with a pastoral staff. Legend, lombardic:

SIGILLUM C ...

Another small seal *ad causas*, in use between at least 1462 and 1501, is a pointed oval $1\frac{1}{2}$ by 1 in., depicting Our Lord crowned, seated under a Gothic canopy of three arches, lifting His right hand in benediction and holding an orb surmounted by a cross in His left.[55] In the base, under a pointed arch, is a bishop (presumably St. Chad) with hands joined in prayer and with a pastoral staff under his right arm. Legend, black letter:

SIGILLUM DECANI ET CAPITULI ECCLESIE
CATHEDRALIS LICHFELDIE AD CAUSAS

In his statutes of 1526 Blythe followed his injunctions concerning the seal *ad causas* with an order that a seal should be provided for the communar. This was to be used to seal letters of acquittance, letters missive, summonses, suspensions, and excommunications. The following year the chapter was shown a newly made seal *ad causas* and the communar's seal.[56] No impression of the communar's seal is known to exist, but a seal *ad causas* in use in 1545 and 1550, and almost certainly

[41] Ibid.
[42] Ibid. Supplement.
[43] Ibid. Supplementary Vol. 1901–11.
[44] *S.H.C.* 1939, pp. xx–xxii.
[45] *Lich. Dioc. Mag.* 1939, 125, 181; ibid. 1952, 82–83, 92 sqq.   [46] *Lond. Gaz.* 15 Jan. 1954 (p. 378).
[47] Dugdale, *Mon.* vi(3), 1256. For the statutes see above p. 142.   [48] Dugdale, *Mon.* vi(3), 1264–5.
[49] S.R.O. 996/1; cast labelled 'John Derby, dean, 1309' among W.S.L. Seals. An impression of this seal, stated to be from a document of 1309, is noted and illustrated (with some omissions and inaccuracies) in Shaw, *Staffs.* i. 286 and plate facing p. 270. Shaw, followed by the cataloguer of the W.S.L. cast, wrongly states that this is the seal of Dean John of Derby, who did not become dean until 1280: see above p. 197. For the legend see D.(W.) 1734/J.1636 and the entry in P.R.O. Cat. of Seals for D.L. 27/67; no legend survived on the latter seal in 1965. In each case the impression is from an *inspeximus* by the dean and chapter, and the seal is stated to be *sigillum capituli nostri*.
[50] *S.H.C.* vi(2), p. xv; undated cast among W.S.L. Seals.
[51] Inf. from the Chapter Clerk (1965).

[52] *S.H.C.* 1924, pp. 44, 189.
[53] E 329/332; S.R.O., D.(W.) 1734/J.1738; W. de G. Birch, *Cat. of Seals in B.M.* i, p. 250. What appears to have been the bronze matrix of this seal was stated in 1849 to have been picked up on or near the village green at Cavendish (Suff.) 'many years since, shortly after a crowd had passed during some riotous commotion': *Arch. Jnl.* vi. 198. See also *Archaeologia*, xxviii. 461; *Proc. Suff. Inst. of Arch., Statistics and Nat. Hist.* ii. 95, 225–6 (stating that at the time of writing (the 1850s) the matrix was in the possession of the Revd. T. Castley, Rector of Cavendish), and plate facing p. 225. The legend is wrongly given in *S.H.C.* vi(2), p. xiv, followed by J. H. Bloom, *Eng. Seals*, 206.
[54] D. & C. Lich., Vicars' Mun. A.8, stating that the seal is *sigillum nostrum commune ad causas*; B.M., Woll. Ch. ii. 78.
[55] S.R.O., D.(W.) 1734/J.1122. In 1831 the silver matrix of this seal was in the possession of Sir Herbert Taylor: note with B.M. Seal xxxv. 83.
[56] Dugdale, *Mon.* vi(3), 1265; D. & C. Lich., C.A. iv, f. 41.

used until the Civil War, was probably the new seal *ad causas* of 1527.[57] It is a pointed oval about $2\frac{1}{8}$ by $1\frac{1}{4}$ in., depicting the Virgin, crowned and holding a sceptre in her right hand, seated under a Gothic canopy of three arches. In the base, between two pillars, is St. Chad in pontificals, facing right and holding a pastoral staff with both hands. Legend, lombardic:

[SI]GILLUM DECANI *ET* CAPITULI ECCLESIE CATH*EDRALIS* LICHFELDIE AD CAUS[AS]

A 17th-century decanal seal, a pointed oval $2\frac{1}{2}$ by $1\frac{7}{8}$ in., depicts the Virgin, crowned, standing with the Child on her left arm; to their left, in profile, stands St. Chad, in pontificals and holding a pastoral staff.[58] The group is framed by a pinnacled round-headed arch. In the base is the shield of arms of the see. Legend, roman:

SIGILLUM DECANI ECCLESIE CATHEDRALIS LICHFEILD*IE*

The vicars choral had a common seal by at least 1315.[59] The earliest known impression of their seal dates from 1368. The seal in use at that date (probably that mentioned in 1315) was still in use in 1508 and apparently continued to be used until the Civil War.[60] It is a pointed oval $1\frac{5}{8}$ by 1 in., depicting St. Chad in pontificals, half-length, with his right hand raised in benediction and a pastoral staff in his left. Over his head is a rounded trefoiled arch with a pinnacle on either side. In the base are seven heads in profile, evidently representing vicars. Legend, lombardic:

S*IGILLUM* COMM*UNE* VICARIORUM LICHESFELDIE

The matrix appears to have been lost during the Civil War or the Interregnum, and after the Restoration a new matrix was cut. This remained the vicars' corporate seal until the dissolution of the corporation in 1934.[61] It is a pointed oval $1\frac{7}{8}$ by $1\frac{1}{8}$ in. and follows the design of the earlier seal, though St. Chad is now under a pointed arch, holds his pastoral staff in his right hand, and rests his left in his lap; in the base the seven heads of the earlier seal have been replaced by seven roundels. Legend, roman:

S*IGILLUM* COMM*UNE* VICARIORUM ECCLESIE LICHFELDIE

A 17th-century seal of the officiality of the spiritual jurisdiction of the dean and chapter is a pointed oval $1\frac{1}{2}$ by $1\frac{1}{8}$ in.; it depicts a hand issuing from the clouds and holding a balance.[62] In the field is the inscription 'Iustitia Reipublicae Basis'. Legend, roman:

SIG*ILLUM* OFFIC*IALITATIS* DEC*ANI ET* CAP*ITULI* LICHFELDIE PRO SP*IRI*TUALI IURISD*ICTIONE* TANTUM

HOUSES OF BENEDICTINE MONKS

2. THE ABBEY OF BURTON

THE earliest religious foundation at Burton is associated with St. Modwen, an Irish abbess who is said to have come to England in the 7th century.[1] She came to the Burton area with two companions and built two churches there, one on an island in the Trent that became known as Andressey, evidently because the church was dedicated to St. Andrew, and later another on the east bank of the river. After some years, most of them spent at Burton, St. Modwen returned to Ireland, leaving one of her companions at Andressey as abbess. The saint is supposed to have died in Scotland and to have been buried at Andressey; her bones were later translated to a shrine in Burton Abbey.

It is likely that any surviving religious house would have been destroyed during the Danish incursion into the area in the 870s.[2] At any rate it was a Benedictine monastery on a new site on the west bank of the Trent at Burton that was built at the beginning of the 11th century. The founder was Wulfric Spot, a king's thegn possibly descended from King Alfred, who owned extensive property in the Midlands and the area to the north-west.[3] The Annals of the abbey give 1004 as the date of foundation, and King Ethelred's charter of freedom and confirmation granted to the abbey in that year show it as already in existence; Matthew Paris, however, gives 1003 and John Brompton 1002.[4] On his death (which according to one source took place in 1010 as a result of a wound received at the battle of Ringmere) Wulfric was buried in the abbey cloister where his wife already lay.[5]

In his will Wulfric appointed the king as lord of the abbey and Archbishop Alfric and Alfhelm, brother to Wulfric, as 'guardians and friends and advocates'. He gave Dumbleton (Glos.) to the archbishop and 'Northtune' to Ufegeat, possibly his nephew, in the hope that each might 'the better be a

[57] S.R.O., D.(W.) 1734/J.1584b and 1588b.
[58] Birch, *Cat. of Seals in B.M.* i, p. 252; undated cast among W.S.L. Seals.
[59] *S.H.C.* 1924, p. 96.
[60] Birch, *Cat. of Seals in B.M.* i, p. 253; W.S.L. 132/8/47, deed of 1 July 1508; *S.H.C.* vi(2), 159–60, stating that the earliest known impression is on a document of 1340. The document referred to is D. & C. Lich., Vicars' Mun. A.2 (see *S.H.C.* vi(2), 168); but the seal on it is not that of the vicars and there is no sign that there was ever any other seal on the document. For the legend (wrongly given in *S.H.C.* vi(2), 160, followed by Bloom, *Eng. Seals*, 212) see D. & C. Lich., Vicars' Mun. A.9 and loose undated impression.
[61] *S.H.C.* vi(2), 160–1, stating that at the time of writing (the 1880s) the matrix was in the custody of the

subchanter. There is a cast of an undated impression among W.S.L. Seals.
[62] Birch, *Cat. of Seals in B.M.* i, p. 251; undated cast among W.S.L. Seals.
[1] For this para. see H. A. Rye, 'St. Modwen', *Trans. Burton-on-Trent Nat. Hist. & Arch. Soc.* iv(2), 37–48; Dugdale, *Mon.* iii. 33; see below p. 212. Other versions of her life place her in the 5th and 9th centuries.
[2] *Trans. Burton Arch. Soc.* iv(2), 42.
[3] *S.H.C.* 1916, 1 sqq., 116; Dorothy Whitelock, *Anglo-Saxon Wills*, 152–3.
[4] *S.H.C.* 1916, 2; Whitelock, *Anglo-Saxon Wills*, 152.
[5] *S.H.C.* 1916, 3, 64–66; Whitelock, *Anglo-Saxon Wills*, 153. He was buried under a stone arch near the door to the upper church and his wife under a stone arch near the door to the lower church: see below p. 211, n. 48.

friend and support to the monastery'.[6] The first abbot and monks came from Winchester — a connexion that was maintained for over a century and a half, seven of the first eight abbots being monks of Winchester.[7] The house was described as the monastery of St. Benedict and All Saints in royal charters of 1008 and 1012[8] but as the abbey of St. Mary in Domesday Book.[9] Its dedication to St. Mary and St. Modwen occurs fairly frequently in the later 12th century,[10] and although there are occasional references to St. Mary alone in the 13th century,[11] the double dedication continued for the rest of the abbey's existence.

The community was never large; in fact the monks stated in 1310 that theirs was the smallest and poorest Benedictine abbey in England.[12] The earliest available figure is that given in the History of the Abbots which states that under Abbot Laurence (1229–60) there were 30 monks.[13] In 1295 there were 31 professed monks.[14] The numbers in the earlier 14th century were evidently between 15 and 30.[15] In 1377 there were 15 monks (including the abbot) and three novices[16] and in 1381 17 monks (including the abbot).[17] Nineteen monks took part in the election of Ralph Henley as abbot in 1433, including Henley himself.[18] Visitations of 1518, 1521, and 1524 show a community of respectively 17 monks and 3 novices, 15 monks and 5 novices, and 22 monks.[19] At the dissolution in 1539, however, the community seems to have numbered only 12: 7 monks, including a deacon and a novice, received pensions, while the abbot and probably 4 other monks were appointed to the new college at Burton.[20] The abbot's household in 1539 numbered 27.[21]

Burton was by far the most important of the Staffordshire religious houses. Its estates, lying in the main on either side of the Staffordshire-Derbyshire border in the Burton area but also extending further afield, produced a gross revenue in 1535 more than double that of the next richest houses in the county, Tutbury Priory and Dieulacres Abbey.[22] The abbot of Burton was not only a secular lord but also exercised an independent spiritual jurisdiction. He was a figure of some standing, regularly serving on papal and royal commissions and acting as a collector of clerical taxes within the diocese.[23] In 1257 he was summoned to the Great Council held at Westminster on the eve of the departure of Richard, Earl of Cornwall, newly elected King of the Romans.[24] He was regularly summoned to Parliament between 1295 and 1322; after that, however, he was not summoned again until 1532.[25]

The abbey's position on a main road by a river-crossing automatically give it some importance. In the late 14th century the monks claimed that this situation involved them in hospitality for 'a multitude of passers-by'.[26] Among these visitors were many of the kings of England, the patrons of the abbey — one of the rooms in the abbey was still called the King's Chamber in the 16th century.[27] William I came on a visit to the shrine of St. Modwen;[28] Henry II was at Burton in 1155,[29] John in 1200, 1204, and 1208,[30] Henry III in 1235 and 1251,[31] Edward I in 1275 and 1284,[32] and Edward II in 1322 during the campaign against Thomas, Earl of Lancaster.[33] The royal treasure was lodged at Burton in 1186 en route for Chester in connexion with John's proposed mission to Ireland,[34] and in 1232 and 1235 the proceeds of taxes collected in Staffordshire were ordered to be sent to Burton.[35]

The Annals of Burton state that Wulfric gave the abbey all his paternal inheritance, worth £700.[36]

[6] S.H.C. 1916, 12, 13, 16, 24–25; Whitelock, Anglo-Saxon Wills, 47, 51, 153–4.
[7] See below p. 213, n. 83. Dom David Knowles points out that between the late 11th and late 12th centuries St. Swithun's, Winchester, 'was second only to Christ Church as a nursery whence abbots were drawn for monasteries all over England': Monastic Order in Eng. (2nd edn.), 178.
[8] S.H.C. 1916, 122, 124.
[9] V.C.H. Staffs. iv. 43. A charter of Wm. I grants land 'to God and St. Mary in the church of Burton and Andreseya': S.H.C. v(1), 9.
[10] S.H.C. 1937, pp. 18, 20; ibid. v(1), 51 (apparently 1160–6: ibid. 10; Dugdale, Mon. iii. 48). Between 1159 and 1175 a certain Simon gave his service and homage to the abbey 'for the love of God and in honour of the holy virgin Modwenna': S.H.C. 1937, 15.
[11] e.g. in Hen. III's charter of confirmation of 1227 (Dugdale, Mon. iii. 43) and on the common seal (see below p. 213). Even in 1418 the abbot spoke of his church of St. Mary of Burton while a letter of 1470 referred to the Abbot of St. Modwenna: S.H.C. 1937, pp. 160, 176.
[12] Cal. Close, 1307–13, 335. They were, however, using it as an argument for their inability to support a royal pensioner: see below p. 206.
[13] Dugdale, Mon. iii. 48.
[14] Burton Corp., Anglesey MSS., J. 271, summarized in S.H.C. 1937, 88, where the date is wrongly given as 1294. The figure includes the abbot and prior.
[15] S.H.C. 1937, pp. xxi, 125, 131.
[16] E 179/20/595.
[17] E 179/15/8b. The figure given in J. C. Russell, 'The Clerical Population of Medieval Eng.' Traditio, ii. 189, and followed in D. Knowles and R. N. Hadcock, Medieval Religious Houses: Eng. and Wales, 61, omits the abbot.
[18] Hist. MSS. Com. Middleton, 252.
[19] Lich. Dioc. Regy., B/V/1/1, pp. 24–25, 72, p. 43 (2nd nos.).
[20] See below pp. 210, 297. Traditio, ii. 190, citing visitation records at the time of the Dissolution, gives the size of the community as 9.
[21] L. & P. Hen. VIII, xiv(1), p. 291.
[22] Hibbert, Dissolution, 64.
[23] See e.g. W. E. Lunt, Financial Relations of the Papacy with Eng. to 1327, 632, 634, 635, 637; Cal. Papal Regs. i. 45–46; ii. 325, 376, 386; Close R. 1227–31, 400; Cal. Pat. 1452–61, 409; 1494–1509, 379; L. & P. Hen. VIII, i(2), pp. 996, 1325.
[24] Annales Monastici (Rolls Ser.), i. 384.
[25] F. Palgrave, Parliamentary Writs (Rec. Com.), i. 510; ii(3), 622; D. Knowles, Religious Orders in Eng. ii. 304, 306; Hibbert, Dissolution, 47–48; L. & P. Hen. VIII, vi, p. 52.
[26] S.H.C. N.S. viii. 142.   [27] Hibbert, Dissolution, 263.
[28] Trans. Burton Arch. Soc. iv(2), 45; Dugdale, Mon. iii. 47; S.H.C. v(1), 9.
[29] R. W. Eyton, Court, Household and Itin. of King Hen. II, 6.
[30] Rot. Litt. Pat. (Rec. Com.), i(1), itin. of King John.
[31] Cal. Chart. R. 1226–57, 213; Cal. Pat. 1247–58, 119.
[32] Cal. Pat. 1272–81, 100; 1281–92, 116, 140.
[33] S.H.C. v(1), 97. The abbey had evidently suffered at the hands of the rebels who occupied Burton Bridge in an attempt to hold the passage of the Trent against the royal troops. When these forded the river above Burton, Earl Thos. burnt the town and withdrew. In addition the abbot was accused of having retained the earl's treasure, which appears to have been stored in the abbey, and he had some difficulty in proving his innocence. See ibid. 96–97; S.H.C. 1937, pp. xl, 122; Dugdale, Mon. iii. 47–48; May McKisack, The Fourteenth Century, 66. For the possibility that Abbot Sudbury may have been in sympathy with Owen Glendower's rebellion see S.H.C. 1937, pp. xl, 157. For the suggestion that the abbey may have favoured the Lancastrians during the Wars of the Roses see ibid. pp. xl–xli, 174, 177.
[34] S.H.C. i. 125, 126.
[35] Close R. 1231–4, 157; 1234–7, 189.
[36] Annales Monastici, i. 183.

Wulfric's will[37] does not substantiate this, but it does show that his endowment was extensive: in Staffordshire Burton, Stretton, Bromley, 'Bedintun' (evidently near Pillaton in Penkridge), Gailey, Whiston (in Penkridge), Darlaston (in Stone), Rudyard, 'my little land at Cotwalton [in Stone]', Leigh, Okeover, Ilam, Calton, Castern, and a hide at Sheen; in Derbyshire Winshill (now part of the borough of Burton), Sutton-on-the-Hill, Ticknall, Morley, Breadsall, Morton, Pilsley, Ogston, Wingfield, 'Snodeswic' (evidently near Morton), the 'little land' at 'Niwantune' (probably Newton Solney), and 'that land at Appleby [now in Leicestershire] that I bought with my money'; in Leicestershire land at Shangton and Wigston Parva and a hide at Sharnford in Wigston Parva; in Shropshire Longford, Stirchley, Romsley, Shipley, and 'Suthtune' (probably Sutton Maddock); in Warwickshire Weston-in-Arden, Burton Hastings, and Harbury. Other places whose identification is more uncertain were 'Actune' (possibly Acton Round in Shropshire) granted for two lives, 'Halen' (probably Halesowen, Worcs.), 'Niwantun at the Wich' (possibly Newton near Middlewich, Ches.), 'Tathawyllan' (possibly Tathwell, Lincs.), 'Ealdeswyrthe' (either Awsworth, Notts., or Aldsworth, Glos.), 'Alfredingtune' (either Alvington, Glos., or Alfreton, Derb.), and 'Eccleshale' (possibly Exhall, Warws., Ecclesall, Yorks W.R., or Eccleshall, Staffs.), and 'Waddune' (possibly Whaddon, Glos.). 'Waededun' has not been identified at all. The abbey was also given a reversionary interest in Elford and Oakley, both in Staffordshire, Wibtoft (Warws.), and 'Twongan' (either Tong, Salop., or Tonge, Leics.). Half the usufruct of 'Langandune' (probably Longdon, Staffs.) was assigned to the monks, and also the enjoyment 'of meat and of men and of all things' on the land of the bishop at 'Bubandune' (evidently Bupton, Derb.). Wulfric's lands between the Ribble and the Mersey and on the Wirral were left to Alfhelm and Wulfage 'on the condition that when the shad shoals come in, each of them give 3,000 shad to the monastery at Burton'; similarly Conisbrough (Yorks. W.R.) went to Alfhelm provided that the monks had a third of the fish every year. Finally Wulfric left the abbey 100 wild horses and 16 tame geldings 'and besides this all that I possess in livestock and other goods except those which I have bequeathed'. Most of these lands were mentioned in the royal charter of 1004 confirming Wulfric's endowment.[38]

Either Wulfric's intentions were never fully carried out, or else the abbey soon lost much of its original property, perhaps during the Danish Conquest in the early 11th century. At any rate many of the estates given by Wulfric were not in the abbey's possession at the end of the Confessor's reign, and what remained was confined to Staffordshire and Derbyshire.[39] In Staffordshire the losses had not been great, and the property there still included Burton, Stretton, Bromley, 'Bedintun', Whiston, Darlaston, Leigh, and Okeover; Ilam, Calton, and Castern, though not mentioned in Domesday Book, were held by the abbey in the early 12th century and may have been included under Okeover in the Domesday Survey. In Derbyshire only Winshill, Sutton, Ticknall, and Appleby remained. 'Ealdeswyrthe' and 'Alfredingtune' had been exchanged by Abbot Wulfgeat in 1008 with the king for Rolleston in Staffordshire, but Rolleston too had been lost by 1066.[40]

There were, however, several permanent additions to the Burton estates during the 11th century. In 1012 Abbot Wulfgeat bought Wetmore from the king.[41] Between 1042 and 1050 Edward the Confessor gave the abbey Willington and Stapenhill in Derbyshire, each apparently with a church; the lands at Brizlincote and Stanton, held by the abbey in the early 12th century, may have been included with Stapenhill.[42] Earl Leofric (d. 1057) gave part of Austrey (Warws.) to the abbey.[43] Coton-in-the-Elms (Derb.) was given by Earl Morcar, taken by William I, and restored by him while on his visit to Burton.[44] In addition William gave the abbey Cauldwell and Mickleover, both in Derbyshire;[45] the latter included the berewicks of Littleover, Findern, and Potlocks, and within the soc of the manor there lay Snelston, Bearwardcote, Dalbury, Hoon, Rodsley, Sudbury, Hilton, Sutton-on-the-Hill, and Rough Heanor (Henovera).[46] In the town of Derby he gave 2 mills, 3 houses, 13 acres of meadow, and apparently the church of St. Mary; by 1086 the abbot also enjoyed a share of the church-scot rendered to the king by the burgesses on the feast of St. Martin.[47] Branston in Staffordshire was held by Countess Godiva before the Conquest but had passed to Burton by 1086.[48] The abbey held 5 messuages in Stafford borough in 1086,[49] but there is no indication when it acquired them. It is likely that the abbey also held Horninglow, Anslow, and Field by this time, the first two as appendages of Wetmore and the third as part of Leigh; Horninglow and Field were among the abbey's possessions in the early 12th century, and Anslow appears by 1180.[50] In fact the Conquest

[37] Whitelock, *Anglo-Saxon Wills*, 46–51, 151–60; *S.H.C.* 1916, 1 sqq.

[38] *S.H.C.* 1916, 58–61, 115–19.

[39] *V.C.H. Staffs.* iv. 43–44, 58; *V.C.H. Derb.* i. 334–5. The statement in the abbey chronicles that Wm. I took several estates away, giving others in exchange (Dugdale, *Mon.* iii. 47), cannot apply to Wulfric's endowments, even if it is true; such of the lost lands as can be identified are shown by Domesday Bk. to have been lost before the Conquest: *S.H.C.* 1916, 41–42. One of the 5 carucates at Appleby had been given by Abbot Leofric to Countess Godiva.

[40] *Ann. Mon.* i. 184; *S.H.C.* v(1), 8. It was held by Earl Morcar in 1066: *V.C.H. Staffs.* iv. 48, no. 149.

[41] Dugdale, *Mon.* iii. 43 (citing the Annals which give the price as £70), 47 (citing the History of the Abbots which gives it as £60).

[42] Dugdale, *Mon.* iii. 47; *S.H.C.* 1916, 293–4 (which seems to have misread the History of the Abbots in stating that the gift was made by Briteric, abbot at the time); ibid.

1937, p. 7. A church at Stapenhill, however, was granted to Abbot Niel (1094–1114) by Geoffrey de Clinton: see below p. 202.

[43] *V.C.H. Warws.* i. 306; iv. 9. It had been left by Wulfric Spot to Ealdgyth, wife of Morcar: *S.H.C.* 1916, 14, 23, 41.

[44] *V.C.H. Derb.* i. 298–9, 335.

[45] Ibid. 334; Dugdale, *Mon.* iii. 47 (where the gift of Coton and Caldwell is wrongly ascribed to Wm. II).

[46] This is to be distinguished from Heanor, a parish in the east of Derbs.: K. Cameron, *Place-names of Derbs.* (Eng. Place-names Soc. xviii), 469, 484.

[47] Dugdale, *Mon.* iii. 47; *V.C.H. Derb.* i. 310, 327, 328. Domesday Bk., however, mentions only 1 mill; nor does it show any of the town's 6 churches as held by the abbey, although 2 were held by the king. By the early 12th cent. the abbey had a church there: see below p. 202.

[48] *V.C.H. Staffs.* iv. 43, no. 89.

[49] Ibid. 37.

[50] Ibid. 43n., 44n., and the further references given there.

seems to have benefited the abbey. The English Abbot Leofric died a few months after the Conquest, but there were English priors well into the 12th century.[51] It is also noteworthy that Burton was one of the few houses which did not hold by military service at the time of Domesday Book.[52]

The century following Domesday saw both gains and losses, and two abbots were expelled during this period for dissipating the lands and goods of the abbey — Abbot Geoffrey Mauland (Malaterra) in 1094 and Abbot Robert in 1159.[53] The gains included Stretton-on-Dunsmore (Warws.), which was given by Alan fitz Flaald probably during the time of Abbot Niel (1094–1114),[54] and Wolston nearby, which was given to Abbot Niel by Alan's widow Adeliza.[55] Land at Hampton in Blithfield was given by Meriet and land at Waterfall by Aschetill the sewer (dispensator); both gifts were probably made about 1120 since both occur in the later of the two surveys of the abbey's property, made respectively between 1114 and 1118 and between 1116 and 1127 or 1133.[56] Shobnall too appears in the second survey.[57] Tatenhill and Sheen had been added to the estates by 1185 when they occur among the possessions of the abbey as confirmed by Pope Lucius III.[58] Estates which were lost included Coton, alienated by one of the abbots, presumably Geoffrey Mauland, by the time of the two surveys.[59] 'Bedintun' disappears after the reign of Henry I, but it may have been absorbed into Pillaton (in Penkridge) with which it was associated and which the abbey held by the time of the first survey.[60] Calton, Waterfall, and Sutton had presumably been lost by 1185 since they do not appear in the papal confirmation.

A feature of the 12th century is the abbey's tendency to make more and more grants of its estates in perpetuity at fixed rents instead of the leases, often for two lives, common in the earlier part of the century.[61] The major 12th-century grants in perpetuity included: under Abbot Geoffrey (1114–50) Ticknall,[62] Rough Heanor,[63] and apparently the manor of Leigh with all its appurtenances except Field;[64] under Abbot Robert (1150–9) Okeover[65] and land at Horninglow;[66] under Abbot Bernard (1160–75) Stretton, Brizlincote, Willington (including the advowson), Darlaston, part of the property in Derby, Pillaton,[67] Wolston, and Stretton-on-Dunsmore;[68] under Abbot Roger (1177–82) Potlocks and Anslow;[69] under Abbot Nicholas (1187–97) Field[70] and probably at this time Ilam and Castern.[71]

By 1185 the abbey was also in possession of numerous churches, chapels, and tithes. Although most of these are not mentioned until various times during the 12th century, the papal confirmation of 1185 seems to ascribe the majority to the gift of Wulfric Spot and the rest to that of William I.[72] Only in the case of Stapenhill and Willington is there evidence to the contrary, but in view of the early date of Wulfric's endowment it seems more than likely that the churches ascribed to his gift were in fact gradually founded on the estates that he had given to the abbey.[73] Burton itself is the only church which can be assumed to date from the original foundation — although even there the first record of provision for a priest to serve the parish dates from the early 12th century.[74] According to the History of the Abbots the churches at Stapenhill and Willington, stated by the papal confirmation to have been given respectively by Wulfric and William I, were given by Edward the Confessor. If so, Stapenhill was subsequently lost for early in the 12th century Geoffrey de Clinton, treasurer and chamberlain of the king, gave to Abbot Niel the church of Stapenhill and tithes in nearby Stanton in return for enfeoffment with the part of Stanton owned by Burton.[75] Pope Lucius mentions the church at Mickleover with its chapels at Littleover, Findern, and Potlocks, and also St. Mary's, Derby, as gifts of William I; churches at Mickleover and Derby both occur among the abbey's possessions in the first of the early-12th-century surveys,[76] although the three chapels are mentioned apparently for the first time about 1180 when Abbot Roger granted them with the church at Mickleover to John the priest. Churches at Bromley and Ilam were listed in the second survey,[77] and within half a century or so there were several chapels dependent on Ilam: Blore (where, however, the abbey's claim to the patronage was surrendered between 1180 and 1187 in return for an annual pension of 1 mark), Grindon (surrendered about 1183 for a pension of 14s.), Sheen, Okeover, and Cauldon.[78] The churches mentioned in a confir-

[51] V.C.H. Derb. i. 298; S.H.C. 1937, pp. 8, 10.
[52] D. Knowles, Monastic Order in Eng. 609. The abbot was, however, among the tenants summoned to Berwick in 1303 and to Carlisle in 1308: S.H.C. viii(1), 25, 29.
[53] Dugdale, Mon. iii. 47, 48. Robert was restored in 1176 after the death of Abbot Bernard. For a sketch map showing the abbey estates in the early 12th cent. see S.H.C. 1916, facing p. 211.
[54] S.H.C. 1916, 247; 1937, p. 11.
[55] Ibid. v(1), 32–33; ibid. 1937, p. 10.
[56] Ibid. v(1), 32; ibid. 1916, 223–4, 225, 257–61. For the dating of the surveys established by J. H. Round see S.H.C. N.S. ix. 271 sqq.
[57] S.H.C. 1916, 213, 214.
[58] Ibid. v(1), 15; Dugdale, Mon. iii. 42.
[59] S.H.C. v(1), 8–10, 12, 14, 51.
[60] V.C.H. Staffs. v. 118–19; the dating there given has failed to take note of the dating established by Round. The reference to Abbot Richard ibid. 119, col. 1, line 2, is an error for Abbot Robert.
[61] S.H.C. v(1), 31 sqq.; ibid. N.S. ix. 276; ibid. 1916, 265; ibid. 1937, pp. 8 sqq. Many of these grants for 2 lives are described as grants in fee. And see V.C.H. Staffs. iv. 28, 44, for the three estates held by tenants in 1086, possibly for short terms of lives; all three were outlying estates.

[62] S.H.C. 1916, 263. It was granted to Rob. de Ferrers and his heirs at a rent of 10s.; this was the same rent by which his father had held it, presumably on a lease for lives.
[63] Ibid. v(1), 37–38.
[64] Ibid. 35, 37. No mention is made of the heirs of the grantee until the confirmation by Abbot Robert.
[65] Ibid. 69–70; ibid. 1937, p. 13; Dugdale, Mon. iii. 41. It was granted to Ralph fitz Orm and his heirs at the same rent and service as his father had rendered.
[66] S.H.C. v(1), 37.
[67] Ibid. 38, 39, 40. Darlaston had previously been held by the same family on leases for 2 lives: ibid. 35–36, 37; and see V.C.H. Staffs. iv. 28.
[68] S.H.C. 1937, p. 14.   [69] Ibid. v(1), 41.
[70] Ibid. 1937, p. 20.
[71] Ibid. v(1), 69.
[72] Ibid. 15; Dugdale, Mon. iii. 42.
[73] For some discussion of the problems see S.H.C. 1937, pp. li–liii.
[74] Ibid. pp. liv–lv. Married priests served the parish in the 12th cent.: ibid. lv.
[75] Ibid. pp. lvii, 7.
[76] Ibid. 1916, 231, 233; 1937, p. 17.
[77] Ibid. 1916, 222, 224.
[78] Ibid. v(1), 15, 41, 45; ibid. 1937, pp. lxiv, 19, 29.

mation of the abbey's possessions by Bishop Peche (1161–82) included Leigh as well as Bromley, Ilam, Stapenhill, Willington, and Mickleover.[79] The advowson of Willington, however, was granted in heredity with the abbey's other rights there by Abbot Bernard (1160–75),[80] and the advowson of Leigh was granted away in return for a pension of 5 marks by Abbot Roger (1177–82).[81] Pope Lucius mentions three chapels dependent on Stapenhill at Drakelow, Heathcote, and Newhall (all in Derb.).

Burton also held many tithes by the 12th century, though not all by the gift of Wulfric as the papal confirmation of 1185 seems to imply. The tithes of Burton parish were doubtless held from an early date; by the early 12th century part had been assigned to the parochial chaplain.[82] The tithes of Stanton were granted to Abbot Niel by Geoffrey de Clinton as mentioned above. By the time of the first of the surveys the abbey had been given the tithes of Newton in Blithfield by Ralph fitz Urnoi or Urvoi in return for land at Hampton in the same parish;[83] the tenant of Willington manor owed tithes 'in all things' including horses;[84] and the abbey held all the tithes of Mickleover.[85] When Field was leased out by Abbot Geoffrey in 1116 the tenant had to give 'strict tithes for his soul in fruits or in cattle or in cheeses or in any other things' besides rent and service, and a similar stipulation was included in a lease of Potlocks also made by Abbot Geoffrey.[86] By the 1150s the abbey held the tithes of Newhall and Heathcote, and Abbot Robert then granted those of Stanton and Newhall and one-third of those of Heathcote to the priest at Stapenhill.[87] Tithes from Linton in Cauldwell were held by the time of Abbot Roger (1177–82) who granted them to the nearby church of Gresley (Derb.) in return for a pension of 2s.[88] Pope Lucius mentions the tithes of Sheen, 'Truelega' (perhaps Throwley in Ilam), 'Mosedene', part of Waterfall, and Drakelow in addition to those of Newton, Linton, Heathcote, and Newhall.

Although there were comparatively few important changes in the abbey's property subsequently, numerous acquisitions of lands, tithes, and money continued to be made. Among these were a salt-pit and salt-pan at Nantwich secured between 1189 and 1197,[89] Hunsdon (in Thorpe, Derb.) for which property at Wetmore was exchanged in 1242,[90] and further property at Austrey later in the century,

including half the manor and the recognition of the abbey's claim to the advowson.[91] Assarted land at Callingwood was held by the later 13th century.[92] By about 1320 there was 'a place surrounded by a ditch' in Shobnall Park, the later Sinai Park, which was used as a retreat for monks undergoing blood-letting.[93] A house called 'Baconsyne' in the parish of St. Sepulchre without Newgate, London, was left to the abbey by John de Cauntebrigg, fishmonger of London, by will proved in 1377, subject to the life interest of his widow. It had passed to the abbey by 1394 and was known in the 16th century as 'the Abbot of Burton's House'.[94] The abbey was involved in numerous lawsuits to defend its possessions, both temporalities and spiritualities; a notable example is the litigation in connexion with the Austrey property in the late 13th and earlier 14th centuries.[95] The reasons given in 1382 to explain the abbey's poverty included 'lawsuits which it has been obliged to undergo'.[96]

The spiritualities also continued to increase, although St. Mary's, Derby, and some of the tithes mentioned in 1185 do not occur again. In fact the abbey was involved in extensive litigation in maintaining and enforcing its claims to tithe or payments in lieu. In 1250, for example, a dispute with the Rector of Hamstall Ridware over tithes from 'Lichlesaselis' claimed by the monks in right of their church of Bromley was settled in their favour; the rector was to pay a modus of 5s. and a pound of incense. By the 1290s, however, the monks had again gone to law to enforce payment.[97] Similarly they were suing the Rector of Blithfield in 1252 for tithes from Newton and Hampton; the dispute was settled in the abbey's favour but had broken out again by 1321.[98] By the 1530s, however, the Rector of Blithfield was paying the monks £1 a year.[99] The 5 marks due from the Rector of Leigh was another cause of litigation from the later 13th century to the end of the 14th century.[1] On the credit side, the churches of Ilam, Stapenhill, and Bromley were appropriated in the earlier 13th century.[2] By 1280 there was a chapel at Cauldwell, the fourth dependency of Stapenhill.[3] Having secured its claim to the advowson of Austrey the abbey was given royal licence to appropriate the church in 1287; in fact this did not take effect, and appropriation was not finally secured until the early 15th century.[4] Endowments of anniversaries, chantries, and lights in the

[79] Ibid. 1937, p. 41.
[80] Ibid. v(1), 39.
[81] Ibid. 1937, pp. 18, 21, 41.
[82] Ibid. 1916, 214; ibid. 1937, p. lv.
[83] Ibid. 1916, 223–4, 257–8. Ralph paid a 7s. modus.
[84] Ibid. 237.
[85] Ibid. 231; ibid. 1937, pp. lxi–lxii. The tenant owed all the tithe of Potlocks under the terms of a lease from Abbot Geoffrey (wrongly dated ibid. p. lx as before 1113: Geoffrey was abbot 1114–50); the '50 large and good eels of Trent' also due from the tenant may have represented a tithe of the fishery of Potlocks.
[86] Ibid. v(1), 34–35.
[87] Ibid. 1937, pp. 12–13.
[88] Ibid. v(1), 41.
[89] Ibid. 1937, p. 20.
[90] Ibid. v(1), 62–63.
[91] Ibid. 77–80, 86, 88, 90–91; ibid. 1937, pp. lxvii–lxviii, 113; V.C.H. Warws. iv. 9–10.
[92] S.H.C. 1937, p. 113.
[93] H. A. Rye, 'Sinai Park', Trans. Burton Arch. Soc. vi. 79 sqq.; Dugdale, Mon. iii. 49. It was still used for this purpose in the 1380s: S.H.C. 1937, p. 147. The manor of 'Seyne' within the park of 'Shopenhale' occurs in 1410

and Sinai Park is listed among the abbey's possessions in the 16th cent.: ibid. 156–7, 184, 187; Valor Eccl. (Rec. Com.), iii. 144, 147. In the early 16th cent. there were complaints about interference with days of recreation called 'le seignes': Lich. Dioc. Regy., B/V/1/1, p. 72, pp. 43, 44 (2nd nos.).
[94] S.H.C. 1937, p. 149; ibid. 1939, 127; Cal. Pat. 1550–3, 16.
[95] See refs. in n. 91 above.
[96] S.H.C. N.S. viii. 142.
[97] S.H.C. 1937, pp. lxvi–lxvii, 46–47, 48–49, 87, 90. It was paid in the 1530s: Valor Eccl. iii. 145.
[98] S.H.C. 1937, pp. 47–48, 121–4.
[99] Valor Eccl. iii. 145.
[1] S.H.C. 1937, pp. lxvi, 66, 69, 116–17, 120, 132, 149–50. This too was being paid in the 1530s: Valor Eccl. iii. 145.
[2] S.H.C. 1937, pp. lx–lxi, 30–31, 36, 41. Vicarages were ordained at all three and also at Mickleover.
[3] Ibid. p. 80.
[4] Ibid. pp. lxvii–lxviii, 159, 167, 191–2; Cal. Pat. 1413–1416, 167; Dugdale, Mon. iii. 49. For the attempt to secure appropriation in 1322–3 and for a 10-year appropriation in 1382 see Cal. Chanc. Wts. i. 542; Rymer, Foedera, ii(1), 557; S.H.C. 1937, pp. 121, 143; ibid. N.S. viii. 142.

abbey church were further increasing the revenues of the house from at least the 13th century.[5] In 1535 St. Modwen's Chapel at Andressey, which had been attracting pilgrims from an early date, had an income of £2 a year from offerings.[6]

The abbey estates included two boroughs, Burton and Abbots Bromley.[7] Burgage tenure was established at Burton by Abbot Nicholas (1187–97), but it was only under his successor, Abbot Melburne (1200–14), that royal licence 'to make a borough' was granted; in 1200 King John also granted a market and fair. Abbots Stafford (1260–81) and Packington (1281–1305) further enlarged the borough, the latter because of a great famine about 1286. A borough was established at Abbots Bromley by Abbot Richard de Lisle (1222–9) in 1222, also under royal licence; in 1227 Henry III granted a market and fair there.

The abbey enjoyed several other privileges. Henry I granted Abbot Geoffrey (1114–50) sac, soc, toll, team, infangentheof, and full jurisdiction for his court (*curiam suam plenarie de omnibus rebus et consuetudinibus*).[8] Stephen, Henry II, John, and Henry III confirmed many of these privileges, and Henry II added quittance of toll, passage, and pontage, and also free warren as the abbot's predecessors had held it in the time of Henry I.[9] At the Staffordshire *quo warranto* proceedings of 1293 the abbot successfully upheld his claim to view of frankpledge, fines for offences against the assize of bread and ale, free warren, gallows, waif, and infangentheof.[10] At the Derbyshire proceedings of 1330 he maintained his privileges in the manors of Mickleover and Stapenhill but had to pay a fine of 20s. to regain his right to infangentheof at Stapenhill; he had not been exercising this right there, and he was ordered to erect a gallows.[11] In 1468 the king confirmed existing privileges and added the right to goods of felons, fugitives and outlaws within the manor of Burton and its members and to various fines from tenants there; the abbot was to act as a justice of the peace in the town and the bailiff of Burton as king's coroner, and the abbot was to have return of writs; an extra fair at Burton was also granted.[12] This grant was confirmed by the Crown in 1488 and 1510.[13] In 1527 the abbey successfully maintained against the king its right to appoint its own coroner within the liberty of Burton.[14]

The abbey's main economic pursuit was the management of its estates. Granges had been established at Shobnall, Stapenhill, Stretton, and Winshill by 1325 and at Burton and Branston by 1327.[15] A grange at Newton (Derb.) is mentioned in 1391,[16] and one had been established at Hunsdon (Derb.) by the later 15th century.[17] Another existed at Findern at some unspecified period.[18] The granges at Stapenhill, Winshill, Hunsdon, and Findern were leased out in the 1520s and 1530s,[19] and the only other mentioned at that time was Shobnall which was still run directly by the abbey.[20] The monks were also involved in the wool trade by the late 13th century, and there was sheep-farming at Hunsdon Grange in the 15th century.[21] They were evidently engaged in the production of cloth by the early 1340s when Brother Robert of Stapenhill erected a fulling-mill at Burton.[22] The abbey was running its own quarry in the early 13th century, probably at Winshill.[23]

The abbey property as listed in 1542, after the transfer of most of it to the new college at Burton,[24] consisted of the manors of Burton and of Abbots Bromley with Bromley Hurst; Hunsdon Grange; rents from Pillaton, Whiston, Darlaston, Field, Leigh, Branston, Stretton, Wetmore, Anslow, Ilam, Okeover, Stapenhill, Newhall, Stanton, Drakelow, Cauldwell, Mickleover, Littleover, Findern, Willington, Potlocks, Ticknall, Derby, Austrey, Appleby, and property in St. Sepulchre's parish, London; the appropriated churches of Abbots Bromley and Ilam, tithes in Newton (in Blithfield), and pensions from Hamstall Ridware, Grindon, and Blore.[25]

In Domesday Book the abbey's estates were valued at £39 8s. 6d.[26] Three valuations are available for the 13th century:[27] £24 12s. 2d. in 1229, £42 12s. 6d. in 1254 (when some of the property was temporarily in the king's hands and so was not included), and £115 17s. 8d. in 1291. Since each apparently includes items not in the other two, proper comparison is not possible. Some indication of the increase in valuation, however, is given by the assessments of Burton church, which occurs on all three occasions: £7 6s. 8d. in 1229, £9 6s. 8d. in 1254, and £10 in 1291. In 1535 the abbey was the only house to be valued twice: at £357 1s. 3½d. (temporalities £271 16s. 3½d. and spiritualities £85 5s.) and then at £513 19s. 4½d. (temporalities

---

[5] For anniversaries and chantries see below p. 208. For the maintenance of lights see e.g. *S.H.C.* 1937, pp. lvi–lvii and the refs. given there, 26, 50, 52, 54, 57, 146.

[6] *S.H.C.* 1937, pp. 25–26; *Valor Eccl.* iii. 145, 147. For Wm. I's pilgrimage see above p. 200. The chapel was still called St. Andrew's at the time of its rebuilding and endowment c. 1200: *S.H.C.* 1937, pp. 25–26.

[7] *S.H.C.* 1937, pp. xxxiv sqq.; ibid. v(1), 12, 43–44, 73–74; *Rot. Chart.* (Rec. Com.), i. 49; Dugdale, *Mon.* iii. 43, 48–49.

[8] *S.H.C.* v(1), 11.

[9] Ibid. 11–12; *Rot. Chart.* i. 49.

[10] *S.H.C.* v(1), 94.

[11] Ibid. 98.

[12] *Cal. Pat.* 1467–77, 95.

[13] *L. & P. Hen. VIII*, i(1), p. 193.

[14] *S.H.C.* 1937, p. 183.

[15] S.R.O., D.(W.) 1734/2/1/101(a), m. 11; /101(b), m. 12. That at Burton itself may have been at Bond End on the south side of the town: C. H. Underhill, *Hist. of Burton upon Trent*, 160 and plate facing p. 148.

[16] *Cal. Pat.* 1388–92, 426.

[17] Hist. MSS. Com. *Middleton*, 258–9.

[18] S.R.O., D.(W.) 1734/1/4/21, lease of manor-place or grange of Findern 1537.

[19] Ibid. /9, 10, 20, 21, 27. All except Hunsdon are described as mese or grange or as manor-place or grange.

[20] *Valor Eccl.* iii. 144, 147.

[21] For its wool from the late 13th cent. to the 1350s see W. Cunningham, *Growth of Eng. Industry and Commerce* (1922 edn.), i. 639; W. Beresford, *Lichfield*, 109; *Cal. Pat.* 1301–7, 484; 1354–8, 164–5; *Cal. Close*, 1346–9, 269. For 15th-cent. Hunsdon see Hist. MSS. Com. *Middleton*, 259.

[22] *S.H.C.* 1937, p. 134; *V.C.H. Staffs.* ii. 217.

[23] Dugdale, *Mon.* iii. 48; *S.H.C.* 1937, p. 35. A quarry at Winshill supplied stone for work on Tutbury castle in the 1440s and 1450s: *Hist. of the King's Works*, ed. H. M. Colvin, ii. 848. In the 18th cent. there was a quarry on the east side of the river about ¼ mile from the bridge: W.S.L., S.MS. 468, pp. 97, 98.

[24] See below p. 297.

[25] S.C.6/Hen.VIII/3356, m. 49.

[26] Dugdale, *Mon.* iii. 33. The figure there given is £39 8s. 8d. since the valuation of Darlaston is read as 27s. 4d. The reading given in *V.C.H. Staffs.* iv. 44, no. 93, is 27s. 2d. and seems preferable.

[27] For these see W. E. Lunt, *Valuation of Norwich*, 26–27, 478–9, 539–40; *Tax. Eccl.* (Rec. Com.), 65, 67, 242, 243, 253, 264.

£414 14s. 4½d. and spiritualities £99 5s.). Total disbursements in each case were £89 2s. 0½d.[28] In 1541–2 the gross value of the former abbey's possessions was £646 17s. 3d.[29]

The officers of the abbey were those usual in larger houses — abbot, prior, subprior, precentor, sacrist, cellarer, kitchener, chamberlain, infirmarer, hospitaller, almoner, pittancer, and martyrologer.[30] By the mid 15th century there was a 'third prior', and the precentor, sacrist, and cellarer each had a deputy. By the 16th century one person often held several offices. The prior acted as chamberlain and pittancer. The precentor was also almoner and in 1518 held the further office of 'third prior', an office held by the sacrist in 1524. The hospitaller acted as infirmarer. The cellarer was priest in charge of St. Modwen's Chapel at Andressey and one of the chantry priests; the martyrologer was in charge of the other two chantries; the subchanter acted as keeper of St. Mary's Chapel. At the visitations of 1518 and 1521 there was some complaint about the duplication as it affected the cellarer and hospitaller. The office of abbot's chaplain occurs from the 13th century.

The abbot, though supreme ruler of the community, was expected to act to some extent in consultation with the chapter. Up to the time of Abbot Bernard (1160–75) the chapter witnessed many of the deeds of enfeoffment.[31] In 1306 the prior and chapter drew up a set of regulations covering various aspects of the life of the house, including the powers of the abbot.[32] He was not to appoint any obedientiary without consulting the prior and senior monks in chapter; he was not to alienate land or wood without the chapter's approval; he was to render an account of his administration once a year to the prior and two of the brethren. Nevertheless the first of the bishop's injunctions following the visitation of 1323 again had to stipulate that all common business such as alienations and elections must be subject to common deliberation and consent.[33] One of the complaints voiced at the bishop's visitation in 1422 was that the abbot did not hold regular chapter meetings, and the abbot himself stated that he did not render an annual account of receipts and that it was not required.[34] He had his own apartments on the west side of the cloister by the 14th century, with a separate kitchen for his household.[35] It was stated at the 1422 visitation that the abbot did not sleep in the dormitory or eat in the refectory.[36]

There was no formal division of revenues between abbot and convent, nor were the finances of the abbey centralized under a single obedientiary. Instead there were various main departments —

chamber, kitchen, infirmary, almonry — each with certain revenues which were paid directly to it without any central control beyond the abbot's general supervision.[37] This system was taking shape in the late 12th century when Abbot Nicholas (1187–97) endowed the chamber and the kitchen; his successor Abbot Melburne (1200–14) confirmed the arrangement. Abbot Wallingford (1216–22) increased the endowment of the kitchen because 'the badness of the times' had rendered the existing endowment inadequate. Abbot Nicholas's grant to the chamber included skins, fleeces, and other materials and also mentioned a tailor, two servants in the tailor's shop, a shoemaker (corveisarius), and a woman who washed the clothes of the brethren; all these were assigned corrodies and wages. Further grants to both kitchen and chamber were made by later abbots and others. By 1295 the income of the chamber amounted to £16 8s. a year, and the abbot in that year issued an ordinance regulating the amounts issued to the individual monks and the spending of the rest by the chamberlain. By 1535 the kitchener received £8 6s. 8d. a year from property in Burton and elsewhere. Both kitchener and chamberlain had a lay representative outside the abbey who was a burgess of Burton and a person of standing.

The infirmary received a small endowment from Abbot Melburne, and other gifts followed; the infirmarer had a clerk of the infirmary under him by the mid 13th century.[38] The almonry was endowed for the maintenance of the poor and of pilgrims by Abbot Melburne who also mentions gifts from Herbert de Stretton. Abbot Wallingford not only made new grants to the almoner for the poor but assigned to the cellarer 300 loaves, 200 gallons of ale, and 600 herrings from the monks' kitchen, and 3s. 3d. from the sacrist to add to the alms distributed on the anniversary day of Wulfric Spot and his wife. Subsequent abbots and others made new gifts to the almoner, including a 'house of stone next to the church for the reception of the poor' given by Abbot Laurence (1229–60). By 1535 the almoner was in receipt of £8 a year from property in Burton; in addition £23 0s. 11d. a year was being distributed to the poor in money, food, drink, and clothing, £19 8s. of it allegedly by the appointment of Wulfric Spot and the rest in accordance with the wishes of various abbots. The almoner too had his secular counterpart by the 13th century.[39]

The prior was given the chapel of St. Edmund by Abbot Richard de Lisle (1222–9) who had built and endowed it. By the early 14th century the prior had an income of £2 a year from property in Burton, which he still received in 1535.[40] The sacrist and the pittancer were in receipt of regular payments from the time of Abbot Laurence,[41] and the martyrologer

[28] Hibbert, Dissolution, 74 sqq. This (pp. 77–79) corrects the wrongly added totals of the Valor Eccl.
[29] S.C.6/Hen.VIII/3356, m. 49.
[30] For this para. see S.H.C. 1937, p. xx; S.H.C. v(1), 81; Lich. Dioc. Regy., B/A/1/11, f. 56; B/V/1/1, pp. 24–25, 72, and p. 43 (2nd nos.).
[31] S.H.C. 1937, pp. xxi, xlii.
[32] Burton Corp., Anglesey MSS., J. 414.
[33] Lich. Dioc. Regy., B/A/1/3, f. 33.
[34] Ibid. /9, f. 175v. He was accounting by the early 16th cent.: see below p. 207.
[35] See below pp. 208, 212; S.H.C. 1937, p. xxiii.
[36] Lich. Dioc. Regy., B/A/1/9, f. 175v.
[37] For this para. see S.H.C. 1937, pp. xxii–xxiv, 21–22,

25, 33; Burton Corp., Anglesey MSS., J. 271; Valor Eccl. iii. 147. The reference in S.H.C. 1937, p. xxiv, to the confirmatory charter of Nic. II is an error for the charter of Abbot Ric. in 1226. At the visitation of 1516 the income of the kitchen was given as £5 a year: Lich. Dioc. Regy., B/V/1/1, p. 25.
[38] S.H.C. 1937, pp. xxvi–xxvii, 32, 52–53, 101; Dugdale, Mon. iii. 48.
[39] S.H.C. 1937, pp. xxvii, 25, 34; Dugdale, Mon. iii. 48; Valor Eccl. iii. 146, 147.
[40] Dugdale, Mon. iii. 48; S.R.O., D.(W.)1734/2/3/112a, ff. 16 sqq.; Valor Eccl. iii. 147.
[41] S.H.C. 1937, pp. xxi, xxvii, 40, 50, 52, 103.

had an income of £14 from property in Burton and elsewhere by 1535.[42]

Of the lay officials and servants the most important was the steward with his subordinate bailiffs. The first recorded steward is Hernald who witnessed a charter of Abbot Nicholas about 1190; in 1535 the office was held by George, Earl of Huntingdon, at a fee of £6 13s. 4d. and was presumably honorary by that time.[43] The keeper of the abbey gate also seems to have been of some standing. He occurs among witnesses of abbey charters and by the 1240s was provided with food and drink, fodder for his horse, a wage of half a mark a year, and 'a serving-man at the gate' who also received a corrody. The office was granted in heredity in 1247 to Walter son of Ralph de Shobnall, who surrendered his capital messuage and lands in Shobnall in return for the office and a burgage in Burton.[44] The maintenance of Burton Bridge was the abbey's responsibility, and a bridge-keeper occurs from at least the early 14th century and perhaps from 1284 when a monk was in charge of repair work then in progress. By the 15th century the keeper was a layman.[45] The ordinances of 1306 laid down that the abbot and obedientiaries were not to retain any servant who was *obstinatum et irreverenter se habentem erga conventum.*[46]

There were also numerous lay people enjoying a share in the spiritual and material life of the abbey, usually in return for a grant of all or part of their property; in fact Burton's early-12th-century records probably provide the earliest available examples of monastic corrodies.[47] At its simplest the association was a mark of friendship. At some time between 1114 and 1126 Robert de Ferrers, after a dispute with the monks over a grove, came to an agreement with them, 'pricked by the fear of God and admonished by the prayer and order of the king'; he promised to pay 20s. a year, and the monks gave him the grove and received him into their 'fraternity and society . . . as friend and guardian of the church so that they should love him perfectly' and pray for him, his family, and his ancestors.[48] The system was also a means by which maintenance in old age or widowhood could be secured. In 1295 a widow, Maud, daughter of Nicholas de Shobnall, surrendered her hereditary keepership of the abbey gate with the privileges that went with it and received instead a daily grant of food and drink for life with grain, oats, hay, wood, and 1 mark a year. Her son was to have good food and clothing for 10 years according to his needs and afterwards was to serve the abbey, receiving due maintenance; if he was prevented from serving by illness, he was still to receive food, drink, and clothing.[49]

The system could also involve a close association with the life of the abbey.[50] William of St. Albans, on receiving land at Stretton from Abbot Geoffrey (1114–50), was given the food and drink (*procuratio*) of one monk until he died or became a monk, when it was to pass to his wife. He occurs as a lay witness of abbey charters and in the 1150s became a monk at Burton. His son Reynold was debarred from inheriting the *procuratio*, but he was included as heir in the grant of the lands and duly succeeded to them. Subsequently Abbot Bernard (1160–75) granted part of the property to him in perpetuity and the rest to him and his heir. In 1166 Reynold too became closely associated with the abbey. In return for the surrender of the property granted to him by the previous abbot and for the service of his body, Reynold was to be received as a monk when he should so desire and meanwhile be provided with the food and drink of a monk. If he travelled far on the abbey's business he was to have expenses for himself, a squire, and horses, and if he was away on pilgrimage or some other distant business he could assign his corrody to someone else. He was free to take the religious habit anywhere, but 'if he wishes to submit himself to the yoke of religion with us, let him come to us with a third part of his goods when it shall please him'. Reynold is found witnessing abbey charters as a layman under Abbot Roger (1177–82).

From at least the early 14th century it was customary for the king to appoint a royal official to a corrody in the abbey, even though the Crown was wrong in claiming Burton as a royal foundation. In 1310 the monks were ordered by Edward II to provide Sir Thomas de Bannebury with food, drink, clothing, and a chamber within the abbey precincts for life as a reward for his long service to the Crown. The monks excused themselves on grounds of poverty; the king replied that the excuse was 'frivolous, untruthful, and inacceptable' and threatened to confiscate their temporalities.[51] The outcome is not known, but in 1315 the king ordered the monks to provide for Alice de Duffeld for life.[52] The following year aged members of the garrison at Berwick were assigned to various religious houses, and Nicholas of Derby was sent to Burton.[53] For the rest of the abbey's existence the Crown appointed a succession of royal servants and officials to this corrody, which was valued at £3 6s. 8d. in 1535.[54] Since the Crown regarded Burton as a royal foundation, from at least 1316 the abbey on the election of a new abbot had to provide a pension for a royal clerk of the king's nomination until the abbot appointed the clerk to a benefice; the amount of the pension in 1535 was 40s.[55]

Financial troubles are a constant feature of the

---

[42] *Valor Eccl.* iii. 147.

[43] *S.H.C.* 1937, pp. xx, xxx–xxxi, 20; *Valor Eccl.* iii. 146.

[44] *S.H.C.* 1937, pp. xxxi, 43–44, 89; B.M., Stowe Ch. 103. In the 1540s the porter of the college of Burton was described as 'gentleman' and received a fee of 60s. as opposed to the wage-earning 'common servants' such as the bridge-keeper and the parish clerk: Hibbert, *Dissolution*, 270, 271; see below p. 297.

[45] *Cal. Pat.* 1281–92, 116; 1324–7, 61; *S.H.C.* 1937, pp. 98, 142, 168, 180; S.R.O., D.(W.)1734/2/3/112a, f. 22v.; *V.C.H. Staffs.* ii. 280; see below pp. 297, 298. For gifts to the bridge see *S.H.C.* 1937, pp. 98, 100, 180, 183; 1939, 128–9.   [46] Burton Corp., Anglesey MSS., J. 414.

[47] This was the opinion of J. H. Round: *S.H.C.* N.S. ix. 288.

[48] *S.H.C.* 1937, pp. 9–10. For other examples see ibid. p. xxix.   [49] Ibid. p. 89.

[50] For the rest of this para. see ibid. pp. xxviii–xxix, 9, 12, 13, 16, 17, 18; v(1), 31, 37, 38. Wm. became tenant of part at least of the land in the reign of Hen. I.

[51] *Cal. Close*, 1307–13, 331, 335, 343; *Cal. Chanc. Wts.* i. 368.

[52] *Cal. Chanc. Wts.* i. 414.   [53] *Cal. Close*, 1313–18, 446.

[54] Ibid. 564; 1318–23, 116, 694; 1343–6, 108; 1354–60, 505; 1369–74, 610; 1381–5, 246; 1399–1402, 211–12; 1413–19, 97; 1435–41, 369; *S.H.C.* 1937, p. 168; *L. & P. Hen. VIII*, ii(1), p. 800; *Valor Eccl.* iii. 146. In 1382 the new corrodian was appointed to the office of abbey porter by the king: *Cal. Pat.* 1381–5, 205; *S.H.C.* xiv(1), 138–9.

[55] *Cal. Close*, 1313–18, 424; 1327–30, 569; 1339–41, 464; 1346–9, 385; 1369–74, 596; 1399–1402, 298; 1419–22, 221, 222 (where the amount is given as £40); 1429–35, 257; 1468–76, 309; *L. & P. Hen. VIII*, v, p. 130; vi, p. 552; *Valor Eccl.* iii. 146.

abbey's history. As already seen two abbots were expelled early on for dissipating the property of the house, in 1094 and 1159.[56] The large-scale granting of property in fee instead of for lives during the 12th century has also been noted.[57] By 1225 the community sought to relieve the burden of debt by granting one of its manors in fee for 100 marks, binding itself under pain of excommunication not to cancel the grant; since the manor was worth 20 marks a year in rents, it subsequently regretted the transaction, and the Pope had to intervene in 1225 to put the matter right.[58] The appropriation of Abbots Bromley church at this period was allowed by the bishop because the abbey was 'weighted by great debts and altogether collapsed'.[59] It may be a sign of continuing financial problems that in 1295 Abbot Packington issued an ordinance regulating the expenditure of the chamber revenues and providing for three-yearly accounting by the chamberlain to a committee appointed by the abbot.[60] The ordinances of the prior and chapter in 1306 included provisions for annual accounting by the abbot and obedientiaries to the prior and certain other brethren specially appointed for the occasion.[61]

Troubles continued. In 1319 at the request of the community the king took the abbey into his protection because of its indebtedness and appointed a royal clerk as keeper of the house and its possessions for three years; the following year, however, the protection was revoked, again at the request of the community.[62] In 1323 the bishop forbade the granting of further corrodies and annuities without his permission and ordered the keeping of accounts by obedientiaries, removing several from office.[63] The abbey was allowed to appropriate Austrey church for 10 years from 1382 because the house was 'so impoverished through dearness of corn and mortality of cattle and lawsuits which it has been obliged to undergo that the monks can no longer maintain hospitality or even live decently'.[64] Two years later the house was once more taken into the royal protection 'on account of its oppression by rivals and the consequent diminution of divine service and works of charity', and Hugh, Earl of Stafford, and Ralph Bassett were appointed keepers; it was stated that this was to be without prejudice to the abbey in the future.[65] An example of oppression is provided by the powerful Sir John Bagot, to whom Abbot Southam (1366–1400) paid 30s. a year to be the 'friend of the house'; Abbot Sudbury complained that in 1402 Bagot, in order to force a larger bribe, had robbed the park at Abbots Bromley.[66]

The confusion seems to have been even worse during the 15th century. In 1400 the king pardoned the abbey all money due to the Crown as a result of the voidance following Abbot Southam's resignation 'because the abbey has been impoverished by the improvident governance of Thomas, late abbot'.[67]

In 1414 the king once more took the house into his hands, blaming 'the bad governance of its abbots' and 'its notable dilapidation' for the fact that it 'is oppressed with annuities, pensions, and corrodies and debt, and its goods and jewels have been wasted and many of its manors, lands, and possessions improvidently demised at farm and otherwise alienated, and the abbot and convent are so troubled that divine worship and other works of piety are withdrawn'. The running of the house and its lands was committed to the prior and cellarer under the supervision of a commission of four outsiders.[68] The bishop's visitation of 1422 revealed no improvement. Debts amounted to £100. No accounts were kept by abbot, chamberlain, or pittancer, and Abbot Sudbury stated that he had found no inventory of goods when he was elected in 1400 and had made none himself. Complaints were made that the abbot, besides being negligent in his administration, was selling the goods of the house and supporting his own relatives. The bishop committed the administration of the goods to the cellarer and his own sequestrator and ordered the restoration of alienated property, an inquiry into all servants of the abbey, and the drawing up of an inventory, a rental, and a full account of pensions and corrodies.[69] Early in 1424 the abbey, having again been taken into the king's hands, was put under the control of a group of commissioners for a year.[70] Indeed the confusion of its affairs may well have been the reason for Abbot Sudbury's resignation later in 1424.[71] In 1433 the house was still impoverished, and the Crown appointed Humphrey, Earl of Stafford, and four others as keepers for seven years.[72] Among the charges leading to Abbot Henley's suspension in 1454 (see below) were alienation of property and general extravagance.[73] The new privileges bestowed by the royal charter of 1468 were granted 'in consideration of the intolerable things which the abbey daily sustains',[74] and in 1498 the bishop after a visitation was again ordering the proper keeping and presentation of accounts by the abbot and obedientiaries. The cellarer was a particular offender and was suspended from all office for a year; the replacement of the existing sacrist was also ordered.[75] At the visitations of 1518, 1521, and 1524, however, there was no complaint about the financial state of the house; it was in fact stated in 1524 that the abbot and officials rendered accounts every Lent.[76]

Information about the spiritual state of the house is confined mainly to the last 200 years of its existence. Standards in the later 12th century were evidently high enough to satisfy the austere Abbot Bernard (1160–75) who had resigned the abbacy of Cerne (Dors.) 'because of the great embellishments of the same house'.[77] The picture that emerges later, however, is of a house that was frequently as unsound spiritually as it was financially; in fact, as already seen, financial confusion was sometimes

[56] See above p. 202.
[57] See above p. 202.
[58] Cal. Papal Regs. i. 104.
[59] S.H.C. 1937, p. 36.
[60] Burton Corp., Anglesey MSS., J. 271.
[61] Ibid. J. 414.
[62] Cal. Pat. 1317–21, 407, 534.
[63] Lich. Dioc. Regy., B/A/1/3, f. 33.
[64] S.H.C. N.S. viii. 142.
[65] Cal. Pat. 1381–5, 415.
[66] S.H.C. N.S. vii. 244.
[67] Cal. Pat. 1399–1401, 400.

[68] Ibid. 1413–16, 204–5.
[69] Lich. Dioc. Regy., B/A/1/9, ff. 135v., 136v., 175v., 176.
[70] E 28/44/21, /29, /55.
[71] See below p. 213.
[72] Cal. Pat. 1429–36, 286.
[73] Lich. Dioc. Regy., B/A/1/11, ff. 56 sqq.
[74] S.H.C. 1937, p. 176; see above p. 204.
[75] Lich. Dioc. Regy., B/A/1/13, f. 239v.
[76] Ibid., B/V/1/1, pp. 24–25, 72, and pp. 43–44 (2nd nos.). This may have been as a result of the influence of Abbot Flegh (1493–1502): see below.
[77] See below p. 213, n. 87.

blamed for the low spiritual standard. At the bishop's visitation of 1323 the abbot was found to be lax in imposing punishments, and two monks were described as much given to frequenting forbidden places in lay company. To guard against ignorance the bishop ordered the papal 'constitutions' to be read twice a year in chapter.[78] The period of Abbot Sudbury (1400–24) was one of particular disorder. In 1407 he and several others of the community received royal pardon for numerous acts of violence, thefts, and ravishings during the previous few years. Sudbury himself was also declared guilty of having on Christmas Day 1404 'in his chamber at Burton ravished Margery, the wife of Nicholas Taverner'.[79] At the bishop's visitation in 1422 Sudbury was accused of failing to hold regular chapter meetings, inflict proper punishments, eat in the refectory, and sleep in the dormitory. The suspicion was voiced that he spent the greater part of Sunday with women, and the bishop in fact found him guilty of adultery with two women. Laxity was in fact general: attendance at services was slack, and the monks often ate and drank in the town with friends — the abbot was again mentioned as a particular offender in both instances. Two women of ill-fame stayed within the precincts of the monastery, and dogs, hawks, and horses were kept for hunting.[80]

Despite the bishop's injunctions laxity continued. In 1454 Abbot Henley was suspended by the bishop after a visitation that revealed not only his maladministration but his habitual absence from divine service and night office, his gaming, and his drunkenness. He resigned in 1455 and was granted a pension of 20 marks.[81] In the 1460s it was reported that a common whore from Lichfield had gone several times to Burton 'and there admitted the monks to carnal copulation'.[82] In 1498 the bishop forbade the frequenting of 'taverns and other suspect places' in Burton by the monks and the keeping of hunting dogs within the precincts of the abbey, a fault of which the cellarer confessed himself guilty. The abbot was not only to see that the abbey gates were shut at the proper times but also to prevent women from having frequent access to himself and the monks and to have the locks of the outer doors changed.[83] Yet the abbot at this time was William Flegh (1493–1502), who is the only one of the abbots listed in the chronicle to be noted for his good life; the writer also stated that he left the house in a good state.[84] No serious troubles were revealed at the visitations of 1518, 1521, and 1524,[85] and about 1530

the subprior of Burton was on the waiting list for admission to a new cell that was being founded by the Carthusian monastery of Mount Grace (Yorks. N.R.).[86]

On the credit side are the chantry and similar foundations originating from within the community, particularly in the 15th century. It had early on been a custom for mass to be celebrated daily for the souls of deceased abbots, priors, and benefactors, but the practice had lapsed by the time of Abbot Melburne (1200–14). He revived it and endowed a chaplaincy for the purpose with the food and drink of one monk and 10s. for vestments from the offerings of pilgrims. With the consent of the chapter he also assigned 10s. rent from burgages in Burton 'for the redemption of his soul and for an obit'.[87] Abbot de Lisle (1222–9), a monk of Bury St. Edmunds who returned there as abbot in 1229, built and endowed a chapel of St. Edmund in the abbey church during his time at Burton.[88] About the mid 13th century a daily mass was instituted in the new chapel of St. Mary in the church.[89] A daily mass was founded in 1292 for the souls of Sir Richard de Draycott and his son Richard in return for the many benefits received from Sir Richard.[90] In 1349 Abbot Ibstock gave lands and rents to endow an anniversary for himself,[91] and in 1386 another was instituted for Reynold of Ibstock, a monk of Burton, in recognition of his gifts of property and goods.[92] Abbots Southam, Sudbury, and Bronston each endowed a chantry and an obit.[93] Abbot Bronston also founded the weekly Jesus Mass and endowed the singers of a mass in St. Mary's Chapel, including apparently boy choristers.[94] A daily mass was instituted in 1488 in this chapel in memory of James Norres, his wife Alice, and her second husband William Prudhom in consideration of many benefits received from James, who was buried in the chapel.[95] In 1518 three chantries were mentioned: Abbot Bronston's, that of Norres and Prudhom, and one founded by a Nicholas Ward. The last was either the monk of that name who was nearly elected abbot in 1430 or the Nicholas Ward who was professed a monk at Burton in 1433 and was kitchener under Abbot Flegh (1493–1502).[96] A fourth chantry was founded by Abbot Bene (1502–1530 or 1531).[97] By 1547 there was a brotherhood of priests in Burton church stated to have been endowed by several benefactors to pray for their souls; the number of priests varied between two and four.[98] This may perhaps represent the survival of the former monastic chantries.

[78] Lich. Dioc. Regy., B/A/1/3, f. 33.
[79] *Cal. Pat.* 1405–8, 364–5, 367, 372, 374.
[80] Lich. Dioc. Regy., B/A/1/9, ff. 135v. sqq., 175v. sqq.; B.M., Harl. MS. 2179, ff. 29v.–30v. See *S.H.C.* 1937, p. 192, for an undated letter of the 15th cent. from Walter Griffyth to an Abbot of Burton asking 'whether it shall please you I shall await on you to hunt with you where it shall please you to command me to meet you and at what hour'.
[81] Lich. Dioc. Regy., B/A/1/11, ff. 56 sqq. He had tried to prevent the bishop's visiting the abbey by appealing to Canterbury: see below p. 209.
[82] D. & C. Lich., xviii, f. 3v.
[83] Lich. Dioc. Regy., B/A/1/13, f. 239v.
[84] Dugdale, *Mon.* iii. 50. But he remarks: 'Nec aliquid ab ipso factitatum compertum habemus quod magnopere laudari aut reprehendi possit.'
[85] Lich. Dioc. Regy., B/V/1/1, pp. 24–25, 72, and pp. 43–44 (2nd nos.).
[86] D. Knowles, *Religious Orders in Eng.* iii. 239 n.
[87] *S.H.C.* 1937, pp. 25–26. This may be the chantry

mentioned in connexion with the 1229 taxation: *Annales Monastici* (Rolls Ser.), i. 365.
[88] See below pp. 211, 213.
[89] *S.H.C.* 1937, pp. lvi–lvii and the references there given; see below p. 211.
[90] *S.H.C.* v(1), 58–59.
[91] Ibid. 1937, p. 135. In 1384 the endowments of this and of an anniversary of Rob. Lucas consisted of 3 houses in Burton: *Cal. Pat.* 1381–5, 385.
[92] *S.H.C.* 1937, p. 147.　　[93] Dugdale, *Mon.* iii. 49, 50.
[94] Ibid. 50.　　[95] *S.H.C.* 1937, p. 179.
[96] Dugdale, *Mon.* iii. 50; Lich. Dioc. Regy., B/V/1/1, pp. 24, 25. For the two Wards see Hist. MSS. Com. *Middleton*, 249; *S.H.C.* 1937, pp. 165, 166, 173, 177. At the visitation of 1524 there were complaints that the obit of Abbot Feld was not being observed as he had laid down: B/V/1/1, p. 43 (2nd nos.).
[97] *Valor Eccl.* iii. 147; its income was £8 13s. 4d. The only other chantry mentioned there is Abbot Bronston's, with an income of £4.
[98] *S.H.C.* 1915, 42; S.R.O., D.(W.)1734/2/3/31.

Another sidelight on 15th-century observance at Burton is the permission, granted in 1459 by the Pope in answer to a petition from the abbey, for the occasional celebration of mass even before daybreak, provided matins was over; this was for the benefit of the large number of laymen who went to the church before daybreak in order to hear mass.[99]

In the intellectual sphere the abbey's most notable achievement lay in its Annals which run from the foundation to 1262. Though not of great local interest, they are a particularly important source for the political history of the 13th century.[1] For the history of the house itself the account of St. Modwen's life and miracles written by Abbot Geoffrey (1114–50), who sent to Ireland for material, and the History of the Abbots are important sources.[2] A list dating from the late 12th century of the books owned by the abbey contains 78 titles, several of them works in Anglo-Saxon.[3] In 1309 the Burton archives were used for a certification of the date of the election of Roger Meuland as Bishop of Coventry and Lichfield.[4]

Burton, however, was a consistent defaulter in the duty of sending monks to study at a university. Defaulters were reported at four Benedictine chapters between 1343 and 1426, and Burton is the only house included on each occasion.[5] On the other hand Abbot Sudbury, himself a bachelor of canon law,[6] assigned a yearly pension out of the Austrey revenues to a scholar at Oxford. The terms of the arrangement seem to suggest that the abbey was already paying £7 10s. 4d. to a scholar as a charge on various endowed departments of the house. By 1535 £10 a year was being paid to Gloucester College, the Benedictine house at Oxford.[7]

At the visitation of 1524 there were complaints that the abbey had no instructor in grammar and that the books in the refectory were in a bad state of repair.[8] Abbot Boston (1531–3), however, was a doctor of theology,[9] and in 1535 one of the community was a bachelor of divinity.[10]

As a normal Benedictine house Burton Abbey was subject to episcopal visitation, despite its claim in 1257 to be exempt,[11] and a few such visitations are recorded from the 14th century.[12] Abbot Henley challenged the bishop's right to visit Burton and

appealed to the archbishop. In 1454, however, in Lichfield Cathedral he acknowledged his error and recognized the bishop's right.[13] The bishop was notified by the king of royal assent to the election of new abbots so that he could institute,[14] and in 1329 the king referred a disputed election to the bishop who made his own choice between the two candidates.[15] In 1412 the prior and other monks secured the bishop's support in a dispute with the abbot over privileges,[16] while at the election of a new abbot in 1430 the bishop imposed his own candidate, a monk of St. Albans, in opposition to the majority who favoured one of their own number.[17]

The abbot, however, exercised a peculiar jurisdiction in the parishes of Burton, Abbots Bromley, and Mickleover. In the late 11th or early 12th century the bishop granted that the mother-church of Burton should not pay customs for consecrated oil or 'any parochial thing' nor send any man or woman to chapters and synods but that it should hold its own court for all causes; nor was the chaplain of Burton to pay any custom or exaction to the Archdeacon of Stafford. The only qualification, 'so long as justice is not wanting', presumably implies a right of appeal to the bishop. This episcopal grant was confirmed by Theobald, Archbishop of Canterbury (1139–54), by his successor, Thomas Becket, by Walter Durdent, Bishop of Coventry (1149–59), by the Archdeacon of Stafford about 1180 and again in the early 13th century, by Archbishop Langton in 1215, and by Archbishop Pecham in 1280, who stated that the chaplain of Burton paid nothing to the bishop except 3s. for Peter's pence.[18] The bull of Pope Lucius III in 1185 confirmed existing liberties and recognized Burton's right of presenting clergy to its churches, of receiving bodies for burial within the abbey, of celebrating mass during a national interdict, and of sanctuary; the bishop was to grant chrism, holy oil, consecration of altars and churches, and ordinations.[19] The Archdeacon of Stafford in confirming the privileges of Burton parish about 1180 added the exemption of Bromley and Ilam from attendance at chapters and synods,[20] but in 1293 the abbot paid procurations to the archdeacon in respect of both.[21] Bromley, however, was included in the abbot's exempt jurisdiction by the 14th century.[22] By the 1270s the abbot was exercising a jurisdiction in the parish of Mickleover to

[99] Cal. Papal Regs. ix. 544–5.
[1] Annales Monastici (Rolls Ser.), i; D. Knowles, Religious Orders in Eng. i. 295–6; Hibbert, Dissolution, 200; Hist. MSS. Com. 14th Rep. App. VIII, 211. For the value of the Annals as a source of information on episcopal visitation of monasteries in the 13th cent. see C. R. Cheney, Episcopal Visitation of Monasteries in the 13th Cent. 13–14, 35, 72–74, 75, 87, 98, 107, 139.
[2] Dugdale, Mon. iii. 48 sqq.
[3] Hibbert, Dissolution, 200, 281–5; H. A. Omont, 'Anciens Catalogues de Bibliothèques Anglaises, XIIᵉ–XIVᵉ Siècle', Centralblatt für Bibliothekswesen, ix. 201–3; Medieval Libraries of Gt. Brit. ed. N. R. Ker (1964 edn.), 15–16.
[4] S.H.C. 1924, p. 341.
[5] Knowles, Religious Orders in Eng. ii. 18. The 'flat rate' system was unfair on smaller houses, and this consistent defaulting perhaps supports Burton's claim in 1310 to be the poorest Benedictine abbey in England (see above p. 200).
[6] Dugdale, Mon. iii. 49.
[7] S.H.C. 1937, pp. 159, 167; Valor Eccl. iii. 146. Burton occurs in the list of abbeys and priories which sent students to Gloucester College in Anthony Wood's Survey of the

Antiquities of the City of Oxford (Oxford Hist. Soc. xvii), 255.
[8] Lich. Dioc. Regy., B/V/1/1, pp. 43, 44 (2nd nos.).
[9] See below p. 213.   [10] L. & P. Hen. VIII, ix, p. 28.
[11] S.H.C. 1937, p. 57.
[12] Lich. Dioc. Regy., B/A/1/3, f. 33; ibid./9, ff. 135v., 175v.; ibid./11, f. 56; ibid./13, f. 239v.; B/V/1/1, p. 24. Bp. Langton (1296–1321), who carried out ordinations at Burton in 1300 (B/A/1/1, f. 93v.), evidently held a visitation at some time during his episcopate: Dugdale, Mon. iii. 46. Bp. Stretton is recorded at Burton in 1365 and 1366: S.H.C. N.S. x(2), 166, 216.
[13] B/A/1/11, f. 52.
[14] See e.g. Rot. Litt. Pat. (Rec. Com.), 108–9, 198; Cal. Pat. 1258–66, 82, 83; 1301–7, 392.
[15] Cal. Pat. 1327–30, 410, 442.
[16] S.H.C. 1937, p. 157.
[17] Hist. MSS. Com. Middleton, 248–50; Cal. Pat. 1429–36, 83.
[18] S.H.C. 1937, pp. 11–12, 25, 29, 80; v(1), 54; Acta Stephani Langton (Cant. & York Soc.), 26–27.
[19] Dugdale, Mon. iii. 42.   [20] S.H.C. v(1), 54.
[21] Ibid. 1937, p. 88.
[22] Ibid. pp. 121, 142.

the exclusion of the Archdeacon of Derby, although in 1295 the bishop in confirming the exemption ordered the abbot to pay 3s. a year to the archdeacon.[23] The abbot presumably had the right of parochial visitation within his peculiar, but there is little record of the functioning of his jurisdiction.[24]

Burton had to fight for the maintenance of these privileges. In the mid 13th century the bishop was complaining to the Pope that the abbot was usurping episcopal rights.[25] In the 1270s the jurisdiction in Mickleover had to be defended against the Archdeacon of Derby, and, though the abbot had the support of the papal judges and the Archbishop of Canterbury, the dispute dragged on. As seen above the bishop attempted a settlement in 1295 but evidently without success since in 1298 the Pope again intervened.[26] In 1324 there was a similar dispute between the abbot and the Archdeacon of Stafford over the abbot's jurisdiction in Burton and Abbots Bromley; the abbot's rights were recognized by a later archdeacon about 1350.[27] In the 1320s the bishop himself challenged the abbot's rights in the parishes of Burton, Bromley, and Mickleover, and the suit went to Canterbury and then to the Pope who in 1333 appointed judges to settle it; the result seems to have been in the abbot's favour. In the meantime the abbot complained to Canterbury about the bishop's infringement of the abbey's privileges by using or attempting to use Burton church for general ordinations; the dispute was cited to the archbishop's court in 1325 and again in 1333. There was also a dispute between the abbot and the bishop over the appropriation of Stapenhill; in 1326 this too was cited on appeal to the archbishop's court. In 1367 the bishop was evidently again challenging the abbot's exempt jurisdiction, and he visited Burton parish in 1390.[28] In 1378 the Archdeacon of Derby was summoned before the Court of Arches to answer the abbot's charge of interference with his jurisdiction in Mickleover.[29] By the 1530s the abbot was paying procurations to the bishop for Burton, Abbots Bromley, and Mickleover as well as for Ilam and Austrey; he also paid procurations to the archdeacon for Abbots Bromley and to the bishop for visitations of the abbey.[30] The abbot's probate jurisdiction in Burton eventually passed with the abbey's property to the Pagets, who continued to exercise it until 1858.[31]

The dissolution of Burton was foreshadowed at the election of 1533 following the promotion of Abbot Bronston to be Abbot of Westminster, the highest office known to have been attained by any monk of Burton. Bishop Lee, under instructions from Cromwell, went to Burton in June with Richard Strete, Archdeacon of Derby, and David Pole, the vicar general, and so 'sped the election' that the community agreed to leave the choice of a new abbot to the bishop and the archdeacon, stipulating only that one of themselves should be chosen before 1 August. Cromwell's original candidate seems to have been 'the monk Baylye', but William Edys, the 'third prior', was appointed.[32]

Early in 1538 Francis, Lord Hastings, wrote to Cromwell to point out that Burton Abbey lay 'very convenient' for him, adding that he would have asked for it earlier but for an attack of measles.[33] Later the same year the Crown tried to secure the tithes of Austrey for a royal official, but the abbot replied to Cromwell that the income was 'so necessary to our house that we cannot do without it'.[34] At the same time Sir William Bassett, of Meynell Langley (Derb.), removed the statue of St. Modwen, defaced its tabernacle, and forbade further offerings; he sent the statue to Cromwell by Francis Bassett, his brother, a servant to Cranmer.[35] In February 1539 Dr. John London was at Burton,[36] and on 14 November the abbot and community surrendered their house and its possessions to Dr. Thomas Legh.[37] Pensions ranging from £6 13s. 4d. to £2 were assigned to 7 monks: 5 priests, a deacon, and a novice. The abbot and probably four remaining monks became members of the new college at Burton which was already being planned, though it was not actually founded until 1541.[38] Robert Heathcote, one of the deacons, and Humphrey Cotton, the novice, were recorded as in receipt of their pensions when they died in 1552 and 1563.[39]

The abbey precincts occupied an area bounded on the east by the River Trent and on the west by the present High Street and Lichfield Street.[40] The church stood at the northern end of the site on ground now occupied by part of the Market Place and by the 18th-century church of St. Modwen. The cloister and the conventual buildings lay immediately south of the church, an area now largely covered by the late-19th-century market hall. Further to the south and west was a walled courtyard with an outer court beyond.[41] The latter was approached from the west through the gatehouse. South-east of the cloister and next to the river was a detached building thought to have been the infirmary.

Apart from limited excavations of the later 19th and early 20th centuries and a few surviving architectural features[42] the main evidence of the monastic

[23] Ibid. pp. 79, 82, 83–84, 89.
[24] Ibid. pp. xlv–xlvi. The constitutions noted ibid. pp. xlv, 137, as for the government of abbey and parish do not in fact appear to be particular to Burton.
[25] Ibid. 1924, p. 193.
[26] Ibid. 1937, pp. 79, 82, 83–84, 89, 116.
[27] Ibid. pp. 123, 124, 142.
[28] Ibid. pp. xlvii–xlviii; Lich. Dioc. Regy., B/A/1/6, ff. 40v.–41, 41v. For Langton's ordinations at Burton in 1300 see above n. 12.
[29] S.H.C. 1937, p. 142.   [30] Valor Eccl. iii. 145–6.
[31] A. J. Camp, Wills and their Whereabouts, 68; S.R.O., D.(W.)1734/2/8/1–72; see above p. 74 and below p. 298.
[32] Hibbert, Dissolution, 45–48; L. & P. Hen. VIII, vi, pp. 177, 190, 304, 313, 315–16, 338, 364, 449; vii, p. 233.
[33] L. & P. Hen. VIII, xiii(1), p. 106.
[34] Ibid. (2), p. 36.
[35] Ibid. pp. 95, 101; Hibbert, Dissolution, 158–9.
[36] L. & P. Hen. VIII, xiv(1), p. 86.
[37] Ibid. (2), p. 183.
[38] Ibid.; xv, p. 544; see below p. 297.
[39] E 178/3239, mm. 7, 8.
[40] For a reconstruction of the plan of the abbey site see H. A. Rye, 'The Ground-plan of Burton Abbey', Trans. Burton-on-Trent Nat. Hist. & Arch. Soc. iii(3), plan following p. 258.
[41] For the courts see ibid. 256 and plan following p. 258; C. H. Underhill, Hist. of Burton-upon-Trent (Burton, 1941), 21.
[42] Trans. Burton Nat. Hist. & Arch. Soc. iii(3), 245, 248, 258; H. A. Rye, 'Some Further Notes on Burton Abbey Plan', ibid. v(1), 35–39.

layout is provided by a plan of the church and cloister, probably drawn in the mid 16th century.[43] The church is known to have been divided into an upper and a lower church, that is, a monastic east end or choir and a non-monastic nave to the west, although the plan does not indicate any clear demarcation. It shows transepts on either side of the chancel with a tower above the crossing. A tower is also marked at the west end between two smaller transepts or porches. The nave extends westwards beyond the tower, and it has been suggested that this projection may have been a galilee or large western porch.[44] An engraving of the church from the south-west by Wenceslas Hollar in 1661[45] does not entirely agree with the earlier plan, but some of its discrepancies may be due to inaccurate drawing. The chancel has apparently disappeared, having fallen into ruin after the dissolution,[46] but a south transept is shown, ending in an ornate gable which has angle turrets and may be of late-13th-century date. There is a polygonal central tower as well as an embattled north-west tower with tall traceried windows. Any westward extension of the nave has either disappeared or is hidden by trees. It has been suggested that the curious fenestration of the south wall of the nave may be due to a lowering of the aisle roof after the dissolution, and the consequent exposure of a Norman triforium which was afterwards glazed.[47] The row of five arches, each enclosing a pair of round-headed openings, may represent such a triforium; the clerestory and embattled parapet above appear to be of later medieval date.

It is possible to trace the history of several of these features. The early-11th-century church seems already to have been divided into an upper and a lower church.[48] In 1114, at the end of his abbacy, Abbot Niel began building at the western end of the church, and his successor Geoffrey (1114–50) erected an elegant (*speciosum*) tower, roofed with lead, over the choir.[49] The nave shown by Hollar presumably dates from this period. The east end was remodelled in the late 13th and earlier 14th centuries. The chancel was rebuilt under Abbot Packington (1281–1305), and the work was evidently completed about 1293. A new high altar was dedicated by Abbot Burton (1305–16) at the end of 1305, and Abbot Brykhull (1340–7) was responsible

for a great window over the high altar.[50] The bell-tower (*clocharium*) mentioned in 1340 as adjoining the market-place[51] is presumably the north-west tower of the church, and this is probably the tower mentioned early in the 14th century.[52] Abbot Ibstock (1347–66), possibly while he was still almoner, rebuilt the northern side of the lower or parish church; Abbot Southam (1366–1400) recast the three great bells in the tower of the lower church.[53] Under Abbot Sudbury (1400–24) Richard Creyhton while sacrist carried out some work in stone in the chancel and reroofed the lower church; Richard Babe as prior and sacrist was responsible for some stone work in the tower of the upper church and also for new stalls in the choir.[54] Under Abbot Henley (1433–55) the tower of the lower church was completed and a bell placed in it.[55] In 1474–5 the tower of the upper church collapsed, causing extensive damage in that part of the building. Abbot Feld promptly repaired the damaged walls, rebuilt one of the four pillars of the choir and the arch between the upper and lower church, erected a new high altar with steps to it, reroofed the upper church, and began a new tower.[56]

There were several side chapels and altars in the church. The altar of Holy Cross is mentioned in the early 13th century and again in 1254.[57] Abbot de Lisle (1222–9), having come from Bury St. Edmunds, built and endowed a chapel of St. Edmund. This was repaired by Prior Richard Lythum shortly before 1428 when the bishop granted an indulgence to all who said prayers and masses there for the dead, and especially for the souls of Richard and his parents.[58] The chapel of St. Mary was begun under Abbot Laurence (1229–60), and in 1254 money was assigned to the sacrist for the maintenance of a lamp before the altar of St. Mary; probably about the same time a further gift was made for a candle before the statue of St Mary during the celebration of her daily mass. The chapel was evidently completed during the time of Abbot Stafford (1260–81) when Prior Michael 'made' it. It was the most important of the chapels, with its daily mass, its own keeper and, by the 15th century, its own singers; in 1535 its revenue from endowments was £4 a year.[59] The altar of St. Nicholas is mentioned in 1254,[60] and in 1305 Abbot Burton dedicated the altars of the

[43] For a copy by Stebbing Shaw see plate facing p. 212. A view in the W.S.L. allegedly of the ruined interior of the church in 1643 by Hollar is in fact one of the mid-19th-cent. forgeries of John Thompson: see Ida Darlington, 'Thompson Fecit', *Architectural Review*, Sept. 1958. Rye's article in *Trans. Burton Nat. Hist. & Arch. Soc.* v(1), is marred by the fact that it accepts the forgery as genuine.

[44] *Trans. Burton Nat. Hist. & Arch. Soc.* iii(3), 245. Although the existence of a galilee is not proved, the 'vestibulum' near the door of which Abbot Feld was buried in 1493 (Dugdale, *Mon.* iii. 50) may have been a galilee.

[45] See plate facing p. 212.

[46] About 1600 Sampson Erdeswick (*Staffs.* 474) noted the 'very large' ruins of the 'decayed' monastic end of the church.

[47] *Trans. Burton Nat. Hist. & Arch. Soc.* v(1), 40.

[48] Wulfric Spot, like his wife before him, was buried under a stone arch in the cloister, he near the door of the upper church and she near the door of the lower church: Dugdale, *Mon.* iii. 47.

[49] Ibid. 47–48, where Niel's work is described as 'novum opus in occidentali fine ecclesiae'; *Annales Monastici* (Rolls Ser.), i. 186; *S.H.C.* 1937, p. 8; *Trans. Burton Arch. Soc.* v(1), 37. The common seals in use in the 12th and 13th cents. depict what may have been intended as views of the abbey church from the west (see below p.

213); the value of seals as architectural evidence, however, is questionable.

[50] Dugdale, *Mon.* iii. 49. Packington is the first abbot mentioned as buried before the high altar instead of in a side chapel; his two successors and Abbot Brykhull were also buried before the high altar: ibid.

[51] *S.H.C.* 1937, p. 131.

[52] Abbot Burton (1305–16) erected a building between the tower and the long building of the sacristy: Dugdale, *Mon.* iii. 49.

[53] Ibid. This mentions in connexion with Ibstock's rebuilding 'deposita prius ibidem quadam magna synagoga'.

[54] Ibid.

[55] Ibid. 50. The building accounts, including payments for hanging 'the bell of St. Modwen' in the new tower, in S.R.O., D.(W.)1734/J.2022, evidently refer to this work.

[56] Dugdale, *Mon.* iii. 50.   [57] *S.H.C.* 1937, pp. 26, 50.

[58] Ibid. p. 162; see above p. 205.

[59] Dugdale, *Mon.* iii. 48; *S.H.C.* 1937, pp. 50, 52; *Valor Eccl.* iii. 147; see above p. 205. Both Abbot Stafford and Prior Michael were buried there. Abbot Mathew too was buried in the chapel 'supra gradum juxta sedile in muro ibidem'; Abbot Bronston, who endowed the singers there, was buried 'honorifice' in the chapel under a marble tomb: Dugdale, *Mon.* iii. 49, 50.

[60] *S.H.C.* 1937, p. 50.

Apostles and the Martyrs; ex-Abbot Southam was buried in the chapel of the Martyrs in 1401.[61] The chapel of the Confessors was built by Abbot Longdon (1329–40), and ex-Abbot Sudbury was buried there in 1425.[62]

Some time after the foundation of the abbey the remains of St. Modwen were transferred there from the nearby island of Andressey in the Trent.[63] A shrine was built in the abbey; decorated with gold, silver, and jewels, it was 'satis preciosum' by the time of Abbot Leofric (1051–66), who despoiled it to buy food for the poor during a famine.[64] William I visited the shrine.[65] It was rebuilt early in the 15th century by Prior Babe.[66]

Andressey, however, remained sacred to the memory of St. Modwen. A chapel of St. Andrew there was dedicated by the bishop early in the 13th century and endowed by Abbot Melburne.[67] It had its own keeper,[68] and in 1535 its income from offerings was £2.[69] It was rebuilt by Abbot Feld (1473–93) and was by then known as the chapel of St. Modwen.[70] It was evidently here that the statue of St. Modwen was kept 'with her red cow and her staff which women labouring of child in those parts were very desirous to have with them to lean upon and to walk with it'.[71]

Doors from the upper and lower church gave access to the cloister,[72] which the 16th-century plan gives as 100 feet square.[73] Some rebuilding of the cloister was carried out in 1431, beginning 'at the corner against the almonry' — probably the north-western corner. Bishop Heyworth's gifts to the abbey at his death in 1446 included £40 for building the cloister. The chapter-house led off the east walk and was rebuilt by Abbots Longdon (1329–40) and Brykhull (1340–7); traces have been found of the doorway and also of burials inside the building. The doorway to the south (which still survives) probably led into the parlour.[74] According to the 16th-century plan the east range continued southwards beyond the line of the cloister, presumably to accommodate the dorter on the first floor; a stairway

shown at the east end of the south walk presumably gave access to it. It is not clear whether the plan depicts the east range at the same level throughout. The dorter is shown separated from the south transept of the church by three 'chambers'. These chambers may be intended to represent the sacristy, chapter-house, and parlour, or, alternatively, rooms above them, and this part of the east range was evidently roofed separately from the dorter.[75] The dorter is shown with six cells along each side and what is presumably the rere-dorter at its south end. The frater occupied the south range. The west range was given over to the abbot's rooms; Abbot Ibstock (1347–66) added the abbot's private chamber between the great hall and the 'outward' chamber, while Abbot Feld (1473–93) erected what was described as the Abbot's Chamber.[76] The 'house of stone next to the church' given to the almoner by Abbot Laurence (1229–60) for the reception of the poor probably stood in this area.

In 1428 Abbot Mathew began building the southern part of the abbey gate on the west of the precinct opposite the end of the present New Street.[77] Abbot Henley (1433–55) built the northern part.[78] The bases of these two parts were noted at the end of the 18th century by Stebbing Shaw, who also recorded that formerly the gate had 'a lofty handsome arch'; the remains of the gate were demolished in 1927.[79] Abbot Burton (1305–16) erected 'a long building by the gates of the abbey', and in 1326 his successor Abbot Bromley assigned it to the chamberlain for use by the brethren as a common chamber.[80]

'The great hall by the water of the Flete' built by Abbot Bromley was probably part of the infirmary near the Trent.[81] Remains of medieval building in this area are incorporated in the house now called The Abbey. They include what is thought to have been a chapel which originally had a large pointed window at each end; a range at right angles to it was found in the late 19th century to be a partly timber-framed structure with an open roof.[82]

[61] Dugdale, *Mon.* iii. 49.

[62] Ibid. Abbot Longdon was buried 'sub arcu inter altare [*sic*] apostolorum et confessorum'.

[63] H. A. Rye, 'St. Modwen', *Trans. Burton Nat. Hist. & Arch. Soc.* iv(2), 43 (citing Abbot Geoffrey's Life of St. Modwen), 48. The 'second feast of St. Modwen' celebrated by 1229 (ibid. 46–47; *Ann. Mon.* i. 245) may refer to such a translation.

[64] *Trans. Burton Nat. Hist. & Arch. Soc.* iv(2), 43–44; Dugdale, *Mon.* iii. 47.

[65] See above p. 200.   [66] Dugdale, *Mon.* iii. 49.

[67] *S.H.C.* 1937, pp. 25–26. The Annals record that in 1201 'St. Wulstan of Worcester and St. Modwen of Burton shone with many and great miracles': *Ann. Mon.* i. 209. The History of the Abbots states that in Abbot Melburne's first year (1200–1) 'there was made a revelation of the relics of the church of Burton as appears in the book of the same revelation': Dugdale, *Mon.* iii. 48. The building of the chapel may well be connected with these events.

[68] Burton Corp., Anglesey MSS., J.46. The warden is not mentioned in the calendared version of the charter in *S.H.C.* 1937, pp. 25–26.

[69] See above p. 204. 'Andreseya' was included among the abbey's taxable property in 1229: *Ann. Mon.* i. 365.

[70] Dugdale, *Mon.* iii. 50. 'The measure of lead' upon it was given in 1546 as 60 ft. in length and 27 ft. in breadth: S.R.O., D.(W.)1734/2/3/9, f. 15v.

[71] Hibbert, *Dissolution*, 158–9; *L. & P. Hen. VIII*, xiii(2), p. 101. For the removal of the statue and the defacing of its tabernacle in 1538 see above p. 210.

[72] Where Wulfric Spot and his wife were buried shortly after the foundation of the monastery: see above n. 48. For this para. in general see Rye's article in *Trans.*

Burton Nat. Hist. & Arch. Soc. iii(3); Dugdale, *Mon.* iii. 48–50; Hibbert, *Dissolution*, 262–3. For some account of the dimensions of the buildings, courts, and garden in 1546 and 1562 see S.R.O., D.(W.)1734/2/3/9, ff. 15–16; /2/3/29.

[73] The measurement of the lead on the roof, in S.R.O., D.(W.)1734/2/3/9, f. 15v., is only 72 ft. in length.

[74] Shaw, *Staffs.* i. 9, mentions 'several curious old arches' still visible in this area and shows them on the plate facing. See also W.S.L., Staffs. Views, ii, p. 192.

[75] The survey of the lead on the roofs of the abbey buildings in 1546 distinguishes the roof of the chapter-house (66 ft. long) and the roof of the dorter (123 ft. long): S.R.O., D.(W.)1734/2/3/9, f. 15v.

[76] 'The King's Chamber' was evidently in this part of the abbey: Hibbert, *Dissolution*, 263. The house known as The Priory, which was demolished to make way for the market hall of 1883, evidently incorporated remains of the abbot's house: Underhill, *Burton-upon-Trent*, 175.

[77] Dugdale, *Mon.* iii. 49. He also began the 'causetum novi vici ante portas abbatiae' as well as a new pavement with a gutter in the middle of the 'high town'.

[78] Ibid. 50. He also pulled down 'hiemalem aulam et stabulum hospitum'.

[79] Shaw, *Staffs.* i. 9 and plate facing; W.S.L., Staffs. Views, ii, p. 181; Underhill, *Burton-upon-Trent*, 21.

[80] Dugdale, *Mon.* iii. 49; *S.H.C.* 1937, p. 125.

[81] Dugdale, *Mon.* iii. 49.

[82] *Trans. Burton Nat. Hist. & Arch. Soc.* iii(3), 255–6 and plate III; W.S.L., Staffs. Views, ii, pp. 181, 199. The measurements of the lead on the various abbey buildings in 1546 include 'the fermery cloister', 75 × 12 ft., a larger measurement than that given for the main cloister, 72 × 12 ft.: S.R.O., D.(W.)1734/2/3/9, f. 15v.

A view of the church from the south-west in 1661

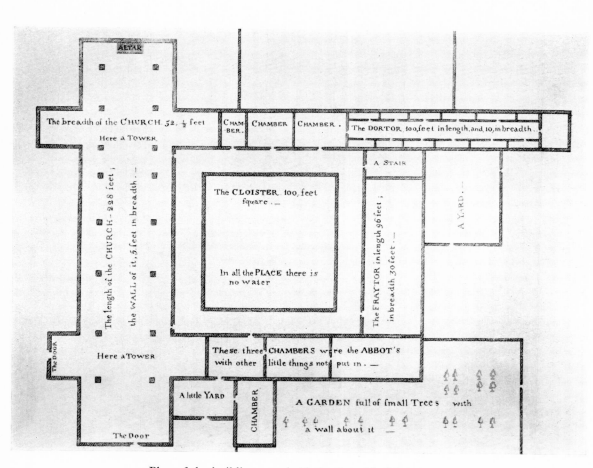

Plan of the buildings, probably in the mid 16th century

BURTON ABBEY

SEAL OF ROCESTER ABBEY

SEAL OF BURTON COLLEGE

THE FRANCISCAN FRIARY, LICHFIELD, 1782

THE PRIORY CHURCH, FAREWELL, IN THE 1740S

ABBOTS[83]

Wulfgeat, by 1004, died 1026.

Brihtric, succeeded 1027, died 1050.

Leofric, arrived 1051, died 1066.[84]

Brihtric, succeeded 1066 or 1067.[85]

Geoffrey Mauland (Malaterra), succeeded 1085, expelled 1094.

Niel, succeeded 1094, died 1114.

Geoffrey, succeeded 1114, resigned 1150.[86]

Robert, succeeded 1150, deposed and expelled 1159.

Bernard, arrived 1160, died 1174 or 1175.[87]

Robert, returned 1176, died 1176 or 1177.[88]

Roger Malebranche, elected 1177, died 1182.[89]

Richard, succeeded 1182, died 1187.[90]

Nicholas, succeeded 1187, died 1197.[91]

William Melburne, arrived 1200, died 1214.[92]

Roger the Norman, elected 1214, died 1216.[93]

Nicholas of Wallingford, elected 1216, died 1222.[94]

Richard de Lisle (de Insula), elected 1222, elected Abbot of Bury St. Edmunds 1229.[95]

Laurence of St. Edward, elected 1229, died 1260.[96]

John of Stafford, elected 1260, resigned 1281.[97]

Thomas of Packington, elected 1281, died 1305.[98]

John of Burton, *alias* of Stapenhill, *alias* Fisher, elected 1305, died 1316.[99]

William of Bromley, elected 1316, died 1329.[1]

Robert of Longdon, appointed by the bishop in 1329 after a disputed election, died 1340.[2]

Robert de Brykhull, elected 1340, died 1347.[3]

John of Ibstock, elected 1347, died 1366.[4]

Thomas of Southam, elected 1366, resigned 1400.[5]

John Sudbury, B.Cn.L., elected 1400, resigned 1424.[6]

William Mathew, elected 1424, resigned 1430.[7]

Robert Ownesby, imposed by the bishop 1430, resigned 1433.[8]

Ralph Henley, elected 1433, resigned 1455.[9]

William Bronston, elected 1455, died 1473.[10]

Thomas Feld, elected 1473, died 1493.[11]

William Flegh, elected 1493, died 1502.[12]

William Bene, elected 1502, died 1530 or 1531.[13]

William Boston, D. Th., elected 1531, elected Abbot of Westminster 1533.[14]

William Edys, appointed 1533, surrendered the abbey in 1539.[15]

The earliest known seal of the abbey is that in use under Abbot Geoffrey (1114–50), depicting what may be intended as a view of the church from the west; there are two flanking towers and what may be the tower over the crossing.[16] No legend has survived.

The seal in use by the early 13th century and until at least 1284 is a pointed oval, $3\frac{1}{8}$ by $2\frac{1}{4}$ in.[17] It depicts a woman, probably the Virgin, crowned and seated on a throne formed by a church with four towers; she holds a book in her left hand and a fleur-de-lis in her right. Legend, lombardic:

SIG[I]LLUM SANCTE MARIE D[E] [B]URTONA

An impression of the 1220s has as reverse an oval counterseal, $1\frac{5}{8}$ by $1\frac{1}{8}$ in., depicting the head and shoulders of St. Modwen. Legend, lombardic:

SANCTA MODWENNA

The common seal in use in 1493 is a pointed oval, about $1\frac{1}{2}$ by about 1 in.[18] It depicts the Virgin seated with the Child on her left knee, and in the base the head and left arm of a man, probably an abbot, under a canopy. Legend, lombardic:

... ET CO ... E ... U ...

3. THE PRIORY OF CANWELL

THE priory of monks at Canwell, in the parish of Hints, was founded by Geva, illegitimate daughter of Hugh I, Earl of Chester, and widow of Geoffrey Ridel, a justice under Henry I who was drowned in 1120 in the wreck of the White Ship.[1] The exact date of the foundation is unknown, but it can be assigned to about 1140. The priory was a Benedictine

---

[83] Unless otherwise stated, the list is based on the Burton Annals (in *Annales Monastici* (Rolls Ser.), i), the less accurate History of the Abbots in Dugdale, *Mon.* iii. 47–50, and from 1214 the Patent Rolls (the king as patron gave permission for elections and approved the abbots-elect).

[84] *V.C.H. Wilts.* iii. 215n.   [85] Ibid. 215.

[86] Prior of Winchester. He died in 1151.

[87] *Letters and Charters of Gilbert Foliot*, ed. A. Morey and C. N. L. Brooke, pp. 531–2. Formerly a monk at Gloucester, he became Abbot of Cerne but withdrew 'because of the great embellishments of the same house'.

[88] *Letters and Charters of Gilbert Foliot*, p. 537.

[89] Ibid.; Benedict of Peterborough, *Gesta Regis Henrici Secundi* (Rolls Ser.), i. 180. He was Prior of Gt. Malvern.

[90] Prior of Rochester. He may have d. 1188: the History of the Abbots gives Apr. 33 Hen. II (1187) and 1188.

[91] Prior of Abingdon. He may have succeeded 1188: see above n.90.

[92] Monk of Reading. In 1199 the monks of Burton gave the king 200 marks 'ut idoneus pastor domui sue proficiatur sine dilatione et ut interim sit abbatia illa in manu eorum': *Rot. de Ob. et Fin.* (Rec. Com.), 31.

[93] Prior of Winchester.

[94] Prior of Burton and thus the first monk of Burton to become abbot there. He is stated to have resigned in *Rot. Litt. Claus.* (Rec. Com.), i. 494.

[95] Prior of Bury St. Edmunds.

[96] Kitchener at Burton.

[97] Prior. He died a month after his resignation.

[98] Prior.   [99] Prior.   [1] Cellarer.

[2] Prior of Tutbury and previously monk of Burton. For the election see above p. 209.

[3] Cellarer acc. to Dugdale, *Mon.* iii. 49; prior acc. to *Cal. Pat.* 1338–40, 443.

[4] Almoner.

[5] Chaplain of the abbot. He died in 1401.

[6] Sacrist. He died the year following his resignation; Dugdale, *Mon.* iii. 49, wrongly dates his death as in 1439, describing this as the year following his resignation.

[7] Almoner. He died in 1431.

[8] Monk of St. Albans. For the election see above p. 209.

[9] Monk of Burton. His resignation followed his suspension by the bishop: see above p. 208.

[10] Cellarer.

[11] Monk of Burton.   [12] Kitchener.

[13] Prior. He was dead by 8 Feb. 1531 when royal permission was granted for the election of his successor: *L. & P. Hen. VIII*, v, p. 55.

[14] Ibid. pp. 81, 129. Monk of Peterborough. He occurs as Benson *alias* Boston in a general pardon of 1547: *Cal. Pat.* 1548–9, 159.

[15] See above p. 210. He was 'third prior'.

[16] *S.H.C.* 1921, plate facing p. 1.

[17] W. de G. Birch, *Cat. of Seals in B.M.* i, pp. 471–2; B.M., Stowe Ch. 143; B.M. Add. Ch. 27314–16; *S.H.C.* 1913, plate facing p. 300; Shaw, *Staffs.* i, plate facing p. 6.

[18] Burton Corp., Anglesey MSS., J.742; Shaw, *Staffs.* i, plate facing p. 6.

[1] *D.N.B. sub* Ridel; W. Farrer, *Honors and Knights' Fees*, ii. 269–70.

house dedicated to St. Giles.[2] There was a spring near the site, and this was known in later times at least as St. Modwen's Well.[3]

There are two early charters relating to the foundation, both issued by Geva. In the first[4] she announces the foundation as being for the souls of herself, her ancestors, and her kinsmen and as made 'by the authority of Bishop Roger of Chester [1129–48] and by the assent of Ranulf, Earl of Chester [1129–53]' and grants the monks the land of 'Stichesleia',[5] a meadow called 'Litemersia',[6] the mill of Fazeley, 5 virgates at Dunton Bassett (Leics.), including a virgate given by Osbert, Geva's chaplain, and a mill in Dunton Bassett called 'le Corre'. The foundation was made with the assent of Geva's grandsons and heirs, Geoffrey Ridel and Ralph Bassett, and this shows that the charter was issued after the death of her son-in-law Richard Bassett who married her daughter Maud in 1123.[7] Richard was still living in 1131,[8] and therefore Geva's foundation must be dated between 1131 and 1148.

Geva's second charter[9] granted part of a grove at Canwell and a house and lands at Drayton Bassett to the monks and the previous grants were restated. Furthermore she gave them the churches of Dunton Bassett and Ragdale (Leics.). The monks were also to hold a court. This second charter cannot have been issued before 1143 as one of the witnesses was Richard, Abbot of Leicester (elected 1143–4).

In 1148 the Pope confirmed the monks in their possession of all that had been granted to them by Geva and also of a meadow in Elford granted by Robert of Weeford and 60 acres in 'Witemore' near 'Sticeleia'.[10] Other early grants included 3 virgates at Hill in Sutton Coldfield (Warws.) given by Roger, Earl of Warwick (1123–53), and confirmed by his son Earl Waleran (1184–1204);[11] land at Langley in Sutton Coldfield and the mill at Bitterscote in Tamworth parish given by Ralph Bassett of Drayton, the grandson of Geva who died shortly before 1166;[12] and a virgate and meadowland adjoining in Curdworth (Warws.) given by Cecily, sister of Hugh of Arden about 1150.[13]

These slender resources, even with some later additions, could not have supported a very large establishment, and it is doubtful whether there were ever more than a very few monks at Canwell, which remained a poor and insignificant monastery. The patronage was retained by the Drayton branch of the Bassett family down to 1390, and several confirmations were issued by successive members of the family. After the extinction of the line of the Bassetts of Drayton the Beauchamp family, earls of Warwick, inherited the patronage. Finally it passed to the Lisle family who retained it until the dissolution of the priory.[14]

Canwell evidently remained undisturbed in its possession of the church of Dunton Bassett, which had been appropriated to the priory by 1220.[15] On the other hand the advowson of Ragdale was lost in 1261 at an assize of *darrein presentment* where there were three contending parties — the Prior of Canwell, Beatrice de Coleville, and Ralph Bassett of Drayton. After the prior had withdrawn his claim judgment was given by the jury in favour of Ralph Bassett, who thereupon exercised his right of presentation.[16] The outcome of this case is somewhat surprising in view of Geva's grant, of the patronage exercised by the Bassett family over the priory, and of the statement in the *matriculus* of Hugh de Welles, Bishop of Lincoln (1209–35), that the Prior of Canwell was the patron of the church of Ragdale and that the parson paid the prior *ab antiquo* 3 marks and a lump of wax.[17] Over a century later the rights of Canwell were restored when in 1389 Ralph Bassett, the last of the Bassetts of Drayton, granted the monks in free alms the patronage of the church of Ragdale.[18] In 1414 the priory recovered the advowson from Sir Ralph Shirley, Ralph Bassett's kinsman and heir.[19] From this time the monks retained the right of presentation until the dissolution, but they seem to have been remiss in exercising it. In 1538 old men of Ragdale affirmed that 'there hath been neither parson nor vicar by the space of nine score years now last past'.[20] Ragdale was appropriated to the priory by the 15th century, the monks paying the Bishop of Lincoln 1 mark from the church.[21] The only other church in which the priory had any interest was that of Ashby Parva (Leics.), from which in the 13th century at least the monks received 4s. annually.[22]

A substantial addition to the endowments of the priory was made about the mid 13th century on the death of Philippa Marmion. A hundred marks were assigned to the monks from her estate on condition that Ralph Bassett — who was later killed at the Battle of Evesham in 1265 — and his heirs should present a secular clerk to the prior and convent to

---

[2] *Sir Christopher Hatton's Bk. of Seals*, ed. L. C. Loyd and Doris M. Stenton, pp. 35–36; Dugdale, *Mon.* iv. 106–7; Lich. Dioc. Regy., B/A/1/2, f. 197; ibid./11, f. 61; C 142/76/36. Geva founded the priory in honour of St. Mary, St. Giles, and All Saints: Dugdale, *Mon.* iv. 105.

[3] Shaw, *Staffs.* ii. 22*.

[4] Dugdale, *Mon.* iv. 105.

[5] A survey *temp.* Hen. VIII mentions a piece of ground near Canwell called 'Olde Stycheleys': ibid. 109.

[6] The copy of the charter in B.M., Harl. MS. 2060, f. 21, gives 'Littlemersia'. In Geva's second charter (see below) as given by Dugdale the meadow is called 'Litlemers'.

[7] F. M. Stenton, *First Century of Eng. Feudalism* (2nd edn.), 33 sqq.

[8] J. H. Round, *Geoffrey de Mandeville*, 265.

[9] Dugdale, *Mon.* iv. 106; *Cal. Pat.* 1408–13, 269–70.

[10] Dugdale, *Mon.* iv. 106.

[11] Ibid. In 1220 Alan de Morcote tried to dispossess the monks at Hill but the attempt failed: *Curia Regis R.* ix. 367.

[12] Dugdale, *Mon.* iv. 106–7.

[13] *Sir Christopher Hatton's Bk. of Seals*, pp. 35–36.

[14] T. Madox, *Formulare Anglicanum* (1702), 16; *Cal. Inq. p.m. Hen. VII*, i. p. 339; Shaw, *Staffs.* ii. 3–5, 12–13; Hibbert, *Dissolution*, 24–25; Dugdale, *Mon.* iv. 106–7; E 327/30.

[15] *Rot. Hugonis de Welles* (Cant. & York Soc.), i. 241, 274; *Rot. Roberti Grosseteste* (Cant. & York Soc.), 415; *Rot. Ricardi Gravesend* (Cant. & York Soc.), 152.

[16] *S.H.C.* iv(1), 147; *Rot. Ric. Gravesend*, 142. His son presented in 1275: ibid. 158. Beatrice was claiming dower in the manor of Ragdale.

[17] *Rot. H. de Welles*, i. 260.

[18] *Cal. Pat.* 1408–13, 270.

[19] Bodl. MS. Staffs. Charters 20; Shaw, *Staffs.* ii. 5 and n.

[20] *L. & P. Hen. VIII*, xiii(1), p. 72.

[21] Lich. Dioc. Regy., B/A/1/11, f. 10; *L. & P. Hen. VIII*, xiii(1), pp. 16, 412; ibid. xix(1), p. 632.

[22] *Rot. H. de Welles*, i. 243; *Tax Eccl.* (Rec. Com.), 63. The church was appropriated to the Knights Hospitallers.

be made a monk and to celebrate divine service for the souls of Philippa and her family.[23] The only indication of the priory's wealth in the assessment of 1291 is the value of £9 8s. placed on its temporalities in the deanery of Guthlaxton in the archdeaconry of Leicester and the pension of 4s. from Ashby Parva.[24] In 1292 William de Meynill was given licence to alienate 4 acres of land in Hints to the priory.[25] By will of 1389 the last Ralph Bassett of Drayton (d. 1390) left £200 and property in Lichfield and Walsall; part of this was to be used for the augmentation of the community by five monks — a provision which was probably never carried out — and 'to make a wall towards the water and a new belfry'.[26] At an episcopal visitation in 1453 the prior gave the annual yearly value of the lands of the priory, including meadow and pasture, as 100s.; the annual income, including the tithes of the appropriated churches, amounted to £21 4s. 8d.[27]

Little is known of the internal history of the priory. At least four priors were Cluniacs.[28] In the mid 1230s, 1313, and 1315 priors of Canwell are found acting as papal judges delegate.[29] In 1272 a monk of Canwell, William de Sutton, killed a man, fled, and was outlawed; the prior was fined 1 mark for having let him escape, and Ralph Bassett stood surety for the prior.[30] The community consisted of the prior and three monks in 1377.[31] In the 15th and early 16th centuries it appears that there were never more than two or three monks in the priory. Often there was only one, and the death of Prior Sadeler in 1456 left the house without any monks at all.[32] The frequent resignations from the priorate suggest that the resident monks took it in turn to be prior. On resignation the prior received a pension. For instance in 1400, when John Molton resigned for the first time, it was arranged that he was to have lodgings in the part of the priory lately built by Ralph Bassett and to receive good food at the prior's table and an annual allowance of 33s. 4d. in silver pennies for dress and other necessaries.[33] At the episcopal visitation of 1453 John Bredon, who while he was prior (1443–7) had been imprisoned and then pardoned for murder, was stated by the prior to be the only other member of the community; he was not resident and was in receipt of an annual pension of £4. The vicar general ordered that the pension should cease to be paid and that John should return to the priory; the £4 was to be spent on immediate repairs to the church.[34]

In the 14th and 15th centuries there were a number of petty disputes between the local inhabitants in Hints and Drayton Bassett and the priory, generally over the cutting down of trees and underwood. The priors were invariably the defendants.[35]

In 1517 the prior brought a case to Star Chamber, complaining bitterly of the violence of the men of Drayton Bassett.[36]

Canwell was one of the 21 monasteries scheduled for dissolution in 1524 in pursuance of Cardinal Wolsey's project for founding Cardinal College, Oxford.[37] Only one other of these houses was poorer than Canwell; its spiritualities were valued in 1526 at £10 and its temporalities at £15 10s. 3d. The possessions of the priory consisted of the manor and demesne at Canwell and, elsewhere in Staffordshire, lands in Drayton Bassett, Fazeley, Hints, Weeford, Packington (in Weeford), Bitterscote, Whittington, and Elford; in Warwickshire lands in Little Sutton, Hill, Tamworth, and Nether Whitacre; and in Leicestershire the rectory of Dunton and lands there and the rectory of Ragdale. At an inquest held at Walsall in 1525 it was stated that the prior and the only other monk at Canwell had freely resigned the priory into the hands of Wolsey and had gone to other monasteries. One of them was evidently the old priest who was farming the church at Ragdale in 1538. The property was conveyed by the king to Wolsey in January 1526 and by Wolsey to the Dean of Cardinal College in February. In 1530 the college drew £14 6s. from the Canwell property. After the fall of Wolsey Canwell's possessions reverted to the king. The process of dissolution was completed in 1530 when Thomas Cromwell and William Burbank spent three days at Canwell and sold goods to the value of £8. The bells were valued at £13 6s. 8d. The former prior was paid £1 and the other monk 6s. 8d., while the prior's father and the servants received £2 between them and the valuers ('praysors') 3s. 4d. In 1532 much of Canwell's property passed to St. George's Chapel, Windsor.[38] The rectories of Dunton and Ragdale were granted to the Oxford college in that year but were in the king's hands in 1538.[39] The manor of Canwell was held by John Veysey, Bishop of Exeter, at his death in 1554.[40]

A survey of Canwell manor made in 1526[41] described the priory church as 84 feet long and 23 feet wide, the nave and chancel being under a single roof covered with tile. The Lady Chapel on the north side of the chancel, 42 × 14 feet, was ruinous, and all but one side of the cloister had fallen down. There was a house on the west side of the manor partly tiled and shingled and partly thatched. It was 69 × 15 feet and contained three parlours and three upper chambers; 'an entry like a gallery' adjoined the house, and the timber throughout was in a bad state. A hall recently repaired and a ruinous kitchen were also mentioned. At the south end of the entry was a stable, 36 × 12 feet, with three chambers. At the east end of the

[23] Dugdale, *Mon.* iv. 107. The priest was to provide his own vestments.
[24] *Tax. Eccl.* 63, 67, 74.
[25] *Cal. Pat.* 1281–92, 484.
[26] Dugdale, *Baronage of Eng.* i (1675), 381. See below for a ref. in 1400 to the part of the priory lately built by Ralph Bassett. The bequest was also intended to endow a chantry priest in Lichfield Cathedral and an obit. In a will of 1383–4 he left Canwell 200 marks to secure certain lands and a mill in Warws.: ibid. 380.
[27] Lich. Dioc. Regy., B/A/1/11, f. 10.
[28] See below nn. 51, 59, 62, 65. It was perhaps this that gave rise to the erroneous statement sometimes found in medieval documents that Canwell was a Cluniac priory; see e.g. the documents relating to its suppression (E 21/3).
[29] *S.H.C.* 1924, pp. 42, 236, 248–9.
[30] Ibid. iv(1), 214.
[31] E 179/20/595.
[32] See below nn. 62, 63, 65, 66, 67.
[33] Lich. Dioc. Regy., B/A/1/7, f. 164v.
[34] Ibid./11, f. 10; *Cal. Pat.* 1446–52, 107.
[35] *S.H.C.* xiii. 40; xvii. 71, 103, 110; N.S. iii. 151.
[36] Ibid. 1910, 8.
[37] For this para, unless otherwise stated, see Hibbert, *Dissolution*, 22–26; *L. & P. Hen. VIII*, iv, pp. 848, 888, 2792; v, p. 86; xiii(1), pp. 16, 72; C 142/76/36; E 36/164, pp. 95, 96 (summarized in Dugdale, *Mon.* iv. 108); E 36/165, ff. 1–17v. (part of which is given in Dugdale, *Mon.* iv. 108–9).
[38] *L. & P. Hen. VIII*, v, p. 579.
[39] Ibid. p. 411; xiii(1), p. 412.
[40] Shaw, *Staffs.* ii. 22.
[41] Dugdale, *Mon.* iv. 108–9 (transcript of E 36/165, ff. 1–3v.); *L. & P. Hen. VIII*, iv, p. 985.

hall was a ruinous building, 41 × 24 feet, with a kiln, a bolting-house and an upper room for corn. There was also mention of a decayed dovecote and a ruinous barn 112 × 28 feet. In the later 18th century the new stables of Canwell Hall were erected on what was said to be the site of the priory, using the remaining ruins.[42]

PRIORS

William, occurs 1148.[43]

Denis, occurs about 1150.[44]

Hugh, occurs about 1184.[45]

H., occurs 1209 and at some date between 1200 and 1216.[46]

Hugh, occurs 1247–8.[47]

Thomas, occurs about 1289 and in 1295.[48]

Walter, occurs 1315.[49]

Henry de Roulegh, died by April 1355.[50]

John de Kyngeston, elected 1355, occurs to 1369.[51]

John Molton, occurs 1386, resigned 1400.[52]

Robert de Atterton, appointed by the bishop with the consent of the monks 1400.[53]

John Molton, resigned 1407.[54]

Robert de Atterton, elected and presented to the patron 1407, occurs to 1423.[55]

Thomas, occurs 1425.[56]

Robert de Atterton, occurs 1426, resigned 1433.[57]

Henry Sadeler *alias* Assheburn,[58] elected 1433, resigned 1443.[59]

John Bredon, elected 1443, resigned 1447.[60]

Henry Sadeler *alias* Assheburn, appointed 1447, died 1456.[61]

John Rakkis, appointed 1456, died 1468.[62]

John Tyttewell, appointed 1468, resigned 1469 or January 1470.[63]

Hugh Lempster, appointed 1470, resigned 1503.[64]

Robert Bentley, appointed 1503, died 1511.[65]

John Muchelney, appointed 1511, resigned by February 1516.[66]

John Alston, appointed 1516.[67]

William Becham, occurs 1517, surrendered the priory in 1524 or 1525.[68]

The priory seal in use in the early 15th century depicts the Annunciation with the head and shoulders of a praying figure below.[69] Legend, lombardic:

AVE MARIA GRATIA PLENA

4. THE PRIORY OF SANDWELL

SANDWELL Priory in West Bromwich was evidently preceded by a hermitage associated with the spring, still in existence, from which the priory took its name. Nothing more, however, is known of this stage of religious life at Sandwell. The founder of the priory was William, son of Guy de Offeni, a principal tenant of Gervase Paynel, lord of Dudley.[1] The date usually given for the foundation is about 1190,[2] but there seems no reason why it could not have been at least ten years earlier.[3] Sandwell was a house of Benedictine monks dedicated to St. Mary Magdalen[4] with the successive lords of West Bromwich manor as patrons.[5]

No foundation charter is known to have survived, but a confirmation of William's foundation by Gervase Paynel gives details of the original endowment of the priory.[6] William gave the monks dwelling in the hermitage by the spring called

---

[42] Shaw, *Staffs.* ii. 22*.

[43] Dugdale, *Mon.* iv. 106.

[44] *S.H.C.* 1939, pp. 182–3.

[45] Ibid. xvii. 242, 251.

[46] Ibid. 250; *Cartulary of Oseney Abbey, vol. v* (Oxford Hist. Soc. xcviii), 96; Dugdale, *Mon.* iv. 112.

[47] *S.H.C.* xv. 37, 38.

[48] Dugdale, *Mon.* iv. 104; Bodl. MS. Staffs. Charters 17.

[49] *S.H.C.* 1924, p. 42.

[50] Lich. Dioc. Regy., B/A/1/2, f. 197.

[51] Ibid.; *S.H.C.* xiii. 40; Bodl. MS. Staffs. Charters 18. He was a Cluniac of Bermondsey (Surr.). He occurs as Prior of Sandwell from 1370 to 1379: see below p. 219.

[52] Bodl. MS. Staffs. Charters 19; see above p. 215.

[53] Lich. Dioc. Regy., B/A/1/7, f. 51v. He was a monk of Canwell.

[54] Ibid. f. 64v.

[55] Ibid.; Madox, *Formulare Anglicanum*, 16; *Cal. Pat.* 1408–13, 269; *Cat. Anct. D.* i, B. 1349. The community in 1407 numbered 3, including Molton and Atterton: E 327/30.

[56] *S.H.C.* N.S. iii. 157.

[57] *S.H.C.* xvii. 110; Lich. Dioc. Regy., B/A/1/9, f. 63.

[58] For this *alias* see B/A/1/11, f. 61.

[59] Ibid./9, ff. 63, 70v. He was a Cluniac of Bermondsey.

[60] Ibid. f. 70v.; Lambeth Palace Libr., Reg. Stafford, f. 93. He was a monk of Canwell.

[61] Reg. Stafford, f. 93; Lich. Dioc. Regy., B/A/1/11, f. 61. He was a monk of Canwell, appointed by the Archbishop of Canterbury during a vacancy at Lichfield. He was described as a monk of Burton in 1453: ibid. f. 10.

[62] B/A/1/11, f. 61; ibid./12, f. 45v. He was a Cluniac of Lenton (Notts.). The bishop appointed as there were no monks left at Canwell. A document of 1461 (Bodl. MS. Staffs. Charters 21) gives the prior as John Chetforde.

[63] B/A/1/12, f. 45v. The bishop appointed as there were no other monks at Canwell.

[64] Ibid.; ibid./14, f. 21v. He was admitted to the guild of Lichfield in 1474: Harwood, *Lichfield*, 406. He was said to be aged 60 in 1516: *S.H.C.* N.S. x(1), 99, 101.

[65] B/A/1/14, ff. 21v., 22. He was a Cluniac of Lenton.

The bishop appointed him as there were no other monks at Canwell apart, presumably, from the ex-prior. He was admitted to the guild of Lichfield in 1503: Harwood, *Lichfield*, 411.

[66] B/A/1/14, f. 22, 22v. The bishop again appointed as there were no other monks.

[67] Ibid. f. 22v. He was a monk of Worcester brought in by the bishop as Canwell was 'destitute of monks'. He had been a scholar of Gloucester College, Oxford, and in 1507 had been admitted to oppose for B.Th.: A. B. Emden, *Biog. Reg. of Univ. of Oxford to A.D. 1500*, i. 28.

[68] *S.H.C.* 1910, 8; C 142/76/36.

[69] J. Nichols, *Hist. and Antiquities of the County of Leics.* iii(1), 386 and plate facing p. 383. The specimen there illustrated does not seem to have survived, but a fragment possibly of the same seal is attached to a document of 1407: E 327/30.

[1] For Wm. see *S.H.C.* i. 198.

[2] Shaw, *Staffs.* ii. 128; Dugdale, *Mon.* iv. 189; D. Knowles and R. N. Hadcock, *Medieval Religious Houses: Eng. and Wales*, 76.

[3] The founder occurs in 1166 (see ref. in n. 1) while Payne de Parles, who occurs as 'dapifer de Parles' among the witnesses of Gervase Paynel's confirmation of the foundation, occurs in 1166 and 1179–80: *S.H.C.* i. 96, 168. Wrottesley gives the date of foundation as *c.* 1180: ibid. 198.

[4] *S.H.C.* xvii. 56; *Cal. Inq. p.m.* (Rec. Com.), iv. 177, 234; Lich. Dioc. Regy., B/A/1/12, ff. 56, 59; C 142/60/62; see below p. 219. A document of 1218 describes it simply as the priory of St. Mary: *Cal. Feet of Fines for Bucks.* (Bucks. Rec. Soc. iv), 37. In 1436 it is called the priory of Holy Trinity and St. Mary: B.M., Harl. MS. 2179, ff. 137v.–139.

[5] Mary Willett, *Hist. of West Bromwich* (West Bromwich, 1882), 4 sqq.; *Cal. Inq. p.m.* (Rec. Com.), iv. 177, 234; *L. & P. Hen. VIII*, iv, pp. 1594, 1711; Hibbert, *Dissolution*, 25; and see below p. 217.

[6] Dugdale, *Mon.* iv. 190. The original of this confirmation too seems not to have survived, and Dugdale's text is evidently corrupt.

Sandwell all the land round the spring, some of his tenants in West Bromwich, 'Wavera' (perhaps a weir or horse-pond) in Handsworth, the assart of 'Ruworth', 'Duddesrudding', land between 'Petulf Greene' and the king's highway as far as 'Waver' and the stream called 'le Burne', a well or pit (*puteum*) at 'Wich' (presumably West Bromwich), and a mill at 'Grete' (near Greets Green in West Bromwich). He also granted the monks tithes of his pannage, hunting, mills, bread, ale, and dishes (*ferculorum*) from the kitchen of his house, wood for fuel and timber, and pasture throughout his manor of West Bromwich at all times of the year for all animals. Finally he gave them the church of Ellesborough (Bucks.) and a dwelling there, 'as much as is of our fee of the barony of Dudley' — in fact a moiety of the church.[7]

In the 13th century the priory was involved in disputes with three generations of the Parles family. In 1211 William de Parles sued the prior for 10 acres in Sandwell and in 1212 for 10 acres in Handsworth. Richard, son of the founder and advocate of the priory, was called upon by the prior to warrant his title and duly did so. The result of the Handsworth dispute is not known, but in 1222 William de Parles remitted his claim to the 10 acres in Sandwell and Richard gave him £5.[8] In 1224 William de Parles sued Richard's brother and heir William for half the advowson of the priory and claimed to have presented Prior Reynold during the reign of King John. On the death of the defendant in the same year, with a minor as his heir, the case was adjourned *sine die*.[9] More serious for the monks themselves was the dispute between John de Parles and the Prior of Sandwell over the advowson of Handsworth, which Sandwell claimed to share with Lenton Priory (Notts.). Here John de Parles was successful, and in 1230 the Prior of Sandwell acknowledged his right to half the advowson. For abandoning his claim he was compensated by John de Parles with a messuage in Birmingham yielding 1 mark a year.[10] The climax of the priory's relations with the Parles family was reached in 1260 when William de Parles led an armed band of assailants against the prior, who was fortunate to escape.[11] An inquisition of 1280, however, taken after William had been hanged for felony, shows that he had enfeoffed the priory with 20s. rent from his mill at Hamstead (in Handsworth).[12]

The priory also had some difficulty during the 13th century in maintaining its rights in distant Ellesborough where by the 1220s Alan de Maidewelle was claiming half the advowson. In 1224, however, he renounced his claim.[13] In 1276 Richard de Seyton and his wife claimed the advowson of Ellesborough against the prior as the heirs of William Brito who had presented in the time of Henry II. They lost the case not because they had no right but because their moiety of the church was not then vacant.[14]

In or shortly before 1230, however, the priory made an important acquisition when the church of West Bromwich was farmed to it in perpetuity by the monks of Worcester for an annual payment of 6 marks and responsibility for maintaining the church, providing books and ornaments, and paying dues to the bishop and archdeacon. This was confirmed in 1230 by the bishop, who also allowed the church to be served by a chaplain appointed by Sandwell, and in 1283 the Pope added his confirmation.[15] In 1291 the church was valued at £4, the exact equivalent of its farm. The priory's share of the church of Ellesborough was valued at £6 13s. 4d., and the monks also received £1 13s. 4d. from the other half. The priory's temporalities at Sandwell were assessed at £4 16s. 8d.[16] In the constitutional crisis of 1297 the priory's lay fees were confiscated by royal order, but they were restored on payment of the subsidy.[17] The prior contributed £1 9s. towards the tenth of 1306.[18]

A glimpse of the internal life of the priory is given by the provision made for an aged prior, evidently Richard de Eselberg in 1330.[19] After receiving the prior's resignation during a visitation, the bishop ordered that he was to have the newly built chamber next to the dormitory, attendance, and the food of two monks, the 'broken meat' being given to the poor; he was also to have 20s. a year for clothing. In addition he was to be assigned some land near the graveyard with a fishpond and dovecote; after his death these were to be used for the support of the brethren in the infirmary.

The history of the priory is undistinguished save perhaps for its turbulence. In the 14th century at least three of the elections of a prior were annulled by the bishop,[20] while the death of the prior in 1349 (presumably of the plague) and in 1361 left only one other in the community on each occasion and the bishop duly appointed him to the vacancy.[21] In a poll tax list of 1377 only the prior is mentioned.[22] In 1380, however, there was one other monk besides the prior, and when the prior resigned in that year the right of appointment was granted to the bishop who brought in a monk from Shrewsbury to fill the vacancy. In 1391 there was only one monk at Sandwell; he elected a monk of Shrewsbury as prior, but the bishop quashed the election and brought in a monk of Coventry.[23] After the resignation of the prior in 1487 the monks claimed to be unable to proceed to an election because of their 'simplicity' and the bishop once more appointed; with a new vacancy the following year the monks again appealed to the bishop to appoint.[24]

It is thus not surprising to find disorders within

[7] *V.C.H. Bucks.* ii. 338. By 1218 the priory had 2 messuages and land in Ellesborough which it then leased out: *Cal. Feet of Fines for Bucks.* 37.

[8] *S.H.C.* iii(1), 150 sqq., 156; iv(1), 11, 15, 218. In 1222 a jury was ordered to investigate an accusation by Ralph Tyrell that the prior had enclosed part of the common pasture of Handsworth: ibid. 23.

[9] Ibid. iv(1), 28, 30, 31.   [10] Ibid. 77, 222–3; ibid. i. 195.

[11] Ibid. iv(1), 143.   [12] Ibid. 1911, 174.

[13] Bodl. MS. Staffs. Charters 41; *Rot. Hugonis de Welles*, (Cant. & York Soc.), ii. 65, 67.

[14] *V.C.H. Bucks.* ii. 338.

[15] B.M., Harl. MS. 3868, ff. 2–3; *Valor Eccl.* (Rec. Com.), iii. 226.

[16] *Tax. Eccl.* (Rec. Com.), 33, 243, 251.

[17] *S.H.C.* 1913, 308; *Cal. Chanc. R. Var.* 51.

[18] *Cal. Pat. 1301–7*, 451.

[19] Lich. Dioc. Regy., B/A/1/3, f. 39. The entry is undated and refers to Prior R. de H.; he is almost certainly to be identified as Ric. de Eselberg.

[20] Lich. Dioc. Regy., B/A/1/1, f. 55v.; /2, f. 147; /6, f. 38v.

[21] Ibid. /2, f. 181; *S.H.C.* N.S. x(2), 108. In 1341 there is mention of Edmund, the prior's priest, of Sandwell: *S.H.C.* xi. 122.   [22] E 179/20/595.

[23] *S.H.C.* N.S. x(2), 147–8; Lich. Dioc. Regy., B/A/1/6, f. 38v.; see below.

[24] Lich. Dioc. Regy., B/A/1/12, ff. 56, 59.

the priory. About 1324 the bishop addressed a stern letter to the monks admonishing them to show proper obedience to the prior. He also stated that one of the brethren was wandering about in secular garb under pretence of a visit to the papal Curia.[25] By 1355 the administration of the priory left much to be desired, and the bishop complained that the monks were committing waste of woods and hedges, granting long leases, and alienating their property.[26] By the 1370s Prior John de Kyngeston's position was being challenged by Richard Tudenham who claimed to be the rightful prior; it was probably in this connexion that John de Kyngeston was attacked by five men in 1370 and shot in the arm with an arrow.[27] This was followed by a dispute with the Abbot of Shrewsbury, against whom John de Kyngeston started legal proceedings. The nature of the dispute is not known, but it may be that an attempt was being made to subordinate the priory to the abbey. In 1379 the Abbot of Shrewsbury, two of his monks, the Rector of Handsworth, and others forcibly removed John de Kyngeston from Sandwell to Sleap (Salop.), a manor belonging to the abbot, and there compelled him to resign the priorate before a notary public and to abandon the proceedings which he had initiated against the abbot.[28] In 1380 Richard Westbury, one of the Shrewsbury monks involved in the attack on John de Kyngeston, was appointed prior by the bishop.[29] Tudenham, however, had not abandoned his hopes of the office and in the meanwhile had procured a papal provision to the priory. He therefore began an action against Westbury in the ecclesiastical courts, hoping to displace him. But the supplanter of John de Kyngeston proved more than a match for Tudenham. The little-applied Statute of Provisors of 1351 was invoked and Westbury's rival was arrested and brought before the Council.[30] What may be termed the Shrewsbury party suffered a reverse in 1391 when the election of a monk of that abbey, William Pontesbury, as Westbury's successor was annulled by the bishop, and a monk of Coventry, John of Tamworth, was appointed.[31] In 1397 Tamworth was ejected by Alexander Leddesham, described as an apostate monk and abetted by a warlike band; by the following year, however, Tamworth was back in office.[32] In 1401 John de Acton, a monk of Shrewsbury, was appointed as his successor by Archbishop Arundel during his visitation of the diocese.[33] In 1436 John Atton, also a monk of Shrewsbury, was elected.[34]

Relations with laymen were also stormy. About 1324 the prior obtained letters of excommunication from the bishop against 'certain sons of iniquity' who had invaded the priory lands, taken fish, cut wood, and oppressed the tenants and were also detaining tithes and burial fees.[35] In 1341 the prior and his priest were among several people whose arrest was ordered by the Crown because of their attempted interference in the appointment of a prebendary of Codsall in the king's free chapel of Tettenhall.[36] Relations with the advocate of the priory had degenerated by 1387 when John Marnham sued Prior Richard Westbury to secure delivery of a bond.[37] In 1414 the prior was accused of sheltering murderers and robbers; together with others similarly accused he was admitted to bail and pardoned.[38]

On the credit side Sandwell was extending its property in the later 14th century. In 1365 it acquired a messuage and virgate in Padbury (Bucks.).[39] Between 1388 and 1390 Prior Westbury, with some help from William Pontesbury, the monk of Shrewsbury who nearly succeeded him as prior, attempted to obtain the farm of the alien priory of Alberbury (Salop.), which was in the royal custody. Although he achieved some temporary success, the original keeper, Geoffrey Stafford, a canon of Ranton, was restored in 1390.[40] In 1398 Prior Tamworth obtained papal sanction for the appropriation of the priory's share of Ellesborough church, which it was to be allowed to serve with one of its own monks or a secular priest on the death of the existing rector. Whatever the advantages to Sandwell of this appropriation it certainly did not redound to the benefit of the inhabitants of Ellesborough. By 1519 the church had fallen into decay and services were rarely held, there being no vicar, but the priory drew regularly 10 marks a year and 4 quarters of wheat. In the 15th and 16th centuries the advowson and half the rectory were leased out by the priory.[41] In the 1450s the priory owned a fulling-mill at Fazeley which it leased out.[42]

Sandwell was among the 21 religious houses scheduled for suppression in 1524 for the benefit of Cardinal Wolsey's Cardinal College at Oxford.[43] The suppression took place in February 1525; provision, however, was made for the continuance of religious services. The prior and one other monk only made up the community, and they were transferred to other Benedictine houses.[44] The possessions of the priory then consisted of buildings and lands in Sandwell, the advowson and tithes of West

---

[25] Ibid. /3, f. 17v. In 1339 Rob. Ingheram, an apostate monk of Sandwell, was seeking to be reconciled: *Cal. Papal Regs.* ii. 545.
[26] B/A/1/3, f. 137v. Timber was evidently of some importance in the economy of Sandwell; in 1466 the prior supplied wood to the church of All Saints, Walsall: *S.H.C.* 1928, 201.
[27] *S.H.C.* xiv(1), 130, 132.
[28] *Cal. Pat.* 1377–81, 423; *Cal. Close,* 1377–81, 343.
[29] *S.H.C.* N.S. x(2), 148.
[30] *Cal. Pat.* 1377–81, 567.
[31] Lich. Dioc. Regy., B/A/1/6, f. 38v.
[32] *S.H.C.* N.S. vii. 288; see below.
[33] Lambeth Palace Libr., Reg. Arundel, i, f. 487.
[34] See below p. 219.
[35] Lich. Dioc. Regy., B/A/1/2, f. 17.
[36] *Cal. Pat.* 1340–3, 147, 183–4, 320; *S.H.C.* xi. 122. They alleged papal provision.
[37] *S.H.C.* xv. 5.
[38] Ibid. xvii. 24.

[39] *Cal. Inq. Misc.* iii, p. 235.
[40] *Cal. Pat.* 1385–9, 438–9; 1388–92, 352; *Cal. Fine R.* 1383–91, 136, 206, 214, 340, 351. On Geoffrey's temporary restitution in 1388 he was stated to have been removed on the false suggestion of the priors of Alberbury and Sandwell who had then secured the custody.
[41] *Cal. Papal Regs.* v. 263; *V.C.H. Bucks.* i. 300; ii. 338; C 142/76/10.
[42] C 1/26/446.
[43] For this para. see Hibbert, *Dissolution,* 22–26 (where the date of suppression is given as Feb. 1524 instead of Feb. 1524/5); E 21/3; E 36/165, ff. 127–40; C 142/76/10 and 35; *L. & P. Hen. VIII,* iv, pp. 971, 987, 1777, 1778, 2245; v, p. 735; vi, p. 101; *Stat. Realm,* iii. 352–4; *S.H.C.* xi. 266; xii(1), 183; *V.C.H. Bucks.* ii. 338; *V.C.H. Surr.* ii. 96.
[44] For Cromwell's attempt in 1528 to oust the curate of West Bromwich in favour of 'Sir William, the prior's monk that was', see *L. & P. Hen. VIII, Addenda,* i(1), pp. 202, 215–16.

Bromwich, two water-mills at West Bromwich, the advowson and half the rectory of Ellesborough, and lands and rents in Sandwell, West Bromwich, Dudley, Tipton, Great Barr, Little Barr, Harborne, 'Wernell', 'Coston' (presumably Coston Hackett, Worcs.), Wombourn, Wednesbury, Handsworth, and 'Feccham'. The spiritualities were valued at £12 and the temporalities at £26 8s. 7d.[45] The priory and its property were conveyed by the king to Wolsey in January 1526 and by Wolsey to the Dean of Cardinal College in February; a further double transaction involving more property took place in 1528. In 1530 the college drew £31 7s. from the Sandwell property. After the fall of Wolsey the property reverted to the Crown. In 1530 Thomas Cromwell and William Burbank stayed five days at Sandwell and sold goods there for £21; the bells were valued at £33 6s. 8d. In 1531 the manor of Sandwell was granted to Lucy Clifford and the advowson of Ellesborough to the Carthusian priory of Sheen (Surr.). Another portion of the property seems to have been granted to St. George's Chapel, Windsor, by 1532.

A survey of Sandwell's possessions in 1526 included the priory buildings which by then were largely ruinous.[46] The chancel was 41 feet long and 18 feet wide, while the nave was 57 × 18 feet with a south aisle 9 feet wide. Between chancel and nave was a 'bellframe', presumably a tower, 18 × 16 feet, on the north side of which were two chapels.[47] The cloister and priory buildings lay north of the church. These included a house adjoining one of the side chapels and measuring 80 × 20 feet; it had three 'low' parlours, three upper chambers, and a chimney. There was a hall adjoining the cloister; 'buylded chaumber wise', it was 57 × 21 feet. A building at the west end of the hall, 60 × 21 feet, included the kitchen and two upper chambers with various outhouses. Other buildings included a gatehouse and chamber, a barn 72 × 24 feet, an adjoining hayhouse 64 × 21 feet, a kilnhouse, a stable, and a water-mill built of timber and thatched. To the west of the priory was a dried-up moat with an overgrown orchard inside it.[48]

PRIORS

John, occurs some time between 1194 and 1218[49] and is probably the Prior John who occurs in 1218.[50]

Reynold, admitted *temp.* King John.[51]

William, occurs 1230 and is probably the Prior W. who was appointed a judge delegate by Archbishop Langton (1206–28).[52]

Richard, predecessor of Thomas.[53]

Thomas, occurs 1293 and is probably the Prior Thomas who resigned 1316.[54]

John de Duckebroc, appointed by the bishop 1316, resigned by March 1323.[55]

Richard de Eselberg, appointed 1323, resigned 1330.[56]

William de la Lee, appointed 1330.[57]

William Harell, appointed 1333.[58]

Richard le Warde, occurs 1341, died 1349.[59]

Nicholas de Cumpton, appointed 1349.[60]

William del Ree, died 1361.[61]

Henry of Kidderminster, appointed 1361.[62]

John de Kyngeston, occurs 1370, resigned 1379.[63]

Richard Westbury, appointed 1380, occurs to 1390.[64]

John of Tamworth, appointed 1391, resigned 1400.[65]

John de Acton, appointed 1401.[66]

Richard Dudley, occurs 1413 and 1416.[67]

William Pruyne, resigned 1436.[68]

John Atton, elected 1436, occurs 1461.[69]

John Newport, occurs 1484, resigned 1487.[70]

Thomas Wynnysbury, appointed 1488, resigned same year.[71]

John Sawer, appointed 1488.[72]

William, occurs 1518.[73]

John Baylye, surrendered the priory in 1525.[74]

A 15th-century copy of a 12th-century matrix belonging to Sandwell Priory has survived.[75] It is o s bronze, pointed oval about 3 by 2 in., and depict Our Lord with cruciferous nimbus, seated with Hi s right hand raised in benediction and holding an open book in His left hand. Legend, lombardic:

SIGILLUM COMMUNE SANCTE MARIE MADALENA
DE SANDWELLE

[45] It was stated in 1526 that the income had included 'much offerings' to St. Mary Magdalen: E 36/165, f. 130v.

[46] Ibid. ff. 127v.–128v. (transcribed in Dugdale, *Mon.* iv. 191). The date is given in *L. & P. Hen. VIII*, iv, p. 987. Little now (1968) remains of the priory. Shaw, in his account of Sandwell Hall (*Staffs.* ii. 130), states that 'some of the foundation etc. [of the priory] is still traceable in the back part and offices'. For a photograph of 1928 showing a wall with windows on 2 stages see W.S.L., F. A. Homer, 'Collections for the History of the Priory of Sandwell'.

[47] It has been suggested that the reference to the two north chapels is an error and that one of the chapels was in fact on the south: inf. from Mr. J. W. Whiston, citing *West Bromwich and Oldbury Chronicle*, 16 Aug. 1901.

[48] E 36/165, f. 129v.

[49] He witnessed a charter also witnessed by Hen., Abbot of Merevale, Warws. (elected 1194), and Rob. Marmion (d. by 1218): Dugdale, *Mon.* iv. 107; *V.C.H. Warws.* ii. 78; C.F.R. Palmer, *Hist. of the Baronial Family of Marmion* (Tamworth, 1875), 118.

[50] *Cal. Feet of Fines for Bucks.* 37.   [51] *S.H.C.* iv(1), 28.

[52] *S.H.C.* iv(1), 77; xvi. 271; B.M., Harl. MS. 3868, f. 2.

[53] *S.H.C.* vi(1), 220.

[54] Ibid. 220, 224, 236; Lich. Dioc. Regy., B/A/1/1, f. 55v.

[55] B/A/1/1, f. 55v.; ibid. /2, f. 137. He was a Cluniac of Wenlock (Salop.); his election by the monks of Sandwell earlier in 1316 had been annulled by the bishop.

[56] Ibid. /2, ff. 137, 147. He was a monk of Sandwell.

[57] Ibid. f. 147. He was a monk of Sandwell; his election by the monks earlier in 1330 had been annulled by the bishop.

[58] Ibid. f. 153. He was a monk of Thorney (Cambs.).

[59] Ibid. f. 181; *Cal. Pat.* 1340–3, 320; *S.H.C.* xi. 122.

[60] B/A/1/2, f. 181. He was a monk of Sandwell.

[61] Ibid. /4, f. 51v.

[62] Ibid. He was a monk of Sandwell.

[63] See above p. 218. He occurs as Prior of Canwell 1355–69: see above p. 216.   [64] See above p. 218.

[65] See above p. 218; Lambeth Palace Libr., Reg. Arundel, i, f. 487.

[66] See above p. 218. He was a monk of Shrewsbury.

[67] *S.H.C.* xvii. 24, 56.

[68] B.M., Harl. MS. 2179, f. 137v.

[69] Ibid. ff. 137v.–139v.; E 36/165, f. 133. He was a monk of Shrewsbury.

[70] C 142/76/10; Lich. Dioc. Regy., B/A/1/12, f. 56. On resignation he was granted a pension of £8 by the bishop: ibid. ff. 56, 59.

[71] B/A/1/12, ff. 56, 59. He was a monk of Evesham (Worcs.).

[72] Ibid. 59. He was a Cluniac of Lenton (Notts.).

[73] He was admitted to the guild of Lichfield that year: Harwood, *Lichfield*, 412.

[74] C 142/76/35; see above p. 218.

[75] A. B. Tonnochy, *Cat. of Brit. Seal-Dies in B.M.* 182.

5. THE PRIORY OF BLITHBURY

A RELIGIOUS house was established on the south bank of the Blithe at Blithbury in the parish of Mavesyn Ridware during the episcopate of Roger de Clinton (1129–48). This house, like that at Farewell founded at the same period, was at first for hermits or monks and was afterwards transformed into a nunnery. The founder was Hugh de Ridware or Malveysin who made two grants to Blithbury. By one of them he gave Blithbury to two monks there named Guthmund and Saxe; the bounds of the property ran from the oak at their gate to 'Holebrocke' and thence to the Blithe and from the river to 'Sichbrooke', with a wood and common pasture.[1] The other grant was to Guthmund, Saxe, and the nuns of Blithbury and gave them Blithbury with its appurtenances to hold in free alms for the service of God and St. Giles — an indication that the house was dedicated to St. Giles. The bounds were now given as running from 'Holebrock' to 'Sikebrock' and thence to 'Blaklake' and so to the Blithe, and the grant included the right to timber for the repair of the house.[2] It was witnessed by Bishop Roger who himself confirmed the holdings of the house, excused it from all synodal and episcopal dues, and granted an indulgence of 21 days to benefactors.[3]

William, son of the founder, in restoring to the house the lands between 'Blakelake' and the Blithe which he had taken from it, mentioned only the nuns. His son, another William, granted the nuns his share of Hammerwich, the other part of which they held already.[4] Meanwhile Rennerius, son of Edricht of Wolseley, granted his lands and woods at Gailey (in Penkridge) to the nuns at some date between 1158 and 1165; by 1189, however, Gailey had passed to the Benedictine nunnery at Brewood.[5] Like certain other nunneries Blithbury received gifts from King John of £2 in 1200 and 2 marks in 1204.[6]

There is evidence that soon after its foundation Blithbury was closely associated with the nuns at Brewood and that it was eventually absorbed by them. Mention has already been made of the transfer of Gailey from Blithbury to Brewood in the reign of Henry II. About 1170 the nuns of the two houses made an agreement with William de Ridware concerning land at Ridware which they held, apparently jointly.[7] About 1275 Mabel, Prioress of Brewood, with the consent of Alice, Prioress of Blithbury, granted half a virgate and some meadow in Little Pipe to Robert de Pipe; both prioresses sealed the grant.[8] References in 1306 to a lane at Blithbury leading *versus nonales* and in 1315 to the road *versus monales*[9] may indicate the continuing

existence of the priory, but no trace has been found in later records. It seems likely that after having been closely associated with Brewood from the later 12th century Blithbury had been merged with it by the 14th century. Certainly the largest item in the revenues of Brewood in the 1530s was its income from land at Blithbury.[10]

By the end of the 18th century a farmhouse occupied the supposed site of the priory. Two buildings dismantled at that time were thought to have been part of the priory, one of them being identified as the chapel.[11]

The only prioress recorded is Alice who was in office about 1275. The seal attached to the deed of that date mentioned above was already lost at the end of the 18th century,[12] and no other impression is known.

6. THE PRIORY OF BREWOOD
(BLACK LADIES)

THE priory of Benedictine nuns at Brewood, dedicated to St. Mary but often known as Black Ladies, lay some 2½ miles west of the village.[1] It may have been founded by Roger de Clinton, Bishop of Coventry and Lichfield (1129–48), who was founder of the nunnery at Farewell, but there is no positive evidence. The fact that the priory was situated within the episcopal manor of Brewood[2] suggests that one of the bishops may have been concerned in the foundation. It was, however, in existence by about the mid 12th century when Ralph Bassett of Drayton gave the nuns half a virgate from his demesne at Pattingham and another half virgate at Hardwick nearby, with common of pasture and woods and free of all secular services.[3]

The next known deed relating to the priory is an agreement made about 1170 by the nuns of Brewood and Blithbury (in Mavesyn Ridware) with William de Ridware concerning land at Ridware which they had through one Godfrey. This land the nuns restored or granted to William for an annual rent of 2s. and he confirmed to them meadowland which they held already.[4] The chief interest of this deed is its indication of the close relationship between the priories of Brewood and Blithbury which apparently ended in the absorption of Blithbury by Brewood by the 14th century.[5] Another instance of the relation is the fact that Gailey (in Penkridge) granted to Blithbury between 1158 and 1165 had passed to the nuns of Brewood before 1189.[6]

Gailey, however, was seized by Henry II, and in 1200 King John granted the nuns the manor of Broom (Worcs., formerly Staffs.) instead. As a result

---

[1] Dugdale, *Mon.* iv. 160; *S.H.C.* 1939, 201. For the site see Shaw, *Staffs.* i. 203, 204, 205.
[2] Dugdale, *Mon.* iv. 160.
[3] B.M., Harl. MS. 2044, p. 100.
[4] Dugdale, *Mon.* iv. 160.
[5] Ibid.; *S.H.C.* ii(1), 244–5; see below.
[6] *S.H.C.* ii(1), 91, 96, 119, 123. Brewood was included in 1204.
[7] See below.
[8] *S.H.C.* 1939, 201–2.
[9] Shaw, *Staffs.* i. 204.
[10] See below p. 222.
[11] Shaw, *Staffs.* i. 204.

[12] Ibid. Blithbury is confused with Blythburgh in W. de G. Birch, *Cat. of Seals in B.M.*
[1] A house of Augustinian canonesses dedicated to St. Leonard and often known as White Ladies lay further west just over the Shropshire border. These nuns too were frequently mentioned as the nuns of Brewood, and it is not always clear which house is meant.
[2] See *V.C.H. Staffs.* v. 25, 36.
[3] *S.H.C.* 1939, 182–3.
[4] Ibid. 202–3.
[5] See above.
[6] *V.C.H. Staffs.* v. 114.

in 1203 the prioress successfully claimed the advowson of Broom against the parson of the mother-church at Clent (Worcs., formerly Staffs.).[7] In 1204 Brewood and Blithbury were among the nunneries which received a gift of 2 marks each from the king.[8] About the same time Sir William de Rudge gave lands in Rudge (Salop.), formerly held by Leovenad de Hetha, to the nuns for a palfrey and 3 marks and an annual rent of 12d. He also confirmed their possession of two meadows 'under Whitehul' given by his father and gave them pasture rights in Rudge and Pattingham; for this the nuns had to make a cash payment of 4 marks with an annual rent of 4d. and also surrender a virgate in Rudge 'which we had given them previously'.[9] At some time between 1211 and 1216 the nuns exchanged the half virgate in Pattingham given by Ralph Bassett for an assart in Chillington owned by Ralph's widow Isabel de Pattingham; the nuns paid Isabel 20s. for the transaction.[10] About 1225 a mill at Chetton (Salop.) was granted to the nuns by Sybil de Broc, lady of the manor of Chetton.[11]

In response to a petition from the priory Pope Gregory IX (1227–41) took it under his protection.[12] He confirmed the community in all property which they already held or might acquire in the future, particularly the site of the house with its appurtenances; the newly tilled lands which they cultivated themselves and the livestock which they reared were to be tithe free. The Pope recognized the sisters' right to elect their prioress, and the bishop was to confer benediction on the nuns and ordination on their chaplain. The bull granted such usual rights as those of receiving outsiders for burial in the priory's graveyard, admitting into the community free women wishing to withdraw from the world (none of whom was to leave after profession without the permission of the prioress except to take stricter vows), and of celebrating the divine offices during time of national interdict.

During the reign of Henry III there were a number of royal grants to the nuns of Brewood but without any indication whether Black Ladies or White Ladies was intended. The grants included three acres of assart in Sherwood Forest in 1241 and of oaks from Kinver Forest in 1256 and 1267.[13] Black Ladies received a gift of 1 mark from the king in 1241 in order that they might redeem their chalice which was in pledge[14] — a sign of the poor financial state of the priory. About 1260–70 the nuns exchanged lands in the manor of Brewood with the bishop in return for an inclosed plot of wood and waste near their house,[15] and in 1267 the king confirmed the charter of 1200.[16] In 1272 half a virgate of land and 16d. rent in Horsebrook in Brewood were granted to the priory by two of the daughters and heirs of Sir Ralph de Coven and their husbands.[17] But the nuns were still recognized as

poor in 1286 when they were convicted of the theft some 10 years before of a stag. The animal had been drowned in the priory fish-pond after escaping from the royal huntsman in Gailey Hay, and the nuns had then divided it with John Giffard of Chillington. Whereas Giffard was imprisoned and fined, the king pardoned the nuns because they were poor.[18] By 1291 the priory's mill at Chetton was worth 16s. a year.[19] In the same year the Pope granted an indulgence of one year and 40 days to all who should visit the priory on each of the four feasts of the Virgin Mary and the anniversary of the dedication of the church there;[20] the nuns would of course benefit from the offerings made by such visitors. At some time before 1318 the nuns had been involved in a dispute with the Vicar of Brewood over tithes of wool and lambs from flocks belonging to other people and folded and pastured on the priory's lands in Brewood parish. The vicar eventually gave the tithes to the nuns as a favour but in 1318 they decided to pay these tithes to the vicar.[21] The nuns were assessed at 2s. for the subsidy of 1327, the lowest assessment in Brewood, but for the subsidy of 1333 they were assessed at 3s., one of the higher assessments in the area.[22] In 1394 the priory received a gift of £100, made to secure prayers for Thomas de Brinton, lord of Church Eaton (d. 1382), and his ancestors.[23] This was probably the largest gift in the history of the priory but also the last of any great value.

Bishop Northburgh held a visitation of the priory, probably in 1323.[24] The injunctions reveal some financial confusion and general laxity. The bishop forbade simoniacal payments by women wishing to join the community, though free-will offerings were allowed; because of the poverty of the house numbers were to be kept at their existing level. He also forbade the granting of corrodies, liveries, and pensions without his licence and ordered the prioress and others holding office to present accounts before the whole house or the senior members. Anabel de Hervill, the cellaress, and Robert de Herst, the keeper of the temporalities, were to be removed from office. A rent received annually by one of the nuns was in future to be used for the whole house. The prioress was ordered to eat in the refectory and sleep in the dormitory, and a damsel of the prioress was to be removed from the house. No secular persons were to be allowed to reside in the priory, and the nuns were forbidden to converse with either secular persons or regulars. Nuns not holding office were not to go outside the cloister without leave — Emma of Bromsgrove was mentioned in particular. A Franciscan was appointed to hear the confessions of the prioress and nuns.

In 1442 and 1452 the bishop appointed a new prioress of Black Ladies, the right having come to him as a result of long vacancies.[25] At the next

---

[7] V.C.H. Worcs. iii. 33, 34; S.H.C. 1939, 194 sqq.
[8] S.H.C. ii(1), 119, 123.
[9] S.H.C. 1939, 183–5.
[10] Ibid. 183, 194.
[11] Ibid. 203.
[12] S.H.C. 1924, pp. 336–7.
[13] Close R. 1237–42, 273; 1254–6, 344; 1264–8, 331.
[14] Cal. Lib. 1240–5, 71.
[15] S.H.C. 1939, 205–6.
[16] Cal. Chart. R. 1257–1300, 79.
[17] S.H.C. 1939, 204–5, 206–7. For the family see V.C.H. Staffs. v. 30.
[18] S.H.C. v(1), 163.

[19] Tax. Eccl. (Rec. Com.), 162. This is the only mention of the priory in the 1291 assessment.
[20] Cal. Papal Regs. i. 536.   [21] S.H.C. 1939, 210.
[22] Ibid. vii(1), 236; x(1), 121.
[23] Ibid. iv(2), 15n.; ibid. N.S. ii. 153; V.C.H. Staffs. iv. 93. In 1346 the prioress and nuns of Brewood — whether Black Ladies or White Ladies is not stated — received licence to appropriate the church of Rode (Som.) at the request of Thos. de Swynnerton (Cal. Pat. 1345–8, 475), but it seems that nothing was done. Alice de Swynnerton was prioress until her resignation in 1332.
[24] Lich. Dioc. Regy., B/A/1/3, ff. 96–97.
[25] Ibid. /9, f. 69v.; /10, f. 20.

vacancy in 1485 the bishop again made the appointment, this time in response to an appeal from the subprioress that he should do so.[26] A visitation of 1521 shows a community of four. All was found in good order, although one of the nuns commented that small girls slept with the sisters in the dormitory. The prioress stated that the annual income of the house was £20 13s. 4d. and that there were no debts.[27]

In 1535 the priory had lands and rents in Brewood parish, including Chillington and Horsebrook, and in Bradley; in Broom and Kidderminster (Worcs.); and in Albrighton, Dawley, and Tong (Salop.).[28] The total value was given as £11 1s. 6d., but the list was certainly incomplete. A rental of 1537[29] and the Minister's Account of 1539–40[30] mention a number of additional places — Blithbury, Shredicote (in Bradley), Stretton, and Hampton Lovett and Hunnington, in Halesowen (both in Worcs.). Apart from the demesne lands near the priory, the most valuable estate was Blithbury, worth £3 12s. in 1537. The total net income from the estates was then £17 2s. 11d.

Brewood was accordingly dissolved with the lesser monasteries, the prioress surrendering it to Dr. Thomas Legh on 16 October 1538.[31] She was given a reward of £2 and a pension of £3 6s. 8d. while each of the other three nuns of the priory received half those amounts. The eight servants of the priory, including the chaplain, received rewards amounting to £3 18s. 2d., of which £1 10s. went to the chaplain.[32] The site and precinct of the priory, with the church, churchyard, a water-mill within the site, and certain pastures in Brewood, valued in all at £7 9s. 1d. a year, were sold in 1539 to Thomas Giffard of Stretton (in Penkridge) for £134 1s. 8d. 'Mr. Littleton', presumably Edward Littleton of Pillaton (in Penkridge), had also been attempting to secure the property.[33] The goods and chattels of the dissolved priory, valued at £7 6s. 1d., included the somewhat meagre furnishings of church, vestry, chapter-house, hall, parlour, chief chamber, bailiff's chamber, buttery, kitchen, larder, brewhouse, 'yelyng' house, cheese-loft, and 'kylhouse'. There were three bells in the tower of the church, and the plate consisted of a silver chalice and three silver spoons. The inventory also mentions a little grain,

one horse, one wain, and one dung cart.[34] No part of the priory buildings has survived.[35]

PRIORESSES

Isabel, occurs at some time during the period 1258–95.[36]
Mabel, occurs 1272.[37]
Emma, occurs 1301.[38]
Alice de Swynnerton, occurs 1324, resigned 1332.[39]
Helewis of Leicester, elected 1332, occurs 1373.[40]
Parnel, occurs 1395 and 1412.[41]
Margaret Chilterne, appointed 1442, resigned by 1452.[42]
Elizabeth Botery, appointed 1452, died 1485.[43]
Margaret Cawardyn, appointed 1485.[44]
Isabel Lawnder, occurs 1521, surrendered the priory 1538.[45]

The priory seal in use in the 14th century was a pointed oval, and showed the Virgin seated with the Child and holding a branch of palm in her left hand.[46] Only the fragment of an impression is now known to survive. Legend:

SIGILLUM CONVENTUS SANCTE MARIE NIGRARUM DOMINARUM

A seal in use in 1538 is a pointed oval, 2¼ by 1¼ in., and shows the Virgin seated under a canopy with the Child on her left arm and holding a fleur-de-lys sceptre in her right hand.[47] Legend, black letter:

[S]IGILLUM COMMUNE NIGRARUM MONIALIUM DE BRE...

7. THE PRIORY OF FAREWELL

A RELIGIOUS house was founded at Farewell, 2½ miles north-west of Lichfield, by Bishop Roger de Clinton (1129–48) and endowed with several episcopal estates. Like Blithbury, which also dates from this period, it began as a foundation for monks or hermits but soon became a nunnery;[1] the bishop may have been patron.[2]

Bishop Roger's original grant gave to the church of St. Mary at Farewell and the canons and lay brothers there the site of the church, the land which they had assarted and as much woodland as they

[26] Ibid. /12, f. 57.
[27] Ibid. B/V/1/1, p. 83.
[28] *Valor Eccl.* (Rec. Com.), iii. 103.
[29] L.R. 2/183, ff. 177–9.
[30] S.C.6/Hen. VIII/3354, m. 42.
[31] *L. & P. Hen. VIII*, x, p. 515; xiii(2), pp. 243, 244; Hibbert, *Dissolution*, 171–2.
[32] *L. & P. Hen. VIII*, xiii(2), pp. 243, 348; xiv(1), p. 600; Hibbert, *Dissolution*, 227, 228. The four nuns were still receiving their pensions in 1540: *L. & P. Hen. VIII*, xvi, p. 731.
[33] *L. & P. Hen. VIII*, xiii(2), pp. 228, 244; xiv(1), p. 159. Thos. had been granted a lease of the priory in 1538: ibid. p. 609. He succ. his father John at Chillington in 1556: *V.C.H. Staffs.* v. 36.
[34] *S.H.C.* 1939, 216–18.
[35] *V.C.H. Staffs.* v. 37.
[36] *S.H.C.* 1924, p. 292.
[37] Ibid. 1939, 204.
[38] Ibid. 186.
[39] Ibid. ix(1), 101, 104; Lich. Dioc. Regy., B/A/1/2, f. 151.
[40] B/A/1/2, f. 151; *S.H.C.* 1939, 187, 197. She was a nun of Brewood.
[41] *S.H.C.* iv(2), 15n.; ibid. N.S. ii. 153; ibid. 1939, 189–91.
[42] Lich. Dioc. Regy., B/A/1/9, f. 69v.; /10, f. 20. She was a nun of Chester.
[43] B/A/1/10, f. 20; /12, f. 57. She was a nun of Brewood,

appointed by the bishop after a long vacancy. She stood as godmother to Ric. son of Ralph Lane at his baptism in Brewood church in 1474: *Cal. Inq. p.m. Hen. VII*, i, p. 550; *V.C.H. Staffs.* v. 34.
[44] B/A/1/12, f. 57. She was subprioress.
[45] B/V/1/1, p. 83; *L. & P. Hen. VIII*, xiii(2), p. 243. She was probably Isabel dau. of Ralph Launder of Beech (in Stone) who at the time of her death in 1551 was living as a paying guest with her sister Agnes Beech and nephew John Beech: *S.H.C.* 1939, 212–13.
[46] *S.H.C.* 1939, 202, 213–14.
[47] W. de G. Birch, *Cat. of Seals in B.M.* i, p. 457; *S.H.C.* 1939, 213–14; E 322/29.
[1] It is described as Benedictine in the bp.'s reg. in 1398 (Lich. Dioc. Regy., B/A/1/6, f. 50v.) and as 'of the Benedictine order or another' at its dissolution in 1527 when the nuns were all transferred to Benedictine houses: see below p. 224. It is given as Cistercian in the bp.'s reg. in 1425: B/A/1/9, f. 52. In the 12th century its daughter-house at Langley (Leics.) claimed to be exempt from tithe in accordance with the privileges of the Cistercians but was unable to maintain its claim: *V.C.H. Leics.* ii. 3.
[2] The bishop evidently played a special part in the dissolution and the subsequent disposal of the property: see below p. 224. In 1398 the Crown stated that it held the patronage (*Cal. Pat.* 1396–9, 293), but no other evidence for this is known.

could assart, a holding called 'Chirstalleia' (probably Chestall on the Cannock-Longdon boundary), and pannage and pasture rights. About 1140 the bishop made a new grant, this time to the nuns of Farewell at the request of three hermits and brothers of Farewell, Roger, Geoffrey, and Robert, and with the consent of the chapter of Lichfield. By it he gave the nuns the church of St. Mary at Farewell, with a mill, a wood, pannage, the land between the stream of 'Chistalea' and 'Blachesiche', and six serfs (coloni), formerly his tenants, with their lands and services. In addition, at the request of Hugh, his chaplain, and of the canons of Lichfield, he granted all the land which Hugh had assarted de bosco and the land which Hugh held of the bishop at Pipe. Bishop Roger further granted the half hide held by Haminch (or possibly Hamon) de Hammerwich at Haminch's own request; half of this estate was to be held by the nuns in demesne and the other half by Haminch's heir as tenants of the nuns. Finally the bishop granted the alms given for the dedication of the church and urged the parishioners to make gifts to the house and generally love and support it. His charter was confirmed by his successor Walter Durdent (1149-59) with the addition of the lands and services of Alvrich de Quadraria and his sons, which were valued at 6s. annually.[3]

The nuns received a charter from Henry II, probably in 1155.[4] The king confirmed to God and St. Mary of Farewell and the nuns there the site of their house at Farewell in Cannock Forest, 3 carucates of land in demesne at Farewell with homage and mills, 8 acres there given by Robert the reeve and Thomas his son[5] and rendering 2s. a year, moorland there for conversion into meadow (moras ad facienda prata), a carucate at Pipe assarted from Cannock Forest, and a carucate at Hammerwich with villeins and a franklin named Hamon the fiddler (vielarius) and their lands and also a plot of pasture. In addition the king granted 40 acres of assarted waste in the forest at Lindhurst within the royal manor of Alrewas with all liberties and customs belonging to the manor. A confirmation was added of all legitimate gifts which the priory might receive in the future. The nuns were to hold their lands free of all secular service. The charter was confirmed in full in 1200 by King John,[6] who also included Farewell in the nunneries receiving a gift of £2 each in that year and 2 marks in 1204.[7] Another grant was made probably about 1170 by Geoffrey Peche who gave the nuns his land at 'Morhale', with his man

there, as the dowry of his daughter Sara on her becoming a nun at Farewell. At this time there were chaplains at Farewell.[8]

In 1251 Henry III ordered the steward of Cannock Forest not to take pannage dues for the pigs of the priory as the nuns were exempted by their charters.[9] Chorley near Farewell was evidently held by the priory by about this time: before 1275 the prioress granted a nief named Henry Aylmond of Chorley with his heirs and chattels to Walkelin de Houton, canon of Lichfield, for 40s.[10] In 1279 the Prior of Llanthony (Glos.) was claiming that the nuns of Farewell had for some time held a house and land in Longdon of his priory for 2 marks a year and the duty of finding a priest to serve a chapel at Radmore (in Cannock); the prioress, however, denied the claim.[11] By 1283 the priory had also acquired a house in Lichfield and had apparently assigned the rent to the fabric fund of the cathedral.[12] In 1293 the prioress successfully sued a Thomas de Hulton for land in Curborough.[13] By the earlier 14th century the priory was in receipt of rents from a compact group of estates in the vicinity at Chorley, Hammerwich, Abnalls, Ashmore Brook, Elmhurst, Longdon, and 'Bourne',[14] while at Farewell, Curborough, and Hammerwich there was demesne farming.[15] The nuns were engaged in sheep-farming as well as arable farming by at least the 1370s.[16] Leet jurisdiction was exercised over Hammerwich, Chorley, 'Halsey', Ashmore Brook, and Bourne.[17] In 1321 Philip de Somerville, lord of Alrewas, had licence from the Crown to give the nuns 20 acres of waste there.[18] In 1367 the prioress sued Humphrey, son of Simon de Rugeley, for 10 acres of land and 2 acres of moor in Longdon, recovering them in 1370 from Humphrey's son Thomas.[19] The king confirmed the charter of Henry II in 1375,[20] and in 1398 the nuns received royal licence to acquire unspecified lands and rents, not held in chief, to the value of 10 marks a year.[21]

A house was founded at Langley near Breedon (Leics.) with nuns from Farewell about 1150. By 1209 a dispute had arisen between the two concerning Farewell's rights over Langley, and the Pope appointed arbitrators. It was agreed that in future the prioress of Farewell should be summoned to preside over elections at Langley but that if she failed to come or to send a representative the election should nonetheless be held. Langley was to retain a Farewell nun called Alice de Hely for five years and then return her to Farewell unless another

[3] Dugdale, Mon. iv. 111. For Chestall see V.C.H. Staffs. v. 57.

[4] Dugdale, Mon. iv. 111; Cal. Pat. 1374-7, 182. The charter is dated at Radmore (in Cannock) which Hen. II visited in 1155: V.C.H. Staffs. v. 57. It was issued in a longer and a shorter version.

[5] Given as his brother in the confirmation of 1200 (see below) but as his son in the confirmation of 1375 (see below).

[6] Rot. Chart. (Rec. Com.), 42.

[7] S.H.C. ii(1), 91, 96, 119, 123.

[8] B.M., Cott. Ch. xxviii. 56. The land had been given to Geoff. by Bp. Ric. Peche (1161-82), and Geoff.'s son Ric. was associated in the grant. The chaplains witnessed the charter.

[9] Close R. 1251-3, 12-13.

[10] S.H.C. 1924, p. 264. The canon set him free and gave his services to the dean and chapter. In 1366 the Prioress of Farewell made a grant of the goods, chattels and services of her villein Thomas son of John Aylmond of Chorley: ibid. 1939, 82.

[11] S.H.C. vi(1), 94.

[12] S.H.C. 1924, p. 267.

[13] J.I. 1/805, m. 12.

[14] S.R.O., D.(W.)1734/2/3/52 (extent of Farewell property 1318). In 1353 the prioress claimed that the West family of Elmhurst held of her by military service: S.H.C. xii(1), 118.

[15] S.R.O., D.(W.)1734/J. 2035 (acct. of bailiff of Farewell 1335-6).

[16] D.(W.)1734/3/3/34 (bailiff's acct. 1377-8); D.(W.) 1734/J. 2037 (bailiff's acct. 1378-9). The acct. of the bailiff 1335-6 includes the sale of wool but the cash figure has been erased: ibid./J. 2035.

[17] D. & C. Lich., C.4, Farewell Ct. Roll 7 Oct. 1367.

[18] Cal. Pat. 1317-21, 565.

[19] S.H.C. xiii. 62, 65. Simon de Rugeley of Hawkesyard (in Armitage) evidently held Chestall (probably the 'Chirstalleia' of Bp. Roger's endowment: see above) in 1333 and Jas. de Rugeley in 1370: V.C.H. Staffs. v. 57.

[20] Cal. Pat. 1374-7, 182.

[21] Ibid. 1396-9, 293.

agreement was made. Farewell renounced its other claims on Langley, but in 1246 the Pope found it necessary to appoint further arbitrators. Farewell then abandoned its claim to any rights over Langley apart from those of the earlier agreement in return for a payment of 4 marks, and the settlement was confirmed by the prioress and convent in 1248.[22]

The records of two 14th-century episcopal visitations afford evidence of conditions in the priory. The first was carried out by Roger Northburgh apparently in 1331, and the subsequent decree concerning corrections was written in French. This was usually done in the case of nunneries, but the bishop specifically stated that he was using French because the nuns had pleaded their difficulty in understanding Latin as their excuse for not fully obeying the decree after the previous visitation. The prioress was instructed to do her utmost to recall Alice de Kynynton, who had left the nunnery and put aside her habit; the bishop added that 'en eyde de vous nous userons la verge de discipline'. Cecily of Gretton, who had also forsaken the nunnery and her habit, was treated more gently; she was to be placed in the charge of a good and wise nun nominated by the prioress to instruct her in her duty and to be with her day and night. The officials of the house were to render accounts. The nuns were not to use girdles and 'burses' of silk but were to wear their habit; they were to elect a nun of experience to be in charge of provision of items of dress. The bishop found that the nuns were sleeping two in a bed in the dorter and with young girls in their beds; he forbade such practices as 'contre regulers constitutions et contre honeste de religion'. No secular women over 12 years of age were to live in the house unless they were going to become nuns there. Nor were secular persons to be received by the nuns in their rooms. Agnes of Lichfield and Margaret of Chorley, apparently servants, were ordered to be put out of the house, and henceforth only women of good fame and honest conversation were to be employed. Finally the door at the back of the garden leading to the fields was in future to be kept locked, several scandals having arisen.[23]

The next bishop, Robert Stretton, visited the priory in 1367. He gave orders that his decree should be read and explained to the nuns 'in the vulgar tongue' by a literate ecclesiastic on the day after it was received. He repeated Northburgh's injunction forbidding secular women, apart from servants, to live in the priory. The nuns were enjoined to observe their threefold vow. They were forbidden to keep more than one child each for education in the priory, and no boy over seven years of age was allowed. The prioress and obedientiaries were to account at least once a year to the whole community or to the senior nuns. All were to eat in common in the prioress's hall because the individual distribution of food had tended to impoverish the

house. There was to be no fire except in the building assigned for the infirmary and called the 'gesthall.' No lands or rents were to be granted away until the bishop had been consulted. The nuns were not to go into Lichfield without leave of the prioress; each had to be accompanied by two other nuns and there was to be no 'vain or wanton' delay. The permission of the prioress in fact was necessary for all departures from the priory, but the bishop stressed that this order was not intended to interfere with 'the laudable custom' whereby the nuns went out walking together on certain days to take the air.[24]

The priory did not survive until the general Dissolution. In 1526 Cardinal Wolsey carried out a visitation of Lichfield Cathedral and evidently discussed the suppression of the priory with Bishop Blythe. In March 1527 at the cardinal's instance a commission was issued to Richard Strete, Archdeacon of Salop, and Dr. William Clayborough, a canon of York, to disperse the nuns and dissolve the priory. The property was to go to the Dean and Chapter of Lichfield for the support of their choristers, evidently in order to extinguish a payment due to the chapter from Wolsey's new college at Oxford.[25] By the end of April the prioress and the other four nuns then making up the community had been transferred to different Benedictine nunneries. The possessions of the priory were then listed as the manor of Farewell with its view of frankpledge and the advowson of the church and property at Chorley, Curborough Somerville, Elmhurst, Lindhurst, Alrewas, Hammerwich, Ashmore Brook, Lichfield, King's Bromley, Water Eaton (in Penkridge), Pipe, Abnalls, Cannock, Burntwood, Rugeley, Brereton, Handsacre, Oakley (in Croxall), Tipton and Longdon. The total annual value was £33 6s. 8d.[26]

In August 1527 the Crown granted the Chapter of Lichfield all the possessions of the dissolved priory, including the house and church, the capital messuage or grange of Curborough Somerville, and property at Frankley (Worcs.) which was not mentioned in the earlier survey.[27] The property was assigned to the twelve choristers of Lichfield, and in 1535 their endowments consisted largely of the possessions of the former priory; out of their total revenue of nearly £40, just under £25 came from rents of the priory estates, £3 5s. 10d. from the tithes and other spiritualities of Farewell, and 10s. from the profits of the court there.[29]

The only part of the priory buildings which remained in the 18th century appears to have been the parish church. This was largely rebuilt in the 1740s, and the only medieval portion now surviving is the east end.[30]

PRIORESSES

Serena, occurs 1248.[31]
Julia, occurs *temp.* Henry III.[32]

[22] *V.C.H. Leics.* ii. 3; Dugdale, *Mon.* iv. 112; E 135/2/28. The first papal commission included the Dean of Lichfield, the precentor, and one of the canons; the 1246 arbitrators were the Treasurer of Lichfield and the Archdeacon of Stafford.
[23] Lich. Dioc. Regy., B/A/1/3, f. 29.
[24] *S.H.C.* N.S. viii. 118–19.
[25] D. & C. Lich., Chapter Acts iv, ff. 43, 47; ibid., uncatalogued 17th-cent. misc. bk., f. 74; Hibbert, *Dissolution*, 27–28; see above pp. 164–5.
[26] S.R.O., D.(W.)1734/J. 1601. One of the nuns, Felicia

Bagshawe, was sent to Brewood nunnery where she remained until its dissolution in 1538. She was probably a member of the Bagshawe family of Farewell: *S.H.C.* 1939, 83, 104, 155.
[27] Hibbert, *Dissolution*, 28.
[28] Ibid.
[29] *Valor Eccl.* (Rec. Com.), iii. 135.
[30] Shaw, *Staffs.* i. 229, 229*; see above plate facing p. 213.
[31] Dugdale, *Mon.* iv. 112.
[32] *S.H.C.* vi(1), 94.

Maud, occurs before 1275, probably early 1270s.[33]
Margery, occurs 1293.[34]
Mabel, died 1313.[35]
Iseult of Pipe, elected 1313, resigned 1321.[36]
Margaret de Muneworth, appointed 1321 after a disputed election and occurs 1353.[37]
Sibyl, occurs 1357.[38]
Agnes Foljambe, occurs 1366 and 1368.[39]
Agnes Turville, resigned 1398.[40]

Agnes Kyngheley, elected 1398.[41]
Margaret Podmore, died 1425.[42]
Alice Wolaston, elected 1425, occurs 1462.[43]
Anne, occurs 1476.[44]
Elizabeth Kylshaw, occurs 1523, transferred to Nuneaton on suppression of Farewell 1527.[45]

No seal is known.

HOUSES OF CISTERCIAN MONKS

8. THE ABBEY OF RADMORE

THE first Cistercian foundation in Staffordshire grew out of a hermitage at Radmore in Cannock Forest near the present hamlet of Cannock Wood, some 3 miles east of Cannock.[1] King Stephen granted Radmore, probably between 1135 and 1139, to Clement, Hervey, and their companions as the site for a hermitage; he also gave them land at 'Melesho' for tillage and pasture. Bishop Roger de Clinton confirmed this grant and gave the hermits permission to follow any rule they wished and to receive and instruct any holy women who came to them after adopting a rule.[2] At some time between 1143 and 1147 the hermits secured a charter similar to Stephen's from the Empress Maud, presumably as a precaution in view of the civil war.[3]

About the same time Maud, who had a great love for the Cistercian rule, persuaded the hermits to join the Cistercian order, and St. Mary's hermitage at Radmore thus became the abbey of St. Mary. New grants followed. Several of these were in Warwickshire, notably at Radway, where a grange was established.[4] William Croc, the steward of Cannock Forest, gave all his rights in Great Wyrley (in Cannock) to the monks on condition that he should be received 'into their fraternity and into the society of the benefactors of the Cistercian order' and his body buried in the abbey.[5] In 1153 Henry,

Duke of Normandy and Aquitaine, the son of Maud, became a benefactor of the monks at his mother's instigation. He confirmed them in their possession of Radmore as 'the site and foundation of the abbey' with Melesho and Wyrley 'for cultivation and pasture' and Hednesford (in Cannock) as pasture free from pannage dues. In the same year he granted most of the royal property in Staffordshire to Ranulph, Earl of Chester, who then gave the monks the vill of Cannock; Duke Henry confirmed this, mentioning also the mill of Wyrley and stating that the grant was to enable the monks to erect a church and domestic buildings.[6]

The monks, however, were finding Radmore an unsuitable site as a result of the oppressions of the foresters who rode there every week.[7] With Maud's support the brethren approached Henry on his coronation day in December 1154 and secured the exchange of Radmore for the royal manor of Stoneleigh in Warwickshire. They arrived there the following June. A royal hunting-lodge was established at Radmore soon after the monks' departure.

ABBOT

William, described as prior of the hermits, became first abbot of Radmore and then of Stoneleigh, dying in 1159.[8]

---

[33] S.H.C. 1924, p. 264. There may have been a prioress named Sibyl at some time between the 1260s and 1280s (ibid. xiii. 13; V.C.H. Glos. ii. 91), but the evidence, which dates from 1357 when the prioress was named Sibyl, is confused and may well be referring to the 14th-century Sibyl.
[34] J.I. 1/805, m. 12.
[35] Lich. Dioc. Regy., B/A/1/1, f. 46.
[36] Ibid.; /2, f. 1.
[37] Ibid. /2, f.1; S.R.O., D.(W.)1734/2/3/53; S.H.C. xii(1), 118. She was provided by the Archbishop of Canterbury, the see of Coventry and Lichfield being vacant. She was subprioress.
[38] S.H.C. xiii. 13.
[39] Ibid. 62; ibid. 1939, 82.
[40] Lich. Dioc. Regy., B/A/1/6, f. 50v.
[41] Ibid. She was a nun of Farewell.
[42] Ibid. /9, f. 52.
[43] Ibid.; S.H.C. N.S. iv. 120. She was a nun of Farewell.
[44] She was admitted to the guild of Lichfield that year: Harwood, Lichfield, 406.
[45] Ibid. 413; S.H.C. 1939, 82. She too was admitted to the guild in 1523.
[1] The whole chronology of Radmore is obscure. For a discussion of it see Stoneleigh Leger Bk. ed. R. H. Hilton (Dugdale Soc. xxiv), pp. xii–xvi. The dating given there is in the main followed in this account, which supersedes that in V.C.H. Staffs. v. 57, and V.C.H. Warws. ii. 78–79.
[2] Stoneleigh Leger Bk. 10–11.

[3] Ibid. 10. The terminal date given ibid. p. xiv, is 1148, but since Bp. Roger mentioned the monks in a charter witnessed by the Abbot of Buildwas and left on the Crusade in 1147 never to return (ibid. p. xv), 1147 must be the terminal date. Maud's grant stipulated that there was not to be excessive assarting of woodland.
[4] Ibid. 13, 14, 17; V.C.H. Warws. v. 142. The land at Radway was given by Bp. Clinton and his tenant, Geoffrey de Clinton; the bishop also confirmed the monks in their possession of Radmore. While travelling from Radmore to Radway Grange the monks were often entertained by the Cistercians of Bordesley Abbey (Worcs.), and a strong friendship developed between the two houses; it was therefore to Bordesley that the new Cistercians turned for instruction in the rule, probably after the move to Stoneleigh in 1155: Leger Bk. 15; V.C.H. Worcs. ii. 154.
[5] Leger Bk. 13; V.C.H. Staffs. v. 79.
[6] Leger Bk. 12–13; S.H.C. ii(1), 221; V.C.H. Staffs. v. 53.
[7] For this para. see Leger Bk. pp. xv–xvi, 15–16, 249–50, and map facing p. liv; V.C.H. Staffs. ii. 341–2; W. H. Duignan, 'On the King's House and the Priory at Radmore, on Cannock Chase', Midland Antiquary, iii. 58 sqq., 141–2. The monks surrendered all their Staffs. property to the Crown: V.C.H. Staffs. v. 53, 57, 59. Hen. II was at Radmore in 1155: R. W. Eyton, Court, Household and Itinerary of King Henry II, 6. For a chapel at Radmore in 1279 see above p. 223.
[8] Leger Bk. 12–16, 17, 249–51.

9. THE ABBEY OF CROXDEN

IN 1176 Bertram de Verdun, lord of Alton, a baron of the Exchequer and a royal justice, granted land at 'Chotes', probably Cotton near Alton, to the Cistercians of Aunay-sur-Odon in Normandy as the site for an abbey.[1] The first abbot, an Englishman, was elected in 1178, but the following year the monks moved to a new site at Croxden a few miles to the south. This was in a remote but fertile valley beside a tributary of the Dove, and the house was styled the abbey of the Vale of St. Mary of Croxden. The site (*locus*) was not dedicated until 1181.

Bertram founded Croxden Abbey for the souls of his predecessors and successors and in particular of his father and mother, of himself, and his second wife Rose, and of Richard de Humez *qui me nutruit*.[2] The endowment consisted of Bertram's lands at Croxden (evidently including a mill),[3] Alton, Madeley Holme (in Checkley), Crakemarsh (in Uttoxeter), and Musden, and also at Oaken (in Codsall) in the south of the county; a grove at Great Gate near Croxden and half a wood at Crakemarsh; land at Tugby (Leics.) and a carucate called Lees at Hartshorne (Derb.); a salt-pit at Middlewich (Ches.); a mill at Stamford (Lincs.); the service due from Achard of Stamford for land there and at Casterton (Rut.) and the 7s. due from Ralph de Normanvile for land at Burton Overy (Leics.); and the churches of Alton and Tugby. Henry II's confirmation of Bertram's charter included also Tugby's dependent chapels of East Norton and Keythorpe.[4] The Verduns remained patrons of the abbey, with the Furnivalles succeeding them in the early 14th century; members of both families were buried in the abbey church.[5]

During the 13th century the abbey's possessions steadily increased. Before he came to the throne in 1199 John gave the monks land in Ireland, and in 1200 he exchanged it for an annuity of £5 from the Exchequer of Ireland;[6] in 1206 he gave the monks Adeney in the manor of Edgmond (Salop.) in place of this annuity.[7] The monks themselves exchanged Adeney with Buildwas Abbey (Salop.) in 1287 in return for Caldon Grange a few miles to the north of Croxden.[8] After the foundation of Dieulacres in 1214 the abbots of Croxden and Dieulacres agreed that Croxden should be allowed to acquire lands and

pastures within a mile of Dieulacres and should be exempt from payment of tithes on lands in Leek parish which it cultivated itself; Dieulacres, on the other hand, was not to acquire any lands or pastures within a mile of Croxden, except in the manor of Leek and the demesne of the Earl of Chester.[9] By 1251 a dispute had arisen because Dieulacres had acquired land at Field. A settlement was then reached by which Croxden agreed that Dieulacres should hold land in Field and promised not to accept land there without the permission of Dieulacres. In return Croxden was freed from tolls and market dues at Leek and was allowed certain inclosures at Onecote and 'Puthullis'; Dieulacres in addition promised not to acquire any land nearer to Croxden or 'the grange of Leyes' without the abbey's consent.[10] From the late 12th century the abbey was acquiring property in the Dog Cheadle area of Cheadle mainly from Rose de Verdun, the Sacheverell family, and the Bassetts of Sapcote, and a grange had been established there by 1275.[11] By the 1230s Henry de Audley had given the monks a pasture on Morridge to the east of Leek.[12] Tugby church was appropriated to the abbey by the Bishop of Lincoln in 1224,[13] and Alton church had been appropriated probably by 1263 and certainly by 1291.[14] A dispute with the Rector of Uttoxeter over payment of tithes from abbey property was settled in 1263; the rector renounced all claim and in return the monks agreed to pay him 12s. a year.[15] By 1291 the abbey had acquired property at Riston (in Bradbourne) and Trusley, both in Derbyshire, and there was a mill at Caldon. Granges had been established at Musden, Oaken, and Riston as well as at Caldon, Cheadle, and Croxden. The total value of the temporalities and spiritualities in 1291 was some £140.[16] At the beginning of the 14th century a jury stated that all the Staffordshire property was held in free alms.[17]

The 13th and early 14th centuries were evidently a time of general prosperity for the abbey — the chronicler noted the period of Abbot Billisdon (1284–93) as one of particular prosperity.[18] The abbey's wealth was drawn partly from sheep-farming. This may have started by the 1230s: in an agreement with the burgesses of Alton in 1239 the monks promised not to erect a sheepfold on the burgesses' land.[19] It was certainly in progress before the end of

---

[1] For this para. see Dugdale, *Mon.* v. 661; *Annales Monastici* (Rolls Ser.), i. 187; *D.N.B. sub* Verdon. For the suggestion that Cotton was never intended to be more than a temporary settlement pending the completion of the first buildings at Croxden see F. A. Hibbert, 'The Date of Croxden', *T.N.S.F.C.* xlviii. 139–41.

[2] For the foundation charter see Dugdale, *Mon.* v. 662; facsimile in C. Lynam, *The Abbey of St. Mary, Croxden*, from Bodl. MS. Staffs. Ch. 47.

[3] Except for the assarts made by his men at 'Wodehuses'; his men were also exempt from suit at the mill at Croxden, and he reserved certain rights in the land above the stream dividing Croxden from Bradley.

[4] Dugdale, *Mon.* v. 662. By 1220 East Norton was served by a resident chaplain and enjoyed full sacramental and parochial privileges, paying 18d. for synodals; Keythorpe was served 3 days a week: J. Nichols, *Hist. and Antiquities of Leics.* i(1), p. lx; ibid. iii(1), 483.

[5] Dugdale, *Mon.* v. 661–2; *S.H.C.* 1913, 22; *Cal. Inq. p.m.* vii, p. 497; Sister Mary Laurence O.P., 'St. Mary's Abbey, Croxden', *T.N.S.F.C.* lxxxv, pp. B3–4, and lxxxvii, pp. B53–56, 60; Lynam, *Croxden*, chronicle, p. x; *Complete Peerage*, v. 583; see below.

[6] *Rot. Chart.* (Rec. Com.), 61.

[7] Ibid. 162; *Bk. of Fees*, 146.

[8] 'Extracts from the Annals of Crokesden Abbey', *Collectanea Topographica et Genealogica*, ii (1835), 309; *Cal. Chart. R.* 1257–1300, 419.

[9] *S.H.C.* N.S. ix. 355–6.

[10] Ibid. 358. 'The grange of Leyes' was evidently in Crakemarsh: see below p. 228. In 1540 'Puttelles' was described as 'by the water of Hanse': S.C.6/Hen. VIII/3353, m. 48.

[11] *S.H.C.* iv(1), 50; v(1), 118; vi(1), 265; 1923, 38–40; 1947, 50; S.R.O., D. 593/A/2/23/2–4, 6–9, 11, 12, 14–24.

[12] B.M., Cott. MS. xi. 38.

[13] Nichols, *Leics.* i(1), p. lx; iii(1), 483.

[14] B.M., Harl. MS. 3868, f. 13; *Tax. Eccl.* (Rec. Com.), 243. In 1331 when visiting Alton and staying at Croxden, the bishop satisfied himself that Alton had been canonically appropriated: *Coll. Top. et Gen.* ii. 306.

[15] B.M., Harl. MS. 3868, ff. 12v–14v. The *Valor Eccl.* (Rec. Com.), iii. 125, shows Croxden as paying 15s. to Uttoxeter church in 1535.

[16] *Tax. Eccl.* 63, 72, 243, 253, 262.

[17] *Coll. Top et Gen.* ii. 302.

[18] '. . . pinguedine terre, id est, frumento, vino et oleo, in toto tempore suo sufficienter habundavit': ibid. 299.

[19] S.R.O., D. 593/A/2/23/1.

the century, and in 1294 the chronicler complained that as a result of the outbreak of war with France that year it was difficult to sell a sack of the abbey's wool even for 7 marks.[20] Some 20 years later, however, Croxden was supplying more wool for the foreign market than any other Staffordshire house,[21] and the monks were evidently still engaged in the Florentine trade in the 1420s.[22] Charcoal burning in the abbey's woodlands is recorded several times between 1291 and 1369; £22 5s. was realized in 1316 from a wood at Cheadle called 'the Neweheye'. Timber was also sold: underwood from the park at Oaken fetched £24 in 1329.[23] The prosperity is reflected in the constant building operations. The first abbot, Thomas of Woodstock (1178–1229), was noted for his building, while under the energetic (*strenuissimus*) Walter London (1242–68) the church was completed and very extensive work was carried out on the conventual buildings. William de Houton (1269–74) continued the work, notably by erecting the abbot's house.[24] William of Over (1297–1308) bought the abbey a house in London for £20, apparently in the parish of St. Peter the Less in the ward of Castle Baynard.[25]

There is very much less evidence available for the internal history of the abbey. Some idea of the size of the community can be formed from the lists of admissions: 80 in the 26 years of Abbot London (1242–68) and 25 in Abbot Houton's 5 years (1269–74), and thereafter a decline — 14 in 1274–84, 14 in 1284–93, 2 in 1294–7, 9 in 1297–1308.[26] Little can be said about observance. Abbot Twyford (1294–7) was noted for his great devotion to the Trinity.[27] The abbots went occasionally at least to general chapters at Cîteaux. Abbot Ashbourne evidently died on the return journey in 1237, while Abbot Houton died at Dijon, presumably on the way to the chapter, and was buried at Cîteaux in the presence of over 400 abbots.[28] Abbot Billisdon evidently went in 1284 after his election and also in 1285. In 1298 Edward I forbade all Cistercian abbots, including those of Croxden, Dieulacres, and Hulton, to attend the general chapter and ordered them to pay to the Crown the money which they would otherwise have taken to Cîteaux. A similar ban was imposed in subsequent years.[29] In 1308, however, when apparently there was no royal ban, Abbot Over was summoned to attend but failed to go, whereupon the chapter deposed him.[30] A visitation was evidently carried out by the mother-house in 1313.[31] Several of these early abbots gave some attention to learning. Thomas of Woodstock

wrote two large volumes containing most of the Bible, and William de Houton bought a Bible of nine volumes from Master Solomon, Archdeacon of Leicester, for the sum of 50 marks. William of Over made additions to the abbey's collection of books.[32] It was probably in the late 13th century too that the compilation of the abbey's chronicle was begun.[33]

The 14th century was a time of increasing difficulty for the abbey. For the first time a serious dispute arose with the patron.[34] The last of the Verduns died in 1316 and was buried at Croxden. The patronage passed with Alton to Joan, his eldest daughter, and her husband Thomas de Furnivalle. Thomas insisted on the abbey's stabling his horses and hounds, feeding seven of his bailiffs every Friday in a room specially set apart for them, and distributing alms daily at the gates. He confiscated a cart belonging to the monks and impounded sheep, oxen, and horses. Eventually 'no one dared to ride freely through the gates of the abbey across the fee of Alton', and the monks barricaded themselves in the abbey for 16 weeks from March to July 1319. They erected two thorn fences at the gates to prevent direct access and made a small gate in the south wall so that they could pass through unobserved. At last, with the aid of several magnates, they secured a writ of novel disseisin and vindicated their rights in July. Peace was restored, and in 1321 the abbot baptized the daughter of Thomas and Joan. In 1334 Joan was buried before the high altar of the abbey church by the abbot, assisted by the Abbots of Burton, Dieulacres, Hulton, Combermere, and Beauchief and the Priors of Worksop and Ecclesfield, and in 1340 Thomas was buried at Beauchief Abbey (Derb.) by the Abbot of Croxden.

More serious were the abbey's economic difficulties. Royal exactions became heavier — the loan of supplies for the Scottish expedition in 1310, the imposition of a corrodian in 1318, the distraint of the abbot in 1322 for refusing to pay his share of the expense of a foot-soldier in respect of the property at Dog Cheadle, subsidies, more loans in 1337 and 1347.[35] Bad harvests, plague, and murrain all had an adverse effect.[36] Extensive repairs to property, notably the reroofing of the conventual buildings, much of it in lead instead of wood, in 1332, 1333, and 1334, and the rebuilding of the abbot's house in 1335–6 at great expense were a further drain on resources.[37] So desperate was the abbey's financial state that in 1368 the Abbot of Aunay, the mother-house, sent the Abbot of Garendon and Brother

[20] *Coll. Top. et Gen.* ii. 300.
[21] 30 sacks as against 25 from Burton and 20 from Dieulacres, the next largest suppliers: F. A. Hibbert, 'Croxden Abbey and Musden Grange', *T.N.S.F.C.* lii. 47.
[22] Ibid. lxxxvii, p. B52.
[23] *Coll. Top. et Gen.* ii. 300, 302, 303, 305, 306, 307, 308.
[24] For buildings see below p. 229.
[25] *Coll. Top. et Gen.* ii. 302; Sister M. Laurence O.P., 'St. Mary's Abbey, Croxden', *T.N.S.F.C.* lxxxvi, p. B42. The abbot was regularly summoned to Parliament between 1295 and 1307: F. Palgrave, *Parliamentary Writs* (Rec. Com.), i. 559.
[26] *T.N.S.F.C.* lxxxv, pp. B9–13.
[27] Lynam, *Croxden*, chronicle, p. v.
[28] *Coll. Top. et Gen.* ii. 298, 299.
[29] *T.N.S.F.C.* xlviii. 131 (which contains some errors).
[30] *Coll. Top. et Gen.* ii. 302.
[31] Ibid. 303.   [32] Ibid. 297–8, 299, 303.
[33] *T.N.S.F.C.* lxxxv, pp. B4 sqq. It continued until 1377,

with a register of monks and abbots until the 16th century.
[34] For this para. see *Coll. Top. et Gen.* 304–5, 307; Dugdale, *Mon.* vi. 661–2; *T.N.S.F.C.* lxxxvii, pp. B55–56. There had been a dispute with Theobald de Verdun in 1282 when the abbot sued him for £8 arrears of rent for the use of Alton mill and Theobald replied with a claim for £40 for a plot of waste; the abbot won: ibid. pp. B53–54. When Theobald's son demanded an aid in 1298 for the knighting of his eldest son, the chronicler recorded: 'we gave nothing at all' (*Coll. Top. et Gen.* ii. 301); but there is no mention of a dispute.
[35] *T.N.S.F.C.* lxxxvii, pp. B51–53, B61; *S.H.C.* ix(1), 92. The corrodian in fact stayed only 3 months: *Cal. Close, 1318–23*, 116.
[36] *T.N.S.F.C.* lxxxvii, pp. B59–60, B61; Lynam, *Croxden*, chronicle, pp. vii, xi, xii; see below p. 249.
[37] *Coll. Top. et Gen.* ii. 306, 307. Some 75,000 shingles were used in the reroofing. The outline of the roof can still be seen on the south face of the south transept. Abbot Walton reroofed the abbey *c.* 1500: ibid. 310.

Henry Foky from Aunay to investigate. The two visitors deposed Abbot Colbeley, and William Gunston was elected in his place. The abbey's debts amounted to £165 2s. 3d.[38] The new abbot made some attempt to improve matters. He recovered Caldon Grange which had been mortgaged, and within a few years he had raised 119 marks by the sale of charcoal.[39] New problems soon faced him, however. There was evidently a bad harvest in 1368, and the following year there was another outbreak of plague.[40] In 1369 also part of the abbey adjoining the church collapsed. Abbot Gunston rebuilt it in 1370 and in 1372 renewed the ditches in the neighbourhood of the abbey. In that year a great flood ruined grass and grain growing by the Churnet, and in 1372 a violent storm damaged the fabric, uprooted trees in the orchard, and damaged barns at Croxden and Musden. Abbot Gunston continued to repair the damage.[41] It is not surprising to find him in debt: in 1371 he was sued by the executors of Philip de Lutteleye for a debt of 40 marks and in 1376 by the Warden of the Chapel Royal at Windsor for three years' arrears of rent amounting to 36s.[42] Yet in 1379 the abbey had to lend the Crown 100s.[43] The great impoverishment of the abbey was stated as the reason for the king's permission, given in 1405, for the appointment of monks of Croxden as vicars of Alton.[44] The general decline is reflected in the small size of the community — an abbot and six monks in 1377 and 1381.[45]

The 14th century brought, however, certain additions to the abbey's property. By 1331 90 acres of waste at Bradnop had been acquired from Hulton Abbey.[46] Royal licence was secured for the acquisition of two small plots of arable and meadow in Combridge (in Rocester) and Sedsall (Derb.) from Robert de Combridge in 1342,[47] a house and 60 acres of land in Alton from Robert Shaw in 1346,[48] 'Verdon maner' in Ellastone from John Pyghtesley in 1392,[49] and a house in Ashbourne from Henry Blore in 1402.[50] In 1398 the Crown granted a licence, for 25 marks, for the appropriation of the vicarage of Alton, and the bishop gave his approval in 1402.[51] In 1403, however, the monks endowed the vicarage, undertaking to build a house for the vicar;[52] this may be connected with the fact that two years later, as seen above, the Crown gave the abbey permission to appoint its own monks as vicars.

Croxden never recovered its former prosperity, but there is some record of achievement in its later days. Abbot Walton, who occurs between at least 1467 and 1507, was engaged in building; the chronicler, indeed, describes him as the good abbot and a peacemaker (concordator) among both the great and the poor, despite the fact that he was involved in lawsuits. Abbot Shipton, who succeeded

in 1519, was a divine of some learning and a benefactor of the poor, and his many good works included the rebuilding of the chancel of Alton church.[53] In addition the number of the community had risen to 13 by 1538.[54]

In its last years the abbey was still poor. In 1533 the abbot was asked by Thomas Cromwell to lease Musden Grange to Francis Meverell, but he gave the excuse that 'neither God's service nor hospitality' could be maintained without the grange, which had not been leased out for 40 years.[55] The gross income of the abbey in 1535 was given as £103 6s. 7d. — £8 16s. 4d. from spiritualities, £57 13s. 7d from rents, and £36 16s. 8d. from demesne at Croxden, Musden, Caldon, and Onecote. Expenditure came to £13 0s. 8d. including £7 in fees to 7 lay officials — the steward of Tugby, the bailiff of Tugby who was also collector of rents in Leicestershire, the steward and the collector of Oaken, the steward of Croxden, Ashbourne, and Caldon, the bailiff of Ashbourne and Caldon, and the collector of Croxden and its members.[56] The income as given was thus lower than in 1291, but there is evidence that the valuation of 1535 was incomplete; a fuller account of the abbey's property in 1538-9 gives the gross value for that year as £163 8s. 10d.[57] Its estates were then listed as the manor and grange of Oaken, Lee Grange in Crakemarsh, and granges at Musden, Caldon, and Trusley; lands and rents in Croxden, Combridge, Great Gate, Ellastone, Alton, 'Whytley' in Leek, Onecote, Cotton, Dog Cheadle, Uttoxeter, Denstone, Calton, Caldon, Stafford, Orberton (in St. Mary's, Stafford), Walton (Staffs.), Ashbourne, Doveridge, Derby, Hartshorne, Thurvaston (in Longford), Langley (Derb.), Burton Overy, Tugby, Mountsorrel (in Barrow-upon-Soar and Rothley, Leics.), Casterton, Stamford, Misterton (? Leics.), London, and 'Sutton Maney'; the appropriated churches of Croxden, Alton, and Tugby and the tithes of Oaken, Lee, Musden, Caldon, and Trusley Granges; and a 'wichehouse' in Middlewich and Hungarwall smithy in Dog Cheadle.

Croxden came within the terms of the Act of 1536 for the suppression of religious houses worth less than £200 a year, but in 1537 the abbey received a licence to continue for a fine of £100.[58] In August 1538 Archbishop Cranmer wrote to Cromwell asking for a commission to be sent to Croxden, and on 17 September Dr. Thomas Legh and William Cavendish received the surrender of the abbey from the abbot and twelve other monks.[59] A month later parts of the fabric were sold for £9 9s. 8d.; the largest items were the roofs of the church and dorter, which realized £6 and £1 13s. 4d. respectively, and 'a little gatehouse on the north side of the common way' which went for 13s. 4d.[60] In 1539 the site, with a water-mill, lands, and the rectory

[38] Ibid. 307-8.
[39] Ibid. 308.
[40] Lynam, Croxden, chronicle, p. xii.
[41] Coll. Top. et Gen. ii. 308-9.
[42] S.H.C. xiii. 79, 124.
[43] Cal. Pat. 1377-81, 637.
[44] Ibid. 1401-5, 490.
[45] J. C. Russell, 'The Clerical Population of Medieval Eng.' Traditio, ii. 195 (which, however, omits the abbot in 1381: see E 179/15/8b).
[46] S.H.C. 1913, 35-36.
[47] Ibid. 92-93; Cal. Pat. 1340-3, 535.
[48] S.H.C. 1913, 111.
[49] Cal. Pat. 1391-6, 109.
[50] Ibid. 1401-5, 88.
[51] Cal. Pat. 1396-9, 446; Lich. Dioc. Regy., B/A/1/7, f. 177.
[52] B/A/1/7, f. 185.
[53] Coll. Top. et Gen. ii. 310; S.H.C. N.S. iv. 152, 155, 192.
[54] The deed of surrender was signed by the abbot and 12 monks: Hibbert, Dissolution, 222.
[55] L. & P. Hen. VIII, vi, p. 16.
[56] Valor Eccl. (Rec. Com.), iii. 125.
[57] Hibbert, Dissolution, 99-100; S.C. 6/Hen. VIII/3353, mm. 43-50.
[58] Hibbert, Dissolution, 138, 145-6, 214-19.
[59] Ibid. 160, 168, 220-3.
[60] Ibid. 255.

THE DIEULACRES CHRONICLE: FOLIO WITH THE STORY OF EARL
RANULPH'S DREAM

THE ST. CHAD'S GOSPELS, LICHFIELD CATHEDRAL: THE EVANGELISTS'
SYMBOLS

Above: West front of the church. *Upper right:* South transept and east range of the cloister. *Lower right:* Interior of the chapter-house from the east

CROXDEN ABBEY

of Croxden, was leased for 21 years to Francis Bassett, servant to Cranmer, on whose behalf the archbishop had put in a plea when asking for the commission to be sent to Croxden. This estate and other property were sold by the Crown to Godfrey Foljambe in 1545.[61] The abbot was granted a pension of £26 13s. 4d. a year. Pensions were assigned to all the monks,[62] and four still occur as pensioners in 1557–8.[63] One of these, John Stanley, was Vicar of Alton from 1546 until his death in 1569 when he was drawing a pension of £5 13s. 4d.[64]

The site lay on the north side of the valley with the stream providing a water supply, a means of drainage, and power for the mill.[65] Although the area is now crossed by a road and part of it is occupied by a farmhouse and farmyard buildings, there are more remains at Croxden than at any other monastic site in the county. In 1936 the site passed into the care of what is now the Ministry of Public Building and Works. In some places the walls of the church and of the conventual buildings are still standing; in others their foundations have been exposed, making it possible to reconstruct much of the original lay-out of the abbey.

The site was dedicated in 1181, two years after the move from Cotton. Building occupied much of the attention of the first abbot (1178–1229), but the church was not dedicated until 1253, in the time of the fifth abbot, Walter London (1242–68).[66] Copied from the church at Aunay, the mother-house, it was more elaborate in plan than most Cistercian churches in England. It was 240 feet long and consisted of an aisled nave of eight bays, transepts, a tower over the crossing, and an apsidal presbytery with a chevet of five radiating chapels. The altar of the Holy Trinity, probably in the north transept, is mentioned in the later 13th century, that of St. Benedict in 1312, and that of St. Lawrence in 1326; two altars, evidently in the south transept, were mentioned in 1334.[67] A bell was hung in the tower in 1302; broken on Holy Saturday 1313, it was recast later the same year.

The modern road runs diagonally across the nave and south transept of the abbey church. To the north of the road only part of one of the five radiating chapels is left above ground; nearby are the remains of four stone coffins. To the south of the road much of the south wall of the church has survived, incorporating evidence that the south aisle was originally vaulted. The west wall, with two west doorways and three tall lancet windows above them, is almost complete. Also standing to their full height are the west and south walls of the south transept. All this work is of the 13th century with no sign of later alterations.

The conventual buildings lay on the south side of the church, the cloister being entered through a door at the east end of the south aisle. Most of the buildings were erected or completed by Abbot London, though the cloister and parlour were rebuilt by Abbot Walton about the end of the 15th century. No remains of the cloister arcade are left standing. The ground floor of the east range, much of which survives, consisted of the sacristy and bookroom, the chapter-house (partly built by 1229 when Abbot Woodstock was buried there), the parlour, and a slype or passage. The chapter-house was a vaulted rectangular building, occupying the centre of the range and projecting eastwards beyond it. To the south of the slype was the vaulted undercroft of part of the dorter; this was probably the noviciate (probatorium) built by Abbot London. The southward extension may have contained the abbot's 'lower chamber' with his dormitory above it, both built by Abbot Houton (1269–74).[68] Projecting eastwards from the south end of this building was the rere dorter. The upper floor of the east range, now destroyed, contained the treasury and the monks' dormitory; the doorway of the night stair from the latter is still visible at a high level in the south wall of the south transept.

The southern range is thought to have consisted of the day-stairs up to the dorter, the warming-house, the frater (which originally projected southwards but was reduced in size to the line of the rest of the range, evidently in the late 15th century), and the kitchen. There was a bell-tower over the frater. Part of the south wall of this range, which is all that remains, shows signs of the 15th-century alterations and also of conversion to a dwelling-house after the dissolution. The modern farmhouse and its outbuildings cover the site of the kitchen and the south end of the west range. The latter was presumably devoted to the lay brothers; at the northern end part of a vaulted undercroft survives with a door leading straight into the church. A building called 'Botleston' — possibly a corruption of Billisdon, which would suggest a building of Abbot Billisdon's time (1284–93) — evidently adjoined the church; in 1369 it collapsed 'from the church as far as the door of the hall' and was rebuilt in timber in 1370.[69]

The abbot's lodging built by Abbot Shepshed in 1335–6 replaced the accommodation built by Abbot Houton probably at the southern end of the east range. The new lodging was a detached building standing south-east of the rere-dorter; two of its walls and part of a third survive. To the north of this was the infirmary, built by Abbot London. The site, partly covered by the modern road, was determined by excavations in the 19th century; further work to expose the foundations was in progress in 1968.

The abbey gatehouse, also built by Abbot London, lay to the north-west of the church, and there

[61] L. & P. Hen. VIII, xiii(2), pp. 65, 450; xx(1), p. 216.
[62] Ibid. xiv(1), p. 598; xvi, pp. 411, 731; E 178/3239, m. 8.
[63] S. W. Hutchinson, Archdeaconry of Stoke-on-Trent (1893), 166 (giving no source). One of these, Ric. Wilcox, does not appear among the monks who signed the surrender; the name may be an alias of Ric. Meyre, one of the signatories.
[64] E 178/3239, m. 8; S.H.C. 1915, 13–14.
[65] Unless otherwise stated the following account of the site and buildings is based on D. Knowles and J. K. St. Joseph, Monastic Sites from the Air, 104–5; Lynam, Croxden (including extracts from the chronicle not printed

in Coll. Top. et Gen. ii. 297–310, or Dugdale, Mon. vi. 661–2); P. K. Baillie Reynolds, Croxden Abbey (Min. of Public Building and Works). For views see plate on facing page.
[66] B.M., Cott. MS. Faustina B. vi, f. 74v.
[67] For these altars see Lynam, Croxden, chronicle, pp. v, vi, viii, x.
[68] According to the chronicle Houton 'edificavit egregie cameram abbatis superiorem et inferiorem': B.M., Cott. MS. Faustina B. vi, f. 75v.
[69] Lynam suggested that this building was the west range and also put the guest-house in that range.

was a chapel to the east of the gatehouse.[70] The chapel, a mid-13th-century building about 50 ft. long, survived as Croxden parish church until 1886, when it was replaced by the present church on a site a little further north.[71] The stone wall round the 70-acre precinct was begun by Abbot London and finished by Abbot Measham (1274–84); some of it can still be seen.

ABBOTS[72]

Thomas of Woodstock, elected 1178 while still a deacon, died 1229.[73]

Walter de Chacumbe, elected 1230.[74]

William of Ashbourne, elected 1234, died 1237.[75]

John de Tilton, elected probably in 1237, resigned 1242.

Walter London, elected 1242, died 1268.[76]

William de Houton, elected 1269, died 1274.[77]

Henry of Measham, elected 1274, resigned 1284.[78]

John de Billisdon, elected 1284, died 1293.[79]

Richard of Twyford, elected 1294, died 1297.[80]

William of Over, elected 1297, deposed by the general chapter in 1308 for failing to obey the summons to its meeting.[81]

Richard of Ashby, elected 1309, resigned 1313.[82]

Thomas of Casterton, elected 1313.[83]

Richard of Ashby, re-elected 1320, resigned 1329.[84]

Richard of Shepshed, elected 1329, occurs 1336.[85]

Alexander de Colbeley, deposed by the visitors in 1368.

William Gunston, elected 1368, occurs 1398.[86]

Philip Ludlow.

Roger Prestone, occurs 1433.[87]

John Dronefeld.

William Burton.

Ralph Leylonde, occurs 1439 and 1450.[88]

John Walton, or Checkley, occurs 1467 and 1507.[89]

Stephen Cadde, occurs 1509 and 1514.[90]

John Shipton, succeeded 1519, occurs 1521.[91]

Richard Snape, occurs 1529, died 1531.[92]

Thomas Chalner, or Chawner, elected 1531, surrendered the abbey 1538.[93]

A common seal was brought into use in 1313.[94] On the election of Thomas of Casterton in May the abbot's counterseal was broken in the presence of the visitors and community and it was decided that a common seal should be made and placed in the custody of four monks. This was duly done in November. It was evidently the seal in use in 1538. This is a pointed oval, $1\frac{3}{4}$ by $1\frac{1}{8}$ in., depicting the Virgin seated beneath a pinnacled ogee arch with the Child on her left knee; to the left is a shield bearing the Verdun arms and in the base under an ogee arch an abbot, three-quarters length, with a pastoral staff in his right hand and a book in his left. Legend, lombardic:

SIGILLUM ABBATIS ET CONVENTUS VALLIS S*ANCTE* MARIE DE CROKESDEN

10. THE ABBEY OF DIEULACRES

THE Cistercian abbey of Dieulacres beside the Churnet a mile north of Leek was founded in 1214 by Ranulph de Blundeville, Earl of Chester, possibly on the site of a former hermitage. The story is that Ranulph, after the dissolution of his first marriage in 1199 followed by a second marriage in 1199 or 1200, had a vision, while in bed, of his grandfather, Ranulph de Gernon, Earl of Chester. The elder Ranulph told his grandson to go to 'Cholpesdale in the territory of Leek' and found a Cistercian abbey on the site of the former chapel of St. Mary the Virgin there, providing it with buildings and ample possessions. Ranulph went on to command that in the seventh year of the interdict that was to be laid on England his grandson was to transfer to this new site the Cistercians of Poulton (in Pulford, Ches.); this was a daughter-house of Combermere (Ches.) and had been founded in the elder Ranulph's name by Robert the Butler between 1146 and 1153. When Ranulph told his wife Clemence about his vision and the proposed foundation she exclaimed in French: 'Deux encres' — 'May God grant it increase'. Ranulph thereupon fixed the name of the place as 'Deulencres' and gave it this name when he laid the foundation stone of the abbey. He transferred the monks from Poulton in 1214. The abbey chronicle states that the transfer took place particularly because of the attacks of the Welsh at whose hands the monks of Poulton suffered

---

[70] In 1719 the gate-house was 'almost entire': T. Barns, 'Mr. Edward Arblaster's Note-book 1719', *T.N.S.F.C.* xlvi. 146–7.

[71] *Kelly's Dir. Staffs.* (1892); Lynam, *Croxden*, plates 70, 71.

[72] Unless otherwise stated the details of the abbots are taken from the abbey chronicle (B.M., Cott. MS. Faustina B. vi).

[73] Buried in the chapter-house.

[74] Believed to have been buried in the chapter-house.

[75] Believed to have died on his way back from Cîteaux.

[76] Prior of Stratford-Langthorn (Essex) at time of election.

[77] Died at Dijon and buried at Cîteaux.

[78] Resigned because of infirmity; died 1286.

[79] Buried in the chapter-house.

[80] Buried in the chapter-house 'supra pulpitum'.

[81] Buried in the cloister 'outside the door of the church, beside the bench'.

[82] Prior at election.

[83] Prior at election.

[84] Resigned 'propter suam evidentem impotenciam'; died 1333.

[85] He built the abbot's lodging in 1335–6: see above p. 229.

[86] *S.H.C.* N.S. vi(2), 183.

[87] *T.N.S.F.C.* lxxxvii, p. B59 (no source given).

[88] *S.H.C.* N.S. iii. 150, 186.

[89] Ibid. N.S. iv. 152, 192; *L. & P. Hen. VIII*, xv, p. 288. His surname is given as Chekkele Walton in the chronicle. A John Blundell, described as Abbot of Croxden, was admitted to the Lichfield Guild in 1476: Harwood, *Lichfield*, 406.

[90] *L. & P. Hen. VIII*, i, p. 208; xv, pp. 286, 287. He was admitted to the Lichfield Guild in 1510: Harwood, *Lichfield*, 411.

[91] Lynam, *Croxden*, chronicle, p. xv; *L. & P. Hen. VIII*, xv, p. 287. He was Abbot of Hulton at the time of his election. In 1522 the Abbot of Croxden, unnamed, was stated to be very ill: ibid. iii, p. 1013.

[92] *L. & P. Hen. VIII*, iv, p. 2700; Lich. Dioc. Regy., B/A/1/14, f. 31.

[93] B/A/1/14, f. 31; see below p. 236; Hibbert, *Dissolution*, 222. He was buried in Checkley church in 1544: Sister Mary Laurence O.P., 'St. Mary's Abbey, Croxden', *T.N.S.F.C.* lxxxviii, p. B89.

[94] For this para. see *Coll. Top. et Gen.* ii. 303; W. de G. Birch, *Cat. of Seals in B.M.*, i, p. 525; Lynam, *Croxden*, chronicle, p. vi; E 322/66.

many injuries.[1] It has also been suggested that the foundation may have been a condition of the dissolution of Ranulph's first marriage in 1199.[2]

Poulton had been given extensive property in Cheshire — half the vill of Poulton, the manor of Byley (in Middlewich) with woods and a mill, land at Alderley, Bradford (in Davenham), Churton (in Aldford), Hull (in Great Budworth), and Wettenhall (in Over), pasture at Chelford and Withington (in Prestbury), and fishing rights in the Dee.[3] Ranulph made a number of new grants in free alms. He gave the monks Rudyard as the site of the abbey; the manor of Leek with its recently established Wednesday market and eight-day fair; the church of Leek with its chapels; land at Wetwood and 'Cocsuche'; a salt-pan at Middlewich (Ches.) free of toll and of suit at the 'wichmote'; and exemption from the payment of pannage dues, toll corn at Chester mills, and toll on all goods bought and sold on his estates.[4] He also granted the monks mills at Leek and Hulme in exchange for more distant property.[5] About 1230 Ranulph granted the advowson of Sandbach (Ches.) to the monks, and in 1254 they vindicated their right against the claim of Roger de Sandbach.[6] In 1256 the bishop appropriated the church to Dieulacres subject to the ordination of a vicarage and the payment of 40 marks a year to Adam de Stanford, Archdeacon of Chester, for life.[7] By 1223 the bishop had appropriated Leek church to the monks, subject to the appointment of a vicar.[8] At Ranulph's instigation King John granted 'the pasture' of Rossall (in Poulton-le-Fylde, Lancs.) to Dieulacres in 1216; though subsequently seized by the Crown it was restored in 1227, and in 1228 Henry III granted 'all the land' of Rossall to the monks for 700 marks to hold in free alms instead of at the royal pleasure.[9] When Ranulph died in 1232 his heart was buried at Dieulacres at his own wish;[10] his widow was buried there in 1253.[11]

Some rights of patronage were evidently claimed by the family of Robert the Butler. William of Measham, Robert's grandson, opposed the move from Poulton, and his agreement was not secured until some 25 years later. About the same time, in 1241, he remitted (for 16 marks) the 20s. rent which the monks had been paying for Poulton, and he also gave his body for burial at Dieulacres.[12] The patronage remained with the earldom of Chester, and in the early 16th century Henry VIII acted as patron in right of the earldom.[13]

Several other donors made grants of land in the earlier 13th century, most of it in the Leek area but some in Cheshire (at Pulford, Dodleston, and Macclesfield, and salt-pans at Middlewich and Nantwich) and in Lancashire (at Great Eccleston in St. Michael-on-Wyre, at Thornton in Poulton-le-Fylde, and at Little Bispham in Great Bispham); pasture was acquired at Saltney (Flints.). The advowson of Cheddleton was granted by Hugh de Cheddleton. The abbey was also buying or otherwise acquiring land around Leek during the 13th and 14th centuries, including land that had been granted in perpetuity to tenants. About 1270 it received a fee-farm grant from Shrewsbury Abbey of the vills of Norbreck (in Great Bispham) and Little Bispham at a rent of 8 marks a year.[14] By the 1240s Dieulacres had been granted an estate in London by Everard the goldsmith, son of Edmund de Angulo; it then sold this property for 100 marks except for a house in Wood Street which it retained as its London house.[15] The abbey was also granted a house in Stafford.[16] The abbey's possessions were confirmed by the Pope in 1246.[17] In 1291 its Staffordshire estates were valued at £37 13s. 8d. with Leek church worth another £28,[18] its Cheshire estates at £29 15s. with Sandbach church worth another £22 13s. 4d., and those at Rossall at £61 10s.[19] By this time Dieulacres was engaged in the wool trade — its sheep at Rossall are mentioned as early as 1228 — and the Black Prince was buying its wool in 1347.[20] By the mid 13th century numerous granges had been established in the Leek area, in Cheshire, and at Rossall; by the

[1] Dugdale, Mon. v. 627–8; Complete Peerage, iii, 'Chester'. The source of the story was the abbey chronicle and not a history of England by Hen. of Huntingdon as stated by Dugdale: see M. J. C. Fisher, 'Dieulacres Abbey' (Keele Univ. M.A. thesis, 1967), 16–18; plate facing p. 228 above. The chapel of St. Mary may have been a hermitage and may be identifiable with a cavern which can still be seen near the abbey site: Fisher, 'Dieulacres Abbey', 27–28; M. H. Miller, Olde Leeke, i. 150–2. For the Irish Premonstratensian abbey known as Dieulacresse see Dictionnaire d'histoire et géographie ecclésiastiques, ed. R. Aubert and E. van Cauwenbergh, xiv. 452–3. For the date of Poulton's foundation see Fisher, 'Dieulacres Abbey', 15–19.
[2] S.H.C. N.S. ix. 294.
[3] Ibid. 329–39. The monks had formerly held land at Aldford (Ches.) but exchanged it for land at Bradford and Wettenhall.
[4] Ibid. 310, 311, 315, 316, 328, 353, 354, 363–4; Fisher, 'Dieulacres Abbey', 28 sqq. 'Gonedun' was associated with Wetwood in that particular grant.
[5] S.H.C. N.S. ix. 310–11.
[6] G. Ormerod, Hist. of County Palatine and City of Chester (1882 edn.), iii. 96, 105; S.H.C. iv(1), 130; Cal. Pat. 1247–58, 431; Reg. Johannis Pecham (Cant. & York Soc.), i. 145.
[7] B.M., Harl. MS. 3868, ff. 31–32. This was the settlement of a dispute over the church between the monks and the archdeacon.
[8] S.H.C. N.S. ix. 311–12.
[9] Rot. Litt. Claus. (Rec. Com.), i. 284, 474; ii. 160; Pat. R. 1225–32, 125; Close R. 1227–31, 62–63; Cal.

[10] Chart. R. 1226–57, 78; Fisher, 'Dieulacres Abbey', 70–71.
[10] J. Sleigh, Hist. of Leek (2nd edn.), 41; S.H.C. N.S. ix. 363–4; Fisher, 'Dieulacres Abbey', 34–35. Ranulph died at Wallingford (Berks.), and his entrails were buried there; his body was buried at Chester.
[11] Fisher, 'Dieulacres Abbey', 37, 208. The only miracle recorded at the abbey was said to have happened at her tomb when a blind monk received his sight back: ibid.
[12] S.H.C. N.S. ix. 361–2; Fisher, 'Dieulacres Abbey', 33 (based on Facsimiles of Early Cheshire Charters, ed. G. Barraclough, 5).
[13] Fisher, 'Dieulacres Abbey', 106–7, 135–6; Black Prince's Reg. i. 70, 129; see below p. 232.
[14] S.H.C. N.S. ix. 305–9, 312–27, 339 sqq.; S.H.C. 1911, 186–7, 326–7; ibid. 1913, 43–44; Cal. Pat. 1281–92, 137; 1313–17, 332; 1330–4, 562; 1391–6, 144–5; V.C.H. Lancs. vii. 235, 246, 279.
[15] S.H.C. N.S. ix. 328. One of the witnesses of the sale was Michael Tony, Mayor of London in 1244 and 1248: B. B. Orridge, Citizens of London and their Rulers, 210.
[16] S.H.C. N.S. ix. 327.
[17] Lambeth Palace Libr., Papal Docs. 40.
[18] This did not include Cheddleton church, valued separately at £8. By this time, and for many years after, the advowson was in dispute between the abbot and the Chetelton family: Fisher, 'Dieulacres Abbey', 102–6.
[19] Tax. Eccl. (Rec. Com.), 243, 248, 252, 259, 329. The valuation of Rossall was reduced to £16 13s. 4d. in 1318 after the Scots invasion.
[20] W. Cunningham, Growth of Eng. Industry and Commerce (1922 edn.), i. 632; Close R. 1227–31, 35; S.H.C. N.S. ix. 350; Black Prince's Reg. i. 81, 137, 145.

dissolution there were seven or eight granges, mostly in the Leek area.[21]

The development of the Staffordshire Moorlands led to clashes with other interests there, notably those of other religious houses. Early on Dieulacres agreed not to accept lands and pastures within a mile of Croxden Abbey, and in 1251, after a dispute had arisen, a further agreement was made with particular reference to the rights of Dieulacres in Field.[22] A dispute with Trentham Priory ended in 1244 with an agreement granting the abbey right of passage through the priory's land at Wall just south of Leek and allowing it to build a bridge over the Churnet there.[23] A dispute over tithe in Wall was settled in 1257 when Dieulacres waived part of its claim in return for recognition of the remainder and the payment by Trentham of 2s. a year.[24] A quarrel with Hulton ended in 1252 in an agreement setting out the rights of the two abbeys, mainly in connexion with pasture and tithes, at Mixon, Bradnop, and Morridge and in Leek parish generally.[25] In the same year another dispute with Combermere Abbey over pasture rights and *vicinitas grangiarum* in the manor of Leek ended in a full recognition of the rights of Dieulacres which in return agreed to pay Combermere 1 mark a year.[26] A dispute with William de Ipstones was settled in 1244 when Dieulacres secured pasture rights in Ipstones but recognized William's inclosures there, while the following year the abbey secured a payment in lieu of tithe of hay from William and his tenants at Ipstones.[27]

The abbot was in fact a great landowner, second only to the Abbot of Burton among the heads of Staffordshire houses.[28] In 1293 he was claiming view of frankpledge, gallows, markets, fairs, waif, and free warren in the manor of Leek.[29] His hunting rights covered a wide area north from Leek to the county boundary.[30] As late as 1504 a lease of Poulton manor stipulated that the tenant must entertain the abbot and 12 mounted companions for six days twice a year and the cellarer and other abbey servants whenever they came to Poulton.[31] At the Dissolution, besides the normal officials on the estates, there was a 'forester of the forest of Leek'. The abbey buildings included a rider's chamber and a butler's chamber, and there were 30 servants there.[32]

Quite apart from the 13th-century disputes over property rights the abbey had a specially turbulent history. By 1339 it had even been seized by the Crown on the plea that it had been acquired in defiance of the Statute of Mortmain, but the abbot had no difficulty in proving that it had been founded long before the Statute.[33] The main cause of friction

with the Crown at this time was the royal claim to the right of imposing a corrodian.[34] In 1344 the king requested the monks to maintain Richard de Preston for life at Dieulacres in succession to Robert de Carmenton; the king alleged that Robert had at the request of Edward I been granted the food and drink of a monk, 18s. 9d. a year for clothing, and a room with fuel, lighting, and a bed. The abbot denied that Robert had been so maintained and also that the king had any right to impose a corrodian, the abbey being in the patronage of the earls of Chester. The king based his claim on the fact that the earldom was now in his hands, but a jury upheld the abbot.[35] Nonetheless corrodians continued to be imposed by Edward III, Richard II, and Henry VI.[36]

Royal grants of protection were frequent in the 13th and earlier 14th centuries: in 1334, for instance, two years' protection was granted to the monks and the servants whom they were sending to buy victuals in Staffordshire, Cheshire, and Lancashire — the abbey was described as 'situated in a lonely waste on the confines of the county of Stafford'.[37] The Black Prince as patron extended his protection to the abbey in the 1340s and 1350s.[38] In 1351 he ordered the justiciar of Chester to protect Dieulacres, along with three Cheshire abbeys founded by the prince's ancestors, from all annoyance; in particular he was to put an end to the impoverishment of the abbeys 'by the frequent visits of people of the country with grooms, horses, and greyhounds'.[39]

In fact the abbey appears as aggressor as much as victim in numerous breaches of the peace in the area during the later Middle Ages, the abbot maintaining armed bands like any troublesome lay magnate. A royal commission of inquiry in 1379 recited 'information that one William, Abbot of Dieulacres, desiring to perpetrate maintenance in his marches and oppress the people', had kept a band of 21 retainers 'to stay with him . . . to do all the mischief they can to the people in the county of Stafford and that they have lain in wait for them, assaulted, maimed, and killed some, and driven others from place to place until they made a fine with them'.[40] In 1380 a similar group was indicted for having beheaded John de Warton at Leek by command of Abbot William. The abbot surrendered and was imprisoned, but he was soon pardoned and released.[41] At the beginning of Henry V's reign the county was in a very disturbed state, and among the many indictments was one involving a monk of Dieulacres and a servant of the abbot. They were accused of being members of a group of 80 who had broken into William Egerton's park at Cheddleton

[21] Lambeth Palace Libr., Papal Docs. 40; *S.H.C.* v(1), 118; ibid. N.S. ix. 325–6, 342, 345; *Tax. Eccl.* 252; see below p. 233.
[22] See above p. 226.
[23] *S.H.C.* N.S. ix. 359–60.
[24] Ibid. 358–9.
[25] Ibid. 356–8. [26] Ibid. 356.
[27] Ibid. 360–1.
[28] On the evidence of the *Valor Ecclesiasticus* of 1535: Hibbert, *Dissolution*, 64. In the *Taxatio* of 1291 Dieulacres has a higher assessment than Burton: Fisher, 'Dieulacres Abbey', 56. The Abbot of Dieulacres was regularly summoned to Parliament between 1295 and 1305: ibid. 100.
[29] *Plac. de Quo Warr.* (Rec. Com.), 713, 714
[30] Mary Bayliss, 'Dieulacres Abbey', *N. Staffs. Jnl. of Field Studies*, ii. 83.

[31] Sleigh, *Leek*, 57.
[32] Hibbert, *Dissolution*, 238, 240, 242.
[33] *Cal. Pat.* 1338–40, 333.
[34] For examples of 13th-century corrodies in exchange for land see *S.H.C.* N.S. ix. 316; *S.H.C.* 1911, 429. For another granted by the monks of Poulton to Hen., son of Hugh the Jew, see *S.H.C.* N.S. ix. 336.
[35] *Cal. Pat.* 1345–8, 83–84; *Cal. Close*, 1343–6, 486; *S.H.C.* xiv(1), 65–66.
[36] *Cal. Close*, 1381–5, 418; 1392–6, 292; 1441–7, 47; 1447–54, 27.
[37] *Cal. Pat.* 1334–8, 9. For grants of protection by the founder see *S.H.C.* N.S. ix. 354, 355.
[38] *Black Prince's Reg.* i. 95, 97, 129; iii. 341.
[39] Ibid. iii. 18.
[40] *Cal. Pat.* 1377–81, 362.
[41] Ibid. 516; *S.H.C.* xiv(1), 153–4.

in 1413 and stolen ironstone. The abbot, Richard Whitmore, was also accused of being privy to their action and of maintaining them afterwards at the abbey.[42] Abbot John Godefelowe was involved in various lawsuits connected with breaches of the peace, including the quarrel between the Meverells and the Bassetts in the 1440s when he supported the Meverells.[43] In 1517 Abbot William Albion and eight monks of Dieulacres were accused of having been involved the previous year in a serious riot at Leek. This aimed at preventing the arrest of Thomas Hyde, who was a servant of the steward of Leek and was accused of complicity in a murder. At one point the abbot was seen to 'take his bow from his monk Whitney and take an arrow from under his girdle and nick it into his bow'. William Egerton of Wall Grange, who had come to arrest Hyde, took sanctuary in Leek church, and the abbot's servants set up a road block of 'trees, poles, and ladders' and tried to prevent all access to him.[44] Both Albion and his successor were deposed,[45] while the last abbot, Thomas Whitney, was involved in several acts of violence against tenants of the abbey.[46]

There is little evidence about the internal life of Dieulacres, although its turbulent history must have affected the standard of observance. The size of the community seems to have dropped during the 14th century: in 1351 it was stated that only a small number of monks were serving God there.[47] In 1377 the number, including the abbot, was 7, but it had risen to 11 by 1381.[48] It was 13 at the dissolution.[49] There is little record of attendance on the part of the abbots at the general chapter at Cîteaux, although they seem to have attended in 1284, 1287, and 1333.[50] The last reference to Dieulacres in the Cistercian statutes is in 1344.[51] There is some evidence of literary activity. The abbey chronicle continued until the reign of Henry IV and is a valuable source for the history of Richard II's deposition.[52] A case has been made for connecting the 14th-century poem 'Sir Gawain and the Green Knight' with Dieulacres.[53]

In 1535[54] the abbey's gross income was £243 3s. 6d.[55] — £174 13s. 2d. from temporal property and £68 10s. 4d. from spiritualities. Most of this latter was from Leek and its four chapels, but part was from Sandbach and its two chapels. The net income was £227 5s. The demesne, estimated at £8 18s. 6d. in value, was reserved for the use of the abbey guest-house. Fees of £5 6s. 8d. were being paid to three collectors, one of whom was also steward of the courts. At some time between 1536 and 1538 Abbot Thomas Whitney stated that his predecessor John

Wodlande had wasted the wealth of the abbey and in particular had granted blank pieces of parchment, sealed with the abbey seal, to various friends so that they 'might well at their liberty and pleasure write and convayn such matter as might be the utter distention and undoing of the said monastery for ever'. Abbot Thomas was then suing at law for the return of some of these blanks,[56] but in 1565 John Whitney, chamberlain of the abbey at the time of the dissolution and evidently the abbot's brother, stated that Abbot Thomas had himself issued sealed blanks shortly before the surrender of the abbey.[57] Whatever the truth, the abbot wrote to Cromwell shortly before the dissolution stating that he had fulfilled a request made by Cromwell on behalf of a servant and adding: 'We have no more churches but one adjoining our monastery, to which belongs no corn but oats, and no granges or demesne lands in our own hands, only a few closes to keep our horses and a few cattle. We beg therefore that such small things as we have may remain in our occupation, for divers gentlemen make great labour to the king to have them from us'.[58] The abbey's debts at the dissolution stood at just under £172.[59] The community consisted of the abbot and 12 other monks, with 30 servants, 8 'lauders and poor bede women', and 19 lay officials.[60] In 1538–9, the year following the dissolution, the abbey estates consisted of the manor of Poulton; granges in the Leek area at Swythamley, Birchalls, Westwood, Woodcroft, and Cheddleton and also New Grange, and two other granges at Byley and Rossall; lands and rents in Leek, Heaton, Leekfrith, Tittesworth (including Thorncliff), Longnor (in Alstonefield), Lowe, Birchalls, Cheddleton, Gratton (in Horton), Bradnop, Field (in Leigh), Stafford, Middlewich, Sandbach (including Hulme and Goosetrey), Newbold (in Astbury, Ches.), Alderley, Knutsford (Ches.), Great Eccleston, Thornton, Norbreck, and Little Bispham; the appropiated churches of Leek and Sandbach and the chapel of Poulton; and salt-pans in Middlewich. These estates were then valued at £285 14s. 2½d. gross.[61]

The abbey was surrendered to Dr. Thomas Legh on 20 October 1538.[62] The next day goods, furnishings, corn, and cattle were sold for £63 14s. 10d. to Edward, Earl of Derby, the steward of the abbey and of the town and manor of Leek; he was also put in possession of the abbey buildings and demesnes on behalf of the Crown. A certain amount of plate (including three gilt chalices), 175½ tons of lead valued at £720, and six bells worth £37 10s. remained unsold.[63] Alms of 26s. 8d. were given to the

[42] S.H.C. xvii. 7, 23.
[43] N. Staffs. Jnl. of Field Studies, ii. 82–83; S.H.C. N.S. iii. 163, 182, 185.
[44] S.H.C. 1912, 9–13.   [45] See below p. 235.
[46] See Fisher, 'Dieulacres Abbey', 138–42.
[47] Black Prince's Reg. iii. 18.
[48] J. C. Russell, 'The Clerical Population of Medieval Eng'. Traditio, ii. 195 (which, however, omits the abbot in 1381: see E 179/15/8b).
[49] See below.
[50] Fisher, 'Dieulacres Abbey', 94–99; Cal. Pat. 1281–92, 130, 269.
[51] Fisher, 'Dieulacres Abbey', 99.
[52] Ibid. 172 sqq. The history of 1399 and the early years of Hen. IV's reign was written by a supporter of Ric. II.; the chronicle is then taken over by an equally strong supporter of Hen. IV.
[53] By Professor R. W. V. Elliott: see The Times, 21 May 1958. See also Sir Gawain and the Green Knight, ed.

J. R. R. Tolkien and E. V. Gordan (2nd edn.), pp. xiii–xiv. It is suggested, for example, that the country round the abbey's grange at Swythamley was the scene of the hunting episodes and that the climax of the poem took place at Lud's Church to the north-east of Swythamley. It is also suggested that the beheading of John de Warton at Leek in 1380 (see above) may have inspired part of the poem.
[54] Valor Eccl. (Rec. Com.), iii. 123.
[55] This corrects the figure given ibid.
[56] C 1/930/42.
[57] Hibbert, Dissolution, 173–4. Thos. mentions 'my brother John Whytney' in his will of 1558: Sleigh, Leek, 64.
[58] L. & P. Hen. VIII, xiii(2), p. 515.
[59] Hibbert, Dissolution, 243–4.   [60] Ibid. 239–43.
[61] S.C. 6/Hen. VIII/3353, mm. 34–42.
[62] L. & P. Hen. VIII, xiii(2), p. 251.
[63] Hibbert, Dissolution, 237–9, 241.

8 lauders and bede women, rewards of £14 5s. 10d. to the 30 servants, and fees and annuities of £34 to the 19 officials, including £2 to Lord Derby.[64] Rewards were paid to the monks: £6 to the abbot, £2 10s. to the prior and two others, and £2 to the remainder. In addition the abbot received a pension of £60, the prior and two others £6 each, four others £5 6s. 8d. each, two others £5 each, and the remaining three £2 each.[65] In 1552 the site of the abbey and other property in the area, all of it in the hands of tenants, were granted to Sir Ralph Bagnall at an annual rent of £105 11s. 7½d.[66]

The monks had some difficulty in securing regular payment of their pensions, and by December 1540 Thomas Whitney, the former abbot, was evidently in some financial difficulty. He then wrote from Leek to John Scudamore, a receiver of the Court of Augmentations, asking for his pension due the previous Michaelmas and for 'the pensions of my poor brethren that are not able to labour for them'. He also requested that his pension should be paid regularly.[67] Five of the monks, including the abbot, were still drawing pensions in 1557–8.[68] The abbot, who died in 1558, was able to make several bequests, including his house in Mill Street, Leek; another legacy was a silver-gilt chalice left to his nephew 'on condition that if the monastery of Delencres be hereafter re-edified the said chalice to be restored to the said monastery'.[69] Three monks of Dieulacres are recorded as drawing pensions when they died — two of them in 1567 and 1569; the third, the date of whose death is not given, was buried at Dieulacres.[70]

Very little now remains of the abbey, but the buildings seem to have been on the normal Cistercian pattern.[71] The church, which consisted of nave, side aisles, transepts, crossing-tower, and chancel, was rebuilt in the 14th century; the work was begun by 'the good king Edward', and in 1351 the Black Prince visited the abbey and gave 500 marks towards the work. The inventory of 1538 shows '4 old altars in the aisles, 4 altars of alabaster in the body of the church', and this may indicate two altars in each of the transepts; there were also 12 candlesticks on the rood-screen. The conventual buildings lay on the south side of the church. The 1538 inventory mentions a glazed cloister with seats for the monks and a laver, the dorter, frater, and infirmary, a hall, 'the corner chamber' with an inner chamber, 'the rider's chamber', 'the butler's chamber', 'the laborars chamber', and the kitchen with its associated offices. The remains were uncovered in 1818, and much of the stone was used in the erection of outbuildings for the neighbouring farm.

ABBOTS

Richard, the first abbot.[72]
Robert, occurs by the early 1220s and in 1228.[73]
Adam, occurs some time between 1230 and 1232.[74]
William, occurs at some time between 1237 and 1240.[75]
Stephen, occurs 1244.[76]
William, occurs 1251.[77]
Ralph, occurs some time between 1257 and 1266.[78]
Hamon, occurs 1266.[79]
Walter de Mortone, occurs 1272.[80]
Ranulph, occurs 1279.[81]
Robert, occurs 1282–3.[82]
Elias, occurs 1287.[83]
Richard, died or resigned 1292.[84]
Robert le Burgulun, occurs from 1294 to 1302.[85]
Nicholas, occurs 1318.[86]
Peter, occurs 1330.[87]
Ralph, occurs 1345.[88]
Robert de Brigge, occurs 1353.[89]
William of Lichfield, occurs from 1379 to 1382.[90]
Richard Whitmore, occurs from 1402 to 1424.[91]
John Godefelowe, occurs from 1443 to 1450 and in 1470.[92]
William, occurs 1472.[93]
John Newton, occurs 1490 and 1504.[94]

---

[64] Ibid. 240, 242–3. The fees and annuities were described as 'granted out by convent seal before the dissolution of the said late monastery'. One of the 'servants' was drawing an annuity of 26s. 8d. at his death c. 1560 and a Thos. Woodland (presumably a kinsman of Abbot Wodlande) was still receiving the same sum out of Dieulacres, as well as £4 out of Hulton, in 1574: E 178/3239, mm. 8, 13.
[65] Hibbert, *Dissolution*, 239, 242.
[66] *Cal. Pat.* 1550–3, 440–1. See *S.H.C.* N.S. ix. 301–4, for its subsequent owners.
[67] *L. & P. Hen. VIII*, xvi, p. 152. He stated that he had had to borrow £8 from his brother.
[68] S. W. Hutchinson, *Archdeaconry of Stoke-on-Trent* (1893), 166 (no source given).
[69] Sleigh, *Leek*, 64. In his will he expressed a wish to be buried in Westminster Abbey.
[70] E 178/3239, m. 8. Only one of these was among those listed 1557–8.
[71] For this para. see *Gent. Mag.* 1819, lxxxix(1), 120–2 (suggesting that the whole was of 5 bays and some 160 ft. long, with the nave and aisles 63 ft. broad and the chancel 29 ft. broad); Sleigh, *Leek*, 72–73 and plate facing p. 60; *T.N.S.F.C.* 1878, 29–30; ibid. 1889, 73; ibid. 1903, 150; Hibbert, *Dissolution*, 237–9. For the 14th-cent. rebuilding see Fisher, 'Dieulacres Abbey', 114–15, citing *Chronicon Hen. Knighton* (Rolls Ser.), ii. 75. This mentions 'miram structuram fabricae ecclesiae' in 1351.
[72] *S.H.C.* 1913, 73.
[73] B.M., Harl. MS. 3868, f. 7; *Coucher Bk. of Whalley Abbey*, vol. i (Chetham Soc. x), pp. 43–44; *Final Concords of County of Lancaster* (Lancs. and Ches. Rec. Soc. xxxix), p. 55. Sleigh, *Leek*, 63, citing Rossall deeds, gives 1229–38.

[74] *S.H.C.* 1911, 423; Sleigh, *Leek*, 63.
[75] *S.H.C.* 1911, 425 (no source given).
[76] *S.H.C.* N.S. ix. 360.
[77] *S.H.C.* iv(1), 244–5; *S.H.C.* 1911, 428.
[78] *S.H.C.* 1911, 425 (no source given).
[79] Sleigh, *Leek*, 63.
[80] *S.H.C.* iv(1), 200. He had become a monk at Croxden some time between 1242 and 1268: 'Extracts from Annals of Crokesden Abbey', *Collectanea Topographica et Genealogica*, ii (1835), 309.
[81] *S.H.C.* 1911, 34.   [82] C 66/102, m. 23d.
[83] *Cal. Pat.* 1281–92, 269.
[84] *S.H.C.* vi(1), 205, 267.
[85] Eaton Estate Office, Eccleston (Ches.), Eaton Charters/ Edw. I/17 (reference supplied by Mr. M. J. C. Fisher); Sleigh, *Leek*, 63; *S.H.C.* 1911, 433; ibid. xi. 51. He was perhaps the abbot who was elected late in 1292: ibid. vi(1), 267.
[86] *S.H.C.* 1911, 433.
[87] Sleigh, *Leek*, 63.
[88] *S.H.C.* xiv(1), 65.
[89] *Black Prince's Reg.* iii. 130.
[90] *S.H.C.* xi. 153–4.
[91] *Cal. Papal Regs.* v. 398; *S.H.C.* xv. 98; xvii. 56.
[92] *S.H.C.* N.S. iii. 163, 182, 185; Lich. Dioc. Regy., B/A/1/10, f. 45v.; Harwood, *Lichfield*, 404 (admission of John, Abbot of Dieulacres, to the Lichfield Guild, 1470).
[93] *S.H.C.* N.S. iv. 180.
[94] Harwood, *Lichfield*, 409 (admission to Lichfield Guild, 1490); Fisher, 'Dieulacres Abbey', 130–1 (which also mentions a lease made by him around 1510). Dugdale, *Mon.* v. 626, gives an Abbot Thos. in 1499, and Sleigh, *Leek*, 64, an Abbot Adam de Whytmore in the same year.

William Albion, occurs 1516, deposed 1519–20.[95]

John Wodlande, occurs 1520, deposed apparently for wasting the abbey's wealth.[96]

Thomas Whitney, occurs 1523, surrendered the abbey 1538.[97]

The common seal in use in the 16th century is a pointed oval, 1⅞ by 1½ in., depicting the Virgin standing crowned beneath a Gothic canopy and holding the Child on her left arm and a fleur-de-lis sceptre in her right hand; in the base under an arch is an abbot with a pastoral staff.[98] Legend, apparently lombardic:

... DELACRIS

11. THE ABBEY OF HULTON

THE Cistercian abbey of St. Mary at Hulton, a daughter-house of Combermere Abbey in Cheshire, was founded by Henry de Audley for the souls of himself and his family. The site, in what was then a remote part of the county, is just over 2 miles east of Burslem in a valley beside the Trent not far from its source. The first brethren were professed in 1219,[1] but Henry's foundation charter was not issued until 1223. His endowment consisted of the vill of Hulton, the vill of Rushton to the south of Burslem with 'Manesmore', a wood at Sneyd 'with the enclosed hay' at Carmount near Hulton, all his land at Bucknall and Normacot, meadow called 'Bukkeley', and in the north-east of the county the vill of Mixon and 'the vills and tenements' of Bradnop, Middle Cliff, Apesford, 'Ruhegh', and 'Mulnesley' with a pasture at Morridge and a wood at 'Witherward'; the grant also included a yearly pension of 10 marks from Audley church.[2] Henry made a new grant of the vills of Mixon and Bradnop with the services of all the inhabitants within five years of the death of Ranulph, Earl of Chester, in 1232; describing Ranulph as his lord, Henry made the grant subject to the daily celebration of mass by thirteen monks at Hulton 'all the days of the world' for the souls of Ranulph, Henry, Henry's predecessors and successors, and all the faithful departed.[3] Further land at Normacot was given by Simon de

Verney[4] and apparently at Bucknall also by Henry de Verdon and his wife Hawise.[5] In 1256 the king confirmed the gifts of Henry de Audley and Simon de Verney, mentioning in addition a mill and a fishery.[6]

Henry de Audley was described as patron and advocate of the abbey in 1242,[7] and his grandson William, who held the family estates from 1276 to 1282, is said to have given the monks land at Swinfen (in Weeford).[8] By 1291 the abbey had acquired tithes at Biddulph and had mills at Normacot and Mixon; the total value of its temporalities was then given as £20 4s. 2d., much of it from rents, while a further £6 13s. 4d. was received from Audley church.[9] About 1300 Sir William de Mere appears to have given the monks land at Meir near Normacot.[10] Other grants are said to have included land near Apesford from William son of Thomas of Rudyard and Normacot Heath from Robert de Caldwal, but no dates are given.[11]

The Audleys continued as benefactors. In 1348 royal licence was given for James, Lord Audley, to grant the monks the advowson of Marwood (Devon) and for the monks to appropriate the church.[12] In 1349 they acquired the advowson of Audley from James with the right to appropriate. Royal licence had not been secured, and in return for a 200-mark fine the monks were allowed to retain the church.[13] In 1354 the Pope gave permission for the appropriation,[14] but in fact appropriation took place only after the death of the existing rector in 1369. A vicarage was ordained in 1370 and the monks duly presented.[15] In 1373, however, James claimed and secured the right of presentation.[16] He exercised it again in 1381,[17] but the next presentation, in 1385, was made by the monks who secured royal confirmation of the 1349 licence a few days later.[18] James, who died in 1386, left the monks £10 for prayers for his soul and directed that he was to be buried in the choir of the abbey in front of the high altar.[19] His son and heir Nicholas, who was buried in the abbey in 1391,[20] secured the appropriation of Biddulph church to the monks earlier the same year; a vicarage was not ordained until 1433.[21] Nicholas's widow Elizabeth paid for the royal licence of 1395 allowing the monks to acquire from the abbey of Blanchelande in Normandy the alien priory of

[95] S.H.C. 1913, 10; Sleigh, Leek, 64. He was deposed after a visitation by the Abbot of Combermere: Fisher, 'Dieulacres Abbey', 134–6.

[96] Eaton Estate Office, Eccleston (Ches.), Eaton Charters/ Hen. VIII/14 (reference supplied by Mr. Fisher); C 1/930/42; see above p. 233.

[97] E 315/93, f. 148 (reference supplied by Mr. Fisher); see above p. 233. He was admitted to the Lichfield Guild in 1536: Harwood, Lichfield, 416.

[98] W. de G. Birch, Cat. of Seals in B.M. i, p. 533; E 326/9052. Dugdale, Mon. v. 627, gives the legend as:

S' COMMUNE MON ... DE DELACRES

The seal shown in Sleigh, Leek, 63, bears no resemblance to the 16th-cent. seal.

[1] L. Janauschek, Originum Cisterciensium, i. 223. Some of the other sources cited there give 1218.

[2] B.M., Harl. MS. 2060, f. 4; Dugdale, Mon. v. 715–16; V.C.H. Staffs. viii. 116, 130, 248, 249, 250, 251. The V.C.H. wrongly mentions (p. 251) the wood of Sneyd as 'within the enclosed hay'; the charter simply says 'with'.

[3] B.M., Cott. Ch. xi. 38.

[4] Dugdale, Mon. v. 716. The land had formerly been Hen. de Audley's; he had exchanged it with Hervey de Stafford who granted it to Simon.

[5] S.H.C. N.S. xii. 30; S.H.C. 1933(2), 127.

[6] Cal. Chart. R. 1226–57, 453. The mill would appear to have been at Hulton, but mills at Normacot and Mixon only are mentioned in 1291: see below.

[7] S.H.C. xi. 314. He was associated with a grant of protection to the abbot by the king in 1235: Cal. Pat. 1232–47, 87.

[8] S.H.C. N.S. xii. 30; Complete Peerage, i. 338.

[9] Tax. Eccl. (Rec. Com.), 242, 252. For leases in the Bradnop-Morridge area see S.H.C. 1911, 438–9, 442–3.

[10] S.H.C. N.S. xii. 31, 245.   [11] Ibid. 31.

[12] Cal. Pat. 1348–50, 48.

[13] S.H.C. N.S. xii. 31; Cal. Pat. 1348–50, 413. They had presented by 1350: ibid. 444. The fine was halved in 1351: see below.

[14] Cal. Papal Pets. i. 258; Cal. Papal Regs. iii. 536; S.H.C. i. 282; ibid. N.S. viii. 123.

[15] S.H.C. N.S. viii. 120–1, 122–3; ibid. N.S. x(2), 128.

[16] S.H.C. xiii. 100, 115; ibid. N.S. x(2), 53. He claimed, wrongly, that he had presented the last rector.

[17] Ibid. N.S. x(2), 150.

[18] Ibid. 155; Cal. Pat. 1381–5, 527; W.S.L., H.M. Aston 6/1.

[19] S.H.C. N.S. xii. 30.

[20] Complete Peerage, i. 340.

[21] Lich. Dioc. Regy., B/A/1/6, ff. 76, 120v.–121; /9, f. 171.

Cammeringham (Lincs.) and the advowson and appropriation of the church.[22] Elizabeth, who died in 1400, also left the monks of Hulton 400 marks for the purchase of lands and £2 to each monk for prayers for her soul and her husband's; she directed that she was to be buried in the abbey 'with my very honourable husband Lord D'Audeley'.[23]

The monks were engaged in sheep-farming by the mid 13th century.[24] Granges were established at Rushton and Hulton soon after the foundation of the abbey,[25] and there is mention of the abbey's sheep-fold at Normacot in 1242 and another at Mixon in 1251.[26] The monks had a tannery at Hulton by the late 13th century and evidently a fulling-mill there at some period. They seem to have produced encaustic tiles, but there is no evidence that they produced pottery, although Potter was a family name at Hulton in the early 15th century. They were running an iron smithy at Horton in 1528 and owned coal mines at Hulton and Hanley by the 16th century.[27] Although in 1535, as in 1291, much of the abbey's income was derived from rents, there was extensive demesne farming at Hulton, Normacot, Bradnop, and Cammeringham in 1535.[28]

The abbey was poor and small. In 1351, 'out of compassion for the poverty of the house', the king remitted half of the 200-mark fine imposed in 1349 for the unlicensed acquisition of the advowson of Audley.[29] The monks based their case for the appropriation of Audley church in 1354 on the fact that their income had fallen to £14 as a result of the Black Death; it had been £26 17s. 6d. in 1291.[30] By 1535 it had risen to £87 10s. 1½d., but this was the smallest of any of the Staffordshire monasteries except Brewood nunnery.[31] The community numbered only 5 (including the abbot) in 1377 and 1381;[32] the abbot and eight monks signed the surrender deed in 1538.[33] There is very little evidence about the spiritual life of the house or its local influence. In 1386 the king ordered the arrest of one of the monks, William de Bynnynton, as a 'vagabond, apostate monk' who had left the abbey without permission and had been excommunicated more than six months before.[34] In 1417 the abbot, Richard Billington, was sued by Sampson Meverell for abducting Joan Condale who was in Meverell's service at Hulton.[35] In the late 1520s the abbot was accused of controlling the neighbourhood and preventing justice from being done; he replied with charges of assaults on his iron smithy at Horton.[36]

During the vacancy in 1534 the Earl of Shrewsbury wrote to Thomas Cromwell informing him that William Chalner, a monk of Hulton, was the candidate supported by most of the brethren 'for his

good living and wisdom.'[37] Sir Philip Draycott' steward of the abbey's Staffordshire manors, wrote to Cromwell stating that Chalner was supported by Shrewsbury, the bishop, and his brother Thomas Chalner, Abbot of Croxden. Draycott, however, writing on behalf of 'the wisest priests in the house, as Johnson and Cradok', stated that 'instead of being a good man, as he will be reported, he is very vicious and exceedingly drunken . . . There is none in the house fit to hold that room but is too old or too young. It is so poor and ruinous that, seeing the variance amongst them, it would be better to put over them some good monk of another house that will bring them in good rule; and because I tender its welfare more than its money or the favour of any I am bold to write the truth.'[38] Chalner was evidently not elected as an Abbot John occurs in 1535.[39]

Sir Philip's reference to the poverty of the abbey is borne out by the returns of 1535.[40] The gross income was given as £87 10s. 1½d. (£20 10s. from spiritualities and £67 0s. 1½d., from temporalities) and the net income as £76 14s. 10½d. Of the disbursements spiritual dues accounted for £3 11s. 9d., while the remaining £7 3s. 6d. went in various annual charges including payments to Sir Philip Draycott, chief steward of the Staffordshire manors (£1 6s. 8d.), and his under-steward (13s. 4d.), Sir Richard Sutton, chief steward of Cammeringham (£1), and the bailiffs of Hulton (£1), Bradnop (10s.), Normacot (10s.), and Cammeringham (£1). In 1538–9, the year following the dissolution, the abbey estates, valued at £108 2s. 1½d. gross, consisted of the manors of Bradnop, Normacot, Cammeringham, and Fillingham (Lincs.) including 'Cotes'; Rushton Grange; lands and rents in Hulton, Newcastle-under-Lyme, Stoke, Burslem, Sneyd, the Burslem part of Milton, Ubberley (in Bucknall), and Meir; the appropriated churches of Audley, Biddulph, and Cammeringham and tithes in Fillingham; and a coal mine in Hulton, rents from a 'wychehouse' in Northwich (in Great Budworth, Ches.), and a rent from St. Leonard's Chapel, Bridgnorth (Salop.), for the maintenance of a light in the chapel of St. Mary at Hulton.[41]

As an abbey worth less than £200 Hulton should have been suppressed under the Act of 1536, but the following year the Crown granted an exemption for a fine of £66 13s. 4d.[42] In August 1538 Sir Brian Tuke, Treasurer of the King's Chamber, wrote to Cromwell asking him to grant the abbey to Tuke's son-in-law 'young Mr. Audley' who at present had only the manor of Audley 'and no house but an old ruinous castle' (Heighley Castle). Tuke claimed that the abbot was willing to resign if Mr. Audley were

[22] Dugdale, *Mon.* v. 716; *Cal. Close*, 1392–6, 490–1.
[23] *Complete Peerage*, i. 340; J. Ward, *Boro. of Stoke-upon-Trent* (1843), 292–3. For the suggestion that the medieval stone coffin now in Burslem churchyard was Elizabeth's see ibid. 223.
[24] *S.H.C.* xi. 306; *Cal. Chart. R.* 453. Hulton appears in a Florentine list of wool exporters of *c.* 1315: see below p. 258.
[25] *V.C.H. Staffs.* viii. 116, 251.
[26] *S.H.C.* xi. 314; ibid. N.S. ix. 356.
[27] *V.C.H. Staffs.* viii. 132, 252; *T.N.S.F.C.* li. 143–4. For the smithy see below and *V.C.H. Staffs.* ii. 109.
[28] Hibbert, *Dissolution*, 107.
[29] *Cal. Pat.* 1350–4, 41.
[30] *Cal. Papal Pets.* i. 258; *Cal. Papal Regs.* iii. 536; see above p. 235 for 1291.
[31] Hibbert, *Dissolution*, 64; and see below.

[32] J. C. Russell, 'The Clerical Population of Medieval Eng.' *Traditio*, ii. 195 (which, however, omits the abbot in 1381: see E 179/15/8b).
[33] *L. & P. Hen. VIII*, xiii(2), p. 147.
[34] *Cal. Pat.* 1385–9, 178.
[35] *S.H.C.* xvii. 57.
[36] Ibid. N.S. x(1), 174; ibid. 1912, 25–26.
[37] *L. & P. Hen. VIII*, vii(2), p. 423.
[38] Ibid. p. 425.
[39] See below p. 237. Chalner was described in 1541 simply as 'late one of the monks of Hulton': L.R. 2/183, f. 142v.
[40] *Valor Eccl.* (Rec. Com.), iii. 107–8.
[41] S.C. 6/Hen. VIII/3353, mm. 12–16.
[42] *L. & P. Hen. VIII*, x, p. 515; xii(2), p. 349; xiii(2), p. 177.

granted the abbey.[43] On 18 September the abbot and eight other monks surrendered Hulton to the Crown,[44] but none of the property went to the Audleys. In October the moveables, including three bells, were bought by Stephen Bagot who in 1539 received a lease of the site and some other property.[45] The site and the manor of Hulton were sold with other neighbouring lands of the abbey to Sir Edward Aston in 1543.[46] The monks were granted pensions, the abbot one of £20;[47] two of the monks are recorded as drawing pensions of £4 when they died in about 1556 and 1566.[48]

The abbey site is on the east side of the road from Stoke to Leek by Carmountside Junior High School. The conventual buildings lay on the south side of the church which consisted of nave, aisles, chancel, transepts (each with two east chapels), and a tower over the crossing. Traces of the abbey fish ponds are visible near the Trent on the west side of the road.[49]

ABBOTS

Adam, occurs about 1230.[50]
Robert, occurs 1240 and 1241.[51]
William, occurs 1242 and 1244.[52]
Simon, occurs 1245–6 and 1254–5.[53]

William, occurs about 1265 and about 1286.[54]
Richard, occurs about 1286. [55]
Henry, occurs about 1288 and about 1302.[56]
Stephen, occurs 1306.[57]
Henry, occurs 1317.[58]
Nicholas of Kesteven or of Tugby, had become Abbot of Combermere (Ches.) by 1324.[59]
William, occurs 1332.[60]
Henry, occurs 1349 and 1375.[61]
Denis, occurs 1389.[62]
Richard Billington, occurs 1395 and 1417.[63]
Nicholas, occurs 1432.[64]
Richard, occurs 1449 and 1450.[65]
John Shipton, occurs 1517, became Abbot of Croxden in 1519. [66]
John Harwood, occurs 1527, became Abbot of Vale Royal (Ches.) in 1534.[67]
John, occurs 1535.[68]
Edward Wilkyns, occurs 1536, surrendered the abbey in 1539.[69]

The seal in use in 1538 is a pointed oval, $2\frac{1}{2}$ by $1\frac{1}{2}$ in.[70] It depicts the Virgin crowned and seated on a panelled and canopied throne with the Child on her right knee and a sceptre in her left hand. In the base is a shield bearing the Audley arms. Legend, black letter:

SIGILLUM COMMU[NE] . . . TE MARIE DE HULTON

HOUSES OF AUGUSTINIAN CANONS

12. THE PRIORY OF CALWICH

THE little priory of Calwich in Dovedale on the Derbyshire border of the county originated as a cell of Kenilworth Priory. The *heremitorium de Calwich* was given to Kenilworth by Nicholas de Gresley *alias* fitzNiel and his wife Margery, the latter having been the ward of Geoffrey de Clinton, founder of Kenilworth. The founders, who held Longford

(Derb.), also gave the church of Longford.[1] The date of the foundation of the priory lies after *c.* 1125 when the mother-house of Kenilworth was founded; about 1130 'the brethren of Calwich' are mentioned in a confirmation of the gift of Longford church.[2] The list of Kenilworth properties confirmed by the king in 1163 mentions Ellastone church as having been given by Nicholas and Margery but makes no mention of Longford, Kenilworth having

[43] Ibid. xiii(2), p. 84. The family name was in fact Tuchet at this time; George, the son-in-law in question, succ. his father as Ld. Audley *c.* 1557: *Complete Peerage*, i. 343.
[44] *L. & P. Hen. VIII*, xiii(2), p. 147.
[45] *V.C.H. Staffs.* viii. 249; Hibbert, *Dissolution*, 257.
[46] *V.C.H. Staffs.* viii. 249.
[47] *L. & P. Hen. VIII*, xiv(1), p. 598; xvi, p. 731.
[48] E 178/3239, m. 8. A third was drawing a pension in 1557–8: S. W. Hutchinson, *Archdeaconry of Stoke-on-Trent* (1893), 166 (no source given).
[49] *V.C.H. Staffs.* viii. 248, 250, 251; C. Lynam, 'Recent Excavations on the site of Hulton Abbey', *Jnl. Brit. Arch. Assoc.* xli. 65–71; *T.N.S.F.C.* (1885), 98–102; ibid. lxv. 149–55; ibid. lxxxv. 84–85; A. R. Mountford, 'Hulton Abbey . . . Excavation & Restoration 1959–1966', *City of Stoke-on-Trent Museum Arch. Soc. Reps. No. 2.*
[50] *S.H.C.* 1911, 425 (no source given).
[51] B.M., Harl. MS. 280, f. 77v. (no source given).
[52] *S.H.C.* xi. 314–15; ibid. 1911, 425, giving 1244 without a source.
[53] Ibid. xi. 306, 315.
[54] Ibid. 1911, 438, 439.
[55] Ibid. 443.
[56] Ibid.
[57] Ibid. 439.
[58] Ibid. 433.
[59] 'Extracts from the Annals of Crokesden Abbey', *Collectanea Topographica et Genealogica*, ii (1835), 309; G. Ormerod, *Hist. of County Palatine and City of Chester*

(1882 edn.), iii. 403. He had become a monk at Croxden some time between 1242 and 1268.
[60] Hutchinson, *Archdeaconry of Stoke*, 35 (no source given).
[61] *S.H.C.* xiii. 100; ibid. N.S. xii. 31.
[62] *Cal. Close*, 1385–9, 675.
[63] Ibid. 1392–6, 491; *S.H.C.* xvii. 57.
[64] *S.H.C.* xvii. 140.
[65] Hutchinson, *Archdeaconry of Stoke*, 35 (no source given); Lich. Dioc. Regy., B/A/1/10, f. 45v.
[66] *S.H.C.* 1912, 12 (Jan. 1517); see above p. 230.
[67] *S.H.C.* 1912, 25–26; *L. & P. Hen. VIII*, vii(2), p. 423; Ormerod, *Cheshire*, ii. 151. He may be the John Wyche who occurs as abbot in D. and C. Lich., 'Census', f. 34. A John Harrower, described as late Abbot of Hulton, occurs *c.* 1540: C 1/1068/10.
[68] *Valor Eccl.* iii. 107.
[69] *L. & P. Hen. VIII*, xii(2), p. 349.
[70] W. de G. Birch, *Cat. of Seals in B.M.* i, p. 590; Ward, *Stoke*, 294; E 322/106.
[1] Dugdale, *Mon.* vi(1), 224; *S.H.C.* N.S. i. 21. The site may have been a hermitage or merely a secluded spot; it is not mentioned in Domesday Bk.
[2] Dugdale, *Mon.* vi(1), 224. The document mentions the consent of Geoffrey de Clinton and of the bishop, Roger de Clinton (1129–48), Geoffrey's nephew. It may be a year or two later than the gift. *V.C.H. Warws.* ii. 86, wrongly gives the founder of Kenilworth as Godfrey de Clinton.

relinquished its claim in return for a pension of 40s.[3] Ellastone was so near Calwich that it could, if necessary, be served by one of the canons, and this factor may have inspired an exchange. In 1391 the dedication of the priory is mentioned as to St. Margaret.[4]

Later evidence shows that the priory was planned to be dependent on Kenilworth, whose prior had power to appoint and remove four canons there, presenting one of them as canon-in-charge on the nomination of the lord of Longford.[5] According to the usual practice a canon was seldom resident at a cell of this nature for more than a few years at a time. This close dependence of Calwich on Kenilworth meant that the former had no separate legal identity. Consequently the growth of its property at this time cannot be traced, but Calwich was certainly never even moderately wealthy, partly perhaps because of its proximity to the abbeys of Croxden and Rocester.

For the aid of 1235–6 Calwich was assessed at 10s., the same amount as Rocester but considerably less than Stone and Trentham.[6] In 1274 the house received one of its larger benefactions when Nicholas le Chamberleyng and his wife Elizabeth gave it a messuage in Ellastone with 2 bovates, 4 acres of land, and the services of two tenants there in return for 'the benefits and prayers of the house'.[7] In 1291 the *custos domus de Calewich* was holding temporalities valued at £2 10s. while the appropriated church of Ellastone was worth £9 6s. 8d.[8] At the *quo warranto* inquiry of 1293 Calwich disclaimed all right to pleas of the Crown and other franchises in its manor of Ellastone.[9] The house appears as one of many given royal protection in 1297.[10]

As often happened in such cases the dependent status of Calwich engendered friction. In 1293, in the course of a lawsuit over pasture rights in Wootton (in Ellastone), it was stated that the 'prior' of Calwich was removable at the will of the Prior of Kenilworth; the 'prior' denied this, but a local jury decided against him on this point.[11] In 1334, perhaps because of some further disagreement over status, the keeper of Calwich was recalled by the Prior of Kenilworth, and the bishop upheld the prior's right to do this.[12] In 1349, however, Calwich acquired its independence,[13] and a long document in a Kenilworth cartulary has preserved details of the settlement.[14] After reciting the original constitution of the cell, the document goes on to relate that the right of the Prior of Kenilworth to transfer brethren whenever he found it desirable had led to complaints that stability was being thereby disturbed. In response to frequent requests and to terminate frequent dissensions with the patron, the bishop now ordained that the cell of Calwich was henceforth to be known as a priory and was to be

completely free from Kenilworth; it was to have the right to elect its own prior, subject to confirmation by the ordinary, and was to have the status of a conventual church. In return for this independence it was to pay Kenilworth priory an annual pension of 60s. When a vacancy occurred, the brethren of Calwich were to obtain licence to elect from their patron, the lord of the manor of Longford, if he was in residence, otherwise from the custodian of the manor. The next deed in the cartulary is an *inspeximus* by Sir Nicholas de Longford of an elaborate and stringent agreement between the two priories to ensure the payment of this pension which was charged on property in Calwich, Stanton, and Ramshorn (all in Ellastone).[15]

Small monastic establishments like Calwich were always a difficult problem for those in authority over them, and it is doubtful whether the new arrangement at Calwich was advantageous, as it solved some problems only by creating others. The time had gone past when the priory was likely to augment appreciably either its numbers or its possessions, and the large pension to Kenilworth must have been a heavy charge on its limited resources. The later history of the house was clearly precarious, and there were never more than a handful of brethren. The community numbered four (including the prior) in 1377 and 1381.[16] A petition of 1385 shows the poor estate of the house. In this the prior sought to be relieved from collecting a royal tax on the ground that there were then in the priory only himself and two canons; he claimed that this was the number required by the terms of the foundation but that they were too feeble through age to labour and too poor to hire others to labour for them, except for their necessities.[17] The success of the petition suggests its substantial accuracy. A similar sign of need is given by the papal indulgence granted in 1391 to those visiting the priory of St. Margaret, Calwich, on certain days and giving alms to its fabric.[18] There are few signs of any acquisitions at this time though in 1386 the priory was pardoned for acquiring in mortmain without licence two cottages and some land in Staffordshire and Derbyshire.[19] In 1449 two canons, John Stone and John Leder, sought the appointment of a prior from the bishop; Stone and Leder were the only canons of the house at the time. John Stone was nominated. His resignation in 1461 left only one other canon in the house, and the new prior was again appointed by the bishop.[20]

By the early 16th century the house was clearly in a tottering condition. A visitation of 1518 reveals a community of two, the prior and a canon named John Deane.[21] At the General Chapter of the order in 1518 the prior was cited to appear with Deane, who was said to have been professed at Trentham; he had probably been lured to Calwich in a desperate attempt to maintain a convent there. The prior

[3] Dugdale, *Mon.* vi(1), 223–4; B.M. Add. MS. 47677, ff. 101, 124v.–125.

[4] See below.

[5] The details are recorded in a deed in a Kenilworth cartulary: B.M. Add. MS. 47677, f. 116v.; see also f. 100v.

[6] See below p. 248.

[7] *S.H.C.* 1911, 28–29.

[8] Ibid. vi(1), 226.

[9] *Tax. Eccl.* (Rec. Com.), 243, 251.

[10] *Cal. Pat.* 1292–1301, 278.

[11] *S.H.C.* vi(1), 226.

[12] Ibid. i. 266.

[13] For this date see list of custodians and priors below.

[14] B.M. Add. MS. 47677, ff. 116–117v.

[15] Ibid. ff. 117v.–118v. It is followed by a shorter deed providing for security in case of nonpayment: ibid. ff. 118v.–119. See also *S.H.C.* 1913, 178; *Cal. Pat.* 1364–7, 252.

[16] J. C. Russell, 'The Clerical Population of Medieval Eng.' *Traditio*, ii. 200 (which, however, omits the prior in 1381 and wrongly gives the date as 1383: see E 179/15/8b).

[17] *S.H.C.* N.S. viii. 152.

[18] *Cal. Papal Regs.* iv. 356.

[19] *Cal. Pat.* 1385–9, 152.

[20] Lich. Dioc. Regy., B/A/1/10, f. 17; /12, f. 41v.

[21] Ibid., B/V/1/1, p. 12.

promised to regularize the situation, Deane being either returned to Trentham or made a member of Calwich.[22] In fact he was still at Calwich in 1524.[23]

The death of the prior in 1530, left but a single canon at the priory.[24] The patron, Sir Ralph Longford, who had a technical right to be consulted over elections, claimed the right of presentation, but the ordinary's 'accustomed provision' was also urged.[25] By 1531 the suppression of the house had been decided upon,[26] not a surprising decision in view of the temper of the time and the lack of a community. What is, however, worthy of note is the complete secularization of the priory's property which followed. In April 1532 an agreement was made between the king and the patron for the suppression of St. Margaret's Priory; Longford was to have the lands of the monastery in tail male, subject to 'a rent agreed by indifferent persons'.[27] In the inquest that followed local interests threatened the royal pleasure,[28] but by October the king's agent, Richard Strete, could write that all was well.[29] A sale followed and Cromwell's accounts for March 1533 included £30 'for goods of Calwyche'.[30] The next month Strete wrote that 'the priory of Calwich, now void, rests in the king's pleasure'.[31] Arrangements were made to dispose of the cattle and corn, and Strete was informed that he might translate the surviving canon of Calwich to 'some good house of that religion' nearby, giving him 'something after your discretion such as may stand with the king's honour and also to his honest contentation'.[32] By mid-May Strete had made an inventory of the goods of the house and had committed the custody of the priory to the Abbot of Rocester, the nearest Augustinian house. A canon was sent from Rocester 'to overse them who hath kept the sequestre syns the departur of the late prior'.[33] The inventory values the household goods, 'very course', at £15 13s. 2d., livestock at £79 15s. 4d., growing corn at £11 6s. 8d., 'stuff for the church, as chales and vestments etc.' at £10 9s. 8d., making a total of £117 4s. 10d. The desmesne lands around the priory were assessed at £23 12s. yearly, tithes at £17 8s. 1½d., and the appropriated church of Ellastone, 'besyde the vicar indoment', at £13 6s. 8d. 'In these is no harde peneworth,' commented Strete; 'the house and other byldinges be in mean good state of reparacion. I have dischargyd and put forth such persons as were not mete to be ther and laft such as be husbaundes, and I have made sure the convent saill [seal] and the evidence.'[34] The suppression of Calwich is of some interest as a gross example of secularization, anticipating the general suppression of small monasteries in 1536 and evidently effected without the careful ecclesiastical supervision hitherto normal in such cases.

The site was leased to Sir Ralph Longford but was granted by the Crown to Merton Priory in Surrey in 1535–6 in exchange for the manor of East Molesey (Surr.); Merton renewed Longford's lease. On the dissolution of Merton in 1538 Calwich passed back to the Crown which then renewed Longford's lease once more. He was, however, already in debt; in 1541 the escheators distrained on the property, and in 1543 he was in the Fleet prison.[35] In that year the property was granted to John Fleetwood.[36] Erdeswick, about the end of the century, stated that he had heard that the Fleetwoods had converted the priory church into a dwelling, making 'a parlour of the chancel, a hall of the church, and a kitchen of the steeple'.[37] Remains of buildings on the site appear to belong to a later period.

KEEPERS[38]

Henry, occurs about 1200.[39]
Nicholas, resigned 1259.[40]
Hugh, occurs 1274.[41]
Thomas de Boweles, appointed 1305.[42]
William of Sheldon, probably appointed 1309.[43]
John of Leicester, appointed 1311.[44]
Richard de Keten, appointed March 1312.[45]
John of Leicester, appointed May 1312.[46]
Geoffrey de Whitewell, appointed 1318.[47]
Nicholas de Blacgreve, appointed 1323.[48]
William Boydyn, appointed 1333.[49]
Thomas de Helyden, appointed 1337.[50]
Robert de Sakerston, appointed 1340.[51]
Geoffrey de Hampton, appointed 1346.[52]
Roger of Birmingham, appointed August 1349.[53]
Henry de Bradewey, appointed September 1349.[54]

[22] Chapters of the Augustinian Canons (Oxford Hist. Soc. lxxiv), 136–7. By will of 1517 Sir John Fitzherbert of nearby Norbury (Derb.) left 12d. to the Prior of Calwich, 4d. to every chantry there, and 6d. to the ringers: J. C. Cox, 'Norbury Manor House and the Troubles of the Fitzherberts', Jnl. Derb. Arch. Soc. vii. 227. As Sir John did not die until 1531 Calwich presumably did not in fact benefit.
[23] Lich. Dioc. Regy., B/V/1/1, p. 51 (2nd nos.).
[24] L. & P. Hen. VIII, iv(3), p. 2836.
[25] Ibid.
[26] Ibid. v, p. 126, where arrangements for the sale of the priory's cattle are mentioned.
[27] Ibid. p. 453.
[28] Ibid. pp. 537–8.
[29] Ibid. p. 615.
[30] Ibid. vi, p. 101.
[31] Ibid. p. 178.
[32] Ibid. p. 294.
[33] Ibid. x, p. 354; Hibbert, Dissolution, 34.
[34] Hibbert, Dissolution, 34. The visitations of 1518 and 1524 show that most of the livestock were sheep: Lich. Dioc. Regy., B/V/1/1, p. 12 and p. 51 (2nd nos.).
[35] Hibbert, Dissolution, 39–41; L. & P. Hen. VIII, xviii(1), p. 205.
[36] L. & P. Hen. VIII, xviii(1), p. 66.
[37] Erdeswick, Staffs. 489–90.

[38] Most of the keepers from 1305 are recorded in the bishops' regs. as 'instituted' or 'admitted', sometimes to the cell of Calwich, sometimes to its custody. Houses of the order often had the right to instal 3 or 4 brethren in any of their churches, one of whom was to be presented to the bishop for institution. Henry is described as prior in the list of witnesses to a deed c. 1200 (see n. 39 below), and some of the keepers are loosely called priors, and the cell a priory, in documents of the later 13th and earlier 14th centuries (S.H.C. i. 266; vi(1), 226, 246; 1911, 28–29; Lich. Dioc. Regy., B/A/1/1, f. 32v.).
[39] F. Taylor, 'Hand-list of the Crutchley MSS. in the John Rylands Library', Bull. of the John Rylands Libr. xxxiii. 155. He witnessed a document also witnessed by Wal., Abbot of Darley (c. 1197–1210): Cartulary of Darley Abbey, ed. R. R. Darlington, i, p. lxxx.
[40] He became Prior of Kenilworth in this year: Cal. Pat. 1258–61, 21, 27.
[41] S.H.C. 1911, 28–29.
[42] Lich. Dioc. Regy., B/A/1/1, f. 16.
[43] The patron's approval of his nomination was asked in a letter of 20 July of this year: S.H.C. 1939, 125–6.
[44] Lich. Dioc. Regy., B/A/1/1, f. 44v.
[45] Ibid. f. 45v.   [46] Ibid. f. 32v.   [47] Ibid. f. 89.
[48] B/A/1/2, f. 138.   [49] Ibid. f. 154v.   [50] Ibid. f. 160.
[51] Ibid. f. 166.   [52] Ibid. f. 178.
[53] Ibid. f. 184.   [54] Ibid. ff. 184v.–185.

PRIORS

Richard Mayel, elected November 1349.[55]

Thomas de Farnecote, occurs 1386, died by January 1392.[56]

Thomas Aleyn *alias* of Trentham, elected 1391 or 1392, resigned 1402.[57]

Robert Holynton, elected 1402, died 1449.[58]

John Stone *alias* Hardy, appointed 1449, resigned 1461.[59]

Lawrence Whalley, appointed 1461.[60]

John, occurs 1463.[61]

Robert Ellerbeke, died 1500.[62]

Thomas Dakyn *alias* Dawson, appointed 1500, resigned 1507.[63]

Ralph Snelston, elected 1507, still prior 1524; he was probably the prior who died 1530.[64]

No seal of the priory has been traced, though it is known that one existed in the early 16th century.[65]

13. THE PRIORY OF STONE

THE priory of Stone was founded in an existing church dedicated to St. Wulfad. The identity of the saint is uncertain. The *Historia Fundationis*[1] claims him as a son of Wulfhere, King of Mercia (657–74), and states that, with his brother Ruffinus, he was converted to Christianity by St. Chad and martyred by his father; remorse for this act is said to have led to King Wulfhere's own conversion by St. Chad and to his foundation of a monastery at Stone. This legend, however, cannot be accepted. Wulfhere was already a Christian when he became king,[2] and the story on which it is probably based is set by Bede in another part of the country over ten years after Wulfhere's death.[3]

It is possible that the regular canons at Stone were preceded by another religious community. Domesday Book records the gift of a carucate of land in Walton (in Stone) made by Achil, a freeman, to his sister; it has been suggested that this was a gift to some small community of nuns, possibly a hermitage.[4] The only corroborative evidence,

however, is provided by some late-medieval verses:

... two nunns and one preest lived in this place
The which were slayne by one Enysan ...
This Enysan slue the nuns and priest alsoe,
Because his sister should have this church thoe.[5]

Although the value of these verses as evidence for an early religious community is slight, they may preserve a confused tradition of the circumstances in which the Austin priory was founded at Stone. Enisan was Enisan de Walton, the son of the Ernald who held Walton under Robert de Stafford in 1086, but it is Enisan's son, another Ernald, who appears in the Pipe Roll of 1129–30 as owing a fine of 10 silver marks for 'the men whom he killed'.[6] It was perhaps the need to raise this sum that led to the sale to Geoffrey de Clinton of the property on which Stone Priory was founded.[7] Soon after his foundation of Kenilworth Priory (about 1125) Clinton acquired the church of Stone from Enisan de Walton and, with the assent of Enisan's superior lord, Nicholas de Stafford, conveyed it to the canons at Kenilworth.[8] In a deed of about 1131 Enisan and Ernald II confirmed the church to Kenilworth Priory and added to it land in Stone and Walton; at the same time they confirmed the sale to Kenilworth of other land in Walton by Enisan's daughter and her husband.[9] In return Clinton gave 50s. and a palfrey worth 20s. to Ernald and a grey cloak and a palfrey to Enisan.[10] These gifts were confirmed by Nicholas de Stafford and his heir, Robert,[11] but were the subject of some litigation in the king's court.[12] They were subsequently confirmed again by Ernald de Walton.[13]

The first mention of a daughter-house of Kenilworth at Stone[14] is in a charter of 1138–47 by which Robert de Stafford II granted 'to the church of Stone and the canons serving God there' considerable spiritual and temporal property.[15] It is possible that this is in fact the foundation charter of Stone Priory; Robert was the overlord of much property which Geoffrey de Clinton secured for his foundation at Kenilworth,[16] and after the death of the powerful Clinton he may well have wished to see a

[55] Ibid. f. 186; B.M. Add. MS. 47677, f. 118v. He was a canon of Calwich. He is mentioned in C 142/81/292 as prior at the time of the agreement with Kenilworth.

[56] *Cal. Pat.* 1385–9, 152; B/A/1/6, f. 39v.

[57] B/A/1/6, f. 39v., conf. of his election Jan. 1391/2 (so that his election may have taken place late in 1391). Aleyn was a canon of Trentham. Thos. of Trentham, described as late Prior of Calwich, became Prior of Trentham in 1402: see below p. 260. As no intervening prior is known and medieval religious are sometimes known by their surname and sometimes by their place of origin, he is probably to be identified with Thos. Aleyn.

[58] B/A/1/7, f. 54; /10, f. 17. He was a canon of Calwich.

[59] Ibid. /10, f. 17; /12, f. 41v.; *S.H.C.* N.S. iv. 109.

[60] B/A/1/12, f. 41v.

[61] *S.H.C.* N.S. iv .126.

[62] B/A/1/13, f. 212.

[63] The former name is given in 1500 (ibid.) and both in 1507 (ibid. /14, f. 21v.). He was a canon of Trentham.

[64] Ibid. /14. f. 21v.; B/V/1/1, p. 12 and p. 51 (2nd nos.). The death of the last prior occurred in 1530 (see above p. 239), but his name is not known.

[65] B/V/1/1, p. 64 and p. 51 (2nd nos.); see above p. 239.

[1] Dugdale, *Mon.* vi(1), 226–30.

[2] *Dict. of Christian Biog.* ed. W. Smith and H. Wace, iv. 1194–5.

[3] *Venerabilis Baedae Historia Ecclesiastica Gentis Anglorum*, ed. C. Plummer (1896), i. 237–8; ii. 229; W. Beresford, 'Stone Priory', *T.N.S.F.C.* (1881), 24–25; W. Beresford, *Lichfield*, 21–22.

[4] *V.C.H. Staffs.* iv. 49, no. 163 and n.; *S.H.C.* i. 178; ii(1), 200.

[5] Dugdale, *Mon.* vi(1), 230–1.

[6] *V.C.H. Staffs.* iv. 31; *S.H.C.* i. 3, 10, 178.

[7] *S.H.C.* ii(1), 200–1, 205.   [8] Ibid. 199–201.

[9] This had been her marriage portion: ibid. 204.

[10] Ibid. 201–4. These transactions are very typical of the methods which Clinton used to endow his foundation: R. W. Southern, 'The Place of Henry I in Eng. History', *Proc. Brit. Acad.* xlviii. 137–9.

[11] *S.H.C.* ii(1), 204–7.

[12] Ibid. 207–9.   [13] Ibid. 209–10.

[14] The verses cited above ascribe a part in the foundation of Stone Priory to Rob. de Stafford I, but he had in fact died before even Kenilworth Priory was founded. Nic. de Stafford, although he confirmed Enisan's gifts to Kenilworth and was buried at Stone, was not a benefactor of Stone Priory. If, as seems likely, Rob. de Stafford II was instrumental in bringing canons to Stone, the foundation of the priory must have occurred between the death of his father (c. 1138) and Bp. Clinton's departure from England (1147). What seems to be an earlier reference to the priory (*S.H.C.* vi(1), 22–23), is suspect, being dated 'Easter A.D. 1136, 36 Hen. I', although Easter 1136 fell in Stephen's reign.

[15] *S.H.C.* ii(1), 210–13.

[16] Besides the property of Enisan and Ernald de Walton which eventually passed to Stone, Clinton gave the manor of Idlicote (Warws.) to Kenilworth: *Proc. Brit. Acad.* xlviii, 138; Dugdale, *Warws.* i. 606.

daughter-house set up in the church where his father, Nicholas, had been buried. Robert's charter stresses his relationship to the priory as 'brother and patron of the same church of Stone' and expresses his desire to be buried there. The patronage remained in the Stafford family.[17] Robert gave to the canons by this charter 'my chapel' of Stafford,[18] the churches of Madeley,[19] Tysoe (Warws.), and Wolford (Warws.), a mill at Wootton Wawen (Warws.), a villein at Stafford castle with his holding, and a tithe of 'all my hunting'. Other gifts made by Robert included half of the church of Wootton Wawen, a villein, Godfrey of Ullenhall, with his holding, part of the wood at Ullenhall (in Wootton Wawen) and the manor of Horton.[20]

Spiritual endowments accumulated fairly quickly thereafter but involved the priory in considerable litigation. The church of Milwich was given by Nicholas de Milwich; this gift was confirmed by his overlord, Robert de Stafford, between 1138 and 1147,[21] though the title was not finally secured until 1233.[22] About 1155 Walter de Caverswall, with the consent of his overlord, Robert de Stafford, gave the canons their half share of the church of Stoke-upon-Trent. By the early 1220s the Earl of Chester, who then held the other half, was claiming the priory's share also; he asserted that it had been wrongfully alienated by Walter.[23] In 1223 the priory surrendered its share to the earl in return for 2 virgates of land in Seabridge (in Stoke parish).[24] The priory early claimed Swynnerton church, and their claim was long resisted by the two clerks there. About 1157, however, with the assent of the lord of Swynnerton, the two clerks conceded that the church was subject as a parochial chapel to Stone Priory[25] and that it should provide the priory, as 'mother-church', with an annual pension of 2s.[26] Nothing was said about the advowson of the church in this agreement. The canons evidently claimed it and succeeded in exercising the right when, during John's reign, the lord of Swynnerton was outlawed.[27] In 1218, however, Kenilworth Priory recognized the lord of Swynnerton's claim to the advowson in return for a pension of 2 marks to be paid to Stone by the parson of Swynnerton.[28] Ruald de Dilhorne gave the church of Dilhorne to the canons, and his grant was confirmed by Robert de Stafford and Bishop Richard Peche (1161–82).[29] The priory also acquired a claim to the church of Bradley, perhaps by a grant of the Stafford family; together with the church of Dilhorne it was confirmed to the priory by Pope Alexander III (1159–81).[30] Bradley church, however, involved the canons in considerable litigation as it was claimed as appurtenant to the church of Gnosall. Although this contention was abandoned about 1165, the priory had to agree to share equally with the Chapter of Lichfield[31] all the revenues of Bradley church except the tithes on the lordship of Bradley and those belonging to St. Nicholas's Chapel within Stafford castle. By 1223, however, both Stone Priory and the Chapter of Lichfield had lost the church of Bradley to the Stafford family.[32] In 1196 the priory was accused of disseising Basile de Loxley of the church of Loxley (Warws.), but the prior successfully delayed proceedings by pleading his subjection to Kenilworth.[33] Soon afterwards the priory's title had confirmed by a final concord.[34] Kenilworth was some right in the church of Checkley but surrendered it to Alice de Hopton in 1196 in return for a rent of 20s. and the tithes of Normacot;[35] Stone Priory established its title to these tithes in 1238.[36]

The priory was granted quittance of all synodal customs for its churches by Bishop Clinton (1129–48), and by Bishop Peche (1161–82) all the liberties which the abbeys of Burton and Rocester possessed in their parishes.[37] Occasional glimpses are afforded of the relations between the canons and their parishes. Landowners who desired to have private chapels or services had to secure the permission of the priory. About 1200 the canons granted to Eleanor de Verdon permission to maintain a chapel in her house at Kibblestone (in Stone parish).[38] In 1226, when Hervey de Stafford fell ill at Tysoe, the canons permitted him to have private services in his chamber there from Christmas to Epiphany taken by Brother Peter, one of their number; it was, however, stipulated that this was not to be a precedent for worship there.[39] To what extent the canons served their parish churches themselves or by secular vicars is uncertain. In 1259, however, a papal indult, after noting that the church of Stone was a parish church and conventual and had hitherto been served by the religious and two secular priests appointed by them, allowed that the canons should not be compelled to institute a vicarage there.[40]

[17] See below p. 244.
[18] Taken by Eyton to be the church of St. Mary in Stafford Borough but in fact St. Mary's, Castle Church: *V.C.H. Staffs.* v. 95 (which, following *S.H.C.* iv(1), 113, assigns the original gift to *temp.* Hen. II). The church was lost to the Dean and Canons of St. Mary's, Stafford, in 1253–5.
[19] Probably simply the advowson of Madeley church; if so, this gift seems to have been contested by Robert's heirs for in 1272 Nic. de Stafford remitted all claim to the advowson in consideration of a payment of £10: *S.H.C.* iv(1), 256–7. The church was not appropriated until the 14th cent.: see below p. 243.
[20] *S.H.C.* vi(1), 6, 7, 28; *Place-Names of Warws.* (Eng. Place-Names Soc. xiii), 245. The grant of Horton manor was ultimately ineffective; in 1227 it passed, with the agreement of Hervey de Stafford, to the Audley family: *S.H.C.* iv(1), 226–7.
[21] *S.H.C.* ii(1), 217–18.   [22] Ibid. iv(1), 228.
[23] *V.C.H. Staffs.* viii. 188. The case aroused the interest of Bracton: *De Legibus et Consuetudinibus Angliae* (Rolls Ser.), i. 426.
[24] *S.H.C.* iv(1), 222–3. In 1291 the priory held property in Seabridge worth £1 13s. 6d.: *Tax. Eccl.* (Rec. Com.), 252.

[25] *S.H.C.* iii(1), 185–6.   [26] Ibid. 1926, 169–70.
[27] Ibid. 170.
[28] Ibid. iv(1), 218–19. This pension of 2 marks seems often to have been in arrears. The priory obtained judgment against the parson of Swynnerton in the bishop's court in 1295 and in the king's court in 1303: ibid. vi(1), 26–27; vii(1), 112. In 1452 the pension was again in arrears: ibid. N.S. iii. 204.
[29] *S.H.C.* vi(1), 19–20.
[30] Ibid. 15.
[31] Presumably because Gnosall church had been granted to the Dean and Chapter of Lichfield: *V.C.H. Staffs.* iv. 128.
[32] Ibid. 85–86. For the Chapel of St. Nicholas see also *S.H.C.* viii(2), 114 n. 2; Dugdale, *Mon.* vi(1), 232.
[33] *Cur. Reg. R.* i. 20.
[34] B.M. Add. MS. 47677, f. 253.
[35] *S.H.C.* i. 161; iii(1), 166; vi(1), 25.
[36] Ibid. iv(1), 235; vi(1), 25.
[37] Ibid. vi(1), 15; ibid. 1924, p. 31; see also above p. 209 and below p. 247.
[38] *S.H.C.* vi(1), 22.
[39] Ibid. 6. In return Hervey promised for himself and his heirs never to claim 'jus cantariae' in his court of Tysoe.
[40] *Cal. Papal Regs.* i. 367.

The temporal possessions of the house did not increase greatly in the course of the 12th century, though Henry II's confirmation shows a few additions to its original endowment.[41] The canons never owned much land outside Stone and Walton but did acquire small properties in Darlaston, Stoke-by-Stone, and Stallington (all in Stone parish).[42] Some property was also acquired at Coppenhall (in Penkridge parish)[43] and Tysoe.[44]

Privileges and gifts from the Crown helped to augment the priory's resources during the 13th century. In 1251 the canons purchased a charter granting them a market at Stone on Tuesdays, a yearly fair there on the eve, feast, and morrow of St. Wulfad (23–25 July), and free warren in their demesne lands in Stone and Stallington provided these were not within the royal forest.[45] In 1266 the king ordered 12 timber oaks to be sent to the priory from Cannock Forest. In 1282 he granted the canons a buck from the forest.[46]

During the Barons' Wars of Henry III's later years the priory seems both to have suffered from, and to have taken advantage of, the disturbed state of the country. Early in 1263 royalist forces under William la Zouche, Justiciar of Chester, and David, brother of Llewelyn, Prince of Wales, took the town of Stafford and Chartley castle. As they returned they burnt the town of Stone, plundered the priory, and destroyed its muniments.[47] In 1265 the Abbot of Hulton impleaded the Prior of Stone and others for impounding 300 of his sheep at Stallington, ill-treating his shepherd, and seizing his growing corn; it was reported that the sheriff had been prevented by the war from distraining the prior to appear.[48] At this time also the cellarer of the priory and others were accused of theft from the house of Adam de Arderne when he was 'in prison for the king and Edward his son'.[49]

From an early date Stone was evidently semi-independent of the mother-house, in fact if not in theory, and was not, like Calwich (another cell of Kenilworth), a place where a keeper presided for short periods over a handful of brethren.[50] Though the parish church of Stone was evidently a wealthy one, the decisive factor in the growth of the priory was probably its adoption as the family monastery by the barons of Stafford. As a result of this Stone was not destined to remain one of those small houses of Austin canons which were characteristic of the order in England. Whether or not the original establishment of a cell at Stone had been due to Robert de Stafford II,[51] it is evident that his successors considered that they had a claim to the advowson of the priory. After litigation over the priory between Robert de Stafford IV and the Prior of Kenilworth in 1242 and 1243, Robert remitted this claim in return for 40 acres of land in Stafford.[52] In 1259, when the Prior of Stone died during a vacancy in the mother-house, the king confirmed the right of the Prior of Kenilworth to appoint (ordinare) the Prior of Stone, saving royal rights when Kenilworth was vacant.[53]

Daughter-houses of regular canons, however, normally attained their independence in the long run, and Stone became independent of Kenilworth in the later 13th century. In 1260 an agreement between the priories of Kenilworth and Stone stated that the latter was to be 'free from all subjection to the prior and convent of Kenilworth'. The agreement, however, reserved and defined the rights of prior and canons of Kenilworth as patrons of Stone Priory. During a vacancy at Stone the custody of the priory was to be exercised by one of the canons or servants of Kenilworth; the canons of Stone were to obtain licence to elect a new prior from the Prior of Kenilworth and two canons of Kenilworth were to be present at the election. The Prior of Stone, if he had been professed at Kenilworth, was to be present at the election of a prior of Kenilworth and was to have a place in the chapter and choir. Apart from the rights of patronage the Prior of Kenilworth reserved only the right to hospitality at Stone for himself and a train of ten horses during a two-day visit each year. The Prior of Stone was to be free to receive and profess canons and to dispose of the possessions of the priory. Copies of all the charters of Kenilworth which related to Stone were to be delivered under the seals of the bishop and the Prior of Kenilworth, and when necessary the originals were to be produced.[54] By an indenture of 1292[55] a division of the property of the two priories was made. Kenilworth released to its daughter-house all its right in the priory and church of Stone with its chapels, lands, tithes, and other appurtenances. The churches of Madeley and Milwich, the chapel of St. Nicholas in Stafford castle, half the church of Stoke-upon-Trent,[56] the Warwickshire churches of Wolford (with its chapel)[57] and Tysoe, and the tithes of Barton[58] were all confirmed to Stone, but the church of Loxley was retained by Kenilworth. Stone was also confirmed in its possession of temporal estates in Stone parish[59] and at Coppenhall, Fradswell (Colwich parish), 'Herdewick' (probably Hardiwick in Sandon parish), and

41 Dugdale, Mon. vi(1), 232.
42 S.H.C. vi(1), 7–11, 17–18. Stallington was sold to the canons for 7 marks at some time between 1149 and 1159 by Nic. de Mauvesin: ibid. iii(1), 194–7.
43 Ibid. vi(1), 23–24.
44 Ibid. 5–7. In 1201 a grand assize found that the priory held 4 acres of land in Tysoe: Curia Reg. R. i. 471.
45 Cal. Chart. R. 1226–57, 364; Close R. 1247–51, 476. For the date of St. Wulfad's feast see Dugdale, Mon. vi(1), 229, 230.
46 Close R. 1264–8, 206; Cal. Close, 1279–88, 172.
47 Annales Cestrienses (Lancs. and Ches. Rec. Soc. xiv), 86, 87. David had recently abandoned his brother for Hen. III: ibid. 82, 83.
48 S.H.C. iv(1), 158, 159, 160.   49 Ibid. 160.
50 See above pp. 238, 239.
51 See above p. 240.
52 S.H.C. iv(1), 95, 100, 236–7.
53 Close R. 1256–9, 402.
54 J. C. Dickinson, Origins of the Austin Canons and their Introduction into Eng. 159–60; Reg. of Bp. Godfrey Giffard (Worcs. Hist. Soc.), ii. 105. Previously to this agreement the Prior of Kenilworth had often appeared as plaintiff or defendant, either alone or with the Prior of Stone, in suits concerning the property of Stone Priory: S.H.C. iii(1), 29, 36, 166–7; iv(1), 66–67, 100; above p. 241.
55 Cal. Pat. 1334–8, 308–9.
56 For an explanation of this moiety see V.C.H. Staffs. viii. 188 n. 55, and above p. 241.
57 The advowson of Wolford church had in fact been sold in 1267: V.C.H. Warws. v. 217.
58 Probably Barton in Bidford parish (Warws.), a parish which belonged to the canons of Kenilworth until the Dissolution: V.C.H. Warws. iii. 56. The tithes of her demesne in Barton had been given to Stone Priory by Cecilia de Freford, possibly descended from a daughter of Enisan de Walton: S.H.C. i. 187; ii(1), 208–9; vi(1), 7.
59 At Aston, Darlaston, Fulford, Stallington, Stoke-by-Stone, Walton and 'Oldeton' (probably Oulton, also in Stone parish).

Stafford. Outside the county Stone retained temporalities at Tysoe, Wootton Wawen, Ullenhall, and Weston-under-Wetherley (Warws.).[60] Kenilworth, as well as retaining Loxley church, expressly reserved the patronage of Stone Priory and an annual pension of 12½ marks out of the revenues of the daughter-house.[61] Despite these reservations the agreement probably marks the effective independence of Stone. The priory's title to certain estates which had belonged to the great-grandson of Enisan de Walton was further strengthened in the following year (1293) by a final concord between the prior and Roger de Pyuelsdon and his wife Joan, heiress of the Walton family.[62]

Stone Priory was assessed at 2 marks for the aid of 1235–6 but was probably wealthier than Trentham which was assessed at the same amount.[63] None of the other Augustinian houses of Staffordshire approached this figure.[64] The *Taxatio* of 1291 shows that Stone Priory was worth £79 6s. 10d. Temporal possessions were worth £10 6s. 10d. and all were within Stone parish except the property at Seabridge (in Stoke parish).[65] Spiritual possessions were worth much more: Stone church was valued at £40, Tysoe church at £20,[66] and Milwich church at £5 6s. 8d. Pensions of £2, £1, and 13s. 4d. were received from the churches of Swynnerton, Checkley, and Madeley respectively.[67] At the *quo warranto* inquiry of 1293[68] the Prior of Stone claimed free warren in all the priory's demesne lands of Stone, Stoke-by-Stone, and Stallington, and the weekly market and yearly fair at Stone. For these liberties he produced the charter of Henry III granted in 1251.[69] The prior also claimed the right of gallows on the authority of a charter of Henry I,[70] which he produced. This confirmed the possessions of Kenilworth Priory which were to be held 'whole, quiet and free . . . with soc, sac, toll and team, and infangentheof'. The Prior of Stone claimed that his house, a cell of Kenilworth, was entitled to enjoy these rights in its possessions, and the jury agreed that the prior and his predecessors had always enjoyed them since the time of the charter.

The priory was evidently in some financial difficulty in the late 13th century. In 1273 it owed 16 marks to Thomas de Basinges, citizen of London,[71]

in 1294 £12 to William of Doncaster,[72] and in 1305 £24 to Ralph de Hengham.[73] It is possible that these debts were unpaid corrodies; there is, at any rate, plenty of evidence that the priory was defaulting on the payment of corrodies at this time. In 1281 Maffeo Spinelli sued the prior for the arrears of an annual rent' of 2 marks due to him from the priory; the arrears amounted to 27 marks, but Spinelli remitted his claim to these arrears and to the rent in return for a payment of 30 marks.[74] In 1288 Thomas de Melewych remitted his claim to a corrody from the priory in return for a payment of 18 marks.[75] In 1294 William, son of Robert de Cotes, sued the prior for disseising him of a corrody at Stone which consisted daily of a loaf of bread, a gallon of ale, broth (*pottagium*), and the same ration of food as a canon received; two candles each night during November, December, and January; and each year four cartloads of wood, a robe worth 1 mark, and sustenance for a horse and groom on three nights. William's plea was successful; he was awarded 30s. damages[76] and was presumably reinstated in his corrody. The priory's general obligation to provide hospitality was also found onerous; the canons alleged that the location of the priory on a main highway caused a heavy burden of hospitality and on this account, in 1343, they were allowed by the bishop and the king to appropriate the church of Madeley.[77] The king, however, exacted as well as conferred favours. In 1315 the priory was burdened with the maintenance for life of William de Blakelowe, a soldier who had been maimed at the recent siege of Carlisle.[78] In 1339 wool belonging to the priory worth 22½ marks was pre-empted by agents of the Crown in return for a promise of repayment the following year.[79]

In 1312 the priory was granted a general licence to acquire lands and rents to the annual value of £20 'on account of the devotion which the king bears to St. Wulfad whose body rests in the church of the priory of Stone'.[80] Acquisitions by the priory in respect of this licence, however, seem to have been few: in 1326 the priory was allowed to acquire 10 messuages in Stone[81] and in 1335 a messuage, land, and rent in Fulford and Meaford worth 26s. 2d.[82] The last acquisition under the licence was in 1402

[60] Given as Weston-by-Honingham. For the identification see *Place-Names of Warws.* 189; *V.C.H. Warws.* vi. 117. There is no further trace of this among the priory's possessions.

[61] For the pension see also *S.H.C.* vi(1), 25.

[62] Ibid. 237; ibid. 1911, 50–51. For the Walton family see *V.C.H. Staffs.* iv. 31; *S.H.C.* i. 178–9; ibid. 1911, 421.

[63] *Bk. of Fees*, i. 558.

[64] See pp. 238, 248. There are no assessments for Ranton and St. Thomas's.

[65] *Tax. Eccl.* (Rec. Com.), 252. This list, however, is not complete; it omits e.g. the small estates at Coppenhall (granted to the priory in the later 12th cent. and still among its possessions in 1535: see above p. 242; *Valor Eccl.* (Rec. Com.), iii. 113) and at Tysoe. It is possible that all the small temporal endowments acquired by the priory in Tysoe had, like the gift there of Matilda de Stafford (*Cal. Pat.* 1334–8, 309), become confounded in the possessions of Tysoe church. The *Valor Ecclesiasticus* shows no temporal estate there in 1535.

[66] The church of Tysoe, appropriated to the priory by Archbp. Becket, 1162–70 (Dugdale, *Warws.* i. 544; *Reg. Giffard*, ii. 105, 106, 439), was not noted among the priory's possessions in 1291.

[67] *Tax. Eccl.* 219, 242, 243. The pensions from Swynnerton and Checkley churches continued to be received until

the Dissolution: *S.H.C.* N.S. x(2), 219; *Reg. Simonis Langham* (Cant. & York Soc.), 90; *Valor Eccl.* iii. 114. Madeley church was later appropriated: see below.

[68] *Plac. de Quo Warr.* (Rec. Com.), 708; *S.H.C.* vi(1), 242.

[69] See above p. 242.

[70] He is simply referred to as Henry, the king's 'proavus', but the quotation seems to identify the charter as that granted by Hen. I to Kenilworth and printed in Dugdale, *Mon.* vi(1), 223.

[71] *Cal. Close*, 1272–9, 51.

[72] Ibid. 1288–96, 439.

[73] Ibid. 1302–7, 318.

[74] *S.H.C.* vi(1), 126.

[75] Ibid. 174.

[76] Ibid. 293.

[77] Ibid. i. 264; *Cal. Pat.* 1340–3, 417. For this road see *V.C.H. Staffs.* ii. 277.

[78] *Cal. Close*, 1313–18, 311.

[79] *Cal. Pat.* 1338–40, 297. Edw. III was granted 20,000 sacks of wool by the Parliament of Feb. 1338, but collection was slow and only about 3,000 sacks had been gathered when Edw. left Eng. (16 July 1338): *Foedera* (Rec. Com.), ii(2), 1051; *Handbk. of Brit. Chron.* 36, 520. Collection was evidently still proceeding in Staffs. in 1339: *Cal. Close*, 1339–41, 96, 165, 301; *V.C.H. Staffs.* i. 235.

[80] *Cal. Pat.* 1307–13, 458.

[81] Ibid. 1324–7, 259. Their value is not stated, but they were in respect of 13s. 4d. of the licence of 1312.

[82] Ibid. 1334–8, 76. They were in respect of 40s. of the licence of 1312.

when the canons were granted permission to acquire messuages, rent, and land worth £4 6s. 8d.[83] The value of the lands acquired under this licence was thus only a nominal £20; in reality they were worth little more than £5.[84] In 1366 the Pope granted an indulgence for penitents who visited the priory and helped to keep it in repair.[85]

The history of the priory in the 15th century is better documented than might be expected. When in 1439 the priory of Christ Church, Aldgate, fell on evil days, the Prior of Stone was one of three Augustinian priors who, with the Abbot of Leicester, president of the order, were appointed to keep the house and its revenues for two years.[86] In 1446 the Pope allowed the priory to serve the church of Stone by one or two canons because 'for the most part secular priests are hard to find and it is not distant from the said monastery'.[87]

During the priorate of Thomas Wyse grave dissension between the prior and canons led to litigation at Canterbury and Rome and to a visitation of Stone by the heads of four neighbouring Augustinian houses.[88] It appears that Prior Wyse had encountered disobedience and hostility from his canons as a result of certain disputes about the canons' salaries and their plots in the conventual garden. In the absence of regular discipline petty disputes were doubtless magnified; the prior reacted harshly and the community was divided by 'schisms . . . insults, hard and unjust words . . . prolonged malice and wickedness'. Matters came to a head when three canons brought the disputes into the archbishop's Court of Audience. The Auditor of Causes made 'a number of injunctions and rules' for the welfare and government of the priory and compelled Prior Wyse to swear to observe them. Wyse, however, did not do so and was excommunicated by the auditor. The prior then appealed to Rome, and in the summer of 1450 the sentence of excommunication was conditionally lifted. Bishop Booth and Prior Holygreve of Kenilworth[89] were ordered to exact a promise from Wyse that, if the sentence were found to be just, he would obey their mandates; they were then to call before them the canons and others who were involved and to settle all the matters in dispute. The quarrels were not, however, settled in this way. Early in December 1450 the abbots of Darley (Derb.) and Lilleshall (Salop.) and the priors of Arbury (Warws.) and Ranton visited the priory 'by the express wish, mandate and authority' of Humphrey, Duke of Buckingham, and the bishop.

This change of plan may have been due to the initiative of Buckingham, the patron, for the visiting abbots and priors in their injunctions several times stressed the obligations of the community to lay society and in particular to the founders and benefactors of the priory.[90]

As the quarrels within the community had given rise to 'scandals and slanders offensive to God and man, and also to great expenses and losses', the visitors applied themselves to the reform of both the spiritual and the temporal government of the priory. Their detailed regulations were designed both to reform specific abuses[91] and to re-establish proper observance of the Augustinian rule generally; they thus give a clear picture of the spiritual state of the community at Stone before 1450 and of the day-to-day routine in a small Augustinian house at this time. It is clear that the common life of the community had largely broken down. This was a not uncommon feature of late-medieval monastic life,[92] and at Stone the symptoms were much the same as elsewhere: the choir and cloister were neglected, the canons associated too freely with secular persons, the refectory was no longer used for meals, and drinking and gossiping after compline were usual.[93] The visiting superiors noted all these faults and made regulations against them, but they showed no inclination to analyse the deeper causes of this crisis beyond attributing a part in it to the Devil.[94]

At Stone as elsewhere the breakdown of the common religious life seems to have been due in large part to the obedientiary and wage systems; these were, however, unaffected, or even strengthened, by the injunctions of 1450. The worst effects of the obedientiary system were the inroads which it made into the service of the choir and cloister. At Stone the visitors provided against these by enjoining the prior and cellarer to be personally present at matins, vespers, and mass each Sunday and solemn feast day and by ordering all canons in priest's orders to celebrate mass daily. In essentials, however, the obedientiary system was confirmed: officials were to be appointed and under the prior's supervision were to employ revenues assigned to them. One common effect of the obedientiary system — the uncertain distribution of the common revenues[95] — had perhaps been made worse at Stone by Prior Wyse's attempts to interfere with the canon's salaries; this had evidently been a principal cause of the crisis. Under the new regulations each canon was to receive an annual salary of £1 13s. 4d. for his clothing and

[83] Ibid. 1401–5, 47. This property was in respect of 18 marks of the licence of 1312.

[84] See preceeding notes.

[85] Cal. Papal Pets. i. 533. The indulgence was available for 10 years (1366–76). In the same year the prior was made an honorary papal chaplain (ibid. 534), and one of the canons, John of Lichfield, was given a dispensation for illegitimacy (ibid. 536).

[86] Cal. Pat. 1436–41, 280.

[87] Cal. Papal Regs. ix. 475–6. Previously the priory had exercised the cure through 2 secular priests removable at will.

[88] For this and the following 5 paras. see (except where otherwise stated) Cal. Papal Regs. x. 467–8; Lich. Dioc. Regy., B/A/1/10, ff. 76–78.

[89] Holygreve was Wyse's predecessor as Prior of Stone: see below.

[90] e.g. 'Nil . . . irregulare de cetero reperiatur in vobis . . . nichilque fiat quod cuiusquam offendat aspectum . . . et tunc coram Deo et hominibus laus vestra crescet cum

honore.' When all canons who were priests were ordered to celebrate mass daily, they were to do so for their founders and benefactors 'pro temporalibus bonis vobis ab eis collatis spiritualia, prout tenemini iugiter, rep018 dentes'.

[91] 'Quarum quidem iniunctionum et ordinationum singule . . . medicine morbis singulis . . . et defectibus predictis sunt apponende . . .'

[92] D. Knowles, Religious Orders in Eng. ii. 209–10, 218, 240.

[93] This last practice was 'almost universal' according to Prof. Knowles (ibid. 209); see also below p. 250.

[94] 'Sane quia inter vos, satore zizanniorum in agro dominico ipso videlicet diabolo insagante, orta fuit noviter materia dissensionis gravis . . .'

[95] D. Knowles, Monastic Order in Eng. 433–4. At Stone, according to the visitors' injunctions, four-fifths of a canon's salary was to be paid to him by the prior or a canon specially appointed to act for the prior, while another fifth was to be paid by the sacrist.

necessities.[96] In addition the canons were to have such gifts, legacies, and offerings as were made for the burial of the dead,[97] while the epistoler and gospeller on the major feasts were to receive rewards of a penny. Though the wage system with its encouragement of possessiveness thus remained, some of its worst manifestations at Stone were checked by the visitors. In their settlement of the disputes between the prior and canons over the conventual garden the visitors ordered that it was to be held in common and that plots there were to be assigned each year to the canons; the profits of cultivation, however, were no longer to be applied to private purposes but to the common uses of the priory. Similarly the profits from bee-keeping in the garden and cemetery were no longer to be privately retained but were assigned to the sacrist's revenues.

Other regulations concerning the secular affairs of the priory were designed to ensure that its business was conducted with unanimity. The officers were to be appointed on the advice of the community and were all, including the prior, to render annual accounts. The common seal was to be kept under three locks, the keys being held by the prior, sub-prior, and sacrist; no corrodies were to be granted, the goods of the house were not to be alienated, and farms were to be granted under the common seal only after due deliberation in chapter. The canons' shaving and the laundering of their clothes were to be paid for out of the common revenues, and the canons were strictly forbidden to employ private laundresses.

It seems clear that the visiting superiors were above all concerned to raise the standard of regular observance, and to this end they made a number of provisions which illuminate in some detail the daily routine of the small community. The canons were to live in 'charity, peace and concord' and to show reverent obedience to the prior at all times, and the prior was urged to be modest and kind to his brethren. Silence was to be strictly observed in the choir, cloister, and dormitory, as laid down in the *liber ordinis*. After compline all the canons were to go together to the dormitory where each in his own cell was to prepare himself for rest by prayer and meditation 'so that the canons who must rise in the middle of the night[98] are more disposed to pay due worship to God'. Attendance at the monastic offices was to be improved and canons who missed matins were to be punished by fines and penitential diets. On Mondays, Tuesdays, and Thursdays the community was to have an hour of recreation before vespers; instead of remaining in the cloister for study and contemplation the canons were to go into the orchard within the monastery precincts; here they could stroll about, read, or play suitable games. All canons were to avoid suspect places and persons, and no secular person was to be admitted to their dormitory or even to their recreation. No canon was to leave the precincts without the prior's special permission.

The most detailed regulations were those concerned with the meals and diet of the canons. Friday and Saturday were the chief days of abstinence, but food was also to be less on Monday and Wednesday unless an important feast occurred. Meals were to be eaten in common in the prior's hall until the refectory had been repaired 'for where there is a community of religious without a refectory . . . religion is not well served'. Eating and drinking in the dormitory cells, which had evidently been usual, was forbidden, and only the infirm or those invited to the prior's table were to eat apart from the community. For infirm canons there had been no proper provision for some years, and the visitors ordered an infirmary to be built and an infirmarer appointed without delay.

The visitors' injunctions were ratified early in 1451 by the Duke of Buckingham as patron, by Bishop Booth, and by Archbishop Stafford.[99] Under the Augustinian rule they were clearly designed to be the basis of the priory's daily life. To what extent they improved the observance of religion there is not known. At many points — as for example the system of fines for being absent from choir and rewards for singing the Epistle and Gospel — they seem to reinforce a mercenary view of the religious life. At others they seem to allow for little zeal on the part of the brethren for whom they were drawn up; thus the infirmarer is urged to attend conscientiously to the needs of the sick, 'reflecting that a similar thing may happen to him in the same way, and therefore let him do for another what he would wish to have done for himself'.[1] The orderly life envisaged by these regulations was evidently hard to attain in the turbulent conditions of the 15th century. In 1458 the suffragan bishop was commissioned to bless and reconcile the priory church, which had been polluted by bloodshed.[2] In 1472 the prior was ordered to pay £6 damages for his part in disseising Richard Whalley of the manor of Darlaston;[3] later in the same year the prior was imprisoned by the sheriff.[4] The following year the prior sued a miller of Walton for breaking into his close at Aston and depasturing cattle there; he also sued a John Heywood for 6½ marks.[5] In 1484 a John Bilstone was sued for stealing 190 sheep worth £20 from the priory.[6]

The community (including the prior) numbered six in 1377 and 10 in 1381.[7] A visitation of 1518[8] shows that there were then six canons and two novices; this number was considered by the visitor to be too low. The prior expressed his desire to increase the number of brethren but alleged that the other canons were unwilling for this to be done. In 1521[9] there were eight canons and two novices. At this period the officials were the subprior, sacrist, and cellarer.[10] In 1521 the novices stated that there

---

[96] This is stated to be the same amount as that paid in larger houses such as Darley, Lilleshall and Kenilworth. For comparative figures see Knowles, *Religious Orders in Eng.* ii. 240–1.

[97] For this kind of payment see ibid. 242–3.

[98] This seems to suggest that the first office was sung at an early hour, although Prof. Knowles says that 'the hour of rising for the Austin canons is nowhere stated': ibid. 238.

[99] Lich. Dioc. Regy., B/A/1/10, f. 78–78v.

[1] A verse jingle was quoted to reinforce the point: 'Quod tibi vis fieri michi fac, quod non tibi noli/Sic potes in terris vivere iure poli' (ibid. f. 78).

[2] Lich. Dioc. Regy., B/A/1/11, f. 93.

[3] *S.H.C.* N.S. iv. 181–2.

[4] Ibid. N.S. vii. 270–1.

[5] Ibid. N.S. iv. 188.

[6] *S.H.C.* vi(1), 157.

[7] J. C. Russell, 'The Clerical Population of Medieval Eng.' *Traditio*, ii. 200 (which, however, omits the prior in 1381: E 179/15/8b).

[8] Lich. Dioc. Regy., B/V/1/1, p. 35.

[9] Ibid. p. 82.

[10] Ibid. pp. 35, 82. This had been so in 1316: D. & C. Lich., Vicars' Mun. A 1.

was no one to teach them Latin except the sacrist.[11]

The visitations of 1518 and 1521[12] reveal that the house was troubled by hostility between the prior and subprior. The main cause of dispute was the presence in the monastery of one Onyon, a glover, and his family, who were evidently protégés of the prior. In 1518 the subprior stated that Onyon's wife and daughters lived at the top of the bell-tower and were maintained out of the goods of the house. In 1521 he claimed to have been attacked and threatened by Onyon and his son and insulted by one of his daughters;[13] he added that the wife and a daughter were a source of scandal.[14] Other members of the community, however, supported the prior and the Onyon family; one of them stated that the subprior was a drunkard and much given to hunting.

At the visitation of 1518 the prior claimed that during his period of office he had increased the value of the priory's goods and livestock to 1,000 marks. In 1518 and 1521 the house was free from debt, and in the latter year the prior stated that the annual income was 360 marks.[15] Neither the *Valor Ecclesiasticus* of 1535 nor the account of the Crown's minister in 1537 suggests an income of this size. It is, however, possible that the prior's figure includes some estimate of the annual income from fines for granting leases of the priory property. The *Valor* gives the total gross income as £130 2s. 11d. a year.[16] Temporal possessions were stated to produce £54 12s. 11d., the major part deriving from the manor of Stone (£27 13s. 2d.) and property at Stallington (£16). Various payments reduced this to £50 19s. 6d.; these included a fee of £1 6s 8d. a year to Sir Edward Aston, chief steward of the priory's temporalities, and a fee of the same amount to Geoffrey Walkeden, bailiff of Stone. Spiritual possessions produced £75 10s. of which the church of Stone produced £40 (principally from tithe) and the church of Tysoe £24 (from glebe and tithe). The annual pension of £9 to Kenilworth Priory and other payments reduced this to £59 15s. 5⅓d.[17] The gross annual value of the priory property as listed in 1537 after it had passed to the Crown was £199 19s. 1½d. The spiritual endowments, worth £87 0s. 8d. a year, consisted of the appropriated churches of Stone, Tysoe, Madeley, and Milwich and pensions from the churches of Swynnerton and Checkley. The temporal endowments, worth £112 18s. 5½d. a year, consisted of the manor of Stone and lands and rents in Aston, Darlaston, Stoke-by-Stone, Burston (in Stone), Oulton, 'Doreslowe', Hilder-

stone (in Stone), Meaford, Walton, Stallington, Stafford, Coppenhall, and Seabridge.[18]

The last prior, William Smyth, seems to have been optimistic about the fate of his house, although Stone came within the terms of the Act of 1536 for dissolving the lesser monasteries.[19] Smyth had bought some timber from the bishop who, apparently seeing the shape of things to come, delayed delivery, whereupon the prior wrote anxiously in February 1537: 'If I have not the said timber, I know not where to be provided for my great work now in hand'.[20] In March Lord Stafford wrote to Cromwell that the royal commissioners were expected the following Sunday but that 'the Prior of Stone thinks his house shall stand, whereof the country is glad'. Lord Stafford had been trying to secure a grant of the priory's land but now asked for Ranton instead.[21]

The house was evidently suppressed in the spring of this year, the prior receiving a pension of £20.[22] He seems to have mortgaged 'a shrine of silver gilt',[23] perhaps to raise money to avert the suppression of the house; chattels of the priory, which were said to have been embezzled, included four standing cups and two 'salts' of silver.[24] Lord Stafford transferred the alabaster tombs of his family from the priory to the Austin friary at Stafford,[25] but in vain since that house too was dissolved the year after Stone. The site of Stone Priory was bought in 1538 by William Crompton, citizen and mercer of London.[26]

Little remains of the priory buildings. Part of a sub-vault of the western range is incorporated in the cellars of the house called The Priory.[27] To the east of it are some slight remains, possibly of the chapter-house.

PRIORS

Ralph, occurs before 1147.[28]

Roger, occurs 1162 and some time between 1174 and 1176.[29]

Sylvester, occurs 1194 and 1196.[30]

Richard, occurs before 1198 and in 1203.[31]

Reynold, occurs 1227.[32]

Gilbert, elected Abbot of Haughmond 1241.[33]

Humphrey, occurs 1245–6.[34]

Roger of Worcester, occurs 1260 and 1288.[35]

John Tiney, occurs 1292 and 1294.[36]

Thomas of Milwich, died by March 1309.[37]

John de Attelberge, elected 1309, died 1327.[38]

John of Stallington, elected 1327, probably died 1349.[39]

Walter of Podmore, elected 1349, died 1391.[40]

[11] Lich. Dioc. Regy., B/V/1/1, p. 82.   [12] Ibid. pp. 35, 82.
[13] She called him 'false' and 'a Lollard'.
[14] According to the subprior's testimony the wife, who was suspected of theft, 'manet ex altera cubiculi prioris ita ut possit prior ex fenestro eam contemplari', and one of the daughters had 'suspect access' to the priory. The subprior added that he had caught one of the brethren with the wife of a townsman in the monastery precincts; the woman had entered through a gap in the cemetery paling which the prior persistently refused to repair.
[15] Lich. Dioc. Regy., B/V/1/1, pp. 35, 82.
[16] *Valor Eccl.* (Rec. Com.), iii. 113, 114.
[17] This figure is incorrectly given as £68 15s. 5⅓d.
[18] S.C. 6/Hen. VIII/3352, mm. 12–19.
[19] *L. & P. Hen. VIII*, x, p. 515.
[20] Ibid. p. 124.   [21] Ibid. xii(1), p. 285.
[22] Ibid. xiii(1), p. 583.   [23] Ibid. xiii(2), p. 176.
[24] Ibid. xii(2), p. 245.
[25] Leland, *Itin.* ed. L. Toulmin Smith, v. 21.
[26] S.R.O., D.649/1/2, p. 102.

[27] Illustrated in W. H. Bowers and J. W. Clough, *Researches into Hist. of Stone* (Birmingham, 1929), plate facing p. 292.
[28] *S.H.C.* ii(1), 215–16.
[29] Ibid. 252; iv(1), 267; W. Holtzmann, *Papsturkunden in England*, i(2), 136.
[30] *S.H.C.* ii(1), 263; iii(1), 166.
[31] Ibid. vi(1), 12; S.R.O. 938/7922, deed of 1203. The church was dedicated in his time.   [32] *S.H.C.* iv(1), 53.
[33] *Cal. Pat. 1232–47*, 256; R. W. Eyton, *Antiquities of Shropshire*, vii. 300. He may be the *frater Gill, dictus prior*, mentioned in *S.H.C.* vi(1), 13.
[34] *S.H.C.* N.S. xii. 101 (no source given).
[35] *Reg. of Bp. Godfrey Giffard* (Worcs. Hist. Soc.), ii. 105, 323.
[36] *Cal. Pat. 1334–8*, 308–9; *S.H.C.* vi(1), 14, 293.
[37] Lich. Dioc. Regy., B/A/1/1, ff. 41v.–42.
[38] Ibid.; B/A/1/2, f. 142v. He was subprior at election.
[39] B/A/1/2, f. 142v. He was subprior at election.
[40] Ibid. f. 186v.; ibid./6, f. 39v. He was a canon of Stone.

William Madeley, elected 1391, died 1402.[41]

Ralph of Stamford, elected 1402, resigned 1423.[42]

Thomas Holygreve, B.Cn.L., elected 1423, elected Prior of Kenilworth 1439.[43]

Thomas Wyse, elected 1439, occurs 1473.[44]

Robert Wyse, occurs 1477, resigned 1493.[45]

Thomas Fort, or Ford, M.A., Bishop of Achonry, elected 1493, elected Prior of Huntingdon 1496.[46]

William Duddesbury, died by March 1507.[47]

Richard Dodicote, elected 1507, died 1524.[48]

William Smyth, occurs 1529, prior at the dissolution in 1537.[49]

The seal of the house in use in the 13th century is a pointed oval 2½ by 1½ in. and shows the Virgin crowned and seated with the Child on her left knee and holding a flower in her right hand.[50] Legend, lombardic:

SIGILLUM ECCLESIE SANCTE MARIE ET SANCTI W . . . [M]ARTIRIS DE STANIS

14. THE ABBEY OF ROCESTER

THE abbey of St. Mary at Rocester in Dovedale was founded at some time between 1141 and 1146 by Richard Bacon, a nephew of Ranulph, Earl of Chester. Few English houses of Austin canons ranked as abbeys, and those mostly the larger ones, so that it is surprising to find Rocester, a small house, among them.

According to the foundation charter Richard gave to Thurstan, the first abbot, and to his canons the church of Rocester together with the vills of Rocester and East Bridgeford (Notts.) and the lands and tenements belonging to them.[1] A much more detailed account of Richard's endowment is given in another charter[2] which, although not genuine,[3] may have been drawn up simply to preserve a fuller account of his gift than that in the more laconic foundation charter. According to this second charter Richard gave the canons the church of Rocester with its chapels of Bradley-in-the-Moors and Waterfall; the vills of Rocester and Combridge and his demesnes there and at Wootton,[4] with appurtenances and liberties in Nothill (in Croxden), Denstone (in Alton), Quixhill (in Rocester), Roston (Derb.), Bradley-in-the-Moors, Waterfall, and Calton; and, in East Bridgeford, 8 carucates and 2 bovates of land and the third part of 2 mills. Rocester was evidently the centre of a large manor,[5] for the second charter states that the men of Rocester, Combridge, Nothill, Wootton, Roston, Waterfall, and Bradley were to continue to render the services and suit of court at Rocester which they had rendered successively to Earl Ranulph and to his nephew. The abbey evidently acquired an extensive jurisdiction with these estates: the second charter mentions sac and soc, toll and team, infangentheof, waif, and wreck. Richard's gift was confirmed by Earl Ranulph de Blundeville about 1200.

Details survive of some early privileges and benefactions.[6] Bishop Clinton freed Rocester church 'from all episcopal custom' and, with the assent of Robert, Archdeacon of Stafford, granted the abbey the same liberty in its parish as Burton Abbey possessed in its parishes.[7] The advowson of the church of Woodford (Northants.) was acquired from Osmund and William Bassett in the late 12th or early 13th century.[8] In 1230 the abbot and convent received an annual pension of £3 from the church, but by 1254 (when the rectory was worth 20 marks) this had dropped to £2.[9] About 1200 one Fulk fitz Fulk gave the church of St. Peter, Edensor (Derb.).[10] The gift was made to the Abbot of Rocester and the canons of 'Leyes' obedient to the

[41] B/A/1/6, f. 39v.; /7, f. 54. He was a canon of Stone.

[42] B/A/1/7, f. 54; /9, ff. 48v.–49. He was subprior at election. The bishop granted him a pension in 1423: ibid. ff. 140v.–141v., undated entry between items of Apr. and July 1423. He resigned because of age and weakness, in particular because 'the light of his eyes' was dulled.

[43] Ibid. /9, ff. 48v.–49; B. M., Harl. MS. 2179, ff. 139v.–140; V.C.H. Warws. ii. 89. He was a canon of Kenilworth before his election as Prior of Stone.

[44] Lich. Dioc. Regy., B/A/1/9, f. 67v.; S.H.C. N.S. iv. 188. He was a canon of Stone.

[45] Cal. Pat. 1476–85, 65; Lich. Dioc. Regy., B/A/1/13, f. 144v. The bishop assigned him a pension of £23 6s. 8d. from the priory's property in Stallington. The ex-prior was also to have bread, ale, and fuel and the use of the new building which he had lately put up within the priory precincts: R. Churton, Lives of Wm. Smith . . . and Sir Ric. Sutton (Oxford, 1800), 72n.

[46] B/A/1/13, f. 143v.; A. B. Emden, Biog. Reg. of Univ. of Oxford to A.D. 1500, ii. 711; Emden, Biog. Reg. of Univ. of Cambridge to 1500, 237–8. He was Bp. of Achonry, Ireland, 1492–1508 and suffragan to the Bp. of Coventry and Lichfield 1494–6 and to the Bp. of Lincoln 1496–1505: see above p. 41; Handbk. of Brit. Chron. 344; Margaret Bowker, Secular Clergy in the Dioc. of Lincoln, 1495–1520, 24. He was also described at his election to Stone as lately a canon of Bodmin (Cornw.).

[47] B/A/1/14, f. 21v. His name is given as Robert in a document of 1542: S.R.O., D.(W.)1721/1/9, f. 52v.

[48] B/A/1/14, f. 21v.; L. & P. Hen. VIII, iii, p. 1263; W.S.L., D.1850/2/14 (transcript of Barlaston Ct. R.). He was a canon of Stone.

[49] L. & P. Hen. VIII, iv, p. 2700; xii(1), p. 583. He was dead by 1538: S.R.O., D.(W.) 1810, [f. 141].

[50] W. de G. Birch, Cat. of Seals in B.M. i, p. 759; B.M. Seal Cast lxii. 43.

[1] For a transcript of what is almost certainly the authentic foundation charter see G. Barraclough, 'Some Charters of the Earls of Chester', A Medieval Miscellany for Doris Mary Stenton (P.R.S. N.S. xxxvi), ed. Patricia M. Barnes and C. F. Slade, 26 n. 1. It is addressed to Wm., Abp. of York (1141–7, 1153–4), and Wm. fitz Nigel, Constable of Chester, among others. Wm. fitz Nigel was dead by Easter 1146: ibid. 27–28.

[2] For the rest of this para., except where otherwise stated, see Dugdale, Mon. vi(1), 410–11.

[3] Medieval Miscellany for Doris Mary Stenton, 26.

[4] Presumably either Wootton in Ellastone or Woottons in Croxden.

[5] In 1086 Rocester was worth £8, a value greater than that of any other manor in North Staffs. except Uttoxeter, also valued at £8: V.C.H. Staffs. iv. 39, no. 18. It was an extensive manor with appendages in Derbs.: ibid. 10n.; V.C.H. Derb. i. 341, 342.

[6] No cartulary has survived, but some early deeds are given in Dugdale, Mon. vi(1), 410–12, from an old roll belonging to Fra. Trentham of Rocester.

[7] B.M., Harl. MS. 3868, f. 35v. For Burton see above p. 209.

[8] Dugdale, Mon. vi(1), 411. Their gift was confirmed by Wm.'s son, another Wm., and his confirmation was witnessed by Thos., Abbot of Croxden (1178–1229).

[9] J. Bridges, Hist. of Northants. i. 131. An attempt in the late 13th cent. by one of the Bassett family to reclaim the advowson of Woodford was unsuccessful: ibid.

[10] Dugdale, Mon. vi(1), 411; J. C. Cox, Notes on the Churches of Derbs. ii. 178–9. From Fulk fitz Fulk's nephew were descended the Iretons of Ireton (Derb.). The canons' right to present to the church was contested in 1225 by Rucherus de Ireton, apparently unsuccessfully: Pat. R. 1216–25, 601.

church of Rocester. No other mention of this community is known;[11] it is possible that some brethren from Rocester were temporarily at Lees Moor near Edensor, but if Rocester did establish such a cell it must have been short-lived. In the time of Bishop Muschamp (1198–1208) Patrick of Mobberley founded a small house of regular canons at Mobberley (Ches.) which he endowed with half the church there.[12] This foundation was soon handed over to Rocester, but there were irregularities in the endowment and the cell seems to have been given up.[13] Between 1245 and 1254 William, son of Geoffrey de Gresley, gave the canons the advowson of Kingstone and all the land which Richard the forester held of him there.[14]

In 1229 Bishop Stavensby gave the abbey permission to appropriate the church of Rocester, with its chapels and appurtenances. The bishop's charter states that the canons of Rocester then suffered greater poverty than any other religious in the diocese, and his grant was made on this account and because their 'immoderate poverty . . ., their holiness of life, their gravity of demeanour, and the grace of their virtuous religious life' had been commended to him. The immunities granted by Bishop Clinton were further defined as freedom 'from all episcopal custom' except 3s. for Peter's pence, and the right to determine all causes involving their chaplains and parishioners. Stavensby also granted the canons the right to serve their parish church by one of their own brethren, provided that he was first presented to the bishop.[15]

The patronage of the abbey belonged to the earls of Chester until the death of Earl John in 1237.[16] In 1246 the earldom was annexed to the Crown,[17] and the patronage of the abbey evidently passed to the Crown at the same time. In the same year the abbey received royal confirmation of Richard Bacon's gift and of liberties which Earl Ranulph had granted.[18] In 1399 the abbey was described as 'of royal foundation and patronage as of the principality of Chester'.[19]

The house never became wealthy. Its comparative poverty is shown by its assessment at 10s. for the aid of 1235–6: Calwich, the smallest Augustinian house in the county, was similarly assessed at 10s., while the priories of Stone and Trentham were assessed at 2 marks.[20] Even the character of the gifts which the abbey received from its royal patrons seems to

reveal the poverty of the house. In 1240–1 the sheriff was ordered to give the canons 12 marks for their clothing and 2 marks to buy a pipe of wine for the celebration of divine service.[21] In 1246 the king presented a silver-gilt communion cup, and in the next year he gave the abbey 10 marks.[22] In 1269 the prior and canons secured the right to keep the temporalities of their house during the next vacancy of the abbey; in return, however, they had to pay the king 10 marks when they sued for a licence to elect.[23] In 1277 the abbey was given royal protection for a year; the effect of this grant seems to have been to exempt the abbey from contributing to the supply of the king's army in Wales under a recent purveyance order.[24]

In the later 13th century the abbey received more substantial grants which probably improved its economic condition considerably. In 1283 the canons were granted the right to hold a Thursday market at Rocester and a yearly fair on the vigil, feast, and morrow of St. Edmund (15–17 November).[25] The abbey's right to this market and fair was upheld at the quo warranto proceedings of 1293, as was its right to view of frankpledge in 'Wystanton'.[26] In 1284 Bishop Meuland granted the canons the right to appropriate Kingstone church on the next vacancy. He had evidently found during a visitation that the abbey was burdened with debt and was maintaining hospitality for poor travellers beyond its means. A few weeks later the then rector, Henry of Marchington, assigned the abbey an annual pension of £2 from the church.[27] The importance of the abbey's spiritual endowments appears from its assessment in the Taxation of 1291. It is clear that parish churches provided over half of the abbey's total income which was then £28 16s. 4d.; temporal property accounted for only £11 9s. 8d. of this, while the parish church of Rocester was valued at £13 6s. 8d. and annual pensions of £2 were received from the churches of Kingstone and Woodford.[28] The church of Edensor was appropriated to the abbey at some time after 1291.[29]

In 1299 the abbot, about to travel overseas, was granted protection for two years and power to appoint attorneys.[30] He evidently visited the papal Curia for in 1300 a confirmation of the possessions and privileges of Rocester was granted by Pope Boniface VIII.[31] The spiritual possessions of the abbey consisted of the site of the monastic church

[11] Except the doubtful reference c. 1160 in Tanner, Notitia Monastica (1787 edn.), Staffs. no. xvi.
[12] Dugdale, Mon. vi(1), 478.
[13] Ibid.; G. Ormerod, Hist. of the County Palatine and City of Chester (1882 edn.), i. 421–5. The moiety of Mobberley church also appears to have been lost and does not appear again as one of the abbey's possessions except in the papal confirmation of 1300: see below p. 249.
[14] Dugdale, Mon. vi(1), 411; S.H.C. N.S. i. 37–38.
[15] B.M., Harl. MS. 3868, f. 26v. A canon serving the church of Rocester was to do so during the abbot's pleasure: ibid. For canons serving the church in the 14th cent. see below n. 45.   [16] Close R. 1231–4, 220.
[17] Complete Peerage, iii. 169–70.
[18] Cal. Chart. R. 1226–57, 292. For the first royal licence for the election of an Abbot of Rocester (29 June 1256) see Cal. Pat. 1247–58, 485.
[19] Cal. Pat. 1396–9, 508. See also S.H.C. v(1), 117.
[20] Bk. of Fees, i. 558. No assessments survive for the priories of Ranton or St. Thomas's near Stafford.
[21] S.H.C. 1911, 9.   [22] Cal. Lib. R. 1245–51, 46, 140.
[23] Cal. Pat. 1266–72, 323, 360–1.
[24] Ibid. 1272–81, 224.
[25] Cal. Chart. R. 1257–1300, 267.

[26] Plac. de Quo Warr. (Rec. Com.), 716; S.H.C. vi(1), 248–9. The Record Commission transcript is defective and should read (bottom of col. 1, p. 716): '. . . in crastino Ascens' ubicunque fuerit etc. De libertate de Wystanton. Et quo ad . . .': J.I. 1/804, m. 35d.
[27] B.M., Harl. MS. 3868, ff. 27–28. The bishop stipulated that a vicarage was to be ordained. The appropriation was confirmed by the Pope in 1300 (see below) and Bp. Langton in 1305 (Lich. Dioc. Regy., B/A/1/1, f. 26v.). Hen. of Marchington is perhaps to be identified with the Hen. de Mertington who at some time between 1224 and 1284 was Vicar of Woodford, another of the abbey's churches: Bridges, Northants. i. 131.
[28] Tax. Eccl. (Rec. Com.), 38, 47, 67, 73, 243, 251. The abbey's chantry chapel in Churchover (see below) appears among the temporalities of the abbey in the Archdeaconry of Leicester and is recorded twice (pp. 67, 73).
[29] J. C. Cox, Notes on the Churches of Derbs. ii. 178–9.
[30] Cal. Pat. 1292–1301, 444.
[31] B.M., Harl. MS. 3868, ff. 29–30v.; W. Hamper, 'Observations on the Site of . . . Halywell in Warws.' Archaeologia, xix. 77. Hamper had probably seen the version of the bull now W.S.L., S.MS. 263. This wrongly gives the year of grace as 1301.

with all its rights and appurtenances; the separate parish church of St. Michael, Rocester, and its chapels at Waterfall and Bradley; the church of St. Giles, Holywell, in Churchover (Warws.), in which the canons were bound to maintain divine service; and the privileges which had been granted to the abbey by bishops Clinton and Stavensby. Other spiritualities confirmed to the abbey were the churches of Edensor, Kingstone, Mobberley,[32] and Woodford,[33] with their appurtenances in various places, and a small part of the tithes of Haddon Vernon (Derb.). The temporal property of the abbey consisted of the vills of Rocester and Combridge; lands in Wootton, Nothill, Denstone, and Quixhill; 1 bovate of land in Bradley and 4 bovates in Waterfall; and land in Kingstone, Swinscoe (in Blore), and Stanton (in Ellastone). Outside the county the abbey possessed temporalities in Edensor, Chatsworth, Clownholme, and Somersal (all in Derb.). These lands were confirmed to the abbey together with whatever other lands, rents, jurisdictions, and rights the house possessed in the dioceses of Coventry and Lichfield and of Lincoln.

The church of St. Giles, Holywell, mentioned in the privilege of 1300, although sometimes called a priory, seems in fact to have been a chantry chapel.[34] It was founded, probably in the mid 13th century, for the souls of Robert of Coton and Richard Fiton, and in 1291 was worth £1 6s. 8d. a year. In 1318 Richard de Bruggeford was licensed to grant a messuage, 3 virgates of land, and 2 acres of meadow in Holme (in Clifton-on-Dunsmore, Warws.) to Rocester Abbey; this was probably in effect a grant to the chantry of Holywell.[35] The chantry, however, was causing the canons some trouble about this time. In 1320 an inquisition revealed that the abbot had ceased to maintain services in the chapel because his canon, Geoffrey Spagurnel, had been robbed there. The chantry and its lands were taken into the king's hands for a short time.[36] In 1325 the king allowed the canons to transfer the chantry to the precincts of their house from its former lonely situation near Watling Street where robbers abounded. The bishop gave his approval to this arrangement in the following year.[37]

In 1318 the canons of Rocester alleged that cattle plague and bad harvests had reduced them to such poverty that they were obliged to go out and seek alms 'like beggars';[38] they were doubtless victims of the famine and plague which had ravaged all Europe during the previous three years.[39] Rocester was engaged in the wool trade by the early 14th century, but whatever profit the abbey had derived from wool was probably wiped out by the animal pestilences of these famine years which attacked sheep as well as cattle.[40] There were, however, other reasons for the continued poverty of the canons in the earlier 14th century. In 1315 they were fined £20 for having appropriated the church of Kingstone without royal permission, and in 1333 they were in trouble again for having acquired 400 acres of land in the Peak without royal licence.[41] In 1327 the Crown licensed the appropriation of Woodford church, and in 1329 the canons secured a bull from the Pope commissioning the Bishop of Lincoln to appropriate this church to them and to ordain a vicarage. This was done, apparently in 1331.[42] In 1334, however, during a visitation, Bishop Northburgh found that the canons were in debt and that this was caused by the expenses of seeking this appropriation.[43]

In 1331 a glimpse is provided of the relations between the canons and their parishioners. The inhabitants of Rocester claimed that on Easter Day by ancient custom they should receive the sacrament in the parish church of St. Michael, not in the conventual church as the canons claimed. The bishop decided that the parishioners might attend either church.[44] The canons, occasionally at least, served the parish church by one of their number.[45]

The communal life of the canons seems to have been much troubled in the mid 14th century. In 1334 the abbot complained at the General Chapter of the order that one of his canons, sent to the king's court on business, had neglected his work and, contrary to his obedience, was wandering about spending much of the abbey's money and retaining its documents.[46] The canon's initials are given as G.S., so that he may be the Geoffrey Spagurnel mentioned above. If so he was soon in trouble again, for in 1337 Geoffrey was accused, along with the abbot (perhaps cited for technical reasons) and a number of laymen, of breaking into Bolingbroke castle and, among other things, of imprisoning there Alice, Countess of Lincoln, and taking away 20 horses.[47] The result of the case is not known. In 1375 another canon, Richard of Foston, was causing trouble. He was said to be wandering from place to

[32] See above n. 13.
[33] Woodford church was not appropriated to the abbey until about 30 years later. The canons probably drew a £2 annual pension at this time. See above p. 248 and below.
[34] V.C.H. Warws. vi. 64. For references to a Prior of Holywell see J. Nichols, Hist. and Antiquities of Leics. iv(1), 336.
[35] Archaeologia, xix. 75; Tax. Eccl. 67, 73; Cal. Pat. 1317–21, 105.
[36] Cal. Close, 1318–23, 275.
[37] Cal. Pat. 1324–7, 202; Lich. Dioc. Regy., B/A/1/3, f. 23; S.H.C. i. 255. On the topography of Holywell see Archaeologia, xix. 75–78. The endowment of the chantry in 1325 was said to be 2½ virgates in the parishes of Churchover and Clifton (Cal. Pat. 1324–7, 202), though land may also have been held in Shawell (Leics.): Nichols, Leics. iv(1), 336. Leicester Abbey also held property in Clifton parish, and at some indeterminate date an exchange of lands there was made between the two houses: Rocester granted to Leicester 2 roods of land in 'Centelemedwe' in exchange for 2 roods in Newbiggin and various pasture rights: V.C.H. Warws. vi. 67 and authorities there cited.
[38] Hibbert, Dissolution, 109.

[39] H. S. Lucas, 'The Great European Famine of 1315, 1316 and 1317', Speculum, v.
[40] Ibid.; W. Cunningham, Growth of Eng. Ind. and Commerce (1922 edn.) i. 639.
[41] Cal. Pat. 1313–17, 257; Cal. Fine R. 1327–37, 370. In 1327, however, the abbey had had a general licence to acquire lands and rents to the annual value of £10: Cal. Pat. 1327–30, 127.
[42] Cal. Pat. 1327–30, 105; Cal. Papal Regs. ii. 287; Bridges, Northants. i. 131.
[43] Lich. Dioc. Regy., B/A/1/3, f. 71. At this visitation the bishop forbade the canons to grant corrodies or to keep hunting dogs; his regulations, however, were not observed: S.H.C. i. 266, 270. In 1322 an intended visitation had been cancelled because of the Scots invasion of northern Eng.: B/A/1/3, ff. 8, 9v.
[44] Lich. Dioc. Regy., B/A/1/3, f. 25v.; S.H.C. i. 256.
[45] A canon was serving St. Michael's in 1312 and 1316: B/A/1/1, ff. 32v. Thos. of Rocester was vicar when he was elected abbot in 1364, and other canons were appointed in 1373 and 1376: S.H.C. N.S. x(2), 138, 143–4.
[46] Chapters of the Augustinian Canons (Oxford Hist. Soc. lxxiv), 147–8.
[47] Cal. Pat. 1334–8, 450.

place posing as Abbot of Rocester.[48] It may have been some aftermath of this that in 1385 led to an order for the arrest of three canons of Rocester — Walter Osbern, Richard Foster (perhaps the Richard of Foston just noted), and Robert of Bakewell.[49] The abbot, John Cheswardine, had earlier been accused of harbouring men guilty of killing one William Verneye, though by 1385 he had established his innocence. The accusation seems to have been connected with the hostility towards the abbot of some of the canons who had expelled him from the abbey and hoped to elect a new abbot in his place. Cheswardine in fact resigned in 1386 and Robert of Bakewell was elected.[50] There seems also to have been some dispute over the election of Bakewell's successor, Henry Smyth. Although the bishop confirmed the election in 1407, there was an appeal to the Archbishop of Canterbury who confirmed it in 1408; the temporalities were not restored by the Crown until after the archiepiscopal confirmation.[51]

Little is known of the finances of the abbey. Occasionally it was burdened with the maintenance of a royal servant.[52] In 1399 the abbey was said to be heavily in debt owing to the negligence and default of its canons, officers, and ministers and grievous oppression by neighbouring malefactors. Royal commissioners were given custody of the place and ordered to examine its condition and to inspect, audit, and control its finances.[53] The resources of the abbey were increased in 1440 by the grant of a market at Rocester on Fridays, a fair there on Whit Monday and the two days following, and another on the feast of St. Maurice (22 September) and the two days following.[54]

The community (including the abbot) numbered 6 in 1377, 5 in 1381, 7 in 1524, and 9 at the dissolution in 1538.[55] A visitation of 1524 shows that the house was being efficiently run, but it was £60 in debt as a result of payments to the Crown. Observance was generally satisfactory, although the abbot complained that the brethren visited alehouses after divine service. There was also some dissension among three of the brethren.[56] Three years after this visitation one of the canons, John Hulme, was admitted Vicar of Woodford and must have ceased to live as a member of the community.[57]

The valuation of 1535 shows that the gross annual income of the house was £111 11s. 7d. (£100 2s. 10½d. net). Spiritual possessions produced £46 13s. 10d. while temporal property produced £64 17s. 9d., of which £23 16s. was reserved for the guest-house. In addition to this money spent on hospitality £1 17s. 4d. ex fundacione monasterii was set aside each year for doles of food to the poor. Other regular payments included a pension of £3 6s. 8d. to a chantry in Lichfield Cathedral, a fee of 13s. 4d. to the steward of the court at Rocester and one of £2 to the receiver.[58] The abbey property as listed in 1539 after it had passed to the Crown[59] consisted of the manor of Rocester, lands and rents in Combridge, Quixhill, Ellastone, Stanton, Denstone, Swinscoe, Kingstone, Clownholme, Hognaston (Derb.), Sedsall (in Doveridge, Derb.) and Scropton, and land near Somersal Heath (in Doveridge);[60] the appropriated churches of Rocester (with chapels at Waterfall, Calton, and Bradley-in-the-Moors), Kingstone, Edensor, and Woodford and tithes at Denstone. The gross annual value of the abbey estates was then £131 12s. 2d.

Although under the terms of the Act of 1536 the abbey was liable to dissolution, by March 1538 exemption had been purchased for £100.[61] Nevertheless in August of the same year Cranmer wrote to Cromwell urging that commissioners be sent to suppress Rocester, Tutbury, and Croxden.[62] Action followed quickly, and in September Abbot Grafton and eight other canons surrendered the monastery with all its possessions to the Crown.[63] A pension of £13 6s. 8d. was assigned to the abbot.[64]

An account has survived of the sale of St. Michael's Chapel, Rocester, in October 1538.[65] The glass and iron in its windows were sold to John Forman for 3s. 4d., the timber to William Loghtonhouse for 7s. 6d., and 'the shyngle' of the chapel to William Bagnall for 8d. The parishioners claimed the three bells, alleging that these had been used for parochial services as well as for those of the abbey. The 'house and site' of the monastery, leased in March 1539 for 21 years to Edward Draycott, one of Cromwell's servants, was sold the following July to Richard Trentham.[66]

There are no remains of the abbey above ground,

[48] Ibid. 1374–7, 159–60.
[49] Ibid. 1381–5, 597; 1385–9, 83.
[50] Ibid. 1385–9, 71, 193, 216, 242, 302; Cal. Close, 1385–9, 101–2, 108, 111, 112. Because of the disturbances the king took the abbey into his hands for a short time early in 1386: Cal. Pat. 1385–9, 77, 100.
[51] Cal. Pat. 1405–8, 371, 455.
[52] Cal. Close, 1313–18, 275; 1402–5, 381; 1447–50, 202.
[53] Cal. Pat. 1396–9, 508.
[54] Cal. Chart. R. 1427–1516, 8.
[55] J. C. Russell, 'The Clerical Population of Medieval Eng.' Traditio, ii. 200 (which, however, omits the abbot in 1381: see E 179/15/8b); Lich. Dioc. Regy., B/V/1/1, p. 50 (2nd nos.); see below.
[56] Lich. Dioc. Regy., B/V/1/1, p. 50 (2nd nos.). The abbey was assessed at £66 13s. 4d. for the loan of 1522: L. & P. Hen. VIII, iii(2), p. 1047.
[57] Bridges, Northants. i. 131. He was not among the canons who signed the deed of surrender in 1538 and did not receive a pension, but he seems to have continued as Vicar of Woodford until his death in 1563: ibid.; Hibbert, Dissolution, 168; L. & P. Hen. VIII, xiv(1), p. 598.
[58] Valor Eccl. (Rec. Com.), iii. 124 (where the chantry pension is wrongly given as £4 6s. 8d.: see ibid. 140).
[59] S.C. 6/Hen. VIII/3353, mm. 17–20.
[60] This land is given as 'Denston Ryddyng in Somersall'.

Henry of Denstone held land in West Broughton (in Doveridge, Derb.), about ½ mile from Somersal Heath, in the early 13th cent. and was making assarts (or riddings) there. He may also have held land in Somersal Herbert (Derb.). See S.H.C. 4th ser. iv, pp. 157–8, 232–3, 264–6; J. C. Cox, Notes on the Churches of Derbs. iii. 287. The field name 'ridding' is found in the parishes of Doveridge and Somersal Herbert: Place-Names of Derbs. Pt. III (E.P.N.S. xxix), 552, 605.
[61] Hibbert, Dissolution, 137–9; L. & P. Hen. VIII, xiii(2), p. 177.
[62] L. & P. Hen. VIII, xiii(2), pp. 64–65.
[63] Hibbert, Dissolution, 167–8.
[64] L. & P. Hen. VIII, xiv(1), p. 598. Seven of the canons besides the abbot were assigned pensions: ibid. And see ibid. xvi, p. 731. In 1557–8 John Britchbank, a former canon of Rocester, was still drawing his pension: S. W. Hutchinson, Archdeaconry of Stoke-on-Trent (1893), 166.
[65] Hibbert, Dissolution, 169, 256. Evidently part of the abbey church was retained as the parish church: Erdeswick, Staffs. 491–2.
[66] L. & P. Hen. VIII, xiv(1), pp. 27, 590. Among the reservations from this grant in fee to Trentham were 'a chamber and churchyard belonging to the vicarage of Rocester'.

but the site evidently lies on the south side of the present churchyard.[67]

ABBOTS

Thurstan, abbot at the foundation.[68]

Ivo, occurs probably 1155.[69]

Richard, occurs probably 1155[70] and at some time between 1161 and 1176.[71]

Henry, occurs 1210.[72]

William, occurs at some time between 1215 and 1224.[73]

Philip, occurs at some time between 1233 and 1238 and in 1251.[74]

Richard, elected 1256.[75]

Walter, elected 1258, resigned 1269.[76]

Walter de Dodele, elected 1269, resigned 1285.[77]

Robert, elected 1286, died 1289.[78]

Roger of Loughborough, elected 1289, resigned 1316.[79]

Walter of Aston, elected 1316, died 1324.[80]

Gilbert de Bosco, elected 1324, resigned by January 1335.[81]

Henry of Hopton, elected 1335, died 1349.[82]

William of Cheadle, appointed 1349, died 1364.[83]

Thomas of Rocester, elected 1364, died 1375.[84]

John Cheswardine, elected 1375, resigned 1386.[85]

Robert of Bakewell, elected 1386, resigned 1407.[86]

Henry Smyth, elected 1407, resigned 1443.[87]

John Hambury, elected 1443, resigned 1466.[88]

Robert Twys, elected 1466.[89]

John Quinten or Quynton, occurs 1475, resigned 1486.[90]

George Caldon, elected 1486, occurs 1496.[91]

William John, died 1507.[92]

Roger Rolleston alias Stathum, elected 1507, occurs 1510.[93]

Thomas Bromley, occurs 1521.[94]

William Grafton, occurs 1524, surrendered the abbey in 1538.[95]

A seal of the abbey in use in 1490 is circular, $2\frac{1}{2}$ in. in diameter. It shows an abbot standing in a canopied niche. He holds a pastoral staff in his right hand and a book in his left. On either side in similar niches are eight canons surmounted by an estoile. The Virgin, with the Child on her knee, is enthroned above the abbot's canopy; on either side, above the canons' niches, are censing angels.[96] Legend, lombardic:

SIGILLUM CONVE . . . CE BEATE
[?M] . . . ESTR . . . LE

15. THE PRIORY OF RANTON

THE priory of Ranton was founded about the mid 12th century by Robert fitz Noel of Ellenhall,[1] whose father had been granted Ranton in fee by Nicholas de Stafford.[2] The foundation charter[3] refers to the house as St. Mary des Essarz, an indication that the house was established on assarted land. Besides the site Robert fitz Noel gave 8 virgates of land in 'Cuccessone' (perhaps Cooksland in Seighford) and the mill of Coton Clanford (in Seighford), both free

---

[67] The 4-sided feature shown in this area by Cambridge Univ., Cttee. for Aerial Photography, nos. RI 64, 65, is probably post-medieval. [68] See above p. 247.

[69] S.H.C. xi. 301, charter of Bp. Durdent (1149–59) with Ivo among the witnesses. Also among the witnesses was Wm., Abbot of Radmore, who moved his abbey from Radmore to Stoneleigh between Dec. 1154 and June 1155: see above p. 225. The King Henry mentioned in the charter is Henry II.

[70] R. W. Eyton, Antiquities of Shropshire, viii. 216–17, charter of Bp. Durdent to Lilleshall Abbey with Ric. among the witnesses. Wm., Abbot of Radmore (see previous note), is again among the witnesses. Eyton dates the charter 1149–52, arguing that the reference in it to Ric. de Belmeis as Dean of St. Alkmund's must make the charter earlier than Ric.'s accession to the see of London (1152). The reference is in fact to the part played by Ric., when Dean of St. Alkmund's, in the foundation of Lilleshall Abbey, several years before this charter was issued.

[71] Eyton, Shropshire, viii. 227 and n. Eyton assigns the charter of Bp. Peche (1161–82) cited there to 1161 but gives no reason for this. The witnesses included Abbot Ric. and Wm. de Lega, Dean of Lichfield, who was succeeded as dean in 1176.

[72] Hist. MSS. Com. 16th Rep. Rutland, IV, 34.

[73] S.H.C. N.S. ix. 311, 312. In 1227–8 there is a reference to Hen., Prior of Rocester: S.H.C. iv(1), 67. The abbey was vacant in 1233: Close R. 1231–4, 220.

[74] S.H.C. viii(2), 156; W. Farrer, Honors and Knights' Fees, ii. 258. He witnessed several undated docs. in the Stone cartulary: S.H.C. vi(1), 11, 17, 19.

[75] Cal. Pat. 1247–58, 485, 488, 490. He was a canon of Rocester.

[76] Ibid. 614, 618; ibid. 1266–72, 360–1. He was Prior of Rocester.

[77] Ibid. 1266–72, 367; ibid. 1281–92, 214.

[78] Ibid. 1281–92, 214, 221, 312. He was Prior of Gresley (Derb.).

[79] Ibid. 314; ibid. 1313–17, 569. He was a canon of Rocester.

[80] Ibid. 1313–17, 603; ibid. 1321–4, 406. He was a canon of Rocester.

[81] Ibid. 1321–4, 410; ibid. 1334–8, 54–55. He was a canon of Rocester.

[82] Ibid. 1334–8, 56; ibid. 1348–50, 368. He was a canon of Rocester.

[83] Ibid. 1348–50, 413; ibid. 1364–7, 38. He was a canon of Rocester. The prior and canons left the choice to the bishop on this occasion but recommended William: Lich. Dioc. Regy., B/A/1/2, f. 186.

[84] Cal. Pat. 1364–7, 53–54; ibid. 1374–7, 80; Cal. Fine R. 1369–77, 286. He was a canon of Rocester and also vicar there at the time of his election: see above n. 45.

[85] Cal. Pat. 1374–7, 113, 120; see above p. 250. A canon of Ranton, he had been Vicar of Seighford from 1369 to 1375: see below p. 253.

[86] See above p. 250; Cal. Pat. 1405–8, 347. He was a canon of Rocester.

[87] See above p. 250; Cal. Pat. 1441–6, 183. He was a canon of Rocester: ibid. 1405–8, 371.

[88] Cal. Pat. 1441–6, 184; ibid. 1461–7, 550. He was prior at the time of his election.

[89] Ibid. 1461–7, 523.

[90] S.H.C. N.S. vi(1), 96; Lich. Dioc. Regy., B/A/1/12, f. 54. He was a canon of Rocester in 1466 when he was appointed Vicar of Rocester: ibid. f. 44.

[91] B/A/1/12, f. 54; S.H.C. 1939, 77. He was a canon of Rocester. He was admitted to the Lichfield Guild as Geo. Chadon in 1487: Harwood, Lichfield, 408.

[92] B/A/1/14, f. 21v.

[93] Ibid. He was a canon of Rocester. He was admitted to the Lichfield Guild in 1510: Harwood, Lichfield, 411.

[94] He was admitted to the Lichfield Guild that year: Harwood, Lichfield, 413.

[95] Lich. Dioc. Regy., B/V/1/1, p. 50 (2nd nos.); see above p. 250. He was evidently buried at Rocester in 1576: Hibbert, Dissolution, 193.

[96] W. de G. Birch, Cat. of Seals in B.M. i, p. 720; B.M., Stowe Ch. 87; cast among W.S.L. Seals; see above plate facing p. 213.

[1] S.H.C. iv(1), 264–7.

[2] Ibid. ii(1), 219. Most of the family property, however, was held of the bishop: V.C.H. Staffs. iv. 27, 34.

[3] Dugdale, Mon. vi(1), 257–8.

of secular service, with another virgate in Coton Clanford held by 'castle service'. The foundation charter states that the canons of Ranton were living 'under the rule and obedience' of Haughmond Abbey (Salop.), and this helps to fix the date of foundation. Ranton must have been founded after the establishment of the mother-house at Haughmond (between 1130 and 1138)[4] and by 1166 when some of the witnesses to the foundation charter were dead.[5] The founder subsequently increased the endowment of his priory by giving the church of Seighford with its dependent chapels of Ranton, Ellenhall, and Derrington ('Doddington') and the church of Grandborough (Warws.).[6] For some unknown reason the little Suffolk priory of Bricett sued Haughmond in the later 12th century for its daughter-house of Ranton and was paid 40s. to remit its claim.[7]

The founder's son, Thomas Noel, added land in Bridgeford (in Seighford), Ranton, and Coton Clanford and arranged to be buried in the priory.[8] The land in Bridgeford, however, was detained by his daughter and coheir, Alice, and her husband, William de Harcourt. Eventually, in her widowhood, Alice regranted this land to the priory with her own body for burial and added more land from her demesne of Seighford.[9] Richard de Harcourt of Great Sheepy (Leics.) gave the priory 9 virgates of land in Great Sheepy with fishing rights and 2s. rent from his mill there; this property was the priory's most important temporal estate outside Staffordshire.[10]

Other benefactions included a virgate of land in Stockton (in Longford, Salop.) given by Richard de Stockton in the later 12th century;[11] a grant in 1221 by Bishop Cornhill of 120 acres of waste land in his manor of Eccleshall for an annual rent of 6s. 8d.;[12] and several grants from successive heads of the Knightley family in the late 12th and earlier 13th centuries. The Knightley grants included quarrying rights in Knightley manor (in Gnosall), right of way over the family lands between the priory and its granges, and 'the spring of Witewell'.[13] Later in the 13th century the priory inscribed in its martyrology the name of Richard of Flashbrook, a benefactor and the son of a benefactor; the canons promised to observe his anniversary like that of one of their own community and contributed 40s. for the redemption of his lands under the terms of the Dictum of Kenilworth of 1266.[14] By about this time a hospital of St. Anne had been established within the priory precincts, and Richard of Flashbrook was among its benefactors.[15] Between at least 1255 and 1290 the priory was much involved in protracted disputes with the Doyly family, lords of Ranton,[16] over 'lands, rights of pasture, and various injuries'. Part of the trouble may have been due to the inevitable obscurities of title following clearance of waste in the area, but other matters in dispute included the private chapel of the Doyly family and the evidently extensive watercourses which connected with the priory's mills and fishponds.[17] By 1291 the priory had acquired a temporal estate in Grandborough parish which was distinct from the appropriated church.[18]

The priory may have had fairly widespread commercial interests in the later 13th century. During this period the burgesses of Stafford admitted the canons to all the 'liberties and free customs' of the borough,[19] while the priory was given a house 'in the new market of Newcastle-under-Lyme'.[20] A burgage and land in Newport (Salop.) were also acquired, some of the property having formerly belonged to William Randolf, a prominent merchant of the town.[21] The acquisitions in Newport, which lies on the road from central Staffordshire to Wales, may have been connected with the priory's development of commercial interests in Wales. About this time Griffith ap Gwenwynwyn (d. 1286), lord of Southern Powys, gave the priory quittance of tolls in his markets, a grant which was confirmed by his son Owen (d. 1293).[22]

The most important development in the early history of the house was its emancipation from Haughmond. The priory's observance of 'the rule of Haughmond' is mentioned in a charter of Archbishop Baldwin (1184–90).[23] A charter of Archbishop Hubert (1193–1205) notes that Ranton was subject to Haughmond.[24] This latter charter may have been occasioned by some friction between Ranton and the mother-house, and an undated agreement between the houses[25] perhaps belongs to the following years. The canons of Ranton were evidently held to be canons of the mother-house, for they were to participate in the election of abbots of Haughmond. The abbot was to visit Ranton at least once a year. The canons of Ranton, however, were empowered to admit new members to their community, though all were to profess obedience to the Abbot of Haughmond. When the priorate of Ranton fell vacant, the canons were to present one of their brethren and another from Haughmond to the abbot, who was to make the final choice. This settlement was clearly a compromise. It suggests that Ranton was larger than most cells of the order

[4] R. W. Eyton, 'Haughmond Abbey', *Arch. Jnl.* xiii. 145 sqq.
[5] *S.H.C.* i. 155. The founder is believed to have died *c.* 1171: ibid. ii(1), 256.
[6] Dugdale, *Mon.* vi (1), 258.
[7] R. W. Eyton, *Antiquities of Shropshire*, vii. 366.
[8] *S.H.C.* iv(1), 267–8.
[9] Ibid. 268.
[10] Ibid.; J. Nichols, *Hist. and Antiquities of County of Leicester*, iv(2), 923–4; *Tax. Eccl.* (Rec. Com.), 73; *Valor Eccl.* (Rec. Com.), iii. 115.
[11] *S.H.C.* iv(1), 279.
[12] Ibid. 287–8. This grant was witnessed by A[lexander], Archdeacon of Salop (from 1221), and confirmed by the Pope in 1221: Le Neve, *Fasti* (1854 edn.), i. 573; *S.H.C.* iv(1), 289.
[13] *S.H.C.* iv(1), 274. For the Knightley family see *V.C.H. Staffs.* iv. 119. At the Dissolution the priory owned 7

granges, of which 6 were leased out: S.C. 6/Hen. VIII/ 3352, mm. 8, 9.
[14] *S.H.C.* iv(1), 284.
[15] Ibid. 287.
[16] *Feudal Aids*, v. 4, 11, 21. They held Ranton of the Harcourts who in turn held it of the barons of Stafford.
[17] *S.H.C.* iv(1), 269–71, 278.
[18] *V.C.H. Warws.* vi. 97.
[19] *S.H.C.* iv(1), 290.   [20] Ibid. 275.
[21] Ibid. 279; Eyton, *Shropshire*, ix. 139.
[22] *S.H.C.* iv(1), 289. Griffith and his son owned land in the Derb. Peak District. All their markets, however, seem to have been situated in central Wales. See G. T. O. Bridgeman, *The Princes of Upper Powys*, 14, 24n., 43–44, 51, 53, 128–9, 129–30, 132, 141–2; *Cal. Inq. p.m.* iii, pp. 62–63.
[23] Dugdale, *Mon.* vi(1), 257.
[24] Ibid. vi(2), 750.   [25] Ibid.

in this country but that it was by no means independent. A further dispute between Ranton and Haughmond occurred, and the matter was referred to papal delegates who in turn referred it to the bishop and his advisers. A final settlement was reached in 1247. Ranton was to have complete independence from Haughmond in all matters spiritual and temporal, but a 'customary payment' of 100s. was to be made to Haughmond each year.[26] It is not clear how these events affected the rights of the Harcourt family who in 1209 possessed what was described as the advowson of Ranton.[27] The family, however, evidently exercised the right of confirming elections throughout the rest of the priory's history.[28]

The Taxation of 1291 gives Ranton's total income as £59 14s. The temporal income was £26 7s. 4d.; all the property from which this was derived lay within the county except for estates at Great Sheepy and Grandborough.[29] Spiritual property was worth £33 6s. 8d. which derived from the appropriated churches of Grandborough (£20) and Seighford (£13 6s. 8d.).[30]

By the early 14th century the priory had acquired lands at Knighton, Flashbrook, and Batchacre (all in Adbaston), and at Milwich. Granges at some distance from the priory had also been established by the same date: Hewall Grange (in Dilhorne) and Oldhall Grange (in Caverswall). In 1313 the king granted the priory free warren in its demesne lands in these places and at Ranton, Seighford, and Ellenhall.[31] In 1320 the bishop ordained a vicarage for the priory's church of Seighford[32] and in the following year reconstituted the vicarage of the appropriated church of Grandborough.[33] In the 1330s the priory was granted licences to acquire property in Dilhorne, Stafford, Apeton (now in Church Eaton), and Hadnall (Salop.).[34]

The internal life of the priory in the 14th century was somewhat turbulent. In 1325 the bishop wrote to the prior that a brother of the house, John de Dumpelton, when absent in charge of its goods, had put off clerical garb and resumed that of a layman. The prior was to admonish him to seek a papal dispensation from the major excommunication which he had incurred.[35] A little later the bishop ordered that John should be transferred to Burscough Priory (Lancs.) where he was to be maintained on a diet of bread, ale, and vegetables.[36]

About 1357 there was violent opposition to the bishop when he tried to carry out a visitation of the priory. In that year he secured the issue of a commission of oyer and terminer to hear his complaint that during his attempted visitation he had been attacked by John, son of Robert de Knightley, and others. The bishop's attackers had planned to prevent him from exercising his jurisdiction, besieging him and his men in the priory so that none of them dared to come out of it to buy food or other necessities. Afterwards the malefactors had withdrawn into a wood and ambushed the bishop as he was going to his manor of Haywood. It was claimed that without the aid of the men of the neighbourhood the bishop would have been killed. As it was he had been robbed and one of his servants had been assaulted.[37]

In 1372 the king revoked orders committing the priory and its possessions to the sheriff and William de Halughton.[38] It is not clear what lay behind this, but it may have been financial mismanagement. The priory then seems to have tried to augment its resources by farming the property of alien priories which were in the king's hands as a result of the war with France. In 1386 Geoffrey Stafford, canon of Ranton, was granted the custody of Alberbury Priory (Salop.).[39] Soon afterwards Geoffrey was removed from the custody — fraudulently, as it was said. In 1388, however, his restitution to the custody was ordered for the duration of the war; the yearly rent was 20 marks.[40] In 1390 Geoffrey was accused of dilapidations and waste,[41] and by 1392 Alberbury had passed to other hands.[42] Geoffrey, however, became joint keeper of the priories of Lapley and of Modbury (Devon) and was also a collector of a clerical tenth.[43]

It may also have been financial considerations which led the priory to serve the church of Seighford by one of its own brethren: John Cheswardine, a canon, was vicar there from 1369 to 1375 and was succeeded by a fellow canon, John of Woollaston.[44] To what extent this practice was recent is uncertain, but it evidently continued: in 1414 John Wilde, a canon of Ranton, resigned the vicarage and was succeeded by his fellow canon, Thomas Halfhide.[45] A visitation of 1518 shows one of the canons as serving the church of Seighford,[46] and in 1530 Bishop Blythe refused to institute a canon of Ranton to Seighford because he was 'unlearned and unworthy'.[47] In 1401, again perhaps for financial reasons, the priory appropriated the endowed vicarage of its church of Grandborough.[48]

The community (including the prior) numbered

---

[26] Ibid.; *S.H.C.* 1924, pp. 49–50, 154. In 1252 the Abbot of Haughmond allotted this pension, with other income, to his brethren for pittances: Dugdale, *Mon.* vi(2), 750.

[27] *S.H.C.* iii(1), 174–5. Alice, daughter and coheir of Thos. Noel, married Wm. de Harcourt: see above p. 252.

[28] In the 1290s and in 1490 the patron's consent was given to the appointment of a new prior: *S.H.C.* 1911, 213; Lich. Dioc. Regy., B/A/1/12, ff. 61v.–62.

[29] *Tax. Eccl.* 73, 251–2, 256.

[30] Ibid. 242. Grandborough church was not noted as belonging to Ranton. The endowed vicarage of Grandborough was worth £4: ibid. 244.

[31] *Cal. Chart. R.* 1300–26, 219; *S.H.C.* N.S. xii. 278; Erdeswick, *Staffs.* 495.

[32] Lich. Dioc. Regy., B/A/1/1, f. 91v.

[33] *S.H.C.* N.S. viii. 124–5; Dugdale, *Warws.* i. 313.

[34] *S.H.C.* 1913, 26–27, 60–61; *Cal. Pat.* 1330–4, 225; 1334–8, 307. Two of these transactions were under a licence of 1318 to acquire property to the annual value of 100s.: ibid. 1317–21, 251.

[35] Lich. Dioc. Regy., B/A/1/3, f. 18v.

[36] Ibid. ff. 19v.–20.

[37] *Cal. Pat.* 1354–8, 556.

[38] *Cal. Close*, 1369–74, 270.

[39] *Cal. Pat.* 1385–9, 146.

[40] Ibid. 438–9; *Cal. Fine R.* 1383–91, 136, 351.

[41] *Cal. Pat.* 1388–92, 352; *Cal. Fine R.* 1391–9, 44, 221, 306; Dugdale, *Mon.* vi(2), 1031 n.

[42] *Cal. Fine R.* 1391–9, 44.

[43] Ibid. 44, 221, 306.

[44] *S.H.C.* N.S. viii. 37; N.S. x(2), 124, 141. Cheswardine was elected Abbot of Rocester: see above p. 251.

[45] *Reg. Chichele*, ed. E. F. Jacob, iii. 338. At the same time another canon of Ranton was instituted to the neighbouring rectory of Haughton, a living never in the priory's patronage: ibid.

[46] Lich. Dioc. Regy., B/V/1/1, p. 27. The visitations of 1521 and 1524 make no mention of Seighford.

[47] Hibbert, *Dissolution*, 112 (no source given).

[48] *Cal. Pat.* 1399–1401, 537; Dugdale, *Warws.* i. 313.

six in 1377 and seven in 1381.[49] Visitations of 1518, 1521, and 1524 show a community of six, said by one of the brethren to be the full complement.[50] The income of the house was not given, but the priory was free from debt; the prior stated in 1518 that 20 marks received from Edward Davenport *pro liberatura sua* had been spent on lead for the house. The prior also complained in 1518 of the low standard of observance on the part of three of the canons; two of these, Robert Parker and Humphrey Huett, had each fathered a child. The brethren were in the habit of leaving the priory without permission, particularly in order to hunt. The visitor ordered the prior on pain of deprivation to report the incorrigible brethren to the bishop or chancellor so that they could be transferred. The prior had also complained that one of the canons went to confession only once a year,[51] and the visitor ordered the brethren to confess at least twice a week. The 1521 visitation shows that no transfers had taken place although Huett was still leading an irregular life. The subprior complained that silence was not properly observed. By 1524 Huett had left for Rome, and the only complaint was from the subprior who alleged the continued breaking of silence.

The valuation of 1535 gives the priory's gross annual income as £102 11s. 1d. The gross temporal income was £56 9s. 7d. a year, almost all the property being in Staffordshire. Deductions, including a fee of £2 to the chief steward, Sir John Harcourt, amounted to £5 15s. 4d. The spiritualities produced a gross income of £46 1s. 6d. a year. Deductions, including the annual pension of 100s. to Haughmond Abbey, amounted to £6 12s. 10⅔d.[52] The gross annual value of the priory property as listed in 1537 after it had passed to the Crown[53] was £117 3s. 9d. About half of this income was derived from the spiritual endowments, which consisted of the appropriated churches of Ellenhall, Seighford, Ranton, and Grandborough and tithes at 'Bircheford' (in Church Eaton). The temporal property consisted of the manor of Great Sheepy; Hethcote[54] and Clanford Granges (both in Seighford), Knighton, Ellerton, and Batchacre Granges (all in Adbaston), Hewall Grange, and Oldhall Grange; lands and rents in Ranton, Seighford, Bridgeford, Ellenhall, Dilhorne, Grandborough, and Woolscot and Walcote (both in Grandborough); and many small properties and rents (whose combined annual value did not reach £10) in Apeton, Aston (in Seighford), Cowley (in Gnosall), Gnosall, Billington (in Bradley), Orslow (in Church Eaton), Adbaston,[55] Stafford, Knightley, Haughton, Eccleshall, Newcastle-under-Lyme, Whitgreave (in St. Mary's,

Stafford), 'Launde'[56] Offley,[57] Stockton, Walford (in Standon), Milwich, Wood Eaton (in Church Eaton), Newport, and Nantwich (Ches.).

Ranton came within the terms of the Act of 1536 for dissolving the lesser monasteries, and a scramble for its possessions ensued.[58] On 2 April 1536 Sir Simon Harcourt wrote to Cromwell:[59] 'I beg you will be a mediator to the king for me, that the house may continue, and he shall have £100 and you £100 if you can accomplish it, and £20 fee out of the said house. If the king is determined to dissolve it I desire to have it as it adjoins such small lands as I have in that country, and I and my heirs will pay so much as the rent of assize cometh to and give you 100 marks.' On the 27th of the same month Henry, Lord Stafford, wrote to Cromwell begging 'the farm of the abbey of Ranton if it be dissolved; it is within four miles of my house and reaches my park pale, and I will give as much for it as any man . . . I heard that George Blount endeavours to obstruct my suit'. The next day Lord Stafford wrote to the Earl of Westmorland urging his claim against Blount's but intimating his willingness to take White Ladies (in Boscobel, Salop.) instead.[60] In May Richard Cromwell wrote to him: 'As to the abbey you wrote about my uncle says that he will not fail to obtain it for you when the surveying of the abbeys is at an end.'[61] A further begging letter from Lord Stafford followed on 12 March 1537, stating that the commissioners were due in Stafford the next Sunday and urging his claims against those of Harcourt: 'I have 12 children and my living £40 a year less than it has been.'[62] But his importunity was in vain. The house was dissolved, and in November the site was leased to Harcourt for 21 years. In 1538 the Crown sold it to John Wiseman and his wife, who soon afterwards exchanged it with Harcourt for the manor of St. Mary Hoo (Kent).[63] The prior was receiving a pension of 20 marks at his death in 1555 at Seighford.[64]

The chief remains of the monastic buildings are a fine western tower of the 14th century, which is intact, and a portion of the adjoining south wall of the church. References in 1663 to 'the cloister at Ranton Abbey', 'the great chamber window', and 'another chamber window'[65] indicate that other parts of the priory were then still standing.

PRIORS

Ralph.[66]

O., occurs at some time probably between 1198 and 1203.[67]

Alfred, occurs 1221 and 1247.[68]

[49] J. C. Russell, 'The Clerical Population of Medieval Eng.' *Traditio*, ii. 200 (which, however, omits the prior in 1381 and wrongly gives the date as 1383: see E 179/15/8b). The community numbered six in 1372: *S.H.C.* xiii. 95.

[50] For the rest of this para. see Lich. Dioc. Regy., B/V/1/1, pp. 27, 63, and p. 42 (2nd nos.).

[51] The subprior said: 'vix septies in anno'.

[52] *Valor Eccl.* iii. 114–16.

[53] S.C. 6/Hen. VIII/3352, mm. 8–10.

[54] Given as 'Heythehouse' Grange in *Valor Eccl.* iii. 114. It was probably situated in the neighbourhood of the modern Grange Farm in the north-west of Seighford parish.

[55] Given as 'Conventes Parrok between Adbaston and Knighton'.

[56] Perhaps Lawnhead (in Ellenhall). See W. H. Duignan, *Notes on Staffs. Place Names*, 90.

[57] Evidently Bishop's Offley (in Adbaston): *S.H.C.* iv(1), 288; ibid. 1914, 81–82.

[58] *L. & P. Hen. VIII*, x, p. 515.

[59] Ibid. p. 248.   [60] Ibid. pp. 312, 314.   [61] Ibid. p. 367.

[62] Ibid. xii(1), p. 285.

[63] Ibid. xiii(1), p. 588; xiii(2), p. 405; Erdeswick, *Staffs.* 136.

[64] E 178/3239, m. 8. In his will of 1555 he expressed a wish to be buried in Seighford church and left vestments to Seighford and Grandborough churches: *S.H.C.* 1926, pp. 11–12.

[65] Bodl. MS. Ashmole 853, f. 22v.

[66] Dugdale, *Mon.* vi(1), 257. In W.S.L., S.MS. 237/M, pp. 8, 13, Ralph is said to have been prior during the founder's lifetime and probably the first prior.

[67] *Letters of Pope Innocent III*, ed. C.R. and Mary G. Cheney, p. 149; Eyton, *Shropshire*, viii. 225, 241.

[68] *S.H.C.* iv(1), 295; ibid. 1924, pp. 49–50; Dugdale, *Mon.* vi(2), 750.

Gilbert, occurs 1253 and 1267.[69]

Thomas, occurs 1272 and 1279.[70]

Peter.[71]

Thomas of Evesham, occurs 1293 and 1298.[72]

Henry de Tywe, occurs 1301 and 1313.[73]

Robert de Bradele, appointed 1326, probably died 1349.[74]

Richard of Milwich, elected 1349, died 1359.[75]

John Harcourt, elected 1359, resigned by 1372.[76]

John of Eccleshall, occurs 1372, died 1380.[77]

Thomas de Went, elected 1380, died by March 1413.[78]

John Bukenale, elected 1413, resigned 1433.[79]

John Bromley, elected 1433, appointed Prior of Arbury 1456.[80]

Roger Beche, elected 1456.[81]

Thomas Sutton, probably occurs 1480.[82]

John Welynton, occurs 1488, resigned 1490.[83]

Roger Smyth, appointed 1490, elected Abbot of Dorchester about 1510.[84]

Thomas Alton, elected 1511, prior at the dissolution in 1537.[85]

Three seals of the house are known. The first,[86] a common seal in use in the 13th century, is a pointed oval about 2½ by 1⅝ in. It depicts the Virgin seated with the Child in her lap; the Child's hand is raised in blessing. Legend, lombardic:

... IE [DE] RAN ...

The second,[87] also a common seal, is a pointed oval about 2⅜ by 1¾ in. It depicts the Virgin crowned and seated on a panelled and canopied throne, with the Child on her left knee; in the base is a trefoil. Legend, lombardic:

... CAP ... [M]ARIE DE RON ...

The third,[88] in use in the 16th century, is a seal *ad*

causas. It is a pointed oval 2½ by 1½ in. and depicts the Virgin crowned and seated on a panelled and canopied throne with the Child on her left knee; in the base is a cinquefoil. Legend, lombardic:

SIGILLUM SANCTE MARIE DE [R]ANTONE AD CAUSAS

16. THE PRIORY OF TRENTHAM

IT has been alleged that St. Werburgh, daughter of Wulfhere, King of Mercia, was founder and abbess of a nunnery at Trentham.[1] This connexion with the saint, however, rests on an identification which is now rejected.[2] The later priory of Austin canons was believed about 1251–2 to have originated 'in the time of William Rufus, through Hugh, Earl of Chester'.[3] If a religious house was founded at Trentham in the 11th century, however, it was evidently not properly established, for with one important exception the 12th-century deeds of the priory make no mention of a previous house. Any foundation of Earl Hugh, moreover, would almost certainly not have been intended as an Augustinian monastery[4] since the Austin canons were barely established in England in his time.[5] Nevertheless the foundation charter of the priory speaks of 'the restoration of an abbey of canons'[6] and supplies the 13th-century tradition with its only support. It is just conceivable that the word *abbathia*, used in the foundation charter, does not necessarily imply that the house was presided over by an abbot, and it may thus refer to a pre-Conquest minster, or house of secular canons, at Trentham.[7]

The establishment of a permanent religious house at Trentham was the work of Ranulph de Gernon, Earl of Chester (d. 1153). In his foundation

[69] *S.H.C.* iv(1), 293, 295; B.M., Cott. MS. Vesp. cxv, f. 39. The latter, a deed of 1267, mentions Prior G.; it is wrongly dated 1277 in *S.H.C.* iv(1), 284.

[70] *S.H.C.* 1924, p. 242; ibid. iv(1), 270, 280.

[71] *S.H.C.* iv(1), 276. *S.H.C.* 1914, 94 (citing no source), gives Peter *c.* 1205 and a Prior John in 1284.

[72] *S.H.C.* iv(1), 278; vi(1), 231.

[73] Ibid. iv(1), 285; ibid. 1924, p. 236.

[74] Lich. Dioc. Regy., B/A/1/2, f. 141v. The bishop quashed his election as invalid and then re-appointed him. He was a canon of Ranton.

[75] B/A/1/2, f. 187; *S.H.C.* N.S. x(2), 13. He was a canon of Ranton.

[76] *S.H.C.* N.S. x(2), 13; *S.H.C.* xiii. 95. He was a canon of Ranton.

[77] *S.H.C.* xiii. 95; ibid. N.S. x (2), 149.

[78] Ibid. N.S. x(2), 149; Lich. Dioc. Regy., B/A/1/7, f. 75. He was a canon of Ranton.

[79] B/A/1/7, f. 75; ibid. /9, f. 62. He was a canon of Ranton. On his resignation the bishop assigned him a house called 'le Newhall', food, drink, fuel, candles, and 6 marks a year for clothing and other needs: ibid. ff. 168v.–169.

[80] Ibid. /9, f. 62; ibid. /11, ff. 15v., 23v.–24. He was a canon of St. Thomas's near Stafford.

[81] Ibid. /11, f. 15v. He was a canon of Ranton.

[82] W.S.L., S.MS. 237/M, pp. 8, 13.

[83] Harwood, *Lichfield*, 408, showing him admitted to the Lichfield Guild in 1488; B/A/1/12, f. 61v. The bishop assigned him a pension of 20 marks on his resignation: ibid. f. 62. His name is given as Wenlock *alias* Wellington in W.S.L., S.MS. 237/M, pp. 8, 13 (where he is said, wrongly, to occur as prior in 1499).

[84] B/A/1/12, ff. 61v.–62; *V.C.H. Oxon.* ii. 90 and n. 13; Erdeswick, *Staffs.* 136n. He was a canon of Ranton. In 1508 he was admitted to the Lichfield Guild: Harwood, *Lichfield*, 411. In 1514, as Bishop of Lydda, he was commissioned as a suffragan in the diocese of Lincoln, and he was briefly employed as such in Coventry and Lichfield diocese in 1521: Margaret Bowker, *Secular Clergy in the Dioc. of Lincoln, 1495–1520*, 24; see above p. 41.

[85] B/A/1/14, f. 22; *L. & P. Hen. VIII*, xvi, p. 731. He was a canon of Ranton. He is given as Thos. Dalton in 1531 (*S.H.C.* iv(1), 292), as Thos. Damport in his will of 1555 (see above n. 64), and as Thos. Damporte *alias* Alton in a pension list (E 178/3239, m. 8).

[86] S.R.O., D.798/1/1/5 (grant of Prior Alfred to which this impression is affixed). On the reverse of the impression is an oval counterseal of the prior.

[87] W. de G. Birch, *Cat. of Seals in B.M.* i, p. 723; B.M. Seal Cast lxxii. 48. Birch dates this seal to the 13th cent.

[88] Birch, *Cat. of Seals in B.M.* i, p. 723; B.M. Seal Cast lxxii. 49; Dugdale, *Mon.* vi(1), 257. Two impressions of this seal, affixed to documents dated 1526 and 1535, survive in S.R.O., D. 798/2/1/7 and D. 798/2/1/9/1. Birch dates this seal to the 13th cent.

[1] *The Life of Saint Werburge of Chester*, by Henry Bradshaw (E.E.T.S. lxxxviii), ed. C. Horstmann, pp. 86, 105–6, 111, 115–16, 118–19, 139; T. Tanner, *Notitia Monastica* (1787 edn.), Staffs. xxix; W. Camden, *Britannia* (1695 edn.), col. 530; *S.H.C.* N.S. xii. 74.

[2] The nunnery was at 'Tricengeham', now thought to be Threckingham (Lincs.): *Chartulary or Reg. of Abbey of St. Werburgh, Chester, Pt. I* (Chetham Soc. N.S. lxxix), pp. x–xiii.

[3] *Bk. of Fees*, i. 1285; *Cal. Pat.* 1338–40, 34.

[4] Earl Hugh died in 1101 as a monk at the Benedictine abbey of St. Werburgh, Chester: *Complete Peerage*, iii. 165. He may have made a vow to found a cell of St. Werburgh's at Trentham, which death prevented him from carrying out. His son and heir, Richard, was a minor in 1101 and in adult life no friend to the Benedictine order: ibid.; R. V. H. Burne, *The Monks of Chester*, 6–7.

[5] See J. C. Dickinson, *Origins of the Austin Canons and their Introduction into Eng.* 97–108.

[6] Dugdale, *Mon.* vi(1), 397.

[7] See W. Page, 'Some Remarks on the Churches of the Domesday Survey', *Archaeologia*, 2nd ser. xvi. 94.

charter[8] Earl Ranulph gave to God, St. Mary, and All Saints 100s. worth of land in Staffordshire, namely 'Trentham . . . and all those appurtenances whence King Henry had 100s.' It has been claimed that Earl Ranulph's charter was drawn up when he was on his deathbed.[9] This is quite feasible. A deathbed fulfilment of a longstanding but neglected obligation is likely enough, and the charter certainly belongs to the mid 12th century and was granted at Gresley (Derb.) where Ranulph died.

On Ranulph's death in 1153 the earldom passed to his six-year-old son, Hugh. Henry II then seems to have obtained permanent possession of the manor of Trentham and with it the patronage of the priory.[10] Earl Ranulph's foundation charter was confirmed by the king probably in mid January 1155 when the earl's gift was more precisely defined as '100s. worth of land of lay fee in the . . . vill of Trentham and in its appurtenances, viz. Blurton and Cocknage.'[11] A few days later the king regranted Trentham church to the canons,[12] and by a writ of about the same date he extended his protection to 'my canons of Trentham.'[13] In yet another charter[14] the king granted the canons more property in Trentham: 'tofts for cultivating and for building their barns'; all the woodland in Trentham manor; and two marshes (moras) to be reclaimed as meadows 'for the maintenance of the brethren and the hospitality of their house.' The new foundation was also confirmed, probably in 1155, by Bishop Durdent, who granted the house immunity from synodal payments with the other privileges which his predecessors had granted to Rocester and other churches of the order.[15]

Like the other Augustinian houses in Staffordshire Trentham never became wealthy and its early acquisitions were not considerable. These are listed in a privilege granted by the Pope in 1162 confirming the status and possessions of the priory.[16] What was evidently the parish church of Trentham with its dependencies was placed first among the priory's possessions; these dependencies included Barlaston, Betley, half of Balterley, and Newcastle-under-Lyme. The priory also held the 100s. worth of land in the parish 'which Henry the King of the English gave to the church at the institution of the order and confirmed by his writing';[17] the hermitage of the well of Tunstall with the land that Walter the hermit cultivated;[18] three carucates of land in Sutton[19] given by Gundred, Countess of Warwick; a carucate of land in Gaddesby (Leics.) of the Earl of Chester's fee;[20] the church of Barkby (Leics.); a bovate of land in 'Honus' (perhaps Hoon in Derbyshire); and six bovates of land in Barkby given by Robert le Poer. Not all these endowments, however, were retained. The church of Barkby was also claimed by Leicester Abbey, to which it was confirmed by the king in the same year.[21] The land given by Robert le Poer was evidently a gift to Barkby parish church,[22] and it too was lost by Trentham. The priory eventually had to be content with a pension of £5 13s. 4d. out of Barkby church.[23]

Some of the priory's subsequent endowments were gifts of the founder's heirs or of officials or tenants of the earls of Chester. Half of the church of Belchford (Lincs.) was given by the founder's son Hugh, Earl of Chester (d. 1181), while the mill and fishing rights of Belchford were given by the founder's grandson Ranulph, Earl of Chester (d. 1232).[24] By the early 13th century the priory had also acquired Wall Grange (in Leek), probably from one of the earls of Chester.[25] Philip de Orreby, Justiciar of Chester from about 1209 to 1229,[26] gave the priory a boat on the River Dee at Chester which he had himself received as a gift from Earl Ranulph (d. 1232);[27] in effect this amounted to the right to fish the river.[28] The advowsons of the Lincolnshire churches of Donington and Stenigot and of St. Paul in the Bail, Lincoln, belonged to the priory by the earlier 13th century. The advowson of Donington had probably been given by one of the earls of

[8] Dugdale, Mon. vi(1), 397.

[9] S.H.C. ii(1), 48–49; D.N.B. sub 'Randulf'. W. Farrer, Honors and Knights' Fees, ii. 266, suggests that Earl Ranulph founded, or refounded, Trentham between Mar. 1153 (when the Treaty of Devizes legitimized his title to the Trentham estate) and his death the following Dec.

[10] Farrer, Honors and Knights' Fees, ii. 7, 266.

[11] S.H.C. xi. 301–2; R. W. Eyton, Court, Household and Itinerary of Henry II, 2.

[12] S.H.C. xi. 300–1.   [13] Ibid. 300.

[14] Ibid. 302; Cal. Chart. R. 1300–26, 217. It is dated from Brill (Bucks.) where Hen. is known to have been in Oct. 1157 and in 1179: Eyton, Itin. of Hen. II, 31, 227.

[15] S.H.C. xi. 301; see also ibid. 312–13, 335–6. For the dating of Durdent's charter see above p. 251 n. 69. For the spiritual privileges see above p. 247.

[16] S.H.C. xi. 303–4; B.M., Harl. MS. 3868, ff. 33–34.

[17] This ambiguous phrase refers to Hen. II (see above) and seems to make the king responsible both for the original endowment and for its confirmation; it probably reflects the dispute between the Crown and the earls of Chester for possession of the large estate at Trentham on which the priory was founded: R. W. Eyton, Domesday Studies Staffs. 49; S.H.C. ii(1), 48–50; xi. 295–6. Eyton, probably following a mid-13th-cent. inquisition (Bk. of Fees, ii. 1261 n. 8, 1285), states that the Earl of Chester obtained Trentham from Wm. II. In this case the property must later have reverted to the Crown, for Earl Ranulph's foundation charter implies that Hen. I had held Trentham. In fact the earl probably acquired or regained it c. 1139: in that year the Empress Maud presented to Trentham church John the chaplain (S.H.C. xi. 322), who may be identifiable as the Earl of Chester's chaplain (ibid. 299); John succeeded Richard pincernus 'who held the aforesaid church of King Henry, after whose death he did

not wish to hold it'. See also above n. 9 and below n. 93.

[18] See above p. 136.

[19] Tentatively identified as Sutton-on-the-Hill (Derb.) in S.H.C. xi. 303. A more likely possibility is Sutton Coldfield (Warws.), which was held by the earls of Warwick. No further trace of this land is found among the priory's possessions.

[20] The ambiguous phrasing of the privilege at this point makes it difficult to link donors and gifts, but it is likely that the gift of the land at Gaddesby, of the Earl of Chester's fee, was made by the Bishop of Lincoln. If so, the Earl of Chester's Domesday estate in Gaddesby must have passed to the bishop, and not to the Earl of Leicester as suggested in V.C.H. Leics. i. 347; see also C. F. Slade, The Leics. Survey c. A.D. 1130, 40.

[21] V.C.H. Leics. iii. 13.

[22] J. Nichols, Hist. and Antiquities of the County of Leicester, iii(1), 48.

[23] Ibid. i(1), p. lix; Rot. Hugonis de Welles (Cant. & York Soc.), i. 257. Another dispute between Trentham and Leicester Abbey, over the church of Brackley (Northants.), had been settled by 1191: Nichols, Leics. i(2), App. xvii, 68.

[24] S.H.C. xi. 316–17; ibid. N.S. xii. 177; Farrer, Honors and Knights' Fees, ii. 173.

[25] S.H.C. xi. 333; J. Sleigh, Hist. of the Ancient Parish of Leek (2nd edn.), 145–6.

[26] G. Ormerod, Memoir on the Cheshire Domesday Roll, 11, 21 (included in G. Ormerod, Miscellanea Palatina, priv. print. 1851); Annales Cestrienses (Lancs. and Ches. Rec. Soc. xiv), 54, 55, 56, 57.

[27] S.H.C. xi. 305. Phil.'s gift was confirmed by Earl Ranulph.

[28] H. J. Hewitt, Cheshire under the Three Edwards, 40; S.H.C. N.S. xii. 75.

Chester, while that of Stenigot may have been acquired from the Wake family who held Stenigot of the earls. The priory also acquired pensions from these churches: £5 a year from Donington in 1217; 10s. a year from Stenigot by 1219; and 6s. 8d. a year from St. Paul in the Bail by at least 1291.[29]

Other early endowments, both spiritual and temporal, were acquired from less important land-owners. Probably soon after 1162 the church of Trusley (Derb.) was granted to Trentham, possibly by Robert de Beausay, lord of the manor of Trusley.[30] In the time of Bishop Richard Peche (1161–82) the church of Sutton-on-the-Hill (Derb.) was given to the priory by Ralph de Boscherville.[31] At some time before 1291 Trentham also acquired an annual pension of £2 from Trusley church and another of £1 from Dalbury church (Derb.).[32] Some of the temporal estates acquired from lesser landowners in the late 12th or early 13th centuries were situated far from Trentham and were relinquished by the mid 13th century. About 1196 Adam de Stocton and his wife Maud gave the priory 200 acres and 13 virgates of land in Fenny Compton (Warws.); shortly afterwards, however, this estate was granted in fee to Richard Peche, lord of Wormleighton (Warws.), for an annual rent of 20s.[33] Land in Frisby (in Galby, Leics.) granted to Trentham by William, the chaplain of Quenby (Leics.), was acquired from the priory in 1255 by St. John's Hospital, Leicester,[34] while land in Bradbourne (Derb.) given by Jordan de Tok was granted in fee about 1250 to Henry of Tideswell for an annual rent of 20s.[35]

Most of the substantial temporal estates accumulated by the priory were in fact situated fairly near to Trentham. More property in Blurton, where some of the priory's original endowment lay, was acquired during the 13th century,[36] and in Hanchurch (in Trentham) the priory secured property which included pasture land and the mill.[37] Various grants of arable, meadow, and services in Longton were made to the priory throughout the 13th century by the Bevill family, lords of the manor of Longton;[38] in 1291 the priory's property there was valued at £1 6s. 8d. a year,[39] and at the dissolution it comprised two farms and certain small rents.[40] Geoffrey Griffin gave the priory considerable property in Elkstone (in Alstonefield) about 1215.[41] In 1253 and

1272, however, the prior was sued for the manor of Over Elkstone, and on the second occasion judgement was given against him. The prior then called on Geoffrey Griffin's heir, another Geoffrey, to warrant his father's gift. Geoffrey pleaded that the gift had been made while the donor was of unsound mind, but a jury decided against this plea and awarded the prior compensation out of his estate at Clayton.[42] Litigation, however, dragged on into the next century,[43] and at least some of the priory's property at Clayton was granted away to St. Thomas's Priory near Stafford. This was, however, recovered by Trentham in the late 13th century,[44] and in 1337 some at least of the property in Elkstone which had been in dispute was granted to the priory.[45] In 1535 Trentham held property in all these places, and two of its more important temporal estates were those at Clayton Griffith and Elkstone.[46]

The canons were careful to protect their parochial rights from which the major part of their income was drawn,[47] but as time went on local landowners sought to build new chapels. Barlaston, part of the parish of Trentham,[48] evidently had its own chapel in the patronage of the lord of Barlaston by the early 13th century. About 1225 John fitz Philip, lord of Barlaston, granted the advowson of this chapel to the canons on condition that they maintained a resident chaplain at Barlaston to celebrate divine service there, to bury 'those dying within the parish of the same chapel', and to baptize 'the children of the parishioners there.' John granted them at the same time sufficient pasture in Barlaston for eight oxen, ten cows, and two bulls.[49] In 1229 Geoffrey Griffin, clerk, was allowed to set up a chantry in his chapel at Clayton, but his chaplain was to swear not to retain offerings belonging to Trentham parish church and compensation was to be provided for any loss incurred by Trentham.[50] In 1282 Adam de Chetwynd was given permission to erect a chapel with a bell-tower at Hartwell near Barlaston; the priest there was to take a yearly oath not to defraud the mother-church of Trentham of any tithes or offerings.[51] The canons were not, however, always successful in protecting their rights. They possessed chapels at Newcastle and Whitmore by the later 12th century and had granted some right in them to Robert de Costentin. A dispute arose between

[29] Farrer, *Honors and Knights' Fees*, ii. 170, 175; *Rot. H. de Welles*, i. 78, 86; iii. 94, 187, 215; J. W. F. Hill, *Medieval Lincoln*, 96; *Rot. Roberti Grosseteste* (Cant. and York Soc.), 60; *Final Concords of the County of Lincoln* (Linc. Rec. Soc. xvii), 226; *Tax. Eccl.* (Rec. Com.), 57.
[30] J. C. Cox, *Notes on the Churches of Derbs.* iii. 335.
[31] Ibid. 327; *S.H.C.* xi. 315.
[32] Cox, *Churches of Derbs.* iii. 107, 336.
[33] *V.C.H. Warws.* v. 48; *S.H.C.* xi. 317–18; B.M. Add. Ch. 21442.
[34] *V.C.H. Leics.* ii. 40; v. 98.
[35] *S.H.C.* xi. 313. Land in Marston Jabbett (in Bulkington, Warws.), given by Hen., son of Hen. of Marston (ibid. 335), was another of the priory's acquisitions which was not permanently retained.
[36] Ibid. 309–11.
[37] Ibid. 325, 326.
[38] Early in the cent. the priory was granted the mill-stream and the land of Rob. the Miller: *V.C.H. Staffs.* viii. 238; *S.H.C.* xi. 320. By *c.* 1247 the priory's estate in Longton consisted of 3 acres of arable and 1 acre of meadow: *Bk. of Fees*, ii. 1185. (*V.C.H. Staffs.* viii. 230, 232, wrongly states that this was the substance of a grant in 1250.) This estate was subsequently increased: in 1249 by a grant of meadow (*S.H.C.* xi. 321); in 1250 and later

by the grant of that part of their manor which, between 1236 and *c.* 1247, the Bevills had alienated in fee (*Bk. of Fees*, i. 143; ii. 1185; *S.H.C.* xi. 318–20, 321, 322), and by a rent of 12d. (*S.H.C.* xi. 319). In the later 13th cent. the priory acquired the right to build a mill and enforce suit to it (ibid. 321–2), and the estate of Hen. of Longton, miller (ibid. 320).
[39] *Tax. Eccl.* 252. *V.C.H. Staffs.* viii. 232, states incorrectly that the priory's Longton estate in 1291 was worth 10s.
[40] *V.C.H. Staffs.* viii. 232.
[41] *S.H.C.* xi. 331–2.
[42] Ibid. iv(1), 126, 192, 197–8, 200; vi(1), 83; xi. 327–8, 331 n. 2; 1911, 180. *S.H.C.* xi. 331 n. 2, states that there was another suit in 1256, but this seems to be a mistake for 56 Hen. III (1271–2): no suit involving Trentham is calendared for 1256 in *S.H.C.* iv(1), 134–5.
[43] *S.H.C.* vi(1), 76, 83, 84, 143, 146, 163, 164–5, 185, 219, 225–6; x(1), 5; B.M., Campb. xxviii. 9.
[44] *S.H.C.* xi. 327.
[45] See below p. 258.   [46] *Valor Eccl.* (Rec. Com.), iii. 108–9.
[47] See below p. 258.
[48] *S.H.C.* xi. 322; see above p. 256.
[49] *S.H.C.* xi. 323–4; S.R.O., D.(W.)1721/1/1, f. 57.
[50] *S.H.C.* xi. 330–1.   [51] Ibid. 332.

Robert and the priory. As part of the settlement made between 1175 and 1182 the chapel of Whitmore was granted for life to Robert's proctor, Vivian, Rector of Stoke.[52] During the course of the next century both chapels finally became dependent on the church of Stoke.[53]

By the middle of the 13th century the priory, if not wealthy, was at least one of the richer houses of the order in Staffordshire. For the aid of 1235–6 Trentham Priory, like the wealthier house at Stone, was assessed at 2 marks,[54] while the other two Augustinian houses for which assessments survive were rated at only 10s.[55] For the aid of 1242–3 Trentham was assessed at 40s. — once again the same assessment as a wealthier house, Ranton.[56] To some extent at least this comparative prosperity seems to have owed something to the agrarian activity of the priory. In the later 12th century the canons were probably improving the land in the immediate neighbourhood of their house, and in 1200–1 they owed the Crown one mark for permission to enclose their woodland.[57] In 1242 the canons acquired from Hulton Abbey the right to take new land into cultivation and to make assarts at Normacot (in Stone).[58] Like Hulton, Trentham was engaged in sheep-farming by the mid 13th century: an agreement was made between the two houses in 1246 whereby Trentham granted to Hulton common of pasture for 400 sheep in Blurton and Cocknage in return for a similar concession in Normacot.[59] Both houses appear in a Florentine list of about 1315 as exporters of wool.[60] The value of the priory's estates was also increased by privileges granted or allowed to the canons by the Crown. In 1251 they were granted free warren in the demesne lands of their manors of Trentham, Wall, and Elkstone;[61] this right was upheld by the priory during the *quo warranto* proceedings of 1293. The canons' right to hold two courts a year at Trentham for the pleas of the sheriff's tourn and their rights of gallows and waif there were also upheld by a jury.[62] According to the *Taxatio* of 1291 the priory's income amounted to £42 6s. 9d.; of this £30 3s. 4d. was derived from spiritual possessions and £12 3s. 5d. from temporal property. The spiritual possessions consisted of the appropriated church of Trentham (£13 6s. 8d.) and pensions from the churches of Barkby, Donington, Belchford, Trusley, Dalbury, Stenigot, St. Paul in the Bail, Lincoln, and Cold Overton (Leics.). The only temporal possessions of the priory listed in the *Taxatio* are those in Leicestershire and North Staffordshire.[63] Within ten years of the compiling of the *Taxatio* the priory's

resources had been augmented by the appropriation of the church of Sutton-on-the-Hill.[64]

The priory obtained two licences to acquire property in mortmain in the earlier 14th century. The first, granted in 1312, allowed the alienation to the priory of two half-virgates of land, one in Trentham and one near Leek; the second, dated 1336, allowed acquisitions worth £10 a year.[65] It was in respect of the second licence that the canons were permitted to acquire extensive lands in Elkstone in 1337 and some in Trentham early in the following year.[66] In 1330 the priory was granted various rents and villein tenements with their holders in Hanchurch.[67]

In the late 13th century the earls of Lancaster claimed the patronage of the priory as an appurtenance of their manor of Newcastle-under-Lyme.[68] Their claim was, however, resisted by the Crown. In the earlier 14th century the priory suffered considerably from the active prosecution of these claims by both parties to the dispute. In 1322 the recently elected prior was in trouble with the king for having done fealty after his election to Thomas, Earl of Lancaster, who during the vacancy had compelled the subprior and convent to obey him as patron. The prior was fined 40 marks. This large fine, however, was remitted, and the prior performed his fealty to the king.[69] In 1327 a jury investigated the matter and declared cautiously that the priory, like the manor of Newcastle-under-Lyme, had belonged to Henry III, who had given the manor to his son Edmund, Earl of Lancaster. The jury, however, professed to know nothing about the priory 'except that the late king had one voidance' and Thomas of Lancaster another.[70]

The trouble caused by the matter was evidently not merely theoretical. In October 1343 it was stated that Prior Dilhorne was on the point of death and that local men had seized the opportunity to occupy the priory and its manors and granges and to collect its rents, cut down its trees, and carry away its goods and chattels. These events were evidently no new experience for the canons, as it was alleged that similar depredations had taken place during earlier vacancies in the priorate. In view of the state of affairs the escheator was ordered to take charge of the house and its possessions. Soon afterwards an inquest found that the constable of Newcastle-under-Lyme and three others had taken possession of the priory in the name of the Earl of Lancaster, against the will of the canons and in defiance of the escheator, who had been present. On this occasion, however, they had not taken away any goods except

---

[52] Ibid. 322–3. The agreement can be dated by the reference to Alan, Archdeacon (of Stafford), not by any reference to Bp. Peche as stated in *V.C.H. Staffs.* viii. 16 n. 7.

[53] *V.C.H. Staffs.* viii. 16; *Cal. Pat.* 1247–58, 560. In 1272 there was further litigation over this: *S.H.C.* iv(1), 188.

[54] *Bk. of Fees*, i. 558.

[55] These were Rocester and Calwich: see above pp. 238, 248.

[56] *Bk. of Fees*, ii. 1134; *Close R.* 1237–42, 421.

[57] See *S.H.C.* ii(1), 105; xi. 302; above p. 256. The priory's woodland lay within the king's New Forest (see *V.C.H. Staffs.* ii. 336, 348) and the canons had to allow the king's deer to pass in and out unhindered.

[58] *S.H.C.* xi. 314–15. This was one of the articles of agreement which settled various controversies between the two houses over property.

[59] Ibid. 306.

[60] W. Cunningham, *Growth of Eng. Ind. and Commerce*

(1922 edn.), i. 632, 639. In 1340 the king owed the priory 36 marks for 4 sacks of wool taken by his officials: *Cal. Pat.* 1338–40, 297.

[61] *S.H.C.* xi. 304–5; *Cal. Chart. R.* 1226–57, 370.

[62] *Plac. de Quo Warr.* (Rec. Com.), 705, 709 (where it also appears that the priory claimed a fair and market in Trentham, although these did not appear in the jury's award), 715, 717; *S.H.C.* vi(1), 241, 243, 247–8, 249.

[63] *Tax. Eccl.* 57, 59, 63, 65, 67, 74, 242, 247, 252.

[64] Cox, *Churches of Derbs.* iii. 327.

[65] *Cal. Pat.* 1307–13, 494; 1334–8, 252.

[66] Ibid. 1334–8, 455, 568.

[67] *S.H.C.* xi. 326–7. In the later 13th cent. the priory's pasture rights had clashed with those of Sir John de Swynnerton; the terms of settlement (1280), however, led to disputes with the church of Swynnerton: ibid. 325.

[68] *Cal. Pat.* 1266–72, 186; 1292–1301, 253.

[69] Ibid. 1321–4, 92.

[70] *S.H.C.* 1913, 4–5.

some victuals.[71] In April 1344 the priory was given royal protection during pleasure. It was then said to be greatly impoverished as a result of the injuries done to it. Ralph, Lord Stafford, and a royal clerk were given the custody of the house and its possessions 'to order the same for the profit and advantage of the priory'.[72] The Crown retained the patronage, and, as one consequence of this, the canons continued to be burdened with the maintenance of old soldiers and servants retired from the royal service.[73]

In 1407 the bishop sanctioned the appropriation of the church of Trusley. The canons were to provide for the proper conduct of divine service there by a suitable secular chaplain or one of their own number as the prior desired.[74] It was perhaps in connexion with this appropriation that the canons agreed to make an annual payment of 2 marks to the bishop.[75] Nevertheless the appropriation was not effective, and the priory eventually lost both the patronage of the church and the pension from its revenues.[76] An unusual grant by the Pope in 1453 perhaps temporarily augmented the resources of the canons. One of their number, John Hawkin, a nephew of Thomas Bourchier, Bishop of Ely, was permitted to hold for life any benefice with cure normally held by secular clerks and to resign it simply or in exchange as often as he pleased.[77] In the later 15th century the priory seems to have acquired more property in Clayton,[78] and in 1503 and 1527 it received royal permission to acquire several estates in North Staffordshire.[79]

The community was never large. It numbered 8 in 1307, 7 in 1377, and 8 in 1381.[80] In 1518 there was a community of 5 which on the instructions of the visitor had been raised to 7 by 1521. Although the community was small there seems normally to have been a subprior.[81] In 1518 the prior himself was acting as sacrist and kitchener; by 1521, however, a separate sacrist had been appointed.[82] Early-16th-century visitations[83] show that the house was in good order, and Prior Stringer was much praised by his canons. In 1518 the prior gave the income as £100 over and above the issues of the demesne lands.

He was then rendering no accounts but began to do so by order of the visitor.

The gross income of the house in 1535 was £122 3s. 2d.[84] Temporal possessions produced £83 19s. 10d., the manor of Trentham accounting for £39 6s. 6d. and property in Clayton Griffith, Blurton, and Hanchurch for just under £20. Net income from temporalities amounted to £75 14s.; the deductions included fees of £1 and £2 respectively to the chief steward, William Chetwynd, and the receiver, Laurence Bradwall, and a corrody of £2 a year still paid to a royal nominee. Spiritual endowments produced £38 3s. 4d.,[85] but various payments reduced this to £31 9s. 9d. The priory property as listed in 1537 after it had passed to the Crown consisted of Trentham manor, Wall Grange, and lands and rents in Blurton, Cocknage, Hanchurch, Newstead (in Trentham), Longton, Chorlton (in Eccleshall), Clayton Griffith, Whitmore, Meaford (in Stone), Newcastle, Seabridge (in Stoke), Elkstone, Fenny Compton, Bradbourne, and Gaddesby; the appropriated churches of Trentham, Barlaston, and Sutton-on-the-Hill; and a pension from Barkby church. These estates were then valued at £156 7s. 10d. gross.[86]

Curiously little is known of the last days of the priory. It was one of the lesser monasteries whose suppression was ordered under the Act of 1536,[87] and it was evidently dissolved in 1537. The prior was granted a pension of £16.[88] The site was leased out by the Crown in November 1537 and sold to Charles, Duke of Suffolk, in 1538. He sold it soon afterwards to Sir Thomas Pope, who in 1540 sold it to James Leveson of Wolverhampton.[89] The medieval buildings have disappeared, but the parish church, which was largely rebuilt in 1844, incorporates remains of the conventual church.[90]

PRIORS

John, occurs 1155[91] and at some time between 1161 and 1176,[92] may have died at some time between 1193 and 1195.[93]

[71] Ibid. 104–5; *Cal. Inq. Misc.* ii, p. 465.
[72] *Cal. Pat. 1343–5*, 252.
[73] *S.H.C.* x(1), 26; *Cal. Close, 1313–18*, 422; *1339–41*, 219; *1354–60*, 619; *1360–4*, 124; *1374–7*, 247; *1441–7*, 65–66, 364. There was still a royal corrodian on the priory's establishment in 1535: see below.
[74] Lich. Dioc. Regy., B/A/1/7, f. 191v.
[75] Ibid.
[76] Cox, *Churches of Derbs.* iii. 336–7.
[77] *Cal. Papal Regs.* x. 246. Two years later Hawkin was appointed honorary chaplain to the Apostolic See: ibid. xi. 192.
[78] *S.H.C.* xi. 330.
[79] *Cal. Pat. 1494–1509*, 266, 319–20; S.R.O., D. 593/B/1/23/1/5.
[80] *S.H.C.* vii(1), 187; J. C. Russell, 'The Clerical Population of Medieval Eng.' *Traditio*, ii. 200 (which, however, omits the prior in 1381: see E 179/15/8b).
[81] See above p. 258; and below notes 1, 6; Lich. Dioc. Regy., B/V/1/1, pp. 19, 81, and p. 54 (2nd nos.).
[82] Lich. Dioc. Regy., B/V/1/1, pp. 19, 81.
[83] Ibid. pp. 19, 81, and p. 54 (2nd nos.).
[84] *Valor Eccl.* (Rec. Com.), iii. 108–9. See also below n. 85.
[85] The figure given in *Valor Eccl.* iii. 109, is £37 3s. 4d., but this omits the pension of £1 from Dalbury church (ibid. 167).
[86] S.C. 6/Hen. VIII/3352, mm. 1–7. This account does not list the £1 pension from Dalbury church. It was, however, considered as part of the priory property after the dissolution: *L. & P. Hen. VIII*, xiii(1), p. 586.

[87] *L. & P. Hen. VIII*, x, p. 515.
[88] Ibid. xiii(1), p. 577; xvi, p. 731. John Brasnell, a canon, had a pension until his death in 1560: E 178/3239, m. 8. He was buried at Trentham: *S.H.C.* 1915, 291.
[89] *L. & P. Hen. VIII*, xiii(1), p. 587; xiii(2), pp. 491, 495; xv, p. 284; xvi, p. 360.
[90] *S.H.C.* N.S. xii. 77; [W. Molyneux], *Trentham and its Gardens* (1857), 16–17 (copy in W.S.L. Pamphs. *sub* Trentham); Constance E. Graham, *Notes on the Hist. of the Church of S. Mary & All Saints, Trentham* [1928], p. 12 (copy in W.S.L. Pamphs. *sub* Trentham). For views of the church before the rebuilding see Plot, *Staffs.* plate between pp. 266 and 267; W.S.L., Staffs. Views, xi, pp. 56, 59.
[91] *S.H.C.* xi. 300–1.
[92] Ibid. 312–13, a charter of Bp. Ric. Peche (1161–82) witnessed by Wm., Dean of Lichfield, who succeeded in that office in 1176 (see above p. 197). See also a charter of Hugh, Earl of Chester (*Cal. Chart. R. 1257–1300*, 310), which was witnessed by Prior John. This must be dated between 1172 (birth of the earl's heir) and 1181 (the earl's death).
[93] The grantee of the priory's original endowment appears on the Pipe Rolls from 1156 to 1160 as John, chaplain of the Earl of Chester (*S.H.C.* i. 26; *Pipe R.* 1160 (P.R.S. ii), 25), and thereafter, from 1161 to 1193, simply as John the chaplain (*Pipe R.* 1161 (P.R.S. iv), 55; *S.H.C.* ii(1), 24). He was apparently dead by 1195 (ibid. 43) and has been identified with the chaplain who was presented to Trentham church in 1139 and with the first prior (see above n. 17; *S.H.C.* ii(1), 48–50; xi. 296–7).

Samson, prior probably about 1200.[94]

Alan, occurs in or after 1203.[95]

Richard, occurs at some time after 1233 and in 1234.[96]

Roger, occurs 1242, 1255, and 1267.[97]

Richard, occurs about 1272.[98]

John de Conyngston, occurs 1277, resigned 1297.[99]

Richard de Lavynden, elected 1297, occurs 1305.[1]

Richard of Dilhorne, occurs 1319, died 1343.[2]

Richard de Whatton, elected 1343, died 1352.[3]

Nicholas of Mucklestone, elected 1352, resigned 1402.[4]

Thomas of Trentham, elected 1402, resigned 1421.[5]

John Clyfton, elected August 1421, resigned by November 1421.[6]

Thomas Madeley, elected 1421, died late 1441 or January 1442.[7]

William Rossynton, elected 1442, died 1445.[8]

Stephen Brown, elected 1445, occurs 1478.[9]

Alexander Greyhorse, elected 1481, died 1486.[10]

Thomas Williams, elected late 1486 or January 1487, died 1499.[11]

Robert Stringer, occurs 1501, died by March 1530.[12]

Thomas Bradwall, elected 1530, prior at the dissolution.[13]

A seal in use in 1280 and 1526 is a pointed oval, $3\frac{1}{4}$ by $1\frac{7}{8}$ in., depicting the Virgin enthroned and crowned, her head surrounded by a nimbus.[14] Legend, lombardic:

SIGILLUM ...C... MARIE [DE] TRENTAHAM

The 1280 impression carries also the impression of a smaller counterseal of which only part has survived. Pointed oval, it depicts the Virgin with the Child on her left arm. The fragment of legend, lombardic, apparently reads:

Another, in use in 1369, is a pointed oval, about $1\frac{3}{4}$ by $1\frac{1}{8}$ in., depicting the Virgin crowned and seated with the Child in a carved and canopied Gothic niche; in the base under an arch is a canon kneeling. The fragment of legend appears to be lombardic.[15]

17. THE PRIORY OF ST. THOMAS NEAR STAFFORD

THE priory of St. Thomas the Martyr on the north bank of the Sow two miles east of Stafford was founded about 1174 by Gerard fitz Brian, who was evidently a burgess of Stafford.[1] Gerard's foundation charter[2] shows that he had obtained some canons from Darley Abbey in Derbyshire and provided them with a site on land which he held from the bishop. Gerard stipulated that the house should be independent of any other and that he should be its patron and protector. The charter cannot be later than 1175 since it was witnessed by Ralph, Archdeacon of Stafford, who ceased to hold office in that year;[3] it cannot be much earlier since St. Thomas of Canterbury, to whom the priory was dedicated, was canonized in 1173.

Gerard's original gift consisted of almost 70 acres called Sheepwash Meadow and as much of the River Sow as belonged to it.[4] The only land, apart from this, which Gerard gave the priory was some property in Stafford subject to a yearly rent of 8s. due to his heirs.[5] It seems that, although Gerard lived for some years after the foundation of St. Thomas's and continued to take an interest in it,[6]

[94] Dugdale, *Mon.* vi(1), 411; *S.H.C.* xi. 297n., 299.

[95] A canon named Alan was in charge of the vacant priory in 1203 (*Bk. of Fees*, ii. 1337) and may be the prior of that name who witnessed an undated early-13th-cent. deed (*S.H.C.* xi. 297, 320).

[96] *S.H.C.* vi(1), 11; Farrer, *Honors and Knights' Fees*, ii. 170.

[97] *S.H.C.* xi. 314–15.

[98] Ibid. 299, 318.

[99] Ibid. 307–8; *Cal. Pat.* 1292–1301, 248. The surname is given in *S.H.C.* vi(1), 225.

[1] *Cal. Pat.* 1292–1301, 253; 1301–7, 347. He was subprior.

[2] S.R.O., D.593/B/1/23/8/2/11 (not 1318 as in *S.H.C.* xi. 331, where this deed is calendared); C 66/210, m. 25 (where the prior's name is given as Ric. 'de Dulverne', i.e. Dilhorne, not 'de Bulmere' as in *Cal. Pat.* 1343–5, 125).

[3] *Cal. Pat.* 1343–5, 135, 140; 1350–4, 294; Lich. Dioc. Regy., B/A/1/2, f. 174v. He was a canon of Trentham.

[4] *Cal. Pat.* 1350–4, 308; 1401–5, 110; Lich. Dioc. Regy., B/A/1/2, f. 192v.; ibid. /7, f. 54. He was a canon of Trentham.

[5] *Cal. Pat.* 1401–5, 112; 1416–22, 395; Lich. Dioc. Regy., B/A/1/7, f. 54; ibid./9, f. 46v. He was Prior of Calwich at his election. He resigned because of infirmity, and the bishop granted him a pension in 1422: ibid. f. 130v.

[6] *Cal. Pat.* 1416–22, 395, 399; Lich. Dioc. Regy., B/A/1/9, ff. 46v.–47. He was subprior at his election.

[7] *Cal. Pat.* 1416–22, 400, 402; 1441–6, 58; Lich. Dioc. Regy., B/A/1/9, ff. 46v.–47, 69. He was a canon of Trentham.

[8] *Cal. Pat.* 1441–6, 46, 342; Lich. Dioc. Regy., B/A/1/9, f. 69. He was a canon of Trentham.

[9] *Cal. Pat.* 1441–6, 354–5; S.R.O., D.593/B/1/23/8/2/13 (not 1479 as in *S.H.C.* xi. 330, where this deed is calendared). He was a canon of Trentham.

[10] *Cal. Pat.* 1476–85, 281; 1485–94, 142. He was a canon of Trentham.

[11] Ibid. 1485–94, 159; 1494–1509, 167. He was a canon of St. Thomas's near Stafford.

[12] Ibid. 1494–1509, 266; Lich. Dioc. Regy., B/A/1/14, f. 27v. In 1524 one of the canons had suggested that Stringer was ailing and in need of a coadjutor: Lich. Dioc. Regy., B/V/1/1, p. 54 (2nd nos.).

[13] Lich. Dioc. Regy., B/A/1/14, f. 27v.; *L. & P. Hen. VIII*, xiii(1), p. 577. Bradwall's rise had been rapid for in 1521 he was still a novice: B/V/1/1, p. 81. Laurence Bradwall, receiver of all the priory's manors, lands, and tenements in 1535 (see above p. 259), was presumably his kinsman. In 1537–8 Hugh and John Bradwall held leases of certain small properties formerly belonging to the priory: *L. & P. Hen. VIII*, xiii(1), p. 585; xiii(2), pp. 491, 492.

[14] S.R.O., D.593/B/1/23/7/2/4 (1280 impression); ibid, B/1/23/2/17 (1526 impression). And see *S.H.C.* xi. 298. 314, 325.

[15] W. de G. Birch, *Cat. of Seals in B.M.* i, p. 779; B.M. Add. Ch. 21442.

[1] *S.H.C.* viii(1), 131–2, gives some particulars of his property there. In 1968 792 deeds relating to the priory and a survey of the priory estates made in 1543 became available at the Staffs. Rec. Office (S.R.O. 938). Over a hundred of these deeds were abstracted or noted in *S.H.C.* viii(1), 123–201.

[2] The original is in W.S.L. (S.MS. 593).

[3] Le Neve, *Fasti* (1854 edn.), i. 570.

[4] *S.H.C.* viii(1), 131–2. For the name (variously spelt 'Scepeswach' and 'Scepewas') and other details of the site see ibid. 134, 135; Sir T. Clifford and A. Clifford, *Topographical and Historical Descrip. of the Parish of Tixall* (Paris, 1817), 11, 33–34, 40; O.S. Map 1/2,500, Staffs. XXXVII. 12 and 16 (1901 edn.).

[5] *S.H.C.* viii(1), 132. This property evidently consisted of burgages: ibid. 135–6. See also ibid. 185.

[6] Gerard witnessed other early grants to the priory, one of which has been dated 1185–9: ibid. 159, 169–70, 172, 173. For a deed witnessed by his bro. Wm. see ibid. 169–70.

he did not finish what he had begun. His foundation was completed by Bishop Richard Peche (1161–82) who referred to it in a grant as 'the church of St. Thomas the Martyr of Stafford . . . which we have founded'.[7] Later, in his confirmation of the canons' possessions, the bishop referred to the site of the priory as 'that place . . . in which, by Gerard's own concession, we have founded their church'.[8] In 1182 Bishop Peche resigned his see, took the habit of a regular canon of St. Thomas's, and was buried there the same year.[9] By later chroniclers he was regarded as the founder and builder of the priory,[10] and the patronage of the house remained with his successors in the see of Coventry and Lichfield.

The bishop's first grant to the canons[11] consisted of a burgage in Lichfield; housebote,[12] haybote, and firebote from his woodland in Cannock Forest; common of pasture in his manor of Baswich; and 'the whole River Sow' from Stafford to the 'Watur Wending'[13] (evidently a grant of fishing rights) with a marshy place called 'le Kocholme' and a thicket near the confluence of the Sow and the Penk. By the time the bishop confirmed the canons' property a few years later[14] his benefactions to the priory had increased, and the canons had received from him land called 'Estmora' in Baswich on the opposite bank of the Sow from the priory, land at Orberton (in St. Mary's, Stafford), another burgage in Lichfield, and quittance of pannage in Baswich manor. Another of the bishop's gifts recorded in this confirmation is noteworthy as indicating the improving activities of the canons. The bishop had given them a meadow which had belonged to his manor of Eccleshall and which was 'often ruined by frequent flooding'; in return the canons 'by their own labour reclaimed to [the bishop's] use another meadow . . . in Eccleshall better and more fertile'. The canons had by this time acquired the right to fish the River Penk as well as the Sow and had also

been allowed to construct fish-ponds on the Sow and the Kingston Brook.

It seems clear from the bishop's confirmation of their property that the canons possessed two mills in the immediate neighbourhood of the priory from an early period. One of these stood on the Sow at the south-west corner of the precinct and was erected by permission of the bishop. The other stood on the Kingston Brook, less than half a mile north-west of the priory; it was erected with the permission of local landowners who had rights in the area.[15]

Much of the priory's early landed endowment, listed in the bishop's confirmation and in a papal confirmation a few years later,[16] came from local manorial lords or lesser landowners, typical members of the class which patronized the Augustinian order in the later 12th century.[17] Thus Alan of Hanyards gave a *cultura* beside the Kingston Brook and another on Tixall Heath;[18] Nicholas de Mauvesin, lord of Coton (in St. Mary's, Stafford), gave 7 acres of land there;[19] Eudes (or Ives) de Mutton gave 6 acres of land in his manor of Ingestre;[20] Reynold le Waite, of Rickerscote (in Castle Church), gave meadow there;[21] Alice de Hopton and her son, Robert de Bek, gave lands and pasture rights in their manor of Hopton (in St. Mary's, Stafford);[22] and Robert de Whyston gave 3 acres of land with a house and garden in Oulton (in Stone).[23] The priory also acquired property in Orberton,[24] Stafford,[25] and Donisthorpe (Leics., then in Derb.),[26] near Gnosall[27] and in 'Falmerisham'.[28]

The canons continued to receive small benefactions of this sort; before 1194 they had acquired land in Acton Trussell and Bishton (in Colwich),[29] and about the same time a rent in Callowhill (in Kingstone).[30] In the early years of the 13th century Simon the cook gave the canons land in Stockton (in Baswich).[31] On the basis of half a virgate in Whitgreave (in St. Mary's, Stafford) which they bought for 5½ marks from Walter Geri, the canons

[7] Ibid. 134.
[8] Ibid. 133.
[9] Ibid.; *S.H.C.* i. 108, 109; *Annales Monastici* (Rolls Ser.), ii. 242.
[10] Dugdale, *Mon.* vi(1), 472; vi(3), 1242; H. Wharton, *Anglia Sacra*, i. 435. See also below n. 12.
[11] *S.H.C.* viii(1), 134.
[12] The bishop's grant specifies housebote as 'timber for repairing their said church, the belfries, and all other buildings now built within the bounds of the priory . . . and their grange of Orberton'.
[13] Near the confluence of the Penk and Sow.
[14] For the rest of this para. and the following para. see ibid. 133–4.
[15] In 1543 the priory possessions, then owned by Brian Fowler, still included 'two cornmills under one roof with Kingston Mill and fishings at the flood gates' and 'fishing upon Sow': 1543 survey in S.R.O. 938.
[16] *S.H.C.* viii(1), 135–6. It was granted by Celestine III (1191–8); as it does not mention the lands in Acton Trussell and Bishton which the priory had acquired by 1194 (see below), it may be datable to the early years of Celestine's pontificate.
[17] J. C. Dickinson, *Origins of the Austin Canons and their Introduction into Eng.* 138–42.
[18] *S.H.C.* viii(1), 133, 135, 172–3, 192. For the probable location of the 'culturam circa Quennedale' on Tixall Heath see Clifford, *Tixall*, 86–87. Alan's gift was confirmed by Rob. de Stafford, the chief lord, and (for 10s.) by Hugh, Alan's son, who remitted a rent of 12d. from the Quennedale land and expressed a desire to be buried in the priory: *S.H.C.* viii(1), 173, 192–3.
[19] *S.H.C.* viii(1), 133, 135; it was confirmed by his overlord Wm. FitzAlan: ibid. 159. For Nic. and his family see Shaw, *Staffs.* i. 168; *S.H.C.* 1914, 114–16. Nic. was

kinsman of the Nic. de Mauvesin who sold Stallington to Stone Priory: see above p. 242 and n. 42.
[20] *S.H.C.* viii(1), 135, 172; xii(1), 271. When Eudes made this grant he stated that he had handed himself over 'living and dead' to the priory. For later benefactions by the Mutton family see ibid. 182, and below pp. 262, 263.
[21] *S.H.C.* viii(1), 135, 181. Reynold was probably descended from a family which played a part in the foundation of Stone Priory: *V.C.H. Staffs.* v. 89; *S.H.C.* ii(1), 207–9.
[22] *S.H.C.* viii(1), 135, 170–1. For this fam. see *V.C.H. Staffs.* iv. 31. Rob. was also a benefactor of Stone Priory: *S.H.C.* vi(1), 11.
[23] *S.H.C.* viii(1), 135, where the donor is called Rob. de Kincester; the identification, however, is certain: ibid. 139; ibid. iv(1), 123.
[24] Ibid. viii(1), 133, 135, 176–7.
[25] Ibid. 133–4, 135–6; for some of the original grants of these Stafford properties see ibid. 185, 187.
[26] Ibid. 135, 166–7. Geoff. Savage gave 4 virgates here. For this fam. see Dugdale, *Warws.* i. 228–9.
[27] *S.H.C.* viii(1), 134, 135, 169–70. These gifts, made by Phil. de Nugent and Steph. de Davenport, were probably from the estate near Gnosall later known as Brough Hall, which was at this time in the possession of a cadet branch of the Noel fam., founders of Ranton Priory: *V.C.H. Staffs.* iv. 125. Phil. de Nugent also gave the priory a rent due to him from Geoff. le Mercer which may have been in this area: *S.H.C.* viii(1), 185 and n. 4; but see also ibid. iv(1), 279. [28] *S.H.C.* viii(1), 135.
[29] Ibid. 137–8, 147. Rob. de Brok gave the land in Bishton and witnessed one of the grants in Acton Trussell. He was dead by 1194: *V.C.H. Staffs.* v. 79.
[30] *S.H.C.* viii(1), 147.
[31] Ibid. 142–3; *V.C.H. Staffs.* v. 5.

built up quite an important estate out of small gifts and purchases during the earlier 13th century.[32] One William, son of Adam de Whitgreave, gave them an acre of land in Whitgreave about 1210.[33] Clement, son of Herbert de Whitgreave, sold the canons 8 acres of land there about 1220 and gave them another 3 acres;[34] a little later Avice de Sogenhull gave 10 acres in Whitgreave which she had bought from Clement.[35] About 1252 Philip le Poer, a canon of St. Mary's, Stafford, gave the priory another 3 acres of land there.[36] At the end of the 13th century the estate at Whitgreave was evidently worked in demesne as a member of the priory's grange at Orberton.[37]

In 1194 the canons acquired their first considerable property when, for 35 marks, they bought the manor of Drayton (in Penkridge) from Hervey Bagot and his wife, Millicent de Stafford.[38] More large properties were acquired during the course of the 13th century. About 1200 Walter de Gray gave the canons that half of the vill of Fradswell (a detached portion of Colwich parish, near Chartley) which he held as one-tenth of a knight's fee. A condition of Walter's gift was that the canons were to receive him and his three children *in concilio suo* and were to keep them in food and clothing.[39] In the later 13th century the priory acquired lordship over the whole of Fradswell.[40] Another important estate acquired in the earlier 13th century lay at some distance from St. Thomas's, in the north-west of the county at Maer. Eudes de Mere gave the priory all his lordship there and his capital messuage with an orchard, a garden, buildings, fishponds, and the wood, meadows, and pastures belonging to the lordship.[41] This was probably a quarter of the manor of Maer of which Eudes seems to have been one of four coparceners;[42] the canons later acquired another quarter of the manor from Thomas, Rector of Standon.[43] Eudes also gave the priory half of the advowson of Maer church;[44] the other half was later acquired by the canons from two of his coparceners.[45] In 1203 Oliver Meverell gave the priory

land in Drointon (in Stowe).[46] Other property was acquired there during the 13th century; Oliver's daughter Alice gave the priory a rent of 10s. and one Geoffrey de Drengeton and his son Robert gave land there.[47] In 1257 Hugh, lord of Weston-under-Lizard, granted the priory 2¼ virgates of land, various smaller properties and all his common pasture rights in his lordship of Newton (in Blithfield) just over a mile south-east of Drointon.[48] About 1275 the canons acquired a small estate in Lea about a mile to the south of Drointon.[49]

By the mid 13th century the priory had received other small grants in Billington (in Bradley), Blithfield, Bradley, Brocton (in Baswich), Chorlton (in Eccleshall), Colton, Dilhorne, Stowe (in St. Chad's, Lichfield), and Silkmore (in Castle Church).[50] Outside the county it acquired an estate in Quinton (then in Glos.) from Philip de Mutton, the grandson of an earlier benefactor.[51]

The priory also received gifts from the Crown. In 1245 Henry III gave the canons £10 to buy a chasuble of red samite with orphreys;[52] in 1255 and 1269 he gave them six timber oaks from Teddesley Hay in Cannock Forest and in 1272 ten from Kinver Forest.[53] In 1257 the priory was exempted on account of its poverty from providing transport for the expedition against Llewelyn, Prince of Wales,[54] in 1263 it received a grant of protection,[55] and in 1272 it was exempted from jury service in the county.[56]

During the Barons' Wars in the later years of Henry III's reign the priory received a number of grants from Robert de Ferrers, Earl of Derby, a leading opponent of the king.[57] In 1261 the earl granted the priory a considerable estate at Pendleton (in Eccles, Lancs.).[58] About two years later he gave the advowson of the church of Stowe-by-Chartley with 2 messuages and 17 acres of land in Chartley and expressed a wish to be buried in the priory; in 1278 the church was appropriated to the canons by the bishop.[59] Other small grants followed,[60] including a toll which had belonged to the Hospital

---

[32] *S.H.C.* viii(1), 200. This sale was confirmed by his brother, Ernald de Orberton, by Ernald's son, Geoff., and by the Prebendary of Whitgreave of whom the land was held: ibid. 199.

[33] Ibid. 200.

[34] Ibid. 198, 199. He evidently held this land of Ernald fitz Geri (*alias* de Orberton) who later remitted a rent of 12d. due to him from the 8 acres: ibid. 200.

[35] Ibid. 198.   [36] Ibid. 200.

[37] *Tax. Eccl.* (Rec. Com.), 253.

[38] *S.H.C.* viii(1), 160; *V.C.H. Staffs.* v. 113.

[39] *S.H.C.* viii(1), 167.

[40] From Hugh Tynmore: *S.H.C.* viii(1), 167, 168. His grandfather had confirmed Walter de Gray's grant: ibid. 167–8.

[41] Ibid. 175. Eudes also gave the priory various lands which he held of Elias de Chorlton and of the church of Chorlton; these were probably in this area of the county, but not part of his lordship of Maer. Other lands which Eudes gave the priory (ibid.) were probably near Apeton and Cowley (both in Gnosall); Eudes seems to have been acquiring interests in this area, at Woollaston, in Bradley (ibid. 200–1; iii(1), 60; ibid. N.S. xi. 15–16).

[42] Eudes's grant to the priory was confirmed (for 10 marks) by the other 3 coparceners: *S.H.C.* viii(1), 175–6.

[43] Ibid. 174–5, 176.

[44] *S.H.C.* viii(1), 174, 175. He had acquired one quarter from his kinsman and coparcener, Wm. de Befurd: ibid. 176. And see ibid. N.S. xii. 250 (where the earlier stages in the descent seem to be conjectural).

[45] *S.H.C.* viii(1), 174, 175.

[46] Ibid. 162, 163; ibid. N.S. xii. 186.

[47] *S.H.C.* viii(1), 162, 163. It seems likely that the lordship of Drointon was divided between the Meverell and Drengeton families: ibid. N.S. xii. 187. Eleanor, Countess of Derby, gave the priory leave to improve the waste which they held in Drointon: *S.H.C.* viii(1), 163; the grant was made before the death of Sir Wm. de Caverswall in or before 1293: *V.C.H. Staffs.* iv. 77, n. 39.

[48] *S.H.C.* viii(1), 144–6. This was in fact an exchange; the priory gave up all its lands in Weston-under-Lizard (for which see ibid. 194) in return for this property in Newton. Hugh kept only some woodland, a moor, and a fishery in the old mill pool in Newton: ibid. 146.

[49] Ibid. 163–4.

[50] Ibid. 143–4, 147–8, 151, 154–8, 159, 174, 183.

[51] Ibid. 180; xii(1), 275. He was the grandson of Eudes de Mutton who gave land in Ingestre: see above p. 261; *S.H.C.* N.S. xii. 152.

[52] *Cal. Lib.* 1245–51, 6.

[53] *Close R.* 1254–6, 290; ibid. 1268–72, 84, 481.

[54] *Cal. Pat.* 1247–58, 573; *S.H.C.* viii(1), 137.

[55] *Cal. Pat.* 1258–66, 263.

[56] *Close R.* 1268–72, 562.

[57] *Complete Peerage*, iv. 198–200. For other benefactors of the priory who were opponents of Hen. III see below p. 264 and notes 72, 80.

[58] *S.H.C.* viii(1), 178–9; *V.C.H. Lancs.* iv. 393.

[59] *S.H.C.* viii(1), 153–4; ibid. 1924, pp. 155–7. The appropriation was in recognition of the canons' almsgiving and hospitality 'even beyond their resources, by reason of the stream of the needy and of guests that pours in upon them'.

[60] *S.H.C.* viii(1), 152, 153, 169.

of St. John the Baptist, Ashbourne (Derb.), and which the earl had obtained by force during the wars.[61] The priory's connexion with the earl, however, seems to have been without any harmful consequence; the canons retained the property at Ashbourne,[62] and the earl's other gifts were ultimately confirmed to them.[63] Moreover the priory continued to receive gifts from the Crown and other marks of royal favour. In 1275 Edward I gave the canons 10 timber oaks for the roof of their church, and in 1290 another 6 for the same purpose.[64] The priory was again exempted in 1282 from providing transport for a royal expedition into Wales, and in 1294 it received a grant of protection.[65] In 1284 the Crown granted the canons free warren in all their demesne lands providing these were not within the royal forest.[66]

The priory acquired a number of important estates in the later 13th century. William de Caverswall gave the canons land and houses in Caverswall and also the advowson of the church there.[67] He also gave them the manor of Coton which he had bought from Saer de Mauvesin.[68] In 1277-8 John de Pendeford sold his manor of Pendeford (in Tettenhall) to the priory. He had recently committed a serious forest offence and fled abroad, but by the time of the sale he seems to have returned and to have sought refuge in the priory. It was evidently a condition of the sale that the canons should keep John in food and clothing and pay him a pension of 40s. a year.[69] In 1281 Archbishop Pecham granted the church of Audlem (Ches.) to the priory. In April and July of the previous year he had stayed at the priory in the course of his visitation of the diocese,[70] during which he had evidently found that Audlem church had long been vacant. By presenting one of his own clerks the archbishop had obtained the advowson and the rectory; he granted the advowson to St. Thomas's Priory and shortly afterwards allowed the canons to appropriate the church.[71] About 1285 Philip de Mutton, descended from a family who had been benefactors of the priory in the earlier 13th century,[72]

gave estates in Reule (in Bradley) and Apeton (in Gnosall).[73] The canons never seem to have obtained effective possession of Reule,[74] but the manor of Apeton was retained until the Dissolution.[75]

In the Taxation of 1291 the annual value of the priory's possessions was given as £49 0s. 9d.;[76] temporal estates were worth £20 0s. 9d. while the appropriated churches of Audlem, Caverswall, Maer, and Stowe-by-Chartley were worth £29. These figures, however, give an incomplete notion of the priory's endowment; its temporal estates in Ashbourne, Donisthorpe, Quinton, and Pendleton are not mentioned, and in 1535 the last of these was the priory's most valuable single possession.[77] It was thus one of the wealthier houses of the order in Staffordshire. At the *quo warranto* inquiry of 1293 the prior claimed the right of free warren in Coton, Orberton, Hopton, Fradswell, Drointon, Haywood, Lea, Colton, Whitgreave, Maer, Drayton, Stockton, Acton, Pendeford, and Shredicote (in Bradley).[78]

As a result either of conditions attached to various gifts made during the 13th century or of agreements with benefactors, an unusually large proportion of the community came to be nominated by outside patrons. In the earlier 13th century Sir Adam de Mutton and his heirs were granted the right to present a canon to the priory who was to celebrate mass for the soul of Philip de Mutton.[79] Similar agreements were made about 1260 with Giles de Erdington,[80] in 1281 with Thomas de Audlem, and in 1292 with Rose de Standon.[81] The size of the early community is not known before the 14th century. Including the prior it numbered 13 in 1342,[82] 7 in 1377, 6 in 1381, and 11 in 1389.[83] Although the priory was not a royal foundation requests for a corrody were made from time to time by the Crown. In 1316 the canons were asked to receive William Deuros, an infirm royal servant, into their house and to feed and clothe him during his lifetime.[84] A similar request was made on behalf of William le Ferour two years later.[85] A demand was made by Bishop Meuland that the priory should grant a 40s. pension to his barber; in 1280, however,

[61] Ibid. 142; *Rot. Hund.* (Rec. Com.), ii. 298.

[62] *S.H.C.* viii(1), 142 n. 2; *Valor Eccl.* (Rec. Com.), iii. 111.

[63] *Cal. Pat.* 1292-1301, 146; ibid. 1317-21, 246.

[64] Ibid. 1272-81, 105; *Cal. Close,* 1272-9, 211; ibid. 1288-96, 98.

[65] *Cal. Chanc. R. Var.* 225; *Cal. Pat.* 1292-1301, 90.

[66] *Cal. Chart. R.* 1257-1300, 272; *S.H.C.* viii(1), 136-7.

[67] *S.H.C.* viii(1), 149-50. Caverswall church had been appropriated to the priory by 1291: *Tax. Eccl.* (Rec. Com.) 243.

[68] *S.H.C.* viii(1), 158-9. Saer had inherited the manor from Nic. de Mauvesin, an early benefactor of the priory: Shaw, *Staffs.* i. 168; and see above p. 261.

[69] *S.H.C.* viii(1), 177; ibid. v(1), 162; *Reg. Epist. Fratris Johannis Peckham* (Rolls Ser.), ii. 505; iii. 1072. Abp. Pecham ordered the prior to pay this pension to John's wife, presumably because the flight of her husband and the sale of his lands had left her without support. The prior was also to absolve John from the excommunication which he had incurred for neglect of his wife. See also Hibbert, *Dissolution,* 114-15; *S.H.C.* i. 318-19.

[70] *Reg. Epist. Peckham,* i. 112-13, 127-9, 392g-392h, 392o-392p; iii. 1003, 1020.

[71] *Reg. Johannis Pecham* (Cant. & York Soc.), i. 117-18, 193-4; *S.H.C.* 1911, 106-7. See also *S.H.C.* vi(1), 118.

[72] See above p. 261. Phil., like Rob., Earl of Derby, was an opponent of Hen. III: *S.H.C.* viii(1), 5.

[73] *List of Inquisitions Ad Quod Damnum Pt. I* (P.R.O. Lists and Indexes, xvii), 15; W.S.L., S.MS. 330(i), pp.

[73 cont.] 195-6; *Cal. Pat.* 1281-92, 234; *S.H.C.* viii(1), 140-1, 180-1.

[74] *V.C.H. Staffs.* iv. 82. In 1296 the canons surrendered all their title to any estate in Reule to Isabel de Mutton's husband, Phil. de Chetwynd.

[75] Ibid. 117; *S.H.C.* viii(1), 142; H. E. Chetwynd-Stapylton, *The Chetwynds of Ingestre,* 46-48. Another gift of Phil.'s, of 4 virgates at Alton, made in 1288 (*Cal. Close,* 1279-88, 516), seems to have been ineffective.

[76] *Tax. Eccl.* 242, 243, 253. This figure includes the appropriated church of Audlem (£10), although this is not noted as belonging to the priory: ibid. 248.

[77] *Valor Eccl.* iii. 111.

[78] *Plac. de Quo Warr.* (Rec. Com.), 709; *S.H.C.* vi(1), 243.

[79] *S.H.C.* viii(1), 180; xii(1), 275. For Phil.'s gifts see above p. 262.

[80] *S.H.C.* viii(1), 183. Although he is stated (ibid. n. 4) to have been 'a considerable benefactor' to the priory, it is not clear what property the priory acquired from him. His father, Thos., may have given some Stafford burgages: ibid. 184; xii(1), 312. Giles, like Rob., Earl of Derby, was an opponent of Hen. III: ibid. viii(1), 5; iv(1), 160, 165.

[81] Ibid. 1911, 166-7; ibid. viii(1), 187-8; W.S.L., S.MS. 412.

[82] *S.H.C.* viii(1), 129 n. 3.

[83] J. C. Russell, 'The Clerical Population of Medieval Eng.' *Traditio,* ii. 200 (which, however, omits the prior in 1381: see E 179/15/8b); see below n. 95.

[84] *Cal. Close,* 1313-18, 447.

[85] Ibid. 1318-23, 117.

Archbishop Pecham forbade the prior to pay this and castigated such use of monastic revenues as sacrilegious.[86]

In the later Middle Ages St. Thomas's Priory seems to have increased its possessions rather more than might have been expected. About 1300 the priory was given a rent of 10s. from the mill of Bupton (in Longford, Derb.) by Sir Geoffrey de Gresley, a former companion in arms of Robert de Ferrers, Earl of Derby.[87] In 1335 the Crown granted the canons a licence to acquire property worth £10 a year.[88] Small acquisitions followed. In 1347 grants of land in Hopton and Pendeford were permitted by the Crown; these were worth 5s. a year.[89] In 1383 the Crown allowed the acquisition under the licence of 1335 of various properties worth altogether £1 a year;[90] these included messuages, shops, gardens, and 6s. rent as well as arable land and meadow and were situated in Stafford, Salt (in St. St. Mary's, Stafford), Hanyards (in Tixall), Silkmore, Walton-on-the-Hill (in Baswich), and Acton Trussell and in Amerton (in Stowe), Lea, and Newton.[91] The licence of 1335 was not used up until 1404 when the priory was allowed to acquire lands worth £3 6s. 8d. in Salt and Enson and in Stafford.[92] The annual value of the lands granted under the original licence was thus a nominal £10; in reality they were worth only £4 11s. 8d. Nevertheless the priory did acquire other more valuable properties during the 14th century under separate licences from the Crown. In 1351 Ralph, Earl of Stafford, gave the priory a messuage and an acre of land in Bushbury and also the advowson of the church;[93] the church was appropriated to the priory in 1356 by Bishop Northburgh.[94] In 1389 Sir Robert Ferrers gave the priory the advowson of the church of Weston-upon-Trent and also stipulated that the brethren should receive 52s. a year from its revenues to augment their pittances every Wednesday by 1d. each. The church was appropriated to the priory in the following year.[95]

Bishop Northburgh visited the priory in March 1347 and found much to criticize. The frequent absences of the subprior on business had led to a breakdown of regular discipline and had encouraged waste and needless expense. No accounts and no inventory of the priory's goods were available. Three of the canons had kept hounds in the priory and gone hunting in the company of laymen. Some canons,

considering themselves better born than their brethren, had adopted worldly fashions in their dress and had gone about in tunics and peaked boots and with knives at their belts. The bishop forbade the prior to employ the subprior on business outside the priory and ordered that annual accounts were to be kept by the obedientiaries and by any canon who was given charge of the priory's goods. In future no canon was to hunt or keep hounds or hawks and all were to adopt the regular dress. Any canon wishing to visit his family or friends was to do so only once a year for eight days, and only if accompanied by one of his brethren. The bishop also ordered that his visitation decrees were to be read in chapter four times a year. The prior's resignation later the same year was presumably a consequence of the unsatisfactory state of affairs which the visitation had revealed.[96]

In 1400 a papal indulgence was issued to penitents who visited the priory church and gave alms for its support.[97] The priory continued to acquire property in the 15th century.[98] In 1408 Bishop Burghill gave the canons the advowson of the vicarage of Baswich church; a few days later he appropriated it to them and allowed them to serve it either by a suitable secular chaplain or by one of their own number.[99] The bishop's grant states that the priory was poverty-stricken and burdened with much almsgiving being situated on the road to Stafford. In 1411 Henry IV, who had stayed in the priory before his victory at Shrewsbury eight years previously,[1] granted the canons licence to acquire property worth £10 a year; once again the grant was made on account of the poverty of the house.[2] In 1414 the canons received property in Rickerscote, Orberton, and Stafford under this licence,[3] and in 1416 they purchased land in Stafford and Marston from Sheen Priory (Surr.).[4]

Little is known of the priory during the last century before the Dissolution. An early-15th-century book of Augustinian observances, once belonging to St. Thomas's Priory,[5] is one of only three such English custumals to have survived. Apart from this and the records of lawsuits[6] there is no light on the internal history of the community before the visitation of 1518.[7] The community then numbered 8 including a novice; according to the subprior this was one below the complement of brethren. The officials were the subprior, precentor,

[86] *Reg. Johannis Pecham*, i. 143.
[87] *S.H.C.* viii(1), 148–9, where it is wrongly dated; the grant must have been made between the knighting of Geoff. (c. 1290–2) and his death (by 1306): ibid. N.S. i. 40, 41.
[88] *Cal. Pat.* 1334–8, 122.
[89] Ibid. 1345–8, 353; *S.H.C.* viii(1), 171–2.
[90] *Cal. Pat.* 1381–5, 297; *S.H.C.* viii(1), 185 (which incorrectly gives Coton instead of Acton: C 66/316, m. 38).
[91] For the original grants of some of these properties see *S.H.C.* viii(1), 139–40, 193–4.
[92] *Cal. Pat.* 1401–5, 402.
[93] *List of Inquisitions Ad Quod Damnum Pt. II* (P.R.O. Lists and Indexes, xxii), 461; *Cal. Pat.* 1350–4, 187; *S.H.C.* viii(1), 149.
[94] *S.H.C.* i. 283. Northburgh endowed a vicarage in the church; this endowment was reconstituted by Bp. Burghill in 1406: Lich. Dioc. Regy., B/A/1/7, f. 189v.
[95] *S.H.C.* viii(1), 105–6; Lich. Dioc. Regy., B/A/1/6, f. 75v.; *S.H.C.* 1924, p. 364. Ferrers's gift implies that the community normally numbered 12; it was witnessed, however, by the prior and only 10 canons. If the size of the community increased, the sum paid from Weston was to be raised proportionately.

[96] Lich. Dioc. Regy., B/A/1/3, f. 110; *S.H.C.* 1914, 127–9; see below p. 267.
[97] *Cal. Papal Regs.* v. 406.
[98] For the 1404 grant of lands in Salt and Enson and in Stafford see above. For another small acquisition see *Cal. Close, 1405–9*, 31.
[99] Lich. Dioc. Regy., B/A/1/7, ff. 194v., 205; *Cal. Pat. 1405–8*, 445. *S.H.C.* viii(1), 143 (followed by *V.C.H. Staffs.* v. 7), wrongly dates this grant to 1407.
[1] J. H. Wylie, *Hist. of Eng. under Henry the Fourth*, iv. 201, 291.
[2] *Cal. Pat. 1408–13*, 269.
[3] Ibid. 1413–16, 290–1; *List of Inquisitions Ad Quod Damnum Pt. II*, p. 462; W.S.L., S.MS. 329(i), pp. 227–9; *S.H.C.* viii(1), 181, 182.
[4] *S.H.C.* viii(1), 176.
[5] Cambridge Univ. Libr., Add. MS. 3572. It has affinities with an imperfect custumal from Llanthony (Glos.), now at Corpus Christi Coll., Oxford (MS. 38, ff. 1–225).
[6] *S.H.C.* N.S. iii. 212–13, 220; N.S. iv. 148; C 1/443/31; Req. 2/11/57.
[7] Lich. Dioc. Regy., B/V/1/1, p. 26.

and sacrist. The prior ruled the house autocratically but well. He gave the income of the priory as £140 a year, which he claimed to have increased by 20 marks a year. The house was £49 in debt but was owed £100. He stated that the standard of observance was satisfactory, and that there was daily reading of the Benedictine constitutions as well as of the Augustinian rule.[8] According to the precentor the prior relied too much on the advice of Richard Hervy, one of the brethren.[9] The truth behind this complaint may be that a few senior brethren had obtained an undue influence over the prior's conduct of business; the subprior stated that the inventory of the priory's goods was not read out before the whole convent, while the prior himself admitted that his account 'was delivered each year to the senior brethren, not before the whole convent'. A few irregularities were noted: some brethren did not sleep in the dormitory; the canons had ceased to use the refectory for meals and ate each day with the prior;[10] according to the precentor the prior's servants did not show proper respect towards the brethren, and since the last visitation the number of hunting dogs had increased. The visitor ordered the prior to render his annual account before the whole convent, to make a new inventory of the priory's goods, to take the advice of his brethren only and not that of laymen, and to secure payment of the debts owed to the priory, if necessary by process of law. The number of brethren was to be increased; three of them were to eat with the prior each day, the other five eating in the refectory. The prior's servants were to behave more suitably towards the brethren and the hunting dogs were to be removed. Another visitation in 1524 shows that some of the instructions of 1518 had not been complied with:[11] some brethren still did not sleep in the dormitory, the complaint about the neglect of the refectory was repeated, some of the servants were alleged to be dishonest, the number of brethren had not increased, and the prior did not render an account or keep an inventory. Nevertheless the prior's rule was praised by his brethren, and the visitor merely repeated his previous instruction about rendering an annual account.

In 1535 the *Valor Ecclesiasticus* gave the gross annual value of the priory's possessions as £180 18s. 9½d., a figure which made it the wealthiest house of the order in the county.[12] Gross temporal income amounted to £130 16s. 5½d. and was derived mainly from estates within the county; the most valuable single estate, however, was the manor of Pendleton valued at £18 18s. 6d. Net income from temporalities amounted to £115 12s. 6½d. after deductions which included an annual fee of £4 to Lord Ferrers, of Chartley, steward of the priory's Staffordshire manors, and one of £1 to Sir Alexander Ratclyffe, steward of Pendleton manor. Gross spiritual income amounted to £50 2s. 4d., but various payments reduced this to £26 0s. 7⅔d. Total net income was

thus £141 13s. 2⅙d., almost exactly the figure given by the prior in 1518. An extent of most of the priory estates,[13] made early in 1543 after they had passed to Brian Fowler, gives the gross annual income from the property as £208 5s. 2d. The spiritual possessions, then worth £47 10s. 8d. a year, consisted of the appropriated churches of Stowe-by-Chartley, Bushbury, Caverswall, Weston-upon-Trent, Gayton, Maer, and Audlem, and the appropriated vicarage of Baswich. The temporal property, producing £160 14s. 6d. a year, consisted of the priory site and the demesnes belonging to it (by then known as Lees Grange), Orberton Grange, the manors of Coton, Drayton, Maer, Apeton, and Pendleton, and lands and rents in Stafford, Marston (in St. Mary's, Stafford), Tillington, Amerton, Drointon, Grindley (in Stowe-by-Chartley), Newton, Lea, Acton Trussell, Hopton, Shredicote, Whitgreave, Admaston (in Blithfield), Rickerscote, Lichfield, Bishton, Oulton, Marchington (in Hanbury), Bednall, Walton-on-the-Hill, and Stockton (all in Baswich), Ashbourne, Kniveton (Derb.), Donisthorpe, Quinton, Nantwich (Ches.), Weston-upon-Trent, Charnes (in Eccleshall), Stowe-by-Chartley, and Audlem. The extent does not include the manors of Fradswell and Pendeford which had by this time passed to William and James Fowler respectively, or the priory lands in Colton and Salt which had passed to Roland Fowler;[14] in 1535 the gross annual value of these properties had been £29 12s. 4½d.[15]

Early in 1536, when the dissolution of the priory seemed imminent, there began a scramble for its property. In April Rowland Lee, Bishop of Coventry and Lichfield and patron of the priory, wrote to Cromwell:

> . . . I pray you remember my suit for the priory of Saint Thomas, and if it shall stand the king's highness shall have not only a certain sum but you also for your goodness. And if that will not be, then my trust is that forasmuch as the demesnes came from the mitre that I may have the preferment of the house and demesnes for one of my kinsfolk . . .[16]

By June Lee had evidently received assurances that he would obtain the priory's lands.[17] In July, however, St. Thomas's was exempted from suppression under the Act dissolving the lesser monasteries,[18] probably in return for the £133 6s. 8d. which the canons had promised to the Crown for 'toleration and continuance'.[19] The payment of this large sum, almost a whole year's net income, evidently created difficulties. In 1537 the prior sent Cromwell £20; in an accompanying letter he recalled that £60 had been sent earlier in the year and asked for another £20 to be respited.[20] It was perhaps the canons' efforts to buy exemption which led to Bishop Lee's accusation in 1538 that the prior was making 'unreasonable waste'. The bishop repeated his request for the possessions of the priory

---

[8] 'Constitutiones tam Benedictini quam regule quotidie leguntur.'

[9] The precentor alleged that Hervy's brother had obtained an unduly advantageous farm from the priory.

[10] One of the brethren, however, alleged that this was done by order of the bishop.

[11] Ibid. p. 53 (2nd nos.).

[12] *Valor Eccl.* (Rec. Com.), iii. 110–12.

[13] S.R.O. 938.

[14] C 142/69/119.   [15] *Valor Eccl.* iii. 110.

[16] *L. & P. Hen. VIII*, x, p. 316; S.P. 1/103, f. 194.

[17] *L. & P. Hen. VIII*, x, p. 491.

[18] Ibid. xii(2), p. 166.

[19] Ibid. xiii(2), p. 177.

[20] Ibid. xii(2), p. 225. The prior also informed Cromwell that the canons had given Mr. Leyke, a Derbyshire gentleman, a 50-year lease of Audlem church as Cromwell had evidently requested. They had received only 6s. 8d. from Leyke for the lease, whereas from one of the king's servants they might have had 40 marks.

'at an easy rent that the poor boys my nephews may have some relief thereby'.[21]

In October 1538 Prior Whytell and five canons surrendered the priory and its possessions to the Crown.[22] The prior received an annual pension of £26 13s. 4d. and the five canons pensions ranging from £6 to £5. One other canon, William Boudon, did not sign the surrender; he received the smallest gratuity of any of the brethren and no pension. Gratuities were paid to 29 servants of the priory as well as to the prior and brethren.[23] The following year the ex-prior became Vicar of Audlem, and he retained this living until his death some 18 years later.[24] On the day following the surrender Bishop Lee paid over £87 for part of the fabric of the priory church, the cloister, and the chapter-house, for the furnishings and fittings of the priory, for timber and hay there, and for grain, farm implements, and cattle at the nearby granges of Baswich and Orberton.[25] Plate weighing 28½ ozs. remained unsold while other plate had been mortgaged for more than £43, doubtless to raise the money for continuance.[26] Lead worth £40, four bells worth £54, and the fabric of certain buildings within the priory precinct also remained unsold.[27] The priory's debts amounted to almost £236.[28] In October 1539 the priory and all its landed possessions and churches were granted in fee to Bishop Lee. On his death in 1543 the site and most of the property passed to his nephew Brian Fowler under a settlement of 1540; three other nephews received most of the remainder.[29]

The present entrance to Priory Farm is almost certainly on the exact site of the medieval entrance to the precinct.[30] The most considerable remains are those of the conventual church and the western and southern ranges of the cloister court.[31] Part of the conventual church is to be seen in a stretch of walling some 39 feet long on the north side of the garden of Priory Farm. The work is without doubt of the earlier 13th century and is part of the north wall of the north transept; two main features of the wall are a respond standing to full height with its original capital and, immediately to the east, a plain aumbry. These were probably parts of a chapel against the east wall of the transept.[32] The west end of the church may have been in line with the west wall of

the present house.[33] The cloister lay on the south side of the church and was almost certainly — and unusually—rectangular rather than square.[34] Priory Farm incorporates medieval features and rooms which probably belonged to the western range of the cloister. The inventory of 1538 mentions the Water Chamber, the Great Chamber, two inner chambers, a chamber over the chapel, and the carter's chamber, all of which were probably in or near the western range. The Prior's Parlour, also mentioned in the inventory, was probably on the first floor of the western range. Of the southern range of the cloister the best preserved part is its south wall, the greater part of which remains to about first-floor level. This range evidently projected well beyond the western range of the cloister and probably contained the buttery, kitchen, brewhouse, and bakehouse mentioned in the 1538 inventory. The frater was probably on the first floor at the east end of the southern range. Nothing is now to be seen of the eastern range of the cloister, which probably contained the chapter-house and dorter and through which a passage led to the cemetery near the east end of the church.[35] At the south-western corner of the precinct the bridge (which retains a little medieval work) and the present Mill Farm certainly stand on medieval sites.[36]

PRIORS

Walter, occurs by 1181 and at some time between 1184 and 1197.[37]

Adam, possibly occurs at some time between 1189 and 1216.[38]

Robert, occurs at some time between 1198 and 1208 and in 1199.[39]

Ralph, occurs 1203.[40]

Philip, occurs probably at some time between 1215 and 1225, in 1221 and 1227, and at some time before 1242.[41]

Richard, occurs 1248.[42]

Nicholas, occurs 1255 and 1276.[43]

Richard, occurs 1277 and 1277–8.[44]

Nicholas of Aspley, occurs 1278 and 1294.[45]

[21] Ibid. xiii(2), p. 285. For other efforts by Bp. Lee and his brother to provide for their orphaned Fowler nephews and nieces see below p. 282; J. L. Hobbs, 'Some Letters of Wm. Fowler, Steward of Shrewsbury, 1593–1595', *Trans. Shropshire Arch. Soc.* lvi. 273–4.

[22] *L. & P. Hen. VIII*, xiii(2), p. 245.

[23] Hibbert, *Dissolution*, 172, 232–3, 235.

[24] G. Ormerod, *Hist. of the County Palatine and City of Chester* (1882 edn.), iii. 470.

[25] Hibbert, *Dissolution*, 229–32.

[26] Ibid. 234. A fine chalice and paten, dating from c. 1530 and now in the V. and A. Museum, may have belonged to St. Thomas's. They were discovered during the demolition of Pillaton Hall in the later 18th century; other items of plate are known to have been mortgaged by the priory to the Littletons, who held Pillaton from the early 16th century. See *31st Ann. Rep. of the Pilgrim Trust* (1961), p. 36; Hibbert, *Dissolution*, 234; *V.C.H. Staffs.* v. 119.

[27] Hibbert, *Dissolution*, 234. The lead was surveyed again by the Court of Augmentations early in 1539: *L. & P. Hen. VIII*, xii(1), p. 362. This letter is wrongly dated as 1537; it was written after the surrender of St. Thomas's in Oct. 1538.

[28] Hibbert, *Dissolution*, 235–6.

[29] C 142/69/119; *V.C.H. Staffs.* v. 5; *S.H.C.* iii(2), 78–80.

[30] J. C. Dickinson, 'The Priory of St. Thomas by Stafford', *T.O.S.S.* 1963–5, 5.

[31] Ibid. 6.

[32] Ibid. 6–7. For a plan of part of the site, showing the position of this wall, and for an elevation showing the wall with its respond and aumbry see *T.N.S.F.C.* 1879, plates 1 and 2 between pp. 40 and 41; these plates are based on a more detailed sketch by Chas. Lynam in W.S.L. 110/38. A chapel of St. John the Baptist 'prope cancellum ecclesie conventualis' is mentioned in 1478: Lich. Dioc. Regy., B/A/1/12, f. 51.

[33] *T.O.S.S.* 1963–5, 6.

[34] Ibid. 9.

[35] Ibid. 7–9. The position of the cemetery, to the east of the eastern range, was indicated in 1965 when a number of burials were uncovered during the construction of a cesspit: inf. from Staffs. County Planning and Development Officer (1968).

[36] *T.O.S.S.* 1963–5, 4–6. Mill Farm occupies the site of the priory mill.

[37] Dugdale, *Mon.* iv. 221–2; B.M., Harl. MS. 3868, ff. 6v.–7; *S.H.C.* iv(1), 267 (for dating of which see *V.C.H. Essex*, ii. 170; *Cartulary of Darley Abbey*, ed. R. R. Darlington, p. lxxx).

[38] *S.H.C.* viii(1), 129.

[39] *S.H.C.* 1924, p. 67; iii(1), 166–7.

[40] *Cur. Reg. R.* ii. 223, 229, 233.

[41] *S.H.C.* viii(1), 161–2; iv(1), 220, 224–5; xii(1), 275; Chetwynd-Stapylton, *Chetwynds of Ingestre*, 47.

[42] *S.H.C.* iv(1), 238–9.

[43] S.R.O. 938/7922.

[44] *S.H.C.* 1911, 30–31; viii(1), 149.

[45] Ibid. vii(1), 34, 134; S.R.O. 938/7931, deed of 1294.

Richard of Hilderstone, occurs 1295, died 1343.[46]

Thomas of Tittensor, elected 1343, resigned 1347.[47]

Robert of Cheadle, elected 1347, occurs 1358.[48]

Richard de Mere, elected probably in 1365.[49]

Nicholas de Huxton, occurs 1374 and 1403–4.[50]

Thomas Swyneshede, elected 1405, died 1412.[51]

Richard Bowyer *alias* Stafford, elected 1412, occurs 1445.[52]

Richard Colwich, elected 1447, resigned 1478.[53]

William Chedull, elected 1478, occurs 1488.[54]

John Messyngham, occurs 1504 and 1533.[55]

Richard Whytell, occurs 1534, surrendered the priory 1538.[56]

A seal of the priory in use by about the end of the 13th century, possibly a counterseal,[57] is a pointed oval, 1 by 1½ in. It depicts the martyrdom of St. Thomas Becket by the four knights; in the base under a trefoiled arch is the head and shoulders, in right profile, of an ecclesiastic praying. Legend, lombardic:

[TRINE DEU]S *PRO* ME MOVEAT TE PASSIO [THOME]

A seal in use in 1433–4[58] and at the time of the surrender[59] is a pointed oval, 1⅝ by 2½ in. It depicts St. Thomas seated on a panelled throne under a three-arched canopy; his right hand is raised in blessing and his left hand holds a crozier. In the base is a corbel. Legend, black letter:

SIGILLUM *COMMUNE* PRIORATUS *SANCTI* TH[OME] MARTIRIS IUXTA STAFFORD

HOUSE OF KNIGHTS TEMPLARS

18. THE PRECEPTORY OF KEELE[1]

AN estate in Keele worth £2 3s. 7d. was given to the Knights Templars by Henry II, probably in 1168–9. By 1185 the Templars were also holding land at Onneley (in Madeley) worth 2s., likewise a gift of Henry II.[2] Richard I confirmed Henry's gifts in 1189 as the vill of Keele and its appurtenances.[3] From at least 1206 the Templars were letting the Keele property.[4]

At some time during the 13th century Keele became a preceptory. By the 1250s the 'Templars of Keele' were holding half a virgate at Stanton upon Hine Heath in Shropshire (probably at Booley) by gift of Richard of Stanton and land at Adeney (in Edgmond, Salop.) by gift of Clement of Adeney, who had become their man.[5] A Preceptor of Keele occurs in 1271.[6] At the *quo warranto* proceedings of 1293 the Master of the Templars upheld his claim to view of frankpledge, assize of bread and ale, and 'theng' in Keele.[7] By 1308 the Templars held rents in Newcastle-under-Lyme, Onneley, Stanton, and Nantwich as part of the manor of Keele.[8]

In 1308, after the condemnation of the Order, the Crown seized Keele with the rest of the Templars' property, retaining it until 1314.[9] Although it should have passed to the Knights Hospitallers, Keele was

[46] *S.H.C.* viii(1), 153, 188–9; Lich. Dioc. Regy., B/A/1/2, f. 171v.

[47] Lich. Dioc. Regy., B/A/1/2, ff. 171v.–172v., 178v. He was subprior.

[48] Ibid. f. 178v.; S.R.O. 938/7963. He was a canon of St. Thomas's. In 1355, when he was allowed to choose a confessor to give him plenary remission at the hour of death, he was simply described as a canon of St. Thomas's: *Cal. Papal Regs.* iii. 580.

[49] Lich. Dioc. Regy., B/A/1/4, f. 57, where it appears that there had been a double election; the bishop quashed that of Rob. of Hilderstone and confirmed that of Ric. de Mere. Both were canons of St. Thomas's.

[50] S.R.O. 938/7910, deed of 1374; *S.H.C.* viii(1), 183, 196.

[51] Lich. Dioc. Regy., B/A/1/7, ff. 60v., 73. He was a canon of St. Thomas's.

[52] Ibid. f. 73; *S.H.C.* viii(1), 188; S.R.O. 938/7930, deed of 1419; /7922, deed of 1445. He was a canon of St. Thomas's.

[53] Lich. Dioc. Regy., B/A/1/10, f. 14; ibid./12, f. 51. He was a canon of St. Thomas's. In 1469 he was admitted to the Lichfield Guild: Harwood, *Lichfield*, 405. After his resignation he may have become Master of St. John's Hospital, Stafford: *Cal. Papal Regs.* xi. 565; see below p. 293.

[54] Lich. Dioc. Regy., B/A/1/12, ff. 51, 172. He was a canon of St. Thomas's. In 1485 he was admitted to the Lichfield Guild: Harwood, *Lichfield*, 408. According to *S.H.C.* viii(1), 130, Chedull was succeeded by Wm. Smith who became prior in 1494, but no contemporary evidence for him has been found; the source cited (B.M. Add. MS. 5828, f. 90v.; Add. MS. 5846, f. 112) forms part of the collections of the 18th-cent. antiquary, the Revd. Wm. Cole, who was himself doubtful about the existence of this prior.

[55] Harwood, *Lichfield*, 411 (his admission to the Lichfield Guild), 414.

[56] S.R.O. 938/7902, deed of 1534; see above p. 266. In 1535 the bailiff of the priory's Coton and Stafford estates was Edw. Whythell (*Valor Eccl.* iii. 111; Hibbert, *Dis-*

solution, 235); he also held certain small properties on lease from the priory in these places (1543 survey in S.R.O. 938). Ric. and Harry Whittall (or Whytell) also held some priory property on lease (ibid.). Ric. and Kath. Whytell (or Whyttyll) received rewards at the surrender as servants of the priory (Hibbert, *Dissolution*, 233). All were presumably the prior's kin.

[57] W. de G. Birch, *Cat. of Seals in B.M.* i, pp. 753–4. Other, more fragmentary, impressions of this seal are attached to E 326/8503, and to S.R.O., D.593/B/1/23/8/1/8 (calendared in *S.H.C.* xi. 327, and to be dated in or before 1293 when Sir Wm. de Caverswall, one of the witnesses, was dead: see above p. 262 n. 47).

[58] B.M. Seal Cast lxxii. 41. Another fine impression is attached to E 329/373 (dated 1435).   [59] E 322/220.

[1] Thanks are due to Miss L. M. Midgley for providing details from documents in the British Museum and the Public Record Office.

[2] *S.H.C.* i. 55 sqq.; Beatrice A. Lees, *Records of the Templars in Eng. in the 12th Cent.* 31; *Bk. of Fees,* i. 143. The value of the Keele property is taken from the Pipe R. (which from 1190–1 give it as £2 3s. 4d.: *S.H.C.* ii(1), 11 sqq.); the Templars' own survey of 1185 gives the value as £5 6s. 8d. (Lees, op. cit. 31). This survey also mentions small properties elsewhere in Staffs. given by other benefactors than the king: ibid. 30, 31.

[3] Lees, *Records of Templars,* 141.

[4] B.M., Cott. MS. Nero E. vi, f. 167.

[5] *Rot. Hund.* (Rec. Com.), ii. 55, 65. R. W. Eyton, *Antiquities of Shropshire,* ix. 293, suggests that Ric. of Stanton may have been the Ric. fitz Halufri who was living in the late 12th cent. Booley is mentioned from 1331, when Stanton has disappeared from the accounts: B.M., Cott. MS. Nero E. vi, f. 168. Adeney does not occur after the 1250s among the Templars' lands.

[6] See below.

[7] *S.H.C.* vi(1), 267.

[8] E 358/18, m. 4.

[9] Ibid. /19, m. 36.

in fact secured by Thomas, Earl of Lancaster, evidently as lord of Newcastle-under-Lyme, and on his execution in 1322 it reverted to the Crown. It was only in 1324 that Keele was granted to the Hospitallers.[10] Instead of establishing a new preceptory they made the manor part of their Commandery of Halston (Salop.).[11]

PRECEPTORS

Roger de Boninton, occurs 1271.[12]
Henry Damary, occurs as commander in 1292 and 1293.[13]
Ralph de Tanet, occurs 1308.[14]

No seal is known.

FRIARIES

19. THE FRANCISCAN FRIARS OF LICHFIELD[1]

FROM the autumn of 1237 come the first signs that the Grey Friars were beginning the 'construction of their dwellings and chapel' at Lichfield,[2] but no contemporary evidence has survived to show who gave them their site. Royal letters patent 20 years later in date spoke of the house as 'founded by the king's predecessors',[3] but the friars did not reach England until Henry III's own reign. When Leland made his tour of England about 1540 he found that local tradition, probably correctly, credited Alexander Stavensby, Bishop of Coventry and Lichfield (1224–38), with being 'the first founder' and with having given the friars 'certain free burgages in the town for to set their house on'.[4]

In 1237 King Henry assigned the friars ten oaks from each of the hays of Alrewas, Bentley, and Hopwas in Cannock Forest,[5] but he raised the contribution from Alrewas to twenty when the friars informed him that there was no timber in Hopwas Hay suitable for building their church.[6] In 1239 the king made them two grants of 10 marks and £5 from the revenues of the bishopric, then vacant;[7] in 1241 the sheriff was authorized 'to clothe the friars minor of Lichfield',[8] and in 1244 they were assigned £5 'to pay their debts' from the issues of the bishopric, once again vacant.[9] Free passage in

Whittlewood Forest (Northants.) was granted them for five years from 1258.[10] In 1286 Edward I gave eight oaks from Cannock Forest.[11]

Five years later 'almost all the town of Lichfield and the habitation of the friars minor' were destroyed in a great fire.[12] This disaster roused wide sympathy within the Franciscan order, comparable with that which had been felt when Winchelsea (Suss.) was destroyed by the sea in 1287. It is not surprising therefore to find that when in 1294 the English Franciscans accepted a sum of 60 marks from the monks of Westminster as the settlement of a dispute between the two, the money was assigned to the houses of Lichfield and Winchelsea to be paid in instalments to relieve their indigence.[13]

The next recorded benefaction was the provision of a water-supply by Henry Bellfounder, son of Michael of Lichfield, bellfounder, who in 1310 granted the friars for their 'use and comfort' his springs at Fowlewell near Aldershaw south-west of the city. The friars were empowered to erect a conduit head there and construct pipes to convey the water 'to their own place', but they were not to give away even a small vessel (*vasum*) of the water without the donor's special permission.[14] In 1329 Ralph Bassett of Drayton received royal licence to assign the friars 2 acres of land adjoining their house for its enlargement.[15] Philip de Turvill, Prebendary of Curborough in Lichfield Cathedral (d. 1337),

[10] E 358/15, mm. 11, 14; /16, mm. 8, 9; S.C 6/1146/11, m. 3. It was described as a member of the earl's manor of Newcastle-under-Lyme in an inquisition into his estates in 1327: *S.H.C.* 1913, 3. During this period the rents in Nantwich were evidently lost. Rents in Balterley (in Barthomley) occur by 1352: Univ. of Keele, Sneyd MSS., S. 2/44.
[11] Univ. of Keele, Sneyd MSS., S. 2/1, Ct. Roll, Mar. 29 Edw.III.
[12] *S.H.C.* vi(1), 49.
[13] *Sel. Bills in Eyre* (Selden Soc. xxx), 43–44.
[14] E 358/18, m. 4.
[1] The writer wishes to acknowledge Miss M. T. Rashleigh Toone who in 1952 generously placed at the disposal of the Staffs. V.C.H. her large collection of notes on the Franciscans of Lichfield, made while she was resident at Lichfield, and a paper embodying the results of her researches which she read in 1929 to the Walsall branch of the Historical Assoc.
[2] *Close R.* 1234–7, 502.
[3] *Cal. Pat.* 1247–58, 651.
[4] *Itin.* ed. L. Toulmin Smith, ii. 100. Stavensby opposed the settlement of the Grey Friars at Chester, but apparently only because he doubted whether sufficient alms would be forthcoming to support them as well as the Black Friars already established there: *Letters of Rob. Grosseteste* (Rolls Ser.), 121–2; *De Adventu Fratrum Minorum*, ed. A. G. Little, 80 n.
[5] *Close R.* 1234–7, 502.
[6] Ibid. 1237–42, 106.
[7] *Cal. Lib.* 1226–40, 373, 407.

[8] Ibid. 1240–5, 71.
[9] Ibid. 283.
[10] *Cal. Pat.* 1247–58, 651. The writ was addressed to the prior and monks of the priory of Lichfield, but this confusion between friars and monks can be paralleled by many similar slips on the part of clerks in the royal chancery and elsewhere; Austin canons, for instance, 'are referred to as monks in medieval documents of all kinds': H. M. Colvin, *White Canons in Eng.* 30 n.
[11] *Cal. Close,* 1279–88, 390.
[12] *Annales Monastici* (Rolls Ser.), iii. 365. Possibly the annalist chose the word 'habitatio' to indicate that the church itself escaped damage.
[13] *Monumenta Franciscana* (Rolls Ser.), ii. 60. The final instalment of the sum due was paid by 2 July 1295. See ibid. 31–62 for docs. illustrating the whole course of the dispute. For a clear summary see E. H. Pearce, *Walter de Wenlok, Abbot of Westminster*, 37–40.
[14] *S.H.C.* 1924, pp. 252–3; Harwood, *Lichfield*, 488, 565. At the dissolution there was a conduit of lead in the cloister and a little conduit 'at the revestrye door': Hibbert, *Dissolution*, 254. Leland soon afterwards noted the 'conducte of water out of an hill brought in lead to the town' and the 'two castelets in the town, one in the east wall of this friars' close on the street side, another about the market place': *Itin.* ii. 100. The Crucifix Conduit near the gates of the friary still stood in the early 19th cent.: Harwood, *Lichfield*, 489.
[15] *Cal. Pat.* 1327–30, 465. In 1449 the subchanter and vicars of the cathedral leased the friars a garden adjoining the friars' orchard for 3 years at a rent of 3s. 4d.: D. & C. Lich., Evidence Bk. of Vicars, ff. 21–22.

included the friary among the 33 religious communities entrusted with providing 100 masses a year for his soul and the souls of his relatives and friends. Three of these masses were assigned to the Lichfield friars, and as each celebrant was to receive 5 marks this made an addition of £10 a year to their income.[16] Other legacies included £20 from Catherine, Countess of Warwick (d. 1369), 6s. 8d. from Isabel de Sutton (d. 1397),[17] and 10s. from John Comberford of Tamworth by will of 1414.[18] The Lichfield friary was one of the mendicant houses which benefited under the will of Roger Horton, justice of the King's Bench; for years he was active on commissions of the peace in Staffordshire and adjacent counties, and by his will of 1422 he left 6s. 8d. to each of several mendicant houses in the area.[19] Richard Martin, a suffragan bishop to the Archbishop of Canterbury, in disposing of his books in his will of 1498, allotted four to the friars at Lichfield.[20] As late as 1537 Nicholas Rugeley, who died that year at Dunton in Curdworth (Warws.), left the friary 12d.[21]

Relations with the outside world were not always good, however. In the 1320s and 1330s there occur two cases of violent attack on Lichfield friars who had been sent on a journey by order of their superior. The first occurred in or before 1325. As the friars were going on their way *ad conventum Novi Burgi* — possibly the house of Austin Friars at Newport in Shropshire — they were beaten and imprisoned by 'sons of iniquity' unknown to them.[22] The second assault evidently took place in or before 1338. The friars were on their way to the house at Worcester when the assailants fell upon them, carried off a novice in their company, stripped him of his habit, and clothed him as a layman.[23] This abduction and the fact that begging friars can have offered little inducement to any ordinary robber make it not unreasonable to suspect that some special factors were at work on these occasions.

The Lichfield house was one of the nine friaries forming the custody of Worcester.[24] Information concerning the size and personnel of the house is scanty. During the episcopate of Robert Stretton (1360–85) over 60 candidates described as friars minor of Lichfield were ordained, but this gives only a rough indication of the size of the community.[25] As to individuals, the warden of the friary was associated in 1337 with two canons in an inquiry into a dispute between the Archbishop of York and his dean and chapter.[26] A Lichfield friar named

Thomas Joys was ordained deacon in 1414 or 1415; he was subsequently for some years chaplain to Humphrey, Duke of Gloucester, on whose recommendation he was dispensed from his vows and in 1442–3 given permission to hold any benefice with cure of souls.[27] In 1451 the warden of the Lichfield house was Richard Leeke or Leech, who between 1430 and 1438 had been provincial minister.[28] The Lichfield friars played their part as confessors during the 14th and 15th centuries. William de Otteley was appointed penitentiary for two years to Sir John de Clinton, his wife, and his household in 1379, and the following year William Blunt was made a penitentiary during the bishop's pleasure.[29] In 1392 the warden, John London, and in 1405, another of the community, Thomas Schawbery, received licence to hear confessions.[30] One of the brethren was in trouble in 1531 for having preached a sermon which many people in Lichfield interpreted as an attack on tithes and oblations. He and the warden, Richard Mason, came before the cathedral chapter to apologize and were rebuked. The chapter took the opportunity to order the removal of the seats which were in the nave of the friars' church, hoping to stop the friars from attracting the inhabitants of the city into their church.[31]

An early case of burial in the precincts of a person outside the order desiring it was that of Richard the merchant. His coffin lid, believed to date from the late 13th century and bearing an inscription in Latin verse,[32] is built into a wall of the Friary School. There used also to be an epitaph in the friary recording the death in 1464 of John Harpur, lord of Rushall.[33] Sir William Dugdale during his Staffordshire visitation of 1663 and 1664 saw at Lichfield a tombstone which showed a man in a surcoat kneeling before Christ and St. Francis; an inscription over his head asked for prayers for the souls of 'Master Roger Illari and the Lady Mar . . .', probably Sir Roger Hillary and his wife Margaret, who was sister and coheir of Nicholas, Lord Audley, and who died in 1410–11.[34]

On 7 August 1538 Richard Ingworth, Bishop of Dover, received the surrender of the house in the presence of Richard Wetwode, a warden of the town guild, and of the two constables; to suit the accepted formula the surrender was certified as made 'voluntarily, without any counsel or constraining, for very poverty'.[35] Ingworth gave the friars letters permitting them to visit their friends and left the

---

[16] *Sede Vacante Wills, Canterbury* (Kent Arch. Soc. Records Branch, iii), 119; Le Neve, *Fasti Ecclesiae Anglicanae, 1300–1541* (new edn.), x. 27.

[17] N. H. Nicolas, *Testamenta Vetusta*, i. 78 (not p. 54 as given in A. R. Martin, *Franciscan Architecture in Eng.* (Brit. Soc. Franciscan Studies, xviii), 164 n.); *Complete Peerage*, xii(2), 374; Lich. Dioc. Regy., B/A/1/6, f. 49; *S.H.C.* ix(2), 57.

[18] *Reg. Chichele*, ed. E. F. Jacob, iii. 321. He also left 10s. to the Carmelites of Coventry. For legacies to Tamworth church see below p. 314.

[19] *Reg. Chichele*, ii. 256–7. The will was proved in 1423.

[20] C. Cotton, *Grey Friars of Canterbury*, 96. His will was proved in 1503. He left 4 books to the Franciscans at Worcester and 10 to those at Canterbury of whom he was guardian: ibid.; *D.N.B.*

[21] Details of will supplied to Miss Toone in 1928 by the Revd. L. Mitchell, Rector of Curdworth; *V.C.H. Warws.* iv. 64. Nic.'s ancestor Nic. Rugeley of Hawkesyard, in Armitage (Staffs.), bought the manor of Dunton in 1422.

[22] Lich. Dioc. Regy., B/A/1/3, f. 18.

[23] Ibid. f. 56v.

[24] See the list prepared for the general chapter at Perpignan in 1331, printed in *E.H.R.* xxxiv. 206.

[25] *S.H.C.* N.S. viii. 159–396.

[26] *Cal. Papal Regs.* ii. 536.

[27] *Reg. Chichele*, iii. 328, 332; *Cal. Papal Regs.* ix. 410. He was ordained deacon during the vacancy in the see between May 1414 and Feb. 1415. The writer's attention was drawn to the ref. in the *Papal. Regs.* by the Rt. Revd. Dr. J. H. R. Moorman.

[28] Harwood, *Lichfield*, 275; A. G. Little, *Grey Friars in Oxford*, 259 (not p. 359 as given in Martin, *Fran. Architecture*, 172 n.). He was buried at Lichfield.

[29] *S.H.C.* N.S. viii. 78, 81.

[30] Lich. Dioc. Regy., B/A/1/6, f. 128v.; ibid. /7, f. 156.

[31] D. & C. Lich., Chapter Acts iv, f. 74.

[32] Martin, *Fran. Architecture*, 171; Shaw, *Staffs.* i. 321–2 and pl. facing p. 320; Harwood, *Lichfield*, 487–8.

[33] Martin, *Fran. Architecture*, 171.

[34] Ibid.; Shaw, *Staffs.* i. 321 and pl. facing p. 320; *Complete Peerage*, i. 340 n.

[35] For this para. see *L. & P. Hen. VIII*, xiii (2), pp. 15, 17, unless otherwise stated.

house and goods in the keeping of Wetwode and the two constables. He also gave them the inventory of the property, sending a copy of it to Cromwell next day when reporting to him. According to this report the warden, hideously disfigured in the face by a skin disease — 'whether of a canker or a pock or a fistula I know not' — had been little at home of late, but now having returned he was loath to give up his house, 'though it is more in debt than all the stuff that belongs to it will pay, chalice, bells, and all, by 20 nobles'. Debts included 20s. due to the bishop for 5 years' rent and 30s. borrowed 'for building of the choir'. The warden, Richard Mason, received a pension of £5 which was evidently still being paid at his death in 1558.[36]

Bishop Lee and Dr. Thomas Legh tried to secure the house for Wetwode, who had 'formerly shown great pleasure' to both of them.[37] Their attempt, however, was unsuccessful, and in October the house and its contents were put up for sale.[38] The items ranged from a friar's mass book, sold for 4d., and a holy water stoup, which went for 1s. 8d., to the entire stock of copes, vestments, and tunicles, which fetched £2. The household furnishings were of the simplest; for instance, a press, a bedstead, and a door, sold as a single lot, went for 4d. Such things as timber, stone and tiles from the structure and pavements found ready buyers. 'The glass that is loose in the new lodging' was sold for 3s., but 'the long new house' on the east side of the inner cloister with the church and choir, the cloister quadrangle, the frater, and 'the chambers stretching to the kitchen' went for £42 13s. 4d. to a group of eight purchasers; lead, bells, paving (except that in the church), and gravestones were reserved. It was stipulated that unless the purchasers secured a licence to the contrary they must deface tower, cloister, 'and choir forthwith the church' within 4 months and pull down the rest of the buildings in 3 years. In 1544 the site and certain lands were sold by the Crown to Richard Crumbilhome of Dutton near Blackburn (Lancs.); the church and the conventual buildings were excluded from the sale, but 'an inn called le Bishop's Lodging or le Great Chamber' was included. Crumbilhome was evidently a middleman for a few days later he received licence to sell the property to Gregory Stonyng and his wife, who were already in occupation.[39]

The friary stood in the south-west part of the city on the west side of Bird Street and St. John Street. The site is crossed by Friary Road, built in the 1920s,[40] but the portion formerly occupied by the church and some of the conventual buildings is preserved as an open space. The references in 1538, already noted, to 'the new lodging', to 'the long

new house' on the east side of the inner cloister, and to the debt of 30s. contracted in the building of the choir indicate that building was in progress on the eve of the dissolution. The church was large: the nave was of five bays and measured 110 × 60 feet, while the chancel was 95 × 28 feet. The tower was probably at the crossing. The cloister, 80 feet square, lay on the south side of the church, and Friary Road follows the line of its south wall. The Bishop's Lodging on the southern part of the site was enlarged by Gregory Stonyng, in 1545 and is now incorporated in the Friary School.

WARDENS

John London, occurs 1392.[41]
Richard Leeke or Leech, D.Th., occurs 1451.[42]
Dr. David Rules, occurs 1470.[43]
John Eton, occurs 1484.[44]
John Wyllnall, occurs 1525.[45]
Richard Mason, occurs 1531, warden at the dissolution.[46]

No seal is known.

20. THE FRANCISCAN FRIARS OF STAFFORD

THE Friars Minor were settled in Stafford by 1274 when the bishop granted 20 days' indulgence to all who visited the friars' church on certain days and said there the Lord's Prayer and the Hail Mary for the king, the kingdom, and the faithful departed.[1] The founder of the house may have been one of the Staffords of Sandon.[2] The friars secured the friendship of Edmund, Baron of Stafford (d. 1308): a Franciscan became his confessor, and he chose the Stafford friary as his place of burial instead of the Augustinian priory at Stone where members of his family were usually buried.[3] Archbishop Pecham celebrated orders in the friars' church in 1280, being unable to do so in St. Mary's which was under an episcopal interdict.[4] At first the friars were hindered in buying their daily victuals by regrators who would even 'snatch what they have bought out of their hands', but in 1282 they secured a licence from the Crown for one year to 'buy without molestation of the king's ministers'.[5] In 1306 a certain Henry Grucok was proposing to grant the warden and friars a piece of his land in Foregate on the north side of Stafford borough, worth 4s. a year and 200 × 100 feet in area, where they could make a courtyard (*curtilagium*).[6]

[36] E 178/3239, m. 8. He evidently became one of the guild priests at Lichfield and may have been Vicar of St. Mary's there; he died at Rolleston in 1558: ibid.; *S.H.C.* 1915, 170, 171, 216.

[37] *L. & P. Hen. VIII*, xiii (2), p. 30.

[38] For this sale see Hibbert, *Dissolution*, 252–4.

[39] *L. & P. Hen. VIII*, xviii(1), p. 366; xix(1), pp. 378, 386. In 1552 Stonyng was licensed to assign the property to trustees: *Cal. Pat.* 1550–3, 430. He was a civil lawyer who became one of the first two bailiffs of the city on its incorporation in 1548: Harwood, *Lichfield*, 419.

[40] For this para. see P. Laithwaite, 'The Lichfield Friary', *Trans. Birm. Arch. Soc.* lviii. 53–55; Martin, *Fran. Architecture*, 168–72; Shaw, *Staffs*. i. 321. For medieval buildings still standing in 1782 see above plate facing p. 213.

[41] See above p. 269.

[42] See above p. 269; A. B. Emden, *Biog. Reg. of the Univ. of Oxford to A.D. 1500*, ii. 1125.

[43] When he was admitted to the Lichfield Guild: Harwood, *Lichfield*, 405. Harwood also gives him as warden in 1471: ibid. 482.

[44] When he was admitted to the guild: ibid. 407.

[45] A friar minor of this name was admitted to the guild in 1525: ibid. 413.   [46] See above pp. 269, 270.

[1] W.S.L., S.D. Beck 1.

[2] Erdeswick, *Staffs*, 144 n., 153–5. He is wrong in favouring Sir Jas. Stafford since he was not born till c. 1300: *S.H.C.* 1917–18, 52.

[3] Dugdale, *Mon.* vi(1), 231; *Complete Peerage*, 'Stafford'.

[4] *Reg. Epist. J. Peckham* (Rolls Ser.), i. 111.

[5] *Cal. Pat.* 1281–92, 25–26.   [6] *S.H.C.* 1911, 283-4.

When an official list of Franciscan provinces, custodies, and houses was prepared for a general chapter of the order held at Perpignan in 1331, the Stafford house appeared with eight others in the custody of Worcester, and thus it remained throughout its existence.[7] It may be confidently surmised that its numbers were never large, and no striking incidents or outstanding personalities connected with it have come to light. During the episcopate of Robert Stretton (1360–85) about 14 of its members were ordained subdeacon or deacon, without mention of any further advance, while 6 proceeded to the priesthood.[8] The names show that the community was recruited not only from English counties in the diocese but from Wales also.[9] In 1405 a Franciscan of Stafford named David Sant received a licence to hear confessions, and this was renewed in 1406 and 1407.[10] Stafford was one of the mendicant houses in the area to which Isabel de Sutton (d. 1397) and the justice Roger Horton by will of 1422 each left 6s. 8d.[11] A number of letters of confraternity survive, issued by Brother John, the warden, in 1479.[12]

The community's existence came to an end on 9 August 1538 when Richard Ingworth, Bishop of Dover, came to the house and read the injunctions which he had framed. Rather than accept these the community, 'with one assent, without any counsel or coaction', surrendered the house into his hands for the king's use. Inventories were made 'of the houses and implements' and each friar was given 'a letter to visit his friends'. Income from rents at this time amounted to only £1 6s. 8d.; debts totalled £4. Ingworth removed a chalice and six spoons; the rest of the property was delivered to the two bailiffs of Stafford.[13]

On 27 September a sale took place of the buildings and the goods in the church, hall, kitchen, buttery, and brewhouse.[14] The total receipts from this sale were £34 3s. 10d. All the buildings within the precinct, with their materials except for the lead, were sold to James Leveson of Wolverhampton for £29 1s. 8d. The friars' wall 'next unto the town' was bought by the town for 3s. 4d. Two bells, one of them a sanctus bell, were excluded from the sale but remained in Leveson's keeping; the bailiffs of the borough were entrusted with the custody of the

lead upon the choir and a chapel — possibly that of St. Francis, mentioned elsewhere in the inventory. The friars' warden bought two brass pots and six plates, while the buyers of items from among the furniture and ornaments of the church included a friar named Wood who bought for 6d. 'a vestment of blue fustian and one of white diaper' and another friar, unnamed, who paid 4d. for 'a cope of linen cloth stained'. A statue of St. Catherine stood in the church which also contained an old pair of portable organs and four tables of alabaster.[15] 'Old books' were found in the library and the vestry. A noteworthy statement in the inventory was that the friars 'have in the field 6 londs yearly worth 16d.', which shows that the Stafford friary must be reckoned among the number, probably small, engaged in husbandry outside the precinct; 'the field' was presumably Foregate Field, which was one of the common fields of the town and adjoined the friary.[16] Other sales included the lead (£45), the bells (£10), and 16 oz. of plate.[17]

The friary lay on the east side of the main road from Stafford to Stone north of what is now the junction with Browning Street; the main road is still known as Grey Friars in this area. In 1610 a house called Grey Friars stood here on an extensive walled site approached through a gatehouse. Despite its distance from the town walls it was evidently pulled down as part of the demolition of buildings within musket shot of the walls under the order of the Parliamentary Committee in 1644 to facilitate the defence of the town.[18]

WARDENS

Richard Depedale, occurs 1392.[19]
John, occurs 1479.[20]
Richard Offeley, occurs 1501.[21]

The seal of the friary,[22] a pointed oval about $1\frac{5}{8}$ by $1\frac{1}{8}$ in., depicts a standing female figure, crowned and holding a raguly cross in her left hand and a book in her right. The figure may represent Our Lady or a virgin martyr. The legend, lombardic, evidently reads:

SIGILLUM FRATRUM MINORUM STAFFORDIE

[7] A. G. Little, *Studies in Eng. Franciscan Hist.* App. vi.
[8] *S.H.C.* N.S. viii. 159 sqq. But see below p. 273 n. 10.
[9] Adam Codsale, Ric. Depedale and Rob. de Leek (*S.H.C.* N.S. viii. 200, 202, 306) presumably came from Staffs. and Wm. de Chesewardyn (ibid. 206, 222) from Salop.; Howell de Aber and Hugh Aber (ibid. 291, 293) were presumably Welshmen. Franciscans were freely moved about from one house to another. Thus Theobald Kyngew was at Stafford when ordained deacon in 1379 and at Worcester when priested in 1380: ibid. 344, 351; John Tyso, at Stafford when ordained subdeacon in 1364, was at Bridgnorth, Salop., when ordained deacon in 1366: ibid. 192, 195.
[10] Lich. Dioc. Regy., B/A/1/7, ff. 156, 158, 195. He is presumably the same as the friar of that name who when ordained was at Lichfield: *S.H.C.* N.S. viii. 358, 373, where he appears as priested in both 1380 and 1382.
[11] Lich. Dioc. Regy., B/A/1/6, f. 49; *S.H.C.* ix(2), 57; see above p. 269.
[12] S.R.O., D.593/A/1/32/16–18; S.R.O., D.(W.) 1082 (33)/8; W.S.L. 152/40.
[13] *L. & P. Hen. VIII*, xiii(2), pp. 19–20.
[14] Hibbert, *Dissolution*, 245–8. The total value of the property exceeded that of the Austin friars of Stafford by

roughly £1 7s. but fell below that of the Franciscans of Lichfield by £8 9s. 6d.
[15] Such tables often stood upon altars, 'apparently forming a reredos': A. R. Martin, *Franciscan Architecture in Eng.* (Brit. Soc. Franciscan Studies, xviii), 26. Four are mentioned in the inventory but only two in the sales list.
[16] Ibid. 39; *L. & P. Hen. VIII*, xiii(2), p. 20. The friars also had half a meadow worth 20s. a year, given for an obit by Rob. Quytgrave (Whitgreave); 'this not kept, he asks for it back': ibid.
[17] Hibbert, *Dissolution*, 185–6 (without giving source).
[18] See J. Speed, *Theatre of the Empire of Great Britaine* (1614), map between pp. 69 and 70; *S.H.C.* 4th ser. i. 35, 72, 76, 82, 98, 105–6.
[19] Lich Dioc. Regy., B/A/1/6, f. 128.
[20] See above.
[21] S.R.O. 938/7902, will of John Askeby 1501.
[22] H. S. Kingsford in *Franciscan Hist. and Legend in Eng. Medieval Art*, ed. A. G. Little, 98 and plate vii. The seal there shown is 13th- or 14th-cent., but the impression of it cited is on a document of 1479. For other impressions of the same period see S.R.O., D.593/A/1/32/16 and 17, and W.S.L. 152/40. The B.M. has a cast of an impression on a charter of 1529, acquired since the completion of the *Cat. of Seals in B.M.* (1887–1900): Kingsford, op. cit. 98. In all these impressions the legend is much defaced.

21. THE DOMINICAN FRIARS OF NEWCASTLE-UNDER-LYME

THERE were Dominican friars in residence at Newcastle-under-Lyme by July 1277 when Edward I, then nearby at Eccleshall, sent them alms of 6s. 8d. for one day's food in the ensuing week. As the cost of one day's food was 4d. a head, the community then numbered at least twenty.[1] Twelve was the minimum necessary for a priory, but most of the houses had a larger community than that required by the Constitutions.[2] It is not known how long the Newcastle house had been in existence or who founded it.[3]

Nor is much known about the progress of the Newcastle friars. Edward II, on a visit to the town in 1323, found only 12 friars there — he bestowed 4s. for one day's food;[4] this, however, may mean no more than that others normally resident were temporarily absent on their ordinary avocations. The house belonged to the 'visitation', or administrative division, of Oxford.[5] It received two early endowments. Nicholas de Audley in his will left the friars £8 8s. 6d. owed to him by the Crown, though they had some difficulty before securing this in 1280.[6] In 1291, after the death of Queen Eleanor, the prior provincial received £5 for the Newcastle house from her executors.[7] Between 1351 and 1361 Henry, Duke of Lancaster, gave the friars licence to buy 'for the enlargement of their house' 3¾ burgages adjoining it, and released to them the annual rent of 3s. 9d. by which the property was held of the duchy. The grant was confirmed by John of Gaunt in 1363, and both grant and confirmation were ratified by Henry IV as Duke of Lancaster in 1404.[8] In this instance the friars profited from having settled in a town which had been within Lancastrian territory since Henry III created the earldom of Lancaster for his son Edmund in 1267. There is no evidence, however, that the friars were ever involved politically on the Lancastrian behalf or that use was made of their services as preachers to assist Lancastrian propaganda. The energies of the house were newly stimulated in 1390 when the master general appointed William de Barleton his vicar with power to gather into the Newcastle house 'the devout brethren of the Observance' — friars belonging to the section within the order which clung to original standards and rejected later mitigations.[9] The provincial chapter met at the priory in 1471.[10]

By the time of the dissolution in 1538 the house was very poor. The visitor, Richard Ingworth, Bishop of Dover, found the priory 'all in ruin and a poor house, the choir leaded and the cloister lead ready to fall down, the rest slate and shingle'. All that could be done with most of it was to 'save the lead and slate and take the profit of the ground'. Income from rents came to 40s.[11] The friars owed over £14 to various people and stated that for this 'all their substance lay in pledge, and yet all not worth the debt; so that no store was in the house but all gone'.[12] Earlier the same year most of the buildings and lands were leased to Henry Broke, who already held property in the area in right of his wife.[13]

Ingworth came to Newcastle on 10 August 1538. In the presence of the mayor, the two bailiffs, and others he received the surrender of the priory. He took a small chalice, five little spoons, and 'two narrow bands of masers' for the king's use but left everything else in the hands of the bailiffs.[14]

The surrendered buildings were leased to John Smith, a yeoman of the guard, and Henry Broke at an annual rent of 13s. 4d.[15] The other lands were let to various tenants for 32s. 1d. a year. The inventory taken of the priory's goods and chattels reflects its poverty. Apart from three sets of silk vestments, only two of which were complete, everything in the church was old, or of inferior material, or in some way defective. The furnishings included a 'fair table of alabaster' for the high altar, one notable copper-gilt crucifix, with Mary and John, a latten censer, and a latten holy-water stoup, but most of the other ornaments were poor and old. There was a pair of organs and two bells in the steeple. In the bed-chambers the friars had two old feather beds, with an old bolster and coverlet. The hall contained two tables, two forms, and four trestles. The kitchen and brewhouse had a minimum of crockery and utensils. A closing memorandum stated that all the property detailed was in the hands of the bailiffs and also mentioned three chests of documents, 'the one of the king's, the other of other gentlemen's, the third of the convent's'.

A sale held a few weeks later brought in £3 11s. 2d. for the goods, £7 6s. 8d. for the materials from superfluous buildings, and 12s. 4d. for lead from small pieces which pilferers had melted down but afterwards returned.[16] In John Smith's keeping there remained the two bells (weighing 2 cwt. and valued at 40s.) and the lead of the choir and part of the cloister (valued at £30). The lead had been estimated

[1] W. A. Hinnebusch, *The Early Eng. Friars Preachers*, 118. In this book Dr. Hinnebusch has combined the results of his own research with absorption of, and full tribute to, the pioneer work done by C. F. R. Palmer, O.P., in the 19th century. Palmer's account of the Newcastle priory appeared in *The Reliquary*, xvii. 130–4.

[2] Hinnebusch, *Early Eng. Friars Preachers*, 275 and n.

[3] Ibid. App. III, where 48 English Dominican priories are classified according to the status of their founders — royal, episcopal, noble, burgess, doubtful. Six only are left in the 'doubtful' category, and Newcastle is one of these.

[4] *Reliquary*, xvii. 130.

[5] It thus appears in a 15th-cent. list printed by A. G. Little in *E.H.R.* xxxiv. 208.

[6] *Reliquary*, xvii. 130. Adam de Chetwynd had been ordered to pay the sum out of debts due from him to the king, but, as the friars complained that he delayed, instructions to pay were given in Nov. 1280 direct to the sheriff who claimed allowance for it in his account the following year.

[7] *Reliquary*, xvii. 130. A later legacy was the 6s. 8d. left by Isabel de Sutton (d. 1397): Lich. Dioc. Regy., B/A/1/6, f. 49; *S.H.C.* ix(2), p. 57.

[8] *Reliquary*, xvii. 130–1.

[9] Ibid. 131.

[10] Ibid.

[11] *Letters relating to Suppression of Monasteries* (Camden Soc. xxvi), 204–5, 206.

[12] *Reliquary*, xvii. 132.

[13] *L. & P. Hen. VIII*, xiii(2), pp. 27–28; *Letters relating to Suppression of Monasteries*, 205. Broke evidently tried to bribe Ingworth to sell him the property.

[14] *Reliquary*, xvii. 131–2.

[15] For this para. see ibid. 132–3, where it is also stated that 'such inventories . . . are not lists of all that the visitor found on his arrival but only what he left in the hands of some agent for the royal use after he had sold on the spot as much as he could readily dispose of'. There is, however, no evidence of such a preliminary sale at Newcastle.

[16] For this para. see ibid. 133–4; S.C. 6/Hen. VIII/7444, m. 30.

at 9 fodders, each worth £3 6s. 8d., but in fact in June 1540 John Scudamore, receiver for the Court of Augmentations, was able to have cast from it no less than 13 fodders 8 cwt. 3 qrs. Meantime in May 1540 a grant for life, rent-free, of this and other church property and buildings had been made to John Smith and his son Richard, backdated to Michaelmas 1539. Within the site, besides the conventual buildings and their gardens, orchards, barns, and stables, there was a hall called Kingsley Hall and a chamber adjoining the church and called the New Chamber, with buildings above and below. The New Chamber was occupied by Henry Broke, who was also still the tenant of the Friars' Wood, the Friars' Meadow, and other plots of land. A tenement with gardens was let to Thomas Byrkes, another to Ellen Browne, widow, and a barn and garden to Ralph Harrison. The grant to the Smiths also included 'the interest and term of years' which the king had in a tenement in Lower Street, now occupied by Richard Brette, which used to belong to the friars. The property of the former friary was valued at £2 5s. 5d. gross in 1538–9.

The site of the priory lay a little to the east of the castle in the angle at which Blackfriars Road on the south-west meets Goose Street on the south-east and where the Smithfield Cattle Market is now situated.[17] Adjacent streets are known as Friarswood Road and Friars Street, the name given in recent years to what used to be Friars Lane. The Lyme Brook, a tributary of the Trent, is believed to have flowed through the friars' precinct.[18]

PRIORS

William of Bromley, occurs 1282–3.[19]
Thomas de Hunstretton, occurs 1323.[20]
William Peppelowe, occurs 1406.[21]

No seal is known.

22. THE AUSTIN FRIARS OF STAFFORD

THE only house of Austin friars in the county was that in Forebridge, a suburb to the south of Stafford

borough in the parish of Castle Church. It was founded in 1344 by Ralph, Lord Stafford, for the good estate of himself, his ancestors and heirs, his wife, and their children, and of Humphrey de Hastang, Archdeacon of Coventry and apparently brother-in-law to Ralph. In November 1343, in answer to Ralph's petition, the Pope gave permission for a foundation in Forebridge provided that twelve friars could be maintained there. In June 1344 the king granted a licence for the foundation and its endowment with 5 acres as the site of the church and other priory buildings; at the same time Humphrey de Hastang was given licence to alienate to the friars a well in Forebridge from which an underground aqueduct could be built.[1] A prior and brethren were there by 1346 when Henry de Caverswall sued Prior John for a toft in Forebridge.[2] William le Heustere, chaplain, son of Richard le Heustere of Forebridge, made a grant of land in Forebridge in 1348,[3] and in 1352 Ralph, now Earl of Stafford, granted the friars a plot of land there which he had acquired from the neighbouring Hospital of St. John.[4]

The house survived until the Dissolution[5] and was a member of the administrative area (limes) of Ludlow.[6] Its first prior, John of Wirksworth, apparently continued to guide its fortunes until at least 1375.[7] Two other friars of Stafford named Wirksworth — Nicholas who was ordained deacon in 1365[8] and Robert who occurs as a penitentiary four times between 1375 and 1382[9] — may perhaps have been kinsfolk drawn into the order by John's influence. Twenty-four of the community were ordained during the episcopate of Robert Stretton (1360–85), six of whom attained the priesthood. Such totals, however, give merely a hint of the size of the community from which they came.[10]

The house remained obscure and received no striking benefactions. It did, however, produce men able to preach and hear confessions on the lines laid down by Boniface VIII in the bull Super Cathedram (1300) which was designed to minimize friction between mendicants and seculars. The bishop admitted one Austin friar of Stafford in accordance with that bull in 1384,[11] and on seven occasions between 1373 and 1383 friars of this house were appointed penitentiaries.[12] In 1403 the friars

---

[17] For the site see V.C.H. Staffs. viii. 8, 47, and map facing p. 78. Although part at least of the conventual buildings survived in the early 18th cent., no traces now remain above ground. When the cattle market was being laid out in 1870–1 remains of the foundations were exposed; in further excavations in 1881 skeletons and a gravestone were found.
[18] Hinnebusch, Early Eng. Friars Preachers, 118, states rather vaguely that the site was 'intersected by the river'; this could be wrongly interpreted as an allusion to the Trent.
[19] C 66/102, m. 18d.   [20] Reliquary, xvii. 130.
[21] Lich. Dioc. Regy., B/A/1/7, f. 195. By 1408 he was prior at Shrewsbury: ibid. f. 198.
[1] Cal. Papal Pets. i. 27; Cal. Papal Regs. iii. 137; S.H.C. 1913, 106; Cal. Pat. 1343–5, 321. Humphrey is elsewhere described as Ralph's brother; Ralph's first wife was the daughter of Sir John Hastang of Chebsey: V.C.H. Staffs. iv. 86 and n.; Cal. Papal Pets. i. 20. Humphrey, a former rector of Bradley, founded a chantry there in 1344 for himself, Ralph, Lord Stafford, and Ralph's family: V.C.H. Staffs. iv. 86, 87.   [2] S.H.C. xii(1), 54.
[3] Cat. Anct. D. ii, B 3631. In 1350 Wm.'s brother Ric. renounced all claim to the land: ibid. B 3635.
[4] S.R.O., D. (W.) 1721/1/1, f. 140. He granted it to the friars for the foundation of their church, dormitory,

refectory and other offices for the souls of his heirs and ancestors, his two wives, and Humphrey de Hastang and for the life of Edw. III.
[5] This deserves note for of 6 Austin foundations licensed later in the century 2 proved abortive and a third, if indeed it ever existed, was soon extinct: D. Knowles and R. N. Hadcock, Medieval Religious Houses: Eng. and Wales, 198–202.
[6] Thus assigned in a 17th-cent. list printed by A. G. Little in E.H.R. xxxiv. 209.
[7] See below p. 274.
[8] S.H.C. N.S. viii. 198.
[9] See below n. 12.
[10] S.H.C. N.S. viii. 194 sqq. It is not easy to arrive at a precise total. Vigilant scrutiny is necessary, in view of variant spelling, to avoid the inclusion of the same man twice over. Moreover, descriptions are sometimes ambiguous: 'John Gregory of Stafford convent' (ibid. 325) could have been either a Franciscan or an Augustinian. Finally, another dozen Austin friars figure in Stretton's ordination lists without indication of the house from which they came.
[11] Ibid. 90.
[12] The prior in 1361, 1373, 1375, and 1379 (ibid. 15, 66, 71, 76) and Rob. of Wirksworth in 1375, 1378, 1379, and 1382 (ibid. 71, 74, 76, 84).

entertained Henry IV after his victory at Shrewsbury, and the Stafford house was one of several mendicant houses in the area to which Isabel de Sutton (d. 1397) and the justice Roger Horton by his will of 1422 each left 6s. 8d.[13]

The passing in 1536 of the Act suppressing the smaller monasteries seems to have aroused locally little or no suspicion that further measures might be in contemplation or that these might proceed from monks to friars. When the house of Austin canons at Stone was dissolved in 1537, Henry, Lord Stafford, removed his family monuments thence to what he evidently supposed to be a safe refuge with the Austin friars at Stafford.[14] In due course, however, on 9 August 1538, Richard Ingworth, Bishop of Dover, came to the house and read the injunctions which he had prepared; rather than accept them the friars, 'with one assent, without any counsel or coaction', gave their house into his hands for the king's use. He made inventories 'of the houses and implements', gave each friar 'a letter to visit his friends', and departed, leaving the possessions of the friary in the charge of William Stanford of Rowley nearby and Richard Warde of Tillington.[15] These inventories,[16] together with the details of the sale which followed on 27 September,[17] confirm Ingworth's statement that 'the Austin friars there is a poor house, with small implements, no jewels but one little chalice, no lead in the house, in rents by year 51s. 8d.'[18] The church ornaments, just adequate to meet minimum requirements, were scanty and well worn. They included four sets of vestments, old or stained altar-cloths, 'one plain cross of copper with a little image of Christ, silver, upon it', 'one little wooden cross plated over very thin with silver', a chalice weighing 13 oz. (which Ingworth took), a pair of organs, a mass book which was sold for 1s., and 'old books in the choir' which fetched 6d. The tower held one large bell valued at £8 and one small one worth 8s. There were the barest supplies of furniture and pots and platters in the hall, brewhouse, and kitchen. The total receipt from the sale of goods and buildings was £32 6s. 8d. One large purchaser of tile, shingle, timber, glass, iron, paving, and some vestments was James Leveson of Wolverhampton. In 1542 20 loads of stone from the demolished church were sold to the church of Bradley to the west of Stafford where the fine 14th-century nave arcade may well have been erected as part of a 16th-century reconstruction using this stone from Stafford.[19] In 1544 the site, such buildings as remained, and lands belonging to the former priory were granted by the Crown to Edward Stanford of Rowley.[20]

The friary site extended south-west from the Green in Forebridge, and street names on that side of Wolverhampton Road preserve the memory of the friars. The Roman Catholic church of St. Austin is so named because it stands on part of the site; the land was leased for the building of the first church in 1788 by the Berington family, who had bought the Stanfords' property in 1610.[21]

PRIORS

John of Wirksworth, occurs from 1346 to 1375.[22]
John Goldycar, occurs 1393 and 1395.[23]
John Stocton, occurs 1399 and 1404.[24]

No seal is known.

HOSPITALS

23. THE HOSPITAL OF ST. MARY, CANNOCK

BY 1220 there was a hospital at Cannock dedicated to St. Mary and comprising a prior and brethren. In that year they were granted the right to bring into cultivation up to 15 acres of heath in Broomhill (in Cannock) and 'Fernifurlong' and to hold them until the king came of age.[1] The hospital in fact retained the land after Henry III came of age in 1227: in 1230 the prior owed 2s. a year to the Crown for 12 acres of heath in Cannock.[2] This annual sum was still owed to the Crown in 1242 but was then 12 years in arrears.[3] The rent remained permanently in arrears after 1230,[4] a fact which suggests that the hospital ceased to exist soon after that date.

24. THE HOSPITAL OF ST. LEONARD, FREEFORD

THE leper hospital of St. Leonard, Freeford (in St. Michael's, Lichfield), was in existence by the mid 13th century. It may have been founded by a prebendary of Freeford; the patronage was certainly

[13] J. H. Wylie, *Hist. of Eng. under Henry the Fourth*, iv. 205, 291; Lich. Dioc. Regy., B/A/1/6, f. 49; *S.H.C.* ix(2), 57; see above p. 269.
[14] Leland, *Itin.* ed. L. Toulmin Smith, v. 21. Leland also noted that 'in this friars hung a pedigree of the Staffords'.
[15] *L. & P. Hen. VIII*, xiii(2), pp. 19, 20.
[16] Ibid. 20.
[17] Hibbert, *Dissolution*, 249–51.
[18] *Letters relating to Suppression of Monasteries* (Camden Soc. xxvi), 204.
[19] *V.C.H. Staffs.* iv. 88.
[20] Ibid. v. 92. In 1538–9 the gross value of the property of the former friary was given as £2 18s. 4d.: S.C.6/Hen. VIII/7444, m. 31.
[21] M. Greenslade, *St. Austin's, Stafford* (Stafford, 1962), 13.

[22] See above p. 273; *Cat. Anct. D.* ii, B 3631, 3635; *S.H.C.* N.S. viii. 15, 66, 71. In 1346 and 1348 the prior is named only as John, but it seems safe to assume that he was the same as the prior described as John of Wirksworth in 1350. In his appointment as penitentiary in 1379 John of Wirksworth was identified only as of the order of Austin friars: ibid. 76.
[23] Lich. Dioc. Regy., B/A/1/6, ff. 129v., 132v.
[24] F. Roth, *The Eng. Austin Friars, 1249–1538*, i. 338.
[1] *Rot. Litt. Claus.* (Rec. Com.), 417.
[2] *Pipe R.* 1230 (P.R.S. N.S.iv), 234.
[3] *Pipe R.* 1242 (ed. H. L. Cannon), 10.
[4] By 1287 the arrears amounted to 114s. (E 372/132, m. 21d.) and by 1292 to 124s. (E 372/137, m.8). By the latter date, as a long-standing debt, it was being entered among the sheriff's *nova oblata* (ibid. m. 8d.).

held by the prebendary in the late 15th century.[1]

In the 13th century several grants and casual gifts were made to the hospital by the Crown and its officers. In 1246 Henry III gave to 'the lepers of Lichfield' 15 carcasses of salt pork from the stores at Nottingham castle.[2] In 1257 the lepers of St. Leonard's Hospital received a grant of protection for five years from the Crown.[3] A further grant, for one year, was made in 1266 to the master and brethren of the hospital.[4] In 1280–1 William Trumwyn, keeper of Cheslyn Hay in Cannock Forest, gave the lepers the salted carcass of a buck which had been killed by wolves in the forest.[5]

Little is known of the endowments of the hospital. By the later 13th century it possessed some land in Burway Field, one of the common fields of Lichfield.[6] In the mid or later 13th century Robert Talecok granted the hospital a rent of 1d. from a parcel of land outside Tamworth Gate, Lichfield.[7] The hospital also held two half-messuages in the town itself during the reign of Henry III.[8] By 1333–4 it possessed land which was probably near Greenhill (in St. Michael's, Lichfield).[9]

By 1366, when its warden was an absentee, the hospital may have lost whatever eleemosynary character it had possessed a century earlier. The plurality returns of that year show that Adam de Eyton, Rector of Berrington (Salop.), was warden of the hospital;[10] he was normally obliged to reside in Berrington.[11] The wardenship of the hospital was then worth 40s. a year.[12]

In 1485 George Dawne, Prebendary of Freeford, granted to the bishop the next presentation to the free chapel of St. Leonard, Freeford. In 1490 the warden, Ranulph Worthyngton, resigned and was given an annual pension of 33s. 4d. for his food and clothing. John Paxson was collated by the bishop in his place.[13] In 1496 Paxson freely resigned the wardenship of St. Leonard's Hospital and, with the assent of the Prebendary of Freeford, it was united

to St. John's Hospital, Lichfield.[14] In return Dawne and his successors in the prebend were granted the right to nominate one of the thirteen almsmen in the the new foundation. The prebendaries retained this right until 1927.[15]

The hospital seems to have stood near to Freeford Manor about a mile from St. Michael's Church along the road to Tamworth. No buildings now remain but the site of the hospital was indicated by the discovery of the chapel burial ground in 1917–1918.[16]

WARDENS

Robert de Suthwode, occurs *temp.* Henry III.[17]

John of Dunchurch, occurs 1314.[18]

Adam de Eyton, occurs 1366.[19]

Ranulph Worthyngton, probably warden in 1485, resigned 1490.[20]

John Paxson, collated 1490, resigned 1496.[21]

No seal is known.

25. DR. MILLEY'S HOSPITAL, LICHFIELD

THE almshouse in Lichfield now known as Dr. Milley's Hospital[1] seems to have been founded on property given by Bishop Heyworth in 1424 for the use of the poor.[2] The bishop's grant makes no mention of the foundation of a hospital, but two circumstances suggest that Dr. Milley's Hospital did originate in the bishop's benefaction and that it was therefore founded about 1424. First, Heyworth gave the property to the cathedral sacrist and the master of St. Mary's Guild, and until recent years the sacrist has had a special responsibility for Dr. Milley's Hospital.[3] Secondly, the property on which the hospital now stands — a long narrow

[1] Harwood, *Lichfield*, 548.
[2] *Close R.* 1242–7, 425–6.
[3] *Cal. Pat.* 1247–58, 572.
[4] Ibid. 1258–66, 637.　　　[5] *S.H.C.* v(1), 163.
[6] *S.H.C.* 1924, p. 208, where 'the land of St. Leonard's Hospital of Freeford' (evidently lying beside the road from Lichfield to Tamworth) is mentioned.
[7] Ibid. p. 197.
[8] *S.H.C.* ix(1), 47. At some unspecified period the hospital possessed a tenement in Wade Street called the Goose House (Anon. *Short Account of the Ancient and Modern State of the City and Close of Lichfield* (Lichfield, 1819), 169) which is possibly to be identified with these or one of them.
[9] Harwood, *Lichfield*, 536 and n. 63. It evidently lay beside the road from Lichfield to Burton-upon-Trent.
[10] *S.H.C.* N.S. x(2), 218. Eyton had been presented to the rectory of Berrington by the Crown in 1361 during a vacancy in Shrewsbury Abbey: *Cal. Pat.* 1361–4, 90.
[11] In May 1367 Eyton was granted leave of absence from his rectory for two years, and in the following March (as an acolyte) received letters dimissory for all orders: *S.H.C.* N.S. viii. 35, 42.
[12] *S.H.C.* N.S. x(2), 218.
[13] Lich. Dioc. Regy., B/A/1/12, f. 61. In the event of one Roger Bilston's dying during Worthyngton's lifetime Worthyngton's pension was to be increased to 5 marks a year; this suggests that Bilston may formerly have been warden of the hospital. Bilston was a vicar choral, but by 1487, possibly through old age, was incapable of looking after his own affairs and they were put in the hands of two other vicars, John Paxson and Wm. Webbe: D. & C. Lich., Chapter Act Bk. ii, f. 26.
[14] Lich. Dioc. Regy., B/A/1/13, f. 165; Harwood, *Lichfield*, 548–9.

[15] See below pp. 281, 285.
[16] A. D. Parker, *A Sentimental Journey in and about the Ancient and Loyal City of Lichfield* (Lichfield, 1925), 53; *T.N.S.F.C.* lii. 135; *Staffs. Advertiser*, 16 Feb. 1918. Some buildings were still standing in 1508 when Ric. Egerton, Master of St. John's Hospital, Lichfield, leased 'a messuage and certain lands at Freeford called the Spyttell Howse' to Wm. Wryght: Sta. Cha. 2/34/143, m. 6.
[17] *S.H.C.* ix(1), 47.
[18] Ibid.
[19] See above.
[20] See above. For a possible predecessor of Worthyngton see above n. 13.
[21] See above. He was named as an executor in the will (1489) of Sir Hen. Willoughby, of Wollaton (Notts.), and there described as 'Sexton of the Close of Lichfield': Hist. MSS. Com. *Middleton*, 122. In fact Paxson was the cathedral sacrist until 1495: D. & C. Lich., Chapter Act Bk. iii. f. 27; *S.H.C.* 1915, 168.
[1] For 'Dr.' Milley see below n. 13. Until the 19th cent. the hospital seems to have been known simply as the Women's Hospital: see e.g. below p. 277; *7th Rep. Com. Char.* H.C. 129, p. 381 (1822), x; Harwood, *Lichfield*, 512. In 1687 the Archdeacon of Stafford, in a return of Staffs. hospitals, referred to it as 'St. Katherine's Hospital in Lichfield founded by one Wills': Bodl. MS. Tanner 131, f. 214. No other reference to this dedication is known, but see following note.
[2] D. & C. Lich., Chapter Act Bk. i, f. 109. The bishop's gift, made on the feast of St. Katherine (25 Nov.), was confirmed by the dean and chapter in the following year. The date of the gift is confused with that of its confirmation in H. Wharton, *Anglia Sacra*, i. 453.
[3] See below.

piece of land running back from Beacon Street and curving south to the Leamonsley Brook[4] — is almost certainly that which Heyworth gave in 1424. The ground seems once to have been a ditch which formed the town defences between the north-west corner of the fortified Close and the bishop's fishponds.[5] The ground floor of Dr. Milley's Hospital is now well below the level of Beacon Street, and this is undoubtedly due in part to its situation in the town ditch.

The hospital's endowment was increased by various other benefactions made during the 15th century. Probably at some time before 1438 a house in Beacon Street and a croft in Sandford Street were given by Hugh Lache who, as sacrist, was doubtless responsible to some extent for the running of the hospital.[6] Thomas Heywood, Dean of Lichfield (1457–92), gave a pasture in King's Bromley; Thomas Reynold, a canon of the cathedral from 1471 until his death in 1497,[7] gave a house in Wade Street; and some time before 1504 the hospital acquired land in Lichfield called Godscroft[8] from Thomas Atwell. By 1504 the cathedral chantry chaplains were making an annual payment to the hospital out of the revenues of an obit founded in memory of John Meneley, Prebendary of Offley (d. 1480).[9]

It is clear that at the beginning of the 16th century the hospital was not well endowed. In 1504 the annual income from these early benefactions amounted to only £2 1s. 10d.[10] Fines for entry on leases may have increased the average annual income from the landed part of this property, but with so small an endowment any such increase cannot have been very great. Money, however, may have been available from other sources. Four of the chantries in the cathedral, for example, are known to have provided money for the poor, and in at least one case the money was specifically assigned to the poor

in almshouses.[11] Moreover the sacrist and the authorities of St. Mary's Guild, both associated with the origin of the hospital, had charitable funds at their disposal[12] and may have been able to subsidize the hospital.

The hospital was re-endowed and probably rebuilt in 1502–4 by Thomas Milley, a canon residentiary of the cathedral.[13] In 1502 he gave to twelve feoffees, who included three of his fellow residentiaries and the sacrist, houses and land in Lichfield and lands at Borrowcop, Pipehill (both in St. Michael's, Lichfield), Elmhurst (in St. Chad's, Lichfield), Birchills (in Walsall), and Chorley (in Farewell). The rents from this property amounted in 1504 to £8 13s. 8d. Taken with the income from the earlier endowments they thus brought the hospital's gross income in that year to £10 15s. 6d.; chief rents, however, reduced this to £9 17s. 3d. net. According to an indenture drawn up in 1504, a few weeks before Milley's death, the feoffees were to allow the sacrist to use the income from this property for the support of fifteen almswomen; they were to live in the hospital and receive 5s. or 6s. a quarter if possible, in money and household necessities. The sacrist was also to keep the hospital in a good state of repair. He was to receive 13s. 4d. a year for carrying out these duties and was to be responsible to the Dean of Lichfield.

The hospital continued to be governed in this way until modern times: the property has been vested in successive bodies of feoffees[14] and the income received and expended by the sacrist. The sacrist's duties with regard to the hospital were such that he became known as its 'master'[15] or 'steward'.[16] During vacancies in the office of sacrist the cathedral chapter seems to have made temporary arrangements for the custody of the hospital. In October 1664, for example, the chapter instructed the subchanter to carry out the sacrist's duties and ordered the appointment of 'a sufficient able man' to receive the

---

[4] Behind the hospital's garden is a slang of land belonging to the hospital and running down to the Leamonsley Brook. This land, variously estimated as 7 or 9 perches, has long been held by the occupier of the property to the north for 5s. a year: map and annual accounts in Char. Com. files; 7th Rep. Com. Char. 384.

[5] The land given by Heyworth in 1424 was described as 'situatum in le Baconstrete ... inter tenementa vicariorum ... ex utraque parte'. It is almost certainly identifiable with the land 'iacentem inter terram vicariorum ... ex utraque parte' which Bp. Scrope leased to Sir Thos. de Aston in 1393 or 1394. It was then also described as 'a garden outside the Bacon Street gate opposite the tower with the statue of Bishop Walter' and was said formerly to have been called 'le Ellerendych'. See D. & C. Lich., Chapter Act Bk. i, ff. 33v., 109.

[6] For this para. see Harwood, Lichfield, 513. Lache seems to have given this property while he was still sacrist. He must have resigned this office by 1438 when he became subchanter: D. & C. Lich., Chapter Act Bk. i, f. 148; and see above pp. 148, 163. Lache later became Master of St. John's Hospital, Lichfield: see below p. 287.

[7] Le Neve, Fasti Ecclesiae Anglicanae, 1300–1541 (new edn.), x. 24, 28, 51, 62, 64, 66.

[8] Harwood, Lichfield, 512, seems to suggest that Godscroft was the hospital's site; it is, however, clear from 7th Rep. Com. Char. 384, that this was not the case.

[9] This obit was supported by a pension from Darley Abbey (Derb.): Valor Eccl. (Rec. Com.), iii. 139, 154. The hospital presumably received an income from this source until the suppression of the obit in 1548: S.H.C. 1915, 153; S.C. 12/28/12, f. 6v.

[10] Harwood, Lichfield, 513.

[11] These were Bp. Langton's chantry (S.H.C. 1915, 157), Dean Mancetter's chantry (ibid.; S.H.C. 1924, pp. 18,

[13] (113), John Kynardessey's chantry (ibid. 1915, 158), and Peter of Radnor's chantry (ibid. 1924, p. 114; Valor Eccl. iii. 135, 138). It was Kynardessey's chantry which assigned money to the almshouses. The charitable funds of Mancetter's and Radnor's chantries seem to have been controlled by the sacrist.

[12] For the sacrist see previous note; S.H.C. 1924, p. 164; Valor Eccl. iii. 136, 138. For the guild see S.H.C. 1915, 171.

[13] For this para. see 7th Rep. Com. Char. 381–2; Harwood, Lichfield, 208, 512, 513–14. Milley was Archdeacon of Coventry and Prebendary of Dasset Parva and had held a prebend in the cathedral since 1457: Le Neve, Fasti (new edn.), x. 15, 31, 44, 66. He was one of the university men promoted by Bp. Hales (see above pp. 31, 159), but there seems no authority for calling him 'doctor' except the inscription on the tablet at present over the hospital entrance (the text of which is given in Harwood, Lichfield, 513). He was usually called 'magister' in contemporary records: see e.g. D. & C. Lich., Chapter Act Bk. iii, ff. 68, 78, 82.

[14] Lists survive for 1585 and 1613 (Harwood, Lichfield, 514 n. 38), 1687 (Bodl. MS. Tanner 131, f. 214), 1700 and 1719 (S.R.O., D.239/M/2800 and /2801), 1732 (ibid. /2908), 1818 (S.R.O., D.(W.) 1702/7/5), 1821 (7th Rep. Com. Char. 382), and 1852 (S.R.O., D.(W.) 1702/7/5).

[15] [J. Jackson], Hist. of the City and County of Lichfield [1795], p. 30 (2nd nos.); Harwood, Lichfield, 512; Lich. Dioc. Ch. Cal. (1869), 96.

[16] Lich. Dioc. Ch. Cal. (1870), 96; and see later edns. In 1719 the sacrist was referred to as 'the Steward or Receiver of the rents belonging to the said Almshouse or Hospital': S.R.O., D.239/M/2800. Since 1957 the chaplain of the hospital has been known as such: Lich. Dioc. Dir. (1957), p. 54; and see later edns. and below p. 278.

rents of 'the Women's Hospital', to pay the almswomen their salaries, and to assume responsibility for the cure of their souls and for the fabric of the hospital. The following month the subchanter was ordered personally to take charge of the rental and to receive and expend the hospital's income himself.[17]

The landed endowment remained substantially the same during the three centuries following Milley's refoundation.[18] Nevertheless the almswomen's income was increased by a number of late-16th- and early-17th-century benefactions. The almswomen benefited jointly with the almsmen of St. John's Hospital from legacies made by John Feckenham and George Saturford in 1585 and 1586. Feckenham's Charity has continued to produce an income for the almspeople of the two foundations. Saturford's benefaction, however, which paid £1 16s. a year to the almswomen and £1 4s. to the almsmen until 1815, was realized as capital in that year by the feoffees of Dr. Milley's Hospital.[19] Other benefactions made at this period consisted of four gifts and legacies of money to the corporation of Lichfield; the interest on two of these sums was to be given to the almswomen, while that on the other two was to be shared between them and the almsmen of St. John's Hospital. In the later 17th century the corporation paid the almswomen £7 19s. a year in respect of these benefactions, while since the same period the almsmen of St. John's have received £1 8s.[20]

During the 18th century the almswomen continued to receive gifts and legacies. George Hand left them £5 in 1745, and in 1780 his son, another George, devised £100, which was invested by the feoffees.[21] In 1771 the feoffees were given £90 by a Mrs. Sandford; they distributed £10 to the almswomen and lent out the rest at interest.[22] Jane Gastrell gave the hospital £100 in 1786 and this was committed by the feoffees to Henry White, the cathedral sacrist, for investment.[23] A few years later she left another £100 to the hospital, which was spent by the feoffees on repairs and improvements.[24]

In 1786 the reserved rents from the hospital lands amounted to £87 16s.[25] By 1821 rents from landed property had increased to £346 2s. 10½d. a year.[26] This increase was due to the energetic measures undertaken by a new body of feoffees appointed in 1808. The following year a select committee of the feoffees discovered that some of the hospital's lands had been lost and that rents were considerably in arrears. The committee recommended the appointment of an agent or accountant to assist the sacrist in the administration of the hospital. The feoffees duly appointed an agent so that from 1809 the sacrist's responsibility for the hospital's financial affairs was exercised by a professional assistant.[27] In 1809 also the hospital's landed property was surveyed, and the feoffees resolved to discontinue the granting of long leases for nominal rents and high entry fines. By 1821 almost all leases of hospital lands which did not include houses had been reduced to terms of 21 years at rack rents, and the feoffees had by then decided to follow the same policy with regard to the leasing of houses belonging to the hospital.[28] In addition to landed income the hospital drew interest of £30 a year from invested capital in 1821, which brought the revenues in that year to a gross total of £376 2s. 10½d.[29]

In 1786 each of the fifteen almswomen received £1 1s. a quarter from the hospital, which also bore various other 'necessary expenses' on their behalf.[30] Their income at this time was still augmented by independent charities founded two centuries or so earlier.[31] The value of the pensions increased at this time in proportion with the increase in the rents from the hospital property. In 1805 each almswoman received 1s. 6d. a week and an additional £1 11s. 6d. a quarter;[32] by 1821 these amounts were 5s. a week and £1 every quarter, while payments from the independent charities then raised each almswoman's weekly income to about 7s. 5d.[33] The yearly stipend of the sacrist had also increased from the original 13s. 4d. of 1504. By 1781 he was receiving £5,[34] and in 1798 this was raised to £8, which remained the chaplain's stipend until 1955.[35] In the early years of the 19th century the sacrist's duties as chaplain to the almswomen seem to have consisted of reading prayers in their chapel and once a year

[17] Lich. Dioc. Regy., DC/C/1/2, chapter acts Oct. 1664, 10 Nov. 1664.

[18] *7th Rep. Com. Char.* 382. Some property had, however, been lost by the beginning of the 19th cent.: ibid.; and see below. According to *Staffs. Advertiser*, 5 Nov. 1796, 'a considerable estate' devolved on the hospital on the death of Cornelius Nevill of Pipehill; his death had presumably terminated a lease of the hospital's property at Pipehill.

[19] *7th Rep. Com. Char.* 385–6, 392–3. Since 1815 the feoffees of Dr. Milley's Hospital have been responsible for paying the £1 4s. a year to the almsmen of St. John's in respect of Saturford's benefaction: see below n. 33. For payments by Feckenham's Charity at the present time see below n. 39. A full account of the charities mentioned in this para. is reserved for a future volume of this *History*.

[20] *7th Rep. Com. Char.* 393–4. The payments to the almsmen have remained the same since the later 17th cent., but those to the almswomen were subsequently increased: see below notes 33, 39.

[21] A. L. Reade, *Johnsonian Gleanings* (priv. print.), iv (1923), 195; *7th Rep. Com. Char.* 385.

[22] *7th Rep. Com. Char.* 386. The loan was repaid in 1815.

[23] Ibid. 385.

[24] Ibid.; Reade, *Johnsonian Gleanings*, v (1928), 252–3. Her will was dated 31 May 1790, and she died on 30 Oct. 1791. In a codicil dated 23 Sept. 1791 she left an

annuity of £10 to one of the almswomen, Sarah Lovely.

[25] *Abstract of Returns of Charitable Donations, 1786–8,* H.C. 511, pp. 1158–9 (1816), xvi(2).

[26] *7th Rep. Com. Char.* 386.

[27] Char. Com. files. The annual salary of the sacrist's assistant was 12 guineas in 1815; it was increased to £21 in 1833, and this sum was still being paid in 1874. See also *7th Rep. Com. Char.* 386.

[28] *7th Rep. Com. Char.* 382, 383–5. After the 1809 survey timber felled on the hospital's estates was sold for £543, of which £400 was subsequently invested.

[29] Ibid. 385, 386. The capital (£600 invested at 5 per cent.) consisted of the £400 raised by the sale of timber (see previous note), Geo. Hand's £100, and Jane Gastrell's £100 (see above).

[30] Jackson, *Lichfield*, p. 30 (2nd nos.); W.S.L., M.849.

[31] Jackson, *Lichfield*, p. 30 (2nd nos.); see above.

[32] Harwood, *Lichfield*, 512.

[33] *7th Rep. Com. Char.* 386. Payments from independent charities then consisted of £25 4s. from Feckenham's Charity and £9 4s. from the Lichfield corporation. Saturford's benefaction had been realized as capital in 1815 by the feoffees who have since paid the almsmen of St. John's Hospital £1 4s. a year in respect of this benefaction: ibid. 386, 393; Char. Com. files.

[34] Char. Com. files. See also W.S.L., M. 849.

[35] Char. Com. files; see below and n. 36.

preaching and administering the sacrament to them.[36]

No important changes to the hospital's constitution were made until the present century. Since 1893 it has been governed under Schemes of the Charity Commissioners.[37] The 1893 Scheme provided for the maintenance of fifteen resident almswomen; in 1902, however, when the trustees were proposing to rebuild the hospital, this was amended to provide for nine residents. When the building was restored and reduced in size in 1906–7 the Scheme was further amended to provide for only eight resident almswomen.[38] The hospital is now administered under a Scheme of 1953.[39] Its management and the appointment of the almswomen are vested in a body of seven trustees, of whom the Dean of Lichfield is normally one. The only land now owned, apart from the ground behind the building, is at Chesterfield (in Shenstone); the greater part of the annual income, which in recent years has been just over £630, is now derived from investments. Eight almswomen reside in the hospital, and the trustees may grant pensions to them and to out-pensioners. The scheme permits the trustees to pay the sacrist of the cathedral for acting as chaplain. The office of sacrist, however, has been vacant since 1940, and since 1948 the chaplaincy has usually been exercised by one of the two priest vicars in the cathedral.[40] The chaplain's stipend was raised from £8 to £15 15s. in 1955.[41] Services for the almswomen are held in the hospital chapel each Thursday, and there is a monthly communion service also on Thursday.[42]

The hospital building appears to date largely from the early 16th century.[43] It is a two-storied structure of red brick, with a stone plinth and stone dressings. Originally the building was L-shaped in plan: from the southern end of the front range a long rear wing extended back along the southern boundary of the property.[44] The front range, which faces eastwards into Beacon Street, contains a central stone porch giving access to a wide entrance hall flanked by rooms for the matron and almswomen; on the first floor the space above the porch forms the east end of the almswomen's chapel.[45] The rear wing has a corridor on each floor, and these corridors originally gave access to almswomen's rooms on the south. North of the corridors is the staircase and also a two-storied addition, probably of the late 18th century, containing two rooms. The internal partitions are of heavy close-studded timbering and incorporate many of the original early-16th-century doorways.

A view of the front, drawn in 1841,[46] suggests that a number of alterations had been made in the 18th century. These included the facing of the exterior with plaster, the insertion of wood casement windows, and the addition of gabled dormers to the roof. The pedimented tablet above the entrance, which commemorates Thomas Milley's refoundation of the hospital, is also of this period.

By the beginning of the present century the hospital was in need of modernization and repair. In 1900 the trustees, on the advice of a local architect, proposed a complete reconstruction of the building.[47] The Charity Commissioners, however, advised instead a careful restoration of the existing structure, and their recommendations were carried out in 1906–7 under the direction of Charles Lynam of Stoke-upon-Trent.[48] The rear wing was made narrower by moving its south wall back from the boundary of the property;[49] the truncated rooms to the south of the corridors were converted into small fuel stores, pantries, and lavatories. These alterations allowed for only eight resident almswomen, who were however more comfortably accommodated than their predecessors. New stone-mullioned windows were inserted on the front elevation, and the external plaster was stripped away to reveal the brickwork. The general appearance of the hospital buildings has remained the same since the alterations of 1906–7, though further restoration and repairs were carried out in 1953–4 and 1967–8 by J. A. Chatwin & Son of Birmingham.[50]

No seal is known.

[36] Harwood, *Lichfield*, 512; *7th Rep. Com. Char.* 386. In 1845, at the feoffees' suggestion, the Revd. H. I. Cotton, the sacrist, agreed to hold a weekday service and to celebrate Holy Communion on 3 Sundays in the year; his salary was accordingly raised to £20 p.a. These arrangements were not continued in his successor's time. See Char. Com. files.
[37] Char. Com. files; Char. Com. Scheme, 27 Jan. 1893; *Lichfield Mercury*, 2 and 9 Sept. 1892 (advts.).
[38] Char. Com. files; Char. Com. Schemes, 4 Feb. 1902, 15 Mar. 1907; *Staffs. Advertiser*, 12 Oct. 1901, 2 Feb. 1907 (advts.); see below.
[39] Except where otherwise stated, the rest of this para. is based on Char. Com. files; Char. Com. scheme, 23 Oct. 1953; inf. from Mr. R. D. Birch, Steward of Dr. Milley's Hospital (1967). The hospital has received just over £100 a year from Feckenham's Charity in recent years and continues to receive £9 4s. from the corporation of Lichfield. Payments, averaging just under £140 a year, have also been made to the hospital in recent years from Haworth's Charity and Lowe's Charity; accounts of these two charities are reserved for a future volume of this *History*.
[40] *Lich. Dioc. Dir.* (1940–1 and later edns.). The sacrist's office was always held *ex officio* by the Treasurer's Vicar: see above p. 148. Both offices lapsed after 1940. The sacrist's office has never been revived, and, although there was a Treasurer's Vicar from 1951 to 1954, he did not act as chaplain to the hospital. From 1940 to 1948 the Revd. H. L. Muriel, Prebendary of Weeford, acted as chaplain: *Lich. Dioc. Mag.* (1948), 36.
[41] Char. Com. Scheme, 18 Oct. 1955.
[42] Inf. from the Revd. C. E. Davis, Dean's Vicar and chaplain to the hospital (1967).
[43] The following account of the hospital's architecture has been written by Margaret Tomlinson.
[44] See O.S. Map 1/2,500, Staffs. LII. 15 (1882 edn.).
[45] For a view of the front range see below plate facing p. 286.
[46] W.S.L., Staffs. Views, v, p. 253.
[47] Char. Com. files. Various proposals considered by the trustees between 1900 and 1906 are set out in a letter from the chairman of the trustees to the *Lichfield Mercury*, 16 Feb. 1906.
[48] For the rest of this para., except where otherwise stated, see Char. Com. files. An unfavourable report (dated 20 Mar. 1902) on the trustees' plan was made by W. D. Caroë and contains a valuable account of the buildings. The files also contain a report on the buildings (dated 6 May 1901) by Hen. Bowyer, an assistant commissioner. It appears from both reports that the buildings were structurally sound. A drawing of the hospital (dated 11 Aug. 1906) by Lynam survives in W.S.L. 334/38. There are also scattered jottings about the hospital in Lynam's notebks. 1905–7: W.S.L. 117/39/128–130.
[49] See O.S. Map 1/2,500, SK 1109 (1966 edn.). This is the first 25″ map to record the 1906–7 alterations to the hospital buildings.
[50] Inf. from Mr. A. B. Chatwin, of J. A. Chatwin & Son (1967); inf. from Mr. R. D. Birch (1968).

26. THE HOSPITAL OF ST. JOHN THE BAPTIST, LICHFIELD

TRADITION assigns the foundation of St. John's Hospital, Lichfield, to 'Bishop Roger'.[1] If this tradition is correct the founder must have been Bishop Roger de Clinton (1129–48), for the hospital was certainly in existence before the time of Bishop Roger Weseham (1245–56). A grant of 1208 refers to the hospital as 'the House of the Hospital of the Holy Spirit and St. John the Baptist.'[2] This double dedication[3] is not found subsequently, and the house was usually known, from its situation outside Culstubbe Gate, as the Hospital of St. John the Baptist without the Bars of Lichfield. In the 13th century the hospital community, apart from the poor who were maintained there,[4] evidently consisted of a prior, brethren, sisters, and lay brethren living under a religious rule and a number of chaplains and servants.[5]

The hospital chapel, as well as serving the hospital community, was a place of public worship from at least the earlier 13th century. Elaborate precautions, however, were taken to protect the rights of St. Michael's Church, Lichfield, in whose parish the hospital stood. By an agreement made in Bishop Stavensby's time (1224–38) with the Prebendary of Freeford[6] the prior and brethren of the hospital and their chaplains promised to maintain the rights of the prebend, to which St. Michael's church was evidently then appropriated. They and such of their servants and tenants as lived in St. Michael's parish were to pay all customary tithes to the prebendary and all customary offerings to his chaplain. The parishioners might worship in the hospital chapel on holy days and the hospital was allowed to have a small bell to summon them; on the great festivals, however, the prior and brethren and their servants were to receive the sacraments in the parish church. The lay brothers, servants, and other inhabitants of the hospital were to be confessed only by the prebendary's chaplain unless licensed by him to go elsewhere, and they were to devise the customary mortuaries to the parish church. All who died in the hospital were to be buried in the parish church.

In return for these promises to maintain the rights of his parish church the Prebendary of Freeford allowed the establishment of a chantry in the hospital chapel.[7] This, however, did not take place

until the heirs and executors of Ralph de Lacok, Canon of Lichfield (d. 1257), combined to found a chantry in the hospital. The chantry chaplain was to wear the habit of the hospital brethren; in the first instance he was to be appointed by Lacok's executors, but thereafter by the bishop either from within the hospital or elsewhere. The endowment of the chantry, which was said to be for the support of the poor and sick inmates of the hospital and those who sought hospitality there, consisted of lands and rent in Stychbrook and Elmhurst (both in St. Chad's, Lichfield).[8] The dean and chapter also gave Lacok's body to the hospital for burial there, but the prior and brethren had to guarantee that this would not prejudice the rights of the church of Lichfield or any of its chaplains; they further promised that they would not claim any burial rights on account of this grant 'until by the help of the Lord they obtain a more generous favour by authority of their superiors'.[9] It is, however, clear that, despite the earlier agreement with the Prebendary of Freeford, the hospital had by this time acquired the right of burying the habited brethren and sisters of the foundation. The hospital cemetery probably lay to the south of the chapel,[10] and by the mid 1340s there was a preaching cross or open-air pulpit there from which Dean FitzRalph is known to have preached.[11]

Apart from the foundation of Ralph de Lacok's chantry little is known of the early endowments or privileges of the hospital.[12] In 1240 Henry III gave to the poor there 8 quarters of wheat.[13] The prior and brethren received letters of protection from the Crown in 1251, 1257, and 1297.[14] In the later 13th century William Young, a Lichfield goldsmith, gave a burgage and a half in Lichfield, a messuage, 6s. 6d. rent, and 3 acres of land in Burway Field to the brethren and sisters for the repair of the hospital; a daily mass for his soul was to be said by one of the brethren.[15]

In the earlier 14th century the hospital acquired a number of more valuable properties. In 1315 John de la Bourne, chaplain, was licensed by the Crown to grant the prior and brethren 7 acres of land and £10 of rent in Lichfield and Pipe (in St. Michael's, Lichfield), and Reynold le Bedel to grant 3½ acres of land worth 12d. a year in the same places.[16] In 1322 the hospital was given 2 messuages and a carucate of land in Rushall and 'Ordeseye' worth 13s. 4d. by Henry of Lichfield, chaplain.[17] In 1349

[1] F. Godwin, *De Praesulibus Angliae Commentarius* (Cambridge, 1743), 313. It has been asserted that Bp. Clinton established Augustinian canons in the hospital (W. Beresford, *Lichfield*, 64–65, 174), but there seems to be no evidence for this. The regular clergy of the hospital seem always to have been known as 'brethren', not 'canons': see below and p. 280 and J. C. Dickinson, *Origins of the Austin Canons and their Introduction into Eng.* 146–7. The writer's thanks are due to Miss Marjorie Anderson, Prebendary H. Baylis, and Canon G. N. Strong for their assistance during the preparation of this article.

[2] *S.H.C.* 1924, pp. 19–20.

[3] Dedication to the Holy Spirit was rare in English hospitals: Rotha M. Clay, *Medieval Hospitals of Eng.* 245–246.

[4] See below.

[5] A prospective lay brother is mentioned in 1208 (*S.H.C.* 1924, pp. 19–20), and this suggests that the hospital was then ruled by a prior and brethren. Fuller evidence for the hospital community is provided by the agreement of 1224–38 with the Prebendary of Freeford: see following para. Habited sisters are first mentioned in 1257: *S.H.C.* 1924, pp. 320–1.

[6] For this para. see *S.H.C.* 1924, p. 203.   [7] Ibid.

[8] Ibid. pp. 207, 319–20. The foundation was confirmed

in 1259 by Bp. Meuland and the dean and chapter: ibid. pp. 206–7.   [9] Ibid. pp. 320–1.

[10] Remains of a medieval burial were found there during alterations to the almshouses in 1967: inf. from Canon G. N. Strong (1967). Burials were still taking place within the hospital precincts during the 18th and earlier 19th centuries, and gravestones to the south of the chapel are shown in a drawing of 1833; A. L. Reade, *Johnsonian Gleanings* (priv. print.), iv (1923), 152, 153, 154–5; viii (1937), 164; W.S.L., Staffs. Views, v, p. 249a.

[11] G. R. Owst, *Preaching in Medieval Eng.* 12.

[12] The grant of 1208 already mentioned (see above) gave the hospital a prospective title to property in Lichfield, a virgate of land in Barton-under-Needwood, and other tillage ground: *S.H.C.* 1924, pp. 19–20. It seems unlikely, however, that it ever took effect: no subsequent evidence that the hospital held land at Barton has been found.

[13] *Cal. Lib. 1226–40*, 467.

[14] *Cal. Pat. 1247–58*, 119, 572; *1292–1301*, 282.

[15] *S.H.C.* 1924, pp. 207–8.

[16] *Cal. Pat. 1313–17*, 367; *S.H.C.* ix(1), 124; ibid. 1911, 328–9.

[17] *S.H.C.* 1911, 347–8; *Cal. Pat. 1321–4*, 139. This was done under a licence of 1317 for the acquisition of property to the annual value of £10: ibid. 1317–21, 11.

Adam de Eton and John Wylimot, chaplains, granted the prior and brethren property worth 41s. 2d.; it comprised 20 messuages, 60 acres of land, 4 acres of meadow, and 18s. 10d. of rent in Lichfield, Longdon, Pipe,[18] Aldershaw (in St. Michael's, Lichfield), Elmhurst, and Shenstone.[19] Other benefactions, the details of which are unknown, were certainly made about this time. In 1321 the dean and chapter ratified the constitution of a chantry at the altar of St. Thomas the Martyr in the cathedral, which had been founded by the prior and brethren to commemorate the many benefactions made to the hospital by Philip de Turvill, Prebendary of Curborough (1309–37).[20] In 1330–1 John de la Bourne added to his benefactions by founding a chantry in St. Mary's Church, Lichfield, and granting the patronage to the prior, brethren, and sisters of the hospital.[21] Probably about this time too the hospital was given a house at Greenhill (in St. Michael's, Lichfield) and 25 selions of land in the fields of Lichfield by John of Polesworth.[22]

Some light is thrown on the internal history of the hospital in the 14th century by the records of Bishop Northburgh's visitations. The bishop visited the hospital possibly in 1331 or 1332[23] and found that the rule of the house was not publicly read; as a result it was not understood and the brethren were not living according to their vows. Sales of corrodies and pensions had evidently been frequent. One of the brethren, Hugh of Wychnor, had been guilty of disobedience and perjury and of leading an irregular life. The bishop ordered that the rule be read to the brethren three or four times a year, if necessary in English, so that they might not pretend ignorance of their vows. The sale of corrodies and pensions was forbidden for the future except by the express permission of the bishop. Wychnor was to be excommunicated and, in accordance with the rule, confined in a chamber within the hospital; he was to live on bread and water and to read the psalter and other devotional works, but on Sundays he might eat vegetables with his bread and once a week was to be allowed to take exercise out of doors. The bishop also ordered that the brethren were not to be given money when they needed clothes or other necessities but that purchases were to be made for them by a suitable person. The form of vow which the brethren took at this time is given; it comprised promises of perpetual chastity, of obedience to the prior, and of loyalty to the statutes and rights of the hospital.

The bishop visited the hospital again in 1339[24] and evidently found that its finances were in need of regulation. The brethren lacked the necessities of life, especially clothing, and received only a subsistence diet so that they were forced to beg 'to the disgrace of their order'. The bishop ordained specific provision for them: 20s. from the rent of the hospital's mill at Sandford[25] and the income from the house and land given by John of Polesworth were to be reserved to provide the brethren with allowances for clothing and other necessities. In 1345, after another visitation of the hospital, Bishop Northburgh sanctioned the appropriation by the prior and brethren of the chantry in St. Mary's Church granted to them by John de la Bourne. The bishop's ordinance was made without royal licence, but in 1346 the Crown granted a pardon and confirmed the bishop's act.[26]

In the earlier 14th century the brethren of the hospital seem to have tried to secure the right of electing their prior. In 1323, on the resignation of William of Wychnor, the brethren nominated William of Repton as his successor. The bishop protested against their action as an infringement of his right to collate but nevertheless appointed Repton.[27] In 1330, on Repton's resignation, the brethren successfully nominated Richard del Hull to the bishop.[28]

Little more is known of the hospital until the later 15th century. At some time before the mid 15th century it evidently ceased to be a corporate institution comprising a prior and brethren living under a religious rule, for in 1458 Bishop Boulers issued a declaration asserting that it was a benefice without cure of souls which could be held by a non-resident secular clerk and in plurality.[29] At what time this change occurred is uncertain. The hospital ceased to be a corporate body of regular clergy, probably in the late 14th century. It was certainly a secular benefice by the mid 15th century for Hugh Lache, then master, was a secular clerk.[30] Bishop Boulers's declaration certainly regularized an existing state of affairs, for the master in 1458, Thomas Mason, was a pluralist. The mastership was then a valuable piece of preferment and may have been worth about £20 a year — as much as the wealthier rectories in the county.[31] All the masters appointed after Boulers's declaration were secular clerks, and many were pluralists and absentees.[32]

In these circumstances the eleemosynary responsibilities of the foundation may well have been neglected until the hospital was reformed by Bishop Smith in 1495–6. It was alleged in 1539 that at the time of Smith's reformation of the hospital 'there was a master and two brethren and they for their ill living were expelled';[33] if these recollections are reliable they probably indicate that no more than two almsmen were then maintained, for the regular brotherhood had long since ceased to exist. Bishop Smith drew up a new set of statutes and re-endowed

[18] Given as 'Herdewykepipe'; for identification see *List of Inquisitions Ad Quod Damnum Pt. II* (P.R.O. Lists and Indexes, xxii), 540.
[19] *S.H.C.* 1913, 137–8; *Cal. Pat.* 1348–50, 420–1. This too was done under the 1317 licence.
[20] *S.H.C.* 1924, p. 365; Le Neve, *Fasti Ecclesiae Anglicanae, 1300–1541* (new edn.), x. 27.
[21] Harwood, *Lichfield*, 456 n. 59, 541–2; *Cal. Pat.* 1330–4, 223. The endowment of the chantry consisted of 3 messuages and 12 a. of land in Lichfield.
[22] Harwood, *Lichfield*, 539–40; *S.H.C.* i. 262. Polesworth, a vicar choral in the cathedral, occurs in 1315 and 1323: *S.H.C.* 1924, pp. 95–96, 306.
[23] Harwood, *Lichfield*, 540–1; *S.H.C.* i. 265. The bishop's decrees appear between entries dated 1331 and 1332, but there is little order in the entries in the register at this point.
[24] Harwood, *Lichfield*, 539–40; *S.H.C.* i. 262.
[25] This evidently stood on the Trunkfield Brook near where it flowed into the bishop's fish-pool: *S.H.C.* 1950–1, 154 (fig. 4).
[26] Lich. Dioc. Regy., B/A/1/2, f. 176v.; *Cal. Pat.* 1345–8, 48.
[27] Lich. Dioc. Regy., B/A/1/2, f. 137.
[28] Ibid. f. 147. [29] B/A/1/11, f. 95v.
[30] Harwood, *Lichfield*, 542; *S.H.C.* 1939, p. 103; see above p. 276.
[31] *Cal. Papal Regs.* xi. 588; see above p. 42.
[32] See below pp. 287, 288, notes 65, 66, 68–86, and authorities there cited.
[33] Sta. Cha. 2/34/143, m. 9d.

the hospital.[34] The statutes, dated November 1495, remained the basis of the hospital's constitution until the present century, and Smith has been regarded as the second founder of the hospital.[35] The responsibilities of the new foundation were twofold, eleemosynary and educational. Thirteen almsmen were to be maintained, each receiving 7d. a week,[36] and there was also to be a grammar school with a master and usher supported out of the hospital's revenues.[37] The hospital establishment was completed by a chaplain and the master. The chaplain, schoolmaster, and usher and the almsmen were to live in the hospital; the chaplain, schoolmaster, and usher were allowed a month's leave of absence each year,[38] and leave of absence could be granted to an almsman by the master of the hospital or the schoolmaster. Detailed regulations were made for the prayers which the pupils and the almsmen were to attend. The almsmen were to leave their own goods, or at least the greater part of them, to the hospital.

The new statutes emphasized the privileges and responsibilities of the master. He was to appoint the schoolmaster and usher, the hospital chaplain, and twelve of the thirteen almsmen,[39] and all these, on admission, had to swear obedience to him as well as to the bishop and the hospital statutes. The exercise of all the hospital's rights and the disposal of its revenues now clearly belonged solely to the master and no longer to a master and brethren jointly. This had probably been so since the end of the regular brotherhood, or at least since 1458,[40] but the statutes of 1495 provided the first authoritative definition of the change and were probably effective in frustrating later attempts to allege the hospital's corporate character.[41] The master was to be in priest's orders but was not bound to reside in the hospital; on admission he was to swear to observe the hospital statutes, and, if his letters of collation did not record his taking this oath, they were to be held invalid. The right of appointing the master was to remain with Bishop Smith during his life, and thereafter with the bishops of Coventry and Lichfield.[42]

Bishop Smith also rebuilt the hospital and proceeded to augment its endowment. In January 1496 the hospital of St. Andrew at Denhall (in Neston, Ches.), with its appropriated church of Burton (Ches.), and the free chapel or leper hospital of St. Leonard at Freeford were united to St. John's

Hospital. The hospital at Denhall was in the bishop's patronage and that at Freeford in the patronage of the Prebendary of Freeford; both foundations were too impoverished to continue independently. In return for agreeing to unite St. Leonard's Hospital to St. John's the Prebendary of Freeford was to have the nomination of one of the thirteen almsmen.[43] On the day of the union of the three hospitals Bishop Smith granted to the almsmen, schoolmaster, chaplain, and usher two cartloads of firewood a year from Cannock Chase.[44]

During the earlier 16th century the hospital seems to have been reasonably well governed in accordance with Smith's statutes. The almsmen, who wore distinctive black gowns with a red cross,[45] were probably maintained in a fair degree of comfort: in addition to their pensions of 7d. a week they may have received money from John Kynardessey's chantry in the cathedral[46] and it was probably customary for them to receive gifts when a new lease of hospital property was sealed.[47] The statute enjoining the almsmen to leave their goods to the hospital was evidently enforced by the masters and must have helped to improve the standard of living of successive entrants: when one of the almsmen died about 1508 the master took charge of the money which he left (40s.) and ordered the bailiff to share out his goods among the other almsmen.[48] Bishop Blythe visited the hospital in 1519, and everything then seemed to be in good order, though the schoolmaster admitted that he did not sleep in the hospital and the master, Richard Egerton, complained that his statutory responsibilities were too numerous to allow the proper maintenance of the hospital buildings out of the revenues.[49]

The right of visiting the hospital had clearly belonged to the bishop during the Middle Ages,[50] but by the earlier 16th century this was being challenged by the dean and chapter. In 1530 or 1531 Dean Denton, claiming ordinary jurisdiction over the hospital, sent Edmund Stretehay to visit it as his commissary. This was evidently not the first time that a visitation had been carried out in the dean's name, for a few years later Stretehay recalled that he had on this occasion seen 'divers precedents that the master there and other of the house had been punished by the said Dean of Lichfield for the time being, and by his commissary, for their ill living.'[51] The dean's claim may have originated in the changes

---

[34] For this and the following para. see Lich. Dioc. Regy., B/A/1/13, ff. 148–151v.; Harwood, *Lichfield*, 542–7; *7th Rep. Com. Char.* H.C. 129, pp. 387–8 (1822), x.

[35] Harwood, *Lichfield*, 556; H. Baylis, *Hosp. of St. John Baptist without the Barrs of the City of Lichfield* (Lichfield, 1958), 11, 26.

[36] Lepers and the insane were not to be admitted; almsmen who became leprous or insane were to leave, though retaining their 7d. a week.

[37] The school, like the hospital, may have been a refoundation: during the process for uniting the hospitals of Denhall and Freeford with St. John's the proxy of St. John's Hospital stated that 'there had not been (according to the canons) any regular instruction of youth in grammar, gratis, . . . by reason of the insufficiency of the masters, and smallness of their stipends': Harwood, *Lichfield*, 549.

[38] Only one of these three, however, might be absent at any one time, and the schoolmaster had to supply a *locum tenens* at his own expense.

[39] For the appointment of the thirteenth by the Prebendary of Freeford see the following para. See also below n. 42 Certain rights of intervention, to guard against long vacancies, were reserved to the bishop and to the dean and chapter.

[40] See above p. 280.

[41] e.g. Sta. Cha. 2/34/143. And see Baylis, *Hosp. of St. John Baptist*, 26.

[42] Appointment of the schoolmaster, usher, chaplain, and 12 almsmen was also reserved to Smith during his lifetime.

[43] Lich. Dioc. Regy., B/A/1/13, ff. 165–9; Harwood, *Lichfield*, 547, 548–9. For the hospital at Denhall see ibid. 547–8; G. Ormerod, *Hist. of the County Palatine and City of Chester* (1882 edn.), ii. 543–4, 555–6; above p. 143. For the hospital at Freeford see pp. 274–5. The union of the 3 hospitals was ratified by the dean and chapter: Harwood, *Lichfield*, 550.

[44] Harwood, *Lichfield*, 550; Lich. Dioc. Regy., B/A/1/13, ff. 169–170v.

[45] Sta. Cha. 2/34/143, m. 7. Some uniformity of dress may have persisted to the 19th cent. when the master still provided the almsmen with cloaks: see below pp. 283, 284.

[46] See above p. 276 and n. 11.

[47] Sta. Cha. 2/34/143, m. 6; see below p. 283.

[48] Sta. Cha. 2/34/143, m. 6.

[49] Lich. Dioc. Regy., B/V/1/1, p. 21; see below n. 42.

[50] See above p. 280. [51] Sta. Cha. 2/34/143, m. 5.

to the hospital's constitution made by Bishops Boulers and Smith. A few years later Richard Strete, a canon residentiary of Lichfield, giving evidence about the hospital's constitution, denied that the master and brethren were a corporation. In support of this he stated that the dean by reason of his archidiaconal jurisdiction in Lichfield 'hath had the master thereof to appear afore him in his visitation in the town many years, and . . . if there were a corporation he is not accustomed to have any jurisdiction'.[52] The bishop, however, seems to have attempted a visitation about the same time as Denton's commissary and was evidently resisted by the dean and chapter and the master.[53] The master was excommunicated by the bishop, and the dispute was taken to the archbishop's Court of Audience. In 1531 the sentence of excommunication was lifted, and the bishop and the dean and chapter agreed to settle their differences by arbitration before Michaelmas.[54] The bishop's right to visit the hospital remained thereafter unopposed.[55]

The gross annual income of the hospital in 1535[56] was £46 18s. 1d., most of which accrued from property in and around Lichfield and from the property of the former hospital at Denhall. Fees and salaries included £19 15s. 5d. a year paid to the 13 almsmen (at the rate of 7d. a week each), £10 a year to the schoolmaster, £5 6s. 8d. to the chaplain, £2 to the usher, and £2 to the bailiff of the hospital's estates. The value of the master's house[57] and certain properties which he kept in his own hands was given as £1 6s. 8d. These figures, however, which appear to support the master's complaint in 1519 of the insufficiency of the hospital's income, cannot be taken as a complete account of the revenues available to him. Richard Egerton, master from 1508 to 1538, must have received a good income from fines paid for granting or renewing leases, as he seems commonly to have leased the hospital's properties for three lives or terms ranging from 50 to 90 years.[58] Thus in 1513–14 Sir Thomas Smith wished to convert his 39-year lease of the former hospital at Denhall into one for 50 years, and Egerton agreed provided 'he would so pay therefor'.[59]

Towards the end of his long mastership Egerton may have been neglecting the responsibilities laid on him by the 1495 statutes. In 1535 Lord Stafford was suing Egerton for 'misusing' St. John's Hospital at Stafford, of which he was also master.[60] Lord Stafford alleged that Egerton was misusing St. John's Hospital, Lichfield, in the same way, 'for it is said that house is in as great decay as mine is'.[61] Egerton's unsatisfactory conduct was reported to Cromwell,[62] who evidently tried to compel him to grant a lease of the hospital and its 'lands and tenements as they did fall' to William Zouche. Cromwell's efforts were evidently fruitless, for Zouche later asked him to send to the recalcitrant Egerton for a 'true copy of the foundation of the said hospital', alleging that Egerton would 'rather perform [this] grant to me for danger that will follow than send your lordship the copy'.[63] Zouche's attempts to secure this lease, however, were unsuccessful. Within a few months Egerton had died. Bishop Lee collated his brother, George Lee, to the mastership,[64] and their nephew, William Fowler, secured a lease of much of the hospital's property.[65]

One of the effects of Egerton's granting of long leases must have been to impoverish his successor by depriving him of any considerable income from entry fines. Lee, however, on the advice of counsel and evidently with the encouragement of his brother the bishop, adopted the expedient of repudiating Egerton's leases:[66] in 1539 he gave it as his view that the master could make a lease only for the duration of his mastership.[67] Lee's policy inevitably led to litigation. He was himself sued by Sir Thomas Smith's widow, Katherine,[68] and some suits between rival claimants to leaseholds of the hospital's property are known to have occurred.[69] Although some limitation of the master's leasing powers would ultimately have benefited the hospital, none was established until the later 19th century.[70]

Lee's mastership was a crucial period in the hospital's history for only the continuance of its charitable and educational activities seems to have averted the consequences of dissolution under the Act of 1547.[71] According to the 1546 chantry certificate, out of a gross annual income of £54 3s. 10d. fees totalling £40 1s. were paid to the almsmen, schoolmaster, chaplain, and usher.[72] Almsmen were still being maintained in the hospital in 1548,[73] and the Crown seems to have been content to appropriate the salary of the hospital chaplain, who was evidently classed as one of the stipendiary priests whose

[52] Ibid. m. 4.

[53] Ric. Egerton, the master, was Prebendary of Whittington and Berkswich and a residentiary in the cathedral: Le Neve, *Fasti* (new edn.), x. 68; see below n. 57.

[54] D. & C. Lich., Chapter Act Bk. iv, ff. 72v.–73, 74v.–75.

[55] See below pp. 283–4, 285.

[56] *Valor Eccl.* (Rec. Com.), iii. 141–2.

[57] This was presumably let as Egerton, a canon residentiary from 1493, lived in the Close: D. & C. Lich., Chapter Act Bk. iii, f. 9; *L. & P. Hen. VIII*, viii, pp. 40–41.

[58] Sta. Cha. 2/34/143, mm. 6, 7, 8, 9.

[59] Ibid. m. 6.   [60] See below p. 291.

[61] S.R.O., D.(W.) 1810, f. 87v. Nevertheless Leland, perhaps a superficial observer, made no such observation when he visited Lichfield about this time: *Itin.* ed. L. Toulmin Smith, ii. 100.

[62] By Lord Stafford, who was trying to draw him into his suit against Egerton: see below p. 291.

[63] S.P. 1/157, f. 38. This letter is wrongly dated 1540 in *L. & P. Hen. VIII*, xv, p. 18; as it was written during Egerton's life and while Cromwell was Keeper of the Privy Seal, it must be dated 1537 or 1538.

[64] See below p. 287.

[65] C 1/1378/36. This lease included 'one messuage called St. John's in Lichfield' (probably the master's house) and

'all other lands . . . belonging to the said hospital . . . within the city and fields of Lichfield'.

[66] Sta. Cha. 2/34/143, mm. 10–12. Counsel declared, after consulting the episcopal registers and a 'book of the king's statutes for setting of farms', that Egerton's long leases 'were of no more value nor effect but as if a parson had let to farm the lands and tenements belonging to his parsonage'.

[67] Ibid. m.1. Lee was evidently maintaining that the master's leasing powers were no greater than those of a parson: see previous note and R. Burn, *Ecclesiastical Law* (1797 edn.), ii. 363–6.

[68] Sta. Cha. 2/34/143.

[69] C 1/1241/77–79; /1286/28–32.

[70] See below pp. 283, 284–5. See also Baylis, *Hosp. of St. John Baptist*, 26.

[71] 1 Edw. VI, c. 14.

[72] A. F. Leach, *Eng. Schools at the Reformation 1546–8*, pt. ii, 196–7. The hospital then possessed 7½ oz. of plate, parcel gilt, and other ornaments and goods of which an inventory had been made but which were not yet valued. For a list of the hospital's plate at the present day, which includes several 18th- and 19th-century pieces, see Baylis, *Hosp. of St. John Baptist*, 32.

[73] *S.H.C.* 1915, 174.

endowments were annexed to the Crown by the Act of 1547.[74] In May 1550, however, his salary was restored when the Court of Augmentations ordered that £5 6s. 8d. a year should continue to be paid to maintain the minister in the hospital chapel.[75]

The Crown seems subsequently to have tried to suppress the hospital, for its dissolution is mentioned in some Chancery proceedings of the 1550s[76] and in 1571 the hospital with all its property was granted to Thomas, Lord Wentworth, as part of a gift to him of lands concealed from the Crown. Even this grant, however, affords proof that the charitable and educational responsibilities of the hospital were still being carried out, for it expressly reserved £35 a year from the property to support ten almsmen, the schoolmaster, and the usher and to pay the Crown's tenth.[77] With this reservation the lands were probably of little value to Wentworth, and the hospital's continuance was perhaps arranged with his agreement. The grant, however, must have extinguished any Crown title to the property and may thus, ironically, have helped to assure the hospital's future. This was evidently felt to be secure from about this time, for the almsmen were beneficiaries of a number of late-16th- and early-17th-century bequests and devises; from the later 17th century they received, in respect of these gifts, £1 8s. a year from the corporation of Lichfield, £1 4s. a year from the heirs of Alexander Wightwick, and a variable income from Feckenham's Trust.[78] The hospital's existence was also recognized by the Crown in charters granted to the city corporation during the 17th century.[79]

Probably none of the 16th-century masters resided in the hospital,[80] and during the later 16th century and earlier 17th century the master's house was leased to the Weston family.[81] John Machon, master from 1632 to 1671, may have held some position in the bishop's administration, for after Bishop Morton's translation to Durham in 1632 he obtained preferment in that diocese.[82] He continued, however, to hold St. John's and when, in 1642, the church party at Durham fled before the Scots invaders Machon may have returned to live in Staffordshire.[83] There is no evidence of any attempt to interfere with his possession of the hospital during the Civil War and the Interregnum.[84] In 1660 Machon was restored to his Durham preferment and evidently returned there to live; it was probably at this time that a deputy master, William Pargiter, was appointed.[85]

In 1662 the hospital was visited by Bishop Hacket, as a result of a petition to him from the almsmen which amounted to a severe indictment of the master. They complained of their poverty and made five more specific complaints: first, that the hospital chapel was ruined; secondly, that 'their mansion house (wherein formerly hath been kept good hospitality) is now become a cage for owls' and that barns and outhouses adjacent to the hospital were 'totally ruined'; thirdly, that the master was frequently renewing leases and keeping the fines himself or else making leases to his brother, Edward, for his own use; fourthly, that hospital tenants were allowed to fell and dispose of timber which would have been better used to repair the hospital buildings; and finally, that they had not profited from any 'fine or augmentation' since Bishop Bayly renewed various leases and used the fines to give the almsmen new gowns.[86] In August Machon wrote to the bishop's registrar, admitting that 'the ruins of the house and chapel . . . are a common object of pity and compassion'[87] but stating that until lately his own fortunes had been 'as ruinous as that house, both pulled down by the same hands of rapine and sacrilege'. The tone of his letter, however, was placatory: he promised to repair the hospital and hoped that the bishop would not 'judge me to lose my estate because I have lost my health'.[88] Evidence produced at the visitation in October included an account of the reserved rents from the hospital property which amounted to £78 0s. 4d. a year; over one-fifth of this sum was due from Edward Machon.[89] The only known act of the visitation is the removal of two

---

[74] S.C. 12/28/12, f. 24v. [75] E 315/105, f. 132.

[76] In a Chancery suit of c. 1552 Egerton was referred to as formerly master of 'the late dissolved hospital of Saint John' at Lichfield: C 1/1286/28.

[77] Cal. Pat. 1569–72, pp. 397–8, 404. The lands granted in 1571 were in part fulfilment of an earlier grant of concealed lands to the annual value of £200 which he or his heirs should discover: ibid. pp. 5, 405.

[78] For the origins of these benefactions see above p. 277.

[79] The master's rights were protected in royal charters to the city in 1623, 1664, and 1686: Harwood, Lichfield, 347, 350, 550; [J. Jackson], Hist. of the City and County of Lichfield (Lichfield, 1795), 41.

[80] See above n. 57 and below n. 81 and p. 287 notes 71, 73, 74.

[81] At least three generations of Westons lived at St. John's: John Weston, his son Jas. (d. 1589), and his grandson Sir Simon (d. 1637). Jas. and Simon were diocesan registrars and recorders of Lichfield. See Shaw, Staffs. i. 334 and n. 7; S.H.C. 1920 & 1922, 34; Harwood, Lichfield, 270, 345, 437; Lich. Dioc. Regy., B/A/1/16, passim; B/C/3/10, 18 Jan. 1583, 14 Jan. 1589; Erdeswick, Staffs. pedigree facing p. 165.

[82] Machon was collated to the vicarage of Hartburn (Northumb.) 12 weeks after Morton's translation; 4 years later he exchanged it for the mastership of Christ's Hospital, Sherburn: Anon. Collections relating to Sherburn Hosp. (1771).

[83] V.C.H. Durham, ii. 48–49; Collections relating to Sherburn Hosp.; Cal. S.P. Dom. 1660–1, 434.

[84] In 1655 Cromwell presented to the hospital's appropriated church of Burton: W. A. Shaw, Hist. of Eng. Church during the Civil Wars and under the Commonwealth, ii. 276 and n. 2. This was not, however, an attempt to usurp the hospital's rights. In 1631 Burton church had been leased to Sir Thos. Smith, who in 1647, as a royalist, had been forced to settle the rectory and tithes on the minister there: Cal. Cttee. for Compounding, ii. 1319. In 1654 the Trustees for Maintenance of Ministers had acquired responsibility for sequestered rectories, and it was their rights that Cromwell was infringing: Shaw, op. cit. 230, 278.

[85] Cal. S.P. Dom. 1660–1, 434. For Pargiter see below n. 90.

[86] Lich. Dioc. Regy., St. John's Hosp. records (petition by the almsmen to the bp., probably to be dated to the early summer of 1662). The visitation is mentioned by Harwood, Lichfield, 550.

[87] Machon described the almsmen's other charges as 'false or frivolous: frivolous as resting on the bare surmise of their opinion, false as requiring more than the statutes allow'.

[88] Lich. Dioc. Regy., St. John's Hosp. records (letter from Machon to Hen. Archbold, 15 Aug. 1662).

[89] Ibid. ('A particular of the Tenements and Lands, belonging to the Hospital of St. John's in Lichfield'). Machon paid £16 12s. 7d. a year in reserved rents; the only other lessee of property on this scale was Sir Thos. Smith, now restored to his lease of Burton rectory, for which he paid £13 6s. 8d. a year.

almsmen.[90] Machon, however, seems to have carried out at least some repairs to the hospital buildings: in 1668 he claimed to have spent £40 and more on repairing the hospital chapel.[91]

The hospital was again visited by Bishop Hacket in 1668 and by Bishop Wood's vicar general in 1687.[92] In 1690–1 it was included with other hospitals in a royal commission of visitation,[93] and Bishop Lloyd visited it in 1696.[94] The frequency of visitation at this time may have been due to the tendency of the masters to treat the hospital as their personal, and even family, property. Thus in 1668 John Machon petitioned the Crown to be allowed to resign the mastership in favour of his son.[95] A few years later, in 1675, Francis Ashenhurst used the property of the former hospital at Denhall, the hospital's most valuable estate, as part of his future wife's jointure.[96] Bishop Lloyd's visitation followed complaints that one of the almsmen had recently died 'in want of necessaries for his body and . . . spiritual advice and assistance in the time of his sickness' and that the almsmen's pensions were paid by the bailiff in clipped money. The visitor made detailed regulations for the payment of the almsmen by the bailiff, including compensation for their past losses; for the repair, furnishing, and regular inspection of their lodgings; for the supply and laundering of their clothes; and for the duties of the chaplain and the statutory prayers in the hospital.[97]

Little is known of the hospital during the 18th century. Three of its masters during this time were more than locally notable: Edward Maynard (1719–1740) and Edmund Bateman (1740–51) as scholars,[98] and Sneyd Davies (1751–69) as a man of letters well-connected with the political and ecclesiastical establishment.[99] All but one of the masters[1] either held prebends in the cathedral at the time of their collation or later came to do so.[2] The hospital chapel remained a place of public worship, and in 1717 it was used by the parishioners of St. Mary's while their church was being rebuilt; the chapel was fitted up with seats moved there from St.

Mary's and the parishioners paid for the glazing of some of the windows.[3]

In 1786 the reserved rents from the hospital lands amounted to £129 4s. 10d.;[4] by 1821 they were £177 1s. 6d. These rents, however, did not represent the whole income of the hospital; between 1804 and 1821 fines for entry on leases brought the average annual income to £355 1s. 6d.[5] In 1821 the Charity Commissioners stated that the master's 'annual payments to the eleemosynary part of the foundation'[6] exhausted the whole income derived from reserved rents. When deducted from the average annual income these payments and various other small charges[7] left the master with slightly less than £160 a year. Out of this he had to repair the buildings, which were 'old and of very considerable extent'.[8] The Charity Commissioners' findings echo Egerton's complaint, made in 1519; the hospital's ability to meet any considerable casual expenditure had not materially improved in the intervening three centuries.

In 1786 each of the almsmen received from the hospital 2s. 6d. a week for maintenance, 10s. 6d. a year for coal, 1s. a year pocket money, and a gown from the master every 4 years.[9] Their income at this time was still augmented by various independent charities founded two centuries or so earlier.[10] By 1821 each almsman received from the hospital 3s. 6d. a week for maintenance and 1s. a year pocket money, while expenditure on coal had risen by about half of the 1786 figure; the master also supplied them with furniture and cloaks when necessary. The Charity Commissioners contrasted this expenditure with the almsmen's strict entitlement of 7d. a week each.[11] Payments from independent charities raised the weekly income of the almsmen in 1821 to about 4s. 6d.[12]

The antiquated practice of granting long leases of the hospital's estates for low rents and large entry fines persisted throughout the earlier 19th century.[13] The chief disadvantage of this system of leasing, the confusion of capital with income, may nevertheless have been avoided by the masters during this period,

[90] Ibid. (visitation act 23 Oct. 1662, signed by Bp. Hacket and Wm. Pargiter, gent., deputy master). One of the expelled almsmen was married and did not live in the hospital. A set of draft acts survives among the records of this visitation; it includes measures to abolish superstitious prayers (i.e. to the Blessed Virgin Mary and for the dead) and to increase the bishop's power to supervise the granting of leases and the bailiff's payment of the almsmen.

[91] *Cal. S.P. Dom.* 1668–9, 91.

[92] Harwood, *Lichfield*, 550; Lich. Dioc. Regy., St. John's Hosp. records.

[93] *Cal. S.P. Dom.* 1690–1, 240. See also ibid. pp. 162, 473–4, 504. [94] See below.

[95] *Cal. S.P. Dom.* 1668–9, 64, 91. The petition was successful, and his son also succeeded him as Prebendary of Wellington: see below p. 287; Le Neve, *Fasti* (1854 edn.), i. 637. There is a short inaccurate notice of the Machons in *D.N.B. sub* Machin. See also *S.H.C.* vi(2), 48; 1915, 181, 182 n. 11, 219, 221 n. 7.

[96] S.R.O., D. 787/2.

[97] Harwood, *Lichfield*, 550–4; Lich. Dioc. Regy., St. John's Hosp. records (undated visitation acts of Bp. Lloyd).

[98] Maynard was the antiquary responsible for publishing the second edn. of Dugdale's *Hist. of St. Paul's Cathedral* in 1716: *D.N.B.* Bateman had the highest reputation as a tutor at Oxford when the young Samuel Johnson went up in 1728: Reade, *Johnsonian Gleanings*, v (1928), 13, 20; x (1946), 76.

[99] In 1762 Sir Chas. Pratt, who had recently left Newcastle's ministry to become Chief Justice of Common Pleas, wrote to Davies: 'If I regret anything, it is that I shall never now be able to promote you to the Reverend Bench of Bishops.' Davies owed his preferment to his friendship at Eton with Frederick Cornwallis, the future bishop. See G. Hardinge, *Biog. Memoirs of the Revd. Sneyd Davies, D.D.* (1817), 21, 178–9; *D.N.B. sub* Pratt.

[1] Theophilus Buckeridge (1769–1803).

[2] See below notes 80–83.

[3] Baylis, *Hosp. of St. John Baptist*, 24.

[4] *Abstract of Returns of Charitable Donations, 1786–8,* H.C. 511, p. 1160 (1816), xvi(2).

[5] *7th Rep. Com. Char.* H.C. 129, p. 389 (1822), x.

[6] These comprised the £151 16s. 4d. paid to, or spent on behalf of, the almsmen, £20 paid to the hospital chaplain, and £5 paid to the usher of the grammar school: ibid. 389, 391–2.

[7] e.g. the steward's salary, chief rents, and street levies.

[8] Ibid. 389.

[9] Jackson, *Hist. of the City and County of Lichfield,* p. 29 (2nd nos.); W.S.L., M. 849. The master also paid £6 a year to a matron to attend the almsmen and wash their linen.

[10] Jackson, *Lichfield*, 29 (2nd nos.).

[11] *7th Rep. Com. Char.* 389–90. Other payments on the almsmen's behalf included 17s. 4d. for their Christmas dinner, £2 for medical attendance, and £20 for the matron's salary and gratuity.

[12] Ibid. 390.

[13] White, *Dir. Staffs.* (1834; 1851). The practice had been abandoned by the feoffees of Dr. Milley's Hospital in 1809: see above p. 277.

when considerable sums seem to have been spent on improvements and alterations to the buildings. Edmund Outram (1804–21), who evidently devoted close attention to the leasing of the estates,[14] spent £1,200 on improvements to the master's house.[15] J. T. Law (1821–36), although he secured a number of leases of hospital property for himself,[16] did not put his own interests before those of the hospital: he evidently spent a considerable amount on the enlargement of the hospital chapel.[17] Nevertheless the system was a bad one: in the years 1840–55 entry fines brought the hospital's average annual income to just over £598, but reserved rents, the permanent income inherited by one master from his predecessor, amounted during these years to only £176 5s. 2d. a year — less than they had been in 1821.[18] In 1856 the Charity Commissioners set out their objections to the system, though in 1859 they agreed that its reform should be delayed until the end of the then master's incumbency. After George Buckeridge's death in 1863, however, no more long leases for low rents and large fines were granted.[19]

The immediate effect of the reform was to reduce the master's income: Buckeridge's two successors, P. H. Dod (1863–83) and John Allen (1883–6), had almost no income after they had met the statutory charges on the master.[20] It was apparent, however, that as the hospital estates came to be leased for economic rents the annual income would increase. Approaches were therefore made to the Charity Commissioners for a Scheme to govern the application of the expected increased income. A Scheme was eventually sealed in 1908 after lengthy negotiations between the commissioners, the bishop, and the master, D. R. Norman. The master, however, had refused to surrender any of his rights during his incumbency, and the Scheme did not come into effect until his resignation in 1925. Norman was thus the last master to govern the hospital and administer its estates under the statutes of 1495, retaining the surplus income after meeting the various charges on him. This surplus continued to grow: in 1899–1900 it was just over £250, and in 1903–4 just over £570. In 1904–6 the master's income, including the value of his house, averaged £650 a year, and in 1908 he was said to hold 'one of the most wealthy benefices' in Lichfield.[21] There was, however, some local criticism of Norman's administration of the hospital, particularly of the disparity between the master's income and the money devoted to the eleemosynary purposes of the foundation.[22] Moreover, despite his reputation as 'an admirable man of business,'[23] Norman was alleged by the hospital steward to have allowed some of the property to fall into a bad state of repair; the allegation led to the steward's dismissal by Norman and to a visitation of the hospital in 1910 by Bishop Legge; the master's rights were upheld by the bishop.[24]

The Charity Commissioners' Scheme of 1908 came into effect with Norman's resignation in 1925, but lapse of time and changes in the hospital's endowment made it necessary to revise the old Scheme and it was replaced by a new one in 1927. The most notable changes made in 1927 were the reduction of the number of almsmen from thirteen to twelve and the abolition of the Prebendary of Freeford's right to nominate one of them; otherwise the new Scheme embodied the provisions agreed in 1908.[25] The hospital is still administered under the 1927 Scheme.[26] The property of the hospital, its management, and the appointment of the almsmen is vested in a body of twelve trustees, of whom the Bishop of Lichfield is always one. The master is still appointed by the bishop, but his responsibilities are in effect limited to acting as chaplain to the almsmen.[27] Under the 1927 Scheme twelve almsmen, normally members of the Church of England, were to reside in the hospital.[28] As a result of extensions and alterations to the buildings in 1966–7,[29] however, the hospital now accommodates 17 resident almsmen.[30] Their accommodation, heating, lighting, and laundry and a certain minimum of furniture are supplied by the trustees. Although, under the Scheme, the trustees are allowed to grant pensions to the almsmen and to out-pensioners, no new pensions have been granted during recent years.[31]

Prayers for Bishops Clinton and Smith are said each morning (except Friday) in the hospital chapel,[32] and the almsmen are expected to attend these services. The chapel remains a place of public worship, and the master ministers to a regular congregation. During the last forty years or so the services have been of an Anglo-Catholic nature. At the present time there is a Sung Eucharist every

[14] Lich. Dioc. Regy., St. John's Hosp. records (letters of Ric. Congreve and his advisers and of Outram and the hospital steward, John Mott; dated chiefly 1817 and 1819).
[15] 7th Rep. Com. Char. 389.
[16] Lich. Dioc. Regy., St. John's Hosp. records (leases to the steward of the hospital, and the steward's declarations of the interest of Law and his heirs).
[17] See below p. 286.
[18] Lich. Dioc. Regy., St. John's Hosp. records (steward's annual accounts to the master 1840–55).
[19] Char. Com. files.
[20] H. Baylis, 'The Prebends in the Cathedral Church . . . of Lichfield', Trans. Lichfield Arch. & Hist. Soc. ii. 41; R. M. Grier, John Allen (1889), 340.
[21] Char. Com. files; supplement to The Daily Graphic, 21 Nov. 1908. In 1907, during negotiations about the Scheme, Norman offered to resign the mastership for £6,650, or 10 years' income, but this was unacceptable to the Charity Commissioners.
[22] Char. Com. files; A. D. Parker, A Sentimental Journey in and about the Ancient and Loyal City of Lichfield (Lichfield, 1925), 36.
[23] The phrase was Bishop Legge's in a letter to the Charity Commissioners (2 Nov. 1907) commenting on Norman's refusal to give up his right to administer the hospital property: Char. Com. files.

[24] Baylis, Hosp. of St. John Baptist, 28; Lich. Dioc. Regy., St. John's Hosp. records (records of this visitation). Norman may have been increasingly hampered by his great age: he became master in his 71st year and resigned in his 98th: Staffs. Advertiser, 23 May 1925, 13 June 1931.
[25] Char. Com. files.
[26] For the rest of this para. see Char. Com. Scheme, 28 Jan. 1927.
[27] He is also associated with the trustees in the appointment of the almsmen (inf. from Canon G. N. Strong, 1968) and ministers to a congregation attending public worship in the hospital chapel (see below).
[28] Other qualifications required of the almsmen are genuine need and normally at least 5 years' residence in the diocese prior to appointment.
[29] See below p. 286.
[30] Inf. from Canon Strong (1968).
[31] The hospital pensions are held to have been made obsolete by National Insurance retirement pensions: inf. from Canon Strong (1967).
[32] This para. is based on inf. from Canon Strong (1967 and 1968) and Prebendary H. Baylis (1967). See also Baylis, Hosp. of St. John Baptist, 29. Marriage and baptismal registers preserved in the hospital date from 1914 and 1941 respectively: inf. from Canon Strong (1968).

Sunday, and baptisms, weddings, and burial services are held in the chapel.

The chapel is the oldest of the hospital buildings now standing; it contains in its south wall a lancet window dating from the early or mid 13th century.[33] The infirmary hall of this period may have formed a westward extension of the chapel, divided from it only by a wooden screen; a long range of this type, consisting of a structurally undivided chapel and infirmary, would have occupied the north side of what is now the hospital quadrangle.[34] The existing chapel is of six bays and its plan was originally a plain rectangle without aisles. The south wall contains, in addition to the lancet, a square-headed window, probably of the late 14th century, and a large pointed window with Perpendicular tracery. Two other pointed windows, dating from the late 13th or the 14th century, have been rebuilt.[35] The north wall formerly had a similar assortment of windows, but these were destroyed when a north aisle of four bays was added.[36] The present chancel contains a north window (now blocked) and a five-light east window, both late-Gothic in style.

Extensive alterations were made to the chapel during the 19th century. A view of the hospital from the street, drawn in the 1790s, shows that the chapel then had a small bell-cote at its west end and a timber-framed east gable set behind an embattled parapet.[37] A north aisle, containing a gallery, was built in 1829 at the expense of the master, J. T. Law; at the same time the east gable appears to have been faced with stone.[38] Further alterations were made by Law's successor, George Buckeridge.[39] In 1870–1, during the mastership of P. H. Dod, a drastic restoration was carried out.[40] The roof was raised and a stone bell-cote containing one bell was placed above the east end of the north aisle. The gallery in the north aisle was removed, and the arcade was rebuilt in a more orthodox Gothic style. Medieval windows in the south wall of the chapel also appear to have been renewed. The chapel was reseated, and most of the 17th- and 18th-century fittings, which had included a three-decker pulpit, were cleared away.[41]

The main east range of the hospital, fronting on St. John Street, is two-storied and is built of red brick with sparse stone dressings. It has generally been accepted that this building dates from the refoundation of the hospital in 1495, although some of its features are typical of a slightly later period.[42] The range is divided by a cross-passage which is entered from the street by a stone doorway with a four-centred head. The thirteen almsmen and the chaplain, schoolmaster, and usher, who were all bound to reside in the hospital according to the 1495 statutes,[43] were presumably accommodated in this range. Their rooms, originally with windows looking into the street, were served by tall external chimneys which are among the most striking features of the hospital, forming an impressive row of eight buttress-like projections along the street frontage. In 1929 the greater part of this range, lying to the south of the cross-passage and containing six almsmen's rooms on each floor, was thoroughly restored and replanned: on both floors the corridors were moved to the east, or street, side and the reconstructed almsmen's rooms were given bay windows looking west. The range was also extended southwards, and modern sanitation was introduced.[44] In 1966–7 an ambitious scheme of modernization and enlargement was carried out. New ranges were built to enclose a quadrangle on its south and west sides. The former includes a covered entry from Birmingham Road, a common room, and accommodation for the matron. The west range provides flatlets for eight almsmen, each consisting of a bed-sitting-room, a kitchen, and a lavatory. When this building was completed in 1966,[45] alterations were begun to the original east range, to provide similar accommodation there for another nine almsmen. Each was allotted two of the old rooms, one of which was divided into a kitchen and a lavatory. The modernized range was ready for occupation at the end of 1967.[46]

The master's house has been so much altered that its original date is obscure, although there are indications that a medieval building occupied the site.[47] It is possible that the house was rebuilt on its present scale in the late 16th or early 17th century. At this period a long lease was held by members of the Weston family; two of them were men of some local importance who would doubtless have needed a substantial dwelling.[48] Internally there is still some late-Tudor panelling and a doorway with a four-centred head; mullioned and transomed windows and an east gable still survived at the end of the 18th century.[49] The house was altered by Edward Maynard, master from 1719 to 1740;[50] a

[33] The following account of the hospital's architecture has been written by Margaret Tomlinson.
[34] Baylis, *Hosp. of St. John Baptist*, 7. Traces of such a building are said to have been found in the cellars of the master's house, which now adjoins the chapel at its west end. For other examples of this arrangement see W. H. Godfrey, *The Eng. Almshouse* (1955), 20–41.
[35] For a view before late-19th-cent. alterations see W.S.L., Staffs. Views, v, p. 249a (drawing by J. Buckler, 1833).
[36] Shaw, *Staffs*. i, plate facing p. 320. For the building of the north aisle see below.
[37] Shaw, *Staffs*. i, plate facing p. 320.
[38] White, *Dir. Staffs*. (1834); see plate on facing page.
[39] White, *Dir. Staffs*. (1851).
[40] *P.O. Dir. Staffs.* (1872); tablet in chapel.
[41] Watercolours in the master's house show the pulpit and fittings before and after Law's alterations of 1829. See also Reade, *Johnsonian Gleanings*, iii (1922), 81 n.; *Country Life*, 3 Oct. 1957.
[42] See e.g. R. Churton, *Lives of Wm. Smyth . . . and Sir Ric. Sutton* (Oxford, 1800), 78, 84; Harwood, *Lichfield*,

542, 549, 554; *S.H.C.* 1950–1, 173. It may be significant that in 1519 the buildings were described as 'ruinous' (Lich. Dioc. Regy., B/V/1/1, p. 21), suggesting that no wholesale rebuilding had taken place before this date.
[43] See above p. 281.
[44] Inf. from Canon Strong (1968); Char. Com. files.
[45] *Express and Star*, 28 Apr. 1966. The new buildings, when completed, were dedicated by the Bishop of Lichfield and opened by Mr. Julian Snow, M.P.: copy of form of service (21 Oct. 1966) in W.S.L. Pamphs. *sub* Lichfield.
[46] *Express and Star*, 19 Dec. 1967; inf. from Canon Strong (1968). The work of 1966–7 was carried out under the direction of the London architects L. de Soissons, Peacock, Hodges, & Robertson.
[47] See above n. 34.
[48] See above p. 283 and n. 81. In 1607 Sir Simon Weston wrote from St. John's inviting the Earl of Salisbury to visit him in his 'poor habitation': S.P. 14/28/31.
[49] Shaw, *Staffs*. i, plate facing p. 320.
[50] Baylis, *Hosp. of St. John Baptist*, 24. In 1720 Maynard placed over the main entrance to the hospital an oval tablet surmounted by a cartouche of arms; its inscription commemorates the hospital's refoundation in 1495.

St. John's Hospital, Lichfield, in 1833

Dr. Milley's Hospital, Lichfield, in 1942

fine panelled room on the west side, the principal staircase, and other fittings are of his time. Alterations and additions were carried out by Edmund Outram, master from 1804 to 1821,[51] whose work completed the conversion of the exterior to its present Georgian form. In 1958 the house was reduced in size by the demolition of early-19th-century additions which had projected southwards into the quadrangle.[52]

PRIORS, MASTERS, OR WARDENS

Hugh of Derby, occurs 1255 and 1257.[53]

Nicholas, occurs 1259.[54]

William of Wychnor, resigned by March 1323.[55]

William of Repton, elected and collated 1323, resigned 1330.[56]

Richard del Hull, elected and collated 1330.[57]

William de Couton, occurs 1345, resigned by January 1352.[58]

Richard de Pecham, collated 1352.[59]

Richard de Wotton, collated 1388.[60]

Thomas Bradeley, resigned 1404.[61]

Thomas Seggesley, collated 1404, occurs 1424.[62]

Hugh Lache, occurs 1449, resigned by February 1455.[63]

Thomas Mason, collated 1455, resigned 1461.[64]

Master Thomas Eggecombe, B.Cn. & C.L., collated 1461, resigned 1474.[65]

Master Thomas Milley, collated 1474.[66]

William Smith, resigned 1494.[67]

Master Sampson Aleyn, B.C.L., collated 1494, died 1494.[68]

William Smith, M.A., collated 1494, resigned by January 1496.[69]

Master Hugh Oldham, B.Cn. & C.L., collated 1496, resigned by April 1498.[70]

Master Robert Frost, collated 1498, resigned by March 1508.[71]

Richard Egerton, M.A., collated 1508, died by March 1538.[72]

Master George Lee, LL.B., collated 1538, resigned by 1560.[73]

William Sale, M.A., presented 1560, probably deprived by 1587.[74]

Zachary Babington, D.C.L., probably master in 1587 and certainly in 1592 and 1613.[75]

Lewis Bayly, D.D., Bishop of Bangor, occurs 1621 and 1625.[76]

John Machon, M.A., collated 1632, resigned 1671.[77]

Thomas Machon, M.A., collated 1671, died by 1673.[78]

Francis Ashenhurst, M.A., collated 1673, died 1704.[79]

[51] 7th Rep. Com. Char. 389.

[52] Baylis, Hosp. of St. John Baptist, 25. These alterations were carried out under the direction of the Lichfield architects Gray & Ballinger.

[53] S.H.C. 1924, pp. 19, 320–1.

[54] Ibid. pp. 319–20.

[55] See above p. 280.

[56] Ibid.   [57] Ibid.

[58] S.H.C. xii(1), 38; Lich. Dioc. Regy., B/A/1/2, f. 190v. On resignation the bishop assigned him a pension of 20s. and Bourne's chantry in St. Mary's, Lichfield.

[59] Lich. Dioc. Regy., B/A/1/2, f. 190v.

[60] Ibid. /6, f. 33v. He was a member of the Lichfield Guild: Harwood, Lichfield, 400 (where his name is given as Wetton).

[61] B/A/1/7, f. 58.

[62] Ibid.; Harwood, Lichfield, 557; S.H.C. vi(2), 175. He was admitted to the Lichfield Guild in 1406: Harwood, Lichfield, 401.

[63] S.H.C. 1939, p. 103; B/A/1/11, f. 14v.

[64] B/A/1/11, f. 14v.; /12, f. 41. He exchanged the mastership with his successor for the rectory of Lambeth (Surr.). For other benefices held by Mason see Cal. Papal Regs. xi. 588. He was a member of the Lichfield Guild: Harwood, Lichfield, 404.

[65] B/A/1/12, ff. 41, 49. On resignation he was assigned a pension of 10 marks by Bp. Hales. He was commissary general to Bp. Carpenter of Worcester and held many benefices: A. B. Emden, Biog. Reg. of Univ. of Oxford to A.D. 1500, i. 631.

[66] B/A/1/12, f. 49. He was the bishop's registrar and refounder of the women's hospital in Bacon Street: see pp. 159, 276. He was a member of the Lichfield Guild: Harwood, Lichfield, 404.

[67] B/A/1/13, ff. 145v.–146.

[68] Ibid. See also Emden, Biog. Reg. Oxford, i. 23.

[69] B/A/1/13, ff. 146, 147. See also Emden, Biog. Reg. Oxford, iii. 1722, 1723.

[70] B/A/1/13, ff. 147, 210. See also D.N.B.; Emden, Biog. Reg. Oxford, ii. 1396–7.

[71] Harwood, Lichfield, 558; B/A/1/13, f. 210; /14, f. 26. He was chancellor to Arthur, Prince of Wales (Emden, Biog. Reg. Oxford, ii. 731–2), and presumably a non-resident master. In 1501 he was admitted to the Lichfield Guild: Harwood, Lichfield, 410.

[72] B/A/1/14, f. 26; ibid. f. 21 (2nd nos.). Egerton was also Prebendary of Whittington and Berkswich and a canon residentiary in the cathedral (see above p. 282 n. 53) and Master of St. John's Hospital, Stafford (see below p. 293); in 1535 he held 5 parish churches whose gross value was over £124 a year (Valor Eccl. (Rec. Com.), iii. 79, 103, 119, 120; v. 211). See also Emden, Biog. Reg. Oxford, i. 630.

[73] B/A/1/14, f. 21 (2nd nos.); /15, f. 30v. He was a pluralist and presumably a non-resident master: R. Simms, Bibliotheca Staffordiensis, 271; and see above p. 282 and n. 65.

[74] B/A/1/15, f. 30v. The evidence for Sale's deprivation is indirect. Bp. Overton and his chancellor, Babington, seem to have been his enemies, and in 1581 Sale alleged that Babington had boasted 'I will sift him out of his livings': B/V/1/13, 23 Sept. 1581. Sale probably did not reside in the master's house for in 1585 Bp. Overton, reporting Sale's alleged involvement with Ld. Paget to the Privy Council, said that 'he hath two houses to repair unto, one in the country, the other here in the Close': W.S.L., S. MS. 315. Sale died in 1588: G. P. Mander, Wolverhampton Antiquary, i. 65–69. See also J. C. Cox, Notes on the Churches of Derbs. iv. 429, 532; Cal. S.P. Dom. 1581–90, 292.

[75] D. & C. Lich., Chapter Act Bk. v, ff. 60–61v. In 1587 new premises were granted to feoffees for the use of the hospital grammar school; the first 2 feoffees named were Babington and John Bagshawe, then master of the school: Harwood, Lichfield, 497–8; P. Laithwaite, Short Hist. of Lichfield Grammar School (Lichfield, 1925), 25–26, 27. Babington is said to have died in 1613: J. Foster, Alumni Oxonienses . . . 1500–1714, i. 52. He was chancellor of the diocese: Shaw, Staffs. i. 300.

[76] D. & C. Lich., Chapter Act Bk. v, ff. 60–61v. On 21 Oct. 1625 Bayly, as master of the hospital, commissioned Dean Curll and others to receive the resignation of the master of the Lichfield grammar school and to appoint the new master: commission preserved in the master's house (1967). Bayly presumably kept the mastership, like the prebend of Colwich (Le Neve, Fasti (1854 edn.), i. 592), until his death on 26 Oct. 1631 (D.N.B.). See also Shaw, Staffs. i. 218–19; Notes and Queries, 7th ser., vi. 211.

[77] B/A/1/16, f. 86v. As the entry is incomplete the name of the person collated does not appear, but it was certainly John Machon: Harwood, Lichfield, 559; Lich. Dioc. Regy., B/A/4/18, [f. 90v.].

[78] Harwood, Lichfield, 559. See also above p. 284.

[79] Harwood, Lichfield, 559–60. He was also presented to the mastership by the Crown in 1689 and instituted in 1690 'ad corroborandum titulum suum': E 331/Coventry and Lichfield/24; Lich. Dioc. Regy., B/A/3/Lichfield, St. John's Hosp. He was a pluralist and evidently did not reside in the hospital: Simms, Bibliotheca Staffordiensis, 24; Reade, Johnsonian Gleanings, iii (1922), 88 n. See also J. Sleigh, Hist. of the Ancient Parish of Leek (2nd edn.), 111.

Thomas Goodwin, D.D., collated 1704, died 1719.[80]

Edward Maynard, D.D., collated 1719, died 1740.[81]

Edmund Bateman, D.D., collated 1740, died 1751.[82]

Sneyd Davies, D.D., collated 1751, died 1769.[83]

Theophilus Buckeridge, M.A., collated 1769, died 1803.[84]

Edmund Outram, D.D., collated 1804, died 1821.[85]

James Thomas Law, M.A., collated 1821, resigned 1836.[86]

George Buckeridge, M.A., collated 1836, died 1863.[87]

Philip Hayman Dod, M.A., collated 1863, died 1883.[88]

John Allen, M.A., collated 1883, died 1886.[89]

Charles Henry Bromby, D.D., collated 1887, resigned 1892.[90]

The Hon. Adelbert John Robert Anson, D.D., collated 1893, resigned 1898.[91]

Denham Rowe Norman, collated 1898, resigned 1925.[92]

Geoffrey Rowland Wynn Griffith, collated 1925, died 1926.[93]

Ronald Robert Wynn Griffith, B.A., collated 1926, died 1940.[94]

George Kenneth Morgan Green, collated 1940, died 1945.[95]

Reginald Norman Lawson, M.A., collated 1945, died 1956.[96]

Harry Baylis, M.A., collated 1956, resigned 1964.[97]

George Noel Strong, M.A., collated 1964.[98]

In 1257 the hospital possessed no common seal and Prior Hugh, with the assent of the brethren, was using his own seal for the hospital's business.[99] A common seal was, however, subsequently used during the Middle Ages. A suit brought against the master about 1539 turned on the question whether the hospital was a corporation of master and brethren with a common seal. The fullest evidence about the seal then in use came from Richard Walker, who had been schoolmaster in the hospital in the early 1530s. Walker said that there was no common seal but that a seal used by the master alone 'hath written about it *Sigillum Commune Hospitalis Sancti Johannis Lichfeld* as he remembereth'.[1] This seal, appropriate for the time when the hospital was a corporation of religious brethren, had evidently not been changed to accord with the alterations made to the hospital's constitution by Bishops Boulers and Smith.[2] It may perhaps be identified with a surviving brass matrix,[3] oval $2\frac{1}{4}$ by $1\frac{1}{4}$ in., depicting St. John the Baptist standing, a nimbus round his head, his right hand raised in blessing, and what appears to be a book under his left arm. The saint wears a long garment. In the field on each side of him are a lighted candle in a candlestick, the letter I, and a fleur-de-lis. Legend, lombardic:

SIGILLUM COMMUNE HOSPITII SANCTI IOHANNIS BAPTISTAE LICH'

A 16th-century brass matrix,[4] pointed oval $2\frac{7}{8}$ by $1\frac{1}{2}$ in., depicts St. John the Baptist standing, a nimbus above his head and his right hand raised in blessing; he wears a tunic tied with a corded belt ending in tassels. In the field on each side are a lighted candle in a candlestick, the letter I, and a fleur-de-lis. Legend, Roman and reversed:

SIGILLUM COMMUNE HOSP' SANCTI IOHANNIS BAPTISTAE LITCH'

[80] Harwood, *Lichfield*, 560. From 1704 he was also Archdeacon of Derby and held a prebend in the cathedral: Le Neve, *Fasti* (1854 edn.), i. 577, 590, 592, 605, 638.
[81] Harwood, *Lichfield*, 560; B/A/4/28, [f. 70v.]; *D.N.B.* He was precentor from 1700: Le Neve, *Fasti* (1854 edn.), i. 580. See also above n. 98.
[82] B/A/4/32, [f. 47v.]; Reade, *Johnsonian Gleanings*, v (1928), 13 and n. He also became cathedral chancellor in 1740 and had held a prebend in the cathedral since 1734. He was a son-in-law of Bp. Smalbroke. See also above n. 98.
[83] B/A/1/21, p. 16; Hardinge, *Sneyd Davies*, 229. He was Archdeacon of Derby from 1755 and also held a prebend in the cathedral at the time of his death: Le Neve, *Fasti* (1854 edn.), i. 577, 613. See also above n. 99.
[84] Harwood, *Lichfield*, 560, where the date of his collation should be 27 Feb. (B/A/1/22, p. 2). See also Erdeswick, *Staffs.* pp. lxvi–lxix.
[85] Harwood, *Lichfield*, 560; Sir R. F. Scott, *Admissions to the College of St. John the Evangelist in the Univ. of Cambridge*, iv. 406.
[86] B/A/1/29, p. 9; /30, p. 24. See also *D.N.B.*; Simms, *Bibliotheca Staffordiensis*, 269.
[87] B/A/1/30, p. 24; *Staffs. Advertiser*, 19 Dec. 1863. He was grandson to Theophilus Buckeridge: *Miscellanea Genealogica et Heraldica*, 4th ser., v. 355–6.
[88] Lich. Dioc. Regy., B/A/1/32, p. 249A; Baylis, *Hosp. of St. John Baptist*, 31; *Staffs. Advertiser*, 10 Feb. 1883.
[89] Baylis, *Hosp. of St. John Baptist*, 31; Grier, *John Allen*, 341, 359.
[90] Lich. Dioc. Regy., B/A/1/35, pp. 107, 205. He had been Bp. of Tasmania.
[91] Ibid. p. 325; /36, p. 380. He had been Bp. of Qu'Appelle (Saskatchewan, Canada): *Crockford* (1902).
[92] B/A/1/36, p. 170; /39, p. 249. He was Rector of St. Mary's, Stafford, from 1875 to 1898: *Staffs. Advertiser*, 13 June 1931.
[93] B/A/1/39, p. 293; *Lich. Dioc. Mag.* (1926), 119. He

was Vicar of St. Michael's, Tividale, from 1889 to 1925: *Staffs. Advertiser*, 10 Apr. 1926; *Lich. Dioc. Ch. Cal.* (1925), 64.
[94] B/A/1/39, p. 320; /41, pp. 18–19; J. Foster, *Alumni Oxonienses . . . 1715–1886*, ii. 570. He was Vicar of St. Andrew's, Walsall, from 1889 to 1926: *Staffs. Advertiser*, 3 Feb. 1940; *Lich. Dioc. Ch. Cal.* (1926), 74. He was brother to his predecessor: *Lich. Dioc. Mag.* (1940), 47.
[95] B/A/1/41, pp. 18–19; *Lich. Dioc. Mag.* (1945), 18. He was Vicar of Albrighton (Salop.) from 1927 to 1940.
[96] B/A/1/41, p. 190; *Lich. Dioc. Mag.* (1956), 25–26. He was Rector of Cheadle from 1941 to 1945 and had served in the diocese since 1915.
[97] B/A/1/42, pp. 103, 354. He was Vicar of Wednesfield from 1942 to 1956: *Lich. Dioc. Dir.* (1955–6), 68.
[98] B/A/1/42, p. 354. He was Vicar of Hoar Cross from 1944 to 1964: *Lich. Dioc. Dir.* (1964), 55.
[99] *S.H.C.* 1924, pp. 320–1.
[1] Sta. Cha. 2/34/143, m. 2. Walker's evidence about the legend was corroborated by Dr. David Pole, the bishop's chancellor: ibid. m. 3. Thos. Pillyn gave evidence that a seal 'having the print of the picture of St. John with a letter on either side the same picture' had been used by successive masters since at least 1457 and was still in use in 1538: ibid. m. 9.
[2] See above pp. 280–1. According to Pillyn and another witness, Walker had stated that 'the same manner of seal' as that used by Egerton 'had been used sith King Henry's days the Second': Sta. Cha. 2/34/143, mm. 7, 9d. This statement cannot have been literally true but probably indicates long usage.
[3] In Lichfield City Mus. An impression from this matrix is illustrated in Baylis, *Hosp. of St. John Baptist*, 27. The matrix was still in use in 1861: W.S.L. 51/11/46, no. 9.
[4] Among W.S.L. Seals. An impression from this matrix survives in the Brit. Mus.: W. de G. Birch, *Cat. of Seals in B.M.* i, p. 627.

A 17th-century ivory matrix[5] is a pointed oval 2 by 1¼ in. It depicts St. John the Baptist standing in left profile between two candles in candlesticks and the letters I B. Legend:

SIGILLUM COMMUNE HOSP' SANCTI
IOHANNIS BAPTISTAE EXTRA BARRAS LICH'

27. THE HOSPITAL OR HOSPITALS OF NEWCASTLE-UNDER-LYME

By 1266 there was a hospital 'without' Newcastle-under-Lyme dedicated to St. John the Baptist: in that year the master and brethren were granted protection for three years by the Crown. The subsequent history of the hospital is obscure, but it may perhaps be identified with the Hospital of St. John situated on the outskirts of Newcastle in 1409.[1]

This hospital, in the patronage of the Duchy of Lancaster during the 15th and 16th centuries, had probably ceased to serve any eleemosynary purpose before the beginning of the 15th century, perhaps because it was too poorly endowed. An attempt at reform may have been contemplated by the patron when it was granted to Thomas Chamberlayn in 1409: he was given the hospital during pleasure only and apparently on condition that he observed all the eleemosynary obligations 'according to the first foundation'. In fact it is unlikely that any permanent reform was made for Chamberlayn's successors were all granted the hospital for life and they probably enjoyed the whole of its endowment. Nevertheless the hospital's income may be regarded as having afforded some charitable relief while it was enjoyed by Chamberlayn's immediate successor John Ryder. Ryder, probably a retired servant of the royal household, had been disabled in the French wars of Henry V and Henry VI and was unable to support himself.[2] Little is known of Ryder's successors save that at least two of them were members of the royal household. In 1485 Henry VII gave the hospital for life to John, the son of Henry Badeley, in consideration of his father's good and faithful service.[3]

There was considerable uncertainty about the correct dedication of the hospital in the 15th century. In 1409 it was said to be dedicated to St. John, and in 1437 to St. Louis. St. John the Baptist and St. Louis were given as alternative dedications in 1454, 1459, and 1460. In 1479 St. John the Baptist and St. Eloy were alternative dedications, but St. Eloy was given as the sole dedication in 1485 and 1546. The hospital was referred to as the Hospital of St. Leo in 1485, 1516, and 1551.[4]

The chantry commissioners of 1546 reported that the rent of certain lands let for £2 13s. 4d. a year was paid to a priest called the Master of the Hospital of St. Eloy. The incumbent did not know the name of the founder or the purpose of the foundation.[5] It appears that the hospital was not formally suppressed under the Act of 1547,[6] for in 1551 Edward VI granted it to Richard Smith to hold for life after the death of John Badeley.[7] Before the end of the century, however, the hospital was evidently held to have been suppressed, for in 1590 it formed part of a large royal grant of former ecclesiastical property to William Tipper and Robert Dawe.[8]

The hospital seems to have been situated in the present Newcastle Lane within the ancient parish of Stoke-upon-Trent just over half a mile from the Newcastle borough boundary.[9]

Wardens or Masters

Thomas Chamberlayn, appointed 1409, died 1437.[10]

John Ryder, appointed 1437.[11]

John Crecy, appointed 1454, resigned 1459.[12]

Master John Carpenter, appointed 1459.[13]

Nicholas Morley, appointed 1460, occurs 1464.[14]

Thomas Goship, died 1479.[15]

Thomas Newark, appointed 1479.[16]

John Badeley, appointed 1485, resigned 1516.[17]

John Badeley the younger, appointed 1516, occurs 1551.[18]

Richard Smith, appointed in reversion 1551.[19]

No seal is known.

28. THE HOSPITAL OF ST. LAZARUS OR THE HOLY SEPULCHRE, RADFORD

By the mid 13th century there was a leper hospital at Radford, about 1¼ mile south-east of Stafford.[1] The dedication is variously given as to St. Lazarus and to the Holy Sepulchre. It was probably founded by a member of the Stafford family, for by the end of the century the patronage belonged to Edmund de Stafford.[2]

---

[5] A. B. Tonnochy, *Cat. of Brit. Seal-Dies in B.M.* pp. 179–80 and plate XXIV.

[1] *Cal. Pat.* 1258–66, 648; D.L. 42/16, f. 98.

[2] D.L. 42/16, f. 98; /18, f. 100; and see below notes 12–19 and authorities there cited.

[3] See below notes 16, 17, and 19 and authorities there cited.

[4] The dedications are taken from the appointments of the wardens among the Duchy patents (cited below in notes 10–19), from *Rot. Parl.* (Rec. Com.), vi. 374, and from *S.H.C.* 1915, 250. Dedications of hospitals were often uncertain: Rotha M. Clay, *The Mediaeval Hospitals of Eng.* 269–70.

[5] *S.H.C.* 1915, 250; Clay, *Mediaeval Hospitals of Eng.* 225.

[6] 1 Edw. VI, c. 14.   [7] See below.

[8] *V.C.H. Staffs.* viii. 188.   [9] Ibid. 175, 188.

[10] D.L. 42/16, f. 98; /18, f. 100.

[11] Ibid. /18, f. 100. Ryder is probably to be identified with the king's esquire who received a grant in 1413 (*Cal. Pat.* 1413–16, 97), and with the sergeant of the poultry who crossed to France with the royal household in 1415 (J. H.

Wylie, *Reign of Henry V*, ii. 31 and n. 7) and was still alive in 1427–8 (*Rot. Parl.* iv. 325).

[12] D.L. 37/59, nos. 128, 163. In 1458 he was granted the hospital or free chapel of St. John the Baptist, Hungerford (Berks.): R. Somerville, 'Duchy of Lancaster Presentations, 1399–1485', *Bull. Inst. Hist. Res.* xviii. 71.

[13] D.L. 37/59, no. 163.

[14] Ibid. no. 172; /60, m. 4.

[15] D.L. 42/19, f. 135.

[16] Ibid. He was one of the clerks of the king's chapel.

[17] Ibid. /21, f. 109; /22, f. 229. In 1485 his title to the hospital was exempted from the provisions of Henry VII's Act of Resumption: *Rot. Parl.* vi. 374.

[18] D.L. 42/22, f. 229; /23, f. IV.

[19] Ibid. /23, f. IV. He was one of the yeomen of the king's guard.

[1] *S.H.C.* iv(1), 246–7; *S.H.C.* 1911, 269, 271. Radford lies on the Stafford-Lichfield road where it crosses the Penk; the river here forms the boundary between the ancient parishes of Baswich and Castle Church: *V.C.H. Staffs.* v. 1, 2.

[2] See below.

Little is known of the hospital's endowments or privileges, which were evidently meagre. In 1255 Hugh de Doxey granted a moiety of two crofts in Silkmore (in Castle Church) to Walter, Master of the Hospital of St. Lazarus, Radford; this land was to be held in free alms for ever by Walter and his successors.[3] In 1258 the master and brethren of the Hospital of the Holy Sepulchre, Radford, received from the Crown a grant of protection for 5 years.[4]

By the end of the 13th century the hospital's endowments were evidently insufficient for the support of the warden and brethren. Edmund de Stafford, the patron, attempted to grant the hospital to the Trinitarian friars of Thelsford (Warws.), but his plan seems to have failed,[5] and the hospital probably continued independently for a few years at least. At some time before 1320 William of Madeley, 'Prior of the Hospital of Radford', exchanged a piece of marsh in Silkmore with Richard, son of John[6] de Wenlock, for a messuage in Forebridge. This exchange was confirmed in 1320 by Edmund de Stafford's widow, Margaret, and her second husband,[7] and in 1321 by Edmund's son Ralph.[8]

Nothing more of the hospital's history is known, and its site has not been identified.[9] There is, however, some slight evidence to suggest that it was refounded in the mid 14th century on a new site and with a new dedication.[10]

MASTERS, WARDENS, OR PRIORS

Walter, occurs 1255.[11]

William of Madeley, occurs at some time before 1320.[12]

No seal is known.

29. THE HOSPITAL OF ST. JOHN THE BAPTIST, FOREBRIDGE, STAFFORD

THE hospital of St. John the Baptist, Stafford, lay in Forebridge, a southern suburb of the town within Castle Church parish. It was probably founded by one of the Stafford family, to which the patronage belonged until the 16th century.[1] The hospital is first mentioned in 1208 when Hugh, son of Ralph, granted 40 acres of land in Castle Church to Eudes, Prior of the Hospital of St. John at Stafford. The hospital seems then to have been run by a religious brotherhood, for Hugh gave the land in return for the prayers of the prior and brethren.[2]

Other benefactions during the 13th century were evidently few and consisted for the most part of properties situated in Castle Church parish; none of these seems to have been of any great value and many were the subject of litigation.[3] It is thus not surprising that by the close of the 13th century poverty had almost brought the hospital to an end. In 1300 its endowments, together with those of the Hospital of the Holy Sepulchre, Radford,[4] were said to be worth only £5 a year, and the brethren and sisters of the two hospitals had apparently left because of the poverty of their houses. Edmund de Stafford, patron of both hospitals, wished to grant them to the Trinitarian friars of Thelsford (Warws.), probably because of that order's special responsibilities towards the poor.[5] A jury, summoned to an inquisition *ad quod damnum*, found that Edmund's proposal would be to the detriment only of the Prior of St. John's and the Warden of St. Sepulchre's. There seems, however, to have been some resistance to the plan. The first sign of this is probably to be seen in the holding of a second inquisition in 1301. It was then found that the prior and warden had not been bound to keep hospitality but had done so only of their own free will, and that they had in fact been driven from their houses by poverty.

The findings of the second inquisition were doubtless convenient for the patron's plans, and St. John's Hospital seems for a time to have been subjected to the friars of Thelsford. In 1304 John de Haseleye, claiming to be master of the hospital, sued Edmund de Stafford and Brother Simon of Thelsford[6] among others for disseising him of a messuage, a carucate of land, and 40s. rent in the suburb of Stafford. Edmund, however, claimed that John had been deposed from the mastership by the ordinary and one Richard had then been admitted at his presentation; Richard too had been deposed and Roger was now master. A jury found that John had never been master and fined him for a false claim.[7] How long the hospital remained subject to Thelsford, however, is not known. The assessment of the Prior of St. John's, Forebridge, for the subsidy of 1327[8] and an assize of novel disseisin

---

[3] *S.H.C.* iv(1), 246–7; viii(2), 99–100.
[4] *Cal. Pat.* 1247–58, 653.
[5] See following article.
[6] Not Thomas as stated in *V.C.H. Staffs.* v. 93, 94.
[7] S.R.O., D.(W.) 1721/1/1, f. 131v. This exchange is incorrectly stated in *V.C.H. Staffs.* v. 93, to have been between Prior William on the one hand and Margaret and her second husband on the other.
[8] S.R.O., D.(W.) 1721/1/1, f. 131v.
[9] L. Lambert, *The Medieval Hospitals of Stafford* (Manchester, n.d.), 10, suggests that the hospital stood at the S.E. corner of the English Electric Co.'s main works, in the angle formed by Lichfield Rd. and the railway, but the source quoted (*S.H.C.* viii(2), 32) gives no support to this. *S.H.C.* viii(2), 114 n. 1, suggests that the hospital stood near the site of the later Hospital of St. Leonard, Forebridge (see below p. 294); 'Radford', however, suggests a site near the Penk.
[10] See below p. 294.
[11] See above.
[12] See above.
[1] See below and p. 291.

[2] *S.H.C.* iii(1), 172–3.
[3] Ibid. iv(1), 111, 240–1; vi(1), 129; vii(1), 27; W.S.L., S.MS. 328(i), p. 561; 332(i), pp. 433, 493, 498; 332(ii), pp. 73, 292. All these properties, which were situated in Rickerscote, Forebridge, and Rowley (in Castle Church), were the subject of litigation. The hospital was also involved in a lawsuit about common of pasture in Dunston (in Penkridge): *S.H.C.* vi(1), 52, 53. A proposed grant to the hospital of land in Maer (*S.H.C.* 1911, 188–9) seems to have been abortive as no later evidence of hospital property there has been found.
[4] For the rest of this para. see *S.H.C.* 1911, 269, 270–1. For the Hospital of the Holy Sepulchre see above.
[5] Rotha M. Clay, *Mediaeval Hospitals of Eng.* 210–11; D. Knowles and R. N. Hadcock, *Medieval Religious Houses: Eng. and Wales*, 180. It was not unusual for a hospital which had fallen on evil times to be managed by, or granted to, a monastic house: Clay, op. cit. 205, 215, 221.
[6] Probably then Prior of Thelsford: *V.C.H. Warws.* ii. 108.
[7] *S.H.C.* vii(1), 121.
[8] Ibid. 244.

brought against the prior in 1343–4[9] suggest that the house was again independent. A confirmation of the possessions of Thelsford Priory, granted by the Crown in 1329, makes no mention of any Staffordshire property.[10]

In 1352 Ralph, Earl of Stafford, was licensed by the Crown to grant to the master and brethren of the hospital rents in Stafford to the value of £5 for the support of a chaplain who was to celebrate daily in the hospital chapel.[11] The earl's son-in-law, Sir John de Ferrers, seems to have granted the hospital two messuages in Stafford.[12] In 1438–9 Humphrey, Earl of Buckingham, gave the hospital arable land in the Green Field near Rowley and the herbage of certain land near Stafford Pool in exchange for rents and other land.[13] The obit in St. Mary's, Stafford, founded in 1469–70 by William Moore, William Dentith (then master of the hospital), and John Cradock, may have been appropriated to the mastership of St. John's Hospital from its foundation.[14]

In the later 15th century the hospital, though poorly endowed, was still an effective eleemosynary foundation.[15] During Dentith's mastership three almsmen (one of them with his wife) were lodged in the hospital and fed every day from the master's table. Dentith himself supplemented the slender revenues of the hospital by collecting alms: many years later his former servant reported that he 'did use commonly, when gentlemen came to the town, to go to them and gather their alms for the . . . poor people'. The almspeople had their own seats in the chapel, every seat having 'a great pair of beads hanging'. The chapel, however, was not used only by the almspeople but evidently by the public also, for christenings and burials took place there. Mass was said daily during the masterships of Dentith and Colwich.

During the minority (1483–99) of Edward, Duke of Buckingham, the mastership of the hospital was bestowed by the Crown on pluralists and absentees,[16] and it was probably during these years that its revenues ceased to be used for the poor.[17] This was certainly the state of affairs during the mastership of Richard Egerton, who was appointed by Buckingham.[18] Egerton was an absentee,[19] and in 1511 he

leased the hospital and its revenues to his nephew and niece, Randle Egerton of Betley and Ellen Bassett of Lichfield, for £6 13s. 4d. a year.[20] The public services, however, seem to have been maintained, presumably because they were a source of profit:[21] in the 1530s there were many burials at the hospital, and Egerton paid a friar 4 nobles (£1 6s. 8d.) a year to sing mass there once a week.[22]

In 1535 the patron, Lord Stafford, sued Egerton for misusing the hospital 'contrary to the foundation'.[23] Stafford alleged that the hospital chapel was in ruins, with only the walls still standing, and that the graveyard had been ruined by swine. He also stated that the master's house, 'which I think cost 200 marks', was so decayed 'that I know no man of any reputation that will dwell therein'; the houses where the almspeople had once been lodged were occupied by 'very unthrifty persons which may not be suffered to dwell in other places'. Finally Stafford complained about Egerton's non-residence. On the same day that his bill was presented in Chancery, Stafford wrote to Cromwell[24] asking him to use his influence to secure 'some speedy reformation' of the hospital. These allegations seem well founded: a carpenter and a tiler, appointed to survey the buildings of the hospital, certified that £40 'would not re-edify it in such condition as it was in Colwich's days'. The result of the suit is not known, but it seems probable that some repairs were carried out, and some decree may have been made concerning the finances and charitable responsibilities of the hospital.[25]

On Buckingham's attainder in 1521 the patronage of the hospital passed to the Crown.[26] By 1524 it had been restored to Buckingham's son, Henry (later Lord Stafford), who in that year granted the next presentation to Mary, Queen Dowager of France, and her husband Charles, Duke of Suffolk.[27] The grant was possibly an attempt by Stafford to secure political goodwill in influential circles. This motive seems likely to have inspired a later grant made to Thomas Wriothesley and two others,[28] for Wriothesley, who was on friendly terms with Lord Stafford,[29] was a channel of communication with Cromwell.[30] Wriothesley's son William succeeded

[9] W.S.L., S.MS. 332(iv), p. 15.
[10] Dugdale, *Mon.* vi(3), 1564–5.
[11] *Cal. Pat.* 1350–4, 256. The grant may have been, in part at least, an exchange: S.R.O., D.(W.) 1810, f. 88v.; see above p. 273. In the 16th cent. Earl Ralph was reputed the founder of the hospital: *S.H.C.* 1915, 236.
[12] *S.H.C.* xiii. 79.
[13] S.R.O., D.(W.) 1721/1/2, *sub* Forebridge.
[14] W.S.L., S.MS. 369, p. 98; see below p. 293.
[15] For this para. see S.R.O., D.(W.) 1810, ff. 87v.–88v.
[16] See below notes 74, 76, 77.
[17] Menwaryng's mastership is mentioned in S.R.O., D.(W.) 1810, f. 88, but there is no evidence that during his time almspeople continued to be maintained as they were during Dentith's and Colwich's masterships.
[18] *L. & P. Hen. VIII*, viii, pp. 40–41.
[19] He lived in the Close at Lichfield: ibid.; S.R.O., D.(W.) 1810, f. 87v.
[20] *S.H.C.* 1939, p. 117. For his nephew and niece see G. Ormerod, *Hist. of County Palatine and City of Chester* (1882 edn.), ii. 628, 692; *Staffs. Pedigrees, 1664–1700* (Harleian Soc. lxiii), 80–81.
[21] Egerton's lease of the hospital to his nephew and niece included 'the chapel and chief mese place thereunto belonging with all tithes, offerings, meses, profits and advantages': *S.H.C.* 1939, p. 117.
[22] *L. & P. Hen. VIII*, viii, pp. 40–41; S.R.O., D.(W.) 1810, f. 87v.

[23] For this para., except where otherwise stated, see S.R.O., D.(W.) 1810, ff. 87v.–88v.
[24] S.P. 1/89, pp. 104–5.
[25] See below n. 41. The hospital buildings seem to have been repaired for in 1548 Ric. Forsett, surveyor of crown lands and church ornaments in Staffs., reported to the Court of Augmentations that the master's house, with the adjoining chapel, 'is the metest place for to be reserved for the keeping of the king's evidences of the said county': S.C. 12/28/12, f. 33v.; A. F. Leach, *Eng. Schools at the Reformation 1546–8*, pt. ii, 212; *S.H.C.* 1917–18, 324.
[26] *S.H.C.* viii(2), 113. It was then described as a donative, i.e. a benefice which the patron may bestow without presentation to, or investment by, the ordinary. St. John's Hospital was in fact subject to the ordinary jurisdiction of the Dean of St. Mary's, Stafford: S.R.O., D.(W.) 1810, ff. 88v.–89, 89v.; and see above p. 290 and below n. 42.
[27] S.R.O., D.(W.) 1721/1/1, f. 133.
[28] Ibid.
[29] Stafford's son, Henry, was educated in Lord Wriothesley's household until 1546: A. H. Anderson, 'The Books and Interests of Henry, Lord Stafford (1501–1563)', *The Library*, 5th ser. xxi(2), 92. Wriothesley's uncle, the Garter King of Arms, took a friendly interest in Stafford's antiquarian pursuits: A. H. Anderson, 'Henry, Lord Stafford (1501–1563) in Local and Central Govt.' *E.H.R.* lxxviii. 226 and n. 9.
[30] S.P. 7/1/56 and 57.

Egerton as master and like him seems to have been an absentee.[31]

In 1521 the hospital was valued at £10 a year.[32] In 1535 its annual income was £10 10s. a year; a fee of 10s. was paid to the bailiff, William Hethe, the rest of the income apparently being enjoyed by the master.[33] The chantry commissioners of 1546 gave the net income as £9 16s. 10d., of which £2 was paid to the master as his salary and £6 12s. 6d. was used for the poor. It seems likely, however, that the commissioners had been given a false account of the hospital's charitable activity rather than that Lord Stafford had secured any enduring reformation. In May 1548 the commissioners reported that the hospital possessed 5 ounces of plate, parcel gilt, ornaments worth 3s. 6d., and 2 bells in the chapel,[34] and that its net income was £10 0s. 2d. They also stated, however, that no poor had been maintained in the hospital for a long time. In June the commissioners reported that the whole of the net income, then given as £8 12s. 2d., was paid to the incumbent. Although the chantry commissioners considered that Stafford was one of the four towns in the county 'where most need is to have hospitals for relief of the poor', the hospital was suppressed at this time, the master receiving a pension of £6.[35]

In 1550 Edward VI granted the possessions of the suppressed hospital to the burgesses of Stafford as part of the endowment of a free grammar school.[36] This grant, however, seems to have been frustrated by Lord Stafford's attempts, temporarily successful, to revive the hospital of which he had been patron. Stafford was evidently supported in his efforts by the tenants of the former hospital lands, for in 1552 the burgesses sued William Tully and others,[37] whom they described as their tenants-at-will in the property of the former hospital. They alleged that for the 18 months since the royal grant the tenants had detained rents and profits to the clear yearly value of some £10, though they had paid these to the Crown after the hospital's suppression.[38] The tenants, however, maintained that the king had had seisin of the hospital property only 'by the unlawful exaction of His Majesty's officers and ministers', as foundations for the poor had been excepted from

dissolution by the Act of 1547.[39] The burgesses rested their case on the royal grant of 1550 and on their allegation that the hospital was not an eleemosynary foundation[40] but simply a free chapel for a priest to celebrate mass for the founder's soul and say divine service on holy days for the inhabitants of Forebridge. The burgesses would admit only that three or four people had long been 'lodged in certain little cottages adjoining to the said chapel and had their lodgings there freely and were relieved of the charitable alms partly of the said priest and partly of the inhabitants of the said borough and of others resorting to the same and were not found of the revenues belonging to the said chapel'. They added that the chapel's annual income, although recently increased from £6 13s. 4d. to £9 4s. 10d.,[41] was plainly insufficient for the support of poor people in addition to a priest.

The burgesses were unsuccessful in their plea for in 1556 Thomas Chedulton was presented to the mastership of the hospital by Lord Stafford.[42] In 1560, however, Chedulton was deprived of the mastership,[43] and although he evidently maintained his claim to it for some years[44] this was the end of the hospital. At the same time the burgesses compensated Lord Stafford for his loss of the patronage by granting him the right to appoint the master of the grammar school.[45] A compromise also seems to have been reached over the lands of the former hospital; these were granted in fee to Lord Stafford by the burgesses for an annual rent of £9 14s.[46]

The master's house, and presumably the chapel which stood next to it, were still held of Lord Stafford by Thomas Chedulton in 1584.[47] He died in 1589,[48] but what was described as the Free Chapel of St. John the Baptist, with all its lands and tenements, had been granted by the Crown in the previous year to Edward Wymarke of London. In 1592 a similar grant was made to William Tipper and Robert Dawe. These grants were probably made simply in order to compel Lord Stafford to pay for the confirmation of his title to the property,[49] and in 1592 Stafford sold the chapel and its site to Richard Foxe, a Stafford gentleman.[50] By 1611 the house and chapel, with some other properties

[31] In the 1548 chantry certificate it was stated: 'William Wryothesley son to th'erle of South't incombent, but it is doubted whether he be lyvyng or not'. A later note adds: 'he did appere in person before the Commissioners — pens' vj li.' See E 301/44, f. 7v. *Complete Peerage*, xii(1), 126, states that Southampton's only son to survive infancy was named Henry.

[32] *S.H.C.* viii(2), 113.

[33] *Valor Eccl.* (Rec. Com.), iii. 119.

[34] *S.H.C.* 1915, 236. By 1552 the chalice, vestments, and other ornaments of the chapel had been removed by the surveyor, Ric. Forsett, though the bells were still there: *S.H.C.* N.S. vi(i), 175.

[35] *S.H.C.* 1915, 237, 238 n. 7; see above p. 136.

[36] *Cal. Pat.* 1550–3, 21; C. G. Gilmore, *Hist. of King Edw. VI School, Stafford*, 14, 124.

[37] C 1/1268/58–63. The date is about 18 months after the royal grant of Dec. 1550: ibid. /58.

[38] Ibid. /58.

[39] Ibid. /62. There was some justification for this plea: see *Stat. Realm*, iv(1), 27–28. Tully denied having paid rents to the Crown: C 1/1268/63.

[40] For the rest of this para. see C 1/1268/63.

[41] This suggests that some reform of the hospital and its finances was made as a result of Lord Stafford's Chancery suit against Egerton, while the figures here quoted suggest that the reform included cancellation of Egerton's lease to his nephew and niece (see above p. 291).

[42] Lich. Dioc. Regy., B/A/1/15, f. 13v. The hospital was

said to be vacant 'per deprivationem Willelmi Wrythesley ultimi magistri . . . eiusdem'. Chedulton was admitted to the mastership by the bishop's vicar general, the peculiar jurisdiction of St. Mary's, Stafford, having lapsed to the bishop by this date (see below p. 308).

[43] *S.H.C.* 1915, 237, 245 n. 10.

[44] In 1563 he leased to Wm. Tully a pasture called Mynours Grove Field in Forebridge, which had belonged to the hospital. By so doing he evidently ignored the lease of the property which Thos. Chambers had had since at least 1550 (*Cal. Pat.* 1550–3, 21), and probably since Egerton's mastership: *S.H.C.* 1938, 122.

[45] Gilmore, *King Edw. VI School*, 125. This right was sold back to the burgesses in 1596 by Edw., Lord Stafford: ibid. 126; W.S.L. 77/45, f. 123.

[46] W.S.L. 77/45, folio facing f. 1. The rent represented the gross value of the hospital lands in 1548: S.C. 12/28/12, f. 33. He is said to have sold the lands soon afterwards: W. Keen, *Letter to the Inhabitants of Stafford* (Stafford, 1808), 28–29; W.S.L. 77/45, f. 1. In 1584, however, Edw., Lord Stafford, was drawing rents from the property; these may possibly have been rents reserved to the grammar school with, in some cases, small increments: S.R.O., D.641/2/E/1/1; W.S.L. 77/45, ff. 2–3v.; B. M., Hargrave MS. 288, f. 25.

[47] S.R.O., D.641/2/E/1/1.   [48] *S.H.C.* 1915, 245 n. 10.

[49] *V.C.H. Staffs.* v. 91; *Augmentation Office Miscellaneous Books* (List and Index Soc. xvi), pp. 19–20.

[50] W.S.L., S.MS. 591.

formerly belonging to the hospital, had passed to the Cradock family.[51] In 1638 house and chapel were both still standing, being included in a sale of lands by George Cradock as 'one messuage . . . called St. John's House . . . and one chapel called St. John's Chapel'.[52]

The site of the hospital has been supposed to be that of the White Lion Inn at the junction of Lichfield Road and White Lion Street,[53] some 320 yards from the Green Bridge over the Sow. Leland, however, described the hospital as 'a free chapel on the Green at Stafford hard by Sow river'.[54] Leland's words, 15th-century descriptions of the site,[55] and a 17th-century rental of grammar-school lands[56] all suggest a site near the Green Bridge, on the west[57] side of the present Bridge Street and perhaps including the site of the present 'Grapes'.[58] The building shown on the seal of the hospital (see below) may be an approximate representation of the chapel as it was when the matrix was cut.

PRIORS OR MASTERS

Eudes, occurs 1208.[59]
William, occurs 1248.[60]
Peter, occurs 1270 and 1283.[61]
John de Haseleye, probably master 1295, deposed by 1296–7.[62]
Richard, deposed by 1296–7.[63]
Roger de Baggeworth, occurs 1296–7 and 1304.[64]
John, occurs 1352–3 and 1370.[65]
David Fissher, resigned 1397.[66]
William Marche, presented 1397.[67]

William Draper, resigned 1409.[68]
Elias of Woore, instituted 1409, died 1418.[69]
Robert Wright, collated 1419, occurs 1438–9.[70]
Simon, occurs 1442–3.[71]
William Dentith, presented 1459, occurs 1475–1476.[72]
Richard Colwich, died 1485.[73]
Master Edmund Chaderton, presented 1485.[74]
John Menwaryng, presented 1485, occurs 1497–1498.[75]
Master John Brown, presented 1486.[76]
Master John Denbye, resigned 1502.[77]
Richard Egerton, M.A., occurs 1511 and 1535.[78]
William Wriothesley, probably master in 1538, master at the suppression in 1548.[79]
Master Thomas Chedulton, presented 1556, deprived 1560.[80]

The seal of the hospital is circular with a diameter of $2\frac{1}{8}$ ins.[81] It depicts what is evidently a cruciform building of the 13th century. Above the door of the west front is a window of three lancets beneath a trefoil. What appears to be a low wall surrounds the church. Legend, lombardic:

SIGILLUM HOSPITALIS SANCTI IOHANNIS BAPTISTE DE STAFFORDIA

30. THE HOSPITAL OF ST. LEONARD, FOREBRIDGE, STAFFORD

THE hospital of St. Leonard, Forebridge, was in existence by 1386–7; it was then in the patronage of

[51] V.C.H. Staffs. v. 91.
[52] W.S.L. 74/50. It has been suggested that the chapel was still standing in 1686: A. L. P. Roxburgh, Stafford, 1.
[53] V.C.H. Staffs. v. 91. This tradition is based only on surviving fragments of an old stone building. It has, however, been incorporated in the Ordnance Survey maps: see e.g. O.S. Map 1/500, Staffs. XXXVII. 11. 23 (1881 edn.). See also W.S.L. 7/00/10.
[54] Leland, Itin. ed. L. Toulmin Smith, v. 21.
[55] e.g. iuxta muros Stafford' (S.R.O., D.(W.) 1810, f. 89); extra muros Stafford' (ibid. f. 89v.); iuxta pontem australem ville Staff' (S.R.O., D.(W.) 1721/1/2, sub Forebridge).
[56] Gilmore, King Edw. VI School, 131, which mentions the 'great house adjoining to St. John's chapel in Forebridge . . . with three cottages between the said chapel and the messuage of Thomas Withnall'. Withnall's messuage was described as 'in Forebridge within St. John's situate at the bridge end, with a croft on the backside thereof, lying in breadth between the highway on the south side and the river Sow on the north side.' The highway to the south of Withnall's messuage was presumably the road running south-west out of the borough through the Friars area of Forebridge, probably to Rowley Hall: J. Speed, Theatre of the Empire of Great Britaine (1614), map between pp. 69 and 70.
[57] S.R.O., D.(W.) 1721/1/9, f. 193, where it appears that 'St. John's corner' was on the west side of the highway leading south from Stafford.
[58] In 1929 'a quantity of human remains, including several complete skulls', was unearthed during excavations in a yard of the 'Grapes'. They were apparently found in 'a brick structure, which somewhat resembled a vault'; there were no coffins. See Staffs. Advertiser, 13 Apr. 1929. It is known that burials took place at the hospital: see above p. 291.
[59] S.H.C. iii(1), 172–3.
[60] Ibid. iv(1), 240–1.
[61] W.S.L., S.MS. 332 (i), p. 498; S.H.C. vi(1), 129.
[62] S.H.C. vii(1), 27, 121; S.MS. 332(ii), p. 292; see above p. 290.
[63] S.H.C. vii(1), 121; S.MS. 332 (ii), p. 292; see above p. 290.

[64] W.S.L., S.MS. 332 (ii), p. 292; S.H.C. vii(1), 121; see above p. 290.
[65] S.R.O., D.(W.) 1810, f. 88v.; S.H.C. xiii. 79.
[66] Cal. Pat. 1396–9, 59, 60, 62. Fissher exchanged the hospital with Wm. Marche for the church of Wentnor (Salop.).
[67] Ibid. Marche was presented by the Crown because of the minority of the patron, Edmund, Earl of Stafford.
[68] Lich. Dioc. Regy., B/A/1/7, f. 98. Draper exchanged the hospital with Elias of Woore for the rectory of Church Lawton (Ches.).
[69] Ibid.; S.R.O., D.(W.) 1810, f. 89.
[70] S.R.O., D.(W.) 1810, f. 89; D.(W.) 1721/1/2, sub Forebridge.
[71] S.R.O., D.(W.) 1810, f. 88v.   [72] Ibid.
[73] Cal. Pat. 1485–94, 7. He may be the Prior of St. Thomas's who resigned in 1478: see above p. 267.
[74] Cal. Pat. 1476–85, 525. Chaderton, who was chaplain, treasurer of the chamber, and councillor of Ric. III, was an absentee pluralist: A. B. Emden, Biog. Reg. of the Univ. of Oxford to A.D. 1500, i. 382–3.
[75] Cal. Pat. 1485–94, 5, 7; S.R.O., D. (W.) 1810, f. 88v. Chaderton's appointment by Ric. III was evidently ignored.
[76] Cal. Pat. 1485–94, 65, 115. He was a master in Chancery and is perhaps to be identified with the pluralist chancery clerk of that name mentioned in Emden, Biog. Reg. Oxford, i. 284. This appointment was evidently ineffective.
[77] S.R.O., D.(W.) 1721/1/1, f. 134, where he is described as 'egregius vir Magister Johannes Denbye'. He is possibly to be identified with the pluralist, John Denby, M.A. (Emden, Biog. Reg. Oxford, i. 567).
[78] S.H.C. 1939, p. 117; S.R.O., D.(W.) 1810, f. 87v.; and see above p. 291. Egerton was dead by Apr. 1538, but it is not known whether he retained the mastership till death.
[79] See previous note and above pp. 291–2.
[80] See above p. 292.
[81] The matrix was presented to the Soc. of Antiquaries of London in 1935. See V.C.H. Staffs. v. 91; Rotha M. Clay, Mediaeval Hospitals of Eng. 108; Downside Review, vii. 114–15.

the Stafford family.[1] In the 16th century it was believed that the hospital had been founded by Ralph, Earl of Stafford (d. 1372), for the maintenance of a priest and certain poor people.[2] It is possible that St. Leonard's Hospital was in fact a refoundation, for ordinary eleemosynary purposes, of the leper hospital at Radford. The hospital at Radford had been in the patronage of the Stafford family, but nothing is known of its history after the early years of the 14th century.[3]

The patronage of the hospital remained with the Stafford family until the attainder in 1521 of Edward, Duke of Buckingham, when it passed with the rest of the duke's possessions to the Crown.[4] Buckingham's son and heir, Henry, Lord Stafford, evidently recovered the patronage in 1531,[5] and he retained it until the hospital was suppressed in 1548.

In 1393 the hospital was said to be worth 10s. a year;[6] in 1521 it was mentioned in a survey of Buckingham's forfeited property as 'a donative called the Spitell' worth £5 a year.[7] The annual income of the master of the hospital in 1535 was £4 13s. 4d.[8] This income came from arable, meadow, and pasture held of the manor of Forebridge,[9] but it did not represent the true value of the rents deriving from these lands. The hospital and its property seem to have been leased out by 1538 for the lifetime of the master, to whom an annual income of £4 13s. 4d. was reserved.[10] In 1548 the chantry commissioners gave the gross value of the hospital's lands as £7 2s. a year, the net value being £6 19s. 10d.; it is evident, however, that the master's income was still only £4 13s. 4d. and that this was further reduced to £4 1s. 11d. a year by his assessment for the Crown's tenth and by rents due to the lord of Forebridge manor and the master of St. John's Hospital. The hospital possessed one bell at the end of the chapel but no plate or other goods in 1548.[11]

Nothing was paid to the poor in 1548, and the chantry commissioners reported that no poor had been relieved there 'these 20 years past'.[12] Although the commissioners considered that Stafford was one of the four towns in the county 'where most need is to have hospitals for relief of the poor',[13] the hospital was suppressed in 1548; the master, William Stafforton, was granted a pension of £4 1s. 11d. a year.[14] In 1550 the hospital lands were granted by the Crown to the burgesses of Stafford as part of the endowment of the grammar school.[15]

The hospital was situated one mile from Castle Church parish church, according to the chantry commissioners of 1548.[16] The site has not been precisely identified but is probably to the east of Lichfield Road between St. Leonard's Avenue and the railway.[17]

MASTERS OR WARDENS

Richard Caus, presented 1386–7, occurs 1398, died by 1422.[18]

Henry Blounte, appointed 1528.[19]

William Stafforton, occurs 1533, master at the dissolution in 1548.[20]

No seal is known.

31. THE HOSPITAL OF ST. JAMES, TAMWORTH

THE hospital of St. James, Tamworth, was founded by Sir Philip Marmion probably shortly before 1274 or 1275, for it was then reported that 'a religious house' had been newly built on land at Tamworth which Marmion had taken from the inhabitants.[1] In 1294 a jury stated that the land was part of John de Hastings's manor of Tamworth and that Marmion had built a hospital there and placed in it a master and brethren. The hospital was therefore presumably built between 1266, when Marmion was granted Henry de Hastings's demesnes at Wigginton and Tamworth,[2] and 1275. In the latter year Marmion was apparently making determined efforts to strengthen his title to Hastings's land,[3] probably in

[1] S.H.C. xvii. 41; Cal. Close, 1392–6, 48; 1402–5, 220.
[2] S.H.C. 1915, 237.
[3] See above p. 290. The hospitals at Radford and Forebridge were in the patronage of the same family and are not known to have existed contemporaneously. They are also connected by two other circumstances: St. Leonard's Hospital, Forebridge, owned land at Radford (see below n. 9), and its dedication may preserve a memory of the leper hospital at Radford, St. Leonard being the second most popular patron of English leper hospitals (Rotha M. Clay, The Mediaeval Hospitals of Eng. 252, 261).
[4] Complete Peerage, ii. 390–1; S.H.C. viii(2), 114.
[5] Stafford was granted back much of his father's property in Staffs. in 1522, but this did not include the manor of Forebridge to which the advowson of the hospital was probably appurtenant. Forebridge manor was granted back to Stafford in 1531: V.C.H. Staffs. v. 87. In 1528 the Crown appointed Hen. Blounte master of the hospital: see below. Lord Stafford was described as patron of the hospital in 1540: S.R.O., D.(W.) 1810, f. 108.
[6] Cal. Close, 1392–6, 48.   [7] S.H.C. viii(2), 114.
[8] Valor Eccl. (Rec. Com.), iii. 119.
[9] S.R.O., D.(W.) 1721/1/9, ff. 186–7. This survey of the manor of Forebridge is probably to be dated 1543. Among the lands held by the hospital at this date was Edmonds Furlong 'lying by Ratford bridge': ibid. ff. 181, 186.
[10] S.R.O., D.(W.) 1810, ff. 108–9.
[11] S.H.C. 1915, 237; ibid. viii(2), 95; S.C. 12/28/12, ff. 33v.–34.
[12] S.H.C. 1915, 237. If this period of 20 years is to be

[13] See above p. 136.   [14] S.H.C. 1915, 237, 238 n. 9.
[15] Cal. Pat. 1550–3, 21–22.
[16] S.H.C. 1915, 237.
[17] O.S. Map 1/2,500, Staffs. XXXVII. 15 (1881 edn.). The two sites there marked 'St. Leonard's Hospital' and 'Burial Ground' are described in W.S.L. 7/00/10; these archaeological notes, compiled in the later 19th cent. for the Ordnance Survey, give the reasons for connecting the sites with St. Leonard's Hospital. The site of the Burial Ground coincides with that suggested for the hospital in L. Lambert, The Medieval Hospitals of Stafford (Manchester, n.d.), 9–10. See also W.S.L., S. 630, f. 104v.
[18] S.H.C. xvii. 41; Reg. Edmund Stafford, ed. F. C. Hingeston-Randolph, 335.
[19] L. & P. Hen. VIII, iv(2), p. 1865.
[20] S.H.C. 1915, 237, 238 n. 9.
[1] Rot. Hund. (Rec. Com.), ii. 116; C. F. R. Palmer, Hist. of the Baronial Family of Marmion (Tamworth, 1875), 86. Thanks are due to Mr. P. Edden and Mr. J. Gould, both of Tamworth, for drawing the writer's attention to some of the sources used in this article.
[2] S.H.C. vi(1), 294; Cal. Pat. 1258–66, 642, 643. Hastings, having played a prominent part against Hen. III during the Barons' Wars, had forfeited his lands and been excluded from the provisions of the Dictum of Kenilworth: Palmer, Baronial Family of Marmion, 91–92; Cal. Inq. Misc. i, p. 105; D.N.B.
[3] Cal. Pat. 1272–81, 96, 120–1; S.H.C. vi(1), 294.

taken precisely it would indicate that the hospital ceased to be an effective charitable institution while it was in the patronage of the Crown.

order to convey a secure title to his new foundation.

In 1283 Marmion granted St. James's Hospital and its appurtenances to William de Crouebyrihal', chaplain;[4] he was to reside in the hospital and celebrate divine service there for the souls of the founder and his family and all the faithful departed. Marmion apparently added to the endowments of the hospital by including in his grant pasture in 'Asscheland' sufficient for four oxen and two horses. He retained the power to dismiss William from the hospital should he be found guilty of incontinence or of neglecting divine service there. In the event of William's dismissal or death his goods were to be retained for the use of the hospital.

It is evident that at the time of this grant Marmion was planning the foundation of a house of Premonstratensian canons at Tamworth, for William de Crouebyrihal' was to retain the hospital only until the canons of the new monastery were ready to take control of it.[5] The canons were then either to receive William as a canon or brother or else to provide him with the same food and clothing as a canon.[6] Marmion may have intended that the hospital itself should be the nucleus of his new Premonstratensian foundation[7] for in 1285 he was planning a considerable increase in its endowment for the maintenance of five chaplains there. It was, however, found that his proposed alienation would be to the detriment of the Crown, and this seems to have thwarted Marmion's purpose.[8]

Nothing more is heard of Marmion's proposed monastic foundation, and he died in 1291 without having carried his plans into effect. It is also unlikely that he succeeded in further endowing his hospital, for he was in debt during his later years.[9] In fact the master and brethren of his hospital left because of their poverty, and after their departure Marmion took its lands into his own hands and leased them out.[10]

St. James's Hospital nevertheless survived, though it remained poorly endowed — probably too poorly endowed to serve any eleemosynary purpose. The patronage evidently passed to the Frevilles and subsequently, in 1419, to the Willoughby family of Wollaton (Notts.), who were descended from Sir Philip Marmion's grand-daughter and coheir,

Joan.[11] When Sir Henry Willoughby visited the hospital chapel in 1524 he made an offering of 4d. and paid 1s. to a friar there who heard his confession and that of his wife. On the same occasion he paid 1s. 'for bread and ale there' and 1d. 'in alms there';[12] it is unlikely, however, that either of these payments can be taken to indicate that the hospital was still an effective eleemosynary foundation. Indeed the Willoughbys appear at least occasionally to have followed Marmion's example by granting the hospital lands without appointing a master. Sir Henry Willoughby gave the hospital lands to John Marmion, one of his household servants, and after Marmion's death to his chaplain Robert Parrot; Parrot, however, came to be regarded as the beneficed incumbent of the hospital.[13] This use of the hospital lands to provide virtual annuities for the Willoughbys' servants may not have left the chapel entirely without the services of a priest: the friar there in 1524 may well have been a stipendiary priest employed by the grantee of the hospital.[14]

In 1535 the income of the 'free chapel or hospital called Saint Jamys Spytell', amounting to £3 6s. 8d. a year from certain lands and pastures, appears to have belonged wholly to the 'chaplain' of the hospital.[15] In 1546 the chantry commissioners stated that there were no jewels, ornaments, plate, or goods belonging to the hospital.[16] Despite the observation in the 1548 chantry certificate that Tamworth was one of the four places in the county 'where most need is to have hospitals for relief of the poor',[17] the hospital was suppressed in that year; the incumbent, Robert Parrot, received a pension of 60s. a year.[18] In 1548 the chapel and its lands were sold;[19] some at least of the lands seem eventually to have passed to John Voughton, yeoman, of Tamworth, who in 1593 devised 'Spittelfield' and 'Spittelhill' to his son Humphrey.[20]

The hospital chapel stands between the roads from Tamworth to Ashby and Wigginton, about a mile north of St. Edith's Church in Tamworth. Some of the chapel's architectural features, typical of an earlier period than that of Marmion's foundation, suggest that it may incorporate remains of an older building.[21] By the end of the 18th century it had been turned into a barn, and half a century later

4 For this para. see Hist. MSS. Com. Middleton, 77–78.
5 According to the statutes of the Premonstratensians a guest-house or 'hospitale pauperum' was an essential part of any foundation of the order: H. M. Colvin, The White Canons in Eng. 306–7, 309.
6 Hist. MSS. Com. Middleton, 77–78.
7 Two Premonstratensian houses, Cockersand Abbey and Hornby Priory (both in Lancs.), seem to have originated as hospitals: Colvin, White Canons in Eng. 138–9, 144–5, 309.
8 Palmer, Baronial Family of Marmion, 86; List of Inquisitions Ad Quod Damnum Pt. I (P.R.O. Lists and Indexes, xvii), p. 16. Marmion's proposed endowment comprised a mill, various messuages, rents, and lands and the advowson of Wilksby church (Lincs.). These were appurtenances of the manor of Scrivelsby, which was held in chief, and were worth £8 19s. 1½d. a year.
9 Palmer, Baronial Family of Marmion, 83–84, 96; Cal. Pat. 1272–81, 393; 1281–92, 118; Cal. Fine R. 1272–1307, 271.
10 S.H.C. vi(1), 294, where no date is given for the departure of the master and brethren. The likeliest date, however, would seem to be after the inquisition ad quod damnum of 1285. By 1294 the hospital lands had been leased for life to Rob. de Pitchford, a canon of St. Edith's: S.H.C. vi(1), 294; Cal. Pat. 1292–1301, 122.
11 For the descent of the Freville and Willoughby families from Joan see Dugdale, Warws. ii. 1051–2, 1135.

12 Hist. MSS. Com. Middleton, 366.
13 S.H.C. 1915, 271, where Willoughby's name is wrongly given as Hugh. During the years 1497–1500 Marmion was acting as collector, receiver or bailiff in various Notts. manors belonging to Willoughby: Hist. MSS. Com. Middleton, 307, 308. He was a kinsman of Willoughby and an executor of his two wills: ibid. 121–2, 126. Parrot (alias Perot), like Marmion, was concerned in the administration of the Willoughby estates, being a receiver to Sir John Willoughby during the years 1536–46: Hist. MSS. Com. Middleton, 314, 315, 316. Parrot seems to have let the lands to another of the Willoughbys' servants, Isebrand Barnaby: Cal. Pat. 1548–9, 38; Hist. MSS. Com. Middleton, 371, 387, 388.
14 For the employment of a friar in the chapel of St. John's Hospital, Stafford, in similar circumstances see above p. 291.
15 Valor Eccl. (Rec. Com.), iii. 148. The same income was reported by the chantry commissioners in 1546 and 1548: S.H.C. 1915, 272.
16 S.H.C. 1915, 272.   17 See above p. 136.
18 S.H.C. 1915, 272, 275 n. 39.
19 Ibid. 272; Cal. Pat. 1548–9, 38–39.
20 P.C.C. 13 Dixy. For Spittal Field see C. F. Palmer, Hist. of the Town and Castle of Tamworth (Tamworth, 1845), map at frontispiece.
21 J. Gould, 'Spital Chapel, Tamworth' (TS. in possession of Mr. Gould).

it was serving as 'a small dwelling-house and barn'.[22] An attempt was made in 1855 by brethren of the Guild of St. Alban to establish a monastic community in the ruined chapel.[23] This failed, however, and the chapel seems to have become simply a dwelling-house once more.[24]

In 1906, when the remains of the chapel were threatened by plans to build on the site, proposals were made to restore the chapel.[25] The restoration was carried out during 1909,[26] and the chapel was dedicated by the Bishop of Lichfield in 1914. Since then it has served as a mission church in the parish of Wigginton.[27]

MASTERS OR CHAPLAINS

William de Crouebyrihal', appointed 1283.[28]

Thomas ad Crucem, occurs 1319.[29]

Robert Parrot, occurs 1535, chaplain at the suppression in 1548.[30]

No seal is known.

32. THE HOSPITAL OF ST. MARY, WOLVERHAMPTON

THE hospital of St. Mary, Wolverhampton, which may have stood about a quarter of a mile south-east of St. Peter's Church,[1] was founded in 1392–5 by Clement Leveson, chaplain, and William Waterfall.[2] In 1392 they received royal licence to found a hospital in honour of St. Mary for a chaplain and six poor people and to endow it with a messuage and 3 acres in Wolverhampton; part at least of this land was intended as the site.[3] A few weeks after the licence had been granted Waterfall was authorized by the Crown to acquire lands or rents to the annual value of £10 for the further endowment of the hospital.[4] The original endowment evidently formed part of the manor of Stow Heath,[5] as the alienation of the property was also licensed in 1394 by the lord of the manor, Hugh, Lord Burnell.[6] A final licence was granted to the founders in January 1395 by Lawrence Allerthorpe, Dean of Wolverhampton, within whose jurisdiction the hospital was to be situated. Allerthorpe permitted the founders to make suitable statutes and regulations, but he reserved the power to authorize and approve the foundation when it

was completed and to add to and interpret the regulations whenever it should be necessary.[7]

The founders' regulations,[8] presumably drawn up shortly after Allerthorpe's licence was issued, contain elaborate provisions concerning the patronage of the hospital, its relations with Wolverhampton church, and the duties of the chaplain or warden. The patronage was vested in Leveson, Waterfall, and the latter's wife Joan during their lives, with successive remainders to William Waterfall's heirs in tail, and to John Waterfall,[9] Richard Leveson of Wolverhampton, Nicholas Waryng of Wolverhampton, Richard Leveson of Willenhall, Roger Leveson, and Hugh, Lord Burnell, in tail. The patron was to present the chaplain of the hospital to the Dean of Wolverhampton for induction and to nominate the almspeople. Should he fail to do this within 6 months of a vacancy, nomination was to lapse to the dean.

As the hospital lay within the peculiar jurisdiction of Wolverhampton, the responsibility for visiting it was laid upon the dean or his official or upon their commissary. Should the chaplain or any almsperson be convicted more than once of any serious sin, the visitor was to expel him from the hospital and inform the patron.

The chaplain, before induction, was to take an oath of canonical obedience to the Dean of Wolverhampton and was also to swear not to infringe the rights of that church to any of its tithes, offerings, or other revenues. All offerings made to the hospital were to be brought to St. Peter's by the chaplain. The six almspeople, who might be male or female,[10] were the chaplain's special responsibility. Each day he was to say mass, vespers, and 'other divine services' in the hospital chapel. On Sundays and double feasts, however, he was to be present in the mother-church during matins and vespers and at mass until the Gospel had been read; after the Gospel he was to cross to the hospital chapel to say mass for the almspeople. Prayers were to be said daily at mass in the hospital chapel for Clement Leveson, William and Joan Waterfall, Lord Burnell, and Lawrence Allerthorpe, and for all the faithful departed. The rights of St. Peter's Church were safeguarded by a regulation which forbade the almspeople to receive the sacraments from anyone but their parochial chaplain[11] unless licensed by him to do so or in time of necessity. On Sundays and the four principal feasts, moreover, such almspeople as

[22] Shaw, *Staffs.* i. 430; Palmer, *Town and Castle of Tamworth*, 348.

[23] P. F. Anson, *The Call of the Cloister* (1964 edn.), 50–51.

[24] C. Lynam, 'The Chapel of the Hospital of St. James, Wigginton, Tamworth', *Jnl. Brit. Arch. Assoc.* June 1906, 125. For a photograph of the chapel still in the ruinous condition described by Lynam see R. K. Dent and J. Hill, *Historic Staffs.* (1896), 177.

[25] *Jnl. Brit. Arch. Assoc.* June 1906, 126–7; H. C. Mitchell, *Tamworth Parish Church*, 77.

[26] Mitchell, *Tamworth Parish Church*, 78; Rotha M. Clay, *The Mediaeval Hospitals of Eng.* 123.

[27] *Tamworth Herald*, 5 Sept. 1914; *Lich. Dioc. Ch. Cal.* (1915), 130; *Lich. Dioc. Dir.* (1968), 126.

[28] See above p. 295.   [29] D. & C. Lich., AA 3.

[30] *Valor Eccl.* iii. 148; see above p. 295.

[1] The site of the hospital may have been the later Pepper's Croft: *Bilston Par. Reg.* (Staffs. Par. Reg. Soc.), 217. In 1609 it was owned by Sir Wal. Leveson of Wolverhampton and extended eastwards in length as far as Can Lane (now partly represented by Pipers Row): W.S.L. 60/63, p. 1; G. P. Mander and N. W. Tildesley, *Hist. of*

Wolverhampton to the Early Nineteenth Cent. 35 and end-paper map. Thanks are due to Dr. A. K. B. Evans for supplying several of the references used in this article.

[2] Leveson was vicar of the prebends of Wobaston, Hatherton, and Monmore in St. Peter's Church, and he and Waterfall were two of the wardens of the light of St. Peter in the same church: *S.H.C.* 1928, p. 131.

[3] *Cal. Pat.* 1391–6, 139. Leveson and Waterfall paid 5 marks for this licence.

[4] Ibid. 176. Waterfall paid 45 marks for this licence.

[5] C 143/414/12.

[6] S.R.O., D.593/B/1/26/4/4. And see ibid. /B/1/26/6/ 40/4; Shaw, *Staffs.* ii. 166; *Complete Peerage*, ii. 435.

[7] S.R.O., D. 593/B/1/26/4/3.

[8] For this and the two succeeding paras. see ibid. /5.

[9] John Waterfall was perhaps Wm.'s brother: Mander and Tildesley, *Wolverhampton*, 34.

[10] Not women only (as stated in G. Oliver, *Historical and Descriptive Account of the Collegiate Church of Wolverhampton* (1836), 54) or men only (as stated in Mander and Tildesley, *Wolverhampton*, 34).

[11] i.e. not the hospital chaplain.

could do so were to attend St. Peter's; for those who were too infirm to go the hospital chaplain could provide only the ministration of holy bread and holy water.[12]

Little is known of the hospital's subsequent history. William Waterfall presented the first recorded chaplain, one John Pepard, who was inducted in 1402.[13] Waterfall seems also to have increased the endowment of the hospital, for in 1415 Pepard took possession of certain lands which Waterfall had held of the Prebendary of Monmore.[14] These lands were later leased out by Pepard, and the rent included 'one competent carriage of land coals to be drawn with five horses'.[15]

Pepard was still alive in 1440.[16] He may in fact have occupied the chaplaincy of the hospital for a long time and given it his name:[17] in 1529 one Thomas Bradshaw was inducted to the free chapel called 'Pepers Chapell in Wolverhampton'. By that time the patronage had passed to the Leveson family, for Bradshaw was presented by James Leveson.[18]

'Pyper's Chapel' is mentioned in an inventory of goods (apparently relating to the year 1541) of the various chapels and guilds of St. Peter's Church,[19] but nothing more of its history is known. Like the chantries and guilds of St. Peter's the hospital is not mentioned in the Staffordshire chantry certificates.[20] It seems, however, to have been suppressed, and its property probably passed to the Leveson family.[21]

WARDENS OR CHAPLAINS

John Pepard, inducted 1402, probably still warden in 1415.[22]

Thomas Bradshaw, inducted 1529.[23]

No seal is known.

COLLEGES

33. THE COLLEGE OF CHRIST AND ST. MARY, BURTON-UPON-TRENT

IN 1541 the Crown reconstituted the dissolved abbey of St. Mary and St. Modwen, Burton-upon-Trent, as the collegiate church of Christ and St. Mary.[1] It had a dean and 4 prebendaries, whose appointment lay with the Crown,[2] and by 1545 there were also 6 'petty' canons, a gospeller, an epistoler, 5 singing men, 6 choristers, 2 deacons, a parish priest, a schoolmaster, and 4 bedesmen. The 11 'common servants' included a barber, the parish clerk, the bridge-master, a laundress, a turnspit, and an apparitor. The office of 'porter of the gates' was held

by Robert Bradshaw, gentleman, at a fee of 60s. and was presumably honorary. The last abbot was appointed the first dean, and three of the minor canons and the epistoler were former religious, presumably of Burton Abbey.[3] The site and all property of the abbey except the manors of Abbots Bromley and Bromley Hurst were granted to the new college to be held of the Crown at a rent of £63 2s. 4d. in lieu of tithes and first fruits, but the estate was burdened with various pensions, stipends, and fees.[4] The dean was also obliged to spend £20 a year on alms and £20 on highway maintenance.[5] The gross value of the college's property in 1541–2 was £564 5s. 6d.[6]

The college was short-lived. In November 1545 it

[12] For holy bread (eulogiae) and holy water see J. Bingham, Origines Ecclesiasticae, vi (1719), 719–21; S.H.C. 1924, pp. 40, 41, 280; F. M. Powicke and C. R. Cheney, Councils and Synods, ii(1), 211. Able-bodied inmates of hospitals often had to go to the parish church for the sacraments; holy bread and holy water were administered to the infirm: Rotha M. Clay, Mediaeval Hospitals of Eng. 197–8, 201–2; V.C.H. Yorks. iii. 307. These substitutes for sacraments were abolished in the liturgical reforms of 1548–9: J. Ridley, Thos. Cranmer, 275, 294–5.
[13] Bilston Par. Reg. 216–17.
[14] Ibid. 217.
[15] Ibid. 217–18.
[16] Pepard (or Pipard) was a party to a number of property transactions between 1405 and 1440: S.R.O., D.593/B/1/26/6/23/6 and 9; /24/17; /25/2; /37/9. He is referred to as deceased in a document dated 1462–3: ibid. /B/1/26/6/26/1. None of these transactions, however, appears to connect him with St. Mary's Hospital. See also S.H.C. xvii. 150.
[17] Mander and Tildesley, Wolverhampton, 35. This seems a more circumstantial explanation of the chapel's name than that put forward in S.H.C. 1915, 338 n. 4. The suggestion made ibid. 322, that 'Pyper's chapell' was in the south transept of St. Peter's Church is not supported by the source there cited.
[18] S.R.O., D.593/J/5/4/3. The Jas. Leveson who presented Bradshaw would seem, from the pedigree in Shaw, Staffs. ii. 169, to be descended from Ric. Leveson of Willenhall (fl. 1369–1409). But this pedigree is probably incomplete, and the heirs of Ric. Leveson of Wolver-

hampton (who had a prior place in the entail of the patronage) had not died out.
[19] Shaw, Staffs. ii. 161 (citing the MS. now W.S.L., S.MS. 386/2, no. 80).
[20] S.H.C. 1915, 322.
[21] This would seem likely from the fact that the foundation deeds passed to the Leveson family whose archives are now in S.R.O. (D.593). See also above n. 1.
[22] See above.
[23] See above. He was possibly the Thos. Bradshaw who was a vicar choral in St. Peter's in 1533 and who died in 1564–5: S.H.C. 1915, 333, 356, 363.
[1] L. & P. Hen. VIII, xvi, p. 536. It was included in the 1539 list of proposed new bishoprics and colleges: ibid. xiv(2), pp. 151–2.
[2] Ibid. xvi, p. 536; ibid. xviii(2), p. 142 (appointment to vacant prebend); ibid. xix(1), p. 381 (appointment of new dean).
[3] Hibbert, Dissolution, 177, 268–70, 277, 279–80. One of the canons, John Carter, was probably the John Carter who was martyrologer of the abbey in 1524: Lich. Dioc. Regy., B/V/1/1, p. 44 (2nd nos.).
[4] L. & P. Hen. VIII, xvi, p. 638; S.C. 6/Hen. VIII/3356, m. 51. Abbots Bromley and Bromley Hurst were retained by the Crown and granted to Sir Wm. Paget in 1544: L. & P. Hen. VIII, xix(1), p. 41. For details of the rest of the property see above p. 204.
[5] L. & P. Hen. VIII, xx(1), p. 670. Hence, presumably, the presence of the bridge-master among the servants of the college.
[6] S.C. 6/Hen. VIII/3356, m. 51; C 1/1403/55.

was dissolved by Richard Goodrich and John Scudamore who travelled from London for the purpose and remained at Burton for four days. They assigned pensions to the dean (£40, subsequently raised to £66 6s. 8d.), three prebendaries (£12 13s. 4d., £15 and £16), the three petty canons who were former monks (two at £6 and one at £6 13s. 4d.), and the epistoler, also a former monk (£5). The other members of the college and the servants received their wages and in most cases a reward or new appointment — one of the petty canons was made curate of the parish church. The four bedesmen received 'wages' of 25s. each. The bridge-master had no reward presumably because he continued to hold the same office.[7] Further pensions were later awarded to the schoolmaster (at the rate of £20 a year until alternative provision was made for him in 1546) and to another of the petty canons.[8] Goodrich and Scudamore also paid debts owing by the dean and chapter (£9 13s. 8d.) and collected others due to the college (£48 2s. 4d.). They compiled an inventory of the plate, vestments, and household goods. The plate, consisting of 49½ oz. gilt, 24½ oz. parcel gilt, and 93 oz. white, and some of the vestments were taken back to London; the remainder was sold, assigned to the parish, or left on the site.[9] The following January the college and all its possessions, except Burton parish church, its lead, and its bells, were granted to Sir William Paget.[10]

DEANS

William Edys, appointed 1541, died 1544.[11]
Robert Brokke, appointed 1544, dean at the dissolution.[12]

The seal, as reproduced by Stebbing Shaw,[13] depicts Christ, St. Mary, eleven figures probably representing Apostles, another figure seated below Christ, possibly Wulfric Spot, the Holy Ghost in the form of a dove, and the coat of arms formerly used by the abbey. Legend:

SIGILLUM COMMUNE DECANI ET CAPITULI ECCLISIE (sic) COLLEGIATI CHRISTI BURTONIE DE TRENT

34. THE COLLEGE OF ST. MICHAEL, PENKRIDGE

TRADITION in the later Middle Ages attributed the foundation of the royal free chapel of St. Michael[1] at Penkridge to King Edgar (957–75). A safer guide is the evidence of the *Liber Niger*, the register of John Alen, Archbishop of Dublin and Dean of Penkridge from 1528 to 1534; a note written in Alen's own hand and appended to certain records of Penkridge in the register states that the 'original founder' of the church was King Eadred (946–55).[2] The antiquarian learning of the archbishop and his knowledge of early deeds relating to Penkridge favour the acceptance of his statement. In the light of it a charter of King Edgar dated at Penkridge in 958 and describing it as a famous place[3] acquires particular meaning. Another early notice of the church is in the will of Wulfgeat of Donington (Salop.) which is probably of about the year 1000; by it Penkridge received a legacy of two bullocks.[4] It was stated in the 13th century that the church of Lapley had belonged to Penkridge at an early date but that through the negligence of the canons it was lost to the abbey of St. Rémy at Rheims after they had acquired the manor of Lapley in the early 1060s.[5] In 1086 there is evidence of a community at Penkridge in the nine clerks whom Domesday Book records as holding one hide of land there in demesne of the Crown.[6]

King Stephen, desirous of winning the support of the episcopacy, gave the churches of Penkridge and Stafford with their lands, chapels, and tithes in 1136 to Bishop Roger de Clinton and his churches of Coventry and Lichfield for the soul of Henry I.[7] Both Penkridge and Stafford were then held in chief of the king by Jordan, a clerk of Roger de Fécamp, probably by grant of Henry I.[8] Jordan was to continue to hold them for his lifetime of the bishop and his two churches who were to remain owners in perpetuity with rights of soc and sac, toll and team, and infangentheof. Stephen's gift was confirmed by papal bulls in 1139, 1144, and 1152.[9] By the early 1180s, however, Penkridge had been recovered by the Crown and restored to the status of a royal free chapel. Robert, Dean of Penkridge,

---

[7] Hibbert, *Dissolution*, 191, 258–80. The list of servants is headed by John Blount gent. whose wages and award came to 26s. 8d., a higher amount than any other servant except the bridge-master whose wages were 33s. 4d.

[8] *L. & P. Hen. VIII*, xxi(1), pp. 160, 778.

[9] Hibbert, *Dissolution*, 258–67, 271, 278–80.

[10] *L. & P. Hen. VIII*, xxi(1), pp. 76–77; *S.H.C.* 1937, 187–9; S.C. 6/Hen. VIII/3360. Certain annual fees had to be paid from the property. In 1546 Sir Wm. compounded for the rent due to the Crown: *L. & P. Hen. VIII*, xxi(1), pp. 89, 164–5.

[11] *L. & P. Hen. VIII*, xvi, p. 536; ibid. xix(1), p. 381; T. Tanner, *Notitia Monastica* (1787 edn.), p. xlvi, which also mentions an arrangement for his burial on the S. side of the high altar.

[12] *L. & P. Hen. VIII*, xix(1), p. 381; Hibbert, *Dissolution*, 277. He was still living some 13 years after the dissolution of the college: C 1/1403/55–60.

[13] See above plate facing p. 213. For the arms see Tanner, *Notitia Monastica*, p. xxxiii and facing page. No impressions of the seal can now be traced.

[1] The original dedication appears to have been to St. Mary, the style used in a bull of 1259. The seal in use about this time, however, gives the dedication as to St. Michael; the earliest dated use of the new dedication is in 1246. The archbishops of Dublin as deans of Penkridge referred to

the royal free chapel of St. Michael in their official title. See *S.H.C.* 1950–1, 14, 15 n., 16 and n.; *Cal. Pat.* 1232–7, 492; 1385–9, 367.

[2] *Cal. Archbp. Alen's Reg.* (Royal Soc. of Antiq. of Ireland, 1950), 310.

[3] *Cart. Sax.* ed. Birch, iii, p. 246; *S.H.C.* 1950–1, 4 and n.

[4] Dorothy Whitelock, *Anglo-Saxon Wills*, 55, 163, 164, 165.

[5] *S.H.C.* 1950–1, 48–49. In the reign of Hen. I the church of Lapley was disputed between St. Rémy and a royal clerk, who was perhaps a canon of Penkridge: see below p. 340.

[6] *V.C.H. Staffs.* iv. 45, no. 115. These clerks also held 2 hides and 3 virgates in Gnosall, probably because they served the church there; the property was never part of the endowment of Penkridge. For Gnosall church see ibid. 228.

[7] *S.H.C.* 1924, p. 285; *Cal. Chart. R.* 1341–1417, 308. The bishop had recently secured papal recognition of Stephen as king: J. H. Round, *Geoffrey de Mandeville*, 253.

[8] Roger seems to have been a chancery clerk under Roger le Poer, son of Hen. I's justicar, Roger, Bp. of Salisbury: Round, *G. de Mandeville*, 46 n. 4, 263.

[9] See below p. 303.

occurs at some time between 1180 and 1188,[10] and by 1183 a vacant prebend of Penkridge was in the hands of the Crown.[11] The king made an appointment to the prebend of Cannock in the late 12th century,[12] and in 1199 King John appointed to the deanery.[13]

By this time a protracted dispute between Penkridge and Lichfield over the church of Cannock had begun. In 1189 Richard I, in order to raise funds for his crusade, sold to the bishop, Hugh de Nonant, the vills and churches of Cannock and Rugeley regardless of the fact that Cannock church was attached to the prebend of Cannock in Penkridge church.[14] In 1191 the Pope confirmed Bishop Hugh in his possession of the churches of Cannock and Rugeley,[15] and within twelve months Hugh had granted them to the common fund of the canons of Lichfield, reserving to Penkridge an annual payment of 4s.[16] The Dean of Penkridge eventually impleaded the Dean and Chapter of Lichfield, and the case was heard by three papal judges delegate in 1207. It was decided in favour of Penkridge.[17] Lichfield was to pay one mark a year to Penkridge through the chaplain of Cannock; deceased parishioners of Cannock were to be buried at Penkridge which was to receive the mortuaries; the chaplain appointed to Cannock by Lichfield was to swear in the chapter-house at Penkridge to observe the agreement. Penkridge and Lichfield promised to support each other 'without charging expenses', and whenever the Dean of Penkridge visited Lichfield he was to be received as a brother of the church in choir and chapter, and on the day of his death and its anniversary Lichfield was to celebrate the office of the dead as for a canon. The transcript of this settlement in the Great Register of Lichfield is followed by an angry note that the *Pencrichenses* immediately broke the agreement by many vexatious acts against the *Lichefeldenses* who appealed to Rome and broke the seals on the deed.[18] The date and result of the appeal are not known. In 1221, however, the Pope, in response to a petition from the chapter, confirmed a grant made by Bishop Cornhill (1214–23) of several churches including Cannock.[19] The dispute continued until the 14th century.[20]

A notable event in the history of Penkridge was the grant of the advowson of the deanery by King John in 1215 to Henry of London, Archbishop of Dublin, and his successors provided that they were not Irishmen. John also confirmed the archbishop in his possession of the manor and fair of Penkridge which had been granted by Hugh Hose or Hussey. The archbishop had given valuable service to the Crown as Justiciar of Ireland from 1210 to 1215 and had also given generous financial help in the

building of Dublin castle.[21] When the deanery fell vacant in 1226 the archbishop assumed that he became dean by virtue of the 1215 grant, but Henry III appointed a dean of his own, Walter de Kirkeham. Within a few months, however, the king gave way after an examination of John's charter. He quitclaimed the deanery to the archbishop and ordered the canons of Penkridge to render him due obedience.[22] The quitclaim was not, however, intended to be permanent, and when Archbishop Henry died in 1228 the king appointed Richard of St. John, chaplain of Hubert de Burgh, to the deanery, declaring it to be in his gift because of the vacancy in the archbishopric of Dublin. Shortly afterwards Luke, Dean of St. Martin le Grand and Treasurer of the King's Wardrobe, was elected archbishop, but the Pope declared the election uncanonical. Luke was re-elected and received papal approval in 1230. Henry III then set aside his previous appointment and quitclaimed the deanery to Luke, confessing that he had been unmindful of his father's charter.[23]

Though surrendering over the deanery, the king retained his right to collate to the prebends of Penkridge during a vacancy in the see of Dublin. In 1253 Henry granted to William of Kilkenny, Archdeacon of Coventry, the power to collate to the prebends of Penkridge which should fall vacant during the next voidance of the archbishopric.[24] On the death of Archbishop Luke in 1256 the Pope appointed Fulk de Sanford, Archdeacon of Middlesex, to Dublin, but two months later the king made a life grant to Henry of Salisbury, a royal chaplain, of the power of collating to the prebends of Penkridge. In March 1257 the king surrendered the deanery to Archbishop Fulk to hold 'as his predecessor Luke held it, saving to the king and his heirs his right when he wishes to assert it.' Fulk obtained a bull in June confirming to him John's grant of the advowson. He also petitioned the Pope to make the union of the deanery with the archbishopric complete and absolute, claiming that the deanery had no revenues of its own for the support of the dean. A bull of 1259 duly granted that no one in future should be instituted as dean except the archbishop and his successors in the see of Dublin.

The union remained undisturbed until the Reformation, but the Crown continued to collate to prebends during vacancies in the archbishopric. In 1271, shortly after the death of Fulk, Henry III granted to William de la Cornere collations to the Penkridge prebends falling void during the vacancy of the see.[25] Edward III took advantage of the rule of devolution established by the Lateran Council of 1179 by claiming the power to collate to a prebend

---

[10] He attested a grant of R., Abbot of Burton, who has been identified as Roger (1177–82) rather than Richard (1182–8); the grant also mentions Ranulf de Glanvill's justiciarship (1180–9): W.S.L. 84/6/41; S.H.C. v(1), 40–41; ibid. 1937, p. lxiv.
[11] The sheriff accounted for a mark from this prebend, formerly held by Roger the Archdeacon, from Mich. 1183 to Mich. 1189: S.H.C. i. 107, 109, 140.
[12] S.H.C. 1950–1, 51.
[13] Ibid. iii(1), 40; ibid. 1950–1, 51, 52 n.
[14] Ibid. 1950–1, 7–8; V.C.H. Staffs. v. 53, 58, 154, 162.
[15] S.H.C. 1924, p. 128.
[16] Ibid. p. 359. The reason for the payment was that the prebendary, in order to secure succession to his father in the prebend, had mortgaged the chapel of Cannock for a lump sum and 4s. a year: ibid. 1950–1, 51. V.C.H. Staffs. v.

58, is wrong in saying the prebendary had to pay 4s. year.
[17] S.H.C. 1924, p.140; ibid. 1950–1, 51–52. The success of Penkridge may be explained by the fact that the three judges were heads of religious houses in or near Bristol; the Dean of Penkridge was Elias of Bristol, who may well have had some influence there. The agreement is dated at Bristol.
[18] Ibid. 1924, p. 141.
[19] Ibid. pp. 12, 66.
[20] See below p. 300.
[21] S.H.C. 1950–1, 9–11. He had been Archdeacon of Stafford. For Penkridge manor see V.C.H. Staffs. v. 108. The dean soon granted two-thirds of the manor to his nephew Andrew le Blund: ibid. 109, 110.
[22] S.H.C. 1950–1, 11.
[23] Ibid. 11–12.
[24] For this para see ibid. 12–15.
[25] Cal. Pat. 1266–72, 601. Wm. was one of the candidates for the archbishopric but was not successful.

which had been left void by the archbishop for more than six months, and in 1337 he appointed Robert de Kyldesby to the prebend of Dunston.[26]

There is little evidence that the archbishops ever came to Penkridge. In 1257 Archbishop Fulk de Sanford was at Lichfield for the burial of Bishop Weseham.[27] One other archbishop who is known to have been at Penkridge is Robert Wikeford. He held a visitation in 1380 and took the opportunity to raise the weekly pittances of the two chantry priests.[28] The non-residence of the deans made necessary the appointment of an official to exercise the dean's peculiar jurisdiction. In 1288 Stephen of Codnor, the 'vicegerent' of Archbishop John de Sanford, was at Penkridge dealing with the contumacy of Sir Richard de Loges, a parishioner of the dean.[29] In 1321 Richard Hillary, commissary of Archbishop Bicknor, held an inquisition at Penkridge into allegations of wastage of the collegiate revenues by resident commissaries. He then appointed one of the resident priests as the dean's commissary to be responsible for all the revenues of the church and to account at least once a year to the canons or their proctors.[30]

In 1291 the church of Penkridge, valued at £44 13s. 4d., had eight prebends: Coppenhall, Stretton, and Shareshill, each valued at £10, Dunston (£5 6s. 8d.), Penkridge (£4), Congreve (£2 13s. 4d.), Longridge (£2), and the vicarage of Coppenhall (13s. 4d.)[31] An inquisition in 1261[32] carried out by the king's command had mentioned only four of these[33] but included also the disputed prebend of Cannock. Besides the chapel of Cannock there were three chapels, at Coppenhall, Shareshill, and Stretton, dependent on Penkridge. The inquisition also showed that at an earlier time, probably in the late 12th century, the prebends were often treated as hereditary estates. This practice had ceased by 1261, but as already seen the Crown was able to secure many of the prebends for its own nominees. The prebend of Cannock evidently disappeared in the 14th century. The dispute with Lichfield had been renewed in the later 13th century and continued until at least the 1330s. A prebendary of Cannock was appointed in 1313 and 1337, but the absence of the prebend from a list of 1365 seems to suggest that Penkridge lost the fight.[34] There are occasional references to other prebends. A prebend of the chapel of Pillatonhall occurs in 1272 with the prebendary asserting his claim to tithes in Huntington (in Cannock) against the Dean and Chapter of Lichfield claiming as rectors of Cannock.[35] The prebend of Bold occurs in 1342 with the vicarage of

Coppenhall annexed to it.[36] The list of 1365 gives 9 prebends: Coppenhall, Shareshill, Dunston, Penkridge, Congreve, Longridge, the King's Chantry, the Chantry of the Blessed Virgin Mary, and the Sacrist's.[37] This last is mentioned as a prebend in 1349.[38] In 1396 a prebend called Brennydhalle was conferred by the Crown on Thomas de Marton.[39]

The inquisition of 1261 revealed that two of the canons, probably the only two then resident, had usurped powers over the collegiate property to the detriment of the rest.[40] Another inquisition in 1321 revealed a similar state of affairs.[41] Two resident priests, acting as commissaries of the deans, were found to have wasted much of the collegiate property. It was stressed that the two priests were not canons but resided as chantry priests obliged to celebrate mass daily, one for the king and the other in the chapel of the Blessed Virgin. It was ordered that in future one of them was to act as commissary if no canon was resident; he was to account for all the revenues of the church once or twice a year to the proctors of the canons. The two priests were to divide between themselves what was left of the income of the church after the chancel had been repaired, again if there was no canon in residence. They were also to take the place in choir of the vicars if these were prevented from attendance by their duties as chaplains of the churches dependent on Penkridge. As already seen, the two chantry priests were listed as prebendaries of Penkridge in 1365. In 1380 it was stated that by custom they had to be resident 'to support the burdens of hospitality.' They then received only 10½d. a week each from the rents of the college, and since the rest of their income, derived from the chantry endowments, was insufficient to support their burdens, the Archbishop of Dublin raised their weekly income from the common rents by 3½d. each.[42]

The permanent union of the deanery of Penkridge and the archbishopric of Dublin had no effect on the status of the church as a royal free chapel. Henry III showed his interest by his gift in 1251 of a silver chalice and of two oaks from Cannock Forest to make stalls for the church.[43] In 1253 he gave ten oaks for the work then in progress on the fabric of the church.[44] More marked was the Crown's resistance, as in the case of other royal free chapels, to papal attempts to tax Penkridge, except when such taxation was for the benefit of the king.[45] In the 14th century papal provisions to prebends in Penkridge provoked determined opposition from the Crown.[46] The first of these seems to have been the provision of Elias de Janaston to the prebend of

26 *S.H.C.* 1950–1, 14 n. By 1362 the Crown allowed only 40 days as the period of voidance during which the archbishop had the right of collation: ibid.; and see below n. 49.
27 H. Wharton, *Anglia Sacra*, i. 440.
28 *Cal. Pat.* 1385–9, 367–8; see below.
29 *Cal. Doc. Ireland*, 1285–92, 193–4.
30 *Cal. Archbp. Alen's Reg.* 310–11; see below.
31 *Tax. Eccl.* (Rec. Com.), 242. There is an undated valuation of the prebends of Penkridge in Alen's Register (see *S.H.C.* 1950–1, 23) which by reason of the lower rate of assessment for all except two may be presumed to be earlier than 1291. It may be the valuation for the Taxation of Norwich of 1254 or the 'verus valor' begun in 1267. The assessments are 40s. for the dean's prebend (not mentioned in 1291), £10 13s. 4d. for Coppenhall (presumably including the vicarage), £6 13s. 4d. for Stretton, £6 6s. 8d. for Dunston, £4 for Penkridge, £2 16s. 8d. for Congreve and 16s. for Longridge. In 1259 the deanery was stated to have no revenues of its own: see above p. 299.

32 *S.H.C.* 1950–1, 46–52. It is wrongly dated as 1271 in *Cal. Archbp. Alen's Reg.* 309.
33 This is on the assumption that the prebend of La More mentioned in 1261 is to be identified with the prebend of Penkridge.
34 *S.H.C.* 1950–1, 21–23, 24; *V.C.H. Staffs.* v. 58; see below.   35 *S.H.C.* 1924, p. 362.
36 *Cal. Pat.* 1340–3, 353. The vicarage of Coppenhall was still a separate prebend in 1333: *S.H.C.* 1950–1, 28 n.
37 *S.H.C.* 1950–1, 24.   38 *Cal. Pat.* 1348–50, 360.
39 Ibid. 1391–6, 650.   40 *S.H.C.* 1950–1, 47–48, 52.
41 *Cal. Archbp. Alen's Reg.* 310–11.
42 *S.H.C.* 1950–1, 25.
43 Ibid. 1911, 16; *Cal. Close*, 1247–51, 457.
44 *Cal. Close*, 1251–3, 389. For the extensive 13th-cent. work in the church see *V.C.H. Staffs.* v. 131–2.
45 See below p. 305.
46 For what follows on provisions see *S.H.C.* 1950–1, 31–36, unless otherwise stated.

Dunston; in 1315 Elias surrendered the prebend and accepted the royal claim that the papal provision was void. In 1317 the Pope made provisions to two canonries at Penkridge, each in expectation of a prebend there.[47] In the case of the first the archbishop-elect of Dublin who was then at the papal court, promised to appoint to the next vacant prebend. In 1325, however, after the vacancy had occurred, Edward II asserted the complete exemption of the prebends of royal free chapels from all ordinary jurisdiction and from conferment by anyone except himself; he cautioned the Dean and Chapter of Penkridge against proceeding further in the execution of the provision. The archbishop as dean accepted the royal declaration and sent it on to the chapter at Penkridge with his order for it to be observed. In 1333 the Pope provided Thomas Michel, Rector of Berkley (Norf.), to a Penkridge canonry with the expectation of a prebend. Two years later Coppenhall fell vacant and Michel was provided to it by papal mandate. Edward III made a strong protest, but Ralph, Lord Stafford, interceded for Michel and the king agreed to confirm him in possession on condition that he renounced his right by virtue of the papal provision. This renunciation was duly made. Another papal provision, to the prebend of Coppenhall in 1342, seems to have been accepted by the Crown without protest, no doubt because of the war with France. When, however, Thomas Michel died in 1361 at the papal court and the Pope proceeded to provide William Russell to the Coppenhall prebend,[48] Edward III opposed the provision and in 1362 appointed David of Wooler.[49] Thomas de Eltenheved succeeded Russell as the papal nominee in 1363, but he was so violently disturbed by Wooler in enjoyment of the prebend that he appealed to the papacy. Judgement was, of course, given for him and the Bishop of Coventry and Lichfield was ordered to restore to him the prebendal property and, in case of hindrance from Wooler, to put him under sentence of greater excommunication. Finally Wooler resigned, and in 1363 the king appointed Richard de Bedyk, ordering the imprisonment of any persons hindering his collation by the prosecution of appeals in foreign parts. But Eltenheved appears to have retained possession, and in 1365 the king appointed John Edward. Eventually he got possession, his estate in the prebend was ratified by the Crown in 1371, and he died as prebendary in 1381. In 1379, during the papal schism, Urban VI had granted Richard II the right to nominate to two canonries, with expectation of prebends, in every cathedral chapter and collegiate church in the realm, and thus in 1381 the king nominated John de Wendlyngburgh to the prebend of Coppenhall without any friction. Several other royal appointments were made between 1385 and 1400.

The Crown was also involved in a struggle over the exemption of Penkridge, like other royal free chapels, from ordinary and metropolitan visitation.

In 1249 the king forbade Thomas of Wymondham to enter the bounds of the free chapel of Penkridge and to exercise any jurisdiction there.[50] In 1259, however, the Archdeacon of Stafford began a visitation of Penkridge. The king promptly wrote to him stating how perturbed he was to hear that the archdeacon was striving to subdue the chapel to the jurisdiction of the ordinary and to hold chapters there. He ordered the archdeacon to desist from such rash presumption if he wished to stay in the kingdom and the sheriff to prevent him from further activities in the parish of Penkridge.[51] The parishioners were also warned not to allow the bishop, his officials, or the archdeacon to enter the vill of Penkridge for the exercise of spiritual functions or to obey them in any spiritual matters.[52] It is not known how this dispute proceeded, but in 1281 Penkridge was one of the six royal free chapels of the diocese recognized by the bishop as exempt from all ordinary jurisdiction and subject directly to the Pope.[53]

In the meantime a conflict had begun between the canons of Penkridge and John Pecham, Archbishop of Canterbury, who came to the diocese of Coventry and Lichfield on a metropolitical visitation in 1280.[54] In a letter of April to the Archbishop of Dublin as Dean of Penkridge Pecham agreed to defer the visitation of Penkridge until the two prelates had met to discuss the college's claim of exemption. Pecham said that he had seen with astonishment a letter shown him by the dean's commissary and bearing the seal of Henry III, which testified to an apostolic privilege granting the general exemption of the royal chapels. The Archbishop of Dublin was advised to think well over the matter, which Pecham suggested, might be brought before the Dean of the Court of Arches.[55] In July 1280 Pecham reported to the king that the dean and canons of Penkridge had done great wrong to the church of Canterbury in its greatest franchise, the exercise of its tuitory power, during their prosecution of an appeal to Rome against the archbishop.[56] It is not, however, clear how Penkridge had done this wrong. In November the archbishop excommunicated Penkridge along with the other royal free chapels.[57] Penkridge's appeal to the papacy against the archbishop was still being prosecuted in March 1281 and caused Pecham to make an exception of Penkridge when he deferred until Parliament met the sentences of excommunication and interdict upon the other royal free chapels in the diocese of Coventry and Lichfield, in compliance with the king's will.[58] The archbishop was, however, careful to exclude from the sentences pronounced against the canons of Penkridge the Archbishop of Dublin, to whom he explained in a letter in February 1281 that only those who actually resisted his jurisdiction were involved.[59] Twelve months later Pecham again expressly excluded the archbishop from the excommunication still in force against the canons.[60] There is no further evidence of the prosecution of this appeal by the canons of Penkridge. Pecham seems to have

[47] *Cal. Papal Regs.* ii. 148, 149. In the first case the king stated that provision belonged to the Archbp. of Dublin.
[48] He was provided on the petition of his kinsman, the bishop-elect of St. David's.
[49] The see of Dublin was not vacant, but the king claimed the right of collation since more than 40 days had passed since Michel's death. The archbp. confirmed the royal grant.
[50] *Cal. Close,* 1247–51, 223.

[51] Ibid. 1256–9, 427.
[52] *Cal. Pat.* 1258–61, 40.
[53] See below p. 324.
[54] See below p. 324
[55] *Reg. Epist. Fratris Johannis Peckham* (Rolls Ser.), i. 112–13.
[56] Ibid. 392q, 392v.
[57] Ibid. 149, 179–80.
[58] Ibid. 392v.
[59] Ibid. 179–80.
[60] Ibid. iii. 1068.

discontinued the assertion of his claims after the agreement of 1281 between the diocesan and the royal chapels.[61]

A metropolitical visitation of Penkridge and of the other royal free chapels in Staffordshire took place under Archbishop Arundel who appointed two commissaries to carry it out in 1401.[62] There was a secret examination of each member of the chapter or his deputy, as well as of other ministers serving the church. In all things canonical obedience was given to the visitors. They also examined certain parishioners and exercised all their visitatorial powers without meeting resistance.

On the eve of the Dissolution the college of Penkridge comprised the dean and 7 prebendaries, 2 resident canons without prebends, an official principal, 6 vicars, a high deacon, a subdeacon, and a sacrist.[63] Three of the vicars were resident vicars choral, each with a yearly portion of £5 from the prebends of Penkridge, Coppenhall, and Stretton.[64] The other three would have had various duties inside the church itself. The two resident canons were still the priests who served the chantry of the Blessed Virgin and the King's Chantry. The stipends of the two canons were £6 16s. 4¼d. and £6 11s. 2¼d. derived from lands and tithes in Penkridge parish and lands and tenements in Muchall (in Penn).[65] There were, however, charges on these stipends of 10s. for bread and wine, 8s. for bread and ale for the Maundy, and 4s. 4d. for a light before the Sacrament. The sacrist had a house and lands in Penkridge worth 8s. 8d. a year. He also shared with the resident canons the income from the Hay House estate in the Dunston area and from land in Muchall, Moor Hall (in Penkridge), Castle Church, Essington (in Bushbury), Whiston (in Penkridge), Cannock, and 'Malton'. The two canons and the sacrist shared with the vicars choral 42s. rent from three closes in Penkridge.[66] The high deacon received 53s. 4d. a year out of the prebend of Dunston and the subdeacon 40s. out of the prebends of Congreve and Longridge. There was also a morrow-mass priest 'employed by the inhabitants of Penkridge' and endowed with a rent of 3s. 4d. from property at Whiston.

The incomes of the prebendaries were derived mainly from tithes and rents. Only at Coppenhall and Stretton were the prebendal chapels served by vicars; in each case the vicar received small tithes and also had a house and glebe. At Shareshill the curate received a salary of £5 6s. 8d. from the prebendary, and there was presumably a similar arrangement at Dunston, where a chapel had been built by 1445.[67] Between 1291 and 1535 all the prebends except Longridge had increased in value. Coppenhall was now worth £16, Stretton £12, Shareshill £10 16s. 8d., Penkridge £9 6s. 8d., Dunston £6, and Congreve £2 16s. 8d. Longridge

had dropped to 16s., entirely from grain, and it was exempt from the synodal payment of 6s. 8d. due to the dean every third year from each of the other prebendaries. The dean's prebend was valued at £1 6s. 8d. At the dissolution the total yearly value of the college was £82 6s. 8d. By then much of its property was leased out, notably to Edward Littleton of Pillaton. The college house and all the deanery possessions were leased to him in 1543 for 80 years; in 1545 he was granted the farm of the prebend of Stretton for 21 years and the farm of the prebend of Shareshill for 10 years, and in 1547 the prebend of Coppenhall for the life of the incumbent and the prebend of Penkridge for 21 years.

Penkridge College was dissolved in 1548 under the Act of 1547.[68] The minister's account for 1547–1548 shows the prebendaries receiving half a year's income, £41 1s. 8d., up to Easter 1548. In August 1548 the site of the college house and all the deanery possessions, in the tenure of Edward Littleton, were granted to John Dudley, Earl of Warwick; his lands were forfeited to the Crown in 1553. In 1581 the Crown granted the college and its possessions to Edmund Downynge and Peter Aysheton, who sold them in 1583 to John Morley and Thomas Crompton. They conveyed them in 1585 for £604 to Sir Edward Littleton in whose family they then descended with little change until the extensive sales of the 20th century.

Despite the dissolution the peculiar jurisdiction of the former college over the parish of Penkridge survived until the 19th century. The archbishops of Dublin were claiming the right of visitation in the later 17th century. Soon after his consecration in 1661 Archbishop Margetson carried out a visitation, while Archbishop Marsh (1694–1703), in response to a request from Bishop Lloyd of Lichfield and Coventry (1692–9), granted him a process to visit Penkridge in the name of the archbishop. There was great local consternation when the process was delivered to the churchwardens of Penkridge. Word was sent to Edward Littleton who wrote to the bishop. Chancellor Walmesley came to peruse the grants and was satisfied that the archbishop had no power to visit. The bishop himself came to Penkridge and confirmed this; he then dined with Littleton and went back to Lichfield 'without any pretence of visiting'.[69] By 1737 Sir Edward Littleton, as patron of Penkridge, was appointing the incumbent of Penkridge as official of the peculiar jurisdiction, a practice which evidently continued until the jurisdiction was abolished in 1858.[70]

The collegiate buildings may have lain to the west of the church. Some buildings of medieval and possibly early-16th-century date survive in this area, and these may have been connected with the college.[71]

[61] See below p. 324.

[62] Lambeth Palace Libr., Reg. of Archbp. Arundel, f. 482. For this visitation see below p. 325. The free chapels of Wolverhampton, Tettenhall and Stafford were also visited.

[63] For what follows on the property and organization of the college and on its dissolution see (unless otherwise stated) S.H.C. 1950–1, 23–24, 36–43, and the references there given; S.H.C. 1915, 202–8; V.C.H. Staffs. v. 111, 113, 120, 124–5, 140, 147, 179; ibid. iv. 166.

[64] A note by Archbp. Alen in his Register (p. 311) stated that the salaries of the resident vicars had been much diminished.

[65] According to the Valor Eccl. (Rec. Com.). iii. 106, the

2 canons had an income of £1 6s. 8d. from lands and tenements.

[66] Only 2 of the closes yielded an income because each year one close lay in the common field.

[67] V.C.H. Staffs. v. 147.   [68] See below p. 326.

[69] S.H.C.1950–1, 44–45.

[70] St. Michael's, Penkridge, Marriage Reg. 1735–54, f. 4v.; Lich. Dioc. Regy., Penkridge Peculiar; W.S.L., C. B. Penkridge; White, Dir. Staffs. (1834); see above p. 74 The last official, J. A. Fell (incumbent of Penkridge 1852–73), continued to exercise the jurisdiction after 1858: Lich. Dioc. Regy., Penkridge Peculiar, marriage bonds.

[71] V.C.H. Staffs. v. 111.

DEANS

Robert of Coppenhall, occurs *temp.* Henry II and is probably the Dean Robert who occurs 1180–8.[72]

Elias of Bristol, appointed 1199, evidently died in 1226.[73]

Walter de Kirkeham, appointed August 1226; appointment cancelled in view of the right of the Archbishop of Dublin; Walter had resigned by December.[74]

Henry of London, Archbishop of Dublin, succeeded 1226, died 1228.

Richard of St. John, appointed 1228, appointment cancelled 1230.

Luke, Archbishop of Dublin, succeeded 1230, died 1256.

Fulk de Sanford, succeeded 1257.

From 1259 the deanery remained united with the archbishopric of Dublin until the Dissolution.

The college seal in use about the mid 13th century depicts the winged figure of St. Michael.[75] Legend:

... S*ANCTI* MI[CHAELIS] [D]E P ...

A brass matrix of the seal of the peculiar jurisdiction survives from the 17th century. It is oval, some 2 inches long, and depicts a dove on a branch holding another branch in its bill.[76] Legend, roman:

SIG*ILLUM* DAN' PIPER A.M. OFFIC*IALIS* ET COMM*ISSARII* PECULIARIS ET EXEMPTAE IURISD*ICTIONIS* DE PENKRICH

35. THE COLLEGE OF ST. MARY, STAFFORD

THE existence of a group of canons in Stafford before the Conquest is attested only by Domesday Book.[1] In 1086 there were 13 of them, described as the king's prebendary canons, who held 14 messuages in Stafford and 3 hides, probably in Whitgreave and Butterton.[2]

By the beginning of Stephen's reign the church of Stafford, like that of Penkridge, was held in chief by Jordan, clerk to Roger de Fécamp, probably by grant of Henry I.[3] The two churches were given by Stephen in 1136 to the bishop and cathedral churches of Coventry and Lichfield;[4] the bishop's possession of them was confirmed by the Pope in 1139, 1144, and 1152.[5] The church of Stafford, like other royal property alienated by Stephen, returned to the Crown under Henry II[6] who appointed Robert and probably also Robert's predecessor, William de C., the first known deans of Stafford.[7] Although a royal chapel, Stafford was still apparently not claiming exemption from the bishop's authority as late as the end of the 12th century. In 1199 one of the canons appealed to the protection of either the bishop or the dean in a dispute about his prebendal lands.[8] Four years later, however, another canon in similar circumstances invoked the dean alone.[9]

There is no obvious explanation of the tradition, recorded in 1546 and 1548, that King John was the founder of the collegiate church.[10] Canons and deans of Stafford are known before his time, but it is possible that the dedication to St. Mary was due to him: the first mention of it belongs to his reign.[11] The earlier parts of the present church date from the late 12th century.[12] Perhaps John promoted the building and a new dedication.[13] This church may have had a predecessor on the same site, or may have replaced as the collegiate church the adjoining Saxon church dedicated to St. Bertelin[14] which continued alongside St. Mary's and preserved a separate though allied existence.[15]

The king usually appointed to the deaneries of royal chapels clerks in his service whom he wished to reward. This system had advantages, for royal servants, though much occupied, were often influential men of outstanding ability. Henry III sent frequent gifts to Stafford while two clerks of his household chapel, Walter of Lench and Simon of Offham, were deans: timber for repairs to the canons' stalls and the building of a belfry in 1244; more timber in 1246 and 1255; venison, pike, and bream for the dean in 1234, 1249, and 1250.[16] He also backed the dean and chapter's claims to dependent chapels. With royal support, the right of St. Mary's to the burial of the parishioners of the chapel of Tixall and the institution of its chaplain was vindicated in 1247.[17] The advowson of Castle Church was recovered from Stone Priory in 1255, when Henry III declared that it was in the gift of the dean like the prebends of Stafford.[18] In 1258 the king sued on

[72] *S.H.C.* vi(1), 23; see above pp. 298–9.
[73] *S.H.C.* 1950–1, 7, 8, 9 and n., 51, 52 n. He was also Dean of Tettenhall *c.* 1225: see below p. 320.
[74] *S.H.C.* 1950–1, 11. For the remainder of the list see above p. 299.
[75] *S.H.C.* 1950–1, 15 n.
[76] A. B. Tonnochy, *Cat. of Brit. Seal Dies in B.M.* 188.
[1] *V.C.H. Staffs.* iv. 44, no. 100.
[2] Ibid. iv. 37, 44. This is an early example of a prebendal system; for its introduction at Lichfield see above p. 141. The canons held 3 hides in Whitgreave and Butterton in the 13th century (*S.H.C.* vi(1), 215, 287; *S.H.C.* 1913, 220–2), and 9 of their prebends lay in Whitgreave (*Feud. Aids*, v. 19–20).
[3] See above p. 298.
[4] *S.H.C.* 1924, p. 285. The full text is given in Ric. II's *inspeximus: Cal. Chart. R. 1341–1417*, 308.
[5] *S.H.C.* 1924, pp. 126–7, 215–16; Dugdale, *Mon.* vi(3), 1249, 1252.
[6] For the resumption of royal demesne by Hen. II see *Chronicles of the reigns of Stephen, Hen. II and Ric. I* (Rolls Ser.), i. 103.
[7] See below p. 308.
[8] *S.H.C.* iii(1), 51.
[9] Ibid. 76.
[10] E 301/40, no. 16; /54, no. 2.

[11] *S.H.C.* iii(1), 170–1.
[12] S. A. Cutlack, 'St. Mary's Church, Stafford', *T.O.S.S.* 1945–6 and 1946–7.
[13] For a possibly analogous dedication associating St. Mary with St. Bertelin see J. Tait, 'The Foundation Charter of Runcorn Priory', *Chetham Soc.* N.S. vol. c, 8–9.
[14] *The Church of St. Bertelin at Stafford*, ed. A. Oswald, 7, 14–27.
[15] In 1428 a jury stated that St. Bertelin's had the right of burial of the parishioners of the chapels of Tixall, Ingestre, and Creswell, which otherwise looked to St. Mary's as their mother-church (see below p. 306); but a jury of 1247 ascribed to St. Mary's the right to Tixall's burials (*S.H.C.* iv(1), 112–13). The presumption that St. Bertelin's shared the chaplains of St. Mary's is supported by the wording of a grant of the deanery in 1524 (*L. & P. Hen. VIII*, iv(1), p. 169), when it was called the deanery of St. Mary and St. Bartholomew, a not uncommon rendering of Bertelin (*Church of St. Bertelin*, 9).
[16] *Close R.* 1231–4, 516; 1242–7, 160, 462; 1247–51, 244, 254; 1254–6, 233.
[17] *S.H.C.* iv(1), 112–13. See above n. 15 for the statement by a jury in 1428 that the burial of Tixall's parishioners belonged to St. Bertelin's.
[18] *V.C.H. Staffs.* v. 95.

behalf of St. Mary's for the advowson of the chapel of Middle Aston in Steeple Aston (Oxon.), claimed as a dependency of Hopton church.[19]

Even more important was the king's support of the claim to exemption from the bishop's jurisdiction. That this exemption had been taken for granted by the Crown is evident from recorded royal appointments to the deanery (the earliest belongs to 1207),[20] for it was to the sheriff that the king sent his mandate to institute new deans. There was no dispute until 1244, and then it was not the bishop who was involved, for the see was vacant. Henry III appointed three canons of St. Mary's as his proctors to defend the liberties of the church,[21] evidently against the archdeacon.[22] Next year he secured a papal declaration that royal chapels were immune from ordinary jurisdiction.[23] The new bishop, Roger Weseham, almost immediately obtained a papal letter excluding Stafford and some other churches in the diocese from the terms of the bull,[24] and he proceeded to hold an ordination in St. Mary's. Henry III continued to assert the privileges of his free chapels[25] and was said to have established, apparently in a charter, that St. Mary's was a royal chapel enjoying the accompanying immunities. This charter was reported stolen in 1251.[26] Although when the king re-issued it only secular privileges were specified, it was claimed in 1293 that St. Mary's had become exempt from the bishop's jurisdiction by Henry III's consent.[27] Certainly Henry III treated Stafford as exempt. In 1247 his attorney objected to matters concerning St. Mary's being heard in court Christian,[28] and in 1252 he ordered the sheriff to arrest a man excommunicated by the bishop 'unless he be of the liberty of the king's chapel of Stafford'.[29]

The claim to exemption brought the king into conflict with the diocesan. In 1257, before Weseham's successor, Roger Meuland, had even been consecrated, the king appointed canons of St. Mary's as his proctors to defend the chapel's liberties.[30] Soon after Meuland's consecration in March 1258 proctors were again appointed,[31] and in December the bishop came to Stafford with many armed men who, it was claimed, broke down the doors of the church and ill-treated the canons, chaplains, and clerks. The king summoned him before his court, but Meuland claimed benefit of clergy and refused to plead.[32] He suspended the chapter of Stafford, excommunicated the dean and two leading canons, and sequestrated one of the prebends.[33] The king personally ordered a justice to inquire into the bishop's jurisdiction over St. Mary's, but this order was later stayed, probably owing to the shortage of judges in 1259.[34]

Although St. Mary's resisted the bishop's authority, no objection was raised against the archbishop when he came on provincial visitation in 1260.[35] Perhaps the canons hoped that he would support them against the nearer and more oppressive diocesan. Archbishop Boniface heard their complaint and found against them. The canons claimed that they had a recent papal grant of exemption and, after failing to produce it on this and two later occasions, appealed from the archbishop to Rome.[36] Urban IV appointed commissioners in England to hear the case, but as they failed to decide it within a year it was remitted to Rome.[37] Though twice cited the Dean and Chapter of Stafford failed to appear or be represented in Rome, and in 1267 judgment was given in their absence.[38] The chapter remained suspended and the dean excommunicated. They were to render obedience to their bishop until they produced proof of exemption, and they were to pay the expenses incurred by the bishop in sending his proctor to Rome. It is not clear why the canons failed to defend their cause. Perhaps they could not afford the expense. Perhaps they relied on royal influence at Rome: Meuland had joined Simon de Montfort while papal sympathies were with the king. Certainly they must have suffered from lack of an effective dean. Bevis de Clare, son of the Earl of Gloucester, was appointed to the deanery at the age of eleven in 1259;[39] when the final judgment was given in 1267 he was still under 19 and already a notable pluralist.[40]

When Archbishop Pecham came to Stafford in 1280 during his metropolitical visitation the chapter of St. Mary's was still under the papal sentence of suspension and still obdurate. The church was under interdict imposed by the bishop,[41] but enjoyed the support of the townspeople, who had asked the

[19] S.H.C. iv(1), 136. For the connexion of Middle Aston with Hopton see S.H.C. N.S. xii. 139 n. The right to the advowson of Hopton was disputed in 1293: S.H.C. vi(1), 225.
[20] Rot. Litt. Claus. (Rec. Com.), i. 80.
[21] Cal. Pat. 1232–47, 420.
[22] Hen. III named the Archdeacon of Stafford as responsible for an attack on the privileges of the royal chapel of Bridgnorth at this time: T. Rymer, Foedera (Rec. Com.), i(1), 261.
[23] Ibid. The bull is also given in Close R. 1247–51, 99, 226. The king sent a transcript to the Dean of St. Mary's: K.B. 27/178, m. 1; and see Cal. Pat. 1281–92, 360.
[24] Annales Monastici (Rolls Ser.), i. 275–6.
[25] Ibid. 275; Close R. 1247–51, 226; F. M. Powicke and C. R. Cheney, Councils and Synods, ii(1), 446–7.
[26] The theft is mentioned in a new charter (Cal. Chart. R. 1226–57, 368) and in an inquisition of 1293 (J.I. 1/804, m. 75d.).
[27] J.I. 1/804, m. 75d.; part of this is given in S.H.C. vi(1), 287. Hen. III began to refer to St. Mary's as his 'free' chapel in 1244: Cal. Pat. 1232–47, 420.
[28] S.H.C. iv(1), 112.
[29] Close R. 1251–3, 194.
[30] Cal. Pat. 1247–58, 550.
[31] Ibid. 621.
[32] S.H.C. iv(1), 140–1.

[33] S.H.C. 1924, pp. 271–2; Close R. 1256–9, 486.
[34] Close R. 1256–9, 405; this justice was particularly busy (see Cal. Pat. 1247–58, 665). For the pressure of judicial business and shortage of qualified judges in 1258–61 see R. F. Treharne, The Baronial Plan of Reform, 1258–63, 145–6, 196, 249.
[35] W. Prynne, Records, iii. 1234, where the date 1265 is an obvious error for 1260 (see S.C. 1/11/94).
[36] The whole story is contained in a letter from Abp. Boniface to Pope Alexander IV: Prynne, Records, iii. 1234–5.
[37] S.H.C. 1924, pp. 271–2.
[38] Ibid. pp. 268–71.
[39] He was born in 1248: Ann. Mon. i. 136. His father had to appear for him when Bp. Meuland came before the king's court in 1259 to answer for his forcible visitation of St. Mary's: S.H.C. iv(1), 140–1.
[40] Cal. Pat. 1258–66, 40, 42, 449, 498, 510. No one has anything good to say of him: he acquired more benefices than any English contemporary (A. Hamilton Thompson, 'Pluralism in the Mediaeval Church', Assoc. Archit. Soc. Rep. and Papers, xxxiii, 53–56), and neglected them thoroughly (Reg. Epist. Fratris Johannis Peckham (Rolls Ser.), i. 371–2); his personal extravagance and meanness as regards charity are brought out by his household accounts (M. S. Giuseppi, 'The Wardrobe and Household Accounts of Bogo de Clare, 1284–6', Archaeologia, lxx).
[41] Reg. Epist. Peckham, i. 111, 3920–p.

king whether they should join his free chapel in resisting the archbishop's citation.[42] Edward I replied ordering them and the Sheriff of Staffordshire to prevent Pecham from entering St. Mary's, and this they did by force.[43] Despite his conviction that the claim to exemption was baseless,[44] in deference to the king's wishes Pecham reluctantly consented to whatever settlement might be reached between the king, the royal chapels, and their diocesans. Meuland was now old and infirm whereas Edward I was vigorous and unyielding. The long dispute ended in 1281 with the bishop's capitulation. He recognized the exemption of St. Mary's and five other royal chapels in his diocese from all ordinary jurisdiction.[45]

The secular privileges of St. Mary's were set out in Henry III's charter of 1251 replacing the earlier charter of the same king which had been stolen.[46] The dean and chapter had the right to hold a court for themselves and for their tenants in the town of Stafford and in Orberton, Butterton, Worston, and Whitgreave. Their court followed the custom of the king's manors without interference of the sheriff or any other royal officer, and they owed no suit to shire, hundred, or borough courts. They had their own gallows and right of infangentheof and utfangentheof. Their tenants were quit of all customs and tallages except those tallages granted by other exempt churches. In virtue of this charter St. Mary's was declared quit of royal tallages in 1252 and 1253.[47]

In theory St. Mary's was also exempt from ecclesiastical taxes. Henry III had asserted in 1250 that no prelate had power to tax royal chapels,[48] but this exemption was not claimed when papal taxes benefited the king. Like the other royal chapels St. Mary's paid the papal tenths granted in 1266 and subsequently.[49]

The assessments for papal taxes give some indication of the value of the church. In 1268 and 1269 St. Mary's paid £3 6s. 8d., representing a tenth of its assessment, but this valuation of £33 6s. 8d. and all other assessments were superseded by that made for the Taxation of 1291. This gives the total value of St. Mary's as £58 17s.[50] There are no details of the value of the individual prebends, but it is possible to supply most of these from later documents, since the 1291 assessment was not superseded until 1535. An inquisition of 1428[51] quotes the old taxation as follows: the deanery £10 16s. 8d.; the prebend of Marston £6 13s. 4d.; the prebend of Salt £6 13s. 4d.; the prebend of

Coton £6 13s. 4d.; the free chapel of Tixall £6 13s. 4d.; the free chapel of Ingestre £3 6s. 8d.; the free chapel of Creswell £3 6s. 8d.; two prebends in Whitgreave £5 and seven small prebends there £10 10s. These items add up to £59 13s. 4d., which is 16s. 4d. more than the total given in 1291. A possible explanation is that some of the prebends of very little value escaped taxation, although in 1428 they were all said to have paid the tenth. At least two of the nine Whitgreave prebends were worth only 2s. 4d.;[52] one, worth 13s. 4d., was said in 1366 not to have been taxed;[53] another was worth £1.[54]

Obviously the only prebends in St. Mary's really worth having were Marston, Salt, and Coton. It was probably one of these which was annexed to the deanery when in 1247 Simon of Offham was authorized by the king to convert to his own use for life whichever of the prebends he chose.[55] His successors did not enjoy the same privilege: subsequent references to prebendaries[56] show that neither Marston, Salt, nor Coton can have remained attached to the deanery. It became the practice, however, to unite one of the Whitgreave prebends to the prebend of Marston. In the 13th century two successive sub-deans held Marston with a prebend of Whitgreave.[57] Such a practice might explain statements made in the 14th century that Alan of Conisbrough in 1328[58] and Simon Gentyl in 1366[59] held a prebend of Stafford worth £8; no one prebend was valued as highly as that, but Marston (or Salt or Coton) together with a Whitgreave prebend worth 2 marks would make up the total. A Whitgreave prebend was still united to Marston in the 16th century; its property consisted of 40 acres of arable in Whitgreave, known as the Hall prebend.[60] By this time, although the Hall prebend retained its separate name, it had lost its separate identity and was reckoned among the assets of Marston. But there were still nine Whitgreave prebends. This suggests that the Whitgreave property had been further subdivided to keep up the number of prebends, irrespective of their value. Surprisingly these very small prebends seem usually to have been held separately. In 1366 two canons residing in the diocese held prebends of Stafford worth only 2s. 4d. and 13s. 4d. respectively, but each held a parish church in the diocese as well;[61] their prebends perhaps gave them a house in Stafford and added status. It is harder to understand the position of William Dyngell who held in the diocese only a prebend of Stafford taxed at 2s. 4d. and yet resided

[42] Prynne, Records, iii. 1236.
[43] Cal. Chanc. Wts. i. 5–6; Reg. Epist. Peckham, i. 111, 392p.
[44] Reg. Epist. Peckham, i. 180–1, 392t.
[45] See below p. 324.
[46] S.H.C. 1911, 120–1; Cal. Chart. R. 1226–57, 368; see above p. 304.
[47] Close R. 1251–3, 81, 210.
[48] Wilkins, Concilia, i. 697; Cal. Pat. 1247–58, 77.
[49] Cal. Pat. 1266–72, 221, 329; Cal. Close, 1313–18, 172–3; Cal. Fine R. 1319–27, 39–40.
[50] Tax. Eccl. (Rec. Com.), 242. The sum is given here as £58 17s., but the tenth (£5 17s. 8d.), and the sum quoted as the assessment of 1291 in the Nonae Rolls of 1341 (Inq. Non. (Rec. Com.), 128), where it is given as 88 marks 3s. 4d., indicate that the true amount was £58 16s. 8d.
[51] Feud. Aids, v. 19–20.
[52] S.H.C. N.S. x(2), 218–19, 220.
[53] Ibid. 219; Cal. Papal Regs. viii. 528; ix. 6–7.
[54] Cal. Papal Regs. ii. 70–71.

[55] Cal. Pat. 1247–58, 1.
[56] Names of these prebendaries before 1535 may be traced as follows: Marston from the mid 13th cent. in S.H.C. vi(1), 177; Abbrev. Plac. (Rec. Com.), 303; Cal. Pat. 1307–13, 480; 1317–21, 471; 1374–7, 372, 460; 1377–81, 323; Cal. Papal Regs. vi. 512; Coton from the late 14th cent. in Le Neve, Fasti Ecclesiae Anglicanae, 1300–1541 (new edn.), vi. 40; x. 33; Cal. Pat. 1391–6, 467; 1401–5, 158; Salt in 1390 in Cal. Pat. 1388–92, 298. The holders of these prebends in 1531 and 1533 are given in taxation lists for the Archdeaconry of Stafford in Lich. Dioc. Regy., B/A/17/1, and D. & C. Lich. lxiii. There is a full list of prebendaries in 1535 in Valor Eccl. (Rec. Com.), iii. 118–19.
[57] S.H.C. vi(1), 177, 239.
[58] Cal. Papal Regs. ii. 267.
[59] S.H.C. N.S. x(2), 220.
[60] The property of Marston prebend is given in full in S.C. 12/28/12, f. 32 (1547–8).
[61] S.H.C. N.S. x(2), 219, 220.

there, though he had a parish church in Lincolnshire taxed at £24.[62]

The free chapels of Tixall, Ingestre, and Creswell were included in the assessment of St. Mary's because they were within the liberty of the collegiate church. This meant that the dean had jurisdiction over them and instituted their chaplains, but he had no control over the advowsons, which belonged to different individuals.[63] These chapels, it was stated in 1428, were separate churches, and by ancient custom their parishioners buried their dead in St. Bertelin's Church and graveyard and not at St. Mary's.[64]

It might be expected that Castle Church would have appeared with St. Mary's in the Taxation of 1291, since the dean owned the advowson and the property in tithes and lands attached to the living. The lands were claimed by Stone Priory in 1293, when the verdict was in the dean's favour, and again from 1311 until at least 1319.[65] Once more, however, the dean seems to have made good his claim, for he was in possession in 1535.[66] It is likely that the dean had always kept Castle Church for himself, providing a priest but taking the bulk of the revenues as he was doing in 1535. This would explain why Castle Church was not assessed separately in the Taxation of 1291: it would have been included in the assets of the deanery. In the period 1282–6 the bailiff administering Castle Church was liable for 40 marks (£26 13s. 4d.) a year for it.[67] Presumably the priest had to be paid out of this, but a sizeable sum would have been left. In addition the bailiff was accountable for £5 13s. 4d. for the dean's prebend,[68] and the dean had the church of Hopton to his own use by gift of the king.[69] The Taxation of 1291 valued the deanery at only £10 16s. 8d., but a comparable difference between this assessment and the real value of the property is to be found elsewhere.[70] The statement of a jury of 1293 that the church of St. Mary, Stafford, held by Bevis de Clare was worth 50 marks (£33 6s. 8d.) a year[71] was probably nearer the truth.

Royal chapels paid only those papal taxes which were assigned to the king. Against other demands the Crown was their firm defender. Edward I and Edward II repeatedly declared them exempt from all papal exactions[72] and in 1307 and 1317 included St. Mary's when issuing prohibitions against the collection of papal procurations from specified chapels.[73] When in 1318 the papal nuncio was forbidden to exact annates from the king's chapels, Edward II named nine churches with this exempt status; St. Mary's came third on the list.[74]

Since royal chapels were exempt from the jurisdiction of the bishop, their visitation and correction

was the responsibility of the king who delegated this power to special commissioners or the Chancellor. In 1368 commissioners were appointed to visit and correct five royal chapels, including St. Mary's, whose officers were reputed negligent.[75] The deans were accused of failing to safeguard property and privileges, and the clergy of leading dissolute lives and appropriating revenues which should have been used for divine service, works of charity, and repairs. The next visitation of St. Mary's, in 1381, was probably at the request of the new dean, William Pakington, since the inquiry was confined to practical matters: the state of the church's property and the diminution of the number of chaplains.[76] Pakington received compensation for his predecessors' shortcomings, but after his death in 1390 his successor petitioned for an inquiry into what had become of this money and into Pakington's own neglect of the property for which the dean was responsible.[77] Despite the resulting visitation there was no improvement. John Mackworth in 1407 complained of all three deans between Pakington and himself; they had allowed the dean's buildings to fall into total disrepair, and Mackworth's immediate predecessor had misappropriated 50 marks allotted to him to put right the dilapidations that he had inherited.[78] Neglect of the dean's property was not surprising when deans were absentees, but apparently they had kept the chancel and furnishings of the church in good repair, since Mackworth made no complaint about them; nor was neglect of divine service alleged.

By the late 14th century it had become accepted that the king's right of supervision of his chapels was exercised by the Chancellor. It is remarkable that in 1400–1 royal rights were disregarded when Archbishop Arundel's commissioners included the king's chapels in their visitation of the diocese. St. Mary's was the last chapel to be visited and raised no protest. Representatives of the dean, canons, vicars, and chaplains appeared and were examined, each professing canonical obedience to the archbishop.[79] The findings are not recorded. This archiepiscopal visitation did not create a precedent: apparently it was the result of temporary political circumstances.[80] In 1407 St. Mary's was visited by royal commissioners; and at some time between 1467 and 1471 the dean, Thomas Hawkins, appealed to the Chancellor in a dispute about tithes, stating that he and his predecessors had no other judge or protector.[81]

By Hawkins's time St. Mary's was no longer in Crown patronage. In 1446 Henry VI had granted the advowson to Humphrey Stafford, Duke of Buckingham.[82] This made no difference to the

[62] Ibid. 218–19.
[63] For the patrons of Tixall see *S.H.C.* iv(1), 112–13; ibid. xi. 237, 244; ibid. 1911, 103; for Ingestre, *S.H.C.* 1911, 71; *Cal. Pat.* 1396–9, 410; for Creswell, *Cal. Pat.* 1334–8, 32, 42, 45; 1345–8, 67, 86; *Cal. Close*, 1346–9, 29.
[64] *Feud. Aids*, v. 19–20.
[65] *S.H.C.* vi(1), 14, 238; ix(1), 34, 73; *Cal. Close*, 1318–1323, 52–53.
[66] *Valor Eccl.* iii. 117.
[67] *S.H.C.* vi(1), 210.
[68] Ibid.
[69] *Year Bk. 20 and 21 Edw. I* (Rolls Ser.), 408–9; *S.H.C.* vi(1), 225.
[70] The deanery of Wolverhampton was similarly underassessed: see p. 324. Tables showing the real value and the 1291 assessments of selected benefices in the dioceses of

Lincoln, Durham, and Wells and similar evidence for other dioceses are given by Rose Graham, 'The Taxation of Pope Nicholas IV', *Eng. Eccles. Studies*, 285–9.
[71] *S.H.C.* vi(1), 275.
[72] *Cal. Close*, 1288–96, 423; 1302–7, 530; 1307–13, 236; 1313–18, 566, 596; Rymer, *Foedera*, ii(1), 297.
[73] *Cal. Close*, 1302–7, 530; 1313–18, 566.
[74] Ibid. 596.
[75] *Cal. Pat.* 1367–70, 142, 143.
[76] Ibid. 1377–81, 629.
[77] Ibid. 1388–92, 349–50.
[78] Ibid. 1405–8, 352; C 145/285/6.
[79] Lambeth Palace Libr., Reg. Arundel, i, f. 482.
[80] For this visitation see p. 325.
[81] C 145/285/6; *S.H.C.* N.S. vii. 269.
[82] *Cal. Pat.* 1441–6, 413; Dugdale, *Mon.* vi(3), 1439.

status of St. Mary's as a royal chapel, since it claimed to be a royal foundation.[83] Subsequent loss of a direct relationship with the Crown could not alter this. Nevertheless the bishop seems to have considered that it was no longer exempt from his authority, for in 1501, on the death of Hawkins's successor, he appointed commissioners to govern the collegiate church and receive the revenues of the deanery during the vacancy, claiming this right by canonical ordinance and laudable and long-standing custom.[84] If this had become custom, it did not stand much longer, for St. Mary's returned to the Crown in 1521 when Edward, Duke of Buckingham, was executed and his estates forfeited.[85] The surveyors of his property explained the status of St. Mary's, 'which ever hath been *capella regia* and is privileged accordingly', adding that 'albeit the Duke was patron, yet the King was founder'.[86] Although the manor of Stafford was restored to Edward's son Henry in 1531,[87] the advowson of St. Mary's remained with the Crown.

When Buckingham became patron in 1446 he had been licensed to endow a chantry in St. Mary's with lands and rents worth 100 marks.[88] No trace of this appears in the survey of church revenues made in 1535. By this date there was only one chantry in St. Mary's, that of St. Thomas the Martyr, which had been founded by Thomas Counter probably in the late 15th century for a chaplain to celebrate mass daily and keep a school.[89] In 1535 its revenues were £4 7s. a year.[90]

In the survey of 1535[91] separate names were given for the nine prebends of St. Mary's which formerly had shared the name of Whitgreave: Swetnam, Blurton, Hervy, Walsall,[92] Sandall, Orberton, Denston, Potrell,[93] and Croft. Their assessments were low, together amounting to only £5 8s. 8d.; Coton, Marston, and Salt were still the only prebends of real value. The deanery's assets included the chapel of Hopton (here called a prebend), which

was annexed to it, as was Castle Church; the dean also received annual pensions from the prebends of Coton, Marston, and Salt and from the chapels of Creswell, Ingestre, and Tixall. The list of chapels within the liberty of St. Mary's now included not only Creswell,[94] Ingestre, and Tixall but also the hospitals of St. John and St. Leonard in Forebridge and the chapel of St. Nicholas within Stafford castle; these three lay within the parish of Castle Church and had been founded by the ancestors of Lord Stafford, who held the advowsons.[95] St. Nicholas's acted as a parish church for the inhabitants of the castle and its park, except that burial was at St. Mary's, Stafford,[96] since Castle Church (St. Nicholas's mother-church) was appropriated to the deanery.

The surveys of chantries and collegiate churches ordered in 1546 and 1548 as a prelude to their dissolution[97] give a clearer picture of the organization of the college of Stafford and its annexed churches than the surviving evidence for earlier periods can afford. The dean and canons were represented in St. Mary's by four priest vicars; these were paid at the rate of £5 a year by the dean and three of the prebendaries (those of Coton, Marston, and Salt), who maintained one each.[98] Besides these four priests there were four 'lay' or 'clerk' vicars[99] to sing the services; these were said in 1546 to be paid 8s. each a year,[1] and in 1548 to share revenues worth £4 13s. 4d. a year, each taking £1 3s. 4d.[2] The Prebendary of Coton, who was also sacrist, provided at his own cost the wine and wax needed for the services.[3] Thomas Counter's chantry priest sang morrow mass and kept a school in the church.[4] Priests serving Castle Church and Hopton were paid by the dean,[5] who drew the revenues of these churches. Chapels at Marston and Salt were served by priests paid by the prebendaries of Marston[6] and Salt[7] respectively. It seems likely that the holders of the nine Whitgreave prebends did no

[83] Hawkins described himself as Dean of Stafford, 'the which is of the foundation of the King our soverayn lord': *S.H.C.* N.S. vii. 269.
[84] S.R.O., D.(W.) 1721/1/1, f. 17d.
[85] *L. & P. Hen. VIII,* iii(1), p. 510.
[86] Ibid.
[87] *V.C.H. Staffs.* v. 87.
[88] *Cal. Pat.* 1441–6, 413; Dugdale, *Mon.* vi(3), 1439.
[89] The name of the founder, as well as the purpose of the chantry and its value, is given in the Chantry Certificates of 1546 and 1548: E 301/40, no. 16; /54, no. 2. The founder was probably the Thos. Counter, Rector of Ingestre, who was a party to a deed of 1480: *S.H.C.* N.S. vi(1), 130.
[90] *Valor Eccl.* iii. 120. The revenues were said to be worth £4 13s. 4d. in 1546 and 1548: E 301/40, no. 16; /54, no. 2.
[91] *Valor Eccl.* iii. 117–19.
[92] One of the prebends had borne this name since at least 1348: *Cal. Pat.* 1348–50, 214.
[93] A prebend of Powtrell in the church of Stafford is mentioned in a papal bull of 1504: *Diplomatic and Scottish Docs. and Papal Bulls* (P.R.O. Lists and Indexes, xlix), 317.
[94] Here called a prebend, no doubt in error since it does not so appear in the Chantry Certificates.
[95] *V.C.H. Staffs.* v. 83, 85, 91, 97. For the hospital of St. John see above p. 291 n. 26.
[96] E 301/40, no. 40; /54, no. 2; /44(1), no. 41.
[97] Under the Acts of 1545 and 1547: see p. 326. Six returns survive for Stafford, dated 15 Feb. 1546, 30 May 1548, 30 June 1548, 15 Mar. 1549, June 1549, and 19 Sept. 1548: E 301/40; /54; /44(1); /44(2); /43; S.C. 12/28/12. The information which they provide is supple-

mented by a list of pensions granted when the college was dissolved (E 101/75/30, 22 June 1548) and a bailiff's acct. of the revenues in 1547–8 (S.C. 6/Edw. VI/424).
[98] E 301/40, no. 16. Salaries of £5 are recorded for the priest vicars of the dean and the prebendaries of Marston and Coton in E 101/75/30, mm. 1d., 3, 5, and for all four priest vicars in E 301/44(2). A stipend of £6 is given for the Prebendary of Coton's vicar in E 301/40, no. 16, but this seems likely to be an error.
[99] E 301/43.
[1] E 301/40, no. 16.
[2] E 301/44(1), ff 11v.–12. In June 1549 it was explained that these revenues came from oblations, mortuary fees, and Easter offerings in St. Mary's, besides lands and rents in Stafford and Butterton; this year they were assessed at £4 3s. 6d.: E 301/43.
[3] *Valor Eccl.* iii. 118; E 301/40, no. 16. The cost was £2 a year.
[4] E 301/40, no. 16; /54, no. 2; /44(1), no. 49; /43.
[5] E 301/54, no. 2. The dean paid three priests a total of £14 6s. 8d. a year: E 301/40, no. 16. Of this his priest vicar in St. Mary's had £5 and the priest of Hopton £4 6s. 8d.: E 301/44(2). The stipend of the priest of Castle Church was therefore £5.
[6] The Prebendary of Marston paid two priests a total of £9 13s. 4d.: E 301/40, no. 16. Of this his priest vicar in St. Mary's had £5 (see above n. 98), which should have left £4 13s. 4d. for the priest of Marston chapel; but it is possible that, like the chaplain of Salt, he was in fact paid £4 6s. 8d. (see below n. 7).
[7] The chaplain of Salt was paid £4 6s. 8d. (E 301/44(2)), but the salaries of the two priests paid by the Prebendary of Salt (his priest vicar, £5, and this chaplain), were said to amount to £9 13s. 4d. in E 301/40, no. 16.

more than draw their small incomes: in 1548 it was not even known whether the Prebendary of Sandall was still alive.[8]

The college was dissolved in 1548 under the Act of 1547.[9] The pensions granted to its members[10] represented compensation for what they were in fact receiving whether in direct payments or as a result of leases already in force. Dean Leighton had leased the deanery for a pepper-corn,[11] and this meant that he got no pension. The prebendaries of Salt, Coton, and Marston were awarded £1 10s., £5, and £6 respectively. The Whitgreave prebendaries received almost complete compensation, the vicars choral £5 each, and the clerk vicars £1. The Prebendary of Denston and one of the vicars choral were appointed to serve St. Mary's, their stipends being £16 and £8 respectively.[12] The priests of Salt and Hopton chapels were pensioned off, but the chaplain of Marston was retained to serve his chapel at a stipend of £8. Thomas Counter's chantry priest was kept on as schoolmaster at a salary of £4 5s. a year paid by the Crown, and in addition in 1550 revenues worth £20 a year were granted by Edward VI to the burgesses of Stafford to make the foundation into a grammar school, with one master and one assistant.[13]

Some of the college's property was disposed of within a few years; the rest was kept by the Crown until 1571 when Elizabeth I granted it to the burgesses of Stafford. The assets of the deanery, worth £44 8s. 2d. a year, were given to Henry, Lord Stafford, in April 1550.[14] Four of the Whitgreave prebends, Swetnam, Blurton, Walsall, and Hervy, were sold to two gentlemen of London in April 1549,[15] and the disused chapels and graveyards of Salt and Hopton to two other Londoners in July.[16] Three more Londoners bought the house of the vicars choral in the same month.[17] Part of the endowment of Thomas Counter's chantry was sold to two Londoners in March 1549,[18] but the rest, together with property given to maintain lights in the parish churches of Stafford and Castle Church, and the lands of the clerk vicars, went to local buyers, Walter and Edward Leveson, in July 1550.[19] The property in Whitgreave belonging to the prebends of Coton and Marston was sold to speculators in 1553 and 1554.[20] This left in the hands of the Crown five of the Whitgreave prebends (Croft, Potrell, Sandall, Denston, and Orberton), the prebend of Salt, and the prebends of Coton and Marston less their Whitgreave lands and less Marston's tithes in Stafford which had been granted in 1550 to the grammar school. It was this remaining property (and not the whole endowment of the former collegiate church) which Elizabeth gave in 1571 to the burgesses of Stafford. At this date it was worth £41 2s. 10d. a year. Out of it the stipends granted in 1548-9 to the three priests (two for St. Mary's, Stafford, and one for Marston) and the schoolmaster had to be met; the rest was to be applied to the repair of St. Mary's church and to works of charity in Stafford.[21]

Even the privileged jurisdiction belonging to the collegiate church, which in the case of some royal chapels passed to the new owners of the deanery and survived until the 19th century, came to an end in Stafford at the dissolution. It seems likely that this was because Henry, Lord Stafford, did not retain the ownership of the deanery but soon disposed of it to a London merchant among whose heirs it was subsequently partitioned.[22] The jurisdiction lapsed to the bishop.[23]

The collegiate buildings included the deanery house, which formed part of the grant to Lord Stafford in 1550,[24] and the 'capital messuage of the priests of the late collegiate church', so described when it was sold by the Crown to a group of speculators in 1549.[25] The latter stood on the south side of the churchyard and eventually came into the hands of the corporation. Known as the College House, it was normally held by the master of the grammar school from at least 1615 until the 1720s, but by then it was decayed. Most of it was demolished between 1736 and 1738 and a workhouse established in some of the outbuildings.[26]

DEANS

William de C. (predecessor of Robert).[27]
Robert, occurs *temp.* Henry II.[28]
Ralph of the Hospital, occurs at some time between 1184 and 1190, resigned 1207.[29]
Henry of London, appointed 1207, elected Archbishop of Dublin 1213.[30]

---

[8] E 301/44(1), no. 2.
[9] See below p. 326.
[10] E 101/75/30; E 301/44(1), no. 2; /44(2).
[11] For the circumstances of the granting of this lease and subsequent disputes concerning it see C 1/1122/59 and 60; S.C. 12/28/12, f. 31; E 315/219, f. 48; C 1/1193/5; E 315/105, f. 109.
[12] E 301/44(1), no. 2; /44(2).
[13] E 319/9; *Cal. Pat.* 1550-3, 21. The endowment included the possessions of the two Stafford hospitals of St. John and of St. Leonard as well as collegiate property.
[14] *Cal. Pat.* 1550-3, 18.
[15] Ibid. 1548-9, 409-10.
[16] Ibid. 1549-51, 131-2.
[17] Ibid. 126.
[18] Ibid. 1548-9, 420.
[19] Ibid. 1549-51, 362-3. None of the property of the chantry school came into the possession of Stafford grammar school.
[20] Ibid. 1550-3, 316; 1553-4, 506.
[21] J. W. Bradley, *Royal Charters and Letters Patent granted to the Burgesses of Stafford*, 99-107; *Cal. Pat.* 1569-72, 394-5; G. Griffiths, *Free Schools and Endowments of Staffs.* 21 sqq.
[22] *Cal. Pat.* 1550-3, 66-67; *S.H.C.* xii(1), 212-13; W.S.L., S.MS. 402, f. 15v. Lord Stafford took a lease of

[the property: *S.H.C.* 1938, 96-97; *S.H.C.* N.S. ix. 11-14.]
[23] *S.H.C.* 1926, p. 18; Lich. Dioc. Regy., B/C/5; ibid., B/V/5/4 and 9. The borough charter of 1614 included a clause safeguarding the rights of the bishop; there had originally been a scheme to include in the charter a provision reviving the exempt jurisdiction and allowing its exercise by the corporation: S.R.O., D.(W.) 1721/1/4, ff. 13, 24v., 28; Bradley, *Royal Charters*, 174-5.
[24] *Cal. Pat.* 1550-3, 18.
[25] Ibid. 1549-51, 126. It is presumably to be identified with the house 'wherein divers ministers did lie' mentioned in 1546: E 301/40, no. 16; E 101/75/30. The Revd. L. Lambert, however, thought that this referred to a third building: *St. Mary's and the College Quarter of Stafford* (Birmingham, 1925).
[26] See e.g. C. G. Gilmore, *Hist. of King Edw. VI School, Stafford*, 27; J. S. Horne, *Notes for Hist. of King Edw. VI School, Stafford*, 30, 70; S.R.O., D.(W.) 1721/1/4, f. 113v.; W.S.L. 49/112/44; S.R.O., D.(W.) 0/8/18; Town Clerk's Office, Stafford, Corporation Order Bk. 1648-91, pp. 7, 17, 256; ibid. 1691-1739, pp. 412, 449.
[27] *Year Bk. 20 and 21 Edw. I* (Rolls Ser.), 432-3. He was possibly Wm. de Capella: see below p. 311 n. 43.
[28] *S.H.C.* iv(1), 136.
[29] S.R.O. 938/7967, charter of Abp. Baldwin; *Rot. Litt. Pat.* (Rec. Com.), 70.
[30] *Rot. Litt. Pat.* 70; *Handbk. of Brit. Chron.* 336.

Bartholomew, appointed by King John, occurs 1227.[31]

Master Walter of Lench, appointed 1231, occurs 1246.[32]

Simon of Offham, appointed 1247, resigned 1259.[33]

Bevis de Clare, appointed 1259, died 1294.[34]

Master John of Caen (de Cadamo), appointed 1294, died 1310.[35]

Master Lewis de Beaumont, appointed 1310, provided to the bishopric of Durham 1317.[36]

Thomas Charlton, D.C.L., appointed 1317, resigned 1318.[37]

Robert of Sandall, appointed 1318, resigned 1325.[38]

Robert Holden, appointed 1325, deprived 1326 as a supporter of Edward II.[39]

Robert Swynnerton, appointed 1326, died 1349.[40]

Nicholas Swynnerton, appointed 1349, died probably 1356.[41]

James Beaufort, appointed 1356, died 1358.[42]

John of Bishopston, appointed 1358, probably resigned 1366.[43]

Robert More, appointed 1366, resigned by February 1376.[44]

Adam Hartington, appointed 1376, died 1380.[45]

William Pakington, appointed 1380, died 1390.[46]

Master Lawrence Allerthorpe, appointed 1390, resigned 1397.[47]

Master John Syggeston, appointed 1397, died 1402.[48]

Robert Tunstall, LL.B., appointed 1402, resigned 1406.[49]

John Mackworth, appointed 1406, died 1451.[50]

William Wore, occurs 1452, resigned 1463.[51]

Master Thomas Hawkins, appointed 1463, occurs at some time between 1467 and 1471.[52]

Name unknown, died 1501.[53]

John Thower, resigned 1524.[54]

Thomas Parker, D.Can.L., appointed 1524, died 1538.[55]

Edward Leighton, S.T.B., appointed 1538, dean at the dissolution.[56]

No seal is known.

36. THE COLLEGE OF ST. EDITH, TAMWORTH

IT is not known when or by whom the college of priests at Tamworth was founded. Its dedication to St. Edith, however, suggests that it was a royal foundation of the 10th century.[1] The St. Edith to whom it was dedicated was probably a sister of King Athelstan who was married to Sihtric, the Norse King of York, at Tamworth in 926 and widowed the following year.[2] She is said to have retired to Polesworth (Warws.), some 3½ miles south-east of Tamworth, and after her death, which probably occurred in the 960s, she was revered as a saint.[3] It is possible

[31] S.H.C. iv(1), 73. He was a nephew of John's chief adviser and supporter Peter des Roches, Bp. of Winchester, and was probably Bartholomew de camera, a clerk of the king's household: Rot. Litt. Pat. 113; York Minster Fasti, vol. i (Yorks. Arch. Soc., Rec. Ser. cxxiii), p. 2; vol. ii (Y.A.S., Rec. Ser., cxxiv), p. 138; T. F. Tout, Chapters in Admin. Hist. of Mediaeval Eng. i. 161 n. 2.
[32] Pat. R. 1225–32, 424, 426; K.B. 27/178, m. 1.
[33] Close R. 1242–7, 525; Cal. Pat. 1258–66, 42.
[34] Cal. Pat. 1258–66, 42; 1292–1301, 106; and see above p. 304.
[35] Cal. Pat. 1292–1301, 106; Cal. Close, 1318–23, 52.
[36] Cal. Pat. 1307–13, 219; Cal. Close, 1318–23, 52; Handbk. of Brit. Chron. 220.
[37] Cal. Pat. 1313–17, 642; 1317–21, 237; A. B. Emden, Biog. Reg. of Univ. of Oxford to A.D. 1500, i. 392.
[38] Cal. Pat. 1317–21, 237; 1324–7, 110.
[39] Ibid. 1324–7, 110; Tout, Chapters, iii. 4–6. He was pardoned in 1327 (ibid. 6 n.) but did not recover the deanery.
[40] Cal. Pat. 1324–7, 343; S.H.C. vii(2), 36.
[41] Cal. Pat. 1348–50, 363; S.H.C. i. 286. The reference in Cal. Papal Pets. i. 233, to Rob. Swynnerton as Dean of Stafford in 1352 must be a slip for Nic.
[42] Cal. Pat. 1354–8, 409; Le Neve, Fasti (new edn.), iii. 84; x. 69.
[43] Cal. Pat. 1358–61, 3. He resigned his rectory of Cliffe-at-Hoo (Kent) and his prebend at Chichester in 1366, presumably as a result of the inquiry into pluralities (Reg. Simonis de Langham (Cant. & York Soc.), 270; Cal. Pat. 1364–7, 325); he probably resigned Stafford at the same time and for the same reason.
[44] Cal. Pat. 1364–7, 325; 1374–7, 232.
[45] Ibid. 1374–7, 232; 1377–81, 559, 560.
[46] Ibid. 1377–81, 556; Le Neve, Fasti (new edn.), i. 80; v. 46. He was also Dean of Lichfield: see above p. 197.
[47] Cal. Pat. 1388–92, 295; 1396–9, 88, 93. The reference to Allerthorpe as still dean in Aug. 1398 is apparently a slip, for Syggeston is styled Dean of Stafford in July 1397: ibid. 1396–9, 410; Cal. Close 1396–9, 207. Allerthorpe was also Dean of Wolverhampton 1394–1406: see below p. 330.
[48] Cal. Pat. 1396–9, 88, 93, 113, 207; 1401–5, 117. He is referred to erroneously as Ric. Sigston in C 145/285/6.
[49] Cal. Pat. 1401–5, 117; 1405–8, 277, 352; Emden, Biog. Reg. Oxford, iii. 1915. He is not to be confused with

Rob. Tunstall, Sch. Th., of Gonville Hall, Cambridge (Emden, Biog. Reg. of Univ. of Cambridge to 1500, 598).
[50] Cal. Pat. 1405–8, 277; Le Neve, Fasti, viii. 27, 80.
[51] Cat. Anct. D. vi, C 4399; Cal. Pat. 1461–7, 270. In 1446 the right of presentation to the deanery was granted to Humphrey, Duke of Buckingham: see above p. 306.
[52] Cal. Pat. 1461–7, 270; see above p. 306. He was appointed by the Crown during the minority of Hen., Duke of Buckingham. He was evidently the M. Thos. Hawkins who was Archdeacon of Stafford 1459–c. 1467 and held other preferment in the diocese; he died in 1479: Emden, Biog. Reg. Oxford, ii. 891–2, which does not, however, give him as Dean of St. Mary's; Le Neve, Fasti (new edn.), iii. 16.
[53] S.R.O., D.(W.) 1721/1/1, f. 17v.
[54] L. & P. Hen. VIII, iv(1), p. 169.
[55] Ibid., pp. 169, 610; ibid. xiii(2), p. 60. He was also Dean of Tamworth 1525–38: see below p. 315. The Crown had recovered the advowson on the attainder of Edw., Duke of Buckingham, in 1521: see above p. 307.
[56] L. & P. Hen. VIII, xiii(2), p. 490; E 301/44(1), no. 2. He is given as Dr. Leighton in L. & P. Hen. VIII, xvii, pp. 78–79.
[1] Founders claimed for the college in the 15th and 16th cents. included King Edgar (C. F. R. Palmer, Hist. and Antiquities of the Collegiate Church of Tamworth (Tamworth, 1871), 46), William I (C 1/68/135), and the Marmions, lords of the honor of Tamworth in the 12th and 13th cents. (Leland, Itin. ed. L. Toulmin Smith, ii. 104).
[2] Anglo-Saxon Chron. (Rolls Ser.), i. 199; F. M. Stenton, Anglo-Saxon Eng. (2nd edn.), 335. The bride's name is not given in the Anglo-Saxon Chron., and Wm. of Malmesbury, who made a detailed study of the lives of the children of Edw. the Elder, was unable to trace it: Wm. of Malmesbury, De Gestis Regum Anglorum (Rolls Ser.), i. 136. Rog. of Wendover gives it as Edith: Eng. Hist. Docs. c. 500–1042, ed. Dorothy Whitelock, 257.
[3] Eng. Hist. Docs. c. 500–1042, 257. For the date of St. Edith's death see Palmer, Tamworth Church, 8; F. Arnold-Foster, Studies in Church Dedications, ii. 414. The early history of the nunnery at Polesworth is obscure; one late account, for example, makes the Edith who was the patron saint of the nunnery a daughter of King Egbert and a disciple of St. Modwen: V.C.H. Warws. ii. 62.

that Tamworth was, for a time at least,[4] the home of St. Edith and her community,[5] and there is some uncertainty whether Polesworth or Tamworth was the saint's burial-place.[6] It is in any case likely that by the end of the century there was a cult of St. Edith at Tamworth. There was also a religious community there about that time: between 1002 and 1004 Wulfric Spot in his will left it a share in an estate at 'Langandune' (probably Longdon) 'just as they have let it to me'.[7] This community may have consisted of a group of priests attached to St. Edith's. The pre-Conquest church was evidently a substantial building[8] and could well have been a minster.

By the mid 13th century the advowson of St. Edith's was held by the Marmions, lords of the castle and honor of Tamworth since the early 12th century.[9] They may have inherited it, with Tamworth, from Robert *Dispensator*[10] or, possibly, have acquired it during the civil war under Stephen.[11] When, however, Edward I claimed the advowson after the death of Philip, the last Marmion lord of Tamworth, it was alleged that Henry II had held it and had presented his clerk William de Capella to the church.[12] There appears to be no further evidence relating to this episode,[13] but in 1267 Henry III granted Ralph de Hotote the prebend which had been held by Simon, a royal chaplain.[14]

The prebendal system was almost certainly introduced into the college during the period of Marmion patronage. It is likely that the early canons of Tamworth were portioners, sharing between them the tithes of Tamworth parish:[15] it is significant that when prebends were created they were all named from farms or hamlets within the ancient parish of Tamworth. The division of the church into prebends is unlikely to have occurred before the 1140s.[16] The first dean whose name has survived was William Marmion, who died about 1240, a younger son of Robert Marmion III.[17] Prebends are not expressly mentioned until 1267, by which date they were evidently an established feature of the church.[18] Almost certainly the mid-13th-century establishment at St. Edith's was that which is noted in 1292[19] and thereafter remained unchanged until the dissolution of the college: a dean, who held the prebend of Amington, and five canons, who held the prebends of Bonehill, Coton, Syerscote, Wigginton (or Wigginton and Comberford), and Wilnecote.

The college was never rich. Most of its income, throughout its history, evidently came from tithes and other spiritualities from the parish of Tamworth. By the end of the 13th century it was probably the practice for a canon to receive as his share of the tithes of the parish the tithes from the township after which his prebend was named. Later evidence[20] suggests that the tithes of the castle mills and those of the mills at Amington (Warws.) were held to belong to the common fund and were divided among the whole body of canons. The canons also received in common the profits of Tamworth fair, which had been granted to them by 1266.[21]

Besides their rights in and around Tamworth the canons had by the end of the 13th century acquired various privileges and endowments in Warwickshire, Leicestershire, and Staffordshire, most of which evidently came from the Marmions.[22] The earliest evidence of interests outside Tamworth occurs in 1198 and 1199, when the canons were involved, apparently unsuccessfully, in a dispute with the Templars over an acre of land at Olton, in Solihull (Warws.).[23] Elsewhere in Warwickshire the college purchased in 1257 from Philip Marmion the advowson of the church of Middleton,[24] which remained part of its property until the dissolution

---

[4] Whether St. Edith settled at Polesworth or Tamworth the community would have had to make a temporary move in 940, when Olaf Guthfrithson, the Norse king of Dublin, sacked Tamworth and plundered the country around: *Anglo-Saxon Chron.* i. 211; Stenton, *Anglo-Saxon Eng.* 352.

[5] An early version of Goscelin's Life of St. Edith of Wilton, written at Canterbury *c.* 1080, states that among the holy lives which influenced the saint was that of her virgin aunt Edith, Edgar's sister, who 'monasterio Tamwordie provincieque Staffordie meritorum signis, sicut et ipsa Wiltonie, precluit'. Later copies of this passage give 'Polesworth' and 'Warwickshire' instead of 'Tamworth' and 'Staffordshire'. No such sister of Edgar can be traced, and it has been suggested that one of Edgar's aunts, possibly Sihtric's widow, is meant. See A. Wilmart, 'La Légende de Ste. Édith en prose et vers par le moine Goscelin', *Analecta Bollandiana*, lvi. 13, 53–54.

[6] It was stated *c.* 1000 that her body lay at Polesworth (F. Liebermann, *Die Heiligen Englands* (Hanover, 1889), p. 14), and Wendover also implies that her relics were there (*Eng. Hist. Docs. c. 500–1042*, 257). Hugh Candidus in the 12th cent. and the Book of Hyde in the 14th cent. give Tamworth as her burial place: *Chron. of Hugh Candidus*, ed. W. T. Mellows, 62; *Liber Monasterii de Hyda* (Rolls Ser.), 111. Relics could of course be moved, and the Marmions were patrons of Polesworth as well as of Tamworth: *V.C.H. Warws.* ii. 62.

[7] Dorothy Whitelock, *Anglo-Saxon Wills*, 49–50. Domesday Book, which contains only a few incidental references to Tamworth and does not mention a religious community there, does not include Longdon.

[8] See R. Sherlock, 'St. Editha's Church, Tamworth', *Arch. Jnl.* cxx. 296 and plan facing.

[9] *Bk. of Fees*, ii. 1280. For the Marmion inheritance see *Complete Peerage*, viii. 505–6; J. H. Round, *Feudal Eng.* 170; Round, *Geoffrey de Mandeville*, 314.

[10] As suggested by C. F. R. Palmer, *Hist. of the Baronial Family of Marmion* (Tamworth, 1875), 21.

[11] In the early 1140s Tamworth was in dispute between the Marmions and the Beauchamps, joint heirs of Rob. *Dispensator*, and *c.* 1141 the Empress Maud granted the castle and honor to Wm. de Beauchamp: Round, *G. de Mandeville*, 313–15. The Marmions maintained their hold on Tamworth, and it is possible that either Rob. Marmion I or his son Rob. II took the opportunity to extend their rights there.

[12] See below p. 311.

[13] The presentation may have taken place immediately after the death of Rob. Marmion II, in or before 1181, and before his heir received livery of his lands (as suggested by Palmer, *Family of Marmion*, 51), and the record of this transaction may have been taken by Edw. I's attorneys as evidence that at that time the Crown had held the advowson.

[14] *Cal. Pat.* 1266–72, 48. At that date Phil. Marmion was of full age and in favour with the king (*Complete Peerage*, viii. 512), so it is possible that he had sold or granted the presentation to the king.

[15] A. Hamilton Thompson, 'Notes on Colleges of Secular Canons in Eng.' *Arch. Jnl.* lxxiv. 194. This was the system in force at St. Lawrence's, Gnosall, throughout the Middle Ages: *V.C.H. Staffs.* iv. 128.

[16] A full prebendal system was not introduced into Lichfield Cathedral until the 1130s, and prebends were perhaps created at Wolverhampton about the same date: see pp. 141, 322.

[17] See below p. 314.

[18] See above.

[19] *Cal. Inq. p.m.* iii, p. 21, not giving the names of the prebends. For these see e.g. Palmer, *Tamworth Church*, 13.

[20] C 1/68/135.

[21] *Cal. Inq. Misc.* i, p. 105.

[22] It is possible also that the Marmions fostered the cult of St. Edith in their Lincs. lands: Arnold-Foster, *Church Dedications*, ii. 416–17.

[23] *Cur. Reg. R.* i. 38; *Rot. Cur. Reg.* (Rec. Com.), i. 290.

[24] *Warws. Feet of Fines, 1195–1284* (Dugdale Soc. xi), p. 163. The purchase price was £10. In 1291 the church was evidently assessed at £3 6s. 8d.: *Inq. Non.* (Rec. Com.), 445.

of the college.[25] At some date between 1259 and Philip Marmion's death in 1291 it also acquired from him the manor of Middleton, which Philip and his heirs continued to hold of the college until its dissolution.[26] The only other pre-1300 Warwickshire endowment known is a pension of 13s. 4d. which, it was stated in 1291, the college received from the church of Berkswell;[27] no later mention of this pension has been found. In Leicestershire the canons had by 1220 acquired tithe rights in the parishes of Burrough on the Hill, Somerby, and Stoney Stanton,[28] probably by grant of the Marmions,[29] and possibly before the mid-12th century.[30] There appears, however, to be no subsequent mention of these rights.[31] In Staffordshire the canons had by 1300 acquired the right to present to the church of Drayton Bassett a clerk nominated by the lord of the manor.[32]

In 1291 the income of the college was stated to be £36 13s. 4d., all derived from spiritualities.[33] In the following year it was given as £36:[34] the dean's average annual income was £10, the prebend of Bonehill was valued at £7 a year,[35] Wigginton at £6 a year,[36] Wilnecote at £5 a year,[37] and Syerscote and Coton at £4 a year each.[38] Both these assessments were no doubt underestimates, although by how much is uncertain.[39] In 1307 Dean Bedewynde seems to have been able to lease his decanal prebend with all appurtenances for four years at £37 6s. 8d. a year, and after Dean Longavilla's enforced resignation in 1329 his successor was ordered by the bishop to pay him a pension of £20 a year.[40]

The death of Philip Marmion in 1291 began the chain of events which led to the acquisition of the college by the Crown. Philip left four heirs: three daughters — Joan I, who had married William de Morteyn, Maud, the wife of Ralph Butler, and Joan II, a minor who later married first Thomas de Ludlow and secondly Henry Hillary — and a grand-daughter, another Joan, wife of Alexander de Freville and child of Philip's second daughter, Mazera, who had predeceased her father.[41] The heirs divided the advowson of the college between them[42] and before long had to face the first challenge from the Crown. In 1293 Edward I sued Joan de Morteyn, Maud and Ralph Butler, and Joan and Alexander de Freville for the advowson, claiming that Henry II had held it and citing as evidence Henry's presentation of William de Capella.[43] The defendants claimed that they could not plead in the absence of Joan II, the fourth coheir, who was still a minor, and the case lapsed; but the division of the advowson eventually provided a way for the Crown to dispossess the Marmion heirs.

In the late 1320s two unsuccessful attempts were made to intrude royal nominees into the deanery.[44] Finally two minorities in the Butler family, lasting from at least 1342 until 1359,[45] gave the Crown a series of opportunities to intervene. They were put to good use. In 1342–3 the right of presentation to the prebend of Wilnecote was disputed between Baldwin de Freville I, Joan's son and heir, and the king, guardian of the Butler heir. The king's case, that the right of presentation was held in common by Marmion's heirs and that the next presentation fell to the Butlers, was successful, and the royal candidate was duly installed.[46] In 1347, when the prebend next fell vacant, the king again presented, still basing his claim on his custody of the Butler heir; but this time the earlier argument, which in 1347 would have given the right of presentation to Henry Hillary, was abandoned, and the Crown based its case on a royal grant of 1317 allotting the advowson of Wilnecote to the Butlers. The verdict again went

[25] V.C.H. Warws. iv. 160, which follows W. Dugdale Antiquities of Warws. (1730 edn.), ii. 1052, in wrongly stating that Middleton became one of the prebends of Tamworth.

[26] V.C.H. Warws. iv. 156–7. The annual rent was 6s. 8d. Presumably Phil. granted the manor to St. Edith's in free alms and immediately received it back in socage.

[27] Tax. Eccl. (Rec. Com.), 242. The manor and advowson of Berkswell were held in the 12th and 13th cents. by the Amundeville family: V.C.H. Warws. iv. 29.

[28] Rot. Hugonis de Welles, vol. i (Cant. & York Soc.), 244, 269.

[29] V.C.H. Leics. i. 326, 327, 351; J. Nichols, Hist. and Antiquities of Leics. iv(2), 963.

[30] Somerby church was among the endowments given to Langley Priory (Leics.) by its founder, Wm. Pantulf, c. 1150, and the Augustinian abbey of Owston (Leics.) had acquired Burrough church by 1166: V.C.H. Leics. ii. 3, 21. It seems improbable that Tamworth acquired its rights at these places after that date.

[31] They are not, for example, mentioned in a survey of 1344 which covers the three churches: Nichols, Leics. ii(1), 320; ii(2), 529; iv(2), 972.

[32] Lich. Dioc. Regy., B/A/1/1, f. 15. In 1318 it was stated that this was the customary procedure: ibid. f. 89v. See also Cal. Inq. p.m. viii, p. 327, which, however, wrongly states that the canons not only presented but also instituted. The bishop instituted: S.H.C. N.S. x(2), 127, 138, 143; S.H.C. 1913, 101.

[33] Tax. Eccl. 243. The values of the individual prebends are not given.

[34] S.H.C. 1911, 208. Possibly this represents the 1291 figure less the Berkswell pension. The names of the prebendaries are given but their prebends are not identified.

[35] Rob. de Pitchford, holder of the £7 prebend, was prebendary of Bonehill: Lich. Dioc. Regy., B/A/1/1, f. 45v. Palmer, Tamworth Church, 112, wrongly lists him as prebendary of Wigginton.

[36] Ralph de Hengham, holder of the £6 prebend, was

prebendary of Wigginton: B/A/1/1, f. 44v. Palmer, Tamworth Church, 115, wrongly lists him as prebendary of Bonehill.

[37] Hugh de Cave, holder of the £5 prebend, was prebendary of Wilnecote: Palmer, Tamworth Church, 108.

[38] Adam de Waltone and Mic. de Ormesby, holders of the £4 prebends, were prebendaries of Syerscote and Coton respectively: ibid. 105, 111.

[39] Later 'official' valuations correspond more or less to those given in 1292. Coton was valued at £4 a year in 1314 and at £5 a year in 1337: Cal. Inq. p.m. v, p. 272, referring to the prebend of Rog. de Clungeford (this was Coton: B/A/1/1, f. 15v.); Cal. Close, 1337–9, 236–7, referring to the prebend held by Rog. Persone, who is evidently to be identified with Rog. de Clungeford. Wilnecote was valued at £4 a year in 1314 and 1317: Cal. Inq. p.m. v, p. 272; Cal. Close, 1313–18, 411.

[40] E 210/1955; Lich. Dioc. Regy., B/A/1/3, ff. 21v.–22.

[41] S.H.C. vi(1), 247; Plac. de Quo Warr. (Rec. Com.), 715; Complete Peerage, viii. 513–14.

[42] Phil.'s widow Mary also had a life-interest in the college, since as part of her dower she received the presentation to the prebends of Wilnecote and Coton; she died in 1313 seised of the presentation, having, however, transferred her life-interest to Ralph Bassett of Drayton and his heirs; Cal. Close, 1288–96, 270; Cal. Inq. p.m. v, p. 272; S.H.C. xiv(1), 69.

[43] S.H.C. vi(1), 247; Plac. de Quo Warr. 715. Wm. may in fact have been Dean of Stafford: see above p. 308.

[44] Cal. Pat. 1327–30, 301, 420. On the first occasion the king claimed the presentation as custodian of the lands of the late Alex. de Freville; no justification was offered for the second presentation. The proceedings led Joan de Freville to present a petition in Parliament against the Crown's efforts to present to the deancry: Rot. Parl. (Rec. Com.), ii. 403.

[45] Cal. Inq. p.m. viii, pp. 247–8, 407; x, pp. 438, 449.

[46] Lich. Dioc. Regy., B/A/1/2, ff. 171, 173v.; Cal. Pat. 1340–3, 515; S.H.C. xii(1), 22.

to the king.[47] The final stage was reached in 1358 and 1359, when the Crown presented to two prebends, making the wider claim that the advowsons which Philip Marmion had held were now in the king's hands.[48] The claim apparently went unchallenged.

After 1341, in fact, the Marmion heirs made no further presentations to Tamworth, and the unsuccessful attempt made in 1342–3 by Baldwin de Freville I to present to Wilnecote appears to have been the last serious challenge to the Crown. It is true that Baldwin's son, Baldwin II, made at least one effort to recover his rights in the college. Inquisitions taken after his death in 1375 also stated that, although the Crown had made a number of presentations, the advowson of the deanery and of the five prebends belonged to him as lord of Tamworth castle. By this time, however, the king had established himself more firmly as patron and the Chancery clerks had begun to refer to the college officially as 'the king's free chapel of Tamworth'.[49] After the death of Dean Whitney in 1369[50] no canon remained who was not a royal appointee.

There is no evidence to suggest that the Crown's acquisition of the college had much effect on it. The mechanics of presentation and institution remained unchanged: the king presented to each prebend, and the bishop, on receiving the royal mandate, instituted the king's nominee.[51] The bishop retained his jurisdiction over the college. He continued to hold visitations there without, so far as can be seen, any opposition,[52] and when in 1442 Dean Bate drew up some statutes for the college he did so by virtue of a commission from the bishop and ensured that they were formally approved by him.[53] Nor did the composition of the chapter alter appreciably; whatever may have been its character in the mid 13th century or earlier, by the late 13th and early 14th centuries, when it was still in the hands of the Marmion heirs, it was evidently a body consisting in the main of pluralists and absentees, some of whom, such as deans Cliffe[54] and Longavilla,[55] and Ralph de Hengham, Prebendary of Wigginton,[56] held office under the Crown or were attached to the royal household. Services and pastoral duties were left to vicars.[57] This state of affairs was that usually accepted in royal free chapels and duly persisted at

Tamworth until its dissolution, with canons being appointed by the Crown from all branches of the royal households and the royal administration.

By the early 1440s the system had produced a state of crisis at Tamworth. The vicars were poorly paid and, because of their parochial responsibilities, were forced to neglect their duties in the college.[58] Dean Bate (1436–79), one of the few deans who spent much time at Tamworth, took steps to remedy this, the most important being the promulgation of a set of additional statutes[59] for the college in 1442.

One of the main purposes of these statutes was to raise the vicars' stipends and give them security of tenure.[60] Before 1442 each vicar apparently received his stipend in two portions: 6s. 8d. a year out of the revenues of the common fund of the college,[61] and an additional payment from his prebendary. In 1366 the dean and the prebendary of Coton each affirmed that he paid his vicar £4 13s. 4d. a year;[62] this would have brought vicars' stipends up to £5 a year, which may have been the standard rate in 1366. It is evident that stipends did not rise over the next seventy years; moreover they may not have been paid regularly. At any rate Bate emphasized the difficulty which was being experienced in finding suitable, well-qualified vicars. He laid the blame for this on the meagreness of the stipends which for many years vicars had customarily received — they were, he stated, insufficient to give the vicars a suitable standard of living — and on the fact that vicars were usually dismissed when they became old or infirm and then had to drag out their declining years in poverty.

Bate's statutes raised the vicars' stipends to £6 a year and made the payment of them one of the standard charges on the college revenues, thus ensuring that the vicars got their money before the year's income from the common fund was divided among the canons. The £6 was to be made up of 6s. 8d. from the income of Middleton church and the tithes of the mills at Tamworth castle and Amington,[63] and £5 13s. 4d. from all the other tithes and sources of income which were traditionally regarded as part of the common fund and divided annually among the canons. Two vicars were to be appointed each year to act as collectors of the money and goods which went into this annual division and were made

---

[47] S.H.C. xiv(1), 69–70; Cal. Pat. 1345–8, 333; B/A/1/2, f. 179. For the 1317 grant see Cal. Close, 1313–18, 411.
[48] Cal. Pat. 1358–61, 12–13, 14, 192. On the second occasion the king had originally presented by virtue of his custody of the Butler heir: ibid. 186.
[49] Palmer, Tamworth Church, 21; Cal. Inq. p.m. xiv, pp. 131, 132. The first reference to Tamworth as a royal free chapel appears to be one of 1367, and there was another in 1372: Cal. Pat. 1364–7, 418; 1370–4, 190.
[50] S.H.C. N.S. x(2), 126.
[51] Cal. Pat. 1358–61 and later vols. passim.
[52] See e.g. B/A/1/11, f. 90.
[53] Ibid. /9, ff. 189, 190v. For the statutes see below.
[54] Dean Cliffe (1317–19) had been a Chancery clerk who had travelled abroad in the king's service and later became keeper of the Privy Seal and Keeper of the Rolls of Chancery; during the years in which he held the deanery he was also chancellor of Bp. Sandall of Winchester: A. B. Emden, Biog. Reg. of the University of Oxford to A.D. 1500, i. 438–9; Regs. of John de Sandale and Rigaud de Asserio, Bishops of Winchester, 1316–23 (Hants Rec. Soc. viii), pp. xl, lxi, 80.
[55] Dean Longavilla (1320–9) was a royal physician; in 1322 he was described as one of those 'constantly attendant upon the king's service', and in 1329 he was referred to as

Master Isambert Medicus: Cal Pat. 1321–4, 174; 1327–30, 420.
[56] Before his death in 1311 Hengham had added the prebend to his many other benefices: see above n. 36. For Hengham's career see the introduction to Radulphi de Hengham Summae, ed. W. H. Dunham, Jr.
[57] The 6 'chaplains' attached to St. Edith's in 1319 (D. & C. Lich., AA3) were evidently vicars.
[58] The canons, however, evidently found the arrangements satisfactory. The only dispute which has come to light arose in 1404 or 1405 when 4 canons alleged that during the past 3 years they had received nothing from the common fund because Dean Bernard had been embezzling its revenues: C 1/68/135.
[59] No copy of any earlier set of statutes appears to have survived; for evidence of their existence see below p. 313.
[60] For the following paras. see, unless otherwise stated, Lich. Dioc. Regy., B/A/1/9, ff. 189–190v.
[61] C 1/68/135.
[62] Reg. Simonis Langham (Cant. & York Soc.), 33, 42, 63.
[63] In 1422 the Crown had ordered a commission, including the Sheriff of Staffs., to inquire whether the income from these sources belonged to the college, and if so whether they had been subtracted or wasted and by whom: Cal. Pat. 1422–9, 66.

responsible for selling those tithes that were paid in kind. All receipts were to be put into a chest with two locks, the two vicars having the key to one and the dean or his deputy the key to the other. The vicars were to be paid their stipends quarterly from the money in the chest under the supervision of the dean or his deputy. The money was also to be used to pay 20s. a year to each deacon in the college, and what remained at Michaelmas was to be divided among the canons. Should there not be enough money in the chest to pay the vicars and deacons, their stipends were to be made up to the required amount by the canons out of the income of their individual prebends; any canon who refused to pay in such a case was to have the revenues of his prebend sequestrated.

To give vicars security of tenure Bate laid down that in future a vicar was to hold office for life, though he had to provide at his own expense a substitute to act for him if he became too old or ill to serve his cure. No canon was to dismiss his vicar without due cause, and the dismissal had to be ratified by the dean or his deputy. To preserve discipline it was decreed that the dean or his deputy was to dismiss any vicar or deacon who persistently neglected his duties or was found guilty of some serious crime.

The statutes made further provision for easing and regulating the vicars' lives. Each vicar was to have six days' leave a quarter, if this could be done without disrupting services. A common life for the vicars and deacons could now be planned, since Henry Jekes of Tamworth had recently left them a house near the church. Previously the working clergy of St. Edith's had boarded with townspeople, an arrangement which, according to Bate, had been thoroughly unsatisfactory.[64] The dean decreed that as soon as the house was repaired the vicars were to live a full common life, eating and sleeping there. The deacons were to be *semicommunarii*: they had their meals in the house but were to sleep in St. Edith's 'for the defence and safe custody of the church's books and ornaments'.

In order to keep the number of vicars up to strength it was laid down that within two months of a vacancy in a vicar's stall the prebendary or his proxy was to present a new vicar to the dean or his deputy. If this candidate were found, after examination, to be suitable *tam moribus quam sciencia*, he was to be admitted and was to take an oath of obedience to the dean, canons, and college statutes. Should a canon or his proxy fail to present to a vacancy within two months the right of presentation passed to the dean or his deputy.

Worship too was regulated. Services were to be sung daily at the standard times and according to the Salisbury Use; matins was to be preceded by three strokes of the bell to summon vicars and deacons to the choir. Clergy were forbidden to chatter to each other during services. Vicars who, without reasonable excuse, missed matins, high mass, or vespers were to forfeit 1d. for each offence; money collected in this way was to be spent on utensils for the vicars' house. In a further attempt to increase the dignity and formality of worship Bate laid down that in future vicars and deacons were to wear surplices and hoods (*capicia*) during services throughout the year with, in addition, black copes from Michaelmas to Holy Saturday.[65] They were expected to provide the vestments at their own expense, but Bate may have hoped that they would gain some advantage from a further statute, which laid down that within a year of his induction a new dean or canon was to spend £5 on a book, vestment, or piece of plate for the church or to give the church £5 in cash for the same purpose, to be spent by the dean and chapter.

The statutes confirm that among the canons absenteeism was the rule rather than the exception. No mention is made of any earlier statute enforcing a minimum period of residence; the only inducement given to canons to reside was the arrangement, apparently abolished by Bate, whereby part of the income from Middleton church and from the tithes of the mills at Tamworth castle and Amington was divided at Michaelmas among those members of the chapter who had spent two consecutive months in residence during the preceding year. It was the vicars who were usually in charge of day-to-day college administration. Bate laid down that when no canon was in residence a vicar was to be chosen to ensure that the new statutes were upheld, and both the statutes which he drew up and passages which he quoted from the earlier statutes made provision for the management of common fund revenues by two vicars whenever all members of the chapter were away.[66]

The statutes throw little light upon the numbers and organization of the lesser clergy of the college, other than the vicars. The deacons are mentioned only as ringers of bells, attendants at services, and night-watchmen, and there is no reference at all to the stipendiaries, who occur in 1414. A deed of about 1531 gives the number of deacons as two, and a survey of 1533 lists twelve vicars and stipendiaries at the college.[67]

Bate made further efforts to increase the income of the lesser clergy. He announced in his statutes that Henry VI had, at his request, granted the vicars and deacons the rent from four messuages in Tamworth to endow annual requiem masses for the soul of Henry V and to provide in due course for annual requiems for the king's own soul. In 1446 the king, again at Bate's request, founded a chantry at the altar of the Holy Trinity and licensed Bate to found a chantry of St. Edith and St. Katherine at the altar of the Virgin; in addition he granted the vicars and the two chantry chaplains a tun of red wine yearly.[68] The college, however, received little or no

[64] Bate stated that it had damaged the good name of the clergy and had led to slack attendance at services. After a dispute between the bailiffs of Tamworth and the vicars a borough ordinance of 1429 laid down a 6s. 8d. fine for anyone who entertained one of the vicars at his table: Palmer, *Tamworth Church*, 24; H. Wood, *Borough by Prescription: a Hist. of the Municipality of Tamworth* (Tamworth, 1958), 52.

[65] Probably a reflection of the usage at Lichfield Cathedral, where black silk copes were worn in Advent and Lent: Dugdale, *Mon.* vi(3), 1259; W. G. D. Fletcher, 'The Lichfield Sequence', *Lich. Dioc. Mag.* 1910, 74–75.

[66] The two vicars collected the revenues, paid stipends and the church's debts, provided St. Edith's with the necessary ornaments, and saw to the repair of the vestry, chancel, and *domus thesaurarie*. Under the pre-1442 statutes they were the two senior vicars and swore an oath before their fellow-vicars that they would discharge their duties faithfully; under Bate's statutes they were chosen by the dean or his deputy and probably swore their oath before him.

[67] *Reg. of Hen. Chichele*, ed. E. F. Jacob, iii. 322; B.M Add. MS. 28174, f. 466; *S.H.C.* 1915, 269.

[68] *Cal. Pat.* 1441–6, 409–10.

benefit from all this. The vicars obtained their wine in 1447 and 1448, but the royal grants were invalidated by the 1450 Act of Resumption and there seems to be no evidence that Bate's chantry was ever established.[69]

Although the college lost these benefactions it received a steady trickle of gifts and bequests throughout the 15th and early 16th centuries. Most of these came from local people and, with few exceptions, consisted of small pieces of property in and around Tamworth or of small sums of money: the will of John Comberford of Tamworth, for example, proved in 1414, included bequests of 3s. to the high altar, 1s. 6d. to the Holy Trinity altar, and 6d. to each of the other altars.[70] There were a few rather more substantial gifts, such as the rent-charge of 26s. 8d. from property at Claverley (Salop.) which Sir Thomas Ferrers gave the vicars in 1496 and the lands and burgage in Tamworth which Dame Dorothy Ferrers, his grandson's wife, gave them in trust in 1530.[71] The largest single gift appears to have been that given to St. George's chantry by the executors of John Bailey, a native of Tamworth. By the early 1530s the Tamworth guild of St. George had acquired property worth about £5 a year, the income from which was used to pay the stipend of a 'St. George priest' or 'morrow mass priest' who sang mass daily in St. George's chapel. In his will Bailey expressed the wish that his money should be used to purchase land for the endowment of a chantry or, if possible, a free school, and in 1536 his executors obtained a royal licence for St. George's chantry and were granted permission to endow it with further property to the value of £6 a year. With Bailey's money they purchased various pieces of land and property round Tamworth bringing in about £5 10s. a year, directing that the St. George priest was in future to keep a free school in the town besides praying for Bailey.[72]

In the *Valor Ecclesiasticus*[73] the total income of the six prebends is given as £57 6s. 8d., of which £4 7s. 8d came from the glebe and the remainder from tithes, gifts, and other spiritualities. Of this the dean received £21,[74] the prebendary of Bonehill £7, the prebendary of Coton £8, the prebendary of Syerscote £3 6s. 8d., the prebendary of Wigginton £10, and the prebendary of Wilnecote £8. The arrangements which Dean Bate had made for the payment of vicars' stipends were evidently still working satisfactorily, and no money had to be deducted from the prebendal incomes to provide for this: the Prior of Alvecote (Warws.), whose three-year farm of the deanery ended abruptly in

1530 in a dispute with Dean Parker, noted at the time that the vicars' stipends were kept separate and that the 'yearly charges of the aforesaid deanery is little or nothing in effect'. The prior also maintained that the income of the deanery had diminished since the passing of the 1529 Act restricting the payment of mortuaries,[75] 'which mortuaries were one of the greatest profits and advantages coming or growing of the said farm [of the deanery]'.[76]

By 1548 the income of all save one of the prebends had dropped slightly; Wigginton had, however, risen in value since 1535 and was now worth £13 16s. 8d. a year. Four vicars each received £5 13s. 4d. a year, and a deacon had a stipend of £3.[77] The endowments of St. George's chantry were said to bring the priest £11 3s. 0¼d. a year; other endowments included property in Tamworth to support a priest celebrating the service called 'Our Lady of Grace' and a chaplain celebrating 'the First Mass'.[78] The net yearly value of the college was about £105.[79]

The college was dissolved in 1548 under the terms of the Act of 1547.[80] All the canons except for Richard Pigot, a layman who had recently been appointed prebendary of Wilnecote, were granted pensions, as were the four vicars and the deacon who occur in the commissioners' report.[81] As a result of a report submitted later in the year by a further set of commissioners St. Edith's remained the parish church, served by a preacher and two curates, who lived in the house which had belonged to the vicars. The master of the free school was confirmed in office and was granted a stipend equal to that which he had received as schoolmaster and St. George priest before the Dissolution.[82]

The Crown began to dispose of parcels of college property (mainly lands left to endow obits) to speculators early in 1549.[83] The six prebends and the advowson were retained until 1581, when they were granted to Edmund Downynge and Peter Aysheton. Two years later Downynge and Aysheton disposed of the property to John Morley and his servant Roger Rant, who broke it up and sold it prebend by prebend.[84]

The dean's house, only fragments of which now remain, stood on the east side of the churchyard, north-east of the church. The vicars' house was south of the church, on the site of the present College Lane School.[85]

Deans

William Marmion, died about 1240.[86]
Matthew, occurs 1257.[87]

[69] Palmer, *Tamworth Church*, 25–28; *Rot. Parl.* v. 183–99.
[70] *Reg. Chichele*, iii. 321.
[71] Palmer, *Tamworth Church*, 33, 36–38.
[72] Leland, *Itin.* ed. L. Toulmin Smith, ii. 104; *L. & P. Hen. VIII*, xi, p. 87; Palmer, *Tamworth Church*, 28–32; E 321/30/89; *S.H.C.* 1915, 270. For the titles 'St. George priest' and 'morrow mass priest' see e.g. *Cal. Pat.* 1549–51, 124.
[73] For this para. see, except where otherwise stated, *Valor Eccl.* (Rec. Com.), iii. 148.
[74] Dean Parker had leased the deanery for £20 a year in 1528, and Cranmer valued it at that amount when writing to Cromwell in 1538: C 1/666/31; *L. & P. Hen. VIII*, xiii(2), p. 79.
[75] Mortuaries Act, 21 Hen. VIII, c. 6.   [76] C 1/666/34.
[77] *S.H.C.* 1915, 268–9, 273, 274. In 1546 the vicars were said to receive £6 a year each and the deacon £3: ibid. 267.
[78] Ibid. 270–1; Palmer, *Tamworth Church*, 32–36, 39; *Cal. Pat.* 1563–6, 63, 64.

[79] Valuations ranged from £102 9s. 11½d. to £107 5s. 0½d.: *S.H.C.* 1915, 267.   [80] 1 Edw. VI, c. 14.
[81] *S.H.C.* 1915, 268–9, 273, 274. The canons' pensions ranged from £6 13s. 4d. (Dean Symonds and Humph. Horton, Prebendary of Wigginton) to £3 4s. (John Fisher, Prebendary of Syerscote); the vicars received £5 each a year, and the deacon £3 a year.
[82] Palmer, *Tamworth Church*, 49–50; E 117/12/5/3; *S.H.C.* 1915, 267.
[83] *Cal. Pat.* 1548–9, 420–1; 1549–51, 124–5, 125, 126, 363. 'Concealed lands' were still being granted away in the early 1560s: ibid. 1560–3, 257; 1563–6, 63, 64.
[84] Palmer, *Tamworth Church*, 55–57; *V.C.H. Warws.* iv. 160.
[85] Palmer, *Tamworth Church*, 97–98; Wood, *Borough by Prescription*, 80.
[86] Palmer, *Family of Marmion*, 57, 118.
[87] *Warws. Feet of Fines, 1195–1284* (Dugdale Soc. xi), p. 163.

Ralph de Manton, presented *temp.* Edward I, died or resigned by 1291.[88]

John de Teford, presented by 1291, occurs 1292.[89]

Roger le Wyne, presented between 1292 and 1295, died 1305.[90]

Walter de Bedewynde, admitted 1305, resigned 1310.[91]

Hugh de Babynton, admitted 1310, resigned 1315.[92]

Master Henry de Cliffe, admitted 1317, resigned 1319.[93]

Nicholas Isambardi de Longavilla, in office by 1320, resigned 1329.[94]

Baldwin de Whitney, admitted 1329, died 1369.[95]

Walter Pryde, admitted 1369, resigned 1372.[96]

Reynold de Hulton, admitted 1372, resigned 1389.[97]

Thomas Iberye, presented 1389, resigned 1391.[98]

John de Massyngham, admitted 1391, resigned 1399.[99]

John Bernard, Lic.C.L., admitted 1400, resigned 1429.[1]

Clement Denston, M.A., B.Th., presented February 1429, resigned April 1429.[2]

Thomas Rodburn, M.A., Lic.Th., admitted 1429, Bishop of St. David's 1433.[3]

John de la Bere, B.Cn.L., presented 1433, resigned 1434.[4]

William Newport, B.C.L., presented 1434, died 1436.[5]

John Bate, presented 1436, died 1479.[6]

Ralph Ferrers, D.C.L., presented 1479, died 1504.[7]

Thomas Bowd, B.Th., presented 1504, probably held the deanery until his death in 1508.[8]

William Lichfield, D.C.L., D.Cn.L., probably presented 1508, resigned 1512.[9]

Humphrey Wistow, D.Th., presented 1512, died 1514.[10]

William Hone, M.A., presented 1514, died 1522.[11]

Richard Rawson, B.Cn.L., D.C.L., presented 1522, resigned 1525.[12]

Thomas Parker, D.Cn.L., presented 1525, died 1538.[13]

Simon Symonds, presented 1538, dean at the dissolution.[14]

A common seal in use before 1500[15] is described as being oval and bearing a figure, probably St. Edith. Legend:

[SIGIL]LUM COMMUNE EC[CLESIE]...

A common seal cut under Dean Parker (1525–1538), re-using a 15th-century matrix of unknown provenance,[16] is a pointed oval 3⅜ by 2⅛ in. It depicts a bishop in full pontificals lifting his right hand in benediction and holding a pastoral staff in his left. On his right stands an archbishop in full pontificals lifting his right hand in benediction and holding a pastoral staff in his left. On his left stands St. Katherine, crowned, holding her wheel in her right hand and a sword in her left. Each figure stands in a niche under a Gothic canopy. In the central canopy there is a small niche containing a seated figure of the Virgin, crowned and holding the Child on her right knee. In the base, in a niche with pointed arch carved with trefoils, a bishop stands in full pontificals with a pastoral staff and with his hands joined in prayer. On the masonry on either side of this central niche is a shield. That on the left bears the initials T P, apparently replacing the royal arms, vestiges of which are still visible. The shield on the right bears the arms of Parker: on a fesse between three pheons, a stag's head cabossed between two pellets. Legend, lombardic:

*SI*GILLUM COMMUNE COLLEGIATE DE TOMWORTH

37. THE COLLEGE OF ST. MICHAEL, TETTENHALL

THE earliest mention of priests at Tettenhall occurs in Domesday Book, which records that they held two hides of the king in alms.[1] Whether they were thus endowed by William I or had possessed these lands before the Conquest is not clear. A jury of local residents in 1401 attributed the foundation and

[88] Palmer, *Tamworth Church*, 101.
[89] Ibid.; *Cal. Inq. p.m.* iii, p. 21.
[90] *S.H.C.* ix(1), 50; Lich. Dioc. Regy., B/A/1/1, f. 16.
[91] B/A/1/1, ff. 16, 44.
[92] Ibid. f. 44; *S.H.C.* ix(1), 50.
[93] B/A/1/1, f. 89; Emden, *Biog. Reg. Oxford*, i. 438; Le Neve, *Fasti Ecclesiae Anglicanae 1300–1541* (new edn.), vi. 29.
[94] *Cal. Pat.* 1317–21, 452; B/A/1/2, f. 144.
[95] B/A/1/2, f. 144; *S.H.C.* N.S. x(2), 126.
[96] *S.H.C.* N.S. x(2), 126, 137.
[97] Ibid. 137; *Cal. Pat.* 1388–92, 157, 163.
[98] *Cal. Pat.* 1388–92, 157, 163, 402; B/A/1/6, f. 38.
[99] B/A/1/6, f. 38; *Cal. Pat.* 1388–92, 402; 1399–1401, 160. Wm. Cotyngham was presented to the deanery in 1390 (ibid. 1388–92, 301), but despite Palmer's assertion to the contrary (*Tamworth Church*, 103), there is no evidence in the bp.'s reg. that he was ever admitted.
[1] *Cal. Pat.* 1399–1401, 160; 1422–9, 531; A. B. Emden, *Biog. Reg. of the Univ. of Cambridge to 1500*, 56. Wm. Pountfreyt was presented to the deanery in 1404 (*Cal. Pat.* 1401–5, 350) but was never admitted.
[2] *Cal. Pat.* 1422–9, 531, 532; Emden, *Biog. Reg. Cambridge*, 182.
[3] Emden, *Biog. Reg. Oxford*, iii. 1582–3; *D.N.B. sub* Rudborne.
[4] Emden, *Biog. Reg. Oxford*, i. 556–7; *Cal. Pat.* 1429–1436, 296, 332, 347.

[5] Emden, *Biog. Reg. Cambridge*, 423–4; *Cal. Pat.* 1429–1436, 347, 603.
[6] *Cal. Pat.* 1429–36, 604; 1476–85, 159.
[7] Ibid. 1476–85, 159; 1494–1509, 384; Emden, *Biog. Reg. Oxford*, ii. 681.
[8] *Cal. Pat.* 1494–1509, 384; Emden, *Biog. Reg. Cambridge*, 82.
[9] Emden, *Biog. Reg. Oxford*, ii. 1145–6; *L. & P. Hen. VIII*, i (1920 edn.), p. 706.
[10] *L. & P. Hen. VIII*, i (1920 edn.), pp. 706, 1431; Emden, *Biog. Reg. Oxford*, iii. 2065, wrongly giving date of admission to deanery as 1514.
[11] *L. & P. Hen. VIII*, i (1920 edn.), p. 1431; iii(2), p. 940; Emden, *Biog. Reg. Oxford*, ii. 956.
[12] *L. & P. Hen. VIII*, iii(2), p. 940; iv(1), p. 610; Emden, *Biog. Reg. Cambridge*, 473.
[13] *L. & P. Hen. VIII*, iv(1), p. 610; xiii(2), p. 282; *S.H.C.* 1915, 268. He was also dean of the college at Stafford: see above p. 309.
[14] *L. & P. Hen. VIII*, xiii(2), p. 282; *S.H.C.* 1915, 268.
[15] Palmer, *Tamworth Church*, 92–93, describing a much-broken impression.
[16] Ibid. 93 and plate facing, stating that at the time of writing (*c.* 1870) the brass matrix of this seal was in the possession of Wm. Staunton of Longbridge Ho. near Warwick; W. de G. Birch, *Cat. of Seals in B.M.* i, p. 766; cast among W.S.L. Seals.
[1] *V.C.H. Staffs.* iv. 45, no. 105.

endowment of the collegiate church to King Edgar,[2] but there is no reason to believe them better informed about events centuries before their time than those who in 1546 and 1548 ascribed the foundation to Edward III.[3]

Domesday Book does not give the number of priests, but their 2 hides (one in Tettenhall, the other in Bilbrook nearby) were sufficient to support four, since the average glebe holding was half a hide.[4] The earliest known member of this group described himself simply as 'priest of Tettenhall' when witnessing a charter between 1161 and 1165,[5] but half a century later the term 'canon' was in use.[6] A dean is first mentioned about 1176.[7] The second known dean, Elias of Bristol, who was also Dean of Penkridge, was one of Richard I's clerks.[8] His successors were similarly clerks in royal service: they included many officials of the Exchequer, the Chancery, and the king's household. The deanery was worth having not only for its revenues but as a fund of patronage, for it carried with it collation to the prebends;[9] their number, when first recorded in 1255, was five.[10]

From the time of the earliest known royal grants of the deanery (that is, from 1226), mandates were sent to the Sheriff of Staffordshire to put the new dean in possession. This shows that Tettenhall was treated as exempt from diocesan jurisdiction, the bishop having no right of institution. Henry III was insistent that royal demesne chapels were immune from the jurisdiction of the ordinary. In 1245 he secured from Innocent IV a bull declaring royal chapels immediately subject to the Roman church and exempt from diocesan authority.[11] For Tettenhall the effect of this was nullified almost at once since Innocent conceded to the Bishop of Coventry and Lichfield that the exemption did not apply to four churches in his diocese which claimed to be royal chapels, Tettenhall among them.[12] In the struggle with the bishop which followed, the king was the champion of these churches. In 1247 he granted his protection to Tettenhall which he declared was his royal chapel.[13] This document is the earliest to give the dedication of the church to St. Michael and to describe it as a royal free chapel. The privileges of all the royal chapels of the diocese were under attack from successive bishops and archdeacons until 1281 when Bishop Meuland was persuaded to recognize the claims of six of them, including Tettenhall.[14]

Exemption from diocesan jurisdiction did not necessarily mean that royal chapels were also free of the jurisdiction of the archbishop. But when Archbishop Pecham tried to visit the royal chapels

in the diocese in 1280, they all resisted him. Like the others Tettenhall claimed exemption and was required to show proof of its privileges. When this was not forthcoming its members came under a general sentence of excommunication and were cited to submit to archiepiscopal judgment.[15] But at the king's insistence Pecham seems to have accepted the agreement made with Bishop Meuland in 1281.

Tettenhall was among the fourteen royal chapels whose status Pecham's successor, Archbishop Winchelsey, was disposed to recognize.[16] It is therefore surprising that there was an attempt to subject it to metropolitical jurisdiction in 1304. The prebend of Codsall was in dispute, and the Dean of Arches had cited one of the claimants before him, together with the Dean of Tettenhall, who presumably had collated him to it. Edward I would not allow the case to be considered in the court of the province of Canterbury, and the Dean of Arches was inhibited from proceeding further.[17]

Circumstances of the moment prompted Edward II in 1315 to forbid even the Chancellor to meddle with Tettenhall's spiritual affairs or trouble its dean.[18] The dean in question was Ingelard Warley, one of the most hated of Edward II's household officers, who had been expelled from royal service by the Lords Ordainers at the end of 1314[19] and had departed on timely pilgrimage overseas.[20] His return in 1315 was followed by this attack on his conduct of his duties at Tettenhall, through the Chancellor, John Sandall, whom the Ordainers had put in office.[21] To protect his friend Edward II was ready to deny the Chancellor's competence to interfere in royal chapels, although it is likely that this was already established. Certainly it was accepted later in the century.[22] In 1399 it was expressly stated by Richard II that Tettenhall was exempt from ordinary jurisdiction except that of the Chancellor, and on that occasion and in 1411 royal commissioners were appointed to visit it because the Chancellor was too busy.[23]

Royal goodwill towards Tettenhall was shown in other ways besides the defence of its privileges. In 1251 the king gave a silver chalice,[24] and in 1257 six oaks from Ashwood in Kinver Forest to repair the church.[25] In 1265 Henry III intervened to save the endowments of a chantry founded by John Chishull in Tettenhall church, when they were seized by the coroner after the chantry chaplain had been outlawed for a felony.[26] But the king's favour stopped short when his revenues were involved. Despite a royal declaration in 1250 that royal chapels were immune from papal taxes,[27] they were obliged to

[2] C 145/279/8; *Cal. Rot. Chart. et Inq. ad q.d.* (Rec. Com.), 346.
[3] E 301/40, no. 22; /54, no. 6.
[4] R. Lennard, *Rural Eng. 1086–1135*, 329; F. M. Stenton, *Anglo-Saxon Eng.* (2nd edn.), 152.
[5] *S.H.C.* ii(1), 252.
[6] G. P. Mander, *Wolverhampton Antiquary*, ii. 94–95 (dated between 1205 and 1222).
[7] *Cartulary of Oseney Abbey*, vol. v (Oxford Hist. Soc. xcviii), nos. 578, 578a; *S.H.C.* 1923, 265–7.
[8] W. W. Capes, *Charters and Records of Hereford Cath.* 35; see above p. 303.
[9] *S.H.C.* iv(1), 209.
[10] Ibid. v(1), 113.
[11] See above p. 304.
[12] *Annales Monastici* (Rolls Ser.), i. 275–6.
[13] *Cal. Pat. 1232–47*, 499.
[14] See below p. 324.

[15] *Reg. Epist. Fratris Johannis Peckham* (Rolls Ser.), i. 147–50, 155–6.
[16] F. M. Powicke and C. R. Cheney, *Councils and Synods*, ii(2), 1144–6.
[17] *Cal. Close, 1302–7*, 210; see also *S.H.C.* vii(1), 157.
[18] *Cal. Chanc. Wts.* i. 431.
[19] T. F. Tout, *Chapters in Admin. Hist. of Mediaeval Eng.* ii. 231–4.
[20] *Cal. Pat. 1313–17*, 198.
[21] Tout, *Chapters*, ii. 215.
[22] See the foundation statutes of the college of Windsor dated 30 Nov. 1352: A. K. B. Roberts, *St. George's Chapel, Windsor Castle, 1348–1416*, 49.
[23] *Cal. Pat. 1396–9*, 510; ibid. *1408–13*, 314.
[24] *Cal. Lib. 1245–51*, 360.
[25] *Close R. 1256–9*, 94–95.
[26] Ibid. *1264–8*, 160–1.
[27] *Cal. Pat. 1247–58*, 77; Wilkins, *Concilia*, i. 697.

pay when these were assigned to the Crown, for instance in 1268 and 1269.

Tettenhall paid 40s. for the papal tenth in 1268;[28] the assessment of the whole church was therefore £20. Since the church, perhaps even the deanery alone, was valued at £33 6s. 8d. in 1255 and 1272,[29] it is obvious that the assessment was a mild one. In 1269 for some reason the amount paid as tenth by only four of the prebends was recorded; these were the prebends of Tettenhall, Pendeford, Wrottesley, and Perton, and together they paid 26s. 8d.[30] The deanery and the fifth prebend, Codsall, between them must have been liable for the remaining 13s. 4d. The sums suggest that each of the six members of the chapter was liable for half a mark. If so the assessment was conventional as well as mild. The new valuation of clerical incomes in 1291 was more realistic; but it still allowed an unofficial tax abatement, so that the assessment remained well below the real value of the benefices. Tettenhall was assessed at £29 6s. 8d.[31] No details of how this amount was divided between the deanery and the prebends are recorded, but it is apparent that they were not given equal assessments: in 1366 (when this valuation was still in force) the prebend of Codsall was said to have been taxed at 10 marks (£6 13s. 4d.), and the prebend of Tettenhall at £5.[32] Local jurors testified in 1293 that the church was worth 100 marks (£66 13s. 4d.),[33] rather more than twice the assessment of 1291.

Although royal chapels had to pay these papal tenths, they were privileged to pay them directly to the Crown and not through the diocesan collectors. In 1308 the dean paid to the Exchequer the arrears of the triennial tenth granted in 1301.[34] In 1315 Edward II named twelve free chapels with the privilege of appointing their own collectors: Tettenhall was among them.[35] But the king protected his chapels against papal taxes which did not benefit himself. For instance in 1318 the papal collector was forbidden to exact 'intolerable impositions and payments' from nine royal chapels of which Tettenhall was one.[36]

Attempts by the Pope to provide to benefices in royal chapels were firmly resisted by the king. In 1341 the Pope tried to provide to the prebend of Codsall. Edward III prohibited any attempts to dispossess the prebendary who had been collated by the late dean,[37] and when this prohibition was ignored he sued the provisor and his supporters.[38] An attempt by the bishop to intervene[39] and decisions by the papal court in the provisor's favour[40] were without effect. The king's will prevailed.[41]

At the time when this attempt at papal provision was made there were grounds for regarding Tettenhall as no longer a royal chapel. In 1338 Edward III had granted the manor of Tettenhall to his chamberlain, Henry, Lord Ferrers of Groby. With this manor and others granted at the same time went the advowsons of churches belonging to them.[42] When Lord Ferrers died in 1343 leaving an heir under age,[43] the custody of most of his lands, including the manor of Tettenhall, was granted by the king to Queen Philippa.[44] Philippa regarded Tettenhall church as appurtenant to the manor, and when the deanery fell vacant she granted it to Robert Caldwell, one of her clerks. Caldwell was said to have secured peaceful possession of it.[45] This appointment must have occurred between 1343 and 1354, when Lord Ferrers's heir, William, came of age.[46] When William died in January 1371, the advowson of the deanery was reckoned as part of his property.[47] Since the deanery became vacant soon afterwards, the king presented to it in October as guardian of the heir.[48] In November the advowson was assigned to William's widow, Margaret, as part of her dower.[49] But despite the acceptance, implied by these proceedings, of the Ferrers right to the advowson of the deanery, the matter was far from clear.

It is difficult to discover who actually held the deanery between 1338, when the manor of Tettenhall was granted to Lord Ferrers, and 1374, when the problem of the advowson was settled. There seem to have been two series of deans. One line was appointed by the Ferrers family and, during the minority of heirs, by the keepers of their possessions in Tettenhall. A second line was created by the king. Disregarding the grant to Robert Caldwell by Queen Philippa, who represented the Ferrers heir, Edward III made rival appointments.[50] Presumably these appointments did not take effect, for Caldwell was said to hold the deanery in 1361, when he valued it at only 3 marks.[51] But by 1366 Caldwell seems no longer to have been dean, for he was holding the prebend of Pendeford, which he exchanged in July for a prebend of York.[52] The vacancy of 1371 in the Ferrers line of deans was caused by the resignation of 'Edmund'.[53] Presumably he had succeeded Caldwell in the deanery at some date between 1361 and 1366. The king's awareness of the problem was apparently sporadic, for in 1371, as guardian of the Ferrers heir, he appointed a dean in succession to Edmund.

The confusion was not confined to the deanery. What made the question acute was the position of the prebendaries. Not only did title to the prebends

[28] Cal. Pat. 1266–72, 221.
[29] S.H.C. v(1), 113; iv(1), 209. The wording of these valuations of the church of Tettenhall suggests that they refer to the deanery alone; a valuation of 1293 ('the church of Tettenhall to which five prebends are annexed . . . is worth 100 marks': ibid. vi(1), 258) apparently refers to the deanery and the prebends.
[30] Cal. Pat. 1266–72, 332.
[31] Tax. Eccl. (Rec. Com.), 243.
[32] Reg. Simonis de Langham (Cant. & York Soc.), 43, 44. The prebend of Tettenhall and Compton is here misnamed Crowkewelle and Tettenham.
[33] See above n. 29.
[34] Cal. Pat. 1307–13, 142.
[35] Cal. Close, 1313–18, 172–3.
[36] Ibid. 596.
[37] Cal. Pat. 1340–3, 147, 183–4.
[38] S.H.C. xi. 122; Cal. Pat. 1340–3, 320.
[39] S.H.C. xii(1), 13.

[40] Cal. Papal Pets. i. 3.
[41] S.H.C. xiii, 112–13.
[42] Cal. Pat. 1338–40, 110; Abbrev. Rot. Orig. (Rec. Com.), ii. 127.
[43] Cal. Inq. p.m. viii, pp. 315, 316.
[44] Ibid. p. 319; Cal. Pat. 1343–5, 118.
[45] S.H.C. xiii. 112–13.
[46] Cal. Inq. p.m. x, pp. 177–8.
[47] Ibid. xiii, p. 65.
[48] Cal. Pat. 1370–4, 140.
[49] Cal. Close, 1369–74, 274.
[50] Cal. Pat. 1348–50, 47.
[51] Cal. Papal Pets. i. 377. If, as seems possible, the deanery was worth 50 marks in the 13th century, most of its property must have been lost while the Ferrers family was in possession.
[52] Le Neve, Fasti Ecclesiae Anglicanae, 1300–1541 (new edn.), vi. 52.
[53] Cal. Pat. 1370–4, 140.

depend upon the dean who had collated to them, but during a vacancy of the deanery the right to present to the prebends fell to the patron. For instance, in 1371 Edward III took care to fill the prebend of Tettenhall (by then called the prebend of Tettenhall and Compton)[54] before appointing a new dean. The situation was exploited by the Crown in 1373. If every collation to the deanery made by the Ferrers family or its representatives was regarded as invalid, no prebendary had been legally appointed since the resignation of Caldwell's predecessor, William of Shenton.[55] All five prebends were therefore vacant, and Edward III made his own appointments to them.[56] A test case was brought against Thomas of Bushbury who had held the prebend of Codsall since 1361, by Caldwell's collation. The king's attorney claimed that since Tettenhall was a royal free chapel it could not be alienated from the Crown without a special deed of record. No special mention of the advowson of the deanery was made in the grant of the manor of Tettenhall to Lord Ferrers. Consequently it still belonged to the king, and the deanery had been vacant since Shenton resigned. No argument could prevail against this contention, and Thomas withdrew his claim.[57]

Even the king's own appointment to the deanery in 1371 was invalid, since he was then acting as guardian of the Ferrers heir. Another royal appointment was made in January 1374.[58] But the new dean, John Hatfield, found the perquisites of his office much diminished. Although it was only during a vacancy of the deanery that the king had the right to present to the prebends, Edward III continued to dispose of them when they were exchanged or fell vacant,[59] and the advisers of the young Richard II began to follow suit.[60] Hatfield took advantage of the opportunity afforded by the change of king to recover his lost rights. His petition, that the Crown should no longer claim to present to the prebends in respect of the former voidance of the deanery, was granted. In August 1377 collation to the prebends was recognized as belonging to the dean.[61] Nevertheless Henry IV assumed the right to present to the prebends of Wrottesley[62] and Compton[63] in 1402 and 1405, when Thomas Hanley was dean. This intervention might have been justified on moral grounds, for there had been an inquiry into the shortcomings of the prebendaries of Wrottesley and Compton in 1401. They were reputed to have neglected their duties for more than ten years and

to have misappropriated lands and rent belonging to the church.[64] But the king's attempts to replace them were unsuccessful.[65]

While Hanley was dean there were as many as three royal inquiries into the negligence of the ministers of the chapel. The only known visitation of Tettenhall before Hanley's time was in 1368 when it was one of five royal chapels in the diocese to be visited by the king's commissioners.[66] At this time the patronage was in the possession of the Ferrers family, and it is obvious that the bishop regarded the church as no longer exempt from his jurisdiction, for in March 1368 he appointed a penitentiary to exercise jurisdiction over the parishioners of Tettenhall.[67] One of the prebendaries was chosen, but his authority was derived from the bishop. Nevertheless, when the king ordered the visitation in May, he described Tettenhall, like the other four churches, as a royal free chapel exempt from the bishop's jurisdiction. Among the items of inquiry was the loss through negligence of liberties, immunities, and privileges. This applied particularly to Tettenhall and perhaps was the reason for its visitation.

In Hanley's time the inquiries were concerned exclusively with spiritual failings. In 1399, 1401, and 1411 the king was informed that the celebration of divine service and other works of piety in the chapel had long been neglected.[68] At last, after the visitation of 1411, decisive action was taken. Henry IV ordered the revenues of the deanery and prebends to be sequestrated until the dean and prebendaries were willing to do their duty, and cited the obstinate to appear in Chancery.[69] The result was Hanley's resignation. He had avoided possible consequences of the visitation of 1399, which had been ordered by Richard II, by losing no time in securing ratification of his status in his benefices from Henry IV.[70] The inquiry of 1401 had concentrated on the unsatisfactory prebendaries of Wrottesley and Compton. But in 1411 the dean, as well as the prebendaries, was found at fault and there was no convenient revolution to save him from royal reprimand. Nevertheless he withdrew with dignity, exchanging his deanery for a canonry of Windsor in 1412.[71] But Tettenhall had not seen the last of him. Just over a year later he exchanged his Windsor canonry for the prebend of Wrottesley.[72] Canonries at Windsor were profitable only to residentiaries,[73] but Tettenhall's revenues he knew could be enjoyed *in absentia*.

[54] Ibid. 129.
[55] The date of Shenton's resignation is in doubt. In 1341 he was described as 'late dean' of Tettenhall: ibid. 1340–3, 147, 320. On the other hand it was stated in 1374 that the deanery became vacant by Shenton's resignation while Queen Philippa had the custody of the manor of Tettenhall, that is between 1343 and 1354: *S.H.C.* xiii. 112–13. It seems likely that Shenton resigned before 1341 and was replaced by a Ferrers appointment (perhaps Jordan de Gathorp who resigned in 1348), and that this was not mentioned in 1374 because the dispute centred on Caldwell's status and no one wanted to argue about intermediate deans. Shenton died in 1367: *Reg. Ludowici de Charltone* (Cant. & York Soc.), 67.
[56] *Cal. Pat.* 1370–4, 335, 336, 341. The grant of Perton to Wm. Hannay did not, however, take effect, for Thos. Dufford, the prebendary in possession, was not displaced: *Reg. Langham*, 92; *S.H.C.* N.S. x(2), 46, 220; *Cal. Pat.* 1374–7, 19.
[57] *S.H.C.* xiii. 112–13.
[58] *Cal. Pat.* 1370–4, 402.

[59] Ibid. 1374–7, 19, 400.
[60] Ibid. 1377–81, 16.
[61] Ibid.
[62] Ibid. 1401–5, 43; *S.H.C.* xvi. 37.
[63] *Cal. Pat.* 1405–8, 96, 182; *S.H.C.* xvii. 47. The prebend of Tettenhall, which before 1371 had acquired the double name of Tettenhall and Compton, by 1373 was called the prebend of Compton: *Cal. Pat.* 1370–4, 341.
[64] C 145/279/8.
[65] *Cal. Pat.* 1405–8, 96, 182; 1413–16, 101; *S.H.C.* xvi. 37, 38; xvii. 47.
[66] *Cal. Pat.* 1367–70, 142, 143.
[67] *S.H.C.* N.S. viii. 46.
[68] *Cal. Pat.* 1396–9, 510; 1408–13, 314; C 145/279/8.
[69] *Cal. Pat.* 1408–13, 321, 374.
[70] Ibid. 1399–1401, 136.
[71] Ibid. 1408–13, 415. A few weeks before, probably when the exchange was arranged, the king had revoked the sequestration of Tettenhall's revenues: ibid. 405.
[72] Ibid. 1413–16, 101.
[73] Roberts, *St. George's Chapel, Windsor Castle*, 8.

It is strange that Tettenhall's spiritual state was not improved earlier in Henry IV's reign, for in February 1401 the chapel was subjected to metropolitical visitation. Archbishop Arundel and his commissaries had already visited three royal chapels in the diocese before Tettenhall's turn came; Wolverhampton had attempted to resist and failed. At Tettenhall the dean, canons, and ministers appeared and were questioned, and some of the parishioners were similarly examined.[74] The outcome is not known; possibly the royal inquiry of August 1401 was prompted by Arundel's discoveries.

The dean should have been responsible for the correction of his clergy: his position was not a sinecure. But on the other hand his duties were not regarded in the 15th century as incompatible with those of another benefice with cure. John Stopyndon, one of the masters in Chancery of Henry V, was allowed by the Pope to hold the deanery with a parish church, an archdeaconry, four prebends, and the wardenship of a hospital for the poor.[75] His obligations towards Tettenhall could be fulfilled by maintaining adequate deputies to perform his spiritual and administrative functions there: a priest vicar to represent him in the chapel, an official to preside in his peculiar court, and a steward or bailiff to manage his property. But no record proving the existence of any of these deputies is known. By the reign of Henry VIII, when information about the clerical establishment is available,[76] the dean's revenues were negligible and apparently he maintained no vicar. How this state of affairs came about is not discoverable. Perhaps the dean's property had been alienated while the Ferrers family had the advowson;[77] perhaps the deanery had always been ill-endowed, though this seems unlikely.[78] In 1498 the advowson of the deanery was again thought to belong to the Ferrers family, as lords of Tettenhall manor; Sir Thomas Ferrers was said by a local jury to have died possessed of it.[79] It may be that the Ferrers family actually presented to the deanery after this date, for no royal appointments are recorded after Thomas Bowd's in 1489; but this may be fortuitous, for the appointments of only three of the six deans of the 15th century appear on the patent rolls. In 1531 the deanery was

valued at only 2s. 1d.,[80] and in 1535 its rents were worth only 1d., though fees from those subject to the dean's spiritual jurisdiction brought his total income up to an estimated £1 14s. 9d. a year.[81] In 1548 his clear portion, after expenses had been deducted, was said to be 17s. 9d.[82] After the dissolution of the college, when the dean's property was in Crown possession, it consisted of land in Autherley worth 1½d. a year and the profits of his spiritual court worth 10s. a year.[83]

Although the dean provided no vicar for Tettenhall, there were six stipendiary priests on the establishment in the second quarter of the 16th century. One of these was the curate of Codsall chapel, whose salary of £5 a year was paid by the Prebendary of Codsall.[84] Two priests served in chantries in Tettenhall church. Our Lady's Chantry had been founded in the 13th century by John Chishull, who endowed it with land in Tettenhall and farm stock.[85] Other unspecified donors were said to have given property to it; in 1548 it possessed lands in Tettenhall, Compton, and Bilbrook.[86] The priest's stipend was a little over £5 a year.[87] The other chantry was known as Cronkhall's. It was said to have been founded in 1528-9 by Richard Cronkhall and was endowed with lands in Tettenhall which produced a stipend of £4 7s. 2d. for the priest in 1548.[88] Cronkhall's chantry chaplain in 1548 was also vicar of the Prebendary of Pendeford, with a salary of £5 a year.[89] Four of the prebendaries maintained priest vicars:[90] Pendeford, Wrottesley, Codsall, and Bovenhill (by 1535 the name of the prebend formerly known as Tettenhall and Compton).[91] Since the Prebendary of Perton had no vicar, it is to be presumed that he was resident at Tettenhall.

The college was dissolved in 1548 under the Act of 1547.[92] By this date all the prebends were let on long leases at rents well below the real value of the property;[93] no doubt large entry-fines had been paid. The pensions[94] assigned to the prebendaries were closely related to the incomes remaining after the discharge of liabilities such as the salaries of their vicars.[95] Perton's income was highest since it supported no vicar; the clear value was £6 7s. and the pension granted £5. The other prebendaries were given pensions corresponding exactly to their

---

[74] Lambeth Palace Libr., Reg. Arundel, i, f. 482.
[75] *Cal. Papal Regs.* viii. 540.
[76] See clerical subsidy lists of 1531 and 1533 in Lich. Dioc. Regy., B/A/17/1, and D. & C. Lich. lxiii.
[77] See above n. 51.
[78] See above p. 317 and n. 29.
[79] *Cal. Inq. p.m. Hen. VII*, ii, p. 159. Sir Thos. was heir male of Wm., Lord Ferrers of Groby (d. 1445): *Complete Peerage*, v. 333.
[80] Lich. Dioc. Regy., B/A/17/1.
[81] *Valor Eccl.* (Rec. Com.), iii. 106.
[82] E 301/44(1), no. 10.
[83] S.C. 12/28/12, f. 4.
[84] E 301/44(1), no. 10.
[85] *Close R.* 1264-8, 160-1. Chishull became Bp. of London in 1274. His chantry was said in 1265 to have been founded long before.
[86] S.C. 12/28/12, ff. 4v.-5.
[87] The revenues were assessed at £5 6s. 8d. in 1535, and the same, less 2s. 6d. reprises, in 1546 (*Valor Eccl.* iii. 105; E 301/40, no. 22); in 1548 they were valued at £5 7s. 4d. and the priest's clear portion was assessed at £5 0s. 8d. (E 301/44(1), no. 46; E 301/54, no. 6; S.C. 12/28/12, f. 5).
[88] *S.H.C.* N.S. vi(2), 286; E 301/44(1), no. 47; E 301/54, no. 6; S.C. 12/28/12, f. 5.
[89] E 301/44(1), no. 10.
[90] Ibid.; /44(2).
[91] Shaw's identification of Bovenhill with Barnhurst

(*Staffs.* ii. 201), followed by later writers, is unfounded. J. P. Jones's statement (*Hist. of Parish of Tettenhall* (1884), 84) that a Wrottesley court roll (presumably destroyed in the Wrottesley fire of 1897) showed that Sir Wal. Wrottesley died in 1642 seised of lands 'held of the manor and prebend of Bovenhull or Barnhurst' is mistaken: no Wal. Wrottesley died in 1642, and the prebend of Bovenhill did not form part of the Wrottesley property (*S.H.C.* N.S. vi(2), 273, 292, 333). Barnhurst and Bovenhill are named separately in a 1719 list of lands in Tettenhall over which the Wrottesleys and the Creswells disputed lordship rights (*41st Dep. Kpr.'s Rep. App. I*, 531) and in White, *Dir. Staffs.* (1851). A. Hamilton Thompson's identification of Bovenhill with Boningale, Salop. (*Arch. Jnl.* lxxiv. 82 n. 2), has no justification.
[92] See below p. 326. In *S.H.C.* 1915, 281, it is stated that the college was dissolved on 4 July 1542. This, however, is the date of a lease of the prebend of Perton; it has been confused with a reference to the college's dissolution in an account of proceedings concerning the lease: see E 315/105, ff. 97v.-98v.
[93] For the leases and rents see S.C. 12/28/12, f. 4; for clear values in 1535 and 1548 see *Valor Eccl.* iii. 105, and E 301/44(1), no. 10.
[94] For the pensions granted to all members of the college see E 101/75/30 (where the prebend of Wrottesley is given twice, once in error for Perton) and E 301/44(1), no. 10.
[95] Other charges are given in *Valor Eccl.* iii. 105.

clear incomes: Pendeford £4, Bovenhill £4, Codsall £3 9s. 4d., Wrottesley £3. Similarly the dean was allotted full compensation for his meagre revenues: his pension was 17s. 9d. Two of the vicars received pensions of £5, equalling their salaries; the vicar of the Prebendary of Codsall, whose salary was £4 6s. 8d., had a pension of £4;[96] the Prebendary of Bovenhill's vicar was appointed to serve Tettenhall church at a stipend of £13 6s. 8d. The curate of Codsall was retained to serve his chapel.

The property of the deanery and prebends, including the college buildings, was assessed by the king's commissioners at £50 17s. 0½d. a year.[97] In May 1549 Walter Wrottesley bought it at the standard purchase price of 22 years' rent: £1,118 14s. 11d. The lands lay in Tettenhall, Autherley, Pendeford, Wergs, Compton, Perton, Trescott, Bilbrook, Wrottesley, Wightwick, Oaken, and Codsall.[98] A few weeks later Wrottesley disposed of three of the prebends, keeping for himself the prebends of Wrottesley and Codsall, of which he held the leases.[99] Perton[1] he sold to his nephew Edward Leveson; the Levesons already held the lease of the major part of Perton's property.[2] Pendeford and Bovenhill[3] were bought by Richard Creswell (who held the leases) and Henry Southwick, formerly Prebendary of Bovenhill.[4]

The properties which endowed chantries, obits, and lights in Tettenhall church were not included among the assets of the college as sold to Wrottesley but were assessed and sold separately. Two tenements belonging to St. Mary's Chantry and two of the obit endowments were bought by John Hulson and William Pendred of London in 1549.[5] The purchase price was 22 years' rent in each case: £31 14s. 4d. for the chantry lands and £6 12s. for the obit endowments.[6] It is likely that most of the other chantry and obit lands had been sold off piecemeal in this way before any that remained to the Crown of the Tettenhall properties were granted in 1588 to Edward Wymarke of London together with any remaining of a large number of former religious houses in various counties.[7]

Walter Wrottesley's purchase of the college had included the deanery, of which almost the sole assets were the profits of spiritual jurisdiction.

Consequently the Wrottesleys were entitled to hold a peculiar court for the whole area formerly under the dean's jurisdiction. Their right to hold a secular court for this area, as lords of the manor of Tettenhall Clericorum, was periodically contested by the Creswells,[8] who held the former prebends of Pendeford and Bovenhill; but their right to spiritual jurisdiction seems to have been unchallenged. It survived until the 19th century, when all such peculiars were abolished. The last wills proved in this court and the latest marriage bonds made before its official belong to 1858.[9]

Some at least of the collegiate buildings seem to have stood to the east of the church, although this was only a memory about 1800.[10] There was a house for the vicars by the 16th century.[11]

DEANS

William, occurs about 1176 and at some time between 1177 and 1182.[12]

Elias of Bristol, occurs about 1225.[13]

Thomas Blundeville, appointed September 1226, elected Bishop of Norwich November 1226.[14]

Walter of Brackley, appointed November 1226, elected Bishop of Ossory 1232.[15]

Nicholas de Neville, appointed 1232, vacated deanery by March 1245.[16]

Peter Chaceporc, appointed 1245, died 1254.[17]

Henry Wingham, appointed 1254, retained deanery while Bishop of London from 1259, died 1262.[18]

Peter of Winchester, appointed 1262, occurs 1272.[19]

Walter Langton, resigned by January 1291.[20]

Master William Burnell, appointed 1291, occurs 1293.[21]

John Benstead, appointed 1297, resigned 1300.[22]

Geoffrey Stokes, appointed 1300, occurs 1304.[23]

Ingelard Warley, appointed 1314, resigned 1318.[24]

William of Shenton, B.C.L., appointed 1318, resigned probably by March 1341.[25]

Jordan de Gathorp, resigned by April 1348.[26]

Stephen Broxbourne, appointed 1348.[27]

Robert Caldwell, appointed by the queen between 1343 and 1354, occurs 1361, had evidently resigned by 1366.[28]

[96] E 301/44(2); E 101/75/30. His pension of £5 (S.H.C. 1915, 286, 351) was not in connexion with Tettenhall but as chaplain of Bilston chantry.

[97] S.C. 12/28/12, f. 4v.; S.C. 6/Edw. VI/424, m. 33. This sum includes an estimated 10s. for the profits of the dean's spiritual court, although nothing was in fact received from this source in the year (1547–8) covered by these accounts. It excludes endowments for chantries, obits, and lights.

[98] Cal. Pat. 1548–9, 305.

[99] He also retained the vicars' house and garden, of which he held the lease (S.C. 12/28/12, f. 4v.). Two receipts survive for Wrottesley's rent for Codsall prebend in 1541: S.R.O., D. 593/F/1/3.   [1] Cal. Pat. 1549–51, 55.

[2] E 315/105, ff. 97v.–98v.; S.C. 12/28/12, f. 4v.

[3] Cal. Pat. 1549–51, 54.   [4] Valor Eccl. iii. 105.

[5] Cal. Pat. 1549–51, 131.   [6] E 36/258, f. 110.

[7] C 66/1310, mm. 2, 11.

[8] In 1591 and 1705 (S.H.C. N.S. vi(2), 284–6), and again in 1719 (41st Dep. Kpr.'s Rep. App. I, 531).

[9] A. J. Camp, Wills and their Whereabouts, 69; S.H.C. 1931, 52 sqq.; see above p. 74.

[10] Shaw, Staffs. ii. 195.

[11] E 301/54, no. 6; see above ii. 99.

[12] See above p. 316; S.H.C. iii(1), 227–8; S.H.C. 1937, pp. 17–19.

[13] Hereford Cath. Libr. nos. 783, 980; W. W. Capes, Charters and Records of Hereford Cath. 59 n.; B. M. Seal Cast xliii. 56. In W. de G. Birch, Cat. of Seals in B.M. i,

p. 242, Elias is wrongly described as treasurer of Hereford Cath., and the seal is wrongly dated as c. 1145 (see Capes, op. cit. 35 n.). The legend reads:

SIGILLUM HELIE DECANI DE PENCRIZ
ET DE TETEHAL'.

[14] Pat. R. 1225–32, 63; Handbk. of Brit. Chron. 242.

[15] Pat. R. 1225–32, 92; Handbk. of Brit. Chron. 341.

[16] Cal. Pat. 1232–47, 1; Close R. 1242–7, 290.

[17] Close R. 1242–7, 290; 1254–6, 19.

[18] Close R. 1254–6, 19; Cal. Pat. 1247–58, 394; 1258–66, 31; Handbk. of Brit. Chron. 239.

[19] Cal. Pat. 1266–72, 731; S.H.C. iv(1), 209.

[20] Cal. Pat. 1281–92, 416.

[21] Ibid.; S.H.C. vi(1), 258; Le Neve, Fasti (new edn.), vi. 27.

[22] Cal. Pat. 1292–1301, 321, 559.

[23] Ibid. 559; Cal. Close, 1302–7, 210.

[24] Cal. Pat. 1313–17, 114; Cal. Chanc. Wts. i. 393; Reg. R. Baldock, G. Segrave, R. Newport et S. Gravesend (Cant. & York Soc.), 184–5; Cal. Pat. 1317–21, 126. He was reported dead in Oct. 1317 but certified as still alive a few days later: ibid. 37, 41.

[25] Cal. Pat. 1317–21, 126; 1340–3, 147; see above n. 55. A. Hamilton Thompson identified 'Sheynton' with Shenton (Leics.) in Arch. Jnl. lxxxiv. 61.

[26] Cal. Pat. 1348–50, 47.

[27] Ibid.   [28] See above p. 317.

Edmund, resigned 1371.[29]
John of Harewood, appointed 1371.[30]
John Hatfield, appointed 1374, resigned 1383.[31]
William Hermesthorp, appointed 1383.[32]
John Lincoln of Grimsby, Sch.Cn.L., appointed 1385, resigned 1386.[33]
Nicholas Slake, appointed June 1386, resigned July 1386.[34]
John Nottingham, appointed July 1386, resigned 1389.[35]
Thomas Hanley, appointed 1389, resigned 1412.[36]
Robert Wolveden, appointed 1412. [37]
John Stopyndon, occurs 1435.[38]
Richard Well, resigned 1465.[39]
Ralph Hethcote, B.Cn.L.,appointed 1465, occurs 1473.[40]
John Vernham, died 1489.[41]
Thomas Bowd, B.Th., appointed 1489.[42]
William Capon, D.Th., occurs 1531, dean at the dissolution.[43]

The seal of the peculiar jurisdiction in use in the 18th century is a pointed oval, $2\frac{1}{8}$ by $1\frac{1}{4}$ in., depicting a figure in robes in the upper part and the arms of the Wrottesleys in the base.[44] Legend, roman:

SIGILLUM PECULIARIS IURISDICTIONIS ECCLESIAE
COLLEGIATAE TETENHALL

38. THE COLLEGE OF ST. PETER, WOLVERHAMPTON

THE foundation of the College of Wolverhampton has been attributed to the Lady Wulfrun since the

discovery, about 1560, of a charter by which she endowed a minster at Hampton.[1] If this charter is authentic,[2] the date of the foundation (or refoundation) is 994.[3] Wulfrun's connexion with the minster is attested by the fact that it added her name to its own; by about 1080 it was called 'the church of Wolvrenehamptonia'.[4] From this the name Wolverhampton is derived.[5] In Wulfrun's time the church was dedicated to St. Mary. It was still St. Mary's in 1086,[6] but by the middle of the 12th century the change to St. Peter had occurred.[7]

According to the charter Wulfrun's endowment consisted of 30 hides of land, in Upper Arley (now in Worcs.), 'Eswich' (perhaps Ashwood in Kinver Forest),[8] Bilston, Willenhall, Wednesfield, Pelsall, 'Ocgintun' (probably Ogley Hay near Pelsall),[9] Hilton (near Ogley),[10] Hatherton, Kinvaston, 'the other Hilton' (near Featherstone), and Featherstone. The lands in Upper Arley were probably those granted by King Edgar to Wulfrun's kinsman, Wulfgeat, in 963;[11] other lands, which belonged to the community in 1086, were probably among those given by Ethelred to Wulfrun herself in 985.[12]

It is not clear from the charter whether Wulfrun's minster was to consist of monks or clerks. Presumably she decided in favour of clerks, if the phrase 'my priests at Hampton' used in a writ of Edward the Confessor can be accepted; the writ is spurious in its present form but may have an authentic basis. The phrase suggests a close royal connexion, a status recognized by the diocesan in the early 12th century as anciently belonging to Wulfrun's church.[13] Perhaps it even enjoyed the freedom from episcopal jurisdiction which later characterized royal chapels.[14]

[29] See above p. 317.
[30] Cal. Pat. 1370–4, 140.
[31] Ibid. 402; 1381–5, 327. [32] Ibid. 1381–5, 327.
[33] Ibid. 1385–9, 14, 154; A. B. Emden, Biog. Reg. of Univ. of Cambridge to 1500, 368–9.
[34] Cal. Pat. 1385–9, 154, 195.
[35] Ibid. 195, 536.
[36] Ibid. 536; 1408–13, 415.
[37] Ibid. 1408–13, 415; Le Neve, Fasti (new edn.), vi. 14. He was also Dean of Wolverhampton: see below p. 330. He became Dean of Lichfield in 1426: see above p. 197.
[38] Cal. Papal Regs. viii. 540; Le Neve, Fasti (new edn.) iii. 8; vi. 43; viii. 48. He died in 1447.
[39] Cal. Pat. 1461–7, 378.
[40] Ibid.; S.H.C. N.S. iv. 191; A. B. Emden, Biog. Reg. of Univ. of Oxford to A.D. 1500, ii. 923. He held this degree by 1475; by 1493 he was B. Cn. & C.L. He died in 1499: Le Neve, Fasti (new edn.), x. 48.
[41] Cal. Pat. 1485–94, 293.
[42] Ibid.; Emden, Biog. Reg. Cambridge, 82. He became Dean of Tamworth in 1504: see above p. 315.
[43] Lich. Dioc. Regy., B/A/17/1; E 301/44(1), no. 10; E 101/75/30, m. 3; Emden, Biog. Reg. Cambridge, 122–123.
[44] Lich. Dioc. Regy., Tettenhall Peculiar, impressions of 1741, 1779, 1784.
[1] The anonymous 'Historia Ecclesiae Lichfeldensis', written in 1575 (printed by H. Wharton, Anglia Sacra, i. 444 sqq.), states that the charter was discovered c. 1560 in the ruins of a wall. According to a Chancery suit of c. 1572 (C 2/Eliz. I/L 12/50), John Leigh, one of the vicars choral, had delivered it to the dean's steward. It was transcribed by Dugdale in 1640 from a text now lost (Mon. vi(3), 1443). In 1548 King Edgar was thought to be the founder: E 301/54, no. 1.
[2] Its authenticity has been doubted. See P. H. Sawyer, Anglo-Saxon Charters, no. 1380; recently Mr. E. E. Barker of Notre Dame College of Education, Liverpool, has suggested that it is a 12th-century forgery making use of a set of boundaries from a pre-Conquest survey. Thanks are due to Mr. Barker for placing his notes at the writers' disposal.

[3] Dugdale gives the date as 996, but this is an obvious error for 994 (S.H.C. 1916, 43, 114).
[4] See below n. 15. Wulfrun may be the mother of the founder of Burton Abbey, and may also be the Wulfrun captured by the Danes at Tamworth in 943: S.H.C. 1916, 9–10, 47; Dorothy Whitelock, Anglo-Saxon Wills, 45, 152.
[5] E. Ekwall, Oxford Dict. of Eng. Place-Names.
[6] V.C.H. Staffs. iv. 45, no. 112.
[7] Shaw, Staffs. ii. 152. A jury of 1393 referred to the church as dedicated to St. Mary temp. Hen. I: Cal. Inq. Misc. vi, p. 20. If their statement is accurate, the implication is that the dedication probably changed in Stephen's reign. From 1327 to 1504 the church is occasionally described as dedicated to St. Peter and St. Paul: S.H.C. 1913, 8–9; Cal. Pat. 1330–4, 24; G. P. Mander, Wolverhampton Antiquary, i. 31; ii. 101–2; Cal. Inq. p.m. Hen. VII, ii, p. 222.
[8] S.H.C. 1916, 110–13.
[9] So identified by W. H. Duignan (Charter of Wulfrun to Wolverhampton, 1888), who noticed that 'a certain wood called Hogeley' belonged to the Dean and Chapter of Wolverhampton in the 13th century (Mander, Wolverhampton Antiquary, i. 296); he pointed out that 'Hogeley' is probably Ogley Hay in Cannock Forest and to be identified with 'Ocgintun'.
[10] S.H.C. 1916, 112–13.
[11] Ibid. 99–100. Wulfgeat's soul was to share the spiritual benefits of Wulfrun's endowment.
[12] Ibid. 101–4; Cod. Dipl. ed. Kemble, iii. 213–16. A virgate at Trescott and a hide probably at Wolverhampton, mentioned in the Domesday Survey of the college's property, are likely to have been part of Ethelred's grant.
[13] F. E. Harmer, Anglo-Saxon Writs, 403–7, 527; Shaw, Staffs. ii. 152.
[14] That this was a liberty granted to highly privileged religious communities of the time is demonstrated by Wm. I's charter of 1068 in favour of St. Martin-le-Grand, where the Bishop of London gave his consent to the exemption: W. H. Stevenson, 'An Old-English Charter of William the Conqueror', E.H.R. xi. 740–3. But at this date St. Martin's was not a royal chapel; it became one in Hen. II's reign: V.C.H. London, ii. 555.

William I gave the church of Wolverhampton and its possessions to his chaplain, Samson.[15] As Samson's tenants the priests of Wolverhampton at the time of the Domesday Survey held ten estates from him.[16] Seven remained of Wulfrun's grant: 2 hides in Upper Arley, together with a half hide in 'the other Arley' withheld from them by force; 5 hides in 'Haswic' (probably Ashwood), then waste on account of the king's forest; 5 hides in Wednesfield; 2 hides in Willenhall; a half hide in Pelsall, then waste; 3 virgates in Hilton (near Ogley); and a hide of waste in 'Hocintune' (probably Ogley). They also held from Samson a hide probably in Wolverhampton, a virgate in Bushbury, and a virgate in Trescott. In all, their estates were said to be worth £6 a year.[17] Of the rest of Wulfrun's endowment Bilston (2 hides) was in the king's hands,[18] while Hatherton (3 hides), Kinvaston (one hide), the other Hilton (2 hides), and Featherstone (one hide, then waste) were held from Samson by two priests, Edwin and Alric. It was, however, noted that Hatherton and Kinvaston had belonged to the church of Hampton in the Confessor's time. Domesday Book also recorded that the priests of Hampton claimed part of the wood of Sedgley manor[19] and still held 2 hides worth 15s. at Lutley (Worcs.) which they had held before the Conquest.[20] By 1300 the canons of Wolverhampton had regained Hatherton, Kinvaston, Featherstone, and Hilton.[21]

Early in Henry I's reign Samson, now Bishop of Worcester, granted the church of Wolverhampton to his cathedral priory; its privileges were still safeguarded even though it no longer enjoyed direct royal patronage.[22] In Stephen's reign the monks of Worcester lost possession of Wolverhampton. It was first seized by Roger, Bishop of Salisbury; after his death in 1139, in spite of his declared intent to restore it,[23] it was granted by Stephen to the bishop and cathedral church of Lichfield.[24] The canons of Wolverhampton[25] complained to Eugenius III, and by 1152 their church had been restored to the monks of Worcester.[26]

Shortly after the monks of Worcester recovered Wolverhampton they lost it to the heir to the Crown, and after a lapse of almost a century the church again became a royal chapel. Henry, Duke of Normandy and Aquitaine, soon to become Henry II of England, in a charter[27] issued in 1153 or early 1154,[28] referred to it as 'my chapel', restored all privileges it had held in the time of Henry I, and recognized its freedom from secular taxation.[29] After Henry became king a second charter[30] specified the right of the canons to hold a court for their tenants. Although these charters did not mention freedom from episcopal jurisdiction, it is likely that Wolverhampton enjoyed it, for Peter of Blois, dean by 1191[31] and probably appointed by Henry II whom he served for many years, described the church as subject only to the Archbishop of Canterbury and the king.[32]

It is not known for how long Wolverhampton had possessed a dean and prebendaries before the time of Peter of Blois. A dean was possibly introduced when the church was in the possession of Lichfield, as a dean is first found at Lichfield at that time.[33] Prebends were perhaps introduced at the same time, as part of the general reorganization of English chapters on the continental model.[34]

Peter of Blois found the canons vicious, intent on keeping their prebends in the possession of their families, and so linked by marriage as to present a united resistance to his attempts at reform.[35] He therefore resigned, probably in 1202, and persuaded Archbishop Hubert Walter, with King John's approval, to dissolve the college and replace it with a community of Cistercian monks. This project was confirmed by Innocent III.[36]

King John consented to the new foundation in January 1203 and at the same time granted the deanery and prebends of Wolverhampton to the

---

[15] H. W. C. Davis, *Regesta Regum Anglo-Normannorum*, i. 57, 125. The grant belongs to a date between 1074 and 1085; in it is the earliest recorded reference to Hampton as Wolverhampton ('Wolvrenehamptonia').

[16] *V.C.H. Staffs*. iv. 44–45.

[17] It has been suggested that this valuation does not include the hide in Wolverhampton: ibid. 28–29.

[18] Ibid. 38, no. 5.

[19] Ibid. 54, no. 224. The manor was held by Wm. fitz Ansculf.

[20] *V.C.H. Worcs.* i. 308.

[21] *S.H.C.* v(1), 177–9.

[22] Shaw, *Staffs.* ii. 152. The date of the grant is between 1100 (since Hen. I is mentioned as approving it) and 1108 (the date of the death of Urse d'Abitot who witnessed Hen. I's charter confirming the grant). According to a jury of 1393 (which may not have been well-informed about events nearly three centuries earlier) Hen. I endowed the church with lands and rents worth £26 13s. 4d. a year: *Cal. Inq. Misc.* vi, p. 20.

[23] Shaw, *Staffs*. ii. 152.

[24] Dugdale, *Mon.* vi(3), 1252 (Latin text); *S.H.C.* 1924, p. 284 (Eng. summary). Dated to Dec. 1139 by R. L. Poole in Hist. MSS. Com. *14th Rep. App. VIII*, 223.

[25] The priests of Wolverhampton were also called canons in Domesday Bk.: *V.C.H. Staffs*. iv. 44, no. 101.

[26] Shaw, *Staffs*. ii. 152. It was omitted from the papal confirmation of the bishop's possessions in Feb. 1152 (*S.H.C.* 1924, pp. 126–7); in the confirmation of 1144 it had been included (ibid. p. 216).

[27] Dugdale, *Mon.* vi(3), 1446.

[28] Henry was in England from Jan. 1153 to the beginning of Apr. 1154; it was during this visit that he added the style 'Duke of Aquitaine' to his titles. His charter to Wolverhampton was issued in England, at Dudley, after he had assumed the new title: L. Delisle and E. Berger, *Receuil des Actes de Henri II*, i. 60–66; ii, Introduction, 130–1.

[29] Apparently, however, it was not exempted from scutage, for the king's chapel of Wolverhampton paid 31s. 8d. when scutage was levied in 1172: *S.H.C.* i. 66, 67.

[30] Dugdale, *Mon.* vi(3), 1446.

[31] Peter was already Dean of Wolverhampton when he wrote to the Chancellor, Wm. Longchamp, Bp. of Ely and papal legate, for protection against the Sheriff of Staffs. who was contravening Wolverhampton's ancient privileges: Migne, *Patrologia Latina*, ccvii, col. 332. Wm. was appointed legate in June 1190 and left the country in disgrace in Oct. 1191.

[32] Ibid., col. 444.

[33] See above p. 197.

[34] W. Page, 'Some Remarks on the Churches of the Domesday Survey', *Archaeologia*, 2nd ser. xvi. 94; A. Hamilton Thompson, *The Eng. Clergy*, 85; Kathleen Edwards, *Eng. Secular Cathedrals in the Middle Ages* (1949 edn.), 12, 18–19.

[35] One of the canons whom Peter of Blois attempted to displace was Robert of Shrewsbury on the occasion of his election as Bishop of Bangor in 1197. Robert's attempt to retain the prebend provoked an angry letter from Peter: Migne, *Pat. Lat.* ccvii, cols. 434–6.

[36] R. de Coggeshall, *Chronicon Anglicanum* (Rolls Ser.), 160.

archbishop for its use.[37] In January 1204 he freed these properties of all forest restrictions and dues[38] and as additional endowments granted the manors of Wolverhampton (July 1204)[39] and Tettenhall (May 1205)[40] and the wood of Kingsley in the forest of Kinver (June 1205).[41] He also prepared a comprehensive charter of liberties for the new monastery.[42] Meanwhile the archbishop had taken steps to secure the consent of the General Chapter of the Cistercian order[43] and, in anticipation of it, had already established some monks at Wolverhampton.[44] In July 1205, however, the archbishop died. King John cancelled his charter of privileges,[45] and the project was abandoned. Within a month the king appointed a new dean of Wolverhampton.[46]

Throughout the 13th century the royal chapels were struggling to establish their exemption from episcopal jurisdiction. The church of Wolverhampton secured this privilege with less difficulty than other royal chapels of the diocese. It owed its success principally to Giles of Erdington who first appears as Dean of Wolverhampton in 1224.[47] Erdington made his career in the royal service and became one of the most distinguished of Henry III's judges.[48] His legal skill is evident in the agreement he negotiated with the new Bishop of Coventry and Lichfield, Alexander Stavensby, immediately after the bishop's consecration in 1224.[49] This formalized the traditional but unwritten privileges asserted earlier by Peter of Blois. It recognized the dean's right to appoint to the prebends in his church, institute his clergy, and correct them; it admitted the bishop's intervention only on neglect of correction and after an official admonition, and even then allowed him no right to procurations. On the other hand it recognized that the bishop was entitled to be received with honour, to celebrate, preach, and confirm in the church, and to hear difficult cases and appeals from the parish.

Under the protection of this agreement Wolverhampton enjoyed its privileges unchallenged during the episcopates of Stavensby and his successors until 1260 when Bishop Meuland attempted visitation. Erdington obtained a royal prohibition and in order to defend the agreement of 1224 invoked a papal bull which Henry III had obtained in 1245, exempting royal chapels from episcopal jurisdiction.[50] The dispute ended finally in 1292 when the bishop recognized that all seven royal chapels of his diocese were exempt from ordinary jurisdiction and directly subject to Rome, and reserved only his right to be received with honour, to preach, ordain, consecrate, and confirm in them.[51]

Erdington also defended the financial interests of the college. He had boundaries perambulated,[52] transactions recorded,[53] and property rights defended in the courts.[54] In 1258 he obtained from the king the valuable grant of a weekly market and an annual fair to be held at Wolverhampton.[55] He secured the goodwill of local landowners by concessions of privilege and of land[56] and promoted good relations with the townsmen by granting his burgesses in 1263 the right to hold their burgages freely by hereditary title with the same privileges and liabilities as the burgesses of Stafford.[57] Perhaps the last benefit the college received from Erdington was an endowment for the maintenance of a chaplain at Wolverhampton.[58] He died probably at the end of 1268, after having held the deanery for at least 44 years.[59]

The next dean, Theodosius de Camilla, was, like Erdington, prominent in the royal service.[60] He seems rarely, if ever, to have been in Wolverhampton.[61] His financial interests, however, were well served by his bailiffs, notably Andrew of Genoa, one of the canons, who was also his proctor.[62] They used high-handed measures to collect his dues and plundered the deanery woods for his benefit.[63] They increased his revenues by allowing tenants to inclose the waste,[64] so that whereas the deanery had been valued in 1272 at 40 marks a year[65] Camilla was able in 1293 to farm it out (excluding the collation of prebends) at 50 marks a year.[66] His right of collation was used to endow at least three of his relatives, and

[37] Lambeth Palace Libr. MS. 1212 (Canterbury Cartulary), p. 19. Tanner's reference to the charter (*Not. Mon.* (1744), 491) must be to the 16th-cent. Canterbury Cartulary now in the Bodl. Libr. (Tanner MS. 223) which took its material from the Cartulary at Lambeth. Apparently John had already appointed another dean for Wolverhampton, on Peter of Blois' resignation, since 'Nicholas, Dean of Wolverhampton', appeared in the list of essoins taken at Lichfield in Sept. 1203 as the defendant in a local plea, but in subsequent proceedings in this suit Nic. was no longer called dean: *S.H.C.* iii. 87, 118, 226. The possibility that Nic. was described as dean in error must be dismissed since a later dean, Theodosius de Camilla, referred to 'Nicholas my predecessor': *S.H.C.* ix(1), 53.
[38] *Rot. Chart.* (Rec. Com.), 115.
[39] Ibid. 135; Dugdale, *Mon.* vi(3), 1446. The manor of Wolverhampton was farmed at £6 12s. a year: *S.H.C.* ii(1), 125, 130.
[40] *Rot. Chart.* 152. The manor of Tettenhall had in fact been given to the archbishop for his abbey in the preceding year, and he received its revenues from midsummer 1204; the manor was farmed at £4 a year: *Rot. Litt. Claus.* (Rec. Com.), i. 8; *S.H.C.* ii(1), 119, 122, 125, 130.
[41] *Rot. Chart.* 153.   [42] Ibid. 154.
[43] J. M. Canivez, *Stat. Cap. Gen. Ord. Cist.* i. 285, 303.
[44] *Rot. Chart.* 135; Dugdale, *Mon.* vi(3), 1446.
[45] *Rot. Chart.* 154.   [46] Ibid. 156; *Rot. Litt. Claus.* i. 44.
[47] *S.H.C.* 1924, pp. 282–3 (dated to 1224 by the reference to Bp. Stavensby's first arrival from overseas after his consecration).   [48] *Cal. Pat.* and *Close R. passim.*
[49] *S.H.C.* 1924, pp. 282–3.
[50] *Cal. Pat.* 1258–66, 126; T. Rymer, *Foedera* (Rec.

Com.), i(1), 261; *Annales Monastici* (Rolls Ser.), i. 275.
[51] Lincs. Archives Office, Dean and Chapter, Carte Decani, f. 55.   [52] *Close R.* 1247–51, 50; 1251–3, 262.
[53] *S.H.C.* iv(1), 232–3; *Bk. of Fees,* ii. 1186, 1246, 1257, 1291; *Close R.* 1247–51, 545.
[54] *S.H.C.* iv(1), 45, 124, 126; *Close R.* 1253–4, 161–2; *Pat. R. 1225–32,* 356.   [55] *Cal. Chart R. 1257–1300,* 7.
[56] *S.H.C.* iv(1), 249, 250–1; Mander, *Wolverhampton Antiquary,* i. 296.   [57] S.R.O., D. 593/B/1/26/6/34/1.
[58] Mander, *Wolverhampton Antiquary,* i. 237.
[59] His deanery was granted to Theodosius de Camilla on 10 Jan. 1269 after his death: *Cal. Pat. 1266–72,* 310.
[60] Frequent references in *Cal. Pat. 1266–72.*
[61] After Henry III's death he spent much time abroad: ibid. 1272–81, 41; 1281–92, 226, 318, 410, 413.
[62] S.R.O., D. 593/B/1/26/6/34/3; *S.H.C.* vi(1), 233, 239.
[63] *Close R. 1268–72,* 179; *Cal. Pat. 1292–1301,* 24; *S.H.C.* i. 175; ibid. v(1), 153; ibid. vi(1), 66, 70; ibid. 1911, 228–32.
[64] *S.H.C.* vi(1), 152, 233; ibid. 1911, 229–32; ibid. 1928, pp. 139–40; S.R.O., D. 593/B/1/26/6/34/3.
[65] *S.H.C.* iv(1), 209.
[66] E 159/66, m. 28. The lessees were the Abbot of Westminster and a canon of Wells. In *Trans. Birm. Arch. Soc.* lx. 82, this lease is confused with another (E 159/67, m. 87) by which Theodosius farmed his prebend of Salisbury to the abbot and convent of Milton (Dors.) and John of Stafford, clerk. Further evidence of the increase of the dean's rents is provided by Camilla's grant of a plot of land in Prestwood, part of the original endowment of the college, to Geoffrey of Bilston, for two silver pennies a year: *Cal. Pat. 1374–7,* 282.

like him they enjoyed their prebends largely *in absentia*.[67] Since other known canons of this period were royal clerks, it seems likely that few resided at Wolverhampton.[68]

The lease of 1293 illustrates the difference between the real revenues of benefices and the lenient assessment made by the clergy for the purposes of taxation. For the Taxation of 1291 the deanery was valued at 20 marks. The prebends, named for the first time, were assessed as follows (no doubt, like the deanery, at well below their true value): Featherstone at £6 13s. 4d.; Willenhall £6 13s. 4d.; Wobaston £4 13s. 4d.; Hilton £6; Monmore £4 13s. 4d.; Kinvaston £8. Besides these there was the chantry of St. Mary in Hatherton (which by 1294 had become a seventh prebend),[69] valued at £4 13s. 4d. The total value of the church was £54 13s. 4d.[70]

While Camilla was dean the college successfully defended its privileges against the claims of the Archbishop of Canterbury to visit it. Metropolitical visitation was an innovation, introduced into the province of Canterbury in 1250 by Boniface of Savoy; it had been applied to the diocese of Coventry and Lichfield in 1260, but of the royal chapels there it seems that Stafford alone was visited.[71] Archbishop Pecham, however, was intent on enforcing the decrees of the Council of Lyons (1274) against pluralism and non-residence, of which the canons of the royal free chapels were flagrantly guilty. He therefore determined to visit them all, even in defiance of the king's prohibition.[72] When on 27 July 1280 he tried to visit the church of Wolverhampton the doors were shut against him; and when he summoned the canons to meet him on 31 July to produce proof of their exemption they, like those of the other royal chapels of the diocese, ignored him and were publicly excommunicated. Canonical proceedings were launched against the seven chapels. This provoked the king to protest. Under royal pressure the archbishop made concessions; and at last, after conversations with the king at the Easter Parliament of 1281, he agreed to accept what the king, in consultation with the bishops and chapters concerned, should decide about the privileges of the royal chapels in the dioceses of Coventry and Lichfield and of London.[73] This conference presumably produced the agreement of June 1281 by which Bishop Meuland recognized that six of the royal chapels in his diocese, including Wolverhampton, were not to be visited by any ordinary. In

return, however, he was to be honourably received when he came by invitation to preach, ordain, consecrate oil and chrism, and confirm.[74] Although the archbishop was not among the named parties to the agreement, he seems to have respected his promise to abide by it.

This agreement did not settle Pecham's difference with Camilla whose non-residence continued to give offence. In 1282 the archbishop excommunicated him, deprived him of two of his churches, and even maintained that he had no right to Wolverhampton, as it was properly in the patronage of Canterbury.[75] Camilla, who had influential friends,[76] was not easily defeated. In 1286 he secured a handsome money compensation for the two churches[77] and continued to hold the deanery until his death in 1295 without apparently changing his habits.

The college property suffered in the 14th and early 15th centuries from wastage by a number of deans. Philip of Everdon (1295–1303) and his successor John of Everdon inclosed plots of the deanery waste and alienated them.[78] Moreover both these deans displeased the king, Philip by accepting a papal provision to one of the prebends,[79] and John by making grants of the college's lands without licence.[80] Hugh Ellis, who died in 1339, not only alienated land[81] but made prodigal gifts of the stock and utensils of the deanery and left the dean's buildings in disrepair.[82] The next dean, Philip Weston, was ill served by his bailiff.[83] It is perhaps not surprising that after Weston's resignation in 1368 the king ordered a visitation of Wolverhampton, together with four other royal chapels of the diocese, to investigate alienation of property, loss of privileges, misappropriation of funds, disappearance of books, vestments and ornaments, neglect of services, and the conduct of the church's ministers.[84] Not all the charges applied to Wolverhampton, for instance the neglect of privileges; for John of Melbourne, though dean for only a few months, had secured royal confirmation of the college's ancient charters in 1328.[85]

The investigation of 1368 appears to have had little effect on subsequent deans. Richard Postell (1373–94) embezzled annually an income of £26 13s. 4d. said to have been intended for the maintenance of six priests celebrating divine service;[86] he was, however, careful of his church's privileges, securing confirmation of its charters from both Edward III and Richard II.[87] Inquiries into dilapidations followed the deaths of two successive deans,

[67] *S.H.C.* vi(1), 180–1; *Cal. Pat.* 1292–1301, 346, 347; 1301–7, 239.
[68] e.g. Geoffrey of Aspall, Keeper of the Wardrobe of Queen Eleanor, who was 'continually engaged in the king's affairs' as well as those of the queen: T. F. Tout, *Chapters in Admin. Hist. of Mediaeval Eng.* v. 236–8; *Cal. Pat.* 1272–81, 469; *Cal. Close,* 1279–88, 129.
[69] *S.H.C.* 1911, 229.
[70] *Tax. Eccl.* (Rec. Com.), 243. In 1255 the jury of Seisdon hundred stated that the value of the church of Wolverhampton with its seven prebends was 60 marks: *S.H.C.* v(1), 115–16. Presumably this estimate includes Hatherton chantry as the seventh prebend. The total sum appears too small as the deanery alone was estimated to be worth £25 c.1249: *S.H.C.* 1911, 144.
[71] See above p. 304.
[72] Decima Douie, *Archbp. Pecham,* 98–101; *Reg. Epist. Fratris Johannis Peckham* (Rolls Ser.), i. 109–10, 392n–o.
[73] *Reg. Epist. Peckham,* i. 130–1, 147–50, 154–6, 178–84, 196, 392s–v.
[74] *S.H.C.* 1924, pp. 251–2.
[75] *Reg. Epist. Peckham,* i. 384–7; ii. 419–20, 559–60; *Cal. Papal Regs.* i. 450, 451.

[76] e.g. Cardinal Benedict Gaetani (later Pope Boniface VIII), who attempted to intercede with Pecham: *Reg. Epist. Peckham,* ii. 558–60, 602–4, 629–30, 693.
[77] Ibid. 692–4; *Cal. Papal Regs.* i. 467, 473, 489.
[78] Proofs of unpublished article by G. P. Mander for *Wolverhampton Antiquary,* ii, no. 4, in W.S.L., D. 1806/19; *Cal. Pat.* 1307–13, 342; 1321–4, 227; 1374–7, 282; S.R.O., D. 593/B/1/26/6/34/6 and 8.
[79] *Cal. Close,* 1302–7, 66, 71; *Select Cases in the Court of King's Bench, vol. iii* (Selden Soc. lviii), 120–2.
[80] *Cal. Fine R.* 1319–27, 201.
[81] S.R.O., D. 593/B/1/26/6/34/9.
[82] *Cal. Pat.* 1338–40, 482, 488; 1340–3, 306; *Cal. Inq. Misc.* ii, p. 434 (also in *S.H.C.* 1913, 82–83, with some misreadings).
[83] *S.H.C.* xii(1), 110, 143; *Cal. Pat.* 1354–8, 532.
[84] *Cal. Pat.* 1367–70, 142, 143.
[85] *Cal. Chart. R.* 1327–41, 83. Dugdale printed the text of the four charters confirmed but erroneously attributed the *inspeximus* to Edw. I: *Mon.* vi(3), 1446.
[86] *Cal. Inq. Misc.* vi, p. 20. See also *S.H.C.* xv. 82, for Postell's unsatisfactory financial dealings.
[87] *Cal. Pat.* 1377–81, 336.

Lawrence Allerthorpe in 1406 and Thomas Stanley in 1410.[88] In Postell's and Allerthorpe's time there were conflicts with the local inhabitants arising from dissatisfaction with the way the dean's agents managed his business affairs and his spiritual jurisdiction.[89] The dean and all the canons were apparently absentees in 1366 and 1385;[90] probably this was usual. Between them the seven prebendaries maintained five vicars to serve St. Peter's in 1385;[91] in 1531 they maintained one each.[92]

Other priests were supported in St. Peter's and its dependent chapels by pious endowment. In St. Peter's there were two chantries, one founded in 1311 by Henry of Prestwood with lands and rents worth 23s. 10d. a year,[93] and the chantry of St. Mary, mentioned in 1398 and 1405,[94] which may be that founded by Giles of Erdington. The dependent chapel of Pelsall had a curate endowed by William le Keu in 1311,[95] and a priest was maintained in the prebendal chapel of Willenhall by the income from property given in 1328 by Richard Gervase of Wolverhampton.[96] In 1447 Sir Thomas Erdington gave lands and rent to support a curate in the dependent chapel of Bilston.[97] Two other benefactions were connected with the college. By 1385 a light in honour of St. Peter was maintained in the collegiate church by an income from land managed by a body called 'wardens of the light',[98] and in 1395 Clement Leveson, one of the vicars, and William Waterfall of Wolverhampton established a hospital which was placed under the dean's jurisdiction.[99]

Under Dean Allerthorpe Wolverhampton's immunity from archiepiscopal visitation was surrendered with only a token struggle. Archbishop Arundel sent his commissaries to the college in February 1401. Half-hearted legal objections were presented, but when they were dismissed the visitation was allowed to proceed.[1] As Allerthorpe enjoyed royal favour, being appointed that year Treasurer of England,[2] and could well have enlisted the king's support, this capitulation must be attributed to the political difficulties of Henry IV, who could not afford to oppose the archbishop at this point.

The importance to the college of its dean's interest was demonstrated after John Barningham was appointed in 1437. He twice went to law to put Wolverhampton's affairs in order;[3] and in his will of 1457[4] he remembered both the church and its people, leaving £5 to the fabric of the nave, 40s. for his obit, and 66s. 8d. to be distributed among the poor. Under his successor, William Dudley, the college's charters were again confirmed,[5] and the rebuilding of the church, already under way in 1439, was continued.[6]

Dudley was the first dean of Wolverhampton to be also Dean of St. George's Chapel, Windsor Castle. Although he vacated both deaneries in 1476 their union was made permanent in 1480 by Edward IV. The Dean of Windsor was to be dean and prebendary of Wolverhampton and to possess all the rights of the deanery. These included an important emolument which he lacked at Windsor, the right to collate to prebends.[7] An attempt made by the chapter of Windsor in 1480 to limit that right by restricting the dean's choice to canons of Windsor[8] had little effect. For fifty years about half the known canons of Wolverhampton were already canons of Windsor;[9] by 1535 there was not a single canon in common,[10] and subsequently only three[11] are known, despite the reissue of the decree in 1637.[12] The two colleges, though having the same dean, remained distinct institutions, with separate statutes, seals, and revenues.

In the 16th century it was the practice for the dean to lease his Wolverhampton property to local men of substance. The first such lease to be recorded belongs to 1516–17;[13] like later leases[14] it probably did not include the profits of market, fair, and court. The rent then agreed of £38 may be compared with the £40 6s. 4¼d. clear which the dean's rents and rights produced in 1416–17, when the profits of the market and fair were £3 19s. 9d. and the court brought in £5 5s. 3d. less expenses.[15]

One of the two lessees of 1516–17, James Leveson, merchant of the Staple, retained the deanery lease at the same rent for at least 25 years, and his family continued to hold it after his death.[16] He also bought up deanery lands, acquiring more than twenty holdings,[17] and leased from the dean a prebend

[88] Cal. Close, 1405–9, 55; Cal. Pat. 1408–13, 223.
[89] Cal. Pat. 1377–81, 401; 1381–5, 59, 91; 1391–6, 357; Cal. Close, 1381–5, 32; S.H.C. xv. 104–5.
[90] Reg. Simonis de Langham (Cant. & York Soc.), 62, 107; Reg. Simonis de Sudbiria, vol. ii (Cant. & York Soc.), 160, 164, 174, 177; S.H.C. 1928, pp. 131–2. Postell was a residentiary at St. George's Chapel, Windsor Castle, where he was steward in 1381–2 and treasurer in 1383–4: A. K. B. Roberts, St. George's Chapel, Windsor Castle, 1348–1416, 57, 198, 240; Cal. Pat. 1377–81, 601.
[91] S.H.C. 1928, pp. 131–2. The prebendaries of Wobaston, Hatherton, and Monmore shared a vicar; the other four had one each.
[92] Lich. Dioc. Regy., B/A/17/1.
[93] Cal. Pat. 1307–13, 357; S.H.C. 1911, 308–9.
[94] Cal. Pat. 1396–7, 387; Bilston Par. Reg. (Staffs. Par. Reg. Soc.), 213, 218 (Ric. Ames's notes).
[95] S.H.C. 1911, 309–10. The income was 30s. 6d.
[96] Ibid. 1913, 8–9; Cal. Pat. 1327–30, 231. The income was 40s. in 1328; in 1535 it was £5 2s. 7d. clear: Valor Eccl. iii. 100.
[97] Cal. Pat. 1446–52, 77; Cal. Rot. Chart. et Inq. a.q.d. (Rec. Com.), p. 390; Cal. Inq. p.m. (Rec. Com.), iv, p. 298. The income was 40s. in 1447; in 1535 it was £4 19s. 10d. clear: Valor Eccl. iii. 100.
[98] S.H.C. 1928, pp. 131–2.   [99] See above p. 296.
[1] Lambeth Palace Libr., Reg. Arundel, i, f. 481.
[2] Tout, Chapters, iii. 456 n. 2; Cal. Pat. 1399–1401, 8, 489.

[3] S.H.C. N.S. iii. 157, 200.
[4] Testamenta Eboracensia, vol. ii (Surtees Soc. xxx), pp. 203–9.
[5] Cal. Pat. 1461–7, 61.
[6] Ibid. 1436–41, 312; S.R.O., D. 593/B/1/26/6/26/11.
[7] Cal. Pat. 1476–85, 175; St. George's Chapel, Windsor, Records (hereafter referred to as W. R.), Denton Black Bk., ff. 102v.–103v.
[8] W. R., Arundel White Bk., f. 161.
[9] For a full list of the canons of Windsor see S. L. Ollard, Fasti Wyndesorienses. Canons of Wolverhampton between 1480 and 1535 can be traced mainly in the rolls of the prebendal courts (S.R.O., D. 593/J/5/6, 7, 8, and 9; G. P. Mander's list (Wolverhampton Antiquary, ii. 108–14) is unreliable.
[10] Valor Eccl. (Rec. Com.), iii. 104–5.
[11] John Robins, Canon of Windsor 1543–58 and Preb. of Monmore 1555–8; Godfrey Goodman, Canon of Windsor 1607–56 and Preb. of Hatherton 1617–21; and Francis Brown, Canon of Windsor 1713–24 and Preb. of Kinvaston 1719–24.
[12] S. Bond, Chapter Acts of the Dean and Canons of Windsor, 1430, 1523–1672, 176, 182.
[13] Shaw, Staffs. ii. 154.
[14] S.C. 12/28/12.
[15] S.R.O., D. 593/F/1/1.
[16] Ibid. F/1/2; S.C. 12/28/12.
[17] S.R.O., D. 593/J/5/4/2 and 3.

called Our Lady Prebend or the prebend of Wolverhampton, first mentioned in 1530 and probably to be identified with the chantry of Our Lady in Wolverhampton.[18] He also acquired property in the prebends of Willenhall, Hatherton, and Wobaston.[19] As the canons, following the dean's example, farmed out their prebends also, the Leveson family gradually increased the number of leases in its possession. By 1538 James Leveson was farming Wobaston prebend;[20] by 1544 Richard Leveson held Hatherton and Hilton;[21] and in 1550 members of the family held four of the prebends as well as the deanery.[22] A lease of Featherstone prebend in 1537[23] provides an example of the conditions: while the lessee was entitled to all profits, he had to pay a vicar and meet all extraordinary charges. These were not easy terms, for the rent was £7 a year and the clear value of the prebend was estimated in 1535 at only £8 13s. 4d.[24]

In 1545 the college was threatened with dissolution under the first Chantries Act,[25] but this expired without effect at the death of Henry VIII. The threat was renewed in 1547 by the second Chantries Act,[26] and, in spite of the dean's argument that the exemption explicitly granted by the Act to St. George's, Windsor, ought also to protect Wolverhampton,[27] the college was dissolved and replaced by a vicarage endowed with £20 a year to support a preaching minister and curate.[28] The pensions paid to the dispossessed clergy were evidently calculated on the basis of their former net incomes, which were as follows: the dean £38 4s.; the prebendaries: Wobaston £8 11s. 4d.; Hilton £8 0s. 9¼d.; Monmore £8; Willenhall £4 17s. 9½d.; Featherstone £7; Kinvaston £6; Hatherton £2; the curates: Willenhall £4 12s. 3d.; Pelsall £4 10s. 8d.; Bilston £5 3s. 3d.; the vicars choral (only five were recorded): Willenhall and Wobaston £5 13s. 4d. each and Hatherton, Featherstone, and Kinvaston £5 each; the morrow-mass priest (who was probably the chaplain of St. Mary's Chantry) £2 8s.[29] The properties of the college, which had an annual value assessed variously at £113 4s. 7¼d., £111 7s. 11d., and £111 8s. 1¼d.,[30] were first confiscated to the Crown, then in 1553 granted to the Duke of Northumberland.[31]

The accession of Mary led to the restoration of the college of Wolverhampton as an act of royal favour to St. George's, Windsor. Her letters patent of 1553 maintained that the dissolution was invalid on account of the exemption granted to St. George's, ordered the college to be reconstituted, nominated the dean, prebendaries, and sacrist (of whom all except two had previously been associated with St. Peter's), and took advantage of Northumberland's attainder to restore all its properties, now assessed

at an annual value of £113 13s. 0¼d.[32] After a few years of uncertainty following Mary's death this restoration was finally confirmed by the grant of a royal charter in 1564.[33]

The establishment of the restored college remained much as it was before the dissolution. The chapter, which was supposed to meet once a quarter, consisted of the dean, seven prebendaries, and the sacrist; it possessed a chapter seal and employed a registrar to keep its records. The dean being inevitably an absentee, his jurisdiction was normally exercised by his substitute, the official, who was usually, but not invariably, one of the prebendaries. The prebendaries had the duty of attending morning and evening prayer on Sundays and festival days; and each had to deliver a sermon every quarter. In practice these duties, preaching excepted, were performed, as in the past, by the permanent, salaried substitutes, the vicars choral, who served each stall. The requirement that the vicars choral should all be at least in deacon's orders proved difficult to maintain on account of the low stipends offered; and by the end of the 17th century the seven vicars choral had evolved into an establishment of three curates or readers, who presumably had some ministerial qualifications, three lay 'singing men', and an organist.[34]

The parochial duties of St. Peter's fell on the sacrist. His office was not new, for there is evidence that it existed in the 13th century,[35] but its name and function seem to have been absorbed into that of the stipendiary or morrow-mass priest mentioned in the surveys of Edward VI's reign.[36] Mary's letters patent not only revived the title of sacrist but elevated his status by making him a member of the chapter, a dignity which he does not appear to have enjoyed before the restoration. The sacrist's estate, which probably included the endowments of the former morrow-mass priest, produced, in the middle of the 17th century, an annual income of £26. This sum did not include fees; and it would therefore seem that the sacrist had adequate provision.[37] It would seem too that the office was adequately served, for the critical Puritan survey of 1604 made no comment on it.[38] It was otherwise with the other pastoral clergy of the parish, the three curates who served the townships of Bilston, Pelsall, and Willenhall. Although their former chantry chapels had survived the dissolution with at least part of their endowments in the hands of trustees who nominated and paid the curates, the stipends amounted to no more than £4 or £5 each a year and could hardly have attracted an able preaching ministry. The Puritan survey of 1604 noted all three curates as non-preachers and drunkards. It was not until later in the 17th century and in the early 18th century that

[18] Ibid. F/1/2.
[19] Ibid. J/5/6 and 7.
[20] Ibid. F/1/2.
[21] S.C. 12/28/12.
[22] W. R., Dr. Evans' Bk. A, ff. 28v., 31, 33–34.
[23] S.R.O., D. 593/J/5/7.
[24] Valor Eccl. iii. 104.
[25] 37 Hen. VIII, c. 4.
[26] 1 Edw. VI, c. 14.
[27] C 2/Eliz. I/L 12/50.
[28] Cal. Pat. 1550–3, 401; E 301/44(1), no. 1.
[29] E 101/75/30; E 301/44(1), no. 1; 44(2).
[30] E 301/44(1), no. 1; E 301/54, no. 1; S.C. 6/Edw. VI/ 424, m. 32; S.C. 12/28/12, ff. 1–2.
[31] Cal. Pat. 1553, 179.

[32] Ibid. 1553–4, 230–1.
[33] W. R. X3 7/13.
[34] Lich. Dioc. Regy., Wolverhampton Peculiar, Dean Day's Orders (of which Miss L. M. Midgley supplied a transcript); C 2/Eliz. I/L 12/50; W.R. iv. B 26, f. 36.
[35] Mander, Wolverhampton Antiquary, ii. 58 (1242). And see S.R.O., D. 593/B/1/26/6/14/2, 5 and 8.
[36] It seems likely that the sacrist's estate as surveyed in 1847 (C.C. 14532) was the same as the estate of the morrow-mass priest as surveyed in 1548 (S.C. 12/28/12, f. 2v.).
[37] Bodl. MS. 323, f. 266v. A figure of £40 a year is given by Erdeswick, Staffs. 263.
[38] A. Peel, 'A Puritan Survey of the Church in Staffs. in 1604', E.H.R. xxvi. 338–52.

the stipends and standards of these curates showed any real improvement.[39]

In the 17th century the college experienced in good measure the conflict between Puritans and Laudians. This came to a head under Matthew Wren, appointed dean in 1628,[40] and his brother Christopher, who succeeded him in 1635.[41] They attempted to silence the Puritan faction in the chapter, particularly Richard Lee, Prebendary of Willenhall since 1622, whose influence was the more odious to them because he actually resided in Wolverhampton and maintained an active preaching ministry in the parish.[42] In 1635, as the dean's disciplinary powers had proved insufficient, Christopher Wren invoked the authority of Laud himself; waiving the ancient immunities of the college, he welcomed the process of metropolitical visitation and by this potent means had Lee suspended and forbidden to preach.[43] Having followed up this success with measures against the Puritan laity of the parish,[44] Wren celebrated his triumph by a thanksgiving service in St. Peter's, where a new high altar was dedicated with incense, music, and a lavish ritual.[45]

The Puritans soon had their revenge. Lee's suspension provided one of the charges brought against Laud in 1644; and Lee's brother, Leonard, together with William Pinson, a Puritan layman of Wolverhampton, testified at Laud's trial.[46] Meanwhile the college had been doomed in principle by the decision, taken in 1643, to abolish all deans and chapters.[47] Accordingly, after Parliament had won the Civil War, the college was dissolved and its possessions sequestrated.[48]

The endowments of the college were now vested in trustees with the intention of making all its revenues available for evangelical purposes. In 1646 £100 a year was granted to support a minister at St. Peter's; and, by a symbolic act of restitution, the post was given to Richard Lee, the silenced prebendary. Another £50 a year, together with the £26 formerly belonging to the sacrist, was provided to maintain an assistant.[49] The surviving surveys of this time, those of the deanery and the prebend of Kinvaston, show that these two properties alone had an annual value of £270 2s. 4d. and £70 9s. respectively;[50] these grants therefore still left money to spare to augment other livings. Accordingly the minister of Wednesbury received £50 a year, and the income of Shareshill, near Hilton, was raised to £100 a year.[51] In practice, however, these grants were vitiated by the circumstance that six of the prebends

had long been alienated into the hands of the Leveson family, and enjoyment of the other properties was limited by existing leases. For a while these obstructions were obscured by the fact that the Levesons and other lessees happened to be royalists, so that their estates had been sequestrated and their revenues temporarily freed for spiritual purposes; but the time came, after 1652, when the sequestrations were discharged and the owners claimed their rights.[52] Then it became apparent that the promised stipends could not be met from the collegiate revenues,[53] and other sources had to be found.[54]

The restoration of the college in 1660 did not require legislation, as the abolition of chapters was regarded as an invalid act. The former sacrist, Robert Dyott, claimed his old office, vacant prebends were filled, and the college tried to return to normal.[55] But it was not easy. The wars and troubles had done severe damage. What mattered was not the damage caused to the fabric of St. Peter's — though this was serious enough and was not made good until the reign of James II[56] — but the loss of most of the college's deeds, destroyed or stolen when the chapter-house was ransacked by a royalist garrison under the command of Col. Leveson.[57] This loss gravely compromised the future of the college. Without documents, it was ill equipped for the next round in the long legal battle which it had been fighting with the Leveson family to regain valuable properties lost in the 16th century.

The story of these lost properties had begun in 1550. By that time it was evident that, in spite of the dean's protests, the college could not escape dissolution. Accordingly the whole chapter, except the dean, sealed new leases, all on the same day, of their prebendal estates, reserving only their prebendal houses with the lands attached to them. These transactions are remarkable in several respects. They took place when the properties in question were about to be confiscated to the Crown and when the existing leases had not expired. Except for Kinvaston, where the new lease was taken by the holder of the old lease, the former lessees were ignored and all the properties leased to John Leveson and Robert Brooke, whose families were shortly to be united in marriage. The rents to be paid were set at half, and in some cases much less than half, the rents reported in the surveys made at the dissolution; but, as the tenants had to meet all charges, including payment of the vicars choral, their total obligation was probably not less than in the

[39] Ibid. 351; C 93/3/5 and 28; C 22/215/27; Lich. Dioc. Regy., B/A/13/II/1705, Wolverhampton, Queen Anne's Bounty; N. W. Tildesley, *Hist. of Willenhall*, 58.
[40] Ollard, *Fasti Wyndesorienses*, 46.
[41] *Cal. S.P.Dom.* 1635–6, 69. *D.N.B.* and Ollard, *Fasti Wyndesorienses*, 47, evidently err in dating his appointment 1639.
[42] C 2/Chas. I/L 24/28; Bodl. MS. 323, f. 266v.; Joseph Hall, *Observations of some specialities of Divine Providence in the life of Jos. Hall, Bishop of Norwich. Written in his own Hand*, 31.
[43] Bodl. MS. Tanner 140, f. 169; *Hist. of the Troubles and Tryal of . . . William Laud . . . wrote by himself . . .* (1695), 371, 527; W. Prynne, *Canterburies Doome* (1646), 380–1, 537.
[44] *Cal. S.P.Dom.* 1637–8, 382–3; 1640, 379; 1640–1, 349, 383, 388, 392.
[45] W. Prynne, *A Quench-Coale* (1637), 196–9.
[46] Hist. MSS. Com. *MSS. of the House of Lords, New Ser. XI*, 400, 406, 441; *Troubles and Tryal of Laud*,

287, 301, 371; Prynne, *Canterburies Doome*, 380, 537–8.
[47] *L.J.* v. 581–3.
[48] Bodl. MS. 323, f. 266v.
[49] Ibid.; *Wolverhampton Par. Reg.* (Staffs. Par. Reg. Soc.), i. 93; *Cal. S.P.Dom.* 1655–6, 142.
[50] B.M. Add. MS. Ga. 1A, ff. 46–77v.; Lambeth Palace Libr. MS. 903, Parliamentary Surveys, ii, ff. 12–19.
[51] *Cal. Cttee. for Compounding*, iv. 2484.
[52] Ibid. 2485–6, 2915; Lambeth Palace Libr. MS. 903, ff. 12–19.
[53] *Cal. Cttee. for Compounding*, iv. 2485; *Cal. S.P.Dom.* 1655–6, 142.
[54] Lambeth Palace Libr., Augmentation Books, vol. 972, ff. 162, 320; vol. 995, f. 83.
[55] *46th Dep. Kpr.'s Rep. App. I*, 47; Hist. MSS. Com. *7th Rep. App. I*, 104; C 5/40/71.
[56] E 134/23 & 24 Chas. II Hil./9; S.R.O., Q/SR, E 1641, ff. 11–13; Shaw, *Staffs.* ii. 155, 158; Mander, *Wolverhampton Antiquary*, i. 330–41.
[57] C 2/Chas. I/L 24/28; C 5/40/71.

past. More important was the duration of the leases. The lease of Kinvaston was exceptional in being limited to 40 years; the six other prebends were all leased in perpetuity. Finally, this transaction was completed with a manifest irregularity, through a confirmation by the chapter of St. George's, Windsor, a body which had no standing in the matter, as only the deaneries, not the colleges, were united.[58]

In engaging in these dubious proceedings the prebendaries believed, or so they maintained later, that they were safeguarding the interests of the college as the leases were granted only on condition of being cancelled should the college be restored;[59] the lessees evidently intended to gain what advantage they could before the estates came into new hands. In the event it was the college and the prebendaries who suffered. For when the college's property was granted to the Duke of Northumberland it seems that the new leases remained in tactful abeyance;[60] but when the college was restored and the prebendaries regained their estates John Leveson and his fellow-lessees, disregarding any promises that might have been made, enforced their rights. By 1560 at the latest Leveson and his son Thomas, who had acquired Brooke's interest by marriage, were in possession of all the prebends except Kinvaston.[61] Thus the college was restored to a wasted inheritance, the greater part alienated to lay hands. From now on six of the seven prebends were diminishing assets: apart from the small revenues that could be raised from the prebendal houses with their adjoining lands, they produced only fixed rents which became worthless over the years and, because the leases were perpetual, lacked the compensation of renewal fines.

It was to be expected that when these effects began to make themselves felt attempts would be made to have the leases set aside. The first attempt was made in 1572,[62] a second in 1614–20,[63] a third by Dean Christopher Wren after his appointment in 1635,[64] and a fourth by Richard Lee in 1641.[65] The struggle was resumed after the Restoration, but the loss of the college's deeds during the Civil War and the Levesons' influence in Staffordshire brought failure once more. The case was dismissed from Chancery in 1667 and Robert Leveson awarded

costs.[66] This failure virtually marked the end of any serious hope of regaining the alienated prebends. In 1705, when Robert Leveson sold his Wolverhampton estates to the Earl of Bradford, the chapter collectively started proceedings, but these broke down at the first hurdle.[67] The chapter abandoned a similar project in 1811 after the dean had taken counsel's opinion.[68]

As hopes of restoring the fortunes of the college faded, so the attractions it offered to men of distinction diminished. Only the deanery and the prebend of Kinvaston — at least when they had recovered from the depredations of the Interregnum and inconsiderate leases — offered a substantial income.[69] In the 17th century the low rents, between £2 and £7 a year, of the other prebends had at least been accompanied by hopes of improvement; and they had therefore been thought suitable rewards for clergy on the road to higher preferment, like Joseph Hall and Godfrey Goodman,[70] or for a foreign scholar like Cesar Callendrine.[71] In the next century the prebendaries were mostly local clergy who made their careers in Staffordshire and the neighbouring counties; the only one to attain distinction was John Cradock, who succeeded his father in Kinvaston and rose to become Archbishop of Dublin.[72] In these conditions the chapter enjoyed long tenures and stable membership.

Even in the harmonious circumstances of the 18th century some of the issues that played their part in the final dissolution of the college began to make themselves felt. The growth of population imposed new pressures on the organization of this extensive parish and raised doubts about the college's contribution — financial and spiritual — to its religious life. The chapels of Bilston, Pelsall, and Willenhall and the new district churches built in the course of the century tended to resent their dependence on the mother-church of St. Peter, which the deans continued to assert. Bilston, for example, which, like Willenhall, enjoyed the right to choose its curate by popular election, openly defied the dean's, attempts to encroach on its privilege in 1730 and 1735.[73] The obligation imposed on the inhabitants of the dependent districts, under which they had to pay fees both to their own curate and to the sacrist of Wolverhampton and had to contribute to the

[58] Featherstone was leased to Rob. Brooke at a rent of £7, Hilton to John Leveson at £2 13s. 4d., Willenhall to Leveson at £6 6s. 8d., Monmore to Brooke at £3 6s. 8d., Wobaston to Leveson at £4, Hatherton to Leveson at £2 4s. 10d., and Kinvaston to John Howlett at £6: W.R. iv. B 16, f. 31v.

[59] C 2/Eliz. I/L 12/50.

[60] Ibid.

[61] C 6/94/53; G. Oliver, *Historical and Descriptive Account of Collegiate Church of Wolverhampton* (Wolverhampton, 1836), 71, 79; *S.H.C.* xiii. 277.

[62] C 2/Eliz. I/L 12/50.

[63] Hall, *Observations*, 26–29; C 33/129, ff. 243v.–244v.; C 2/Chas. I/L 24/28; C 5/40/71; W.R., Frith's Old Reg., ff. 131–6.

[64] C 2/Chas. I/L 24/28; C 5/40/71; *Cal. S.P.Dom.* 1635–1636, 69; ibid. 1636–7, 525; ibid. Apr.–Nov. 1637, 83; ibid. Addenda, 1625–49, 515–16; Hall, *Observations*, 29–30; Lich. Dioc. Regy., Wolverhampton Peculiar, bdle. 12(d), General Chapter of 20 Mar. 1637; W.R. iv. B 16, f. 161; Bond, *Windsor Chapter Acts*, 176, 182.

[65] H. Burton, *For God, and the King* (1636), 161; C 5/40/71; *L.J.* iv. 158.

[66] C 5/40/71; C 33/220, ff. 450v., 583v., 643, 797v.; /222, ff. 67, 250; /224, ff. 152, 266, 274v., 282, 288, 423v., 529, 561v., 828; /226, f. 370; /228, ff. 506v., 528.

[67] C.C. 9737, Wolverhampton Deanery, Surveyor's Report, 1848; Oliver, *Church of Wolverhampton*, 81.

[68] Lich. Dioc. Regy., Wolverhampton Peculiar, Commissions to Collate to Prebends, Peter Thoroton to John Mott, 22 Jan. 1811; ibid., Preb. of Kinvaston, Mott to Rob. Leeson, 1819; W.R. iv. B 27, citation for the chapter to appoint an attorney, 28 Aug. 1811; G. Robinson, *Letter to His (Late) Majesty's Commissioners* (1837), 5–6.

[69] E 134/16 Chas. II Mich./10; /20 Chas. II Mich./27 and East./11; /23 Chas. II East./20; /23 & 24 Chas. II Hil./9; C 6/94/53; C 8/101/13; Lich. Dioc. Regy., Wolverhampton Peculiar, box 2, Prebend of Kinvaston, 1654; Lambeth Palace Libr. MS. 903, Parliamentary Surveys, ii, ff. 12–19; *S.H.C.* 1915, 343.

[70] Ollard, *Fasti Wyndesorienses*, 111.

[71] Collated to Hatherton prebend 1621: C 5/40/71; see also A. Wood, *Athenae Oxonienses* (ed. P. Bliss, 1815), ii. 394, 863; iii. 269. For two other scholars, Andrew Durell and Samuel de l'Angle, collated to Kinvaston prebend 1679 and 1684, see W.R. iv. B 26 and 28.

[72] W.R. iv. B 28; *D.N.B.*

[73] Lich. Dioc. Regy., B/A/3, Bilston and Willenhall Polls; B/A/3, 14 Nov. 1730, 4, 12, and 13 Feb. 1736; W.R. iv. B 26, ff. 32–33; Robinson, *Letter to His (Late) Majesty's Commissioners*, 15–16.

repairs of St. Peter's as well as to those of their own church, provided a frequent source of dispute.[74]

The sacrist clung to his financial rights all the more tenaciously because fees from burials, marriages, and christenings provided a large part of his income. The difficult relationship with the dependent churches could therefore be resolved only if he could be provided with a satisfactory income from other sources. At one point it seemed that the development of the local coal industry would make this possible. In 1811 an Act was obtained for increasing the income of the sacrist — or perpetual curate as he was henceforth to be called.[75] It provided that a quarter of the royalties to be obtained from exploiting the coal under the dean's estate should be invested on the sacrist's behalf up to a total value of £8,000, which would yield an income rising eventually to £266 a year. The Act also abolished the three readerships and by transferring their stipends to the sacrist added a further £30 a year to his income.[76] The Act did not, however, fulfil expectations; it did too little too slowly. By 1835 the income from the invested royalties reached only £15,[77] and by 1843 it was no more than £60.[78] Consequently fees continued to supply a considerable part of the sacrist's income. In 1843, while rents and interest produced £270, fees produced about £200.[79] Therefore, as long as the college survived, the controversy about fees continued to embarrass relationships between St. Peter's and the other churches of the parish.[80]

Even before the end of the 18th century the traditional pre-eminence of the collegiate church, which the dean and sacrist were trying for financial reasons to preserve, was gradually being undermined. Ceremonies like the Rogationtide procession and the solemn perambulation of the parish bounds, which used to maintain the dignity of the mother-church and assert its presence, had been abandoned.[81] The independence of the peculiar had been diminished by frequent episcopal intervention;[82] and even the peculiar court came to be held at Lichfield rather than at Wolverhampton.[83] Furthermore the Act of 1811, suppressing the readerships and establishing a perpetual curacy, in effect made St. Peter's virtually indistinguishable from its daughter-churches. These changes made the claims of the collegiate church even less palatable.

In an evangelical age the college was susceptible to criticism which drew attention to the contrast between the spiritual contribution which it made to the parish and the large revenues which it took out. It was not only that it imposed a double burden of fees, but that its other revenues had increased. This was not true of the six alienated prebends, and hardly of Kinvaston, which produced little more than £100 a year;[84] but the exploitation of mineral resources had greatly increased the value of the deanery, and the last dean must have drawn on average more than £600 a year from his Wolverhampton estates.[85] The dean of course was an absentee; but so also during the college's last fifty years were most of the chapter in contrast with the practice of the previous century. In 1835 only two of the prebendaries held livings in the county.[86] These absentees not only contributed little to the spiritual life of the parish; they also hampered its material development. Their estates, which in most cases consisted only of their prebendal houses and the lands attached to them, were laxly administered and their properties badly maintained. The clergy's preference for a system of long leases and occasional fines, together with their lack of capital and incentive, stood in the way of long-term improvements. Until after the middle of the 19th century the effective development of the centre of Wolverhampton was hindered by the slum dwellings and vacant lots of which the collegiate estates largely consisted.[87]

The last dean and the last perpetual curate did nothing to restore the standing of the college. Dean Hobart, who held his office from 1816 to 1846,[88] lacked the influence at court and in the Church that might be expected of a dean of Windsor and Wolverhampton. Dr. Oliver, who was appointed perpetual curate in 1834, engaged in a succession of rather sordid and very public disputes with the other clergy of the parish and ended by quarrelling, also publicly, with his own churchwardens.[89]

In these circumstances it is not surprising that after the establishment of the Ecclesiastical Commission in 1836 had prepared the way for reform no attempts were made to save the college, even in some modified form. The Cathedrals Act of 1840 provided that, on the dean's death, the deanery and peculiar were to be suppressed;[90] and after Hobart's death in 1846 the college was speedily wound up.[91]

[74] *Bilston Par. Reg.* (Staffs. Par. Reg. Soc.), 4, 5, 93, 121; Lich. Dioc. Regy., B/A/3, 17 Aug. 1709, Chapter Act 10 Oct. 1718, and undated petition of Wm. Cradock, Thos. Hall, and churchwardens of St. Peter's; C 12/2329/67; Tildesley, *Willenhall*, 74–75; [R. N. Bissell], *Story of St Leonard's Church, Bilston, passim* (copy in W.S.L. Pamphs. *sub* Bilston).
[75] 51 Geo. III, c. 182 (local and personal act).
[76] C.C. 14532.
[77] *Rep. Com. Eccl. Revs.* H.C.54, pp. 84–85 (1835), xxii.
[78] C.C. 23398 (in Lich. Dioc. Regy.).
[79] Ibid.; C.C. 14532; Robinson, *Letter to His (Late) Majesty's Commissioners*, 8–10, 15.
[80] G. Oliver, *Candid Statement of the Question relating to St. George's Church* (1835); G. B. Clare, *Address to the Congregation and Parishioners of St. George's* (1835).
[81] Shaw, *Staffs.* ii. 165; Oliver, *Church of Wolverhampton*, 179–80.
[82] Lich. Dioc. Regy., Wolverhampton Peculiar, Commissions to Collate to Prebends, Hobart to Mott, 31 Jan. 1825; ibid., Wolverhampton Act Book 1819–39, 24 Aug. 1832; ibid., Nominations and Licences to Perpetual Curacies: agreement between Oliver and Clare about fees, 4 July 1834; Oliver, *Candid Statement*, 7; *Wolverhampton Chron.* 5 Feb. 1840.

[83] Lich. Dioc. Regy., Wolverhampton Peculiar, Act Bk. 1752–1818; ibid., Court Bk. 1822–45; Shrewsbury Peculiar, Act Bk. 1722–1854 (under heading Wolverhampton).
[84] *Rep. Com. Eccl. Revs.* 84–85; Lich. Dioc. Regy., Wolverhampton Peculiar, Kinvaston; C.C. 14391; C.C. 23398 (in Lich. Dioc. Regy.); Robinson, *Letter to His (Late) Majesty's Commissioners*, 7.
[85] *Rep. Com. Eccl. Revs.* pp. vii, 30–31; W.R. iv. B 26, f. 31; iv. B 27, ff. 20, 23; C.C. 9737; C.C. 23398 (in Lich. Dioc. Regy.).
[86] *Rep. Com. Eccl. Revs.* 84–85.
[87] C.C. 13866, 14391, 14534; C.C. 23398 (in Lich. Dioc. Regy.); Anon. *Wolverhampton Church Property* (1855), 1–2.
[88] Ollard, *Fasti Wyndesorienses*, 53.
[89] Oliver, *Candid Statement*; *Second Pastoral Address* (1835); *Address to the Inhabitants of Wolverhampton in Reply to the Misrepresentations in a Circular issued by Messrs. Thorneycroft and Parks on the 25th April 1840* (1840); Clare, *Address to Congregation and Parishioners of St. George's*; *Wolverhampton Chron.* 13, 20 May, 9 Aug. 1840; G. P. Mander and N. W. Tildesley, *Hist. of Wolverhampton*, 174–6; *D.N.B.*
[90] 3 & 4 Vic. c. 113, secs. 21, 51, 63.
[91] *Wolverhampton Chron.* 13 May 1846.

Already prebends had been kept vacant as their holders had died.[92] In October the jurisdiction of the peculiar was transferred to the bishop.[93] In 1847 Dr. Oliver resigned and the office of perpetual curate was suspended.[94] Finally in 1848 the Wolverhampton Church Act dissolved the college and transferred its possessions to the Ecclesiastical Commissioners. St. Peter's was established as a rectory, with a living worth £750 a year. It lost its ancient pre-eminence, as the old parish was broken up and the daughter-churches acquired independent status.[95] From the revenues of the former college the commissioners were able to augment the stipends of all thirteen incumbents of the old parish and contribute to the repair of their churches.[96] By these means the aims of the Edwardian and Cromwellian reformers were at last achieved.

DEANS

Peter of Blois, probably appointed by Henry II, occurs 1190–1, resigned probably 1202.[97]

Nicholas, occurs 1203.[98]

In January 1203 the deanery was granted to Hubert, Archbishop of Canterbury, who planned to dissolve the college. The grant was cancelled when the archbishop died in 1205.[99]

Henry, son of Geoffrey, Earl of Essex, appointed 1205.[1]

Giles of Erdington, occurs 1224, died 1268 or 1269.[2]

Master Theodosius de Camilla, appointed 1269, died 1295.[3]

Master Philip of Everdon, appointed 1295, resigned 1303.[4]

Master John of Everdon, appointed 1303, probably resigned 1323.[5]

Godfrey of Rudham, appointed 1322, perhaps held the deanery from 1323 to 1326.[6]

Robert of Silkstone, appointed 1326, resigned 1328.[7]

John of Melbourne, appointed April 1328.[8]

John of the Chamber, appointed October 1328, resigned November 1328.[9]

Master Hugh Ellis, appointed November 1328, died 1339.[10]

Philip Weston, appointed 1339, resigned 1368.[11]

John of Newnham, appointed 1368, died 1369.[12]

Amaury Shirland, appointed 1369, held the deanery until 1373.[13]

Richard Postell, appointed 1373, resigned 1394.[14]

Master Lawrence Allerthorpe, appointed 1394, died 1406.[15]

Thomas Stanley, appointed 1406, died 1410.[16]

Robert Wolveden, appointed 1410, presumably resigned 1426.[17]

William Felter, B.C.L., D.Cn.L., appointed 1426, resigned 1437.[18]

John Barningham, appointed 1437, died 1457.[19]

Master William Dudley, appointed probably 1457, provided to the bishopric of Durham 1476.[20]

Master Lionel Woodville, appointed 1477, probably resigned 1480.[21]

From 1480 the deanery of Wolverhampton was united with the deanery of Windsor.[22]

The chapter seal in use in the late 13th century[23] is a pointed oval, 2¾ by 1¼ in. It depicts St. Peter standing, with a pastoral staff in his right hand and two keys in his left; on his head is a close-fitting cap. Legend, lombardic:

SIGILLUM SANCTI PETRI DE WLFRUNEHAMTUNE

The seal in use in the late 15th century[24] is a pointed oval, 2½ × 1½ in. It depicts St. Peter and St. Paul standing in a double niche with canopies; St. Peter holds a book and keys, St. Paul a sword and book. In the base under a round arch is the three-quarter figure of a cleric praying, surrounded by five

[92] Eccl. Comm. *1st Rep.* 1845, 12.
[93] *Wolverhampton Chron.* 18 Nov. 1846.
[94] Eccl. Comm. *3rd Rep.* 1851, 63; *Wolverhampton Chron.* 12 Apr. 1848.
[95] 11 & 12 Vic. c. 95 (local and personal act); Eccl. Comm. *3rd Rep.* 11.
[96] Eccl. Comm. *3rd Rep.* 80; *5th Rep.* 1853, 31; *6th Rep.* 1854, 33–34.
[97] See above p. 322 and n. 31.
[98] See above p. 323, n. 37.
[99] See above pp. 322–3.
[1] See references in n. 46 (above p. 323).
[2] See references in nn. 47 and 59 (above p. 323).
[3] *Cal. Pat.* 1266–72, 310; 1292–1301, 147. He appears as 'Master' ibid. 1266–72, 306, 322.
[4] Ibid. 1292–1301, 147; 1301–7, 149. He is styled 'Master' in *Cal. Papal Regs.* i. 601; *S.H.C.* 1924, p. 4.
[5] *Cal. Pat.* 1301–7, 149; A. B. Emden, *Biog. Reg. of Univ. of Oxford to A.D. 1500*, i. 654. Abortive grants of the deanery were made to M. Wal. of Islip in 1318 and Godfrey of Rudham in 1322 (*Cal. Pat.* 1317–21, 113; 1321–4, 91, 180). John was still dean in Dec. 1322 (ibid. 227) and was trying to recover the deanery from Rob. of Silkstone in 1328 (K.B. 27/271, m.69d.).
[6] *Cal. Pat.* 1321–4, 91, 180; see above n. 5.
[7] *Cal. Pat.* 1324–7, 315; 1327–30, 288, 380–1.
[8] Ibid. 1327–30, 257.
[9] Ibid. 325, 334.
[10] Ibid. 334; Emden, *Biog. Reg. Oxford*, i. 639. An abortive grant of the deanery was made by Edw. III to Ric. Castle in Dec. 1330, but Ellis successfully asserted his right to it in Jan. 1331: *Cal. Pat.* 1330–4, 24, 85; *Cal. Close*, 1330–3, 107.
[11] *Cal. Pat.* 1338–40, 397. Weston was described as former dean in July 1369 (*Reg. Sudbiria, vol. i*, 72); he

died soon afterwards (Assoc. Archit. Soc. *Rep. & Papers*, xxxvi. 23).
[12] *Cal. Pat.* 1367–70, 112; A. Gibbons, *Early Lincoln Wills*, 62–63; Assoc. Archit. Soc. *Rep. & Papers*, xxxv. 226; Hist. MSS. Com. *Cal. MSS. of Dean and Chapter of Wells*, ii. 14.
[13] *Cal. Pat.* 1367–70, 306; *Cal. Papal Regs.* iv. 193.
[14] *Cal. Pat.* 1370–4, 333; 1391–6, 373.
[15] Ibid. 1391–6, 373; 1405–8, 206. He was Dean of Stafford 1390–7: see above p. 309.
[16] *Cal. Pat.* 1405–8, 206; 1408–13, 223.
[17] Ibid. 1408–13, 169. He was Dean of Tettenhall from 1412 and Dean of Lichfield from 1426: see above pp. 197, 321.
[18] *Cal. Pat.* 1422–9, 381; 1436–41, 32; Emden, *Biog. Reg. Oxford*, ii. 675.
[19] *Cal. Pat.* 1436–41, 32; Le Neve, *Fasti Ecclesiae Anglicanae, 1300–1541* (new edn.), vi. 14.
[20] The date of his appointment must lie between 1447, when Hen. VI granted the next presentation to John, Ld. Dudley (*Cal. Pat.* 1446–52, 54), and 1461, when his estate as dean was ratified by Edw. IV (ibid. 1461–7, 60). For his provision to Durham see Le Neve, *Fasti* (new edn.), vi. 109. For his degree see Emden, *Biog. Reg. Oxford*, i. 599.
[21] *Cal. Pat.* 1476–85, 17; Emden, *Biog. Reg. Oxford*, iii. 2083.
[22] A list of deans of Windsor is given in Ollard, *Fasti Wyndesorienses*, but there are some inaccuracies.
[23] W. de G. Birch, *Cat. of Seals in B.M.* i, p. 813; Mander, *Wolverhampton Antiquary*, i. 199–200 and plate facing p. 192. These authorities state that the seal is 12th-cent.
[24] Birch, *Cat. of Seals in B.M.* i, pp. 812–13; Mander, *Wolverhampton Antiquary*, i. 201–2 and plate facing p. 192; cast among W.S.L. Seals.

heads; this probably represents the dean and canons. Legend, black letter:

SIGILLUM COIE (sic) CAPITALI (sic) DE WOLVERNHAMPTON

In 1872 the brass matrix of this seal, then in private possession, was restored to St. Peter's Church.

A chapter seal struck in the 17th century,[25] circular with a diameter of 1⅜ in., depicts St. Peter standing; in his left hand he holds two keys, and his right rests on a shield bearing the royal arms;[26]

round his head is a nimbus. Legend, roman:

SIGILLUM DECANI ET CAPITULI LIBERAE CAPELLAE REGIAE SANCTI PETRI DE WULFRUNHAMPTON

The silver matrix was purchased by the British Museum in 1868.

The chapter seal in use in the later 18th and earlier 19th centuries[27] is an oval, about 1¾ by 1½ in.; it depicts a bishop in pontificals. Legend:[28]

SIGILLUX (sic) SANCTI PETRI DE WLFRUNHAXTUN (sic)

The matrix was of silver.

ALIEN HOUSES

39. THE PRIORY OF TUTBURY

ON the authority of a couplet found in the Tutbury Cartulary[1] the foundation of Tutbury Priory, a dependency of the Benedictine abbey of St. Pierre-sur-Dives in Normandy, is generally accepted to have been in 1080.[2] Some confirmation of this is to be found in Domesday Book where it is recorded that 'the monks' were holding the Derbyshire manors of Doveridge and Marston-upon-Dove from Henry de Ferrers.[3] It is equally possible, however, that 'the monks' were not the monks of Tutbury Priory but those of the abbey of St. Pierre-sur-Dives and that a priory had not yet been founded at Tutbury, the *caput* of the Ferrers honor. At any rate there is no mention in Domesday Book of monks at Tutbury.

The charter of Henry de Ferrers which gives recognition to the existence of Tutbury Priory was issued in the reign of William II.[4] It records the extensive endowment given by Henry and his wife Bertha to the priory, which was dedicated to the Virgin Mary. In Staffordshire the monks were granted the parish of Tutbury castle and the tithe of tolls collected there, the tithes of vineyards, hunting, pannage, and honey, free supplies of firewood and timber, fishing rights, the demesne tithes of Rolleston and Tutbury, and the church and tithes of Mayfield with one villein. Their most extensive possessions were to be found in Derbyshire where they received the vills of Marston-on-Dove (except 11 bovates and a quarter of the meadowland), Doveridge, and West Broughton, the church and tithes of Norbury with one villein, two-thirds of the demesne tithes of Scropton, Barton Blount, Sapperton, Mugginton, and Duffield, the tithes of Brassington and Tissington, and a villein at Scropton and Duffield. In Leicestershire they were given two-thirds of the

demesne tithes of Orton-on-the-Hill, Stapleford, and Coston, with a villein at each place, and in Northamptonshire two-thirds of the demesne tithes of Potterspury with one villein.

Bertha had also granted the monks the vill of Stanford-in-the-Vale (Berks.), but after the death of Henry de Ferrers his son Robert exchanged it for the Derbyshire vills of Church Broughton, Norbury, and Edlaston, in view of the remoteness of Stanford-in-the-Vale.[5] Robert made further grants in Derbyshire — 19 bovates in Mercaston (in Mugginton) and the demesne tithes of Hartshorne.[6] The tithes of the burgage rents of the new borough which Robert had founded near Tutbury were granted to the priory by his son Robert (II). Robert (I)'s brother Eugenulph and others further contributed to the endowment of the priory, which by 1159 was also in possession of the whole vill of Mayfield, tithes at Hollington (Derb.), at Stanford-in-the-Vale, and at the Leicestershire vills of Wymondham and Edmondthorpe, and one villein at Stanford-in-the-Vale, Coston, Wymondham, and Edmondthorpe.[7]

Robert, Earl of Derby, the son of Robert de Ferrers, confirmed the grants of his predecessors between 1150 and 1159. He also confirmed and exemplified the numerous grants of his tenants. Among these may be mentioned Osmaston (Derb.) and the church of 'Wibalditone' in Berkshire.[8] An attempt by the priory to gain the advowson of the more important church of Didcot (Berks.) was, however, frustrated at an assize of *darrein presentment* in 1220.[9]

William, Earl of Derby, who succeeded Robert before 1160, had the body of his great-grandfather, the founder of Tutbury, translated and buried on the south side of the high altar of the priory church. At the same time he granted the priory a bovate of land at Marston-upon-Dove.[10] His son William,

---

[25] Birch, *Cat. of Seals in B.M.* i, p. 813; Mander, *Wolverhampton Antiquary*, i. 202 and plate facing p. 192; A. B. Tonnochy, *Cat. of Brit. Seal-Dies in B.M.* 169.
[26] The royal arms are those borne 1603–88 and thus help to date the striking of the matrix: J. and J. B. Burke, *Encyc. of Heraldry or General Armoury of Eng., Scotland and Ireland* (3rd edn.).
[27] Mander, *Wolverhampton Antiquary*, i. 203, where a sketch of a fragmentary impression is reproduced; Oliver, *Church of Wolverhampton*, 89.
[28] Mander, *Wolverhampton Antiquary*, i. 203, suggests that the erroneous *x*'s are the result of an attempt to copy the lombardic *m* of the 13th-cent. seal.
[1] Dugdale, *Mon.* iii. 392; Sir Oswald Mosley, *Hist. of Castle, Priory, and Town of Tutbury* (1832), 7, 249.

[2] D. Knowles and R. N. Hadcock, *Medieval Religious Houses: Eng. and Wales*, 79, gives +1080.
[3] *V.C.H. Derb.* i. 302–3, 338.
[4] Dugdale, *Mon.* iii. 391. For a detailed discussion of the priory's possessions see *S.H.C.* 4th ser. iv, pp. 5 sqq.
[5] *S.H.C.* 4th ser. iv, pp. 99–100; but cf. *Bk. of Fees*, i. 295, which shows that Tutbury still had possessions in Stanford in 1220.   [6] *S.H.C.* 4th ser. iv, pp. 64, 65.
[7] Ibid. pp. 64–66, 75. The 'new borough' founded by Rob. I is distinct from the later Newborough (founded 1263): *V.C.H. Staffs.* ii. 349 n. 14.
[8] *S.H.C.* 4th ser. iv, pp. 64–66; *V.C.H. Berks.* iii. 472.
[9] *Cur. Reg. R.* viii. 4, 22, 184, 300; and see *S.H.C.* iv(1), 80.
[10] *S.H.C.* 4th ser. iv, pp. 66–67. The charter states that the founder's body was reburied 'in dextera parte majoris altaris'.

Earl of Derby (1190–1247), gave the monks the hermitage of Agardsley, the hamlet of Thorney Lane, and 172 acres of land. These properties were in Needwood Forest where William also gave the monks rights to pasture, firewood, and timber.[11] About 1260, however, at the request of the then earl, Robert, the monks exchanged Agardsley for the mills of Scropton and other neighbouring properties.[12] William (I) also confirmed the monks in their possession of the churches of Edmondthorpe, Wymondham, and Stapleford in Leicestershire granted by his kinsman William de Ferrers.[13] About 1200 William (II) confirmed the monks in these churches and added the church of Coston which the monks had also acquired.[14] He further gave them all the tithes of his forests of Needwood and of Duffield (Derb.).[15]

It will be seen that much of the revenue of the priory was drawn from tithes, but these were not always easy to collect, largely because of the opposition of the parish priests. The rights of Tutbury were buttressed by mandates of Archbishops Theobald, Becket, and Richard to the bishops and archdeacons concerned, ordering them to support the priory by excommunicating offenders.[16] In 1163 Pope Alexander III took the priory under his protection and confirmed its possessions.[17]

There is little evidence available about the internal organization of the priory, but it appears that the prior followed the prevailing practice among heads of religious houses of maintaining a separate establishment. In 1230 an agreement was drawn up between the prior and the monks in respect of the monks' kitchen.[18] For this purpose 26 marks a year were assigned, to be drawn from various sources; if any of these failed the prior was to make up the deficit out of his own funds. He was also to provide the monks with 29 live pigs in a year when acorns were plentiful or 10 live oxen in a bad year, 6 sextaries of lard, 20 large cheeses, 25 small cheeses, 3 pounds of pepper, 3 pounds of cummin, a sextary of salt, 10 bushels of white beans, with a further quarter at Easter, and 2 quarters of oatmeal. The prior was to provide 'a great feast' on the Assumption (15 August). He was further to supply all kitchen utensils. His right to eat with the monks was safeguarded, and he was allowed to bring three or four companions with him to the monks' refectory and one or two to the monks' parlour. These arrangements were to remain in force so long as the number of monks did not exceed fifteen. An incidental reference shows that a supply of fish for the priory came from the Derwent at Derby as well as from the Dove fishery at Tutbury.

In view of the difficulties with which the priory had to contend on account of its alien status, some account must be given of its relations with the abbey of St. Pierre-sur-Dives. Tutbury was held to be a 'conventual' and not a 'dative' priory, and it therefore enjoyed a large measure of autonomy: a conventual priory had a common seal and the prior could govern the monastery and administer and dispose of its possessions without any interference from the mother-house. On the other hand a regular payment ('apport') was sent abroad.[19] There are, however, few early references to the relationship between St. Pierre and Tutbury. In 1145 the Abbot of St. Pierre sent a long account of the rebuilding of his church and the miracles occasioned thereby to his fellow monks at Tutbury.[20] In the 1160s the Abbot of St. Pierre, followed by the Prior of Tutbury, witnessed a charter of William, Earl of Derby.[21] For the first century of the priory's existence the appointment and deposition of the prior was evidently in the hands of the mother-house, the Ferrers as patrons having no rights in the matter. An agreement of about 1180, however, between Earl William and the abbot gave the prior reasonable security of tenure and the patrons a strong voice in appointments and removals.[22] By a further agreement concluded by the mid 13th century the abbot nominated three candidates out of whom the patron was entitled to present one to the bishop; if the patron did not fulfil his duties within four days the abbot was entitled to make the final choice.[23] Under this system the chances were strongly in favour of the prior's being a Frenchman. It is also probable that at first the majority, if not all, of the monks were also French. It is only during the prolonged French wars that English monks are first found. Even as late as 1410 the Prior of Tutbury received a royal licence to bring over six monks from St. Pierre-sur-Dives,[24] which must almost certainly have restored the French preponderance in the priory. The priors of Tutbury were supposed to visit the mother-house once every three years, and visits by the priors or their representatives to their superiors in Normandy are in fact recorded; similarly representatives of the French abbey came to Tutbury.[25] William, Earl of Derby (1190–1247), challenged the right of visitation by the mother-house, and at the beginning of 1244 the abbot sued the earl for denying him free ingress to the priory. The abbot appointed Brother Albinus as his attorney — perhaps a Tutbury monk. Three months later the abbot abandoned the suit, having apparently received satisfaction from the earl.[26]

During the 13th century the Prior of Tutbury was sometimes appointed by the Abbot of St. Pierre as his attorney or agent for his affairs in England, and such appointments were accepted by the king as being valid in the English courts.[27] Thus among the other duties of the Prior of Tutbury was the supervision or control of the smaller dependent priories of St. Pierre-sur-Dives, Wolston (Warws.), and Modbury (Devon), in the absence of any direct

[11] Ibid. pp. 79–80. [12] Ibid. pp. 89–91.
[13] Ibid. pp. 73–74.
[14] Ibid. p. 70.
[15] Ibid. pp. 68–69, 77.
[16] Ibid. pp. 27–30.
[17] W. Holtzmann, Papsturkunden in England, i. 360. The bull was evidently addressed to the abbey of St. Pierre-sur-Dives: S.H.C. 4th ser. iv, p. 24.
[18] S.H.C. 4th ser. iv, pp. 16–17, 207–8. For the fishery at Tutbury see ibid. p. 221.
[19] C. W. New, Hist. of the Alien Priories in Eng. 37; D. J. A. Matthew, Norman Monasteries and their English Possessions, 44–51.

[20] L. Delisle, 'Lettre de l'Abbé Haimon', Bibliothèque de l'Ecole des Chartes, xxi (1860), 113. A translation is given in N. Edwards, Medieval Tutbury, 56 sqq.
[21] Matthew, Norman Monasteries, 47.
[22] S.H.C. 4th ser. iv, pp. 12–14.
[23] Dugdale, Mon. iii. 395–6; Cal. Pat. 1436–41, 52.
[24] Cal. Pat. 1408–13, 213.
[25] S.H.C. 4th ser. iv, p. 13; Lich. Dioc. Regy., B/A/1/1, f. 23v.; Cal. Close, 1333–7, 692; ibid. 1341–3, 124.
[26] K.B. 26/132, m. 6d.; /133, m. 5d.
[27] Pat. R. 1225–32, 137; Cal. Pat. 1232–47, 73; Close R. 1261–4, 283.

control from the mother-house. In the case of Wolston the Abbot of St. Pierre granted control to the Prior of Tutbury in 1226 in consideration of a payment of £10 a year; the patronage of the vicarage of Wolston, however, remained in the hands of the monks of Wolston.[28] John of St. Aubyn, a Prior of Wolston, became Prior of Tutbury in 1329 despite the opposition of the Tutbury monks.[29] Much less is known about the relations between Tutbury and Modbury. In 1399 John Roger, a monk of Tutbury, was appointed Prior of Modbury.[30] This may have given rise to some dispute because five years later another monk of Tutbury, Thomas Matieu,[31] received a pardon of outlawry for not appearing to answer John, Prior of Modbury, touching a trespass.[32]

The rights of the patron have already been discussed with regard to the appointment of the prior. His right to levy an aid on the priory for feudal reasons was recognized by the monks in 1125.[33] On coming of age and receiving his lands in 1260 Robert, Earl of Derby, destroyed the priory buildings.[34] The background to the violent action was probably a dispute over the rights of the patron. In 1262 Robert relinquished his right of exacting a *compotus* from the priory and recognized the monks' right to alienate their property without interference from him or his heirs; he also confirmed the status of the priory as it was at the time when he obtained seisin of his estates. As patron he agreed in 1263, in consideration of the monks' abandoning their legal proceedings against him, that neither he nor his heirs would interfere with their property during a vacancy.[35] As early as 1261 he had granted to the priory the rents and services of his men at Coston, a virgate and a villein at Rolleston and the advowson of the church there, all fines from priory tenants in the Appletree Hundred court (Derb.), and the priory's customary rights in Needwood Forest.[36] A staunch supporter of Simon de Montfort, Earl Robert suffered forfeiture in 1266. His possessions, including the patronage of Tutbury, were transferred to Edmund, Earl of Lancaster. Although the stream of donations to Tutbury now dried up, the Lancastrian house was not unfavourably disposed towards the priory. Edmund himself maintained the customary annual offering of 4s. 4d. which had been made by the earls of Derby.[37]

The right of compelling the priory to grant a corrody or pension to one or more of his adherents was also recognized to belong to the patron. In the

15th century, when the king issued such 'requests' to the priory, they were put out under the seal of the Duchy of Lancaster,[38] perhaps to stress that he was applying for the corrody as patron of the monastery. It may be doubted, however, whether this apparent example of rectitude was in fact anything more than an administrative convenience, for the rights of the monarch were recognized by the Church. In 1280 Archbishop Pecham forbade the Prior of Tutbury to accede to the request of the Bishop of Coventry and Lichfield to grant a pension and accommodation to his cook, pointing out that only the king, the queen, or the patron could properly exercise this right.[39] In 1238 Henry III asked the prior for a vacant benefice for one of his clerks,[40] and so did the Prince of Wales in 1305.[41]

In the assessment of 1291 the temporalities of Tutbury amounted to £42 4s. 11d. and the spiritualities to £40 6s. 8d. These were to be found in Berkshire,[42] Derbyshire,[43] Leicestershire,[44] Northamptonshire,[45] Staffordshire,[46] and Warwickshire.[47] As might have been expected, Derbyshire accounted for nearly two-thirds of the temporalities with £27 4s. 8d.; Staffordshire yielded £10 18s. With regard to the spiritualities, however, Staffordshire, with the appropriated churches of Mayfield and Tutbury, was assessed at £17 13s. 4d. while Derbyshire with the church of Duffield and tithes from other parishes could reach only £15 11s. 4d. The assessment in Leicestershire shows that Tutbury was drawing tithes from Coston and Stapleford and pensions from the churches of Stapleford, Wymondham, and Edmondthorpe. Although there is evidence that Tutbury presented to these churches in the 13th century,[48] it had lost the advowsons of Wymondham, Stapleford, and Edmondthorpe by 1316, in which year Thomas, Earl of Lancaster, obtained licence to alienate them in mortmain;[49] there is, however, no evidence that he did so. In the *Quo Warranto* proceedings of 1293 the priory claimed free warren in Tutbury by charter of Henry III.[50] This particular charter does not seem to have survived, but there is another charter of Henry III which granted the priory free warren in Staffordshire in Mayfield and Wetton, and in Derbyshire in Doveridge, Marston-upon-Dove, Broughton, Ednaston, Hollington, Osmaston, and Edlaston.[51] The priory also claimed view of frankpledge of its tenants twice a year but made no claims to any other franchises.

The priory led a very unhappy existence during

[28] Dugdale, *Antiquities of Warws.* (1730), i. 36, 37–38; *V.C.H. Warws.* ii. 132.
[29] See below p. 335.
[30] *Cal. Pat.* 1396–9, 480.
[31] Probably Thos. Masse who, by the date when the pardon was issued, had become prior.
[32] *Cal. Pat.* 1401–5, 443.
[33] F. M. Stenton, *First Century of Eng. Feudalism* (2nd edn.), 175.
[34] *Annales Monastici* (Rolls Ser.), i. 491. Another example of turbulence during the baronial wars is the invasion of priory lands at 'Mosemere' in Sudbury (Derb.) by 19 men including the Rector of Sudbury; the case was heard Mich. 1266: K.B. 26/177, mm. 11, 16d.
[35] *S.H.C.* 4th ser. iv, pp. 14, 91–92.
[36] Ibid. pp. 83–84. In 1324 the priory was claiming the right to amerce its tenants in Appletree Hundred, stating that it had held this right since the foundation; at an inquisition that year the jurors upheld the right: *Cal. Inq. Misc.* ii, p. 174.
[37] *S.H.C.* 4th ser. iv, pp. 245–6.

[38] Ibid. pp. 211–14; D.L. 37/60, m. 7.
[39] *Reg. Epist. Fratris Johannis Peckham* (Rolls. Ser.), i. 115. In 1296 Abp. Winchelsey ordered that pending the ordination of a vicarage for Tutbury the vicar should continue to have his existing corrody from the priory: *Reg. Roberti Winchelsey, vol. i* (Cant. & York Soc.), 93–94.
[40] *Close R.* 1237–42, 132.
[41] *Letters of Edward, Prince of Wales* (Roxburghe Club, 1931), 89.
[42] *Tax Eccl.* (Rec. Com.), 191.
[43] Ibid. 246, 247, 261–2.
[44] Ibid. 65, 67, 71.
[45] Ibid. 53.
[46] Ibid. 243, 251.
[47] Ibid. 241.
[48] *Rot. Hugonis de Welles, vol. i* (Cant. & York Soc.), 267–8, 288, 304, 321; *Rot. Roberti Grosseteste* (Cant. & York Soc.), 387, 389, 403–4, 407–8, 433.
[49] *Cal. Pat.* 1313–17, 512.
[50] *S.H.C.* vi(1), 241.
[51] *Cal. Chart. R.* 1226–57, 403.

the long period of French wars which opened in the reign of Edward I. In 1294 on the beginning of hostilities the king ordered a survey to be made of the possessions and rights of the priory. The Derbyshire possessions were valued at £208 16s. 0¼d. and those in Staffordshire at £60 8s. 10d. In 1295 the king took over the lands and goods of the priory as an alien foundation.[52] These were restored to the prior in 1296 on condition that he rendered each year a sum at the Exchequer. This was fixed to begin with at £60,[53] and the prior made two payments of £30 in 1297.[54] In 1298 and 1299 payments of £40 were made,[55] and in 1300 a payment of £30 is recorded.[56] Tutbury was among the alien priories which petitioned at the Parliament of 1302 against excessive royal exactions.[57]

By 1301 matters had apparently returned to normal and Prior Walter was able to make a short visit to St. Pierre-sur-Dives.[58] The purpose of this visit may have been to regularize his position in relation to the abbey, as there is some evidence that he was elected by the monks of Tutbury without reference to the rights of the mother-house.[59] On his return Walter had to contend with the open hostility of his patron, Earl Thomas. The earl's retainers were doing great damage on the priory lands and were terrorizing the bailiffs and other officials of the priory, who were afraid to remain in its service.[60] In 1305 a commission of oyer and terminer was sent to deal with the complaints of the priory, and the prior and convent petitioned Parliament to extend the term of the commission.[61]

When Edward II marched against the Scots in 1310, he issued a request to the Prior of Tutbury, among others, to lend him supplies for the campaign.[62] The contribution of Tutbury was 40 quarters of wheat, 60 quarters of oats and 50 quarters of malt, together with 10 oxen and 50 sheep.[63] The priory played a somewhat doubtful part in the events of 1322, culminating in the battle of Boroughbridge and the execution of its patron, Earl Thomas.[64] In the short interval between the abandonment of Tutbury castle by the earl and its occupation by Edward II and his forces, a large amount of money, jewellery, and other goods was taken from the castle to the priory by some of the local inhabitants and deposited there with the connivance of the prior. This apparent conspiracy to defraud the king could not be kept secret and on 13 March, three days before the battle of Boroughbridge, an order was issued that all the jewels, goods, and chattels of Earl Thomas and the other rebels which were in the priory were to be brought to the king.[65] The following year three officials of the late earl were charged with having conveyed £1,500 from the castle to the priory. The jury accepted their

plea that they had no other intent except to deposit the money for safety in the priory. The prior was accused of harbouring seven cartloads of gold cloth, silver vessels, and other ornaments to the value of £300 but was acquitted. On another charge of failing to deliver up £40 worth of goods and a barrel of sturgeon, the jury would not accept the prior's plea that the king 'out of kindness' had allowed him to keep this property unless he could obtain the personal corroboration of the king.[66] This apparently was not forthcoming, and the prior was accordingly fined £70. After paying £20 he addressed a petition to Parliament asking for the restitution of this sum and the remission of the rest of the fine, but the petition was rejected.[67]

In the same year, 1323, the prior was excommunicated for not having paid the annual pension of 10 marks due to the Dean and Chapter of Lichfield from the appropriated church of Mayfield.[68] After having paid this, he was threatened with renewed excommunication unless he met the arrears which had accumulated. Faced with these demands, with the continued provision of a royal corrody,[69] and with a robbery of the priory's goods and chattels estimated at a value of nearly £80,[70] Prior Robert de Longdon fell into debt. In 1325 he acknowledged that he owed £100 to a Florentine[71] and a further sum of 20 marks to another merchant.[72] He also acknowledged a debt of three sacks of wool worth £20.[73]

Meanwhile an unavailing struggle by the monks of Tutbury, led by the subprior, for the right of freely electing their prior had begun. The dispute reached its height in 1336 at the time of the appointment of Alexander de Portu to the priorate. Henry, Earl of Lancaster, who had recovered his brother Thomas's titles and possessions in 1326 and 1327, took out a writ of *quare impedit* against the subprior and convent, claiming that they had impeded his right of presenting to the priory.[74] The monks claimed that in the time of Edward I they had freely elected Walter as their prior, that Earl Thomas had accepted their nominee and presented him to the bishop, and that Walter's status had remained unchallenged. This assertion was rejected by the earl who maintained that Thomas himself had nominated Walter and presented him. The arguments of both sides seem to be inaccurate in view of the occurrence of Walter as prior in 1297.[75] Although Thomas's father, Edmund, died in June 1296, Thomas did not attain his majority for another two years. If any irregularity had been committed by the monks, it may have been during this interval. There is of course the bare possibility that there may have been two successive Walters holding the priorate at this time.

[52] *S.H.C.* 4th ser. iv, p. 229; Matthew, *Norman Monasteries*, 81–82.
[53] *Cal. Pat.* 1292–1301, 177.
[54] E 106/1/4, 4/2.
[55] Ibid. 1/1.
[56] Ibid. 1/2.
[57] Matthew, *Norman Monasteries*, 85.
[58] Lich. Dioc. Regy., B/A/1/1, f. 23v.
[59] See below.
[60] *Cal. Pat.* 1301–7, 353, 405–6.
[61] *Rot. Parl.* i. 477.
[62] *Cal. Close*, 1307–13, 263.
[63] W. Beresford, *Lichfield*, 109.
[64] A century and a half earlier Tutbury castle had played an important part in the rebellion of 1173–4 against Hen.

II, but the priory does not appear to have been affected on that occasion.
[65] *Cal. Fine R.* 1319–27, 106.
[66] *S.H.C.* ix(1), 95 sqq.
[67] *Rot. Parl.* ii. 387.
[68] *S.H.C.* 1924, p. 306.
[69] *Cal. Close*, 1323–7, 325.
[70] *S.H.C.* x(1), 61.
[71] *Cal. Close*, 1323–7, 349.
[72] Ibid. 513.
[73] Ibid. 488.
[74] *S.H.C.* xi. 72; Dugdale, *Mon.* iii. 396; *Year Bk. 11–12 Edw. III* (Rolls Ser.), 16 sqq.
[75] E 106/4/2.

Strangely enough, after the death of Walter none of the interested parties seems to have made any move to replace him, and it was left to the Bishop of Lichfield to take the necessary action to fill the vacant priorate. In May 1308 he ordered the sequestration of the spiritualities of Tutbury, and in July he collated Robert of Longdon, a monk of Burton Abbey, who was duly installed by the vicar general.[76]

After a disputed election at Burton in 1329 the bishop appointed as abbot Robert of Longdon, who had been one of the candidates.[77] To replace him at Tutbury the monks held an election and presented Giles de Longford (or Giles de F.) to Earl Henry. The latter, however, would not receive him and accepted the nominee of the Abbot of St. Pierre-sur-Dives. This was John of St. Aubyn, originally a monk of St. Pierre and now Prior of Wolston. He was presented to the bishop by the earl in September 1329 and was duly installed as prior. The subprior and the monks thereupon sued their new prior in the ecclesiastical courts.[78] Seeing the case going against him John resigned in 1335. The monks then elected Ralph of Coventry, a monk of Tutbury, while the Abbot of St. Pierre-sur-Dives submitted his three nominees to Earl Henry, who chose Alexander de Portu, a monk of St. Pierre.[79] The Tutbury monks seem to have resorted to violent action, for on his way back from his presentation to the bishop, Alexander was seized and carried off and for some time his whereabouts were unknown.[80] The following year, however, the Court of King's Bench decided in favour of the earl[81] and Alexander took up his difficult position, apparently little the worse for his unfortunate experience, which is not alluded to again.

Behind this desire for independence from the French mother-house can be discerned the activity of the English monks at Tutbury. The priory was now divided into two bitterly opposed factions. Prior Alexander was supported by three monks from St. Pierre whom he had admitted as brethren of Tutbury. The subprior, Ralph of Derby, had the support of eight English monks, including Ralph of Coventry, whom they had elected prior. Having lost their case in the secular courts, the English party now brought an action against the Abbey of St. Pierre at the papal Curia. The judges delegated by Benedict XII at first favoured the abbey, but in 1342 the final decision was given in support of the claims of the English monks. Accordingly Clement VI issued a bull confirming the right of the monks of Tutbury to elect their own prior without any interference from the Abbey of St. Pierre.[82]

Alexander and his French supporters took no notice of the bull, and in 1344 the English monks applied to the king, who gave them permission to publish it.[83] Shortly afterwards, however, he revoked

this licence,[84] presumably on the representations of Alexander who, although apparently defeated, was in a much stronger position than the English monks as he was holding the farm of the priory from the king. A last attempt by the English monks at the Curia evoked a mandate from the Archdeacon of Norwich, who from the safety of Avignon ordered some of the leading ecclesiastics of Lichfield diocese to excommunicate Alexander and his supporters. This mandate, dated December 1344,[85] was received after the king had expressed support for Alexander, and it appears that no action was taken. During this period the Abbot of St. Pierre-sur-Dives was doing his best to maintain contact with the priory. In 1336, at a critical moment, two of his monks came to Tutbury.[86] In 1341, despite the state of war between England and France, two of the monks of Tutbury received licence to visit the abbey, providing they took no letters or 'apport';[87] the object of their visit was no doubt to provide evidence for the trial of the rival claims.

These internal disputes clearly must have had a bad effect on monastic discipline. The only available evidence, however, comes from about 1329 when the bishop was investigating charges against the monks of Tutbury. They were accused of bearing arms, hunting, general disorder, and incontinence.[88] The results of the inquiry are not known.

The opening of the Hundred Years' War in 1337 added to the troubles at Tutbury. The priory was taken into the king's hands and then farmed out to Prior Alexander for the sum of 100 marks a year, about a third of the annual revenue.[89] The advowsons of Tutbury, however, remained with the king.[90] The prior, being an alien, received the king's protection, at first for a year,[91] and then for as long as he held the custody of the priory.[92] He also undertook to make a special payment of 57½ marks for the custody.[93] He had great difficulty in finding this additional sum, and in August 1337 his arrest was ordered.[94] He was, however, exempted from the payment of a tenth in 1338 in view of the heavy burdens already laid on the priory.[95] In 1339 the experiment was tried of the direct administration of the priory by the king's ministers, but this was abandoned and the farm restored to the prior in April 1340.[96] The officials sent to the priory had done a great deal of damage, and in consequence royal revenue had suffered. Furthermore the prior had contracted a debt of 90 marks to John de Rivers.[97] The Earl of Lancaster was able to obtain a pardon for the prior of the arrears of 40 marks due to the king which had accumulated while the priory was under direct royal administration.[98] These continual heavy payments must have had a grave effect on the economy of the priory, and the prior was described by Earl Henry as 'very grievously depressed by poverty'. On the restoration of the

[76] Lich. Dioc. Regy., B/A/1/1, ff. 28v., 29.
[77] Cal. Pat. 1327–30, 410; see above pp. 209, 213.
[78] S.H.C. xi. 72; Year Bk. 11–12 Edw. III, 16 sqq.; Dugdale, Mon. iii. 396; Lich. Dioc. Regy., B/A/1/2, f. 145v.; S.C. 6/1127/18, m. 1.
[79] Year Bk. 11–12 Edw. III, 20; B/A/1/2, f. 159.
[80] S.H.C. i. 267.
[81] Ibid. xi. 72.
[82] Mosley, Tutbury, 264 sqq.
[83] Cal. Pat. 1343–5, 215.
[84] Ibid. 329, 334.
[85] Mosley, Tutbury, 270 sqq.
[86] Cal. Close, 1333–7, 692.

[87] Ibid. 1341–3, 124.
[88] S.H.C. i. 273.
[89] Cal. Fine R. 1337–47, 28.
[90] Cal. Pat. 1338–40, 128, 201, 318, 321.
[91] Ibid. 1334–8, 479.
[92] Ibid. 484.
[93] Cal. Close, 1337–9, 163.
[94] Ibid. 176, 251.
[95] Ibid. 336.
[96] Cal. Fine R. 1337–47, 175.
[97] S.H.C. xi. 102.
[98] Cal. Pat. 1340–3, 232.

custody of Tutbury to the prior, he mistakenly thought that the advowsons also had been restored to him, and accordingly the priory presented to Doveridge.[99] In April 1342 the king too made a presentation to Doveridge, but he withdrew it and ratified the action of the priory in view of the exceptional circumstances.[1]

A thorough investigation of the finances of the priory, instituted in December 1341, led to a reduction in the annual farm from 100 to 60 marks the following March.[2] Although the king might have been expected to support the English monks, especially in war-time, his financial interest in the priory inclined his favour towards the prior, as has already been seen. About the same time as he withdrew permission from the English monks for the publication of the bull authorizing free elections, in July 1344, he reaffirmed the committal of the priory to Alexander de Portu and complained of the financial deterioration at Tutbury owing to the activities of the English monks. Richard Passemere and Richard de la Pole were appointed to survey and reform the estate of the priory and to correct the English monks; in this way the payment of the farm would be safeguarded and divine service maintained.[3]

Alexander de Portu resigned in December 1347.[4] A few days previously Henry, Earl of Lancaster, had presented Peter Vasseur or Vausser to the bishop on the nomination of the Abbot of St. Pierre-sur-Dives.[5] It seems that Peter was the choice of the retiring prior.[6] In the following February the custody of the priory was committed to Peter; the farm remained at £40.[7] In 1349 one John Vasseur, probably a relation of the prior, was appointed by the king to the church of Marston-upon-Dove.[8] He resigned this vicarage in 1353.[9] In the following year the prior acknowledged for himself and the convent that they owed Vasseur £60.[10] Although, as has been seen, the priory was pardoned the payment of a tenth in 1338 in view of the heavy annual farm, 40s. was paid by the prior in 1350 towards a subsidy granted by the alien priories.[11] In 1356 the priory granted an annuity of £10 to Nicholas de Denston;[12] the transaction may be connected with the litigation at this period between the priory and Nicholas over property at West Broughton.[13]

After the conclusion of peace between England and France, the priory recovered its independence in February 1361.[14] Shortly afterwards it fell vacant. Before his death in 1361 Henry, Duke of Lancaster, had settled his possessions on a group of trustees[15]

who in 1362 presented William Beloc, a monk of St. Pierre-sur-Dives, to the bishop on the nomination of the abbot and convent.[16] He was able to administer the priory in peace for seven years and even to present to benefices,[17] but with the renewal of the war in 1369 the priory was once more taken into the king's hands.[18] In the following year the farm was committed to the prior at the old rate of £40 a year.[19]

The next prior, John Bellocier, a monk of St. Pierre-sur-Dives, was presented in 1377 by John of Gaunt,[20] who had succeeded to the Lancastrian heritage of his father-in-law in 1362. The farm of the priory was committed to the new prior at £40 a year.[21] The growing poverty of the priory seems to be indicated in a survey of the spiritualities and temporalities of the house in Staffordshire made in 1379–80; their value amounted to £45 6s. 5½d.,[22] which shows a decline of £15 since 1348. In addition the size of the community had dropped to four by 1377.[23] To repair the fortunes of his priory John obtained papal permission in 1398 for the appropriation of the church of Church Broughton (Derb.).[24] The priory was, however, compelled to pay 80 marks for a royal licence for appropriation in mortmain,[25] while in 1401 the bishop reserved to his see an annual pension of 13s. 4d. to be paid by Tutbury to compensate for the episcopal dues lost at Church Broughton.[26] It was also agreed that the vicar to be appointed there should have a stipend of 10 marks, the burial dues, and payments at confession. The priory was to provide a suitable house containing a hall, two rooms and a stable, with a curtilage annexed, but the vicar was to be responsible for its upkeep.[27] In April 1399 the farm of Tutbury was raised to its original amount of £60; possibly on account of the growing infirmity of Prior Bellocier, the custody of the priory was removed from his sole administration and the bishop and two clerks, Ralph Canon and William Pollard, were associated with him.[28]

The first years of Henry IV were a period of great confusion for the priory. At the outset of his reign all the alien priories were freed from royal control.[29] Accordingly in December 1399 Tutbury was restored to John Bellocier together with its advowsons.[30] In 1400 the prior obtained a licence to grant an annuity of 52 marks to Master Henry Davy, clerk.[31] A year later the bishop appointed Thomas Masse, a monk of Tutbury, to be the co-adjutor of the prior on account of his infirmity.[32] Meanwhile a new threat was developing to the newly-gained

[99] Ibid. 493.
[1] Ibid. 399.
[2] *Cal. Close,* 1341–3, 358, 361; *Cal. Fine R.* 1337–47, 294.
[3] *Cal. Pat.* 1343–5, 329.
[4] Lich. Dioc. Regy., B/A/1/2, f. 179v.
[5] Ibid.
[6] Alexander, on submitting his resignation to the bishop, asked him to admit Peter Vasseur: ibid.
[7] *Cal. Fine R.* 1347–56, 73.
[8] *Cal. Pat.* 1348–50, 358.
[9] Ibid. 1350–4, 397.
[10] *Cal. Close,* 1354–60, 55.
[11] Ibid. 1349–54, 167.
[12] *Cal. Pat.* 1354–8, 465.
[13] *S.H.C.* 4th ser. iv, pp. 231–4; B.M. Add. MS. 6714, p. 134.
[14] *Cal. Pat.* 1358–61, 560.
[15] Ibid. 580.
[16] *S.H.C.* N.S. x(2), 111.
[17] Ibid. 125.

[18] Ibid. 128; *Cal. Pat.* 1367–70, 316.
[19] *Cal. Fine R.* 1369–77, 82.
[20] *S.H.C.* N.S. x(2), 144, which gives his name as Philip; John is given in subsequent refs. In 1383 John of Gaunt granted timber from Needwood Forest to the priory: *John of Gaunt's Reg. 1379–83, vol. ii* (Camden Soc. 3rd ser. lvii), 283.
[21] *Cal. Fine R.* 1377–83, 82.
[22] E 106/11/5.
[23] J. C. Russell, 'The Clerical Population of Medieval Eng.' *Traditio,* ii. 196 (where the source cited should be E 179/20/595).
[24] *Cal. Papal Regs.* v. 153.
[25] *Cal. Pat.* 1396–9, 407.
[26] Lich. Dioc. Regy., B/A/1/7, f. 171.
[27] Ibid. f. 180.
[28] *Cal. Fine R.* 1391–9, 300.
[29] New, *Alien Priories,* 81; Matthew, *Norman Monasteries,* 120–1.
[30] *Cal. Pat.* 1399–1401, 71.
[31] Ibid. 320.
[32] Lich. Dioc. Regy., B/A/1/7, f. 170v.

independence of Tutbury. Sentiment in Parliament had for a long time been most violent against the alien priories. In 1377 the Commons had secured an Act expelling French monks from England. The conventual priories were exempted, but it was laid down that even in these only English monks should henceforth be admitted.[33] In 1402 the Commons petitioned for the seizure of the dative priories, and the royal assent was granted.[34] In December the Prior of Tutbury was ordered to come in person before the king and council to prove the conventual status of his priory in order that it should be exempt from seizure.[35] Although the prior rightly claimed exemption from the provisions of the Act,[36] John de Fynderne, a professional farmer of alien priories, and John Cokeyn falsely represented that Tutbury was a dative priory and the prior's claim was rejected. Accordingly in February 1403 the priory was seized and committed to the custody of the prior, his co-adjutor Thomas Masse, John Cokeyn, and John de Fynderne at a farm of 100 marks a year.[37] Shortly afterwards the prior resigned, and in July a new set of farmers was appointed — the ex-prior, Sir John Dabriggecourt, and Bernard of Ridware, the Vicar of Tutbury.[38] They had offered an additional 50 marks over and above the regular farm of 100 marks. The machinations of the farmers were at length detected, and in 1404 the king revoked his seizure of the priory,[39] which now remained unmolested down to its dissolution in 1538.

In 1404 the king, in his capacity as Duke of Lancaster, nominated Thomas Masse as Prior of Tutbury and he was duly admitted by the bishop.[40] In 1410 the king granted the prior a licence to bring over six monks from St. Pierre-sur-Dives.[41] There seemed, therefore, to be no question of Tutbury's following the example of many of the other conventual priories and seeking denization.[42] The link with St. Pierre was never formally broken. As late as 1437 an *inspeximus* of a charter of Robert de Ferrers, Earl of Derby, of 1263 was put on the Patent Roll, exemplifying the rights of the abbey at the election of a prior.[43] Despite this there was undoubtedly a marked decline in French influence at Tutbury during the 15th century. The decline may have been accentuated by an Act of 1413, which reaffirmed that henceforth only English monks should be admitted into the alien priories.[44] There was only one more French prior after Thomas Masse, Adam Preaux (1429–33). His successor, Thomas Gedney, had a register compiled of the charters of Tutbury,[45] and not one document included in this cartulary refers to the Abbey of St. Pierre. At the surrender of Tutbury the prior and all the monks were Englishmen,[46] and at no time during the process of dissolution was there any mention of the abbey.

On the death of Thomas Masse in 1424 presentation was made on behalf of the king under the Duchy of Lancaster seal of Thomas Derby, a monk of Tutbury, who was duly admitted by the bishop in June.[47] Derby had a stormy career. About three weeks before his installation a robbery took place at Marston-upon-Dove, and eventually in 1429 Derby was accused of having committed this felony and stolen a 'trussing-coffer' containing 40 marks in cash and other goods to the value of £40. He was sent to prison but was released on bail and afterwards acquitted.[48] In the meanwhile he had been in serious trouble with his bishop. A letter testimonial of Bishop Heyworth of August 1429 announced the absolution of Thomas Derby, 'formerly Prior of Tutbury', from ecclesiastical censure incurred by his having violently resisted the sequestration of the goods of the priory made on the bishop's authority.[49] It is most probable, therefore, that he had been deposed. He failed to obtain any pension and in 1444 obtained a licence to sue the Pope for a benefice, as his annual income was less than 6 marks.[50]

His successor Adam Preaux,[51] a monk of St. Pierre, was the last French prior. He did not hold office for long, and on his resignation in 1433 Thomas Gedney, a monk of Westminster, was admitted, having been presented by the king.[52] Gedney's priorate of twenty-five years was noteworthy for the compilation of the Tutbury Cartulary at some time between 1452 and 1458.[53] Most of the documents contained in it are of the 12th and 13th centuries, although a few of the later priors are also represented. Many of the documents are concerned with litigation over tithes, the most troublesome part of the Tutbury endowments. In some cases the priory had disposed of outlying rights of tithe to other monasteries or to the local incumbents in return for an annual pension.[54]

Gedney also made a vain attempt in 1440 to resist the royal corrodies. He did, however, achieve the minor success that the beneficiary on that occasion was to serve at the monks' table.[55] The corrodies went on until the dissolution of the priory: in 1532 the Duke of Richmond, illegitimate son of Henry VIII, wrote to the priory from Calais, quartering on the monks the clerk of his jewel-house, Robert Amyas.[56] In June 1458 Gedney resigned, receiving a competent pension, and a month later his successor Richard Burton, a monk of Tutbury, was appointed by the bishop as Queen Margaret, the patron, had on this occasion conceded her right of presentation to him.[57] Burton resigned in 1461, receiving a pension of £40 and the food of two monks, and in

[33] *Rot. Parl.* iii. 22.
[34] New, *Alien Priories*, 81.
[35] *Cal. Close*, 1402–5, 25.
[36] *Cal. Pat.* 1401–5, 366.
[37] *Cal. Fine R.* 1399–1405, 198–9.
[38] Ibid. 214.
[39] *Cal. Pat.* 1401–5, 366.
[40] Lich. Dioc. Regy., B/A/1/7, f. 58v.
[41] *Cal. Pat.* 1408–13, 213.
[42] See New, *Alien Priories*, 77. Matthew, *Norman Monasteries*, 136, states that Tutbury became denizen but gives no authority.
[43] *Cal. Pat.* 1436–41, 52.   [44] *Rot. Parl.* iv. 13.
[45] Mosley, *Tutbury*, 276.
[46] *L. & P. Hen. VIII*, xiii(2), p. 134.
[47] Lich. Dioc. Regy., B/A/1/9, f. 50v.

[48] *S.H.C.* xvii. 124.
[49] Lich. Dioc. Regy., B/A/1/9, f. 163.
[50] *Cal. Pat.* 1441–6, 268.   [51] See below p. 339.
[52] B/A/1/9, f. 63.
[53] For a discussion of the Cartulary see *S.H.C.* 4th ser. iv, pp. 1 sqq.
[54] Ibid. pp. 96–98 (tithes of Tissington and Brassington, Derb., to Dunstable Priory, 1364), 98–99 (tithes of Buttsbury, Essex, to nunnery of Stratford-at-Bow, 1371), 103–4 (tithes of Harbury, Warws., to Kenilworth Priory c. 1200). A list of pensions paid to Tutbury is given in *Valor Eccl.* (Rec. Com.), iii. 143; and see *S.H.C.* 4th ser. iv, pp. 250–6.
[55] *S.H.C.* 4th ser. iv, pp. 212–14.
[56] *L. & P. Hen. VIII*, v, p. 644; and see D.L. 37/60, m. 7.
[57] Lich. Dioc. Regy., B/A/1/11, f. 16v.

October Thomas Longdon, a monk of Tutbury, was admitted by the bishop on the presentation of Edward IV.[58]

After this little of note is recorded in connexion with the priory. Five priors of Tutbury were admitted to the guild of Lichfield — Thomas Longdon in 1468, William Coventry in 1487, William Whalley in 1492, Thomas Rolleston in 1492 while he was still a monk, and Arthur Meverell in 1535.[59] A community of 9 monks and 3 novices was recorded at the visitation of 1518. There were 10 monks in 1521 and 10 monks and 3 novices in 1524. In addition to the prior and subprior, the officials in 1518 consisted of precentor, master of novices, sacrist, and cellarer. There was no subprior in 1521, and the appointment of one was apparently ordered at the visitation of 1524.[60] The only evidence of any educational activities at the priory is provided by a petition of Thomas Alenson to the Chancellor in 1530. He claimed that he had served the priory as singing-man from 1496 to 1527, when he had been expelled from the priory by the 'malice' of Prior Heth, then cellarer. He claimed 40 marks' arrears of pay and 53s. 4d. in lieu of livery gowns. In the course of his petition he described the nature of his work, which was to keep and attend to the divine service and to teach six children at the priory plainsong, 'prick-song', and descant. For this he received 4 marks a year, lodging at the priory and a livery gown each year. In addition Alenson stated that he had spent money of his own on behalf of Prior Madeley, which he had never recovered.[61]

An event of some note at Tutbury was the annual bull-running which continued down to 1778 and of which full descriptions survive.[62] Until the Dissolution the priory played an important part in the bull-running, which was held on 16 August, the morrow of the Assumption. The prior had to provide a bull for the minstrels of Tutbury, who had been incorporated as a court or guild by John of Gaunt. If the minstrels could catch the bull on the Staffordshire side of the Dove, they were to have it, or alternatively the prior could give them 40d. The origin of this custom is unknown; its first mention seems to be in 1414.[63] While folklorists have claimed an ancient pagan origin,[64] there is something to be said for the view that it was introduced by John of Gaunt, together with the organization of the minstrels' court and the office of king of the minstrels.[65]

In the early 16th century the priory was in some financial confusion. In 1518 Prior Rolleston gave the annual income as £400, but his successor stated in 1521 that Rolleston had left the house £140 in debt while he himself had had to pay the Crown 100 marks for his temporalities. The debt had been reduced to £100 by 1524, but numerous complaints were then made by the monks about the size and extravagance of the prior's household.[66] The *Valor*

Ecclesiasticus of 1535 gave Tutbury's receipts from temporalities as £170 18s. 4d., with outgoings of £20 14s.[67] The priory received £73 18s. 4d. from spiritualities, with outgoings of £21 7s. 10d. Disbursements for charitable purposes were given as £3. Thus the gross annual receipts were valued at £244 16s. 8d. and the net income at £199 14s. 10d. Some of the annual payments made by the priory in 1535 are of interest. The chief steward, George, Earl of Shrewsbury, who had been the steward of the honor of Tutbury since 1529,[68] received £3 6s. 8d. The clerk of the priory's courts received £1 6s. 8d. and the auditor £2. Seven bailiffs earned £10 between them, and the receiver, Humphrey Meverell, presumably a kinsman of the prior, Arthur Meverell, was paid £2. In 1538–9, the year immediately following the dissolution, the gross value of the priory's property was given as £353 7s. 9¾d.[69] Its estates outside Tutbury were stated to be the manors of Mayfield, Church Broughton (Derb.), Doveridge (Derb.), and Marston-upon-Dove (Derb.); lands and rents in Duffield, Edlaston, Ednaston (in Brailsford), Foston, Hollington and Lower Thurvaston (both in Longford), Mercaston (in Mugginton), Norbury, Osmaston, Scropton, Shirley, Sudbury, and Sutton (all Derb.), Saxby and Stapleford (both Leics.), and Wetton; the appropriated churches of Church Broughton, Doveridge, Marston-upon-Dove, and Mayfield with its dependent chapels of Butterton and Wetton; tithes in the parishes of Ashbourne, Aston-upon-Trent, Dalbury, Duffield, Egginton, Hartshorne, Longford, Osmaston, Scropton and Foston, Shirley, and Sudbury (all Derb.), Edmondthorpe, Saxby, Stapleford, and Wymondham (all Leics.), East Leake (Notts.), and Ilam; and pensions in lieu of tithes from the Hospitallers, the abbeys of Kenilworth (Warws.) and Welbeck (Notts.), the priories of Dunstable (Beds.), Langley (Leics.), Repton (Derb.), Stratford-at-Bow (Mdx.), and Trentham, Newark College at Leicester, and the church of Mugginton. The priory had fishing rights on the Dove and owned several mills, including a fulling-mill on the Dove at Church Mayfield (in Mayfield).

The priory came within the terms of the Act of 1536 for the suppression of the lesser monasteries.[70] In 1537, on payment of £100, it received licence to continue in existence.[71] Archbishop Cranmer, however, showed an unfriendly interest in its fortunes and in August 1538 wrote to Cromwell, reminding him about the proposed suppression of the 'abbey'.[72] He was not to wait long for the fulfilment of his wishes. In September Dr. Thomas Legh, the renowned suppressor of religious houses, made a rapid tour of the Midlands. On the 14th he arrived at Tutbury and accepted the surrender of the house from Arthur Meverell, the prior, and eight other monks.[73] Meverell, a member of a well-known local family, received a pension of £50, which may

[58] Ibid. /12, f. 41v.

[59] Harwood, *Lichfield*, 404, 408, 410, 415.

[60] Lich. Dioc. Regy., B/V/1/1, pp. 20, 68, p. 52 (2nd nos.). In 1521 and 1524 the precentor was also acting as sacrist. It would appear from these three visitations that 13 was regarded as the full complement of the priory.

[61] C 1/603/1.

[62] Mosley, *Tutbury*, 84. The basic description is in Plot, *Staffs.* 439–40.

[63] D.L. 42/4, f. 125v.

[64] *Folk-lore*, vii. 346. There were similar customs at Stamford and Rochdale.

[65] This is Sir Oswald Mosley's view.

[66] Lich. Dioc. Regy., B/V/1/1, pp. 20, 68, and p. 52 (2nd nos.).

[67] *Valor Eccl.* iii. 142–4.   [68] *Complete Peerage*, xi. 708.

[69] S.C. 6/Hen. VIII/3353, mm. 21–31.

[70] Hibbert, *Dissolution*, 138–9.

[71] Ibid. 145–6; *L. & P. Hen. VIII*, xii(1), pp. 514, 602. This was provided for by clause 13 of the Act.

[72] *L. & P. Hen. VIII*, xiii(2), p. 65.   [73] Ibid. p. 134.

be compared with the pension of £40 and the food of two monks received by Prior Burton on his retirement in 1461. The other pensions were one of £7, three of £6 13s. 4d., and four of £6.[74] Fifteen years later Meverell and five of the other monks were still drawing their pensions.[75] Meverell became Vicar of Tutbury in 1543 but resigned in 1544; he may well be the Arthur Meverell who was Vicar of Tideswell (Derb.) from 1544 until his resignation in 1547.[76]

The site of the priory was leased to Sir William Bassett.[77] In 1552 it was granted to Sir William Cavendish together with many of the possessions of the former priory,[78] and he built a house on the site, using priory stone for it.[79]

The priory occupied an area of 4 acres on the hillside below the castle with the monastic buildings lying on the north side of the church.[80] Only the church — the parish church of St. Mary — remains standing, and that has been much reduced in size. Before the Reformation there seem to have been two further bays at the east end of the nave as well as transepts, choir, and a tower over the crossing. Most of what remains evidently dates from about 1160–70 with the two easternmost piers about 1100; the west front exhibits the earliest known use of alabaster in England. The south aisle was probably added as part of the work begun in 1307, which was itself probably the restoration made necessary by Earl Robert's destruction of the priory in 1260.[81] The water supply would originally have come from the fleam to the north-east of the priory, but by the 13th century there was a piped supply from wells in the neighbourhood.[82] Building timber came from Needwood Forest.[83]

PRIORS

Herbert.[84]
Ralph.
William, occurs 1125.[85]
William, occurs some time between 1136 and 1138 and twice between 1140 and 1152.[86]

Richard, occurs some time between 1149 and 1159.[87]
Fulk, occurs in the 1160s, c. 1170, and possibly later.[88]
William, occurs some time between 1161 and 1182.[89]
Richard, occurs some time between 1177 and c. 1195.[90]
William le Deneys, occurs some time between 1191 and 1197.[91]
Bartholomew, occurs by 1209 and some time between 1222 and 1226.[92]
Nicholas, occurs from 1226 to 1231.[93]
Fulk, occurs 1234 and c. 1245.[94]
William de Truard, occurs c. 1245.[95]
    There was a Prior William in 1248 and 1256. Prior William de Sentellys and Prior William de Mentall occur temp. Henry III.[96]
William de Favers, died 1262.[97]
Geoffrey de Beumes or de Bovinis, appointed 1262, occurs 1266.[98]
Robert, occurs not later than 1286.[99]
Walter, occurs 1297, died by 1308.[1]
Robert of Longdon, appointed 1308, elected Abbot of Burton 1329.[2]
John of St. Aubyn, appointed 1329, resigned 1335.[3]
Alexander de Portu, admitted 1336, resigned 1347.[4]
Peter Vasseur or Vausser, presented 1347, occurs until 1361.[5]
William Beloc, admitted 1362, occurs until 1371.[6]
John Bellocier, admitted 1377, resigned 1403.[7]
Thomas Masse, Masceewe or Maucieu, admitted 1404, died 1424.[8]
Thomas Derby, admitted 1424, deposed or resigned by August 1429.[9]
Adam Preaux, presented 1429, resigned 1433.[10]
Thomas Gedney, admitted 1433, resigned 1458.[11]
Richard Burton, admitted 1458, resigned 1461.[12]
Thomas Longdon, admitted 1461, died 1478.[13]

[74] Ibid. p. 178; xiv(1), p. 598; E 315/233, ff. 19–20v. For Prior Burton see above p. 337. For Meverell's family see L. & P. Hen. VIII, viii, pp. 4, 19; Cal. Inq. p.m. Hen. VII, ii, p. 403. In Nov. 1538 Thos. Meverell was appointed bailiff of the priory lands: L. & P. Hen. VIII, xiv(1), p. 593.
[75] Hibbert, Dissolution, 190–1. For three Tutbury monks still drawing pensions of £6 when they died see E 178/3239, mm. 7, 8.
[76] S.H.C. 1915, 292; J. M. J. Fletcher, 'Sir Sampson Meverill of Tideswell, 1388–1462', Jnl. Derb. Arch. Soc. xxx. 20.
[77] L. & P. Hen. VIII, xiv(1), p. 609.
[78] Cal. Pat. 1550–3, 290.
[79] Shaw, Staffs. i. 52, 59; Erdeswick, Staffs. 534.
[80] Mosley, Tutbury, 243–4; S.H.C. 4th ser. iv, p. 220.
[81] Edwards, Medieval Tutbury, 85, 88; V.C.H. Staffs. ii. 198, 201.
[82] Edwards, Medieval Tutbury, 84; S.H.C. 4th ser. iv, pp. 148–9. The grant of the site to Sir Wm. Cavendish in 1553 included a well, a conduit, pipes, and leaden channels.
[83] See V.C.H. Staffs. ii. 356; S.H.C. 4th ser. iv, pp. 93–94; above p. 332.
[84] The names of what are probably the first 4 priors of Tutbury are given in an Okeover charter of 1136–8: S.H.C. N.S. vii. 128.
[85] S.H.C. 4th ser. iv, p. 85.
[86] Ibid. pp. 74–75; S.H.C. N.S. vii. 128–9; R. W. Eyton, Antiquities of Shropshire, viii. 216–17.
[87] S.H.C. v(1), 16.
[88] Ibid. 4th ser. iv, pp. 69, 118, 131; Matthew, Norman Monasteries, 47.

[89] S.H.C. 4th ser. iv, p. 30.
[90] Sir Christopher Hatton's Bk. of Seals, ed. L. C. Loyd and Doris M. Stenton, p. 101.
[91] S.H.C. 4th ser. iv, pp. 102, 183–4.
[92] Letters of Pope Innocent III, ed. C.R. and Mary G. Cheney, p. 141; Derbs. Charters, ed. I. H. Jeayes, p. 325.
[93] S.H.C. iv(1), 80; ibid. 4th ser. iv, pp. 70, 202–3.
[94] Cal. Pat. 1232–47, 73; S.H.C. v(1), 50.
[95] S.H.C. 4th ser. iv, p. 181.
[96] Ibid. pp. 146, 204; S.H.C. xiii. 192; P.R.O., Transcripts 31/8/140B, p. 10.
[97] Annales Monastici (Rolls Ser.), i. 500.
[98] Ibid.; Close R. 1261–4, 283; Cal. Pat. 1436–41, 52; S.H.C. 4th ser. iv. 201; K.B. 26/177, m. 11.
[99] S.H.C. 4th ser. iv, p. 96.
[1] See above p. 334.
[2] See above p. 335.
[3] See above p. 335.
[4] See above pp. 335, 336.
[5] See above p. 336; Cal. Close, 1360–4, 261.
[6] See above p. 336; S.H.C. 4th ser. iv, pp. 98–99.
[7] See above pp. 336–7; Cal. Fine R. 1399–1405, 198, 214.
[8] See above p. 337; Cal. Pat. 1401–5, 443; 1408–13, 213.
[9] See above p. 337.
[10] R. Somerville, 'Duchy of Lancaster Presentations 1399–1485', Bull. Inst. Hist. Res. xviii. 68; Lich. Dioc. Regy., B/A/1/9, f. 63. He was a monk of St. Pierre-sur-Dives.
[11] See above p. 337.
[12] See above p. 337.
[13] See above p. 338; Bull. Inst. Hist. Res. xviii. 68.

William Coventry, presented 1478, died 1492.[14]

William Whalley, admitted 1492, occurs 1503, dead by 1507.[15]

Thomas Rolleston, admitted by 1507, occurs 1518.[16]

John Madeley or Mawdeley, occurs 1521, died by 1528.[17]

Richard Heth, elected 1528, died 1535.[18]

Arthur Meverell, appointed 1535, surrendered the priory 1538.[19]

The priory seal[20] in use about 1230 is a pointed oval, about $2\frac{1}{4}$ by $1\frac{5}{8}$ in., depicting the Virgin seated with the Child, the right hand of the Child raised in benediction and the left hand holding a book. The surviving fragment of legend appears to be lombardic.

A seal[21] in use in 1400 is a pointed oval, about $2\frac{1}{4}$ by $1\frac{1}{2}$ in. It depicts a standing figure holding a cross or a sword in its right hand and a book in its left; on each side is a diapered field with a shield. No legend has survived.

A seal[22] in use in the 16th century is round, $2\frac{1}{2}$ inches in diameter, depicting beneath three canopies the Coronation of the Virgin who is seated between the Father and the Son with the Dove overhead; there is a shield of arms on either side, that on the right the arms of the Ferrers, that on the left a saltire vairy between four crescents. Legend, black letter:

SIGILLUM COMMUNE PRIORIS ET CONVENTUS MONESTERII B . . .

The reverse shows the Virgin crowned and seated beneath a canopy; she holds the Child on her right knee and a sceptre in her left hand. In a canopied niche on either side is an angel, and in the base under an arch is the prior kneeling. Legend, black letter, a rhyming verse:

. . . A PIA SERVOS INTENDE MARIA

40. THE PRIORY OF LAPLEY

IN 1061 Burchard, son of Alfgar, Earl of Mercia, fell ill at Rheims on the return journey from Rome whither he had accompanied Aldred, Archbishop of York, on an embassy. When he realized that he was dying Burchard expressed a wish to be buried in the Benedictine abbey of St. Rémy at Rheims and promised that land should be given to the abbey on his behalf. Very soon after his son's death Earl Alfgar gave to St. Rémy four estates in Staffordshire — Lapley, Hamstall Ridware, Meaford, and a hide at Marston in Church Eaton — and one in Shropshire — Silvington — for the welfare of Burchard's soul.[1] It was stated in 1415 that the original grant was made to St. Rémy 'to find two chaplains celebrating divine service daily in the infirmary of the abbey before the infirm there'.[2]

Henry I confirmed St. Rémy in its property at Marston and in Shropshire and granted the monks exemption from attendance at hundred and shire courts.[3] He also confirmed the church of Lapley, with tithe and burial rights, to the monks after Godric, a monk of St. Rémy, had gone before the king at Tamworth and proved the claim against Robert, a royal chaplain; Godric contended that the church had formed part of Alfgar's grant.[4] St. Rémy secured confirmation of all its possessions from Pope Alexander, probably Alexander III (1159–81); the English property comprised Lapley with the church, Wheaton Aston (in Lapley parish), the hide at Marston, 'half of Wilnifort, Wilifort, and the vill of Ridware', all in the diocese of Chester, and Silvington and the tithe 'de Roniaco' in the diocese of Hereford.[5] Although Meaford was not mentioned, it continued among the abbey's possessions.[6]

A medieval abbey which held distant estates normally administered them by establishing a small cell or priory of two or three monks to manage a manor or group of manors and send the profits to the mother-house. The hide at Marston was held in 1086 by two men of St. Rémy,[7] and this may indicate that a cell of two monks had already been established by St. Rémy in England. The Godric of Henry I's reign may well have been an early prior. Lapley, the most central of the manors and the one in which St. Rémy also held the church, was the natural place for the monks to establish a priory. It is not, however, until the time of Peter of Celle, Abbot of St. Rémy (1162–81), that the existence of a priory at Lapley can be proved.[8] The priors of Lapley administered all the English possessions of their mother abbey and were normally instituted by the Bishop of Coventry and Lichfield on the presentation of the Abbot of St. Rémy.[9]

[14] *Bull. Inst. Hist. Res.* xviii. 68; Lich. Dioc. Regy. B/A/1/13, f. 131. He was subprior.

[15] B/A/1/13, f. 131; ibid. /14, f. 21v.; *Cal. Inq. p.m. Hen. VII*, ii, p. 403. He was a monk of Tutbury.

[16] B/A/1/14, f. 21v.; B/V/1/1, p. 20.

[17] B/V/1/1, p. 68, p. 52 (2nd nos.); C 1/603/1. He was subprior in 1516: B/V/1/1, p. 20.

[18] See above p. 338; *S.H.C.* 1917–18, 325; C 1/603/1; *L. & P. Hen. VIII*, viii, pp. 4, 19. He was cellarer from at least 1516: Lich. Dioc. Regy., B/V/1/1, pp. 20, 68, p. 52 (2nd nos.).

[19] *L. & P. Hen. VIII*, viii, p. 19; Hibbert, *Dissolution*, 125–6. He was subprior of Tutbury and was recommended to Cromwell by the Earl of Shrewsbury: *L. & P. Hen. VIII*, viii, pp. 4, 19. For his career after the Dissolution see above.

[20] W. de G. Birch, *Cat. of Seals in B.M.* i, p. 781; B.M., Wols. Ch. ix. 76.

[21] E 135/10/21/13. The P.R.O. Cat. of Seals suggests that the figure is St. Paul, that the left-hand shield may bear the arms of England, and that the right-hand shield is vairy.

[22] Birch, *Cat. of Seals*, i, p. 781 (wrongly giving 'abbatis' for 'prioris'); E 322/247; cast among W.S.L. Seals. The reconstructions in Shaw, *Staffs.* i. 51, and Dugdale, *Mon.* iii. 391, are inaccurate.

[1] R. W. Eyton, *Domesday Studies, Staffs.* 41–42; Eyton, *Antiquities of Salop.* iv. 378–9; Dugdale, *Mon.* vi(2), 1042; *S.H.C.* 1916, 126–9; *V.C.H. Staffs.* iv. 28, 44, 59, 94, 146; *V.C.H. Salop.* i. 311.

[2] *Cal. Pat.* 1413–16, 334–5.

[3] Dugdale, *Mon.* vi(2), 1043. In granting immunity from attendance at hundred and shire courts the king added: 'sed incopolitos suos vel unum ex hominibus suis mittant.'

[4] Ibid. Lapley church seems earlier to have belonged to Penkridge church: see above p. 298.

[5] Dugdale, *Mon.* vi(2), 1043. Dugdale cites it as a bull of Pope Alexander, 1154. 'Wilnifort', 'Wilifort' and 'Roniaco' have not been identified; the last may be Ronhill in Cleobury Mortimer (Salop.).

[6] *S.H.C.* vi(1), 28; xiii. 62.   [7] *V.C.H. Staffs.* iv. 59.

[8] Migne, *Pat. Lat.* ccii, col. 596. *V.C.H. Staffs.* iv. 146, cites the Pipe R. of 1129–30 to show that the men of Lapley then paid 20s. fine for a breach of the peace but that St. Rémy was excused its share, a further 20s. The *V.C.H.* states that this definitely proves the existence of a priory at Lapley by 1130; the conclusion does not in fact seem to follow.

[9] *Close R.* 1231–4, 337; Lich. Dioc. Regy., B/A/1/1, f. 90v.; ibid. /2, f. 136; *S.H.C.* N.S. x(2), 110; *Cal. Inq. Misc.* ii, p. 355.

Unlike the outlying manors Lapley and the land at Marston were never leased out; Marston in fact probably came to be regarded as part of Lapley manor. An inquiry in 1272, made on a complaint by the prior that his privilege of exemption from the courts of hundred and shire was being infringed, showed that for the hide in Marston the monks of St. Rémy owed suit, worth ½ mark a year to the Crown, to the county court every month and the hundred court of Cuttlestone every three weeks; for Lapley and Wheaton Aston, however, they had never done suit, being acquitted by royal charters from time immemorial. For a long time they paid nothing for this exemption. After 1248 the sheriff sometimes took 10s. 'by extortion', and from 1258 he exacted 5 marks a year.[10] Hamstall Ridware, Meaford, and Silvington were leased out, presumably being too far from the priory to be worked directly by the monks.[11] Ridware was held by serjeanty, the tenant being bound to come to the priory each Christmas Eve and perform the service of marshal there on 24, 25, and 26 December; on the 27th he placed 5s. 4d. on the table and left after breakfast.[12]

It was part of Godric's claim in the early 12th century that Earl Alfgar had given a church at Lapley with the vill; certainly Henry I recognized the appropriation of the church.[13] A vicarage had been ordained by 1266 when the bishop, having found it inadequately endowed, secured a more generous provision for the vicars from the prior.[14] The right of presenting the vicar lay with the prior, but during the long periods of the 14th century when alien priories were in the king's hands the presentation was made by the Crown.[15] The priory's right to the church and also to a dependent chapel at Wheaton Aston was confirmed by the bishop in 1319 after a visitation.[16]

The prior paid 3 marks towards the tallage of 1199, although he did not complete payment until 1201–2.[17] To the aids of 1235–6 and 1242–3 he paid 4 marks and 40s.[18] In 1291 the temporalities in Lapley and Wheaton Aston were valued at £28 19s. and Lapley church at £13 6s. 8d.[19] The king granted a new charter in 1292, conferring on the abbey of St. Rémy a Tuesday market and a fair on 31 July and 1 August in the manor of Aston and free warren in all the demesne lands in Lapley, Aston, Edgeland (in Lapley), and Marston.[20] In the following year, however, when the prior was called upon to show his title to pleas of the Crown, free warren, a fair, and a gallows in these places, he claimed free warren in Marston only and the right to view of frankpledge and a gallows in Lapley manor and its members, Edgeland and Aston. He produced the charter and

the king allowed it, also accepting the view of frankpledge since the sheriff received 5 marks a year for it.[21]

As an alien priory Lapley was frequently in the hands of the king. After the loss of Normandy in 1204 King John seized the priory, and in 1205–6 the prior acknowledged that he owed three palfreys as a fine for recovering seisin and paid 10 marks in respect of two of them; in the following year he paid off the remainder of the fine, 5 marks.[22] In 1288 the escheator was ordered to take the priory into the king's hands because the prior had gone overseas without licence;[23] in 1318 the prior was granted letters of protection to go abroad.[24] Presumably these journeys were visits to the mother abbey. In 1325, after the outbreak of war with France the previous year, the priory was again in the king's hands; the prior secured restoration by agreeing to pay the Crown 55 marks a year. An inventory made at the restoration shows the priory in possession of a store of grain, pots and pans, a psalter, a missal, and the furnishings of the chapel.[25] During the Hundred Years' War the priory was repeatedly seized by the Crown.

Shortly before the outbreak of war in 1337 the priory was troubled by a dispute between two rival claimants to the office of prior, Baldwin de Spynale and Gobert de Lapion. Gobert and another monk, John Lange, had evidently been sent by the Abbot of St. Rémy to administer the priory,[26] but in 1334 Baldwin upheld his claim in the bishop's court and Gobert was excommunicated.[27] Each of them, however, received a grant of royal protection for one year in 1335, and each was described as Prior of Lapley in his grant.[28] In the same year the king appointed a commission of inquiry as a result of Baldwin's complaint that a number of people, including the Vicar of Lapley, had broken into his house and driven off 40 oxen, 15 bullocks, 15 heifers, and 40 swine, cut down trees, broken 12 chests and carried off 30 deeds and other muniments.[29] Later in 1335 Baldwin complained of a further raid; this time Gobert, his clerk and his servant appear amongst the raiders, and their presence shows the real reason for the raids. The king thereupon appointed a second commission of inquiry,[30] followed by a third two months later,[31] but the dispute continued.

With the outbreak of the Hundred Years' War in 1337 the Crown seized Lapley as an alien priory and committed it to Gobert and Robert de Shareshull as the proctors of the Abbot of St. Rémy for a farm of 55 marks.[32] Baldwin petitioned the king and in 1338, after another inquiry, not only obtained

[10] S.H.C. 1911, 142–3; Cal. Inq. Misc. i, p. 135.

[11] See e.g. S.H.C. iv(1), 95, 98; C 145/135/12; Dugdale, Mon. vi(2), 1042–3.

[12] The details were given by the prior in a lawsuit in 1286: S.H.C. vi(1), 170–1.

[13] See p. 340.

[14] V.C.H. Staffs. iv. 149–50.

[15] Ibid. 149; S.H.C. N.S. x(2), 146; Cal. Pat. 1381–5, 161.

[16] Dugdale, Mon. vi(2), 1043; V.C.H. Staffs. iv. 149, 152.

[17] S.H.C. ii(1), 83, 88–89, 102, 109.

[18] Bk. of Fees, 558, 1134.

[19] Tax. Eccl. (Rec. Com.), 243, 251.

[20] V.C.H. Staffs. iv. 144, 146.

[21] S.H.C. vi(1), 247. Marston was included in the view in 1382: ibid. xiv(1), 160.

[22] Ibid. ii(1), 137, 139–40, 143, 149; Rot. de Ob. et Fin. (Rec. Com.), 334.

[23] Cal. Fine R. 1272–1307, 248. In 1282 the king appointed a comm. of inquiry into the removal of the prior's goods by persons claiming to be the king's bailiffs and accusing the prior of receiving stolen goods: Cal. Pat. 1281–92, 48.

[24] Cal. Pat. 1317–21, 153.

[25] E 106/8/12.

[26] Cal. Inq. Misc. ii, p. 355.

[27] S.H.C. i. 266.

[28] Cal. Pat. 1334–8, 75, 91.

[29] Ibid. 136.

[30] Ibid. 145.

[31] Ibid. 211; Cal. Inq. Misc. ii, p. 355.

[32] Cal. Fine R. 1337–47, 36.

possession but also secured a reduction of the farm to £26 5s. 7½d., this being the value placed on the property by the commissioners; knights' fees and advowsons were reserved to the king. The bishop stood surety that Baldwin would pay the farm, be of good behaviour, not withdraw the goods of the priory, and not send revenue abroad. Two months later the farm was reduced to 10 marks on the ground that the priory had suffered severely at the hands of the previous keepers; the prior had to meet the cost of supporting the monks and servants of the priory.[33] The farm was raised to 20 marks in 1341.[34] A month later the king announced that others were offering 30 marks for the custody of the priory but that he was unwilling to remove the prior provided he paid as much.[35] The prior, however, surrendered the priory which was then committed to Henry, Earl of Derby, still at 20 marks.[36] By the end of 1342 Robert de Shareshull again held the custody,[37] but in 1346 it was once more committed to Baldwin, still at a farm of 20 marks.[38] The grant was made at the request of Isabel, the queen mother, and it was perhaps her patronage that enabled Baldwin to survive as prior. In 1347 the king summoned him to France 'upon certain special affairs', and he was allowed to defer the payment of his farm.[39] Later the same year £18 arrears were remitted altogether.[40]

In 1354 Baldwin claimed that he was impoverished as a result of the recent plague and a fire which had burnt down all the priory buildings except for one chamber and three barns; the church too had suffered. He was promptly pardoned arrears amounting to £77 13s. 3¾d. and granted a new inquiry. This revealed that the total annual value of the manor of Lapley, including 6 marks from the church, was £11 14s. 10d., and a further half-year's farm was remitted.[41] In 1356, again at the request of Queen Isabel, Baldwin was excused payment of the farm for three years, after which he was to pay 10 marks instead of 20.[42] Finally in 1357 he was excused another 40 marks of arrears.[43]

In 1361 after the restoration of peace with France the prior was allowed to resume full possession without payment and the arrears were remitted.[44] Baldwin probably died the same year: the priory became vacant in November 1361, and Peter de Gennereyo, monk of St. Rémy, was presented to Lapley by the abbot and instituted the following January.[45] The resumption of the war in 1369 once more brought alien priories into the king's hands, and the prior was given custody of Lapley at the old farm of 20 marks; this was raised to 25 marks in 1377.[46] The prior was evidently among those exempt from the expulsion of foreign monks in 1378. Another general survey was made of the priory's possessions in 1379. Their total annual value was given as £26 17s. 8d. from demesne lands, rents and other revenues at Lapley, Wheaton Aston, Bickford (in Lapley and Penkridge), Marston, Hamstall Ridware, and Silvington.[47] In 1384 the king granted the priory for the duration of the war with France to his esquire, Robert de Hampton, rent free.[48] Peter, 'sometime prior', secured a lease from Hampton two years later at the greatly increased farm of £40 13s. 4d.[49] In 1388, however, the king once more committed Lapley to Peter as prior at a rent of £20 for the duration of the war.[50] It was committed to Peter and to Geoffrey Stafford, canon of Ranton, in 1397, and later the same year to Peter, John Bally his fellow monk at Lapley, and Thomas Marton, clerk.[51] The £20 farm was assigned to another royal esquire, William Walshale, for life in 1398, a grant which was confirmed in 1404; he was still receiving the £20 in 1413.[52]

In 1402 Prior John Bally, who had succeeded in 1399 after the death of Prior Peter, was summoned before the Council to show whether his priory was conventual and so not liable to be taken into the king's hands with non-conventual priories.[53] He was unable to do this, and in 1403 the priory was committed to him and two others at a farm of 40 marks.[54] In 1413 it was committed to Bally, William Kanc his fellow monk, and Richard Knightley of Brough in Gnosall at a farm of 42 marks.[55] Ten marks from the farm was granted to the queen in 1409; this was raised to 12 marks in 1414, whilst in 1415 the remaining £20 was granted to another esquire, John Vale.[56]

In the 14th century the connexion with the mother abbey of St. Rémy must have been less important to the priors than their relations with the Crown. In 1367 during the period of peace the prior gave a bond for 120 marks to St. Rémy,[57] but the abbey can have had little profit from its English lands. The history of the priory ended in 1415 when all its possessions were granted to Tong College (Salop.), founded in or soon after 1410 by Isabel, widow of Sir Fulk Pembrugge.[58] In 1417 the king pardoned John Bally and other late keepers of the priory all arrears.[59]

The priory buildings evidently adjoined the church on the north side, and part of the site is now occupied by the timber-framed Old Manor House. The church itself contains much 12th-century work. The priory site and the church were enclosed within a moat.[60]

[33] Ibid. 75–76, 87.
[34] Ibid. 1337–47, 212.
[35] Cal. Close, 1341–3, 125.
[36] Cal. Fine R. 1337–47, 230.
[37] Cal. Pat. 1340–3, 590–1.
[38] Cal. Fine R. 1337–47, 473; Cal. Close, 1346–9, 90. The 20 marks was assigned to Hen. of Lancaster in part payment of royal debts.
[39] Cal. Close, 1346–9, 176, 285.
[40] Cal. Pat. 1345–8, 297.
[41] Ibid. 1354–8, 11–12; Cal. Close, 1354–60, 26; Cal. Inq. Misc. iii, pp. 59–60.
[42] Cal. Close, 1354–60, 301; Cal. Fine R. 1356–68, 2.
[43] Cal. Close, 1354–60, 356.
[44] Cal. Pat. 1358–61, 558–9.
[45] S.H.C. N.S. x(2), 110. From 1377 until 1399 the prior is referred to as Peter Romelot; it seems possible that this is the same Peter.
[46] Cal. Fine R. 1369–77, 25, 395; 1377–83, 18.

[47] E 106/11/5. Meaford, or a moiety of it, was held by the Trussell family in 1367: S.H.C. xiii. 62.
[48] Cal. Pat. 1381–5, 476.
[49] Cal. Close, 1385–9, 145.
[50] Cal. Fine R. 1383–91, 273–4.
[51] Ibid. 1391–9, 221, 237.
[52] Cal. Pat. 1396–9, 385, 405; 1401–5, 383–4; E 106/12/7.
[53] Cal. Close, 1402–5, 25.
[54] Cal. Fine R. 1399–1405, 196–7. A month before it had been committed at the same rent to Bro. Ralph Wybunbery: ibid. 194.
[55] Ibid. 1413–22, 44–45; Cal. Pat. 1416–22, 104–5.
[56] Cal. Pat. 1408–13, 86; 1413–16, 165, 281.
[57] E 135/15/10.
[58] Cal. Pat. 1413–16, 334; Eyton, Antiquities of Salop. ii. 250, 253; D. Knowles and R. N. Hadcock, Medieval Religious Houses: Eng. and Wales, 314, 343.
[59] Cal. Pat. 1416–22, 104–5.
[60] V.C.H. Staffs. iv. 144, 150, and plate facing p. 139.

Priors

Godric, possibly prior *temp.* Henry I.[61]

P., prior at some time between 1162 and 1181.[62]

Absalon, replaced Prior P. by 1181.[63]

Inganus, occurs by 1181 and in 1206–7.[64]

John, presented 1233.[65]

Walcher, occurs 1266.[66]

Reynold, occurs 1297.[67]

Peter de Passiaco, resigned 1305.[68]

John de Tannione, admitted 1305, resigned 1320.[69]

Gobert of Brabant, admitted 1320, resigned 1322.[70]

John de Aceyo, admitted 1322, resigned by 1328.[71]

Baldwin de Spynale, prior probably from 1328 and certainly from 1332; occurs to 1357, probably in office until November 1361; Gobert de Lapion occurs as rival prior 1334 to 1337.[72]

Peter de Gennereyo, admitted 1362; he may be the Peter Romelot who occurs as prior from 1377 and was dead by 1399.[73]

John Bally, admitted 1399; prior until the suppression.[74]

No seal is known.

[61] See p. 340.
[62] Migne, *Pat. Lat.* ccii, col. 596.
[63] Ibid.
[64] Ibid. col. 597; *S.H.C.* ii(1), 143.
[65] *Close R.* 1231–4, 337.
[66] *S.H.C.* 1924, pp. 154–5.
[67] E 106/4/2.
[68] Lich. Dioc. Regy., B/A/1/1, f. 16.
[69] Ibid. ff. 16, 90v. He was a monk of St. Rémy. It is either this or the earlier John who is referred to as John Tanyer in 1367 as holding *temp.* 'King Henry the king's grandfather' (*S.H.C.* xiii. 62): the grandfather of Edw. III was Edw. I; Hen. III was his great-grandfather.
[70] B/A/1/1, f. 90v.; ibid. /2, f. 136. He was a monk of St. Rémy.
[71] Ibid. /2, ff. 136, 143v.–144. He was a monk of St. Rémy.
[72] Ibid. ff. 143v.–144, 152; see above pp. 341–2. He was a monk of St. Rémy.
[73] See above p. 342 and n. 45; *Cal. Pat.* 1399–1401, 42.
[74] *Cal. Pat.* 1399–1401, 42; Lich. Dioc. Regy., B/A/1/7, f. 50v.; see above p. 342.

INDEX

PRINTED IN GREAT BRITAIN
BY ROBERT MACLEHOSE AND CO. LTD
THE UNIVERSITY PRESS, GLASGOW